ENCYCLOPEDIA OF WORLD BIOGRAPHY

SUPPLEMENT

35

ENCYCLOPEDIA OF WORLD BIOGRAPHY

SUPPLEMENT

$\dfrac{A}{Z}$ **35**

GALE
CENGAGE Learning·

Farmington Hills, Mich • San Francisco • New York • Waterville, Maine
Meriden, Conn • Mason, Ohio • Chicago

Encyclopedia of World Biography Supplement, Volume 35

Project Editor: James Craddock

Editorial: Tracie Moy, Jeffrey Muhr

Image Research and Acquisition: Lynn Vagg

Manufacturing: Rita Wimberley

For product information and technology assistance, contact us at
Gale Customer Support, 1-800-877-4253.
For permission to use material from this text or product,
submit all requests online at **www.cengage.com/permissions.**
Further permissions questions can be emailed to
permissionrequest@cengage.com

Gale
27500 Drake Rd.
Farmington Hills, MI, 48331-3535

ISBN-13: 978-1-57302-955-1
ISSN 1099-7326

This title is also available as an e-book.
ISBN-13: 978-1-57302-957-5
Contact your Gale sales representative for ordering information.

Printed in Mexico
1 2 3 4 5 6 7 19 18 17 16 15

CONTENTS

INTRODUCTION

The study of biography has always held an important, if not explicitly stated, place in school curricula. The absence in schools of a class specifically devoted to studying the lives of the giants of human history belies the focus most courses have always had on people. From ancient times to the present, the world has been shaped by the decisions, philosophies, inventions, discoveries, artistic creations, medical breakthroughs, and written works of its myriad personalities. Librarians, teachers, and students alike recognize that our lives are immensely enriched when we learn about those individuals who have made their mark on the world we live in today.

Encyclopedia of World Biography Supplement, Volume 35, provides biographical information on 175 individuals not covered in the 17-volume second edition of *Encyclopedia of World Biography (EWB)* and its supplements, Volumes 18 through 34. Like other volumes in the *EWB* series, this supplement represents a unique, comprehensive source for biographical information on those people who, for their contributions to human culture and society, have reputations that stand the test of time. Each original article ends with a bibliographic section. There is also an index to names and subjects, which cumulates all persons appearing as main entries in the *EWB* second edition, the Volume 18 through 34 supplements, and this supplement—more than 8,000 people!

Articles. Arranged alphabetically following the letter-by-letter convention (spaces and hyphens have been ignored), articles begin with the full name of the person profiled in large, bold type. Next is a boldfaced, descriptive paragraph that includes birth and death years in parentheses. It provides a capsule identification and a statement of the person's significance. The essay that follows is approximately 2,000 words in length and offers a substantial treatment of the person's life. Some of the essays proceed chronologically while others confine biographical data to a paragraph or two and move

on to a consideration and evaluation of the subject's work. Where very few biographical facts are known, the article is necessarily devoted to an analysis of the subject's contribution.

Following the essay is a bibliographic section arranged by source type. Citations include books, periodicals, and online Internet addresses for Web pages, where current information can be found.

Portraits accompany many of the articles and provide either an authentic likeness, contemporaneous with the subject, or a later representation of artistic merit. For artists, occasionally self-portraits have been included. Of the ancient figures, there are depictions from coins, engravings, and sculptures; of the moderns, there are many portrait photographs.

Index. The *EWB Supplement* index is a useful key to the encyclopedia. Persons, places, battles, treaties, institutions, buildings, inventions, books, works of art, ideas, philosophies, styles, movements—all are indexed for quick reference just as in a general encyclopedia. The index entry for a person includes a brief identification with birth and death dates *and* is cumulative so that any person for whom an article was written who appears in the second edition of *EWB* (volumes 1-16) and its supplements (volumes 18-34) can be located. The subject terms within the index, however, apply only to volume 35. Every index reference includes the title of the article to which the reader is being directed as well as the volume and page numbers.

Because *EWB Supplement,* Volume 35, is an encyclopedia of biography, its index differs in important ways from the indexes to other encyclopedias. Basically, this is an index of people, and that fact has several interesting consequences. First, the information to which the index refers the reader on a particular topic is always about people associated with that topic. Thus the entry "Quantum theory (physics)" lists articles on people associated with quantum theory. Each article may discuss a person's contribution to quantum theory, but no single article or group of articles is intended to provide a comprehensive treatment of quantum theory as such. Second, the index is rich in classified entries. All persons who are subjects of articles in the encyclopedia, for example, are listed in one or more classifications in the index—abolitionists, astronomers, engineers, philosophers, zoologists, etc.

The index, together with the biographical articles, make *EWB Supplement* an enduring and valuable source for biographical information. As school course work changes to reflect advances in technology and further revelations about the universe, the life stories of the people who have risen above the ordinary and earned a place in the annals of human history will continue to fascinate students of all ages.

We Welcome Your Suggestions. Mail your comments and suggestions for enhancing and improving the *Encyclopedia of World Biography Supplement* to:

The Editors
Encyclopedia of World Biography Supplement
Gale, a Cengage Learning company
27500 Drake Road
Farmington Hills, MI 48331-3535
Phone: (800) 347-4253

ADVISORY BOARD

OBITUARIES

The following people, appearing in volumes 1-34 of the *Encyclopedia of World Biography,* have died since the publication of the second edition and its supplements. Each entry lists the volume where the full biography can be found.

AGNEW, HAROLD MELVIN (born 1921), American physicist, died in Solana Beach, CA on September 29, 2013 (Vol. 32).

ANGELOU, MAYA (born 1928), American poet, author, playwright, and stage and screen performer, died in Winston-Salem, NC on May 28, 2014 (Vol. 1).

ATTENBOROUGH, RICHARD SAMUEL (born 1923), English actor and filmmaker, died in London, England on August 24, 2014 (Vol. 18).

BACALL, LAUREN (born 1924), American actress, died in New York, NY on August 12, 2014 (Vol. 29).

BAKER, HOWARD HENRY, JR. (born 1925), U.S. Senator and White House chief of staff, died in Huntsville, TN on June 26, 2014 (Vol. 18).

BARRY, MARION SHEPILOV, JR. (born 1936), African American mayor and Civil Rights activist, died of hypertensive cardiovascular disease in Washington, DC on November 23, 2014 (Vol. 2).

BRINK, ANDRE PHILIPPUS (born 1935), South African author, died on February 6, 2015 (Vol. 22).

BYRNE, JANE (born 1933), the first woman mayor of Chicago, died of complications from a stroke in Chicago, IL on November 14, 2014 (Vol. 3).

CARO, ANTHONY (born 1924), English sculptor, died in London, England on October 23, 2013 (Vol. 3).

CLANCY, TOM (born 1947), American author, died in Baltimore, Maryland on October 1, 2013 (Vol. 4).

CORNFORTH, JOHN WARCUP (born 1917), Australian chemist, died in Sussex, England on December 8, 2013 (Vol. 24).

CUOMO, MARIO (born 1932), Democratic New York state governor, died of heart failure in New York, NY on January 1, 2015 (Vol. 4).

DECROW, KAREN (born 1937), American journalist and activist, died in Jamesville, NY on June 6, 2014 (Vol. 31).

DEE, RUBY (born 1922), African American actress, died in New Rochelle, NY on June 11, 2014 (Vol. 4).

DJERASSI, CARL (born 1923), Austrian-American chemist, died of complications of bone and liver cancer in San Francisco, CA on January 30, 2015 (Vol. 34).

DOI TAKAKO (born 1928), Japanese politician, died in Hyogo Prefecture, Japan on September 9, 2014 (Vol. 5).

EDELMAN, GERALD (born 1929), American neuro-scientist, died of Parkinson's Disease in La Jolla, CA on May 17, 2014 (Vol. 27).

ENGELBART, DOUGLAS (born 1925), American inventor, died of kidney failure in Atherton, CA on July 2, 2013 (Vol. 31).

FITCH, VAL LOGSDON (born 1923), American physicist, died in Princeton, NJ on February 5, 2015 (Vol. 24).

FOLEY, TOM (born 1929), Democratic representative from the state of Washington and Speaker of the U.S. House of Representatives, died of complications from a stroke in Washington, DC on October 18, 2013 (Vol. 5).

GOODLAD, JOHN INKSTER (born 1920), American education researcher, died of cancer in Seattle, WA on November 29, 2014 (Vol. 6).

GORDIMER, NADINE (born 1923), South African author, died in Johannesburg, South Africa on July 13, 2014 (Vol. 6).

GRAVES, MICHAEL (born 1934), American Post-Modernist architect, died in Princeton, NJ on March 12, 2015 (Vol. 6).

GRAY, WILLIAM H, III (born 1941), first African American to be elected House Whip for the U.S. House of Representatives, died in London, England on July 1, 2013 (Vol. 6).

HEANEY, SEAMUS (born 1939), Irish poet, author, and editor, died in Dublin, Ireland on August 30, 2013 (Vol. 7).

HESBURGH, THOEODORE MARTIN (born 1917), activist American Catholic priest who was President of Notre Dame, died in South Bend, Indiana on February 26, 2015 (Vol. 7).

HOWARD, ELIZABETH JANE (born 1923), British author, died in Bungay, England on January 2, 2014 (Vol. 29).

JACOBSON, DAN (born 1929), South African author, died in London, England on June 12, 2014 (Vol. 22).

JAMES, P.D. (born 1920), British crime novelist, died in Oxford, England on November 11, 2014 (Vol. 8).

JARUZELSKI, WOJCHIECH WITOLD (born 1923), career soldier who became Poland's head of state (1981-1990), died of complications from a stroke in Warsaw, Poland on May 25, 2014 (Vol. 8).

KEMAL, YASHAR (born 1923), Turkish novelist, died in Istanbul, Turkey on February 28, 2015 (Vol. 8).

KWOLEK, STEPHANIE (born 1923), American chemist, died in Wilmington, DE on June 18, 2014 (Vol. 31).

OGOT, GRACE (born 1930), Kenyan author and politician, died in Nairobi, Kenya on March 18, 2015 (Vol. 11).

PAISLEY, IAN K. (born 1926), political leader and minister of religion in Northern Ireland, died in Belfast, Northern Ireland on September 12, 2014 (Vol. 12).

PANNENBERG, WOLFHART (born 1928), German theologian, died on September 5, 2014 (Vol. 12).

REYNOLDS, ALBERT (born 1932), prime minister of Ireland (1992-94), died of Alzheimer's disease in Dublin, Ireland on August 21, 2014 (Vol. 13).

SCHLESINGER, JAMES R. (born 1929), American government official, died in Baltimore, MD on March 27, 2014 (Vol. 14).

SHEVARDNADZE, EDUARD AMVROSEVICH (born 1928), Soviet foreign minister (1985-1990) and president of Georgia (1995-2003), died on July 7, 2014 (Vol. 14).

SMITH, DEAN (born 1931), American college basketball coach, died in Chapel Hill, NC on February 7, 2015 (Vol. 18).

STONE, ROBERT ANTHONY (born 1937), American novelist, died in Key West, FL on January 10, 2015 (Vol. 14).

STRAND, MARK (born 1934), fourth Poet Laureate of the United States, died in Brooklyn, NY on November 29, 2014 (Vol. 14).

TOWNES, CHARLES HARD (born 1915), American physicist, died in Oakland, CA in January 27, 2015 (Vol. 15).

Sani Abacha

The Nigerian general Sani Abacha (1943–1998) was Nigeria's head of state from 1993 until his death. His rise to power and rule have been widely described as ruthless and corrupt.

Abacha came to prominence as part of a group of military officers who ousted a civilian-ruled Nigerian government in 1983. He became president in 1993 after he imprisoned a democratically elected leader who was preparing to assume power, and he suppressed the protests that followed his actions, killing many of the protesters. In 1995 Abacha drew international condemnation after the execution of environmental activist Ken Saro-Wiwa. Abacha's personal style verged on the paranoid; never seen without dark glasses, he was accompanied wherever he went by a Special Bodyguard Unit numbering between 2,000 and 3,000 soldiers. United States general and future secretary of state Colin Powell, on learning about Abacha's life and careers, said, as quoted by Cameron Duodu and David Harrison in the London *Observer*, "Abacha's psychological bio-history is the worst I have ever read." Although some credited Abacha with stability that led to economic growth in Nigeria, it became apparent after his death in 1998 that he had skimmed off hundreds of millions of dollars in Nigerian riches for himself.

Unhealthy During Childhood

Sani Abacha was born on September 20, 1943, in Kano in northern Nigeria. His Muslim family was of the Kanuri ethnic group. Abacha suffered from a series of childhood diseases in infancy, any of which could have killed him. During his first years in school he remained sickly and was often picked on by bullies. But he survived and was educated at the Kano Provincial Secondary School (now known as Government College), graduating in 1962. Next, Abacha joined the army of the young nation of Nigeria, which had gained independence from the United Kingdom in 1960. He attended the Nigerian Military Training College in 1962 and 1963, was appointed a second lieutenant, and impressed his superiors enough to be sent to the Defense Officers' Cadet Training College in Aldershot, United Kingdom, in 1963.

In 1966, the first in a series of military coups against civilian government occurred in Nigeria, and Abacha prospered, winning a promotion to lieutenant. Civil war broke out in 1967 as eastern Nigeria, populated predominantly by the Igbo ethnic group, seceded and formed the independent nation of Biafra. Abacha saw action in the brutal war that ensued, during which one million people are estimated to have been killed. He is reputed to have fought bravely, and he advanced rapidly through the Nigerian officer corps, reaching the rank of major in 1969.

After peace was restored, Abacha continued with his preparations to assume top-level command posts, as Nigeria prospered along with other oil exporting nations. Several times he was sent abroad for further study; in 1982 he was a member of the Senior International Defense Course in Monterey, California. Nigeria flirted with a return to civilian rule between 1979 and 1983, but the country's economy stagnated as oil prices fell in the early 1980s, and President Shehu Shagari was viewed as corrupt in many quarters.

Announced Coup to Nation

On December 31, 1983, the Nigerian military overthrew Shagari's government, and it was Abacha who was heard on the radio with the actual announcement, telling Nigerians

Issouf Sanogo/AFP/Getty Images

that their economy had been badly mismanaged and that Nigeria had become a beggar nation. When the government of General Muhammadu Buhari failed to bring things under control and was in turn overthrown in 1985, Abacha was once again the face of the military, this time appearing on television in combat camouflage garb. Under the new government of General Ibrahim Babangida, Abacha entered the ruler's inner circle. He became army chief of staff and chairman of the Joint Chiefs of Staff, and in 1989 he survived a purge of top military officers carried out by Babangida.

After successfully squashing a coup against Babangida in 1990, Abacha became head of Nigeria's defense ministry. Once again he personally announced the coup's failure in Nigerian broadcasts, and by this time he was the second most powerful figure in Nigeria. When Babangida announced plans to return the country to civilian rule, Abacha initially seemed sympathetic, explaining the plan in a major annual lecture. The Nigerian elections in June of 1993, though, did not turn out to the satisfaction of Babangida and Abacha; the apparent winner was a Yoruba-speaking business executive, Moshood Abiola, who had little connection with the northern Nigerian military culture of which Abacha was part. Babangida unilaterally annulled the election results, turning over power instead to an appointed civilian leader, Ernest Shonekan. When Abiola tried to assume power himself, Abacha had him imprisoned, and his security forces were later implicated in the street murder of Abiola's wife.

Shonekan attempted to liberalize the Nigerian political situation and to implement a series of financial shock treatments prescribed by the International Monetary Fund (IMF). This precipitated a nationwide general strike, giving Abacha the opportunity he had been waiting for. On November 17, 1993, he demanded that Shonekan resign, and he seized control of the Nigerian state. Within a year he had dissolved the machinery of Nigerian democracy, outlawing some political parties and installing military commanders at the heads of those that remained. Fearful that he, too, would become a victim of the coup cycle, Abacha adopted a paranoid style, rarely appearing in public (and heavily guarded even then). He regularly dismissed and often imprisoned staff members he suspected of turning against him.

Had Environmental Activist Executed

These actions were tame compared with those undertaken against dissenters who directly challenged Abacha's actions. The best-known of these was Ken Saro-Wiwa, a leader of Nigeria's Ogoni ethnic group in the oil-rich Niger River delta region. In 1990 Saro-Wiwa launched a campaign protesting against environmental degradation resulting from the activities of international oil firms in the area. After increasingly violent military repression of the group's activities, Saro-Wiwa was jailed in 1993. In 1995, in spite of international appeals for clemency (even Shell Oil appealed for lenient treatment), Saro-Wiwa and eight other defendants were executed after a trial before a military tribunal.

The result was international condemnation for Abacha and his regime: Nigeria's membership in the British Commonwealth was suspended, and the United States suspended arms sales to Nigeria. Many countries recalled their ambassadors to Nigeria, but Abacha was unmoved. Nor were human rights appeals from African leaders, including South African president Nelson Mandela, any more successful. Even an appeal for the release of a group of political prisoners by Pope John Paul II in 1998 met with no response, although Abacha did promise that year to resume a process leading to the restoration of civilian rule. In fact, the opponents against whom Abacha planned to run were ones he had selected himself.

Before the election could take place, Abacha died on June 8, 1998, at his villa in the Nigerian capital city of Abuja. The official cause given was a heart attack; rumors held that it had been brought on by the use of the sexual stimulant Viagra, and that Abacha had been in the company of Indian prostitutes at the time of his death. Still more rumors flared the following day when Moshood Abiola, too, died in his prison cell, again after a cardiac episode.

Abacha was married to Maryam Jidah and had 11 children, one of whom, Ibrahim, died in a plane crash in 1996. His oldest surviving son, Mohammad, was arrested in 1999 on a variety of charges that included the murder of Abiola's wife and a variety of financial counts. Over the next several years the Nigerian government tried to recover Abacha's embezzled wealth from his family; although no complete accounting of Abacha's loot was ever made, a deal was finally reached in which the family was allowed to keep $100 million of its inheritance.

Books

Contemporary Black Biography, Vol. 70, Gale, 2009.

Periodicals

Economist, April 6, 1996.
Guardian (London, England), June 9, 1998.
Independent (London, England), June 10, 1998.
New Republic, May 18, 1998.
New York Times, June 9, 1998.
Observer (London, England), November 12, 1995.
Times (London, England), June 9, 1998.
World and I, July 1999.

Online

''Biography of Sani ABACHA,'' *African Success: People Changing the Face of Africa,* http://www.africansuccess.org/visuFiche.php?id=414&lang=en (October 1, 2014).□

Print Collector/Getty Images

Frederick Abel

The British chemist Sir Frederick Abel (1827–1902) was the co-inventor of cordite, a smokeless type of gunpowder. His innovations in that field grew out of his work with guncotton (nitrocellulose), whose manufacture he was the first to make safe and practicable on a large scale.

A bel was a mainstay of British engineering for decades, and he made important contributions in a variety of fields including the military applications of electrical fuses and the process of steel manufacturing. He was best known, however, for his work on explosives, which, Britain's *Dictionary of National Biography* noted drily, was ''carried out at great personal risk.'' Abel was both a friend and a rival of the Swedish chemist and engineer Alfred Nobel, the inventor of dynamite (nitroglycerin). The explosive substances developed by Abel were different from Nobel's dynamite, but their work overlapped, and Abel was sued for patent infringement by Nobel in the 1890s. Cordite remained a common military explosive for decades, and it remains in use today.

Descended from Artists and Musicians

Born on July 17, 1827, Frederick Augustus Abel was a native of Woolwich, England, now part of southeast London, and lived there for most of his life. His family background was artistic: his paternal grandfather was a German artist who served as the official painter of miniatures to the Grand Duke of Mecklenburg-Schwerin, and his father was a musician and music teacher. Abel himself was a talented musician. But on a family trip to visit a mineralogist uncle, A.J. Abel, in Hamburg, Germany, he became interested in science. He was 14 at the time, and back in England he enrolled at the Royal Polytechnic Institute, one of the few college preparatory high schools in the country with a strong science curriculum. In 1845 he became a member of an inaugural class numbering 26 at the Royal College of Chemistry.

Abel impressed his teacher, the great German chemist A.W. Hoffman, who had been brought to England by Prince Albert and Queen Victoria, and in 1846 he became a teaching assistant at the college. He remained there for five years, in 1851 becoming a chemistry demonstrator at a hospital. The following year he was hired as a lecturer in chemistry at the Royal Military Academy at Woolwich, and in 1856 he added the post of ordnance chemist to his responsibilities. In 1854 he and his assistant and successor, Charles Loudon Bloxham, published a *Handbook of Chemistry: Theoretical, Practical, and Technical.* The book went into a second edition in 1858.

Abel's designation as Chemist to the Office of Ordnance effectively made him the chief authority on explosives for the British military. The job was later renamed Chief Chemist to the War Office. He retained that status until his retirement from the Royal Military Academy in 1888. He also served as professor of chemistry at the Academy. Over the second half of the 19th century, military explosives underwent fundamental change, and Abel contributed to the application of many new materials and techniques. His first major experimental accomplishment, however, was his development of guncotton as an explosive that could be safely and reliably manufactured.

Combined Earlier Innovations

Abel's genius in developing guncotton consisted in putting together small innovations made earlier by others. The Austrian officer and chemist Wilhelm Lenk von Wolfsberg had suggested that washing guncotton thoroughly would remove acid and impurities that made it less stable. Another procedure developed prior to Abel's innovations came from John Tonkin, the British manager of a small plant, the Cornwall Blasting Powder Company, who suggested that the guncotton (not cotton but a flammable compound produced by acid treatment of cellulose) could be worked with more easily if it were first pulped by putting it through a set of revolving blades. According to G.I. Brown, writing in *The Big Bang: A History of Explosives,* "Abel generally gets most of the credit for bringing guncotton into safe, regular use," but he relied on the work of these two predecessors.

In 1866 Abel summarized his findings in a pair of lectures titled "Gun Cotton" and "The Modern History of Gunpowder." By that time, the manufacture of guncotton was already underway, although it grew slowly, and in 1865 Abel had taken out a patent for the procedure. By 1871 a new plant at Waltham Abbey was set up to produce 250 tons of guncotton per year. Abel's method was not substantially improved upon until 1905, although a new variant, Tonite, was used in blasting several railroad tunnels in Britain and was introduced in the United States by the DuPont Corporation in 1892.

Abel's work on cordite grew out of his development of guncotton, augmented by his observations in his military post of new technologies emerging in other countries, particularly the new explosive compounds under development by Alfred Nobel in Sweden. He received a new stimulus to his efforts in 1888, when the British government established a new Explosives Commission. In 1889 he and the Scottish chemist James Dewar patented a new mixture of nitroglycerine, guncotton, and petroleum jelly, produced in long rods that looked like cords; it was thus given the name cordite. Cordite was the commonly used propellant for British military guns through both world wars and remained in production in Britain until the end of the 20th century.

Sued by Nobel

Nobel had also been at work on explosive nitroglycerine mixtures and had developed a compound called ballistite that had been rejected by British planners as too unstable because it contained camphor as an ingredient. Nevertheless, it was similar to Abel's cordite, and Nobel filed suit against Abel and Dewar for patent infringement. The House of Lords ruled in favor of Abel and Dewar, partly because of the wording of Nobel's patent, and cordite went into full production.

Abel was active in many other areas relating to explosives. He developed the Abel test for the flash point (the temperature at which vapors above a volatile combustible substance ignite when exposed to flame), refining it through two devices known as the Abel open-test apparatus and Abel close-test apparatus. He worked on military applications for electrical fuses, and his work on the steel manufacturing process was significant enough to win him

the Bessemer medal of the Iron and Steel Institute in 1893. He served as president of that body from 1891 to 1893.

In 1888 Abel retired from his post at the War Department, but he remained active in a variety of scientific societies and continued to conduct research. Throughout his career his organizational skills and the variety of his scientific interests had led him to high positions in research and industry organizations, including the presidencies of the Chemical Society from 1875 to 1877, the Institute of Chemistry from 1881 to 1882, and the Society of Chemical Industry in 1883, as well as of the Institute of Electrical Engineers. He maintained his artistic interests, serving as chairman of the Society of Arts in 1883 and 1884. During his retirement years, Abel served as the director and recording secretary of the Imperial Institute from 1893 to 1901. He married Sarah Selina in 1854 and Giulietta de la Feuillade in 1889 but had no children.

Abel was the recipient of numerous awards, including honorary degrees from both Oxford and Cambridge universities. Abel was knighted in 1883 and made a baronet ten years later. He published 65 scientific papers and contributed a number of articles to the massive ninth edition of the *Encyclopedia Britannica.* In 1860 he was elected a fellow of the Royal Society, and in 1887 he received the prestigious Royal Medal. Abel died at his London home on September 6, 1902.

Books

Brown, G.I., *The Big Bang: A History of Explosives,* Sutton, 1998.

Lee, Sir Sidney, ed., *Dictionary of National Biography, Second Supplement,* Macmillan, 1912.

World of Invention, Gale, 2006.

Online

"Frederick Abel," *Grace's Guide: British Industrial History,* http://www.gracesguide.co.uk/Frederick_Abel (January 6, 2015).

"Frederick Abel Biography," *How Products Are Made,* http://www.madehow.com/inventorbios/2/Frederick-Abel.htm (January 6, 2015).

"Sir Frederick Augustus Abel," *S9.com,* http://www.s9.com/Biography/Abel-Frederick-Augustus-Sir (January 6, 2015). ☐

Abu al-Abbas As-Saffah

Abu al-Abbas Abdullah as-Saffah (c. 722–754) was the first caliph of the Abbasid dynasty and descendant of the Prophet Muhammad. His proclamation as leader of a new Islamic state in 750 CE marked the end of the Umayyad dynasty that had guided and enlarged the Muslim faith in the century after the prophet's death. As-Saffah served as caliph for just a few years, but his Abbasid heirs remained in power until the 1250s in a half-millennium period often deemed the Golden Age of Islam.

slamic scholars are uncertain of the exact date of the birth of Abu al-Abbas Abdullah as-Saffah, whose ''As-Saffah'' name is sometimes translated from the Arabic as ''the Blood Spiller.'' The Abbas part of his name refers to one of his forefathers and would be used to denote the new caliphate and its ruling dynasty.

Descended from Powerful Quraysh Chiefs

As-Saffah was likely born in the early 720s, about 90 years after the death of Muhammad. He is thought to have been born and raised in an Arab-populated settlement in Syria. The family were Banu Hashim, a kin group of the Prophet Muhammad's family. The Banu Hashim were also ethnic Quraysh, a prosperous merchant tribe on the Arabian peninsula. As-Saffah and his older brother Abu Jaffar Abdullah al-Mansur were sons of a man also named Muhammad, but known as Muhammad ibn Ali ibn Abdullah. Their father's great-grandfather was Al-Abbas ibn Abd al-Muttalib, who was uncle to the Prophet Muhammad. As-Saffah and possibly Jaffar were sons of their father's union with a Berber woman named Salama.

The emergence of Islam and the respect accorded to the Prophet Muhammad and his family was linked to the Hashim family and the Quraysh group's influence in Mecca, a holy city on the Arabian peninsula. Mecca was an ancient place of worship even in the pre-Islamic period and home to a massive black stone called the Kaaba. Before Islam, the ancient Arab Nabatean kingdom participated in organized religious rituals involving the large stone, whose origins as an object of veneration are obscured by the passage of time. The Nabateans were mentioned in Greek and Judaic texts of the pre-Christian era but their kingdom was subdued by the Roman Empire in the first century CE. Nabateans dispersed and were among the many Arab-origin groups that lived in what became present-day Syria, Iraq, Jordan, Egypt, Saudi Arabia, and other parts of the Middle East.

Mecca eventually became a holy city of Islam and its access was restricted to followers of the faith. During the Prophet Muhammad's lifetime tensions in Mecca, his birthplace, eventually forced him to establish a second base in Medina, another city on the Arabian peninsula. When Muhammad died in 632, his father-in-law Abu Bakr was chosen to lead the Muslim faithful. Abu Bakr became the *khalifa,* or successor to Muhammad, though he was not considered a prophet himself but rather a steward for the followers of the founder's teachings. For the remainder of the seventh century CE a series of civil wars, ideological divisions, and internal tensions roiled the sect as it expanded across key cities and territories of the Middle East. That expansion sometimes occurred through swift and brutal military force.

Islam Roiled by Dissent

Abu Bakr and the caliphs who succeeded him made impressive territorial gains in the 630s and 640s, taking larger chunks of the Arabian peninsula, Iraq, and Egypt. They pushed back the once-powerful Sassanids, a Persian empire that had previously dominated this region, and the

emerging Muslim state also proved a formidable challenge to the Byzantine Empire, the successor of the long-vanquished Roman Empire.

The internal power battles within Islam were tied to factions of the Prophet Muhammad's family. On one side was his widow Aisha, whose father was Abu Bakr. Aisha emerged as an influential scholarly figure in Islam who worked diligently to promote her late husband's teachings, said to have been revealed to him in a series of visions by Allah, or god. Another key figure was Muhammad's first wife, Khadijah. From that union a daughter named Fatima was born in Mecca around 605. Fatima married her cousin, Ali ibn Abi Talib, who was the son of the prophet's important Hashim-chief uncle and protector Al-Abbas ibn Abd al-Muttalib.

Muhammad's son-in-law is known simply as Ali and was said to have been the first male to convert to Islam. During his lifetime Ali was revered as an imam, or holy leader, and known as the Lion of God for his role in the religion's early years. In 656 there was an epic clash between Ali on one side and factions loyal to Aisha and her followers on the other. This took place near Basra, Iraq, and is known as the Battle of the Camel or Battle of Jamal. Ali won, and his followers became known as *shiat Ali,* an Arabic-language term that means ''party of Ali.'' They are called Shiite to distinguish them from the Sunni Muslim sect, who wielded power in the first decades after the Prophet Muhammad's death.

As-Saffah Descended from Revered Ali

Ali, the Lion of God, was murdered in 661. Neither of his sons—the Prophet Muhammad's grandsons—were appointed to succeed him. Instead one of his foes, a tribal chief and military commander named Muawiyah, became caliph. It is from Muawiyah's name that the Umayyad Caliphate, the first major Islamic state, derives is name. Founded in 661, the Umayyad Caliphate had a fairly impressive 20-year rule under Muawiyah's rule, expanding its borders and securing key cities in the Middle East.

All of these events occurred decades before As-Saffah's birth but would play a crucial role in the rise of his own family branch and its establishment of the Abbasid Caliphate. The internal divisions inside Islam prompted multiple assassination plots and forced believers to choose sides for the safety of their own families and their communities. As-Saffah and his brothers were the sons of a grandson of Al-Abbas ibn Abd al-Muttalib, the uncle of the Prophet Muhammad.

Rose Against Umayyads

Muawiyah's successor as caliph was his son Yazid, who ruled the Umayyad Caliphate until his death in 683. Abd al-Malik ibn Marwan became caliph in 685 and, like Muawiyah, had a fairly long and stable reign of twenty-odd years. Known as al-Malik or Marwan I, the caliph brutally suppressed insurrections but also carried out a major expansion program to secure the caliphate. Its borders moved west into Africa, northward to Turkey, and in a very successful easterly campaign into former Persian lands then southwest Asia and Central Asian cities, which were important stops on the valuable Silk Road trade route. Marwan's two sons succeeded him as caliph in the waning years of the Umayyad period, when its wealthy and powerful leaders were nevertheless unable to organize a successful-enough tax-collection and military apparatus to control an ever-growing, multinational territory.

As-Saffah and his brother joined a secret underground movement to oust the Umayyad dynasty. They were aligned with a canny military leader in Khorasan, a province of the Umayyad caliph that comprises parts of Iraq, Afghanistan, Turkmenistan, and Uzbekistan. This leader was rebel army commander Abu Muslim, who declared himself in opposition to the declining Umayyad Empire in 747. Abu Muslim famously unfurled a war banner that was a field of pure black, and that ominous banner would be used centuries later as the symbolic flag and color of Islamic revolutionaries.

Took Kufa and Damascus

As-Saffah and his brothers took part in Abu Muslim's cavalry-mounted battles against the Umayyads and their base in Damascus, the Syrian city that is one of the world's oldest urban settlements. Abu Muslim cleverly said that he represented the family of the Prophet Muhammad, but did not reveal which branch whose allegiance he had secured. His armies took large sections of Khorasan and Iran by mid-749 and then seized the strategic city of Kufa, Iraq, in September of 749. The city had an enormous mosque, but back in 661 Ali—the son-in-law of the Prophet Muhammad—had been slain inside its walls by a sword-wielding assassin.

Ali's death was avenged on November 28, 749, when As-Saffah was proclaimed the new caliph inside the Great Mosque of Kufa. The Abbasid Caliph came into existence formally on January 25, 750, when Abu Muslim's army defeated the Umayyad descendants of Marwan at the Battle of Zab River, a tributary of the Tigris River, near Mosul, Iraq. The Umayyad caliph, known as Marwan II, was forced to flee. Marwan II was turned away at Damascus then slain en route to Egypt. His severed head was couriered to As-Saffah as proof of the ignominious end of the Umayyad dynasty.

The Infamous Banquet Table

As-Saffah ruled from Kufa, whose immense mosque was one of the first major worship sites in Islam constructed after those in Mecca and Medina. Like many of his predecessors as caliph, As-Saffah dealt ruthlessly with potential saboteurs and traitors. Islamic historian Ziauddin Sardar gives an account of one formal banquet to which As-Saffah had invited the remaining Umayyad family members and courtiers as a display of his newfound power. As Sardar wrote in *Mecca: The Sacred City,* a veiled person appeared at the palace and asked to speak to the new caliph just before the meal was to begin. The unknown visitor was a poet who spoke in verse and warned As-Saffah to "cut the accursed tree at its root and branches," according to Sardar.

In response, As-Saffah turned to the defeated Umayyad guests and spoke these words: "Criminal brood, I see before me the images of my kith and kin that you have murdered. And you still breathe and enjoy life," Sardar quoted the caliph as saying. As-Saffah then ordered his loyal Khorasani guards to club the defeated Umayyads to death. A carpet was thrown over their bodies, and the caliph ordered the banquet to begin atop this pile of corpses. Another oft-old incident from this era was another massacre of Umayyads in Damascus; one escapee was Abd al-Rahman, who managed to flee all the way across North Africa and by boat across the Strait of Gibraltar, where he established the Emirate of Córdoba in 755.

As-Saffah remained in power for just a few years and is known only as the first caliph of the Abbasid era. He died of smallpox in June of 754. His brother Jaffar was his designated successor and took the formal name Abu Jaffar al-Mansur. It was al-Mansur who decided to build a new and lavish walled city to serve as capital of the Abbasid caliphate. The site chosen was near an ancient Persian city called Ctesiphon. The new city was named Baghdad and the Abbasids ruled from it for nearly 500 years until 1258, when an invading Mongol army sacked it and slaughtered thousands of civilians.

The black banner under which As-Saffah and his family members fought was later adopted by Islamic jihadists, and the dream of a multinational, single-religion Islamic caliphate has been revived many times. His brother al-Mansur was eventually succeeded by a grandson named Harun al-Rashid, the fifth caliph. In the 790s al-Rashid erected a fortress in Ar-Raqqa, Syria. In 2014, the militia armies of the new Islamic State (IS; also known as ISIS, or Islamic State of Iraq and Syria) mounted a significant campaign against parts of Iraq and Syria. After several military victories IS leaders announced that Ar-Raqqa would be the geographical capital seat of their proposed caliphate.

Books

Glassé, Cyril, *The New Encyclopedia of Islam,* Rowman & Littlefield, 2008.

Pryor, John, "The Mediterranean Breaks Up: 500–1000," in *The Mediterranean in History,* edited by David Abulafia, Thames & Hudson, 2003.

Sardar, Ziauddin, *Mecca: The Sacred City,* Bloomsbury, 2014. □

Abu Hanifah

The Sunni Islamic theologian Abu Hanifah (700–767), born in present-day Iraq, was one of the first scholars to attempt to codify Islamic law after the death of the Prophet Muhammad. He founded what became known as the Sunni hanafi school of fiqh, or Islamic jurisprudence.

Abu Hanifah was essentially a generation removed from the Prophet. He may have met some of Muhammad's companions, whose testimony regarding proper Islamic conduct was especially prized, but in most matters of law he faced the challenge of applying the Prophet's teachings and actions systematically, deriving a body of jurisprudence from the Quran and from the principles that followed the paths laid down by the Prophet in his own life. Several basic principles marked Abu Hanifah's teachings. He believed that Islamic law was not an abstract body of principles but had to apply to the challenges people faced in their everyday lives. He stressed the value of debate and analogy in determining the law and its correct application. And he had no hesitation in speaking truth to power, a tendency that often got him in trouble and may have cost him his life.

Worked in Family Silk Business

Abu Hanifah was born in the year 700 in Kufa, in what is now Iraq. He was probably of Persian ancestry. Kufa, home to one of the world's oldest mosques, was a major center of early Islamic learning. His birth name was Numan ibn Thabit ibn Zuta ibn Ham; Abu Hanifah, which has been transliterated in several ways, was a patronymic or a name derived from that of his father, a prosperous silk merchant. The region's governor at the time was a dictatorial figure named al-Hajjaj ibn Yusuf who was hostile to intellectuals and scholars, and Abu Hanifah focused as a young man on learning the family business.

Abu Hanifah's father died in 713, and Abu Hanifah took over the family business. Even before his involvement with the law began, Abu Hanifah was the subject of an unusually large number of anecdotes pertaining to his honesty and high ethical character. Once a woman brought him a silk dress to sell, offering what Abu Hanifah considered the unreasonably low price of 100 dirhams. He demanded that he be allowed to pay her more, and a reverse bargaining session ensued in which the woman repeatedly professed herself ready to accept a lower price, but Abu Hanifah continued to offer more. Finally he brought in an expert who valued the dress at 500 dirhams, and he paid that price. Abu Hanifah chastised dealers who resold commodities from his show at higher prices, claiming that they were cheating their customers. Once he noticed a man who was avoiding him on the street; after learning that the man was embarrassed because he owed Abu Hanifah 10,000 dirhams he could not pay, Abu Hanifa forgave the debt and even apologized for causing the man distress.

The ascent to power of Caliph Sulaiman in 714 was accompanied by a new emphasis on learning and scholarship, which might have turned Abu Hanifah's mind in that direction. And perhaps word of his ethics had spread to local teachers as well. According to a story of the time, Abu Hanifah was walking one day past the house of one al-Sha'bi, a noted scholar, who stopped him and asked where he was going. Abu Hanifah answered that he was going to meet a certain businessman, whereupon al-Sha'bi told him that he showed signs of intelligence and should turn toward a life of study. Abu Hanifah apparently accepted the scholar's suggestion.

May Have Known Prophet's Companions

The nature of Abu Hanifah's Islamic education is not entirely clear. At the time it was said that he had known between eight and ten of the Prophet Muhammad's companions, men whose direct contact with the Prophet lent them great credibility. But the Prophet died in 632, and some Islamic scholars have questioned whether Abu Hanifah could actually have known any of his companions, who would all have been very old by the second decade of the eighth century. What is clear is that Abu Hanifah studied with al-Sha'bi and some of the other leading Islamic scholars in the city. At the beginning he lagged behind his fellow students, but he soon exceeded them in reasoning skills and breadth of knowledge.

Abu Hanifah attended lectures by Qatada and Shu'ba, two scholars who had learned the teachings of the Prophet directly from the Prophet's companions. At this point, he could probably have prospered by opening a school of his own and beginning to teach, but instead he resolved to continue learning and to reach the highest intellectual level of which he was capable. He undertook the hajj to Mecca and stayed on there for study with some of the top Islamic scholars in the holy city. In 720 he moved on from Mecca to Medina, attending further lectures there. He asked some of his teachers to write down the body of hadiths, oral reports of the teachings, acts, and sayings of Muhammad, and thus played an important role in the transmission of the Prophet's teachings.

By the time he had completed all these travels, Abu Hanifah had learned hadiths from an estimated 4,000 sources, and he had gained a reputation as a great scholar and teacher himself. He did not abandon his silk business but took a partner who carried out most of the day-to-day activities of the enterprise. Abu Hanifah wrote a book, the *Kitabul-Athar,* and he amassed a large body of students. In fact, according to a biography on the website of Pakistan's *Renaissance* journal, "It redounds to the credit of Imam Abu Hanifa that he left behind the greatest number of pupils in the world of Islam, including Qazi Abu Yusuf, Imam Muhammad, Hafiz Abdur Razzaq, Abdullal Bin Al Mubarak, Abu Naeem Faza, and Abu Asim who acquired great fame in their days." Beyond the world of Islamic scholarship and study, Abu Hanifah was greatly admired by ordinary people in his part of the world.

Codified Islamic Teachings

His accomplishment was to organize the legacy of the Prophet and his companions, and to begin to make that legacy into a set of law codes. His primary method was dialogue: he would ask questions that derived answers to new questions from Islamic texts and from what was known to have been said by the Prophet. "In fact," noted the *Lost Islamic History* website, "the concept of using debate and logic became a cornerstone of his methodology for seeking Islamic laws." His efforts coalesced during his life and after his death into a system of Islamic jurisprudence (or *fiqh*) called the Hanafi school, the largest and most influential of the four schools of jurisprudence in the Islamic world.

The book *The Muslim 100* noted that "he pioneered a new legal interpretive methodology based on the two fundamental sources of Islam [the Quran and hadiths] and used this fresh, innovative, and dynamic legal methodology to formulate Islamic answers to the problems and challenges which confronted the Muslims of his time." As an innovator, Abu Hanifah faced criticism both from within Muslim scholarly circles and from political leaders, whom he clearly mistrusted. When the Caliph Mansur offered Abu Hanifa a high legal post in his empire, the scholar (according to *Renaissance*) responded, "Supposing a complaint is lodged against you in my court and you wanted it to be decided in your favour otherwise I would be thrown into the river: Please rest assured that I would prefer to be drowned in the river rather than tamper with justice."

These attitudes apparently brought Abu Hanifah into serious difficulties with authorities at the end of his life. It is unclear exactly what happened to him. According to one story, he was imprisoned by Mansur after refusing to accept the post as judge. But another account holds that he became enmeshed in factional fighting. He died in prison in 767, perhaps poisoned by one of the leaders of whom he had run afoul. It was said that 50,000 people gathered for his funeral and mourned for several days. He is memorialized by the Abu Hanifah Mosque in Baghdad and by a large mausoleum built there by Ottoman Turkish rulers, on whose judicial world Abu Hanifah had exerted a strong influence.

Books

Hallaq, Wael B., *The Origins and Evolution of Islamic Law,* Cambridge, 2005.
Khan, Muhammad Mojlum, *The Muslim 100,* Kube, 2009.

Online

"Abu Hanifa," *Living Islam,* http://www.livingislam.org/ahanifa_e.htm (January 11, 2015).
"Imam Abu Haneefah," *Muslim Heritage,* http://www.muslimheritage.com/article/imam-abu-haneefah (January 11, 2015).
"Imam Abu Hanifa," *Renaissance,* http://www.renaissance.com.pk/feletfor96.html (January 11, 2015).
"The Life of Imam Abu Hanifa," *Lost Islamic History,* http://www.lostislamichistory.com/the-life-of-imam-abu-hanifa/ (January 11, 2015). □

Abul Fazl

Abul Fazl (1551–1602) was a chronicler and courtier in the Mughal Empire, a Persian-ruled state that controlled much of the Indian subcontinent.

Abul Fazl served Akbar, the third emperor (1542–1605) of the Mughals and one of the greatest in the dynasty, enlarging the empire in the military arena but also adopting a sympathetic stance toward the cultures of the people he conquered, and even departing considerably from the orthodox Islamic faith of the cultures that had birthed the empire. Abul Fazl chronicled the military and administrative affairs of the empire under Akbar's rule in considerable detail in two large volumes, one of them cut short by his assassination, and in a number of smaller writings. But, in the words of the *Story of Pakistan* website, Abul Fazl "was much more than Akbar's courtier. He was counselor, confidant, chief secretary, official chronicler, legislator, and master of the Dewani Department [a regional administrative unit]." He is thought to have done much to shape Akbar's liberal and tolerant attitudes.

Descended from Religious Seekers and Intellectuals

Abul Fazl traced his ancestry to a family of seekers and the intellectually curious who had come from Yemen and made their home in the Sindh region of what is now Pakistan. His grandfather, Shaikh Khizr, in the words of an old Persian biography appearing on the *Persian Literature in Translation* website, followed "the yearnings of a heart imbued with mystic lore, [and] emigrated to Hindustan. There he traveled about visiting those who, attracted by God, are known to the world for not knowing it...." Shaikh Khizr traveled to Hijaz on the Arabian peninsula and then returned to India. His son, Shaikh Mubarak, was Abul Fazl's father; Shaikh Mubarak was recognized as a genius at the age of four and likewise traveled widely before settling in Akbarabad (now Agra), the capital of the Mughal Empire later the site of the Taj Mahal.

There Abul Fazl was born on January 14, 1551 (6 Muharram 958 in the Persian calendar). Like his father he showed precocious intellectual gifts. He claimed that he learned to speak shortly after the age of one, and by five he was both reading and writing in the Arabic language, learned from his father. He was given a complete course in the lore of the Islamic faith and the sciences the Mughals inherited from the Arab world, recalling that he would study so hard that he might go two or three days without eating. For a period of time he apparently was subject to what would now be called depression, and set his studies aside, but he later resumed them. As a youth he astounded other scholars with various intellectual feats, among them the reconstruction of a dictionary that had mostly been eaten by ants. Finally the original book was discovered, and it was found to differ from Abul Fazl's reconstruction only slightly.

Apparently because of his reputation for knowledge, Abul Fazl was asked to join Akbar's court in 1574 or 1575. His brother Abul Faiz, a poet, joined the court at about the same time. Akbar already had a reputation for religious tolerance and for the encouragement of religious pluralism, and these seem to have only strengthened under the influence of Abul Fazl and Abul Faiz. Akbar seems to have rejected, at least in part, the strictures of Islam, "for which both brothers have been branded by Muhammadan writers as atheists, or as Hindus, or as sunworshippers, and as the chief causes of Akbar's apostasy from Islam," in the words of the *Persian Literature in Translation* biography.

Achieved Military Victories

In the words of *India NetZone,* "The relationship between Akbar, a soldier of Turkish descent, and Abul-Fazl, an Indian Muslim brought up in the Persian school of science and administration, epitomizes the strengths of the Mughal Empire itself.'' Abul Fazl was one of the nine Navratna, or gems, of Akbar's court, and he served the emperor in a variety of fields. He was a skilled general, leading Akbar's troops into battle on the Deccan plateau, and his writings examine in detail the military strategies of the Mughals and their enemies. His writings about the administrative structure of the Empire reveal a deep familiarity with its workings.

Abul Fazl seems over time, in fact, to have become perhaps Akbar's most trusted advisor. Although his only official title was head of the emperor's correspondence office, he traveled with the emperor extensively, including on a 1598 pilgrimage to Punjab to meet the Sikh teacher Guru Arjan. He and Abul Faiz seem to have helped Akbar shape the syncretic new religion of Din-i-Ilahi that he attempted to implement in the empire, incorporating elements of Islam, Hinduism, and other faiths, including Christianity. Abul Fazl aided in this enterprise by translating the Bible into Persian.

His best-known accomplishment, however, was the *Akbarnama* (Book of Akbar), a giant chronicle whose first part occupied seven years of Abul Fazl's life. The first part is thought to have been written between 1590 and 1596. Commissioned by Akbar himself, who wished to leave a record of his accomplishments, the book was lavishly illustrated with more than 100 miniature paintings. It is housed today at the Victoria & Albert Museum in London.

The *Akbarnama* was written in flowery prose festooned with lavish praise for Akbar, and its mixture of erudite Persian sentence structure, turning at times into poetry, combined with an extraordinary density of detail, has posed problems for English translators. The entire *Akbarnama* was translated early in the 20th century by Henry Beveridge, with several layers of corrections in new editions up to the 1930s; Beveridge made no secret of his discomfort with Abul Fazl as an observer. The *Ain-i-Akbari* was translated again by H.S. Jarrett in the 1940s, and a new translation of the whole, by Wheeler M. Thackston, began to appear in 2015.

Chronicle Provided Detailed Accounts of Empire

The *Akbarnama* is the most detailed document to have survived, and it provided a direct record of the workings of the Mughal Empire. The first part of the *Akbarnama* filled two volumes, each requiring well over 500 pages of text, plus numerous notes, in modern translation. The first part devoted considerable space to Akbar's background and ancestry, tracing it back to the Mongol emperor Timur (or Tamerlane), who died in 1405. Abul Fazl went on to detail the first 17 years of Akbar's reign, covering the diplomatic and economic bases of the empire as they evolved under Akbar's rule.

The second part of the *Akbarnama* was called the *Ain-i-Akbari* (Constitution of Akbar), which examined in detail the Mughal administrative system during Akbar's rule up to the emperor's 46th year. Abul Fazl detailed the sizes of specific territories, prices and price trends of commodities, the lives of allied princes and the strength of their armies, taxes, biographies of imperial officeholders, and the functions of administrative departments. He included an *Account of Hindu Sciences* that tried to explain the Hindu faith to Muslims and thus to promote religious tolerance.

After Abul Fazl's death, the *Ain-i-Akbari* was completed by Inavat Ullah.

Abul Fazl was at work on the later chapters of the *Ain-i-Akbari* when, on August 12, 1602, he was assassinated while returning to Agra from the Deccan Plateau by a clan chieftain, Bir (or Vir) Singh Bundela. His severed head was delivered to the man who instigated the plot, Prince Salim (1569–1627), Akbar's eldest son, who was aware that Abul Fazl opposed his succession to the emperorship (the plot was successful and Salim became Emperor Jahangir). Akbar was said to be inconsolable over Abul Fazl's death, and to have reacted more strongly to it than he would have to the death of his own children.

Books

Coetzee, Daniel, and Lee W. Eysturlid, eds., *Philosophers of War*, ABC-CLIO, 2013.
Smith, Vincent A., *Oxford History of India*, Oxford, 1958.
Thackston, Wheeler M., trans., *The History of Akbar, Volume 1*, Harvard, 2015.

Online

"Abul Fazl," *The Sikh Encyclopedia*, http://www.thesikhencyclopedia.com/muslims-rulers-and-sufi-saints/abul-fazl (December 6, 2014).
"Abul Fazl," *Story of Pakistan*, http://www.storyofpakistan.com/abul-fazl/ (December 6, 2014).
"Abul-Fazl, Mughal Historian, *India NetZone*, http://www.indianetzone.com/43/abul-fazl_mamuri.htm (December 6, 2014).
"Biography of Shaikh Abulfazl I'Alla'Mi'," *Persian Literature in Translation*, http://www.persian.packhum.org/persian/ (December 6, 2014).
"The Reign of Akbar," https://www2.stetson.edu/secure/history/hy10430/abulfazl.html (December 6, 2014).
"12th August 1602: Abu'l Fazl, Akbar's Vizier was Assassinated at the Instigation of Akbar's Son, Prince Salim," *Maps of India*, http://www.mapsofindia.com/on-this-day (December 4, 2014). □

Adelheid, St.

Adelheid (931–999) was one of the most powerful and influential women of late tenth-century Europe. Crowned as Holy Roman Empress alongside her husband Otto I, she held the rare title of queen of Italy and of a newly unified German *reich,* or kingdom. She was connected by both blood and marriage to several aristocratic dynasties in France, Germany, and Italy, and in her lifetime gave generously to abbeys and monasteries in those lands.

A delheid was descended from the royal line that controlled one of the fief kingdoms of greater Francia, the precursor state of the Kingdom of France. Born in 931 in present-day Orbe, Switzerland, she was the daughter of Burgundian King Rudolf II and Bertha of

Interfoto/Alamy/Alamy

Swabia. Adelheid lived during a time of major political and territorial upheavals in western Europe, as the proliferous descendants of Charlemagne, the first Holy Roman Emperor, vied with one another for control of various lands and trade routes.

Family Ties to Carolingians

Adelheid's paternal great-great grandfather was Conrad I. Conrad's sister Judith had married Charlemagne's son Louis the Pious, also known as Louis I. The Kingdom of Burgundy, into whose ruling family Adelheid was born, switched allegiances on several occasions, siding first with the Frankish empire, and later with the Lombardians who held parts of southern France and northern Italy.

Ecclesiastical sources assert that Adelheid's father Rudolf made an arrangement for his two-year-old daughter to eventually marry Lothar II, son of Hugh of Arles, Rudolf's rival for power, in order to secure peace between the two states. Modern historical sources place the date of this marital transaction to a later year, more likely after the death of Rudolf II in July of 937. Four months later, in December of 937, Adelheid's widowed mother Bertha married Hugh of Arles and moved with her daughter to Pavia, where Hugh's Italian court was situated. Adelheid spent her formative years at Pavia and married Lothar on December 12, 947. A daughter, Emma, was born from the union in 948.

Husband Poisoned

Into the unceasing battle for control of the Italian peninsula stepped another player in northern Italy, the Margrave Berengar of Ivrea. Descended from Charlemagne, Berengar was also a claimant to the *rex Italia* title, or king of Italy. He was grandson and namesake of Berengar I, himself the grandson of the aforementioned Louis the Pious and his wife Judith. In 950, the younger Berengar made a bold move to secure the title King of Italy: after forcing Hugh to abdicate, he was said to have invited Lothar to a banquet, after which Adelheid's young husband died. Berengar then demanded that the newly widowed Adelheid marry his own son, Adalbert of Ivrea, to cement the Berengarian claim to northern Italy. When she refused and attempted to cross the Alps to the safety of Burgundian lands, Berengar's forces pursued her entourage and took her by force, detaining her at a castle on an island in the middle of Lake Garda, near Como.

Adalbert's mother, Willa of Tuscany—the wife of Berengar II—was said to have been exceedingly cruel to Adelheid and even physically assaulted her in an attempt to coerce her into the marriage. After a few months, Adelheid managed to escape the island fortress via a water tunnel and fled to the protection of Bishop Adalard of Reggio. Adalard sent an emissary to Otto I, the Duke of Saxony and a figure of emerging power and influence in the bitterly divided fiefdoms of France, Germany, and Switzerland.

Otto was the grandson of the first Duke of Saxony, also called Otto. The second Duke of Saxony—son of the elder Otto and father of the younger—was Henry the Fowler, who worked assiduously to unify the warring fiefdoms of East Francia, the rump state once ruled by Louis the Pious and other descendants of Charlemagne. Adelheid's mother Bertha had been the daughter of one of Henry's most trusted courtiers. Otto continued his father's mission to bring Germanic and Frankish lands under a single rule. Through war as well as diplomacy, Otto united a large section of what became modern Germany into the Kingdom of Germany in 936. Otto was crowned Otto I, King of Germany, in the same cathedral in northern German, at Aachen, that had been built by Charlemagne more than a century before. The site was significant because Charlemagne had been granted the title Holy Roman Emperor by the pope in Rome, which made him successor to the Roman emperors that had ruled both pre-Christian and late-antiquity Western Europe.

Rescued by Future Husband

Otto controlled vast parts of Germany and had enacted major reforms to stabilize his realm. Previously he had been involved in the dispute between Adelheid's father Rudolf II and Hugh of Arles, and through this secured the allegiance of the Kingdom of Burgundy, Adelheid's homeland. It was this link that prompted Adelheid to request help from the German king after Berengar II's ruthless assassination of her husband Lothar. Otto set out with an army, crossed the Alps, and entered Lombardy in northern Italy in the late summer of 951; his son

Liudolf had already secured parts of this area on behalf of his father. Their combined armies marched southward and entered Pavia on September 23, 951. Otto, too, sought the title *rex Italia,* and with it the crown of the Holy Roman Empire. Berengar I, who died in 924, had been the last king of Italy who had also secured the title Emperor of the Romans, bestowed at the time only by the reigning pope in Rome.

Like Adelheid, Otto had lost his first spouse, Eadgyth of England. Eadgyth was the granddaughter of King Alfred the Great, the famed Anglo-Saxon leader who was one of England's earliest monarchs of a united realm of formerly warring chieftaincies. Seizing the opportunity presented to unite their families, Adelheid and Otto were married on Christmas Day of 951 in Pavia. Adelheid's dower of lands in the Kingdom of Burgundy, which she inherited upon the death of her father, were restored to her through Otto's intercession, as were her Lombardian possessions that came through her first marriage to Lothar.

Otto kept a roving court, but spent much of his time in Memleben in northern Germany, near present-day Magdeburg. The couple began a family, with sons Henry and Bruno born, respectively, in 952 and 953. Neither survived childhood. A daughter Matilda was born in 954, followed a year later by Otto II. During this period Adelheid's husband crisscrossed Germany several times on diplomatic and military missions. In 955, he led a massive army against an incursion of Magyars, or Hungarians, who were laying siege to Augsburg in southern Germany. Coming from deep inside Central Asia, the Magyars had been making westward incursions through the former Byzantine Empire and the loosely organized lands of the Slavs for the past two centuries. Their power grew steadily, and they remained one of the last Central European peoples to practice paganism.

Sent Missionaries to East

Otto's victory over the Magyar army near Lechfeld in 955 was a decisive turning point for his realm and for the Holy Roman Empire he sought to restore to power. After that, the Hungarian ruling dynasty was allowed to keep their previous territory—centered in present-day Hungary—on the condition that they formally accepted Christianity. A later Hungarian ruler, Istvan, married Gisela of Bavaria, whose great-grandfather was Henry the Fowler. Istvan is revered as St. Stephen, the first King of Hungary who more firmly imposed Christian rule on his nation.

After years of preparation, Otto led an army into Italy and marched to Rome. It is known that Adelheid and their young son accompanied him, and Pope John XII crowned the couple as co-regents of the Holy Roman Empire on February 2, 962. Their son Otto II was crowned co-Holy Roman Emperor five years later, in 967. Another providential match was arranged, this one between Otto II and Theophanu, a princess of Byzantium. The couple were wed at St. Peter's Basilica in Rome in 972. Adelheid had already become a grandmother at the age of 36, when the daughter from her first marriage, Emma, married a different Lothar, this one king of West Francia, and gave birth to a boy named Louis V around 967. That Louis would be the last direct descendent of Charlemagne to wear a crown, and he died childless, ending the Carolingian dynasty in Europe.

Regent for Grandson

In 973, Adelheid was widowed a second time when Otto died in Memleben. Adelheid bears the unusual distinction of being the wife, mother, and grandmother of a Holy Roman Emperor—arguably the most powerful figure in Western Europe during a period when the papacy was in a dramatically weakened state—as well as holding the title *coimperatrix,* or co-emperor, as Latin-language documents of the era designated her. Her son Otto II died in Rome in 983 during an outbreak of malaria, and Adelheid served as regent for her three-year-old grandson Otto III until his coronation in May of 996. Both her son and grandson spent much of their adult lives battling rival armies and claimants to their rule from various distant relatives, including the Bavarian line descended from Otto I's brother. They also expanded the *reich* founded by Otto into Poland and Baltic lands, and worked to bring these late pagan nations, too, into the Christian realm. Adelheid's grandson Otto III is also responsible for installing the first German-heritage pope, who took the name Gregory V. That pope was also Otto III's cousin and great-grandson of Otto I through Liutgarde, a daughter of Eadgyth and Otto I.

Patron of Cluniac Reformers

Holy Roman Empress Adelheid gave generously to monasteries and abbeys in the former Frankish and Burgundian lands, and to those in the Kingdom of Germany, too. Both she and Otto supported the sweeping ecclesiastical reforms of religious communities that began in the early tenth century in Cluny, France. She established a nunnery in Seltz in 991, located in the Alsace region on the Rhine River, where she died on December 16, 999.

Adelheid's lands, titles, and family connections made her the most powerful woman in late tenth-century Europe. Reports of her piety and charity were written by several notable figures, including a *vita* written by Hroswitha of Gandersheim, a Benedictine nun, and Bishop Odilo of Cluny. Liudprand, who became Bishop of Cremona, had spent his youth at the Pavian court of Hugh of Arles, and provided much of the information concerning Adelheid's first marriage, early widowhood, and imprisonment on the island in Lake Garda. Adelheid's second daughter, Matilda, became Princess-Abbess of Quedlinburg, the convent founded by Otto I's mother, St. Matilda of Ringelheim. Adelheid was canonized in 1097 by Pope Urban II.

Books

Liudprand, Bishop of Cremona, *The Complete Works of Liudprand of Cremona,* translated by Paolo Squatriti, Catholic University of America Press, 2007.

Queenship and Sanctity: The Lives of Mathilda and the Epitaph of Adelheid, edited by Sean Gilsdorf, Catholic University of America Press, 2004.□

Guido Adler

The Austrian music scholar Guido Adler (1855–1941) was a key founder of musicology as an academic discipline. He was among the first to use the word "Musikwissenschaft," the German equivalent of "musicology," to describe the formal academic study of music.

Adler's influence on the study of music was enormous. He transformed what had been a largely amateur field, devoted to biography and aesthetic appreciation, into a systematic science with clearly defined branches. For Adler, the history of music developed something like that of an organism, and he favored a holistic view of creativity in which a composer's life and music were not seen as separate realms but as part of the same historical phenomenon. Part of Adler's conception of musicology involved the creation of fixed, well-researched scholarly editions of musical works, based not on received traditions but on careful research into a composer's intentions. This activity still makes up a substantial portion of musicological research today, and the structure of the academic discipline of musicology, especially in Germany and in the United States, where many of Adler's students fled during the era of German fascism, still bears the stamp of Adler's ideas.

Impressed Priest

Guido Adler was born in the small town of Eibensch-tz in Moravia, then part of the Austro-Hungarian empire (it is now Ivančice, Czech Republic), on November 1, 1855. His father, a doctor, died when Adler was young, and the family moved to the larger city of Iglau (where composer Gustav Mahler also grew up). Although the family was Jewish, Adler caught the attention of a local priest who noticed his studious ways and gave him recommendations for continued schooling. The Adler family moved to Vienna in 1864, and Adler attended the *Akademisches Gymnasium*—in American terms a good college preparatory high school—and also a local monastery school.

At first Adler planned to become a lawyer. As early as 1868 he studied music at the Gesellschaft der Musikfreunde music conservatory with the great Austrian composer Anton Bruckner as one of his teachers, but by his own testimony he did so without enthusiasm. Adler enrolled at the University of Vienna in the mid-1870s, majoring in law and graduating in 1878. But while he was there he attended lectures by the philosopher Franz Brentano, who probably introduced him to new currents in the philosophy of science. In 1878 Adler got a job as a law clerk but left after three months, realizing that his true interest lay in music, not law, but that it was in scholarship, not composition, where his talent lay.

Working largely on his own and sometimes with only a piece of bread for dinner, Adler managed to publish a paper called "The Basic Classifications of Western Christian Music Before 1600." Among its readers was the Vienna music critic and professor Eduard Hanslick, who encouraged Adler,

DeAgostini/Getty Images

allowed him to attend his lectures and gave him advice on his *Habilitationsschrift*, a kind of thesis that would qualify Adler to teach music in an Austrian university or high school. Adler successfully defended this thesis, about the history of harmony, in 1881 and was appointed a *Privatdozent* or private teacher at the University of Vienna two years later.

Founded Journal

This was still a poorly paid position on the edge of the academic world, and over the next decade Adler set about producing a set of publications that would build his academic reputation. In 1884–1885, with two senior scholars, he founded the *Vierteljahrsschrift fül Musikwissenschaft* or Musicology Quarterly, the world's first academic journal devoted to musicology. The lead article in the journal was by Adler himself, and it was titled "The Scope, Method, and Aim of Musicology." Adler based his definitions of the young field largely on the study of natural sciences, and his rigorous explication earned him a professorship at the University of Prague in 1885.

The implications of Adler's article are still being felt today. For the first time, the study of music was seen as more than telling the stories of the lives of great composers and explaining the beauties of their works. Adler viewed the history of music as a developmental process in which compsers' lives and music were fundamentally intertwined with each other and with the larger historical forces among which they lived. In Adler's own words, as translated by Benjamin Breuer in *The Birth of Musicology from the Spirit of Evolution*,) "one ought to stress that the task of music historiography lies not in exploring the Beautiful in art but in discovering the development process of music in works and creators." Although Adler himself thought of musicology as devoted solely to the European classical tradition, later researchers began to apply his idea of systematic musicology to the traditions of world music as well.

A new and important part of musicology in Adler's view was the production of scholarly editions of music: bound library volumes of works by famous composers or music in a specific historical tradition, designed to give an accurate rendering of how composers intended their music to sound and to strip away decades or centuries of distortions introduced in commercial sheet-music editions. Adler took the lead himself in this regard as editor of the series *Denkmäler der Tonkunst in Österreich* (Monuments of Musical Art in Austria), whose first volume appeared in 1894 and which continued until 1952. Adler remained the series' editor until the *Anschluss* or unification of Nazi Germany in Austria in 1938.

Overcame Anti-Semitism

Although he was himself an unorthodox and liberal Jew who often celebrated the Sabbath by taking long nature walks, Adler had begun to suffer negative consequences resulting from anti-Semitism long before that. At each stage of his rise up the academic ladder, he faced resistance from German nationalists who conspired against him because of his Jewish faith. His patrons, however, included the influential Hanslick, who had emerged as the primary critical opponent of the intensely German-centered operatic music of composer Richard Wagner. In 1898, Adler succeeded Hanslick as professor of music at the University of Vienna. This finally brought Adler a measure of material success, and he moved his wife and three children into a substantial house on a streetcar line connecting Vienna and one of its new suburbs.

Adler's opponents were irritated not only by his Jewish background but also because he committed what was to them the cardinal sin of championing non-German music. In 1892 Adler organized the music division of an International Music and Theatre Exhibition in Vienna, taking the opportunity to mount a production of the Czech-language comic opera *The Bartered Bride*, by Bedrich Smetana; the work was little known at the time, but Adler had encountered it in Prague. Germanic purists howled, but the opera went on to become one of the most popular in the standard repertory. Never retreating to the ivory tower, Adler had a flair for mounting large public music festivals that showcased the latest scholarly discoveries. In 1909 he staged a festival marking the bicentennial of the birth of Joseph Haydn, most of whose music was little known at the time. Adler did not return the hostility shown him by German nationalists; among his books was a series of lectures on Wagner, published in 1904. He also wrote a book about Mahler and an autobiography, *Wollen und Wirken* (Desires and Accomplishments, 1935).

In 1927 Adler was a central figure in the organization of the International Musicological Society, which is still active today. His influence in the field of musicology lived on partly through his students, some of whom fled Austria in the 1930s and began to set up American university music departments along the lines Adler had suggested. The famed Haydn biographer Karl Geiringer was among Adler's students, and his University of Vienna lectures, popular despite what is reputed to have been his unpleasant temper, attracted the avant-garde composer Anton Webern among others.

One of Adler's children died in a Nazi concentration camp, and he himself was saved only by advanced age from a similar fate; orders were given for his arrest, but his housekeeper met the solider tasked with the job at the door and protested that Adler was 84 years old. The soldier departed. Adler remained in Vienna, but his family managed to send his personal papers to the United States; an archive is housed at the University of Georgia. Adler died in Vienna on February 15, 1941; his death was ignored, but after World War II he was reburied in Vienna's Central Cemetery, the resting place of various prestigous Austrians. In the words of the *New Grove Dictionary of Music and Musicians,* "Modern musicology owes a great debt to Adler."

Books

Sadie, Stanley, ed., *New Grove Dictionary of Music and Musicians,* 2nd ed., Macmillan, 2001.

Slonimsky, Nicolas, ed. emeritus, *Baker's Biographical Dictionary of Musicians,* centennial ed., Schirmer, 2001.

Online

Breuer, Benjamin, *The Birth of Musicology from the Spirit of Evolution: Ernst Haeckel's Entwicklungslehre as Central Component of Guido Adler's Methodology for Musicology* (Ph.D. dissertation, University of Pittsburgh, 2011), http://www.d-scholarship.pitt.edu/7236/1/Breuer2011.pdf (October 5, 2014).

"Guido Adler, 1855–1941," Hargrett Rare Book & Manuscript Library (University of Georgia Libraries), http://www.libs.uga.edu/hargrett/manuscrip/adler/ (October 5, 2014).

"Guido Adler's 'The Scope, Method, and Aim of Musicology' (1885): An English Translationwith an Historico-Analytical Commentary," *Yearbook for Traditional Music,* 1981, http://www.web.ff.cuni.cz/ustavy/mus/pdf/gabrielova/Mugglestone_AdlersTheScopeMethod AndAimOf Musicology.pdf , (October 5, 2014). □

Samuel Akintola

Nigerian politician Samuel Akintola (1910-1966) was elected as the premier of the Western Region three times, for two different political parties. Deeply involved with the divisive politics of Nigeria in the mid-20th century, Akintola was assassinated during a military coup that removed President Benjamin Azikiwe from office.

Keystone Pictures USA/Alamy

Born July 6, 1910, in Ogbomosho, Nigeria, Samuel Ladoke Akintunde Akintola was the son of Akintola and Akanke. Both of his parents were members of the Yoruba ethnic group. His father's family had been traders of goods and slaves for centuries, while his mother was the daughter of a chief, Oyeniya from Oje-ile. He had a title, Oloye Aare Ona Kakanfo XIII of the Yorba.

Educated at Christian Schools

Aktinola's father moved the family to Minna, in northern Nigeria, when Akintola was four years old. There, he attended local schools run by the Christian Missionary Society. His father went missing in 1918, on his way to Lagos to buy merchandise. Though his family was unsure of his fate, he had been caught up in a rebellion of the Egba people, and had to escape the situation. He returned to his family in 1919.

After the end of World War II, Aktintola's attendance at school became more sporadic because his father did not see the benefits to regular attendance and wanted to teach his son about his business. Akintola's education became more regular after 1922, when his father sent him to live with Akinbola, Akintola's grandfather, in Ogbomosho. There, Akintola attended the Baptist Day School from 1922 to 1925, then entered Baptist College in 1925. The latter institution was both a seminary and teacher's college. Akintola focused on teaching, and also became a voracious reader of literature in English.

Became a Teacher

When Akintola graduated from Baptist College in 1930, he was hired as a science teacher at the Baptist Academy in Lagos. In addition to teaching biology and general science, he was an instructor in scripture and religious instruction. As a teacher, Akintola had a reputation for strictness and demanding the best of his students.

While employed as a teacher, Akintola also was active in the Baptist Teachers' Union, serving as secretary. He was the editor of the *Nigerian Baptist* from 1939 to 1943 as well. In this period, Akintola was married to a nurse, Faderera Awomolo, with whom he would have five children.

In 1942, Akintola resigned from his position after the school fired several teachers who presented a petition for better working and living conditions. Explaining his decision, Akinjide Osuntokun wrote in *Chief S. Ladoke Akintola: His Life and Times,* ''Being Secretary of the Baptist Teachers' Union, Ladoke therefore felt that continued stay in the employment of the Baptist Mission ran counter to his commitment to collective responsibility for an action taken by the union, and one of which he was Secretary.''

Unprepared for unemployment, Akintola took a civil service exam and briefly worked in general administration for the Nigerian Railways department. He also gave lectures around Lagos. He then joined the editorial staff of the *Nigerian Service Daily,* and became its editor in 1943. Akintola held this position until 1946, withstanding criticism for opposing a general strike called in 1945. He also continued to speak in Lagos, appearing before many literary societies in the city.

Educated in England

After leaving the *Nigerian Service Daily,* Akintola founded and edited a weekly Yoruba newspaper, the *Irohin Yoruba.* He also won a British Council Scholarship in 1946. While working for the *Nigerian Service Daily,* he had studied to take the University of London matriculation examination that needed to be passed so he could enter an English university. Mastering the exam, he used the scholarship to attend a college of journalism for one year.

When Akintola began attending the school in England, he realized he had wider ambitions and wanted to further his education there. Garnering financial support from friends in Nigeria, he spent three years studying the law at Barnet House and Lincoln's Inn. To support himself, he worked at the British Rail station in Euston. During this period, Akintola also became interested in Communism and attended party meetings for a time.

After being called to the bar in England in 1949, Akintola returned to Nigeria to practice law in March of 1950. Primarily based in Lagos, he handled cases there and in Yorubaland. Many of his cases involved land disputes. By 1952, Akintola established a partnership with Chris Oladipo Ogunbanjo and Michael A. Odesanya, forming the law firm of Samuel, Chris, and Michael.

Became Involved in Politics

Also during this period, Akintola became more actively involved in politics after being interested in and affiliated with various movements, including the Nigerian Youth Movement. In the early 1950s, he played an active role in the founding of the political party, Action Group, helmed by Obafemi Awolowo. The party was intended to present a united front for the people of Western Nigeria at the British conferences related to Nigeria's constitution and future. It was also to counter the vast influence of the National Council of Nigeria and the Cameroons party and its leader Nnamdi Azikiwe.

In elections held in the 1951, Awolowo became the premier of the Western Region of Nigeria while Akintola was elected to the federal House of Representatives of Nigeria. In the Nigerian House, he served as the leader of the opposition Action Group parliamentary party. He also held a number of posts in various ministries, including the Ministries of Labour, Health, and Welfare. While part of Labour, he made speeches and appearances around Nigeria, further raising his public profile.

By 1953, Akintola became active in the Nigerian independence movement. He called for Nigeria to be free by 1956, and to that end, toured the hostile northern region of Nigeria to promote his cause. His backing of this movement only increased after elections held in 1954, when he became the deputy leader and national vice president of the Action Group because of his widely recognized qualifications and leadership actions. By 1957, he played a key role in getting the motion to support independence passed in Parliament.

Elected Western Region Premier

Building on his popularity and higher profile, Akintola became the premier of the Western Region in 1960. His tenure in this position was short-lived, ending as a result of political intrigue. When Akintola became premier, he had a disagreement with his Action Group political party and Awolowo in what amounted to a power struggle. Both Awolowo and Akintola had strong personalities, and their differing visions came into conflict at this time.

The clash manifested itself in several ways. Akintola refused to give some of the best positions in his government to members of his party. One such incident focused on an economic mission to Europe helmed by Akintola. Awolowo, by then head of the Action Group party, wanted certain candidates to accompany Akintola, but the premier turned them down and brought his own choices. Other disagreements focused on renewing board appointments as well as ideological differences.

Though there were attempts in 1962 to come to an understanding, Akintola's party ordered him to resign as a result of such disagreements, but he flatly refused. Akintola tried to maintain control and diffuse the situation by asking the parliamentary speaker to summon the legislative body. He wanted a vote of confidence in the house of representative. The speaker in turn refused.

Addressed Political Intrigue

Next, Akintola petitioned the governor to dissolve parliament and hold elections, but the governor would not agree to this idea. To avoid dismissal, he looked to the constitution

of Western Nigeria. The document gave him the right to give advice directly to the British monarch on appointing and removing the governor, even though Nigeria was now a former British colony. Akintola wanted to exercise this right to Queen Elizabeth II.

Before he could, Akintola was dismissed in 1962. Nonetheless, Akintola offered his advisement to the queen. He argued that he could not be dismissed under the constitution without a vote of no confidence in parliament. Furthermore, he took the case to court. The queen declined to intervene because Akintola had already been dismissed. The Supreme Court of Nigeria ruled that Akintola was correct, however, and he had been illegally dismissed. Because of the ruling, the queen was compelled legally to accept his advice.

The intrigue continued because the federal government in Nigeria had declared a state of emergency in the meantime. The offices of premier and governor had been suspended. The governor still made an appeal to the British Privy Council, which held that Akintola had been legally removed from office. The Privy Council's decision was not completed in time as the state of emergency ended and Akintola was restored as premier in 1963.

Became Leader of New Political Party

The situation grew even more complex. Queen Elizabeth took Akintola's advice and removed the governor from office. To address the decision rendered by the Privy Council, Akintola ensured that the constitution had a retroactive amendment that would not allow his dismissal without a vote of no confidence. As a result of this crisis, Akintola switched political parties by the mid-1960s, becoming the leader of his own Nigerian National Democratic party. Representing this party, he was re-elected as premier of the Western Region in 1965.

Shortly before national elections in late 1964, Nigeria experienced a difficult period where its economic and political development essentially ended. This was the first general election held after the country achieved independence. Anti-government violence ensued during this election as well as the Western Region election in which Akintola was elected again as premier of the region.

There was widespread opposition to Akintola and his government, which became an open revolt by December 1965. Though Akintola believed that it was outside agitators causing most of the problems, the violence and persistence of the opposition led to the import of police personnel from the north region to address the issues. Arson and the killing of Akintola's supporters was widespread. By this time, Akintola was unsure he could manage the crisis and considered resigning. He believed Fani-Kayode would do a better job.

Assassinated During Coup

Despite extraordinary efforts to protect himself, Akintola was soon a victim of violence. In early 1966, a military coup led by anti-government forces and coordinated by Major Chukwuma Nzeogwu removed Nigerian president Benjamin Azikiwe from office. In the process, a number of

Nigerian national and regional officials were injured or lost their lives. The three leaders assassinated that day included the federal prime minister, Sir Abubakar Tafawa Balewa; the Northern region premier, Ahmadu Bello; and Akintola. He died on January 15, 1966, at the age of 55.

After their deaths, a new head of state took office, Major General Aguiyi-Ironsi. More unrest continued as the coup did not solve fundamental tensions within Nigeria, and soon erupted into civil war. By 1967, the Biafran War broke out.

Though controversial, Akintola's legacy was not forgotten. According to *All Africa,* professor Jide Osuntokun described Akintola as an important Nigerian and an important Yoruba. Osuntokun stated, "He was the last premier of Western Nigeria, public orator, polyglot and a great exponent of the Yoruba language and heritage."

Books

The Columbia Electronic Encyclopedia, Columbia University Press, 2013.

Vance, Jonathan F., ed. *Encyclopedia of Prisoners of War and Internment,* 2nd ed., Grey House Publishing, 2006.

Osuntokun, Akinjide, *Chief S. Ladoke Akintola: His Life and Times,* Frank Cass, 1984.

Periodicals

All Africa, January 15, 2014.

The Australian, October 12, 2012. □

Giulio Alberoni

Italian-born Cardinal Giulio Alberoni (1664–1752) was best known not for his activities as a religious official but as a court official and statesman. From 1716 to 1719 he was Spain's prime minister.

Alberoni came to Spain during the War of the Spanish Succession (1701–1714), a period of intense instability that drew in most of the major European powers of the day. He had no roots in Spain but came there with a French military commander. Nevertheless, he moved easily among the top circles of the Spanish nobility and, by ingratiating himself with the right people at the right time, emerged as the country's leader. Over his three years as prime minister he instituted several important reforms but also launched ill-considered attacks on southern Italy and the island of Sardinia in a futile effort to recover lost Spanish power and prestige. In his later years he was active in Catholic church affairs in his native Italy. Although sometimes compared with the cardinals who were active in French state affairs, Alberoni became a high church official only as a result of political pressure, and many years separated his election as cardinal and his consecration (or ordination) in that post.

Quagga Media/Alamy

Worked as Bell-Ringer at Cathedral

Giulio Alberoni was born on May 31, 1664, in Firenzuola d'Arda near Piacenza, Italy, in what was then the Duchy of Parma. He was of modest origins: his father was a gardener, and his mother, as Simon Harcourt-Smith put it in *Alberoni or The Spanish Conspiracy,* "a seamstress disturbed by frequent pregnancies." He was one of six children. Alberoni was put to work in local gardens himself as a child. His introduction to church life came when he was hired as a bell-ringer at Piacenza's great Romanesque cathedral. In 1674 his father died, and he was forced to support his family through whatever work he could get. In his early teens he worked as a clerk at the church of Santi Nazzaro e Celso in the nearby town of Agazzano.

Alberoni's escape from dire poverty came thanks to a group of Piacenza priests of the Barnabite order who undertook to give him a basic religious and literary education. By 1680 he was studying philsophy at a Jesuit religious school, and he made friends with a lawyer from Ravenna, Ignazio Gardini, who made him an assistant. Gardini was, for unknown reasons, expelled from Piacenza in 1685, and Alberoni followed his employer to Ravenna. There he met a church leader, Giorgio Barni, who in turn was chosen as bishop of Piacenza, brought Alberoni back to his home area, and served as his mentor. In the late 1680s or early 1690s Alberoni was ordained as a priest, and in 1691 he became the pastor at Santi Nazzaro e Celso.

Bishop Barni then hired Alberoni as a tutor for his nephew Giambattista Barni, who later became an important Catholic leader himself. Alberoni accompanied the younger Barni to Rome in 1696. Barni was supposed to further his education there, but unconfirmed contemporary reports from several sources suggest that he spent most of his time with girls with whom Alberoni set him up. Alberoni himself, however, took advantage of the great city's educational resources while he was there: he learned to speak French, which at the time was a smart move for a man with ambitions.

Sent on Diplomatic Mission

Back in Piacenza, Alberoni obtained a prebend—an ecclesiastical stipend connected with a senior church post—at the city's cathedral, where he had once rung the bells, in 1698. His reputation as a rising church leader with strong administrative skills snared him an appointment as private secretary to a member of the Duke of Parma's ambassadorial staff. This led to his being asked to undertake a diplomatic mission to the Duke of Vendôme, the commander of France's army in Italy, in 1702. According to the French memoirist Louis de Rouvroy (1675–1755), known as Saint-Simon, Alberoni was sent as a replacement for the Duke of Parma, whose own mission had ended ignominiously: the Duke of Vendôme, who had a fondness for a kind of rough humor he associated with ancient Rome, received the Duke of Parma while seated on the toilet and then compounded the insult by turning his back and wiping himself. The Duke of Parma, aghast, departed and returned home to Parma.

Alberoni, according to Saint-Simon, handled the situation better. When the Duke of Vendôme repeated his performance, Alberoni cried (as quoted in a translation of Saint-Simon by Robert Wernick) ''O culo di Angelo!'' (oh, angelic ass!) and proceeded to kneel and kiss the duke on the posterior. The duke was delighted. Alberoni returned to Parma to take up a post as canon at Parma Cathedral in 1703, but the Duke of Vendôome remembered the churchman who had gotten his joke and offered him a job as his private secretary. Alberoni returned to Paris in 1706, and when the duke began to travel frequently in the later stages of the war, Alberoni went with him.

From 1706 to 1711 Alberoni lived in the Netherlands, part of which was still under Spanish control. Alberoni accompanied the duke to Spain in 1711. The following year the duke died, and Alberoni, by now a consummate insider, was named Parma's ambassador to Spain. He used this post intelligently to advance his ambitions still further: he arranged the marriage of Spain's widowed King Philip (Felipe) V to Elisabetta Farnese, the niece of the duke of Parma. They married, by proxy, in 1714. When she finally arrived in Spain, Elisabetta set about establishing her own influence at court and demanded that her countryman Alberoni be made prime minister. In 1716 the king complied.

Instituted Transcontinental Mail Service

As prime minister, Alberoni instituted economic and social reforms that were intended to streamline Spanish economic activity and restore the nation's competitiveness. He reduced the influence of the grandees, or nobility, in Spanish society, and he took steps to ease import regulations for materials coming from Spain's colonies in the Western hemisphere. Under Alberoni, a regular mail service between Spain and the Americas was instituted. He was also responsible for several domestic economic reforms. With an eye toward future conflicts, and knowing that Philip wanted to restore Spanish holdings in Italy lost under the Treaty of Utrecht that had ended the war, he reorganized Spain's army and navy.

Unfortunately, Philip pressured Alberoni to act before he was ready. Alberoni ordered Spanish invasions of Sardinia in 1717 and Sicily in southern Italy the following year, and he tried to obtain international support for the restoration of the Stuart dynasty to the British throne, backing Jacobite forces in Scotland who supported the move. These acts of aggression proved disastrous for Spain. The British initiative came to nothing, and the combined forces of France, England, the Netherlands, and the Holy Roman Empire expelled the Spanish from Sardinia and invaded the Spanish province of Navarre. With most of the European powers arrayed against him, Philip V gave up, removed Alberoni as prime minister, and expelled him from Spain. Alberoni arrived in Italy in 1720 and was arrested by forces loyal to Pope Clement XI, to whom he had pledged not to invade Italy. He escaped from confinement but had to go into hiding in the mountains.

Alberoni was saved by the death of Clement XI in 1721. He had been elected as a cardinal in Málaga, Spain, in 1717, but his consecration ceremony did not take place until 1725. Nevertheless, he was allowed to participate in the conclave of cardinals that chose Innocent XIII as pope. Alberoni was sentenced to four years in prison for his part in the Spanish military operation, but the new pope issued a brief clearing him of his crimes. Mostly he lived quietly, participating in several more papal conclaves, but he dabbled once again in politics, accepting an appointment as papal legate (or representative) to the Romagna region in 1735. He remained there until 1739.

Returning to Piacenza in old age, Alberoni died a wealthy man there on June 26, 1752. He founded the Collegio S. Lazzaro in Piacenza; still in existence, it is now named the Collegio Alberoni. Renowned as a gourmet whose advice on cuisine was sought at the Spanish court, Alberoni lives on in memory as the namesake of the Timballo Alberoni, a baked macaroni-and-cheese dish with shrimp.

Books

Harcourt-Smith, Simon, *Alberoni: or, The Spanish Conspiracy,* Faber & Faber, 1943.

Harcourt-Smith, Simon, *Cardinal of Spain: The Life and Strange Career of Giulio Alberoni,* Knopf, 1955.

Online

''Alberoni, Giulio (1664–1752),'' *The Cardinals of the Holy Roman Church,* http://www2.fiu.edu/~mirandas/conclave-xviii.htm (January 7, 2015).

''Gossip Redux,'' http://www.robertwernick.com/articles/Gosslittwo.htm (January 7, 2015).□

Richard Aldington

The writings of British author Richard Aldington (1892–1962) covered an unusually broad range from poetry to novels, essays, and literary biography. Collectively they form a detailed portrait of British society in the early 20th century, including the all-important experience of World War I.

In the first part of his career, Aldington was known as a member of the Imagist movement, a group of British and American poets who pared their poetic language down to minimalist, economical images. He experienced trench warfare in World War I, suffering the effects of poison gas deployed by Germany against entrenched British forces. The experience permanently shaped Aldington's art, showing up first in his poetry, then in the autobiographical novel *Death of a Hero,* and generally in a sharply critical attitude toward British society. Later in life Aldington favored neither poetry nor fiction, putting much of his energy into a series of often controversial biographies of other writers. Aldington lived much of his life outside his native Britain, whose literary establishment he gradually antagonized. Partly as a result, his works are less often read today than they were formerly, although they offer vivid portraits of British literary life and of the genteel world that World War I swept away.

RIA Novosti/Alamy

Became Engrossed in Literature

Richard Aldington was born on July 8, 1892, in Portsmouth, England, and grew up partly in Dover. Aldington's father was a lawyer, prosperous for a time, and Aldington attended private schools where he learned to read French and Latin and studied the literary classics, helped along by a large library his father had at home. He was bitten by the poetry bug at 15 when he read the long John Keats poem "Endymion," and he began to think of literature as a refuge from dull small-town life. Reading ever more voraciously, he scored an unheard-of 98 out of a possible 100 points on an entrance exam he took prior to matriculating at the University of London in 1910.

What seemed to be a brilliant academic career was cut short the following year as Aldington's father suffered financial setbacks. The 19-year-old Aldington had the chance to take a financially reliable position as a clerk, but instead chose the riskier course of trying to make a living as a writer. For a time he earned a living as a part-time sports reporter, but he also translated writings from French, began to land reviews and essays in literary journals, and had a few of his own poems published. This process brought Aldington into the social circle of other struggling young writers, and in 1913 he married one of them, the American-born Hilda Doolittle, who used the pen name H.D.

Among the couple's friends were another American poet, Ezra Pound, who became perhaps the best-known figure of the Imagist movement. In 1914 Pound published an anthology called *Des Imagistes* that included some of

Aldington's poems. Aldington, H.D., Pound, and the other Imagist poets rejected the dense, allusion-filled poetry of the Victorian era in favor of depicting ideas as much as possible through a series of simple images, connected by a minimum of syntactical devices. "The heavy musty air, the black desks, / The bent heads and the rustling noises / In the great dome / Vanish... / And / The sun hangs in the cobalt blue sky," Aldington wrote in "At the British Museum." Another important friend Aldington made was the editor Harold Munro, who published Aldington's first book, *Images (1910–1915),* in 1915.

Joined Military

Aldington had already begun to extend his literary tendrils beyond London. Some of his poems were published in *Poetry* magazine in Chicago, and he traveled through France and Italy, on one occasion dressing up in a futuristic cloth costume to go to hear the Italian poet Marinetti. From 1914 to 1916 Aldington himself edited an Imagist magazine, *The Egoist.* These heady literary adventures came to an end in 1916 when Aldington enlisted in the British army, was sent to the front, and suffered a poison gas attack while stationed in a trench. By 1918 he had reached the rank of captain, but emerged with a case of shell shock, which today would be called post-traumatic stress syndrome.

Back in England after the war, Aldington succeeded in resuming his literary career. He published several more books of poetry, but *Images of War* (1919) had a grim tone that reflected his wartime experiences, and he eventually gave up writing poetry altogether. That year he separated from Doolittle; the two were eventually divorced, and in 1938 Aldington married Netta McCullough. The pair had a daughter, Catherine. Although his view of human nature had darkened, Aldington was a prolific writer who became successful enough to live where he chose; in 1928 he left England and lived mostly in France and Italy for the rest of his life, except for a stint of several years in the United States during World War II.

In the late 1920s Aldington turned to the novel as a way of expressing his experiences. *Death of a Hero,* the first of his eight novels, appeared in 1929 and has remained one of his best-regarded works. Drawing on Aldington's own experiences during the war, although it is clear from the beginning that its hero does not survive, the novel has been likened to Erich Maria Remarque's *All Quiet on the Western Front* and Ernest Hemingway's *A Farewell to Arms* in its unsparing depiction of the horrors of trench warfare— and also of the alienation experienced by war veterans. Part of the novel takes place as the hero, George Winter-bourne, returns home on a leave of absence.

Another section of *Death of a Hero* satirizes the literary scene before the war; Aldington had come to see the literary world of which he himself had been part as out of touch with the dangers and social trends that led to war. Several of his other novels, although they do not deal with the war, likewise trace the decline of older English ways of life; *The Colonel's Daughter* (1931) and *Women Must Work* (1934) examine the situation of women whose horizons are constricted by traditional gender roles. Only *The Romance of Casanova* (1946) does not have a contemporary English setting.

Wrote Controversial Biographies

After *The Romance of Casanova,* Aldington once again abandoned a genre in which he had experienced considerable success. Many of the books from the last 20 years of his life were biographies, and this new turn in his career again attracted considerable attention. The first was *The Duke: Being an Account of the Life & Achievements of Arthur Wellesley, 1st Duke of Wellington* (1943); this account of the life of the general who defeated Napoleon at Waterloo, won the James Tait Black Memorial Prize. Aldington followed that with biographies of British novelist D.H. Lawrence and American poet Robert Louis Stevenson. Most controversial was his 1955 book about T.E. Lawrence, *Lawrence of Arabia: A Biographical Inquiry,* which was condemned for the then-shocking suggestion that Lawrence was gay. That, and other assertions in the book, remain live topics in research on Lawrence's life.

The summary of Aldington's works presented here does not come close to covering the volume and variety of his writings. He also wrote books of literary criticism, an autobiography (*Life for Life's Sake,* 1941), plays, and short stories, and he translated and edited a wide variety of writings, including collections of letters of his own and other writers. Over his 45-year publication career he was the author, co-author, or translator of more than 90 books.

Feeling that he had been given short shrift by Britain's literary establishment, Aldington visited Moscow in 1962 to accept an award from the Soviet Writers' Union although his own politics were somewhat conservative by that time. His novels were widely known in the Soviet Union. Shortly after his return to his home in Sury-en-Vaux, France, he became ill and died suddenly on July 27, 1962. Many of Aldington's personal materials are housed in U.S. collections at Southern Illinois, Harvard, and Yale universities, and the University of Texas. Critical studies of Aldington since the 1970s have been sparse.

Books

Aldington, Richard, *Life for Life's Sake: A Book of Reminiscences,* Viking, 1941.

Dictionary of Literary Biography, Gale, Volume 20: *British Poets, 1914–1945,* 1983; *Volume 36: British Novelists, 1890–1929: Modernists,* 1985; *Volume 100: Modern British Essayists,* 1990; *Volume 149: Late Nineteenth- and Early Twentieth-Century British Literary Biographers,* 1995.

Gates, Norman, *The Poetry of Richard Aldington: A Critical Evaluation and an Anthology of Uncollected Poems,* Pennsylvania State, 1974.

Online

"Richard Aldington," *Poetry Foundation,* http://www.poetry foundation.org/bio/richard-aldington (October 4, 2014).

"Richard Aldington: Biographical Sketch," University of Texas Libraries, http://www.lib.utexas.edu/taro/uthrc/00005/hrc-00005.html (October 4, 2014).□

Franz Alexander

Hungarian-born American Franz Alexander (1891–1964) was a leading 20th century psychoanalyst and helped spread the discipline throughout the United States. The founder of the Chicago Psychoanalytic Institute, Alexander published a number of important texts on psychoanalysis. He was particularly interested in the study of juvenile crime.

Franz Gabriel Alexander was born on January 22, 1891, in Budapest, Hungary, the son of Bernard and Regina (Broessler) Alexander. His father was Jewish, and a philosophy and history professor at the University of Budapest. Alexander's academic and intellectual interests were impacted by his father and his uncle, who was a chemical engineer and exposed his nephew to the meticulousness of scientific discipline.

Had Early Interest in the Humanities

Early on, Alexander was interested in the humanities, languages, and aesthetics. By high school, he was more focused on science, though the humanistic pursuits continued to be of interest. Brain-related research also emerged as a favored pursuit. Alexander earned his B.A. from the Humanistic Gymnasium in Budapest in 1908.

Pursuing medical studies, Alexander first attended the University of Göttingen in Germany. There, Alexander also took notice of new knowledge in the areas of mathematics, theoretical physics, and philosophy. Returning to Budapest to finish his medical training, Alexander also focused on biochemistry and physiology research. The latter pursuit especially centered on brain-related physiology. He completed his M.D. at the University of Budapest in 1913. As he completed his training, World War I broke out.

During the war, Alexander served in the Austro-Hungarian Army and spent some time stationed at a field laboratory dedicated to bacteriology. In addition to acting as a bacteriologist, he was a military physician who served on a number of battlefronts. After the war ended in 1918, Alexander continued to pursue brain physiology research at the University of Budapest's neuropsychiatric clinic.

Pursued Education in Psychoanalysis

In the post-war period, Alexander became increasingly interested in psychoanalysis and its viability in a clinical setting. During medical school, he had read *The Interpretation of Dreams* by Sigmund Freud, who had formulated the theories and early practices of psychoanalysis. But it was not until Alexander worked in the psychiatric clinic that he came to see the examinations and testing that were part of psychiatry as less effective than psychoanalysis.

Changing his career path, Alexander moved to Berlin, Germany, in 1919, to pursue training in psychoanalysis. There, he did post-graduate work at the University of Berlin's psychiatric hospital. When the Berlin Psychoanalytic Institute was founded, Alexander became its first student. His instructors included Hanns Sachs, who also served as Alexander's analyst. Alexander soon became an assistant there as well. He later became a clinical associate and a lecturer. As he began training others in analysis, Alexander came to believe that psychoanalysis was a branch of psychiatry and became quite skilled in the techniques of psychoanalytic therapy.

Alexander's abilities in, and depth of understanding of, psychoanalysis soon attracted the attention and support of Freud. In 1921, the same year Alexander was admitted to the German Psychoanalytic Society, his study "The Castration Complex in the Formation of Character," won an award from Freud. A few years later, in 1924 and 1925, Alexander gave lectures at the Berlin Institute which further stretched the theory of the superego. Such work impressed not only Freud, but others in the psychoanalytic community as well.

Published Noteworthy Books

Remaining affiliated with the institute through the 1920s, Alexander conducted research and began publishing books. Further expanding his theory of the superego, he considered the psychology of the psychoanalytic ego by reformulating the study of neuroses in his 1927 book, *Psychoanalyse der Gesamtpersönlichkeit; neun Vorlesungen über die Anwendung von Freud's Ich-Theorie auf die Neurosenlehre* (Psychoanalysis of the Total Personality). This book was greatly informed by his experiences in Berlin.

Alexander's next book built on the ideas about the superego presented in *Psychoanalysis of the Total Personality*. He believed that psychoanalytic principles could be applied to criminology. Working with a lawyer, Hugh Staub, as a co-author, they wrote a book that offered information on understanding and diagnosing criminal personalities. Their definitive study of criminology from a psychoanalytic perspective was published in 1929 as *Der Verbrecher und seine Richter*. (It was published in English as *The Criminal, the Judge, and the Public: A Psychological Analysis*.) This book garnered wide attention in Europe and the United States.

Throughout the 1920s, many of Alexander's key ideas about analysis were being formed. For Alexander, psychoanalysis should provide patients with a means of exploring their minds to achieve more fulfilling lives. He developed an interest in psychosomatic symptoms, believing they originated in neurotic conflicts from childhood. Alexander also argued that dreams occurred in complementary pairs to achieve wish fulfillment. Perhaps of greater controversy, especially later in his career, were Alexander's theories on lessening the amount of therapy needed through such means as the transference relationship between patient and analyst.

Took Positions in the United States

In the 1930s, Alexander's career would shift from Europe to the United States. Because of the book *The Criminal, the Judge, and the Public: A Psychological Analysis*, Alexander was asked to come to the International Congress for Mental Hygiene, held in Washington, D.C., in 1930. While at the conference, Robert Hutchins, the new president of the University of Chicago, offered him a one-year visiting psychiatry professorship at the University of Chicago Medical School as a means of introducing psychiatry into the curriculum. Alexander wanted to be a visiting professor of psychoanalysis instead.

An agreement was reached between officials at the University of Chicago and Alexander, whereby a first university chair in psychoanalysis in the world was established. Alexander became the first to hold it and moved to Chicago in 1930. He taught only psychoanalysis and psychoanalytic psychiatry during his year in the post. Academics and students in social science, philosophy, and law were more interested in Alexander's classes than doctors, though a few showed interest.

After leaving Chicago, Alexander went to Boston as a research associate at the Judge Baker Foundation. He conducted research with the foundation's director, William Healy, on issues related to juvenile delinquency and criminology. Like Alexander, Healy was a psychoanalyst. Alexander's experiences here informed his 1935 book *The Roots of Crime*, written with Healy.

In this book, the pair focused on exploring why individuals, especially juveniles, commit crimes and are impacted by crime causation. In this context, they looked at how people were affected by economic and other environmental variables based on their personalities. They also considered individuals' perspectives on law and authority figures. The co-authors drew their data from psychoanalytic case studies on juveniles from the foundation. The treatment and understanding of juvenile crime would be a particular focus for Alexander throughout his career.

Founded the Chicago Psychoanalytic Institute

During the this period, Alexander also emerged as a public face of medicine focusing on psychoanalysis. His activity in this area increased in this period, before the publication of *The Roots of Crime.* In 1932, Alexander returned to Chicago and founded the influential Chicago Psychoanalytic Institute. For two decades, until 1952, he served as director of the institute. While leading the organization, he was known for his authoritarian administrative attitude, ruling as something of a benevolent ruler.

Modeling the center on the Berlin Psychoanalytic Institute, Alexander envisioned the Chicago Psychoanalytic Institute as a training center for psychoanalysts who also conducted research and held clinical practices—all outside of a university. The institute also offered credentialing for analysts. The institute's home building included classrooms, a library, and a dining room for staff to facilitate communication.

Inviting analysts already in Chicago while also recruiting those from other cities and countries to come to the institute, Alexander implemented a structure that included lifetime appointments for some analysts and ensure collaboration for training and research. He also reached out to the medical community in Chicago, and trained its leaders in the principles of psychoanalysis.

In addition, Alexander ensured that the institute was organizationally separate from the Chicago Psychoanalytic Society, which admitted Alexander as a member in 1933. As a result of his organizational decisions, many conflicting and divergent viewpoints were tolerated in the institute. It also was key to the spread and acceptance of psychoanalysis. Some of those who received training and credentials there founded similar organizations in other cities like Topeka, Kansas, and Los Angeles, California.

Conducted Research in Psychosomatic Medicine

For Alexander, the institute provided support for his own research. Through his large grants gained from the Rockefeller Foundation, he explored various areas of psychosomatic medicine and other topics in psychoanalysis. His research into psychosomatic medicine was especially influential into the 1950s.

While affiliated with the institute, Alexander also worked elsewhere. In 1938, Alexander took on a new academic position. He joined the faculty of the University of Illinois as a professor of psychiatry. He would remain on staff until 1956. In 1939, Alexander was the co-founder of a new journal of review, *Psychosomatic Medicine.* The journal offered analysis of the nature and causes of psychosomatic (emotionally caused or based) illnesses and related theories.

By the early 1950s, Alexander's theories became more out of step with others at the Chicago Institute and the popular techniques of the time. For example, Alexander promoted treatment options such as undergoing analysis only three times per week. He also believed in what he termed a corrective emotional experience. For such reasons, as well as new opportunities in California, Alexander moved on.

Moved to California

After spending much of two decades based in Illinois, Alexander left the institute in the mid-1950s and moved to California. He was replaced as director of the Chicago Institute by Gerhart Peters. Beginning in 1955, he spent a year at the Palo Alto-based Center for Advanced Study in Behavioral Science. After his year term was completed, he became the head of Mount Sinai Hospital's newly established psychiatric department in 1956. At the same time, Alexander became a professor of psychiatry at the University of Southern California, and became affiliated with the Southern California Psychoanalytic Institute.

While holding these posts, Alexander used Ford Foundation funding to establish a research project that analyzed the nature of the psychotherapeutic process. It was conducted by observing the interactions between patients and therapists. He was especially interested in the impact of the therapist's personality in the therapeutic process. He also conducted research in other areas of psychosomatic studies, psychotherapy, and psychodynamic treatment.

Also in 1956, Alexander was one of the founders of the American Academy of Psychoanalysis. He also would served as the president of the organization. Alexander also would become the president of the American Psychoanalytical Association and the president of the American Society for Research in Psychosomatic Medicine.

While based in California, Alexander published more books including *The Western Mind in Transition* (1960) and *The Scope of Psychoanalysis* (1961). Alexander died on March 8, 1964, in Palm Springs, California. At the time of his death, he had papers and books, ready or nearly ready for publication focusing on such topics as the history of psychiatry and psychosomatic medicine. Several books by Alexander were published posthumously, including *Psychosomatic Medicine* (1965) and *Psychosomatic Specificity* (1968).

Books

Contemporary Authors Online, Gale, 2002.

Dictionary of American Biography, Charles Scribner's Sons, 1981.

Encyclopaedia of Criminological Theory, edited by Francis T. Cullen and Pamela Wilcox, SAGE Reference, 2010.

Encyclopaedia Judaica, 2nd ed., Volume 1, edited by Michael Berenhaum and Fred Skolnik, MacMillan Reference USA, 2007.

International Dictionary of Psychoanalysis, Volume 1, edited by Alian de Mijolla, Macmillan Reference, 2005.

International Encyclopedia of the Social Sciences, Volume 1, edited by David L. Sills, MacMillan, 1968.□

Hugh Allan

Scottish-born shipping tycoon Hugh Allan (1810–1882) was a figure of enormous political and financial influence in 19th-century Canada. The bulk of his fortune came from his family's stake in the Allan Shipping Line, which carried cargo and immigrants across North Atlantic waters for decades, but Allan also invested heavily in real estate, banking, railways, and other ventures in Montreal and the province of Quebec.

Hugh Allan was the grandson of a carpenter in the Ayrshire region of Scotland. His father, Alexander "Sandy" Allan, was a shoemaker-turned-ship carpenter who prospered after becoming a merchant-ship captain and ship owner. Born on September 29, 1810, in Saltcoats, Ayrshire, Allan was the second of five sons born to Captain Allan and his wife Jean Crawford Allan. At age 13 he followed his brother James into the family business with a clerk's job at a counting house—a form of private bank that also offered bookkeeping services for import-export companies and ship owners—in Greenock, a seaside area adjacent to Glasgow's main port. At 16 he sailed for Canada to work for a business partner of his father's in Montreal, the grain merchant William Kerr. By that point his father had already launched the Allan Shipping Line, whose ships carried goods between Glasgow and Montreal, a former French fort on the St. Lawrence River that became part of the British Empire in the 1760s.

Became Steamship Operator

In 1831, Allan joined a Montreal shipping and export firm and spent the rest of the decade there, becoming a partner in 1835. He learned the art of brokering deals with shipbuilders, maritime insurers, cargo captains, and local merchants, and his willingness to become bilingual boosted his business ties to the city's Francophone population. With the help of his father and brothers he was able to acquire his first ship, the *Thistle,* and rapidly leveraged his holdings to add to the fleet. He commissioned new ships from Glasgow builders and smaller ones from Montreal yards, where access to abundant Canadian timber reduced construction costs. The larger vessels carried immigrants from Scotland and two other main ports, Londonderry in Northern Ireland and Liverpool, on England's west coast, to British North America. Allan also accurately forecasted an increase in trade and passenger travel between Montreal and other cities on the St. Lawrence River, which connected the ports on the five Great Lakes—also a booming economic sphere during this era—to the Atlantic Ocean.

Allan married Matilda Caroline Smith in Montreal in 1844 and began his own branch of the Allan dynasty. She, too, was from a Scottish family and was the daughter of a successful dry-goods merchant in Lower Canada, as Quebec was called during this era. Matilda's sister Isabella married a younger Allan son, Andrew, who was also a partner in the Allan maritime fleet. Eldest brother James stayed in Glasgow, while another junior brother, Bryce, ran the Liverpool office. The fifth and youngest brother was Alexander Jr. and worked with James in Glasgow. Their father Sandy died in 1854 and left a thriving, well-managed business to his five sons, who enlarged it over subsequent decades to become the largest privately owned shipping line in the world.

Secured British Mail Route

In the 1840s and '50s Allan expanded his entrepreneurial realm and rose to a position of civic prominence in Montreal. He sat on the board of directors of the Bank of Montreal after 1847 and in 1851 was elected president of the Montreal Board of Trade. The family's Allan Shipping Line, meanwhile, dominated the passenger-immigration route between Britain and North America, dropping off English, Irish, and Scottish workers and families in Montreal and Quebec City in Lower Canada; its ships also made stops all the way down the Atlantic seaboard, from Halifax, Nova Scotia, and Portland, Maine, to Boston, New York, Philadelphia, and Baltimore.

Allan was a savvy entrepreneur who recognized that royal charters and government subsidies would yield phenomenal revenue growth. To secure the regular Royal Mail route between Britain and North America in the 1850s, he had two fast steamers built as the flagships of his newly formed Montreal Ocean Steamship Company, which he founded with his brother Andrew. When Britain went to war in the Crimea in the 1850s, he offered his ships for military and cargo transport. Allan presciently invested in new technologies, too, taking over the Montreal Telegraph Company just as Canada was expanding westward, and was involved in scores of other business enterprises. Writing in the *Dictionary of Canadian Biography,* Brian J. Young and Gerald J.J. Tulchinsky described the Montreal tycoon as "one of Canada's first monopoly capitalists. Despite some false starts and without the rationalization of later industrial organization, Allan developed an integrated financial, transportation, and manufacturing empire. His ships carried immigrants, his factories hired them and made the material for their clothes, his land companies sold them land, and his financial agencies insured them and lent them money."

Courted Politicians

After several years as a director of the Bank of Montreal, Allan founded Merchants' Bank of Canada in 1864. Four years later, it acquired another bank and with that buyout Allan also came into possession of the personal debt obligations of one of Canada's most famous historical figures, John A. Macdonald. Of Scottish heritage, too, Macdonald had successfully wrangled with his political party to unite with other groups in Upper and Lower Canada to form a confederation; Macdonald then led tough negotiations with Britain to secure independence for Canada in 1867. As head of the Conservative Party, Macdonald became the first prime minister of Canada, and though he had proved a masterful defense attorney, attorney general, legislator, and political power-broker, the fellow Scot was an incautious speculator and was forced to make payment arrangements with Allan's bank to repay a sum that had ballooned to $80,000.

Macdonald and the Conservative Party faced stiff opposition from Canada's Liberal Party in the 1872 election, at a time when Allan was attempting to build the first trans-Canada railroad. The new provinces of Ontario and Quebec were already connected to states in New England via the Grand Trunk Railway line, and Allan was unhappy with a slim profit he made after Grand Trunk extracted its freight and transit fees at various points along the route. Allan had invested in the Detroit and Milwaukee Railway, but it was not profitable, but he had managed to take over the Montreal Northern Colonization Railway in 1871, which carted timber from Quebec's vast forests in the Laurentian Mountains to meet the growing demand for housing and fuel in Montreal, Quebec City, Ottawa, and Toronto.

Blamed in the Pacific Scandal

Biographers of Canada's first prime minister assert that it was Macdonald's wily political ally, George-Étienne Cartier, who promised Allan the Conservative Party's support in exchange for campaign contributions in the 1872 election. At the time, Allan was competing with a Toronto tycoon to secure the Canadian government charter to build and operate a railroad that would connect Ontario all the way to the Pacific Ocean in the new province of British Columbia. It was an ambitious effort on all fronts: the transcontinental line would require enormous start-up costs, but right-of-way and land deals that came with the route would ensure that investors saw a quick profit as towns sprang up across the Canadian prairie.

Allan had formed a railroad syndicate with American investors, and this "alien" presence was greeted with alarm in Ottawa, the new federal capital, as well as in London, where Canada still retained close political and economic ties as part of the British Commonwealth. Cartier extracted a large campaign contribution from Allan, which went into Conservative Party coffers just ahead of the crucial general election in August of 1872. The suspect funds were likely used to bribe voters at the polls in Quebec Province, and the subsequent scandal resulted in a revision to Canadian election law that required the use of the secret ballot from that point forward. Macdonald was said to have been aghast at the overt bribe and demanded that Cartier rescind any pledges and return the funds, and Cartier told the incumbent prime minister that he had done so.

Macdonald and the Conservative Party narrowly won the election, and Allan was pressed to shed himself of his American railroad investors and seek British financing instead. One of those spurned investors was George McMullen, who contacted the prime minister and threatened to reveal the campaign donation. A powerful Montreal lawyer and politician named John Joseph Caldwell Abbott, who also had close ties to Allan, returned some funds to McMullen at Macdonald's behest. In April of 1873, a Liberal Party legislator brandished evidence in the Canadian House of Commons that he claimed linked Macdonald and Cartier to Allan and the railroad deal, including one telegram asking for another $10,000.

The Pacific Railway Scandal, as the bribery debacle came to be called, dominated newspaper headlines for months in 1873. Allan hastily returned to Montreal from London, where he had been courting new railroad investors, and later testified before a Royal Commission established to investigate the matter. Macdonald's cabinet collapsed and he was forced to resign in November of 1873, several months after Cartier's death from kidney disease. Correspondence between Allan and Cartier was presented as evidence before the Commission, but Allan told the panel of judges he was unsure about what the letters and telegrams actually documented. "It is difficult to explain what Sir George meant by them," Allan said in his defense, according to the *Times* of London. "He was not a man with whom you could talk very much, because in all the interviews with him he generally did most of the talking himself and you could with difficulty say anything. I never understood exactly what he meant on any of these points."

Built Palace-Sized Villa

Macdonald was reelected in 1878, and died in office in 1891 as one of Canada's longest-serving prime ministers. Apart from the failed railroad deal, the Pacific Scandal had little long-term impact on Allan's fortunes, either. He remained one of Montreal's most prominent figures and one of Canada's wealthiest men, and had been knighted by Queen Victoria in 1871. His marriage to Matilda produced four sons and nine daughters, and he built an enormous Italianate Renaissance-style chateau on Montreal's Mount Royal called Ravenscrag. Completed in 1863, its ballroom could host 500 guests and from its tower windows were views all the way to Vermont, where Allan owned marble quarries. His extensive holdings also included ironworks, the Citizens' Insurance Company of Canada, silver mines in the Great Lakes region, and even seal-hunting operations in Newfoundland. Allan died on December 9, 1882, while visiting one of his daughters in Edinburgh, Scotland. On the day of his funeral in Montreal, the Montreal Stock Exchange closed for the afternoon, and the city's mayor led the procession to the cemetery. The Allan Shipping Line was run by his son Montagu, who donated Ravenscrag to the Royal Victoria Hospital in 1940, and it subsequently became part of the Allan Memorial Institute of Psychiatry of McGill University.

Allan's children produced many notable Canadians and Americans. His son Montagu married the daughter of the Hudson's Bay Company president. Their two teenaged daughters were killed during World War I when a German submarine torpedo hit and sank the RMS *Lusitania*, owned by the rival Cunard line.

Periodicals

The Beaver: Exploring Canada's History, October-November 2007.

New York Times, December 28, 1882.

Times (London, England), November 6, 1873.

Online

Young, Brian J., in collaboration with Gerald J.J. Tulchinsky, "Allan, Sir Hugh," in *Dictionary of Canadian Biography,* vol. 11, University of Toronto/Université Laval, 2003, http://www.biographi.ca/en/bio/allan_hugh_11E.html (July 23, 2014).□

Alphonse Alley

The Dahomean military leader Alphonse Alley (1930–1987) was a key player in the sequence of unstable military governments that ruled the new Republic of Dahomey in the first decade of its existence. He served as the country's head of state in 1967 and 1968.

Dahomey (renamed Benin in 1975) gained its independence from France in 1960. Like other African countries of the period, it suffered from problems caused by underdevelopment, corruption, ethnic and regional rivalry, and leftist unrest. Alley avoided association with some of these problems; he was a member of a small tribe in the north of the country that stood apart from the country's large ethnic divisions, and he was popular among members of the country's military, which seized power several times in the 1960s. He rose to the rank of chief of staff of the Dahomean army. Finally he picked the wrong side in one of Dahomey's ongoing military power struggles, was imprisoned, and then went into exile in France. He was pardoned before his death and returned to his homeland.

Fought in Vietnam

Alponse Amadou Alley was born on April 9, 1930, in Bassila in central Dahomey near the border with Togo. At the time, Dahomey was a French colony, and Alley grew up in a military family loyal to the country's French overlords. His father fought for the French army in the Middle East during World War II. Alley attended schools in Dahomey and several other French West African colonies. In 1950 he enlisted in the French army himself and was sent to Vietnam (known as French Indochina), where he was involved in fighting between 1951 and 1953 as France tried to hold onto its colony in the face of leftist rebels led by Ho Chi Minh. His term of service ended just before a large French force was pinned down by a Vietnamese siege in the city of Dien Bien Phu.

This experience qualified Alley to attend an officer training school in France, at Saint-Maixent. He fought on the French side against rebellions in Morocco (1955–1956) and Algeria (beginning in 1959), serving as a paratrooper. But the era of French colonialism was drawing to a close, and when France withdrew from Dahomey, he was seen as a figure who could help ensure a peaceful transition and was sent home. (Independence in Dahomey, unlike other French colonies, came without bloodshed and proceeded peacefully through a period of self-governance to full independence in 1960.) Alley was given the rank of lieutenant in the new army of the Republic of Dahomey and headed up a unit of commandos as paratroopers in Ouidah. In 1962 he became a captain, and in 1964 a major. That year he led a platoon of troops to the border with Niger during a brief boundary dispute.

Alley's rise into Dahomey's inner circle occurred because he hitched his star to that of his commanding officer, General Christophe Soglo. He urged Soglo to overthrow Dahomey's government and seize power in 1963 and 1965. The second attempt was successful, and Alley was installed as chief of staff of the Dahomean army. At this point, the French wanted stability in their former colony, and Alley was allowed to come to France for senior staff training.

Popular Among Troops

Alley was a reasonable choice for a leadership post. When the European powers pulled out of Africa, they often left national boundaries that did not correspond to the area's longstanding cultural histories. Dahomey's country, and military, were fractured along regional north-south lines among Fon and Yoruba speakers to the south and Dendi, Bariba, and Fula (or Fulani) to the north. Alley was a northerner, but he was a member of a small ethnic group, the Widji, and he was popular among southerners in the army as well. Over the two years of Soglo's rule, however, a rivalry developed between Alley and another northerner, the military officer and cabinet chief Maurice Kouandété.

The years 1967 and 1968 were perhaps the most unstable in the young country's history. Disagreements between Alley and Kouandété flared in cabinet meetings, with Alley remaining loyal to Soglo in spite of his own reservations about Soglo's leadership. Kouandété and a group of about 60 junior officers planned a coup against Soglo, keeping Alley in the dark about their intentions. In December of 1967, after a series of crippling strikes, they overthrew Soglo and placed Alley under house arrest.

The plotters quickly realized, however, that they did not have the support to control the government. "Overthrowing Soglo's regime was far easier than resolving the civic and military cleavages that had led to its demise," noted Samuel Decalo in *Coups and Army Rule in Africa: Studies in Military Style.* France, where President Charles de Gaulle had just received Soglo on a state visit, cut off aid to Dahomey; Kouandété was forced to release Alley and, even worse (from Kouandété's point of view) to appoint him interim leader. On December 20 Alley became president, also taking over Kouandété's role as chief of staff.

It was not just his neutral ethnicity that made Alley a popular figure, but his outgoing personality as well. According to Decalo (writing in the *Historical Dictionary of Dahomey*), he was a dashing figure that foreign diplomats dubbed the "wine, women, and song" officer. Alley remained in power as the military announced plans for a new constitution, to be voted on in a national plebiscite.

The vote on the constitution went well, with 76 percent of Dahomeans approving it, but by May of 1968 conflicts had flared once again. Although both Kouandété and Alley hoped that they could install a figurehead who could be easily controlled, the military unilaterally announced that former officeholders would be ineligible to run for president, and ignored a Supreme Court decision that annulled that restriction.

Tried to Purge Rival's Supporters

Accordingly, the elections held in the summer of 1968 were a fiasco, and ordinary Dahomeans felt no stake in the result. Turnout was a dismal 27 percent, and the army felt no compunction about ignoring the elected winner, Dr. Basile Adjou, and going into a set of meetings to try to decide on the next course of action. During this period, Alley tried to engineer a purge of Kouandété and his supporters from the government, but he was unsuccessful. After Emile Derlin Zinsou was appointed president as a compromise candidate acceptable to Kouandété, Alley was removed as army chief of staff and appointed military attaché in Washington, D.C., in an apparent attempt to get him out of the way.

Alley refused this appointment, and he was ejected from the army entirely and arrested on charges of planning to kill Kouandété, a potential capital offense, in the summer of 1969. Zinsou spoke on his behalf, but in October he was sentenced to ten years' hard labor. The tables turned once again after Kouandété seized control of the government at the end of that year and found once again that he needed support from the faction of the army that supported Alley, who then became Secretary-General of National Defense.

After more controversies, Alley's luck finally ran out after a 1972 coup by army major Mathieu Kerekou. The new military regime feared the clique of older officers who had for so long divided power among themselves. Alley was given the largely meaningless title of commissioner of the national oil mills, and in 1973 he was arrested once again and given a 20-year prison sentence for anti-regime plotting. During riots in 1975, supporters helped him to escape from prison and to go into exile in France, where he remained for nine years. He was released in 1984 during a general amnesty and died in Cotonou, the capital of the country by then named Benin, on March 28, 1987.

Books

Daggs, Elisa, *All Africa*, Hastings, 1970.

Decale, Samuel, *Coups and Army Rule in Africa, Studies in Military Style*, Yale, 1976.

Decalo, Samuel, *Historical Dictionary of Dahomey (People's Republic of Benin)*, Scarecrow, 1976.

Decalo, Samuel, *Psychoses of Power: African Personal Dictatorships*, Westview, 1989.

Ronen, Dov, *Dahomey: Between Tradition and Modernity*, Cornell, 1975. □

Lilí Álvarez

A multi-sport master, Spain's Lilí Álvarez (1905–1998) excelled at ice skating, skiing, tennis, and car racing. She was best known for tennis and gained fame for a series of near-wins at the Wimbledon Championships. Álvarez made the finals three years in a row (1926-28) but failed to come away with the top prize. She won a doubles championship at the 1929 French Open, then parlayed her popularity into a successful career as a journalist and women's rights advocate.

Elia Maria González-Álvarez y López-Chicheri was born May 9, 1905, at the Hotel Flora in Rome, Italy. Her formal name was shortened to Lilí. Álvarez was born in Rome while her wealthy, Spanish parents were visiting the city. She was born into a devout Roman Catholic family and was baptized at one of the most ancient churches in the world—Rome's Basilica of St. John Lateran.

Enjoyed Affluent Upbringing

Because her parents were well-off financially, Álvarez grew up traveling to tourist resort areas around the world. During the winter, her family lived in Switzerland, which allowed Álvarez to skate and ski in the Alps. In the spring, her family visited cities around Lake Maggiore, the lake that runs between Switzerland and Italy. During this season, Álvarez concentrated on cycling and horseback riding. She spent summers in the French Riviera, visiting Cannes, Nice and Monte-Carlo and perfected her tennis skills. Her first competitive endeavor was billiards, which she started playing at the age of four.

As Álvarez traveled across Europe, she learned several languages and enjoyed an upper-class lifestyle that afforded her the opportunity to participate in many sports. She won her first ice skating event at age 11, besting the reigning French champion. At 14, she captured her first tennis title. At 16, Álvarez earned her first international gold medal in skating, winning a competition at St. Moritz, Switzerland. In 1924, she won a prize at Spain's Catalan Automobile Championship, racing her Peugeot to victory through the 250-mile course. She also participated in golf, fencing, and equestrian events.

When Álvarez was 18, the family settled in the French Riviera, allowing Álvarez to run with a crowd that included famed artists, European royalty and politicians. Sweden's King Gustaf V was one of her tennis partners. Around this time, Álvarez decided to focus on tennis. In 1924, at age 18, she qualified for the Olympic Games, held that year in Paris. She advanced to the quarter-finals and finished tied for fifth place. Though Álvarez did not return home with a medal, her participation was noteworthy because she was the first female from Spain to compete in the Olympics.

©Underwood & Underwood/Corbis

Made Mark at Wimbledon

In 1926, Álvarez played her way to the finals at England's famed Wimbledon Championships. In the finals, she faced Britain's Kitty Godfree. Godfree won the first set 6-2. Álvarez battled back to take the second set 6-4, and took a lead in the third and final set. At one point she was up three games to one and leading 40-15 in the next game with victory on the horizon. Spain's King Alfonso XIII and Queen Victoria Eugenie sat in the crowd cheering her on, but Álvarez lost that set, and with it the match. She returned to Wimbledon in 1927 and once again made the finals. This time she faced Helen Wills of the United States, but lost in two quick sets. In 1927, she had another near-win when she teamed with U.S. tennis star Bill Tilden in the mixed doubles competition at the French Open Championships. They made the finals, only to lose to the French duo of Marguerite Broquedis and Jean Borotra—6-4, 2-6, 6-2. In 1928, Álvarez again faced Wills in the Wimbledon finals, but once lost in two sets.

In 1927 and 1928, London *Daily Telegraph* tennis correspondent Wallis Myers ranked Álvarez number two on his list of top ten female players. Myers complimented Álvarez, writing that as a stroke-maker she was beyond compare to any of her peers.

Álvarez created a stir with her natural Mediterranean beauty and sophisticated style. To stay warm between matches, she wore a white fur-trimmed coat. During matches, she appeared in the required white linen shirt and skirt, but placed a fashionable turban on her head to keep her short, dark hair from flapping in her eyes. The British public swooned for Álvarez and the papers published her picture frequently, dubbing her "the Señorita." Fans lined up for autographs and admirers followed her around the city to restaurants and theaters, hoping for a glimpse of the celebrity.

In 1929, Álvarez was eliminated in the fourth round at Wimbledon and did not compete in 1930. In 1931, she made a run to the third round at Wimbledon before losing to Britain's Dorothy Round Little, who went on to capture a Wimbledon Championship in 1934. During the 1931 Wimbledon games, Álvarez took center stage—not for her playing, but for her clothes. She dropped the conventional dress code that had female tennis players competing in modest, calf-length skirts that flapped around and restricted movement. Italian fashion designer Elsa Schiaparelli designed Álvarez a "pant-skirt" outfit that made movement easy. The silk outfit was basically a pair of billowy Bermuda pants covered by a skirt, a sort of precursor to the modern skort. Previously, women had only worn skirts, which were considered proper feminine attire. Álvarez, however, challenged the established norm with her outfit. Newspaper columnists wrote that her attire proved women had a masculine fixation because they wanted to wear trousers. The outfit flew in the face of the day's modesty norms.

While a Wimbledon title evaded her, Álvarez enjoyed success elsewhere. In 1929, she teamed with Dutch star Kea Bouman to win the ladies' doubles title at the French Open, defeating South Africans Bobbie Heine and Alida Neave 7-5, 6-3. Álvarez made it to the semifinals at the French Open in ladies' singles in 1930, 1931, and 1936. She won the ladies' singles championship at the Italian Open in 1930, the first year that tournament was held. In fact, she won three events that year, also placing first in ladies' doubles and mixed doubles. She won Spain's singles championship in 1929 and 1940. In addition, she won both the singles and mixed doubles championships in Argentina in 1930.

Launched Journalism Career

Over the years, Álvarez's fame led to numerous assignments as a journalist. After she won the Argentine International Championships in 1930, the Argentinian paper *La Nación* sought her articles. In 1931, she began writing for the London *Daily Mail*, covering mostly Spanish politics and highlighting women's changing role in society. She made contributions to the *Daily Mail* through 1936. During the mid-1930s, she was involved with Spain's Sección Femenina (Women's Section) of the Falange political movement, working to promote sporting opportunities for young girls.

In 1927, Álvarez published *Modern Lawn Tennis,* a 116-page treatise on how to play the game. In the book she warned players that one important aspect was that of finding a proper racket that feels right to them: "No matter what special advantages a racket may be advertised to have, no matter how many championships have been won by that particular kind, unless the *'feel'* of it is comfortable to *you,* don't have it."

During the 1940s, Álvarez settled in Spain and wrote sports columns for the Spanish dailies *Arriba* and *La Vanguardia*. Many of her articles encouraged women to enter sports. She often argued that participating in sports would increase their well-being and open up opportunities. During the 1940s, she turned her attention to skiing. She entered a 1941 ski race at Candanchú, a ski resort in Pyrenees, Spain. She created controversy at the competition, however, after complaining about the preferential treatment given to the male skiers.

Álvarez spent the next three decades writing about feminism, spirituality, and women's equality. In 1946, she published *Plenitud,* an essay on women, sports and religion. In *Plenitud,* she expounded on her belief that sports were the key to an enriching spiritual life. She wrote that she believed an athlete was a whole person because of developing both the "inner" and "outer" life, whereas poets and other spiritual seekers tended to develop only their inner selves. She held that a person could achieve harmony by developing the physical body for athletic pursuits, which in turn would enhance the soul. She went so far as to describe the athlete as a godlike figure.

In *Plenitud* Álvarez also wrote that for her, the goal was not to win but to find a state of joy and "plenitude" (completeness or fullness) through the pursuit and process of preparing for and competing in athletic events. These statements lend some light on why Álvarez refused to turn professional during her heyday. In 1926, U.S. sports agent Charles C. Pyle—known as "Cash and Carry Pyle"—offered Álvarez a blank check to turn pro, but she turned him down, explaining that amateur athletes were superior to professional ones because it was nobler to play, not for the paycheck but for the sake of the game.

Focused on Feminism/Spirituality

In 1951, Álvarez created a stir with her speech "La Batalla de la Feminidad" (The Battle of Femininity) at the Fifth Latin American Feminist Congress. In the speech, she suggested that it was imperative for women to participate in sports if they wanted to see advancements in other areas of society. She believed that participating in sports would help women develop skills like initiative and self-motivation, necessary to advance their status and role in society. In her 1956 book *En Tierra Extraña* (In a Strange Land), she called on religious institutions to expand women's roles in the church.

Álvarez furthered this idea in 1959, publishing *El Seglarismo y su Identidad,* in which she denounced prohibitions that prevented women from participating in certain religious endeavors. She felt that both women and men were "complementary" figures in earth's humanity. She went on to criticize the Catholic Church's moral code, which she felt treated men's and women's sexuality differently. In Spain, she was well-known for her spiritual books. Author Lorenzo Gomis noted in the *Australian,* "She considered herself 'atypically pious.' Her books combined militant feminism with intellectual religiosity."

For the rest of her life, Álvarez continued her quest to advance women's spirituality through articles, books, and discussions. In 1965, though, she returned her attention to

tennis, covering the Davis Cup in Australia for *Blanco y Negro* as Spain's national men's team advanced through the rounds to make the finals. Álvarez made her last public appearance in May 1998, upon the release of her book *The Great Explanation Concerning Life and Sport.* Álvarez died in Madrid on July 8, 1998. She was 93. She left no survivors. In 1934, she wed a French diplomat, the Count of Valdène, but they separated after five years of marriage after Álvarez had a miscarriage. At the time of her death, Álvarez had been tapped to receive the Golden Medal for Merit from the Higher Sports Council in Madrid.

Books

Álvarez, Lili, *Modern Lawn Tennis,* Butler & Tanner Ltd., 1927.

Periodicals

Argus (Melbourne, Australia), September 20, 1928.
Australian, July 22, 1998.

Online

"Lili Álvarez: Star Athlete, Writer, and Feminist: 'a su Manera,'" Texas State University, http://www.modlang.txstate.edu/letrashispanas/previousvolumes/vol7/contentParagraph/0/content_files/file0/Bellver.pdf (December 11, 2014). □

Nalini Ambady

Indian-born social psychologist Nalini Ambady (1959–2013) devised groundbreaking methods of measuring human nonverbal behavior and cues. Best known for her work on predicting the accuracy of snap judgments, Ambady taught at Harvard and Stanford universities and was the first Indian-American woman to teach psychology at both schools. Her promising career was cut short by leukemia after a much-publicized effort to find a lifesaving bone-marrow transplant donor.

Nalini Ambady was born on March 20, 1959, in Kolkata, India's third largest city. As a young woman she studied at the Lawrence School, a private academy in the state of Tamil Nadu, and progressed on to Lady Shri Ram College, a single-sex undergraduate school affiliated with the University of Delhi. In the 1980s she moved to Williamsburg, Virginia, to attend the College of William and Mary, which awarded her a master's degree in psychology in 1985.

Investigated Snap Judgment Phenomenon

Ambady entered Harvard University's doctoral program in social psychology and was awarded her Ph.D. in 1991. Her teaching career began at the College of the Holy Cross in Worcester, Massachusetts, and later included faculty slots at Tufts University in Boston as well as Harvard University, which hired her as an assistant professor in 1994 and elevated her to associate professor in 1999.

Ambady's first two professional papers as primary author were also credited to her Harvard mentor, Dr. Robert Rosenthal, chief of the psychology department at the time and a pioneer in nonverbal communication. The first of the papers appeared in a 1992 issue of *Psychological Bulletin* under the title "Thin Slices of Expressive Behavior as Predictors of Interpersonal Consequences." She expanded her findings for a 1993 article published in the *Journal of Personality and Social Psychology*. This one bore the title "Half a Minute: Predicting Teacher Evaluations from Thin Slices of Nonverbal Behavior and Human Attractiveness" and cemented Ambady's professional reputation on the phenomenon of thin-slicing, a term she and Rosenthal coined to describe how people make snap judgments about others, especially in school and workplace interactions.

A few years, later Ambady explained her methodology to writer Malcolm Gladwell in an article that appeared in the May 29, 2000, issue of *New Yorker.* Her original plan for her first thin-slicing study was to have research volunteers give an estimation of a teacher's effectiveness, and measure that parameter against end-of-semester evaluations by students that delivered concrete opinions on how effectively the instructor had performed. Ambady found some videos that Harvard used in the teacher-training process, but was dismayed that they had scarce footage of just the instructor; for a proper study she needed to edit or manipulate the tapes that showed the teacher plus the class. "I didn't want students in the frame, because obviously it would bias the ratings. So I went to my adviser, and I said, 'This isn't going to work,'" she told Gladwell. Her adviser urged her to use the 30-second clips.

Believed Brain's Response "Very Primitive"

Ambady went ahead with the survey, and found that a clip rated by observers did in fact correlate to how actual students had judged the same instructor. When Ambady reduced the footage to ten-, six-, and finally two-second clips, her participants' initial judgments continued to match up well. Ambady then went and asked her study-participants to reflect more carefully on how they judged a potential instructors' effectiveness, and with that they became confused and the accuracy of their assessments declined when compared against the end-of-semester evaluations. Ambady expanded her study to eliminating almost everything from the tapes of the instructors except a patch of skin, and was astonished that these, too, correlated with actual teacher evaluations. "The brain structures that are involved here are very primitive," she told Gladwell. "All of these affective reactions are probably governed by lower brain structures."

Ambady and Rosenthal's initial joint work on thin slicing roused the interest of other social-psychology researchers, who expanded on the Harvard duo's first experiments. *Psychology Today* writer Jena Pincott defined the phenomenon of thin slicing as an "ability to infer something about a person's personality, character, or other traits after a very brief exposure," Pincott wrote. Pincott

then went on to describe those lower-brain structures Ambady had mentioned to Gladwell. "Thin-slicing relies on a brain network that includes the fusiform gyrus, which perceives faces," Pincott wrote, "and the amygdala, which filters that information for anything that might be useful or threatening to survival."

Data Mined for *Blink*

Ambady made thin-slicing the basis of her promising career. With other researchers she conducted scores of new studies exploring facial-expression cues, gender stereotypes, and even the ability to predict religious affiliation and political party membership. Her work received wider attention when Gladwell's original article in the *New Yorker* expanded into book form. *Blink: The Power of Thinking Without Thinking* was published in 2005 and spent 20 months on the *New York Times'* hardcover bestseller list. "It is important to note that she does not say that people can necessarily judge actual teaching *effectiveness,* or objective teaching ability," remarked Melanie Tannenbaum, a writer for *Scientific American,* about Ambady's field of study. "Rather, she shows that our snap judgments or evaluations are remarkably resistant to change over time." Tannenbaum, also a social-psychology researcher, went on to explain the significance of Ambady's work. "Given that we live in a world where perceptions shape reality, this is not a finding to be taken lightly. For example, are politicians truly elected because they are objectively competent, or because people *perceive* them to be competent?"

Ambady's other research into thin-slicing queried whether or not someone could judge a married couple's likelihood of future divorce, and whether or not a doctor had been the defendant in medical malpractice lawsuits. One of her more widely publicized studies was first presented at a Toronto symposium in 1997 and involved the ability of "in-group" members, a social psychology term, to judge another person's sexual orientation. This is commonly referred to as "gaydar," a portmanteau word created by combining "gay" and "radar" to refer to a gay person's ability to accurately recognize a like-minded stranger. Her first paper on the topic, written with other researchers, appeared in 1999 and she returned to the topic several more times.

Ambady joined the faculty of Stanford University in 2011, becoming the first professor of Indian origin in the school's psychology department. At the elite California university Ambady launched SPARQ, a research laboratory whose focus was to attack larger societal questions—like racial bias or gender-linked income inequality—using tools based on social psychology findings. "She said, 'Let's take our academic research and findings and see if we can apply it to make changes in the real world,'" her husband Raj Marphatia told Bjorn Carey, a writer for States News Service.

Career Cut Short

Ambady had met her husband at Harvard when Marphatia was enrolled at Harvard Law School. The couple had two daughters and a close network of bicoastal friends and family in both the Cambridge/Boston and Palo Alto/San Francisco Bay areas. Ambady was briefly hampered by a diagnosis of leukemia in 2005, but it was successfully treated and went into remission. She suffered a recurrence in late 2012 and as her treatment options diminished, Ambady sought a bone marrow transplant. There is a national donor registry in the United States, but as her physician-friend Liz Gaufberg wrote in a blog post, "a South Asian like Nalini has a 1-in-20,000 chance of finding a match, while for Caucasian recipients the chance is 1 in 8" in the U.S. Bone Marrow Registry.

Gaufberg penned her appeal for CommonHealth, a Web page hosted by Massachusetts public radio station WBUR-FM, and explained that she and Ambady had been longtime friends and mothers of teen daughters who were also close friends. In the article Gaufberg added that blood-marrow "donation is generally safe and painless—the chief barriers are psychological and cultural. There is a diversity of opinions about biological donation across cultures, with some more traditional ones considering the practice taboo." Marphatia, Gaufberg, and friends and family back in Kerala, India, attempted to enlarge the pool of potential donors via a fundraising and awareness drive they called "Nalini Needs You." They asked for financial donations to purchase test-swab kits and urged their social-media network contacts to spread the word and submit to a preliminary swab in a kit that could then be mailed off to a lab, who would add those results to a database of potential bone-marrow donors.

Over several months in 2013 the story of Ambady's plight featured some optimistic turns and unfortunate setbacks. One potential donor match was located in India, but family members dissuaded that person from the procedure. In her CommonHealth blog post, Gaufberg reflected that there was a grim irony in this, for "no one knows better than Nalini about the social and psychological factors that mitigate helping behavior....Whenever an appeal is made to a large group of people, as Nalini's friends are doing through social media, it's easy to convince yourself that someone else will step up to the plate," Gaufberg reflected.

Ambady died on October 28, 2013, at age 54 in Boston, Massachusetts, before a willing donor could be found. Tributes appeared in dozens of media sites around the world, from the *Times of India* to the *New York Times*. Her employer Stanford University also lamented her passing in an official news release. A colleague in Palo Alto, Hazel Markus, recalled Ambady's "incredible energy [and] very positive spirit," the psychology professor told Carey, the States News Service writer. "She was brilliant and held herself and others to very high standards. She loved social psychology so much that people were very attracted to working with her."

Periodicals

New York Times, November 5, 2013.
New Yorker, May 29, 2000.
Psychology Today, November-December 2012.
States News Service, October 31, 2013.
Times of India, April 28, 2013.

Online

Gaufberg, Liz, "Saving Nalini: Leading Psychologist Seeks Bone Marrow Donor To Survive," *CommonHealth,* WBUR-FM, May 3, 2013, http://commonhealth.wbur.org/2013/05/saving-nalini-ambady (February 8, 2015).

Tannenbaum, Melanie, "Rest In Peace, Nalini Ambady," PsySociety, *Scientific American,* http://blogs.scientificamerican.com/psysociety/2013/10/29/nalini-ambady/ (February 8, 2015). □

Bettina von Arnim

German writer Bettina von Arnim (1785–1859) was closely acquainted with some of the top creative figures of the early 19th century, and she became famous for writing about her encounters with the poet Johann Wolfgang von Goethe in particular.

Bettina von Arnim, wrote Jan Swafford in the London *Guardian,* "was a supreme muse, a one-woman literary movement, at once among the singular and most representative figures of the Romantic century." She had an eventful life, much of which was reflected in letters she wrote and received; when she published those, she became a celebrity who attracted admirers as far-flung as Ralph Waldo Emerson in the United States. Arnim was a contributor to *Des Knaben Wunderhorn* (The Youth's Magic Horn), one of the most important Romantic-era folklore publications, and she was a vigorous polemicist in favor of socially progressive causes, something that nearly led to her imprisonment during the last years of her life. Arnim was, in short, a fascinating figure who played a central role in German culture of the Romantic era.

Raised Partly in Convent

Bettina (in German often spelled Bettine) von Arnim, born Catarina Elisabetha Ludovica Magdalena Brentano, was born in Frankfurt, then part of the Holy Roman Empire, on April 4, 1785. She was one of 20 children born to an Italian-German businessman. Bettina was not the first writer in her family nor the first to travel in literary circles; her grandmother Sophie LaRoche was noted as a sentimental novelist, and her mother had dated Goethe when both were young. After Bettina's parents died, she was sent to a convent but then moved with two of her sisters to LaRoche's home in the city of Offenbach. There she got to know her older brother Clemens Brentano, who introduced her to Goethe's writings and to the literary world in general.

The effect on Bettina was immediate and startling. She began to identify in the extreme with the character of Mignon in Goethe's famous novel *Wilhelm Meisters Lehrjahre* (Wilhelm Meister's Apprenticeship)—a young dancer abducted by circus performers. She began to dress as Mignon and to emulate scenes from the novel. She worshiped Goethe, Mignon's creator, from afar—for now. She

Interfoto/Alamy

also made friends with a young poet, Karoline von Günderode, who lived in a convent but was in unrequited love with a married man and finally committed suicide over the failed affair.

In 1807, after making friends with Goethe's mother, who knew about her through the earlier relationship between the poet and Bettina's own mother, Bettina was introduced to the 58-year-old Goethe himself. Asked what she was interested in, Bettina replied (as quoted by Swafford), "Nothing interests me but you," and sat down on the poet's lap. Despite this physical introduction, Goethe and Bettina are not thought to have consummated a physical relationship. Instead, she wrote frequently to him, proposing herself as a kind of creative muse. Goethe wrote back noncommittally, but Bettina began to read much more into his replies than was actually there.

Flirted with Beethoven

Meanwhile, Bettina began to pursue the other great German genius of the age, composer Ludwig van Beethoven, sneaking up behind him, putting her hands on his shoulders, and introducing herself as a relative of her half-brother Franz Brentano. She apparently accompanied Beethoven on some of the long walks on which he often sought musical inspiration, and she also tried to introduce the composer to Goethe (they finally met but did not get along well). Bettina has been proposed as candidate for the

identity of the Immortal Beloved, the woman to whom Beethoven wrote a passionate ten-page letter that was never sent and that did not name the intended recipient. A more likely candidate, however, is Franz's wife, Antonie Brentano.

Bettina's brother Clemens continued to encourage his sister's intellectual adventures, and the two worked together on collecting the folktales included in *Des Knaben Wunderhorn,* a book that inspired several generations of German creative figures. She herself was a composer who, among other accomplishments, was the first to set the writings of the radically experimental German poet Friedrich Hülderlin to music. She also set poetry by Goethe and by Achim von Arnim, a young poet to whom Clemens, hoping to see her safely married, had introduced her. After Bettina was barred from the Goethe household due to an argument she had with Goethe's wife, Arnim and Bettina were married in 1811.

The marriage produced four sons and three daughters, several of whom launched literary careers of their own. Apparently the marriage was not entirely happy; after the birth of her children Bettina took them to live in Berlin while Arnim lived on his family's country estate. He died in 1831, and after that Bettina resumed her creative career. Her most famous book in her own time was *Goethes Briefwechsel mit einem Kind* (Goethe's Exchange of Letters with a Child), published in 1835, three years after the great poet's death. She had designed a Goethe memorial while he was still alive; it showed herself, as Mignon, kneeling in front of the poet with a lyre. (The monument stands today in the city of Frankfurt.) The book was widely read—and difficult to classify. At first it was taken as genuine, but close readers noted inconsistencies and suggested that it was a literary fraud. One of those inconsistencies was that the 21-year-old Bettina was hardly a child when she met Goethe. Still later, Goethe scholars concluded that the materials in the book were mostly authentic but had been treated with creative freedom, and some suggested that Bettina intended the book as an epistolary novel (a novel made up of letters).

Published Semi-Fictional Letters

Bettina followed that up with another set of letters that blurred the line between fantasy and reality: *Die Günderode* (1840) drew on her relationship with Karoline von Günderode. She turned her attention toward her brother in *Clemens Brentanos Frühlingskranz* (Clemens Brentano's Spring Garland, 1843) and toward Achim von Arnim in *Ilius Pamphilus und die Ambrosia* (Ilium Pamphilus and Ambrosia, 1848), a made-up correspondence between Arnim and a young poet.

By the 1840s a second, more political strand of Bettina's creative personality began to develop. *Dies Buch gehört dem König* (This Book Belongs to the King, 1843) argued in favor of equal treatment for Jews, and still more controversial were a pair of books arguing for the liberalization of Prussia's monarchical rule. In 1842 she met Karl Marx. Inspired by volunteer work she had done during a cholera epidemic in Berlin, she began work on a large collection of writings called the *Armenbuch* (Book of the

Poor) but never finished it, and when unrest broke out among Silesian weavers in 1844 she was accused of supporting Communism. These accusations apparently led to an order for her arrest, but since the Prussian king was a fan of her earlier writings, it was never carried out. Even so, the Clemens Brentano and Ilius Pamphilius books were suppressed, a ban that was lifted only when Bettina appealed personally to the king.

Bettina's celebrity might have saved her in any case. The embroidered Goethe letters, especially, were internationally popular. The American philosopher Ralph Waldo Emerson wrote (as quoted on the website *The Hedonistic Imperative*, which published an English-language version of the Goethe book): "She is a finer genius than George Sand or Mme. De Stael, more real than either, more witty, as profound, & greatly more readable. And where shall we find another woman to compare her with." Even as speculation waxed and waned as to exactly what the relationship between Goethe and Bettina had been, her books remained popular through the 19th century and were rediscovered at the end of the 20th as readers and scholars began to investigate the creativity of women during the Romantic era.

In her later years, Bettina edited many of her husband's writings and published one more book, *Gespräche mit Dämonen* (Conversations with Demons, 1852), a socially progressive fantasy in which she describes conditions in Berlin's prisons and slums, and depicts herself as a ghost whispering what she has seen into the king's ear. In 1854 she suffered a stroke that left her mute. She recovered partially but died in Berlin on January 20, 1859, surrounded by her children, with a bust of Goethe in front of her. The vast majority of critical and biographical writings about Bettina von Arnim are in the German language.

Books

Hardin, James N. and Christophe E. Schweitzer, eds. *German Writers in the Age of Goethe, 1789–1832,* Dictionary of Literary Biography, Vol. 90, Gale, 1989.

Online

"Bettina von Arnim, Born Brentano," *The von Arnim Family: An Old German Dynasty,* http://www.von-arnim.net/files/portr_bettina_engl.pdf (October 14, 2014).

"Editorial Preface to the English translation of Goethe's correspondence with a child by Bettina von Arnim–1837," *The Hedonistic Imperative,* http://www.hedweb.com/bgcharlton/preface-bettina.html (October 14, 2014).

"A Virtuoso Muse," *Guardian* (London, England), http://www.theguardian.com/books/2003/aug/23/classicalmusicandopera (October 14, 2014).□

B

Laura Battiferri

Italian poet Laura Battiferri (1523–1589) was celebrated in her lifetime as one of the rare female writers to publish works in 16th-century Europe. An eyewitness to extraordinary times as a citizen of Florence and Rome, Battiferri was married to another prominent figure of the Italian Renaissance, the architect-sculptor Bartolomeo Ammannati.

The circumstances of Laura Battiferri's birth are as unique as her later status in Florentine society as a woman of letters. Literary scholars pinpoint her likely birthdate as November 30, 1523, based on a poem she wrote many years later in which she referenced that date and a saint associated with it in the Christian religious calendar. She came from Urbino, a wealthy city in the Marche region of Italy, and her mother was Maddalena Coccapani, the lover of a high-ranking church official. Almost nothing is known about Coccapani, whose name survives only on two real estate documents of the 1530s which cite her as mother to a son, Ascanio, and daughter Laura. Both children were educated by private tutors, and Battiferri proved to be a gifted student of classical languages and literature.

Daughter of Prelate

Battiferri's father was Giovanni Antonio Battiferri, a prelate who rose in the Roman Catholic Church through his service to several influential cardinals. One was Giulio di Giuliano de' Medici, who became Pope Clement VII in 1523; another was Alessandro Farnese, who succeeded Clement VII as Pope Paul III in 1534. It was Farnese—himself a father of several children—who signed a document dated February 9, 1543, legitimatizing Battiferri and her brother Ascanio as legal heirs of Giovanni Antonio.

Battiferri would have been 19 years old when that document was filed. Her father was protonotary in the Apostolic Chamber, a key office in the Vatican. Functioning as a type of administrative branch of the papacy, the Chamber controlled several lucrative and security-related arms of Church business, including funds due to it through the granting of benefices, a form of patronage, and the Mint of Rome, where coins of the realm were smelted.

Battiferri's family surname is sometimes spelled as Battiferra or Battiferro. Around 1544 she married musician Vittorio Sereni of Bologna. Little is known of Sereni, but his deathbed will of 1549 states that his worldly possessions should be divided between his brother and his wife, and also mentions the dowry amount paid by Battiferri's father. A widow at age 25, Battiferri assuaged her grief in sonnets to her late husband.

Remarried Prominent Artist-Architect

Battiferri's father remained in his post at the Apostolic Chamber in the 1550s under Paul's successor Pope Julius III. Thirty years earlier Giovanni Antonio had built an impressive residence in the Borgo neighborhood of Rome, and its exterior featured allegorical paintings from workshop of Raphael that referenced the meaning of the Battiferri surname, which translates as pounder of iron, or blacksmith. There was also another Roman residence, a smaller one in the Campo Marzio district, where Battiferri was thought to have grown up and to which she likely returned after Sereni died. At one point her brother Ascanio attempted to falsify a real-estate transaction involving this second property and for that their father disowned him. Giovanni Antonio's last

De Agostini Picture Library/Getty Images

will and testament bequeaths his assets to Battiferri and specifically omits Ascanio. Correspondence that survives the centuries reveals that Battiferri had long-lasting legal troubles related to both inheritances: in the first matter the brother of Vittorio Sereni refused to allocate funds due to her; in the other case Ascanio challenged the terms of their father's will after Giovanni Antonio's death in 1561.

Battiferri's father was thought to have aided in matching her to a particularly well-suited second husband. This was renowned sculptor and architect Bartolomeo Ammannati. Twelve years her senior and also from Urbino, Ammannati came from a family of *scarpellini,* or stone carvers, from the ancient marble quarries of Settignano near Florence. Ammannati had trained under one Renaissance master, the sculptor-architect Jacopo Sansovino, and maintained a cordial relationship with one of the most famous names of the Italian Renaissance, Michelangelo, who had childhood ties to Settignano.

The dowry for Battiferri's second marriage was a stunning 2,000 *scudi,* an impressive amount for a woman not of royal rank. The wedding date was April 17, 1550, and the widowed writer and the 38-year-old Ammannati were wed at the famous Basilica della Santa Casa in Loreto, which was built over the original structure said to have been the childhood home of the Virgin Mary, the mother of Jesus. Already a famous pilgrimage site for a few hundred years by then, Loreto's Casa Santa had been disassembled by

Crusaders in the Holy Land and rebuilt in the more guardable confines of northern Italy. Battiferri possibly chose this site for its symbolic significance, for her first marriage had not produced any children and she likely hoped her second one would.

Flourished Under Tuscan Sun

The first five years of Battiferri's marriage to Ammannati were spent in Rome, where the sculptor and architect executed important commission work for Julius III. After the death of this pope in 1555 the couple moved to Florence, where Ammannati had a more extensive network of professional contacts. Battiferri loved living in Rome, dubbed the Eternal City for its long history in Western Christendom as seat of the Church, and had some misgivings about relocating to Florence, one of the powerful city-states of northern Italy.

In Florence, Battiferri continued to write poetry in her study and eventually adjusted to the move as her career began to build momentum. The couple had a city residence and a country home. The former was in the Via dei Ginori, and the other a villa near Maiano, a quiet enclave adjacent to the hill town of Fiesole above Florence, a city prone to epic floods. The Duke of Florence, Cosimo de' Medici, became an influential patron of the arts during his long tenure in that role and as Grand Duke of Tuscany. The duke's Spanish-born wife, Eleonora de Toledo, was also a generous benefactor and it is to her that Battiferri dedicated *The First Book of Tuscan Works,* an anthology of verse published in Florence in 1560.

Battiferri's poetry had been circulating privately for several years by then, a convention of the pre-modern, correspondence-heavy era. Her *Primo libro della opere toscane,* as the original title of her debut work reads, was printed at the Giunti house, founded by brothers Filippo and Bernardo Giunti. Its pages feature 187 poems—including verse from other writers—that portray Tuscany and its history through various forms of meter.

The fact that Battiferri's own writings were openly published under her full name in *Primo libro* was a remarkable achievement for a woman in Europe in 1560. "After preliminary salutes to princely readers and other notables, her sonnets take an autobiographical turn, sharing meditations that wrestle with the move" from Rome to the Tuscan capital, remarked contemporary scholar Victoria Kirkland in an essay that appeared in *Renaissance Quarterly.* "As she prepares to depart, the poetess asks the blessed souls whirling above with the stars and the planets to intercede on her behalf, that her name might be remembered among monuments surviving through time and the great people ('treasures') who over the centuries have given Rome its glory."

The year 1560 proved a fortuitous one for both Battiferri and her husband. Battiferri received an invitation to join the selective Accademia degli Intronati of Siena, whose talented members held social events and drafted collectively authored works that shaped the Italian commedia dell'arte tradition. There were several private societies for creative types in late-Renaissance Italy, and Battiferri was the first female member formally inducted into one of them. Her husband was also one of the Intronati (the

Dazed) and was busy with multiple commissions. One of them was for the Medici ruling family and involved a rear courtyard extension of their Pitti Palace. Ammannati was also contracted to sculpt a massive Fountain of Neptune for the Piazza della Signoria in Florence and designed a storied bridge over the city's Arno River, which had flooded in September of 1557—an event Battiferri commemorated in a poem. Ammannati's elliptical-arched Ponte Santa Trinità, completed in 1570, became an iconic symbol of Florence and so vital a cultural landmark that it was rebuilt faithfully according to the architect's original design after it was destroyed during World War II.

Battiferri's husband celebrated his wife's success with a portrait of her he commissioned from Agnolo Bronzino, also know as Il Bronzino. One of the leading painters of the late-Renaissance Mannerist style, Bronzino also executed commemorative works for the Medici family members, all of which bear the same realistic, somber tone of *Portrait of Laura Battiferri,* which hangs in Florence's Palazzo Vecchio. She is depicted in profile and with a book of sonnets by the 14th-century Italian master Petrarch.

Donated to Jesuits in Florence

In 1564 Battiferri's second published work as an author, *I sette salmi penitenziali di David con alcuni sonetti spirituali* (The Seven Penitential Psalms of King David), was printed in Florence at the house of Giunti. "Every Psalm has an individual preface," wrote Kirkland in *Laura Battiferra and Her Literary Circle: An Anthology.* "These take the form of dedicatory letters from Laura, who speaks as a scriptural commentator to well-born women in nunneries of Florence and Urbino, explaining why each text is appropriate for its recipient."

Battiferri, Ammannati, and their Medici patrons had all come of age during the tumultuous twilight years of the Italian Renaissance and onset of religious wars that scarred the European continent for generations. There would be no more popes with children, nor Vatican prelates wealthy enough to build Roman villas alongside Borgo aristocrats. The Protestant Reformation became a defining force in late 16th-century Europe and Rome responded with the Counterreformation. This was a period of demonstrable piety and sober reflection as the Roman Church enacted major reforms. Much of footwork of this new era was carried out by a disciplined new religious order founded by St. Ignatius of Loyola of Spain. These were the Jesuits, or members of the Society of Jesus.

Eleonora, the Medici by marriage, was an important patron of the Jesuit presence in Italy. Battiferri and Ammannati followed suit. Ammannati designed the order's spiritual home in Florence in a new Church of San Giovannino, whose cornerstone was laid in 1579. About a decade later the artist Alessandro Allori, commissioned for San Giovannino's interior work, portrayed both Battiferri and her husband in the *Christ and the Canaanite Woman.* The inscription in the church's funeral chapel cites her date of death in 1589 at age 66, and her husband's death three years later at age 82.

Battiferri was working on a third volume at the time of her death, *Rime.* "The incomplete manuscript," noted Kirkland in her *Renaissance Quarterly* essay, "still survives at the Biblioteca Casanatense in Rome, with marginal instructions to the printer that seem to be in her own hand...From a period when Laura's literary activity was thought to have ceased, it is an unsuspected trove of several hundred poems, many of them deeply spiritual and never seen by the public, before or since." Ammannati hired a Jesuit writer to complete it, but then fell ill himself and the manuscript was abandoned.

"Be Astonished with Me, Heaven"

In her later years Battiferri and her husband lived at a small former abbey of the Camaldolese monks at Camerata, just outside Florence's city gates. It had a private chapel she used daily. Later generations of Italian scholars wrote of her exceptional writing talent, starting with Bernardino Baldi, an academic who lived and worked in Battiferri's birthplace of Urbino until his death in 1617. Kirkland, Battiferri's biographer and primary translator, cited one verse from *Rime* as a choice example of Battiferri's maturation as a poet. Kirkland translated this in the *Renaissance Quarterly* survey as "Stupisci meco, Ciel; stupisci, terra; poiche vedi la terra ir sopra 'l Cielo, e per me terra il Ciel porto sotterra (Be astonished with me, Heaven; be astonished, earth; for you see the earth go above Heaven, and for me earth Heaven carried beneath the earth)."

Books

Battiferra degli Ammannati, Laura, *Laura Battiferra and Her Literary Circle: An Anthology: A Bilingual Edition,* edited and with an introduction by Victoria Kirkland, University of Chicago Press, 2006.

Cox, Virginia, *The Prodigious Muse: Women's Writing in Counter-Reformation Italy,* Johns Hopkins University Press, 2011.

Periodicals

Renaissance Quarterly, Summer, 2002.□

Anatole De Baudot

French architect Anatole de Baudot (1834–1915) possessed a vast knowledge of historical building methods but is best known for promoting the use of reinforced concrete as a modern, cost-efficient construction material. His most enduring work is a minor Paris Art Nouveau landmark, the Church of St.-Jean-de-Montmartre. Completed in 1904, it was the first public structure in France to use reinforced concrete as its primary building material.

B orn Joseph-Eugène-Anatole de Baudot on October 14, 1834, the future architect and professor of art was a native of Sarrebourg in the Moselle département of France. As a young man he won a place at the prestigious École des Beaux-Arts (School of Fine Arts) in

Paris. Among his mentors there was the architect and professor Eugène Viollet-le-Duc, best remembered for this restoration of the Notre Dame Cathedral of Paris. It was Viollet-le-Duc, a champion of the Gothic Revival style, who added the signature gargoyle and chimera figures on the façade of the famous Roman Catholic cathedral. Baudot also trained under Henri Labrouste, a pioneer in the use of iron frames in large-building construction.

Restored Medieval Church

In 1865 Baudot joined the faculty of the newly formed École Spéciale d'Architecture, a private academy that sought to break with the tradition-bound rules of Beaux-Arts architects. Other leading figures at the new École included Viollet-le-Duc and Ferdinand de Lesseps, the builder of the Suez Canal. Baudot taught at the school while maintaining auxiliary career pursuits: he wrote extensively on architectural theory while also seeking architectural commission work from public and private sources. One of his first important completed works was the rebuilding of a church in Saint-Lubin in Rambouillet, near Paris. Named after the sixth-century French bishop canonized as Saint Leobinus in the Roman Catholic faith, the original house of worship dated back to the 12th century and was badly in need of renovation. Baudot designed a Gothic Revival edifice that used iron bars in the flying buttresses, which are one of the signature elements of traditional Gothic architecture. He completed the project in 1869, two years following the publication of his first book, a survey on town and village houses of worship titled *Église du bourgs et de villages*.

Baudot's professional mentor, Viollet-le-Duc, also recruited Baudot to work on an important restoration project in Paris, the Château de Vincennes. One of the most historically significant castles in France, the structure dated back to the 1340s and once included the tallest fortified guard tower in all of Europe. Viollet-le-Duc died in 1879, and Baudot took over the supervision of the project, which lasted another 40 years. By that point he had been hired by the French government ministry that oversaw education and religious organizations as the architect for diocesan buildings. During this period he also secured an official appointment to a seat on France's Historical Monuments Commission.

Spoke at 1889 Paris Exhibition

Baudot was excited by rapid innovations in science and industry that occurred in his lifetime. He wrote extensively on architecture and urged its practitioners to lead 19th century France forward in building design. In 1889 he spoke before an international gathering of architects assembled as part of the 1889 Exposition Universelle, held to commemorate the centenary of the French Revolution. "A long time ago the influence of the architect declined, and the engineer, *l'homme moderne par excellence,* is beginning to replace him," he said, according to Sigfried Giedion's *Space, Time and Architecture: The Growth of a New Tradition.* "It will not be [arbitrarily chosen] shapes which will form the basis of the new architecture: in urban planning, in the real application of modern construction, the taking into account of the new

situations which must be reckoned with will lead us to the shapes so long sought in vain."

In 1882 Baudot won a prestigious architectural commission to design the campus of a new high school in Sceaux, a suburb of Paris. The Lycée Lakanal was named after a leading figure and educational reformer in the French Revolutionary period, Joseph Lakanal. Baudot designed a series of classroom buildings, dormitories, and administrative and recreational facilities for the competitive-entrance high school. It was completed in 1885 and Baudot designed two more schools like it, the Lycée Edmond-Perrier in Tulle, which was completed in 1887, and the Lycée Victor-Hugo in Paris. All three institutions were still educating students a hundred years after their architect died in 1915.

Designed Montmartre Landmark

Baudot joined the faculty of his own alma mater, the École des Beaux-Arts, in 1887 as a professor of medieval and renaissance architecture. A few years later he won a major commission from the Roman Catholic diocese of Paris to construct a new church in Montmartre, the rapidly expanding quarter of the city in which an immense, new white-travertine landmark of Paris, the Sacré-Cœur Basilica, was under construction.

Baudot worked with a French building engineer named Paul Cottancin who had devised a way to reinforce concrete with iron. Baudot later said that his bid for the Montmartre church was accepted simply because the costs involved were so much lower—concrete was a much cheaper material than granite or other load-bearing materials. Work began on the site at 19 rue des Abbesses in 1894, but municipal building authorities cast doubts about the safety of reinforced concrete. "The novelty of the technique involved him in all sorts of wearisome litigation," remarked Peter Collins in *Concrete: The Vision of a New Architecture* about Baudot's audacious plan, "but this at least had the advantage of giving well-merited publicity to his enterprise and courage.".

As Collins further revealed in the book, Baudot's trouble with Paris authorities began a few years into the job and was related "to some obscure contravention of a regulation concerning building alignments, whereby the curé of Montmartre should have obtained prior municipal dispensation for the site he chose, the police tribunal fined him a nominal five francs and then ordered the half-constructed church to be torn down," Collins wrote. Baudot and the curé battled for several more years, working with Cottancin to prove that the building's walls, floors, and other potentially lethal structural elements were indeed safe. The house of worship was consecrated in 1904 as the Church of St. Jean l'Evangéliste de Baptiste, but is better known as the Church of St.-Jean-de-Montmartre. It was the first church to be built with reinforced concrete anywhere in the world, though Baudot designed an exterior façade that features brick, glass, and ceramic elements.

Exhorted Use of New Spaces, Forms

Baudot wrote extensively about the construction methods he and Cottancin used for the Church of St.-Jean-de-Montmartre and on another project, a municipal theater in Tulle, the same city where Baudot's Lycée Edmond-Perrier was located. As a theorist Baudot's most widely read titles are *L'Architecture et le ciment armé* (Architecture and Reinforced Concrete), published in 1905 and *L'Architecture: Le passé, le présent* (Architecture, Past and Present), which appeared posthumously. In the latter work, Baudot exhorted designers to embrace the progress of the Industrial Age. "Do we not have one of the most useful and interesting examples in the new expressions of terrestrial and marine vehicles?" he argued, according to *Changing Ideals in Modern Architecture, 1750–1950,* another book by Collins. "Have these been given the forms of carriages or ships of the time of Louis XIV? Not at all; the inter-relationships and appearances were deduced from scientific and industrial data. Why therefore are fixed shelters, that is to say, buildings, not designed in a similar way?"

Baudot was among several pioneers working with various methods of reinforced concrete. Besides Cottancin, other engineers were patenting ways of shaping concrete around iron rods and wire mesh to give both tensile strength and strructural integrity. Concrete had been used as a building material by the ancient Romans, who perfected the mixture of stone, water, and a binding element to erect large arches and domes, but it had fallen out of favor for centuries. Builders began experimenting with other recipes in the 1700s. Baudot was not the first architect to use reinforced concrete, but his Montmartre church was the first-ever building designed for public use with a frame made entirely from iron-infused cement.

Baudot served as president of France's Historical Monuments Commission from 1907 until his death eight years later. He died in Paris at the age of 80 on February 28, 1915. One of his most influential followers in the use of reinforced concrete was Auguste Perret, a Belgian architect who worked in Paris for many years and designed some notable landmarks, including as the Église Notre-Dame du Raincy and the Théâtre des Champs-Élysées. Perret hired a young Swiss man named Charles-Éduard Jeanneret-Gris, who had not yet chosen a career path. Working in the Perret architectural firm inspired Jeanneret-Gris to take up the profession, and he later adopted the pseudonym Le Corbusier and became one of the 20th century's most daring visionaries. Le Corbusier designed epic works out of reinforced concrete and inspired generations of architects whose Modernist works are found in cities around the world.

Books

Collins, Peter, *Changing Ideals in Modern Architecture, 1750–1950,* McGill-Queen's University Press, second edition, 1998.

Collins, Peter, *Concrete: The Vision of a New Architecture,* McGill-Queen's University Press, second edition, 2004.

Giedion, Sigfried, *Space, Time and Architecture: The Growth of a New Tradition,* fifth edition, Harvard University Press, 1967.

Online

"Anatole de Baudot," *Structurae.net,* http://structurae.net/persons/data/index.cfm?id=d001484 (July 15, 2014) . □

Bruno Bauer

German philosopher and historian Bruno Bauer (1809–1882) showed much promise early in his career as a scholar of the origins of Judeo-Christian theology. His legacy is intertwined with that of Karl Marx, on whom Bauer was a decisive influence when Marx was still a university student in Berlin.

Bruno Bauer was the eldest of four sons born to Caroline Wilhelmina Reichardt Bauer, the daughter of an advokat, or legal professional, in Saxony. She was married to a porcelain painter and the couple was living in Eisenberg, a town in the present-day German state of Thuringia, when their first son was born on September 6, 1809. Three more brothers followed, named Edgar, Egbert, and Egino.

The eldest Bauer boy benefited significantly from his family's move to Berlin, the capital city of the Kingdom of Prussia, around 1824. He attended schools in the city's royal-palace district of Charlottenburg, and from there he entered Friedrich Wilhelm University, a major center of science and progressive scholarship in Germany during this period. He spent four years as a student of theology and in 1829 penned a prize-winning essay on philosopher Immanuel Kant, a major figure of Germany's Age of Enlightenment.

Promoted by Hegelians

At Friedrich Wilhelm University, Bauer was a protégé of the highly regarded professor Ernst Wilhelm Hengstenberg, a Lutheran theologian who wrote extensively on the sources of the Bible. Young theologians of Bauer's generation were also profoundly influenced by the work of German philosopher Georg Wilhelm Friedrich (G.W.F.) Hegel who, with Kant, became a major force upon 19th century German scholarship.

Another influential figure in Bauer's years at Friedrich Wilhelm University was Philip Marheineke, a theology professor who helmed a faction of followers of Hegel known as the Old Hegelians, or Right Hegelians, in the years following the philosopher's death in 1831. Bauer would eventually become part of a faction that divided followers of Hegel into two opposing camps: the Old Hegelians like Marheineke were more closely associated with the staunchly conservative German Lutheran church. Young Hegelians, by contrast, shared few commonalities except the belief that Hegelian critical theory could be used to examine—and hopefully dismantle—the Christian underpinnings of the Prussian state. The Young Hegelians are sometimes called Left Hegelians.

In 1834 Bauer was given a teaching position in the faculty of theology at Friedrich Wilhelm University and began voicing more radical views on religion. Just 25 years old, he gained renown as a riveting lecturer and soon gathered his own circle of acolytes. There was a *stammtisch,* or weekly drinking club, and it was there in 1836 that a young newcomer to Berlin, Karl Marx, found comradeship and encouragement for his literary ambitions. The 18-year-old Marx was from Trier, a city on the Rhine River, and came from a prosperous family who were relatively recent converts from Judaism.

Encouraged Marx toward Political Philosophy

Marx was ostensibly in Berlin to pursue a law degree at Friedrich Wilhelm University in accordance with his father's wishes. He balked at this, however, and became increasingly devoted to writing poetry, fiction, and essays that focused on philosophy and religion. He took Bauer's course on the Old Testament book of the Hebrew prophet Isaiah, and Bauer invited Marx to help edit a new edition of Hegel's seminal *Philosophy of Religion*. Marx also became involved in plans for a yearbook of literary criticism with another member of the stammtisch circle, Adolf Rutenberg, who was related to Bauer through marriage.

The Young Hegelians urged a reexamination of works from the religious, historical, and literary canon using a firmly Rationalist approach. Following his mentor Hengstenberg, Bauer became active an area of theological study that involved parsing the books of the Old and New Testaments. Another well-known figure from this period was David Friedrich Strauss, whose 1835 tome *Das Leben Jesu* (The Life of Jesus) was a major influence on Bauer. Like Strauss, Bauer and others studied the oldest known fragments of the Bible in ancient languages like Greek and Aramaic, and compared them to other documents from the same historical period. This approach was an emerging field and slightly daring for its examination of the books of the Hebrew prophets and the gospels attributed to followers of Jesus Christ; Bauer and others regarded them less as reverence-worthy sacred texts to be considered the word of God as transmitted through prophets but rather as historical documents that reflected the political realities and aspirations of the Hebrew and early Christian peoples of the ancient Middle East.

Bauer published a spate of weighty tomes during his years at Friedrich Wilhelm University. One of his first important contributions to scholarship was an 1838 book, *Kritische Darstellung der Religion des Alten Testaments* (Critical Exhibition of the Religion of the Old Testament). Two years later he produced *Kritik der evangelischen Geschichte des Johannes* (Critique of the Evangelical History of John). By that point he had taken a teaching position at the University of Bonn, a post that came to him through his ties to Karl von Altenstein, Prussia's education minister. Von Altenstein was a progressive who promoted Bauer and two other Young Hegelians, Arnold Ruge and Ludwig Feuerbach, to secure university posts in the 1830s. When von Altenstein died in 1840 and was replaced by a much more doctrinaire government minister, a brief period of academic freedom for the Young Hegelians in Prussia in the 1830s came to an end.

Debated Historical Accuracy of Gospels

Bauer, like Ruge and Feuerbach, took a firm view on the role of religion in German society and protested the new era of academic censorship that followed under Johann

Eichhorn, von Altenstein's successor. He also openly professed his atheist beliefs, which was deemed incompatible with his role as a lecturer in Protestant theology. Bauer spent just two years at the University of Bonn. During that time he completed *Kritik der evangelischen Geschichte der Synoptiker* (Critique of the Evangelical History of the Synoptics) and began work on *Hegels Lehre von der Religion und Kunst* (Hegel's Doctrine of Religion and Art). His writings grew increasingly strident in their rejection of several key tenets of biblical theology. In one astonishing paper he contended that a rebel sect leader named Jesus or Yeshua had not existed in that time period that the Gospels recount, from the birth of a messiah in the Year 0 to that sect leader's crucifixion and resurrection 33 years later. Bauer asserted that early adherents of Christianity had instead concocted a series of interconnected stories that closely matched previous Jewish prophecies that a son of God, or messiah, would arrive on earth at some future date.

Bauer was not the first historian to venture that an individual named Jesus of Nazarene had never actually existed, but his writings were the among the first of their kind to be widely disseminated and discussed in Germany. His arguments were not uncommon for his generation, but they did imperil his position as a government-salaried teacher of theology. Eichhorn, von Altenstein's successor, ordered him to publicly retract some of his more radical views or resign. This battle was waged through much of 1841, and attracted enormous attention in Bonn, Berlin, and cities where Hegelian ideas had taken root. When Bauer refused to resign, arguing in support of his right to academic freedom, Eichhorn suggested he return to Berlin and take a research position instead. Bauer refused, and for that his teaching license was revoked by the Ministry of Education. This was a grave setback to his career in German academia, and one from which he would never recover.

Rode Donkeys with Marx

The dismissal of Bauer from his university post also had dire implications for Marx, who had become one of his most promising protégés. Bauer encouraged Marx to finish his doctoral dissertation—a philosophical tract deemed too controversial for the University of Berlin in the late 1830s—and offered networking advice to secure a university-teaching position. Bauer also urged Marx to come to Bonn and promised to use his influence to help Marx find a spot on the faculty at its university. After the University of Jena granted Marx his Ph.D. in 1841 the newly minted Herr Doktor Marx went to Bonn to work with Bauer, whose career was swiftly disintegrating in the midst of his months-long battle with Eichhorn and the Ministry of Education. Biographers recount one infamous incident that was said to have occurred around Easter weekend of 1842 in which Bauer and Marx, after drinking prodigiously, rented donkeys and rode them through the streets of the resort town of Bad Godesberg outside Bonn. This mimicked the entry of Christ into Jerusalem and was said to have scandalized visitors and residents of Bad Godesberg during the holiest week on the Christian liturgical calendar.

After losing his university-teaching license in the spring of 1842, Bauer went to Berlin to petition the Ministry of Education for reinstatement. Marx, meanwhile, was faced with the removal of his most high-ranking mentor and was devastated by the prospect of not securing a respectable and well-paid teaching post. Marx went to a nearby city of Cologne and worked under Rutenberg, Bauer's brother-in-law, who was editor of the *Rheinischer Zeitung*. Rutenberg drank heavily, however, and Marx eventually took over the job. Around this time Marx met another young revolutionary from prosperous background similar to his own, Friedrich Engels, who had fallen in with the Young Hegelians while stationed in Berlin for military service. Marx and Engels began writing together and eventually produced the pivotal *Communist Manifesto* of 1848.

Biographers of Bauer, Marx, Engels, and the others in their circle cite a government crackdown as instrumental in the direction of their careers. Marx and others, denied jobs for their beliefs, became even more radical and called for an overthrow of the old regime, much in the same way that philosopher-writers of 18th-century France had spurred a populist uprising against the *ancien régime* in 1789 and instituted a republican parliamentary system. Marx also made a firm break with the Young Hegelians, as did Engels. The group's repeated attacks on Christianity as a way to destabilize the Prussian state were futile, Marx came to believe. Marx instead argued that economic power—the capital in capitalism—was a much more powerful force of control on the masses than religion.

Wrote Anti-Semitic Screeds

The actual episode and paper trail related to the epic unfriending between Bauer and Marx is lost to history. It is known that once Bauer returned to Berlin and was unsuccessful in petitioning for reinstatement of his teaching license, he took up writing to support himself. In 1843 he wrote an inflammatory work about the status of Jews in Germany, who had historically been denied key civil-rights protections in most of Christian-ruled Europe since the Middle Ages. Bauer's *Die Judenfrage* (The Jewish Question) contended that because observant Jews were bound by certain Talmudic law, they could never be fully integrated into a modern, democratic society. Marx penned a blistering retort with Engels, *The Holy Family, or Critique of Critical Criticism against Bruno Bauer and Company,* which appeared in 1845. They continued to assail Bauer's writings in an 1846 book, *German Ideology*.

Bauer's generation, and it's the slightly younger one that followed as guided by peers like Marx and Engels, nearly succeeded in pushing many German states, plus France and multiple other European lands, into full-scale revolt in the spring of 1848. Bauer had no involvement in any of its activities, but his brother Edgar was an writer active and an enthusiastic proponent of terrorist acts.

Bauer died in the Berlin-Rixdorf district on April 13, 1882. He remains a largely forgotten figure in biblical scholarship, but references to his anti-Semitic writings began to turn up in the 21st century in debates about Islam in Europe. Conservatives who argued that Muslims' respect for their own shariah religious laws meant they could never

be fully integrated within a free and democratic society were reminded that a once-influential theologian had made the same contentions in the 1840s about Europe's large Jewish population.

Books

Rosen, Zvi, *Bruno Bauer and Karl Marx: The Influence of Bruno Bauer on Marx's Thought,* Martinus Nijhoff, 1977, reprinted by Springer Science & Business Media, 2012.

Sperber, Jonathan, *Karl Marx: A Nineteenth-Century Life,* W.W. Norton & Company, 2013.

Periodicals

New York Times, September 3, 2011.□

Bayezid I, Sultan of the Turks

Bayezid I (1354–1403) was one of the founding figures of the Ottoman Empire. Ruling an inherited sultanate for a crucial period in the 1390s, the Turkish prince and warrior led conquering armies across Eurasia and westward into the Balkans. In the Turkish language he is remembered as "Yildirim," or the Thunderbolt, for military campaigns that included an epic, eight-year-long siege of Constantinople.

B ayezid came of age at a time when the once-powerful Byzantine Empire was gradually enfolding itself into an emerging Ottoman successor state. Byzantine rule flourished between 500 and 700 CE, with Constantinople its center of power, but conflicts with neighboring Arabic and Persian rival empires diminished Byzantium's size and influence.

Fourth of 36 Osmanoğlu Rulers

Bayezid was born in 1354 during the reign of his grandfather Orhan I. Orhan's father was Osman I, who established the foundation state of the Ottoman Empire in 1299 after taking the Seljuk Sultanate of Rûm in eastern Turkey. Rûm was once part of a larger Seljuk Empire that had flourished for nearly two centuries between the 1030s and late 1190s. Sunni Muslim in faith and merging highly mobile Central Asian military prowess with advanced elements of Persian-Arabic culture, the Seljuks held a large part of Anatolia—the name generally given to a large portion of modern-day Turkey's Asian-continent provinces—after the decline of Byzantine power. The name Rûm, in fact, referred to the Eastern Roman Empire, an alternate name for Byzantium.

Anatolia was a vital gateway land between Europe and Asia, and Bayezid was born in the same year his father took advantage of a regional earthquake to seize Gallipoli, a strategic peninsula on the European side of present-day

Lebrecht Music and Arts Photo Library/Alamy

Turkey, also known as Eastern Thrace. Like Anatolia, Thrace and its environs were important land and sea routes that provided Europe with its only access to the Middle East and Asia until long-distance navigators began to sail south and east around the African continent. Europe lay on one side of Thrace, and on the opposite flank in Anatolia were routes to the Black Sea and Greater Rus, to the Levant and the important religious sites like Jerusalem, and to Central Asia. Beyond Anatolia, to the south and east, were to powerful Persian, Arabic, and Mongol empires. The Ottoman Turks, in fact, had originally come to Anatolia from the ancient city of Merv in Turkmenistan under the battle flag of Bayezid's great-grandfather, whose army came to aid the Seljuk Turks in one skirmish.

Captured Balkans, Sought Venice

It was Bayezid's father Murad I who first adopted the title of sultan in 1362 after conquering other lands and establishing a capital at Edirne in Thrace. Bayezid's mother was Gülçiçek, said to have been a former concubine taken by Orhan's armies when they seized the Karasid kingdom on one military excursion in Anatolia. Bayezid had one older half-brother and at least one younger full brother, Yahsi. All of the brothers likely began training for war at a very young age. Much of his teen and young-adult years were likely spent engaged in various military campaigns led by Murad. As the sultan's son he was likely schooled in good governance and administration at some point. It is known that he

served for a time as governor of the interior province of Kütahya in Anatolia.

In June of 1389, Bayezid took part in one of the most important battles on European soil of that century. This was the Battle of Kosovo Polje, an episode of major historical importance for the Serbian kingdom on the Balkan peninsula. The Serbs were a southern Slavic people and had staved off Greek and then Roman invasions over successive centuries. They eventually adopted Christianity and were granted the right to self-rule in the mid-twelfth century. They, too, went to war frequently, and began to clash with Bulgarians on their northeastern flanks and Greek Byzantine armies moving westward into Europe. There were multiple events that led to the Battle of Kosovo Polje, but Murad's end goal succeeded: he secured Ottoman control of the Balkans lands and that victory served to introduce Islam to this part of southern Europe.

Bayezid's father Murad led this famous battle and died on the "Field of the Blackbirds," the Serbian-language translation of Kosovo Polje. Murad was either slain in battle or shortly afterward by a Serbian knight, Miloš Obilić, in retaliation for the death of Serbian nationalist figure Prince Lazar Hrebeljanović. According to long-burnished tales, Bayezid reportedly killed his elder half-brother Yakub during this battle to remove Yakub from the line of succession.

In one of his first acts as sultan, Bayezid moved to cement his authority in the newly conquered Serbian lands by taking Olivera Despina, daughter of Prince Lazar, as his fourth wife. He also appointed her brother, Stefan Lazarević, as ruler of Serbia, which became a vassal state of the Ottoman Empire. As the fourth Ottoman sultan, Bayezid continued his late father's expansion campaign. His vision was to bring a vast stretch of territory under Ottoman control, from the Euphrates River in Iraq and Syria to the Danube, a symbolic water border that was also the gateway to the lands of the Holy Roman Empire in Western Europe. He also sought the riches of Venice, an early and active player in a new global mercantile empire that linked Europe to Asia.

Seized Macedonia and Bulgaria

Bayezid already had several progeny by a woman named Devlet, whose father Süleyman Shah had ruled the Germiyanids in Kütahya province. More significantly, Devlet was descended from the mystics who founded the Sufi branch of Islam. One of her sons with Bayezid eventually became the hereditary ruler of the Ottoman caliphate, and the family's hold stretched into the 1920s.

Bayezid spent much of his 13-year reign as sultan at war. In the early 1390s he took the region of Karaman in Anatolia as well as its great city Konya, once the Roman Empire outpost known as Iconium. On another front, he sent armies into Thrace and beyond to quash Greek, Macedonian, and Bulgarian rivals to Ottoman rule. In some cases the bitter enmities were religious in nature—the Greeks and others remained faithful to Eastern Rite Christianity and to the weakened Byzantine emperors.

Bayezid had grand ambitions to move further into Europe. In 1394 his army crossed the Danube River to seize Wallachia, a province on the other side of Bulgaria located in what is present-day Romania. Wallachia lay south of the Kingdom of Hungary, a buffer state between the Muslim

Ottomans and the rest of Christian-oriented Europe. At the Battle of Rovine in 1394, a Wallachian army forced the Ottomans back across the Danube in what proved to be only a temporary stay; Bayezid's descendants would later succeed in expanding Ottoman Muslim rule on a significant portion of southern Europe and very nearly took Vienna, Austria, in 1529 and again in 1683.

Besieged Constantinople

As an Ottoman sultan, Bayezid is chiefly remembered for his tenacious campaign to take the city of Constantinople, the last remaining holdout of the Byzantine emperors and another strategic prize and symbolic gem. In the late eleventh century, armies of Crusaders from Western Europe began moving through Byzantine lands on their way to retake Jerusalem from Muslim Arabic rule. In the disastrous Fourth Crusade of 1204 the mercenary army opted against the Middle East venture altogether and simply retook Constantinople. The new Latin Empire established there lasted for a little over a century, but it was a weak power and its inability to secure the rest of Turkey permitted figures like Bayezid's great-grandfather to move into Anatolia and establish a base of power there. Constantinople was eventually retaken by the 1320s by a new generation of Greek dynastic rulers, and those Palaiologos descendants remained in power in Constantinople for 125 years. These were the last of the Byzantine emperors, identifying themselves as both Greek and Christian, and they were the last non-Turks to hold the city.

Bayezid's siege of Constantinople began in 1394 and lasted eight years. It was not successful, but 50 years after his death his heirs captured the capital and made it the center of Ottoman rule that lasted until World War I. Bayezid's siege preparations include construction of Güzelcehisar, or Beauteous Castle, an immense fortress he constructed on the Bosphorus.

Bayezid had a more decisive victory in 1396 with the Battle of Nicopolis, a Bulgarian episode that concluded his conquest of Macedonia. The battle at this fortress site on the Danube is also considered the final chapter in the western Europe's Crusades to retake former Byzantine lands and holy sites in the Levant. The battle pitted nearly 10,000 soldiers on both sides and was epic in its bloody finality. Bayezid's foes were a combined force led by Sigismund, the King of Hungary, plus French and German armies under John II, Duke of Burgundy. The Ottomans slaughtered nearly all combatants after retaking Nicopolis, and even captured John. The Burgundians paid an enormous ransom for his return.

Legend of Caged Caliph

Bayezid himself was taken prisoner six years later in July of 1402 during the Battle of Ankara, an ancient city in Anatolia. Ankara had previously been under Roman, Greek, and even late Bronze Age Hittite rule, and was flourishing once again during Bayezid's lifetime as a center of mercantile and maritime power. Like the rest of Anatolia, Ankara was newly threatened by Mongol armies from Central Asia. Led by Timur—also known as Tamerlane, a successor of Genghis Khan—the Mongols were marauders of

the first order and feared from the Russian steppes down to the Indus River Valley on the Asian subcontinent.

Timur established his Timurid dynasty as a rival to Ottoman power and pushed from Central Asia into Anatolia by securing alliances with minor princes who had long-standing grievances against Bayezid and his predecessors. Bayezid was taken prisoner during the Battle of Ankara and possibly transported to Timur's court in Samarkand in an iron cage. Bayezid's wife Despina was also said to have been publicly humiliated, and these stories absolutely riveted Western Europe, who knew of Bayezid as the son of a Muslim king who had killed a Christian prince, Lazar, on Christian soil in the Balkans; he was also infamous for seizing John II, the Duke of Burgundy.

Bayezid died in Akşehir, Anatolia, on March 8, 1403. He was the last Ottoman sultan ever to marry—his successors took only concubines, to forestall the tendency to fratricide and inheritance wars carried out in Bayezid's own generation and among his sons. Those princely rivals were Süleyman, İsa, Mehmed, and Musa, and they fought one another during what became known as the Ottoman Interregnum after Timur and his armies retreated from Anatolia. Mehmed eventually prevailed and became Sultan Mehmed I in 1413.

Bayezid also holds a singular place as the Ottoman sultan ever taken as a prisoner of war. His descendants remained in power for a period of astonishing longevity that stretched from 1299, when his great-grandfather took the title of Sultan, to 1922, when the last sultan of Anatolia was deposed. The site of his crushing defeat at Ankara was also selected that same decade as the new capital and symbolic heartland of the Republic of Turkey.

Books

Finkel, Caroline, *Osman's Dream: The History of the Ottoman Empire,* Basic Books, 2006.

Kastritsis, Dimitris J., *The Sons of Bayezid: Empire Building and Representation in the Ottoman Civil War of 1402–1413,* Brill, 2007.

Necipoğlu, Nevra, *Byzantium Between the Ottomans and the Latins, Politics and Society in the Late Empire,* Cambridge University Press, 2009.

Periodicals

Europe, May 1999. □

Achille François Bazaine

French military officer Achille François Bazaine (1811–1888) reached the rank of the Marshal of France and played a key role in mid-19th century conflicts as the Crimean War and the Franco-Prussian War. Though he had served with distinction from the 1830s to the 1860s, his less than stellar actions during the Franco-Prussian conflict led to a censure, court-martial, and imprisonment.

Georgios Kollidas/Shutterstock.com

Born on February 13, 1811, in Versailles, France, Achille François Bazaine was the son of an engineer. Not academically gifted and from relatively humble origins, Bazaine failed the entrance examination to the Ecole Polytechnique. After this disappointment, he enlisted in the French Army. He joined the 37th Infantry Regiment in March 1831, starting his military career as a mere private. Less than a year later, Bazaine transferred to the French Foreign Legion. By 1833, he was commissioned a second lieutenant in the Foreign Legion.

Served in Algeria and Spain

Bazaine was first exposed to combat during the 1830s. He was involved with the First Carlist War, which lasted from early 1834 to August 1839. As part of his duties during the war, he took part in a military mission to Spain. He also served as a soldier during the French conquest of the North African country of Algeria, which lasted much of the 1830s. He was wounded in the process, and was honored with the Cross of the Legion of Honor. After the conquest of Algeria ended, Bazaine remained active in the Algerian region for much of the 1840s. He focused on political and counter-insurgency operations there.

By the early 1850s, France became involved in the tensions in Crimea. By the time war broke out in 1853, Bazaine had reached the rank of colonel. He was sent to Crimea in 1854 and put in command of a brigade, the First Regiment of the Foreign Legion. On September 6, 1855, he took part in the final assault on the key Russian fortress at Sevastopol. When the city was captured, Bazaine became its military governor. In the next month, Bazaine also took part in the attack on Kinburn to take these forts.

At the end of the 1850s, Bazaine was involved in the Piedmontese War, also known as the Italian war. The short-lived conflict—lasting a few months in mid-1859—was fought between the Kingdom of Sardinia, which included Piedmont-Sardinia, and their French allies against Austria. Bazaine lead a division in the corps of Baraguay d'Hillier, and was wounded in the head while taking part in fighting in Melegnano in the Lombardy region. In the June 1859 battle at Solferino, his actions were considered particularly honorable. He suffered a near injury as he was shot with a bullet through his saddle-holster. Bazaine was promoted to brigadier general in this period.

Was Effective in Mexico

In the early 1860s, France, led by Napeolon III, focused on intervening in Mexico, perhaps for colonial purposes. In 1862, Bazaine was sent to Mexico as a divisional commander and again showed his skills as a military leader. On May 17, 1863, he was able to capture the city of Puebla. Because of this key victory, he was appointed commander of all the expeditionary corps in Mexico in July 1863 by the order of Napoleon III. Bazaine replaced General Élie-Frédéric Forey.

For the next eight months, Bazaine essentially ruled Mexico until Napeoleon's chosen emperor arrived, Archduke Maximilian. During this period, Bazaine was charged with gaining the support of moderates in Mexico, while reconciling competing factions. He also followed Napoleon III's policy of stopping any reversal of key Reform Laws supported by France. On his own, Bazaine showed his disdain for conservatives in Mexico and, later, the indecivsiveness of Emperor Maximillian.

By September 1864, Bazine's impressive military work in Mexico led to his promotion to marshal of France. Early the next year, he had another military victory in Mexico, successfully conduting a siege on Oaxaca. This victory was considered a high point of his military career as he took the city with 8,000 toops and captured the Mexican military commander, Porfirio Díaz. Bazaine remained in Mexico for two more years, but because of diplomatic pressure from the United States, France evacuated Mexico beginning in 1866. Bazaine oversaw the evacuation and left on the last convoy, which departed Mexico on March 12, 1867. Because Napoleon considered the Mexican campaign an embarrasement by its end, Bazaine received no military honors despite his outstanding service.

Failed Leadership in Franco-Prussian War

Bazaine returned to France for several years, and when the Franco-Prussian War broke out in 1870, he returned to action. Prussia, led by minister-president Otto von Bismarck, was working to unify the German states under Prussian leadership, but had decieved France and used French communications to further his unification cause. Prussian actions—such as trying to secretly place a German prince on the throne of Spain—further inflamed tensions. As the situation grew worse, the French government declared war on July 19, 1870, and Prussia responded by positioning three armies along the French frontier in the Rhineland.

In August 1870, Bazaine was handed command of the Third Army Corps and its 103,000 men. Because of two major defeats of the French army under the control of an ill French emperor Napoleon III, he gave Bazaine command of the reorganized French Army of the Rhine. Also known as the left wing of the French Army, it included the Second, Third, and Fourth Army Corps. Though Bazaine was essentially an army commander, he had no army staff and could not compete with superior Prussian organization and preparation, which may have impacted subsequent mistakes.

Bazaine and his troops struggled during the rest of the conflict. Prussia had a number of military successes on the frontier, and his troops fell back toward Chalons. In August 1870, he tried to make a stand against Prussia at Borny but was wounded. Despite his injuries, he led his troops in battles at Mars-la-Tour and Rezonville, but the battles proved inconclusive.

Errors at Gravelotte-Saint-Privat

On August 18, 1870, Bazaine could have made a serious breakout effort from Prussian troops at the key battle of Gravelotte-Saint-Privat, but did not. The Prussian forces wanted to destroy the French, and threw 188,000 Germans with 732 guns at the 112,000 French troops and their 520 guns. Additional German forces did not arrive because they became trapped in a ravine. If Bazaine had made a focused attempt to better position and employ his troops, many historians believe he would have most likely achieved victory and bested German forces that day.

Bazaine also made an error when he failed to support the Sixth Army Corps, led by Marshal François Certain Canrobert, at the same battle that day. Canrobert's Sixth Army Corps of 23,000 men were holding off 100,000 German troops, but needed reinforcements to maintain their hold. Bazaine would not do so. When another German force arrived and was in a position to cut off Canrobert's forces, he was forced to withdraw to Metz.

After Bazaine's own withdrawal to French headquarters at Metz and its entrenched camp, he was quickly beseiged by Prussian troops and cut off from any escape routes. The seige lasted for 70 days. Though he had several opporunities to improve his situation after this point, he could not see or capitalize on them. Bazaine failed to break out of Metz, and two attempts proved half-hearted at best.

France itself suffered further setbacks. Its military lost at Sedan, and MacMahon surrendered his 100,000 men, including Napoleon III, on September 1, 1870. The Second Empire was overthrown that same day, and Napoleon III was deposed. A new regime—the Government of National Defense helmed by Leon Gambetta—took power. Bazaine did not try to establish communications with the so-called Paris Commune, but instead started negotations with Prussian leader von Bismarck himself.

As part of the negotiations, the idea that Bazaine be allowed to use his troops to save France from this new

Third Republic was discussed. Instead, Prussian forces made their way to Paris and put the city under seige until January 1871. Negotiations between Bazaine and the Prussians reached their end, though historians believed that Bazaine could have held out until at least mid-November 1870 and perhaps saved the French army.

Surrendered to Prussia

On October 28, 1870, Bazaine formally surrendered Metz and his army—which included some 130,000 to 173,000 troops—to Prussia. He was then held captive by the Prussian army in Germany. Bazaine rejected the Prussian offer of honors of war. As part of his surrender, he failed to order the destruction of his army's remaining weapons, so the Prussians gained some 600 working firearms as well. This particular decision flummoxed future historians because destruction of an army's firearms was a common part of surrender agreements.

When Bazaine's captivity ended and he returned to France, he was roundly criticized for his actions during the Franco-Prussian conflict. Though he had been a brave and able soldier during previous military excursions, he was perceived to be quite the opposite during this last conflict. He was timid, indecisive, and inept, and his performance considered not above reproach despite extenuating circumstances such as Prussian military and organizational superiority.

Indignant, Bazaine demanded a court of inquiry because he believed that there was no legitimate authority from which to take orders. The outcome was not what Bazaine expected. In the spring of 1872, he was severely censured. Because Bazaine was not pleased with this outcome, he asked for a court martial. This sentence was even more harsh. Convicted of treason because of his actions during the war, he was sentenced to military degradation and death on December 10, 1873. Bazaine was spared this fate by the president of the Third Republic, Marshal Patrice de MacMahon. The president commuted Bazaine's sentence to 20 years of seclusion in prision.

Escaped Prison

Bazaine was held in a prison on Ile Sainte-Marguèrite, located on the Mediterranean coast near the city of Cannes. On August 10, 1874, Bazaine escaped with the assistance of his wife. She supplied him with ropes which he used to climb down the 300 foot cliffs outside the prison. There, a sailboat—hired by his wife in Cannes—awaited him. After fleeing captivity, Bazaine first went to Italy, then later settled in Spain. He spent the rest of his days in poverty in the latter country. He died in Madrid on September 20, 1888.

Despite the many mistakes that Bazaine made in the Franco-Prussian War, some subsequent historians believed he was unfairly blamed for the defeat at the hands of the Prussians. In a London *Financial Times* review of Wolfgang Schivelbusch's *The Culture of Defeat: On National Trauma, Mourning, and Recovery*, Michael Glover argued that Bazaine was a scapegoat. Glover stated, ''How . . . do you make yourself feel better when you have been humiliated?...France dealt with the shock of defeat at the hands of the Prussians by blaming the mob rule of the Paris Commune....A little later it found a scapegoat in the person of one particularly treacherous French general, Achille-François Bazaine, who had surrendered to the Prussians instead of leading his men back to Paris—in doing so he had done no worse than Napoleon III himself."

Books

Dupuy, Trevor N., Curt Johnson, and David L. Bongard, *The Harper Encyclopedia of Military Biography,* HarperCollins, 1992.

Encyclopedia of Invasions and Conquests: From Ancient Times to the Present, 2nd ed., edited by Paul Davis, Grey House Publishing, 2006.

Encyclopedia of Latin American History and Culture, Volume 1, 2nd ed., edited by Jay Kinsbruner and Erick D. Langer, Charles Scribner's Sons, 2008.

A Global Chronology of Conflict: From the Ancient World to the Modern Middle East, Volume 4: 1861-1981, edited by Spencer C. Tucker, ABC-CLIO, 2010.

Tucker, Spencer C., *Battles That Changed History: An Encyclopedia of World Conflict,* ABC-CLIO, 2011.

Periodicals

Defence Studies, Spring 2005.

Financial Times (London, England), November 15, 2003. □

Franz Anton Beckenbauer

Nicknamed "Der Kaiser" (The Emperor), German soccer star Franz Beckenbauer (born 1945) remains the only soccer player to both captain (1974) and coach (1990) his country to World Cup victories. Widely considered one of the best defenders to ever play the game, Beckenbauer was named to the World Cup All-Star team in 1966, 1970, and 1974.

Franz Anton Beckenbauer was born September 11, 1945, in Munich, Germany, to Franz and Antonie Beckenbauer. His father was a postal worker. As early as age nine, Beckenbauer attracted attention for his playing style. By 13, he was the star of his local junior team, SC Munich 06, and aspired to join team 1860 Munich as soon as he came of age. At the time, 1860 was a prestigious placement and the team most German boys aspired to play for. However, Beckenbauer's team played the youth team from 1860 and the players treated him so poorly he vowed never to join the team.

Beckenbauer played forward at the time and had a rough match against the 1860 Munich defender tasked with marking him. "He was maybe twice my size, and he hit me a few times; then he hit my face," Beckenbauer recalled to *Sports Illustrated* reporter Grant Wahl. "After the game, I said to my teammates, 'I'm not going to 1860. I'm going

Hans-Guenther Oed/vario images GmbH & co.KG/Alamy

to Bayern.' And all my teammates, who also wanted to go to 1860, came with me to Bayern."

Joined Bayern Munich

In 1959, Beckenbauer joined the FC Bayern München (Bayern Munich) junior club. He was 14. Over the next few years he developed his skills and played so well he made the West German national youth team for 1964. Beckenbauer, however, was kicked off the squad because his girlfriend became pregnant and the 18-year-old Beckenbauer refused to marry her, which caused outrage in the German Football Association, better known as the DFB. He was later reinstated after his coach, Dettmar Cramer, interceded on his behalf.

In 1964, Beckenbauer was elevated to the Bayern senior team. At this time, he quit the insurance salesman trainee program where he was enrolled, in order to pursue professional soccer. He made his debut at left wing on June 6, 1964. At the time, Bayern competed in a regional league. In 1963, when the German leagues consolidated to form a premier professional league called the Bundesliga, Bayern was not admitted to the league. With Beckenbauer on the roster, however, Bayern had a successful 1964-65 season. That year the team also added goalkeeper Sepp Maier and striker Gerd Müller. The three would later earn the collective nickname "the axis." Because of the team's success, Bayern achieved promotion into the Bundesliga in 1965.

During its first season in the Bundesliga, Bayern Munich played strong and remained in title contention throughout most of the year. In the end, however, Bayern came up three points short and finished in third as cross-town rivals 1860 Munich went on to win the title. However, Bayern was successful in winning the 1966 German Cup (DFB Cup) a few weeks after the season ended. The tournament started with Germany's top 32 teams and Bayern Munich came out on top. In 1967, Bayern won the UEFA (Union of European Football Associations) Cup Winners' Cup, an inter-European club competition.

Dominated in World Cup

In 1966, Beckenbauer made 12 appearances with the German national team and played in his first FIFA World Cup. Beckenbauer had traditionally played defense for Bayern Munich, but was placed as a midfielder on the German team, helping to stabilize the midfield. Germany faced Switzerland in its first match, winning five to zero. Beckenbauer scored two goals in the match—one from a distance of 40 feet and the other from 52 feet out. Just 20, he was the youngest player on the German squad.

In a quarter-final match against Uruguay, Beckenbauer scored another goal as the Germans went on to win 4-0. He also scored in a 2-1 semifinal victory over the Soviet Union, helping Germany advance to the final against England. Tied 2-2 after regulation play expired, extra time was added to the match and England came out on top after a dramatic overtime. Beckenbauer scored four goals and was named young player of the tournament.

In 1968, Beckenbauer took on the role of captain for Bayern and returned to defense. Led by Beckenbauer's skills at sweeper and Müller's offensive play-making (Müller scored a league-leading 30 goals), Bayern won its first Bundesliga title during the 1968-69 season and repeated as league winners in 1972, 1973, and 1974. Bayern also won the German Cup (DFB Cup) in 1968, 1969, and 1971.

Earned Nickname *Der Kaiser*

During his heyday, Beckenbauer was credited with revolutionizing the sweeper position, also known as the *libero*, which is Italian for "free." The sweeper was tasked with "sweeping up" the ball when the opposing team broke through the defensive line. Most sweepers stayed put with the defensive line. Beckenbauer, however, liked to roam free and would advance into an offensive position whenever his side went on the attack. In this way, Beckenbauer organized his team from the back, using his pace, vision and deft passing ability to create offensive opportunities for his team. Instead of holding back, he always pressed ahead with the forwards.

During the mid-1960s, Beckenbauer earned the nickname "Der Kaiser." Accounts vary as to how he earned the moniker. One story says that while touring Austria, Beckenbauer posed with a bust of former Austrian Emperor Franz Joseph I. The press, when printing a caption for the picture, referred to Beckenbauer as the "football Kaiser" and the name later dwarfed to Der Kaiser. Other stories suggest the press gave Beckenbauer the nickname because he loosely resembled mad King Ludwig of Bavaria—in both looks and style.

Another account says the nickname came about during the 1969 German Cup final. In this match, Beckenbauer stole the ball from FC Schalke 04's star player, Reinhard Libuda, with a tackle that many thought should have earned a foul. Schalke fans booed Beckenbauer, who was nonplussed and dribbled the length of the pitch with the ball. Beckenbauer went deep into Schalke territory and proceeded to keep the defenders from taking the ball by juggling it for about 30 seconds until the hissing fans had to recognize his obvious talent. At the time, Libuda was widely hailed as the "König von Westfalen," or King of Westphalia. As Beckenbauer had "de-throned" Libuda in the match, the press dubbed Beckenbauer "Der Kaiser."

In 1970, Beckenbauer helped deliver West Germany through a strong run at the World Cup. The German squad won its first three matches and faced England in the quarter-finals. England led 2-0 until Beckenbauer scored a goal in the 69th minute, causing a shift in momentum that allowed Germany to tie the game before match time expired. Germany went on to win in extra time. In the semi-finals, Germany faced Italy in a grueling match during which Beckenbauer suffered a dislocated shoulder while getting fouled. He finished the game with his arm in a sling, but in the end, Germany could not overcome the Italians. West Germany's 4-3 loss to Italy knocked the Germans out of contention for first place. Instead, Germany played a consolation match against Uruguay and won to finish in third.

Four years later, Beckenbauer was captain of the 1974 German squad that made it to the World Cup finals. West Germany beat The Netherlands 2-1 in the final to secure the second World Cup victory in West German history. Beckenbauer became one of the few players to earn a complete collection of World Cup medals, having won gold (1974), silver (1966), and bronze (1970) during his years representing Germany.

Played in United States

In 1977, Beckenbauer stunned his homeland when he went to play soccer on the other side of the Atlantic Ocean, joining the New York Cosmos, which played in the now-defunct North American Soccer League. At the time, the Cosmos had been acquiring aging European soccer stars to increase attendance. The 1977 Cosmos roster featured Brazilian superstar Pelé, former Italian striker Giorgio Chinaglia, Dutchman Johan Neeskens and Belgian forward François Van der Elst. The star-studded international cast of players attracted crowds of 70,000 to Giants Stadium in New Jersey. It was reported that the transfer fee from Bayern, coupled with Beckenbauer's four-year contract, cost the Cosmos $2.8 million.

At the time, Beckenbauer said he transferred to the United States so he could enjoy some anonymity. A poll conducted around that time found that more Germans could identify Beckenbauer's face than could ID West German Chancellor Helmut Schmidt. Because of his skill and charm, Beckenbauer had become Germany's first poster boy for soccer. With Beckenbauer in the ranks, the Cosmos won the NASL championship in 1977, 1978, and 1980.

In 1981, Beckenbauer returned to native soil and joined Hamburger SV for the 1981-82 season. The 35-year-old defender helped the team to its second-ever Bundesliga title that year. Beckenbauer returned to the Cosmos for the 1983 season with a short-term, five-month contract. In addition to playing soccer, the deal included an agreement for the star to do promotions for Warner Communications, the company that owned the Cosmos. By this time, Beckenbauer was 37 and well beyond his prime.

Beckenbauer acknowledged to *New York Times* writer Alex Yannis that his best years were behind him and that he felt he was at his prime between 25 and 30. Cosmos forward and Yugoslavian Vlado Bogicevic told Yannis he was happy to have Beckenbauer on the team playing defense. ''Franz is good for the Cosmos and good for the N.A.S.L. I think the ball will get to midfield from the back faster, that's for sure. He has a better pass than most people. The ball comes at the right time. The guy knows the game. There is nothing you can teach him.'' After the 1983 season, Beckenbauer retired from soccer. In 105 appearances with the Cosmos, Beckenbauer scored 17 goals.

Worked as Soccer Ambassador

As a player, Beckenbauer enjoyed a phenomenal two-decade career. On the international stage, he represented West Germany from 1964-77. During that time, Beckenbauer became the first German player to exceed 100 caps. In soccer, a ''cap'' signifies each international match played. In sum, the star player had 103 caps with 14 goals scored. On the international field, Beckenbauer helped his teams to 69 wins, 19 draws, and 15 losses. In three World Cup tournaments, Beckenbauer scored five goals in 18 games. He had a hand in 14 wins, 1 draw, and three losses in World Cup play.

After hanging up his cleats, Beckenbauer became a coach. In 1986, he coached the West German squad to the World Cup title match, which ended in a 3-2 loss to Argentina. Beckenbauer had better luck as coach of the 1990 German squad, which once again faced Argentina in the final. West Germany scored in the 84th minute and went on to win the title. This win marked the final World Cup win for West Germany as German reunification soon followed.

Beckenbauer stayed with soccer, becoming a manager for Bayern Munich during the 1990s and later serving as president of the organization. He also worked as a sports commentator for the German tabloid *Bild*. In 2000, Beckenbauer oversaw Germany's bid to host the 2006 World Cup, and the organizing committee ended up choosing Germany over South Africa as the tournament site. Beckenbauer then served as president of the German organizing committee for the World Cup and, serving as an ambassador for the game, visited the 31 other countries participating in the Cup Finals. He traveled 75,000 miles in 117 days to make contact with the other teams.

In the days before the 2006 World Cup commenced, Beckenbauer went to the Austrian Alps to marry Heidi Burmester. He had divorced his second wife in 2004 and separated from his first wife while with the Cosmos. From his three marriages, Beckenbauer had five children. In 2010, Beckenbauer served on FIFA's executive committee, which decided the 2018 and 2022 World Cup venues.

Books

Beckenbauer, Franz, *Franz Beckenbauer's Soccer Power*, Simon and Schuster, 1978.

Kuper, Simon, *Soccer Men: Profiles of the Rogues, Geniuses, and Neurotics Who Dominate the World's Most Popular Sport*, Nation Books, 2011.

Periodicals

Age (Melbourne, Australia), March 22, 2006.
New York Times, June 19, 1980; July 2, 1980.
Observer (London, England), July 9, 2006.
Sports Illustrated, November 17, 2014.
Washington Times (D.C.), June 30, 2006.

Online

''Beckenbauer Is Set For Cosmos Opener,'' *New York Times,* http://www.nytimes.com/1983/05/01/sports/beckenbauer-is-set-for-cosmos-opener.html?pagewanted=print (December 18, 2014). □

Alexandre-Edmond Becquerel

The French physicist Edmond Becquerel (1820–1891) made critical discoveries in the fields of luminescence and phosphorescence. It was he who first explored the ways in which light could produce chemical reactions that in turn produce energy, a process later known as the photovoltaic effect.

Once harnessed, the photovoltaic effect would make it possible to convert sunlight into electricity and thus to construct the solar cells of today. Becquerel did not build solar cells, but he did a great deal of the basic research that first led to an understanding of how substances reacted to exposure to light. He devised instruments to measure light intensity resulting from chemical reactions, and the time it took for materials to react to the absorption of light, and he experimented with substances as coatings for tubes into which he would discharge electricity (a step in the direction of electric lighting, although he did not reach that milestone). In the middle of the 19th century, Becquerel was the most important scientist, in any country, working on the phenomenon of light produced by electrochemical reactions.

Part of Multigenerational Physics Family

Alexandre-Edmond Becquerel, who used the first name Edmond, was born on March 24, 1820, in Paris. He was part of a French family that made groundbreaking discoveries in a variety of fields over several generations. His father, Antoine Cé Becquerel (1788–1878), was a physics professor who devised a way of using electrolytes—broadly, liquids that conduct electricity—to separate

World History Archive/Alamy

metals from mined ore. Becquerel's son Antoine Henri Becquerel (1852–1908) was the discoverer of radioactivity, and his grandson Jean Antoine Becquerel did noted experimental work connected with the Theory of Relativity. Alexandre-Edmond was trained as a scientist by his father, turning down admission to two of France's top technical schools, the Ecole Polytechnique and the Ecole Normale Supérieure, to continue his studies with his father.

Eventually Becquerel signed on as his father's assistant in his physics classes at the Museum of Natural History, and then took a similar assistantship at the University of Paris, where he received a doctor of science degree in 1840. After teaching for a short time at the Agronomic Institute of Versailles, he became the chair of the physics department at the Conservatory of Arts and Trades (Conservatoire des Arts et Métiers) in 1852.

For much of the first part of his life, Becquerel worked in his father's laboratory, and he began to make significant discoveries while still in his teens. As early as 1839 he made a crude photovoltaic cell from a pair of electrodes (sometimes silver, then, when he got better results, platinum) enclosed in a black box, placed in an acid bath, and illuminated and placed under light. Becquerel found that the apparatus generated a small electric current. He immediately recorded his observations, varying not only the composition and coating of the electrodes but also the light source, using blue light, ultraviolet light, or sunlight.

Refined Faraday's Laws

Over the next years and decades, he worked to elaborate on this discovery, investigating related phenomena in electricity, magnetism, and the measurement of light. At a time when electricity was poorly understood, he was fascinated by electric current when it occurred. In 1843 he proposed a modification to Joule's Law, showing that an electrical current could generate heat in a liquid as well as a solid, and he also conducted experiments that expanded the reach of Michael Faraday's laws of electrolysis, proposed in 1834. He was also intrigued by the early form of the battery known as a voltaic pile (after its Italian inventor, Alessandro Volta, for whom the volt is named). Becquerel used a device of his father's invention, called the electrostatic balance, to measure the electric currents generated by voltaic piles, and he systematically investigated the effects of such variables as metallic and liquid composition, temperature, and electrode polarization on the power generated by voltaic piles.

For much of the period between 1845 and 1855, Becquerel worked on the problem of diamagnetism, a property of many common materials (water included) that causes them to repel an external magnetic field. Becquerel was troubled by Faraday's belief that diamagnetism was an essentially different phenomenon from usual magnetism, and he labored in vain to construct a theory that would connect the two. Devising an ingenious experiment involving condensed oxygen in a charcoal-filled glass tube, he was able to show that the magnetic force of the oxygen could be manipulated. But he was frustrated by the fact that the same effects could be observed in a vacuum, which should have altered them if his theory, which posited the relationship between a substance and its surroundings as a significant variable, were correct. He tried to explain the discrepancy with reference to the now-discredited idea of the ether, a supposed fifth element thought to transmit light other electrical phenomena.

Becquerel had more success when he worked on problems associated with light and its measurement. He was interested in the differences between luminescence, flourescence, and phosphorescence, which are closely related and can be distinguished from each other partly through close measurements of the speed at which substances react to light. Becquerel invented the phosophoroscope, a box sealed with rotating discs into which holes had been punched. This allowed him to observe substances in increments of fractions of a second after they had been exposed to light. He also invented another instrument, which he called an actinometer; it grew out his early experiments with the photovoltaic effect, and it related the intensity of light to electrochemical reactions and their heat intensity. The actinometer for the first time made it possible to determine the temperature of hot bodies by observing them optically.

Became Museum Director

In 1860 Becquerel began teaching chemistry (at the time, chemistry and physics were more closely related than they are today) at the Chemical Society of Paris, and he rejoined the staff of the Museum of Natural History there in 1863. In 1878, after his father's death, he became the museum's director. These promotions perhaps resulted from the publication of the 1859 book *Recherches sur les divers effets lumineux qui resultent de l'action de la lumiäre sur les corps* (Investigations into the Diverse Luminous Effects That Result from the Action of Light on Bodies), which described the phosphoroscope and summarized much of Becquerel's research over the years up to that point.

Becquerel's research covered a variety of other subjects related to light and energy. Interested in spectroscopy because it involved the composition of sunlight, he demonstrated the presence of Fraunhofer lines (dark lines that appear in the optical spectrum of sunlight) in the ultraviolet portion of the spectrum. He was interested in photography as it applied to phenomena in physics, and he was able to produce crude color photographs of the spectrum, although the images he created disappeared almost immediately after they were exposed to light. He found a unique method of developing photographs that involved the exposure of silver halides to light; although technically innovative, his method has rarely been used.

A second large publication, *La lumière: ses causes et ses effets* (Light: Its Causes and Effects), appeared in 1868. By that time Becquerel was a well-known physicist. He had been elected to France's Academy of Sciences in 1863, and the organization's journal, *Comptes Rendus,* published many of his papers. In 1886 Becquerel was elected to the Royal Swedish Academy of Sciences, the body that chooses the recipients of the Nobel Prizes in physics and chemistry. The Becquerel Prize, for outstanding achievements in photovoltaics research, was established in 1989 and named for Becquerel.

Becquerel died in Paris on May 11, 1891, and the following year his son Henri, born in 1852, became the third member of the family to serve as physics chair at the Museum of Natural History. "In the middle years of the nineteenth century," noted the *Complete Dictionary of Scientific Biography,* Becquerel "virtually monopolized the significant discoveries made" in the field of luminescence.

Books

Complete Dictionary of Scientific Biography, Scribner's, 2008.

Harvey, E. Newton., *A History of Luminescence from the Earliest Times Until 1900,* American Philosophical Society, 1957.

World of Invention, Gale, 2006.

Online

"Alexandre Edmond Becquerel (1820–1891)," *Molecular Expressions* (Florida State University), http://www.micro.magnet.fsu.edu/optics/timeline/people/becquerel.html (October 17, 2014).

"Alexandre-Edmond Becquerel Biography," *How Products Are Made,* http://www.madehow.com/inventorbios/25/Alexandre-Edmond-Becquerel.html (October 17, 2014).□

Menahem Mendel Beilis

Ukrainian factory manager Menahem Mendel Beilis (1874–1934) was accused of murder in one of the 20th century's most ignominious episodes of "blood libel," an anti-Semitic myth. The superintendent of a brickworks in Kiev, Beilis narrowly escaped conviction in a court case that aroused international attention and brought condemnation of human rights abuses in Tsarist Russia.

Menahem Mendel Beilis was born in 1874 into a family of Hasidic Jews in present-day Ukraine. At the time, Ukraine was part of the Russian Empire, a state so immense that an enormous standing army was required to maintain security. Jews were first conscripted into the Russian military in the 1820s, but the reformer Tsar Alexander II instituted a universal draft and shorter lengths of service than the mandatory 25-year stint for most conscripts. Beilis was among those who benefited from these new rules, which included a relaxation of residency laws for Jewish veterans. As a young man, Beilis settled in Mezhigorye, a distant suburb of Kiev, and married a woman named Esther and began a family. One of Esther's uncles owned a brick-manufacturing enterprise, and Beilis's first job was with that firm.

Respected Figure in Neighborhood

Around 1896, Beilis accepted a job offer much closer to Kiev as the superintendent of a new brick factory. The kilnworks was part of a philanthropic network established by the Jewish Zaitsev family, who were successful sugar merchants. The Zaitsevs had founded a hospital to serve the city's poorest Jews, and the Kiev brickworks was established as a commercial enterprise whose profits went toward staffing and supplies for the hospital.

Beilis worked for 15 years as the superintendent and was well liked by his largely non-Jewish workforce. The kilnworks was located on Yurkovskaya Street in a hilly, northern part of Kiev that was also near ancient caves uncovered by road builders some decades earlier. The Lukianovka caves, named for the Kiev district, were rumored to have been the hiding place of a long-buried treasure taken by Cossack forces or others over the years, and were a favorite haunt of adventurous youth.

Beilis was not an especially observant Jew. He often worked on Saturdays, for example, which is the traditional day of rest and religious observance in the Jewish faith. In his 1926 memoir *The Story of My Sufferings,* he recalled that he was treated cordially by his non-Jewish neighbors, and was even singled out for added protection by a Russian Orthodox priest when a wave of anti-Semitic violence erupted in Kiev and other parts of the Russian Empire in 1905.

Targeted by Black Hundred Group

Beilis repaid the favor when the same priest asked for bricks to build a school at a Russian Orthodox orphanage.

Beilis conferred with the owner, Zaitsev, and they sold the materials below cost. Such exchanges helped eradicate longstanding enmity between religious groups in Russia at a time when the tsarist regime still imposed restrictions on Jews' freedom of religion and of movement. There were calls for Alexander's grandson, Tsar Nicholas II, to eliminate the boundaries of the Pale of Settlement, the area in which Jews were legally bound to live and work. There were strong anti-Semitic elements in imperial Russia, however, and an ultranationalist group called the Union of the Russian People—also known as the Black Hundred—agitated against any reform. The group sought to scapegoat Jews and foment grass-roots resistance to any liberalization measures that did not designate ethnic Russians and adherents of the Russian Orthodox faith as protected citizens of the Empire.

Saturday was both a workday and a schoolday for Russians of the early 20th century. On the morning of March 12, 1911 (March 20 according to the New Style revised Gregorian calendar adopted by most of Europe in the sixteenth century), a 13-year-old boy named Andrei Yushchinsky left his house in another part of Kiev and headed to visit a friend in the Lukianovka district, where Andrei had previously lived with his impoverished family. He deliberately cut class that day at his Russian Orthodox-affiliated school and went instead to the home of his friend, a 13-year-old named Zhenya Cheberyak. Zhenya's mother Vera lived in a flat above a wine store next to the Zaitsev brickworks. The two boys were seen hanging around the street that morning by a neighbor named Kazimir Shakhovsky and his wife Ulyana.

Eight days later, a group of boys exploring the Lukianovka caves came across the corpse of a young boy and alerted authorities. The body was that of Yushchinsky, who had never returned home on March 12, and it was riddled with stab wounds. Kiev police detectives immediately questioned the Cheberyak family. Vera was shown the body and said the boy looked familiar, but she did not know him. She was already known to authorities, however, who had suspected her of being involved in both a sex-worker ring and part of a group of petty criminals who dealt in stolen merchandise. A few years earlier, a French musician with whom Vera was romantically linked was blinded in a sulfuric acid attack, but no charges were brought against her.

Detained and Demanded Fair Trial

When Vera Cheberyak, her brother, and two other men were taken into police custody, the Black Hundred rallied to their defense. The stab wounds on the boy, they claimed, were a sign that Yushchinsky had been killed by Jews in a heinous secret ritual. This accusation is called the blood libel, and was first mentioned in the 1140s when a young boy was found slain in Norwich, England, in a case that was never resolved. A Benedictine monk named Thomas of Monmouth wrote that a converted Jew had told him about a secret part of the Jewish holy book, the Talmud, that required Jews to kill a Christian child in order to fulfill a prophecy to return to their Holy Land.

Thomas of Monmouth's Latin text circulated through Europe in the later Middle Ages and was further embellished by new and equally fabulist accounts of crimes supposedly committed in secret by Jews. In the more superstitious and backward parts of Europe, it was even claimed that the blood of a Christian child was required to make matzoh, the unleavened bread that Jews eat during the week of Passover. Scholars familiar with Jewish law and Hebrew texts, and even senior figures in the Christian church, dismissed the blood libel rumors as factually incorrect as well as a most odious expression of anti-Semitism. The persecution appeared to die out following the Age of Enlightenment, but made a surprise resurgence in the Russian Empire in the 19th century, where a few cases inspired mob violence against Jewish homes, businesses, and synagogues.

Police Conspired to Frame Beilis

Kiev police officials released Cheberyak and the others, and agitators from the Black Hundred group pressured authorities to find the supposed Jewish culprit. Shakhovsky and his wife were brought in several more times for police questioning, and eventually gave false evidence that they had seen the two boys on the grounds of the Zaitsev works, where children were known to trespass. Shakhovsky eventually claimed that he had seen a Jewish-looking man drag the victim toward the kiln. The Black Hundred group circulated pamphlets around Kiev showing a photograph of the still-boyish Yushchinsky in his coffin with incendiary text blaming his death on "the Yids."

Beilis was arrested at his home on July 21, 1911, and questioned relentlessly by police and Ministry of Justice officials. He had a solid alibi for the morning on which Yushchinsky had been slain—he was busy at work, as scores of his employees told police. There was even paperwork for deliveries that he had signed that day. At one point, he was offered a pardon if he confessed, but he demanded a trial. As word of his detention spread through Kiev and to the capital, St. Petersburg, prominent attorneys came to his defense and decried the case as an embarrassing episode of anti-Semitism that showed the rest of the Western world just how uncouth and medieval Tsar Nicholas's empire remained.

Beilis's lead attorney was a prominent defense litigator named Oscar Gruzenberg, who swiftly demolished the state's case against Beilis when the trial began at Kiev's Circuit Court on September 25, 1913. Gruzenberg introduced scholars who carefully explained that the Talmud and other religious texts firmly disavowed the shedding of any human blood, and that the age-old "blood ritual" was a medieval superstition resurrected by the more noxious adherents of anti-Semitism. The claims of the Shakhovskys were disputed, and they eventually testified that police detectives had plied them with vodka to elicit their statements. Journalists from around the world came to Kiev to cover the Beilis trial, and details of expert-witness testimony and defense cross-examination proceedings were chronicled daily in the *New York Times* and other newspapers. On October 28, 1913, the jury voted to acquit Beilis of the crime, though contending that the boy's murder was probably a ritual slaying.

Died at Saratoga Springs Spa

Freed but facing death threats, Beilis moved his family to Tel Aviv in what was then called Palestine. In early 1921 they relocated to New York City, where he wrote a memoir in Yiddish whose English translation, *The Story of My Sufferings,* was published in 1926. He spent his final years as a seller of life insurance policies and died in Saratoga Springs, New York, on July 7, 1934, at age 62. Thousands of mourners came to pay their respects at his funeral at the Eldridge Street Synagogue on Manhattan's Lower East Side, and his final resting place is in a Jewish cemetery, Mount Carmel, in Queens, New York.

Beilis died just as the most rabidly anti-Semitic political state in modern times emerged in Germany under Nazi Party leader Adolf Hitler. Over the next decade, Nazi officials disseminated propaganda listing Beilis as among the supposed "child-killers" involved in ritual murders of non-Jews. "During World War II, there were signs that the Kiev case had survived in the collective memory," wrote Edmund Levin, author of a 2014 nonfiction account, *A Child of Christian Blood: Murder and Conspiracy in Tsarist Russia: The Beilis Blood Libel.* "Residents of German-occupied Poland called the product rumored to be made from human fat in the Auschwitz concentration camp 'Beilis Soap.'"

A Kiev police detective named Nikolai Krasovsky, who had been dismissed from the department for pursuing the Cheberyak crime ring as the likeliest culprits in the Yushchinsky murder, presented credible evidence the youth had been killed by Vera Cheberyak and her accomplices after Andrei and her son Zhenya argued, and Yushchinsky threatened to tell police about the stolen-goods racket at the Cheberyak flat. Bolstering Krasovsky's suspicions was the fact that Zhenya and his younger sister Valentyna died not long after Beilis was arrested in the summer of 1911, thought to be the victims of a deliberate poisoning at their home. Vera Cheberyak survived the 1917 Russian Revolution, but was shot by its Cheka secret police in 1919.

Beilis's case was said to have inspired *The Fixer,* a 1966 novel by Bernard Malamud, which won the Pulitzer Prize for Fiction and a National Book Award—though Beilis's family objected to the characterization of the persecuted brickworks superintendent Malamud named "Yakov Bok" in his novel. Even contemporary anti-Semitic works reference the 1913 case, wrote Levin in an excerpt from *A Child of Christian Blood* that was published on *Slate.com.* "A century after the trial, the Beilis case remains a rallying point for the extreme right fringe in Russia and Ukraine," and added that the spurious blood libel has resurfaced in some parts of the Middle East within political regimes that deem Israel an illegally established sovereign state. "The ordeal of Mendel Beilis," Levin remarked, "stands as a cautionary reminder of the power and persistence of a murderous lie."

Books

Levin, Edmund, *A Child of Christian Blood: Murder and Conspiracy in Tsarist Russia: The Beilis Blood Libel,* Schocken Books, 2014.

Weinberg, Robert, *Blood Libel in Late Imperial Russia: The Ritual Murder Trial of Mendel Beilis,* Indiana University Press, 2013.

Periodicals

New York Times, July 10, 1934.
Sunday Times (London, England), May 12, 1912.

Online

Levin, Edmund, "The Last Blood Libel Trial," *Slate.com,* October 8, 2013, http://www.slate.com/articles/news_and_politics/history/2013/10/mendel_beilis_and_blood_libel_the_1913_trial_in_kiev_russia.html (June 25, 2014). □

Jacopo Bellini

The Italian artist Jacopo Bellini (c. 1400–c. 1470) made daring advances in painting, perspective, and representation of the human figure during his long career. His Venice workshop trained several prominent painters, among them his son Giovanni and son-in-law Andrea Mantegna. Art historians place Bellini among the chief creative forces in Europe who propelled the static style of late-Gothic religious painting forward into more dynamic and dazzling imagery of the Italian Renaissance.

The exact birthdate of Jacopo Bellini is lost to history, though scholars of the Venetian Renaissance generally place it around 1400, perhaps as early as 1395. It is known he was born in Venice and that his father Niccolò's occupation is listed as that of *stagnero,* or caster of tin and pewter. The earliest document definitively tied to the Bellini family is Niccolò's last testament and will, dated 1424. It reveals that the name of Bellini's mother was Franceschina and that he had a sister, Elena. Franceschina may have been the daughter of a boatman, one of the men who worked as cargo and passenger navigators on the city's extensive network of canals. Obscuring the available information about Bellini is the fact that his father apparently had a son by another woman, a half-brother to Bellini named Giovanni, which was also the name Bellini gave to one of his own sons later in life.

Apprenticed to Umbrian Master

Bellini's career as an artist began when Gentile da Fabriano, a talented fresco artist from Umbria, came to Venice in 1408 to execute a commission inside the Doge's Palace, the famous Venetian waterfront landmark. This particular ducal palace dates to the 1340s, replacing earlier fortresses and buildings, and was the official residence of the doge, or ruler of Venice. Gentile created since-lost frescoes for the Sala di Maggior Consiglio, or meeting room of the Great Council, at the Doge's Palace. The young Bellini trained under him and then may have gone with his master to Brescia in 1414 and possibly on to Florence, the Tuscan city-state that was a major rival to the Republic of Venice.

Years later Bellini would credit Gentile for the excellent artistic training he provided, and named another son after his former teacher.

Gentile completed his most famous work, *The Adoration of the Magi*, in the early 1420s for a church in Florence, the Santa Trinita (Holy Trinity). If Bellini was indeed with Gentile in Florence during this period, as art historians surmise, he was eyewitness to works in progress by several leading artists of the Florentine Renaissance. These include magnificent bas-relief bronze doors by sculptor Lorenzo Ghiberti for the Florence Baptistry, which took years to finish, and the actual start of construction on the Duomo, or dome, of the city's signature-skyline cathedral, in 1420. This distinctive red-brick dome of the Basilica di Santa Maria del Fiore was designed by architect Filippo Brunelleschi and became one of the largest constructed works ever built by human hands when it was finished in 1436.

Established Venice Workshop

By 1424 Bellini had returned to Venice and established a *bottega*, or workshop, with his half-brother Giovanni. These *botteghe* emerged as an influential element of the Italian Renaissance, serving as successful commercial enterprises as well as impressively regulated apprentice schools for aspiring artists. They competed against one another for official government commissions for decorative elements in all public buildings such as legislative chambers, courts of law and commerce, and churches. Bellini's workshop was located in the center of Venice, near the Piazza San Marco, which was also near his residence at the Procuratie Vecchie complex. He was married by 1429, a fact established through another early document, a will made by his wife Anna Rinversi, whose family was of Lucchese origin. The Rinversis were wealthy silk merchants, and the bride had brought to her marriage a dowry of 250 ducats, a not-insignificant sum. Anna Bellini's will is dated February 6, 1429, and it notes that she is expecting a child, though it is unclear which of her children was born that year. It may have been the son Gentile, named after the master painter, or her daughter Niccolosia.

Bellini lived in an oligarchy that had been in existence seven centuries by the time of his birth and was in full force as a global maritime and commercial center when he set up his bottega. Founded in 697 CE, the Most Serene Republic of Venice, or "La Serenissima" had been a major stopping point for armies from Western Europe on their way to Crusades to reclaim the Holy Land from Muslim rule; it was also a longstanding transit hub for merchants who traded with Byzantium and points even further east in Asia. Wool, precious stones, silks, spices, and valuable commodities all passed through Venice and influenced its cosmopolitan outlook, storied affluence, and advances in the visual arts. As an independent republic, Venice possessed an impressive navy and its rulers used that, plus a skilled militia and equally deft corps of diplomats, to move aggressively against neighbors who posed a threat to its safety and security. As the Republic expanded from its original lagoon archipelago at the head of the Adriatic Sea into other parts of Italy on its western flank and onto the Balkan peninsula to the south and east, opportunities for new commissions on the newly conquered *terraferma* multiplied.

Renowned for Madonna Portraits

One of Bellini's first significant commissions came from one of these new terraferma lands. This was the recently incorporated lands belonging to the Duchy of Ferrara, and the work was commissioned by the head of its ruling house, Niccolò III d'Este. In the early 1430s Bellini visited the ducal seat at Este and painted a portrait of the duke's son and heir Leonello d'Este, who later became a generous patron of the arts himself. This portrait of Leonello is one of Bellini's many lost works, but the artist also completed another work in Este for Niccolò, *Madonna of Humility Adored by a Prince of the House of Este*. The portrait of the Virgin Mary and an infant Christ, a ubiquitous artistic theme of the Gothic and Renaissance eras, shows a prince kneeling before the holy mother and son. The prince may be Leonello or one of his several brothers. The painting eventually became part of the permanent collection of the Musée du Louvre in Paris.

During his lifetime Bellini gained some early renown as the painter of an enormous *Crucifixion* scene installed at the cathedral in Verona, Italy. The work was finished in 1436 and remained in the church until the 1750s, when Verona's archbishop ordered it removed; it was later destroyed, though other artists sketched it for many years and its original composition does survive in reproductions. One work that bears a rare full signature by Bellini is his *Virgin and Child*, a commission for a church of the Servite religious order in Casalfiumanese in Bologna, another northern Italian land. Bologna was aligned with the Duchy of Milan intermittently during the Renaissance era and this work of Bellini's is preserved in the Pinacoteca di Brera in Milan. The most authoritative modern biographer of the Bellini clan is the German art historian Oskar Bätschmann, whose 2008 work *Giovanni Bellini* discusses this particular religious painting from 1448 and the elder Bellini's use of linear perspective. Bellini, wrote Bätschmann, "emphasized the solidity of both figures by means of a pronounced relief effect. The illusion that the figures project in the front of the picture plane is heightened by the way in which the crown overlaps the frame."

Bellini produced several other notable Madonna paintings. *Madonna and Child Blessing*, completed before 1460, hangs in Venice's treasure-filled Gallerie dell'Accademia Museum. An earlier *Madonna and Child* is part of the permanent collection of the Metropolitan Museum of New York. The Met also owns Bellini's portrait of *Saint Bernardino of Siena*, painted in the 1450s. The Los Angeles County Museum of Art has a prized Bellini, too, his 1465 *Virgin and Child*. Most of these are tempera on wood and featured actual gold embellishment; Bellini's son Giovanni would later master the new medium of oil paint, which represented a significant advancement in Western art.

Protégés Flourished during Renaissance

Bellini's daughter Niccolosia married the artist Andrea Mantegna in 1453. The Paduan-born Mantegna was influenced by Bellini and went on to become one of Renaissance Italy's most masterful painters. Bellini also trained sons Giovanni and Gentile, and the family workshop completed some notable commissions for major churches in Venice and elsewhere. In the 1460s they created four altar triptychs for the Santa Maria della Carità in Venice, which are preserved in the Gallerie dell'Accademia. They depict the saints Lawrence and Sebastian, the Nativity scene, and other standard religious iconography.

Bellini is thought to have died around 1470. Again, sources provide this estimation based on a last will and testament, this one dated November of 1471, and specifying the bequests of his widow Anna. It mentions her sons Gentile and Niccolò, but omits Giovanni; the absence of his name and the bequest of her estate to Gentile leads Renaissance scholars to surmise that the famous Giovanni was probably born to a woman other than Anna Rinversi Bellini. Gentile was an artist as well as a diplomat and was sent by the Doge as Venice's emissary to the Ottoman Empire in the 1470s. While there Gentile painted *The Sultan Mehmet II,* another work deemed important enough to earn a place in the Musée du Louvre. Known as Mehmet the Conqueror, the Turkish leader seized the great city of Constantinople and reestablished Islamic Ottoman rule over large parts of the Middle East. When Gentile painted Mehmet, the Sultan was arguably the most powerful figure in Eurasia, rival only to the Pope in Rome. Another work widely attributed to Gentile Bellini shows *Seated Scribe,* a portrait of a white-turbaned youth in the Sultan's court shown in profile and bent over in concentration at his work. The enigmatic image, with superb coloration and magnificent fabric detail, hangs in the Isabella Stewart Gardner Museum in Boston. Gentile died in 1507.

Left Enormous Trove of Drawings

Much of the elder Bellini's work is known to art historians from two enormous volumes of drawings, one of which is in the Louvre; its companion resides in London at the British Museum. Their 300 leadpoint drawings on parchment show his keen interest in linear perspective, architecture, and even landscape design. The Bellini bottega continued to prosper under the guidance of son Giovanni, who trained several leading masters of the Italian Renaissance, among them Titian and Tintoretto. Before he died in 1516, Giovanni Bellini served as curator of the Doge's Palace art collection, a position reflecting his enormous stature in La Serenissima. The mastery of color and tone Giovanni displayed in his most famous works later inspired a signature cocktail of cosmopolitan modern Venice, the Bellini, whose pale-pink color reminded the proprietor of Harry's Bar—the Venice watering hole that catered to an elite clientele for decades—to dub the white-peach and Prosecco-wine cocktail the "Bellini."

Books

Bätschmann, Oskar, *Giovanni Bellini,* Reaktion Books, 2008, translated by Ian Pepper from the original German edition, *Giovanni Bellini: Meister der venezianischen Malerei,* C. H. Beck, 2008.

Eisler, Colin T., *The Genius of Jacopo Bellini: The Complete Paintings and Drawings,* Abrams, 1989. □

Andrey Bely

The Russian writer Andrey Bely (1880–1934) was the leading representative of the Symbolist artistic movement in Russia. He is best known for the ambitious and experimental novel *Petersburg* (1913).

That novel, which has been compared in scope and technique with James Joyce's *Ulysses,* is difficult to translate into other languages. The same is true of many of Bely's other writings, which contain puns, figurative language, coloristic and musical details, and local references that pose deep problems for a translator. That may be one reason Bely has been less renowned outside Russia than several of his contemporaries. Yet in his own time he was a cutting-edge figure whose own ideas benefited from confrontation with several of the major intellectual currents of the day, not only Symbolism. With fresh translations of his work into English and a renewed interest in the culture of the years on either side of the founding of the Soviet Union, Bely's reputation has been on the rise.

Product of Unhappy Marriage

Andrey (or Andrei) Bely was born Boris Nikolayevich Bugayev (or Bugaev) on October 14, 1880, in Moscow. His father was a distinguished mathematics professor of strongly conservative views, his mother an attractive socialite who, in the words of the online *Russiapedia,* "had an irrational attraction to the arts, despising both her husband's professional activity and ugly looks." Bely was apparently scarred psychologically by his upbringing and, exceptionally among the writers of the Symbolist school, devoted several major works to the theme of childhood later in life.

Despite problems at home, Bely received a superior education. He attended a prestigious private school, the Polivanov Gymnasium, where he immersed himself in philosophy and literary classics. Literary figures who met him, including the poet Zinaida Gippius, were impressed by how much he knew for a student in his early teens. When Bely was 15 he made friends with another student, Sergei Soloviev, who was a nephew of the noted poet and philosopher Vladimir Soloviev. The Soloviev household became for Bely a place where he could participate in intense discussions of literature and the world of ideas.

Bely matriculated at Moscow University in 1899. At his father's urging he majored in physics and mathematics, but his mother, backed by the Soloviev family, encouraged him to follow his bent toward literature and music. As he began to write, he was especially influenced by the latter, coming under the spell of the fashionable idea that aspects of the various arts could come together in a single work. He began writing four works that he called symphonies, attempting to capture in prose the four symphonies of German composer Robert Schumann and dedicating one of them, called *Vtoraia Simfoniia,* to his girlfriend at the time, socialite Margarita Morozova. His career took a major step forward when the Solovievs, impressed, supported the

Heritage Image Partnership Ltd/Alamy

publication of the four symphonies. Worried about his father's reaction, he accepted the Solovievs' suggestion that he use a pen name, Andrei Bely ("Andrew White"). He would later use other pen names, including 2 B and Alter Ego, but it was as Andrei Bely that he became known.

Became Member of Argonauts Group

The symphonies included satirical depictions of contemporary Muscovites and Moscow types and were not easily classifiable as either poetry or prose. Talked-about and controversial, they put Bely on the literary map, and he capitalized on his newfound fame with a series of essays in which he lampooned mainstream Russian literary tastes. For a time he was associated with a group of Moscow writers called the Argonauts, who presented themselves—sometimes on business cards—as mental reincarnations of mythological animals such as unicorns and centaurs.

Bely's romantic life during this period was as colorful as his literary career. After a bad breakup with fellow writer Nina Ivanovna Petrovskaya (who took up with Bely's publisher Briusov), he had an affair with Liubov' Dmitrievna Blok, the wife of poet Alexander Blok. Blok had been among Bely's strongest supporters, but the episode led each to challenge the other to a duel. The tension receded, however, when Bely fell in love with 18-year-old Asia Turgenieva, a niece of the novelist Ivan Turgenev.

Bely differed from the other Symbolists in that he was able to use these experiences in his creative work, sometimes

dressed up in mythological themes. *Urna,* a 1909 volume of love poems, seems to have been directly inspired by the affair with Blok's wife. After the failure of the 1905 revolution in Russia, however, Bely departed somewhat from the idealistic themes of Symbolist poetry and began to turn toward longer forms. He published a novel, *The Silver Dove,* after which he began to travel through Europe, the Middle East, and North Africa with Turgenieva. The pair married in Switzerland during this trip, possibly to avoid breaking Swiss laws relating to the cohabitation of unmarried couples. Through Turgenieva, Bely became interested in the works of Austrian philosopher and educational reformer Rudolf Steiner and in the Russian occult writer Helena Petrovna Blavatsky, known as Madame Blavatsky.

During the trip, Bely worked on *Petersburg* (or *St. Petersburg*), which was refused by the publisher who had commissioned it. The novel appeared in a yearbook and was revised several times as Bely tried to meet the requirements of publishers in the new Soviet Union; it first appeared in book form in 1916. The novel revolves loosely around an assassination plot during the 1905 revolution, with the politician victim modeled on Bely's father and the assassin on Bely himself. But much of the novel consists of a panoramic depiction of the pre-Revolutionary Russian capital, rendered in a densely allusive, experimental prose that captured the chaos of the dissolving old order in a way that more objective treatments failed to do. The first writer to compare the work to the sprawling experimental writings of Irish novelist James Joyce was *Doctor Zhivago* author Boris Pasternak.

Condemned by Trotsky

Bely returned to Russia, without his wife (they formally separated in 1921), during World War I, supported the provisional government that overthrew the Czarist regime, and was open to the ascent of Communism in the October 1917 revolution though never a strong supporter. After the war he worked as a lecturer in Moscow and then lived in Berlin, where he worked on *Kotik Letaev* (1922), again a difficult work to classify. Drawing partly on the author's own experiences, the book is an evocation of the life and perceptions of a child between the ages of three and five. Influenced by Rudolf Steiner's philosophy, the book has been translated into English by Gerald J. Janecek. In 1923 Bely returned to the Soviet Union, but his writings were condemned by the radical Communist leader Leon Trotsky. Bely was able to partially maintain his position by appealing for help from Trotsky's archrival, Joseph Stalin.

In his later years Bely remained a prolific writer, increasingly turning to literary criticism. He published the biographical *Recollections of Blok* in 1922 and *The Mastery of Gogol,* a study of the satirical 19th-century writer who had been one of his own biggest influences. Bely issued three linked novels set in Moscow, *The Moscow Eccentric* (1926), *Moscow Under Siege* (1926), and *Mask* (1931), as well as three volumes of memoirs that were rich in details of pre-Revolutionary Russian society. In 1931 he married Klavdia (or Ksenia) Vasilyeva, a Steiner adherent who at one point was jailed by the Soviet regime.

Bely died on January 8, 1934, in Moscow, just before Stalin's own repression of creative figures grew more severe. His own apartment and that of the Solovievs were combined into a museum, the Andrei Bely Memorial Museum Apartment, which opened in 2000, and a major Russian literary prize is named for him. Although not widely known among Western readers, Bely has been the subject of extensive research and critical study both in Russia and abroad, and familiarity with his works has grown as they have appeared in English translation.

Books

Alexandrov, Vladimir E., *Andrei Bely: The Major Symbolist Fiction,* Harvard, 1985.

Elsworth, John D., *Andrey Bely,* Bradda, 1972.

Kalb, Judith E., et al., *Russian Writers of the Silver Age, 1890–1925,*(Dictionary of Literary Biography, Vol. 295), Gale, 2004.

Periodicals

Review of Contemporary Fiction, Summer 2000.

Online

"Andrei Belyi," *PoemHunter.com,* http://www.poemhunter. com/andrei-belyi/biography/ (October 15, 2014).

"Andrey Bely (1880–1934)," *Books and Writers,* http:// www.kirjasto.sci.fi/bely.htm (October 15, 2014).

"The Moving Tide of Abundance: Petersburg by Andrei Bely," *Quarterly Conversation,* http://www.quarterlyconversation. com/the-moving-tide-of-abundance-petersburg-by-andrei-bely (October 15, 2014).

"Prominent Russians: Andrey Bely," *Russiapedia,* http:// www.russiapedia.rt.com/prominent-russians/literature/ andrey-bely/ (October 15, 2014).□

Itzhak Ben-Zvi

Ukraine-born Israeli activist, educator, and political leader Itzhak Ben-Zvi (1884–1963) was the second president of Israel. Active in Zionist causes for much of his life, he played a significant role in the Jewish labor movement in Palestine before the founding of Israel, helped found the Ahdut Ha'avodah party, and was elected to the first Knesset. The popular Ben-Zvi was the longest serving Israeli president.

Born Yitzhak Shimsehlevits on November 14, 1884, in Poltava, Ukraine, Itzhak Ben-Zvi was son of Zevi Shimshelevich, a passionate Zionist. Other members of his family were also active in Zionism. At this time, Ukraine was part of the Russian Empire, and the Russian government placed limitations on the number of Jews receiving certain types of education. Because of this situation, Ben-Zvi could not begin attending high school until he was 17 years old. The same year he was accepted to a

Russian gymnasium, 1901, his father went to Palestine and tried to organize a Jewish settlement.

Became Active in Jewish Causes

Three years later, Ben-Zvi went to Palestine himself for a two month visit during a break from school, and returned to Ukraine wanting to emigrate. After completing his studies at the gymnasium in 1905, he entered the University of Kiev. A general strike brought an end to his studies, however. That year, Ben-Zvi began taking part in self-defense groups which defended Jews during the November pogroms (organized killings of Jews).

In 1906, Ben-Zvi attended the founding meeting of the workers' movement, Poale Zion (Workers of Zion, or Zionist Social Democrats) of Russia. At the meeting held in Poltava, Ben-Zvi was part of the small committee that devised the final version of the party's program. He personally wrote the section of the program that addressed Palestine.

Also that year, Russian authorities targeted Ben-Zvi's family. When Russian police conducted a search of his family's home, weapons were discovered. They were the property of a self-defense organization helmed by Ben-Zvi. Because of the discovery, Ben-Zvi's father was arrested and put on trial. After his conviction, Ben-Zvi's father was sentenced to a lifetime of exile in Siberia. By 1922, his father was allowed to leave Siberia, and he then made his way to Palestine. The rest of Ben-Zvi's family were arrested and imprisoned, including his aunt, sister, and brother.

Became Leader of Labor Zionism

Ben-Zvi avoided arrest by going to Vilna, then part of Russia and located in Lithuanian territory. The city had a large Jewish population, and he continued to work on behalf of the Poale Zion's central committee there. Later that year he went to Minsk, another Russian-controlled city in Belarus with a large Jewish population and an active worker's movement: There, he organized a conference related to his Zionist and workers' causes, emerging as a leader of the Labor Zionist movement.

Also in 1906, Ben-Zvi traveled to several European countries—including Germany, Austria, and Switzerland—to convince Jewish students and others to join Poale Zion. After his trip, he returned to Minsk, where he faced further harassment from local police. He was arrested and imprisoned several times over the next few months.

Emigrated to Palestine

At the beginning of 1907, Ben-Zvi was able to immigrate to Palestine, as part of the Second Aliya, a wave of Jewish immigration to Palestine. There, he made his home in Jaffa. He soon served as a delegate representing Poale Zion and his new home at the Eighth Zionist Congress, held in the Hague. In this period, Ben-Zvi also founded the Poale Zion Party in Palestine.

Ben-Zvi soon focused on bridging the divide between the Zionist worker theories and practices he supported in Russia with the realities of Palestine. In 1907, he was a leader in organizing an underground Jewish self-defense group, Bar-Giora. This group trained its members so they could replace the Arab guards often employed to guard remote Jewish agricultural settlements. Bar-Giora later became a part of a larger group, the Hashomer, when it formed in 1909.

Ben-Zvi went on to play an active role in establishing the Jewish presence in Palestine. For example, he was a co-founder of and teacher at a Jewish gymnasia high school in Jerusalem in 1909. This small school focused on teaching Jewish students what they would need to know to live in a modern Jewish society. A year later, Ben-Zvi played a role in the establishment of *Ahdut,* a socialist journal written in Hebrew that served as the voice of the Poale Zion Party. It was the first such journal published in Palestine.

Also in 1909, Ben-Zvi made a trip to Turkey representing Poale Zion Party, after the Turkish revolution that occurred that year. He made connections to Jewish communities and leaders in such cities as Smyrna, Constantinople, and Salonika. As part of this experience, Ben-Zvi visited Beirut and Damascus to create ties with the Jewish peoples there. The excursion also proved important to his later historical work as he first came into contact with the Shabbatean sect, which he further researched in subsequent years.

Studied Law in Constantinople

Ben-Zvi returned to Constantinople in 1912 to further his education and study law, along with his friend David Ben-Gurion. They spent two years there, hoping to enter politics among the Ottomans. They were forced to return to Palestine, however, when World War I broke out in the summer of 1914. Because Palestine was still under the administrative control of the ever-weakening Ottoman Empire and persecution of the Jews in Palestine increased in this period, both men were imprisoned. In 1915, they were deported from the territory for reasons that can be essentially summarized as being regarded as troublemakers by the Ottomans.

From there, Ben-Zvi and Ben-Gurion traveled to Egypt and gained admittance to the United States. Living temporarily in New York City, the pair promoted the Poale Zion movement and managed fundraisers for Zionist groups. They also founded the Hehalutz movement. Hehalutz meant the pioneer, and focused on preparing youth for immigration to Palestine and living on the land there so that an Israeli state could be established. Ben-Zvi and Ben-Gurion also wrote a book in Yiddish, *The Land of Israel, Past and Present,* to further their cause.

During this period, Ben-Zvi and Ben-Gurion actively recruited for the Jewish Legion, which offered military support to Britain during World War I. They volunteered themselves for the legion, returning first to Egypt then to Palestine itself to serve in the British Royal Fusiliers by late 1918. Before the end of the conflict, the British took control of administering Palestine as a mandate, essentially a trusteeship overseen by Britain for the League of Nations.

Ben-Zvi and his close friend Ben-Gurion had an ideological split, though they remained close personal friends. Unlike Ben-Gurion, Ben-Zvi remained committed to the principles of Labor Zionism, as embodied by Poale Zion, and believed that this ideology could bring together all the Jews in Palestine and create a humane Jewish society.

Served on Several Councils

Ben-Zvi soon became more directly involved in politics. In the years after the war, Ben-Zvi was named to the Government Advisory Council by Sir Herbert Samuel, the British high commissioner for Palestine. After the Arab riots in the spring of 1921, the British administrators began restricting the number of Jewish immigrants to Palestine. Because of this action, Ben-Zvi resigned from his post.

In subsequent years, Ben-Zvi was elected to the Jerusalem Municipal Council, where he formed relationships with Arab members of the council. He served on the council from 1927 until 1929, when he resigned because of the city's position on riots that occurred in 1929; he returned in 1934 for another stint. Later, Ben-Zvi was first a member and then the chair of the Va'ad Le'umi, or National Council.

Over the next two decades, Ben-Zvi was also an active member of the Haganah, an underground Jewish self-defense group he co-founded with David Ben-Gurion. He also became deeply involved with the Jewish labor movement in Palestine. He was a member of the Histadrut secretariat after he and Ben-Gurion helped form it in 1920 as an organization of Jewish trade unions. Additionally, Ben-Zvi was a co-founder of the Ahdut Ha'avodah, or Labor Union, party.

In this period, Ben-Zvi became known as an expert on Jewish history and ethnology, and a highly productive journalist. Because he understood there were fundamental differences in the national interests of Zionists and Palestinians, he especially focused on analyzing the history of

Palestine under the Ottomans. Another area of research centered on Jewish communities in ancient times and in remote places. Among his published books in this period was *The Jewish Yishuv in Peki'in Village* (1922).

Founded Institute, Joined Israeli Government

After Israel became its own state in May 1948 and triumphed in a war on its independence day, an Israeli government formed. That year, Ben-Zvi helped found an institute dedicated to the study of Jewish communities in the Middle East and their history. The establishment of the Institute for the Study of Oriental Jewish Communities in the Middle East was achieved with the help of the Jewish Agency, the Israeli ministry of education and culture, and the Histadrut. (It was re-named the Ben-Zvi Institute in 1952 and became affiliated with the Hebrew University of Jerusalem.)

Ben-Zvi also entered Israeli politics. He was elected to the first Knesset, or parliament, in January 1949. He was a member of the Mapai Party. In December 1952, the first president of Israel, Chaim Weizmann, died, and Ben-Zvi was elected by the Knesset to take his place. Ben-Zvi bested three others who sought the post, winning the first of his three five-year terms in office.

Though the Israeli presidency was primarily ceremonial—political power primarily resided in the office of prime minister—the position offered a chance to be influential. When he took office, Ben-Zvi chose to lead by example and be inclusive by living a very down to earth life. For example, he debuted events that became traditions, including a public open house on the Sukkot festival and an informal reception on Israeli independence day for all visitors.

Lived Frugally

In this period, Israel mandated rations by law because of limited availability of certain foodstuffs. Because of this situation, when Ben-Zvi moved the residence of the president to Jerusalem, he chose to live in two simple wooden prefabricated buildings which included living space, reception rooms, and his offices. Ben-Zvi took other frugal measures, including owning only one pair of shoes, refusing to buy a new suit, and hosting simple dinners for diplomats.

Ben-Zvi also went for a decade without a pay raise, and by the early 1960s, his driver was making more money than he was. Ben-Zvi was upset that a committee of the Knesset was voting on tripling his pay rate. Though he spoke out against the raise—citing the need to keep the standard of living low in Israel to better absorb the Jewish population emigrating to Israel—his pay was increased. He donated the pay increase to charity.

While serving as president, Ben-Zvi also continued to publish books on history and other topics in Jewish scholarship. Titles published in this period included *Eretz-Israel under Ottoman Rule* (1955) and *The Exile and the Redeemed* (1957). Very popular among Israeli voters and politicians, Ben-Zvi was elected to two more terms as president, with the last election coming in December 1962. Because the presidency was later limited to only two terms, Ben-Zvi held the presidency longer than anyone in the history of Israel.

Ben-Zvi died while still serving as the president on April 23, 1963, in Jerusalem, at the age of 79. He was succeeded as president by Shneur Zalman Shazar. More works by Ben-Zvi were published posthumously. They included a collection of letters by Ben-Zvi, *The Hebrew Legion: Letters* (1969). In subsequent years, Ben-Zvi would be regarded as one of the most popular and effective presidents to hold the office.

Books

Encyclopaedia Judaica, 2nd ed., edited by Michael Berenbaum and Fred Skolnik, Macmillan Reference USA, 2007.
The Encyclopedia of the Arab-Israeli Conflict: A Political, Social, and Military History, Vol. 1, edited by Spencer C. Tucker and Priscilla Roberts, ABC-CLIO, 2008.
Encyclopedia of the Modern Middle East and North Africa, edited by Philip Mattar, Macmillan Reference USA, 2004.

Periodicals

The Australian, May 23, 2013.
The Jerusalem Report, February 14, 2000.
St. Louis Post-Dispatch, April 26, 1998. □

Hans Berger

The German neurologist Hans Berger (1873–1941) was the discoverer of the electroencephalogram, or EEG for short. The EEG was for many years a tool of critical importance in the diagnosis of epilepsy and other brain disorders, and it is still widely used.

B erger's discovery came late in his life, and his route to it was circuitous. He began doing research on the brain because, as a result of events connected with an accident he suffered as a young man, he was convinced that psychic phenomena existed, and he hoped to find a physical basis for them. Much of his life's work, in an era when the available instruments for the measurement of brain phenomena were rudimentary, came to nothing. Berger's colleagues considered him odd, and most of the research that led directly to the EEG was conducted in secret, in a small laboratory Berger visited after his day's work was done. It took him several years before he published his groundbreaking results, and several more before he saw other scientists accept them. By the time the medical world woke up to the importance of what Berger had done, the rise of Nazism in Germany made it difficult for him to reap the rewards of what he had found or to see his discoveries applied in practice.

Descended from German Poet

Hans Berger was born in May 21, 1873, in Neuses, near the present-day city of Coburg in southern Germany. His father, Paul Friedrich Berger, was a doctor, and his mother, born Anna Rückert, was the daughter of one of the most

Apic/Getty Images

famous German poets of the Romantic era, Friedrich Rück-ert. Berger devoted his educational and academic career to the sciences, but he maintained a strong interest in philosophy and was always oriented toward ideas that seemed outside strictly scientific boundaries. Berger attended the Gymnasium, or college-preparatory high school, in Coburg and then enrolled at the University of Jena. He planned to major in astronomy, but he was overwhelmed by college life, and in 1892 he dropped out temporarily and enlisted in the German army in the nearby city of Würzburg.

Berger spent a year as a cavalryman-in-training, and during this period he experienced an event that shaped his later interests. Riding a horse one day during an exercise, he was thrown into the air and landed in the path of an oncoming horse-drawn cannon. The driver of the cannon team managed to stop his horses, and Berger emerged unhurt. But Berger's sister was convinced that he was in danger, and she persuaded their father to send a telegram to Berger, asking whether he was safe. Berger wrote, as quoted by Dean Radin in *Entangled Minds*: "This is a case of spontaneous telepathy in which at a time of mortal danger, and as I contemplated certain death, I transmitted my thoughts, while my sister, who was particularly close to me, acted as the receiver."

Returning to the university convinced that hitherto unknown forms of brain energy existed, he applied himself to his studies with renewed vigor. He received a doctoral degree in 1897 and spent several years as an assistant to the

Swiss psychologist Otto Binswanger. In Jena in 1901 his *Habilitationsschrift,* a thesis qualifying him to teach in the German university system, was accepted, and he became a non-staff instructor. He would spend the rest of his life at the University of Jena, except for a stint as an army psychiatrist during World War I. He became a lecturer in 1906, chief doctor at the University Clinic in 1912, and director at the university's Psychiatry and Neurology Clinic in 1919. That year he also became a full professor of psychiatry.

Performed Measurements on Dog's Brain

In the first years of the 20th century, the measurement of brain activity was in its infancy, and Berger made stabs in the dark in terms of technique, equipment, and experimental goals. With plenty of subjects referred from the university clinic, he published papers describing his attempts to measure brain size and activity through the volume of blood circulation and the brain's temperature, as well as the effects of substances such as cocaine and caffeine on brain pulsations. In 1902 he tried to measure the electrical activity of a dog's brain. But by 1910 he became convinced that his research was leading nowhere, and he abandoned his work. He married a young noblewoman and lab assistant, Ursula von Büow, in 1911, and the couple had four children, Klaus, Ruth, Ilse, and Rosemarie.

The poor opinion of his colleagues contributed to Berger's feelings of discouragement. His appointment as professor and as director of the clinic was backed by Binswanger, but the older scientist seemed to value Berger mostly as an administrator, and upon retirement he passed on his prestigious private practice on to another assistant. Several of Berger's colleagues openly criticized his research, and Berger became further depressed by Germany's defeat in World War I. After the war, he seems to have experienced a kind of crisis in which his public self and his inner thoughts split into carefully limited spheres.

Berger's colleagues knew him as punctual, strict, conservative, and a bit dull. He put in a full day each day as an administrator, setting aside his own research completely when his posts demanded it. But most of the time he worked from 5 to 8 p.m. on experiments of his own, carried out in secret in a small building on the university clinic grounds. To distract people from what he was doing, he gave public lectures on telepathy, which even his own assistants considered nonsensical. His own work he kept strictly to himself.

Recorded First EEG

In the early 1920s Berger resumed his research on the brain, using two methods: stimulation of the motor cortex (the part of the brain that controls physical movement) through a skull defect, to try to measure the time until the body reacted, and direct measurement of electrical activity on the brain's surface, at first when an open skull exposed part of the brain, then through the intact skull. Over time, as Berger learned more about what earlier scientists (such as the British surgeon Richard Caton) had noticed about the brain's electrical activity, the second of these methods became more important. Finally, in 1924, experimenting on a 17-year-old student named Zedel who had undergone two operations to remove a brain tumor, he attached two electrodes bandaged to the young man's head to a galvanometer and was able to record actual brain waves in a rudimentary way on a sheet of photographic paper. He called the new image an *Elektrenkephalogramm,* in English an electroencephalogram, or EEG.

Berger's first EEGs noted only tiny swings in brain activity. Over the next several years he experimented, with varying degrees of success, with the equipment he used for his measurements, and by 1929 he had hundreds of EEGs in hand, some of them from patients with epilepsy, dementia, and other brain disorders. In epileptics he noted particularly strong brain waves preceding a seizure. He had no clinical goals in mind and still thought of his research in almost metaphysical terms. But he decided to begin publishing his results, noting only "purely concrete facts and findings," according to an article in *Perspectives in Biology and Medicine.* His first paper, *On the Human Electroencephalogram,* appeared in April of 1929 and was followed by 13 others over the next several years.

Berger may have thought that he was still measuring a kind of divine energy, and in fact he did not live to see the days when EEGs were a common item in a hospital's medical arsenal. But others realized the importance of his discoveries almost immediately. By 1937, at the International Congress of Psychology in Paris, he was hailed as a distinguished scientist. He told the crowd that unfortunately in Germany he was not so famous, and he made plans to visit the United States and began practicing his English for the occasion.

It was not to be. Thought to be hostile to Adolf Hitler and his Nazi party, Berger was forced to retire in 1938, according to hitherto accepted accounts, and was placed in a kind of internal exile in a small town called Bad Thuringia. He was not allowed to do research. His physical condition worsened, due to a condition variously reported as depression and congestive heart failure. This account of Berger's last years has been challenged by German historians who have uncovered evidence of his involvement in Nazi euthanasia programs. Not under debate is the fact that Berger committed suicide by hanging himself on June 1, 1941, in Jena, and that the brain waves he discovered (one of which, the so-called alpha wave, was named Berger's wave) became central to neurology in the second half of the 20th century.

Books

Complete Dictionary of Scientific Biography, Scribner's, 2008.

Fields, R. Douglas, *The Other Brain,* Simon & Schuster, 2009.

Radin, Dean, *Entangled Minds,* Simon & Schuster, 2009.

World of Health, Gale, 2007.

Periodicals

Perspectives in Biology and Medicine, Autumn 2001.

Online

"Hans Berger," *Who Named It?,* http://www.whonamedit.com/doctor.cfm/845.html (December 14, 2014).

"Hans Berger (1873–1941)—The History of Electroencephalography," National Institutes of Health (translation of article in Croatian), http://www.ncbi.nlm.nih.gov/pubmed/16334737 (December 14, 2014).□

Alexander Berkman

Russian anarchist Alexander Berkman (1870–1936) was reviled and respected in equal measure during the 31 years he spent in the United States as one of the left's fiercest polemicists. Nearly half of that time was spent in prison for his role in a shocking assassination attempt on industrialist Henry Clay Frick. Released in 1906, Berkman spent another decade as a strident critic of capitalism before he and longtime collaborator Emma Goldman were deported to the Soviet Union.

Ovsei "Alexander" Berkman came from a prosperous Jewish family living in Vilnius, Lithuania, at the time of his birth on November 21, 1870. The city was then part of the Russian Empire and home to a sizable Jewish population, due in part to tsarist-regime residency laws that restricted the rights of even non-observant Jews. Berkman's father was a successful merchant of shoe and boot leather and eventually received permission to move the family to the glittering, rich capital city of St. Petersburg.

Nephew of Nihilist Writer Maxim Natanson

Berkman was the youngest of four children and emerged as a rebellious teenager after the untimely death of his father, which forced his mother Yetta to take them to Kaunas, Lithuania, where her banker-brother Nathan lived. In a dichotomous biographical detail, Berkman's other maternal uncle was a renowned radical who spent years in Siberian penal colonies for his involvement in anti-tsarist activities.

A gifted student and insatiable reader who questioned authority at every opportunity, Berkman came to loathe his conformist uncle Nathan, who exercised financial control over the family. The teenager also had epic arguments with his mother over her punitive treatment of their household staff, and at his elite private high school subverted the rules so brazenly that he was eventually expelled. In early 1888 Berkman traveled with his brother Max to Leipzig, Germany, where Max was to begin medical school, and from there opted to go on to Hamburg, where he booked a steerage-class passage on a ship bound for the New York City harbor.

Everett Collection Inc/Alamy

"There Is No 'Dignity of Labor'"

A near-penniless immigrant to America, Berkman struggled to find steady work and affordable shelter. At times he slept rough in Union Square Park in between arduous and low-paying factory jobs he loathed. He found solidarity with other impoverished immigrants from eastern and central Europe and happily involved himself in various leftist causes. In 1889 he met Russian immigrant Emma Goldman at a Lower East Side café. Goldman was, coincidentally, also from the city of Kaunas, and shared Berkman's conviction that the democratic-capitalist system favored in the West was little better than the police-state absolutism of tsarist Russia. "Life in the tenements is sordid, the fate of the worker dreary," he wrote, according to the joint biography *Sasha and Emma: The Anarchist Odyssey of Alexander Berkman and Emma Goldman.* "There is no 'dignity of labor.' Sweatshop bread is bitter."

Berkman learned some rudimentary typesetting skills and worked for publications that promoted anarchist ideology. A Greek term for "without rule," anarchy embraced the tenet that power corrupts even the most well-intentioned human beings, and people should be free to opt out of all types of political, religious, and economic control and become loosely self-governing units. Predictably, the loosely organized anarchist movement was riven by deleterious squabbles, with Berkman and Goldman hewing to the more extreme left. To start anew, they moved to the textile-mill city of Worcester, Massachusetts, to live with a cousin of

Berkman's. Their time there was notable for the friends' brief but surprisingly successful foray into entrepreneurship as operators of a lunchroom that served deli food to Jewish-immigrant workers.

The Plot Against Frick

In June of 1892 Berkman was 21 years old, had broken completely with his family back in Russia, and was growing increasingly disenchanted with life in America. Two of the most dangerous industries, coal mining and steel production, were growing exponentially as the United States prospered during its Gilded Age. The demand for labor in those industries was intense and there were attempts to leverage this into collective-bargaining agreements and legally sanctioned trade unions. The coal and steel companies fought labor-union organizers and work-stoppage attempts with a variety of tactics, many of them later outlawed. One was the hiring of out-of-town strike-breakers who "broke" through picket lines with the aid of company-paid private security forces. In 1892 these and other brazen acts by Carnegie Steel executives to quash a bold strike at a plant in Homestead, Pennsylvania, dominated newspaper headlines across the United States for weeks. The Carnegie Steel executive in charge of operations in Homestead was Henry Clay Frick, who misgauged the commitment of the Amalgamated Association of Iron and Steel Workers union that summer—and public sympathy for the strikers and their families as the labor action near Pittsburgh dragged on through June. After a day-long standoff on July 6, 1892, that left 16 dead, Berkman decided to publicly assassinate Frick and then kill himself.

Berkman's mission was inspired by an anarchist principle known as the *attentát* in French, or propaganda by deed. An attention-getting act of violence was necessary, some anarchists asserted, in order to spur disruptive social change. Berkman first tried to make a bomb, but he had limited technical skills and decided to use a .38-caliber revolver to kill Frick in his office; he also carried a steel blade laced with poison and hid in his mouth a dynamite capsule by which he planned to self-destruct. Berkman took a train to Pittsburgh, bought a new suit, and entered Frick's office on July 23, 1892, firing two shots. Frick was struck by both bullets, but not fatally injured, and the gun jammed when Berkman tried to fire a third shot. Others in the Carnegie Steel office came running and attempted to grab Berkman, who struggled and managed to stab Frick, too. Berkman, who still spoke only passable English, was taken into custody and the dynamite device discovered and choked out of him before it detonated.

The Homestead strike leaders decried Berkman's violent act and publicly distanced themselves from it. As a defendant, Berkman refused the right to counsel and instead penned a lengthy statement that the presiding judge cut short when a translator read it at trial. The jury did not even bother to sequester themselves for deliberation and voted unanimously in the box, declaring Berkman guilty of several felony charges. He was sentenced to 21 years in prison and remanded to the massive, fort-like Western Penitentiary in Allegheny Pennsylvania, on the banks of the Ohio River.

Agitated for Prison Reform

After a failed suicide attempt Berkman found like-minded friends behind bars and even produced an underground newsletter, *Zuchthausblüthen* (Prison Blossoms). He also used the time to improve his English and read books in the prison library. Periodically his activities landed him in trouble and he spent long periods in the dungeon, the dreaded underground pits that served as solitary confinement cells at Western Penitentiary. One year-long stint in solitary was the result of his refusing to name the outside co-conspirators in a daring but failed escape attempt that once again made Berkman the subject of newspaper headlines across the United States. A house near the prison grounds had been rented in 1900 and its tenants secretly began digging a tunnel from its cellar toward the prison yard, but the plan was foiled when some adventure-seeking children roamed around the unoccupied house and discovered the vast underground route.

In 1905 Berkman's sentence was reduced and he was released to the Allegheny County Workhouse. He was freed on May 18, 1906, after nearly 14 years in prison, and a posse of journalists was there to interview him. Emma Goldman and other longtime friends rallied to his side, but the newly freed ex-convict was plagued by anxiety attacks and found himself ill at ease around crowds. "The comrades are sympathetic and attentive, but their very care is a source of annoyance," he wrote about this time in his 1912 autobiography *Prison Memoirs of an Anarchist*. "I long for solitude and quiet. In the midst of people, the old prison instinct of escape possesses me."

Berkman eventually returned to New York City with Goldman and settled into a new role as editor of the leftist magazine she founded, *Mother Earth*. The illustrated monthly promoted anarchist ideas, freedom of speech, women's reproductive rights, and workers' movements around the world. Federal law-enforcement authorities targeted it for years, and finally managed to shut it down in the summer of 1917 after the United States formally entered World War I. Berkman and other writers had been critical of new military-draft laws, specifically the Selective Service Act of 1917 that required all male citizens in the United States between the ages of 21 and 30 to register in advance of possible conscription into the U.S. armed forces. In May of 1917 Berkman and Goldman founded the No Conscription League of New York.

Jailed, Then Deported

On June 15, 1917, U.S. President Woodrow Wilson also signed into law the Espionage Act of 1917, which permitted federal charges to be brought against persons who publicly encouraged others to flout the Selective Service Act. That same day, the *Mother Earth* offices in New York City were raided and Berkman and Goldman were arrested. In July of 1917 they were found guilty and Berkman returned to prison for another two-year-stint. This sentence was served at the Atlanta Federal Penitentiary in Georgia, a much harsher place than the Pennsylvania prison, and Berkman endured another long stretch of solitary confinement.

Berkman was freed on October 1, 1919, and he and Goldman now faced a new legal battle in the U.S. government's attempt to deport them back to their homelands under the Anarchist Exclusion Act of the 1917 Espionage Act. Their legal team argued that the pair would likely be targeted by White Guard forces in the Russian Civil War, which erupted after Russian Communists forced the abdication of the tsar at the end of World War I, then seized firm control of the remnants of the Empire in a 1917 Bolshevik revolution. Berkman lost his case and Goldman chose to sail with him, along with hundreds of other "foreign instigators" in December of 1919. The pair were initially feted in the new Soviet Russia but soon discerned that the tsarist-era levels of corruption, bungling, and police-state climate of fear were still very much in place. They ran afoul of authorities for backing a strike by malnourished sailors in the Kronstadt port city near St. Petersburg that ended violently.

Criticized Soviet Dictatorship

Berkman and Goldman left Soviet Russia in December of 1921. Forced to petition other nations for political asylum, they were technically stateless persons without any citizenship rights. They eventually settled in Berlin, Germany, where both wrote of their time in the Soviet Union. Goldman's book *My Two Years in Russia* was published in 1923, and Berkman wrote *The Bolshevik Myth* in 1925. That same year he moved to France, where the last decade of his life was marked by financial hardships and health problems. He committed suicide on June 28, 1936, in Nice, France.

Berkman was a marginalized figure for some years after his death, a curious anarchist footnote in the history of the labor union movement in the United States. His writings and speeches were rediscovered in the 1960s by a new generation of anti-war protesters and academics. "I have always said things that everybody can hear," Berkman said in one of his most famous speeches, delivered to an agitated, heckling crowd at a 1917 anti-draft meeting and reprinted in *Life of an Anarchist: The Alexander Berkman Reader*. "And what is more important, I want the police and the soldiers to hear what I have to say. It will do them good." Addressing the New York City crowd and, more specifically, males of eligible draft age on the matter of whether or not to register for service, Berkman urged them to "use your own judgment and rely upon your own conscience. It is the best guide in all the world. If that is a crime, if that is treason, I am willing to be shot."

Books

Avrich, Paul, and Karen Avrich, *Sasha and Emma: The Anarchist Odyssey of Alexander Berkman and Emma Goldman*, Harvard University Press, 2012.

Berkman, Alexander, *Life of an Anarchist: The Alexander Berkman Reader*, notes and introduction by Gene L. Fellner, Seven Stories Press, 1992, updated with foreword by Howard Zinn, 2004.

Berkman, Alexander, *Prison Memoirs of an Anarchist*, Mother Earth Publishing Association, 1912.

Periodicals

Times (London, England), July 25, 1892. □

Folke Bernadotte

Swedish diplomat Count Folke Bernadotte (1895–1948) was instrumental in managing a humanitarian relief effort that saved thousands of disabled British and American prisoners of war in Nazi Germany during World War II. Nephew of the reigning Swedish monarch and head of the Swedish Red Cross, Bernadotte was appointed by the United Nations to mediate troubles in the newly declared State of Israel in 1948, where he was assassinated by an extremist group.

Keystone Pictures USA/Alamy

F olke Bernadotte, Count of Wisborg, was born on January 2, 1895, in Stockholm, Sweden. The last of five children in his family, at the time of his birth he was also the grandson of the reigning monarch of Sweden, King Oscar II. Bernadotte's father, also named Oscar, had given up his title as Prince of Sweden to marry a commoner, Ebba Henrietta Munck af Fulkila. Their 1888 engagement caused a minor scandal and aroused intense public sympathy across Scandinavia, and Bernadotte's father was able to marry his fiancée only if he removed himself from the line of succession to the Swedish throne.

Descended from Kings of Sweden

The Bernadotte family dynasty in Sweden dated back to the Napoleonic era and was a mix of French, Swedish, and German bloodlines. Bernadotte's great-great-grandfather was Jean-Baptiste Bernadotte, a high-ranking French military leader in the service of Napoleon Bonaparte. That Bernadotte had a long record of service in the Baltic region and took part in Napoleon's ambitious military offensive across Europe. At the time, the Swedish throne was at risk, for its king was advanced in age and without an heir. In a surprise move, the Swedish parliament chose General Bernadotte as the designated Crown Prince in 1810, and he accepted the offer. In an even more surprising move, the newly ennobled French general broke with Napoleon, launched his own military offensive, and in 1818, was crowned king of a united Sweden and Norway as King Charles XIV. His son inherited the throne in 1844, and ruled for 15 years as Oscar I. The next in line was Charles XV, king of the still-unified Scandinavian realms until 1872, followed by Bernadotte's paternal grandfather, who took the name Oscar II and ruled until his death in 1905.

Bernadotte's maternal grandmother was born Sophia of Nassau and descended from a German princely family with generations-old links to aristocratic dynasties in the Netherlands and Luxembourg. Members of Sophia's family married into several other European dynasties, including Tsarist Russia's ill-fated House of Romanov.

Despite the princely lineage, Bernadotte and his brother Carl and sisters Maria, Ebba, and Elsa were raised in a spartan household in Stockholm with a focus on religious observance and service to others. Oscar and his children were granted the *Greve af Visborg* title as a courtesy title,

bestowed in similar circumstances to other Swedish princes who had removed themselves from the line of succession. In the summer of 1904, the family traveled to England and a nine-year-old Bernadotte easily picked up a new language on the vacation. He struggled in school, however, and was thought to have been dyslexic. Adaptive in other learning strategies, he later became fluent in French and German, which would prove crucial to his later career as a diplomat.

Married American Heiress

In his teens Bernadotte entered the Military Academy Karlberg in Stockholm and trained to become an officer in the Royal Life Guards, a cavalry unit of the Swedish Army. He graduated tenth in his class in 1915, but poor eyesight restricted his actual military service. In any case, combat was not an option, as Sweden had adopted an official policy of neutrality in the perennially simmering wars on the European continent.

In 1918, Bernadotte was commissioned a lieutenant in the Swedish Army and spent the next decade as a cavalry officer in the Royal Life Guards. While on vacation in France in 1928, he met American heiress Estelle Romaine Manville. Her family fortune was derived from asbestos, a flame-retardant mineral that was widely used in building-construction materials for decades. The couple wed on December 1, 1928, at an Episcopal church in Pleasantville, a village in Westchester County, New York. The nearby

Manville estate was large enough to host a wedding reception attended by a thousand guests.

The newlyweds returned to Sweden in 1929 after a long honeymoon, settling in Stockholm, and the first of their four sons was born in January of 1930. Their second son, Folke, was born in United States in February of 1931. A third son, Fredrik, died in infancy in Stockholm in the summer of 1934, followed by the death of first-born son Gustaf at the age of six in 1936. The Bernadottes' fourth son, Bertil, was born in the fall of 1935 in Sweden.

Found Calling During Wartime

Bernadotte and his American wife were popular ambassadors for the Swedish crown in the United States in the 1930s. The Count was an official emissary to the 1933 World's Fair in Chicago, and also served as the Swedish commissioner-general at the 1939 New York World's Fair. His longtime military service also made him a natural fit for the Svenska Scoutförbundet, or Swedish Boy Scouts, and in 1937 he became director of the organization. When World War II began in the summer of 1939, Bernadotte oversaw the formation and training of Boy Scout units for civil defense and medical assistance in Sweden.

Sweden was able to remain neutral during the six-year war, but neighboring Denmark and Norway were invaded by Nazi Germany in the spring of 1940 and came under punitive occupation rule. In Copenhagen, Oslo, and other Danish and Norwegian cities, those deemed hostile to the right-wing Nazi ideology were deported to labor camps in other parts of conquered Europe. Denmark's king, Christian X—a blood relation to the House of Bernadotte—and other top officials worked to allow Danish Jews to flee to the safety of Sweden. By contrast, Norway, whose nine-decade-long union with Sweden was dissolved in 1907, cooperated with Nazi occupiers to deport its small Jewish population, though some were able to reach asylum in Sweden.

Britain led the fight against the Nazi regime at first, and were eventually joined by the Soviet Union and the United States as the combined Allied Forces after 1941. Casualties and combat wounds were catastrophic on both sides, and there were reports emerging that the labor and detention camps located deep inside Hitler's newly created Reich, or empire, were actually death factories set up to exterminate all European Jews. In 1943, Bernadotte was appointed vice-chair of the Swedish Red Cross and began devoting his efforts to helping the Allied prisoners of war, or POWs, captured by German troops and held at "Stalag" camps under similarly abhorrent conditions.

Risked Life to Arrange Relief

The first POW exchange between the Allies and Germany began in the third week of October of 1943. Bernadotte had worked with International Red Cross officials to broker the exchange, which freed nearly 5,200 British Empire soldiers from German POW camps. Most of the men had been classified as unfit for military service, meaning they were badly maimed or disabled. They boarded relief ships in Sassnitz, a German port city on the Baltic, for transport to Göteborg, Sweden, where they were to remain under medical supervision. Several weeks later Bernadotte made the first of several trips into the Third Reich for further talks about additional POW exchanges. In late November he was one of several to emerge from the Swedish Legation on Tiergartenstrasse after a particularly heavy aerial bombardment that was, to date, the worst attack on the Nazi capital city of the war.

Bernadotte oversaw another POW exchange in September of 1944, but as the Allies made significant land advances to liberate Nazi-occupied parts of Europe there were fears that German Chancellor Adolf Hitler and his equally ruthless military commanders would abandon any idea of a "peace with honor" and instead enact a scorched-earth policy, leveling towns and cities as they retreated. The safety of the remaining POWs, which now included many American troops, was also a concern, as was the fate of Danish, Norwegian, and Swedish Jews and political prisoners in the Nazi death camps.

In February of 1945, Bernadotte began making visits to Germany again to arrange the White Buses humanitarian relief effort. With the help of Norwegian diplomat Niels Christian Ditleff, Bernadotte negotiated with the Nazi regime to secure the release of Scandinavian civilians in the camps and bring them to safety in Sweden. Bernadotte traveled with the dozen whitewashed buses, which carried only a Red Cross emblem to shield it from Allied bomber planes whose pilots targeted anything that even looked like a military convoy. Bernadotte brought with him 250 Swedish Army personnel plus Red Cross nurses and doctors; the White Buses also had to bring food, medical supplies, and even gasoline reserves, because the Nazis were not obligated to provide any assistance. The White Buses program brought out 2,000 Danes and Norwegians from the Sachsenhausen camp, another 600 from Dachau, and roughly 1,600 from other grim sites. The effort continued for several weeks as the war descended into its final and bloodiest days.

Bartered for Time with Himmler

Bernadotte's highest-ranking contact inside the Nazi regime was Heinrich Himmler, a close aide to Hitler and a top army, police, and cabinet official in the Reich. They met several times at the White Buses headquarters at Friedrichsruh Castle in Schleswig-Holstein, Germany, and in Berlin. By late April Himmler believed that Hitler had given up hope and planned to die in his underground bunker in Berlin, refusing to surrender Germany to its enemies at any price—even high civilian casualties. Himmler asked Bernadotte to pass on his offer to negotiate a surrender deal in which German troops would lay down their arms against British, French, and American troops on the western front, but keep fighting the Soviet Union in the east. The Allied powers, however, had already agreed upon a postwar plan to divide Europe and demanded Germany's unconditional surrender.

Hitler committed suicide on April 30, 1945, as Stalin's Red Army was entering Berlin, and Himmler fled and attempted to disguise himself as an ordinary German. He was discovered by Soviet troops, handed over to British commanders, and committed suicide in custody with a cyanide capsule hidden in a tooth.

Bernadotte had written reports to the Swedish Foreign Ministry as the White Buses program was underway, and published them with some commentary as *The End: My Humanitarian Negotiations in Germany in 1945 and Their Political Consequences* in 1945. On January 1, 1946, he was named president of the Swedish Red Cross. In May of 1948, he accepted a request from the United Nations Security Council to serve as mediator for the Arab-Israeli conflict in Palestine. The request came just five days after Jewish settlers and militia had declared victory and established the State of Israel. He visited Palestinian refugee camps and worked with officials on both sides, and his first proposal for a single state solution—an Arab-Israeli union comprised of two equal members—was summarily rejected. On September 17, 1948, Bernadotte was en route to a meeting in the Jewish district of Jerusalem when his U.N. vehicle was ambushed; a right-wing extremist pointed a gun inside the car and fired off six shots. Bernadotte's aide, a French colonel named André Sérot, was also killed.

The 53-year-old Bernadotte's murder prompted international outrage and was later linked to a group headed by future Israeli prime minister Yitzhak Shamir. Swedish Boy Scouts carried Bernadotte's coffin at a somber funeral service in Stockholm.

Books

Bernadotte, Count Folke, *Last Days of the Reich: The Diary of Count Folke Bernadotte, October 1944–May 1945,* Frontline Books, 2009, originally published *The Fall of the Curtain: Last Days of the Third Reich,* Alfred A. Knopf, 1945.

Periodicals

Daily Mail (London, England), February 17, 1944; April 30, 1945.
Times (London, England), November 25, 1943; April 30, 1945; May 2, 1945; May 3, 1945; September 18, 1948.□

Portrait of a young man (oil on panel), Spanish School, (15th century) / Museo Lazaro Galdaniano, Madrid, Spain/Bridgemena Images

joined with the Corona de Aragón through the marriage of Ferdinand and Isabella. The joint monarchs' newly unified and more firmly Catholic Kingdom of Spain would shape Berruguete's career as an artist, as alliances with Italy and the Holy Roman Empire were bolstered abroad, while at home churches were lavishly restored through generous royal patronage.

Pedro Berruguete

Spanish artist Pedro Berruguete (c. 1450–1503) is among the influencers who brought elements of Italian Renaissance painting to the Iberian peninsula. Working at a time when Spain was emerging as a new global empire, Berruguete is believed to have spent several years in Italy and later became a favored court painter to King Ferdinand II and Queen Isabella I, joint rulers of the Kingdom of Spain.

Pedro Berruguete's exact date of birth is unknown but is usually placed around 1450 by art historians. It is known that he came from Paredes de Nava, a village in the Palencia province of Castile. At the time, the Corona de Castilla (Crown of Castile) was a kingdom ruled with the adjacent Kingdom of León and by 1479 would be formally

Made Artistic Pilgrimage

Paredes was one of several stopping points along the route to Santiago de Compostela, a pilgrimage site that had attracted the faithful for half a millennium by Berruguete's lifetime. Located in the northwestern tip of the Iberian peninsula, Santiago was named in honor of St. James, whose remains were said to have been brought to the Galician city in 813. This James was one of the 12 apostles and was said to have preached in Galicia before returning to the Middle East. The Camino de Santiago, or Way of St. James, led directly to the cathedral built around the burial place in Santiago de Compostela. Paredes and nearby villages provided food, lodging, health care, and consumer goods to pilgrims en route to the city, and that early religious tourism exposed Spanish peasants in places like Paredes to customs and ideas from other parts of Europe. During his early years, the town was a thriving agricultural center, though little is known about his family or his forebearers' professions.

Berruguete may have shown enough early promise as a young artist to work on some altar panels and other objects inside the Church of San Juan in Paredes. He is thought to have traveled to Italy in the early 1470s, and was there until as late as 1483, though parish logs in Paredes de Nava record his 1478 marriage, which produced at least six children.

Berruguete's name is closely associated with that of Federico III da Montefeltro, the Duke of Urbino during a flourishing period of that city and commune of the same name. Urbino itself is a walled hillside city in Italy's Marche, a region wedged between the Adriatic Sea and two more powerful entities of Umbria and Tuscany. In 1444, the young Federico—scion of the Montefeltros, a northern Italian noble family—ascended as the newest duke in Urbino. He had been born illegitimate but seized power and amassed a considerable fortune through a mixture of warfare and diplomacy. As a young man Federico had first gained fame as a *condottiero,* or leader of his own militia band, in service to more powerful personae on the Italian peninsula. These included Pope Pius II, who named him Gonfalonier, or Supreme Commander of Christian Forces in service to the church in Rome.

Influenced by Flemish Art

As Duke of Urbino, Federico successfully remade the otherwise isolated duchy into a center of scholarship and the arts. He invited writers, artists, and philosophers to Urbino and built an impressive library of nearly a thousand rare manuscripts that would later be acquired by the Vatican. Federico also endowed churches, monasteries, and schools, and commissioned a majestic ducal palace for himself that became a UNESCO World Heritage Site.

Berruguete is generally accepted to have been one of those artists whose early career was shaped by his time in Urbino, though the specific extent of his work and that of another foreign painter there, Justus van Ghent, remains a point of art-historical debate centuries later. Van Ghent is counted among several notable artists from Flanders—more specifically the cities of Ghent and Bruges in present-day Belgium—who belonged to a distinct and vivid artistic style known as the Flemish School, which evolved independently from Italian Renaissance art but shared several features and figures. Jan van Eyck was among the most prominent of the early Flanders portraitists, and his 1434 *Arnolfini Portrait,* which depicts a wealthy Italian merchant in Bruges and his spouse, is one of the best-known examples of the Flemish School.

The fresh, naturalistic style of Flemish painting migrated to Italy and came to dominate through the patronage of wealthy figures like Federico and other secular leaders. The duke became one of the most prominent supporters of the Italian Renaissance during his lifetime, and his fervor for the new and the splendid was on full display in Urbino. His private chamber and study in the Palazzo Ducale, for example, features magnificent inlaid wood carvings done by Sandro Botticelli, a Florentine painter better known for his *Birth of Venus* masterpiece. Both Berruguete and Justus van Ghent were in Urbino at the same time and were thought to have worked under the

guidance of Piero della Francesca, one of the Italian Renaissance's most revered painters. Berruguete and van Ghent may have worked jointly, or separately, on a series of 28 portraits of *Uomini famosi* (Famous Men), another epic commission from Federico for his Ducal Chamber.

Painted Duke and Son

In that same Ducal Chamber hangs *Portrait of Federico da Montefeltro with His Son Guidobaldo,* one of Berruguete's best-known works. The full-length portrait, dated roughly 1475, shows Federico with his young son Guidobaldo, whose mother Battista Sforza had died in 1472. The duke wears a suit of armor as well as the Order of the Garter, bestowed on him by England's King Edward IV. "Four-year-old Guidobaldo leans against his father's knee, holding the ducal sceptre,'' commented Adrian Mourby, a journalist for the *Independent on Sunday.* "Although the portrait celebrates Federico's award of the garter from England and ermine from Naples, its tone is domestic and brings home the loneliness of father and son.''

Federico commissioned many portraits of himself, nearly all of which are in profile. The duke lost his right eye during a jousting tournament and later had to have part of his distinctive nose removed. In the British arts journal *Apollo,* Russell Chamberlin also wrote about Berruguete's *Portrait* of the duke and his son, noting that it is one of the few that bears evidence of the scar that ran down the side of the elder Montefeltro's face. Chamberlin characterized the work as one of the more dramatic examples of Renaissance portraiture, depicting "a man totally at ease with himself who combined strength with tolerance, who would be surprised by nothing, expected nothing, and was well able to defend his own.''

Federico died in 1482 and the Duchy of Urbino passed to Guidobaldo, who allied with the powerful Borgia family and was involved in multiple wars on the Italian peninsula. Urbino's place as an important city of the Italian Renaissance was by then surpassed by Florence, along with Venice and Rome.

Berruguete returned to Spain around 1482. Historical evidence confirms that he lived and worked in the city of Toledo later in the 1480s and into the early 1490s. More specifically, he was involved in the final stages of embellishment for the magnificent Toledo Cathedral, an important ecclesiastical seat of Christianity in Spain. Construction on the Gothic-style masterpiece began in the 1220s, but the site's history as a place of worship dated back to the sixth century and the Visigoth kings of early-medieval Spain. The new cathedral replaced an Islamic mosque built over the original church during the era of Moorish rule in Spain. Berruguete is believed to have painted several frescoes in the cathedral.

Taunted Torquemada's Legacy

Berruguete lived in Ávila, another important cathedral city in Spain, after 1499, after accepting some major commissions. These include the main altar paintings for a new Dominican monastery in Ávila dedicated to St. Thomas Aquinas, an important theologian of the early Christian era. The Santo Tomás monastery project was supervised by Fray Tomás de Torquemada, Spain's Grand Inquisitor. It was Torquemada, determined to reaffirm the Kingdom of Spain as a firmly Christian polity, who is most closely associated with the worst excesses of the Spanish Inquisition, a period of religious persecution. The Inquisition followed the full *Reconquista* of the Iberian peninsula after several centuries of Moorish Muslim rule. The *Reconquista* is also linked to Ferdinand and Isabella's formal expulsion of Spain's longtime Jewish population.

Torquemada was a friar of the Dominican order whose name became synonymous with the Spanish Inquisition's human-rights abuses, which included torture and capital punishment. The devout priest was also close to Ferdinand and Isabella, who endowed the Santo Tomás monastery and gave it *real,* or royal status. "The importance of the new foundation and its powerful patrons was not lost on Berruguete, and he rose to meet the challenge," wrote Jonathan Brown in his 1998 tome *Painting in Spain: 1500–1700.* "The paintings in the principal altarpiece are especially sumptuous, in part because of the lavish, if somewhat anachronistic use of tooled gold backgrounds, which was probably stipulated in the contract." Brown also noted that the monarchs selected the Santo Tomás monastery as the burial site of their first-born son, Crown Prince Juan of Castile, who died at age 18.

Brown also attributes to Berruguete one particularly grand work in the collection of Madrid's famed Prado Museum. Painted for the Santo Tomás monastery and completed in 1500—two years after the death of the much-feared Torquemada—it shows the founder of Torquemada's order, St. Dominic, presiding over one of the ecclesiastical courts that were precursors to the Grand Inquisition. Berruguete's *St. Dominic Pardons a Heretic* ostensibly takes place sometime before the saint's actual death in 1221, but Berruguete "makes the connection with the contemporary world practically inevitable by clothing the figures in the costume of his time," Brown wrote, and went on to describe "the disarmingly informal tone," with sleepy, indifferent clerics and ruthless executioners. "Berruguete steps out of his comfortable role as the faithful painter of exemplary sacred stories and offers a bitter taste of contemporary life," Brown remarked.

Son Alonso Carried On

Berruguete was completing a major work for the main altar of the Ávila Cathedral when he died in late 1503. The job was completed by one of his assistants, Juan de Borgoña, also known as John of Burgundy. Berruguete probably trained his son Alonso, who went on to a fairly prominent career. Born around 1486, the younger Berruguete studied in Italy at the height of the Renaissance and returned to Spain inspired by Michelangelo, whose atelier he had visited. Alonso's monumental works include the choir stalls at the Toledo Cathedral, and several other acclaimed examples of late-Renaissance Mannerist art in Spain.

In 2003, Berruguete's birthplace of Paredes de Nava honored the 500th anniversary of his death with a special exhibition at the Iglesia de Santa Eulalia. On loan from the Palazzo Ducale in Urbino was *Portrait of Federico da Montefeltro with His Son Guidobaldo,* the first time the artwork had left Italy in its 528-year history.

Books

"Berruguete, Pedro," in *The Grove Encyclopedia of Medieval Art and Architecture,* Volume 2, edited by Colum Hourihane, Oxford University Press, 2012.

Brown, Jonathan, *Painting in Spain: 1500–1700,* Yale University Press, 1998.

Periodicals

Apollo, September 2003.

Independent on Sunday (London, England), November 11, 2001. □

Theodore Beza

French theologian Theodore Beza (1519–1605) was a prominent figure in 16th-century Europe's Protestant Reformation. As one of the leading French Huguenots, he worked closely with John Calvin for many years and, like Calvin, spent much of his career in Switzerland. In the city of Geneva, which became known as the "Protestant Rome" in Beza's time, he taught theology and classical languages for decades at its Academy, an important training school for future ministers in the Reformed Church.

Theodore Beza was born on June 24, 1519, in Vézelay, a town in Burgundy in central France. He was baptized Dieudonné de Bèze in the traditional French Roman Catholic faith. Vézelay was a particularly strong center of the Roman Catholic faith: it was home to Vézelay Abbey, an old Benedictine monastery, and the town's main cathedral was named in honor of Mary Magdalene and claimed to house her relics. Beza's father Pierre held a royal appointment as governor of the local jurisdiction, and his father's brother served in the Parlement in Paris, an advisory body to the king. Another Beza uncle was Claude, a Cistercian friar who became abbot of a monastery in Fromont.

Trained for the Law

In his childhood Beza demonstrated an obvious talent for Greek and Latin, and was sent to live with his uncle Nicholas in Paris for further tutoring. In 1528, a nine-year-old Beza moved to Orléans to study under a renowned German scholar of Greek, Melchior Wolmar. Beza's teacher was receptive to the ideas coming out of Germany at the time that challenged the doctrines and practices of the Church in Rome. The movement had many roots, but is most closely connected to a dissident priest in the German cathedral city of Wittenberg named Martin Luther. Excommunicated in 1521, Luther went on to establish his own "reformed" church while his followers turned up elsewhere in Western Europe and launched their own breakaway religious communities.

One of the most influential of Luther's adherents was a gifted French student named Jehan Cauvin, who later Anglicized his name to John Calvin. Like Beza, Calvin came from a prosperous, respected family and seemed destined for a rewarding career in the French civil-service or ecclesiastical realms. In 1529, Calvin began studies at the University of Bourges, a new center of Protestantism in France. When Wolmar was invited to teach at Bourges, Beza went with him and through this met Calvin.

A dutiful son, Beza obeyed his father's wishes and began law studies at the University of Orléans. On August 11, 1539, a 20-year-old Beza received his law degree and soon thereafter moved to Paris to begin his career. He was a diffident lawyer, preferring scholarly pursuits and writing poems in Latin, and lived off a decent annual income from benefices, or guaranteed stipends tied to service in the Roman Church. These came from his uncle the abbot, and when Beza's brother died in 1541, he began to receive his late sibling's benefice, too. In Paris Beza met a young woman named Claudine Denosse, and the two were wed in secret in 1544. The wedding did not take place in a church nor was it registered with local authorities, for Beza was apparently fearful of losing his benefice income.

Self-Imposed Exile

In 1548 Beza published his first volume of verse, *Juvenilia,* a collection of Latin poems that also appeared under the later title *Poemata.* His pride in the achievement was dampened by guilt over his relationship with Denosse and the hypocrisy of his gilded life in Paris, linked as it was to his family's allegiance to the Roman Church. Stricken by an illness, he suffered a crisis of conscience and religious awakening that prompted him to break with his family, his benefices, and with the bonds that tied him to France and the Church. He and Denosse departed Paris in October of 1548, and the two were wed in Geneva, Switzerland, which was becoming home to a growing community of French Protestants, among them John Calvin. Several months later the Parlement of Paris issued an official judgment on Beza's actions, charging him with simony—a financial crime related to his benefices—and with Lutheranism.

Beza was welcomed in Germany and in Switzerland, both of which had active Protestant movements. He reconnected with Wolmar, visiting his former teacher in Tübingen, a German university town not far from the Swiss border. For several years Beza and Denosse—whom he had married openly in Switzerland in late 1548—lived in Lausanne, another Swiss city, where he was hired to teach Greek at a relatively new academy established there to train French-speaking Protestant men for the ministry. During Beza's time in Lausanne he produced an important play, *Abraham Sacrifiant,* a dramatization of the Old Testament story of the Hebrew patriarch Abraham from the Book of Genesis.

Switzerland was a refuge for scores of French Protestants like Beza at a time when freedom of religion was drastically curtailed by French law. The kings of France ruled with absolute authority, and they were beholden to the pope in Rome and to their various allies across Europe.

Both the Holy Roman Emperor and the ruling houses of Spain, Italy, and other European powers were all related through marriages and formal political alliances to France, which itself was a formidable maritime, economic, and military power of the 16th century. Like Calvin, Guillaume Farel, and Pierre Viret, Beza was among the most respected defectors from the French *ancien reégime* to establish themselves in Switzerland, a land with a deeply entrenched sense of independence and self-governance.

Translated Famous Psalter

Beza worked closely with Calvin for many years and finally began to apply his legal training to writing tracts on good governance, the rights of citizens, and the role of civic magistrates and local office-holders. He also penned scores of tracts on theology and the plight of French Huguenots who remained in France and were growing in number. He traveled to the German cathedral city of Worms in 1557 to take part in a colloquy, which failed to resolve some crucial doctrinal differences between the Reformed Church clerics and representatives of the Roman Church. Also present in Worms was Philip Melanchthon, a close associate of Luther's and a German theologian with whom Beza corresponded for many years. Luther had died in 1546, and Calvin became the most prominent and influential of Luther's followers over the next two decades.

In 1558, Calvin established a *collège* or Academy of Geneva, and a year later appointed Beza its first rector. Beza also chaired its Greek-language faculty and delivered theology lectures. He also produced an impressive amount of scholarly works and translations during these years. His knowledge of classical languages was an invaluable resource on the team that produced the first English-language Geneva Bible, which appeared in 1560. He also completed the first French-language translation of the Old Testament's Book of Psalms. This French Psalter, began by another poet Clément Marot and completed by Beza after Marot's death, was first published in 1562 and became a work of immense significance for French Protestants. The Psalter remained in use, in the original French metrical translation, more than four centuries later.

Beza wrote a personal essay declaring his adherence to the Reformed Church—a standard practice for Protestant theologians and clerics—in 1559. *Confession de la foi chrétienne* was dedicated to Wolmar, his first tutor, but written with Beza's aged father in mind. In 1561 Beza took part in the Colloquy of Poissy, representing the interests of French Protestants, and was also present at the Colloquy of St. Germain in January of 1562. He was particularly aggrieved at France's worsening religious strife, which had erupted in multiple wars in the years since he had come to Switzerland. The French Huguenot leader Louis, the Prince of Condé, secured a 1563 peace treaty that guaranteed some religious freedoms to Protestants in France, and Beza was among those who opposed its terms and warned that it would only prompt deeper enmity and clashes at a later date, which proved true.

Succeeded Calvin in Geneva

Calvin, Beza's longtime mentor, died a year later in 1564. Beza succeeded him as Moderator of the Venerable Company of Pastors in Geneva, a council that had helped cement the city's reputation as the Protestant Rome, and he also took over as theology chair at the Geneva Academy, which eventually morphed into the University of Geneva.

Beza's fears about future civil strife in France between Catholics and Protestants proved well founded. On the night of August 23-24, 1572, a wave of attacks was carried out in Paris and other French cities on French Huguenot leaders, including military officers who had served with Condé. Thousands died in what was known as the St. Bartholomew's Day Massacre and the remaining French Huguenots fled France en masse. As Moderator of the Company of Pastors, Beza offered shelter and alms to the refugees. Religious tensions in neighboring France—and elsewhere in Europe—roiled the Continent and the British Isles for the next century and beyond.

Targeted by Jesuits

On the side of the papacy in Rome was an influential Roman Catholic order, the Society of Jesuits. Known for their intellectual rigor and fierce defense of the Throne of St. Peter, they produced reams of anti-Protestant propaganda and even fomented rumors that key leaders and defenders of the Protestant faith had clandestinely returned to the fold of the Church in Rome. This was one of the most scurrilous of all accusations against a religious leader and was aimed at destabilizing flocks of Protestant faithful in Switzerland and elsewhere. Pamphlets claiming Beza's premature death and deathbed renunciation appeared in the 1590s and compelled Beza to produce his own strongly worded defenses repudiating the Jesuits' claims.

Beza's 40-year marriage to Denosse ended with her death in 1588. They had no children. Several months later, he married a widow from Genoa named Catharina del Piano. He retired from teaching posts and duties as rector of the Geneva Academy in steps over the next decade. He died in Geneva on October 13, 1605, at age 86. In his adopted city he is remembered on a piece of monumental public art carved out of the old city walls. In the bas-relief Reformation Wall, erected in 1909 to mark the 400th anniversary of the birth of Calvin, Beza appears alongside Calvin, Farel, and John Knox, a Scottish reformer.

Among the voluminous works left behind by Beza and preserved by his students and acolytes was his *Annotationes*, his 1598 retort to the Jesuits. "I am still healthy and, though almost eighty years old, completely sound in mind and body," it read, according to his biographer Scott M. Manetsch in *Theodore Beza and the Quest for Peace in France: 1572–1598*. "Having served forty of my eighty years in the army of the ministry, I continue to teach the very holy truth of God purely and from his holy word...and, God willing, I will continue to attack that detestable Roman prostitute seated in the seven-hilled city until my very last breath."

Books

Manetsch, Scott M., *Theodore Beza and the Quest for Peace in France: 1572–1598*, Brill, 2000.
"Théodore de Bèze," in *Encyclopedia of the Renaissance,* edited by Paul F. Grendler, Charles Scribner's Sons, 2000.

Periodicals

Renaissance Quarterly, Spring 2008.□

Georges Bidault

An active member of the French Resistance during World War II, French politician Georges Bidault (1899–1983) was a prominent member of post-war governments. Holding such posts as prime minister, defense minister, and foreign minister, Bidault played an active role in forming French policies in the 1940s and 1950s. Disgraced later in his career because of his outspoken opposition to the independence of the French colony of Algeria, Bidault spent his last years in exile, then obscurity.

Georges-Augustin Bidault was born on October 5, 1899, in Moulins, France, the son of a wealthy insurance official. He was educated at an Italian Jesuit school. At the end of World War I, Bidault briefly served in the French Army. In 1919, he took part in the occupation of the Ruhr.

Was a Catholic Activist

After the war ended, Bidault entered the University of Paris. At the Sorbonne, he earned degrees in both history and geography, and was active in a Catholic Action movement. When he completed his education, he began his professional career as a history teacher. He also continued to be a Roman Catholic activist.

By the early 1930s, Bidault began working as a journalist for the Christian Democratic press. In 1932, he founded a Catholic leftist daily newspaper, *L'Aube (The Dawn)*. In addition to serving as editor, Bidault wrote for the paper and penned the foreign affairs column. In his pieces, he spoke out against appeasement of Nazi Germany in the 1930s, including the Munich Agreement in 1938. He was a columnist for the newspaper until 1939, when Nazi Germany invaded and occupied France.

During the Occupation, German authorities targeted Bidault as a high profile leftist in France. Initially, Bidault evaded them and volunteered for military service during World War II. Reaching the rank of sergeant, he served at the front as a volunteer. Bidault was captured in 1940, and spent some time as a prisoner of war in Germany. In 1941, Bidault was repatriated after being in German custody for about a year with a group of soldiers who had all served during World War I.

Pictorial Press Ltd/Alamy

Became Involved in the Resistance

After his return to France, Bidault became a secondary school teacher in Lyons, France. He also took an active and leading role in the French Resistance against the German Occupation. In May 1943, Jean Molin formed the National Council of Resistance, and Bidault was a co-founder and charter member of the group. When Moulin was captured, tortured, and murdered by the Gestapo (the Nazi secret state police), Bidault assumed leadership of the National Council of Resistance and coordinated the Resistance movement in France. In the same period, Bidault backed the Free French provisional government formed by General Charles de Gaulle in London.

Though Nazi Germany learned of Bidault's place in the Resistance in 1943, Bidault was able to avoid all their attempts to capture him again. When Paris was liberated in August 1944, he marched down the Champs-Éylsées with de Gaulle. As World War II ended, Bidault became involved in French politics. In November 1944, he founded a Christian Democrat political party, the Mouvement Républicain Populaire (Republican Movement/Popular Republican Party). This political group was especially focused on representing Roman Catholic interests.

When de Gaulle formed the first post-war provisional government in 1944, he served as the first president and prime minister of France. Elected to the French National Assembly, Bidault served as de Gaulle's foreign minster in this government from 1944 to 1948, except for a brief period as prime minister from July to December 1946. International issues would become a special area of focus for Bidault, as he balanced France's interests with the need to compromise.

Focused on International Issues

During Bidault's term as foreign minister, he took part in major post-World War II events representing France. In 1945 alone, he was a signee of the Franco-Soviet alliance and supported the Yalta Agreement which reorganized post-war Europe. He also formed economic agreements with Belgium, the Netherlands, and Luxembourg. In addition, Bidault was the chief of the French delegation to the founding meeting of the United Nations, held in San Francisco in 1945. Because of Bidault's skilled negotiating efforts, France gained a high-profile place in the United Nations. Bidault signed the Charter of the United Nations as well.

Bidault further advanced French interests when he represented his country at the Conference of Foreign Ministers at meetings in 1945 in London and in 1946 in Paris. He also supported the formation of the Marshall Plan, also known as the European Recovery Program. This U.S. economic plan was to help rebuild a devastated Europe after the end of World War II. Bidault helped coordinate the European response to the Marshall Plan throughout 1947 and 1948. The Marshall Plan began its economic support in 1948 and ran through 1951.

During this period, Bidault's politics evolved, becoming more right leaning. Bidault became an outspoken opponent of decolonization because he believed it would lessen France's standing in the world. He firmly believed that France should have and maintain a world empire. In the mid-1940s, Bidault tried to prevent Premier Pierre Mendes France from giving up Indochina through political measures but failed. Bidault also authorized Georges Thierry, d'Argenlieu, the French High Commissioner to Indochina, to use forced if needed against Vietnamese nationalist forces after the French cruise *Suffren* bombarded the port of Haiphong. This led to the Indochina War, fought from 1946 to 1954. Issues that simmered eventually led to the Vietnam War, which began in 1955.

Because of his earlier left-leaning politics, Bidault initially was not hostile to the Soviet Union. However, his opinion changed after the Soviets brought Czechoslovakia into its sphere of influence in 1948. Bidault came to believe that Western Europe needed its own defensive and economic alliance, and supported the formation of the North Atlantic Treaty Organization (NATO). Economic cooperation came in the form of the Coal and Steel Pool, formed in 1951 by France, Germany, Italy, and several other countries. From this organization, the European Economic Community eventually emerged. He also played a role in the formation of the Council of Europe and the European Defense Community.

Held French Government Positions

During the late 1940s and early 1950s, Bidault held a number of positions in the French government. He was prime minister from October 1949 to June 1950, then defense minister from 1951 to 1952. He again served as foreign minister, from 1953 to 1954. Bidault tried and failed to form his own government in June 1953. He ran for president in December 1953, but failed to gain the post. He remained a part of French legislature, however.

By the early 1950s, the issue of Algeria had begun to be more prominent. In 1954, Muslim nationalists started a revolt in the French colony. Independence was sought, and the war continued for several years. Two years later, Bidault backed a group called the Union for the Safety and Resurrection of French Algeria. This group wanted Algeria to remain under French control.

By 1958, Bidault was outspoken in his belief that de Gaulle should return to office to address this issue. Bidault incorrectly believed, however, that de Gaulle backed the concept of Algeria remaining part of France. In May 1958, the Algerian conflict took on a new dimension when French officers and settlers in Algeria staged an uprising, an event supported by Bidault. The leadership of the French government was transformed soon after, and de Gaulle came out of retirement to helm the next government. Also in 1958, Bidault founded a new, right-wing version of the Christian-Democratic Party.

Bidault and de Gaulle soon had a major disagreement over Algerian independence. In a speech he gave in 1959, de Gaulle publicly backed Algeria's desire for freedom and believed independence was the best way of solving the Algerian crisis. Bidault maintained his belief that France should continue to control Algeria, and supported the rebellious French officers there.

Acted Against Algerian Independence

Unhappy with French policy, Bidault became increasingly militant about Algeria in the early 1960s. Bidault was a co-founder of the Vincennes Committee, which wanted to retain French Algeria. Other prominent French politicians and personalities backed the committee's intent as well. The committee was believed to have supported terrorist activities in Algeria and France meant to undermine de Gaulle's efforts to bring independence to Algeria. The Vincennes Committee was banned by late 1961.

Bidault persisted in his work against Algerian independence in 1962, going underground to do so. He was believed to be the designated successor of the head of the Organisation de l'Armee Secrete (OAS, or Secret Army Organization). This violent terrorist group acted against the French government's backing of a free Algeria. Bidault denied that he was affiliated with the group and the successor of General Raoul Salan, who was arrested in April 1962. Still, many believed that Bidault served as the national director of the OAS.

Bidault also publicly called de Gaulle's government both illegal and illegitimate. Because of his actions, he was put on a list of persons who were believed to be plotting against the French government in 1962. The immunity he gained by being a member of the French National Assembly was taken away and a warrant was issued for his arrest. He was charged with conspiracy.

Went into Exile

Labeled a criminal, Bidault fled France in 1962 and went into exile to avoid arrest. He lived in Switzerland, Italy, Germany, Portugal, Belgium, and Brazil. From these countries, Bidault called on the French people to resist de Gaulle, and denounced him over and over again. Bidault also tried to create another National Council of Resistance, echoing World War II, but it was of no interest to the French. Overall, Bidault's actions were considered politically embarrassing when he was in Europe.

During his time in exile, Bidault also penned his memoirs, *Resistance: The Political Autobiography of Georges Bidault.* Often taking an acrimonious tone, Stanley Hoffman noted in the *New York Review of Books,* "One does not hope for serenity from an exile, and one fully expects bitterness. But what has the reader done to deserve the deluge of resentment that Bidault has poured over these bloated pages? Can it all be explained by a passionate devotion to a cause which may have been the wrong one, but which he deemed sufficiently noble to justify acts that denied his past?"

Bidault went to Brazil in 1967, but was able to return to France when de Gaulle gave amnesty to those accused of crimes related to Algerian independence in May 1968. After his return, Bidault lived a quiet, relatively marginalized life in France. He had a brief return to politics as the founder of the far right wing political party, *Mouvement pour las Justice et la Paix* (Movement for Justice and Peace). The party had no impact on French politics. Often in poor health, he spent much of his last years defending his subversive actions. His only honor came in 1977 when he was named the honorary president of the Christian-Democratic Party.

In December 1982, Bidault suffered a stroke at his home in Paris. To receive treatment, he was taken to a specialized hospital in the southwestern French city of Cambo-les-Bains. Bidault died there on January 27, 1983. He was 83 years old. He was buried at Lasalle-les-Bordes.

Books

Cold War: A Student Encyclopedia, Volume 1, edited by Spencer C. Tucker, ABC-CLIO, 2008.

The Encyclopedia of American Business, Volume 2, edited by W. Davis Folsom, Facts on File, 2011.

The Encyclopedia of the Vietnam War: A Political, Social, and Military History, Volume 1, 2nd ed., edited by Spencer C. Tucker and Paul G. Peirpaoli, ABC-CLIO, 2011.

Axelrod, Alan, *Encyclopedia of World War II,* Volume 1, edited by Jack A. Kingston, Facts on File, 2007.

Raymond, Gino, *History Dictionary of France,* 2nd ed., Scarecrow Press, 2008.

Periodicals

Associated Press, January 27, 1983.

Financial Times (London, England), January 28, 1983; June 3, 1997.

Globe and Mail (Toronto, Ontario, Canada), January 28, 1983.

New York Times, January 28, 1983.

United Press International, January 27, 1983.

Online

"Memoirs of a Disappointed Man," *The New York Review of Books,* http://www.nybooks.com/articles/archives/1968/feb/01/memoirs-of-a-disappointed-man/ (January 1, 2014). ☐

Max Bill

Max Bill (1908–1994) was a revered figure in 20th-century modernism. The Swiss-born architect, artist, and industrial designer studied with the original Bauhaus visionaries in Germany in the 1920s and went on to co-found the similarly influential Ulm School of Design after World War II.

SZ Photo/Friedrich, Brigette/DIZ Muenchen GmbH, Suedddeutsche Zeitung Photo/Alamy

Max Bill lived through two world wars that physically and psychologically scarred the nations of Europe, and a fair portion of his career was spent working to bring a new, pan-European design ethos that would transcend outmoded nationalist sentiments. Born on December 22, 1908, he was from Winterthur, a city northeast of Zürich and en route scenic Lake Konstanz. His father was the stationmaster of the Winterthur train station and the family lived in quarters above the depot. At age 15, Bill began a silversmithing course at the School of Applied Arts in Zürich.

Emerged as Teen Prodigy

Bill was just 16 years old in 1925 when a silver jug he designed was included in the Swiss section of the International Exposition of Modern Decorative and Industrial Arts exhibition in Paris, France. This event's longer French name, the *Exposition Internationale des Arts Décoratifs et Industriels Modernes,* was later used in shortened form to designate the style known as Art Deco. The Paris trip exposed Bill to the work of significant new theorists on art, architecture, and the applied arts, and Bill was especially enamored with the cube-like purity of the controversial L'Esprit Nouveau (The New Spirit) pavilion at the International Exposition. The pavilion was the work of a visionary French-Swiss architect, Le Corbusier (born Charles-Édouard Jeanneret-Gris), and Bill became an acolyte of the renegade architect who was emerging as a pioneer in the use of reinforced concrete as a building material.

In 1927, Bill moved to Dessau, Germany, to begin studies at the Bauhaus school of design, a major force in 20th-century modernism. The school's founders and graduates would go on to create landmark buildings around the world, plus the appropriate furnishings and art to fill them. Bauhaus faculty members included Ludwig Mies van der Rohe, Wassily Kandinsky, and Paul Klee. Bill studied architecture at the Bauhaus school under Hannes Meyer, also from Switzerland, who went on to work in the Soviet Union and Mexico City. "Bill shared Meyer's Utopian conviction that architecture and design could create a new society if only informed by science and shaped by technology," wrote Frank Whitford in the London *Independent.* "Like Meyer, Bill was also unconvinced by the claim, made by several Bauhaus teachers, that the fine arts deserved special status because of their spiritually regenerative properties."

Settled in Zürich

Bill eventually joined the informal group painting classes led by Kandinsky and Klee and would continue to create abstract art for the remainder of his professional life. The Bauhaus instructor who proved the most influential on the course of his career, however, was László Moholy-Nagy, a Hungarian émigré who taught sculpture, photography, and metalwork. A dalliance with a dance troupe led by another well-known Bauhaus figure, Oskar Schlemmer, ended with a collision with a trapeze artist. Bill lost part of a tooth and there was also damage to his palate, which required expensive reconstructive dental surgery. Back in Zürich in 1929, he met a dancer named Nusch Éluard, but Bill's family objected to the romance, and she moved on to Paris, where she sat for Pablo Picasso and Man Ray.

In 1932, Bill married Binia Spoerri, a photographer, and completed his first building as lead architect, a house in the Höngg quarter of Zürich, over the following year. In the early years of their marriage, he and Spoerri supported themselves by collaborating on graphic design jobs, and his Bauhaus architecture training led him into exhibition design, echoing the path of Le Corbusier. In 1936 Bill's Swiss Pavilion at another decorative-arts and architecture exposition, the Milan Triennale, won top honors. Two years later Bill was admitted as a member of the Congrès internationaux d'architecture moderne (International Congress of Modern Architecture, or CIAM), a prestigious group of modernist builders founded by Le Corbusier.

Promoted Constructivist Art

The outbreak of World War II marked an abrupt but temporary break in European modernism in art and architecture. With much of Western Europe overtaken by right-wing Nazi Germany, works of modern art were banished, deemed "degenerate," and dismissed as insufficiently nationalist; instead Nazi propagandists favored a monumental neo-Classical style in public buildings and visual art that bolstered claims of ethnic German superiority. The Bauhaus school had already been shut down, and many creative professionals had fled Europe altogether. Bill was able to remain in Switzerland, which was an officially neutral non-combatant nation, as it had been since 1815. In 1944, Bill began teaching at his alma mater, Zürich's School of Applied Arts. That same year he organized the first international exhibition of Concrete Art—also called Constructivist art—in the Swiss city of Basel.

The Basel *Konkrete Kunst* exhibit showcased the work of emerging new three-dimensional artists whose work was crafted from reinforced concrete as well as metal and granite. Their style was rigorously abstract and organized around spatial concepts of geometry or the laws of physics when applied to kinetic sculpture. In 1948 Bill established the Institute for Progressive Culture in Zürich to promote his ideas, and he also served as president of the Swiss Work Federation, or Werkbund, an organization for industrial designers and makers of decorative-arts objects. With the end of World War II came ambitious plans to rebuild a war-ravaged landscape, and Bill was among the thought leaders who advocated for a drastic remodeling based on egalitarian principles.

Co-Founded Ulm School

As president of Swiss Werkbund, Bill launched an annual exhibition in the late 1940s that heralded the newest entrants in what was titled *Gute Form*, or "Good Design." The exhibits attracted notice from a cadre of young German designers, linked initially by their family ties to one of the Nazi era's underground resistance movements, *Die Weisse Rose* (The White Rose), founded by a few students at the University of Munich. Inge Aicher-Scholl lost two of her siblings to summary executions by Nazi authorities. After the war she married the artist Otto "Otl" Aicher, taking a joint surname. They began the Geschwister Scholl Foundation to honor the slain students' memory. That, in turn, led to the idea for a new art school, based partly on the Bauhaus theories, as a site that would serve as an ideological beacon to creative professionals committed to a new, more egalitarian society. This became the Hochschule für Gestaltung Ulm (Ulm School of Design), known by its German language acronym as HfG.

Bill moved to Ulm to serve as the founding rector of the HfG. His direct association with the original Bauhaus

teachers made him one of the top candidates for the post, in addition to the fact that he was not averse to relocating to post-World War II Germany—a place still strewn with piles of rubble from heavily bombed cities, and territory few progressive-minded thinkers wished to make their home after the full crimes of the Nazi era were revealed. From 1951 to 1957, Bill served as HfG rector as well as head of its architecture and industrial design departments.

Bill designed the famous HfG campus, upon which many other university-housing complexes across Germany were later modeled. HfG's series of low-slung modernist cubes hugged a scenic hillside, and their concrete-and-glass square shapes were built to be free of status hierarchies and encourage communication and collaboration. Following the Bauhaus ideal, they were designed to maximize daylight and featured a marked absence of extraneous decorative elements. Despite the good intentions of Bill, the Aichers, and other key figures at HfG, the school administration was wracked by ideological battles and its state funding increasingly imperiled by political interference. Bill resigned in part because of this turmoil, and the Ulm School was eventually shuttered altogether in 1968.

Bill had a multifaceted and prolific career both before and after his HfG tenure. In the 1940s, he found success as an industrial and consumer-product designer, which prompted him to codify and publish his theories about art, architecture, and the decorative arts. One of his most widely read treatises dated back to 1952 and was published in English translation as *Form: A Balance Sheet of Mid-twentieth Century Trends in Design*. His mass-produced consumer goods included a popular kitchen clock made by Junghans Uhren, a venerable German timepiece maker. Another top-selling object from the 1950s was Bill's sturdy Ulmer Hocker, or Ulm Stool, on which he is cited as co-designer with HfG colleagues Hans Gugelot and Paul Hildinger. The Ulm Stool delighted minimalists and design purists with its simplicity: fabricated from just three pieces of wood plus a metal rod, the object can be used as a chair, table, or shelf.

Created Modern Colossi

Bill also won important commissions for public sculptures. Some were variations on a recurring motif, the *Endlose Treppe* (Endless Steps), which paid homage to the spatial phenomenon known as the Möbius strip. "Bill derived his rigorously geometric forms and meticulously planned and fashioned compositions from mathematical systems, formulae and other relationships, while his use of colour is reminiscent of charts illustrating theories of colour and its perception," noted Whitford in the London *Independent*. "The temptation to see something quintessentially Swiss in the smooth precision and clipped economy of Bill's work is irresistible."

Bill's most visible projects were commissioned for public spaces in Switzerland and Germany. One was the *Pavillon-Skulptur*, a series of enormous granite arches erected next to the Zürich train station in the early 1980s. He also created the soaring colorful tower blocks for a Mercedes-Benz museum in Stuttgart, Germany. Another major commission came from Deutsche Bank for its headquarters in Frankfurt am Main, Germany. Called *Kontinuität* (Continuity), the 66-ton sculpted knot of Sardinian rock was unveiled in 1986 and is thought to be the largest granite sculpture erected in Europe since the end of the Roman Empire.

Served in Swiss Parliament

From 1967 to 1974, Bill was a professor at the Institute for Fine Arts in Hamburg in northern Germany, and also served as chair of its Environmental Design faculty. His marriage to Spoerri produced one son, Johann Jakob, but the couple separated in the early 1970s and Bill later remarried an art historian, Angela Thomas. An active participant in Switzerland's political scene as an independent candidate, he served on the municipal council of Zürich in the early 1960s and was elected to a seat in the lower house of the Swiss Federal Assembly, which he held from 1967 to 1971. He built a second home in a suburb of Zürich called Zumikon and gave the Höngg house to his son. Despite the rigorous aesthetics of his art and theories on design, Bill was not immune to the lure of a well-made consumer status object and owned a prized collection of luxury cars, including a Rolls-Royce sedan he drove to Federal Assembly sessions.

Bill kept working well into his eighties. After meetings in Berlin in late 1994 to discuss plans for a new Bauhaus Archive building, he collapsed at Tegel Airport and died of a heart attack en route to a Berlin hospital at age 85 on December 9, 1994, less than two weeks before his 86th birthday. Eight years earlier, a journalist from Britain's *Sunday Times* visited Bill at his home in Zumikon; the photographs that ran with correspondent John McEwen's 1986 article were shot by Lord Snowdon, the ex-husband of Queen Elizabeth II's younger sister Princess Margaret. "Bill's clear and constructive thinking has had a clarifying effect on the thought and practice of the visual arts worldwide" since the 1920s, McEwen asserted. "When we praise some particularly well-designed object by saying, 'It's probably Swiss,' we probably mean, without realizing it, that it bears the influence of Max Bill."

Periodicals

Building Design, June 24, 2011.
Guardian (London, England), December 31, 1994.
Independent (London, England), December 15, 1994.
New York Times, December 14, 1994.
Sunday Times (London, England), December 14, 1986.□

Gilles Binchois

Gilles Binchois (c. 1400–1463), from one of the small noble states in what is now Belgium, was one of the most famous and influential composers of the Renaissance era (c. 1400–1600) in music.

The music of the Renaissance differs from music of our own time in ways that art and literature do not, and it remains known mostly to specialists and to fans who have become acquainted with it. Even among those groups, Binchois has been less frequently performed

World History Archive/Alamy

than that of his Netherlandish contemporary Guillaume Dufay and the English composer John Dunstable. Research has shown, however, that Binchois's music was more widely copied that that of either Dufay or Dunstable—an accurate indicator of popularity in the days before music was reproduced on printing presses. Other indicators, too, show that Binchois was highly esteemed in his own time, and groups specializing in Renaissance music have begun to perform his songs and religious music more frequently.

Used Pen Name

The lives of Renaissance composers were only sparsely documented, and what is definitively known about Binchois fills perhaps a page of text. His real name was apparently Gilles de Bins, and Binchois was a pen name or other appellation that he acquired later; one manuscript calls him Gilles de Bins dit Binchois (Gilles de Bins, known as Binchois). His date of birth is unknown, but based on the dates in the late 1410s when he first begins to show up in court and cathedral payroll records (one of the few reliable ways of determining a composer's activity), he is thought to have been born around 1400 in Mons, in what is now Belgium. His father, Jean de Binche, was a well-off Mons businessman who served as an advisor to the local ruler, Duke Guillaume IV of Hainaut.

Who trained Binchois as a composer is not known, but in musically rich Mons there would have been many possibilities: an Italian traveler remarked on the unusual skill of the singers in the area, and soon wealthy Italian families began to vie with each other to hire the best singers and musicians from the Low Countries. Binchois was probably a choirboy, perhaps at the Hainaut court in Mons, and he also acquired skills as a keyboardist: the first proof of his existence is an account book showing he was paid for organ-playing services at the St. Waudru cathedral in Mons in 1419.

In addition to providing Binchois with a solid musical grounding, Mons was ideally situated to acquaint him with the hottest musical trends of the early 15th century. Dufay, whom Binchois met later and may have known quite early in life, grew up in Cambrai in nearby Burgundy, where a fresh style had been imported from England and dubbed the "contenance Angloise" or English countenance. In addition, English forces were active in northwestern Europe during those years, and the nobles who headed them brought music with them. Binchois is thought to have paid a fee in 1423 allowing him to leave Mons for the city of Lille on what is now the French-Belgian border, and there or in Paris he entered the service of William de la Pole, the Earl of Suffolk.

Became Soldier-Composer

Binchois's duties for the Earl were various. A piece written in his honor after his death refers to him as an honorably chivalrous soldier, but he also apparently had musical duties: a legal deposition mentions that de la Pole commissioned a "Binchoiz" to compose a song called *Ainsi que a la fois m'y souvient* (And at the Same Time Remember Me). Binchois is also thought to have composed his most famous song, *De plus en plus* (More and More), during these years. Unlike most of his composer contemporaries, Binchois never became a priest or obtained a university degree that would have qualified him for higher religious offices. Nevertheless, in the late 1420s he left the Earl's service and joined the musical staff of the Burgundian court chapel in Brussels. He may have been rewarded for supporting the Duke of Burgundy against an English rival in an argument over some French servants.

Binchois's presence in Burgundy is attested by his composition, in 1431, of a motet, *Nove cantum melodie* (New Songs), marking the birth of Prince Anthoine of Burgundy. The text of the motet incorporated the names of the 19 singers who performed it, including Binchois himself. He remained in the court's service for the rest of his life, composing the bulk of his music there and gradually acquiring more influence. In 1437 he was made honorary court secretary, and he also was given prebends or stipends from churches around the Low Countries: in Bruges, Mons, Soignies, and Cassel. He also appears to have had some skills as a doctor or dentist; in 1437 he was paid for a ring that he had given to the Burgundian duchess in hopes of curing her toothache.

The largest group of Binchois's compositions were songs in a form called the rondeau, an intricate poetic structure in which halves of a refrain were interleaved with new verses. The rondeau was common at the time and had been for a century, but Binchois bent it to his own ends. He broke up the poetic structure with unprecedented interludes that seemingly were intended for instrumental performance (on a lute, for example), and he simplified the texture he had inherited, focusing primarily on a melodic top line. To musical listeners today, the texture of a melodic line plus simpler accompaniment seems natural, but it has not always existed in the Western tradition, and Binchois was one of its pioneers.

Wrote Both Secular and Sacred Music

Some of the texts of Binchois's songs were apparently written by the composer himself, others by court poets of the day. For the most part they follow the conventions of so-called courtly love: they are poems in which a knight pines for the love of an unattainable woman and nevertheless declares his undying loyalty to her. An exception is the off-color *Je ne pouroye estre joyeux* (I Cannot Be Joyous). Binchois's duties also involved the composition of sacred choral music. Much of his output in the sacred field is intentionally simple, employing a texture of parallel vocal lines called fauxbourdon. A few works written for ceremonial occasions were more intricate.

Compared with Dufay, who could write both simple, lyrical songs and pieces in the highly intellectual isorhythmic motet form (Binchois wrote only one isorhythmic motet), Binchois may seem a less versatile composer. Yet by the late 15th century his writings were showing up in collections painstakingly copied out by scribes not only in northwestern Europe but in Italy, where the money and the musical cuttting edge were increasingly located. Even as things stand now, Binchois is better represented in manuscripts than Dufay or Dunstable, suggesting that his melodic style was well loved among musicians and their courtly audiences. One of his songs appeared in seven different versions in the Buxheimer Orgelbuch, a collection of organ arrangements of vocal pieces. His songs also provided the basis for several masses by other composers; settings of the mass at the time often made use of secular material. There is evidence that a good deal of his music has been lost, and a sequence of Renaissance theorists beginning with Martin le Franc tended to mention Dufay and Binchois together, in similar terms.

Binchois moved to Soignies in 1453 to take up a position at St. Vincent cathedral that had been associated with his stipend. He continued to draw a pension from the Burgundian court and apparently was a figure of some renown whose presence attracted several younger composers. He died in Soignies on September 20, 1460.

Much of Binchois's music is still the subject of active research, with even its chronology uncertain, and David Fallows wrote in the *New Grove Dictionary of Music and Musicians* that "the time is not yet ripe for a judicious evaluation of Binchois' position in musical history." Yet Binchois' contemporaries had no doubt of his importance. Two of them, Dufay and Johannes Ockeghem, wrote *Déplorations* or laments after his death, an honor reserved for only those Renaissance composers who were most highly regarded in their own time. Ockeghem's *Mort tu as navré de ton dart*, an ingenious weaving of funeral chants with a précis of Binchois's life, is unlike any other work of its time.

Books

Randel, Don Michael, *Harvard Biographical Dictionary of Music,* Harvard, 1996.

Sadie, Stanley, ed., *New Grove Dictionary of Music and Musicians,* 2nd ed., Macmillan, 2001.

Online

"Gilles Binchois," *Allmusic,* http://www.allmusic.com (October 15, 2014).

"Gilles Binchois—A Discography," *Medieval.org,* http://www.medieval.org/emfaq/composers/binchois.html (October 15, 2014).□

FALKENSEINFOTO/Alamy

Jean-Baptiste Biot

The French physicist, mathematician, and science historian Jean-Baptiste Biot (1774–1862) had one of the most wide-ranging scientific minds of the 19th century. He made major advances in the understanding of the polarization of light.

Beyond that, Biot was active in a large variety of disciplines. He made measurements that increased the precision of the metric system, and early in his career he went aloft in the first balloon ever launched for the purpose of scientific investigation. He helped establish the reality of meteorites and did various other kinds of research into astronomy, electricity and magnetism, mathematics, and the properties of crystals, among many other subjects. Biot was inspired as a young man by the giant of early 19th-century French physics, Pierre-Simon Laplace, and at the end of his own life he inspired Louis Pasteur, whose early research on molecular structure grew directly from Biot's work. Biot lived through the a turbulent period in French history, and, in the words of a biography appearing on the *Pasteur Brewing* website, he "was considered to be the last of a heroic age." His variety of interests marked him as a scientist of an older type, but in his thorough, systematic approach to research he was a forerunner of modern science.

Boredom Led Eventful Life

Born in Paris on April 21, 1774, Jean-Baptiste Biot was descended from peasant stock. His father, Joseph Biot, had landed a job at France's national treasure and hoped that Jean-Baptiste would follow in his footsteps. Biot attended a high school with a classical curriculum, the Collè Louis-le-Grand, and did well. At his father's behest he signed up for private math lessons and took a job as an assistant clerk in the city of Le Havre. That job required him to copy numerous letters by hand, a task that bored him to such a degree that he decided to enlist in the French army.

In the wake of the French Revolution, that was a decision with eventful results. He was wounded in the Battle of Hondschoote on what is now the French-Belgian border in 1793, suffered a complicating infection, and decided to leave the army and return home. Walking to Paris, he was given a ride in a carriage by a well-off stranger who also intervened in his favor when he was charged with desertion; he never learned who the stranger was. Recuperating from his injuries, Biot devoted himself to the study of mathematics. In 1794 he was accepted into the School of Bridges and Roads and then moved to the Ecole Polytechnique, the government's new engineering school, the following year.

As a student there, Biot impressed his teacher, Laplace, with proof he presented in a mathematics class. Laplace asked Biot to come to his office, and when Biot showed up, the teacher laid before him the same proof that Biot had just presented—but unfinished, for Laplace had not been able to complete it. After graduating, Biot became a professor of mathematics at a technical school in Beauvais (his quick advancement was due to the need for competent teachers on the part of France's revolutionary governments in the midst of an expansion of the country's educational system). Then, thanks to Laplace (for whose encyclopedia *Celestial Mechanics* he served as proofreader), he obtained a professorship of mathematical physics at the prestigious Collè de France in Paris. In 1803 he became one of the youngest members of the French Academy of Sciences.

During a time before the nature and origin of meteorites was understood, most scientists ascribed reports of rocks falling from the sky to superstition. Biot traveled that year to L'Aigle in the French region of Normandy, following widespread reports of falling rocks. Carefully tallying eyewitness testimony against rocks he found in the area, Biot argued forcefully in favor of an earlier hypothesis that the rocks were of extraterrestrial origin, a conclusion that has been accepted ever since. In 1804 he and Joseph Gay-Lussac undertook the first balloon ride ever made for scientific purposes. The pair traveled to a height of more than 12,000 feet, measuring the oscillations of a magnetized needle as they went, in order to test a hypothesis that the Earth's magnetic field would diminish away from the surface (it did not). Reportedly, Biot was so frightened by the balloon's bumpy descent that he refused to accompany Gay-Lussac on future trips.

Measured Gases in Fish Air Bladders

In 1806, Biot and his sometime friend and rival Francois Arago traveled to Spain's Balearic Islands to carry out precise measurements with a pendulum connected with the length of the meter, which was originally defined as one ten-millionth of the length of a meridian (or longitude line) along a quadrant (i.e. of the distance from the equator to the North Pole). On this trip, he took time out to measure the composition of gases in the air bladders of local fish. When war between Spain and France broke out, the two scientists, fearful of being mistaken for spies, hastened back to France. Biot became a professor of astronomy in the faculty of sciences at the new University of France, established by Napoleon Bonaparte (whom he personally disliked). He remained there for the rest of his career, serving as dean of the faculty from 1840 to 1849.

Biot had a systematic way of approaching the basic properties of materials and physical phenomena. He and Arago tested gases for their light-refracting properties, and in 1820 he and Félix Savart determined through experimentation that a magnetic field generated by running current through a wire varied proportionally in intensity according to how far it was from the wire. This proportional relationship became known as the Biot-Savart law, and it remains a fundamental principle of electromagnetism.

Over much of his career Biot carried out experiments on light. It was in this area that his research was most far-reaching; it is still reflected in such modern devices as liquid crystal displays, polarized sunglasses, and 3D glasses at movie theaters. Ironically, Biot's research rested on a misunderstanding of the nature of light and partly proceeded from an attempt to show the truth of his own position. The theory that light consisted of waves rather than particles dated back to the 1670s, but in Biot's time many scientists still believed that it consisted of particles. Biot shone light through various substances and invented a new device, the polarimeter, that directed polarized light—light in which the waves line up in a single plane rather than propagating randomly—through various substances, especially those with a crystalline structure, to see how it would behave.

Won English Award

He found that the field in which polarized light waves oscillated might be linear, or, when they passed through certain substances, it might rotate, a phenomenon known as rotary polarization. Arago had noticed that this might occur with quartz, but Biot found that the phenomenon could be demonstrated with many substances and solutions, and could be used to measure the concentrations of saccharine solutions, or solutions containing sugar. For his work in this field, Biot was awarded the Rumford Medal of the Royal Society of London in 1840.

As a mainstay of the French academic world, Biot also wrote various textbooks as well as biographies of major scientists and mathematicians, such as Gottfried Leibniz, Isaac Newton (the first one written), and even Benjamin Franklin. In Beauvais in 1797 he married 16-year-old Gabrielle Brisson, who spoke German; he taught her enough mathematics to assist him with the translation of a German physics book in 1806. Biot himself, however, claimed credit for the translation. They had one son, Edouard, born in 1803, who studied Chinese.

The early work of Louis Pasteur, whose accomplishments included the pasteurization of milk and major advances in the production of vaccines, dealt with molecular structure and grew directly out of Biot's work with rotary polarization. Pasteur carried out an experiment that resolved one issue Biot had left unfinished, wrote to Biot (who had no idea who he was), and demonstrated his results under Biot's supervision. The delighted Biot, known to be cantankerous in old age, said (as quoted on the *Pasteur Brewery* site), "My boy, I have loved science so much during my life that this touches my very heart!" Biot died in Paris on February 3, 1862.

Books

Complete Dictionary of Scientific Biography, Scribner's, 2008.
World of Scientific Discovery, Gale, 2006.

Online

"Jean Baptiste Biot," *MacTutor History of Mathematics* (St. Andrews University, Scotland), http://www-history.mcs.st-andrews.ac.uk/Biographies/Biot.html (January 2, 2015).

"Jean-Baptiste Biot," *Molecular Expressions* (Florida State University), http://www.micro.magnet.fsu.edu/optics/timeline/people/biot.html (January 2, 2015).

"Jean Baptiste Biot," *Pasteur Brewing*, http://www.pasteurbrewing.com/colleagues/biographies/jean-baptiste-biot-1774-1862.html (January 2, 2015).□

Chris Blackwell

Chris Blackwell (born 1937) founded Island Records, a major British independent music label which promoted the careers of artists such as U2 and Bob Marley and the Wailers. Also a record producer, Blackwell remained actively involved in Island until 1997. Later in his life and career, Blackwell was involved in other businesses such as hotels and rum.

Allstar Picture Library/Alamy

B orn Christopher Percy Gordon Blackwell on June 22, 1937, in Westminster, England, he was the son of Joseph Blackwell and Blanche Lindo. Raised in Jamaica, his wealthy family was involved in the producing of rum and was one of the oldest families taking part in rum production in Jamaica. They also were involved in the trade of sugar, coconuts, and cattle.

For the first ten years of his life, Blackwell was primarily raised in Jamaica. Through his parents, he was exposed to the high-flying, international jet set lifestyle and met such luminaries as author Noël Coward and actor Errol Flynn. Sent to England to be educated in public schools, he was expelled from Harrow when he was 17 years old.

Returning to Jamaica, Blackwell worked in various jobs in real estate, motor scooter rental, and water skiing. At 19, James Bond author Ian Fleming gained Blackwell a job as a location scout on the set of the film version of *Dr. No.* After *Dr. No* wrapped, Blackwell had a job offer from the film's production team but was already thinking about starting a record company.

Started Own Label

Blackwell had become more and more interested in music after seeing jazz legend Miles Davis play in New York City. When Blackwell returned to Jamaica, he chose the musical style closest to jazz, ska, and founded his own label, Jamaican Island Records, to sell it. The name of the label was derived from a novel by Alec Waugh, *Islands in the Sun.* In 1959, Blackwell released his first record on Jamaican Island Records, *Lance Heywood at the Half Moon.* Blackwell also recorded and marketed local R&B.

Blackwell was not the only music industry type trying to capitalize on Jamaican music. He found competition among such record producers as Leslie Kong and Sir Coxone Dodd, who also were doing well with Jamaican music. But Blackwell found that his records released on the Jamaican Island Records sold better in Britain than Jamaica. Blackwell then decided to move to England.

Established Island Records

In England in 1962, Blackwell founded Island Records. Through this label, Blackwell sold not only his own, but also the records of his rivals in Jamaica, in the United Kingdom. He found a growing audience among the West Indian immigrant population living in England at the time.

Initially, Island was a specialty label because Blackwell noticed that labels that had long-term success tended to be very focused, while those that were popular music-focused did not last as long. He modeled his label on thriving labels like Motown, which centered on a specific R&B sound, and Blue Note, which focused on jazz.

Describing his early success, Blackwell told Chris Dafoe of the *Globe and Mail,* "What I was doing was specialist music. I wasn't trying to get records on the radio. But then it started to spread out; the English people started to get into the black club scene. It was a cutting edge kind of scene; people were scared of these places and those who went down there were hip and brave, and the word get out: 'This music is great.'"

Found Mainstream Success

Island broke into the mainstream primarily because of one Jamaican artist. Singer Millie Small had a very distinctive voice. The record she made for Island, the ska-pop "My Boy Lollipop," became a big hit, the first for the label. Because of its success, Island was able to move from a limited market to a wider audience.

Over the next few decades, Blackwell guided Island through an expansion of sounds and artists, while retaining an underground vibe. Continuing to focus on Jamaican music in the 1960s and the 1970s, Blackwell tried to capitalize on the growing popularity of reggae, first by molding Jimmy Cliff. The artist left Island for EMI before finding major success.

In 1970, Blackwell took a chance on three reggae musicians, Bob Marley, Peter Tosh, and Bunny Livingston. He signed them and gave them $8,000 to make an album. As Bob Marley and the Wailers, they recorded *Catch a Fire,* which became an important, classic reggae record. Before Blackwell, Bob Marley and the Wailers were regarded as a band that could not be signed.

When Blackwell signed Marley and the Wailers, he only asked that they should move away from their pure form of reggae, and add some wider crossover appeal. The band rewarded Blackwell's confidence in them by agreeing to do so, which contributed to the band's success.

Blackwell later added other reggae artists such as Burning Spear and Toots and the Maytals to the Island roster.

Blackwell's handling of Marley and the Wailers also illustrated his emphasis on packaging and telling the story of the artist through visuals. The original *Catch a Fire* album sleeve folded out in the shape of a Zippo lighter. Chris Salewicz, a British rock journalist who wrote a history of Island Records, told Andrew Perry of the *London Daily Telegraph*, "He always said that if a record looked great from the outside, then you knew there must be something good inside as well, so all their sleeves were absolute works of art."

Moved into Rock, Studio Ownership

Also in the 1960s and 1970s, the Blackwell-led Island moved into various types of rock. After the international success of the Beatles in 1963, Blackwell signed his own version of British pop, the Spencer Davis Group and his discovery, the teenaged phenomenon Steve Winwood. Blackwell also signed Winwood's later group, Traffic. By the early 1970s, Blackwell was championing and helping spread progressive rock. He signed Jethro Tull, King Crimson, and Emerson, Lake and Palmer, among others, to Island.

In 1977, Blackwell added to his empire by founding a recording studio called Compass Point. Not merely a place to record an album, Blackwell intended it to be a retreat for all the recording artists signed to Island so they could relax while recording. He hoped they would share ideas with other musicians and perhaps work together as well. Among the projects that came to fruition at Compass Point was the B-52's' classic song "Rock Lobster" which was part of their 1979 debut album, *The B-52's*. Another was "Once in a Lifetime" by the Talking Heads, released in 1980 and included on their album *Remain in Light*.

The studio also helped Blackwell find new acts, including Jethro Tull. Always a music fan, Blackwell told Gordon Masson of *Music Week*, "When you have a studio, which I think any record company of my kind of era would have, you would find new talent in the confines of the studio. Musicians would come down to the playing of somebody's record and you'd get chatting to them and they'd play for you or hand you a tape of some songs they had. Or they'd say about somebody else who was a friend."

Blackwell continued to diversify his signings in the 1980s and 1990s. In 1980, Blackwell added U2 to Island, and helped build the Irish rock band into one of the biggest bands in the world. He also signed such forward-thinking acts as the androgynous Grace Jones, the glam Roxy Music, and the stylish Robert Palmer. Though Blackwell did not sign many punk artists, Island was the home to the revolutionary Slits for a time. Other noteworthy Island artists included PJ Harvey, Tom Waits, and Melissa Etheridge. In the late 1980s, Blackwell again proved ahead of the curve by capitalizing on the burgeoning world music movement. He added such world music artists as King Sunny Ade, Trouble Funk, and Buckwheat Zydeco to the Island family.

Helmed an Artist's Label

Blackwell's company developed a reputation as an artist's label. Though Island could not match what major labels offered to artists, his company flourished as an independent especially because Blackwell was willing to take risks. He consciously made commitments to acts who truly wanted to be musicians and were not just about the lifestyle. In his quest to develop serious artists, he only signed those who had talent and were committed to working hard to achieve success. Blackwell did not have to know or even understand their sound but thought in terms of long-term development and commitment. He also spent much time in the studio, enjoying the process of recording the artists and developing their talent in the studio as well. Blackwell firmly believed in image, style, and marketing. In the 1980s, he accomplished this through the production and use of music videos. The first video played on MTV was an Island act, the Buggles.

Sold Island, Left the Label

In 1989, Blackwell sold most of his interest in Island Records to Polygram for £272 million. At the time of its sale, Island was considered the most important British independent record label. Blackwell remained involved as a non-executive chairman for nearly a decade. He only left in 1997, in the period after Polygram was acquired by Universal in the 1990s. The name of the label remained in existence, however. Island continued to be vital in the early 21st century, signing such artists as Amy Winehouse.

Blackwell took on new projects after leaving Island. In 1998, for example, he was the force behind the launch of Palm Pictures. Though this multimedia venture failed, it proved that he was also ahead of the curve, as he had been with music. Also in 1998, Blackwell was a backer of an internet music service called Sputnik that was intended to offer music videos and sell music online in the United Kingdom and the United States. He also owned a few cinemas in the United Kingdom.

Primarily living in Jamaica after the turn of the 21st century, Blackwell had several business ventures there. In 2009, he focused on developing a Jamaican property called Goldeneye, located in the resort town of Oracabessa. The estate was the place where Fleming penned a number of his James Bond novels. Goldeneye became a boutique hotel/estate that attracted many celebrities.

Blackwell also founded the Island Outpost hotel group. It ran Goldeneye as well as four other Jamaican boutique hotels, the Caves, Jake's, Strawberry Hills, and Geejam. Of his hotel business, Blackwell told Sathnam Sanghera of the London *Times*, "In the record business you find people to work with—engineers, producers, musicians—and you put together the overall picture. In hotels, you work with architects, designers and painters and create an atmosphere in the same way. Also it's a long process of development, as with artists. And for me, hotels are a way of turning people on to Jamaica. That was my motive with Marley, whose work I am probably proudest of in my career, and it continues to be my aim."

Made Rum

Blackwell had other business concerns as well. He operated Royal Hut, an interiors company that was founded by his late second wife, designer Mary Vinson, who died of bone cancer in 2009. Nodding to his family's heritage, he created his own rum, Blackwell Fine Jamaican Rum. Originally only available in Jamaica, Blackwell Fine Jamaican Rum became available in the United States in 2011 and Great Britain in 2012.

Blackwell essentially stayed out of the music industry, though he took on a few projects here and there. In June 2011, he started a new venture with Simon Fuller, another high profile music industry executive. The company, Blackwell Fuller, Inc., was intended to help with artist development through content and audience management. Through an independent partnership arrangement, the company helped acts take control of their careers.

Though Blackwell had limited dealings with the music industry in the 21st century, his importance and influence were not forgotten. He also appreciated the depth of his career. When Blackwell was named the most influential music industry executive between 1959 and 2009 by *Music Week,* he stated, according to Paul Williams of *Music Week,* "I just loved music. I've been incredibly fortunate to be in the right place at the right time."

Periodicals

Associated Press International, September 12, 2003.
Daily Telegraph (London, England), March 12, 2009.
Globe and Mail, January 5, 1998.
Music Week, October 10, 1998; April 18, 2009.
PR Newswire, June 13, 2011; July 19, 2011.
Sunday Telegraph (London, England), May 6, 2012.
Time Out, May 21, 2009.
Times, November 7, 1997.
Times (London), February 26, 2011. □

Johann Friedrich Blumenbach

The German anthropologist and physician Johann Friedrich Blumenbach (1752–1840) was the creator of the scientific study of race, and one of the founders of physical anthropology.

Blumenbach was a widely respected scientist and one of the most original thinkers of his day. He had a distinguished career that included a stint as court physician to England's king, and his ideas about natural history looked far into the future. Yet he is most often remembered, and often favorably, for his work on the concept of race. He subdivided humans into five varieties, which he designated Caucasians, Mongolians (Central Asians), Ethiopians (African peoples), Americans (Native Americans), and Malays (southeast Asians and Pacific islanders). At a time when it was not even generally

FALKENSTEINFOTO/Alamy

recognized that humans were a single species, Blumenbach's ideas were progressive, and he was a staunch opponent of slavery and racism. Yet his methods laid the groundwork for the use of science to support ideas of European racial superiority. As the idea of race itself has been thrown into question, Blumenbach's position in history has become ambivalent.

Inspired by Lectures on Fossils

Johann Friedrich Blumenbach was born on May 11, 1752, in Gotha in the Thuringia region of central Germany. His father was a teacher and assistant headmaster at a *Gymnasium* (a college preparatory high school with a strong classical and scientific curriculum) located in Gotha. His mother, Charlotte, was the daughter of a town official and the granddaughter of a prominent theological scholar. Blumenbach grew up with a strong scientific and literary education as a primary goal. After graduating from high school in 1769 he enrolled at the University of Jena, planning to major in medicine. A series of lectures by the mineralogist Johann Ernst Immanuel Walch touched on the topic of fossils, which fascinated Blumenbach. He moved to the University of Göttingen early in his university career and changed his major to natural history, finding another inspiring teacher in the globe-trotting linguist Christian W. Büttner.

Blumenbach graduated in 1775 after writing a thesis titled *De generis human varietate nativa* (On the Natural

Varieties of Mankind). It was an initial attempt to formulate an opinion on the question of multiple human races, the issue to which he would devote much of his academic career, and for a 23-year-old it was a remarkable achievement. Blumenbach was appointed extraordinary (or adjunct) professor of medicine at Göttingen in 1776 and was given a full professorship of natural history there several years later. He continued to teach classes in mineralogy, botany, and zoology until his death, and among his students were several of 19th-century Germany's greatest scientists. He wrote books on several subjects, including a physiology textbook that remained in use for nearly 40 years and was translated into several foreign languages. He was also a practicing physician who suggested some advancements in treatment. He posited the idea of a *Bildungstrieb* or developmental drive, and noted that it favored Aristotle's idea of epigenesis, or the development of organisms through cell differentiation, rather than the concept of preformation that was dominant at the time.

It was his work on the subject of race, however, that was most far-reaching, and it was recognized in his own time that his ideas were extremely innovative. They rested in general on a conception of natural history that was modern for its time. Blumenbach's work took place many decades before the appearance of the theory of evolution, but he recognized that plants and animals appeared in historical time (as opposed to having been part of the creation of the world), developed, and became extinct. He gave specific examples; one pig parasite, he noticed, was present only in domestic pigs and thus could not have existed when pigs were exclusively wild. Many of his ideas were summarized in the textbook *Handbuch der Naturgeschichte* (Handbook of Natural History), published in 1830.

Followed Writings of Linnaeus

When it came to human beings, Blumenbach tried to take the same long view and examine the development of human beings as part of natural history. In the late 18th century, many scientists and ordinary well-educated individuals believed that the variety of humans found around the world included more than one species. Among those who accepted the idea that all humans were part of the same species was the Swedish zoologist Carl Linnaeus, who formulated a crude system of racial classification that broke the single human race into subdivisions: white Europeans, dark Asians, red Americans, and black Africans. To each of these Linnaeus assigned basic characteristics; Europeans, he believed, were hopeful, while Africans were naturally calm and lazy.

For Blumenbach, the writings of Linnaeus would have been the most important in the field, and his 1775 dissertation was an attempt to expand upon Linnaeus's ideas. He laid out the arguments for the unity of the human species, pointing out that all humans share a large brain, the power of speech, two free hands, bare skin, upright posture, and, in women, a hymen. He then suggested that the larger human race comprised four races, defined primarily by geographical regions: Europeans Asians, Africans, and Native North Americans. In the second edition of his thesis, which appeared in 1781, he expanded his classification to

five groups, and in the third edition (1795) he arrived at his final scheme, consisting of Caucasians, Mongolians, Ethiopians, (Native) Americans, and Malays.

The common use of the term "Caucasian" to describe white people comes ultimately from Blumenbach, who believed that people from southwestern Asia, in what is now Georgia, were a kind of ideal human type, and that Europeans were descended from them (a conclusion that fit with the conclusions linguists were then drawing about the relationships among European, southwest Asian, and north Indian languages). "I have taken the name of this variety from Mount Caucasus, both because its neighborhood, and especially its southern slope, produces the most beautiful race of men, I mean the Georgian; and because . . . in that region, if anywhere, it seems we ought with the greatest probability to place the autochthones [original forms] of mankind," he wrote, as translated by Stephen Jay Gould in *Discover* magazine.

Collected Skulls

The biggest difference between Blumenbach and his predecessors, and the one that was most important for the future, was that he applied the techniques of anatomical study to racial classification and did much to create the modern science of physical anthropology. The scientists who had taken up the question of race before him had relied heavily on impressions, stereotypes, and simple observations, but Blumenbach brought a wealth of physical data to bear in his arguments. Many of his measurements concerned skulls, of which, beginning during a stint as curator of the University of Göttingen's natural history museum, he acquired a large collection.

Blumenbach himself was remarkably progressive on racial questions for a man of his time. He affirmed not only the essential physical but also the moral similarity of all humans, favored the abolition of slavery, and even argued that slaves were morally superior to those who enslaved them. At his home he collected a library of books by black authors that included the works of the African-American slave Phillis Wheatley, contending that works of writers of African descent exceeded those of many European nations in quality despite the difficult conditions under which black authors worked.

Nevertheless, Blumenbach's work contained the seeds of its own later misuse. As Gould put it, "When Blumenbach presented his mental picture of human diversity in his fateful shift away from Linnaean geography, he singled out a particular group as closest to the created ideal and then characterized all other groups by relative degrees of departure from this archetypal standard. He ended up with a system that placed a single race at the pinnacle, and then envisioned two symmetrical lines of departure away from this ideal toward greater and greater degeneration." From there it was easy for believers in eugenics (the idea of improving the human race through selective breeding) and later Nazi propagandists to suggest the ideal of a master race.

A widely recognized scientist in his time, Blumenbach was a member of 78 different academic and learned societies in various countries, including the prestigious Royal Academy of Paris, to which he was elected in 1831. He died in Göttingen on January 22, 1840. His skull collection remains in the possession of the University of Göttingen, and although his ideas have been largely discredited, many of the questions he asked, such as those pertaining to the migrations of early humans, remain live ones.

Books

Osborne, Richard, *The Biological and Social Meaning of Race*, Freeman, 1971.
Science and Its Times, Gale, 2001.

Periodicals

British Medical Journal, December 22, 2007.
Discover, November 1994.

Online

"Johann Friedrich Blumenbach," *The Embryo Project Encyclopedia* (Arizona State University), http://www.embryo.asu.edu/pages/johann-friedrich-blumenbach-1752-1840 (January 5, 2015).
"Johann Friedrich Blumenbach," *Who Named It?*, http://www.whonamedit.com/doctor.cfm/1247.html (January 5, 2015). □

Mohammed Boudiaf

ABDELHAK SENNA/AFP/Getty Images

A hero of the Algerian war of independence before spending nearly three decades in exile, Algerian political leader Mohammed Boudiaf (1919–1992) served as president of Algeria for six months. Assassinated at an appearance in 1992, Boudiaf was a popular, respected political figure whose death remains a national tragedy in his country.

Mohammed Boudiaf was born June 23, 1919, in M'sila, Algeria. M'sila was a rural region located about 180 miles southeast of Algiers. He received his education in the area.

Joined French Colonial Army

In 1943, Boudiaf was drafted into the French colonial army as an adjunct. He soon became active in Algerian liberation activities. Within the army, he made attempts to form Algerian nationalist cells. A supporter of Algerian nationalism, he backed Messali Hadj and his nationalist ideas. In this period, Boudiaf also joined the Organisation Spéciale, a paramilitary group.

Later in the decade, when Boudiaf was in France—and evading French authorities—he was involved with the Mouvement pour le Triomphe des Libertés Démocratiques as a party organizer. In Algeria, Boudiaf actively supported the launch of the Comité Révolutionnaire d'Unité e d'Action. Through this group, the National Liberation Front (Front de Libération Nationale, or FLN) was formed to seek Algeria's freedom from France.

Boudiaf was involved with the FLN, whose number included urban guerillas from the late 1940s. Impressed by their cause, Boudiaf deserted the French army in 1950 and joined the FLN. He soon rose to a leadership role in the FLN as Algeria began seeking its independence. By 1954, Boudiaf was one of 22 members of the leadership council of FLN, though aligned with an external faction.

Became Leader During War

Also in 1954, Algeria began fighting its war of independence against France. Boudiaf was a hero in the war in which he fought against the French as a member of the FLN. He was considered one of the top five leaders of the FLN in this period, and one of the nine so-called historic chiefs of the war of independence. He is given credit for developing the revolution's ideological theory.

In 1956, Boudiaf nearly lost his life in an incident related to the conflict. He was flying from Morocco to Tunis with the FLN leader, Ahmed Ben Bella, and two other senior members of the FLN, Hocine Ait Ahmed and Mohamed Khider. Their plane was skyjacked by French fighter planes in Algiers. Boudiaf was imprisoned for six years in Paris.

In 1962, when French president Charles de Gaulle announced a cease fire, an end to the conflict, and Algerian independence, Boudiaf and other FLN leaders held by France were freed from captivity. They were flown to Geneva from Paris in a plane provided by the French government.

Named to Provisional Government

Before the end to fighting was declared, Boudiaf was selected to serve as the deputy premier in the proposed provisional government of free Algeria, the Gouvernement Provisoire de le République Algérienne. After the provisional government arrived in Algeria, however, there was an ideological split that led to a power struggle. Boudiaf and Ben Bella, who was to be vice president, became bitter opponents. Ben Bella made an attempt to depose the provisional premier, Benyoucef Ben Khedda.

By July 1962, this struggle led to Boudiaf being kidnapped by Ben Bella's loyal troops. Boudiaf was only held for 24 hours. Ben Bella then took power and put Boudiaf back in place as deputy premier. Boudiaf was also given power over free Algeria's foreign affairs in the politburo.

Only a short time later, the increasingly controversial Ben Bella decided to postpone Algeria's general elections one week before they were to occur. The move was startling and unanticipated by others in the government. When Ben Bella made the announcement, Boudiaf resigned in protest because he believed that Ben Bella's interim, unelected government intended to stay in power indefinitely.

Arrested by Ben Bella

By 1963, Boudiaf was involved with the Socialist Revolutionary Party (Parti de la Révolution Socialiste), a dissident group, in a leadership role. Because of his association, Ben Bella had Boudiaf arrested for contributing to a plot against the Algerian government. Boudiaf was sentenced to death and held at an oasis in the Saharan desert. There, he staged a hunger strike and lost 40 pounds. After five months, Boudiaf was taken to a hospital and released with the understanding that he accept exile.

After going into exile in 1964, Boudiaf remained interested in Algerian politics. He backed a coalition of opposition groups, founded that same year. This group was called the Comité National de Défense de la Révolution.

In 1965, Ben Bella was disposed in a military coup by a military officer, Colonel Houari Boumedienne. The FLN's one-party regime remained intact, however. Boudiaf opposed and criticized this new government as much as Ben Bella's because he believed in democracy with multiple political parties for Algeria. Boudiaf also deemed the FLN corrupt and authoritarian. Because of his stances, Boudiaf was regarded as a politician with integrity who was in touch with the Algerian people. Boudiaf would remain in exile until the early 1990s. He primarily lived in Morocco in relative obscurity. There, he owned a brick factory. Some former FLN officials, including Ben Bella and Ait Ahmed, returned to Algeria after the October 1988 riots forced political liberalization.

Turmoil in Algeria

Events in the early 1990s changed Boudiaf's perspective. The FLN was still ruling Algeria, as it had since the early 1960s, but the years of corruption, authoritarianism, and mismanagement had taken a toll on its leadership. Elections were scheduled for early 1992, and it seemed a Muslim fundamentalist group, the Islamic Salvation Front (Front Islamique du Salut, or FIS), would gain power. The first round of parliamentary elections were held in December 1991, and the FIS posted a decisive victory over the FLN.

To prevent the FIS from actually gaining power, the Algerian government and military took action. The president, Chadli Bendjedid, resigned. After his resignation, the military and political leadership of Algeria canceled elections to ensure the Muslim fundamentalists would not take office. They also asked Boudiaf to return as president.

Returned from Exile

In January 1992, Boudiaf came back to Algeria after 27 years in exile. Upon his return, the London *Times* reported that he said "I felt I could bring something to this country, so I decided to return." Boudiaf was appointed as the head of a five-member high state council, the Haut Comité d'Etat (HCE), a collective executive body. Drawing on his unmarred reputation, he was brought back to the country to become president of the high state council to ensure Muslim fundamentalists would not gain power and to put a positive face on the government. At the same time, Boudiaf was to serve as a respected civilian face on what was essentially a military-controlled government.

When Boudiaf came to Algeria, he publicly stated he had no political affiliation but serving Algeria. However, he agreed to keep the present government organization in place and work with prime minister's Sid Ahmed Ghozali technocratic administration. He also allowed the army to continue to detain thousands of those sympathetic to the Islamic regime in detention camps in the southern Sahara, though he did campaign for the release of hundreds of that number. The FIS party was outlawed, and its leaders were being tried.

Became Increasingly Popular President

As president, Boudiaf wanted to make changes, but not quick or radical ones in the short term. While Boudiaf retained his reputation for pursuing purity in government, he also gave no indication that he would make accommodations for the revival of the Islamic Front. He attempted to talk directly with the public. By April 1992, Boudiaf had also formed the first Conseil Consultatif National (CCN), which was an advisory group.

Putting into practice a suggestion made by those who had brought Boudiaf to Algeria, he launched a non-party gathering, the National Patriotic Assembly (Rassemblement Patriotique National, or RPN), as an alternative to the disgraced FLN and the outlawed FIS. Formed in May 1992, the assembly excluded fundamentalists and old-style politicians, but tried to attract those who did not vote in the general election by offering a viable alternative to the FIS. Some Algerians questioned the attempt to build and capitalize on Algerian patriotism and modernism, but respected that Boudiaf had broken ties with the FLN and wanted to hold elections by 1994.

Though Boudiaf accomplished little in his first few months in office and the government was essentially ineffective, he was respected and popular among most Algerians for his energy and attempts to engage the public. His promise to support all investigations into charges that senior officials—some still with political power—embezzled a total of $30 billion over the previous three decades, brought him wider respect. But his anti-Islamic stance was not particularly popular in certain circles, and he also made enemies with his focus on rooting out official corruption. Overall, Boudiaf was emerging as a national hero, but his time in office was short-lived.

Assassinated in Annaba

Boudiaf was assassinated while making an appearance in Annaba, Algeria, on June 29, 1992, as part of a greater effort to garner support for the council which he helmed. He was 73 years old at the time of his death. One of his own bodyguards killed Boudiaf while he was leading a ceremonial opening of a cultural center hall. Boudiaf was shot in the back and the head, and others standing near him were sprayed with bullets. During the same event, a bomb went off in front of his podium and a grenade was tossed under the president's chair. Forty-one people were injured in the incident.

Moments before his assassination, Boudiaf had spoken these predictive words. According to the London *Times,* he remarked "We must know that the life of a human being is very short. We are all going to die. Why should (the authorities) cling so much to power? Other peoples have overtaken us by technology and science. Islam..." Then gunfire interrupted his speech.

Upon Boudiaf's death, *The Economist* lamented, "He was an honourable man but his job was too ambiguous to count for much. His savage death is expected to do little more than tighten the defensive rule to which he gave his blessing." According to Youssef M. Ibrahim of the *New York Times,* an editorial published in Algeria's largest independent daily, *Al Watan* attributed Boudiaf's death to wider issues in Algeria. The editorial read, "Boudiaf has been a victim of the system. The death of Boudiaf, who fought a solitary battle for a total break with the rotted system that has governed Algeria, has demonstrated that the 'conspiracies of the shadows' remain, unfortunately, very influential and very powerful."

When Boudiaf's assassination occurred, hundreds of policemen and soldiers in Algeria had been killed in similar fashion by those sympathetic to or former members of the Islamic Salvation Front. While authorities originally believed that Boudiaf was killed by someone linked to the FIS, the true reasons why his bodyguard shot him are unknown. The assassin was sympathetic to Islam, but there were also forces within the power establishment who were threatened by Boudiaf. His death deeply impacted Algeria, and the national incident continues to be commemorated annually in the early twenty-first century.

Books

Encyclopedia of the Modern Middle East and North Africa, Vol. 1, 2nd ed., Macmillan Reference USA, 2004.

Periodicals

The Economist, July 4, 1992.
New York Times, July 5, 1992.
The Times (London, England), June 30, 1992.□

Georges Boulanger

The French general and politician Georges Boulanger (1837–1891) became the leader of a popular movement, known as *Boulangisme,* which threatened to destabilize the French political system when it reached its height in 1889.

Boulanger and Boulangisme have been the focus of debate among historians. Boulanger's cult hero status, his reliance on nationalist appeals, and his sloganeering rhetoric have marked him for some as a forerunner of European fascism. Yet much of Boulanger's political support came from working class circles, and his political origins mixed elements from the left and right. French leaders who backed Boulanger and his movement spanned the political spectrum; some were motivated by opportunism in the face of a mass movement that exploded with startling speed, and then, after Boulanger left France, collapsed equally quickly. Boulanger began his rise to power with measures that endeared him to ordinary members of the French military. He was a complex figure who, at the critical moment, seems to have failed in his aims for reasons that were more personal than political, and he was not always comfortable with the movement to which he had given birth.

Named for George Washington

Georges Ernest Jean-Marie Boulanger was born on April 29, 1837, in Rennes, in the French region of Brittany. His father was a lawyer, and his mother a British woman who admired George Washington and gave her son the name Georges in his honor (he usually used Ernest as an adult). Boulanger was sent to English schools for a time; he was unhappy there but gained a knowledge of English that would later serve him well. When he was 17 he entered an officer training program of the French St. Cyr military academy in Brittany.

After graduating two years later, Boulanger began his military career in France's campaign to occupy what became its colony of Algeria. From the start he was a favorite of the men he commanded, at this point as a second lieutenant. In 1859 France joined the Kingdom of Sardinia in its war against the Habsburg Empire of Austria. He was wounded three times during the war, once very seriously, and he was visited in the hospital by the French

World History Archive/Alamy

empress Eugénie and was inducted into the French Legion of Honor. In the 1860s he fought in the French campaign to occupy and colonize Cochinchina, now the southern part of Vietnam.

For several years Boulanger led a quieter life; he was promoted to captain and served as a military instructor at St. Cyr. With the outbreak of of the Franco-Prussian War in 1870, the officer corps was mobilized, and Boulanger participated in the defense of Paris against the Prussians. He was wounded once again as the Prussians laid siege to the city. When the left-wing Paris Commune government was established in the war's wake, Boulanger was one of the officers who planned its overthrow. But when the Commune was violently suppressed by the French army at the end of May of 1871, resulting in the deaths of thousands of its supporters, Boulanger was recuperating and took no direct part in the fighting. He seems to have held no strong political convictions at this time beyond a dislike both for the left and for the forces that plotted to restore the French monarchy.

Visited United States

In the 1870s and early 1880s Boulanger rose through the ranks of the French military, becoming a colonel in 1874, brigadier-general in 1880, and Director of Infantry at the French war ministry in 1882. The previous year, he had a taste of celebrity when the French government sent him to the United States for the centenary of the British surrender

at Yorktown during the Revolutionary War; with his knowledge of English, sharp red uniform, and reputedly dashing figure, he was greeted by admiring crowds. He gained a modest reputation as a military reformer and minister of war in 1886; his sponsor was the future Prime Minister Georges Clemenceau, who had been his high school classmate but would soon resist his growing influence.

As war minister, Boulanger was a hit among the troops. He replaced the traditional straw mattresses with spring beds, allowed soldiers to keep or grow beards, and founded a massive parade, the Bastille Day review, that served as a platform for his own growing ambitions. At the inaugural review on Bastille Day (July 14), 1886, he was more warmly applauded than president Jules Grévy. In late 1886 and early 1887, Boulanger took a hard line against Germany in several controversies, championing the cause of a French spy, Guillaume Schnaebelé, who had been arrested along the disputed-French-German border. He began to emerge as a folk hero among rural French families who had never accepted the loss of the Alsace and Lorraine regions to Germany in the Franco-Prussian War, and many French homes featured a chromolithograph of Boulanger on the living room wall.

Uncomfortable with his growing popularity, the French government removed Boulanger from his post as war minister and placed him in command of a regiment in Clermont Ferrand in central France, more than 250 miles from Paris. When he was preparing to board the train to take up his new post, demonstrators angry about his perceived demotion surrounded the train and tried to block it. Boulanger was pleased with the show of support, but backed down when, according to historian Elizabeth Wormeley (writing in *France in the Nineteenth Century*), a friend warned him that "these twenty thousand friends will make you forty thousand enemies."

Met with Napoleon Descendant

Once out of office, however, Boulanger set about gathering support. Conservative figures coalesced around him, and nationalist feeling directed at Germany became ever stronger. Monarchist groups, previously opposed by Boulanger, began to move in his direction after he met with Jérôme Napoléon Bonaparte, an American citizen and nephew of French national hero Napoléon Bonaparte, in Switzerland. The government, alarmed by the fact that Boulanger–without declaring himself a candidate–had received about 100,000 votes in a regional election thanks to the efforts of conservative propagandists, removed him from the army altogether and began to maneuver against him.

Nothing the government did seemed to discourage his growing ranks of admirers, even though the slogans of Boulanger's supporters ("Boulanger is work!" "Boulanger is honesty!") were simplistic even by the standards of 19th-century electoral politics. Boulangist publications sprang up, and songs were written in his support. Many ordinary French voters saw Boulanger as the savior of a country paralyzed by squabbling factions in the national legislature, and as a genuine military hero and a get-things-done administrator untouched by political feuding.

In 1888 Boulanger and a wave of his supporters were elected to France's Chamber of Deputies, and although the Boulangistes remained in the minority, he was probably the most popular political figure in France at the time. Supporters urged him to run for the French presidency, and Boulanger took another step toward the corridors of power in January of 1889 when he ran for a Chamber of Deputies seat from a district in Paris, winning handily with a majority of working class support.

At Boulanger's victory rally at the Café Durand, a boisterous crowd demanded that Boulanger seize power by force. He hesitated, however, partly because he was consumed by an extramarital affair with the likewise married Marguerite Bonnemains. That gave the government time to launch a counterattack, detaining some of his supporters for violating conspiracy laws and threatening to arrest Boulanger himself. In April of 1889, Boulanger fled with Bonnemains to Belgium, and then to the island of Jersey. The movement that bore Boulanger's name quickly withered without his presence, and Boulangists were badly defeated in elections later in 1889. Bonnemains suffered from tuberculosis, and the pair returned to Brussels, Belgium, to try a purported cure that had been developed there. Bonnemains died in Boulanger's arms in July of 1891, and on September 30 of that year he went to Bonnemains's grave, shot himself in the head, and was buried with her.

Books

Irvine, William D., *The Boulanger Affair Reconsidered: Royalism, Boulangism, and the Origins of the Radical Right in France,* Oxford, 1989.

Latimer, Elizabeth Wormeley, *France in the Nineteenth Century,* McClurg, 1905.

Seager, Frederic, *The Boulanger Affair: Political Crossroads of France, 1886–1889),* Cornell, 1969.

Online

"General Boulanger and the Boulangist Movement," *Marxist Internet Archive,* https://www.marxists.org/history/france/boulanger/biography.htm (December 14, 2014).

"Georges Boulanger: The Third Republic's Spy Master?" *Proceedings of the Western Society for French History,* Volume 39, http://www.hdl.handle.net/2027/spo. 0642292.0039.018 (December 14, 2014). □

Matthew Boulton

The British industrialist Matthew Boulton (1728–1809) was among the most important figures in the manufacturing world in the late 18th century. His Soho Manufactory in its time was the world's most famous factory, attracting international tourism.

Boulton's main accomplishments were threefold. According to on the UK Assay Office website, he built the Soho Manufactory into what pottery maker Josiah Wedgwood called "the Most compleat Manufacturer in Metals in England, using modern production

World History Archive/Alamy

methods to bring together a complex of industrial functions under one large factory roof. As partner of the Scottish steam engine designer James Watt, he marketed Watt's substantial improvements in steam engine design to their first major customers, mine owners, and he suggested to Watt the marketability of the rotary-motion steam engine that, when used in textile mills, kicked the Industrial Revolution in Britain into high gear. Finally, he revolutionized the production of coinage in Britain and around the world, essentially creating coins in the form in which they exist today, and in the process devising an early version of the modern production line. Boulton's innovations fed into one another, together showing that Bolton possessed one of the keenest business minds in British history.

Inherited Wife's Fortune

A native and lifelong resident of Birmingham, Matthew Boulton was born on September 14, 1728. His father made small silver objects known at the time as toys—not children's toys, but buckles, buttons, snuff boxes, toothpick cases, graters, and the like. Boulton received only a basic education and then joined the family firm, becoming a full partner at age 21. In 1749 he married Mary Robinson, an heiress. The couple had three children, all of whom died in childhood, and Mary herself died in 1759, leaving her fortune to Boulton. He plowed the money into business enterprises, remarking to a friend, as quoted in a *Spartacus Educational* biography, that he "had had the option of living the life of a gentleman but chose, rather, to become an industrialist.''

Boulton's father died in 1759 as well, leaving Boulton in full control of his silvermaking business. Boulton's first move was to acquire a plot of land outside of Birmingham and begin to construct the Soho Manufactory. Uniting the talents of a variety of workmen in a single large factory, Boulton was able to achieve economies of scale, and the factory's output grew rapidly. It produced jewelry, plates and other tableware, coated ware known as ormolu, medals, and many other decorative objects that found a worldwide market. In turn, the factory proved so popular among visitors that Boulton provided a tea house on the grounds so that tourists would have no need to leave the area to find food.

Boulton was far from a robber baron or heartless industrial overlord. He refused to hire children to work at Soho, and he was one of the first to introduce a workmen's compensation scheme; workers made small contributions to a fund that paid most of the salaries of workers who were injured or ill. Soho was kept clean and well-ventilated, and young apprentices who showed artistic talent were given art lessons and encouraged to attend plays, concerts, and art exhibitions in Birmingham, all of which Boulton supported generously. Although his factory prospered, thanks to Boulton's flair for ingenious workplace design, Boulton was not particularly motivated by wealth; Watt said, according to the *Birmingham Jewellry Quarter* website, that ''the love of fame has been to him a greater stimulus than the love of gain.''

Co-Founded Scientific Society

Although he had limited education, Boulton was, like his personal friend Benjamin Franklin, self-taught and interested in a wide variety of topics, from astronomy and chemistry to music and landscape gardening. In 1766 he co-founded the Lunar Society, a group of enthusiastic scientific amateurs who met each month on the night of the full moon to exchange ideas and sometimes to conduct experiments. Another member was Erasmus Darwin, grandfather of evolutionary biologist Charles Darwin; the elder Darwin was an anti-slavery activist, and Boulton came to adopt that position as well.

After marrying Ann Robinson, Mary's younger sister, in 1760, Boulton started a family (he had a daughter, Anne, and a son, Matthew) and continued to expand the Soho factory, which acquired King George III as a customer in the late 1760s. Between 1773 and 1775 he took his already substantial empire to the next level: he acquired an interest in the new steam engine design patented by James Watt, and in 1775 he invited Watt to become a partner in the Soho operation. In the words of the *Birmingham Jewellry Quarter* website, ''They complemented one another perfectly, the ingenious and inventive Scotsman, and the ambitious, indomitable Brummie [a Brummie is a resident of Birmingham] who, with the skilled and talented team of craftsmen he had gathered around him, never let a practical difficulty defeat him.''

Boulton had realized that Watt's engine had applications in many industrial operations, including his own.

Watt's patent was about to expire, but Boulton numbered lobbying skills among his many talents, and he prevailed upon the British Parliament to extend it until the end of the 18th century. Boulton has historically been thought of as the marketer and Watt as the inventor, but Boulton also had a hand in the installation and operation of the steam engines. The pair's biggest customers were coal mines, which used the engines for the laborious task of pumping water out of the ground. By 1800 Boulton & Watt had sold about 450 steam engines.

Established Mint

In the late 1780s, Boulton had another idea for the use of the steam engine: he planned and executed a complete overhaul of British coinage, and in so doing, according to Richard G. Doty quoted on the Soho Mint website, he ''created the coin as we now know it.'' Coins prior to Boulton's Soho Mint, established in 1789, were irregular and, as a result, easily counterfeited. Boulton was granted a patent for a steam-powered coining press in 1790, and the device, regulated by stringent quality control from Boulton's workers, could quickly produce thousands of standardized coins with grooved or lettered edges, thereby frustrating the ''shavers'' who until then had been able to mill down coins and melt their precious metals for resale. Between 1797 and 1799 alone, the mint is estimated to have produced 45 million coins. Beginning in 1799 the Royal Mint itself was outfitted with Boulton & Watt steam engines.

Just as the Soho Manufactory had, the Soho Mint attracted international attention. In 1800, Catherine the Great of Russia commissioned Boulton to set up a new Russian Mint in the imperial capital of St. Petersburg, and Boulton responded with a streamlined sequence of machinery in which strips of metal were fed into one end of a production line, and finished coins appeared at the other. This is thought to be the first example of the production line, which eventually became a standard way of organizing work in factories of all kinds.

Living in his own Soho House, which he remodeled in the 1790s and which today is open to the public, Boulton became a well-known figure in later life. In the mid-1790s he served as the High Sheriff of Staffordshire. Boulton and Watt opened a new Soho Foundry in 1796 to manufacture steam engines themselves; up to that point they had mostly subcontracted the manufacture of parts, and installed the machines on site according to the needs of clients. In 1800 Boulton and Watt turned their steam engine business over to their sons.

Boulton had numerous smaller accomplishments, including the establishment of an assay (metals evaluation) office in Birmingham. An enthusiastic musical amateur and admirer of the earlier eras of British music (something that was unusual at the time), he promoted early music festivals in Birmingham, with the proceeds going to support the city's General Hospital, which he himself had helped develop. Boulton remained active after retirement, helping to establish the Birmingham Theatre in 1807, at the age of 79. He died at Soho House on August 17, 1809.

Books

Clay, Richard, *Matthew Boulton and the Art of Making Money*, Brewin, 2009.

Mason, Shena, ed., *Matthew Boulton: Selling What All the World Desires*, Yale, 2009.

Tann, Jennifer, and Anthony Burton, *Matthew Boulton: Industry's Great Innovator*, History Press, 2013.

Uglow, Jenny, *The Lunar Men: Five Friends Whose Curiosity Changed the World*, Faber & Faber, 2002.

Online

"Matthew Boulton," *Grace's Guide: British Industrial History*, http://www.gracesguide.co.uk/Matthew_Boulton (December 4, 2014).

"Matthew Boulton," Robinson Library (Birmingham), http://www.robinsonlibrary.com/technology/mechanical/biography/boulton.htm (December 4, 2014).

"Matthew Boulton," *Spartacus Educational*, http://www.spartacus-educational.com/SCboulton.htm (December 4, 2014).

"Matthew Boulton—Biography," The Assay Office, http://www.theassayoffice.co.uk/matthew_boulton_biog.html (December 4, 2014.

"Matthew Boulton Biography," *How Things Are Made*, http://www.madehow.com/inventorbios/48/Matthew-Boulton.html (December 4, 2014).

"Matthew Boulton the Man," *Soho Mint*, http://sohomint.info (December 4, 2014).

"More About Matthew Boulton," *Birmingham Jewellry Quarter*, http://www.jquarter.org.uk/webdisk/moremboulton.htm (December 4, 2014).☐

Ulf Andersen/Getty Images

Pierre Bourdieu

The French sociologist Pierre Bourdieu (1930–2002) was among the most widely read French thinkers of the late 20th century. His book *Distinction: A Social Critique of the Judgment of Taste* (1984), a study of how culture reinforces existing social structures, was a standard text in cultural studies programs even in the English-speaking world.

Bourdieu shaped the theoretical language of social criticism, introducing such influential concepts as habitus, symbolic violence, and symbolic capital. Yet in later life he seemed to reject the status of an intellectual separated from public life, adopting a more direct and committed approach to social change. In France, where philosophers writing about broad themes have always commanded large audiences, he was almost a celebrity, but he vigorously resisted the role of television talking head, and from himself and his students he demanded academic rigor and clarity of thought. Of the great public intellectuals modern France has produced, Bourdieu was perhaps the one most concerned with culture in the forms in which it is most broadly consumed and produced.

Excelled on Rugby Pitch

Pierre Bourdieu was born on August 1, 1930, in the small village of Denguin, in southwestern France. His father was a mailman, and his strongly rural family spoke not French at home but the regional language Gascon. Ironically for someone who would later argue that the place of humans in society is often fixed by culture, Bourdieu began to advance through the hierarchy of French education by dint of intelligence and hard work alone. An enthusiastic rugby player, he excelled academically at the top high school in the city of Pau in the Pyrenees mountain region, and then won admission to a top Paris high school, the Lycée Louis-le-Grand. There he earned a place at the Ecole Normale Supérieure, a Parisian university famous for producing some of France's top intellectual stars. Bourdieu majored in philosophy, studying with the French Marxist Louis Althusser.

Although he graduated at the top of his class in 1954, Bourdieu, with his modest background, felt out of place among his fast-talking prep school classmates. After he passed his *Agrégation* (a civil service education exam), he took a job as a high school philosophy teacher. But then he decided to challenge himself by working abroad in one of the most difficult possible places: Algeria, a French colony whose inhabitants were in open revolt against French. Working as a lecturer at the University of Algeria in 1959 and 1960, Bourdieu studied the region's traditional cultures and published his first book, translated in 1962 as *The Algerians*.

Like other young French intellectuals, Bourdieu was pushed to the left politically by France's brutal tactics in its ultimately unsuccessful war to maintain control over its colony. Returning to France, Bourdieu embarked on a seemingly tranquil academic life. He married Marie-Claire Brisard in 1962, and the couple had three children. Through the 1960s Bourdieu held teaching posts at various French universities, including the University of Paris, the University of Lille, and, from 1964, the Ecole pratique des Hautes Etudes (School of Advanced Studies). In 1968 he was named director of the Centre de Sociologie Européenne (Center of European Sociology), a research-oriented post that allowed him to write and develop his ideas.

Founded Journal

Bourdieu used this opportunity to formulate a broad critique of the dominant cultural forces in French society. Among the first works to show his characteristic way of thinking was *La Reproduction* (The Reproduction), which appeared in 1970 and dealt with the French educational system. Bourdieu contended that the French educational system worked to perpetuate social inequality and introduced the key idea that power structures in society work not by brute force but by finding ways to reproduce themselves with each new generation. In 1975, he founded a new journal, *Actes de la Recherche en Sciences Sociales* (Documents in Social Science Research), which served as a vehicle for his own ideas and those of his increasingly numerous followers.

Perhaps Bourdieu's most widely read work outside France was *La distinction: Critique sociale du jugement* (1979), translated as *Distinction: A Social Critique of the Judgment of Taste* in 1984. The book was a wide-ranging discussion of the relationship between cultural tastes and social class. The book proposed the idea of cultural (or symbolic) capital, possessed by those with high levels of education and status, who are able to deploy that cultural capital to make those of lower status accept their place in the cultural structures that underlie human societies. The International Sociological Association named *Distinction* one of the ten most important works of sociology in the 20th century.

Bourdieu's writings of the 1960s and 1970s introduced several other concepts that have entered the vocabulary of social criticism. These included habitus, which might be defined as the conditioning that leads people to accept existing cultural constraints, and symbolic violence, exerted by social-cultural structures in the absence of physical violence, which is a monopoly of the state. Bourdieu's ideas were ultimately rooted in the class-based analysis of Marxist thinking, but he combined Marxism with sociological and anthropological ideas that showed why power structures were often remarkably stable instead of being threatened by class struggle.

In 1981 Bourdieu ascended to the chair of sociology at the Collège de France, among the most prestigious positions in the field of social science in France. Bourdieu was a prolific writer, issuing about 35 books over his four-decade career. Many of them have been translated into English. Among his later works were *Homo Academicus* (1984), in which he turned his lens on his own academic world, and *Les règles d'art* (The Rules of Art, 1992), which examined the role of literature in public cultural spaces or "fields."

Adopted More Activist Stance

Bourdieu's writings of the 1990s marked a new direction, less theoretical and more oriented toward direct action in support of causes in which he believed. Several of his books became best-sellers in France; *Sur la television* (On Television, 1996) was an attack on that medium that Bourdieu only rarely softened by agreeing to appear on televised interview programs, while *La Misère du Monde* (translated as *The Weight of the World*, 1999) was a collection of interviews with ordinary individuals. Increasingly Bourdieu aimed for audiences beyond the conventional academic sphere, and although critics sometimes questioned this new emphasis, he achieved considerable success as a public intellectual.

Bourdieu also spoke out directly on behalf of causes and individuals he supported. He defended small farmer José Bove, who vandalized a French McDonald's store as part of his larger protest against the incursions of multinational food companies in France, and he backed striking railroad workers and spoke out on behalf of undocumented immigrants. Bourdieu attacked the trend of globalization in general, and he was dissatisfied with the policies of France's Socialist party in this realm. Sometimes he spoke of himself as representing the Left of the Left.

Bourdieu continued to write, issuing more than two dozen books and editing several others. At his death he was at work on several new projects, and two new books, *Esquisse pour une auto-analyse* (Sketch of a Self-Analysis) and *Images de l'Algerie; Une affinité életive* (Images of Algeria: A Chosen Affinity), were published posthumously. Bourdieu died of cancer in Paris on January 23, 2002; by that time such concepts as symbolic capital were part of the ordinary vocabulary of theoretical sociology, even beyond France. In the words of Bridget Fowler of the London *Independent*, Bourdieu's direct engagement with the world around him "gave his sociology an unrivalled depth of theoretical knowledge and mastery of methods. It also gave him a profound sense of the scope and the tensions in the stakes to be fought for, nothing less than a symbolic revolution in sociology." His "choice of theoretical stance was always conditioned by the value of those theoretical positions for humanity as a whole."

Books

Webb, Jen, et al., *Understanding Bourdieu*, Allen & Unwin, 2002.

Periodicals

Australian, February 6, 2002.

Guardian (London, England), January 28, 2002.

Independent (London, England), February 1, 2002.

New York Times, January 25, 2002.

Times (London, England), January 29, 2002.

Online

"Pierre Bourdieu," *Books and Writers*, http://www.kirjasto.sci.fi/bourd.htm (October 21, 2014). □

Charles Boyer

French/American actor Charles Boyer (1899–1978) became a Hollywood star of the 1930s and 1940s. Often appearing in Warner Brothers films, the Academy Award-nominated actor's best known works include *Algiers* (1938) and *Barefoot in the Park* (1967). Boyer began on the French stage where he usually played suave lovers, as he would also do in film.

Charles Boyer was born in Figeac, France, on August 28, 1899. He was the son of Maurice Boyer and Augustine Durand. His father was a wealthy seller of farm machinery and implements. By the age of seven, Boyer was appearing in school plays to counteract his shyness. Though he was focused on stage acting throughout his childhood, it was not until he was a teenager that he was certain about pursuing the craft as a career. During World War I, Boyer served in a medical unit of the French Army and organized entertainments. Positive audience feedback cemented his decision.

Studied Acting in Paris

After attending the local College Champollion, Boyer moved to Paris in 1918. He focused on furthering his education, studying philosophy at Sorbonne. He later trained as an actor at the Paris Conservatory (the Conservatoire National). Before gaining formal admittance to this conservatory, he was auditioning for roles and developed a reputation as a quick study. This lead to his professional stage debut on an opening night production of *Les Jardins de Murcie,* without a rehearsal. Because of the renown he gained from this performance, he was admitted to the Paris Conservatory.

While an acting student, Boyer held part-time jobs as a violinist in a night club and as a Sûreté detective. Boyer graduated from the conservatory in 1922. He then focused on stage roles, becoming a French stage star. One of his early performances in Paris came in a production of *La Bataille.*

During the 1920s, Boyer became one of the best compensated stage actors in France. This was primarily due to his connection to Henry Bernstein, a playwright and producer. Though Boyer decided against taking up Bernstein's offer to become his manager, Boyer did appear in numerous plays written by Bernstein for Boyer. Despite Boyer's professional and financial success as a result of these plays, their relationship was strained in part because of typecasting. Boyer believed he was a character actor but Bernstein saw him quite differently, as a romantic leading man. Bernstein wrote such roles for him, and Boyer would be thrust into such parts for much of the rest of his career.

Made Film Debut

Boyer soon began working in film as well, making his film debut in 1920 in *L'Home du Large.* He made a few silent

AF Archive/Alamy

films, though they hid one of his best assets as an actor, his voice. Among them was the 1923 film *L'Esclave,* his first leading role. It brought his name to the rest of France. He also appeared in *Le Capitaine Fracassé* (1927), after which he avoided films for several years.

Instead, in the late 1920s, Boyer focused on stage work. He went on an extended stage tour, with performances in European countries, as well as Egypt, Syria, and Turkey. By 1929, Boyer was back in Paris, appearing in the stage hit *Melo.* The play was written by Bernstein.

Boyer decided to go to Hollywood for the first time, however, and he left the production to do so. The reason for his departure was the demand in Hollywood for foreign language actors. By this time, talking pictures were emerging. In this early stage of sound and dialogue films, Hollywood films were re-created in other languages for foreign markets. An actor like Boyer, who spoke five languages, had a chance to be successful. At the urging of a friend who had made a splash in American film musicals, Maurice Chevalier, Boyer learned English as well, adding to his marketability for roles.

Attempted to Break Into Hollywood

Each year from 1929 to 1932, Boyer traveled to California to do such work. He did land some roles there, appearing in French-language versions of Hollywood films. In 1931, Boyer made his first major film in English, *The Man from Yesterday.* It also starred actress Claudette Colbert. But he failed to break through into serious Hollywood roles. In the early 1930s, Boyer appeared in French-language versions of German and British films as well. They included an impressive turn in *Le Bonheur* (1934), based on the play by Bernstein. This film was a romantic comedy with political undertones, in which he played a socialist/anarchist newspaper cartoonist.

Later in 1934, Boyer returned to Hollywood and had more success. In addition to meeting and marrying Patricia Paterson, a British actress who appeared in musical comedies, Boyer focused on acting in Los Angeles as a freelance, instead of studio contracted, actor. He landed an agent, Charles Feldman, who supported Boyer's freelance stance. In this time period, studio contracts provided stability and security for actors and actresses who signed them, but also led to studios exercising control over parts they played and their private lives.

With Feldman's assistance, Boyer landed a contract on a bigger Hollywood film. He was paid the princely sum of $40,000 for working on *Caravan* (1934), though the film failed to catch on with audiences. Boyer continued to land major roles throughout the mid-1930s, and was marketed to American audiences as a polished romantic lover, a continental gentleman who dressed well, had perfect manners, and exuded suaveness. Also possessing the attitude and voice to make him a believable man of action, Boyer's classical features and deep-set eyes added to his appeal. Boyer's fans included directors in charge of Warner Brothers cartoons, and Boyer was the inspiration for the classic animated character, Pepe Le Pew.

Typecast in Romantic Roles

This romantic typecasting of Boyer began with his work in the 1935 film *Private World* opposite Colbert. That year he also appeared in two other films, *Shanghai* and *Break of Hearts*. In 1936, he was featured in *Garden of Allah* and became a Hollywood star. Also in 1936, Boyer impressed audiences with his role in *Mayerling* opposite star Danielle Darrieux. Set in 1880s Austria, the film focuses on political intrigue at the Austrian court of Emperor Franz Joseph. As Charles Taylor wrote in the *New York Times,* "When Charles Boyer attempts to wench and drink his heartache away in *Mayerling,* we know we're seeing dissipation as a proof of his undying love." By this point, Boyer was taking roles in both Hollywood and Europe.

Perhaps Boyer's best known film of this period was *Algiers* (1938), in which he played a French super thief, Pepe le Moko. The film co-starred Hedy Lamarr. Other romantic hero roles came in the late 1930s and early 1940s, including a part specifically tailored for him in *Love Affair* (1939). Boyer also appeared in *All This and Heaven Too* (1940), and *Gaslight* (1944). His co-stars in such films included Irene Dunn, Bette Davis, and Ingrid Bergman. Other films in this period included *History Is Made at Night* and *Tovarich.*

Supported France During WWII

Throughout his time in Hollywood, Boyer remained a firm supporter of France and anti-fascist actions in the United

States before World War II broke out. When war began in Europe in 1939, Boyer returned home and enlisted in the French Army. He spent 11 weeks as a private before the French premier released him from service to focus on being a French goodwill ambassador in the United States, including Hollywood.

Boyer used his position as a Hollywood star to encourage and facilitate a relationship between the United States and France. He founded the related French Research Foundation to encourage a cultural exchange. Boyer also co-founded the French War Relief Committee and ensured Hollywood filmmakers had access to information that would make films about France more accurate. Boyer provided assistance to those escaping European territories occupied by the Nazis as well. For these efforts, Boyer was honored with a special Academy Award in 1942.

Though Boyer continued to appear in some films in this period and was Warner Brothers' top paid star in 1945, much of Boyer's time was spent focusing on the war effort in various ways. When Nazi Germany entered Paris in June 1940, Boyer was in France helping family and friends escape. Boyer was also a member of the free French government in exile in London, led by General Charles de Gaulle. He played a role in recording and publicizing de Gaulle's radio addresses in France and the United States. In 1942, Boyer became an American citizen, while retaining his French citizenship.

Boyer's support of France continued after World War II ended. At war's end, there was dissidence between those who resisted the Nazis and those who were collaborated with them or were accused of collaboration. Boyer asked for reconciliation and gave a memorable speech at the Cannes Film Festival to that effect, which was well received. He also appeared in war related films like the 1948 thriller *Arch of Triumph,* set in Paris shortly before the beginning of the conflict. Boyer played a debonair exile seeking revenge on a Gestapo officer.

Returned to the Stage

In the late 1940s, Boyer again began appearing in stage productions. He made his Broadway debut in *Red Gloves,* an adaptation of Jean-Paul Satre's *Les Mains Sales.* Though Sartre was critical of the production, Boyer was well received in the role.

It was through stage work that Boyer's gifts as an actor showed through. As part of the First Drama Quartet—along with Agnes Moorehead, Cedric Hardwicke, and Charles Laughton—Boyer gave platform readings of part of George Bernard Shaw's *Man and Superman,* specifically the interlude *Don Juan from Hell.* In addition to an appearance on Broadway, the group did two tours throughout the United States and England, for more than 700 performances. Boyer played Don Juan, impressing audiences with his verbal and acting skills.

More stage work followed, including appearances in *Kind Sir* in 1951 and *Lord Pengo* in 1962. Lighter stage work followed for Boyer, including *Man and Boy* by Terence Rattigan in 1964. In this production, Boyer made his London stage debut. The production also went to Paris, where Boyer performed on stage for the first time since the 1940s.

Though Boyer became disenchanted with Hollywood in the wake of the anti-Communist activities of the House Un-American Activities Committee, he did expand his career in television in the early 1950s as well. In 1952, Boyer was a co-founder and partner in Four Star Television, along with fellow actors Dunn, Dick Powell, and David Niven. For the next two decades, Boyer appeared in many of their televised dramatic productions. Among them was the 1964 television drama, *The Rogues*, which focused on a group of high-flying jewel thieves and con men.

Relocated to Europe

In 1965, Boyer suffered a personal tragedy when his only child, son Michael, committed suicide. Michael Boyer was employed as an associate producer for Four Star, but could not succeed in other realms. After the loss, Boyer and his wife moved to Geneva, Switzerland. Boyer continued to work in films, including appearances in *Is Paris Burning?* (1966), *How to Steal a Million* (1966), the James Bond film *Casino Royale* (1967), and *Barefoot in the Park* (1967). One of his best known American films of this period was a musical, *Lost Horizon* (1973), in which he played the ancient High Lama. Boyer's last film role came in *Stavisky* (1974) in which he played Le baron Jean Raoul. For his work as Stavisky, he won a New York Film Critics Circle Award.

In ill health with prostate issues in 1977, Beyer also had to manage his wife's illness when she was diagnosed with terminal cancer. Only two days after her death, Boyer committed suicide by overdosing on Seconal on August 26, 1978, in the Scottsdale, Arizona, home of a friend. He was 78 years old, and only two days from his seventy-ninth birthday. As Bruce Bennett wrote in the *New York Sun*, "The end of Boyer's own saga drew a shroud of despair over an enduring real-life romance that was as rare on-screen as off."

Books

Dictionary of American Biography, Charles Scribner's Sons, 1995

Periodicals

Associated Press, August 26, 1978.

Los Angeles Times, August 29, 1978.

New York Sun, May 23, 2008.

New York Times, September 13, 2009.

Times (London, England), August 22, 2003.

Washington Post, August 28, 1978; August 30, 1978.

Online

"Charles Boyer," *AllMovie*. http://www.allmovie.com/artist/charles-boyer-p7830 (December 21, 2014). □

Yvonne Brill

Rocket scientist Yvonne Brill (1924–2013) was the inventor of the electrothermal hydrazine thruster (EHT), an efficient propulsion system which prevented communication satellites from losing their orbits. A patent holder, she worked in rocket science and satellite thruster design from its earliest years in the United States. Brill balanced demanding engineering jobs with raising a family, and regularly supported efforts of girls and women to become scientists.

Born Yvonne Madelaine Claeys on December 30, 1924, in St. Vital, Manitoba, Canada, she was the youngest of three children of recent immigrants from the Flanders region in Belgium to Canada. (St. Vital is a suburb of the major Manitoban city of Winnipeg.) Her father worked there as a carpenter.

Showed Academic Promise

Though her parents did not graduate from high school, Brill showed her brilliance as a student, especially during high school. Her father encouraged her to open a small store, like a dress shop, after her education was complete. Brill had different ambitions, however, which included engineering, science, and college. She became the first in her family to attend an institution of higher learning. Although interested in engineering from an early age, Brill was not allowed to major in the subject at the University of Manitoba. Engineering students had to attend an outdoor engineering camp to do field work, but there were no accommodations for women at the camp. Because they would not allow her to attend the camp, she was barred from the engineering program.

Studying mathematics and chemistry instead, Brill graduated from the university at the top of her class in 1945. After gaining her degrees, she moved to California. Despite her lack of an engineering degree, Brill was able to land a job with Douglas Aircraft in Santa Monica. There, she was employed doing rocket trajectory calculations. She also helped translate documents captured from Germany about rocket technology. Brill was, most likely, the only woman in the United States who was pursuing propulsion in rocket science during this time period. Brill chose to work in rocket engineering because there were no women doing so. She believed that there would be no rules devised to treat just one person unfairly.

Began Working in Propulsion

By 1947, Douglas had a satellite project which served as the foundation for the RAND Corporation, a scientific research group. The project resulted in the first designs for an American satellite, created for the U.S. Air Force. Brill was employed by RAND for three years. While at RAND, she worked on the satellite project and related rocket

AP Images/Pablo Martinez Monsivais

science research. Brill soon specialized in the chemistry of propulsion. According to Martin Childs in the London *Independent*, Brill once said, "I didn't have engineering but the engineers didn't have the chemistry and math."

While employed at RAND, Brill earned a master's degree in chemistry at the University of Southern California, in 1951. She also met her future husband, William Franklin Brill, a research chemist, at a chemistry lecture given by Linus Pauling, a Nobel Prize winner, during this time period. The couple married in 1951 as well.

Though Brill's career would have benefitted from being on the West Coast where rocket science was centered, her husband had better job prospects in the East. In 1952, the couple moved to Connecticut after he landed a job there. The couple eventually had two sons and one daughter, and relocated again for his career to New Jersey. Despite fewer opportunities on the East Coast, Brill found more positions in which she could work on rockets.

One such job was with New Jersey-based Wright Aeronautical in the 1950s. After Brill's children were born, however, she left the company in 1958. She did not cease working entirely. Brill was employed as a part-time consultant for FMC Corporation while raising her children. By 1966, Brill was again working full-time, this time with the rocket subsidiary of RCA, RCA Astro Electronics. It was in this part of her career that she had the most success as an engineer.

Devised EHT

Brill's work became internationally known by the early 1970s. In that time period, Brill devised a propulsion system which ensured that communication satellites remained in their orbits. Named the hydrazine resistojet propulsion system, it was more commonly called the electrothermal hydrazine thruster (EHT). She patented this system in 1972.

The EHT used liquid hydrazine, a combination of nitrogen and hydrogen that was highly volatile. When liquid hydrazine breaks down, it produces heat. During World War II, the Germans used liquid hydrazine as a rocket propellant. The Americans employed liquid hydrazine as a propellant for space travel in the Mercury and Apollo programs.

Brill's innovation came from her discovery that there is greater fuel efficiency when the products of hydrazine's decomposition are heated electrically before discharge. By taking advantage of this and reheating ejected propellant before leaving the nozzle, there was a reduction in the weight of fuel on a satellite. Because of Brill's system, satellites could carry more equipment, 30 percent less fuel, and had less cost. They also were able to stay in space for longer periods of time than previous satellites.

Brill's satellite propulsion system was also distinguished by its efficient rocket thrusters, which put satellites into space, placed them in correct orbit, and helped them to remain there. Her thrusters also made satellites easier to adjust, ensuring that they operated correctly. Engineers could efficiently alter and monitor satellite positions in their geosynchronous orbit circling the Earth.

The first communications satellite using Brill's EHT technology was launched in 1983. The technology proved itself, became the industry standard, and stood the test of time as many satellites stayed functioning and in place for years. EHTs were still being used by telephone and television broadcasting companies into the 2010s.

Contributed to Other Projects

Over the years, Brill helped work on other propulsion systems for a number of noteworthy satellites and rockets. They included the first weather satellites, the Tiros series, and Atmosphere Explorer, the first satellite that reached the upper atmosphere of the Earth. She also contributed to the propulsion systems on Nova rockets, which were intended to be used by the United States for lunar missions. In addition, Brill was part of the team that created the propulsion system of the Mars Observer. In 1992, the observer nearly completed its mission of entering the orbit of Mars.

Brill also worked on other parts of rockets. Employed by NASA (National Aeronautics and Space Administration) in Washington, D.C., from 1981 to 1983, Brill served as the director in the solid rocket motor unit for the space shuttle program. In her time at NASA, she also created the rocket motor for the space shuttle. In 1986, Brill joined the London-based International Maritime Satellite Organisation. She served as the manager of Space Segment Engineering products for combined propulsion systems on certain types of mobile communication satellites. She remained employed there until she formally retired in 1991.

In retirement, Brill remained active in her industry. She served as an aerospace consultant on various projects, primarily related to satellite technology and space propulsion systems. She was also a member of the Aerospace Advisory Panel for NASA. By 2013, she was a member of the Space Studies Board of the National Research Council.

Supported Other Female Scientists

While Brill was unusual in that she was a rocket scientist when few other women were pursuing such science and technical positions, she went out of her way to support other women who wanted to take up science and engineering. In addition to writing letters in support of distinguished female engineers so they would gain recognition, she also encouraged girls to study math and science. She believed that determination was key to the success of women in science, telling Lynda Radosevich of *InfoWorld*, "You need a confidence in your ability, because often you'd question whether you're really on the right path."

Because of the nature of her own career path, including the break she took to raise her young children, Brill struggled at times to balance work and family. An internationally respected scientist, she was also honest about the difficulties that came from pursuing both demanding life pursuits. After Brill's death in 2013, Elizabeth Payne of the *Ottawa Citizen* wrote, "At a time when the question of whether women can 'have it all' is more alive than ever, Brill's accomplishments deserve recognition—both as a groundbreaking scientist and as a woman who found a way to balance her life and have it all—in a fashion—before anyone even thought to ask whether it was possible." For this accomplishment, she was given the Diamond Superwoman Award from *Harper's Bazaar* and the DeBeers Corporation in 1980.

For her work, Brill received numerous awards and honors. In 1987, she was elected to membership in the National Academy of Engineering, when the organization had few female members. In 1999, was inducted into the Women in Technology International Hall of Fame. In addition to gaining the Resnik Challenger Medal from the Society of Women Engineers in 1993, she was given the NASA Distinguished Public Service Medal in 2001, and the Wyle Propulsion Award, American Institute of Aeronautics and Astronautics in 2002. In 2010, she was inducted into the National Inventors Hall of Fame. In 2011, Brill was presented with the National Medal of Technology and Innovation by President Barack Obama.

Served as Subject of Controversial Obituary

Suffering from breast cancer at the end of her life, Brill died of complications related to her cancer in Princeton, New Jersey, on March 27, 2013. She was 88 years old. After her death, Brill's obituary in the *New York Times* became an international source of controversy. As originally written, the obituary emphasized her culinary skills as well as her roles as wife and mother before any mention of her numerous professional accomplishments. Critics called it sexist and indignantly noted that a man's obituary would not have been written in the same way. Though the *New York*

Times edited the offending passage and re-published it, the gaffe brought further attention to Brill's accomplishments and highlighted continuing issues of sexism in science and society.

In the *Financial Times,* Jurek Martin wrote of the snafu, "Brill would probably have been pleased that people took such umbrage on her behalf but, then again, she was always very practical about life. As she said after Manitoba frustrated her engineering ambitions: 'You just have to be cheerful about it and not get upset when you get insulted.' Space, after all, was her final frontier and she did voyage scientifically where few men, or women, had been before."

Periodicals

Daily Telegraph (London, England), June 20, 2013.
Financial Times (London, England), April 6, 2013.
Independent (London, England), June 26, 2013.
InfoWorld, May 3, 1999.
New York Times, March 31, 2013.
Ottawa Citizen, April 4, 2013.
Targeted News Service, March 28, 2013.
Washington Post, April 1, 2013; April 3, 2013.□

Joseph Broussard

Acadian resistance leader Joseph Broussard (1702–1765) led a long and bloody war against British control in Canada's Maritime Provinces. Known by the *nom du guerre* Beausoleil, Broussard belonged to a tight-knit community of French-heritage settlers in Nova Scotia and New Brunswick who were forcibly deported by the British in the 1750s. The dispersed Acadians died out, but Broussard led a small remnant to Louisiana, where they maintained a unique ethnic identity later classed as Cajun, a linguistic corruption of the descriptor "Acadian."

Joseph Broussard was born in 1702 in Port Royal, Nova Scotia, one of France's first permanent settlements on the North American mainland. Founded by the French in 1605 as a small fort and trading post, Port Royal grew along with the surrounding L'Acadie, or Acadia. In its peak years Acadia included lands in what became the Canadian provinces of New Brunswick, Nova Scotia, and Prince Edward Island as well as a slice of Maine in the United States.

Learned Native American Hunting Skills

Broussard's father François—whose surname is spelled in some sources as Brossard—was likely the same person born in Anjou, France, who came to New France in 1671 aboard the ship *L'Oranger.* The elder Broussard was probably 25 years old in 1678 when he married a woman named Catherine Richard in Port Royal. The couple went on to have eleven children, and Broussard was among the younger half of the brood.

At the time of Broussard's birth, Acadia was part of New France and loosely governed from Quebec. French colonial authorities imposed few laws or taxes on the Maritime communities around the Gulf of St. Lawrence and Acadians lived in a largely conflict-free coexistence with the Míqmaq, one of Canada's First Nations. As a youth Broussard and his brothers were encouraged to learn to hunt and fish with their Míqmaq peers—skills that would serve them well in the ground-warfare conflict that later defined their adult lives.

In 1710 France was forced to cede significant territory in the Atlantic Maritime provinces to Britain after losing Queen Anne's War. Broussard's father was among the more outspoken opponents of new British military rule, whose commanders were sent from Boston in British North America. Port Royal was renamed Annapolis Royal in honor of Queen Anne, and the family moved to another site in Acadia. This was on the other side of the Bay of Fundy across from Port Royal, in an area of New Brunswick called Haute Rivière. The original name of the settlement was Beausoleil, and this storied place name became Broussard's *nom du guerre*.

The Beausoleil village was located near a marshy area where three rivers converged. Acadians were expected to give crops, livestock, and other commodities to new British troops in the area, and there was outright subversion and acts of violence. Broussard's father was among the several Haute Rivière men arrested along with their local Roman Catholic priest at the village chapel in January of 1711 after one incident. The elder Broussard was detained for months in little more than a dirt dungeon, and this episode marked the start of a long and grievous battle against British rule in Acadia.

Joined Guerrilla Brigade

French missionary priests of the Récollect order were politically active and, along with some of their colleagues of the Society of Jesus (Jesuit) order, were suspected of fomenting anti-British sentiment in Acadia. As a young man, Broussard and his brother Alexandre fought in Father Rale's War, after Father Sébastien Rale, a Jesuit priest who was killed in action in the third year of this conflict in 1724. They fought for control of disputed territory along the Kennebec River near New Brunswick's present-day border with Maine.

In September of 1725, Broussard married Agnès Thibodeau, whose older sister Marguerite was married to Alexandre Broussard. The marital unions, plus those of the older Broussard siblings, made the brothers part of an extended network of Acadian families who fought British rule most vigorously, often in alliance with Míqmaq and the Wabanaki Confederacy, another First Nations group.

The Thibodeaus were among those who had first settled the Chepoudy Bay area of Albert County, New Brunswick. Around 1730 both Broussard and Alexandre moved there with their wives. Ten years later, in about 1740, the brothers and their families moved further inland to a site where other Thibodeaus family members lived. This was the settlement of LeCran on Stoney Creek, which fed into

the larger Petitcoudiac River. They called it Beausoleil in homage to their original village in Haute Rivière.

Attacked New British Garrisons

Hostilities between the French and British erupted once again in the 1740s, and Broussard and his brother opted to side with the French. They also supported the Míqmaqs' grievances against the British. In January of 1747 Broussard set off with 240 French settlers plus a contingent of Míqmaq and Maliseet, a smaller First Nations group. They wore snowshoes and carried their equipment in sleds across the Isthmus of Chignecto, which connects New Brunswick to the Nova Scotia peninsula. After a 17-day trek Broussard and the war party came to an Acadian hamlet of Grand-Pré on the east side of Gaspereau River on February 10, 1747. This well-protected and fertile area guarded the Minas Basin of the Bay of Fundy. From there Broussard and the men attacked an English settlement on the other side of the river in a stunning 3 a.m. raid during a snow squall. As many as 100 English colonists were slain and half that number were taken prisoner. With this infamous strike the Acadians slowed British encroachment on Nova Scotia, but only temporarily. By 1749 British troops had dispatched units to oversee the building of fortifications across Nova Scotia.

Broussard and Alexandre became local legends for their role in Father Le Loutre's War, which lasted from 1749 to 1755. This was named after French missionary priest Jean-Louis Le Loutre, who organized resistance to British rule in Nova Scotia. Le Loutre and Broussard were the chief commanders of a combined force of French Canadian, Acadian, Míqmaq, and Maliseet units. It was a long guerrilla war and Broussard took part in several violent actions, including a battle at Chignecto in September of 1750 and a raid on Dartmouth the following spring. Revered by then as an elder statesman of the Acadians, Broussard was said to have killed no less than one thousand English soldiers and colonists.

Father Le Loutre's War ended in mid-June of 1755 when British forces took the small French fort of Beauséjour on Isthmus of Chignecto. Broussard and Alexandre were taken into custody. The British victory doomed the remaining Acadians in Nova Scotia and New Brunswick and also marked the start of the much larger French and Indian War between the two European powers in the New England colonies and Maritime provinces. Broussard, his brother, and other Acadian men were offered a chance to swear an oath of allegiance to the British crown, which they declined.

Heroically Resisted Deportation

British colonial authorities, sensing the enduring threat posed by Acadian resistance, dismissed more diplomatic remedies suggested by London and opted instead to begin mass deportations of Acadians from the area. Le Grand Dérangement, the French-language term for the expulsion, began in earnest in August of 1755. The action is often cited as the first instance of European-on-European ethnic-cleansing war crimes in North America. The Acadians were forced to abandon prosperous farms and villages in

Maritime lands that had been cleared, developed, and even irrigated by their ancestors more than a hundred years earlier. British-flagged vessels came to Annapolis Royal and Halifax, a newer Nova Scotia port, to ferry Acadian families to assigned places elsewhere in British North America. Some were ordered to New York, others to Pennsylvania, but the most obdurate resisters were sent the furthest south to plantations in Virginia, Maryland, and the Carolinas. Broussard's son Victor and Victor's uncle Alexandre were among the ringleaders taken in chains in October of 1755 to Sullivan's Island, South Carolina, an infamous landing site for slave ships from Africa.

Broussard was not among that group because he managed to escape from custody at Fort Beauséjour, which had been renamed Fort Cumberland after the British took it. He went inland and met up with some remaining Acadians, including the family of his eldest brother Pierre. The first Broussard son had settled years before in the bustling port of Louisbourg on Île Royale on Cape Breton Island, on Nova Scotia's northern tip. For years Louisbourg remained the sole French seaport on the Atlantic Ocean in North America, and France spent heavily to build a massive fortification there. Broussard and these other Acadians remained in French-held lands, evading the deportation orders for a few more years.

The attempts to resettle Acadians in New England and the mid-Atlantic seaboard had proved disastrous, as revealed by information that filtered back to Louisbourg. Governors in some colonies, fearful of an influx of hundreds of French-speaking, staunchly anti-British refugees and their potential to foment local unrest, refused to permit the Acadians to disembark. The ships remained in harbor under guard for months, turning them into pestilence-ridden prisons. In some cases Acadian children were taken from their parents and placed with adoptive families.

Lived Off the Land

In retaliation for this treatment, Broussard spent three years harrying British shipping in the Bay of Fundy and elsewhere. Alexandre and Victor escaped from a penal colony workhouse in South Carolina and, with about 30 other fugitives, walked the Appalachian Trail back up to Nova Scotia to resume the fight in mid-1756. The French and Indian War still raged and, in the summer of 1758, the British seized the valuable Fort Louisbourg site, the all-weather shipping gateway to Canada. Broussard was taken into custody once again while other family members were deported to France. Many of them died on the perilous west-to-east Atlantic crossing, or succumbed after arriving in St. Malo from dysentery and other diseases.

Broussard eluded capture once again by hiding out in Miramichi, a Míqmaq-controlled area of New Brunswick. His wife Agnès died during a particularly brutal winter of 1756-57. Along with scores of nephews, cousins, and other extended-family members loyal to the cause, Broussard lived off the lands, as he had learned how to do as a boy, but many of the youngest Acadians and similarly persecuted Míqmaq could not survive such conditions and died from lack of shelter. The party moved to the Atlantic Ocean-facing Chaleur Bay site at Restigouche, New Brunswick, before the next winter, but in the fall of 1759 Broussard, age 57, decided to surrender himself to the British lest he subject his family to another deadly winter. He spent three years in military detention in Halifax, though some of it was served under house arrest.

The French and Indian War ended after nine years in 1763. The British were victorious and, as a result, this left the roughly 600 remaining Acadians in Nova Scotia with tenuous legal status under the terms of the Treaty of Paris. Some were allowed to work as indentured servants for English landowners on restored farms in the Haute Rivière, region; others finally accepted offers to resettle elsewhere in French-held territories such as Haiti, a vast Caribbean plantation run with ruthless brutality to maintain control over thousands of slaves required to cut sugar and harvest coffee. Finally, in late 1764 Broussard boarded a ship with about 200 other Acadians and they sailed from Halifax to Cap François, where they found conditions appalling and the tropical heat unbearable.

In his last and most enduring act of leadership, Broussard arranged for a ship to take them across the Gulf of Mexico to Louisiana, a former French colony that had just passed into Spanish hands with the Treaty of Paris but remained staunchly French and a haven for dissenters. Louisiana governor Charles Phillippe Aubry welcomed Broussard and his party, gave them a large parcel of land west of New Orleans, and approved an order bestowing Broussard with authority over his own militia. Both Broussard and Alexandre died later that year after an outbreak of an unknown tropical disease that swept through the Acadian community. A Jesuit priest recorded Broussard's date of death as October 20, 1765.

Books

Faragher, John Mack, *A Great and Noble Scheme: The Tragic Story of the Expulsion of the French Acadians from Their American Homeland*, W.W. Norton & Company, 2005.

Marshall, Dianne, *Heroes of the Acadian Resistance: The Story of Joseph Beausoleil Broussard and Pierre II Surette, 1702–1765*, Formac Publishing, 2011.□

C

John Cairncross

British government official John Cairncross (1913–1995) was dogged for years by rumors that he was the purported fifth traitor among the infamous Cambridge Five espionage ring. He eluded detection for years, and later admitted only to divulging select secrets that aided the Soviet Union's efforts to defeat Nazi Germany on its eastern front during World War II. Some of that espionage work occurred during the period when Cairncross worked at Bletchley Park, the manor home that housed the top-secret wartime Enigma code-breaking effort.

John Cairncross was Scottish by birth. Born on July 25, 1913, in Lesmahagow, Scotland, he was the last of eight children in his family. His father was an iron-monger and Cairncross attended a rigorous secondary school in Lanarkshire, the Hamilton Academy, and went on to the University of Glasgow to study modern languages. He also attended the Sorbonne University of Paris and finished his graduate studies at Trinity College of Cambridge University. Years later he admitted that he had briefly joined the British Communist Party in 1935 while at Cambridge—a not-uncommon political activity for college students and liberal-leaning intellectuals of the era.

Hoped for Diplomat's Career

At Cambridge Cairncross became friends with a registered British Communist Party member named James Klugmann. That association with Klugmann ties Cairncross to the other members of a traitorous ring of Cambridge graduates who provided the Soviet Union with classified information during the early years of the Cold War. The other four were Anthony Blunt, Guy Burgess, Donald Duart Maclean, and Harold "Kim" Philby. All four were said to have been recruited by undercover Soviet agents while at Cambridge, and in later years gave conflicting accounts of Cairncross's involvement in years before World War II. Blunt, Burgess, and Philby actually worked for British intelligence services, a particularly appalling breach of security protocol; Maclean was employed only by the British Foreign Office and did not engage in espionage activities on behalf of the British, only for the Soviets. All four had top security clearances and were well placed to provide the Soviets with a steady stream of classified documents and information.

Cairncross, too, joined the Foreign Office in White-hall, the seat of the British government, after scoring top marks in the British civil service examination in 1936. He spoke fluent French and German, and as a junior-level Foreign Office employee could anticipate a cushy future posting in an embassy elsewhere, with diplomatic perks and the chance to influence foreign policy. Years later, Cairncross said that it was during this first salaried government job that he met Donald Maclean while both were employed in the Spanish Section at the Foreign Office. "Towards the end of my stint with the department, Maclean confided to me that I did not make the right impression because I was too spontaneous and oblivious of conventional behaviour," Cairncross later wrote in his posthumously published memoir with a characteristically grandiose title *The Enigma Spy: The Story of the Man Who Changed the Course of World War II.* Cairncross added that his colleague Maclean explained that "it was not so much a question of having the wrong views, though this was also noted, as not coming from the right background."

©Pascal Parrot/Sygma/Corbis

Cairncross was crushed to learn his chances for advancement were slim. He was transferred to the Treasury Office in October of 1938, just a month after the so-called Munich Crisis involving Nazi Germany's invasion of neighboring Czechoslovakia. In a highly controversial response, British prime minister Neville Chamberlain opted not to support Czechoslovakia, an independent nation with a democratically elected government. In the late summer of 1939, Germany signed a non-aggression pact with the Soviet Union and Nazi troops used the Czech and Slovak lands to move into neighboring Poland. With that act, Britain and Nazi Germany declared war on one another. A technically superior German Luftwaffe launched a bombardment campaign against British cities, including heavy raids on London.

Recruited in Regent's Park

In September 1940, Cairncross was assigned to serve as private secretary to Lord Hankey, a cabinet minister in the government of new prime minister Winston Churchill. An effective strategist and former administrator of the Suez Canal region, Hankey served as Paymaster-General from 1940 to 1941 and had a trusted role in overseeing the secretive work of the British security services. Cairncross's boss was believed to known of clandestine research efforts between British and American scientists involved in plutonium- and uranium-enrichment projects with the goal of creating a new class of deadly atomic weapons. In the early years of World War II

the scientists shared their research discoveries, but the United States' entry into World War II in December of 1941 ended that collaboration when transmitting information across the Atlantic Ocean became impossible. Because of his service to Hankey, Cairncross has sometimes been named as the Atomic Age's first spy, though those with knowledge of the Churchill government's cooperation maintain that as a minor government factotum Cairncross did not possess the required security clearances that would have made him privy to such information inside Hankey's office.

Cairncross steadfastly maintained that he had not been part of the original Cambridge ring recruited in the 1930s, and that his first foray into espionage work came when Klugmann, his friend from Cambridge, arranged a meeting in Regent's Park in London around the time of the Munich Crisis. A third figure greeted them, a shadowy figure introduced only as Otto. This was thought to have been Arnold Deutsch, an Austrian with staunch Russian sympathies who had probably recruited Burgess, Blunt, Philby, and Maclean. Otto "pointed out that the British government was cooperating with Hitler, and appealed to my anti-Nazi convictions and the need for all peace-loving people to unite against the danger from Germany," Cairncross wrote of the incident in his autobiography *The Enigma Spy.* Cairncross said he told Otto that he would provide limited information. "I was eager to work in any way I could for the alliance between Russia and Britain against Nazism," he recalled, "but not as a Soviet agent."

Took Transcripts from Bletchley Park

Cairncross was called up for military service in 1942 and joined the Royal Armoured Corps. His German-language expertise led to a choice assignment at Bletchley Park in Buckinghamshire, England. The Bletchley estate was home to the Secret Intelligence Service (SIS)'s Government Code & Cipher School (GC&CS) and its code-breakers eventually cracked a sophisticated encryption system, known as Enigma, that was used by the German military. Cairncross later admitted that during his translation work in a grim brick building called Hut 3 on the estate grounds, he hid papers in his trousers and passed them on to a handler he met in London he knew only as Henry. "I recruited myself as an independent and voluntary agent, using the KGB as a channel to the Russians," Cairncross boldly declared in *The Enigma Spy.* "If I can be defined as a spy, it is only in this solitary case." Several months later Henry thanked Cairncross and said that the information he had handed over had helped Soviet weaponry designers come up with more effective tools to penetrate the unstoppable Tiger tanks built by Nazi Germany, whose invasion of the Soviet Union was stalled finally at the 1943 Battle of Kursk.

Cairncross's overbearing claims were not isolated to his memoirs. Years later, former co-workers in the Foreign Office, at the Treasury, and at Bletchley Park recalled him as a man prone to peevishness and with a grating personality. After the war he was shunted off to a dismal Ministry of Supply office, a career dead-end. The other Cambridge spies, meanwhile, went on to well-paid and prestigious Foreign Office jobs, though they were known inside the SIS as working field agents. Their separate identities as

Soviet sympathizers and double agents went undetected until a series of missteps involving alcohol and sexual debauchery led to their unmasking. Burgess and Maclean simply vanished in May of 1951, and eventually resurfaced in Moscow, where they lived in relative luxury and were feted as heroes of the Soviet Union.

Detected by Diary Entry

SIS believed Philby was part of the Cambridge ring, too, as was Blunt, but both were by then professional dissemblers and convincingly denied any wrongdoing. Blunt had even managed to remove incriminating evidence from Burgess's home, but investigators found a trunk with papers that include notes about Treasury Office doings that dated back to 1940. "One of the notes referred to a luncheon with Sir John Colville, a senior government official, later to become Churchill's secretary," reported the *Times* of London. "Colville was able to check the date in his diary and help to identify the handwriting as that of Cairncross."

With that revelation, Cairncross was forced to resign from his civil-service job at the Ministry of Supply and lost his pension. He led a curious life in exile for the next 43 years: he lived in Italy and Switzerland, working alternately as a journalist, translator, and United Nations employee. He came to the United States to teach at Case Western Reserve University in Cleveland, where in 1964 an SIS interrogator asked him again about the extent of his involvement with the Cambridge ring after Philby, too, defected to the Soviet Union. Cairncross later returned to Italy, married an Italian woman, and worked in banking while translating fairly well received editions of works by Molière and other French writers. In 1982 he was detained by officials at the Italian-Swiss border and found to have been carrying several thousand British pounds into Switzerland, and spent time in jail on a currency smuggling charge.

Outed as Mysterious "Fifth Man"

Anthony Blunt's double life as a Soviet spy was finally unmasked in late 1979, and he was removed from his post as Surveyor of the Queen's Pictures. Blunt finally revealed more information to SIS interrogators and claimed that he had recruited Cairncross, naming him as the so-called fifth man. Once again, Cairncross denied any involvement. A few years later a high-ranking KGB official, Oleg Gordievsky, defected to the West and provided SIS with a trove of details in exchange for political asylum. Gordievsky confirmed that Cairncross was the long-rumored fifth man.

Cairncross again denied the charges Blunt had made in a sensational news story that dominated headlines in the last week of 1979. Several months later, from his home in France, he revealed that he had passed very limited materials to his Soviet handler during the World War II years when he worked at Bletchley Park. After that he began quietly cooperating with SIS interrogators, who granted him immunity from prosecution. In the 1980s he had even returned several times to Britain to undergo clandestine SIS sessions in which he divulged details about senior government officials who had possibly collaborated with Soviet agents during the World War II years and beyond. Those figures—unlike Burgess, Maclean, and Philby—were still working inside the British government and SIS.

Cairncross lived in France until the spring of 1995, when he boarded a train that passed through the recently opened Channel Tunnel to England. His longtime live-in companion, an American opera singer named Gayle Brinkerhoff, had arranged for a house rental in Oxfordshire, where he completed his memoirs. After the death of his first wife—the Italian woman whom he had never divorced—Cairncross married Brinkerhoff but died a few months later on October 8, 1995, at age 82. In his posthumously published memoirs he admitted he knew Blunt, had had some contact with Burgess over the years, and defended his actions. He took credit only for his transgressions while working at Bletchley Park, and claimed the information had aided the Allies' war effort, especially regarding the pivotal Battle of Kursk. "There is at least one Russian proverb with which I am in agreement," he wrote in *The Enigma Spy*. "'Don't be born handsome. Don't be born rich. Be born lucky.'"

Books

Cairncross, John, *The Enigma Spy: The Story of the Man Who Changed the Course of World War II*, Century Books, 1997.

Hamrick, S.J., *Deceiving the Deceivers: Kim Philby, Donald Maclean, and Guy Burgess*, Yale University Press, 2004.

Macintyre, Ben, *A Spy Among Friends: Kim Philby and the Great Betrayal*, Crown, 2014.

Periodicals

Guardian (London, England), September 27, 1997.

Observer (London, England), October 15, 1995.

Times (London, England), December 24, 1979; October 11, 1995. □

Harry Caray

During a career spanning 53 seasons, American baseball broadcaster Harry Caray (1914–1998) gained a national following for his brash broadcast style and larger-than-life personality. Caray made dull games come to life with his signature phrases of "Holy Cow!" and "It might be . . . it could be . . . it is—a home run!" The highly revered announcer, well-known for his raspy voice, oversized glasses and critical digressions, got his start as an announcer for the St. Louis Cardinals and ended his career in Chicago.

"Harry Caray was Babe Ruth at the microphone," fellow broadcaster Jon Miller told *Sporting News* writer Peter Schmuck shortly after Caray's death. Witty and spirited, Caray electrified the airwaves and roused fans for half a century, broadcasting more than 8,300 games. In 1989, Caray received the National Baseball Hall of Fame's Ford C. Frick Award for his contributions to baseball.

Mickey Pfleger/Sports Illustrated/Getty Images

Orphaned as Child

Caray was born Harry Christopher Carabina on March 1, 1914, in St. Louis to Christopher and Daisy (Argint) Carabina. His mother was of French-Romanian descent, while his father was Italian. Caray never knew his father, who died when Caray was a baby. Caray spent his early years living in downtown St. Louis on LaSalle Street. By age eight, he was working the street corners, persuading laborers and businessmen to buy the *St. Louis Post-Dispatch* on their way home from work. Eager to sell out of his papers, Caray developed a boisterous, attention-grabbing style as he announced the headlines of the day to entice interest.

By ten, Caray was orphaned. After his mother's death he went to live with an aunt. Caray found solace at the ballpark and became a Cardinals fan. He loved watching games at Sportsman's Park—at the time the home field of both the St. Louis Cardinals and St. Louis Browns. As a child, Caray fantasized that he would one day wear a Cardinals uniform. Caray attended Webster Groves High School, playing shortstop and second base. A switch-hitter, Caray earned a full-tuition scholarship to play baseball at the University of Alabama but turned it down because he could not afford to pay for his room and board.

After high school, Caray worked odd jobs. He tended bar, waited tables, sold newspapers, and played semi-pro ball on the weekends for the Smith Undertakers and the Webster Groves Birds. Caray piqued the interest of some scouts, who invited him to a minor league tryout camp. Despite his scrappy style, Caray lacked the eyesight, speed, or arm to make it very far and was quickly cut from the roster. Thereafter, Caray gave up playing baseball and became an assistant to a Medart Manufacturing Company sales manager. Medart made such things as basketball backboards, school lockers, and gymnastics equipment.

When he was in his twenties, Caray married Dorothy Kanz. Dorothy lived in his Webster Groves neighborhood and marrying her meant moving from his aunt's house to the nearby home of Dorothy's parents. Caray and Dorothy had three children; Skip, Patricia, and Christopher. They divorced in 1949. Skip Caray followed in the family tradition, becoming an announcer for the Atlanta Braves. Two of Skip's sons, Josh and Chip, also became baseball announcers.

Sought Job as Sports Announcer

Caray found enjoyment following the St. Louis Cardinals. He loved the excitement of going to the ballpark but could not understand why radio broadcasts failed to produce the same feelings. In 1943, he wrote a letter to KMOX general manager Merle Jones complaining about the situation. KMOX was the St. Louis station that covered baseball. Jones agreed to meet with Caray and, during their meeting, Caray explained why he could do a better job announcing. Jones offered Caray an audition, which he promptly bumbled. Jones, however, liked the timbre of Caray's voice and suggested he get some experience in the business.

Jones passed Caray's name to a colleague at WCLS, a small AM station in Joliet, Illinois. The station hired Caray to work as a sports and special events announcer. Caray dropped his birth name of Carabina, legally changing his name to Caray because he thought Caray was catchier and better suited for the airwaves. Eighteen months later, Caray moved to a bigger station, WKZO in Kalamazoo, Michigan. At WKZO, Caray spent two years working under news director Paul Harvey, who went on to become an acclaimed radio broadcaster.

It was in Kalamazoo that Caray adopted the use of "Holy Cow!," which went on to become one of his signature phrases and the title of Caray's 1989 autobiography. In his book, Caray discussed his love for the phrase: "To me, 'Holy cow!' seemed like the right kind of exclamation. It was forceful, exciting, and certainly couldn't offend anybody. And, of course, more important than any of the above, it was the only exclamation I could come up with that didn't involve profanity." Throughout his career, Caray used the phrase generously—to celebrate everything from home runs and great catches to spectacular throws.

By 1944, Caray was back in St. Louis, working as a staff announcer at KXOK-FM. At the time, most radio stations broadcast a nightly sports show. Caray began listening to the shows and thinking of ways to improve them. Most of the shows featured an announcer simply reporting the day's scores or reading press releases from baseball clubs. When KXOK offered Caray the chance to broadcast his own nightly 15-minute sports show, he was ready. Instead of relying on stories coming off the Associated Press wire, Caray scoured the city for his own sports stories. He also added his own commentary and opinions by condemning and critiquing teams and players as he saw fit. Ratings grew and letters poured into the station.

Sold Beer, Baseball on the Airwaves

Caray got his big break in 1945 when he was hired to call Cardinals baseball games and promote Griesedick Brothers beer, which sponsored the baseball broadcasts on KMOX. Caray was paired with Gabby Street, a former Cardinals' catcher and manager. Caray called the play-by-play action while Street offered analysis. They broadcast their first Cardinals game on April 17, 1945. Initially, they covered only home games.

In 1946, Caray and Street started broadcasting away games. This proved tricky because the duo did not actually travel to the games. Instead, they relied on transmissions from the Western Union telegraph and had to re-create the games on the spot as they read the ticker tape. The information they received was minimal—transcriptions like B1, S1, B2, 1BLF. This meant that the batter took a ball, then a strike, then a second ball before slapping a single to left field.

Using this minimal information, Caray had to set the scene and call the game at a reasonable pace, even when the wire transmissions got interrupted. In 1947, Caray and Street finally started traveling with the team. Caray got to broadcast from legendary parks like the Polo Grounds (home of the New York Giants) and Ebbets Field (home of the Brooklyn Dodgers). Caray frequented the famed nightclubs in every town he traveled to and quickly earned a reputation for his partying, drinking, and gambling. Caray kept a diary of his travels. After his death, when parts of his diary became public, fans were astounded to learn that in 1972, Caray went bar-hopping 288 days in a row.

Involved in Cardinal Controversy

In 1953, Anheuser-Busch bought the St. Louis Cardinals. Caray persuaded team owner August Busch to bring him on board to announce Anheuser-Busch-sponsored broadcasts of the Cardinals on KMOX. At the time, this was controversial because Caray was the face of Griesedieck Brothers beer. During the 1950s, Caray announced Cardinals games alongside Jack Buck and Joe Garagiola. When the Cardinals made it to the World Series in 1964, '67, and '68, NBC put Caray behind the microphone to broadcast games on national television since Caray served as the team's official announcer.

Veteran sportscaster Bob Costas told *St. Louis Post-Dispatch* writer Dave Luecking that he grew up listening to Caray. Costas said Caray was a great technical announcer, always on top of each play. "If you really wanted to know what Harry Caray was about, you'd have to get tapes of him doing the Cardinals in the '50s and '60s on the radio, because then, he was a combination of this great, bombastic, bigger-than-life personality coupled with excellent announcing skills."

At times, Caray offended listeners and players with his candid calls. "He said it like it was," Cardinals' slugger Stan Musial told Luecking. "I guess some of the ballplayers were perturbed, but he was a fan . . . he didn't mean anything by it. A little later, he'd be rooting for you." Some listeners, however, complained about Caray's judgmental nature, his lack of political correctness, and his constant bungling of player names.

Though beloved by some, Caray was fired in 1969 after a falling-out with the Busch family. At the time his dismissal was announced to the public, Caray was at a St. Louis restaurant. Local television stations converged on the scene, awaiting his reaction. Caray, in turn, sent the bartender across the street to find some beer from rival brewer Schlitz. With television cameras rolling, Caray raised the Schlitz beer into the air and drank, hoping to raise the ire of the Busch family as he snubbed their hometown brew.

Ended Career in Chicago

Caray spent 1970 with the Oakland A's, then landed in Chicago in 1971 as an announcer for the White Sox, where he continued his critical approach. Caray never broadcast as an emotionless watcher. He criticized umpires for calls and lambasted players for poor performances. Once, according to *Chicago Tribune* reporter Ed Sherman, when White Sox shortstop Bee Bee Richard was having a rough time, Caray made this remark after the player removed some trash from the diamond: "Richard just picked up a hot-dog wrapper at shortstop. It's the first thing he has picked up all night."

Caray, however, believed in his style, despite what detractors said. Caray once told Charles P. Miller of the *Saturday Evening Post* that he realized he offended people, but he firmly believed his job was to work for the fan and not worry about pleasing the players, managers, or owners. "I am just a big fan," Caray told Miller. "If there's any appeal I have to the people it's that people consider me one of them. I show the same disgust in my voice when something disgusting happens; I'm ecstatic when something good happens. I think the average fan thinks I'm doing the game the way he'd be doing it. I'm talking fan-to-fan."

Caray's approach kept the turnstiles spinning. It was with the White Sox that Caray began his famed seventh-inning slaughter of "Take Me Out to the Ballgame." It started in 1976, when Sox owner Bill Veeck noticed that fans sitting near the broadcast booth joined Caray in singing while the organist played during the seventh inning. Veeck had a microphone installed in the broadcast booth so Caray's off-key, down-tempo rendition could be heard by everyone in the park. From then on, Caray led fans in the song every game he broadcast for the rest of his life.

In 1982, after 11 seasons with the Sox, Caray moved across town to broadcast for the Chicago Cubs on cable superstation WGN-TV. Cubs fans quickly fell in love with Caray and his jovial antics. Some days, Caray appeared at Wrigley Field waving a fishing net from the broadcast booth in an attempt to catch foul balls. Other days, he sat with fans and broadcast games from the bleachers. On really hot days, Caray broadcast the games shirtless, undaunted by his plump and pasty physique. Whenever the game hit a lull, Caray would announce birthdays and anniversaries of fans in the crowd. Caray spent 16 years with the Cubs. He called his last game on September 21, 1997.

Caray suffered a heart attack during the off-season and died on February 18, 1998, at the Eisenhower Medical Center in Rancho Mirage, California. Caray left behind his third wife, Dolores "Dutchie" Goldmann, and five children. He had married Dutchie in 1975. Perhaps Caray's former broadcast pal Jack Buck summed up his legacy best. After Caray's death, Buck told the *St. Louis Post-Dispatch*: "Maybe there have been some better, who knows? But nobody was more unique."

Books

Caray, Harry (with Bob Verdi), *Holy Cow!*, Villard Books, New York, 1989.

Periodicals

Chicago Tribune, February 19, 1998.
St. Louis Post-Dispatch, February 19, 1998.
Saturday Evening Post, October 1989.
Sporting News, March 2, 1998. □

Graham Chapman

A member of the ground-breaking comedy troupe Monty Python's Flying Circus, Graham Chapman (1941–1989) contributed memorable characters and his zany sense of humor to its television series, *Monty Python's Flying Circus,* and feature films. Chapman played in two Monty Python films, *Monty Python's Holy Grail* and *Life of Brian.* Despite dying of cancer at the age of 48, Chapman's contribution to comedy was remembered into the 21st century.

AP Images/J. Langevin

Born January 8, 1941, in Leicester, England, Chapman was the son of a policeman. He was deeply impacted by an incident from his early childhood. Near the end of World War II, when Chapman was only three years old, he was at a park near his home with his mother when a plane flown by Polish airmen crashed near the area. Though his father was first on the crash site, Chapman and his mother came across body parts in the street and observed parts in trees as well. His father worked on putting the bodies together for body bags, and accused someone of stealing a missing head. The horror and absurdity of the experience remained with Chapman for the rest of his life.

Trained as a Doctor

Educated at Cambridge University and Barts (Medical College of St. Bartholomew's Hospital), Chapman received training to become a medical doctor and gained some of the necessary qualifications to practice. The call of comedy proved too strong, however. While still a student at Cambridge, Chapman joined the Cambridge Footlights performance troupe, which launched the careers of many British actors, comedians, and satirists. Chapman met his future writing partner and Monty Python cohort John Cleese when they were part of the Footlights.

By the mid-1960s, when Chapman was still studying at Barts, he and Cleese wrote sketches for British broadcaster David Frost for his show, *The Frost Report.* Chapman

and Cleese met other future members of Monty Python through the experience, including Terry Jones and Michael Palin. Also in this period, Chapman openly came out as homosexual, despite the homophobic nature of the British medical profession at the time. He came to understand his sexuality after a vacation in Ibiza in 1966, and began living with a partner, David Sherlock, who would remain with Graham until his death. Over the next year, Graham told many of his medical and comedy friends and colleagues.

Formed Monty Python

In 1968, Chapman, Cleese, Palin, and Jones formed the comedy team Monty Python's Flying Circus, along with Eric Idle and an American, Terry Gilliam, who was responsible for the animated portions of the troupe's output. The name the group chose was not intended to have any particular meaning. Monty Python was originally put together to develop a television show. The troupe's show, also called *Monty Python's Flying Circus,* debuted in October 1969 on the BBC and aired for the next five years.

Monty Python's Flying Circus was unique and popular, surreal and bizarre. Reflecting the madcap comedy obsessions of each of its members, critics regarded the humor therein as both sophisticated and ingenuous, simple yet irreverent. There were obsessions, fantasies, and nightmares explored in comic fashion. According to Constance L. Hays of the *New York Times,* Chapman once explained,

"The BBC didn't quite know what to do with us, and so they rather nervously gave us a free hand to create our own program."

For *Monty Python's Flying Circus,* Chapman devised some of the troupe's classic characters, such as the Colonel. A pompous army officer who spoke in a posh accent, the Colonel would appear in full uniform to end a sketch because it was deemed too silly. Chapman often played characters that were authority figures like officers, policeman, and business executives. He also was the originator of such skits as "Spam," in which the canned meat is the center of all meals and repeatedly said for comic effect, and "The Ministry of Silly Walks," a recurring bit of physical comedy involving the team's members demonstrating their most bizarre walks.

Of Chapman as a performer, Palin told Mark Edmonds of the London *Sunday Times,* "Graham could play serious characters like a bank manager and then subvert them from underneath. You put a moustache on him and peaked hat and he looked like a general. So he could get away with all these authority characters while having this extraordinary sense of the eccentric, which was really weird in a way."

Complicated Relationship with Cleese

Throughout the years of Monty Python's television show, Chapman continued to write and appear in many sketches with Cleese. Their relationship was quite complex, and had destructive elements. While Chapman was complicated, confused, and even, angst-ridden, he was also free-spirited and off-the-cuff in his comedy and writing methodology. In contrast, Cleese was controlling and precise. As a result, the pair had an intense dynamic, that could result in arguing about a single word in a sketch for days.

This volatile situation was further heightened by Chapman's alcoholism. During the years of *Monty Python's Flying Circus,* his drinking grew worse, relying on large amounts to leave home or to shoot scenes. This situation made filming with Chapman sometimes difficult, as he would regularly forget lines and be late for rehearsals and filmings. Chapman would later quit drinking cold turkey in 1983.

In December 1974, the last original episode of *Monty Python's Flying Circus* aired on British television. Earlier that year, however, Monty Python found a wider audience when Americans began seeing the show on public television stations after the Dallas outlet started airing early episodes. *Monty Python's Flying Circus* became a staple on many public television stations for many years.

Focused on Feature Films

After the end of production on *Monty Python's Flying Circus,* Chapman and the other members of Monty Python remained together and began creating new projects. They started focusing on feature films that continued to feature their off-kilter brand of comedy. For their first film, Chapman played the lead, Arthur, in *Monty Python and the Holy Grail,* a version of the legend of Arthur and the Knights of the Roundtable. The film was released in 1978.

More controversial was Monty Python's 1979 film, *Life of Brian.* It offered the Monty Python take on the story of Jesus

Christ. Chapman played Brian, who was often mistaken for Jesus. Because of the nature of *Life of Brian,* the film was criticized by many religious leaders, especially in the United States. It was even temporarily banned by a Georgia-based judge. Chapman dismissed criticisms by noting that he believed everyone's deity had a sense of humor.

In addition to films, Monty Python also performed live on occasion. In 1982, for example, they put on a series of sketches at the Hollywood Bowl in Los Angeles. The performances were filmed and released as a popular feature entitled *Monty Python Live at the Hollywood Bowl.*

The final Monty Python film, *Monty Python's Meaning of Life,* came out in 1983. This film offered a surreal perspective on each of the seven deadly sins, but was the least successful creatively and critically. Later that year, Monty Python decided to end their working relationship. For the next six years, Chapman pursued other projects, as did the other members of Monty Python.

Published a Memoir

Even before the end of Monty Python, Chapman had already been working on other outsdide projects, though nothing would match the success of Python or the chemistry he had with Cleese. Chapman published his autobiography, *A Liar's Autobiography,* in 1981, co-written with his partner Sherlock and others. Two years later, the screenplay Chapman wrote for *Yellowbeard* was produced and he had the starring role in the comedy. The story focused on a quest for treasure by pirates.

For much of the rest of the 1980s, Chapman worked on scripts for film and television. Though England was still considered his home, he spent much time working in New York City and Los Angeles. He lived in Los Angeles as a tax exile, to avoid the high taxes that came from living in England. In the late 1980s, Chapman played a crotchety knight in a British series, *Jake's Journey,* which also aired on CBS in 1988. In 1987, he had a long lecture tour in North America.

Died of Cancer

During this period, Monty Python's brand of comedy remained important and relevant to audiences in North America, Great Britain, and elsewhere. In September 1989, the members of Monty Python reunited for a television special in honor of the 20th anniversary of their first appearance on British television. Before the program could air, however, Chapman lost his life. A cancerous growth was found on his tonsils in August 1989, and it quickly spread. Later tests showed that cancer was also found on his spine. Chapman died of throat and spinal cancer at a hospital in Maidstone, England, on October 4, 1989, at the age of 48. Both Cleese and Palin were with Chapman when he died. He was survived by his long time partner, Sherlock, their adopted son, John Tomiczek, and a brother.

Monty Python had previously scheduled an anniversary party that was canceled when the seriousness of Chapman's illness was learned. The timing and irony were not lost on the surviving members of Monty Python. According to Leslie Shepherd of the Associated Press, Jones released a statement the following day which said, "Last night we were going to have our anniversary party to celebrate 20 years of Python. It was 20 years today since the first program went out. I think it's the worst case of party pooping I have ever come across. We will all miss him, we love him very much.'' Cleese delivered Chapman's eulogy, which was the first live eulogy ever to air on the BBC.

Remained Important After Death

Decades after Chapman's death, his legacy was not forgotten. In 2000, a play Graham wrote in the mid-1970s but never put on entitled *Oh Happy Day* received its debut in Atlanta. Featuring humor and situations in the vein of Monty Python, Cleese and Palin acted as advisors to the show. Three years later, Chapman's complicated relationship with Cleese was the subject of a play by Adrian Poynton, that was a hit at the Edinburgh Fringe Festival, and later put on at the Soho Theatre in London in 2004. The playwright played Chapman, while Tom Price portrayed Cleese. *A Very Naughty Boy— The Life of Graham Chapman* focused on 20 years in their relationship from 1969 until Chapman's death.

In 2013, the surviving members of Monty Python, save Idle, contributed voices to an animated film based on Chapman's memoir, *A Liar's Autobiography*. Chapman himself also contributed, in the form of recordings created when he did public readings of his autobiography. Like the book, the film did not flinch in looking at his alcoholism, the dark moments in his personal and professional lives, and the physical battles between the Pythons. The project was put together by Sherlock, and was directed by Bill Jones, son of Python Terry Jones, along with Jeff Simpson and Ben Timlett. It included numerous animated sequences contributed by 14 different animators. *A Liar's Autobiography* gained some critical notice for its unusual, but effective, style.

Amidst continued popular culture references to the greatness of Monty Python and the ongoing careers of its other members, Bill Jones told the *Jerusalem Post*, ''Part of the idea behind this film was just to remind people of Graham, and give him an opportunity to step back onto the spotlight, even though he's dead.'' Jones also stated to David Germain of the Associated Press, ''It's just an appreciation of his twisted humor. Not understanding who the man is or finding out any facts about the man's life, but getting a sense of him and getting at his feelings. I think we're just trying to show the sort of thing he enjoyed, because he is sort of the forgotten Python.''

Periodicals

Associated Press, October 5, 1989; October 31, 2012.
Associated Press State & Local Wire, September 17, 2000.
Independent (London, England), April 13, 2004.
Jerusalem Post, January 23, 2013.
Sunday Times (London, England), January 27, 2013.
Toronto Star, April 10, 1987.

Online

''Graham Chapman, 48, Comedy Troupe Founder,'' *New York Times*, http://www.nytimes.com/1989/10/05/obituaries/graham-chapman-48-comedy-troupe-founder.html (November 5, 2014). □

Glafcos Clerides

Greek Cypriot Glafcos Clerides (1919–2013) spent much of his career attempting to solve an intractable political stalemate on his Mediterranean island nation. A veteran legislator, human rights attorney, and diplomat, Clerides served two terms as president of the Republic of Cyprus but is best remembered for his 35-year dialogue with his Turk Cypriot counterpart, Rauf Denktash, to resolve the issue of a Cyprus divided into two antagonist republics.

Cyprus has been at the center of geopolitical drama for millennia. A strategically situated island in the eastern Mediterranean, Cyprus has been a valuable maritime stronghold for centuries. It was first settled by the ancient world's Mycenaean Greeks and later conquered by Alexander the Great; in subsequent epochs it came under Persian, Ottoman, and even Roman and Venetian rule. Turkish settlers arrived in the 16th century during the Ottoman period. In contrast to their Greek neighbors, who tend to adhere to the Eastern Orthodox faith, the newcomer Turkish Cypriots practiced Islam and remained wary of alliances with European powers. Religious and ethnic tensions abated only somewhat in the 1870s, when Cyprus came under British rule.

Captured by Germans

Glafcos Ioannou Clerides was born in Nicosia on April 24, 1919, to Ioannis "John" Clerides, a teacher who had gone on to a university education in London before World War I and later became mayor of Nicosia, the capital. Like his father, Clerides traveled to England for his education, and was caught there when World War II erupted in 1939. He joined the Royal Air Force and became a gunner on Wellington-model bomber planes. In July of 1942, one of those RAF aircraft was downed by German anti-aircraft weaponry, but Clerides was able to eject and parachute down near Hamburg. He spent nearly three years as a prisoner of war.

In 1945 Clerides returned to London at the war's end, and married a Mumbai-born performer named Lilla Erulkar. He earned his law degree from King's College, London, in 1948 and returned to Cyprus in 1951. The next decade would prove a troubled one for Cyprus, which remained in British hands. A Greek Cypriot guerrilla group known by the acronym EOKA (*Ethniki Organosis Kyprion Agoniston*, or National Organization of Cypriot Fighters) agitated for self-determination and *enosis*, or union with mainland Greece. EOKA launched a covert war in the spring of 1955 against British targets, and the British colonial officials' reaction was swift and brutal. As a trained lawyer fluent in both Greek and English, Clerides served as defense lawyer for EOKA members who were arrested and detained by British authorities.

Negotiated for Greek Cypriots

Cypriots of Turkish origin objected to the goal of union with Greece, while Britain balked at handing over the strategically located island with its naval and air bases.

Photoshot/Newscom

Turk Cypriots also raised the idea of a union of their own with mainland Turkey, to which nearly all sides objected strenuously. Finally, an arrangement was brokered in London in 1959 that would let Cyprus become an independent, dual-nationality state. Clerides served on the Greek Cypriot negotiating team at the London Conference that same year, and served as Minister of Justice in the postcolonial transition government. He also led a Greek Cypriot delegation in a newly formed constitutional committee. After all parties—including mainland Greece and Turkey—signed off on the arrangement, the newly independent Republic of Cyprus came into being on August 16, 1960. The first president of Cyprus was Archbishop Makarios III, a primate of the Greek Cypriot Orthodox Church. In elections that year, Clerides stood for and won a seat in the newly created national legislature. His peers elected him to serve as president of the House of Representatives, a job in which he remained for the next 16 years. In the early 1960s, he also served as head of the Cyprus Red Cross.

Internal problems with dual Greek Cypriot and Turk Cypriot rule surfaced early on. The minority Turk Cypriot community raised grievances over official discrimination and unofficial harassment in their residential sections of Nicosia and other cities. Sectarian violence flared in 1963, and the United Nations (UN) sent a small peacekeeping force to the island in 1964. Four years later, with the tensions still simmering, President Makarios asked Clerides to meet with the leader of the Turkish Cypriot

community, Rauf Denktash, whom Clerides had known since childhood. Like Clerides, Denktash was a London-educated lawyer and the two representatives began a series of talks that rolled into the 21st century.

Helmed Nation During Unrest

Both mainland Greece and mainland Turkey inserted themselves into the troubles on Cyprus. Greece had been under a military dictatorship since 1967, while Turkey veered back and forth between democratically elected governments and army-led coups. On July 15, 1974, a Greek Cypriot paramilitary force calling itself EOKA B staged a coup on Cyprus, forcing Makarios from office and into exile. A pro-enosis journalist and EOKA B leader named Nikos Sampson was installed as president, and a hastily forced union with mainland Greece became an imminent possibility. This, in turn, prompted Turkey to act and send an invasion force that landed on July 20, 1974. They seized roughly a third of the island and declared it the Turkish Republic of Northern Cyprus. A small-scale war raged for several days until Sampson was ousted on July 23 and UN peacekeeping forces set up a buffer zone around the Turkish-held section. Denktash—until recently the vice president under Makarios—became the first and longest-serving head of state of the Turkish Republic of Northern Cyprus, but because of the ongoing presence of mainland Turkish army troops, its legitimacy as a sovereign state was recognized only by Turkey.

As president of the House of Representatives, Clerides was constitutionally obligated to serve as acting president of the internationally recognized Republic of Cyprus in the absence of the president and vice president. Makarios remained in London for the next several months, seeking support to oust the Turkish military occupation on Cyprus, while Clerides held the office of president of the distressed nation during its most troubled five months.

UN officials, at a loss, finally partitioned the nation and established a sizable buffer zone around the northern sector. Thousands were forced to relocate: Turk Cypriots in the south unable to join family in the Turkish zone emigrated to Turkey, and Greek Cypriots whose lands and villages were in the northern or near the buffer zone were similarly forced to uproot. Clerides stepped down as acting president on December 7, 1974, when President Makarios returned to Nicosia. The entire debacle actually brought down the military dictatorship in Greece, and over the next two decades Clerides and other Greek Cypriot leaders worked to restore domestic stability and lure vital tourism dollars to its struggling economy. Over time, Cyprus became popular with European vacationers as an affordable alternative to the Greek islands, and later became an attractive place for offshore financial-service providers.

Sought High Office

In 1976 Clerides founded his own political party, *Demokratikos Synagermos,* or Democratic Rally, known by its acronym DISY. The new party failed to attract much voter support in its first appearance in a national election that same year, winning no seats in the national legislature, but gained some ground after the death, in office, of Makarios in 1977. Clerides's main rival for power was Spyros Kyprianou, head of the Democratic Party of Cyprus and his successor as president of the House of Representatives. Clerides entered the coming 1978 presidential race as the DISY candidate to challenge an incumbent Kyprianou. When Kyprianou's 19-year-old son was kidnapped by an extremist EOKA faction, Clerides bowed out of the race. Kyprianou announced his government's refusal to negotiate with the group, and the teenager was released four days later. Kyprianou won the 1978 election.

Clerides ran for president a second time in 1983 but lost to Kyprianou, who was elected to a second five-year term. In 1988, Clerides ran once again as the DISY candidate, losing this time to George Vasiliou of the United Democrat Party. Regarding the breakaway northern part of Cyprus—which remained an international pariah, sharing none of the economic gains of the larger, more prosperous Republic of Cyprus—Clerides had continued to meet with Denktash to resolve the situation since the 1974 crisis. At first, they negotiated pressing matters like prisoner exchanges in the aftermath of the brief coup, but the UN worked with both sides to arrange peace talks that would bring a permanent solution. In 1991 the UN Security Council urged both sides to begin negotiations for a single, federated island state, with no partition and no plans for union with either Greece or Turkey.

In February of 1993, a 73-year-old Clerides finally won election as president of Cyprus, beating Vasiliou by a narrow margin. There were modest hopes that a settlement with Northern Cyprus might finally be reached, but pro-Greek Cypriot sentiment remained strong. When Queen Elizabeth II visited the Republic of Cyprus later that year, her appearance sparked loud protests and even an attack on a parked Rolls-Royce she had recently exited. Further hopes for peace were dashed when Clerides, in one of his first moves as president, placed an order for 40 Russian-made anti-aircraft missiles. The arms purchase remained mired in controversy for several more years while Clerides defended his government's right to protect its sovereignty. "As there are 40,000 Turkish troops (in the north) we have the right to defend ourselves," he told Helena Smith in the *Guardian* in 1997. "These are very expensive toys and unless the Turkish air force attacks me, I'm not going to be firing them. To provoke Turkey I'd have to be ready for a lunatic asylum."

Made Historic Visit

Clerides and Denktash met again several times during his first term in office, in 1996 and 1997, but no agreement was reached. Clerides was reelected in 1998, and sought to end his second term with a successful flourish. He and Denktash, now 82 and 76 years old respectively, met in an abandoned house in the demilitarized zone in December of 2001 and agreed to meet elsewhere. Denktash even extended a surprise invitation, hosting Clerides for a dinner at the Denktash home in 2002—the first time a representative of the Republic of Cyprus had entered the Turkish rebel state since its creation in 1974. The goodwill gestures were merely symbolic, in the end: talks resumed, but no agreement was reached.

Clerides lost the 2003 presidential election to Tassos Papadopoulos, the candidate of a rightwing party known as DIKO. He retired to Larnaca, on the southeast coast, and died

in Nicosia on November 15, 2013, age 94. His wife had died in 2007, and his longtime friendly foe, Denktash, had died in early 2012. Clerides's daughter Katherine followed him into politics and was elected to the House of Representatives. Clerides's four-volume memoir *My Deposition* was published between 1988 and 1991. "Denktash...often quoted from it," the writer of Clerides's *New York Times* obituary, "saying it was a scrupulous record of events."

Periodicals

Guardian (London, England), January 8, 1996; April 7, 1997; November 19, 2013.
New York Times, January 16, 2002; November 16, 2013.
Sunday Times (London, England), June 8, 1975.□

Harold Clurman

American director, producer, theater critic, and author Harold Clurman (1901–1980) spent 56 significant years in theater. Beginning his career as an actor, he was the co-founder of the influential Group Theater in 1931, and became a respected theatrical director of such dramas as *Member of the Wedding*. Clurman also spent decades writing intellectual yet wry criticism for periodicals including *The Nation* and books on theatrical topics such as *On Directing* (1972).

Born September 18, 1901, in New York City, on the Lower East Side of Manhattan, he was the son of Samuel Clurman, a doctor. His father introduced Clurman to the theater, taking his son to see a production of *Uriel da Acosta* at a Yiddish theater in 1907. It starred one of the leading Yiddish actors of the era, Jacob Adler. The memorable experience ignited Clurman's passionate feeling about the theater.

Studied in Paris

Clurman initially attended Columbia University, but left when he was 20 years old to study in Paris. His roommate in Paris was Aaron Copeland, who would later gain fame as a composer. To complete his degree at the University of Paris, Clurman wrote his thesis on a theater topic, the history of French drama in the period from 1890 to 1914. While living in Paris, Clurman had a number of important cultural and theatrical experiences that influenced his future work. One such event was meeting Russian director Constantin Stanislavsky, who employed an ensemble approach with the Moscow Arts Theater's permanent company and developed effective training methods for actors.

In 1924, Clurman returned home to New York City. In the period from 1924 to 1931, he was an actor, play reader, and stage manager. Though he was untrained in acting, Clurman began his acting career as an extra in a 1924 production of Stark Young's *The Saint* at the Greenwich Village Theater. During this period, Clurman became

©Bettmann/Corbis

increasingly interested in theater and further clarified his vision of what he believed it could and should be.

Co-founded Group Theatre

In 1931, Clurman was an original co-founder of Group Theatre, along with Cheryl Crawford and Lee Strasberg. After a series of conversations with the performers, playwrights, and directors who would form its founding core, Group Theatre was conceived to have to a different tone and focus than the commercial theater of the era. The motivation of the members of Group Theater was examining real life in the 1930s, with the moral, spiritual, and energetic as key aspects of the vision for the company. Clurman and others were idealistic in what they believed Group Theater could be. As Group Theater member Robert Lewis told Kathleen Quinn of the *New York Times,* "No matter what anybody thought about the Group Theater and its actors and its methods and its plays, the fact remains that, once upon a time, 25 or so people got together and did something in the theater because they really believed in it. We don't have that anymore."

From the first, Group Theatre was a ground-breaking and trend-setting theater company, and profoundly impacted the American stage. In addition to its original tenor, the company launched the careers of such theater luminaries as actress Stella Adler (who would later come to fame as an acting teacher as well), actors Les Sanford Meisner and Franchot Tone, playwrights Clifford Odets, Irwin Shaw, and William Saroyan, and director Elia Kazan. Group Theatre also spread the use and influence of Stanislavsky's method for training actors.

Known as the Stanislavsky method or method acting, it included drawing on the internal and external resources available to the actor. Originally a way of training actors, the method became a way of interpretive acting in subsequent decades. In the *New York Times,* Quinn summarized, "By broadly disseminating the acting theories of Konstantin Stanislavsky in America, through its actor training programs, the Group created an ever-expanding pool of professionals that has dominated theater and film for more than five decades. And even more significantly, from 1931 to 1941 the Group Theater proved by example that American actors could live their lives as artists in the theater."

In all, Group Theatre had 23 productions on Broadway. Clurman directed several dramas for the company, including *Awake and Sing* and *Golden Boy.* Both were written by Odets, and became definitive productions of the 1930s. Another Clurman-directed production came in 1935, of Odets's *Paradise Lost* which Wendy Smith of the *New York Times Review of Books* called "subtly stylized, emotionally profound." From 1937 to 1941, Clurman served as the managing director of Group Theater as well.

Directed Films, Stage Works

In 1941, the Group Theater was forced to disband due to a lack of funding. For Clurman, his vision was incompletely realized despite the company's impact in subsequent decades. He moved on to new professional experiences. From 1941 to 1946, Clurman primarily worked in Hollywood. He was affiliated with studios such as 20th Century Fox, RKO, and Paramount, and directed one completed film, *Deadline at Dawn.* The screenplay was written by Odets and the film starred Susan Hayward. Clurman married Adler in 1943, but then the couple divorced in 1960. Clurman later married and divorced actress Juleen Compton.

When Clurman again focused on stage work in New York later in the decade, his career was a struggle. He directed four plays on Broadway, without any stand-out successes. Clurman was also a producer of *All My Sons,* written by Arthur Miller. In 1949, Clurman's directing career reached a peak after he read the play *Member of the Wedding,* penned by Southern playwright Carson McCullers. Though she was reluctant to let producer Robert Whitehead put together a production of *Member of the Wedding*—she did not believe it would make any money despite its strong themes and writing—she eventually relented and it was a huge success. A leading actress in the play, Julie Harris, became a star, and, in 1950, Clurman won the Donaldson Award, which honored the best director of the year, for his work on *Member of the Wedding.* In the *New York Times Review of Books,* Wendy Smith dubbed the Clurman-directed production "haunting."

Clurman continued to direct plays through 1969, primarily on Broadway, though some productions were elsewhere. He directed productions of plays by leading playwrights, such as Miller, Jean Anouilh, Tennessee Williams, and Eugene O'Neill. Clurman's last work as a director came in Los Angeles, where he directed a staging of Anton Chekhov's

Uncle Vanya at the Center Theater Group. Over the course of his career, Clurman directed 40 stage productions in all. Esteemed theater critic Walter Kerr wrote of Clurman as a director in the *New York Times*, stating "To me, he was Broadway's best invisible director because he permitted the author's work to absorb his powers and his personality so entirely. Lost not in the clouds, but in another man's creation."

Became Respected Critic

The same year he directed *Member of the Wedding*, Clurman launched a new phase of his theatrical career. From 1949 to 1952, he served as a theater critic for the periodical, *The New Republic*. In 1953, Clurman began serving as the critic for another magazine, *The Nation*, to which he would contribute reviews and other pieces until his death. Over the years, Clurman's criticism and articles would appear in other periodicals such as the *New York Times*.

As a critic, Clurman took a unique perspective. He was known for placing stage works in an intellectual and historical context, yet he was also forward thinking in embracing stage productions that were different from his personal interests. That said, Clurman was not considered an elitist in his tastes, though he could be pithy in his words. Respected for not overly judging plays, Clurman did not offer undue praise or condemnation. While his assessments could be curt, he did not respond negatively or pile on harsh words for problematic plays. At the same time, he rarely used the term "great" except for extremely strong productions deserving the honor. As a critic, then, Clurman was careful in his choice of words, though he was sometimes criticized by others for what they preserved as his lack of objectivity.

According to Mel Gussow of the *New York Times*, Clurman once explained his distinctly informed perspective. Clurman said, "The fact that I am engaged in active stage work does not render me either timid and indulgent or resentful, malicious and vindictive. It makes me scrupulous and responsible." In the *New York Times Review of Books*, Smith added, "Clurman was not a snob in his reviews—he loved a good variety show and raved over the 1960 *Ice Capades*—but theater as entertainment engaged him only marginally. He was primarily interested in a playwright's ideas and how well a production conveyed them."

Published Numerous Books

In the 1950s, as his criticism career was developing, Clurman also wrote book-length works. In 1950, Clurman published the book he had been working on for much of the 1940s, *The Fervent Years: The Group Theatre and the Thirties.* This book provided a history and analysis of the Group Theatre and its importance. Though other books on Group Theatre would follow, Clurman's *The Fervent Years* became the definitive history of the company.

During the 1970s, as Clurman essentially left his directing career behind, he focused more time on writing and publishing books related to theater. One of his most important works was *On Directing*, published in 1972 and influential among theater students for years after its release. In 1974, Clurman published both a book of his essays, *The Divine Pastime*, and his autobiography, *All People Are Famous.* Four

years later, Clurman put out a thoughtful, analytical book on the major Norwegian playwright, director, and poet Henrik Ibsen with *Ibsen*. In the last four years of his life, Clurman had been writing a significant critical study of playwright Eugene O'Neill, which was not completed at his death.

Also in the 1970s, Clurman began teaching and sharing his knowledge of theater with college students. Beginning in about 1970, he annually taught a class on playwriting at Hunter College in New York City. Clurman also taught summer classes related to theater at the University of California at Los Angeles and University of California Berkeley.

Revered After Death

Ill for the last few years of his life, Clurman died of cancer at Mount Sinai Hospital in New York City on September 9, 1980. He was 78 years old. Revered even before his death, he had an off-Broadway theater named after him, the Harold Clurman Theater. Still respected and influential into the 21st century, the first Harold Clurman Festival of the Arts was held in New York City in 2006.

In Clurman's obituary in the *New York Times*, John Corry summarized Clurman's importance and appeal. Corry wrote, "In life, Clurman assumed the roles of advocate and champion, a civilized man constantly in search of the best. Not only did he produce and direct and teach, he also wrote at length, and by the end of his life, perhaps without even thinking about it, he had become his own best creation. He was a link to the theater's past and, until his death, a force in its present. In a career of 56 years, without ever being faddish, he somehow was always new."

Periodicals

Associated Press, September 9, 1980.
Back Stage East, May 18, 2006.
New York Times, September 10, 1980; June 25, 1989; November 19, 1990; April 6, 1994.
New York Times Book Review, April 10, 1994.

Online

"Harold Clurman: About Harold Clurman," *PBS: American Masters*, http://www.pbs.org/wnet/americanmasters/episodes/harold-clurman/about-harold-clurman/557/ (December 9, 2014). □

Mickey Cochrane

American Baseball Hall of Famer Mickey Cochrane (1903–1962) is widely considered one of the best catchers of all time and certainly the best of his era. The hard-hitting receiver played in five World Series, winning two with the Philadelphia Athletics (1929 and 1930) and one with the Detroit Tigers (1935), the latter as a player-manager. Cochrane's career on-base percentage of .419 remains in the top 20 of all players of all time.

The Conlon Collection/Getty Images

Gordon Stanley "Mickey" Cochrane was born April 6, 1903, in Bridgewater, Massachusetts, to parents of Scotch-Irish descent. His father, John Cochrane, worked as a coachman and caretaker for a family of wealthy Boston socialites. One of seven children, Cochrane grew up playing ball with his siblings. One brother, Archie, also played semi-professional baseball. As a child, Cochrane had to hoe the potato patch as one of his chores but often stole away from the field and headed for the town's sandlot to play baseball with his pals. When Cochrane got caught, he got a licking, but he kept risking it because he loved to play ball.

Admired as Multi-Sport Standout

Cochrane graduated from Bridgewater High School in 1920 and headed to Boston University, where he starred as an offensive back on the football team, played third base and outfield on the baseball team and contributed to the success of the basketball team. He also found time for track and boxing. In 1921, Cochrane punted a 53-yard field goal, which stood as a university record for more than six decades. During his college years, Cochrane brushed shoulders with professional baseball players because many teams stayed at the nearby Hotel Brunswick when playing the Red Sox. Seeing them inspired Cochrane to pursue the sport, though most biographical accounts of Cochrane's life note baseball as his weakest sport.

In 1923, Cochrane joined a Dover, Delaware-based minor league team. He was disappointed to discover the team already had a favorite third baseman, so Cochrane started catching to earn playing time. In 1924, Cochrane left college and made his debut with the Portland Beavers in the Pacific Coast League. He spent one season there, smacking 100 hits in 99 games to end the year with a .333 batting average. Philadelphia Athletics owner/manager Connie Mack quickly added Cochrane to the Athletics' roster, where he made his major league debut at age 22.

Joined Philadelphia A's

Cochrane reported to the Philadelphia A's in 1925 but once again found no starting position open. The team already had Jimmie Dykes at third and Cy Perkins as catcher. Perkins took the young rookie under his wing and taught Cochrane how to handle different pitchers. With the help of his steady bat, Cochrane soon took the job from Perkins, who was relegated to back-up catcher. Cochrane caught more than 100 games his rookie season and hit .331. Cochrane threw with his right hand but batted as a lefty. In his rookie year, Cochrane became the first catcher in baseball history to hit three homers in one game.

While the batting came easily, Cochrane had a lot to learn behind the plate. His first year in the majors, Cochrane caught a motley crue of pitchers, including the wild rookie southpaw Lefty Grove and knuckle-baller Ed Rommel, whose pitches came over the plate from every angle. Cochrane also handled the cutting curveballs of George Earnshaw and Rube Walberg. For Cochrane, it was trial by fire as he learned to perfect the position. Initially, Cochrane caught batting practice every day to help learn the fundamentals.

Partway through the 1926 season, Cochrane was put out of commission after one of Grove's fastballs hit his throwing hand. The injury inspired Cochrane to perfect the one-handed catching technique later made famous by Johnny Bench. Cochrane protected the fingers on his throwing arm by making his hand into a fist when taking delivery of the ball, opening his hand only after the ball was in the glove. Cochrane also became adept at calling the game and was one of the first catchers to study opposing batters to learn their weaknesses. Before Cochrane joined the Athletics, Mack called all pitches from the bench. Cochrane, however, displayed a knack for plotting pitching strategies, prompting Mack to relinquish the job of calling pitches. In this way, Cochrane became a prototype for the modern catcher.

A tenacious catcher, Cochrane played the game with a fiery competitive spirit, earning the nickname "Black Mike" for his gritty nature. Cochrane was especially rough with his pitchers and was known to stomp out to the mound and punch or kick Walberg when his pitching flagged. Cochrane used different approaches with each pitcher. With Grove, he spewed insults to get the pitcher's blood pumping. This would cause Grove to get angry and fire the ball harder, in an attempt to hurt Cochrane. As Grove noted in Charles Bevis's book *Mickey Cochrane: The Life of a Baseball Hall of Fame Catcher.* "Sometimes I was a lot madder at Cochrane than I was at the hitters." The technique worked, although sometimes their mound confrontations got so heated teammates had to separate the two.

Cochrane's determination inspired his teammates to fight harder, as did his dugout rants, unleashed when he thought his teammates were giving up on a game. During the 1928 season, as it looked like the Yankees would pull away to win the division, Cochrane inspired his team to play harder. During a streak from mid-July to mid-August, the Athletics won 17 of 18 games. In the end, the Athletics finished second and lost the pennant race to the Yankees, though Cochrane provided inspiration down the home stretch in a run to unseat the Yankees. For his motivation and encouragement, Cochrane won the American League's 1928 Most Valuable Player award. During the off-season that year, Cochrane picked up his saxophone and hit the vaudeville circuit, telling jokes and playing "Take Me Out to the Ballgame" before crowds in Boston, New York, Brooklyn and Philadelphia.

Enjoyed Postseason Success

In 1929, the Athletics' momentum proved unstoppable. Cochrane hit .331 and smacked in 95 RBIs. His defense was also spectacular as he made just 13 errors in 749 defensive plays. The Athletics won the pennant and beat the Chicago Cubs in the World Series. Cochrane hit .400 in the series. The Athletics won the pennant again in 1930, boosted by Cochrane's career-high .357 batting average. They faced the St. Louis Cardinals in the World Series, and Cochrane got the matchup rolling by smacking a home run in the series opener, then followed with another homer the next day. The Athletics won the World Series four games to two as Cochrane guided pitchers Grove and Earnshaw to two wins apiece.

In 1931, the Athletics won the pennant for the third straight year. Cochrane batted .349 that season and hit 17 homers. This time, the A's could not surmount the Cardinals and lost the World Series four games to three. The Athletics played well again in 1932. Cochrane crossed home plate 118 times and drove in 112 RBIs to become the first Major League baseball catcher to score 100 runs and produce 100 RBIs in a single season. Nonetheless, the Athletics finished second to the Yankees.

During the 1933 season, Cochrane hit for the cycle (a single, double, triple, and home run) during an August game against the Yankees. He had also accomplished the feat the season before. Trouble was brewing, however. With the Depression in full swing, the crowds at Shibe Park grew smaller. Mack was forced to trim the budget to stay afloat, and traded Cochrane to the Detroit Tigers.

Landed in Detroit

Cochrane joined the Detroit Tigers in 1934 as manager and catcher and promptly inspired the young team to greatness. In 1934, the Tigers won 101 games and lost only 53—a record that stood 80 years later as a franchise-best winning percentage. That season, Cochrane batted .320 to lead the Tigers to the pennant for the first time since 1909. The Tigers faced the Cardinals in a brutal World Series that went seven games, with the Cardinals coming out on top.

Cochrane endured a spike wound in the third game that sent him to the hospital and was also flattened at the plate during a subsequent game. He was hospitalized in both St. Louis and Detroit but refused to stop playing.

The 1935 season started out rough, with the Tigers in last place as of April. The team fought back to win the pennant and faced the Cubs in the World Series. As player and manager, Cochrane led his team to victory. In game six, with the score tied 3-3 in the bottom of the ninth, Cochrane got on base and was driven home to score the winning run, securing the first World Series title in the Detroit club's history. Cochrane was carted off the field by fans and teammates, becoming a well-loved hometown hero.

When Cochrane landed in Detroit, the city was in trouble because the Depression had caused the automobile industry to collapse and the city's banks to fold. The people of Detroit needed a hero to believe in, and Cochrane assumed the role. As *Time* magazine reported in 1935: "Mickey Cochrane's arrival in Detroit coincided roughly with the revival of the automobile industry and the first signs of revived prosperity. His determined, jolly New England-Irish face grinning from front pages soon came to represent, not only to baseball fans but to all civic-minded citizens, the picture of what a dynamic Detroiter ought to look like." In 1935, season attendance at the Tigers' games was double 1933's figures. Detroit factories broadcast the Tigers' games as inspiration for workers. Cochrane was so popular that at one point he employed a secretary to help answer his fan mail as he received some 200 letters a week.

Faced Tough Times

In 1936, Cochrane became player, manager, and general manager of the Tigers. Besides the job stress, he was worried about his finances because he had co-signed loans for teammates after the stock market crash and now found himself in serious debt. Partway through the season, he suffered a nervous breakdown and had to quit playing. In 1936, he appeared in just 44 games, compared to the previous 11 seasons where he played more than 110 games a year.

The 34-year-old Cochrane returned in 1937. He started the season in good form, batting .306 in his first 27 games. Then, on May 25, Yankee hurler Bump Hadley beaned Cochrane in the head, fracturing his skull. These were the days before helmets, and Cochrane lay in a coma for 10 days. Many speculated that the beaning was intentional, as Cochrane had homered in his previous at-bat. Whatever the case, Cochrane never took the field again and was fired from his position as Detroit manager partway through the 1938 season. Cochrane's managerial record was impressive. During his time in Detroit, he managed the team to 348 wins and 250 losses, as well as two pennants and one World Series win.

In 1942, as World War II erupted, Cochrane enlisted in the U.S. Navy and was sent to the Great Lakes Naval Training Base as an athletic coach. Discharged in 1945, he found work as a scout and coach. In 1947, he was voted into the Baseball Hall of Fame. Cochrane played only 13 seasons, but made the most of them. He caught 110 or more games 11 years in a row, hit over .300 nine times and scored 100-plus runs in four different seasons. In addition, he played in five World Series over seven years, winning three.

In 1961, the Tigers made Cochrane a vice president but the job did not last long, as the heavy-smoking Cochrane was diagnosed with a cancerous tumor and died on June 28, 1962, in Lake Forest, Illinois. Survivors included his wife, Mary, and two daughters. His son, Gordon Jr., had died in battle during World War II. For Cochrane, there was no greater joy in life than baseball. As noted by Al Hirschberg in *Baseball's Greatest Catchers,* one of Cochrane's friends said this after his passing: "It was only mortal death. Mickey really died the day he got hit in the head. If it hadn't been for that he'd still be fighting for ball games and pennants."

Books

Bevis, Charles, *Mickey Cochrane: The Life of a Baseball Hall of Fame Catcher,* McFarland & Co., 1998.

Hirshberg, Al, *Baseball's Greatest Catchers,* G.P. Putnam's Sons, 1966.

Laird, A.W., *Ranking Baseball's Elite: An Analysis Derived from Player Statistics, 1893-1987,* McFarland & Co., 1990.

Periodicals

Collier's, August 16, 1930.

Time, October 7, 1935.

Online

"Mickey Cochrane," *Baseball-Reference.com,* http://www.baseball-reference.com/players/c/cochrmi01.shtml (November 7, 2014). □

AP Images

Willis Conover

As the host of "Music USA" on the Voice of America radio station, U.S. radio broadcaster Willis Conover (1920–1996) served as a worldwide ambassador for jazz, spreading the jazz message of musical freedom to the far corners of the globe. Conover spent four decades hosting and producing the show. He was scarcely heard in the United States, yet gained millions of fans overseas, particularly in Eastern European countries where jazz was banned during the Cold War.

Despite being a non-musician, Conover had an incredible influence on musicians around the world. Conover believed in the power of jazz and thought listeners were drawn to the genre because it exuded an air of freedom. Speaking to *New York Times Magazine* writer John S. Wilson, Conover once speculated on his program's popularity, putting it this way: "Jazz is a cross between total discipline and anarchy. The musicians agree on tempo, key and chord structure but beyond this everyone is free to express himself. This is jazz. And this is America. That's what gives this music validity. It's a musical reflection of the way things happen in America. We're not apt to recognize this over here but people in other countries can feel this element of freedom. They love jazz because they love freedom."

Raised in Military Family

Willis Clark Conover, Jr., was born December 18, 1920, in Buffalo, New York, to Willis Clark Conover Sr. and Frances Estelle (Harris) Conover. The elder Conover served in both the U.S. Navy and Army and earned decorations for combat during World War I, then made a life in the military. The family moved from base to base, leaving Conover little chance to put down roots. He attended more than 20 schools before graduating from high school. To entertain himself—and escape his circumstances—Conover spent his time reading. Conover's father wanted him to attend The Citadel and pursue a career in the military. Conover, however, had other ideas. He was more interested in the expressive arts.

As a teen, Conover had taken an interest in *Weird Tales,* a popular fantasy/horror pulp magazine. He wrote letters to the publication and began corresponding with other fans of "weird" fiction. At age 16, Conover published his own fanzine, titled *Science-Fantasy Correspondent.* Horror fiction writer H.P. Lovecraft submitted work to Conover's zine and the two began corresponding. After Lovecraft's death in 1937, Conover ceased his publication, but continued as an associate editor for *Fantascience Digest.* Later in life, Conover published a book of letters between himself and Lovecraft, titled *Lovecraft At Last* (1975).

Conover attended Maryland State Teachers College in Salisbury from 1938–39. He took an interest in acting and played the role of Edgar Allan Poe at a college production of *Plumes in the Dust* and later appeared in a production of Oscar Wilde's *The Importance of Being Ernest*. In 1939, Conover landed a part-time job at WSAL-AM in Salisbury. He entered an amateur announcer contest and won with his sonorous baritone voice. This led to a job offer at WTBO-AM in Cumberland, Maryland. Conover's job at WTBO was to keep the turntable rolling and the records spinning for the airwaves. He also read news broadcasts, prepared music programs and conducted interviews. At the station, Conover came across "Cherokee," a jazz hit by sax-playing bandleader Charlie Barnet. The discovery led Conover to the record store, where he purchased similar jazz albums and began his lifelong pursuit of collecting jazz music.

Became Jazz Concert Promoter

In 1942, Conover was drafted into the army after the United States joined World War II. During his induction examination, Conover mentioned his radio skills and was appointed a technical sergeant. In this role, Conover was responsible for interviewing new recruits at Fort Meade, Maryland, and never left U.S. soil during his wartime service. This allowed him to continue his explorations of jazz. In 1944, Conover began hosting a weekend jazz show on WWDC-AM. After his discharge in early 1946, Conover started at the station full-time. Conover preferred to call himself a program conductor instead of radio announcer or disc jockey.

With his interest in jazz, Conover became a concert promoter. In this capacity, he got involved with efforts to break down racial barriers related to jazz. After organizing a concert, Conover would escort the black musicians to the event nightclub and insist they be let inside. At the time, many Washington-area clubs were segregated. During the late 1940s and early '50s, Conover arranged "House of Sounds" shows at Washington's Howard Theater.

Conover was upset because black musicians were not allowed to play at the Capitol Theater, so he put together shows at midnight on Saturdays at the Howard Theater so no one would be left out. For instance, when jazz clarinetist Woody Herman, who was white, played at the Capitol, he had to replace his lead trumpeter because the man was black. By arranging shows at the Howard, Conover offered a chance for the full band to play together. For other black musicians, playing at the Howard afforded them the opportunity to play a large venue in the capital city. Conover brought in Miles Davis, Roy Eldridge, Coleman Hawkins, Stan Getz, Thelonious Monk, Charlie Parker, and Buddy Rich. Conover was always present at the events to introduce the artists and forged lifelong friendships with many of them. In 1949, he presented Duke Ellington's first formal concert in Washington, D.C. Ellington had previously played only dances in the area.

With all of his involvement and connections, Conover soon rose to acclaim in U.S. jazz circles. In 1950, he was elected president of the Hot Jazz Society of Washington, D.C. In 1951, he became master of ceremonies for the Newport Jazz Festival and served in that role for more than a decade. During the early 1950s, he helped with the startup of THE Orchestra, a Big Band outfit that was able to attract high-class guest musicians like Lester Young and Charlie Parker.

Earned Voice of America Job

Conover continued his radio show on WWDC but longed for a freer format than commercial radio allowed. He got his break in 1954 when the U.S. Information Agency was looking for broadcasters for its Voice of America (VOA) radio station. Conover applied and was hired as an independent contractor to produce a jazz show for the VOA. The VOA was launched by the U.S. government in 1942 to promote international goodwill and act as a counterforce to Nazi propaganda by providing news and commentary to foreign nations through shortwave radio. During World War II, the VOA served as a foreign policy tool. The VOA began aiming its broadcasts at the Soviet Union around 1947 and continued through the Cold War, employing broadcasters who spoke the native languages of the countries under Communist rule. The programs were intended to combat Soviet propaganda by offering an outside voice to listeners who were shielded from world events by state-censored news agencies. The VOA also promoted, and defended, U.S. policies.

Conover taped his first *Music USA* show for the VOA in December 1954. His commercial-free, two-hour show opened with 15 minutes of news, followed by 45 minutes of popular music. At the top of the next hour, he broadcast 15 minutes of news, followed by 45 minutes of jazz. Conover's first show was broadcast on January 6, 1955. The jazz segment proved highly popular. He chose Ellington's "Take the 'A' Train" as his theme song. Once the program went on the air, it quickly touched a nerve with overseas listeners. Knowing most of them did not speak English, Conover took a slow, highly enunciated approach to his announcing. He modeled his cheery style on former President Franklin D. Roosevelt's weekly "Fireside Chat" radio series.

On the show, Conover played music strictly from his own personal music library of LPs and 78 RPM sound recordings. Conover had 60,000 selections in his collection. He taped the programs in advance and self-produced the show. He once told *World Monitor*'s David Burns that his approach was pretty straightforward: "My formula is simply to play the best music. I don't sell America, which is not for sale. Nor do I sell jazz: The music speaks for itself. I see myself as a kind of messenger. I visualize just one listener, an intelligent person listening carefully, not some crowd out in 'radio land.'"

During the four decades Conover hosted the show, he never used a substitute host. If Conover had to be out of town, he pre-taped the shows or mixed new material with repeats from previous broadcasts. Conover's studio was located at the U.S. Department of Health, Education and Welfare building in Washington, D.C. He kept some 400 music "staples" there—music he turned to frequently, like Louis Armstrong, Ellington and Parker. While Conover carefully selected the music for each show beforehand, he did not select the sequence. Once he began taping, he tried to get in the flow of the moment and play what seemed to fit next.

Conover's show ran six nights a week. He frequently played music by Armstrong, Irving Berlin, John Coltrane,

Ella Fitzgerald, and Dizzy Gillespie, and many of those musicians joined him on the air for interviews. In this way, he introduced jazz music to millions of listeners who lived in countries where jazz had been deemed "subversive" and thus forbidden. Through his shows, Conover planted seeds of promise and possibility. There were many musicians worldwide who taped his show so they could study the music and replicate it themselves. The *New York Times* reported that at one point, Conover had 30 million listeners in Eastern Europe (particularly the Soviet Union) and some 100 million listeners worldwide. Undoubtedly, he had the largest audience of any international broadcast in production.

Known as Worldwide Jazz Ambassador

While Conover's show was not heard in the United States, his presence was felt on the stage. During his lifetime, Conover established jazz programs at the White House, the Smithsonian and the Kennedy Center for the Performing Arts. He narrated concerts at those venues, as well as at Carnegie Hall. In 1969, he put together a White House tribute concert for Ellington's 70th birthday, which found Ellington a guest of then-President Richard Nixon. Conover also helped establish international jazz festivals around the world. In 1959, he visited Warsaw for a jazz festival and was greeted at the airport by a throng of 500 fans. He was well-loved by listeners. According to the book *Friends Along the Way: A Journey Through Jazz*, author Gene Lees noted that Conover once received a letter from a young Russian that read: "You are a source of strength when I am overwhelmed by pessimism, my dear idol." At home, though, some members of Congress were leery about providing funding for Conover's program, thinking jazz frivolous and worrying that it focused on the wrong element of U.S. culture.

Conover produced 20,000 broadcasts during his VOA career. He was noted for being one of the most famous Americans no American had ever heard of. Federal regulations prohibited the VOA to broadcast within U.S. borders, so Conover remained virtually unknown in the United States, though he was a household name overseas in Europe, Asia and Latin America. In 1983, then-President Ronald Reagan formally recognized Conover for his contributions by awarding Conover a presidential citation.

Conover was still taping shows when he died on May 17, 1996, at a hospital in Arlington, Virginia. A lifelong smoker, he succumbed to lung cancer. He left no survivors, though he married five times. Conover was cremated and his ashes were interred at Arlington National Cemetery.

Books

Lees, Gene, *Friends Along the Way: A Journey Through Jazz,* Yale University Press, 2003.

Periodicals

New York Times Magazine, September 13, 1959.
Washington Post, May 20, 1996.
World Monitor, February 1993. □

Martha Coston

American inventor Martha Coston (c. 1828–1904) doggedly pursued her late husband's idea for a chemical-based signal flare for use at sea. In the years just before the American Civil War, Coston taught herself chemistry, pyrotechnics, and the art of procuring lucrative government-defense contracts. Her patented Coston signal flare was widely used in the decades before the development of ship-to-shore radios and other types of electronic maritime communication.

Martha Coston was a young bride and came from a family already struggling financially after the death of her own father. In her later years she penned a autobiography published in 1886 as *A Signal Success: The Work and Travels of Mrs. Martha J. Coston* which reveals an author somewhat unhealthily preoccupied with job titles, financial success, and self-congratulatory remarks. Its pages gloss over some crucial details, such as the date and place of her birth and the exact date of her marriage. She was born either in New York City or Baltimore, Maryland, around 1828 or perhaps earlier. Her mother was from Baltimore and widowed when Coston was still quite young.

Became Teen Mom

By the early 1840s the family was living in Philadelphia, where Coston's mother Rebecca sought suitable husbands for Coston's two sisters, whom she calls her half-sisters in her memoir. At age 14 Coston met 19-year-old Benjamin Franklin Coston, a brilliant inventor-engineer from the Boston area. Her mother thought the young chemistry whiz with enticing career prospects would be a better match for one of her older daughters, who apparently treated Coston with contempt. In *A Signal Success* Coston reports that Benjamin began helping her with her homework and the two fell in love, carrying on a clandestine courtship before her sixteenth birthday. She claims they were secretly wed in Philadelphia after Coston turned 16, an act they initially attempted to conceal from her mother.

Little information about the young inventor and pyrotechnic aficionado Benjamin Franklin Coston survives outside of his widow's 1886 memoir. An 1845 publication from the Franklin Institute of the State of Pennsylvania for the Promotion of the Mechanic Arts in Philadelphia mentions his application for a patent "For Improvements in the Apparatus for Generating, Condensing, and Burning Gas for Oil, Resin, or Coal." Around the same year of his marriage he was hired at the laboratory of the Navy Yard in Washington, D.C.—a potential career move that Coston claimed to have prompted the soon-to-be-separated pair to marry. If they wed in the spring after she turned 16, the vows were spoken in 1844. Benjamin Coston died in late 1848, and Coston notes that she had given birth to four children by then.

A Signal Success devotes several pages recounting the excitement of Washington's social scene and how well-liked both she and her husband were—except by those who were jealous, or attempted to undermine his Navy Yard career. Coston's husband was a civilian employee of the U.S. War Department's Bureau of Ordnance and Hydrography and was said to have worked on the rocket propellant developed by British inventor William Hale and used in the Mexican-American War of 1846–48. According to *A Signal Success* Benjamin also worked on a cannon percussion primer for the U.S. military but there was some strife over patent ownership. Another source reports that Coston's husband devised a new scheme for lighthouse illumination that was tested at the Christiana River Station in Delaware. His plans involved having the lighthouse operator mix his own gas concoction in a separate building to keep an effective, long-distance beacon lamp lit, but this method proved impractical.

Moved to Boston

As Coston reports, her husband quit the Navy Yard laboratory job after a promised elevation to officer's rank and raise in his salary failed to materialize. She also notes that he began to suffer health issues, which were likely the result of exposure to hazardous chemicals in the laboratory. Around 1847 the couple moved to Boston when he was offered a job with the Boston Gas Company, a position that had some ties to an invention he offered for improvements in sylvic gas lamps. At the time of their move, Coston reported that she had three young sons and was pregnant with a fourth child. On a business trip to Washington her husband became ill and broke his journey at Philadelphia to enter a hospital there with a high fever. She hurried there to care for him, but he died on November 24, 1848. Coston eventually decided to stay in the city to be close to her mother, and the stress of the tragedy was compounded by the death of her youngest son, an infant she had named Edward.

When her mother became ill and died, 21-year-old Coston realized she was penniless. In her memoir she blames business associates of her husband's plus family members who, she claimed, likely swindled her out of assets. During his fatal illness her husband had suggested she look in his study for files he kept about potential new inventions. She found the locked trunk, opened it, and found "numerous packets carefully sealed and labelled. One by one I lifted them out, only to be told by the title of the contents of unfinished inventions, inventions too costly to be utilized, and successful experiments in chemistry to be used in different branches of pyrotechnics," as she wrote in her memoir. One of them was an idea for a waterproof chemical signal flare, which used various oxide elements to burn in red, white, or other combinations that could be seen from a distance at night.

Mariners and coastal-living peoples had used various navigational lighting methods for centuries. Ancient Greeks and Romans built enormous hilltop lighthouse towers that were lit by fire. Oil lamps were later used, but as maritime commerce increased in the seventeenth and eighteenth centuries, so did marine disasters and shipwrecks. Ship captains and harbor-pilot professionals required more complex aids that were both waterproof and visible in poor weather or at night. The British were navigation-apparatus pioneers and one famous enthusiast was Captain Frederick Marryat, who developed a system of brightly colored flags in blue, white, red, and yellow, each of which specified a number from zero to nine. Marryat wrote a code book in which commonly used phrases were denoted by specific four-number combinations. The flags could be displayed and their messages deciphered by trained teams on board or on land.

Vanquished Long List of Naysayers

Around 1840 Coston's husband had first experimented with a chemical-tinted flare device that would deploy the standard colors in the Marryat system. His idea had the advantage of being much more visible at night and in adverse weather conditions than flags. He apparently made some prototype flares at the Washington Navy Yard and one of the first challenges Coston faced in starting her company was to retrieve these early devices from her late husband's former job site. Her book hints at a long list of stratagems she deployed in launching a company, including threats and subterfuge, but more often than not Coston displays a steely persistence.

Coston spent most of the 1850s persuading investors, government officials, and chemists to work with her on her late husband's idea. During these years her second son died, leaving her with two growing sons to support, but those surviving boys proved themselves to be earnest allies in their mother's business plans at a young age. Eventually Coston came up with a method of producing a red-colored flare light and a second one that burned white, but she needed a third chemical-supplied color to complete her husband's original adaptation of the Marryat code system. Hoping to create a patriotic-themed blue flare that would give her invention some public-relations sizzle, she tried various chemicals combinations to yield a consistent cerulean-tint light, without success. In August of 1858, in New York City to witness a fireworks event commemorating the transmission of the first successful telegraph message via a recently built transatlantic cable line, Coston thought that pyrotechnicians might provide some insight into producing a blue flare. She began writing them under a male alias. Eventually one of them helped her come up with a stable formula that burned green, and Coston duly filed her patent application.

One of Coston's most crucial allies was U.S. Secretary of the Navy Isaac Toucey, a former governor of Connecticut who served in President James Buchanan's cabinet from 1857 to 1861. Toucey encouraged her to pursue the signal-flare project and promised technical support and a reimbursement of her costs if the patent was approved. It was granted on April 5, 1859, and Coston gave her late husband the proper credit as originator of U.S. Patent No. 23,536, for "Pyrotechnic Night Signals." Toucey fulfilled his pledge and set up the procurement process, putting 3,000 signal cartridges aboard various U.S. Navy vessels for field testing. They worked uniformly well and the Naval Board of Examiners recommended that Coston be paid $20,000 for her work.

Business Remained in Family

Coston initially outsourced the manufacturing of what became known as the Coston signals, which were enthusiastically adopted for use by Union Army warship commanders during the American Civil War. The flares gave the North some technical advantage over Confederate navy ships and ended ruinous nighttime enemy missions in major port cities. They helped the Union side maintain a crucial blockade of maritime shipping to and from the South—preventing cotton exports and essentially starving the Southern states, which were economically reliant on the crop's enormous profit margins overseas—and were also used to keep key Union-held posts on Mississippi River. Once the war ended, the flares proved to be superb rescue aids for wrecks and other maritime disasters. Commissioners of the U.S. Life-Saving Service, the forerunner of the U.S. Coast Guard, suggested they be included as mandatory equipment aboard all ships.

In 1873 Coston petitioned the U.S. Patent committee for an extension on her original 14-year exclusivity deal, and she continued to make improvements in the manufacture and ignition processes of the Coston signal flare, as the device was called. By then her two sons had entered the field, too. William became president of the Coston Signal Company and his brother Henry developed a type of aerial projectile flare during his long service record in the U.S. Marine Corps.

Coston outlived both of her sons. Henry died in 1896 at age 50, leaving a widow Ella whose name turns up a few years later as the recipient of an annual federal pension from her late husband's service in the Marines. In August of 1901 Coston's other son, William, died after a backyard workshop explosion at his family home on Bement Avenue in the West Brighton section of Staten Island, New York.

His widow, Anna, took over management of the company with Coston, whose death on January 12, 1904, in Washington, D.C., went largely unreported. Anna's son, named William after his father, died in 1954 and his business partners and their successors ran the Coston Supply Company until the 1980s. From the 1870s until well into the 20th century reports of Coston lights, flares, or signals turn up with astonishing regularity in newspaper articles about shipping and maritime accidents. Coston flares were used to help rescuers find survivors of the *Titanic* in 1912. The distress-signal flares used by modern-day boaters are descended from Coston's original waterproof device.

Coston's name turns up occasionally in lists of women inventors. The preface to her 1886 autobiography is an enduring testament to her tenacity and business skills. "I am actuated by no idle vanity," she assured readers of *A Signal Success*, "nor yet the wish to pose as a writer, but by the honest desire to encourage those of my own sex who, stranded upon the world with little ones looking to them for bread, may feel, not despair but courage rise in their hearts; confident that with integrity, energy, and perseverance they need no extraordinary talents to gain success and a place among the world's breadwinners."

Books

Coston, Martha J., *A Signal Success: The Work and Travels of Mrs. Martha J. Coston—An Autobiography*, J. B. Lippincott Company, 1886.

Periodicals

New York Times, August 19, 1901; October 30, 1901.

Popular Mechanics, March 1905.□

D

Raymond Damadian

American physician and inventor Raymond Damadian (born 1936) developed MRI (magnetic resonance imaging) technology for use on humans to detect abnormal tissue. Though Damadian successfully capitalized on his patent invention through his FONAR Corporation, he was a center of controversy when the 2003 Nobel Prize in physiology or medicine was awarded for MRI technology and Damadian was not included in the honor.

Damadian was born March 16, 1936, in New York City. His father worked for the *New York World-Telegram* as a photoengraver. Educated in public schools, Damadian was passionate about music. A talented violinist by the age of eight, he received training in the instrument at the Juilliard School of Music. During the summers, Damadian was a tennis professional on Long Island as a teenager. When he realized he would not find success as a violin soloist and had other academic pursuits in his mid-teens, Damadian left music behind.

Attended Medical School

Gifted in math and science in addition to music, Damadian landed a Ford Foundation Scholarship at the age of 15. He then studied mathematics and chemistry at the University of Wisconsin at Madison, and earned his undergraduate degree in mathematics in 1956. Entering medical school at New York City's Albert Einstein School of Medicine, Damadian wanted to find a cure for cancer. He was granted his M.D. in 1960.

After earning his medical degree, Damadian focused on research as a faculty member of the SUNY (State University of New York) Downstate Medical Center in Brooklyn. His early research centered on how potassium and sodium generate electric voltages in human bodies. In 1969, Damadian's research focus shifted when a doctor interested in measuring potassium in bacteria contacted him. After growing the bacteria, the scientists placed it in a common tool for chemists, a nuclear magnetic resonance machine. Damadian was surprised when a signal was instantly produced and the rate of decay of the potassium was measured. In the laboratory, the normal process to determine this decay rate took days.

Damadian's new research focus became the application possibilities of NMR (nuclear magnetic resonance) technology. As he told Kasey Wehrum of *Inc.*, "I thought, if we could do on a human what we just did on that test tube, maybe we could build a scanner that would go over the body to hunt down cancer. It was kind of preposterous. But I had hope."

Developed the Concept of MRI Technology

In the NMR process as applied by Damadian, atomic nuclei in a magnetic field emit radio waves at constant frequencies. By the end of the 1960s, Damadian devised the idea of a NMR (nuclear magnetic resonance) whole-body scanning systems for use on the human body to take advantage of these radio waves. Because of the differences in tissue relaxation between normal and abnormal tissue, the scanner could detect abnormal tissue by the differences in their radio waves.

In 1969, Damadian described how such technology could be used to externally scan the human body and discover early signs of malignancy. As envisioned by

113

© Neville Elder/Corbis

Damadian, large circular magnets would be built and patients would be run through the middle of them. He demonstrated that the concept could work on lab rats to detect cancer by 1970, publishing the results in a 1971 issue of *Science.* After the results became public knowledge, Damadian landed a grant from the National Cancer Institute and he began building the first magnetic resonance scanner, dubbed the Indomitable. It was constructed by Damadian with the help of several post-graduate and laboratory assistants, including Lawrence Minkoff, Michael Goldsmith, and Joel Stuntman.

Filing for a patent in 1972, Damadian was granted his patent for his MRI (magnetic resonance imaging) machine, as his technology came to be called, in 1975. It was the first patent in what would become an important technique for medical imaging. Though Damadian was an innovative researcher, his personality was rude, assertive, petty, and vindictive. Because of such qualities, he pushed away other scientists studying NMR technology. It also turned off those companies, the federal government, and others who could invest in or fund his project.

Damadian continued to do his research and focused on practical medicine. As Grant Fjermedal wrote in the *New York Times,* "His perseverance despite funding crises and professional ridicule is inspiring—at one point the university disconnected his telephones; at another point one of his principal research associates was urged by faculty and friends to abandon his laboratory."

Finished First MRI Machine, Founded FONAR

In the late 1970s, the Indomitable was completed. Damadian's first image was created on July 3, 1977, of the chest of Minkoff. By 1978, the machine was being used on cancer patients on a trial basis. The original machine was donated to the Smithsonian Institute in the 1980s.

Damadian faced roadblocks, however. The first MRI scans looked primitive. Damadian also was accused of making his discovery sound better than it was able to be at that time. This contributed to the lack of research funding. Though corporations were interested after they saw the machine, Damadian wanted to hold a leadership position in any company related to his MRI project. He did not want to give up control of his technology. No one was willing to meet this demand.

Ultimately, Damadian decided to commercialize production on his own and founded his own company. Raising two million dollars among friends, he established FONAR (field focused nuclear magnetic resonance) Corporation in 1978 and served as the company's president. Within two years, the company had produced the first commercially available MRI machine. Called the QED 80, it was used to examine soft tissues and detect a variety of medical conditions. By 1981, FONAR had gone public, and in 1985, FONAR introduced the first mobile MRI.

Filed Patent Lawsuits

During much of the period between the late 1970s and late 1990s, Damadian and FONAR filed a number of patent infringement suits against other companies producing MRI machines. Most were larger than Damadian's small company and started building their own versions of the MRI scanner. The competition was negatively impacting his business because it was hard for his smaller company to compete against corporate giants. There was also some uncertainty about FONAR's ability to last in the face of this competition, compelling some hospitals and clinics to go with well-established corporate giants. Despite such uncertainties, FONAR managed to be profitable by 1987, with sales of $37 million that fiscal year.

Some legal efforts did not have a favorable result, despite Damadian's patent. In 1985, he and his company brought a lawsuit against Johnson & Johnson, which had began working on its MRI scanner in 1979. Though Damadian won the initial case against Johnson & Johnson with a favorable jury verdict, the judge in the case reversed the decision and the judge's opinion was held up by the appellate court.

Lacking funds for more suits, Damadian contacted a lawyer who had been part of a legal team which won a major patent lawsuit for Honeywell over the autofocus lens. The lawyer agreed to take the case on full contingency in 1990, and sue General Electric for patent infringement. Two separate lawsuits were filed, one related to Damadian's original patent and the other for another patented spine imaging technology. In 1995, Damadian won the first case against GE, with an $80 million judgment in his favor.

Damadian turned away a settlement offer from GE in which the second lawsuit would be dropped, GE would pay the $80 million for the second patent, and GE would not appeal the court's decision. Damadian would not accept these terms, and GE petitioned the court of appeals to overturn the ruling. The court ruled unanimously in favor of Damadian and his company, giving them a judgment worth $128.7 million in 1997. The decision against GE was held up by the U.S. Supreme Court, which recognized and enforced his original patent. Other companies, including Siemens and Hitachi, settled out of court with Damadian and FONAR. By 1997, FONAR's annual revenues had reached $13 million.

Received Numerous Honors, Except Nobel Prize

In this period, Damadian received numerous awards and recognitions. For example, in 1988, he was honored with the National Medal of Technology, with Dr. Paul Lauterber, by President Ronald Reagan, for the conception and use of MRI technology for medical uses. The next year, Damadian was inducted into the U.S. Patent Office's National Inventors Hall of Fame. In 2001, he was given the Lifetime Achievement Award by the Lemelson-Massachusetts Institute of Technology Prize Program for inventing the MRI.

More honors came Damadian's way in 2003, including the Man of the Year Award from the Knights Vartan and the Innovation Award in Bioscience from the periodical *The Economist*. A Nobel Prize was given that year for the discovery of MRI technology, but Damadian was not included in the honor. Though a Nobel Prize can be divided by up to three recipients, the honor was only given to a chemist, Paul Lauterbaur, and a physicist, Sir Peter Mansfield. Damadian considered this choice a snub, as did many in the scientific community.

Though many considered Damadian a difficult person with an off-putting personality, he was widely given credit for his originating role in MRI research and many important innovations in the field. This included mentions in respected academic textbooks and journal articles. Advertisements were published in leading American, British, and Swedish newspapers in support of Damadian and his cause. According to the London *Independent*'s Steve Connor, the text of one ad included a quote from the dean of medicine at SUNY Downstate Medical Center, Eugene Feigelson. It read, "We are perplexed, disappointed and angry about the incomprehensible exclusion of Damadian from this year's Nobel Prize. MRI's entire development rests on the shoulders of Damadian's discovery."

It was unclear why Damadian was denied a share of the prize by the Nobel committee, though some attributed it to the more important developments to MRI technology that came from Mansfield and Lauterbaur. The pair improved the quality and usefulness of the images produced by an MRI machine, making it practical in a clinical setting. Despite the loss, Damadian continued to receive accolades, including the Bower Award in Business Leadership from the Franklin Institute in Philadelphia in 2004.

Company Remained Innovative

Despite this snub, Damadian's company continued to innovate. In 2001, FONAR introduced the only commercially available upright MRI machine, used for neck and spine scans.

It remained the only such MRI machine on the market for many years. By 2008, another version of Damadian's MRI machine was introduced, the Upright Multi-Positional MRI. It was named the Invention of the Year by the Intellectual Properties Owners Association Education Foundation. Also in this period, Damadian collaborated with Wilson Greatbatch, who had developed an implantable pacemaker, to develop a pacemaker that was compatible with MRI technology.

FONAR also continued to grow and prosper. By 2011, FONAR had revenues of $30 million. By 2014, Damadian's company had 15 MRI scanning centers in the United States. It was used by at least 60 million patients worldwide. Though he was denied a Nobel Prize for his work on MRI technology, the experience of creating the MRI technology provided an educational experience for Damadian. He told PR Newswire, "What I learned in the process of developing the MR scanner was that criticism is an integral part of the process and always has been. The bolder the initiative, the harsher the criticism."

Periodicals

Inc., April 2011.
Independent (London, England), December 11, 2003.
Market News Publishing, February 24, 2009.
New York Times, February 9, 1986.
Philadelphia Inquirer, March 18, 2004.
PR Newswire, April 24, 2001.
St. Petersburg Times (FL), March 25, 1987.

Online

"Raymond Damadian," *Who Made America?*, http://www.pbs.org/wgbh/theymadeamerica/whomade/damadian_hi.html (December 21, 2014).
"Raymond V. Damadian, MD," SUNY Downstate Medical Center, http://www.downstate.edu/ia/raymond-damadian.html (December 21, 2014).□

Mercedes de Acosta

The American writer Mercedes de Acosta (1893–1968), although active and innovative as a playwright, poet, and novelist, is remembered mostly for her romantic relationships with several of the leading female performers and creative artists of her time, probably including the Swedish-born film star Greta Garbo.

The exact nature of de Acosta's relationships remains difficult to determine, for she lived in a time when lesbianism was generally hidden behind codes and oblique references, and carried out far from the prying eyes of gossip columnists and Hollywood publicity departments. Her *New York Times* obituary described her as a "close friend" of Garbo and Marlene Dietrich. But about de Acosta's own sexual orientation there is no doubt. She came out as a lesbian at a time when there were few of those in the

United States, and she often boasted, according to her biographer Robert Schanke (as quoted on his website) and other sources, that she "could get any woman from any man." Hugo Vickers of the London *Independent* noted that "there is considerable evidence to support her claim," and her love life, regardless of its total extent, was vigorous and varied.

Dressed as Boy in Childhood

Born March 1, 1893, in New York, de Acosta was of Spanish and Cuban background and was the youngest of eight children, six of whom survived. Her mother, Micaela Herríndez de Alba y de Alba, was a Spanish heiress who came to the United States at age 14 and successfully campaigned for her share of the family fortune in a case that went all the way to the U.S. Supreme Court. Her father, Ricardo de Acosta, was said to have been part of a cell of rebels attempting to overthrow Spanish rule in Cuba. As a child, de Acosta experienced gender confusion; she believed she was a boy, and her family, who had hoped for a son, played along and called her Rafael. But a boy who showed her his penis when she was seven disabused her of her belief.

De Acosta was sent to a convent, where it was hoped that she would be taught feminine roles, but as she grew into adolescence she continued to question traditional gender roles.: "I am not a boy and I am not a girl, or maybe I am both—I don't know," she recalled saying to the nuns, as quoted by Vickers. "And because I don't know, I will never fit in anywhere and I will be lonely all my life." De Acosta also had a strong initial attraction to Catholicism, putting stones and nails into her shoes to inflict pain on herself, and kneeling with her arms spread as if crucified. Over time, however, she became more interested in Eastern religions.

Growing up on Manhattan's upper-crust West 47th Street, de Acosta moved in New York's most fashionable social circles, creative and otherwise. Her family's neighbors included former president Theodore Roosevelt. As she entered adulthood, de Acosta cultivated a look of her own, unconventional and distinctive. She dressed in black and/or white, wearing a close-cut jacket or cloak and a tricorne hat. She began to circulate in New York's film and theater worlds, and by 1916 she was in a relationship with the Russian theater actress Alla Nazimova. A year later she had a fling with modern dance pioneer Isadora Duncan, who composed erotic poetry for her. In 1920 de Acosta married artist Abram Poole, who may have been gay himself; the marriage ended in divorce in 1935.

Wrote Play for Romantic Interest

De Acosta had written several books of poetry herself as a young woman, titled *Streets and Shadows*. She also wrote two novels, *Windchaff* and *Until the Day Breaks*. But her most significant writing efforts came in the 1920s, when she was romantically involved with the noted British stage actress Eva Le Gallienne (who while on tour in 1922 was said to have written de Acosta three or four letters each day). One de Acosta play, about Joan of Arc, was performed in Paris with Le Gallienne in the lead role in 1925. The de Acosta–Le Gallienne liaison lasted for five years but dissolved around

1926 when Le Gallienne decided to put her energy into a new theatre to be paid for by a patron she had met.

Stung by Le Gallienne's rejection, de Acosta returned to a play she had been working on called *Jacob Slovak*, which depicted anti-Semitism in a New England village. The play was produced both on Broadway and in London with John Gielgud as the star, and it earned strong reviews. De Acosta was also active as a screenwriter in the late 1920s and early 1930s, losing one job, she recalled, when she refused to fictionalize a scene in a screenplay about Rasputin. As the film industry moved from New York to Hollywood, de Acosta followed in 1931. "Even though she avoided direct representation of same-sex eroticism in her writing," according to Schanke, "she freely 'smuggled in' ideas and issues common to those of us in the homosexual community but she put them in a heterosexual setting."

De Acosta was also rumored to have had affairs with writer Alice B. Toklas and actresses Marlene Dietrich and Eleonora Duse, among others. Her most famous connection was the one with the notoriously secretive Greta Garbo, whom she met in 1931 in Hollywood and apparently fell hard for. Garbo's letters to de Acosta, carefully worded, reveal no conclusive indications of a lesbian relationship, and when she sent flowers to de Acosta, she would not write her name on the greeting card. But in the summer of 1931 the pair took a vacation together in the Sierra Nevada mountains, during which de Acosta took topless photographs of Garbo. When the pair returned to Hollywood, de Acosta moved in next door to Garbo, and the two remained close although subject to frequent stormy disagreements into the 1950s.

Garbo Script Killed

As she had with Le Gallienne, de Acosta worked on a writing project that she intended as a showcase for Garbo's talents. (The idea in this case was Garbo's.) The script was given the title "Desperate," and the story would have required Garbo to dress as a boy for much of the film. The project reached the script-reading stage, but MGM studio executives, who were already investing marketing energy into cultivating Garbo's glamorous image, killed the idea.

De Acosta was ahead of her time in ways beyond her open lesbianism. She held strong feminist beliefs and argued in favor of Isadora Duncan's belief that women should not be burdened with layers of unnecessary clothing such as corset or stockings. Early in her career she was a women's suffrage activist. De Acosta was a vegetarian, once saying that eating meat made human bodies into tombs. Her interest in Eastern spirituality also occurred at a time when such beliefs were much less common in the United States, but she eventually came to believe that each individual should form his or her own religion, taking ideas from various sources. She traveled to India in 1938.

Later in life, even as homosexuality became more open, de Acosta was not a well-regarded figure. M.G. Lord of the *International Herald Tribune* called her "the first celebrity stalker." Years of profligate spending—she threw all-celebrity dinner parties in her Manhattan apartment—brought her into financial difficulties. In 1960, partly to raise funds, she issued a memoir, *Here Lies the Heart*, which hinted at but did not directly state the existence of her lesbian relationships.

Nevertheless, several of the women mentioned in the book, including Garbo and Le Gallienne, terminated contact with de Acosta after its publication, and although the book received positive reviews it failed to sell well.

De Acosta's last years were not happy ones. A leg problem and a brain tumor that required surgery further drained her financial resources. Although she was reputedly offered $10,000 for her correspondence with Garbo, she refused and instead consigned it to the Rosenbach Museum & Library in Philadelphia, stipulating that it not be opened until ten years after Garbo's death. In the 1960s de Acosta lived in a two-bedroom apartment with a small kitchen alcove. She died in New York on May 9, 1968.

Books

Cohen, Lisa, *All We Know: Three Lives,* Farrar, Straus & Giroux, 2012.

Schanke, Robert, *"That Furious Lesbian:" The Story of Mercedes de Acosta,* Southern Illinois, 2003.

Tyrkus, Michael J., and Michael Bronski, *Gay & Lesbian Biography,* St. James, 1997.

Vickers, Hugo, *Loving Garbo,* Random House, 1994.

Periodicals

Curve, December 2006.
International Herald Tribune, October 8, 2012.
New York Times, May 10, 1968.

Online

"Garbo's Letters to Mercedes de Acosta," *Garbo Forever,* http://www.garboforever.com/Letters_to_or_by_Garbo-5.htm (December 20, 2014).

"Loving Garbo: She could be the cruellest of lovers. " *Independent* (London, England), http://www.independent.co.uk/ (December 20, 2014).

"That Furious Lesbian:' The Story of Mercedes de Acosta," www.robertschanke.com/mercedes (December 20, 2014). □

Paco de Lucía

The Spanish guitarist Paco de Lucía (1947–2014) gained international success by mixing traditional flamenco styles with external influences—principally jazz, but also classical music, film music, and even pop and rock.

Flamenco is a music with traditions centuries old, reaching far back into the culture of Spain's gypsy minority. When he began to experiment with it, de Lucía found that flamenco purists rejected his music. His reputation grew stronger as he released best-selling albums with jazz guitarists John McLaughlin, Al Di Meola, and others. It was not simply commercial success that solidified de Lucía's reputation, but also the persistence of flamenco roots in his playing. "I am a purist at the center even though I am a revolutionary, at the vanguard, or a creator. . . . I have

INGO WAGNER/AFP/Getty Images

respect for the essence, the old, what is valid, and memory," he was quoted as saying by the London *Independent.* "What I have tried to do," de Lucía said in a Verve Music Group biography, "is have a hand holding onto tradition and the other scratching and also digging in other places trying to find new things I can bring into flamenco."

Learned from Family

Paco de Lucía was born Francisco Śanchez Gomes on December 21, 1947, in Algeciras, Spain, in the southern flamenco heartland of Andalucía. His father, António Sánchez, was a day laborer who played flamenco guitar to make extra money; the family was poor and sometimes did not have enough to eat. "My father had to earn his living playing for the rich señoritos who got drunk with whores and fancied a party," de Lucía was quoted as saying in the *Times* of London. "That was the highest thing any flamenco musician could aspire to back then." But music was emphasized from the start. He learned the guitar from his father, his older brother Ramó, and a famed flamenco player named Nino Ricardo. He never learned to read music. "You must understand that a Gypsy's life is a life of anarchy. That is a reason why the way of flamenco music is a way without the discipline, as you know it. We don't try to organize things with our minds; we don't go to school to find out. We just live. . . . Music is everywhere in our lives," de Lucía observed in his Verve biography.

Paco is a common Spanish nickname for Francisco, and the guitarist took the name de Lucía in honor of his Portuguese-born mother, Lucia Gomes. Winning a local guitar competition in Algeciras, de Lucía caught the attention of the dancer José Greco and joined his troupe for several years as a teen. This took de Lucía to the United States, where he met another famous flamenco player, Agustín Castellón Campos, known as Sabicas. The older guitarist urged de Lucía not to imitate others but to develop a style of his own. De Lucía later mused that Sabicas was probably expressing annoyance that he, de Lucía, seemed to be a follower of Sabicas's rival Ricardo, but de Lucía nevertheless took the advice to heart.

De Lucía's early albums were in a traditional style. He and his brother Pepe released an album as Los Chiquitos de Algeciras in 1961, and his 1967 album *La Fabulosa Guitarra de Paco de Lucía* contained only modest departures from tradition. Hearing jazz trumpeter Miles Davis and pianist Thelonious Monk at a jazz festival he played in Berlin, Germany, was a major formative experience, and he began to think about ways of incorporating jazz into flamenco music. By the time he released his *Fantasía Flamenca* album in 1969, he had begun to plan out compositions formally instead of relying on the basic theme-and-variations structure of many flamenco pieces. In 1970 de Lucía's profile in the United States was raised with a performance at New York's Carnegie Hall.

Backed Vocalist

It was also in the late 1960s that de Lucía began to collaborate with the vocalist Camarón de la Isla (José Monje Cruz), a partnership that would produce 14 albums (some of them also with the guitarist José Ferríndez Torres, known as Tomatito). Camarón was also experimentally minded when it came to flamenco, and the pair stimulated each other creatively. "My soul left me each time I heard him; he gave to flamenco a wild, savage feeling," de Lucía told the *Times* after his collaborator's death.

However, the strides de Lucía made as a soloist and small-group leader were best known outside Spain. De Lucía began to move in decisively new directions with his 1972 release *El Duende Flamenco de Paco de Lucía* (The Flamenco Spirit of Paco de Lucía). His 1973 album *Fuente y Caudal* (Source and Flow) included a best-selling single, "Entre dos Aguas" (Between Two Waters), a rumba that shocked flamenco purists with its inclusion of bongo drums and an electric bass. De Lucía 1976 album *Almoraima* added Arabic influences to his increasingly jazz-inflected flamenco style. All these albums were supported by live performances that spread the de Lucía legend ever more widely in spite of the performer's severe stage fright—or perhaps because of it. "The night I don't feel nerves," de Lucía was quoted as saying in the *Telegraph Online*, "I will stop playing."

In the late 1970s British jazz guitarist John McLaughlin heard one of de Lucía's recordings on the radio and resolved to perform with him. The virtuoso American jazz guitarist Al Di Meola experienced something similar, and the result was the *Friday Night in San Francisco* trio album of 1981 and tours (as the Guitar Trio) that filled stadium-sized venues. De

Lucía formed a jazz group of his own in the same year, including bass, drums, and saxophone, and he teamed with jazz pianist Chick Corea for the *Zyryah* album in 1990.

De Lucía sometimes said that he felt a spirit in common between jazz and flamenco, although he felt flamenco had a more anarchic quality. Even with his formidable technical skills, the virtuoso jazz musicians he played with kept de Lucía on his toes. "Some people assume that they (Di Meola and McLaughlin) were learning from me, but I can tell you it was me learning from them," he was quoted as saying in the *Times*.

Played Classical Pieces from Memory

The technical challenges likewise proved substantial when de Lucía attempted to perform repertory from the Spanish classical guitar tradition, whose practitioners had long derided flamenco players as amateurs. He released the album *Paco de Lucía Interpreta a Manuel de Falla* (Paco de Lucía Interprets Manuel de Falla) in 1980, and in 1991 he performed Joaquín Rodrigo's *Concierto de Aranjuez*, a pillar of the classical guitar repertory. In both cases, lacking the ability to read music, de Lucía had to play from memory. He appeared unusually nervous during the *Concierto de Aranjuez* performance, but Rodrigo, who was in the audience, is said to have approved of it.

De Lucía continued to challenge himself by moving into new musical areas as his career progressed. Particularly notable was his soundtrack to the 1983 film *Carmen*, in which director Carlos Saura gave the classic George Bizet opera a modern setting while de Lucía reinterpreted the music. De Lucía also joined rock guitarist Eric Clapton on the soundtrack of the 1984 film *The Hit*. In between all these experiments he periodically recorded and performed flamenco in a traditional style, as on the acclaimed 1987 solo album *Siroco*. Perhaps his greatest departure from tradition was his appearance on the 1995 single "Have You Ever Really Loved a Woman," by Canadian rock star Bryan Adams.

De Lucía remained active into the 21st century, winning a Latin Grammy award for his 2004 album *Cositas Buenas* (Good Things). In later years he divided his time between Spain and Mexico, where he enjoyed spearfishing. De Lucía was married twice, to Casilda Varela and Gabriela Canseco, and had three children. He died after a cardiac episode on a beach in Cancún, Mexico, on February 26, 2014. His last album, *Canción Andaluza* (Andalusian Song) was posthumously awarded another Latin Grammy.

Books

Contemporary Musicians, Vol. 51 Gale, 2005.

Periodicals

Daily Telegraph (London, England), February 27, 2014.
Guardian (London, England), February 27, 2014.
Guitar Player, May 2014.
Independent (London, England), February 27, 2014.
Telegraph Online (London, England), March 5, 2014.
Times (London, England), February 28, 2014.

Online

"Biography: Paco de Lucía," Verve Music Group, http://www.vervemusicgroup.com/pacodelucia (December 4, 2014).

"Paco de Lucía," *Allmusic,* http://www.allmusic.com (December 4, 2014).

"Spanish Flamenco Guitarist Paco de Lucía Dies at 66," *BBC News,* http://www.bbc.com/news/world-europe-26351251 (December 5, 2014). □

Henri Decoin

French filmmaker Henri Decoin (1890–1969) wrote and directed such classic films as *Abus de confiance* (Abused Confidence, 1938) and *Razzia sur la chnouf* (Chnouf, 1955). A commercially successful filmmaker who helped build the acting career of his third wife Danielle Darrieux, he had more than 50 films to his credit by the end of his life.

AFP/Getty Images

Henri Decoin was born on March 18, 1890, in Paris, France. For much of his youth, Decoin was a dedicated athlete. Swimming was his primary sport. Competing with the Sporting Club Universitaire de France (SCUF), he was an excellent freestyle swimmer. He first represented France in the 1908 Olympic Games, held in London. He competed in the men's 400 meter freestyle event. Decoin did not finish the first heat of the first round of competition, however.

Competed in Second Olympics

Though he did not compete one heat of his first Olympic experience, Decoin continued to swim with SCUF. In 1911, he won a national event in the men's 500 meter freestyle. He was again named to the French team for the 1912 Olympic Games, held in Stockholm, Sweden. This time, Decoin was a member of the French water polo team. The French team finished tied for fifth with Hungry. This was, essentially, last.

During World I, Decoin served as a pilot and in the infantry. He also married his first wife, Hélène Rayé in September 1915. The couple would later divorce in 1926. After the war, Decoin started a career as a sports journalist. He wrote for such publications as *L'Auto, L'Intransigeant* and *Paris-Soir.*

While continuing to pursue journalism, Decoin branched out into fiction as well. In 1926, he published his first, and best known book. The novel was entitled *Quinze Combats* (Fifteen Fights). It had 15 chapters, echoing both its title and the number of rounds in a boxing match. *Quinze Combats* focused on the behind-the-scenes world of boxing. A year after publishing the novel, Decoin married his second wife, Blanche Montel, an actress, with whom he would have one child.

Wrote Plays and Screenplays

Moving further into the creative arts, Decoin also wrote plays in this period, including *Hector, Normandie Le Téméaire,* and *Jeuz dangereux.* Decoin began working in film in the mid-1920s, starting as a screenwriter and, soon after, assistant director. He co-wrote his first screenplay in 1925, *Le Roi de la Pédale.* This silent film was directed by Maurice Champreux. Decoin also wrote another silent film, *La Ronde infernale* (The Infernal Circle, 1928). Decoin would continue to write screenplays as the transition to sound was made. Among his sound film scripts made by other directors were *Un soir de rafle* (1931), *Roi de Camargue* (1934), and *Poliche* (1934).

By 1931, Decoin was directing and writing films himself. His first film as a director was a short for which he also wrote the screenplay, *A bas les Hommes.* Decoin's first two feature films came out in 1933. *Les requins du pétrole* (The Sharks of Oil) was a French-language film of the German film *Unsichtbare Gogner,* directed by Rudolf Katscher. Decoin wrote the screenplay for his other 1933 film, *Les Bleus du Ciel* (The Blue Ones of the Sky). Another film made in 1933 was *Toboggan,* also scripted by Decoin and made for Gamount. This film focuses on a has-been boxer returning to fighting to again find glory. All were successful.

Decoin greatly admired American culture and filmmakers, and these influences showed through in his films. Often working for UFA, a number of his early films were

French versions of German films. These films were made in Berlin at the Neue Babelsberg studios. The experience not only insured regular employment, but also taught him much about working in many genres and provided better understanding of what made a box office star. As he began making his own films, he employed a number of assistant directors who would become filmmakers in their own right, including Philippe de Broca.

Married Danielle Darrieux

Many of his early films starred his third wife. In 1933, Decoin and Montel divorced. Decoin met his next wife, actress Danielle Darrieux, while working on the film *L'Or est dans la rue* (Gold in the Street, 1934) in Berlin, Germany. Decoin wrote the screenplay for the Kurt Bernhardt-directed production, which starred the 17-year-old actress. Decoin and Darrieux married in 1935.

Decoin and Darrieux would make ten films together, and Darrieux became a quintessentially French film star beginning in the 1930s with some of the films she made with her husband. Among them were the melodramas, *Le Domino Vert* (The Green Domino, 1935), *Mademoiselle ma mére* (1937), and *Retour á l'aube* (She Returned at Dawn, 1938). *Le Domino Vert* was the French language version of a German film, *Der grüne Domino* by Herbert Selpin. The pair went to Hollywood in 1937, where Darrieux appeared in one film, *The Rage of Paris* (1938). The couple returned to France after less than a year.

According to Darrieux, Decoin's support was crucial to her success as a film actress. According to Judith Mayne in *Studies in French Cinema*, Darrieux once said, "He knew how to highlight my good qualities and how to persuade me that I was capable of playing dramatic roles . . . He encouraged me when I lost confidence, when I wanted to give up. It's to him, and him alone, that I owe everything I became." At the same time, Decoin emerged as an increasingly successful, respected filmmaker, in part because of the films he made featuring Darrieux.

During the 1930s, Decoin played a defining role in what came to be considered the golden age of French cinema. In this period, Decoin often made policiers, films that followed police and detective work. Other key films made by Decoin at the time focused on definitive father figures, such as the one played by Charles Vanel in *Abus de confiance* (Abused Confidence, 1938). The melodramatic film was directed by Decoin and starred Derrieux as an impoverished law student, Lydia, without a family and few prospects besides prostitution to make her way in the world. A friend suggests Lydia pass herself off as the daughter of an author, the product of a long-ago affair. Though the author accepts her as his child, his wife does not, learns she is correct, but does not reveal the ruse because of Lydia's skills in the courtroom.

Made Films During the Occupation

While France was occupied by Nazi Germany beginning in 1939, Decoin continued to work in France. One of the films Decoin made during this period was *Battement de coeur* (Beating Heart, 1940). In the film, the penniless, underage orphan Arlette, played by Derrieux, is trained to become a thief, becomes entangled with an older Ambassador out to prove his wife's disloyalty, and marries him after many complications.

Battement de coeur was the last film Decoin and Derrieux made as a married couple. Darrieux became involved with a Dominican diplomat, and Decoin and Derrieux divorced in February 1941. Decoin would go on to marry for a fourth time, to Derrieux's best friend. Decoin and his fourth wife, Juliette, would have two children. Decoin and Derrieux would continue to work together, despite the end to their marriage.

In addition to making films independently during the Occupation, Decoin made three films for Continental Films, a Nazi operated organization helmed by Alfred Greven. Decoin was hired by Continental because he was familiar with the German film industry, having worked a number of German-French co-productions, including *L'Or est dans la rue*, before the war. The films made by Decoin for Continental in this period included *Premier rendez-vous* (Her First Affair, 1941), *Les Inconnus dans la maison* (Strangers in the House, 1942), and *Mariage d'amour* (Love Marriage, 1942). *Premier rendez-vous* starred Derrieux, and was a romantic comedy about the mishaps and misunderstandings that a young couple experiences before finally coming together. *Les Inconnus dans la maison* was a courtroom thriller featuring an alcoholic lawyer and a murder suspect he defends.

Decoin's independent releases made during the Occupation period included *Le Bienfateur* (The Benefactor, 1942), *Je suis avec toi* (I Am With You, 1943), and *L'Homme de Londres* (The London Man, 1943). The last film was an adaptation of Georges Simenon's novella *The Man from London* (1934). This noir focuses on a railway signalman who steals a large sum of money from a murder victim. Decoin set the film in 1930s France.

Explored Noir

In the post-war period, Decoin reflected the more complex state of French cinema. More realistic and serious, he focused on making noirs and, again, policiers. His films of this period included *La Fille du diable* (Devil's Daughter, 1946), *Les Amoureux sont seuls au monde* (1947), and *Au grand balcon* (1949). Decoin also directed and co-wrote *Entre Onze Heures et Minuit* (Between Eleven and Midnight), released in 1949. A policier, the noir-esque crime drama follows Inspector Carrel's efforts to discover who killed well known criminal Vidauban. Because the pair look exactly alike, Carrel takes on Vidauban's identity to discover his killer and becomes involved with Vidauban's lover, Lucienne, among others.

Decoin continued to make films in the 1950s and through the mid-1960s. His films in this period were more commercial yet often still Hollywood noir-influenced policiers. In 1952, he reunited with Darrieux on the film *La Vérité sur Bébé Dongé* (The Truth of Our Marriage). They also worked together on *L'Affaire des poisons* (The Case of Poisons, 1955). In his 1955 film *Razzia sur la chnouf* (Chnouf), Decoin centers on a vice squad cop who assumes the identity of a gangster to break up a crime ring. The film was shot in a documentary realism style. Through such films, Decoin brought the concept of a cop of action, a greater emphasis on the underworld, and a greater use of realism to police thrillers.

Made Musicals

Other key films for Decoin in this late stage of his career included *Folies-Bergère* and *Charmants garçons*, both released in 1957 and both Hollywood-style musicals. Another important film for Decoin in this period was *Tous peuvent me tuer* (Everybody Wants to Kill Me, 1957). As he reached his seventies in 1960, Decoin continued to make films and some works for television, albeit at a slower rate. In 1962, he adapted an Alexandre Dumas novel *Le Masque de fer* (The Iron Mask).

Working only a few years before his death, Decoin's final films were released in 1964 and included *Les Parias de la Glorie* (Pariahs of Glory) and *Casablanca, Nid d'Espions* (*License to Kill*). The latter revisited the escapades of the silent film detective Nick Carter. Decoin died on July 4, 1969, in Neuilly-sur-Seine, France. He was 79 years old. His son, Didier, from his fourth marriage would follow Decoin's impressive creative legacy with his own award-winning career as a novelist and screenwriter.

Books

Directory of World Cinema: France, edited by Tim Palmer and Charlie Michael, The University of Chicago Press, 2013.

Drazin, Charles, *The Faber Book of French Cinema,* Faber and Faber, 2011.

Oscherwitz, Dayna, and MaryEllen Higgins, *The A to Z of French Cinema,* Scarecrow Press, 2007.

Rège, Philipe, *Encyclopedia of French Film Directors,* Volume 1, Scarecrow Press, 2010.

Periodicals

Independent (London, England), November 29, 2004.

Studies in French Cinema, 2004; 2010.

Online

"Henri Decoin," *AllMovie,* http://www.allmovie.com/artist/p87326 (December 30, 2014).

"Henri Decoin," *Internet Movie Database,* http://www.imdb.com/name/nm0213940/ (December 30, 2014).

"Henri Decoin," *SR/Olympic Sports,* http://www.sports-reference.com/olympics/athletes/de/henri-decoin-1.html (December 30, 2014).□

Desmond Dekker

Jamaican singer and songwriter Desmond Dekker (1941–2006) was the first performer who successfully brought the reggae musical style to international audiences.

Pictorial Press Ltd/Alamy

Dekker scored a major hit in Britain, continental Europe, and North America with "Israelites," first released in Jamaica in late 1968. His career was intertwined in its early stages with that of reggae superstar Bob Marley, with whom he remained personally friendly. It was Dekker who paved the way for Marley's later successes, proving the commercial viability of reggae with "Israelites" and making contact with British producer and entrepreneur Chris Blackwell of the Island record label. Through the 1960s Dekker stayed abreast of fast-moving trends in Jamaican music as reggae emerged from ska and a cluster of other earlier styles, and he was quick to sense reggae's capacity for social commentary. In Britain, where he moved in the early 1970s, Dekker influenced a host of young musicians in reggae- and ska-based styles.

Apprenticed as Welder

Desmond Dekker was born Desmond Adolphus Dacres in the Jamaican capital of Kingston on July 16, 1941. Sometimes he gave his birth year as 1942 or 1943, but he was quoted by Pierre Perrone in the London *Independent* as saying he did that just because "I like to keep people wondering." After his mother's death, he was raised by his father on a farm near Seaforth in Jamaica's St. Thomas Parish, where he sang gospel music in church. Dekker's father also died when Dekker was in his early teens, but he was able to enroll for a time at Kingston's Alpha Boys'

School, a Catholic-operated trade training school, and eventually landed work as an apprentice welder.

Dekker enjoyed not only Jamaican music but also the vocal styles of American pop and jazz artists such as Louis Armstrong and Nat "King" Cole, and his co-workers appreciated his frequent on-the-job serenades and encouraged him to pursue music professionally. It was around 1960 that he met Marley, who according to some accounts was one of those co-workers. Dekker auditioned without success for the Studio One and Treasure Isle labels but had more luck at Beverley's, where ska singer Derrick Morgan noticed the gospel power in Dekker's voice and convinced label entrepreneur Leslie Kong to listen to the singer. Kong encouraged Dekker but cannily refused to record him until he returned with a collection of strong original compositions. According to some accounts, it was Marley who paved the way for Dekker's entry into Kong's stable; others hold that Dekker introduced Marley to Kong after getting his own foot in the door. It is clear that both young singers occupied similar spaces in Jamaica's new homegrown music industry.

In any event, Dekker followed Kong's advice and was accordingly allowed to record the single "Honor Your Father and Your Mother" in 1963. That release inaugurated a long run at or near the top of Jamaica's music sales charts for Dekker, who won the Golden Trophy award, given annually to Jamaica's top vocalist, five times in the 1960s. His early release "King of Ska" was optimistic in its title, but as he racked up a series of 20 number-one hits, few quarreled with the claim. Dekker was sometimes known as the King of Bluebeat as well. Early recordings such as "Sinners Come Home" and "Labour for Learning" had a positive, often moralizing tone. It was during this first part of the singer's career that he began to use the stage name Desmond Dekker.

Adopted Rudeboy Image

Part of Dekker's success was due to his ability to stay a step ahead of current trends in Jamaica. From his morally upright early songs, Dekker moved into lyrics reflecting the so-called rudeboy subculture in the mid-1960s, often using the heavier rocksteady beat. Dekker scored a major hit with the Kong-produced "007 (Shanty Town)" in 1967; the song's gangster-oriented Jamaican themes ("Dem a loot, dem a shoot") propelled it not only to the top of the charts in Jamaica but into the top 15 in Britain, where the song was adopted by disaffected youth groups. Sung in a Jamaican patois, the song nevertheless appealed to British listeners. "I was amazed, because I thought people wouldn't understand the lyrics," Dekker said in an interview quoted by Perrone. Another song featuring Jamaican patois was "It Mek" (1968).

Dekker switched stylistic gears once again with "Israelites," released in 1968; the flexible, loping beat featured in the song was by then rapidly acquiring the name of reggae. At that time, Jamaican songs (notably Millie Small's "My Boy Lollipop") had appeared in the United States as novelties, but no Jamaican artist had had a major hit. "Israelites" reached the top ten in the United States, exposing an entire generation to reggae rhythms. In Britain,

Canada, South Africa, Sweden, the Netherlands, and West Germany, it reached the number one chart position.

The song, backed vocally by a group of brothers often included on Dekker's recordings and usually known as the Aces, included a memorable mixture of biblical images of suffering and exile, social commentary, and contemporary references ("I don't want to end up like Bonnie and Clyde"). Dekker drew the song from real life. "I was walking in the park, eating corn," he was quoted as saying in the London *Daily Telegraph*. "I heard a couple arguing about money. She was saying she needed money and he was saying the work he was doing was not giving him enough. I relate to those things and began to sing a little song—'You get up in the morning and you slaving for bread.' By the time I got home it was complete."

Covered Jimmy Cliff Song

Dekker remains best known for "Israelites," but he enjoyed several more years of popularity after its release, especially in Britain. In 1970, inspired by reaching number two on British pop charts with a cover of Jimmy Cliff's "You Can Get It If You Really Want," Dekker moved to Britain permanently. He continued to record, with Kong shipping him rhythm tracks from Kingston.

In the 1970s, however, Dekker went into a creative and commercial decline. Partly it was precipitated by the death of his creative collaborator Kong from a heart attack at age 38, in 1971. After that, Dekker floundered artistically. He recovered somewhat with a British top ten re-recording of "Israelites" in 1975, but the deeper beat and more ponderous spirituality of Marley, who had hardly been known during Dekker's heyday, was by then in vogue, and Dekker's music was bypassed. He had some success with recordings in a reggae-pop hybrid style, such as "Sing a Little Song" (1975).

Venerated by waves of younger British musicians, Dekker remained a strong stage draw. Successive revivals of ska and "2-tone" music in Britain brought Dekker on stage and into the studio with rock bands and producers, including for a time the Graham Parker–led group the Rumour. With that band he recorded the *Black & Dekker* album for the punk label Stiff in 1980. Dekker declared bankruptcy in 1984, attributing his financial problems to bad management, but "Israelites" remained a popular standard. The song was reissued as a single yet again in 1990 after heavy exposure in a Maxell audiotape television commercial.

Later in his life Dekker continued to perform frequently, his reputation bolstered by a series of reissue releases on his British label, Trojan, many of them bringing together material previously available on 45 rpm singles. A U.S. reissue was the Rhino label's *Rockin' Steady: The Best of Desmond Dekker* (1992). Dekker died suddenly of a cardiac episode on May 25, 2006, in Thornton Heath in England's Surrey region, two weeks after a performance in Leeds. London reggae disc jockey Daddy Ernie of the Choice FM radio station told the BBC: "People like Desmond Dekker come along once in a lifetime. This is one of the pioneers that has passed away—his place is definitely cemented in reggae history."

Books

Contemporary Black Biography, Vol. 104, Gale, 2013.
Contemporary Musicians, Vol. 57, Gale, 2006.

Periodicals

Daily Telegraph (London, England), May 27, 2006.
Guardian (London, England), May 27, 2006.
Independent (London, England), May 27, 2006.
International Herald Tribune, May 29, 2006.
Times (London, England), May 27, 2006.

Online

"Desmond Dekker," *Allmusic,* http://www.allmusic.com (October 2, 2014).
"Reggae Legend Desmond Dekker Dies," *British Broadcasting Company,* http://www.news.bbc.co.uk/2/hi/entertainment/5018910.stm (October 2, 2014).□

Toshiko d'Elia

American runner Toshiko d'Elia (1930–2014) was an acclaimed amateur athlete who took up her sport in her forties and set numerous records for times in her age group over the years. Competing in such races as the Boston Marathon and the New York Marathon, she was the first woman over the age of 50 to run a marathon in under three hours. D'Elia continued to competitively run into her eighties, only months before her death.

D'Elia was born Toshiko Kishimoto in Kyoto, Japan, on January 2, 1930, the daughter of a very traditional father and a more independent mother. She and her three siblings had a difficult childhood in Japan, especially in the period after World War II, when the country was in a period of devastation because of the war. In the *New York Times,* Frank Litsky reported d'Elia as saying, "We starved. My mother would stand in food lines all day and come home with a cucumber to feed a family of six. I dreamed of being a bird so I could fly away."

Studied Deaf Education

D'Elia's career path was determined by an experience at a Roman Catholic convent. Working there as an interpreter, she witnessed a deaf teenager fall from a ladder and express his pain by screaming. Until this point, d'Elia had not realized that the deaf possessed voices. She decided to become an educator of the deaf.

To that end, d'Elia entered Tsuda College, a woman's college, where she focused on special education for the deaf. After completing her undergraduate degree, she applied for and won a Fulbright scholarship that allowed her to study in the United States. She asked her father to help fund the experience. Wanting his daughter to have an arranged marriage instead of an education, her father refused to provide financial assistance for her to go to America. He thought it more appropriate to buy a new car than spend money educating a woman. Despite this setback, d'Elia went to the United States in 1951 and studied audiology at Syracuse University.

While a graduate student at Syracuse, d'Elia married her first husband and had a daughter. She completed her master's degree, but her marriage ended after two years. D'Elia returned to Japan with her six-month-old child. Her father disapproved of what had happened, and urged her to put her baby up for adoption. Because her father believed that she had brought shame to the family with her divorce, d'Elia's mother funded her return to America so she could start her own life.

Back in the United States, d'Elia returned to New York. She became a teacher at the New York School for the Deaf, where she worked for decades. In 1961, she settled in Ridgewood, New Jersey, after she had married a second time, to Manfred d'Elia, a classical pianist and piano teacher. It was the couple's focus on outdoor pursuits that led to her serious focus on running.

Began Running for Mountain Climbing

D'Elia and her husband became enthusiastic mountain climbers, and set an initial goal of climbing the top five peaks in North America. The couple eventually traveled around the world to ascend such well known peaks as Fujiyama, Damavand, Monta Rosa, and the Matterhorn. They ultimately climbed every major peak in Europe and the United States.

D'Elia started running reluctantly. After she tried and failed to reach the summit of Mount Rainer, D'Elia was advised to try running to improve her strength and endurance, and decided to try to run a mile. She ran as fast as she could, collapsed after a half mile, and declared she would never run again. Yet she did. Initially, d'Elia ran a mile every morning, then increased to three miles, then five. Her daughter, Erica, would run with her at five a.m. every morning, and helped her mother with some of running's finer points.

It was because of her daughter, who was the team captain of her high school's girls track and field/cross-country team, that d'Elia became interested in competitive running in 1973. When her daughter's team entered a county-wide cross-country meet—a five-kilometer race held at Bergen Community College—she did not want any of her teammates to finish last and convinced her mother to run a race with them to ensure this did not take place. Her daughter finished first, while d'Elia finished third.

The experience inspired d'Elia to train and run in a marathon. She also received some professional coaching, beginning in 1975. D'Elia trained with elite marathon coach Bob Glover. It was Glover who realized her talent, and helped her refine it. D'Elia would continue to work with Glover for decades.

Competed in First Marathon

For her first marathon, d'Elia planned to only run half the race, 13.1 miles, to test her ability to handle the distance.

But the event, held in New Jersey in January 1976, was run on a cold day with snowy and icy conditions. When her ride did not arrive to pick her up at the halfway point, the 46-year-old d'Elia finished the race. Her time was an impressive three hours and 25 minutes. With the time, she qualified for the Boston Marathon, where she posted a time of 3:15. By the end of 1976, d'Elia had competed in the New York Marathon as well. Her time again improved, to 3:08.15. She placed third among all women in the race.

Also in 1976, d'Elia also helped establish and promote the Ridgewood Run, held in her home community. It was organized by North Jersey Masters Track & Field Club, a running club that d'Elia and her husband co-founded. She remained deeply involved with the event—later re-named the Fred d'Elia Memorial Day Ridgewood Run after his death in 2000—for the rest of her life. Her daughter, Erica Deistel, told Ed Mills of the Passaic County, New Jersey *Herald News,* "My mom was never concerned about times or performances of the people, just that they were happy and had a good time. 'In one of the first Ridgewood Runs I was making up entrance tags.... We've come a long way since then and a large part of that is due to my mother...''

By 1988, d'Elia had become a dedicated runner. She ran 90 to 100 miles per week and entered numerous competitions for those over the age of 40. She competed in and won both sprints and long-distance races. She repeatedly set many records, both American and world, in her age group over and over again. A particular focus for d'Elia was the American Masters marathon and distance races as well as many New York Road Runner races. She also regularly competed in the Boston Marathon and the New Jersey Shore Marathon. After nearly every race she entered, d'Elia would perform a ritual of taking off her shoes, thanking her feet for watching out for her, and then consuming a beer.

In 1980, at the age of 50, d'Elia posted an impressive time of 3:09 at the Boston Marathon, only four months after cervical cancer treatments. A Japanese reporter covered the event and interviewed her, putting her story on the front pages of newspapers in Japan. Though d'Elia had vowed never to return to Japan, she accepted an invitation to speak at the Women's World Sports Symposium, held that year in Tokyo. The experience also resulted in the publication of a biography, *Running On,* accompanied by a movie. Though both were originally in Japanese, the movies were translated into English for American audiences.

Set Marathon Time Record

Because of her time at the 1980 Boston Marathon, Glover decided to push d'Elia to run a marathon in under three hours, which no woman over the age of 50 had officially accomplished. Increasing her training to 100 miles per week with a special focus on speed and hills, she became the first woman over the age of 50 to run a marathon in under three hours at the World Veteran's Marathon Championship in Glasgow. D'Elia's time was 2:57:45. Because of this achievement, she was honored by *Runners World Magazine* with its Paavo Nurmi Award.

D'Elia's dominance as a runner continued in the 1990s. When she was competing in an over 65 age group race, she became the first woman to run an indoor mile in under seven minutes. In 1996, she was inducted into the National Track and Field Hall of Fame. She was a member of the first class included for the Masters division.

Captured Records in Her Seventies

More records fell for d'Elia in 2001. In January 2001, she set a new world record for women over the age of 70 in the indoor 1500-meter run. Her time was 6:47.46, more than three minutes less than the previous record. Only a few weeks later, d'Elia set three new records in the 800 meter, five kilometer, and ten kilometer races.

d'Elia continued to set American long distance running records for the 75 and over age division for women. In 2005, she broke her arm during a 12-mile race after a fall. She not only completed the race but set a course record for her age group. In 2008, when she was 78 years old, d'Elia had open heart surgery to fix an aneurism and a heart arrhythmia. D'Elia's running continued after a few weeks of rehabilitation.

Five years later, in 2013, d'Elia's importance in racing was demonstrated when she was invited as an honored guest to the Mini 10K, the first all women's race. She and the first woman to win the Boston Marathon, Nina Kuscik, addressed the 6,000 runners running the race. As she had a number of times before, d'Elia ran in the race herself. This year, d'Elia finished the 10K in 1:47:16.

Whenever she discussed her sport, d'Elia de-emphasized competitiveness in favor of personal fulfillment. Gail Kislevitz, a board member for the New Jersey Masters, told Jay Levin of the Bergen County, New Jersey *Record,* "She encouraged everyone to just go out and have fun. The thing I loved about her, she'd never ask someone who finished a race, 'What was your time?' Instead, she'd say, 'Did you have a good time?' She instilled that spirit of running for fun."

Competed Until the Age of 83

Well into her eighties, d'Elia maintained an intense training focus. In addition to running three miles per day, she also swam and did yoga daily. She kept this schedule until December 2013 when she was diagnosed with brain cancer. D'Elia had run her last race only days before, a five-kilometer race on Thanksgiving held in Upper Saddle River, New Jersey. D'Elia died of complications from her condition about two months after her diagnosis on February 19, 2014, at her daughter's home in Allendale. She was 84 years old.

After her death, many of d'Elia's records, especially those for the women's 75 and older division, remained intact. She was also remembered for encouragement of those new to running. According to Gail Kislevitz of the *Ridgewood News,* d'Elia once said, "I view running as a necessary tool to help me get through life, so I do everything I can to nurture it, take care of it, and appreciate it. I want to hold on to my friend for as long as I live."

Periodicals

Herald News (Passaic County, NJ), May 27, 2014.
New York Times, February 21, 2014.
The Record (Bergen County, NJ), February 22, 2014.
The Ridgewood News (Bergen, NJ), July 12, 2013; February 21, 2014.□

Jacques Demy

Filmmaker Jacques Demy (1931–1990) created the first French musical comedies, including such popular films as *Les Parapluies de Cherbourg* (The Umbrellas of Cherbourg, 1963), for which he won a Palm d'Or at the Cannes International Film Festival. Demy also created other important films such as *Lola* (1960) and *Trois Places Pour le 26* (1988). As a film artist he favored fantasies, often inspired by youth.

Album/Newsom

Demy was born June 5, 1931, in Pontchateau, France, a village on the Atlantic Ocean located near the city of Nantes. Demy's father was an auto mechanic, and he wanted his son to pursue a career as an engineer. To that end, Demy initially studied mechanical and electrical engineering. Yet Demy felt drawn to the creative arts and cinema as well. During his youth, he experimented with puppet theater and stop-action animation. When he was 14 years old, he purchased a film camera. He used classmates to make a film about a young girl named Solange who is kidnapped.

Trained for Film Career

By the age of 16, Demy was receiving an arts-oriented education at the Technical College of Fine Arts in Nantes. While a student there, he met his future set designer, Bernard Evein, who would work on many of Demy's films. Increasingly interested in having a career in film, Demy continued his education in Paris, at the Ecole Technique de Photographie et de Cinematographie (the Technical School of Photography), beginning in 1949. In this time period, Demy also worked for other filmmakers, including the documentarian Georges Rouquier and animator Paul Grimault. With the latter, Demy helped make animated commercials.

In the mid-1950s, Demy began making his own short films, and soon showed his penchant for being very controlling during the production process. The first, *Le Sabotier du Val de Loire,* was completed in 1955 and produced by Rouquier. Shot in documentary realism style, it was inspired by his own childhood memories, and its story was centered on a clog maker and his wife. Two years later, Demy's next short film was an adaptation of Jean Cocteau's sketch *Le Bel Indifferent.* The story was a monologue of a woman who was in love with an indifferent man. Demy made three more shorts before the end of the decade, including *Musee Grevin* (1958), *La mere at l'enfant* (1959), and *Ars* (1959).

Released *Lola*

In 1960, Demy made his first feature-length film, *Lola.* Considered part of the emerging "nouveau cinema" movement that was emerging in France in the 1960s, it starred Anouk Aimee as the titular character, a cabaret dancer with a heart of gold who has been left by her one true love seven years earlier. In the film, her true love returns to renew his relationship with her. Other characters in the film are also searching for their love fantasies, many of which have

some tie to Lola. The melodrama features a melancholy look at love and happiness in the South of France. Its look was bathed in white, from the sea to the sky to the uniform of American naval personnel.

Lola was critically acclaimed and retained its power for decades after its release. Describing the film, *The Times* noted that "While its balletic flow and bitter-sweet tone often echoed the famous director of *La Ronde,* Demy firmly established his own stylistic signature. He also showed himself a marvellous director of actresses: Anouk Aimee, as the abandoned heroine, had never seemed so bewitching."

Next, Demy explored his love of the sea in the drama *La Baie des Anges* (Window of Angels). Set in Nice, it focuses on two gamblers, Jackie and Jean, who ply their passion at the ocean-side city's casinos. *La Baie des Anges* starred Jeanne Moreau, who played a femme fatale compulsive gambler involved with Jean, played by Claude Mann. Like *Lola, La Baie des Anges* emphasized the white and whitewash in the city by the ocean. Unlike *Lola, La Baie des Anges* was considered more problematic by critics.

Some critics saw depth in *La Baie des Anges,* however. Writing about the film in the *New York Times,* Terrence Rafferty stated, "*Bay of Angels* is a dazzling essay on the sensuality of submission to the enigmatic logic of mathematical probability—a logic that, in Jacques Demy's movies, also governs the course of love." Rafferty added, "The beauty of the abrupt, out-of-the-blue happy ending in *Bay of Angels* is its sheer arbitrariness. It's another spin of the wheel...." *La*

Baie des Anges was released in 1962, the same year Demy married Agnes Varda, a film director as well, with whom he had a son Mathieu.

Made First Musical Comedy

While musical comedies had been produced in Hollywood and found audiences worldwide, the genre was not particularly popular in France. Demy brought the genre to his native country and made a number of well-received musical comedies in French. The first and best for Demy was 1963's *Les Parapluies de Cherbourg* (The Umbrellas of Cherbourg), which made him famous and came to be seen as a definitive film of the 1960s. With a musical score written by Michel Legrand, *Les Parapluies de Cherbourg* exclusively featured sung dialogue.

Starring French film icon Catherine Deneuve, this so-called musical novel explored the love story between Deneuve, who played the daughter of an umbrella shop owner, and a mechanic, played by Nino Castelnuovo. Though Deneuve's character wants to marry the mechanic, her mother, played by Anne Vernon, objects. Their love story reaches an end when the mechanic is called to serve by the French Army in Algeria.

Les Parapluies de Cherbourg won the Palm d'Or at the 1964 Cannes Film Festival, cementing Demy's reputation as a filmmaker. Though the film was well received by critics, it was also considered sugary and sentimental. With the success of *Les Parapluies de Cherbourg,* Demy made other significant films in this genre.

Created *Les Demoiselles de Rochefort*

Demy's next film was an even happier musical, *Les Demoiselles de Rochefort* (The Maidens of Rochefort), released in 1966 and again featuring a score by Legrand. It starred Deneuve and also featured her older sister, Francoise Dorleac; they played twins who are looking for love. Along the way, they have encounters with such actors as Gene Kelly, Jacques Perrin, and George Chakiris. At the same time, their mother, played by Danielle Darrieux, misses her own lost love, played by Michel Piccoli, who comes back into her life. On the whole, *Les Demoiselles de Rochefort* celebrated Hollywood musicals, particularly *On the Town.*

With the success of *Les Demoiselles de Rochefort,* Demy decided to pursue his goal of making films in Hollywood. Demy and his wife moved to Los Angeles in 1967. His first film was *Model Shop,* released by Columbia in 1968. The film starred Aimee reprising her role as Lola, who is living in Los Angeles and working as a pin-up model so she can go back to France. Love impacts the world-weariness that Aimee's Lola feels. *Model Shop* did not catch on with American audiences and was a box office failure.

Focused on Fairy Tales

Demy decided to go back to France himself, and follow his creative impulse back to musicals. In 1970, he released *Peau d'Ane* (Donkey Skin), a musical comedy interpretation of the fairy tale by Charles Perrault. Featuring another score by Legrand and starring Deneuve and Perrin, the film was beautifully shot, image-laden, romantic, and sentimental with a happy ending. Though Demy would not return to the genre in the same way again, *Peau d'Ane* was a strong entry into the genre despite French disinterest in the film.

Demy continued to adapt fairy tales and legends for film over the next few years. His 1971 film, *Le Joueur de flute* was based on the legend of the Pied Piper of Hamelin and starred the popular singer Donovan. Filmed in England and Germany, *Le Joueur de flute* celebrated innocence and purity. Demy's next project was based in France, the 1972 release *L'Evenement le plus important depuis que l'homme a march sur la lune* was a modern twist on a fairy tale. Starring Deneuve and Marcello Mastroianni, the latter actor's character is a man who becomes pregnant. Despite praise for its edginess, the film was not a box office success.

Demy spent much of the 1970s creatively frustrated. He wanted to move beyond the musical comedies beloved by the French public, but could not bring many projects to fruition. Taking advantage of the interest shown by Japanese producers, Demy used their funding to make *Lady Oscar.* This English-language film was based on a comic strip by Ryoko Ikeda, *Rose of Versailles.* In 1980, Demy went back to France and made a film for French television, *La Naissance du Jour* based on a novel by French novelist Colette.

Returned to Musicals

In 1982, Demy put out another musical, albeit one that included elements of tragedy with its comedy, *Chambre en Ville* (A Room in the City). While still amusing, the film also included more violence, passion, history, and social commentary than his musicals of the 1960s. Highlighted by a score by Michel Colombier, the film's setting was Nantes in 1955 when the shipyard workers went on strike. *Chambre en Ville* starred Danielle Darrieux, Fabienne Guyon, and Marie-France Roussel, and explored the idea that love and happiness are no longer found hand in hand. Though critics praised Demy's creative triumph, this "musical tragedy" was a box office disaster.

Though Demy's productivity was impacted by the relative failure of *Chambre en Ville,* he continued to make challenging films. His 1985 film *Parking* was a modern version of the legend of Orpheus, based on Cocteau's *Orphee.* The film starred Francis Huster. Demy's last film was released in 1988, *Trois Places Pour le 26* (Three Places for the 26). Set in Marseilles, it was at once a musical comedy, a biopic, and an homage to Broadway. It was noteworthy for focusing on the real life of Yves Montand, a French actor. With a score by Legrand, *Trois Places Pour le 26* explores the theme of love without sentimentality.

Suffering from leukemia, Demy died of a brain hemorrhage on October 27, 1990. He was 59 years old. Upon his death, Jacques Siclier wrote in the *Guardian Weekly,* "Jacques Demy loves cities open to the sea, full of white uniformed sailors, young girls in search of love, men perhaps too handsome to be happy, and mature, nostalgic women still able to dream. He made his audiences love these things, too. He created romantic stories, melodramatic intrigues and enchanted, fairy tale-like worlds, which, when occupied by real life and social truth, could bring sadness to our hearts and tears to our eyes."

Periodicals

Associated Press, October 28, 1990.
The Guardian, October 30, 1990.
Guardian Weekly, November 11, 1990.
The Independent (London, England), October 30, 1990.
New York Times, October 30, 1990; November 11, 2001.
The Times, October 30, 1990.□

Helene Deutsch

An influential theorist, teacher, and pioneer in women's psychology, Austrian-American psychoanalyst Helene Deutsch (1884–1982) studied with Sigmund Freud as an elite member of his famous Vienna Psychoanalytic Society. Deutsch was best known for her two-volume work, *The Psychology of Women.* Published in 1944–45, the book offered a comprehensive look at women's psychological development.

Helene Deutsch was born Helene Rosenbach on October 9, 1884, in Przemyśl, which at the time was part of the Austro-Hungarian empire. She was the fourth child born to Wilhelm and Regina Rosenbach. Deutsch's parents were of Jewish-Polish descent. Deutsch did not bond with her mother and was frequently beaten by her. Later in life, Deutsch wrote extensively about the mother-daughter bond. She was closer to her father, a well-respected lawyer and judge. Deutsch watched him meet with clients at his home office and at times traveled with him to court. At one point, Deutsch wanted to become a lawyer, but women were barred from the field.

Rebelled as Teen

In Przemyśl, there were no educational opportunities for girls beyond age 14. At this age, it was customary for girls from upper-class families to live as "debutantes" and prepare for marriage should a suitable bachelor come around. Deutsch, however, wanted to continue her education and did not want her parents to force her into a "socially appropriate" marriage. Deutsch had watched as her older sister, Malvina, gave up the army officer she loved to marry the Jewish attorney the family had chosen for her. As a teen, Deutsch ran away from home twice and only returned after her father promised to help her attain her *Abitur.* The Abitur was the test students took after secondary school to earn entry into a university. Deutsch's parents sent her to a private girls school in Lwów, Poland (now Lviv, Ukraine), and she also studied in Zürich, Switzerland. After five years of on-and-off schooling and private tutoring, she passed her Abitur.

During this time, Deutsch continued her rebellion against her mother's bourgeois aspirations. Whereas Deutsch's mother spoke German, Deutsch chose Polish as her conversant language and threw herself into the Polish nationalist movement, the workers' movement and social revolution by fighting for women's rights. She organized a workers' strike of women at a shirt collar factory and began writing articles for the local newspaper. Around age 16, she further irritated her mother by engaging in an affair with Polish Socialist Party leader Herman Lieberman, a married man 14 years her elder.

Lieberman encouraged Deutsch's educational pursuits and socialist leanings. Deutsch attended demonstrations and threw herself in front of police horses as authorities sought to control the crowd. She also delivered propaganda to the frontier. "I was always burning to be arrested," she told *New York Times Magazine* writer Suzanne Gordon. "I used to bring *bibua,* you know, forbidden propaganda, to the border so someone could come and take. I was longing to be arrested, but [it] never happened."

Entered Medical School

In 1907, Deutsch earned admittance to the University of Vienna Medical School. She was one of seven women to gain entrance that year. Initially, she thought she might become a pediatrician. During her studies in Vienna, Deutsch discovered Freud after reading *Gradiva,* a novel by German author Wilhelm Jensen. This led her to read Freud's 1907 work, *Delusion and Dream in Jensen's 'Gradiva,'* in which Freud applied his psychoanalytic technique to the main character. "What attracted me to Freud was [his] theory of infantile sexuality and the unconscious, but also his protest against society," Deutsch told Gordon.

In Vienna, Deutsch continued her affair with Lieberman, who had recently been elected to parliament and was living there without his wife. In 1910, the two traveled to the International Socialist Congress, held in Copenhagen. While there, Deutsch met several female socialist leaders who were strong, independent women. She aspired to be like them and realized that her affair with Lieberman left her in a subservient position since he would not divorce his wife or leave his child. Deutsch soon left him to study in Munich and aborted her pregnancy. According to Janet Sayers, author of *Mothers of Psychoanalysis,* Deutsch justified her decision this way: "I was ripe for motherhood, and the nature of our relationship made it out of the question."

On April 14, 1912, she married Vienna physician Felix Deutsch. He went on to become an analyst and a pioneer in psychosomatic medicine, as well as the Freud family doctor. The following year, Deutsch finally graduated from medical school and began working in a hospital for mentally challenged children. However, she found the work unsatisfying because she felt it did not challenge her intellect. After a few months, she found a position at Vienna University's Clinic for Psychiatry and Nervous Diseases working as an assistant to clinic director Julius Wagner von Jauregg, who went on to win a Nobel Prize for his work in neurophysiology.

As a female doctor, Deutsch was only allowed to practice in the women's and children's wards and soon grew restless. In 1914, she left her husband behind and went to Munich to study with German psychiatrist Emil Kraepelin. Under Kraepelin's direction, she conducted word tests to try and determine the effects of feelings on memory. According to Lisa Appignanesi and John Forrester, authors of *Freud's Women,* Deutsch once wrote about her restlessness this way: "We were happy—but my old friend and enemy, the restless desire for excitement and, above all, for learning and achievement, did not let me fully enjoy what we possessed. 'The air was clear,' but somehow I longed for storms. This longing was not silent and from time to time forced me to get away.... I always wanted to learn something that could only be learned somewhere else—I wanted to repeat my adolescent flight from home. Or to say it even more simply, I longed for new longings.''

Deutsch stayed in Munich only a few months, then returned to the Wagner-Jauregg clinic in Vienna and began studying Freud's work. On January 29, 1917, Deutsch gave birth to a son, Martin Deutsch. She had endured several miscarriages since her marriage. Later, in *The Psychology of Women,* Deutsch discussed miscarriage and attributed it to psychological factors, including a woman's unconscious inability to identify with her own mother. Deutsch offered a case study on a patient named "Mrs. Smith," actually a pseudonym for herself.

Studied with Freud, Became Teacher

In 1918, as World War I came to a close and male physicians returned home, Deutsch feared she would soon lose her position at the Wagner-Jauregg psychiatry clinic, so she decided to quit and pursue psychoanalysis. She applied to Freud's Vienna Psychoanalytic Society, a Wednesday evening group that met weekly to study psychoanalysis. In March 1918, she presented her first paper to the group— an investigation and analysis of the memory association research she had conducted in Munich. Within a few months, Deutsch had become a Freud understudy and started undergoing analysis by Freud himself. Since Deutsch was already a respected psychiatrist with sincere ambition, Freud welcomed her in his circle. Many of the anecdotes Freud cited in his work came from his analysis with Deutsch. Freud dropped Deutsch as a patient after about a year to make room in his schedule for more complex cases. She continued to work with Freud on psychoanalysis, and Freud often discussed his cases with Deutsch, using her as a "control" analyst.

In 1924, Deutsch took charge of the Vienna Psychoanalytic Training Institute. She was the first woman to lead the organization. In this capacity, Deutsch evaluated all candidates who came to Vienna for instruction in analysis. Deutsch gained a reputation as a leading lecturer in the field of psychiatry and therapy and trained the next generation of psychoanalysts. In the 1920s, she published *The Psychoanalysis of the Sexual Functions of Women,* followed by several clinical papers. In 1930, she published *Psychoanalysis of the Neuroses,* which was widely used in psychiatric training schools.

At this point, Deutsch was working 12 hours a day. She continued her analysis of her own patients and stayed busy with administrative work and teaching. She taught a popular course on feminine psychology and was known as an engaging teacher. In her seminars, she introduced case studies and sometimes lectured late into the night. Deutsch also formed the Black Cat Card Club, a group comprising young students of psychoanalysis who met every Saturday at Deutsch's apartment to play cards and discuss cases and techniques.

Moved to United States

As the political climate changed in Vienna with the rise of Hitler, Deutsch and her husband relocated to the United States and settled in Cambridge, Massachusetts. Deutsch joined the Boston Psychoanalytic Training Institute in 1935 and became an associate psychiatrist at Massachusetts General Hospital, where she continued training future analysts. She also stayed busy with her own practice and with writing. In 1944–45, Deutsch published the two-volume set *The Psychology of Women,* a comprehensive and analytic account of the issues faced by women.

In the two books, Deutsch moved from girlhood, puberty, and adolescence to motherhood and menopause. Though she relied on Freud's system of thought as a starting point, Deutsch delved into her own observations and insights concerning women's sexuality and psychology as uncovered through her clinical observations and personal experiences. She explored many topics other psychologists had long ignored, such as women's sexuality and many of the conflicts women sometimes felt, such as an inner battle between motherliness and eroticism. Over the years, her views on female masochism and narcissism caused controversy.

During her lifetime, Deutsch wrote several books and presented numerous papers at conferences. She was well-known for identifying the "as-if" personality type, now known as Borderline Personality Disorder. Deutsch first wrote about the "as-if" personality during the 1930s, noting patients who behaved "as if" they were well-adjusted, yet lacked emotional depth. Deutsch was also noted for her work on countertransference. Other books included *Neurosis and Character Types* (1965), *Selected Problems of Adolescence* (1967), and *Confrontations with Myself* (1973).

During the late 1930s, Deutsch and her husband established a farm in New Hampshire, which they dubbed "Babayaga," after the good witch in Polish folklore. In 1963, Deutsch retired from training analysts. Felix Deutsch died in 1964. Deutsch, however, continued writing essays on narcissism, the ego, and mother-son identification. She died on March 29, 1982, in Cambridge, Massachusetts. Her legacy in psychology and the women's movement has long been debated. During her lifetime, Deutsch was vilified by feminists who felt her work parroted Freud in endorsing male chauvinist ideas about women and advancing women's subjugation. Like Freud, Deutsch relied on a theoretical model for women's development that assumed women lived with basic constitutional drawbacks because of biology. She often wrote about female masochism and passivity, and her association with Freud caused her to be dismissed by many feminists.

Deutsch biographer Paul Roazen, however, found Deutsch to be a role model for the independent-minded woman. Roazen pointed out that Deutsch continually fought against the prevailing standards of her society and was writing at a time when women were expected to do no more in life than take care of their families. "In her profession she attained freedom and was not just a subject and disciple of Freud's," Roazen wrote in *Helene Deutsch: A Psychoanalyst's Life.* "His genius was the presence which released Helene Deutsch's most creative talents, but in defining who she was Helene Deutsch did not have to rebel against Freud. She inquired into what interested her.... She could transcend Freud without dishonoring their relationship. Her life demonstrated that women need not be victims, but that their special abilities, based on social and biological sources, can be translated into active doing in the world.''

Books

Appignanesi, Lisa, and John Forrester, *Freud's Women,* BasicBooks, 1992.

Roazen, Paul, *Helene Deutsch: A Psychoanalyst's Life,* Anchor Press/Doubleday, 1985.

Sayers, Janet, *Mothers of Psychoanalysis,* W.W. Norton & Co., 1991.

Periodicals

New York Times Magazine, July 30, 1978.□

Oscar Deutsch

Oscar Deutsch (1893–1941) built the Odeon Cinemas company into Britain's largest chain of movie houses in the span of a just a few short years in the 1930s. Though it was an ancient Greek word he borrowed for his company name, the signature neon-lit "ODEON" letters were jokingly said to be an unofficial acronym for "Oscar Deutsch Entertains Our Nation." His luxuriously furnished Art Deco palaces were beacons for filmgoers in England and Scotland during the tough economic years of the Great Depression.

Born on August 12, 1893, Oscar Deutsch grew up in the Balsall Heath area of Birmingham, England. At the time of his birth, the West Midlands city was experiencing a decades-long industrial boom and Deutsch's father Leopold had a thriving scrap-metal business. Both Leopold and his wife Leah were Jewish émigrés from Central Europe; the Deutsch line was of Hungarian origin while the Cohens, his mother's side, were from Poland. Unfortunately Leopold died in an accident in 1904, the year his son turned 11. His business partners carried on the Deutsch and Brenner metals-dealership and a 17-year-old Deutsch joined it when he finished his education at King Edward VI School at Five Ways, named for the 16th-century Tudor dynasty monarch and the busy Birmingham junction at which the building stood.

The Brenner partner had sons who were poised to take over key management roles in the company. After Deutsch married Lily Tanchan in 1918 and began his own family, he began to seek out new business opportunities in Birmingham. With two friends he formed a film distribution company in 1920, Victory Motion Pictures, and five years later made a bid to take over a failing three-cinema chain in Coventry, England. Deutsch and his new business partner Reginald Noakes decided to sell off one of the properties but kept the

Stevenson/Getty Images

Crown movie palace and its sister site, the Globe. They began renting films from distributors and tidying up the properties; the small management team that ran the two Coventry theaters became key executives in the empire that would emerge under the Odeon name a few years later.

Success Despite Grave Health

Tragically, by 1925 the then-32-year-old Deutsch was already suffering from stomach cancer, the ailment that felled him 16 years later. When his health was restored in periodic remissions, Deutsch maintained an exhaustive work schedule, often working late into the night and on the road. The first movie house he built from the ground up, with the backing of some investors, was the Picture House at Brierley Hill, a town on the outskirts of Birmingham. It had seats for 1,000 patrons and opened on October 1, 1928. The first cinema house bearing the Odeon name was also a newly built property in Perry Barr, another suburb of Birmingham, which opened in August of 1930. The Odeon name was suggested by one of Deutsch's financial backers, who had seen the word used on a recent Mediterranean-region vacation. At the time, early film houses were called nickelodeons'' and the Greek noun ''odeion'' dated back to antiquity, denoting a type of amphitheater used for public performance. Deutsch and his partners liked the sound and would eventually adopted it as a brand name for their growing chain of theaters, which operated as the Cinema Service Ltd. in their first years of existence.

Deutsch's business model involved leasing already-operating movie houses, but as revenues increased he hired a series of architects to design dedicated film-exhibition spaces. This was an emerging field in the 1930s and required significant investment in new technologies. Electricity, heating and cooling systems, and acoustics had to be perfected, and the exteriors needed to meet local requirements and stir public excitement. Deutsch hired a Birmingham architect, Harry Weedon, who created some of the Odeon chain's most noteworthy cinema houses. In 1933 Deutsch opened five new sites, most in the south of England, giving him a total of 26 movie houses. Seventeen theaters were added in 1934, and Deutsch doubled the number of new properties by 1936.

Deutsch's Odeon chain set new standards in design as streamlined Art Deco theater palaces with their modernist ODEON lettering in neon. Often there was a tower that flew his signature Odeon flag, like a ship—which some of the buildings even resembled, especially those close to seaside resorts. Weedon, the company's chief architect along with fellow professional Cecil Clavering, favored enormous fronts with rounded corners, sleek lines, and colored faience as a decorative element. "This type of glazed tile provided Deutsch with exteriors that would remain bright and attractive in Britain's smoke-laden Victorian towns and cities," explained cinema historian Allen Eyles in the first volume of his landmark *Odeon Cinemas* tome. "Smoke abatement was not yet practised and urban sites were very hard to keep clean. Faience was popular because it created an impression of cleanliness and was easily washed down."

Popularized Sleek Art Deco Look

The expansion carried out by Deutsch in the mid-1930s set new industry records, even for the fast-growing entertainment sector. With a flood of films from newcomer British studios, Hollywood powerhouses, and even solid imports from French and German filmmakers, a wide swath of the public began attending the cinema, and did so every week. In 1934, the first year such figures were tracked in Britain, 900 million movie tickets were sold. Deutsch chose high-traffic areas in retail zones in urban areas, or sites that allowed for easy automobile parking. "Deutsch's Odeons were constructed on main roads close to bus and tram stops, or in the new middle-class suburbs," noted Barry Doyle, a writer for *History Today*. "His well-appointed auditoria, moreover, were aimed at a more affluent and respectable audience who would not consider patronising the 'fleapits' which served working-class neighbourhoods."

In the summer of 1937, Deutsch and his company board of directors issued a public offering of stock in Odeon Theatres Ltd., which included by 250 operating cinema houses. Some were renovated older properties, but Deutsch also continued building brand-new showcases, especially in major urban centers, and a few sat up to 1,700 moviegoers at a time. Many of these cinemas later became Art Deco landmarks and displayed a daring modernism and glamour, with beautifully lit exteriors and vast expanses of leopard-print carpeting. "They brought not only the latest British films and Hollywood movies, but

also a standard of contemporary design that was absent from the lives of most people in these determinedly old-fashioned islands," wrote Jonathan Glancey in the London *Guardian* decades later. "With their cloud-piercing towers and sweeping lines, Odeons were a promise of the shapes of things to come. For less than a shilling (five pence), coal miners, railway workers, teachers, nurses, servicemen, typists and clerks could disappear into a shining world of futuristic dreams, a whole dimension away from the grim economic and political reality."

Built Leicester Square Flagship

Deutsch's most opulent cinema was the London flagship Odeon at Leicester Square. In 1936 his company bought and demolished the old Alhambra Theatre vaudeville venue in the heart of the capital's West End theater district and erected a magnificent movie house in its place. An action-adventure film *The Prisoner of Zenda* was shown on its November 2, 1937, opening night, a premiere that marked the peak of Deutsch's career as a cinema magnate. Among the guests were Prince Henry, younger brother to England's King George VI, and the prince's wife Alice, Duchess of Gloucester. "The auditorium," remarked the London *Times* correspondent about the new Odeon landmark, "gives the impression of being made from a single piece of material. . . . In fact the whole construction gives one the sensation of being enclosed inside a machine."

In addition to the cinema business, Deutsch was an enthusiastic investor in other new technologies, such as a burglar alarm system that worked by motion-detecting sensors. He was also involved in an early form of television, called the Scophony System, which was never fully developed for commercial use. The Odeon chief maintained a brisk work schedule when his still-tenuous health permitted. He crisscrossed England and Scotland constantly, either by rail or luxury Daimler sedan, to negotiate deals and inspect new building sites. His permanent staff included a virtual mobile-office team always at his side, with stenographers, typists, and even telegraph operators traveling with him. He was one of the regulars on a newly constructed two-hour express train that traveled from Odeon's offices in London to his family home in the posh Edgbaston area of Birmingham. It was common for entire bundles of correspondence to be tossed off trains at stations bound for Royal Post couriers as Deutsch's staff worked to keep up with his voluminous memos and instructions.

Endured Cutthroat Competition

Deutsch's fast-paced work habits were driven by his own sense of mortality as well as fears that a larger shark was swimming his waters, which indeed was the case. His chief competitors were Associated British Cinemas (ABC) and the Gaumont-British concern. Among all three there was fierce competition to lock down deals on first-run films from Britain's domestic studios like Ealing, plus those from the major Hollywood players, whose big-name new releases generated enormous box-office numbers. The American studios were particularly keen to move into England and other lucrative overseas markets and eliminate the domestic distributorship altogether. Deutsch was appointed to a seat on the United Artists Ltd. board of directors, and even moved into film production himself in a deal with legendary director Alexander Korda.

Only the outbreak of World War II slowed Deutsch's pace and Odeon's dominance in the U.K. movie business. When Britain and Germany declared war in September of 1939, all non-military construction was halted and existing cinemas were ordered to temporarily close as a security measure. They eventually reopened, but adjusted to new wartime blackout laws. Deutsch committed his company resources to the war effort, assigning theater managers to work with civil-defense agencies, encouraging his 7,000-plus employees to participate in war-bond savings programs, and even giving wartime bonuses to keep up with the cost of inflation. One of his proudest triumphs was *The 49th Parallel,* which had a star-studded premiere in October of 1941. Retitled *The Invaders* for its U.S. release, the propaganda thriller featured fugitive Nazi militants attempting to stir up pro-German antiwar sentiment in the United States and Canada.

Left 258-Odeon Chain

In worsening health in the autumn of 1941, Deutsch negotiated deals for a parent company for Odeon Cinemas to ensure that no major Hollywood studio could make an attempt to take over his chain after his death. This new company was run by one of his board members, J. Arthur Rank, who ensured its financial stability and even enlarged Odeon in the coming decades. The 48-year-old Deutsch died after a 17-year battle with stomach cancer on December 5, 1941, at the London Clinic. Odeon Cinemas survived through scores of corporate buyouts and reconfigurations, and was the largest theater chain in Europe well into the 21st century.

Deutsch was said to be a cousin of Arnold Deutsch, a Viennese émigré who is believed to have recruited members of the infamous Cambridge Five espionage ring. Oscar Deutsch's immediate surviving family members were his wife Lily and their three sons. The middle boy, David, had a long career as a film producer in Britain. A nephew, Frederick Dexter, would eventually become the father-in-law of rock guitarist Mick Jones of Foreigner fame, and grandfather to the DJ/musician Mark Ronson and his twin sisters Charlotte and Samantha Ronson.

Books

Eyles, Allen, *Odeon Cinemas,* Volume 1, *Oscar Deutsch Entertains Our Nation,* BFI Publishing, 2002.

Periodicals

Daily Mail (London, England), December 6, 1941.

Guardian (London, England), May 18, 2002.

History Today, February 1998.

Times (London, England), November 3, 1937. □

Shakuntala Devi

Showing genius mathematical skills from an early age, Shakuntala Devi (1929–2013) demonstrated an ability to quickly calculate large numbers. Known as the "human computer," she was an international phenomenon for her gift with math and founded the Shakuntala Devi Educational Foundation Public Trust. Devi also wrote a number of books, including a 1977 book supporting gay rights.

Born November 4, 1929, in Bangalore, India, Shakuntala Devi was raised in an orthodox family of the Brahmin caste (an educated caste of priests and other leaders). Eschewing the priestly focus of much of the family, her father joined the circus, and performed on the trapeze and tightrope. He also was a lion tamer and performed the human cannonball.

Showed Mathematical Abilities as a Toddler

Raised primarily in a ramshackle area of Bangalore, Devi's mathematical genius was demonstrated when she was only a toddler. Playing cards with her father at the age of three, she bested him. He soon figured out that she was not winning by a trick of her hands but because she was memorizing the cards.

Devi's father discovered that she liked numbers and already had a great memory for them. Solving equations and reciting complex numbers were easy for the young Devi, who could figure cube roots and solve other math problems by the age of five. He decided to capitalize on his daughter's abilities and share them with the world for profit. For her part, Devi could not explain exactly how she performed these complex calculations so quickly, save that the numbers would appear in her head instantaneously.

At the age of six, the public learned about Devi's skills. Her parents took her to a public event in Mysore, India, where she showed off her abilities at the local university. When she was eight, she took part in the number games held at the Annamalai University in Chidambaram, India.

Devi also showed off her math skills as part of her father's circus. Road shows and tours, all booked by her father, followed. According to Haresh Pandya of the *New York Times,* Devi once said, "I had become the sole breadwinner of my family, and the responsibility was a huge one for a young child. At the age of 6, I gave my first major show at the University of Mysore, and this was the beginning of my marathon of public performances."

Received No Formal Education

Because of her father's limited income and her many public events and tours, Devi received no formal, conventional education, save for three months in a convent at the age of ten. She had to leave because her parents could not pay her fees. In addition to practicing and learning about numbers and math, she also learned to read and write. Devi resented that she was not allowed to go to school, and even ran

Dallas Morning News/AP Images

away from home and separated herself from her family for a time. Despite her lack of education and, sometimes, food, she was not only naturally skilled in mathematics but also sharp-minded and clever in other intellectual pursuits. Devi also had presence.

Of Devi's performances, Elizabeth Barber wrote in the *Christian Science Monitor,* "There was nothing to see but Devi deliver the final answer, before the public had even managed to take that breath of anticipation—would she be able to answer? Would she get it right? Despite the invisibleness of her act, or perhaps because of it, her almost magical performances of computational adroitness held audience's un-yielding attention."

In 1944, the 15-year-old Devi moved to London with her father to better position her to demonstrate her skills to a wide audience. Devi toured Europe and the United States in the 1950s, sometimes appearing on television. In one appearance, she showed off her skills on the BBC, where she and her interviewer attempted to complete the same calculation. Though they came up with different answers, it was Devi's that proved correct. A similar incident happened at a demonstration at the University of Rome, where one of her answers was thought to be wrong, when in fact it was the academics who had miscalculated.

Devi lived in England for nearly two decades, returning to India in the mid-1960s. She then married an officer in the Indian Administrative Service (IAS), Pritosh Bannerji.

The couple had a daughter before divorcing in 1979. The family lived in Bannerji's native Kolkata.

Bested Computer at Calculating

Devi gained more worldwide recognition for her mathematical skills, beginning in the mid 1970s, through more public demonstrations of her impressive numerical abilities. In 1976, for example, Devi put on a performance in New York City that included giving the cube root of many complex numbers and naming the day of the week of any date from the previous century. At a 1977 event at Dallas's Southern Methodist University, she was able to figure out the 23rd root of a 201 digit number in her head. It took Devi 50 seconds. She was competing against the fastest computer in existence, a Univac computer, which took 62 seconds to calculate the same figure.

In 1980, Devi was at an event at Imperial College in London, where she showed she could multiply two random 13-digit numbers. It only took Devi 28 seconds to come up with her answer to 7,686,369,774,870 x 2,465,099,745,779 (the answer: 18,947,668,177,426,462,773,730). For this accomplishment, Devi was given a place in the 1982 edition of the Guinness Book of World Records.

Devi said in 1987, according to the London *Times,* "I consider myself a goodwill ambassador for my country. I go around the world spreading a mathematical message and also showing that the human mind is still superior to the computer."

Became an Astrologer

In the early 1980s, after the couple divorced, Devi moved back to Bangalore. (Bannerji died in Kolkata in 2010.) When she returned, she began another career as an astrologer. She gave her insights on the stars to anyone who asked, from celebrities and politicians to common people. Devi also went on tours internationally where she displayed her skills in astrology and mathematics.

In 1988, Devi traveled to the United States where University of California, Berkeley, educational psychology professor Arthur Jensen, worked on learning the nature of her abilities. His study focused on the question of where her abilities came from, practice or a natural ability. With the help of volunteers, he conducted tests on mathematical abilities and published the results in *Intelligence* in 1990. Jensen reported that she could solve most of the problems written on a blackboard faster than he could record them in his notebook or before the stopwatch could be stopped.

Through the study, Jensen concluded that Devi's understanding and perception of large numbers was different than most other people. According to the London *Daily Mail,* Jensen wrote, "For a calculating prodigy like Devi, the manipulation of numbers is apparently like a native language, whereas for most of us, arithmetic calculation is at best like the foreign language we learnt at school."

Jensen also noted that Devi was not a stereotypical, antisocial or withdrawn savant. Noting that she was nothing like the autistic character played by Dustin Hoffman in *Rain Man,* Jensen found that Devi was very socially skilled and extroverted. She impressed and charmed not only Jensen, but many others among academics and audiences alike.

Published Numerous Books

In addition to her mathematical skills and astrology business, Devi also was the author of more than a dozen books on these and other subjects. Her published titles include *Fun with Numbers, Astrology for You,* and *Mathability. Figuring: The Joy of Numbers* was particularly important. It offered information on how people could become more proficient with math.

Some of Devi's books were puzzle books, including *Puzzles to Puzzle You.* Novels and cookbooks were among her other publications. One of Devi's most important books focused on a social issue. In 1977, Devi published a book that called for tolerance and acknowledgement of homosexuality in India. The country was extremely socially conservative, and homosexuality was criminalized, but Devi chose to be a pioneer with *The World of Homosexuals.* Devi wrote the book because of personal experience. More than two decades after *The World of Homosexuals* was published, she admitted her husband had been gay and their marriage failed as a result. Her book was a sympathetic reaction to the situation.

The text of *The World of Homosexuals* featured interviews with many Indian men who were gay, as well as a Canadian same-sex couple. The subjects speak in-depth about how they came to understand their sexuality, and the effect it had on their lives. Devi also offers her perspective, arguing homosexuality is not immoral and that gays should not be condemned to live lonely, often false lives.

Quoting the book in the *Bangalore News,* Samuel Jacob states that Devi wrote, "Immorality does not consist in being different. It consists in not allowing others to be so. It is not the individual whose sexual relations depart from the social custom who is immoral—but those are immoral who would penalize him for being different."

Established a Public Trust

Also a philanthropist, Devi established the Shakuntala Devi Educational Foundation Public Trust. Through it, she supported and encouraged the study of these subjects as well as philosophy and astronomy. She wanted to help people improve their aptitude for numbers, and to use her abilities to help think of ways to do so.

Hospitalized in the last weeks of her life, Devi died of heart failure and kidney and respiratory problems on April 21, 2013, in Bangalore. She was 83 years old. Even when she was in the hospital at the end of her life, she was energized and wanted to return home. Her long-time associate, Kavita Malhotra, told the Indo-Asian News Service, "She was a legend. Really, we didn't expect madam to go like this. She was very lively and was looking forward to get well soon. But her health was not good and it's a great loss to all of us."

When she died, Devi owned property in India, London, and New York, and had an estate worth a significant sum of money. After her death, her daughter, Anupama Banerjee, and the secretary of her trust, D. N. Ramamurthy, went to court over the disposition of her estate in November 2013. Banerjee insisted there was no will and she was the sole heir

entitled to the properties, while Ramamurthy claimed he possessed a valid will.

Though the court case impacted her legacy and dragged on for some time, it did not lessen her reputation or memories of her spirit. On what would have been her 84th birthday, Google honored Devi with its daily doodle on its homepage in North America, Asia, and other countries. The image included her picture and the screen of a calculator spelling out "Google."

Periodicals

Christian Science Monitor, November 4, 2013.
Daily Telegraph (London, England), April 23, 2013.
Indo-Asian News Service, April 21, 2013.
Mirror Publications, November 8, 2013.
New York Times, April 26, 2013.
Times (London, England), April 26, 2013.
United News of India, April 21, 2013.

Online

"Google Honours 'Human Computer' Shakuntala Devi with a Calculator-Styled Doodle on her 84th Birth Anniversary," *DNA India,* http://www.dnaindia.com/scitech/ (November 3, 2014).
"India's 'Human Computer' Impresses Students with Calendar Trick," *The Telegraph* (London), http://www.telegraph.co.uk/news/newstopics/howaboutthat/10010612/ (November 3, 2014).
"Shakuntala Devi's 84th Birthday," *Google.com,* http://www.google.com/doodles/ (November 3, 2014).
"The Woman Who Conquered the World of Numbers," *Bangalore News,* http://bangalore.citizenmatters.in/articles/ (November 3, 2014).□

Ophelia DeVore-Mitchell

American modeling agency executive Ophelia DeVore-Mitchell (1921–2014) worked for decades to bring diversity into mainstream consumer advertising. After launching a modeling agency for African-American talent in the 1940s, she worked behind the scenes on Madison Avenue to expand the job market for her models, many of whom went on to trailblazing success in fashion, entertainment, and even television news. "I wanted America to know that beauty isn't just white," her *Times* of London obituary quoted her as saying.

Emma Ophelia DeVore was a product of the segregated, pre-civil-rights-era in the American South. Born in Edgefield, South Carolina, on August 12, 1921, she was one of ten children of two mixed-race parents whose roots included European, African, and Native American ancestry. Her father ran a road construction company and her schoolteacher mother was a church pianist and firm believer in stoic social deportment and the rules of etiquette. Like many black families in the South, the DeVores had relatives who had made the Great Migration north for job opportunities after World War I, and at age 12 DeVore-Mitchell was sent to live in New York City with an aunt. She attended Hunter College High School and took some courses at Hunter College, but married a future New York City firefighter at age 19 and began a family.

"Passed" into Non-Minority World

Tall and poised, with light skin and wide-set eyes, DeVore-Mitchell was a vividly attractive young woman who had earned some money as a model. To improve her chances in the fashion industry, she signed up for a professional training course at the Vogue School of Modeling. It was only when she heard that a darker-skinned African-American woman had been rejected as an applicant that she realized that the school did not admit black students. Realizing how opposed the industry was to minority women as potential models and standard-bearers of beauty, she banded with four friends to launch a modeling agency for women of color.

The Grace Del Marco Agency was set up in New York City in 1946. The name "Marco" was an acronym for the five co-founders' first names; DeVore-Mitchell's Ophelia, which she used instead of Emma, was the "O." The partners started the agency just a year after the launch of *Ebony* magazine. The Chicago-based monthly was not the first national publication aimed at an exclusively African-American readership, but it became a dominant player in its first few decades for its coverage of emerging African-American elites in politics, entertainment, sports, and business. With its sister publication *Jet*, the magazines became a fixture in African-American households and each boasted immense and phenomenally durable circulation figures. Those numbers gave the parent company, Johnson Publications, some clout with potential advertisers, and DeVore-Mitchell began advising executives and ad agency creative teams on how to target the African-American consumer with aspirational images.

The agency addressed a new trend for more racially inclusive advertising campaigns, but DeVore-Mitchell and her partners struggled to bring qualified candidates to potential clients. "We couldn't find trained models," she told journalist Angela Taylor in a 1969 *New York Times* profile. "Few Negro girls had any background in showing clothes. We had to teach them how to do their hair and make-up, how to walk." On the side, in the late 1940s, DeVore-Mitchell set up the Ophelia DeVore School of Self-Development and Modeling.

DeVore-Mitchell taught her first classes in a rented space in a photographer's studio in Queens, then worked out of a renovated basement in the home where she and her parents lived. But by 1950 the burgeoning school had outgrown its modest beginnings and moved into a Manhattan space. She hired a roster of teachers who taught wardrobe styling, makeup application, public speaking, and even courses in "Figure Control with Fencing and Ballet" and "Positive Thinking."

DeVore-Mitchell's school turned out hundreds of graduates, some of whom went on to substantial modeling careers. One of DeVore-Mitchell's greatest success stories was Helen Williams, who became the highest-earning African-American model in the 1950s. "Through a combination of Mrs. DeVore-Mitchell's indefatigability, her considerable charm and Ms. Williams's breathtaking luminosity, the agency placed her in campaigns for major advertisers," recounted *New York Times* writer Margalit Fox, who noted that those print ads "appeared in mainstream publications like the *New York Times, Life* and *Redbook,* feats without precedent for a black model."

"Polishing Black Diamonds"

A full course at DeVore-Mitchell's school, which operated out of the Empire State Building in the 1960s, ran for several weeks and required a $400-plus commitment. The school's impact on a generation of women of color during a transitional period in American culture was subtle but proven. Veteran stage and screen actress Cicely Tyson was an instructor, and future Broadway dancer and television star Diahann Carroll took courses as a teenager. Joan Murray, a pioneering television journalist who began reporting the news for New York City's CBS affiliate in 1965, had been a teen model who also passed through DeVore-Mitchell's academy.

Journalist Angela Taylor's previously mentioned 1969 *New York Times* profile ran under the headline, "Her Name is Ophelia DeVore and Her Specialty is Polishing Black Diamonds." DeVore-Mitchell told Taylor that roughly a tenth of her school's students were modeling hopefuls, adding that a larger share "come for job advancement.... We help them to achieve the goals they set for themselves," she explained. "Negro women have to throw off the stereotype and accept a change of image. We expose them to audiences, arrange trips to teach them how to travel. We teach them to think, 'Don't I look wonderful?' And you know what, they do."

Discovered Major Talent

DeVore-Mitchell's work as a corporate advertising consultant was without precedent. In the early 1970s, when African-American models made enormous strides and even graced the covers of mainstream fashion magazines like *Vogue* and *Mademoiselle,* DeVore-Mitchell's name was regularly cited in media profiles about the new, more diverse generation of celebrity models like Beverly Johnson and Naomi Sims, as well as the women who had laid the foundations before them. DeVore-Mitchell's longtime association with Helen Williams was often mentioned, as were the other avenues of professional achievement traveled by protégés like Carroll, who became the first African-American woman to star in a prime time television series when she debuted as single mom *Julia* on NBC in 1968.

In 1977 novelist Jamaica Kincaid visited DeVore's modeling school to write a piece for the *New Yorker's* "Talk of the Town" section, and reported that for almost 30 years its founder "has taught thousands of young black women how to do just about everything properly." DeVore-Mitchell spoke to Kincaid about her long career as a consultant in the advertising business, which was still struggling to diversify the public's image of the American dream. "I had to tell them how to use blacks without offending whites," she admitted to Kincaid. "At some point, all this will become extinct," she added on an optimistic note.

DeVore-Mitchell's husband, Harold Carter, a former New York City firefighter, became involved in the modeling business, as did her sister Precola DeVore, who ran a modeling school in Washington, D.C., under her own name. Carter launched a "Mr. Carter" division for male models, and future *Shaft* star Richard Roundtree was one of its most successful signees. DeVore-Mitchell's parents and her own five children all helped run the Del Marco Agency and the modeling school. She and Carter divorced, and in 1968 she married newspaper publisher Vernon Mitchell, founder of the *Columbus Times* in the Georgia city of the same name.

DeVore-Mitchell was widowed just a few years later, and took over her husband's publishing duties. Her modeling school stayed in business in the New York area into the 21st century, and for many years she commuted between Columbus and New York City. In 1989 her achievements were recognized as part of a portrait exhibition, *I Dream a World: Portraits of Black Women Who Changed America,* at the Corcoran Gallery in Washington. It featured DeVore-Mitchell alongside other still-living legends like civil rights heroine Rosa Parks and Shirley Chisholm, the first African-American woman ever elected to a U.S. Congressional seat.

Donated Archives to Emory University

DeVore-Mitchell kept meticulous files over the years, including carefully curated clippings that tracked the success of her agency's models and the modeling-school graduates. She donated the trove to Emory University's Manuscript, Archives & Rare Book Library a year before she died. In her later years she lived primarily in Georgia, and her daughter Carol took over publishing duties at the *Columbus Times.* Now into her 90s, DeVore-Mitchell returned one final time to New York City to live nearer to one of her sons. She died there of complications from a stroke on February 28, 2014, at age 92. Later that year, she earned a posthumous place of merit as one of the featured obituaries that ran in the *New York Times Magazine*'s year-end "The Lives They Lived" tribute issue. "It was the vehicle that I used to communicate a positive image of my people," she was quoted as saying about her career as a modeling agency pioneer. "I wanted everybody to be accepted as human beings."

Periodicals

New York Times, August 20, 1969; February 9, 1989; March 13, 2014.
New York Times Magazine, December 28, 2014.
New Yorker, June 6, 1977.
Times (London, England), March 22, 2014.□

Manna Dey

Indian vocalist Manna Dey (1919–2013) was one of the most widely respected singers in the world of Indian cinema. At his death in 2013, Indian prime minister Manmohan Singh, as quoted in *The New York Times,* called him "the king of melody."

© D Chakraborty/Demotix/Corbis

Dey was what is known, especially in India, as a playback singer: he was heard on film soundtracks but was not seen in the films themselves. Within that realm, his versatility was unmatched. His career lasted from 1943 almost until his death in 2013, comprising nearly 3,500 recordings in a large variety of Indian languages. Dey was trained in Hindustani or North Indian classical music, a discipline he maintained throughout his life and one which enabled him to adopt widely varied styles of film music and make them sound natural. The *Cultural India* website expressed a common evaluation of Dey's career when it noted that he "infused the melody of classical music in the frame of pop music." Dey performed everything from pure classical pieces and pop film songs rooted in classical patterns to light comic-romantic duets and Westernized songs, enjoying a career of nearly unprecedented duration as he unveiled new vocal capabilities.

Took Indian Classical Singing Lessons

Prabodh Chandra Dey was born on May 1, 1919, in Calcutta (now Kolkata) in what was then British-ruled India. Manna Dey was a nickname. His father, Purna Chandra Dey, was an accountant, but, according to the *Learning & Creativity* website, he recalled growing up "in an atmosphere drenched in music." Manna attended good schools, including Scottish Church College Collegiate School and then Scottish Church College and Vidyasagar College, from which he graduated. He was an avid boxer and wrestler, and sometimes he would participate in stage shows or entertain his college classmates by singing while drumming on a table top. This alerted his relatives to his musical talent, and he began taking singing lessons from an uncle, Krishna Chandra Dey, and then from a local classical singing teacher, Ustad Dabir Khan. Dey continued taking lessons for much of his career, studying with two renowned masters, Ustad Amad Ali Khan and Ustad Abdul Rahman Khan. Even into his 90s, he would practice his classical technique daily.

Accompanying his uncle on a trip to Bombay (now Mumbai) in 1942, Dey was exposed to the city's growing film industry and signed on for work as assistant music director for several productions. He got his first chance as a performer the following year on a film called *Tamanna* for which his uncle had composed the score. He performed the duet "Jago Aayee Usha Ponchi Boley Jago" with a singer named Suraiya and earned a salary of three dollars. The song became a moderate hit, and Dey made more playback recordings over the next several years, forging the beginning of a long association with the film composer Sachin Dev Burman.

Dey's breakthrough came in 1950 with the film *Mashaal,* like *Tamaan* in the Hindi language. His solo track *Upar Gagan Vishal,* composed by Burman, became a nationwide hit. Two years later Dey furnished playback tracks for the film *Amar Bhupali,* which was produced in versions in the Bengali and Marathi languages. Dey sang in both, and his effort in his native language, Bengali, established him as the top playback singer in that large market. Some of his classical training had been in Bengali music, including the songs of the poet-composer Rabindranath Tagore.

Performed Classical-Style Film Music

Dey married Sulochana Kumaran on December 18, 1953, and the couple had two daughters, Suroma and Sumita. Throughout the 1950s, Dey's reputation as a singer grew; he was seen as the go-to artist for difficult material rooted in India's classical traditions. In 1956 he performed a duet with classical singer Pandit Bhimsen Joshi in the film *Basant Bahar,* which itself took the name of one of the ragas—the melodic patterns that are the basis for North Indian classical music. That duet, "Ketaki Gulab Juhi," became one of Dey's best-known numbers.

"His hallmark," noted the London *Independent,* "was...sheer versatility." In later films, Dey essayed romantic songs, patriotic nostalgia, devotional songs in various religious traditions (and in an era of great tension between India and Pakistan, he achieved popularity in the latter country), and even various Western-influenced styles such as rock and roll. In the words of *Learning & Creativity,* "The classical training set Manna Dey in a genre of his own but that did not any way affect his extensive repertoire of love songs, humorous songs and songs that could move you to tears." His image grew more familiar as he appeared in a piece of trademark attire: a fur hat characteristic of the Punjab region.

The basic seriousness of Dey's style may have kept him for a time outside the very top rank of popularity among Indian singers, but as his career evolved his popularity began to grow. He sang duets with some performers whom he might have considered his rivals, including Kishore Kumar; the pair's "Ek chatur naar" (from the 1965 film *Padosan*) became a comic standard. With his perfect timing and elocution, Dey was a master of comic song in film. Another frequent duet partner for Dey was a female counterpart, Asha Bhosle, whose vocal gifts perhaps equaled his own; they recorded more than 150 duets in the Hindi language between the 1950s and the 1980s.

Recorded Songs in Numerous Languages

Perhaps the most striking demonstration of Dey's versatility and professionalism was his level of accomplishment as a linguist. While the bulk of his output was in India's most-frequently spoken language, Hindi, he recorded songs in an astonishing variety of other Indian languages for films serving the country's various regional film industries. These included more than 1,000 songs in Bengali (many of them in modern popular genres unconnected with films), as well as songs in the Gujarati, Marathi, Bhojpuri, Punjabi, Oriya, Kannada, Malayalam, Assamese, and Nepali languages, as well as single numbers in yet other languages with smaller numbers of speakers. In the south Indian language of Kannada, unrelated to his native tongue, he was sufficiently convincing that the government of Karnataka, the Kannada-speaking state where he died, canceled his medical debts as "a mark of respect to the great singer who had also sung a few songs for Kannada films," according to the *Times of India.* Although as an alumnus of English-language schools he would have spoken English well, he apparently never recorded in that language.

Dey's vocal training and his ability to reveal new facets of his talent allowed him to enjoy an unusually long career. He recorded his last soundtrack music for the film *Umar* in 2006. In his later years, he reduced his film work but continued to give concerts. He made his last concert appearance in Mumbai in early 2012, at the age of 92. In later years he and his wife lived in the south Indian city of Bangalore; Sulochana died of cancer in 2012, and the following year Dey made plans to record four songs in her memory. Later that year, however, he was sidelined by respiratory infections.

Not until later in his career did Dey begin to win major awards, but once recognition came it was significant. He won the first of several National Film Awards for best male playback singer in 1969, for the film *Mere Huzur.* In 1971 he was awarded the Padma Shri, the Indian government's fourth-highest civilian award; in 2005 India's president conferred on him the still-higher Padma Bhushan. In 2007, Dey won the Dadasaheb Phalka Award, India's highest cinematic honor, and the Filmfare Lifetime Achievement Award followed in 2011.

A sampling of Dey's vast recorded oeuvre was released in box set form under the title *Legends: Manna Dey—The Maestro* in the year 2000. Dey died in Bangalore on October 24, 2013. He was, in the words of the *Independent,* "the great all-rounder of the Golden Age of Bombay cinema and had a greater longevity and diversity than his male compeers."

Periodicals

Dawn (Karachi, Pakistan), November 3, 2013.
Hindustan Times (New Delhi, India), October 24, 2013.
Independent (London, England), November 6, 2013.
New York Times, November 1, 2013.
Telegraph (Calcutta, India), October 25, 2013; October 27, 2013.
Times of India, October 26, 2013; November 3, 2013.

Online

"The Life of Legendary Singer Manna Dey, Golden Voice of Indian Cinema," *Hindustan Times,* http://www.hindustantimes.com/entertainment/music/ (October 22, 2014).
"Manna Dey," *Cultural India,* http://www.culturalindia.net/indian-music/indian-singers/manna-dey.html (October 22, 2014).
"Manna Dey: A Rare Voice That Excelled in All Music Genres," *Learning & Creativity,* http://www.learningandcreativity.com/manna-dey/ (October 22, 2014).
"Manna Dey: May 1, 1919–October 24, 2013," *Bollywood Life,* http://www.bollywoodlife.com/news-gossip/ (October 22, 2014).□

Simón Díaz

A popular folk musician and performer in Venezuela, Simón Díaz (1928–2014) was well known throughout the Americas and internationally for his prowess on the cuatro and his support of traditional Venezuelan music. He acted in films, and hosted radio and television programs, including a long-running series for children which earned him the nickname Tio Simón (Uncle Simon).

Michael Buckner/Getty Images

S imón Narciso Díaz Márquez was born on August 8, 1928, in Barbacoas, Venezuela, a small, rural, cattle town located in the northern state of Aragua. His father was a farmer and self-taught amateur musician who played the coronet in a local musical group. As a child, Díaz began pursuing music himself. He learned how to play the cuatro, a guitar-like instrument with four strings, and the six-string guitar.

Exposed to Many Musical Styles

In his youth, Díaz was exposed to and became fond of many music styles, including the many types of folk music found in the cattle-producing regions of Venezuela. It was produced with a cuatro, a guitar, and an arap llanera, a South American harp. He also loved the joropo, a country dance style of music. Throughout his childhood, Díaz played this music at family parties and gatherings.

When Díaz was 12 years old, his father died. Díaz, his seven siblings, and his mother moved to a bigger city, San Juan de los Morros, located in the plains region of Los Llanos, Venezuela. There, Díaz helped support his family by working as a street vendor, and later as a musician and singer. He had to end his schooling for a time to support his family.

Further developing his musical skills, Díaz became proficient on the cuatro. A master of the instrument, he demonstrated a talent for making the complex seem quite simple. In addition to furthering his skills on the guitar, he used the maracas as percussion and a Venezuelan harp in his performances.

By the age of 15, Díaz was performing as a stand-up comedian and storyteller under the performance name of El Chato, which means small nose. In addition, he played with the band Orquesta Sidoney, which performed throughout Latin America from the 1930s to the 1950s. Unlike Díaz's other musical projects, this group focused on Cuban musical traditions and covered Cuban and Cuban-style hit songs.

Studied at a Conservatory

In 1949, Díaz moved to the Venezuelan capital of Caracas, where he spent six years studying at a musical conservatory, Escuela de Musica Jose Angel Lamas. There, he became a classically trained musician. At the same time, Díaz saw his interest in the folk music of Venezuela grow. Díaz would travel around the countryside gathering and annotating such music, focusing especially on tonadas and coplas. Tondas, the work ballads of laborers such as cowboys and fisherman, were especially interesting to Díaz. These songs were often melodic and featured Spanish influences. They were originally used to make cows produce more milk by relaxing them through music.

Díaz was also fond of and promoted the country music of Venezuela, the *musica llanera,* which were songs of the plains region where he spent much of his youth. Musica llanera showed diverse influences from the indigenous peoples, former slaves, and Spanish colonizers. In addition, Díaz studied gaita and later made it commercially popular. Through his influence, it became a South American form of country and western.

According to Larry Rother in the *New York Times,* Díaz once said "Sometimes people would ask why I wanted to dedicate myself to music from the country, but that is where I am from, and that is the music I felt inside of me. It was always a part of who I am. I'm inspired by the people, the work, the land, by the raw materials and the truth of nature, by the simple things that were once important."

Gained Fame on Radio

Díaz's regional fame began in the mid-1950s with the launch of a radio program. He hosted a radio show called *The Plainsman* for about 25 years. The program focused on the country and folk music of his country, and contributed to his reputation as an ethnomusicologist. Through the show, he first garnered attention in Venezuela, and other nearby countries in South America and the Caribbean. Because of its wide popularity, Díaz landed his own recording contract.

Over the years, as a musician, Díaz recorded and released more than 70 albums, beginning with his first in 1963. He continued to record until the early 21st century, with his late albums including *Amorosante,* released in 2001 and focusing on his roots in bolero. In 2005, Díaz put out *Sabaneando.*

Díaz not only recorded and performed traditional and folk songs, he wrote and played more than 200 of his own original songs as well. Many of his songs were covered by other artists throughout the Americas, from Danny Rivera to Mercedes Sossa to Joan Manuel Serrat. Devendra Banhart, an American folk singer and songwriter, was greatly influenced by him and covered his song "Luna de Margarita."

Wrote "Caballo Viejo"

Perhaps Díaz's best known song was released in 1980, "Caballo Viejo" (Old Horse). This song, about an older man who falls in love with a woman much younger, was covered by hundreds of artists in many languages, including Ry Cooder, Plácido Domingo, and Celia Cruz. There were more than 350 recorded versions of "Caballo Viejo."

"Caballo Viejo" was also the source of legal action. In 1987, a French band, the Gipsy Kings, used the song as the basis for their international hit, "Bamboleo," without consulting him. Their use and re-purposing of the song irked Díaz, who threatened to sue the band. Before a trial could begin, the Gipsy Kings agreed to compensation for Díaz, in the form of 50 percent of the royalties, and to give him co-authorship for the song. Though Díaz was upset by what

had been done to the song, the agreement provided him long-term royalties.

Díaz's music was also known in some European circles. In 1995, famed Spanish director Pedro Almodóvar included Díaz's song "Tonada de Luna Llena" on the soundtrack for his film *The Flower of My Secret.* German choreographer Pina Bausch used bits of songs by Díaz in her piece *Nur Du (Only You).*

Though Díaz's influence and popularity was more limited in the English-speaking world, he performed and recorded for English-focused audiences at times. In 2003, Díaz made his concert debut in Britain with a well-received concert in London. Of Díaz's performance at the Barbican, John L. Walters of the London *Guardian* described, "The music is superficially simple and sunny: gentle rhythms, such as the tonada and the merengue, over which he sings with a storyteller's unhurried delivery."

Released *Mis Canciones* (*My Songs*)

In 2005, Díaz released his first album specifically for the American market, *Mis Canciones* (My Songs). The 15 songs on the album were folk songs in Spanish reflecting the breadth of his musical interests. Many were ballads, and a number of them had romantic perspectives on nature and rural life. The album's linear notes include English translations of the Spanish-language songs. Reviewing *Mis Canciones* in *Sing Out!,* Elijah Ward noted "It is appropriate that this album should be titled My Songs. Diaz is a fine singer and his band has an infectious lilt, but it is his imaginative poetry that makes his work stand out...." The following year, Díaz toured the United States.

While Díaz was primarily known for his work as a musician, his success on *The Plainsman* also led to acting and comedy careers. His acting career was launched in 1960 and included five feature films, a few stage roles, and a number of television appearances. When he worked as a comedian, Díaz sometimes was paired with his brother José, who performed as Joselo.

Became Tio (Uncle) Simón

Díaz's high point as an actor came on a television program for children, *Contesta por Tio Simón.* Airing for over a decade beginning in the 1960s, he played a character named Tio (Uncle) Simón. His character was not unlike the popular American children's show host Captain Kangaroo or folk singer Pete Seeger.

Through *Contesta por Tio Simon,* Díaz taught the culture and folklore of Venezuela to children. Describing the show, Robin Denselow wrote in the London *Guardian,* "He may have been a fine musician and composer, but he retained a decidedly non-academic, easygoing approach, mixing songs of the pampas with jokes and light-hearted stories in a style that appealed to different generations across the country."

Firmly ensconced as a national treasure by the early twenty-first century, Díaz owned his own cattle farm in the Llanas region late in life. He was a hands-on owner who rode horses and managed the cattle himself. Still a national folk hero who continued to perform, he drew on this status as his country dealt with political upheavals. Díaz stayed above the difficult political situation in Venezuela, and would not take sides with or against controversial Venezuelan leader Hugo Chávez during his many years in power before his death in 2013.

Yet, in 2002, Díaz appeared on television during a two-month national strike in the form of a commercial which aired regularly for some time. In it, he performed a song in which he asked both sides to listen to each other. His actions reflected his anger and frustration over the situation in the country, feelings shared by many. In his song, he asked for peace and calm as well as an election. His lyrics mention Simon Bolivar, the South American who freed Venezuela and other countries from Spanish control.

Honored by His Government, Latin Grammys

Because of his thoughtful work, Díaz received numerous honors over the course of his life, including many from the Venezuelan government such as the Gran Cordon of the Orden del Libertador (Order of the Liberator). He was the only musician to receive the Order of the Liberator from the Venezuelan government. In 2008, Díaz was honored with the Latin Grammy Award for lifetime achievement.

Near the end of his life, Díaz was suffering from and received treatment for Alzheimer's disease. He died on February 19, 2014, at his home in Caracas, Venezuela, at the age of 85. After his death, both the Venezuelan government and those who opposed it honored the singer. All Venezuelan schools performed a song in his honor a few days after his death.

According to a press release from the Embassy of the Bolivarian Republic of Venezuela in the United States, Díaz said, in reference to his 2006 appearance at Carnegie Hall while in his seventies, "I feel very honored by all these things that are happening in life at my age. To play at Carnegie Hall in my seventies is a blessing that I never imagined. I'm very happy to come to the United States, but this happiness isn't just for me, but also for my country. I am who I am and I cannot separate myself from my music and my cultural heritage."

Periodicals

Associated Press, February 19, 2014.

Daily Telegraph (London, England), February 8, 2003.

Guardian (London, England), February 11, 2003; March 1, 2014.

New York Times, March 5, 2014.

PR Newswire, September 30, 2008.

Sing Out!, Fall 2005.

Times (London, England), March 4, 2014.

Washington Post, September 30, 2005.

Online

"Musical Tribute to Simón Díaz Postponed," Embassy of the Bolivarian Republic of Venezuela, http://venezuela-us.org/2012/12/04/Óensamble-panelaÔ-offers-musical-tribute-to-simon-diaz/ (November 9, 2014). □

Ray Dolby

Best known for his work improving the sound quality of films and recorded music, Ray Dolby (1933–2013) developed such technologies as Dolby Stereo, Dolby Surround, and Dolby Digital. Through advancements introduced and continually improved through his Dolby Laboratories, audio recordings became more clear and realistic with less hiss. Dolby held more than 50 patents in the United States for his work.

Ray Milton Dolby was born January 18, 1933, in Portland, Oregon, the son of Earl Milton and Esther (Strand) Dolby. His father was employed as a salesman and real estate broker. When Dolby was still a child, the family moved to the San Francisco area, where he spent the rest of his childhood. Throughout his youth, Dolby was interested in music, and had a deep curiosity and enjoyment of learning. He also spent time tinkering. From an early age, Dolby was especially curious about sound as well as how various machines and instruments operated. A clarinet player, he was interested in the way the vibrating reeds worked, for example. At one point, he wanted to be a cameraman for Hollywood films.

Hired by Ampex

While a student at Sequoia High School in Redwood, California, Dolby served as a volunteer in the audio-visual department. Through this position, he met one of the founders of Ampex, Alex Poniatoff, in 1949. Poniatoff, who was also an electrical engineer, needed a projectionist for a charity event where he was speaking. At the time, Ampex produced tape recorders. After the event, an impressed Poniatoff hired Dolby, who worked for Ampex part-time through high school and was a top manager before obtaining his diploma.

Dolby continued to work for Ampex after graduation. At Ampex, Dolby showed his ingenuity. Among his accomplishments was serving as the chief electronics designer on what became the first workable recording system for videotapes. In addition to working for Ampex, Dolby began a stint in the U.S. Army after completing high school. Upon completing his time in the military, he entered Stanford University, where he studied electrical engineering. After finishing his undergraduate degree in 1957, Dolby left Ampex and moved to England to pursue graduate studies.

Studied Physics at Cambridge

Funded by a Marshall Scholarship and a fellowship from the National Science Foundation, Dolby studied physics at Pembroke College, Cambridge University. He was the first American to be elected a fellow of the college, an honor which came in 1960. Dolby was granted his doctorate in 1961, but remained in England. In 1962, he married Dagmar Bäumert, a German student whom he met at Cambridge. The couple eventually had two sons.

Allstar Picture Library/Alamy

Also in the early 1960s, Dolby was part of a group from Cambridge that went to India for two years. There, Dolby served as a science advisor as part of UNESCO (United Nations Educational, Scientific and Cultural Organization) project. Though the mission in India focused on helping the Indian government establish a national laboratory that would create scientific and industrial instruments, Dolby pursued his ideas on noise-reduction systems in his spare time.

In 1964, Phillips debuted the first pre-recorded cassette tapes. While in India, Dolby developed a means of addressing one of the main problems with Phillips' tapes, the poor sound quality. Much of the problem came in the form of constant background hiss that was created as part of the recording process and became part of the master tape.

As Dolby was recording native musicians in India by using an Ampex tape recorder, he came up with an idea of getting rid of this hiss, by separating the high and low frequencies. By splitting the sound into two channels after recording, the hiss could be eliminated. Through this audio compression and expansion, he was not only able to eliminate undesired noises but also to maintain the clarity of the recording.

Founded Dolby Laboratories

In 1965, Dolby returned to England, and founded Dolby Laboratories in London. He started the company with $25,000 of his own savings and with funds from friends. With four initial employees, the audio company focused on refining and marketing his noise-reduction system. From the first, Dolby served as the company chairman, a position he would hold until his retirement in 2009. He also was the president of Dolby Laboratories from founding until 1983.

Dolby's noise-reduction technology soon became an industry vanguard. It eliminated the hiss from all tape speeds, and ensured that cassettes had high sound quality. In 1966, the Decca record label bought the first noise-reduction system created by Dolby. The label put Dolby's system in its recording studio in London. Soon, the recording industry was widely using Dolby's tape machines and commercial tapes. By the 1970s, overall cassette quality greatly increased, in large part due to Dolby's developments.

Though he continued to work on audio technology for recorded music, such as 1987's Dolby SR, Dolby's next sonic conquest came in the film industry. His noise-reduction technology was used by filmmakers to improve the sound of their films and make it more realistic. While movie sound had improved after the move from mono, or single source sound, to stereophonic, Dolby's innovations profoundly changed the industry. The first film to use Dolby technology was Stanley Kubrick's adaptation of *A Clockwork Orange,* released in 1971.

Introduced Dolby Stereo

Dolby Stereo, introduced in 1975, as well as other technologies that followed, such as Dolby Surround, vastly increased sound quality for films. Not only were soundtracks more detailed, they were able to be projected at a higher volume and grander scale without hiss. For the first time, they could place specific sounds accurately within an audio spectrum to evoke an affect through the use of multi-channel technology.

Through developments with speakers and speaker placement, movie theater operators were also able to improve sound projection. They embraced Dolby's technology because it was relatively inexpensive and added depth and clarity to the sounds of films. As with cassette tapes, Dolby's film sound developments soon became the standards for the industry.

As Dolby and his company increasingly focused on film, he decided to move himself, his family, and his company to the United States in 1976. A year later, Dolby's film soundtrack improvements found an ideal vehicle through such blockbuster films as George Lucas's international smash, *Star Wars* and Steven Spielberg's *Close Encounters of the Third Kind.*

On *Star Wars'* complex, sophisticated soundtrack, sound was more layered and directional. The *Star Wars* soundtrack sometimes consisted of hundreds of individual tracks, all without hiss. Because of his sonic contributions to *Star Wars,* Dolby achieved wider fame as a household name.

For *Close Encounters,* Dolby's technology made the sound match the film's emotional intensity. Discussing a particularly memorable scene where an alien spaceship hovers over Devils Tower in Wyoming and communicates with scientists via electronic tones. Sidney Ganis, a producer and former president of Paramount Pictures, told

Natasha Singer of the *New York Times,* "The sound of the spaceship knocked the audience on its rear with the emotional content. That was created by the director, but provided by the technology that Ray Dolby invented."

Moved into Digital and Television

During the 1980s, Dolby's company expanded the use of surround sound technology to television, though the company initially hesitated to embrace digital over analog. Both compact discs and laser discs incorporated Dolby technology. After further developing technology in the mid-1990s that brought high-quality digital sound into the home, Dolby Laboratories increasingly concentrated on consumer electronics in the early 21st century. Sound technology was developed for such products as car stereos and high definition televisions. Home theater systems were particularly important to Dolby Labs in this time period.

Later in his career, Dolby continued to refine his audio systems. He held numerous patents in the United States. Among the last was for his Atmos system. With this technology, specific sounds, such as footsteps or raindrops, can be programmed by commands to come through specific speakers in a movie theater to create sonic illusions in various parts of a movie theater.

As the chairman of Dolby Laboratories, Dolby also encouraged his young engineering talent to be innovative in their own right and further improve the quality of the company's products. Dolby Labs continued to improve sound for films and movie theaters. Among the company's later products were refined versions of Dolby Digital and Dolby 3D Digital Cinema.

In addition to being a technological sensation, Dolby's company was also financially successful. Between September 2004 and 2005, Dolby Laboratories had sales of $289 million and a net income of $39.8 million. He took Dolby Laboratories public in February 2005. It raised $495 million in its initial public offering (IPO), while its market value was $1.75 billion. Dolby's share in Dolby Labs was worth $1.2 billion. He retained control of the company after the IPO, but retired as chairman in 2009 and fully retired from working in 2011.

Received Numerous Honors

By the time of his retirement, Dolby had received numerous honors for his work. Not only had Dolby received honorary doctorates from Cambridge University and York University, he was inducted into the National Inventors Hall of Fame. In 1997, he was given the National Medal of Technology and Innovation by President Bill Clinton. In 2004, he was elected to membership in the Royal Academy of Engineers. Additionally, Dolby received both an Emmy and an Oscar. In 2012, the theater where the Academy Awards are held was named the Dolby Theatre in his honor.

Before his death, Dolby and his wife, who was also an active philanthropist, gave away millions of his estimated $2.4 billion (as of 2012) fortune. Much of their giving focused on health care and other types of scientific research. Among their large donations was $36 million given to the University of California, San Francisco, for stem cell research.

Suffering from Alzheimer's, Dolby died of acute leukemia on September 12, 2013, at his home in San Francisco. He was 80 years old. Upon learning of Dolby's death, *Consumer Electronics Daily* quoted the president of Consumer Electronics Association, David Shapiro, as saying that Dolby was "true legend and pioneering visionary." Shapiro added, "His legacy lives on each time we marvel at and are moved by the amazing clarity and immersive sound of our audio and video entertainment."

Periodicals

Broadcasting and Cable, April 16, 2007.

Consumer Electronics Daily, September 16, 2013.

The Daily Telegraph (London, England), September 14, 2013.

New York Times, November 29, 1987; February 17, 2005; September 14, 2013.□

E

Gunnar Ekelöf

Swedish poet Gunnar Ekelöf (1907–1968) is considered the most influential, and innovative, poet in modern Swedish literature. Over the course of his career, he wrote in excess of ten volumes of poetry, as well as numerous books of essays and poetry translations. Ekelöf garnered popular and critical acclaim despite creating demanding, difficult poetry greatly influenced by mysticism, symbolism, and surrealism.

Born on September 15, 1907, in Stockholm, Sweden, Bengt Gunnar Ekelöf was the son of Gerhard Ekelöf and Valborg von Hedenberg. His father was a self-made multi-millionaire stockbroker, while his mother was of noble birth. Gerhard Ekelöf contracted syphilis from a prostitute before marrying his wife in 1906. Though there were no viable treatments for the disease at this time, Gerhard Ekelöf incorrectly thought he had been cured of syphilis before his marriage. The disease emerged from remission around the birth of his son, Gerhard Ekelöf told his wife that he had previously contracted syphilis, and both his marriage and his health went into decline. In Ekelöf's youth, he was quite close to his father, especially when he had periods of lucidity. Gerhard Ekelöf died when his son was eight years old.

Felt Alienated in His Youth

Though Ekelöf spent his childhood in wealth and privilege, including large homes and a comprehensive education at schools in Stockholm, he cultivated an outsider status from an early age because of his life experiences. After his father's death, in June 1916, he was sent away to a boarding school for the summer, as he would be for several more. Ekelöf's mother soon remarried, adding to his sense of alienation and feelings of abandonment.

Despite such personal difficulties, Ekelöf developed strong academic interests in such subjects as music and Oriental mysticism. He was able to pursue higher education in these areas. In 1926, he moved to London to attend the London School of Oriental Studies for a semester. When Ekelöf was accepted here, he cut off contact with his mother, feeling betrayed and disconnected from her. While Ekelöf's personal life was unstable, he also found solace in travel from the mid-1920s to 1930, visiting France, Germany, Italy, and Greece.

In 1927, Ekelöf began his degree studies at the University of Uppsala, where he focused on Persian Studies. Because of regular illnesses and lack of focus, Ekelöf was unable to finish his degree. But his studies influenced his decision to write poetry. While studying at Uppsala, he read the poetry of Ibn el-Arabi for the first time. These mystic poems compelled him to write his own poems. Mysticism would be found in many his works throughout his career.

Wrote First Poetry Volume

Deciding to study music and become a pianist, Ekelöf moved to Paris to pursue his education in this area. Though the language of music and music concepts would later be scattered in his verse, it was the language of poetry and its problems that soon gained more of his attention. While undergoing an emotional breakdown related to the quick end to his first marriage, the desperate Ekelöf wrote the poems that would be included in his first major collection, *Sent på jorden* (Late Arrival on Earth, 1932), in Paris.

epa/Nescom

Ekelöf later claimed to have written the verse while listening to Igor Stravinsky, and the book was dubbed the death book or suicide book. Many of the poems therein are full of anguish, darkness, death, and decay, and were greatly influenced by French Surrealism. Though it would receive little critical attention when it was published, it became hugely influential in its era. This work brought the concept of lyric modernism to Swedish poetry.

Ekelöf soon developed a very distinctive voice and perspective as a poet, very modern and lyrical in its perspective. From his first collection, the poet focused on the difficulties of individuals and the inner self, especially when isolated or imprisoned within themselves. In many ways, Ekelöf's poems challenged readers to give up the conventional perceptions of reality and poetry, and to give credence to the often fantastic thoughts and feelings of the subconscious.

Published First Translations

After *Sent på jorden,* the productive Ekelöf would publish new poetry volumes at least every three to four years. He was particularly prolific in the early to mid-1930s. He published translations of French surrealist poems in *Fransk surrealism* (*French Surrealism*) in 1933, then another book of translations in 1934, *Hundra år modern fransk dikt* (One Hundred Years of Modern French Poetry).

The early 1930s included another project for Ekelöf: serving as co-founder, with Artur Lundkvist, of a surrealist

journal, *Karavan,* in 1933. The publication was short-lived, however. Ekelöf lived in Berlin during the fall and winter of 1933 and 1934, and contributed to many leading newspaper and literary magazines in Stockholm. In addition, he wrote for publications related to both the trade union and cooperative movement in this period.

Ekelöf published another original volume of poetry, *Dedikation* (Dedication), in 1934. This collection included poems influenced by, or a reaction to, the ideas of French symbolism and symbolist poet Arthur Rimbaud, while still retaining a sense of surrealism that was also found in *Sorgen och stjärnan* (Grief and Stars, 1935). *Dedikation* was more positive in tone than *Sent på jorden,* and focused on trying to find truths that lie beyond reality. In contrast, *Sorgen och stjärnan* was the poet's denial of the existence of reality in every way.

Experienced Transitional Period

Ekelöf's poetic voice was in transition with his next two collections, *Köp den blindes sång* (Buy the Blind Man's Song, 1938) and *Färjesång* (Ferry Song, 1941). In the latter work, his tone was more calm, self-assured, and intellectual. Influenced by both symbolism and romanticism, Ekelöf considered ideas related to self and reality as well as the truthfulness of traditional concepts of them. The ideas and verse therein were also influenced by Buddhism, Taoism, mysticism, folklore, and modern rationalism.

Also in the early 1940s, Ekelöf published his first major collections of essays, *Promenader* (Walks, 1941) and *Utflykter* (Excursions, 1947). His personal life was also reaching new realms. In 1943, Ekelöf married his second wife, Gunhild Flodquist, who brought a sense of stability to his life.

Though Ekelöf's next original poetry collection, 1945's *Non serviam* featured a much darker, more subdued mood, there was still joy and a love of nature over conformist culture. The verse included references to authors such as John Milton and James Joyce. Other original collections by Ekelöf were published in the 1940s, including *Dikter I-III* (1949). Overall, his poems in this decade established him as the greatest lyric poem produced by Sweden. Many of his important poems produced in this period were longer, abstract, speculative, and metaphysical.

Brought New Perspective to Poetry

In the 1950s, Ekelöf took a new wife and new perspective on his poetry. He divorced Flodquist and married her sister Ingrid in 1951. The couple later had a daughter, Suzanne. In this period, the poet consciously made his style simpler so that he could make his poetry more depersonalized. Many poems from this period were body-oriented, focusing on such areas as sexuality, eroticism, and obscenity. While Ekelöf's tone varied from collection to collection, most poems included in such books as *Om hösten* (1951), *Strountes* (1955), and *Opus incertum* (1959), were often simple and short, focusing on common objects and situations. A number of poems were absurd and comical as well.

Also in this period, Ekelöf published more collections of essays and translations. His next important book of essays was published in 1957, *Blandade kort* (*A Mixed Deck*). Two major collections of translations came in the 1960s, *Valfrändskaper* (Chosen Kinships, 1960) and *Glödande gåtor* (1966), his rendering in Swedish of Nelly Sachs's *Glühende Rätsel*.

Ekelöf's career as a poet ended in the 1960s with tomes that emphasized the mystical and the complexity of consciousness. His first collection of new poems published in the decade was *En Mölna-elegi* (A Mölna Elegy, 1960). In this work Ekelöf especially focused on life and death, memories of the dead, and inheritances of all kinds from a personal perspective in the poems.

Composed Poetic Trilogy

Influenced by a 1965 trip to Istanbul, the final three original poetry collections published in his lifetime formed a trilogy that further explored the mystic in realms from classical antiquity to the Middle Ages, in civilizations in Byzantium, Greece, and the Middle East. Always a traveler, Ekelöf was particularly interested in and drawn to the Middle East. Through the three volumes—*Dīwān över fursten av Emgión* (1965; *Dīwān over the Prince of Emgión*), *Sagan om Fatumeh* (The Tale of Fatumeh, 1966), and *Vägvisare till underjorden*, 1967 (Guide to the Underworld, 1980)—Ekelöf's poems included expressions of erotic mysticism, an exploration of the nature of love, suffering, and an understanding of a reality that consists of both life and death.

By the end of his life, Ekelöf received numerous accolades. In 1958, he was given an honorary degree by the University of Uppsala. Ekelöf was also elected to the Swedish Academy that year. He was a somewhat active member, though he did not attend all the group's meetings. In 1966, the Scandinavian Council gave him its prize for *Dīwān över fursten av Emgión*.

Suffering from throat cancer by his early sixties, Ekelöf died of the disease on March 16, 1968, in Sigtuna, Sweden. Cremated after death, his ashes were sent to rest in the ancient city of Sardis, located in modern Turkey. After his death, more poetry, essays, letter collections, and other materials gathered from his notebooks and manuscripts were published. His widow was his literary executor and published one such book culled from various sources in 1971, *En självbiografi* (*An Autobiography*) and *En röst* (1973). A book of essays was also published, *Lägga patience* (Playing Solitaire, 1969).

Increased Reputation After Death

Decades after his death, Ekelöf remained relevant. In retrospect, Ekelöf became more critically acclaimed for the depth and breadth of the thoughts behind his poetry and ability to included many diverse influences in his work. While greatly influenced by others, he was also a definitively Swedish poet who allowed aspects of his native country to be found throughout his work. He secured a place in modern literature for his originality and relevancy, and influenced many Scandinavian poets who came after

him. Some critics believed Ekelöf would be even more widely known and studied had he written in English.

In 1993, Ross Sideler stated of Ekelöf in *Scandinavian Studies*, "When he died in 1968, Gunnar Ekelöf left behind a body of poetry that made him one of northern Europe's most powerful and probing lyric voices of this century. Ekelöf's poetry plumbed the depths of human consciousness, and it influenced, with its humor, mysticism, and searing imagery and sound patterns, at least three generations of Scandinavian authors. In the quarter of a century since his death, Ekelöf's reputation, rather than fading as the legends of major authors so often do, has continued to grow."

Books

DISCovering Authors, Gale, 2003.
European Poets, Vol. 1, 4th ed., edited by Rosemary M. Canfield, Salem Press, 2011.
European Writers: The Twentieth Century, Vol. 12, edited by George Stade, Charles Scribner's Sons, 1983.

Periodicals

Scandinavian Studies, Winter 1993.□

Elisabeth, Princess Palatine

Princess Elisabeth of Bohemia (1618–1680) was called "Star of the North" by her contemporaries in northern Europe of the 17th century. A largely self-taught polymath, the German-born royal possessed an uncommonly deep level of scholarship for a well-born woman of her time and was lauded for her mastery of classical languages, advanced mathematics, and the intricate debates that laid the foundations of modern philosophy.

E lisabeth Simmern van Pallandt was born on December 26, 1618, in Heidelberg, Germany. Her royal lineage was impressive: both of her parents were descendants of England's King Henry II, also known as Henry Plantagenet, who ruled from 1154 to 1189. Her father was Frederick V of Bohemia, prince of the Electorate of Palatine at the time of her birth. The Palatine royal seat was Heidelberg Castle, where Elisabeth spent her infancy.

Granddaughter of English King

Elisabeth's mother was Elisabeth Stuart, often mentioned in the historical records as the Winter Queen. Both mother and daughter were named in honor of England's Queen Elizabeth I, who died childless in 1603. The throne then passed to the father of Elisabeth Stuart, King James of Scotland. Seeking a solid union with Protestant rulers in Europe, Elisabeth Stuart was affianced to one of Germany's wealthiest princes, Prince Frederick of the Palatinate lands. Their 1613 wedding in London set a new benchmark for European royal nuptials,

Akg-images/Newscom

with hundreds of titled family members and other guests traveling to England for the festivities at Whitehall Palace, at the time the largest palace in Europe and host to the largest such gathering to that date.

The Stuart-Simmern van Pallandt marriage produced 13 children, of whom Elisabeth was the third child and eldest daughter. The couple and their family were staunch Protestants and both parents had strong blood ties to other leading supporters of the Protestant Reformation across Germany, Britain, Scandinavia, and the Low Countries. Tensions between Protestants and those loyal to the Roman Church and its pope rose noticeably during Elisabeth's childhood and would eventually alter the political landscape of the Continent.

In 1618 German-allied Protestants in the Kingdom of Bohemia invited her father to become their next king. He and Elisabeth Stuart journeyed to Prague for the coronation, but their stay in Bohemia was a short one and, in the end, resulted in tumultuous religious strife. Because of this both Elisabeth's parents are known as the Winter King and Winter Queen for their short reign over Bohemia. Their Prague coronation ceremony sparked an escalation of armed conflict that culminated in the historic Battle of White Mountain in November of 1620. In that contest Elisabeth's father and his Bohemian allies were routed by multinational forces loyal to the pope in Rome.

Sheltered at Berlin Palace

Elisabeth's mother was familiar with the perils of the Reformation and the zeal its opponents provoked: as a child in England she had been targeted by the pro-Catholic organizers of the Gunpowder Plot of 1605, whose plan was to blow up the Houses of Parliament in Westminster when King James formally opened the new session. The plotters hoped to place the then nine-year-old Elisabeth Stuart on the throne and restore Roman Catholicism to its full status as the religion of England and Scotland. That plot was foiled and its discovery is still celebrated every November 5 as Guy Fawkes Night.

Elisabeth was barely two years old when her parents were forced to flee Bohemia when the Thirty Years' War began in earnest after the Battle of White Mountain. In 1622 her father's magnificent Schloss Heidelberg was besieged and fell to pro-Catholic troops, along with his hereditary Palatinate lands. The family sought shelter in the Netherlands, close to powerful cousins on both sides of their marital union.

Elisabeth was not with her parents during these turbulent years. She and her older brother Karl Ludwig remained at Schloss Heidelberg under the care of their paternal grandmother, Countess Louise Juliana, and then when the Thirty Years' War moved west to the Palatinate lands along the Rhine River the children were handed over to their aunt, Elisabeth Charlotte, who was married to the Elector of Brandenburg. Elisabeth Charlotte was the sister of their father Frederick and lived in Berlin. Her namesake niece's earliest childhood memories were of the Berlin palace and the other House of Hohenzollern castles in Brandenburg and Prussia where she grew up with cousins who were roughly the same age as she and Karl Ludwig.

Elisabeth was reunited with her parents in 1628 at age ten, when she was sent to the Dutch city of The Hague, her parents' new residence and close to their influential cousins. Her mother was also descended from house that ruled the Kingdom of Denmark, while Frederick's mother was from the equally influential Dutch house of Orange-Nassau. The young princess now had four younger brothers and three sisters, and the family would continue to grow with two more children, born in 1630 and 1632. Only the death of Frederick in 1632 ended Elisabeth Stuart's prodigious output, having spent nearly an entire decade of her life pregnant by the time she was widowed at age 36.

Siblings Called her "La Grecque"

Elisabeth and her siblings were all taught at home. Elisabeth Stuart's sons and daughters were tutored in history, geography, and other subjects. The first-born daughter proved especially gifted in mathematics and languages and learned Latin and Greek, both of which were requisite for scholarly reading; she also spoke fluent French and English as well as German. Among her instructors were Constantijn Huygens, a poet and composer who was a trusted secretary in the household of the Prince of Orange, and Johan Stampioen, another intellectual figure in The Hague and leading mathematician of the era.

The Stuart-Simmern van Pallandt family remained dispossessed of income after their Palatinate lands were taken in the Thirty Years' War. Elisabeth Stuart took an active role in diplomacy, working to secure the return of the Palatine for her now-fatherless brood, and she also sought to match her ten surviving children to high-ranking future spouses from other royal lines across Europe. Despite the reduced circumstances, her mother's household in The Hague became a lively minor court and the four Palatine princesses—Elisabeth and her younger sisters Louise Hollandine, Henriette Marie, and Sophia—were all renowned for their charm, artistic and intellectual gifts, and conversational skills. Among her family Elisabeth was considered the most learned of the four, and was dubbed *La Grecque* by her family for her proficiency in this difficult classical language, which used a separate alphabet.

Challenged Descartes

Elisabeth was raised in the Protestant faith and there was talk of a marriage to a prince of Poland, Wladislaw IV, which would have required her formal conversion to Roman Catholicism, and Elisabeth resisted this. In 1643, she began an epic correspondence with the French mathematician and philosopher René Descartes, one of the key figures of Renaissance Europe. Born in France in 1596 but a longtime resident of the more tolerant Dutch-held lands, Descartes was a prolific writer whose expositions laid the foundations for Western philosophy and inspired the minds that shaped the Age of Enlightenment. It was Descartes who developed a system of mathematical calculations using x and y axes that enabled significant advances in algebra and geometry and bears his name as the Cartesian coordinate system.

Elisabeth had met Descartes when she was quite young and he visited The Hague court, and later requested from an intermediary a formal introduction by letter. She had read his works to date with some interest, and discussed them with other learned figures in The Hague. In her first letter to Descartes, dated May 6, 1643, she queried him about the mind-body connection, which the French thinker had argued were entirely separate entities. She wondered how this could be, and in her letter—whose English translation appears in the online repository *Early Modern Texts*—she writes: "So I ask you for a definition of the soul that homes in on its nature more thoroughly than does the one you give in your *Meditations,* i.e. I want one that characterizes what it is as distinct from what it does (namely to think)." Elisabeth went on to remark that, "it looks as though human souls can exist without thinking—e.g. in an unborn child or in someone who has a great fainting spell—but even if that is not so, and the soul's intrinsic nature and its thinking are as inseparable as God's attributes are, we can still get a more perfect idea of both of them by considering them separately."

Descartes responded with equal fluency, and the correspondence between the two endured for the next seven years until his death in 1650. His 1644 volume *Principia philosophiae* (Principles of Philosophy) is dedicated to her and extols her gifted intellect. "Neither the distractions of the court nor the customary upbringing which usually condemns girls to ignorance could prevent you from discovering all the liberal arts and all the sciences," Descartes enthused in his 1644 dedication, according to *Pandora's Breeches: Women, Science and Power in the Enlightenment* by Patricia Fara. The French philosopher added in the formal dedication to Elisabeth that "I have so far found that only you understand perfectly all the treatises which I have published up to this time. For to most others, even to the most gifted and learned, my works seem very obscure."

Quickly Solved *Apollonius's Problem*

In addition to her zeal for debating the tenets of modern philosophy, Elisabeth spent her time conducting scientific experiments, solving complex mathematical puzzles, and carrying on a correspondence with other luminaries of her time. She continued to reject potential suitors and was able to return to Germany finally after the Thirty Years' War concluded with the 1648 Peace of Westphalia. Her brother Karl Ludwig restored Heidelberg University in their homeland, while another brother, Rupert, was ennobled in England as the first Duke of Cumberland. Rupert took part in the English Civil War that resulted in the ignominious beheading of their Stuart uncle, King Charles I, in 1649. Her sister Louise Hollandine became a renowned artist and portraitist, and Henriette Marie married into a royal line that produced princes of Poland, Hungary, and Transylvania. The youngest sister, Sophia, became Electress of Hanover and made a sudden advancement to the restored English throne many years later. She died before she could claim it but the title passed to her son, who became England's King George I. This succession marked the end of the House of Stuart rule in Britain and the emergence of the House of Hanover in its place. George's grandson was the English monarch known as Mad King George III, and that George's granddaughter was Queen Victoria. That queen's grandson, King George V, was in turn the grandfather of England's long-reigning Queen Elisabeth II.

In 1660 Elisabeth entered a Lutheran convent in Herford, Germany, with roots dating back to the late eighth century. Her cousin Elisabeth Louise had been its abbess since 1649, and Elisabeth succeeded her Simmern van Pallandt cousin as abbess upon the latter's death in 1667. Under Elisabeth's tenure it became a refuge for Protestants fleeing another eruption of religious and civil conflict in the 1670s. She died there at age 61 in early February of 1680.

Books

The Correspondence between Princess Elisabeth of Bohemia and René Descartes, edited and translated by Lisa Shapiro, University of Chicago Press, 2007.

Fara, Patricia, *Pandora's Breeches: Women, Science and Power in the Enlightenment,* Random House, 2011.

Pal, Carol, *Republic of Women: Rethinking the Republic of Letters in the Seventeenth Century,* Cambridge University Press, 2012.

Online

"René Descartes and Princess Elisabeth of Bohemia," *EarlyModernTexts.com,* http://www.earlymoderntexts. com/pdfs/descartes1643.pdf(November 6, 2014).□

Emma of Normandy

Norman-born English queen consort, Emma of Normandy (c. 985–1052), also known as Elfgifu, was the wife to two English kings and mother to two more. A political power player, she provided the hereditary link between Norman, Danish Viking, and Anglo-Saxon rulers in early English history.

Emma was born c. 985 (some sources say 987), the daughter of Richard I, the Duke of Normandy and his wife, Gunnor of Denmark. Her ancestors were Norsemen who had taken over northern France earlier in the tenth century. Emma's great grandfather, Rolf, also known as Rollo, was a leader among the Vikings. In 911, he formally was given control of the territory of Normandy from a weak French king, Charles III the Simple. This transaction established the Norman dynasty.

Little is known about Emma's life before her first marriage. She had many siblings, conceived both before and after the marriage of her parents. Her father died when she was still a child, in 996. Richard I was succeeded by his son, Richard II, who would later prove a valuable ally for his sister.

Married English King Aethelred

A few years later, on April 5, 1002, when Emma was about 17 years old, she was married to Aethelred II, the Saxon king of England, most likely for political reasons. He was known as Aethelred Unraed, or uncounselled, or Aethelred the Unready. Emma was Aethelred's second wife. (He had married his first wife, Aelfgifu, daughter of Thored of Northumbria, in 985. She died in 1002, and had at least ten children with Aethelred.) Upon her marriage, Emma took the official name of Elfgifu, which she used when she witnessed official documents. Privately, she remained known as Emma for the rest of her life.

Before this union, English kings usually took English women for their wives. The marriage between Emma and Aethelred might have been part of a treaty reached between Richard and Aethelred in 991. This agreement tried to ensure further friendly relations between the Normans and the English. A marriage between the Norman duke's daughter and the British monarch would support such relations.

Also in the 990s, England was suffering from an increase in damaging Viking attacks. A marriage to Emma might have been an effort to convince Normans to deny Viking raiders access to their ports, which facilitated the raids. Though the marriage between Emma and Aethelred was intended to stabilize his kingdom against the actions and violence being committed by the Vikings in some form, the union did not achieve this goal. Instead it ultimately facilitated the ever increasing power of the Normans and that group's ability to acquire property in the north.

Birthed Three Children for Aethelred

Aethelred and Emma had three children together, including two sons, Edward, who was born in 1004 or 1005, then

Culture Club/Getty Images

Alfred. Both boys were sent to Normandy after their births to keep them safe. They spent most of their childhoods and young adulthoods living there. The couple also had a daughter, Godgifu. Beginning in the medieval era, historians believed that Emma did not love Aethelred nor their children. This seems contradicted by Aethelred's gifts to her, including bestowing towns, goods, and estates on throughout their marriage. These properties included Winchester and Exeter.

Early in her marriage to Aethelred, Emma was also given the title of queen, which underscored her status and influence. By holding this title, she, as queen mother, could help position her children better in the line of succession for the English crown. Primogeniture—that is, the oldest son automatically gaining the throne—was not yet in practice, so holding this title gave Emma particular power.

Aethelred's tenure as king was not particularly impressive. During his reign, the English kingdom grew increasingly smaller as control of Saxon territory was lost to Vikings, including the future king of England, the Danish Viking leader Cnut, and his father, Danish king Sweyn Haraldson. The attacks only increased after 1002.

Went into Exile with Aethelred

Most of Aethelred's lands were gone by 1013 or 1014, when he was essentially deposed. At that time, Aethelred and Emma fled England and went into exile at the court of Emma's brother. To address the increasingly chaotic situation in England, Aethelred and one of his sons from his first marriage tried to take action against the invaders but disagreed on what should take place. Nearly all English territory came under Cnut's control by the time of Aethelred's death in April 1016. Emma, however, would remain in Normandy until 1017.

Upon Aethelred's death, one of his sons by his first marriage gained temporary hold of the throne. Edmund "Ironsides" reigned until his death in November 1016. He was able to take the throne because he split power with Cnut. Upon his death, Cnut took control of the whole country. Though Cnut was only 19 or 20 years old when he took control of the English kingdom, the savvy monarch would soon become king of Denmark and Norway as well.

Married Cnut

Though Emma considered mounting a campaign to put her son Edward on the throne, he was too young to be a formidable threat and she was still living in Normandy. Because of his insecure hold on the throne and her links to the successful Normans, Cnut needed validation for his rule and asked Emma to become his wife. They were wed in July or August 1017. By marrying Cnut, she retained her position as the most important, powerful woman in England and put herself in a position to ensure one of her children succeeded him. She was about 11 years older than her second husband.

When they married, Cnut was involved with an Anglo-Saxon woman named Aelfgifu of Northampton. It is unclear if they were married or if she was his concubine. Either way, they had two sons, Harold Harefoot and Sweyn, whom their father considered potential heirs to the throne despite their likely illegitimate birth. Before Emma married Cnut, she insisted on an agreement that any children they would have together would head the line of succession, then Cnut's sons with Aelfgifu, and finally Emma's sons with Aethelred. Aelfgifu and Emma became instant rivals, a situation that would only grow more tense in successive years, as Aelfgifu would outlive Cnut.

With Cnut, Emma had two more children, son Harthacnut, then daughter Gunhild. Gunhild would later become the wife of a German emperor, Henry III. During his rule, Emma was noted for the many charitable donations she made to churches all over England. She also increasingly gained power during Cnut's reign, especially after 1020 when her son and presumed heir was born.

Promoted Interests of Son Harthacnut

Emma unexpectedly faced another succession crisis. While conducting an inspection tour of England, Cnut died suddenly on November 12, 1035, creating another royal power vacuum. The children of Aelfgifu and Emma began competing for the throne of England. Emma's sons by Aethelred were still in Normandy, while Harthacnut, though still young, was on the throne in Denmark. Emma tried to hold on to the throne for Harthacnut, but Harold Harefoot had the advantage of location. Harthacnut could not travel to England because of political tensions in Denmark, as the Norwegian king was threatening an attack.

Ultimately, Harold Harefoot gained the throne, primarily because he was the only one in the country when his father's unexpected death occurred. Though Emma tried political maneuverings to keep Harthacnut's claim active and had some support of English nobles, she was only able to secure Wessex for him. She was also allowed to live on her properties in Winchester.

This deal was made with the assistance of Godwin, Earl of Wessex, who soon betrayed Emma and her family. Though initially allied with Emma, Godwin saw Harold Harefoot's power steadily increase and decided to back Harold instead. In 1036, Emma asked her sons from her first marriage to come to her aid. Alfred answered his mother's call. Godwin ordered Alfred to be seized and had him blinded. Alfred ultimately lost his life from the incident.

Saw Harthacnut Take the Throne

Though Alfred was lost, Harold's tenure proved to be short-lived as well. He was officially recognized as the English king in 1037. At that time, Emma was forced into exile, and she lived under the protection of Count Baldwin of Flanders in the city of Bruges. She asked her son Edward to join her and take action in England, but he declined because he lacked the support of anyone in England. Harthacnut did come to Flanders in 1039, at which time Emma and her son planned an invasion of England.

The need for an invasion was eliminated when Harold died in March 1040. Only a few months later, in June 1040, Emma returned with Harthacnut to England. There, her son claimed the throne and was recognized as the English king.

Published Biography

To promote the interests of herself, her deceased husband Cnut, and her son Harthacnut, Emma commissioned a biography in this period from a cleric living in northern France. *The Encomium of Queen Emma (Encomium Emmae Reginae)* described the lives of Emma and her family in overwhelmingly positive words to impress a secular audience for political gain. At this time in history, most biographies were written as a means of making a case for sainthood.

Like his half-brother Harold before him, Harthacnut's reign was short-lived. Before Harthacnut died unexpectedly in June 1042, he had designated his half brother Edward, Emma's son, as his heir. His word was respected and Edward returned to England to rule later that year. Edward, who was later styled as Edward the Confessor, deprived his mother of her lands, properties, and wealth soon after formally taking the throne, in 1043. The reasons for this decision were not fully clear, but described as Emma's lack of support for him and favoritism for Harthacnut.

Supported Edward's Reign

Within a few years, however, Edward and Emma seem to have reconciled because she again exerted power in 1044 and part of 1045. This is known because her signature can be found on royal documents in this period. Her influence—and signatures—ceased after Edward married Edith, the daughter of Godwin, in 1045. Emma's son Edward proved a popular Saxon king, known for his generosity to the poor and deep religious faith. Edward also had his own struggles as king, including overwhelming internal strife, constant threat of invasion, and inability to produce an heir with his wife.

Living a quiet life in Winchester after 1045, Emma died there on March 6, 1052. She then was buried at the Winchester Cathedral. In retrospect, her legacy centered on how she provided continuity through multiple kings in England. She also was the great-aunt to William, Duke of Normandy, known as William the Conqueror, who captured England in 1066 at the Battle of Hastings. This conflict occurred after Edward's death on January 5 of that year, and ensured that William would beat out rival claimants, Godwin's son Harold and Harold Haadraada. Though Emma of Normandy was largely forgotten in history, she proved to be the major link between England's Danish Viking, Anglo-Saxon, and Norman roots.

Books

Dictionary of Women Worldwide: 25,000 Women Through the Ages, edited by Anne Commire and Deborah Klezmer, Yorkin Publications, 2007.

Koman, Alan J., *A Who's Who of Your Ancestral Saints,* Genealogical Publishing, 2010.

Women in World History: A Biographical Encyclopedia, Volume 5, edited by Anne Commire, Yorkin Publications, 2002.

Periodicals

Guardian (London, England), August 13, 2005.
Publishers Weekly, May 23, 2005.

Online

"Emma Receiving The Encomium, In *The Encomium of Queen Emma,*" British Library, http://www.bl.uk/onlinegallery/onlineex/illmanus/other/011add000033241u00001000.html (December 23, 2014). □

Maggie Estep

Author and spoken word performer Maggie Estep (1963–2014) came to fame in the 1990s as a slam poet featured on such networks as MTV and HBO. Considering herself an author first and foremost, she published novels such as *Hex* and *Flamethrower,* and short story collections including *Soft Maniacs.*

B orn on March 20, 1963, in Summit, New Jersey, Margaret Ann Estep was the daughter of a racehorse trainer father. Because of her father's career, her childhood involved many moves. Her father often trained horses for wealthy clients, but would often get mad at or disagree with the owners and quit, forcing him to seek new opportunities elsewhere. In addition to New Jersey, the

family lived in Canada, France, Colorado, Georgia, Pennsylvania, and New York state.

Moved to New York City

A childhood visit to New York City cemented her future. Estep visited New York City in 1971, and became attracted to city life when she observed people stepping across a dead body on a sidewalk without a second thought. After dropping out of high school at the age of 17, Estep moved to Manhattan. There, she found employment as a go-go dancer for a brief period of time. Joining New York's punk scene, Estep became a heroin addict. By the mid-1980s, she was in drug rehabilitation. At this time, she began writing fiction.

As she worked on getting her life together, Estep's career path was further molded by educational experiences. In Boulder, Colorado, in 1986, she took part in a summer course at Naropa University's Jack Kerouac School of Disembodied Poetics. The course was taught by Beat Generation author William S. Burroughs, one of her favorite authors. Inspired by this experience, she spent two years at the university. Estep returned to New York in 1988 to complete a writing degree at Manhattan's Empire State College.

Making her home in the East Village, Estep lived a bohemian life style as she pursued writing fiction and poetry. To support herself, she worked at menial jobs, such as office manager for a nightclub called The World. Estep was also employed by the National Writers Union, where she performed odd jobs. During this time, Estep became exposed to performing. A small art space in the East Village, ABC No Rio, held open mike nights every Sunday, and Estep became a regular. Though Estep enjoyed performing, she was not at ease performing elsewhere early on.

Discovered Spoken Word Performing

This situation changed when Estep learned of poetry slams at the Nuyorican Poets Cafe. This was one of the launch pads of the slam poetry movement, a hub of the emerging art form that came from such coffee shops. Slam poetry added elements of rap battles, stand-up comedy, and performance art to the live reading of poetry. Performers worked on impressing and persuading audiences to support them. The poet who demonstrated the superior style of speaking, the most confidence, and the most impressive sense of humor often came out on top.

Over the next few years, Estep thrived performing at the Nuyorican. As audiences grew and became more passionate, Estep became one of the break-out poets appearing there. She regularly won slams at the cafe. Estep was a particularly memorable poet and spoken word performer. Her poetry was honest and realistic, featuring her dark sense of humor and post-punk feminist leadings. Estep delivered her poems quickly and insistently, often with a quick tumble of absurd, violent, and allusion-filled images.

Describing her poetry, Neil Strauss wrote in the *New York Times,* "Maggie Estep doesn't have to stray far from her East Village studio to find inspiration. She constructs humorous spoken pieces out of the pointless situations that occur on her doorstep, from the drug dealers who see her every day but persist in their futile efforts to offer her crack and 'smoke" to the male passer-bys who yell 'Hey, baby' in her direction."

For her part, Estep explained her in-your-face showmanship by giving a nod to the popular heavy metal band Kiss. She told Eric Deggans of the *St. Petersburg Times,* "That was the first band I got to see live." Estep added, "It was my first exposure to that kind of big rock 'n' roll thing. It probably explains everything."

Made Famous by MTV

When Estep took part in poetry slams at the Nuyorican, audiences knew the names of many of her poems and screamed them out. As more celebrities showed up at poetry slam events, MTV, the music television and popular culture network, sent talent scouts to the cafe, where they discovered Estep. It was MTV that brought Estep from the poetry slams at Nuyorican to greater fame. Estep soon became a star spoken word performer.

Not only did the network feature Estep performing stand-up poetry on two thirty-second spots that regularly aired in 1993 and 1994, MTV also made her the center of two episodes of its long-running *Unplugged* series which were dedicated to spoken word. Describing her appearance on one of these episodes, Caryn James of the *New York Times* wrote, "The show is full of MTV moments. Maggie Estep stands center stage, wearing tight black jeans,

a black tank top and no shoes. Lights flash in the background, bass-heavy backup music plays and she yells out a self-mocking poem about 'the stupid jerk I'm obsessed with.' . . . Here is poetry as performance, poetry as video. And though most purists would prefer to ignore this truth, here is poetry returned to its roots in song and chant."

In addition to these televised appearances, Estep had a featured role on MTV's spoken word tour, "Free Your Mind" in 1993. The following year, she toured with Lollapalooza, where she performed between Henry Rollins and Green Day, and found the audience divided on the effectiveness of her presence. She also made a live appearance at Woodstock '94, as well as other regional festivals. Additional television program appearances included *Russell Simmon's Def Poetry Jam,* which aired on HBO.

Released Albums and Videos

The Nuyorican capitalized on Estep's popularity. The cafe jointly formed a record label with Imago Records called NuYo. The first album released on the label was Estep's *No More Mr. Nice Girl,* which came out in the spring of 1994. It featured both spoken word and musical songs, with the musical aspect created by her band I Love Everybody.

One song off the record was a novelty hit in 1994. "Hey Baby" was inspired by catcalls from construction workers on the streets of New York and includes her response to these men. Estep gained an even wider audience when the video for "Hey Baby" was mocked by the animated duo of MTV's popular series *Beavis and Butt-head.*

Three years later, Estep put out another album, *Love Is a Dog from Hell.* It was released on Mouth Almighty/Mercury in 1997. As with her previous album, *Love Is a Dog from Hell* included both spoken word and musical tracks. Among the latter was a cover of a song by Lou Reed, "Vicious." Actor Steve Buscemi directed the accompanying music video.

Despite finding success and performing in various other spoken word and poetry reading venues, Estep continued to live simply, though she saw some financial gains from her fame. She was more amused than anything about becoming popular among rock music fans. Estep focused on writing, penning poetry, stories, and travel diaries. She also had an acting appearance in an independent film, *Alchemy,* that aired as a television movie in 1995.

Focused on Writing

By the late 1990s, Estep moved away from spoken word performing and increasingly focused on writing and publishing her fiction. In 1997, her first novel, *Diary of an Emotional Idiot: A Novel,* was published. The book explored a woman's life in a fashion similar to *Bridget Jones' Diary,* but from a more underground perspective. The characters included drug dealers and dominatrixes.

Next, in 1999, Estep put out *Soft Maniacs,* a collection of short stories. The narratives included in the collection are woven together, and primarily focus on the lives of two women; Judy, a psychiatrist with a sex addiction, and Katie, a woman who is emotionally distant. The stories are about each woman's failed relationships, and their quest for a meaningful domestic life. They are told from the perspective of the men in their lives. Discussing the book in *In These Times*, Kristin Kolb noted, "But Estep is optimistic. If we can stop obsessing over and get beyond our sexual demons, a relationship between a man and a woman isn't so suffocating after all. It's the emptiness that confines us."

Estep's fictional works centered on different topics in the 21st century. In 2002, Estep began a trilogy *Hex*, a horse-centered mystery noir featuring the character Ruby Murphy. Murphy is a worker at a museum on Coney Island who has to become a detective among the horse racing set. *Hex* was chosen by the *New York Times* as a notable book of 2003. In 2005, she put out the sequel to *Hex*, entitled *Gargantuan*, followed by *Flamethrower* in 2006. During this period, Estep spent time living in New Smyrna Beach, Florida, where she was serving as an artist-in-residence for the Atlantic Center for the Arts in 2005.

Estep had not forgotten her poetry roots. In 2003, she published *Love Dance of the Mechanical Animals: Confessions, Highly Subjective Journalism, Old Rants and New Stories* which included her spoken-word and nonfiction works. She also contributed fiction and nonfiction to such anthologies as *The Best American Erotica, Brooklyn Noir 2*, and *Goodbye to All That*. In addition, Estep wrote a blog which she regularly updated. While working as an author, she continued to hold other jobs, such as working as a realtor.

Unexpected Death

Though Estep spent much of her adulthood living in Brooklyn, she moved to upstate New York in her later years. By 2012, Estep had moved to Hudson, New York. In early February 2014, Estep suffered a heart attack at her home in Hudson, New York. She died two days later, on February 12, 2014, in Albany, New York. She was 50 years old. She was working on a novel entitled *The Story of Giants* when she died.

At Estep's memorial service, a spoken word artist and friend of Estep's told Art Cusano of the Hudson, New York *Register-Star*, "Maggie Estep was beautiful, standing at the microphone in the early days of slam. She could spit and coo in the same breath. Sometimes it scared me. Other times it made me laugh, along with everyone else. Wit, wisdom and words—she was a Marshall-amped Dorothy Parker, without the gin martini."

Periodicals

Associated Press, July 26, 1993.
In These Times, December 26, 1999.
News-Journal (Daytona Beach, FL), March 25, 2005.
New York Times, July 25, 1993; September 11, 1994; September 25, 1994; February 13, 2014.
St. Petersburg Times (FL), January 26, 1996.

Online

"Friends Recall Maggie Estep as 'Possessed by a God,'" *Register-Star*, http://www.registerstar.com/news/article_a4555662-9695-11e3-9c4c-0019bb2963f4.html (October 29, 2014).
"Gen-X Icon, Poet and Novelist Maggie Estep Dead at 50," *Rolling Stone*, http://www.rollingstone.com/culture/news/gen-x-icon-poet-and-novelist-maggie-estep-dead-at-50-20140213 (October 29, 2014).
"Maggie Estep," *Internet Movie Database*, http://www.imdb.com/name/nm0261602/ (October 29, 2014).
"Maggie Estep, Novelist and Spoken Word Artist, Dies at 50," *Los Angeles Times*, http://articles.latimes.com/2014/feb/12/entertainment/la-et-jc-maggie-estep-has-died-20140212 (October 29, 2014).
"Steve Buscemi Remembers Maggie Estep," *Billboard*, http://www.billboard.com/articles/news/5915779/steve-buscemi-remembers-maggie-estep (October 29, 2014).□

F

Bill Finger

American comic book writer Bill Finger (1914–1974) helped create iconic comic book characters like Batman and the Green Lantern. A gifted scripter, Finger worked for what would become DC Comics for two decades at mid-century. Though Finger originally received no official credit for creating Batman for most his life, his influential role in devising Batman and many aspects of his superhero world eventually came to light.

Born Milton Finger on February 8, 1914, in Denver, Colorado, he was the son of a tailor. Finger changed his name from Milton to William, or Bill, to avoid discrimination as a Jew later in life. His family moved to New York City when he was a child. There, he graduated from DeWitt Clinton High School in 1933. Other comic book legends graduated from DeWitt including Bob Kane, the credited creator of Batman, and Stan Lee, the force behind Marvel Comics. By the time he reached high school, Finger was an enthusiastic reader, favoring pulp and mystery stories.

By the time Finger was in his late teens, the Great Depression was creating economic turmoil for many Americans as the economy in the United States collapsed. The shop owned by Finger's father closed, and Finger sought jobs to give his family needed income. He worked as a clerk in a hat shop and shoe store, for example. Despite harsh circumstances, Finger had ambitions to write himself.

Began Writing with Kane

Finger had not known Kane in high school, though they had attended DeWitt at the same time. By the time Kane had reached his early twenties, he had become a successful comic strip artist and was also creating works for National Periodical Publications (later and better known as DC Comics). After Finger met Kane at a party in 1938, the pair began working together on projects by meeting at New York's Edgar Allan Poe Park. Kane was drawing two featured comics by this time, *Rusty and His Pals* and *Clip Carson,* and Finger worked on them through Kane.

Though Finger was not credited for many years and never received official credit, he helped devise the character of Batman with acknowledged creator Kane. Kane was approached to create a new superhero for National in late 1938. Earlier in the year, the company had found much success when it introduced Superman to the world, and hoped to find another best-selling superhero to feature in comics. At the behest of DC editor Vin Sullivan, Kane was charged with formulating a new superhero. Kane asked Finger for help. Over a weekend in 1938, they hashed out ideas together and came up with Batman, who has become one of the most popular superhero characters in the world. The actual creation process is not fully clear because of differing stories told about the experience over the years by Kane and those who knew Finger.

Played Role in Creating Batman

What is generally accepted about the process was that Kane came up with the idea for a superhero who was like a bird or bat. Kane's original idea included clothing the human hero in wings and red tights. He also originally wanted to make Batman a vehement avenger. Finger molded Batman into something different. Not only did Finger make Batman more of a detective, he contributed many of the best known visual aspects of Batman, including a costume that is black and gray in color and a cowl that underscores Batman's bat name. Finger also devised the Batmobile, the Batcave, Batman's Bruce Wayne alter ego, the term Gotham City, Batman's sidekick Robin/Dick Grayson, and a number of Batman's foes and villains, such as Joker, Catwoman, the Penguin, and Two-Face/Harvey Dent. In addition, Finger wrote the first Batman comic book stories, including, most importantly, Batman's moving and heartbreaking origin story. Unlike many superheroes created in the late 1930s, it was psychologically complex.

Much of what Finger contributed to Batman made the character successful and memorable. As the London *Independent* explained, "From the start, Batman was unlike other heroes. His rivals, Superman and Spider-Man, are festooned in the primary colours of the American flag, whereas Batman dresses in dark blues and blacks. And no other superhero has a story quite as bleak. When Bruce Wayne was a little boy, he watched his parents' deaths at the hands of Joe Chill, a heartless mugger, and vowed to dedicate the rest of his life to gaining revenge on the criminal underworld. Superman's arrival from another planet is kids' stuff in comparison."

In this era of comic book history, writers were generally not given credit for their work or the aspects of the stories they created. Finger did not receive any recognition for his work on the comic for Kane; it was Kane who signed a deal with the publisher in 1939, promoted Batman, and built an audience for the superhero. Kane became known for recognizing and employing talent, like Finger and ghost artists who would draw and ink the Batman comics he created.

As the first Batman comics were being created, Finger continued to refine the look of Batman and the comic as a whole. He had Kane and his ghost artists look at pictures he collected of actor Douglas Fairbanks, Sr., for the acrobatic movements of Batman. Another visual innovation credited to Finger was the use of giant props in the comic. To enhance the look of the comic, he added massive images of clocks and symbols like the Statue of Liberty. For both writing and artistic purposes, Finger kept articles from publications like *Popular Science* to inspire the gadgets in the Batcave and Batmobile. The stories in Batman took their cue from gangster and detective movies and books of the era.

Did Not Press for Credit

Because of the ongoing economic depression, Finger was more concerned with having a steady job and regular income—albeit with low pay—than seeking credit as Batman became increasingly popular. In *Icons of the American Comic Book: From Captain America to Wonder Woman*, Sheldon Moldoff, a former assistant artist for Kane, explained, "He was so overwhelmed that he was getting steady jobs that he never thought of anything else. He just wanted to be a writer. Bill was so happy he was working, he didn't think about royalties, rights, any of that. He was very grateful to Bob."

Finger's personality contributed to the situation. He was introverted, shy, and unassertive, in contrast to the brash Kane. Finger was also usually professionally deferential, steamrolled by editors in other situations as well. Though it came to light that Finger thought it was unacceptable that he

was not credited for his part in creating Batman as the years passed, he chose not to fight for it for reasons unknown.

Sometime after 1946, Kane and DC Comics came to an agreement whereby he was named the creator of Batman. Kane received abundant recognition and immense financial rewards. Kane gained even more wealth when Batman was turned into a television series in the mid-1960s. Finger wrote one episode of *Batman*—"The Clock Cleaner's Crazy Crimes"—in 1966, but received no compensation for his role in creating Batman. The experience was unique, however. He was the only comic book writer to pen a script for the series.

Wrote Other Comics, Scripts

By the mid-1940s, Finger's professional career had moved past Kane. Finger worked for Kane directly on Batman for only a few years, allowing him his break into the comic book business. In 1940, Finger had also helped create another significant superhero, the Green Lantern, with Martin Nodell.

When National Publications discovered that Kane was misrepresenting the creative process for Batman and that Finger, not Kane, was writing the comic, the publisher took action and hired Finger as a freelancer directly in 1941. By this time, Finger was highly regarded as a comic book writer. For National, Finger wrote many issues of Batman, as well as Superman and Green Lantern, among other superhero characters for the next two decades. He also had a hand in the creation of some lesser known comic book characters such as the *Sensation Comics* hero, Wildcat, co-created with Irwin Hansen.

Finger's television script for *Batman* was not his first work for television, however. In the 1950s, he wrote episodes of such series as *The Web* and *Foreign Intrigue*. In addition to *Batman*, Finger wrote multiple episodes of *77 Sunset Strip* during the 1960s. He co-wrote a science fiction film script, *The Green Slime*, produced in 1968.

Gained Public Recognition for Batman

At a comic book convention appearance in New York City in 1965, Finger publicly described the role he played in creating Batman. Though Finger lost out on credit and financial gain, he was not hostile or angry but merely stating his part. In the wake of Finger's appearance, a fan magazine article written by Jerry Bails and published in *CAPA-Alpha* #12 further publicized Finger's previously unknown role. Kane responded in anger with his own article claiming sole credit as creator and dubbed Finger a liar. As a result, Finger was further pushed to the outskirts of comic books.

By the mid-1960s, Finger's comic book writing career was waning for other reasons as well. Long a procrastinator who rarely turned in his scripts on time, he fell victim to a changing of the editorial guard at DC Comics. The new editors became disillusioned and unwilling to overlook his faults despite the quality of his work. Also in this period, he and other long-time DC Comics freelancers demanded royalties, benefits, and tried unsuccessfully to unionize. In the aftermath, those who took part in this movement were given fewer assignments and were gradually forced out.

A few years later, during the early 1970s, Finger did write some freelance scripts for the company for mystery comics like *House of Mystery* and *House of Secrets* on a limited basis. Yet, by the time of his death, Finger was impoverished. He died on January 18, 1974, in New York City, at the age of 59.

Given Credit for Batman After Death

At the time of his death, Finger's role in the creation of Batman was known in certain circles, but he was still officially unrecognized for his contributions. Reprints of some early Batman comics were giving Finger story credit, however. Kane would live for more than two decades longer, but continued to publicly deny Finger's important role on Batman for a number of years. However, in Kane's 1989 autobiography *Batman & Me,* he admitted that Finger could have had a byline on the Batman comics, but Finger had not asked for one nor had Kane offered one. In retrospect, Kane stated, he should have given him credit and acknowledge the important role played by Finger.

Finger's legacy was not forgotten in the early 21st century. In 2005, comic book inker Jerry Robinson helped found the Bill Finger Awards for Excellence in Comic Book Writing. These honors are presented at Comic-Con International, held annually in San Diego, California.

Summarizing Finger's importance, the author of the book *Bill: The Boy Wonder: The Secret Co-Creator of Batman,* Marc Tyler Nobleman, told *Premium Official News,* "Some would call him the greatest martyr in comics history. He created a character that by some sources is the most lucrative superhero of all time and possibly one of the most recognisable fictional characters of the modern era, yet he died poor and unknown, without a proper obituary or funeral. There's a huge disconnect between his contribution to culture and his legacy. It's a cautionary tale for anybody who wants to be in the creative arts. You need to know how important it is to protect your intellectual property."

Books

Icons of the American Comic Book: From Captain America to Wonder Woman, edited by Randy Duncan and Matthew J. Smith, Grenwood Press, 2013.

Periodicals

Independent (London, England), July 22, 2008.

New York Magazine, March 9, 2009.

New York Times, October 6, 2013.

Oklahoman (Oklahoma City, OK), July 18, 2008.

Premium Official News, November 6, 2012.

School Library Journal, August 2012.

Western Morning News (Plymouth, England), December 14, 2006.

Transcripts

All Things Considered, National Public Radio, August 11, 2012. □

Jack Donovan Foley

During the late 1920s as Hollywood studios moved from silent films to "talkies," American sound effects engineer Jack Foley (1891–1967) pioneered innovative ways to capture ambient sounds to enhance the audio quality of a film. Foley spent nearly four decades at Universal Studios, inventing and perfecting the art and craft of creating realistic, synchronous sound effects for film. Later dubbed the Foley technique, "Foley artists" continue his work today.

Jack Donovan Foley was born April 12, 1891, in Yorkville, New York, to Irish immigrant parents. His father died when he was an infant. As a young man Foley worked as a clerk at the Coney Island docks and played semi-professional baseball. He grew tired of the cold Northeast weather so he moved to Santa Monica, California, around 1914 with his wife, Beatrice Rehm. They had four children. Foley's wife was an athlete who excelled at long distance ocean swimming. During World War I, Foley was active with the American Defense Society (ADS). Founded in 1915, the ADS was a nationalist, anti-Communist organization that called for increased armaments to prepare defenses should the German army decide to attack the United States. The ADS feared an attack on U.S. water supplies, so members guarded the Los Angeles water supply during the war to protect it from sabotage.

Joined Hollywood as Location Scout

Foley moved his family to Bishop, California, after falling in love with the Owens Valley and surrounding mountains. Bishop was some 260 miles north of Los Angeles. In Bishop, Foley found work at the local hardware store. He helped stage small theater productions, working as an actor, writer and director. He also wrote and drew cartoons for the local paper. Owens Valley thrived with farmers, but during the 1920s the farmers began selling their property and offering water rights to Los Angeles, which had started to outgrow its water supply. At this point, Foley began to worry about the future of Bishop, fearing it would become a ghost town. As Foley looked at the lush valley and snowcapped mountains surrounding the town, he thought the landscape might be ideal for Hollywood filmmakers, particularly those shooting Westerns. Foley persuaded the Bishop shopkeepers to let filmmakers use their storefronts, and the town was soon thriving again.

At this point, Foley began working as a location scout for the booming movie business. He also became a stuntman and double, eventually working his way up the ladder until he was serving as an assistant to William Kraft. Foley went on to direct short films starring comedian Benny Rubin. Foley directed two shorts in 1929, *Marking Time* and *The Pilgrim Papas.* The latter film starred Rubin. Foley also began selling manuscripts to Universal Studios.

Foley also earned jobs directing "inserts" for various Hollywood film studios. Inserts were close-up shots correlating to an action in a master shot. For instance, in a master shot including a gun battle the insert might consist of a hand reaching for a holster and grabbing a pistol. Typically, inserts were not filmed during a shoot so actors could concentrate on their performance, but were added later to provide more details to a scene. Foley shot inserts by himself, arranging the sets and acquiring the necessary props. Inserts had to be meticulously filmed, using the same lighting and angles as the main take. Foley also worked with title cards during film's silent days. To show what a character was thinking, aesthetically pleasing title cards were periodically placed in front of the camera with phrases depicting the character's thoughts. In 1923, Foley released *How to Handle Women*, which he co-wrote and co-directed.

Added Sound to *Show Boat*

Foley stumbled into sound production in the late 1920s as studios rushed to perfect the new technology. The competition began after Warner Bros. released *The Jazz Singer* in 1927. The film, which offered the first synchronized film dialogue, included Al Jolson singing six songs, as captured by the studio's Vitaphone recording system. The Vitaphone system recorded sound on a phonograph record synced to the film projector. Warner Bros. had exclusive rights to the technology. Soon after *The Jazz Singer* was released, Universal Studios was set to release *Show Boat* as a silent musical. Silent musicals were not uncommon at the time, as moviegoers were eager to catch a glimpse of Broadway even if they could not hear the sounds of Broadway. Universal, however, realized that it could not release another silent musical if it wanted to compete with Warner Bros.

According to *FilmSound.org*, Foley poked fun at Universal for being so far behind the times with regards to sound. In 1952, Foley wrote the following in the *Universal Studio Club News*, according to *FilmSound.org*: "The Warner kids on the neighboring ranch had just come up with a sound picture 'The Jazz Singer' while the hard riding, cliff-hanging shoot-from-the-hip boys on the U ranch were complacently rounding up the last few scenes of the great American musical, 'Show Boat,' a SILENT picture. Faces around here were so red someone yelled 'The Indians are going!' Someone asked, 'Are we still in business?'"

Foley was quickly dispatched to the University of Southern California to learn about the Fox-Case portable sound unit, which Universal planned on using to add sound to *Show Boat*. The unit was available for short trials. After a crash course in using the equipment, Foley played an integral role in retrofitting *Show Boat* with sound. Universal built a primitive sound stage and placed a 40-piece orchestra there under the direction of Russian composer Joseph Cherniavsky. The singers took the stage, as did Foley and his sound-making assistants. As the film rolled along, they recorded the sounds to go with it, adding the music, the footsteps, the clapping hands and background voices in real-time. This was referred to as the "make and sync" technique whereby the effects were done on a sound stage in sync with the action of the picture.

Perfected Art of *Artificial* Sound

As the sound revolution continued, studios began adding sounds to more and more films and Universal called on Foley for help. As a former film stuntman and director, Foley took an interest in this new technology. He realized a film needed more than just dialogue. To sound realistic, it also needed ambient background noises, such as the sounds on the periphery of a person's consciousness. At this point, he grew obsessed with figuring out how to add "realistic" background noises to film. He began developing his own techniques that would work within the constraints of the early sound systems. Foley only had one track to work with to add sounds, so he had to figure out how to layer several sounds into one take.

Foley realized that when people walk, they make more noise than just footsteps. To remedy this situation, Foley kept a piece of cloth tucked into his back pocket whenever he was conducting a sound recording. He pulled the cloth out when he needed to add the sound of a person "moving." Whenever Foley needed to add the footsteps of more than one person, he walked across the sound stage with a cane. It was said that Foley could emulate the sound of three people walking using only himself and a cane. When Foley needed to add the footsteps of a character with a limp, he placed a rock in his shoe. His family often found him in the kitchen with the cooking utensils, dropping and rattling them around to see what kind of sounds they could simulate.

Over the course of his career, Foley figured out ways to use inanimate objects to get the desired sounds needed for a film. Foley artists continue his craft in the 21st century using some of his innovations and constantly creating new ways to make familiar sounds. To make a crackling fire, a Foley artist crinkles cellophane. To make footsteps in the snow, a Foley artist squeezes a box of cornstarch. To get the sound of walking in the mud, a Foley artist squeezes wet, crumpled newspaper. Have a character walking on leaves? A Foley artist will run a finger through some cornflakes. Need to crack a bone? A Foley artist will break some celery. Need the sounds of a dinghy at sea rocking on the water? A creaky floor will do.

As Foley refined his craft, he realized that to sound realistic, the footsteps had to match the character. According to Richard Verrier of the *Los Angeles Times*, Foley once offered these observations to an interviewer: "Rock Hudson is a solid stepper. Tony Curtis has a brisk foot; Audie Murphy is springy; James Cagney is clipped, Marlon Brando, soft." Over the course of his career, Foley estimated he had walked 5,000 miles to capture all of the footsteps needed for the films he worked on. Foley worked with a full crew at his disposal. He had prop people, recording experts and sound assistants. Many of his apprentices went to other studios where they continued to utilize his techniques.

Left Mark on Sound Industry

Many times, Foley came up with a solution to a director's sound problem. Once, a director needed a step to creak whenever a character stepped on it. The director tried again and again to capture the sound of the creaky step as the actress walked across it. He could not get it to work, so Foley stepped in. Foley decided to sit in a rocking chair and rock back slowly whenever the actress hit the step. One of Foley's most innovative sound solutions came in 1960's historical drama *Spartacus*. Director Stanley Kubrick was ready to take the cast and crew back to Spain to re-shoot a large battle scene because the "on-location" sound he had captured during filming did not sound right. The scene in question involved 8,000 Roman soldiers marching into battle. Instead of gathering a large crowd to march and make the footsteps, Foley took some key rings filled with keys and rhythmically jingled them in sync with the marching steps to get the cadenced chink of armor. Innovative methods such as this not only saved time, but also saved money for movie studios.

Speaking to the Toronto *Globe and Mail*'s Jennie Punter, Hollywood sound editor Walter Murch offered his theory as to why sound is so important to a movie. "Film sound is rarely appreciated for itself alone but functions largely as an enhancement of the visuals. By means of some mysterious perceptual alchemy, whatever virtues sound brings to film are largely perceived and appreciated by the audience in visual terms. The better the sound, the better the image."

Besides working on the sound stage, Foley also wrote for the *Universal Studio Club News*. He retired from Universal's sound department around 1964. Although he never edited a clip of sound, the Motion Picture Sound Editors made Foley an honorary member in 1962. Foley died on November 9, 1967, in Los Angeles. Today, Foley artists continue to use Foley's techniques for film, television, radio, commercials, computer games, and audio CDs. The Motion Picture Sound Editors even offer annual Golden Reel Awards for "best sound effects and Foley." During his lifetime, Foley never received any mention for his work in the film credits. Today, credit is given to the "Foley Artist." Foley's story and techniques were given a detailed look in Vanessa Theme Ament's 2009 book, *The Foley Grail: The Art of Performing Sound for Film, Games, and Animation*.

Books

Ament, Vanessa Theme, *The Foley Grail: The Art of Performing Sound for Film, Games, and Animation*, Focal Press, 2009.

Mott, Robert L., *Sound Effects: Radio, TV, and Film*, Butterworth Publishers, 1990.

Periodicals

Electronic Musician, September 2001.

Globe and Mail (Toronto, Canada), January 20, 2003.

Los Angeles Times, April 4, 2006.

Science Now, June 4, 2002.

Online

"The Story of Jack Foley," *FilmSound.org*, http://www.film sound.org/foley/jackfoley.htm (December 31, 2014).□

Redd Foxx

The African-American comedian Redd Foxx (1922–1991) starred in the immensely popular *Sanford and Son* television series in the 1970s. He also found great success, in terms of sales if not financial rewards, with a series of comedy albums featuring frequently obscene material.

Foxx, as Nick Ravo put it in *The New York Times*, was "a bridge between a decades-old burlesque-show tradition of scatological party humor and a younger generation of comics and social satirists from Lenny Bruce to Andrew Dice Clay." His comedy recordings, known as party records (a genre he said that he created), exerted a tremendous influence on later comics and opened the door to the comedy mainstream for off-color humor and in many ways for African-American comics in general. *Sanford and Son*, too, blazed trails with its affectionate depiction of African-American urban life. Christopher Reed of the London *Guardian* quoted Foxx as saying that the show "doesn't drive home a lesson but can open up people's minds enough for them to see how stupid every kind of prejudice can be."

Derived TV Character Name from Brother's

Foxx was born John Elroy Sanford in St. Louis, Missouri, on December 9, 1922. "Red" was a childhood nickname derived from his complexion; once in show business he added a second "d" to match the double x in his stage name, taken (according to the official website maintained by his estate) from that of baseball star Jimmie Foxx. His father, an electrician, and older brother were both named Fred Sanford; the name of Foxx's character on *Sanford and Son* came from his brother, who helped raise him. Foxx's father abandoned the family when Foxx was young, and he grew up poor. By the time he was seven, Foxx knew he had a talent for telling jokes.

He was in and out of school; later he recalled thinking that knowing that George Washington had crossed the Delaware River would not help him in a brick fight in St. Louis. Foxx's mother, Mary Carson, had done preaching on the radio, but during a destitute stretch she moved her family to Chicago, where she found work as a maid. Foxx joined two friends at DuSable High School to form a street band called the Bon Bons. In 1939 the group hopped a freight train and headed for New York City. Foxx scraped together a living as a busboy, garment worker, and dishwasher; in the last-named capacity he met Malcolm Little, later Malcolm X, who called him the funniest dishwasher on earth.

The Bon Bons disbanded during World War II, and Foxx eluded the military draft when he went to register at a draft board office in Harlem: "Those cats weren't hip yet to the soap deal," he recalled, as quoted by Michael Smith Starr in *Black and Blue: The Redd Foxx Story*. I had eaten a half bar of Octagon soap, which causes heart palpitations." So he was rejected for service. Foxx began to find nightclub

Michael Ochs Archives/Getty Images

gigs as a singer, and for two years, from 1943 to 1945, he was master of ceremonies at a club called Gamby's in Baltimore, Maryland. During this period he honed his skills at standup comedy. He formed an act with comedian Slappy White, whose start date has been given in various sources as anywhere between 1941 and 1951. The pair began working $5-a-night gigs in clubs in a set of black-oriented entertainment known as the chitlin' circuit, but soon their fees started to rise.

Agreed to Record Routines

In the early 1950s, having made as much as $450 a week, the pair made their way to California to take an engagement as an opening act for singer Dinah Washington. Foxx remained in Los Angeles after the gig ended, going through another rough financial patch and working as a sign painter when nightclub work was sparse. The next phase of his career began when he met the independent record label executive Walter "Dootsie" Williams (also the discoverer of the musician later known as Papa John Creach), who persuaded him to commit some of his comedy work to recordings. At this point the Foxx-White partnership dissolved.

The first of Foxx's roughly 50 party records, *Laff of the Party*, appeared in 1956, and Foxx was paid $25 for recording it. He later complained that he had never been paid fairly for his work on the party records. Foxx was certainly not the first African-American comic to perform raunchy

material, but a taboo against such material on recordings was broken largely by his releases. The party records sold well in predominantly black neighborhoods; some stores catering to whites sold them under the counter. The records appeared mostly on Williams's Dooto and Dootsie labels and on the independents King, Laff, Loma, and MF. One of Foxx's milder routines, "You Gotta Wash Your Ass," appeared on the major Atlantic label. The party records cumulatively sold some 20 million copies.

Word spread underground about Foxx's records, helping him publicize his nightclub act. His bookings increased in frequency and pay, and by the time Hugh Downs, then host of NBC television's *Today* morning news program, saw a performance by Foxx in San Francisco in 1964, he was reportedly earning $1,250 a week. Downs urged television executives to give Foxx wider exposure. Concerned about the streak of blue in Foxx's humor, they at first agreed to slot him only on the late-night talk shows of Merv Griffin, Steve Allen, and others, where slightly more latitude was permitted with sexual topics. In 1968 Foxx covered for a missed gig by singer Aretha Franklin in Las Vegas; executives at the Hilton hotel were so impressed by his improvised hour-and-40-minute set that he was signed to a $960,000 contract to appear there.

Starred in Sitcom

Foxx's breakthrough to general audiences came when television producer Norman Lear saw Foxx in the film *Cotton Comes to Harlem,* portraying a junk dealer. Putting Foxx's skills together with his idea of adapting a British situation comedy called *Steptoe and Son,* Lear signed Foxx to appear in *Sanford and Son,* which ran from 1972 to 1978 on NBC and was a major ratings success. The show revolved around Los Angeles junk dealer Fred Sanford and his son, Lamont (Demond Wilson), whom Fred manipulated emotionally by feigning a heart attack and shouting "I'm coming to join you, Elizabeth [his deceased wife], I'm coming!" A cast of other family members and eccentric neighborhood characters (including Melvin White, played by Slappy White) provided grist for Foxx's satirical takes on African-American life; several characters on the show were named after friends from Foxx's youth.

Sanford and Son gave white audiences a glimpse of a brand of African-American comedy they had mostly never seen before. In its portrayal of an African-American small businessman it was innovative for its time. The comedian, however, professed little interest in politics, saying at one point that he was more interested in "green power" (money) than in the Black Power movement.

Indeed, Foxx lived luxuriously, buying an assortment of cars and homes. In 1983 he filed for bankruptcy after accumulating large debts to the Internal Revenue Service; at his death he reportedly owed the agency several million dollars more. *Sanford and Son* ended in 1978 after Foxx jumped to the ABC network and created a variety show, *The Redd Foxx Comedy Hour.* That show failed commercially, as did a revamped *Sanford* and several other small projects. Foxx bounced back when the young comic Eddie Murphy, one of many African-American performers of his generation who admired Foxx, cast him and his longtime friend Della Reese in the 1989 film *Harlem Nights.*

The Foxx-Reese routines in *Harlem Nights* inspired a new Foxx television series, *The Royal Family,* which went into production in 1991. Foxx suffered a heart attack on the set in Los Angeles and died on October 11, 1991; other cast members, recalling the heart attack routines on *Sanford and Son,* at first thought he was joking. Foxx was married four times and had one adopted daughter; he was married to his fourth wife, Ka Ho Cho Foxx, at the time of his death.

Books

Starr, Michael Seth, *Black and Blue: The Redd Foxx Story,* Applause, 2011.

Periodicals

Guardian (London, England), October 15, 1991.
New York Times, October 13, 1991.

Online

''Biography,'' *Redd Foxx Official Website,* http://www.reddfoxx.com/about/biography.htm (January 16, 2015).
''Redd Foxx,'' *AllMovie,* http://www.allmovie.com (January 16, 2015).□

Peter Horree/Alamy

Frederick Henry, Prince of Orange

The Dutch political leader Frederick Henry, Prince of Orange (1584–1647) was the stadholder, or head of state, of five of the small principalities of the Netherlands between 1625 and 1647. He was one of the most important Dutch political and military leaders in the first half of the 17th century.

Frederick Henry appears most prominently in Dutch history books as a military leader. In 1629, newly invested with both political and military control, he made his name by directing a successful siege of the city of 's-Hertogenbosch, an important step in the decades-long effort to regain control of the Netherlands from Spain and the Catholic Holy Roman and Habsburg empires. As he assumed the leadership of the regions that had broken away from the Spanish Netherlands, he proved a capable political leader as well, skillfully negotiating the religious and cultural divides of the time and beginning to build the institutions of the golden age that brought the Netherlands international cultural and economic influence.

Raised by Older Brother

Frederick Henry, or in Dutch Frederik Hendrik, was born January 29, 1584, in the Dutch city of Delft, three years after it declared independence from Spanish control. His father was the stadholder William the Silent, also known as William of Orange (the noble House of Orange or Orange-Nassau was a family of rulers so named because they had once controlled the Orange region in southern France). Frederick's mother, Louise, was the offspring of influential French Huguenot (Protestant) leaders. William the Silent had led some of the earlier stages of the Dutch rebellion against Spain in the late 16th century, and he was married several times; Frederick Henry's predecessor as stadholder, Maurice of Nassau, was William's son by an earlier marriage, and thus Frederick's half-brother. It was the much older Maurice who shaped Frederick as a military and political thinker: Frederick never knew his father, who was killed by a Spanish partisan in 1584 and became the first head of state assassinated with a handgun.

Frederick Henry was an army brat of the first order, virtually growing up in military camps and absorbing lessons in the field of the war against Spain. He was also, for several reasons, a natural and popular leadership figure. Good-looking and well-mannered, he made friends easily and was loved by the soldiers under his command. Moreover, he was an authentically Dutch member of the mostly foreign Orange-Nassau clan; he was the first in the family to speak Dutch without an accent, and he showed a feel for the issues that divided the peoples of the Netherlands among themselves.

One more form of adaptation to social norms remained, however, before Frederick Henry's path to the stadholdership became clear. As Maurice's health declined, he pressured Frederick Henry to marry, although he himself had never done so and had had a series of illegitimate children by a Catholic woman, Margaretha van Mechelen. Frederick Henry, in the words of Herbert H. Rowen, writing in *The Princes of Orange*, was a "gay blade, roistering with the wildest of his army camp companions. The thought of binding himself to a wife was distasteful, and he had insisted on retaining the privileges of bachelorhood." Maurice, however, threatened to marry van Mechelen and thus legitimize their children, putting them in line to rule. Frederick Henry capitulated and married his paramour of the moment, a young German-born woman named Amalia van Solms. The marriage turned out to be a long and prosperous one, producing nine children including Frederick Henry's successor, William II

When Maurice died in 1625, Frederick Henry was immediately acclaimed as military leader of the Dutch States Army. His appointment as stadholder took slightly longer, for some of the Dutch provinces wanted to name a local nobleman as stadholder, but by July Frederick Henry had become stadholder of the provinces of Holland, Zeeland, Utrecht, Overijssel, and Gelderland. The Dutch had recently suffered defeats at the hands of the Spanish, and the part of the Netherlands outside of Spanish control was beset by conflicts among Protestant sects. The Netherlands were ready to give their unqualified support to their new leader.

Planned Siege

He did not let them down. After Dutch forces captured the eastern town of Grol (or Groenlo) in 1627, Frederick Henry set his sights on the larger city of 's-Hertogenbosch, defended by a large garrison of soldiers loyal to Spain, in 1629. Frederick Henry assembled an army of 24,000 men and 4,000 horses. Military planners in the Holy Roman imperial capital of Brussels received this news gleefully, for they were sure Frederick Henry would fail. Part of the difficulty in attacking the city lay in the fact that it was largely surrounded by marshes through which few roads ran. Supervising the operation himself, Frederick Henry ordered the construction of a large depot in a nearby village, building huge dikes across the marshes that would support cavalry and artillery.

Frederick Henry's next stroke was even more brilliant. Laying siege to 's-Hertogenbosch, he ordered the construction of dams on two small nearby rivers and flooded much of the surrounding countryside. This cut the city off from the reinforcements coming from Brussels and interfered with the supplies flowing to its defenders. Imperial forces launched attacks against other towns, but Frederick Henry pressed the attack, leading Dutch, French, and English forces on the front lines himself after capturing two smaller side forts. By September the defenders of 's-Hertogenbosch had capitulated, an event that had symbolic value all across Europe and became a key step in the long decline of Spanish power in the Netherlands. The victory is regarded as high point in Dutch history. Returning to the Hague in November, Frederick Henry was hailed as a hero.

In the 1630s, Frederick Henry evolved from heroic general to moderate political leader. In the long-running conflict among Dutch Protestants between the Calvinist church and the dissident Remonstrants (also known as Arminians, after their founder, Jacob Arminius), Frederick Henry personally sided with the Remonstrants in the points of doctrinal disagreement that had led to the exile of some Remonstrant ministers. But, while affirming the authority of the established Calvinist church, he encouraged tolerant attitudes and discouraged repressive religious measures. The result was that some of the exiles began to return to the Netherlands, where the Remonstrant Brotherhood continues to exist and was one of the first European church bodies to sanctify same-sex marriages.

Brought Prosperity to Netherlands

Frederick Henry continued to helm successful military campaigns against the regions still controlled by the Spanish and the Holy Roman Empire. In the 1630s and early 1640s his forces conquered the cities of Maastricht, Breda (earlier the site of a major Spanish victory), Sas van Gent, and Hulst. He broke with his French allies and began negotiations toward a truce with Spain. With the Dutch Republic's seagoing towns near Amsterdam becoming more secure, the Netherlands began a period of spectacular economic growth that would last for the rest of the 17th century and involve the building of a globe-spanning colonial empire through its multinational corporation, the Dutch East India Company.

In later life Frederick Henry tried to build his stadholdership into a major European royal house. He built several substantial country mansions (only one of which still exists) and renovated a palace in The Hague. He began to patronize the Netherlands' growing contingent of fine artists, bringing together various artistic endeavors in the celebration of the marriage of William II to the nine-year-old Mary Stuart of England in 1641.

Despite his growing political status, Frederick Henry continued to lead the Dutch state's military operations. During the campaign to capture Hulst, his health failed, and he returned to The Hague very ill. Meeting with government officials for the last time three days before his death, he passed away on March 14, 1647, and was given an elaborate public funeral memorialized by artists. He did not live to see the signing of the Peace of Münster, which established the Netherlands as a fully independent entity and for which he had paved the way, the following year.

Books

Israel, Jonathan, *The Dutch Republic: Its Rise, Greatness, and Fall,* Clarendon, 1995

Jardine, Lisa, *The Awful End of William the Silent: The First Assassination of a Head of State with a Handgun,* HarperCollins, 2005.

Rowen, Herbert H., *The Princes of Orange: The Stadholders in the Dutch Republic,* Cambridge, 1990.

Online

"Frederick Henry, Prince of Orange," *Cambridge Modern History, Chapter 24,* http://faculty.history.wisc.edu/sommerville/351/CMHFredHen.html (January 3, 2015). □

Elsa von Freytag-Loringhoven

The German poet, artist, artist's model, and aesthetic provocateur Elsa von Freytag-Loringhoven (1874–1927) was a major figure in the Dada artistic movement, especially in the United States. Today she would be called a performance artist, but during her lifetime that concept did not exist.

Freytag-Loringhoven was a pioneer in the fields of experimental poetry and art; among women she had virtually no predecessors. She may have had a hand in Marcel Duchamp's sculpture "Fountain," one of the most famous artworks of the Dada period. But among her contemporaries it was her physical presence that was remembered most. Constantly skirting obscenity laws, she "dressed in what she found, transforming herself into a walking Dada sculpture," noted René Steinke of *The New York Times.* Freytag-Loringhoven appeared on the street wearing a postage stamp on her cheek, teaspoons as earrings, shower curtain rings as bracelets, and, perhaps most spectacularly, a brassiere made of tomato cans. Long known only to connoisseurs of Dada arts, Freytag-Loringhoven has gained stature as cultural observers have come to appreciate her influence on later female experimentalists.

Ran Away from Home

Freytag-Loringhoven was born Else Hildegard Plötz in Swinemünde in the German region of Pomerania (it is now Świnoujście, Poland), on July 12, 1874. Elsa is the English form of her first name. Her father, Adolf, was quick-tempered and hostile. She was close to her mother, Ida-Marie, who was mentally ill and who died of uterine cancer when Elsa was 18; she blamed her father for her mother's death, believing that it had resulted from syphilis that Ida-Marie had contracted from Adolf. After an episode of physical abuse from her father, Elsa ran away from home and stayed for a time with an aunt in Berlin.

It did not take Freytag-Loringhoven long to break into Berlin's art scene. She attended plays and began to model for artist Henry de Vry, falling in with a group of aspiring artists who surrounded the poet Stefan George. Freytag-Loringhoven had numerous short-term relationships, emerging with persistent cases of both gonorrhea and syphilis; the latter left her hospitalized in 1896. She began to travel in Italy with a friend, the artist Richard Schmitz, and once back in Germany, in the culturally fertile Munich area, she began taking art lessons herself.

Everett Collection Inc/Alamy

There she met architect August Endell and traveled to Italy once more with him. The pair married, but she abandoned Endell mid-journey for writer Felix Paul Greve, sticking by him during a year's imprisonment on fraud charges and writing him sexually explicit letters and poetry in prison. They married in 1907. Greve made a reputation with novels, drawing heavily on his relationship with Freytag-Loringhoven, who helped him fake his own suicide. Greve traveled to the United States and Freytag-Loringhoven went with him; the pair settled on a small farm in Sparta, Kentucky. After the couple clashed over Freytag-Loringhoven's colorful sexual history. He left her in Kentucky, hardly able to speak English.

Married German Nobleman

Working as an artist's model and moving from city to city, she made her way to New York. There she caught the attention of the unconventional German nobleman Baron Leo von Freytag-Loringhoven. The pair married in 1913, and Elsa took the title of Baroness. The marriage was a short one: Leo returned to Germany as World War I broke out and was promptly taken prisoner by French forces. Horrified by the war and depressed by his imprisonment, he committed suicide after the war ended. Elsa was left with a noble title but very little money, and she began modeling once again, at the Ferrer Art School and the Art Students' League.

Although she was imprisoned for three months on spying charges in 1917 and 1918, Freytag-Loringhoven found her feet once again. Settling in New York's hip Greenwich Village neighborhood, she met and modeled for various influential artists including Gilbert Dixon, with whom she had an affair (and in whose divorce case she was cited), and George Biddle, in a session with whom she introduced the tomato-can bra in early 1917. The Dada movement first appeared in Zurich, Switzerland, in 1916, and Freytag-Loringhoven quickly grasped its outrageous anti-art aesthetic and began to apply it in her own life.

Another major artist present in New York during this period was Marcel Duchamp, whose famous work "Fountain," consisting of a urinal, was exhibited in New York in 1917. The work may have been partially or completely Freytag-Loringhoven's creation; it resembled a sculpture she created with Morton Schamberg, titled "God" and consisting of an iron plumbing trap mounted on a miter box. Moreover, "Fountain" was signed "R. Mutt," and Duchamp wrote a letter to his sister saying that "one of my female friends, under a masculine pseudonym, Richard Mutt, sent in a porcelain urinal as a sculpture."

A Definite Flair for Self-Presentation

Freytag-Loringhoven also wrote poetry during this period, some of it inspired by her unrequited passion for Duchamp but in a decidedly disjointed Dada mode. An example was "Love—Chemical Relationship," which was published by the *Little Review* in 1918. Other periodicals that published Freytag-Loringhoven's poetry were *Broom, The Liberator,* and *transition.* Freytag-Loringhoven also created two portraits of Duchamp, one a fairly conventional pastel work with collage elements, and the other made up of a collection of feathers and other found objects arranged on top of a wine glass.

Freytag-Loringhoven was not the only artist to practice Dada in the United States; French expatriates Duchamp and Francis Picabia and the American artist Man Ray were equally influential. But writer Jane Heap, as quoted on a University of Maryland Libraries website about Freytag-Loringhoven, wrote that she was "the only one living anywhere who dresses Dada, loves Dada, lives Dada." She was fearless about opposing American censorship, appearing in Ray and Duchamp's 1918 film *The Baroness Shaves Her Pubic Hair,* sculpting a plastic penis, and including frankly erotic imagery in her poems. Other artists may have been more celebrated as artists than Freytag-Loringhoven, but it was she who garnered buzz with such episodes as a physical conflict, variously reported as a fistfight or a boxing match, with poet William Carlos Williams.

Williams's defeat did not stop him from helping Freytag-Loringhoven in her efforts to return to Europe after the war, a difficult enterprise given her chronic lack of funds. Her aim was to make her way to the artistic hotbed of Paris, but the best she could do was to reach Berlin, which in 1923 was in the middle of a disastrous run of currency inflation. Nearly destitute, Freytag-Loringhoven was reduced to selling newspapers on the Kurfürstendam, a major Berlin artery. Her mental health was apparently unstable, for she was institutionalized several times after targeting several famous writers with ill-planned and incoherent blackmail attempts. Still, she maintained a flair for unexpected self-presentation, showing up at the French embassy in Berlin dressed in a birthday-cake hat (with lit candles), stamps as cheek makeup, and false eyelashes made of gilded porcupine quills.

Freytag-Loringhoven succeeded in moving to Paris in the spring of 1926, scraping together a living by working once again as an artists' model. She tried with diminishing success to find publication opportunities for her poetry and began making plans to open a modeling school. On December 14, 1927, Freytag-Loringhoven, along with her dogs, died after unlit gas jets in her apartment were left on all night. Whether the act was suicide or murder has never been definitively determined; her writings from the period mentioned suicide, but there was speculation at the time that a sailor she picked up on the street had turned on the gas, and friends believed that she would never have harmed her pets. Freytag-Loringhoven was for many years known mostly to aficionados of Dada, but the early 21st century has seen a substantial revival of interest in her work, with museum exhibitions and the publication of a biography, *Baroness Elsa: Gender, Dada and Everyday Modernity,* by Irene Gammel (2002).

Books

Gammel, Irene, *Baroness Elsa: Gender, Dada, and Everyday Modernity,* MIT, 2002.

Periodicals

Guardian (London, England), November 7, 2014.
New York Times, May 3, 2002, August 18, 2002.
Women's Review of Books, September-October 2013.

Online

"Baroness Elsa Biographical Sketch," University of Maryland Libraries, http://www.lib.umd.edu/dcr/collections/EvFL-class/bios.html (November 4, 2014).
"The Dada Baroness," *Artnet,* http://www.artnet.com/magazine/features/oisteanu/oisteanu5-20-02.asp (November 14, 2014).
"Daughters of Dada: Baroness Elsa von Freytag-Loringhoven," *Francis M. Naumann Fine Art,* http://www.francisnaumann.com/daughters%20of%20dada/elsa.html (November 4, 2014).□

David Frost

British broadcaster David Frost (1939–2013) gained international fame for his memorable interviews with such luminaries as Richard M. Nixon, John Lennon, George Clooney, and Vladimir Putin. His televised conversation with Nixon, in which the disgraced president apologized to the American people, was considered the most important political interview of all time and became the subject of a play and film, both entitled *Frost/Nixon.* Frost was employed by Al Jazeera English network at the end of his career.

Paul Smith/Featureflash/Shutterstock.com

B orn April 7, 1939, in Tenterden, England, David Paradine Frost was the son of W.J. (Wilfred John) Paradine and Mona (Aldrich) Frost. His father was a Methodist minister who had his own church. Though the family spent some years living in Tenterden, located in county Kent, they eventually moved to a community located in the Midlands region of Britain.

Showed Early Interest in Journalism, Performing

Educated in local schools and at Wellingborough Grammar School, Frost originally considered following in his father's footsteps and joining the Methodist ministry himself. At school, he became interested in journalism and performance while attending Wellingborough. He credited his English teacher for increasing his interest in words and their use. Frost also appeared in a number of school plays. A stand-out athlete, Frost was asked to play professional soccer for a team in Nottingham, England, but turned down the opportunity to go to university.

Entering Cambridge University, Frost continued his writing and performing interests. He served as an editor on a student newspaper and the university magazine, *Granta*. He also was a member of the Footlights Dramatic Club, which launched the careers of many actors and satirists. During these years, Frost discovered he had a talent for performing satire as well.

Began Working on Television

After completing his education, Frost began performing satire in nightclubs. He was soon recruited and hired by the BBC. Beginning in 1962, Frost hosted the show *That Was the Week that Was.* He also served as co-writer. Though a neophyte on television, colleague Christopher Booker told Adrian Higgins of the *Washington Post* that Frost showed an "extraordinary, intuitive feel for television itself. In the studio, he was instantly, nervelessly at home, as if the very presence of cameras and light gave him an extra charge of confidence and energy."

Airing on Saturday nights for two years, That Was the Week that Was offered a satirical take on the news stories of the week—including the dishonesty of politics and religion—through interviews, skits, and music performances. Despite its short run, the show was an influence on other satire-tinged news programs that followed. They included the long-running Comedy Central hit *The Daily Show.* It also gave the young Frost a taste of the high life and greater fame. His quest for personal fame turned off some of his coworkers.

When *That Was the Week that Was* went off the air, Frost moved on to other programs on the BBC. He developed a new show with the creator of *That Was the Week that Was,* but it failed to catch on. Other work included talk shows with an intellectual bent, as well as more entertainment-oriented television such as game shows.

Hosted *The Frost Report*

During the 1960s and 1970s, Frost's work for the BBC included *The Frost Report,* which gave John Cleese his first taste of a wide audience in Britain. It also featured future stars Ronnie Barker and Ronnie Corbett. The sketch show helped pave the way for Cleese and his comic cohorts in Monty Python to develop their BBC series *Monty Python's Flying Circus.*

Later in the 1960s, Frost furthered his interviewing skills on his own current issues show, *The Frost Programme.* He also did many specials such as *David Frost's Night Out in London.* Additionally, he was featured in shows for the London Weekend Television network.

Though Frost's home base remained in Britain, he was also regularly appearing in the United States, where he also did both television series and interview specials, and soon became a regular, respected media presence. In 1968, Frost was twice a fill-in for Johnny Carson on popular late night talker *The Tonight Show.* The following year, Frost was given his own syndicated talk show, *The David Frost Show,* which aired until 1972. He continued to tape five shows a week in New York for the Westinghouse Broadcasting Company until 1979.

Became Expert Interviewer

By this time, Frost had become an expert at effective interviewing techniques which compelled his subjects to make newsworthy statements. His arsenal included penetrating questions and the effective use of silences and pauses, which also encouraged insights. Most of all, Frost believed in preparation for interviews. He told Scott Williams of the Associated Press, "Some people think the more preparation you do, the more it shakles you to a prepared plan. The truth of good homework or good research, is it liberates you to go with the flow of the interview.... The less you know the more you have to stick to your set questions. The other thing is, it saves you from boring the pants off somebody."

Frost's interview technique was widely admired. The managing editor of Al Jazeera English, Al Anstey, told Brian Stelter of the *New York Times,* "No matter who he was interviewing, he was committed to getting the very best out of the discussion, but always doing so by getting to know his guest, engaging with them and entering into a proper conversation."

Interviewed Nixon

Frost's most memorable interview came in the late 1970s with former U.S. president Richard M. Nixon, several years after he resigned in the wake of the Watergate scandal. The interview broke Nixon's long self-imposed silence. Arranging for a series of interviews for a television special airing on American television—for which Nixon was paid $600,000 and a percentage of the broadcast profits—Frost and Nixon talked for nearly 29 hours over a month period. These interviews were condensed into four 90-minute episodes.

The revelations from the Nixon interviews were stunning for Frost and the public. Nixon acknowledged he believed that abusing presidential power was legal. When Frost spontaneously pressed him about the errors around Watergate, Nixon said he was sorry for the impact of his actions on Americans and that he felt the weight of his actions.

When Frost's interview of Nixon aired, they were the most watched political interview in the history of television. The interviews with Nixon were considered by Frost to be the most important to his career. The interviews themselves became the subject of a play, *Frost/Nixon,* written by Peter Morgan and first presented in Britain in 2006.

The play was made into a popular feature film of the same name in 2007, with actor Michael Sheen playing Frost and Frank Langella depicting Nixon. For the film, Frost wrote a book, *Frost/Nixon: Behind the Scenes of the Nixon Interviews,* which offered further insights into the hours he spent with Nixon.

Talked to Other Major Figures

Frost continued to interview important figures on the world stage for the rest of the 20th and into the 21st century for the BBC and American outlets. While he talked such celebrities as John Lennon, Prince Charles, Billy Graham, and Orson Welles, many of Frost's most memorable conversations came with political figures. Frost had a remarkable interview with Nixon's national security advisor and secretary of state Henry Kissinger, for example, as well as the Russian leader, Vladimir Putin.

Frost talked to seven American presidents. Among them was George H.W. Bush, whom Frost found to be astute. Frost interviewed Bush for his short-lived PBS series *Talking with David Frost* in 1991. Frost also talked to many leaders from other countries, including eight British prime ministers. He conversed with British prime minister Tony Blair about the Iraq War in 2006, for example.

Not every person he interviewed was famous, but Frost's skills always shone through. A colleague at Al Jazeera, Charlie Courtauld, told Khushbu Shah, Josh Levs, and Emma Lacey-Bordeaux of the CNN Wire, "What was remarkable about Sir David was his ability to put any interviewee at ease, from the most high and mighty to an ordinary person on the street. He found interest in anybody. Whoever he was interviewing would realise that Sir David was genuinely interested in them and their lives. He was very much a people person."   .

Worked in Early Morning Television

In addition to such interviews, Frost also worked on and contributed to other programming for the BBC and his own production company, David Paradine Productions. In the early 1980s, he introduced early morning shows to British television. His show, *Frost on Sunday,* aired on TV AM from the 1980s until 1992. Frost moved the show to the BBC in 1993 and renamed it *Breakfast with Frost.* This version aired until 2005. In the 1990s, for his production company, Frost was the host of a daytime show, *Through the Keyhole.*

Because of his success as a broadcaster, Frost was named an Officer of the Order of the British Empire in 1970. He also was named a Knight Bachelor, a higher honor, in 1993. The entertainment industry acknowledged Frost's work with an Emmy Award for lifetime achievement, given in 2009.

Joined Al Jazeera English

By the time he was given his Emmy, Frost had left his home broadcasting network, the BBC. In 2006, Frost joined Al Jazeera English. At the time, Al Jazeera, based in the Middle East, launched its first English-language news service. The network aired his programs *Frost All Over the World* and *The Frost Interview.* The former was a weekly current affairs show. Though Frost was no longer employed by the BBC, he continued to be a respected broadcaster and interviewer. Later in life, his interviewees included actor George Clooney and the Turkish prime minster Recep Tayyip Erdogan. The first episode of the 2013 season of *The Frost Interview* featured Buzz Aldrin, the American astronaut.

Frost had an interview with British prime minster David Cameron scheduled for September 2013. However, while traveling from Britain to the Mediterranean Sea on the ship the Queen Elizabeth, Frost suffered a heart attack and died on August 31, 2013. He was 74. His survivors included his second wife, Carina Fitzlan-Howard, and their three sons, Miles, Wilfred, and George. Upon Frost's death, Cameron stated, according to David Pilditch of the *Express,* "Sir David was an extraordinary man with charm, wit, talent, intelligence and warmth in equal measure. He made a huge impact on television and politics."

Periodicals

Associated Press, January 2, 1991.
Broadcast, September 2, 2013.
CNN Wire, September 1, 2013.
The Express, September 2, 2013.
New York Times, September 2, 2013.
Washington Post, September 2, 2013.□

G

Rituparno Ghosh

Widely respected filmmaker Rituparno Ghosh (1963–2013) directed at least 20 feature films about sexuality, gender identity, and the urban middle class in India that were popular in his native country and found international acclaim as well. Primarily working in the Bengali language, he created such classic award-winning films as *Shubho Mahurat*. He also directed several English-language films, such as *The Last Lear*.

Rituparno Ghosh was born August 31, 1963, in Calcutta, India, the son of artist and documentary filmmaker Sunil Ghosh. Ghosh's path to filmmaking was not direct, though both of his parents were involved in filmmaking, and cinema was his first interest. After graduating from South Point High School, he studied economics at Jadavpur University in Calcutta, earning an undergraduate degree in the subject.

Began Career in Advertising

Ghosh began his professional career at an advertising agency in the 1980s. As part of his work at Response, an ad agency based in Kolkata, India, he wrote copy for ads and filmed them. During his time at the company, he showed talent as an adman as he created advertisements for such products as Boroline antiseptic cream and Frooti. Eighteen of his ads won industry awards.

Yet Ghosh was unhappy with just creating to sell. Inspired in part to pursue a feature film career because of another Bengali advertising agency employee turned successful filmmaker, Satyajit Ray, Ghosh once said, according to Ajanta Chakraborty of the *Times of India*, "I was not satisfied. I love to talk, to write and to communicate at length. I was searching for a feature to happen."

Working at Response facilitated Ghosh's transition to feature films. In 1990, one of Response's member companies, Tele-Response, was commissioned to make a documentary on Vande Mataram, the national song of India, for Doorharshan, an Indian public broadcasting network. Ghosh played a major role on the project.

Made Feature Films

Within a few years, Ghosh had reached his goal of creating his own feature film. His first film was 1992's *Hirer Angti* (The Diamond Ring). The film for children was commissioned by the chairperson of the Children's Film Society, Shabana Azmi, after just one meeting. It focused on a man who tries to become part of a wealthy family in order to steal a diamond ring, but fails in his efforts.

After *Hirer Angti,* he made at least 12 more films in the Bengali language before branching out into films in Hindi and English. Many focused on the problems facing the urban middle class in India. Serious and thought-provoking, Ghosh was bold and realistic in his film vision, taking on controversial topics like women's issues, sexuality, divorce, homosexuality, and gender identity. Ever interested in and quite knowledgeable about human behavior and motivations, many of his films focused on women, and their emotional and personal struggles. Ghosh personally had a high regard for women and used the film medium to explore their lives. He also injected and highlighted the humor of life situations in many of his films. In addition, he played a role in every aspect of creating his films. Classical Indian vocalist Shubha Mudgal told Yogesh Pawar of *DNA*, "To an outsider

Raj K Raj/Hindustan Times/Getty Images

he'd seem preoccupied, to the point of impatience but that's also because of his sheer involvement with every aspect of filmmaking."

Won First Film Award

A female character was at the center of his second film, *Unishe April* (The Nineteenth of April). Released in 1994, it focused on the complex life of a dancer who has complicated relationships first with her husband, then with her adult daughter. *Unishe April* was given a best film award, one of many honors he would receive over the course of his career as a filmmaker.

Making 19 films in 15 years, Ghosh was particularly prolific in the late 1990s and the first years of the 2000s. Actress Kirron Kher told *DNA*'s Pawar, "Where there are many who can claim they're equally prolific but none can match his consistency in exceptional brilliance. No wonder a variety of big names from both Bengal and Hindi cinema jumped at the opportunity to work under his baton." As he became widely acclaimed, Ghosh was able to cast the leading actors and actresses in India in his works.

In 2003, Ghosh released *Dust in the Eyes,* an adaptation of the Rabindranath Tagore novel *Chokher Bali.* Many critics consider this film to be Ghosh's best. *Chokher Bali* explores the life of a young, educated Hindu widow, Binodini, living in the Bengal region between 1902 and 1905. Though Indian social conventions were quite conservative at the time and prevented widows from remarrying,

Binodini refused to live a restrained life. This includes her guilt-free sexual desires for a man who once rejected her and is now married to a woman that Binodini is befriending. The actress who played the widow was Aishwarya Rai, a popular Indian actress who once held the Miss World title.

Later, Ghosh admitted he felt quite close to the character of Binodini. As his friend Myna Mukherjee wrote in *Open* after his death, "Binodini stood on a threshold of social transformation as she struggled for social acceptance as a widow after the British had legislated widow remarriage in the face of countrywide resistance. Rituparno felt a strong sense of identification with the tragic isolation of someone caught in the half-light of legitimacy."

Created *Raincoat*

Also in 2003, Ghosh wrote the screenplay for and directed *Shubho Mahurat,* an adaptation of the Agatha Christie novel *The Mirror Crack'd From Side to Side.* Another acclaimed film by Ghosh was released in 2004. The Hindi-language *Raincoat* was a romantic melodrama inspired by early 20th century American literature. It again starred Rai, along with another acclaimed Indian actor, Ajay Devgan.

Rai played a wealthy young wife living a life that is lonely and not particularly happy in an area of Calcutta that is slightly beneath her. One day during monsoon season, her ex-lover, Manoj, played by Devgan, pays her a surprise visit, where they catch up and exaggerate about their lives. As Ann Hornaday wrote in the *Washington Post,* "By the time *Raincoat* concludes in an elegant, bittersweet twist, Ghosh has immersed viewers in a hothouse world that is at once archaic and contemporary, claustrophobically specific and romantically universal."

By the early 21st century, Ghosh had branched out into English language films. In 2007, he released *The Last Lear,* his first foray into English. It focused on a Shakespearean stage actor who has been retired for many years before being convinced to make his film debut playing King Lear in a film version of Shakespeare's *King Lear.* The actor may never be in another film, and *The Last Lear* looks at the contrast between theater and cinema. The film starred Amitabh Bachchan, who had come to fame for his roles in Bollywood films. *The Last Lear* had its premiere at the Toronto Film Festival, and was also shown at the London Film Festival.

Focused on Gay Rights and Gender Identity Issues

Thus, Ghosh not only was commercially and critically success in India, his films were often shown in film festivals in Asia, Europe, and North America, where he was widely respected and his films acclaimed. Ghosh used his fame, especially later in his life, as a creative gay rights activist. Ghosh was personally flamboyant and open about his cross-dressing, especially later in his life. He favored feminine, lush clothes, makeup, and jewelry like dangly earrings. Ghosh said that he was not transgender but considered himself gender fluid, identifying between the genders.

According to the *International Business Times,* the BBC correspondent in Kolkata, Amitabha Bhattasali stated after Ghosh's death, "Initially he wore men's clothes, but in the last few years he completely switched to women's dresses. Film analysts say that through this films, writings, and acting roles, Mr. Ghosh gave a voice to disempowered sexual minorities. Though mocked by many, he lived life on his own terms and never shied from taking up verbal fights with those who mocked him."

One way Ghosh accomplished this was through acting roles. After making his acting debut in the 2003 Oriya-language film *Katha Deithilli Ma Ku,* Ghosh appeared in a trilogy of films that explored gender identity issues. Directed by different filmmakers, he played complex characters in *Areketi Premer Golpo* (Just Another Love Story) and *Memories of March,* both released in 2011. *Areketi Premer Golpo,* directed by Kaushik Ganguly, showcases Ghosh playing a transgender filmmaker who is making a film biography of Chapal Bhaduri, the first gay jatra (folk theater) actor in Bengal.

Ghosh himself wrote, directed, and appeared in the third film in the trilogy, his 2012 release *Chitrangada* (The Crowning Wish). In this semi-autobiographical film, Ghosh played a transgender male dancer in a long-term relationship with a man. So the couple can adopt, Ghosh's character undergoes a sex change operation. *Chitrangada* won a special jury prize at the Indian National Film Awards in 2013.

Ghosh also did not limit himself to film work. He was the editor of a film magazine, *Andandalok,* which was published in the Bengali language. Additionally, Ghosh was the host of two celebrity talk shows, *Ebong Rituporno* and *Ghosh & Co.* He worked at a television network as well, holding a position of leadership.

Died of a Heart Attack

Shortly before his death, Ghosh, a diabetic, was being treated for pancreatitis. Only two days before his death, Ghosh finished work on what would be his last film, *Satyanweshi,* a crime thriller that featured Byomkesh Bakshi, a famous fictional detective in Bengali literature. Ghosh continued his inspired casting, selecting another film director, Sujit Ghosh, to play the role of Bakshi.

Suffering a heart attack, Ghosh died on May 30, 2013, at his home in Kolkata, India. He was 49 years old. Over the course of his career, Ghosh made more than 20 highly respected films. Ghosh's lifestyle also made an impact on stage and screen artists. The Indian theater group Dum Dum Shobdomugdho created a play *Rituparno Ghosh* in March 2014 inspired by his life and the day of his death, using aspects of Ghosh's writings and works to look at the isolation that sexual minorities often faced in India.

Ghosh's death, coming at a relatively early age, was shocking to many of his friends and colleagues. According to the India Blooms News Service, India Information and Broadcasting's Manish Tewari stated after the event, "I am deeply shocked by the tragic and premature death of Shri Ghosh. He was a creative genius who gave a new dimension to film making with every film he was associated with. His films always left a deep imprint on the minds of the audiences who were captivated by the honest portrayal of human emotions."

Periodicals

Associated Press, May 31, 2013.
DNA, May 31, 2013.
India Blooms News Service, May 30, 2013.
International Business Times (U.S. edition), May 30, 2013.
Metro Magazine, Summer 2005.
New York Times, June 5, 2013.
Open, June 6, 2013.
Screen, June 21, 2013.
The Telegraph (India), May 5, 2011.
Times of India, May 31, 2013; March 25, 2014.
Washington Post, April 13, 2005.

Online

"Rituparno Ghosh," *Internet Movie Database,* http://www.imdb.com/name/nm0315916/ (November 10, 2014).
"Indian Director Rituparno Ghosh Dies at 49," *Hollywood Reporter.com,* http://www.hollywoodreporter.com/news/indian-director-rituparno-ghosh-dies-560632 (November 10, 2014).□

H. R. Giger

Working in a style he dubbed biomechanical, Swiss artist H. R. Giger (1940–2014) created surreal, otherworldly, often disturbing images in visual media, furniture, and other designs. Perhaps best known for designing the titular *Alien,* he also fashioned memorable images for album covers for such artists as Emerson, Lake & Palmer and the Dead Kennedys.

He was born Hans Ruedi Giger on February 5, 1940, in Chur, Switzerland, located in the southeastern part of the country. His father was employed as a pharmacist, while his mother, Melli, raised their family. Gloom was part of Giger's life from an early age. He grew up in a dark house with few windows, and regularly went to a local museum which had a mummy. Giger's mother introduced him to the surrealist art of Salvador Dali, via a small postcard of one of his paintings, when her son was young.

Created Art from an Early Age

Giger began drawing at an early age. He entered many competitions throughout his youth and young adulthood, but never won, increasing his personal sense of isolation. Throughout Giger's childhood, he also suffered from disturbing nightmares and night terrors. This experience impacted and informed his burgeoning art style.

After reaching adulthood, Giger completed Switzerland's mandatory military service. He then furthered his education, studying architecture, industrial design, and interior design at a college in Zurich. He studied these subjects at the insistence of his father, who wanted his son to learn a trade. Giger also served an apprenticeship with a furniture maker.

© Louie Psihoyos/Corbis

Throughout this period, Giger continued to paint, though his subjects were eccentric as he focused on sex and death. By the 1960s, he was a full-time artist, influenced by Dali, the fantasy artist Ernst Fuchs, and the horror fiction penned by H.P. Lovecraft. At the same time, his sleep became more relaxed as he worked out his issues through art and eventually no longer had nightmares.

Matured as an Artist

As an artist, Giger developed a mature style of painting he called biomechanical, which included disturbing creatures, human-like forms, mechanical imagery, and erotic and macabre elements. Often depicted in shades of blue-gray and brown, many of his figures were skeletal, tentacled, and/or fused humans and machines. Much of Giger's work was dark. Yet Giger thought he also included elements that were nicer and pleasant amidst the darkness. Similarly, Giger himself preferred to dress in black and only worked through the night, and in person was mild mannered, pleasant, and gentle.

Giger's dim, murky artistic style was not appreciated in his rural region. The host of one of his early exhibitions was reportedly forced to wipe the spit of disgusted neighbors off the gallery windows every morning. It was not until Giger reached the age of 27 that he sold his first major work of art. But by the late 1960s, he gained more positive attention.

In 1966, a book that collected images of Giger's early artworks, *Ein Fressen für den Psychiater* (A Feast for the Psychiatrist), was published. It primarily featured his ink and oil works, though he would soon focus on airbrushing and his own original freehand technique. Later in the decade, many of Giger's paintings were published in poster form by a friend, which brought more attention from galleries and curators. Giger's work became commercially successful, though it was still panned by many critics as being gruesome, vulgar, and tasteless.

By the early 1970s, Giger was financially successful enough to move to Zurich and buy three attached row houses located in a working class suburb of the Swiss city. The homes were interconnected with a labyrinth-like series of passageways and stairs. In them, Giger displayed many of his canvases and the armchairs and furniture he designed, all with his signature biomechanical style.

Began Working in Film

In this period, Giger expanded into film work. In 1974, Chilean filmmaker Alejandro Jodorowsky asked Giger to create the design for his adaptation of the science fiction classic *Dune*. The production ultimately failed, but it allowed Giger to work with one of his idols, Dali.

Three years later, Giger published another book of his airbrush paintings, *Necronomicon* (Masks of the Dead). Like his other works of the era, it was a collection of detailed, surreal images of unearthly forms which were a combination of mechanical and human-like shapes. Though critics were both revolted and seduced by the paintings in the book, it led to Giger's best known professional accomplishment.

One reader of *Necronomicon* was British director Ridley Scott, who chose Giger to design the creature at the heart of his first major film project, *Alien*. Scott wanted Giger to base the alien creatures on the figures featured in "Necronomicon IV." James Cowan, friend of Giger and owner of a Las Vegas art publisher and retailer, told Audie Cornish and Melissa Block of National Public Radio's *All Things Considered*, "It blew Ridley Scott's mind. And he found one or two paintings in there and he just realized that that was the alien essentially, his biomechanical design, the elongated head and all of these aspects that Ridley Scott and Giger worked on to break up the human form so it didn't look like a man in a suit."

Though the film's studio, 20th Century Fox initially rejected the look of Giger's creations, Scott backed him and supported his work. Giger's monsters were memorable and came to define the film. They also won Giger and the other members of the special effects team, including Carlo Ramaldi who helped design the creatures, an Academy Award. For *Alien*, Giger fashioned the creatures in several forms, from birth to queen, and also created some of the settings of the film. The aliens were surreal, with elements that could be regarded as erotic, machine-like, and dragon-like. The skeletal creatures had elongated heads, narrow torsos, and a spiny tail similar to a scorpion. Perhaps their most distinctive feature were the two rows of teeth and a long tongue.

For his part, Giger was influenced by another artist when he created the aliens in *Alien*. He told the *National Post* in 2009, "It was Francis Bacon's work that gave me the inspiration. Of how this thing would come tearing out of the man's flesh with its gaping mouth, grasping and with an explosion of teeth . . . it's pure Bacon."

Giger worked on other films as well, designing creatures and other dark elements. They included the 1986 film *Poltergeist II* and 1995 film *Species*. For the latter, he devised the memorable creature at its center, Sil.

Faced Professional and Personal Struggles

Yet the process for creating films was exasperating for Giger. His version of the creature in *Alien* was also used in the sequels, including *Aliens* (1986), *Aliens 3* (1992), *Alien: Resurrection* (1997), and *Alien v. Predator* (2004), but he received no compensation. Also, the Batmobile that Giger designed for Tim Burton's Batman film was rejected by the filmmaker. By the end of Giger's life, he had renounced much of what he created for film.

Though Giger's career was reaching new heights in his film period, he was dealing with personal struggles. His long-term girlfriend and muse, actress Li Tobler, committed suicide in 1975. He was briefly married to Mia Bonzanigo later in the decade. In 2006, he married Carmen Maria Scheifele, who remained his wife until his death.

Designed Album Covers

Also in the 1970s and 1980s, Giger designed the art for album covers for high profile musical artists. For example, for the progressive rock band Emerson, Lake & Palmer's 1973 release *Brain Salad Surgery*, Giger designed an image of a human skull melded into a machine in an industrial setting. Also acclaimed was his cover for the 1981 solo album by Blondie vocalist Debbie Harry. *KooKoo* centered on the singer's head with four pins horizontally impaling the flesh of her face. *Rolling Stone* considered it one of the best album covers of all time.

Not all of Giger's album covers and art for musicians were embraced. For the punk band the Dead Kennedys, Giger created a poster that was included in the band's 1985 album *Frankenchrist*. A reproduction of one of Giger's paintings, *Penis Landscape*, the images included male and female genitalia taking part in various sex acts. Because of the poster, the group's lead singer, Jello Biafra, was put on trial for distributing pornography. The case was dismissed in 1987. Giger's other work for musicians included a custom designed microphone stand.

Changed Career Focus

In 1992, Giger decided to quit painting, though he continued to draw. He focused more on sculpture as well. Many of his sculptures were constructed using metal, Styrofoam, and plastic. Giger also designed furniture and jewelry. His images were even used on tarot cards and shopping bags for a Swiss chain of grocers. Though he stopped making any new paintings, he continued to exhibit older works. To the delight of the artist, images created by Giger were

popular for tattoos in the 1990s and beyond. The artist was pleased by their use in this context because of their permanency.

Bigger projects for Giger later in life included designing the interiors of Giger Bars, beginning in the early 1990s. These establishments featured images and designs inspired by his biomechanical, dark style. The atmosphere was also inspired by his work for *Alien* and other films on which he worked. The high-backed chairs, for example, were Gothic-like and featured skeletal spinal cords. On the walls, Giger placed full-length sculptures of crying infants.

In 1998, Giger opened up a museum in which many of his works were displayed. It was located in a castle, the Chateau St. Germain, that he bought that year in the city of Gruyères, Switzerland. Giger displayed his own collection of art and other designs, as well as featured pieces by Dali and Dado. In addition, Giger held shows for other artists, such as the Swiss/Canadian painter Rudolf Stussi in 2005. Giger's own mainstream acceptability was cemented by museums in cities such as Paris and Vienna hosting retrospectives of his work. In 2013, he was inducted into the Science Fiction and Fantasy Hall of Fame.

After suffering a fall in his home, Giger died of his injuries on May 12, 2014, in Zurich, Switzerland. He was 74 years old. According to CNN Wire, his friend and manager Leslie Barany released a statement which said in part, "We are absolutely heartbroken over the loss of this loving husband, selfless friend and supremely talented artist. He truly was one of a kind, committed to a craft, to his friends and to his family. His warm personality, incredible generosity and sharp sense of humor were in stark contrast with the universe he depicted in his art."

Periodicals

Associated Press, May 13, 2014.
CNN Wire, May 13, 2014.
Globe and Mail (Canada), May 14, 2014.
Los Angeles Times, May 14, 2014.
National Post (Canada), October 31, 2009; May 14, 2014.
Washington Post, May 14, 2014.

Transcripts

All Things Considered, National Public Radio, May 13, 2014.□

Gilberto Gil

Brazilian singer, songwriter, guitarist, and government official Gilberto Gil (1942–) has been one of the most significant South American musicians of the 20th and 21st centuries.

"There are many ways of singing and making Brazilian music, and Gilberto Gil (pronounced zheel-BEHR-toh Zheel) prefers all of them," poet Torquato Neto was quoted as saying by Larry Rohter in the *International Herald Tribune*. The various stages of Gil's

Pedro Lobo/Bloomberg/Getty Images

career indeed intersected with most of the major styles of modern Brazilian music, including samba, bossa nova, *tropicalismo,* MPB or *música popular brasileira,* and the forró of Gil's native Brazilian northeast, as well as with numerous foreign styles. Yet often he went his own way, not following any single style. Perhaps the thread linking the large volume of music produced by Gil over his long career is a quest for musical and spiritual meaning and a spirit of idealism—idealism that at times led Gil toward direct political action.

Imitated Songs Heard on Radio

Gilberto Passos Gil Moreira was born on June 29, 1942, in Salvador, Brazil, in the culturally heavily African state of Bahia. Many parts of the area were poor, but Gil, the son of a doctor father and a teacher mother, grew up in middle-class surroundings and, like young people all over the world, began to broaden his musical horizons while a college student, at the Federal University of Bahia in the late 1950s. He had already showed a strong interest in music as a child, imitating on the trumpet the music he heard on the radio and then taking up the accordion, the character-istic instrument of Bahia's numerous forró bands. As a teen-ager he performed with a group called Os Desafinados.

Gil's musical transformation from amateur to profes-sional occurred when he heard the major Brazilian hit "Chega de Saudade" (difficult to translate, but issued in English as "No More Blues") in its version by João Gilberto

in 1959. The song, composed by pioneering Brazilian songwriters Antonio Carlos Jobim and Vinícius de Moraes, kicked off the internationally successful style known as bossa nova and inspired Gil to switch from accordion to guitar and to begin performing and writing songs in the new lightly romantic style.

A business administration major at the university, Gil embarked on a career as a management trainee with the multinational corporation Gessy-Lever in the metropolis of São Paulo. But he was already earning money on the side writing bossa nova–style jingles for television commercials, and music became more and more important in his life. He and Caetano Veloso, who met in college and who both became major musical stars, challenged and egged each other on as close friends. Finally Gil broke through as a songwriter with "Louvação" (the word refers to a section of the Brazilian *capoeira* dance) in 1966; the song became a hit for Brazilian vocalist Elis Regina. Gil issued a debut album by the same name the following year. It included not only his own compositions but also songwriting con-tributions from Veloso and future Brazilian experimentalist star Tom Zé

Placed in Solitary Confinement

By the late 1960s Gil and Veloso were heavily involved with artistic movement known as tropicalismo or tropicá-lia, which in the musical realm featured influences from North American and English rock music and a generally free, experimental attitude. The 1968 album *Tropicália ou Panis et Circenses* (Tropicalia, or Bread and Circuses), recorded by Gil, Veloso, Zé, and several other artists, is often thought to have marked the beginning of tropica-lismo. Gil's increasing political advocacy landed him in hot water with Brazil's military dictatorship, which reached its most repressive phase in the late 1960s and early 1970s. In 1969 Gil was involved with left-wing students who were resisting military rule, and he was arrested, placed in soli-tary confinement, released briefly into house arrest (at which time he wrote and released his first major solo hit, "Aquele Abraço—" or "That Embrace," an affectionate hymn to Brazil's cities), and finally exiled to Britain.

Gil was unhappy away from home, but his musical horizons expanded still further over the three years he spent in England. He performed in London clubs with leading rock artists such as Pink Floyd and Rod Stewart, and recorded the stylistically eclectic solo album *Gilberto Gil.* By the early 1970s Gil had added the rising jazz-rock fusion style to his guitar arsenal, and when he returned to Brazil in 1972 he featured that style on his album *Expresso 2222,* a major commercial success.

Gil's music of the 1970s and early 1980s was extra-ordinarily diverse. He toured the United States and released a partly English-language album, *Nightingale,* in 1979. More important in the development of his interna-tional popularity, however, was a double live album he recorded in 1978 at the Montreux Jazz Festival in Switzer-land. Gil began a long religious quest, exploring Asian and African faiths as well as the Theosophical movement before ending up unaffiliated with any organized religion. In the early 1970s he investigated African music and at one point met with Nigerian political firebrand bandleader Fela Kuti and American R&B star Stevie Wonder in Lagos. He was influenced by reggae music and toured with Jamaican star Jimmy Cliff, releasing with him a duo version of the late Bob Marley's "No Woman, No Cry" in 1980. Gil began to identify himself more forcefully as Afro-Brazilian and lent support to the rising movement for black consciousness in Brazil.

Many of Gil's lyrics continued to feature political content, and in the late 1980s he served a term on Salvador's city council. He declined to run for a second term, telling *Billboard* that "I realized that I do not have much talent as a politician. Politics has a guerrilla dimension. I prefer a diplomatic approach, and so I felt a little out of my element being involved in the political process." In 1992 Gil released the album *Paraboliámara*, featuring a kaleidoscope of Brazilian style from the preceding quarter-century; it has been one of his best-received albums critically. The album was supported with a new tour of the United States, raising Gil's profile through appearances in such venues as television's *Late Night with David Letterman*.

Won Major Prizes

Gil remained involved in political activity, joining Brazil's Green Party and leading the environmental group *Onda Azul* (Blue Wave), which worked to protect Brazilian waterways. Gil continued to tour tirelessly and released several successful live albums. One of these, *Quanta Live*, won a Grammy award for Best World Music Album in 1999. Gil later won a second Grammy, for Best Contemporary World Music Album (for the CD *Electracüstico*) in 2005; he has also won two Latin Grammy awards, and Sweden's prestigious Polar Music Prize. Gil was married four times and had five children, one of whom died in an auto crash. His daughter, Preta Gil, is a noted singer.

In 2003 Gil returned to politics as Brazil's Minister of Culture, appointed by the country's new leftist president, Luis Ignácio Lula da Silva, and cutting his trademark dreadlocks. However, he remained a Green and not a member of the president's labor-oriented party. In Brazil he was only the second cabinet minister of African descent; the first was soccer star Pelé, who served as sports minister. "I've gone from being the stone thrower to being the glass," he was quoted as saying by Clive Davis in the *Times* of London. Gil's political opponents tried to restrict his performances, especially abroad, arguing that his work commitments should take priority. But Gil maintained a heavy recording and performing schedule.

Gil resigned as culture minister in 2008, citing health problems, but he has continued to be a strong presence on the music scene. The intersection of music and computers has become a major interest; as early as the 1960s he had written a song about computers, "Electronic Brain." As culture minister he had worked to implement the Creative Commons alternative copyright arrangement in Brazil. Gil returned to the music with which he had begun his career on the 2014 release *Gilbertos Samba*. He has issued a Portuguese-language autobiography, *Gilberto Bem Perto*, but his extraordinarily long and creative musical life (as of this writing he has released nearly 60 albums) has not yet been traced in a book-length English language biography.

Books

Contemporary Musicians, Volume 61, Gale, 2008.
Veloso, Caetano, *Tropical Truth: A Story of Music and Revolution in Brazil*, Da Capo, 2003.

Periodicals

Billboard, November 3, 2012.
Independent (London, England), July 8, 2005.
International Herald Tribune, March 13, 2007.
NACLA Report on the Americas, January-February 2003.
New York Times, May 9, 1999.
Times (London, England), June 28, 2003.

Online

"Bio," Gilberto Gil Official Website, http://www.gilbertogil.com.br (December 14, 2014).
"Brazilian Pop Star Gil Tours U.S.," *USA Today*, http://www.usatoday30.usatoday.com/life/music/2007-03-16-2248300129_x.htm (December 14, 2014).
"Gilberto Gil," *Allmusic*, http://www.allmusic.com (December 14, 2014).□

Anatoliy Golitsyn

Anatoliy Golitsyn (born 1926) was an intriguing figure in the high-stakes espionage game of the Cold War era. The KGB officer turned up one night in Finland in December of 1961 to request political asylum and is believed to have been the top-ranking official ever to defect from the Soviet Union. The assertions Golitsyn made roiled the espionage agencies of the United States and Britain for decades and contributed to a culture of secrecy, suspicion, and counterintelligence errors.

Anatoliy Mikhaylovich Golitsyn was born in August of 1926 in Pyriatyn, a city in the Poltava oblast of Ukraine. At the time, Ukraine was firmly entrenched within the borders of the Soviet Union, which had proclaimed the world's first Communist Party-led revolution just nine years before Golitsyn's birth. His surname was also that of a prominent aristocratic family in the previous tsarist regime, and some of those Golitsyns had fled to the West after the Russian revolution and Russian civil war that followed and altered the spelling of their name to "Galitzine."

Loyal to Stalin and Party

Golitsyn came of age during the calamitous events of World War II. As a youth he attended a military academy and at age 19, in 1945, formally joined the Russian Communist Party. He was also selected for entrance to an elite foreign intelligence-gathering academy established a few years earlier during World War II. This was under the control of SMERSH, an acronym whose full Russian-language name was *Spetsyalnye Metody Razoblacheniya Shpyonov*, which translates as "Special Methods of Spy Detection;" an alternate version of its acronym is *Smiert Shpionam*, or "Death to Spies."

As a young man Golitsyn was deeply committed to the Soviet state and rewarded with military-rank promotions and trusted assignments. He earned a law degree and had advanced training in diplomacy and intelligence-gathering operations. For a time he lived in Vienna, Austria, a city that remained under an unusual postwar occupation-zone arrangement until 1955. Like Berlin, the defeated capital of Nazi Germany, Vienna was divided into zones and jointly administered by Soviet, U.S., French, and British military authorities.

Back in Moscow Golitsyn was assigned to an intelligence-analysis desk at the Kremlin, the seat of government. He held the rank of major inside the KGB, or Committee for State Security (*Komitet gosudarstvennoy bezopasnosti* in Russian), after taking part in the transition team that over-saw the absorption of SMERSH into the agency. The KGB was the Soviets' formidable domestic- and foreign-intelligence gathering apparatus, entrusted with guarding the Soviet Union from threats both internal and external. The KGB monitored Soviet citizens at home and abroad, though few were allowed to travel freely outside its borders.

The KGB's chief counterparts in the West were the U.S. Central Intelligence Agency (CIA) and Britain's MI6 (Military Intelligence, Section 6). All three employed agents who operated under diplomatic cover, in addition to a network of informants who provided valuable information and classified documents about military technology, eco-nomic concerns, and relations with other nations. Golitsyn spent several years of his Kremlin career analyzing data that came to the KGB through these channels. He moni-tored information passed by agents who reported to the KGB's Anglo-American section and he also handled highly classified reports about NATO, or the North Atlantic Treaty Organization. NATO's original mission was to block fur-ther Soviet encroachment in Europe, which had become painfully divided along ideological lines in the decade after the end of World War II in 1945. Not unexpectedly, Eastern European nations occupied by the Soviet Red Army failed at maintaining open elections and quickly fell into the Soviet sphere. NATO was a joint British and American pact to come to the defense of Western Europe in the event of a Soviet military threat.

Fled Finland in Terror

As a high-ranking KGB official, Golitsyn claimed to have vast knowledge of espionage networks and undercover operations across Europe, from the Baltic states in Eastern Europe westward into a divided Germany plus France and Britain. In 1961 he was given a new cover identity, that of Ivan Klimov, Soviet diplomat, and posted as vice consul at the Soviet embassy in Helsinki, Finland. Behind the scenes he was likely in charge of running agents and missions from the strategically located Scandinavian port city. He brought his wife Svetlana and young daughter Tanya with him.

Undaunted by a late-afternoon snowstorm on Friday, December 15, 1961, Golitsyn and his wife and daughter took a taxi to the home of Frank Friberg, the CIA station chief in Finland. Before knocking at Friberg's residence, Golitsyn stashed a cache of classified documents in the snow outside the residence. At the door, in heavily accented English, Golitsyn asked for asylum and told Fri-berg that he was not Ivan Klimov, as his identification papers claimed, but a KGB official with the rank of major. He hoped to defect to the West, providing valuable infor-mation in exchange for protection for himself and his fam-ily. He told Friberg that there was a 8:15 p.m. flight to Stockholm, Sweden, and that he wanted to board it with his family. After Friberg agreed to help, Golitsyn then showed the station chief the documents he had hidden near the driveway.

Golitsyn allegedly refused to board the connecting flight from Stockholm to Frankfurt, West Germany, so fear-ful was he of being tailed by his KGB colleagues and assassinated on the spot. Friberg wrangled access to a U.S. Air Force plane that flew the Golitsyns to London; en route Golitsyn told Friberg that the entire CIA was a com-promised organization, with much of its intelligence-gathering operations against the Soviet Union useless because a top CIA official regularly met with a KGB counterpart to divulge information. This was a mole, in the parlance of espionage—a traitor within an agency whose top security clearance gave him (or her) access to vast amounts of classified data.

Warned CIA of Mole

Golitsyn was adamant that he be allowed to meet with U.S. President John F. Kennedy before he spoke to any CIA officials. The president, however, was on an official visit to Latin America during that third week of December, then flew to Bermuda to meet with British prime minister Harold Macmillan. In between engagements Kennedy spent time in Palm Beach, Florida, where his father Joseph had been hospitalized after a debilitating stroke. Instead, Golitsyn was taken to a CIA safe house in a secluded part of Virgin-ia's scenic horse country and debriefed by one of the CIA's most formidable spymasters, Richard Helms, who at the time held the title Deputy Director for Plans at the agency. Helms was dubious about some of Golitsyn's claims but another high-ranking CIA official, James Jesus Angleton, believed Golitsyn represented a significant intelligence chess move for U.S. foreign policy.

Golitsyn told Angleton that he did not know the exact identity of the mole in the CIA, but provided enough details to bring suspicion on Peter Karlow, a CIA agent in West Germany. Golitsyn met with interrogators from the British intelligence services and told them that they had failed to detect the so-called "Third Man," a high-ranking mole with Soviet sympathies inside its own espionage ranks. Ten years before Golitsyn defected, British diplomats Guy Burgess and Donald Maclean had vanished from England in a case that prompted international headlines. The two men turned up in Moscow after requesting asylum and were revealed to have been double agents. A friend of Burgess and Maclean, another British diplomat and agency operative named Harold "Kim" Philby, was questioned when Burgess and Maclean disappeared but was cleared of any wrongdoing.

Ten years later Philby was living in Beirut, Lebanon, and again working for the U.K. intelligence services when Golitsyn defected. Several months later, after being tipped about another investigation, Philby defected to the Soviet Union. Golitsyn claimed the three men were part of an even-larger "Ring of Five" turncoats Brits who had secretly provided the KGB with troves of information for years after they had been recruited as Cambridge University students back in the 1930s.

Protected by Angleton

Golitsyn also told American and British intelligence officials that the Soviets were planning to assassinate a major political figure in the West. His assertions seemed so preposterous that few took him seriously, and he was never able to meet with President Kennedy, who was slain in November of 1963. Golitsyn's staunchest ally was Angleton, the CIA's director of counterintelligence. The two reportedly spent hours building complex theories involving an intensive, impossible-to-disprove idea of a "long game" played by the Soviet Union with the help of covert allies inside Western democracies. Golitsyn even persuaded Angleton to let him personally review thousands of pages of CIA documents to uncover potential traitors. Later, foes of Angleton claimed that Golitsyn had been a plant and never genuinely defected; critics of Golitsyn maintained that he remained in the employ of his KGB bosses all along and had passed along highly classified information thanks to the trust Angleton placed in him.

Golitsyn's assertions led Angleton, as CIA counterintelligence chief, to launch a secretive, decade-long operation code-named Honetrol within the CIA to root out the suspected mole. Many senior-ranking employees with Russian-language experience or Communist-country postings on their resumés were drawn into this net, subject to persistent interrogations and personnel-file notations that effectively roadblocked their intelligence careers permanently. Angleton was eventually forced out as director of counterintelligence at the CIA in 1974 after *New York Times* reporter Seymour Hersh revealed that Angleton had attempted to infiltrate American political and religious organizations through the planting of undercover operatives.

Theories Embraced by Far Right

Some details about Golitsyn's life in the West remain murky, but his name is attached to a 1984 book warning about the dangers of Soviet communism, *New Lies for Old: The Communist Strategy of Deception and Disinformation.* In it, he argued that Soviet foreign policy had masterfully deluded the West into believing that its ideological disagreements with other Communist nations were little more than carefully stage-managed maneuvers. His second book, *The Perestroika Deception: Memoranda to the Central Intelligence Agency,* was published in 1995. Here Golitsyn asserted that the so-called end of communism that began in 1989 was another elaborate ruse by elite Russian

masterminds. He contended that the Soviets' short-term goal had been to trick the West into nuclear disarmament talks, which had succeeded, and that its long-term goal of a unified socialist state stretching from Britain to the Baltic lands—in other words, the European Union—was well on its way to becoming reality. He also contended that the KGB would never really disappear, but rather return under a new acronym in an even more staunchly authoritarian, heavily militarized Russia.

Golitsyn's theories are beloved by conspiracy theorists who cite them as evidence that Communism "faked its own death" in the early 1990s. An even more outrageous claim adds another layer of subterfuge to the Golitsyn saga: some claim that the KGB defector known as Anatoliy Golitsyn never actually existed. British journalist and intelligence-services analyst Gordon Corera authored a history of the Britain's secret service, *MI6: Life and Death in the British Secret Service,* and spoke to Golitsyn's wife. Their daughter had died years ago, in the early 1970s, and Golitsyn himself lived on near-constant fear of assassination by KGB agents. Svetlana Golitsyn told Corera that her husband had died in December of 2008.

Books

Corera, Gordon, *MI6: Life and Death in the British Secret Service,* Orion, 2011.
Holzman, Michael, *James Jesus Angleton, the CIA, and the Craft of Counterintelligence,* University of Massachusetts Press, 2008.
Macintyre, Ben, *A Spy Among Friends: Kim Philby and the Great Betrayal,* Crown, 2014.

Periodicals

New Yorker, July 28, 2014.
Sunday Times (London, England), March 4, 1984. □

Carlos Gracida

Mexican-born American professional polo player Carlos Gracida (1960–2014) is considered one of the best ever to play the game, with his teams winning the sport's elite tournaments in Argentina, the United States, and Great Britain—polo's grand slam—in the same year an unmatched three times. Known as the "Mexican Maestra," Gracida also taught polo to royalty and other prominent figures, and was the favorite polo player of British Queen Elizabeth II.

B orn on September 5, 1960, in Mexico City, Mexico, he was the son of Guillermo Gracida. His family had a long history in polo. In the 1920s, his grandfather, Gabriel Gracida, Sr., played the sport, was particularly successful in Argentina, and was a trainer of horses and polo ponies. Gabriel Gracida, Sr., had six sons, all of whom

Jennifer Wenzel/Icon SMI 995/Jennifer Wenzel/Icon SMI/Newscom

were taught to play polo by their father. They became a force in international polo, with four of them, including Guillermo Gracida, forming the team that won the 1946 United States Open. Gracida's father reached a ranking of 9-goaler, the second highest possible polo ranking, at his peak. (Polo ratings range from -2 goaler for novices to the elite being ranked 10-goalers.)

Followed in Family Footsteps

Like his father before him, Gracida and his elder brother, also named Guillermo and known as Memo, became elite polo players. They trained in the sport from an early age. Gracida began playing polo on foot at the age of five, and soon moved up to playing on a bicycle. Next, Gracida was trained to ride on horseback and led around on a horse while learning to use a polo mallet. All these steps occurred by the age of ten.

When he turned ten, Gracida began playing on horseback and competing in polo tournaments for novices and younger players. In the late 1970s, the teenaged Gracida was traveling to play in tournaments in other countries, including the United States. By the age of 18, Gracida had achieved a ranking of 3-goaler, and would soon move up. Within a few years, he competed in his first tournaments of highly ranked players. He was part of teams that competed in and won the USPA (United States Polo Association) Rolex Gold Cup and the International Open, held in Palm Beach, Florida.

Gracida achieved greatness in the 1980s. By this time, Gracida and his brother were based primarily in the United States, first in San Antonio, Texas, then in Southern Florida, where the sport of polo became more popular in the 1980s. Influenced by his brother Memo, who was also an elite player—arguably even more gifted than Gracida—Gracida achieved greatness. Beginning in 1985, Gracida achieved the highest ranking possible in polo when he became a 10-goaler. (His brother held the ranking for 21 total years.) Gracida remained ranked a 10-goaler until 2000, and was given a ranking of 9-goaler in 2003. Doing better the following year, he was able to again achieve a 10-goaler ranking in 2006 though he dropped down to 9-goaler again by 2014.

Describing Gracida's skill as a polo player, Jimmy Newman, the International Polo Club Palm Beach's director of operations, told Jimmy Yardley of the *New York Times*, "A polo field is 900 feet long. He might take the ball two or three times a game from one end to the other and go around three or four players. He had a heck of an eye. He got where he wanted to go with the ball." His brother Memo was similarly impressed, telling Kristen M. Daum of the *Palm Beach Post*, "Many times I found myself just watching him do these incredible plays and acts on the polo field that were uncanny. I have never seen and I don't think I will ever see anybody running down the field, throwing the ball in such a gracious, effortless and talented way."

Won Numerous Championships

Gracida demonstrated his talent and gained his high ranking from his excellent tournament play. During the 1980s and beyond, for example, Gracida played in many high profile tournaments in Argentina. He was a member of teams that won national championships there. Sometimes he played with high-profile polo families in Argentina, such as the Heguy polo dynasty. In three separate years—1987, 1988, and 1994—his teams triumphed in the three major annual polo tournaments held in Argentina, the United States, and Great Britain in a calendar year. This grand slam accomplishment was unmatched in polo before or after Gracida, through at least 2014.

By the mid-1990s, Gracida had reached a peak of his game. In 1994, Gracida won nearly every major tournament in polo, in addition to the grand slam. He took the Triple Crown of Argentina that year as well. Some of his victories in 1994 came as a member of the Ellerstina team. Fielded and owned by Kerry Packer, an Australian media mogul, Gracida was paid a salary of about $200,000 per month to play for Ellerstina. Packer also had a secondary agenda to make polo—generally regarded as a sport of and for the wealthy—more accessible to a wider audience through Ellerstina and other efforts. Packer wanted to change some of polo's rules, increase the amount of television coverage, and make the sport more attractive overall. Though Gracida supported his ideas, Packer's attempts did not result in substantive changes to the sport.

Over the course of his distinguished career, Gracida won the Argentine Open six times, the British Open ten times, and the United States Open nine times. (Memo

Gracida won a record 16 United States Opens.) Overall, Gracida won more tournament titles worldwide than any other player. He played in and won many of the major polo tournaments in the world, including the Queen's Cup and Gold Cup in England, the Melbourne Cup in Australia, and the Deauville Gold Cup in France. He also competed in the Mexican Open in his native country. At one point, Gracida served as the captain of England's team.

Played with Brother

Gracida played with a number of high profile players on winning polo teams, and often played with his brother. In 2013, six years after Memo Gracida retired, the brothers again played on a team, La Herradura, which competed in the Herbie Pennell Cup and other tournaments at the International Polo Club Palm Beach. While Memo Gracida's objective for playing again included showing off the horses he trained and having fun, he also appreciated playing again with his brother. Memo Gracida told the *Palm Beach Post,* "Playing with Carlos brings back great memories and great experiences. We still have a lot of good polo in us."

Ponies were also important to Gracida's success as a player. He had two polo ponies he favored. Chesney was his best known mount, and the horse won numerous best playing pony awards. These included the British Open Gold Cup in 1988, 1989, and 1991. Gracida himself favored another horse, Nony Nony, on whom he won British Open Gold Cups seven times. Three other of Gracida's ponies, Calasa, Oca, and Que Linda, were honored with the Hartman Trophy.

Taught Polo to Others

In addition to playing polo, Gracida was a distinguished teacher of the game, not only to his own sons, Carlos Jr., and Mariano who also became professional polo players, but also to leading figures in the world. He served as a coach to a number of members of the British royal family, including Prince Charles, Prince William, and Prince Henry. According to Chris Maume of the London *Independent,* Gracida said, "My experience with the Royal Family was really something special because they are true princes. I remember . . . a training session in which Prince William arrived four or five minutes late for a class and said sorry more than anyone I've ever met in my life. They are fantastic people."

Gracida also taught polo to members of other royal families, including King Constantine II of Greece and Prince Talal of Jordan. In addition to leaders in business, Gracida coached film stars like Sylvester Stallone in the game. Gracida taught the less famous as well. Among his many students were a number of women, though the sport was male dominated.

Polo was also the focal point of another business for Gracida. In 2011, he founded Gracida Polo, in a partnership deal with a New York-based investment group. The company was to be a lifestyle brand that produced polo gear and polo-inspired apparel, and other luxury products. Gracida Polo also had interests in property development and athlete management.

Throughout his renowned career, Gracida was given five player of the year awards as part of the Polo Excellence Awards. He was honored with the inaugural award in 1986, and won again in 1989, 1993, 1995, and 2004. Only one player matched this feat in his lifetime—his brother. Gracida was also a member of the Polo Hall of Fame, inducted in 2012. In addition, by 2014, he had become a legal citizen of the United States, after spending much of his adult life living there.

Died After Polo Accident

Gracida died on February 25, 2014, in Delray, Florida, after suffering an accident while playing polo. He was 53 years old. He had been participating in the Freebooters Classic 14-goal Tournament at the Everglades Polo Club in Wellington, Florida, where he had long made his home. Though eyewitness accounts differ on what happened, it is known that Gracida fell off his horse and the horse fell on top of him or stepped on him. In the process, Gracida suffered a blunt force trauma to his chest as well as head injuries. The cause of the fall is unclear, but his horse may have been accidentally hit on the head by another player's mallet and the horse and Gracida's heads collided.

Before Gracida died, he was aware that polo could be a dangerous contact sport that regularly resulted in injury, and, occasionally, death. The tournament continued after Gracida's accident, as all involved believed he would have wanted, and to honor his memory. The captain of the Flight Options team, Melissa Ganzi, told Sharon Robb of the *Palm Beach Post,* "For all of us and each day that goes by, we realize even more the magnitude of the loss to the polo community. He was so much to so many. He touched the world of polo with his talent, charisma, generosity, knowledge, horsemanship, dignity and grace." In the months after his death, the village of Wellington planned to honor Gracida by renaming a street after him. It was proposed that Wellington's 40th Street be known as Gracida Way.

Upon Gracida's demise, the chief executive officer of the United States Polo Association, Peter Rizzo, told Kristen M. Daum of the *Palm Beach Post,* "Around the world, he is beloved. He is a fierce competitor and one of the top players of all time. He has a record of wins that may never be equaled." The London *Daily Telegraph* concluded, "Gracida came to personify the notion of the dashing, distinguished and daring polo player living the high life on the game's global circuit. . . .His grace in the saddle was drawn from a keen understanding of the game's history and traditions."

Periodicals

Daily Telegraph (London, England), February 27, 2014.

Express (London, England), March 1, 2014.

Independent (London, England), February 27, 2014.

New York Times, March 2, 2014.

Palm Beach Post, January 3, 2013; February 27, 2014; February 28, 2014; March 2, 2014; October 17, 2014.

Online

"Inductee to the Polo Hall of Fame: Carlos Gracida, Inducted February 17, 2012," Museum of Polo and Hall of Fame, http://www.polomuseum.com/hof_inductees/gracida_carlos.htm (December 4, 2014).

"2004 Polo Excellence Awards," *Polo Players' Edition,* http://www.poloplayersedition.com/new/may2005.html (December 4, 2014).□

Camargo Guarnieri

Camargo Guarnieri (1907–1993) was the among the most highly regarded Brazilian classical composers of the 20th century, ranking at the top of the generation following the master Brazilian nationalist, Heitor Villa-Lobos. He also made notable achievements as a conductor and educator.

Guarnieri, like Villa-Lobos, is considered a representative of Brazilian nationalism in music, and his compositions make use of rhythms and melodic traits derived from popular, Afro-Brazilian, and Amerindian musical styles. Brazilian popular musicians, in turn, rewarded Guarnieri by performing his songs and making some of them into standards. Yet Guarnieri's nationalism was of a cosmopolitan kind, influenced by his studies in Europe and mixed with contemporary styles of European music. In the words of Joseph Stevenson of *Allmusic,* Guarnieri "avoids the sense of the mysterious or exotic that is frequently a trait of his older compatriot's works." Guarnieri's career lasted for nearly 70 years, and for most of that period he was a towering figure in Brazil's classical music scene.

Rejected Mozart Name

Camargo Guarnieri was born Mozart Guarnieri in the town of Tietˆ in Brazil's Saõ Paulo state on February 1, 1907. His three older siblings were named Rossine (a misspelling of Rossini), Bellini, and Verdi, all names of Italian composers. Camargo was his mother's maiden name. For a time he used the name M. Camargo Guarnieri, but later he came to consider it presumptuous to use the name of the composer Wolfgang Amadeus Mozart and even became annoyed if the "Mozart" was used on an album cover or concert program. Guarnieri's father, an immigrant of civilian birth, was a barber who also had some musical skills and gave his son his first music lessons. At age ten he began studies with a local teacher named Virginio Dias, and soon he had written his first composition, "Artist's Dream."

The Guarnieri family moved to the city of Saõ Paulo in 1923, and there Guarnieri was able to study piano, composition, and conducting with a variety of immigrant European teachers. At first he had to work in his father's barbershop and play in silent movie houses and cafés to pay for his studies. His most important inspiration was writer and ethnomusicological scholar Mario de Andrade, who introduced Guarnieri to the everyday musical styles of the Brazilian people and encouraged him to incorporate those styles into his own compositions. Andrade and Guarnieri remained friends and associates for many years. Guarnieri made rapid progress on many fronts and was appointed as a teacher of piano at the Saõ Paulo Conservatory in 1927, when he was just 20. Around the same time he began to publish his own compositions, and two early piano pieces, *Brazilian Dance* and *Cancão Sertaneja* (roughly, "Cowboy Song") have remained among his most popular works.

Many of Guarnieri's compositions during this first part of his career were songs for voice and piano, and some of these, too, have remained popular in Brazil. When the city of Saõ Paulo founded a Department of Culture in 1935, Guarnieri, with Andrade's help, found employment as conductor of the civic Coral Paulisto chorus. A government fellowship, obtained on the recommendation of French pianist Alfred Cortot, allowed Guarnieri to travel to Paris for further musical studies in 1938; he remained there until the outbreak of World War II at the end of 1939.

Studied in France

Although only about a year long, Guarnieri's time in France was decisive for his career. He studied composition and aesthetics with French composer Charles Koechlin and conducting with Franz Rühlmann. He also took some lessons with the composition teacher Nadia Boulanger, who served as an inspiration during this period to a large number of composers from both North and South America. Guarnieri soaked up the latest European trends, including the polyphonic craft of the German composer Paul Hindemith, the neoclassic sounds of French composers, and the rigorously worked-out elaborations on ethnic rhythms of the Hungarian composer Béla Bartók. All of these would emerge as layers grafted onto his own Brazilian-flavored style.

When he returned from France, Guarnieri was more comfortable with the idea of handling a symphony orchestra, and he began to write in larger forms such as the symphony and piano concerto in addition to composing smaller works like songs, piano pieces, and chamber music. He created some 700 pieces, including seven symphonies, six piano concertos, two operas (one serious, one comic), and several large works for voice and orchestra, as well as songs, piano pieces, and chamber works. Guarnieri composed five volumes of piano pieces in a uniquely Brazilian genre called Ponteios, a word originally referring to a type of guitar music. His piano works are often heard in concert and played by piano students in Brazil. Guarnieri's first two symphonies, both appearing in 1944, are considered some of his best works.

In 1945 Guarnieri was appointed conductor of the São Paulo Symphony Orchestra. He used his platform as a conductor to promote his own music, leading the Boston Symphony Orchestra in his own Symphony No. 1 in the 1946–1947 season and making several other trips to the United States, where his music found a certain degree of popularity. Among his strongest backers in the United States was the composer Aaron Copland, whose combination of European techniques and native materials in some respects resembled those of Guarnieri. Copland (as quoted on the *Piano Society* website) wrote that "Camargo Guarnieri is in my opinion the most exciting 'unknown' talent in South America. . . . What I like best about his music is its healthy emotional expression—the honest statement of how one man feels. . . . He knows how to shape a form, how to orchestrate well, how to lead a bass line effectively. Most attractive in Guarnieri's music is its warmth and imagination, which are touched by a deeply Brazilian sensibility. At its finest, his is the fresh and racy music of a 'new' continent."

Rejected Serialist Technique

Some of the biggest controversies in the musical world in the 1950s involved atonality and the procedure known as serialism, which organized music according to repeating sets (or "rows") of pitches and later other musical parameters. Guarnieri at first resisted the serialist movement, exhorting his fellow Brazilians to reject it in his *Open Letter to the Musicians and Critics of Brazil* (1950). In the 1960s, however, like Copland, he began to experiment with the technique himself. For several years in the mid-1960s, Guarnieri wrote nothing, seemingly struggling with the varied musical currents that were in the air at the time.

As serialism declined in influence in the 1970s and 1980s, Guarnieri's creativity returned. He was remarkably prolific in his old age, composing two new symphonies in the 1980s and continuing to produce new works as late as the *Chôo* for bassoon, harpsichord, percussion, and strings, in 1992, when he was 85. He was the founder of the String Orchestra of the University of São Paulo, and he remained its conductor until 1992.

Guarnieri was an active participant in Brazilian musical life as an educator and official. Several generations of Brazilian composers, including Aylton Escobar, Almeida Prado, and Osvaldo Lacerda, numbered among his students during his years as a teacher at the São Paulo Conservatory and later the Santos Conservatory. He received several major South American music prizes, including first prize honors in the São Paulo Fourth Centenary Competition in 1954 and the Caracas International Competition in 1957.

The last of these was the Gabriela Mistral Prize, awarded by the Organization of American States in 1993 to the "Greatest Contemporary Composer of the Three Americas." Shortly after receiving the prize, Guarnieri died in São Paulo on January 13, 1993. New recordings of his orchestral works, especially, have appeared at a steady clip in the early 21st century.

Books

Behague, Gerard, *Music in Latin America*, Prentice-Hall, 1979.

Sadie, Stanley, ed., *New Grove Dictionary of Music and Musicians*, 2nd ed., Macmillan, 2001.

Slonimsky, Nicolas, ed. emeritus, *Baker's Biographical Dictionary of Musicians*, centennial ed., Schirmer, 2001.

Periodicals

American Record Guide, March–April 1998; September–October 2005, p. 111; May–June 2013.

Online

"Camargo Guarnieri," *Allmusic,* http://www.allmusic.com/artist/camargo-guarnieri-mn0001950327 (November 2, 2014).

"Maestro Camargo Guarnieri," University of São Paulo, http://www.usp.br/osusp/maestro_camargo.html (November 2, 2014).

"Mozart Camargo Guarnieri (1907–1993)," *Piano Society,* http://pianosociety.com/cms/index.php?section=2172 (November 2, 2014). □

Jesús Guerrero Galván

Mexican realist painter Jesús Guerrero Galván (1910–1973) made a name for himself with his highly individualized approach that blended magical realism, Italian influences, and Mexican folk art and culture into a unified style. Guerrero Galván got his start with Mexico's mural movement, which began in the 1920s and launched the careers of Diego Rivera, José Clemente Orozco, and David Alfaro Siqueiros. Unlike many of his muralist contemporaries, Guerrero Galván, moved away from social and political art and became well-known for his portraits depicting women and children.

Guerrero Galván was born into a family of poor farmers in Tonalá, Jalisco, Mexico, on June 1, 1910. As a child, he went to Texas with his mother and sister. There, Guerrero Galván helped his family at a food stand and spent his free time etching scenes on the sidewalk with pieces of charcoal. One day, a couple passed by and noticed his work. They were so impressed they became benefactors and helped the young man enroll at a fine arts school in San Antonio. Soon, he took an interest in the work of French modernist André Derain, a proponent of Fauvism—an art movement that emphasized the use of vivid, non-natural colors.

Studied Under Vizcarra

After returning to Mexico, Guerrero Galván began studying in Guadalajara with master painter José Vizcarra. Working with Vizcarra, he developed an affinity for Renaissance masters like Raphael. His assignments at this time involved going to the Guadalajara museum and copying works by Spanish religious painter Francisco Zurbarán and the Spanish Baroque masters Bartolomé Esteban Murillo and Luca Giordano.

Guerrero Galván soon fell in with a group of avant-garde artists who painted from a studio at the University of

Guadalajara. Initially, the members of the group explored the Impressionist movement but later moved to a style they called poetic neo-realism, which showed a strong connection to Cubism. Together, the members painted faux murals, often on drywall instead of utilizing plaster in a more traditional al fresco style.

Soon, he joined a collective of artists, writers, and intellectuals known as the Bandera de Provincias. The group published a magazine and organized exhibitions and lectures. Members of the group included Mexican muralists Raúl Anguiano and José Guadalupe Zuno and writer Agustín Yáñez. In 1928, Guerrero Galván enrolled at the Free School of Painting at the Jalisco Museum. By 1932, he was involved with the Young Painters of Jalisco. The group included Anguiano, as well as other up-and-coming Mexican artists. The artists showed their pieces—mostly oils and watercolors—in regional exhibitions.

Painted Government-Commissioned Murals

Guerrero Galván moved to Mexico City in the mid-1930s. At this time, young artists were flocking to the city to hook up with other painters to improve and explore their craft. The city teemed with social and political painters crafting murals for social commentary. During the 1920s, a mural movement exploded in Mexico City as the government began hiring the country's best artists to paint government-sponsored murals to reaffirm the values of the Mexican revolution and strengthen Mexican identity. Many Mexican artists—including Rivera, Orozco and Siqueiros—got their start with the mural movement.

Likewise, Guerrero Galván painted decorative murals in schools and public buildings in Mexico City, though he mostly painted in the schools. In 1932, Mexican painter and architect Juan O'Gorman became head of the architectural office of the Ministry of Public Education. Over the next few years, he designed and built more than 20 elementary schools in Mexico City's working class neighborhoods. The buildings were highly functional, delivering maximum efficiency at a minimal cost. By now, Rivera, Orozco and Siqueiros were busy overseas, so O'Gorman commissioned several young artists to paint the stairwells and corridors.

Along with Julio Castellanos and Pablo O'Higgins, Guerrero Galván was hired by O'Gorman to decorate the buildings. His murals shied away from overtly political themes. Most of them featured children. He painted a large mural at the Escuela Colonia Portales. This mural featured a classroom of students engaged with a teacher who stood at the center of the room. Behind him, people worked math problems on a blackboard. The students were all barefoot and most had papers in their hands. The mural was titled "School Activities." Most of Guerrero Galván's murals were painted in the Alamos and Portales neighborhoods.

During this period, he also painted at the Church Santa Maria de Guido in Morelia, Mexico, and completed frescoes in the cupola of one of the old buildings at the University of Guadalajara. In addition, he worked as a painting instructor in the Ministry of Education's Department of Fine Arts. Guerrero Galván was also involved with theatre, painting backdrops for plays and ballets. He later became a professor of figure drawing at the School of Fine Arts at the National Autonomous University in Mexico City.

By now, Guerrero Galván had established himself with his easel paintings and was especially known for his paintings featuring full-frame women and children. In 1939, he staged an exhibition of his work in San Francisco. In 1940, his work was included in a Museum of Modern Art exhibit titled "Twenty Centuries of Mexican Art." The exhibit included pre-Columbian art, colonial art and folk art, as well as a modern art division. His artwork appeared in the "modern art" segment alongside works by Rivera, Orozco, Siqueiros, and Miguel Covarrubias. The exhibit debuted in New York City, then moved to Albuquerque in a show sponsored by the Art League of New Mexico. In 1941, he held a solo exhibition at the Galería de Arte Mexicano in Mexico City.

Taught in U.S., Mexico

In 1942, Guerrero Galván came to the United States to serve as an artist-in-residence at the University of New Mexico in Albuquerque. The placement came through a grant funded by the Committee for Inter-American Artistic and Intellectual Relations through the Office of Inter-American Affairs (OIAA). The OIAA was founded by the U.S. government to help build relations with Latin American countries in an effort to quell the influence of Germany and other Axis powers.

He arrived at the University of New Mexico for the summer 1942 session and stayed through the first semester of the 1942–43 school year. He taught a technical course on painting and offered a lecture class on contemporary Mexican painters. He also executed a mural at the university's administrative building. Titled "Union of the Americas," the mural depicted a mystical figure of "Liberty" holding a torch of justice. Underneath this figure, he painted a mother and child on each side. The mother and child on the left side represented Latin American countries and in the distance behind them stood pyramids. The figures on the right side had American features with a background of mountains. Unlike many of the artist's early murals from Mexico City, this one remained intact and was still on display some 70 years later.

After leaving the United States, he returned to teaching at the National University of Mexico. In the mid-1940s he executed a series of lithographs to illustrate a book on Quetzalcóatl, a feathered serpent deity from the Toltec and Aztec traditions. Written by Ermilo Abreu Gómez, the 175-page book was published in 1947. In 1952, Guerrero Galván held an exhibition at the Palace of Fine Arts (Palacio de Bellas Artes) in Mexico City. In 1952, he returned to mural painting after receiving a commission to paint a wall at the administration building of the Electric Power Commission. The mural depicted how the earth's natural forces could be harnessed for electricity. The mural also portrayed the many ways people benefit from electricity in modern life.

In 1959, Guerrero Galván joined Anguiano, O'Gorman and Orozco in founding the Unión de Pintores y Grabadores de México (Mexican Painters and Engravers Union). In 1960, he toured the Soviet Union after being invited by several artists. When he returned, he learned that Siqueiros had been imprisoned and he went on a hunger strike in response. Like Siqueiros, Guerrero Galván had ties to the Mexican Communist Party. Siqueiros had been jailed for his work with revolutionaries and labor organizers.

Spent Last Years Painting

While many of Guerrero Galván's fellow painters turned toward political and social commentary with their work, he concentrated on painting figures—mostly women and peasant children. He also tackled paintings involving spirituality and the mysteries of the universe, populating his work with guardian angels, healers, mystical experiences, and dream landscapes, all the while staying true to Mexican art traditions and throwing in a hint of influence from the Italian masters. He tended to execute his portraits in gray-blue tones and violets.

One distinct feature of his work was the way he distorted the proportions. Hands were often oversized with the exaggerated proportions of his gigantic figures, adding a poetic effect. The eyes in his subjects often gave off a serene indifference as they gazed into infinity. The subjects most often looked out off the canvas, never focusing on any elements within the picture. The faces the artist painted were also placid, giving no hints of emotion. The settings were always sparse. Many paintings depicted the bleak realities of Mexican children. Frequently he painted women with their children, although the children often seemed to be drifting in limbo.

In 2006, the *Santa Fe Reporter*'s Zane Fischer attended the *Mexican Modern: Masters of the 20th Century* exhibit at the Museum of Fine Arts in Santa Fe. The exhibit featured work from Rivera, Frida Kahlo, Orozco, Siqueiros, and Guerrero Galván. The exhibit included one of Guerrero Galván's more famous paintings, "Niños con raqueta" (Children with Racket), an oil-on-board painting executed in 1936. The painting featured an ill-proportioned boy and girl. The girl, wearing a semi-translucent tennis dress, holds a tennis racket in one hand and a pink rose in the other. Fisher wrote that the painting offered a glimpse of strange beauty: "Each element is malformed just to a point of indecision about youth vs. age, sex vs. innocence, rich vs. poor. The swollen brown eyes of both figures are on the verge of bursting off the canvas, so stuffed are they with the weight of 1936."

Besides "Niños con raqueta," some of Guerrero Galván's more noted works include "La nina" (1939), a watercolor of a woman holding an unfurled sheet as if to fold it or place it on a clothesline to dry; "La concepción" (1939), a full-frame image of a "glowing" figure seated in a long white shirt with distortions such that a viewer is unable to tell the age or gender of the figure; "Sueño de Juventud" (1946); "Girl in Pink Dress" (1948); and "Niña con paloma" (Girl with a Dove) (1959).

Guerrero Galván was highly prolific. He spent his last years in Cuernavaca, Morelos, Mexico, settling there sometime in the late 1960s. He suffered ill health from complications due to childhood tuberculosis and problems with alcohol, yet he kept painting. He and his wife, Dabaki Garro, had five children. One daughter, Flora Guerrero, became an artist and environmentalist and was known for her paintings focused on nature. Guerrero's father served as her primary teacher, encouraging her to experiment with tones, textures and strokes.

Guerrero Galván died May 11, 1973. He was 62. In 1977, the Museo de Arte Moderno (Museum of Modern Art) in Mexico City held a retrospective of his work. In 2007, "La concepción" sold at Sotheby's for more than $180,000.

Books

Burchwood, Katharine Tyler, *The Origin and Legacy of Mexican Art*, A.S. Barnes & Co., 1971.

Edwards, Emily, *Painted Walls of Mexico*, University of Texas Press, 1966.

Metropolitan Museum of Art, *Splendors of Thirty Centuries*, Little, Brown & Co., 1990.

Periodicals

Albuquerque Journal (NM), March 11, 1942.

McClatchy-Tribune Business News, October 15, 2009.

Santa Fe Reporter (NM), June 7, 2006.

Other

"A Mexican Painter Views Modern Mexican Painting," *Inter-Americana Short Papers, II* University of New Mexico Press, 1942. □

Thich Nhat Hanh

During the latter half of the 20th century, Vietnamese Buddhist monk Thich Nhat Hanh (born 1926) emerged as a potent spiritual teacher, spreading the message of mindfulness to the masses. A writer, poet, and peace activist, Nhat Hanh was well known around the globe and sometimes referred to as "the other Dalai Lama."

Thich Nhat Hanh was born October 11, 1926, in Tha Tien, a village in the central Vietnamese province of Qu'ng Ngai. His birth name was Nguyen Xuân Bao. Early in childhood, Nhat Hanh felt moved to follow in the Buddha's path. In Vietnam, Buddhism is a deeply rooted ancient tradition. Nhat Hanh recounted his "aha!" moment to *Spirituality & Health* magazine, putting it this way: "I saw a drawing of the Buddha sitting on the grass, very peacefully. I was impressed, because people around me were very unhappy and not peaceful. This picture gave me the idea that I could someday be like him, someone who could sit very still and calm."

Became Novice Monk at 16

As Nhat Hanh grew, the desire intensified. At 16, his parents let him enter the Tu Hieu Temple to begin training as a novice monk. After years of study, which included intensive Zen training in the Mahayana branch of Buddhism, he became an official monk in 1949. At this time, he gave up his birth name and was given the new name of Nhat Hanh, which means "one action." The term "Thich" was also added. Thich is a designation used by many monks, meaning "descending from Buddha." Vietnamese is highly phonetic, making name pronunciations hard to render in other languages. In English, his name is commonly pronounced Tik-N'yat-Hawn. Students, however, call him Thay, which is Vietnamese for teacher.

In 1949, Nhat Hanh co-founded the An Quang Buddhist Institute in Ho Chi Minh City (Saigon). A fellow Dharma teacher helped him construct a bamboo and thatch temple for the institute. Nhat Hanh went on to instruct the institute's first class of novices. From the start, he pushed the boundaries of what was considered traditional and proper for a monk. He studied secular subjects at the University of Saigon and rode a bicycle. Early in the 1950s, he hit upon the idea of renewing Vietnamese Buddhism and began writing articles promoting a humanistic, unified Buddhism to bring together the citizens of Vietnam.

During this time, the political climate in Vietnam was unstable. Beginning in the mid-1940s, Vietnamese resistance fighters had been battling the French, seeking to end French rule. Parts of Vietnam and Cambodia had been French colonies known as French Indochina. Finally, in 1954, with the signing of the Geneva Accord, Vietnam was split in two. The Communist-backed Viet Minh took possession of the northern half, while a member of the Nguyen Dynasty became emperor of the south. More than a million refugees fled the north and moved into South Vietnam, causing further unrest.

Promoted *Engaged Buddhism*

Nhat Hanh saw a war of ideologies developing in his homeland so he stepped up efforts to rejuvenate Vietnamese Buddhism. One local newspaper asked him to write from a Buddhist perspective and offer guidance on how to sooth the unrest in the country, and around 1954 he published a series titled "A Fresh Look at Buddhism." It was

179

Peter Kramer/Getty Images

during this series that Nhat Hanh came up with the idea of "Engaged Buddhism," which envisioned a more humanistic Buddhism that could respond to the needs of the people. In other words, he promoted the idea of applying Buddhist teachings in an activist and socialist manner in areas of education, economics, politics, and so forth. These ideas were not very popular with the Vietnamese Buddhist hierarchy, which favored a strict tradition.

Nhat Hanh discussed the idea of Engaged Buddhism (later called Applied Buddhism) in a Dharma talk he delivered much later, during a 2008 retreat in Hanoi, Vietnam. Talk excerpts were printed in *The Mindfulness Bell,* a publication of the Unified Buddhist Church. In the talk, he described Engaged Buddhism as Buddhism that is present in every moment of daily life. "While you brush your teeth, Buddhism should be there. While you drive your car, Buddhism should be there. While you are walking in the supermarket, Buddhism should be there—so that you know what to buy and what not to buy!" Nhat Hanh went on to define Engaged Buddhism as being present in the here and now. "Engaged Buddhism is the kind of wisdom that responds to anything that happens in the here and the now—global warming, climate change, the destruction of the ecosystem, the lack of communication, war, conflict, suicide, divorce."

In 1955, war erupted in Vietnam as factions from the north and south sought control in the country. Foreign nations offered help; North Vietnam received backing from Communist allies (including the Soviet Union and China)

and South Vietnam got support from the United States and other anti-Communist allies. As the war intensified, Buddhist monks and nuns struggled with their role. The traditionalists sought to keep on with their contemplative lives, mostly remaining in their monasteries. Nhat Hanh thought that Buddhist leaders ought to reach out to help those suffering through the chaos of war. Once again, this notion of "Engaged Buddhism" came to the forefront of his thinking. He expounded on the topic in *Vietnam: Lotus in a Sea of Fire* (1965), which introduced the idea of Engaged Buddhism to the wider world.

Nhat Hanh's views caused dissension in the Buddhist community. In 1956, he became editor of *Vietnamese Buddhism,* the journal of the Buddhist General Association. Within two years, publication was suspended because many Buddhist higher-ups did not agree with the journal's content. During this period, Nhat Hanh lived at a small temple in the Blao district, but he was acutely aware of the tension around him.

In August 1957, Nhat Hanh joined a handful of other monks to buy a 60-acre plot for a hermitage in the Dai Lao forest. Here, they founded the Phuong Boi (Fragrant Palm Leaves) Meditation Center. After purchasing the land, they were out of money, so they cleared ten acres to plant tea. Nhat Hanh continued writing and selling manuscripts, using the proceeds to help fund construction at Phuong Boi. At one point, there were about eight people living there. They spent their days working the land, hiking, writing and instructing visitors. Within a couple of years, however, the hermitage came under government suspicion because Nhat Hanh continued to speak out against the war. One of his associates was arrested and questioned. Nhat Hanh decided it was not safe to stay at Phuong Boi so he went to the Bamboo Forest Temple in Saigon.

Pushed for Peace in Face of War

In 1960, Nhat Hanh left Vietnam to study comparative religion at Princeton University. A lifelong student, he became well-versed in several languages and religious traditions. In an interview with Oprah Winfrey, Nhat Hanh joked that the place felt familiar, even though New Jersey was worlds apart from tropical Vietnam. "Well, Princeton University was like a monastery," he quipped. "There were only male students at that time." In 1963–64, he taught Buddhism at Columbia University. Meanwhile, civil war continued in his homeland and by the end of 1964, he was back in Vietnam assisting with the peace movement.

Upon his return, Nhat Hanh founded Van Hanh University in Saigon, as well as the Order of Interbeing (1964). The order was founded to combat the hatred and violence sweeping across Vietnam. The Order of Interbeing included nuns, monks, and lay members who dedicated themselves to following and spreading the Fourteen Precepts (or Mindfulness Trainings). He envisioned the Order of Interbeing as a spiritual resistance movement based on the teachings of the Buddha. In addition, he established the La Boi Press and the School of Youth for Social Service, a grass roots relief organization that trained rural peace workers in the Buddhist principles of non-violence and compassionate action. In 1966, he received the "lamp transmission" from Master Chân Thât, making him an official Dharma teacher.

In his work and writing, Nhat Hanh continued to call for reconciliation and peace in his country. Naturally, his anti-war stance was unpopular as North and South Vietnam, aided by outside allies, continued to engage in an ideological war. In 1966, after Nhat Hanh traveled to the United States to lecture at Cornell University, he found himself barred from returning home. He spent the next 39 years in exile, and initially it was hard for him to endure. Nhat Hanh told Winfrey that he felt "angry, worried, sad, hurt. The practice of mindfulness helped me recognize that. In the first year, I dreamed almost every night of going home. I was climbing a beautiful hill, very green, very happily, and suddenly I woke up and found that I was in exile."

Lived in Exile

Unable to re-enter Vietnam, Nhat Hanh continued his peace efforts abroad. He lobbied foreign governments to end the Vietnam War and led the Buddhist delegation to the 1969 Paris Peace Talks. He continued to write books and lecture. In 1967, he received asylum in France and by 1970 was working as a lecturer and researcher at the University of Sorbonne. In France, he established the Unified Buddhist Church and in 1975 founded the Sweet Potatoes Meditation Center near Paris. In 1982, he moved the training community to southern France and re-established it as Plum Village, which went on to become the largest and most active Buddhist monastery outside of Asia. At Plum Village, resident monks and visitors came to learn about Nhat Hanh's art of mindful living. Over the next several decades, he established monasteries in Australia, Hong Kong, Thailand and the United States, as well as the European Institute of Applied Buddhism in Germany.

In 2005, Nhat Hanh was allowed to return to Vietnam after receiving a special visa. Even after the war ended in 1975, he could not return home because his writings had been banned by the Communist government, which only allowed state-controlled churches. Nhat Hanh spent several months there teaching and visiting Buddhist temples. The year 2006 found him in Paris, where he spoke to the United Nations Educational, Scientific and Cultural Organization (UNESCO), calling for action to end violence, war and global warming. In 2010, Nhat Hanh unveiled an art exhibition titled *Calligraphic Meditation: The Mindful Art of Thich Nhat Hanh*. The exhibition debuted at the University of Hong Kong before making other stops across the globe.

Besides his own personal practice of meditation and mindfulness, Nhat Hanh spent his life teaching Buddhist precepts to followers and addressing political leaders around the globe. Just 5-foot-5 inches tall, Nhat Hanh could nonetheless still a crowd. His lectures have been heard in more than 35 countries, most often selling out the house. "Thich Nhat Hanh is a small, slender man who possesses an aura of stillness and a focus that commands attention," Gustav Niebuhr once wrote in the *New York Times*. Highly sought after as a speaker and teacher, Nhat Hanh visited the United States in 2013 and led mindfulness events at Google, The World Bank, and the Harvard School of Medicine.

Over the course of his life, Nhat Hanh wrote more than 80 books, offering meditations, mindfulness exercises, anecdotes, and personal observations aimed at helping people find peace in their lives. Titles included *Zen Keys: A Guide to Zen Practice* (1994), *Living Buddha, Living Christ* (1995), *Savor: Mindful Eating, Mindful Life* (2010), the best-selling *The Art of Mindfulness* (2012), and *No Mud, No Lotus* (2014).

By the end of 2014, Nhat Hanh was no longer making public appearances. He suffered a brain hemorrhage in November 2014 and spent several weeks in a coma at a hospital in Bordeaux, France. In early 2015, Nhat Hanh was receiving care at a stroke rehabilitation clinic as he had not regained his ability to speak. The nuns and monks from Plum Village stayed by his side. He was able to smile and laugh and recognize familiar faces.

Books

Nhat Hanh, Thich, *Fragrant Palm Leaves: Journals 1962-1966*, Riverhead Books, 1966.

Periodicals

New York Times, October 16, 1999.
O: The Oprah Magazine, March 2010.
Orange County Register (Santa Ana, CA), February 21, 2004.
Spirituality & Health, September/October 2013.
Time International, January 24, 2005.

Online

"Dharma Talk: History of Engaged Buddhism," *The Mindfulness Bell*, http://www.mindfulnessbell.org/wp/2012/12/dharma-talk-history-of-engaged-buddhism/ (5 January 2015).
"Thich Nhat Hanh," Plum Village, http://www.plumvillage.org/about/thich-nhat-hanh/ (5 January 2015).□

Harald zur Hausen

The German medical researcher Harald zur Hausen (1936–) discovered the role of human papilloma virus (HPV) in causing cervical cancer. He shared the 2008 Nobel Prize in Physiology or Medicine for his work.

I t was zur Hausen's research that laid the groundwork for a vaccine against cervical cancer, which was introduced in 2006 and could potentially save the lives of tens of thousands of women a year, many of them in poor countries. Since receiving his award and retiring from his position as chairman of the German Cancer Research Center, zur Hausen has campaigned for wider availability of the vaccine he helped create. The research for which he won the Nobel Prize took place over many years, as zur Hausen began with an unpopular hypothesis—that the HPV causes cervical cancer—and proceeded to demonstrate it step by step. When he began his work, the study of human oncoviruses, or viruses that cause cancer in humans, was in its infancy, as was the science of virology itself.

Miguel Villagran/Getty Images

Early Schooling Interrupted by War

Harald zur Hausen was born on March 11, 1936, in Gelsenkirchen, Germany. Despite the city's location in the midst of Germany's heavily industrialized Ruhr region, he was fascinated by flowers and by birds and other animals, and he soon decided he wanted to be a scientist. His first years of school were interrupted during World War II, when schools were closed as Allied bombing raids destroyed three-quarters of the city. Entering a gymnasium or college-preparatory high school in 1946, zur Hausen had to scramble to catch up. In 1955 he graduated from high school (in the German system, high school studies cover part of what would normally be the first years of college in the United States) and decided to enroll at the University of Bonn with a major in medicine.

At the beginning, zur Hausen encountered difficulties in his studies as he was drawn to classes in biology as well as those in his pre-med sequence. He did extremely well in an exam administered after five semesters, however, and felt more confident about designing his own curriculum. He transferred to the University of Hamburg and then to the University of Düsseldorf Medical Academy, which granted him the M.D. degree in 1960. Although he was sure he wanted to be a scientist, zur Hausen decided to also pursue a license to practice medicine, and completed internships in gynecology and obstetrics. The latter, he recalled in the autobiography he wrote on receiving the Nobel Prize,

"fascinated me tremendously, although it turned out to be physically highly demanding."

Working as a researcher at the University of Düsseldorf, zur Hausen still vacillated between a career in medical research and one as a doctor. But his first exposure to the nascent science of virology, or the study of viruses and their interaction with their host organisms, both fired his imagination and made him realize the extent of the gaps in his knowledge of the field. After marrying and welcoming a son to his family, he moved to the Children's Hospital of Philadelphia, where the German-born husband-and-wife team of Werner and Gertrude Henle, who had fled the Third Reich for the United States, had established a pioneering virology program.

Did Early Research on Viral Cancer Role

In Philadelphia zur Hausen was surrounded by some of the earliest research demonstrating a viral role in a human cancer (the first such link had been demonstrated only in 1964): the Henle lab worked to find a link between the Epstein-Barr virus (EBV) and a cancer called Burkitt's lymphoma. Feeling that he was not yet ready for such research, zur Hausen prevailed upon Henle to let him work on a different virus, adenovirus type 12, and to become familiar with electron microscopy and the latest techniques of molecular-level study. After laying a strong foundation for his own work, he contributed to the Henles' research in its later stages.

Invited to lead his own research group at the University of Würzburg, zur Hausen returned to Germany in 1969. He continued to work on EBV-related topics, and by the end of the year he had demonstrated the presence of EBV genetic material in Burkitt's lymphoma tumors. In further experiments, he found EBV DNA in epthelial (surface) cells in cancers of the nose and throat system. These breakthroughs earned zur Hausen the chairmanship of the new Institute of Clinical Virology in Erlangen-Nürnberg, Germany, in 1972.

At the time, the idea that viruses could cause cancer was generally restricted to a small group of the field's most progressive researchers. Among this group, cervical cancer was a prime suspect for a viral role, but most researchers, based on epidemiological data, believed that a herpes virus, HSV-2, was the culprit. Deciding to devote full time in his research efforts to the question of viruses and cancer, zur Hausen first directed his research staff, using the DNA techniques he had learned, to try to confirm the HSV-2 hypothesis. They found no HSV-2 DNA in a large sample of cervical cancer biopsies.

Meanwhile, zur Hausen had heard anecdotal evidence that the genital warts caused by the human papilloma virus had become cancerous in some cases. Despite the skepticism of most researchers in the field, zur Hausen set out to test the possibility of a link between HPV and cervical cancer. Using a large supply of tumor tissue samples provided by a local dermatology hospital, zur Hausen and his staff set to work looking for HPV DNA or traces of viral particles from genital warts in tissues from cervical tumors. Their initial results were negative, but zur Hausen's work was considered promising enough that he was appointed chairman of the Institute of Virology at the major University of Freiburg. His staff followed him to his new job, and the group continued their work, hypothesizing that their negative results were due to the fact that the papilloma virus existed in a number of different types.

Discovered New HPV Types

In 1979 the group succeeded in cloning DNA from genital warts, but they once again failed to find the virus in cervical cancer tissue. However, they persisted once again, using the insights they gained from their genetic experiments to isolate a new papilloma virus type, HPV-11. Examining a set of 24 cervical cancer biopsies, they found HPV in one of them and became convinced that they were on the right track. Finally, in 1983 and 1984, they isolated two more HPV types, HPV-16 and HPV-18, which were found in 50 percent and 20 percent of cervical cancer biopsies, respectively. In 1983 zur Hausen assumed the chairmanship of the German Cancer Research Center in Heidelberg, making him the leader of Germany's national cancer research effort.

Zur Hausen continued to refine his work in the 1980s, discovering, among other things, why the virus did not always show up in cancer cells (it tended to be genetically deleted as the tumor grew). The group made overtures to pharmaceutical companies, which at first declined to pursue work on an HPV vaccine. Given the sexual transmission of HPV, religious objections have also played a role in limiting the vaccine's implementation. The vaccine was finally released in 2006, and two years later zur Hausen shared the Nobel Prize in Physiology or Medicine with a pair of French AIDS researchers. Allegations that the prize was tainted by the presence of a pharmaceutical company board member on the Nobel Prize committee were denied by the AstraZeneca, the multinational firm involved.

In 2003, zur Hausen retired as director of the German Cancer Research Center. He has remained active as a public face of cancer research, arguing that the price of the HPV vaccine should be reduced so that it can be more readily available to women in poor countries, and warning of a connection between red meat consumption and colon cancer. Given estimates that about 16 percent of cancers may be caused by infection, the field of research zur Hausen helped to develop remains among the hottest in the world of medical research.

Periodicals

New York Times, October 7, 2008.
Sunday Tribune (South Africa), July 20, 2014.
Times (London, England), December 19, 2008.
Times of India, December 3, 2009,

Online

"Harald zur Hausen—Biographical," *Nobel Prize,* http://www.nobelprize.org/nobel_prizes/medicine/laureates/2008/hausen-bio.html (January 15, 2015).
"Nobel Laureate Harald zur Hausen—A Portrait," Federal Ministry of Education and Research (Germany), http://www.bmbf.de/en/18785.php
"Prof. Harald zur Hausen Awarded Nobel Prize for Medicine," University of Heidelberg, http://www.uni-heidelberg.de/presse/news08/press601e.htm (January 15, 2015). □

Elizabeth Hawes

Fashion designer Elizabeth Hawes (1903–1971) made a woefully brief impact on American fashion, but her cannily prescient writings from the 1920s through the '50s reverberate with cultural critics decades later. Hawes, wrote Alice Gregory in the *New York Times Magazine,* "took fashion as a serious and sociologically significant subject when most other people did not. She wrote about its economics, culture and ethics; she maintained, with barely a wink, that being perfectly dressed 'contributes directly to that personal peace which religion is ultimately supposed to bestow.'"

Elizabeth Hawes was born in Ridgewood, New Jersey, on December 16, 1903, exactly one day before brothers Wilbur and Orville Wright made their historic flight a few states down the Eastern seaboard. She had an older sister, Charlotte, and her mother Henrietta Houston Hawes would add another daughter and son to the family. Their father John Hawes was an executive with the Southern Pacific Company steamship company. Hawes's mother was active in her community and had graduated from Vassar College, one of the elite single-sex schools established in New England at a time when the Ivy League schools did not admit women into undergraduate classes. Henrietta Hawes sought to improve public education opportunities in Ridgewood, stood firm on civil rights and integration matters, and in the 1930s would serve as local administrator of a federal social service agency.

Earned Economics Degree

Hawes's mother also taught her daughters the practical household arts. Hawes learned how to sew doll clothes as a young girl and by her teens had progressed to making her own ensembles. After graduating from Ridgewood High School she entered Vassar, in Poughkeepsie, New York, and eventually chose economics as her major. She remained intensely interested in dressmaking, however, and one summer took a short course at the Parsons School of Fine and Applied Arts in New York City. Sensing there was a deep well of potentially lucrative clients in the field who were not serviced by traditional off-the-rack wares, she worked another summer as an unpaid intern at Bergdorf Goodman, the elite Manhattan clothier and luxury-goods seller.

At Vassar, Hawes completed her degree requirements ahead of her graduation date. Her senior thesis examined the role of British politician Ramsay MacDonald, the first Labour Party chief to serve as prime minister. In July of 1925, she and a friend sailed for France, with Hawes having already secured two freelance writing jobs to report back on Paris fashion trends. Through a family connection she also found work at a dressmaker's on the Rue du Faubourg St. Honoré as a copyist. This involved attending invitation-only runway presentations by top Paris fashion houses such as Chanel and Vionnet and committing the new styles to memory; back at the studio she would sketch out the looks and work with dressmaking colleagues to create near identical versions in less costly fabrics. Hawes harbored design ambitions of her own and eventually the stress and guilt prompted her to quit the knock-off atelier job.

Wrote for the *New Yorker*

Hawes was able to remain in Paris for a few more years as a department store buyer, stylist, and fashion writer. She sent dispatches that were published in U.S. newspapers and moved on to a plum post as a contributor to the *New Yorker* magazine using the nom de plume "Parisite." There was a snap and vigor to her prose, typified by one column in January of 1928 in which she recounted a visit to a popular Parisian *boîte,* the Florida. Her fellow revelers, she reported, were "the bigger and better of the élite and refined (and mostly British) Parisians. On the last occasion I went there, a couple of light purple—not lavender—dresses were a good color note." Continuing on, she informed readers of the *New Yorker* that "it seems obvious that some purple coloring is coming in. It hasn't been used to any extent in ages and this business of black and white must come to an end some day, although it is the most becoming and the smartest mode that has ever been successful."

Returning to New York City later in 1928, Hawes went into business with her friend Rosemary Harden and rented a fourth-floor atelier space on West 56th Street. Hawes-Harden carried Hawes's original designs and garnered a fashion-forward clientele, including Broadway stars Lynn Fontanne and Katharine Hepburn. Following the Wall Street crash of 1929 and the subsequent financial duress, Hawes and Harden parted ways and Hawes kept the business under her own name as Hawes, Inc. In July of 1931 she made her runway-collection debut in Paris under her own name with a line of women's dresses and daywear, but as Hawes told an American reporter a few weeks later her work was greeted coolly by the French attendees, a few of whom even hissed. "There was no escaping the realization that my fashions were not wanted in Paris," she resignedly told the *New York Times* reporter.

In 1933 Hawes relocated her showroom to space on East 67th Street, and had some success with an elegant buttoned long suede glove she called the Guardsman that was featured in print advertisements for Lucky Strike cigarettes. She also designed theater costumes on commission and visited the Soviet Union in 1935 as part of a cultural-exchange junket. "They are big women, strongly built, and they should have their own styles," she told a *New York Times* reporter about the Russians she met. "They are beginning to develop their own mode of dress best suited to themselves."

Wrote Bestselling Critique/Memoir

Hawes was convinced that American women should dress to suit their personality, their active lifestyle, and not look to the latest styles from Paris to guide them. She also loathed much of what department stores and garment manufacturers on Seventh Avenue sold to the mass-market shopper. When she became pregnant during her second marriage—to theater director Joseph Losey—she rejected the tentlike maternity dresses available and instead wore loose-fitting silk robes of Chinese import before the birth of son Gavrik in 1938.

The year was a milestone one for Hawes. Her first book, *Fashion Is Spinach,* was published to favorable notice and even became a minor bestseller for its incisive appraisal of the business of fashion. The book's curious title came from a recent *New Yorker* cartoon that showed a child at mealtime arguing with his mother over the vegetable on his plate. Inside the book Hawes recounted her years in Paris and her struggles to work with Seventh Avenue manufacturers, whose factory managers altered her designs. Her chapters also delineated the difference between fashion and style—the former could be bought, while the latter was harder to acquire, she explained. "Now we have the advertising agency and the manufacturer, the department store and the fashion writer all here to tell us that the past, present, and future of clothing depends on fashion, ceaselessly changing," she argued. A reviewer for the *New York Times* pronounced *Fashion Is Spinach* a worthy read. "Her book delights as it debunks," the anonymous critic asserted. "Its frankness is sparkling even in cynicism."

Hawes's decisive pronouncements did little to improve sales at her company, and she shut down Hawes, Inc. in 1940. In the early 1940s she wrote for *PM,* a newspaper that drew a devoted following for its insider-y prose that proved a tastemaking forerunner to the *New York Observer.* Her columns advocated for dress reform for both men and women, especially when the United States entered World War II. Recalling her mother's contributions to the community as a wife and mother, Hawes also argued that more effort should be made to expand reliable child-care services for families of all income levels—an idea espoused by Russian revolutionaries and even some of the more progressive nations of Western Europe.

Worked for U.A.W.

Hawes was enervated by the social changes visited upon the U.S. civilian population during the World War II. With available manpower mobilized for combat and military support positions, federal agencies urged women to contribute to the fight against fascism by filling much-needed labor shortages in factories. This shift, she realized, might result in genuine reform for American women. Hawes even took a factory job herself at the Wright Aeronautical plant in Paterson, New Jersey, not far from her hometown of Ridgewood. She expounded on her ideas in the 1943 book *Why Women Cry, or Wenches with Wrenches.* For a time she even moved to Detroit, Michigan, a city whose automobile manufacturing plants had been converted over to wartime production, and worked as a field educator for the powerful United Auto Workers labor union.

In 1948 Hawes attempted to relaunch her design business in New York City, but her leftist political activism had brought unwelcome attention from domestic-surveillance agents, who maintained a file on her and Losey. The couple had divorced in 1944 and Losey's career was so hampered that he was forced to move to England. Likewise Hawes settled in the U.S. Virgin Islands and continued to write. In 1948 she produced *Anything But Love: A Complete Digest of the Rules for Feminine Behavior from Birth to Death; Given out in Print, on Film, and Over the Air; Seen, Listened to Monthly by Some 340,000,000 American Women,* an exhaustive satire of women's magazines of the day.

Remained Quip-Ready Provocateur

In the mid-1950s Hawes moved to California and published two more books, including *It's Still Spinach,* an update to her groundbreaking 1938 book. Sweeping social changes finally arrived in the 1960s, and Hawes's dictums about practicality and originality had not been forgotten by style-setters who recalled her original designs of the 1930s—items so timeless and well-constructed that her devoted clients wore them for decades. The Fashion Institute of Technology honored Hawes with a 1967 retrospective and she used the occasion to revive the idea of men in skirts, arguing "there's nothing new about the idea," she told *New York Times* fashion reporter Bernadine Morris. "The Moroccans, the Arabs and the Greeks have been at it for years, not to mention the Scots. The only time men blanch is when you call it a skirt. If you say kilt, it's all right."

Hawes moved to the Chelsea Hotel in Manhattan and lived out her final years there. She became one of the long list of famous and semi-famous denizens who called the bohemian address their permanent home. She died on September 6, 1971, at age 67, from cirrhosis of the liver. Decades later her revolutionary ideas about apparel design were still a source of marvel to curators at the Costume Institute of the Metropolitan Museum of New York, which regularly featured them in retrospective exhibits about the history of American fashion in the 20th century. "Her exasperated appraisal of the behind-the-scenes issues of the industry was remarkably provident," remarked Gregory, the author of the 2014 essay on Hawes that ran in the *New York Times Magazine*'s *T Style* supplement. "She castigated unskilled imitation, the tyranny of trends, the extent to which the bottom line determined what was produced when and for whom. Ever self-aware, Hawes asserted that, 'the butt of fashion's dirtiest jokes is the public.'"

Books

Berch, Bettina, *Radical by Design: The Life and Style of Elizabeth Hawes,* Dutton, 1988.

Hawes, Elizabeth, *Fashion Is Spinach,* Random House, 1938.

Periodicals

New York Times, July 25, 1931; July 17, 1935; March 27, 1938; April 6, 1967; September 7, 1971.

New York Times Magazine (*T Style* supplement), June 15, 2014.

New Yorker, January 7, 1928.

Vogue, March 2014. □

Sessue Hayakawa

Coming to fame in the silent film era in Hollywood, Japanese actor Sessue Hayakawa (1889–1973) was the only Asian to become a leading male actor in such films and the first Asian film star. Fighting against stereotypes for Asian performers, Hayakawa successfully founded his own production company to make quality films. Best known for roles in such films as *The Cheat* (1915) and *The Bridge on the River Kwai* (1957), Hayakawa became the first Asian male to be nominated for an Academy Award for his work in the latter film.

Born Kintaro Hayakawa on June 10, 1889, in Minami-boso, Chiba province, Japan, he was the second son of Yoichiro and Kane Hayakawa. His family was distinguished. His father had an aristocratic lineage, served in the Japanese navy, and was the provisional governor of Chiba, while his mother's ancestors including samurai warriors. Hayakawa and his brothers were raised with the ideals of the samurai, including training in the martial arts. Though the family was wealthy, Hayakawa had menial chores to ensure he would not see himself as overprivledged.

Attempted Suicide After Injury

Destined to follow his father's steps in the navy, Hayakawa was educated at the Navy Preparatory School. After graduating in 1908, he entered the Naval Academy, located in Etajim, but he was injured while swimming and ruptured his eardrum. Because of the injury, Hayakawa was dismissed from the academy and not allowed to join the navy. His father was mortified by his son's failure, and their relationship was damaged. Hayakawa even attempted a ritual suicide, the hara-kiri, because of the shame. Hayakawa stabbed himself 30 times, but survived.

In critical condition for weeks, Hayakawa recovered in seclusion in a Zen Buddhist monastery. There he learned the principles of the faith and incorporated its practices into his life. In May 1909, he ended his seclusion when he rescued some Americans whose ship crashed in Tokyo Bay. Hayakawa decided to travel to the United States to further his education as a result of the encounter.

Though his father initially opposed the move, Hayakawa soon traveled to the United States to enter the University of Chicago. There, he majored in political science. He also played American football, and was the university's quarterback. His stint on the team came to an end, however, when he used judo moves to best members of the other teams and he was removed.

Launched Acting Career

Completing his degree in 1913, Hayakawa traveled to Los Angeles with the intention of returning home via freighter and becoming the banker his father wanted. While staying in the city, he learned about the Japanese Playhouse, a

Popperfoto/Getty Images

theater that put on Japanese-language plays. Hayakawa was inspired by the performance he saw, and believed he could be an even better actor. It was at this time that he changed his first name to Sessue.

In addition to acting, Hayakawa took on some technical duties for the Japanese Playhouse. The first play he appeared in was *The Typhoon*, which opened in early 1914.

Hayakawa's work in *The Typhoon* caught the attention of an early film producer, Thomas Ince. The producer wanted Hayakawa to appear in the film version of *The Typhoon*, reprising his leading role. Because Hayakawa was considering furthering his education, he made what he considered an outrageous demand, $500 per week.

Defying Hayakawa's expectations, Ince agreed. The actor starred in the silent film, also titled *The Typhoon* and released in 1914. The film was a hit and Hayakawa was on his way to film stardom. He then appeared in two more films produced by Ince.

Signed with Famous Players Lasky

In 1915, Hayakawa signed a contract with a leading film company of the era, Famous Players Lasky (later known as Paramount). His first two films were released in 1915 and were directed by Cecil B. DeMille, who would become recognized as one of the greatest directors of the silent era. The films were *The Secret Sin* and *The Cheat*.

The Cheat was an especially important film. In it, Hayakawa played Tori, a Burmese ivory trader and art dealer, who helps a white American woman, played by Fannie Ward, who needs to save herself after stealing from a charity. In one memorable scene, Hayakawa's character brands the woman with the iron he used on his other possessions to show his control of her. His character eventually is lynched by a mob. Because of the success of the film, Hayakawa became a well-known film star, highly regarded for his acting skills and good looks. Unlike many silent film stars, Hayakawa's acting style was more subtle and calm without exaggerated emotion or melodramatic touches.

Over the next few years, Hayakawa appeared in a number of films, often playing villains and forbidden lovers in films like *The Secret Game* (1917) and *Each to His Kind* (1917). Prejudice and cultural norms of the times limited what roles he could take. As Donald Richie wrote in *The Japan Times*, "In all of them he was the dashing if sometimes villainous lover, yet all these roles were invariably portrayals of Japanese as seen through Western eyes." Despite these limitations, his stardom was so great—especially among female filmgoers—that he was offered the leading role in *The Sheik* (1921). Hayakawa turned it down to start a new venture, and the role eventually went to Rudolph Valentino, who became a star for his work as a result.

Formed Production Company

Feeling restricted by the roles available to him, Hayakawa formed his own production company in 1918. With a million dollar loan from the parents of a college friend, Haworth Pictures Corporation allowed him to become his own producer. Hayakawa carefully picked roles that showed a wider range of Asian characters, beyond stereotypes and including romantic leads.

Between 1918 and 1922, Haworth Pictures made about $2,000,000 dollars annually—he repaid the loan within two years—and Hayakawa made about $5,000 to $7,500 per week. He appeared in about 40 films, often with his wife Tsuru Aoki, whom he had married in 1914. Another Asian-American actress, Anna May Wong, also made regular appearances in Haworth films.

Among the most creative films produced by Hayakawa and Haworth was *The Dragon Painter* (1919). In the film, directed by William Worthington, Hayakawa played an artist in Japan who was deeply in love with the spirit of a dragon princess. The fairy-tale like *The Dragon Painter* became noteworthy for Hayakawa's lively, naturalistic acting.

Throughout the silent era, critics from around the world acclaimed Hayakawa's formidable acting skills. Yet there was a distinct Hayakawa persona throughout his silent film years. As Matthew Mizenko wrote in *Pacific Affairs*, "the cultured, genteel, disciplined and honourable (bushido and all that) Japanese gentleman who, while able to demonstrate a certain degree of Americanization (thus speaking to the obsession about the assimilation of immigrants), can never quite shake his essential Japaneseness, which contains a certain amount of primitive violence that can erupt at any moment."

Left Hollywood

Hayakawa's success as a film star allowed him to live extravagantly, including owning a 32-room Scottish-style castle in Hollywood known as the Argyle Castle, where he held legendary parties. He was among the first acting stars in Hollywood to live in a mansion. He also owned a gold-plated Pierce-Arrow limousine, and gambled away millions of dollars. His fame was so wide that he was invited to the White House in 1921 to meet the president, Warren G. Harding. This lifestyle came to an end in 1922 when he disbanded Haworth due to an increase in anti-Japanese attitudes in the United States, an attempt on his life, and problems with his partners in the film company.

In the early and mid-1920s, Hayakawa traveled in the United States and Europe, including France and Britain. He performed in plays and on vaudeville, and continued to be a high-roller gambler. He also appeared in some films. Among them was the French film *J'ai tue!* (I Have Killed!). Hayakawa played Hideo, a Tokyo antiques dealer who is mistakenly tried for a murder he did not commit. In this period, Hayakawa also wrote a novel *The Bandit Prince*, published in 1926.

In 1929, Hayakawa went to New York and had a starring role on Broadway in *The Love City*. He eventually went back to Japan. There, Hayakawa made more films—though he was unable to match his success in Hollywood, in part because many of the roles in played in the United States were not always flattering to Japanese—and also appeared in stage productions for several years. In all, he appeared in about 120 silent films.

Made Sound Film Debut

Hayakawa appeared in his first sound film, with Wong, entitled *Daughter of the Dragon*, in 1931. Though the picture was of high quality, Hayakawa had a strong Japanese accent that was deemed unsuitable for non-silent films of the time. He also saw that actors of Japanese descent were being openly discriminated against. After its release, Hayakawa returned to stage acting in Paris and the Far East.

Because Hayakawa's sympathies lay with the West, he was unable to stay in Japan, where nationalism became increasingly strong after the mid-1930s. In 1937, Hayakawa returned to France. His timing was unfortunate, as the country soon became occupied by Nazi Germany and Hayakawa was unable to escape. Supporting himself and his family by painting watercolors on silk, he also took action as part of the French Resistance.

After the war ended Hayakawa's film acting career was revived in 1949 through the support of well-known American actor Humphrey Bogart. The *Casablanca* star convinced Hayakawa to take a role in *Tokyo Joe* (1949). Hayakawa's work in the role led to another stage in his acting career.

Also in 1949, Hayakawa returned to Japan, where he was the producer of a play, *The Life of the Buddha*. Because of this play and his dedication to Zen Buddhism, he was chosen for the Zen Buddhist priesthood. He passed the required test and was formally ordained.

Nominated for Academy Award

Continuing to act in the 1950s, Hayakawa again became a star through his performance as Colonel Sito, the Japanese commander of a prisoner of war camp, in the World War II drama *The Bridge on the River Kwai* (1957). Hayakawa demonstrated his formidable acting skills in a battle of wills with Nicholson, the English colonel played by well-known British actor Alec Guinness. For his work in the David Lean-directed film, Hayakawa became the first male Asian actor to be nominated for an Academy Award for best supporting actor.

Hayakawa continued to work in film, and, to some degree, television, for a few more years. By the end of the 1950s, he returned to Japan where he taught acting and focused on Zen Buddhism. He also wrote an autobiography, *Zen Showed Me the Way* (1960). It focused on his faith and his acting career.

Hayakawa died of cerebral thrombosis on November 23, 1973, in Tokyo, Japan. He was 83 years old. Explaining Hayakawa's unique success in the silent era, Stephen Gong, the executive director of the Center for Asian-American Media, told Anthony Venutolo of *NJ.com*, "He really is sort of extraordinary. Yet, in some ways his rise is very understandable.... The machine was finally in place to create stars, and Hayakawa was seen as very exotic."

Books

Asian and Pacific Islander Americans: Great Lives From History, edited by Gary Y. Okihiro, Salem Press, 2013.
Dictionary of American Biography, Charles Scribner's Sons, 1994.

Periodicals

Architectural Digest, November 2008.
Daily Yomiuri (Tokyo, Japan), June 23, 2007.
The Japan Times, August 12, 2007.
New York Times, September 7, 2007.
Pacific Affairs, Fall 2007.

Online

"Cinema Can't Keep Up with Hayakawa's Strides," *NJ.com*, http://www.nj.com/entertainment/tv/index.ssf/2008/03/cinema_cant_keep_up_with_hayak.html (December 27, 2014). □

Stanley William Hayter

Widely considered the most influential and pioneering printmaker of his era, British-born artist Stanley William Hayter (1901–1988) founded Atelier 17, an experimental workshop for the graphic arts. Launched in Paris in 1927, the workshop later moved to New York before reconvening in Paris. Atelier 17 led to a 20th-century revival in printmaking as an expressive art. Well-known artists from around the globe were drawn to study with Hayter at Atelier

17, including Pablo Picasso, Jackson Pollock, Wassily Kandinsky, Willem de Kooning, and Mark Rothko.

Stanley William Hayter was born December 27, 1901, in London. He came from a long line of painters. Hayter's great-great uncle—George Hayter—served as Queen Victoria's official portrait painter. His great-great grandfather, John Hayter, enjoyed his first exhibition at the Royal Academy at age 15. Hayter's father, William Hayter, was also a well-known British painter. Hayter, naturally, took up painting as a child.

Started Career in Natural Sciences

As a young adult, Hayter departed from the artistic world of his family to pursue science. He took a job as a research chemist at the Mond Nickel Company and enrolled at King's College in London. After earning his chemistry/geology degree in 1921, Hayter landed a job in Abadan, Iran, working for an oil company. He worked in Iran from 1922 to 1925. While there, he completed a series of paintings inspired by his surroundings. These consisted of seascapes, boats, landscapes and the oil refinery plant. He also made pencil portraits of his co-workers. In 1925, he suffered a bout of malaria and returned to London to recuperate. His employers staged a show of his work at their London office and the exhibition proved highly popular, with most of the pieces selling.

Afterward, Hayter did not return to the Persian Gulf. Instead, he went to Paris in 1926 to study at the Académie Julian. Hayter soon met Polish printmaker Józef Hecht, who had set up a studio in Paris. Hecht took Hayter under his wing and taught him the basics of engraving, such as how to use a burin (a specialized chisel) to etch a design into a copper plate. Hayter began experimenting with engraving. He cut designs in copper plates and inked them, then wiped off the excess ink, leaving the toner behind in only the engraved areas. Next, he ran the plates through a printing press to "print" the engraved lines onto paper.

At this point, engraving had fallen out of favor as a preferred art form. Mostly, printmaking was used to render art reproductions. Hayter, however, saw possibility in the black and white medium and began explorations in printmaking. Initially, his engravings featured figures. In 1926, he exhibited his prints and paintings at Salon d'Automne, an annual art exhibition held in Paris. He followed with a show at the Sacre du Printemps Gallery in 1927. The gallery exhibition caught the attention of U.S. sculptor Alice Carr de Creeft, who was studying in Paris. De Creeft stopped by Hayter's studio with a friend to purchase some prints. They returned several days later to ask Hayter if he would teach them printmaking. Hayter suggested that if they could find a few more students, he would be willing to do so.

Launched Workshop in Paris

In October 1927, Hayter set up a workshop to explore the art of printmaking. Tuition from the students helped pay for the press, ink and burins. From the start, he did not envision his establishment as just another art school. From his

perspective, the artist thought teaching was futile because people learned by doing. He preferred to offer a small amount of instruction on basic technique, then let his students explore. In fact, he did not call the artists who studied with him "students." Instead, he called them "associates" because he believed they were all working together. Hayter thought his role as "teacher" was to ask questions to incite and provoke the artists to explore new realms.

Writing in *New Ways of Gravure*, Hayter described his philosophy on "teaching": "I prefer to regard my activities over all these years as unteaching, diseducation, disintoxication. . . . There is no way in which the experience of a teacher can be transferred to a pupil, and the warning given to all beginners in our workshop not to believe a word they are told is necessary in view of the verbal deformations of our current civilization. Only the action of the newcomer can give rise to knowledge, this understood as the extension of his own experience."

Hayter's new "school" revived the workshop conception of the artist. While many artists worked alone, Hayter believed artists did better toiling together in a community where they could pool their collective discoveries and work off of one another's breakthroughs. In 1929, he staged a one-man exhibition at London's Claridge Gallery. He also began showing his work at the Salon des Indépendants, an annual independent art exhibition held in Paris. He also began exhibiting his work with the surrealists and soon came to the attention of Spanish painter Joan Miró,

German-French sculptor Hans Arp, and French surrealist painter Yves Tanguy. They all joined Hayter's workshop.

Found Inspiration from Surrealists

At the workshop, Hayter explored and created alongside the other artists. By the early 1930s, his style had begun to change. Gone were the concrete figures that populated his early work, as he began examining more abstract realms. He drew new inspiration from surrealism, which emerged from the Paris arts movement of the 1920s. Surrealists sought to capture visual images from the subconscious mind through a new mode of expression called "automatism," or automatic drawing. With automatic drawing, artists allowed their hands to move freely across the paper with no preconceived subject or composition in mind.

Hayter began employing this technique with printmaking. Most engravers kept the copper plate fixed in one position, varying the lines by moving the burin around. Hayter began twisting the copper plate from side to side, allowing fluid, freely moving lines and shapes to form. His work was strikingly different from that of others. Previous well known engravers had concentrated on rendering detailed pictures of nature, scenes from the Bible and portraits that resembled drawings. Hayter's pieces were more expressionistic and abstract, with twirling lines and swirly geometric designs.

In 1932, six of Hayter's engravings were printed in a book titled *L'apocalypse*. The book featured text written by French artist George Hugnet, who was so inspired by Hayter's "L'apocalypse" series he felt compelled to add words as commentary. In 1933, the workshop moved to 17 rue Campagne-Première and soon became known as Atelier 17. Atelier is French for workshop. Even when the workshop moved across the ocean, Hayter retained the name Atelier 17. In 1934, the members of Atelier 17 held exhibitions in Paris and London, drawing further interest in the workshop.

In 1934, Hayter produced an engraving called "Oedipus," which revealed another innovation. In "Oedipus," Hayter painted a waxy resist coating onto the plate, then pressed his palm into it to leave a background texture on the plate. The technique involved using an acid-resistant coating made of such things as asphaltum, rosin, beeswax and tallow. The plate was then exposed to acid and the waxy resist prevented the acid from "biting" into the plate in the places where it had been applied. Hayter's background in chemistry allowed him to develop this "soft-ground" etching process, and soon the members of Atelier 17 began pressing crushed paper and silk gauze into their etching plates to create tonal passages.

Around 1934, Hayter and Picasso became friends. The two exchanged prints and Hayter offered technical assistance to Picasso by making some engraving tools for him. Around this time, Hayter completed a series of paintings and prints in response to the ongoing Spanish Civil War. Hayter's most famed print from this collection was "Combat" (1936), a surrealist take on the explosive tension of war. A year later, Picasso unveiled his black, white, and gray painting "Guernica," which he created in response to an aerial attack carried out in Guernica, Spain. Hayter's "Combat" and Picasso's "Guernica" were often mentioned together and raised awareness of the ongoing civil

war in Spain. On a larger note, the art pieces came to symbolize the tragedies of war. In September 1939, after Germany invaded Poland and war erupted in Europe, Hayter and his associates abandoned Atelier 17. Hayter returned to London and worked with the British reserves to organize a camouflage research unit.

Fled to United States

In 1940, Hayter abandoned Europe for New York and soon found a job teaching printmaking at the New School for Social Research, where he set up a new Atelier 17. In 1944, the members of Atelier 17 landed an exhibit at the Museum of Modern Art in New York and the free-flowing, experimental pieces captured widespread interest. Afterward, Hayter was booked for lectures and workshops across the United States. Around this time, Hayter broke with the New School and launched Atelier 17 in Greenwich Village. The workshop became a meeting place for American artists and European exiles and greatly influenced the direction of contemporary art in the United States. American artists William Baziotes, Robert Motherwell, Jackson Pollock and David Smith all studied at the workshop, as did Russian émigré Mark Rothko and Dutch-American artist Willem de Kooning.

During the 1940s, Hayter worked to introduce color into printmaking. Hayter first successfully employed color in the abstract piece "Cinq Personnages" (1946), which included three colors and black. Unlike the traditional printmaking process for books, which used a separate plate for each color, Hayter developed a method for printing several colors from one engraved and etched plate. He called it "simultaneous" printing. With this technique, he used linseed oil to thin the ink to different viscosities. When he applied the inks to the plate, the thinner ink repelled the thicker ink, thus allowing the inks to disperse into the numerous grooves in the plate, with each color coating a different "level" of groove.

Returned to Paris

In 1950, Hayter returned to Paris and reopened Atelier 17. The workshop in New York continued for another five years under various directors. Ultimately, Hayter closed it in 1955 because it had lost sight of its original mission. "The people working in the Atelier began restricting themselves to producing saleable objects," Hayter told Carolyn Paul of *ARTNews*. "Local commercial success is adverse to any serious research."

The workshop in Paris, however, continued. During the 1950s, Indian artists Kaiko Moti and Krishna Reddy studied at the workshop and refined Hayter's color technique, developing a method whereby 50 colors could be printed from a single plate. Other workshop innovations included adding sculptural qualities to prints by pouring plaster onto the plates and etching in it before applying ink. Hayter continued at the atelier for the next three decades, bringing new "students" in and allowing them to stay as long as they kept producing something he had never seen before. He admitted beginners just as often as seasoned artists. In fact, he found the novices to be more innovative, he told Paul. "Most of the big names, like de Kooning, Motherwell, Rothko, Pollock, for instance, didn't do anything outstanding when working with us. And their work doesn't represent the Atelier's best efforts.''

Over the course of his lifetime, Hayter made more than 450 etchings. While he was best known for his prints, he was also an accomplished painter who liked to explore water and its ripples and reflections on canvas. During his lifetime, Hayter's work was featured at galleries and exhibitions around the world. In 1958, Hayter was chosen to represent England at the Venice Biennale. Hayter retrospectives have appeared at the Victoria and Albert Museum in London (1967), the Musée des Arts Décoratifs in Paris (1970), and at the National Gallery of Art in Washington, D.C. (2009). Hayter also wrote two books on printmaking in which he espoused his technical wizardry. The books, *New Ways of Gravure* (1949) and *About Prints* (1962), are considered must-reads for any printmaker.

Hayter died of a heart attack at his Paris home on May 4, 1988. He was 86. Hayter had two children from a marriage to American sculptor Helen Phillips. The two met in Paris when Phillips studied at his workshop. They married in 1940 and divorced in 1970 after having two children, Augy and Julian. At the time of his death, Hayter was married to Irish poet and writer Desiree Moorhead. A first marriage to Edith Fletcher ended in 1929. After Hayter's death, the Paris workshop was renamed Atelier Contrepoint and continued operations in the 21st century.

Books

Hayter, Stanley William, *New Ways of Gravure* (rev. ed.), Watson-Guptill Publications, 1981.
Matisse, Picasso, and Modern Art in Paris, Virginia Museum of Fine Arts, 2009.

Periodicals

ARTnews, September 1978.
Newsweek, July 10, 1944; June 19, 1961.
Smithsonian, September 1978.
Times (London, England), May 7, 1988.
Washington Times (Washington, D.C.), June 7, 2009.

Online

"Stanley William Hayter, 86, Dies; Painter Taught Miro and Pollock," *New York Times,* http://www.nytimes.com/1988/05/06/obituaries (16 January 2015).☐

Perry Henzell

Known as the "father of Jamaican cinema," Jamaican filmmaker and author Perry Henzell (1936–2006) released his first and best known film *The Harder They Come* in 1972. A cult hit that brought Jamaican culture to international attention, it was the first Jamaican feature film and starred future reggae legend Jimmy Cliff. Henzell also published two novels, including *Power Game* (1982).

J. Vespa/WireImage/Getty Images

Born March 7, 1936, in Port Maria, Jamaica, Henzell was the son of a father from Antiguan and a mother from Trinidad. Both were white, wealthy, and came from families who had long histories in island culture. Earlier generations included white sugar cane plantation owners known as the plantocracy. His paternal grandfather had many Huguenot glassblowers in his ancestry but married into an established Antiguan family.

Had Early Directorial Aspirations

Raised on a sugarcane estate, Caymanas, located about 12 miles outside of Kingston, Henzell spent much of his childhood absorbing black Jamaican street culture. Henzell's family sent him to be educated outside of Jamaica as a teenager. At 14, he began attending the Shrewsbury School in England. The rebellious Henzell eventually left Shrewsbury and hitchhiked throughout Europe for a time. Henzell later attended Montreal's McGill University, but dropped out after a short period as a student.

Moving to London to pursue directing, Henzell went to the BBC drama department hoping to become a director, though he lacked any experience. Instead, he worked as a stagehand and scenery shifter for the television drama department, acquiring valuable knowledge about the creative process. Through this position, Henzell became sure that he wanted to work in the dramatic arts. He also felt drawn to Jamaica, and decided to return home.

There, Henzell formed a production company, Vista Productions, which made commercials. Early spots were shown in movie theaters before screenings. After Jamaica gained independence from Great Britain in 1962, the island had its own television station. Vista Productions made commercials for the station. In all, Henzell made more than 200 commercials, while learning his craft and venturing into the experimental.

Made *The Harder They Come*

In the early 1970s, Henzell decided to shift into making films. With a production cycle that lasted from 1970 to 1972, he created Jamaica's first full-length feature film, *The Harder They Come*. It was the first film shot in Jamaica by a Jamaican director with a Jamaican cast and focusing on real life in Jamaica. Henzell raised the $1.5 million to make the film from local investors, including Jamaican music mogul Chris Blackwell. Henzell co-wrote the film with Trevor Rhone, and served as director and producer.

Henzell based the story of *The Harder They Come* on the life and times of a notorious 1940s Jamaican gangster, Ivanhoe "Rhyghin" Martin. Martin came to West Kingston from Linstead, Jamaica, targeted the wealthy in his criminal activities, and gave some of his plunder to families in need before being killed by police in 1948. In Henzell's film, Ivan O. Martin (played by Jimmy Cliff) moves to Kingston from a rural Jamaican community to become a reggae star but struggles financially. Not only is he betrayed by greedy music producers, he becomes involved with crime, drugs, and guns. He grows more desperate as gets into trouble with the authorities despite having a hit topping the Jamaican charts.

Describing the importance of the film in the London *Guardian*, David Katz stated, "It adapted the story of Ivanhoe Martin . . . to make broader points about the harsh realities facing migrants from the countryside in the island's dehumanising capital, taking in the exploitation of the music industry and the illicit lure of the marijuana trade along the way. Jimmy Cliff's sympathetic portrayal of the lead character . . . showed a determined character whose pride would not allow him to be beaten down, but whose desperation led to an inevitably gory demise. Through it, Henzell illuminated the widespread social injustice commonplace in the developing world."

Brought Jamaican Culture to the World

When *The Harder They Come* was first shown in Jamaica in 1972, there were near riots in Kingston. Early showings attracted so many viewers that fences and cinema doors were broken down, and box office records were smashed. One reason for the film's popularity with Jamaican audiences was its depiction of island dwellers, as well as West Indians, not merely as servants or slaves, but as real people of various social classes and with interesting problems. Henzell moved beyond stereotypes to depict the overall culture of Jamaica as complex and raw.

Henzell spent five years distributing *The Harder They Come* throughout Europe and Africa himself. It became a cult hit in many countries, including the United States.

Though it had a slow start in cities like London and Boston, the film ran for months, if not years at many theaters. *The Harder They Come* also found acclaim, winning the Young Cinema Award at the Venice Film Festival in 1973. The soundtrack to *The Harder They Come* also contributed to its popularity, introducing the reggae genre to audiences outside of Jamaica.

In addition to playing Martin, Cliff composed four songs for the soundtrack to the film, including the title song. Cliff became an international musical star for "The Harder They Come," "Many Rivers to Cross," and "You Can Get It If You Really Want." Other reggae and ska musicians contributed to *The Harder They Come* soundtrack, including Toots and the Maytals, the Melodians ("(By the) Rivers of Babylon"), and Desmond Dekker ("007 (Shantytown)"). The soundtrack to *The Harder They Fall* was a best seller in many countries, and was included on lists of the all-time best film soundtracks over succeeding decades.

Both *The Harder They Come* and its soundtrack spread interest in Jamaica, Rastafarianism, and reggae culture, and influenced fashion trends such as dreadlocks. The influence of Henzell's movie opened up a path for Bob Marley to take his reggae music to a bigger audience. Marley had his first tour outside of Jamaica, to North America, shortly after the film's release; he became an international star by the end of the decade. The film and soundtrack also influenced other musicians and genres, such as the British punk band the Clash, who mentioned Cliff's character in their song "Guns of Brixton." Henzell also influenced filmmakers in the Caribbean and Latin America, who saw the potential to make realistic movies about their cultures.

Tried to Make Second Film

The Harder They Come not only brought attention to a real Jamaica and reggae, but also made Henzell a celebrity, especially in his home country. Though he had offers to work in Hollywood, he wanted to make films his way, in a more personal, realistic style. He spent much of the next eight years raising money for and shooting his next feature, *No Place Like Home* beginning in 1973. The film focused on an affair between a television director from New York City visiting Jamaica and a woman from a rural part of the country. A sequel to *The Harder They Come*, the film included a young Grace Jones, who would later become a famous singer in her own right.

Because of funding issues, Henzell had to start and stop production on *No Place Like Home* several times, but completed a significant amount of the film by the end of the 1970s. By 1986, Henzell had shot most of it and had a half million dollars needed to complete it. However, the New York lab that was processing his film went bankrupt and the negative was misplaced when the lab's assets were transferred to a warehouse in New Jersey. It was found in the early 2000s. At that time, Henzell oversaw production of more scenes and editing. *No Place Like Home* received its debut at the Toronto Film Festival shortly before Henzell's death. The first showing in Jamaica occurred at the Flashpoint Film Festival the day after his death in 2006. Though the film was well received at these festivals, his heirs continued to work on and edit the film for several more years.

Published Novels

By the 1980s, the on-going issues with *No Place Like Home* compelled Henzell to make changes. In addition to becoming more of an activist, focusing on such issues as prison reform, he became more reclusive and spent more time writing. Living primarily at Runaway Bay on Jamaica's north coast, Henzell often stayed at Itopia, an isolated villa owned by his family. In 1982, he published his first novel. A political thriller, *Power Game* was set in the Caribbean and focused on corrupt island politics. Though the novel included elements of romance and adventure, it referred to the failings of the 1970s democratic socialist administration of Michael Manley.

Over succeeding years, Henzell worked on the screenplays of others. He also staged a musical about Jamaican political activist and journalist Marcus Garvey in 1988, and wrote the forward to the book *Yes Rasta* in 2000. Despite being diagnosed with bone cancer in 2000, Henzell continued to work while receiving treatments in Jamaica and New York. In 2002, Henzell published his second novel, *Cane,* which was set in 18th century Jamaica and reflected his own family's heritage and discussed the Jamaican plantocracy.

Involved with Musical Version of *Harder*

Though initially reluctant to turn his film *The Harder They Come* into a stage musical when approached by Jan Ryan of the production company U.K. Arts International in 2003, Henzell became enthusiastic and provided much input over the next few years. The production debuted in London in 2006 at the Theatre Royal and did well. Though he was seriously ill, he was able to see a production in the last months of his life.

The Harder They Come moved to a West End theater in 2007. Two additional productions were later staged in London, and *The Harder They Come* had its North American premiere in Toronto in 2009. Ryan, the project's driving force, told Bruce DeMara of the *Toronto Star,* "I saw the film in the 1970s in Brixton in south London, and I absolutely loved it. It was one of the things that turned me on to Caribbean culture. I always thought how wonderful it would be to do a stage version because the songs were so wonderful and iconic...."

Henzell died of cancer on November 30, 2006, in St. Elizabeth, Jamaica, at the age of 70. In the years after his death, his daughter Justine took over managing his creative legacy, including the stage version of *The Harder They Come* and completing the final edit of *No Place Like Home.* Of Henzell, Justine Henzell told Michael Posner of the *Globe and Mail,* "My father believed that Jamaica was the most incredible place on Earth. He felt he didn't rally have to create anything—just set up the camera and capture the talent oozing out in front of him." She added, "He was a great storyteller, my father, but more than anything, he wanted Jamaicans to take control of their own destiny, and part of that was telling our own stories in our voices, and not being reduced to crude stereotypes."

Periodicals

Associated Press, December 1, 2006.
Daily Variety, December 19, 2006.
Financial Times, June 9, 2012.
Globe and Mail, July 21, 2009.
The Guardian (London, England), December 4, 2006.
The Independent (London, England), December 2, 2006.
Times (London, England), December 5, 2006.
Toronto Star, July 18, 2009.
Variety, May 1-7, 1995.□

Melba Hernández

Considered a heroine of Fidel Castro's communist revolution in the 1950s, Cuban activist, lawyer, politician, and diplomat Melba Hernández (1921–2014) assisted Castro in the rebel cause and was rewarded with various posts in his government. Among them, Hernández served as an ambassador to Vietnam and Cambodia as well as the secretary-general of the Organization for the Solidarity of the Peoples of Asia, Africa, and Latin America.

She was born Melba Hernández Rodríguez del Rey July 28, 1921, in Cruces, Cuba, to middle-class parents. She was not the only revolutionary in her lineage. Members of her family had taken part in the movement to rid Cuba of Spanish colonial rule which resulted in the Cuban War of Independence and the Spanish-American War at the end of the 19th century.

Became Lawyer, Met Castro

Attending the University of Havana, Hernández earned an undergraduate degree in social sciences and then a law degree from the University of Havana School of Law. When she completed her education in 1943, she took a position with the government of Carlos Prío Socarrás working as a customs lawyer. Hernández also used her legal knowledge to help the poor and powerless.

After Fulgencio Batista seized power in 1952 and became the dictator of Cuba, Hernández grew unhappy with the corruption in his administration. She was a member of the Ortodoxo Party, which spoke out against the government of Batista and worked to enact changes in Cuba within the existing structure. In this period, she met a fellow lawyer and member of the Ortodoxo Party who shared her perspective, Fidel Castro.

Describing her initial impressions, Douglas Martin of the *New York Times* quoted Hernández as stating in Tad Szule's book *Fidel: A Critical Portrait,* "I felt secure. I felt I had found the way." She added, "Fidel spoke in a very low voice, he paced back and forth, then came close as if to tell you a secret, and then you suddenly felt you shared the secret."

ALEJANDRO ERNESTO/EPA/Newscom

Helped Organize Attack on Barracks

The discontent felt by Hernández and Castro soon led to an organized, active underground rebellion against Batista and his government. Castro emerged as the group's charismatic organizer, and the spirited, outspoken Hernández was among the first to join his cause. According to Georgie Anne Geyer in her book *Guerrilla Prince: The Untold Story of Fidel Castro,* Hernández said, "When we were barely a small group that didn't even number ten, or barely ten, very small, already Fidel was the leader. And we didn't feel as though were ten, we felt like a movement of tremendous force." Hernández added, "He had been born. We were born with him."

Castro soon made plans for his small group of rebels to attack in an attempt to bring down, or at least damage, the Batista regime by armed insurgence. He chose the target of the Moncada Barracks, an army quarters located in the southeastern city of Santiago de Cuba. Hernández was involved with the preparations. Locating an army sergeant who was sympathetic to Castro's cause, she convinced the sergeant to give her at least 100 uniforms; the army member later joined the movement as well.

Along with the other prominent female member of Castro's group, Haydée Santamaria, Hernández helped prepare these uniforms before the attack in the rebel's hideout near the barracks. The women sewed rank patches on their sleeves to better hide the rebels' true identities. She and Santamaria also ironed the uniforms the night before the attack and made those who would take part a final dinner. Hernández also provided Castro and his rebels with fire arms, smuggling them into their hiding location with the types of flower cartons used by florists.

The attack on the Moncada Barracks took place on July 26, 1953. Approximately 130 rebels took part in the direct assault. Hernández and Santamaria were not among them. Though the women wanted to take part, Castro did not want them to. Instead, Hernández and Santamaria were stationed nearby, ready to provide any needed medical assistance to rebels who would become wounded in the attack.

Arrested After Assault Failed

The Castro-led assault on the barracks was a failure. The rebels could not match the fire power or sheer number of Cuban soldiers in the barracks. Nearly half of the rebels were killed or taken as prisoners on site, while 18 police officers and soldiers died. Though the raid failed, it was regarded as the beginning of the Communist revolution in Cuba and made Castro an acknowledged leader of opposition to the Batista government.

In the wake of the attack, many of the surviving rebels were arrested and imprisoned. Their number included both Hernández and Santamaria, who were sentenced to a seven-month prison term. Castro was detained and jailed as well. Hernández and Santamaria were released in February 1954, before Castro and others involved in the operation. Some of the rebels who escaped arrest or were released from custody went into exile in Mexico.

Before Hernández joined them, she furthered Castro's cause in several ways. Hernández, sometimes working with Santamaria, organized rallies of support for those who were still locked up and detained. Castro had letters smuggled out of prison to Hernández. They were written in lemon juice to ensure they remained secret. When heated, the writing on the letters was revealed. In this correspondence, Castro told Hernández what he wanted done to keep what had been dubbed the July 26 Movement moving forward. He also advised her to be careful about not making any unnecessary enemies.

In addition, Hernández and Santamaria ensured the public would know Castro's words and messages. Hernández put together and edited the notes, essays, and other writings Castro compiled in prison. The pair also ensured his works were printed and distributed, usually in underground fashion to build more sympathy and interest in the revolutionary cause. Among their publications in this period was the text of Castro's defense of himself and his cause during his time in court. This speech was published under the title *History Will Absolve Me,* a title that became a rallying cry for the cause.

Lived in Exile in Mexico

By the time Castro and the other rebels were released from prison by order of Batista on May 15, 1955, Hernández had already joined the exiles in Mexico. She moved there with orders to make contact with the rebels and others who were against the Batista regime. Castro ordered her to convince Cubans there who wanted Batista out not to back another emerging opposition leader, the former president Prío Socarrás, but to support Castro instead.

Castro and other revolutionaries went to Mexico to re-organize their cause by July 1955. They formed a guerilla army and made a new plan to bring down Batista. In this period, Hernández married her husband, a rebel named Jesus Montane. He died in 1999.

In Mexico in 1956, Hernández helped Castro organize for the movement's next action, including organizing an army and preparing a vessel for an invasion. The group bought a rundown yacht, the Granma. On December 2, 1956, this ship took 82 rebels—including Castro but not Hernández—to the eastern Sierra Maestra in Cuba. Once onshore, they began a guerrilla campaign against Batista. Though this first military campaign was a failure—the rebels were ambushed and only 20 of the 82 survived—Castro did not give up, and it was the beginning of the end for Batista.

After Castro's revolutionaries began their campaign in Cuba, Hernández returned and joined their cause in person. She became a key member of the army's so-called Third Front and of its national directorate. In this phase of the rebellion, Hernández actively participated in the fighting and served directly under Comandante Juan Almeida Bosque. Despite a number of early setbacks, the rebels made progress over the next few years. In the face of the growing strength and support for Castro and his guerrillas, Batista abandoned Cuba on January 1, 1959, and Castro took power soon after.

Served in Castro's Government

After he took power, Castro did not forget Hernández's important key role in the revolution. She assisted in the formal establishment of the Communist Party in Cuba. She also served in the Cuban national assembly as a deputy from 1976 to 1986. She was re-elected to the assembly in 1993. In another post, she spent a significant period of time in charge of women's prisons. Though exactly when her tenure occurred is unknown, Castro's prisons were accused of violating human rights by groups such as the Organization of American States.

Hernández held numerous other positions in the Cuban government. Many were related to diplomacy, and a number involved Vietnam and surrounding countries in Asia. Hernández was the Cuban ambassador to Vietnam and Cambodia (when it was called Kampuchea). She was given the post in Vietnam after the end of the Vietnam War in the mid-1970s, after the Communists essentially won the conflict. In addition, Hernández served as the president of the Cuban Committee in Solidarity with South Vietnam, which was renamed the Cuban Committee of Solidarity with Vietnam, Cambodia, and Laos after the end of the Vietnam War. After this post, Hernández was involved with the Committee in Solidarity with Vietnam and Cambodia.

One of Hernández's more prominent posts involved serving as the secretary-general of the Organization for the Solidarity of the Peoples of Asia, Africa, and Latin America. This political organization had been founded in Cuba in 1966 and was dedicated to promoting socialism and supporting quests for independence in developing and third world countries. Another high-profile position for Hernández involved her working with the Presidium of the World Peace Council. Among her last posts was serving as the president of the Parliamentary Group for the Cuba-Vietnam Friendship in 2003. Castro and the Cuban government believed it was important to retain ties between the two countries and relied on Hernández's long-standing relationship and familiarity with Vietnam in this sensitive position.

Honored for Her Work

Over the years, Hernández received several honors for her work. In 1997, Libyan leader Moammar Gadhafi honored her with his Al-Gaddafi International Prize for Human Rights. Libya and Cuba had a close relationship, and Gadhafi gave Castro the prize in 1998, the year after Hernández. Closer to home, Hernández was given an honorary doctorate from the University of Havana in 2007.

By the time Hernández received this honor, she only appeared occasionally in public. Most of her appearances were official government events. She died of complications from diabetes on March 9, 2014, in a Havana, Cuba, hospital at the age of 92. Upon her death, she was cremated and her ashes laid to rest in Santiago de Cuba's Santa Ifigenia where other participants in the Moncada Barracks attack had been buried.

Hernández's funeral was attended by more than 70 diplomats from Cuban allies, including Vietnam, and Latin American and South American countries. According to Andrea Rodriguez of the Associated Press, the Communist Party's Central Committee published a statement in its official organ *Granma* upon Hernández's death that said "She is one of the most glorious and beloved combatants of the revolutionary quest, (and an) imperishable example of the Cuban woman."

Books

Geyer, Georgie Anne. *Guerrilla Prince: The Untold Story of Fidel Castro,* Little, Brown & Company, 1991.

Periodicals

Agence France Presse—English, March 10, 2014.

Associated Press, March 10, 2014.

New York Times, March 16, 2014.

The Times (London, England), April 4, 2014.

Xinhua News Agency, August 6, 2003.

Online

"Diplomatic Corps Pay Homage to Melba Hernandez in Havana," *CubaMinRex,* http://www.cubaminrex.cu/en/diplomatic-corps-pays-homage-melba-hernandez-havana (December 2, 2014).

"Melba Hernandez, 93; Leader of the Cuban Revolution," *People's World,* http://peoplesworld.org/melba-hernandez-93-leader-of-the-cuban-revolution/ (December 2, 2014).□

Abigail Heyman

American photographer Abigail Heyman (1942–2013) often took a feminist perspective when photographing the realities of life and culture, especially for women and girls. She published several books of provocative photographs, including her best known collection *Growing Up Female: A Personal Photo-Journal* (1974). Heyman was also a gifted freelance photographer, employed by leading periodicals and picture agencies.

The daughter of Lazarus S. and Annette Heyman, she was born on August 11, 1942, in Danbury, Connecticut. Lazarus S. Heyman was employed as a real estate developer until he died in 1968. Raised in Danbury with her elder brother Samuel, Heyman wanted to become a doctor by the time she completed high school.

Studied Photography

Attending Sarah Lawrence College, located in Bronxville, New York, Heyman initially pursued pre-medical studies. Graduating in 1964, she did not go to medical school, in part because she believed she was unable to take her education seriously. Heyman found that she was greatly influenced and limited by what she perceived as society's expectations for her gender. In addition to being twice married and a housewife for a time, Heyman did work in sales and as a receptionist, as she followed her artistic calling.

By 1967, Heyman was studying photography under Ken Heyman and Charles Harbutt, then began working as a freelance photographer and photojournalist. She took pictures that appeared in such publications as the *New York Times, Life,* and *Time* magazine. She also contributed photos to *Life, Harpers, Ms., Popular Photography,* and *Modern Photography.* In addition, Heyman took on other projects. For the international aid agency UNICEF (the United Nations International Children's Emergency Fund), she took pictures for a study on population and its relationship to children's needs. For this project, she took photographs in India in 1973 and Morocco in 1974.

By the early 1970s, Heyman was considered part of a group of photographers—which included Bruce Davidson and Harbutt—who cultivated a new, hybrid type of photojournalism that blurred the line between illustrating news events and personal expression. Even their non-periodical work would have these qualities. Such photographers would publish the breadth of their photographs in books and display them in galleries. In 1972, Heyman had her first photography show, held in Manhattan, which included such images. Over the course of her career she would have many solo and group shows, including those in New York City, Montreal, Washington, D.C., San Francisco, and other cities in the United States.

In this period, Heyman was becoming well known for developing photography style. In 1974, she became the first woman admitted to Magnum Photos, an esteemed photographer's cooperative. Founded in 1947 by respected photographers like Henri Cartier-Bresson and Robert Capra, Magnum became one of the world's most esteemed photographic agencies in the world. Heyman remained affiliated with Magnum for a number of years.

Published *Growing Up Female*

In 1974, Heyman published her first book of photographic images, *Growing Up Female: A Personal Photo-Journal.* Perhaps her best known work, the book reflected what had become her signature concern as a photographer. A feminist, Heyman offered a distinctly female perspective on gender roles, expectations, and society. She especially focused on concepts like being a girl, being a woman, being a mother, and being an object. The conflicts and contradictions in growing up female and trying to change were especially interesting to her.

Full of pictures that represented the photojournalism style being developed in this time period, *Growing Up Female* was both intensely autobiographical and full of emotion but also journalistic, detailed, and remote. Primarily consisting of black-and-white photographs of women and girls, the book depicted their experiences and struggles growing up in a society that was dominated by men. Many of the pictures showed females taking part in actions and activities that embodied stereotypes. Loneliness, limitations, and dissatisfaction were common themes.

Many of Heyman's images in *Growing Up Female* were considered arresting in their content and composition. Young girls were shown playing with dolls, or taking part in a game in which only the boys are doctors and the girls are nurses. An image of a married couple shows the father eating alone while the young mother takes care of their children. Heyman included women alone as well, in laundromats or shopping for groceries with curlers. One woman is depicted alone at a kitchen table overwhelmed by fatigue. Women were also spectators, watching men take part in activities they enjoyed, while others were objects, such as a strip club dancer on her back. One of the most memorable images was Heyman herself, taken during an abortion procedure.

According to Paul Vitello of the *New York Times,* "Her book, she said, 'one feminist's point of view' of the narrow range of choices women had in their lives, which she hoped her work would help to expand." Highly regarded and widely praised, *Growing Up Female* sold an impressive 35,000 copies, a high number for such a book in this period. It was regularly featured in feminist and women's bookstores of the era.

Created Challenging Works

After *Growing Up Female,* Heyman was part of other memorable projects in the late 1970s and early 1980s. Her feminist photos were included in a 1975 book, *Women of Photography: An Historical Survey,* which was published by the San Francisco Museum of Art. She also contributed images to a book of photographs about working women put together by Wendy Saul. *Butcher, Baker, Cabinetmaker: Photographs of Women at Work* was published in 1978.

Also in the late 1970s, Heyman took part in a photography project called Espejo, which focused on cataloging the mores and traditions of Mexican Americans living in California. As with much of her work, she focused on the lives of women and girls in this culture. Heyman took pictures of weddings and cultural rituals, among other events and every-day occurrences. She especially focused on exploring the tension between a macho male Mexican-American culture and the fashion and perspectives of Mexican-American women. Though some critics noted Heyman's images were more reserved and less personal than other examples of her work, her pictures for Espejo demonstrated her fundamental feminist perspective. The images from this project were collected in a book published by Oakland Museum in 1978 entitled *Espejo: Reflections of the Mexican American: Louis Carlos Bernal, Morrie Camhi, Abigail Heyman, Roger Minick, Neal Slavin.*

Focused on Agency Work, Education

In the 1980s, Heyman expanded her agency work and focused more on teaching others about photography. From 1981 to 1987, for example, she was a partner in Archives Pictures. A picture and photography agency, it was founded by five photographers formally affiliated with Magnum Pictures, including Heyman. The partners in the company self-financed it, and Archive Pictures had strong growth and increasing interest in the 1980s. The images sold by Archives were used by periodicals and textbook publishers, among others. Archives was particularly concerned with allowing its affiliated photographers to practice their art as they saw fit. Photographers were respectful of each other's method of working, while growing what was a profitable, financially successful company. The photographers edited each other, and allowed a balance between personal aesthetics, artistic interests, and what was needed commercially.

In 1986, Heyman took a position at the International Center of Photography in Manhattan. She became the director of the center's documentary and photojournalism department's full time studies program. She remained in the post until 1988. Over the years, Heyman also served on the faculty of other institutions and organizations as well, including New School for Social Research, the Center for Concerned Photography, the Country Photography Workshop, and the Aperion Photography Workshops.

One reason Heyman remained an in-demand educator in this period was the rebirth in interest of the type of photojournalism that Heyman, Davidson, and Harbutt were responsible for developing in the 1970s. In the mid to late 1980s, this style was called new photojournalism. In the late 1980s, Heyman also published books and took part in projects that continued to reflect her distinctive, insightful work in this style of photography.

Published *Dreams & Schemes*

For Heyman's 1987 book *Dreams & Schemes: Love and Marriage in Modern Times,* she attended 200 weddings and took pictures of the small human dramas surrounding and occurring at these family events. She also wrote essays about what she observed, included in the book. Focusing especially on what happened behind the scenes at weddings, one of Heyman's images highlighted a set of parents who were visibly unhappy because the bride was not changing her name after the ceremony. Other memorable photographs and essays included a bride struggling to decide which parent to invite because of their divorce, while another bride had to face two former paramours who showed up at her reception.

Writing about *Dreams & Schemes* in the *New York Times,* Andy Grundberg noted that Heyman successfully "uses a first-person narrative to help pierce another social fantasy." Describing the book in another piece in the *New York Times,* Grundberg stated, "By taking a reportorial approach, Ms. Heyman reveals a slice of reality seldom glimpsed in wedding photography. And believe me, this slice is not what most young bride's parents want to show their friends for the next 40 years." For her part, Heyman told Brit Hume on ABC *Weekend News Saturday* that she found weddings to be infinitely interesting. She stated, "It's like being in a wonderland of emotional relationships." She added, "There is a kind of tension before the ceremony.... People know their lives are about to change...."

Founded the Picture Project

Another photographic program launched by Heyman was also family oriented, the Picture Project, Inc. Heyman was the co-founder of the project and she served as its director, beginning in 1987. One project involved 66 of the most highly regarded photographers in the United States taking very personal family portraits in their own personal style. For this project, family did not always mean nuclear family, but also included pets and wider family groups, from infants to the elderly. The results were published in an anthology called *Flesh and Blood: Photographers' Images of Their Own Families* in 1992. Heyman was an editor of the book, along with Alice Rose George and Ethan Hoffman.

Continuing to work until the early 21st century, Heyman died of heart failure at her home in Manhattan on May 28, 2013. She was 70 years old. Describing Heyman's importance to the feminist movement, Joan Liftin, the former photojournalism director at the International Center of Photography, told the *New York Times'* Vitello, "As a feminist, she was not so much about marching. She took pictures that showed what the marching was about." At the same time, her images were personal and affecting. Jordyn Rozensky further summarized Heyman on the Jewish Women's Archive website, writing "Abby Heyman was a photographer with something to say, one who created a work of consequence through brutally honest and personal photographs. She wove her own identity—that of a woman growing up in a culture not always meant for women—into her photographs."

Books

Contemporary Authors Online, Gale, 2013.
Contemporary Photographers, Gale, 1996.
The Writer's Directory, Vol. 3, 31st ed., St. James Press, 2013.

Periodicals

Guardian (London, England), September 22, 1992.
New York Times, December 18, 1985; April 12, 1987; June 2, 2013; June 9, 2013.
Photo District News, November 1986.
USA Today, December 11, 1992.

Online

"Abigail Heyman: A Feminist & Photography," Jewish Women's Archive, http://jwa.org/blog/abigail-heyman-feminist-photographer (December 8, 2014).

Transcripts

Weekend News Saturday, ABC, June 27, 1987. □

Oscar Hijuelos

American author Oscar Hijuelos (1951–2013) wrote about the Cuban-American experience in such novels as *The Mambo Kings Play Songs of Love* (1989). With this book, Hijuelos became the first Latino to be honored with the Pulitzer Prize for Fiction. He also penned other popular novels such as *The Fourteen Sisters of Emilio Montez O'Brien* (1993) and *Beautiful Maria of My Soul* (2010).

Taylor Hill/Getty Images

Born Oscar Jerome Hijuelos on August 24, 1951, in Manhattan, New York, he was the son of Pascual and Magdalena Torrens Hijuelos. His parents emigrated from the countryside of Cuba in the 1940s. In New York, his father was employed as a cook at the Biltmore Hotel and other hotel kitchens. His mother was a homemaker who secretly wrote poetry. One of his Cuban grandfathers was an opera singer and a poet.

Split from Spanish Roots

Raised primarily in the Manhattan neighborhood of Morningside Heights, Hijuelos's family only spoke Spanish and it was Hijuelos's only language until the age of three. After a trip to Cuba in 1955, he developed a kidney disease, acute nephritis, so severe that he was hospitalized for a year in Connecticut and nearly died. During this period away from his family, he became fluent in English. When Hijuelos was released from the hospital and went back to his family, he primarily spoke English. Hijuelos later looked back at this time in his life and believed it was when he became disassociated with his roots.

Though he was allowed to go home from the hospital, the young Hijuelos was still ill for a time and susceptible to infection. Because he was not allowed to leave home for several months, he taught himself to read, consumed comic books, and trained his mother in English. Once recovered, Hijuelos was educated in public schools in Manhattan. He remained an avid reader, reading books that his mother

had picked up on the Columbia University campus. In this way, the young Hijuelos was exposed to random novels and textbooks. He also suffered tragedy as his father died when he was 17.

After graduating from Louis D. Brandeis High School, Hijuelos attended a number of colleges, including Bronx Community College, Lehman College, and Manhattan Community College. He ultimately completed two degrees—a bachelor's degree and an M.F.A. in creative writing—at the City College of New York. During his college years, he took creative writing courses taught by seminal authors like Susan Sontag and Donald Barthelme.

Published First Novel

When Hijuelos completed college, he began a career as an advertising copywriter, and wrote novels in his free time. In 1983, Hijuelos published his first novel, *Our House in the Last World.* It examines the highs and lows faced by a family that leaves Havana, Cuba, in 1939 and must adjust to life in Spanish Harlem. The novel took inspiration from and drew on his own life and the experiences of his family.

Our House in the Last World set the tone for future works in that Hijuelos often focused on the lives of Cuban émigrés in the United States and Cuban Americans. Overall, his novels usually considered assimilation, including its issues and odd circumstances, instead of the political. Full of heart and insight, Hijuelos composed graceful, earthy prose with a decidedly American rhythm.

Summarizing Hijuelos's focus and skills as an author, Bruce Weber of the *New York Times* stated that the author "wrote about the non-native experience in the United States from a sympathetic, occasionally amused perspective and with a keen eye for detail in his period settings." Weber added, "His characters were not necessarily new arrivals—in Mr. Hijuelos's books, which sometimes ranged over decades, they certainly didn't remain so—but in various stages of absorbing the sometimes assaultive American culture while holding on to an ethnic and national identity."

Wrote Pulitzer Prize-Winning Novel

Though *Our House in the Last World* was successful, Hijuelos continued to work in advertising until the mid-1980s. In 1985, he won a prize from the American Academy of Arts and Letters. It included a year-long residence at the American Academy of Rome and a stipend that allowed him to write full time. This experience led to his next and best novel, *The Mambo Kings Play Songs of Love*, which was begun there. When Hijuelos developed and wrote the novel, he used the woman who would be his second wife as a sounding board. His first marriage ended in divorce, and he met Lori Marie Carlson, a writer and editor, in the early 1980s. The couple married in 1998.

Published in 1989, Hijuelos's second novel, *The Mambo Kings Play Songs of Love* centers on two brothers in the 1950s who come to America from Cuba to start an orchestra. Cesar Castillo is a bandleader, all flamboyance and immorality, while his brother Nestor, a trumpeter, is more thoughtful. The pair have a band, the Mambo Kings, who become briefly famous and appear on the popular situation comedy *I Love Lucy*. *The Mambo Kings Play Songs of Love* is a story of immigrants, but one in which their dreams are not truly fulfilled and they miss needed connections.

For the novel, Hijuelos was given the 1990 Pulitzer Prize for Fiction and became more widely known as an author. *The Mambo Kings Play Songs of Love* was adapted into a 1992 film entitled *The Mambo Kings*. It starred Armand Assante and Antonio Banderas in the title roles. A musical followed in 2005, staged in San Francisco.

Continued to Create Successful Works

Because of the success of *The Mambo Kings Play Songs of Love*, Hijuelos was able to focus on writing full time. Hijuelos continued to produce noteworthy novels in the 1990s. Another major work was published in 1993, *The Fourteen Sisters of Emilio Montez O'Brien*. In this homage to his mother, Hijuelos explores the lives and loves of several generations of a family in small town Pennsylvania. Helmed by an American father and Cuban mother, the couple had 14 daughters. Through the work, Hijuelos explored the mind and voice of women.

Hijuelos suffered a setback before his next novel was published. After Hijuelos's editor at HarperCollins, Robert S. Jones, rejected the manuscript for a joyful Christmas novel, the author took a new angle on a Christmas story. The result was his first novel with a non-Hispanic character at its center. In 1995, Hijuelos published *Mr. Ives' Christmas*, which became a best seller. In this book, he wrote about a father whose life falls apart when his son is killed. Edward Ives is a commercial artist who believes he has a spiritual gift that emerges through his art, and a son, Robert, who wants to become a priest. Shortly before Christmas in 1967, Robert is murdered by a teenager for no discernable reason. For years, Ives suffers because of his son's murder, mourning and pushing his wife away. It is not until he forgives his son's murderer that that he experiences redemption.

Essentially, *Mr. Ives' Christmas* transports the essence of the Biblical story of Job to Morningside Heights in contemporary times. Though the novel focuses on the concepts of religion and suffering, Samuel Freedman of the *New York Times* praised it for its "enormous artistry and insight." Hijuelos's wife, Carlson, told Freedman, "The root of that novel was a real story. When Oscar was growing up in his neighborhood, one of the families that was very close to his family lost their boy. He was shot. And it was a senseless, tragic, horrific murder, and Oscar never forgot it. And the dignity of the family and the way they dealt with it stayed with him."

Put Out *Empress of the Splendid Season*

Four years later, in 1999, Hijuelos published his next novel, *Empress of the Splendid Season*. Returning to Hispanic characters, the story focuses on Lydia Espana, an immigrant from Cuba who lived a life of privilege in her native country but finds life more difficult after moving to New York City in the late 1940s. She works as a cleaning woman for rich families, is married to a husband who is ill, and has troubled relationships with her Americanized children. Throughout her difficulties in life, she remains dignified. Of the novel, Hijuelos told Robert Domingeuz of the New York *Daily News*, "It's intended as a love note to what I call the upper-class poor. It captured some of my feelings the same way a kid from a working-class family suddenly looks around and sees how the rest of the world works."

Hijuelos followed *Empress of the Splendid Season* with two books that were similarly thoughtful and challenging. In 2002, he put out *A Simple Habana Melody (From When the World Was Good)*. The story focuses on a Cuban composer named Israel Levis who lived in Europe for many years before returning home in 1947. Hijuelos explores Levis's experiences, which included being locked up by the Nazis during World War II because they believed he was Jewish. In 2009, Hijuelos moved into young adult novels with *Dark Dude*. In this work, he looks at the life of a sensitive boy from Cuba living in a rough neighborhood in Harlem. This coming of age novel sees this teenage boy removed from New York and sent to the Midwest where he comes to understand himself and his identity.

Taught at Duke University

By the time *Dark Dude* came out, Hijuelos had started another career. Though he had never worked as an educator before, he began teaching at Duke University in 2008. After being recruited by a professor there, Hijuelos taught creative writing, including autobiographies and short stories. His wife was an English professor there, and she told Ryan Zhang of the *Duke Chronicle*, "My husband had no airs about him. His sole interest was making certain that the kids who were in his classes would leave as better writers."

While teaching at Duke, Hijuelos continued to write. In 2010, he put out a book related to *The Mambo Kings Play Songs of Love, Beautiful Maria of My Soul.* This book focuses on one pivotal character from *The Mambo Kings*, the woman who broke Nestor's heart. In the novel, Hijuelos describes what happens in her life after she breaks it off with Nestor. Next, Hijuelos published his memoir, *Thoughts Without Cigarettes*, in 2011. The autobiography looks at his life, personal identity, his faith, and spiritual life. *Thoughts Without Cigarettes* included a tribute to his father.

Unexpected Death

Though Hijuelos was not in obvious ill health, he suffered a heart attack and collapsed while playing tennis. He died on October 12, 2013, in Manhattan at the age of 62 years old. At the time of his death, Hijuelos had been quietly completing a novel he had been working on for more than a decade. Unlike his previous works, this was a historical novel that had nothing to do with the immigrant experience in the United States. Instead, the well-researched 859-page novel explored the 37-year-long friendship between two high profile figures in the 19th century, author Mark Twain and the Welsh explorer Henry Morton Stanley. Hijuelos had finished the novel only days before his death, and died only two days before it was scheduled to be sent to publishers.

After Hijuelos's death, his grieving widow was unable to oversee the publishing process until the following year. Moved by how much time and effort her late husband had put into the novel, she and Hijuelos's literary agent, Jennifer Lyons, arranged for its publication through Grand Central Publishing. *Twain and Stanley Enter Paradise* along with a previously unpublished short story—"Another Spaniard in the Works," which focuses on the meeting between John Lennon and a young musician in 1980—were scheduled to be published in the fall of 2015. A departure from his previous works, Hijuelos was proud of the final product. He also had another 700 page novel that was not finished, about a pair of archaeologists who find love, though his widow was unsure if it would ever be published. No matter what he wrote, Hijuelos wanted to affect his readers. He explained to Paula Span of the *Washington Post*, "In my little way, I try to enchant people, and maybe open their eyes."

Periodicals

Christian Science Monitor, August 1, 2014.
Daily News (New York, NY), February 23, 1999.
The Duke Chronicle, October 18, 2013.
The Guardian (London, England), October 28, 2013.
The Herald (Glasgow, Scotland), December 18, 1995.
Las Cruces Sun-News (New Mexico), October 18, 2013.
New York Times, October 14, 2013; November 30, 2013; July 31, 2014.
Washington Post, March 17, 1993.□

Helen Holmes

One of Hollywood's first stuntwomen, American actress Helen Holmes (1892–1950) rose to notoriety starring in the weekly film serial *The Hazards of Helen* (1914–15). Each episode featured Holmes as a bold, daring, quick-witted heroine leaping to and from trains, bridges, horses and automobiles to save the day. Holmes went on to become one of the most famous "serial queens" of her era.

Helen Holmes was born July 7, 1892. Her exact birthplace has never been verified. Some sources cite Louisville, Kentucky, or South Bend, Indiana, as the city of Holmes's birth, while others note Cook County, Illinois. Her father, Louis Holmes, came from a family of Norwegian immigrants. He worked as a railroad clerk at the Illinois Central Railroad and was later employed by the Chicago & Eastern Illinois Railroad. Holmes's mother, Sophia Barnes, was from Indiana. An alternate birthdate of June 19, 1892, has sometimes been used for Holmes.

Holmes spent her early years in Chicago alongside two siblings. The family struggled financially so little Helen was put to work as a photographer's model to supplement her father's income. Around 1910, tuberculosis swept through the family and Holmes became ill. Soon thereafter, the family purchased a home in the Death Valley area of California and headed West.

Launched *Hazards of Helen*

Around 1911 or 1912, Holmes befriended film star Mabel Normand, who was employed by Keystone Studios. Through Normand, Holmes secured some modeling work and became the face of a Santa Fe Railroad poster campaign. Soon, Keystone Studios founder and director Mack Sennett took an interest in Holmes and gave her small roles in *Kings Court* (1912) and the slapstick comedy *Barney Oldfield's Race for Life* (1913). She appeared in several Keystone films before signing with the Kalem Studio in 1913.

At Kalem, Holmes worked under Australian director J.P. "Jack" McGowan, and at some point, the two married. Working for McGowan, Holmes perfected the daredevil antics that would make her a Hollywood darling. Through 1913, the two made a number of "railroad" dramas. These were films that involved a thinly veiled action plot involving a locomotive or two. Having grown up around the railway where her father worked, Holmes was comfortable in that setting and felt capable at the controls of an engine. One favorite stunt involved Holmes being tied up on the railroad tracks as an oncoming locomotive approached. At the last instant, her hero would rush in and save her from impending doom.

After mild success with their railroad dramas, McGowan and Holmes decided to make a serial. The first episode of *The Hazards of Helen* appeared on November 14, 1914. During this period, it was common for theaters to show short serial films each week before the main feature. Most

Akg-images/Newscom

serials were more like chapter films with each week's episode ending in a cliffhanger. The point was to capture theatergoers' interest so they would return the next week to see how the situation got resolved.

Each *Hazards of Helen* episode lasted about ten to 12 minutes. Unlike the other serials that ended in a cliffhanger each week, *Hazards of Helen* included a resolution. Each episode was its own mini-melodrama; and the clips could be shown out of order and still make sense. As such, some film historians do not classify *Hazards of Helen* as a true serial. The series was highly popular and earned Holmes designation as the "Darling of the Rails." Holmes even directed episodes when McGowan was unavailable, though she never received credit.

Each week, the action-packed *Hazards of Helen* featured Holmes as a clever, tough-as-nails heroine facing runaway trains, broken bridges, fires, bandits and other assorted scalawags. The scenario was often the same. Holmes played a telegraph operator who came into knowledge of impending disasters like runaway trains and fleeing bandits. She then used her brains and brawn to solve the problem. The titles of each episode hinted at the danger to come, with such episodes as "The Girl at the Throttle," "The Open Drawbridge," "The Girl on the Trestle," and "Escape of the Fast Freight."

Gained Fame for Daredevil Antics

Hazards of Helen demanded strength and courage and was physically taxing and dangerous for Holmes. In episode

nine, titled "The Leap from the Water Tower," Holmes dangled from a water tower, then jumped to the top of a moving train as it passed by. In another episode she rode a motorcycle onto an open drawbridge, then plunged into the water below. Another favorite trick involved jumping from a moving horse to a moving train, or vice versa. Holmes also leapt from burning buildings, ran atop boxcars and once dropped from a trestle into an automobile passing below. As such, *Hazards of Helen* did not need to end with a cliffhanger each week because people flocked to the theaters to see what feat Holmes would tackle each week. These were the days of silent film, so the tension was accentuated with music.

Holmes did most of her own stunts and was unfazed by the danger involved. In a 1917 interview with Norah Meade of the *Fort Wayne Journal-Gazette*, Holmes quipped, "Oh, I run no risks. It's all a matter of understanding the idiosyncrasies of inanimate things. Before I let a machine turn a somersault with me in mid-air and plunge into sixty feet of water, you bet I know where and when I am going to exit, and it is not in the same spot as the car."

What Holmes lacked in glamour, she made up for with grit. She was extremely popular and featured frequently in the movie magazines of her day, often on the cover. As the women's suffrage movement gained momentum in the United States, Holmes's trend-bucking character caught on with females who wanted to see women in expanded roles. University of Washington cinema studies assistant professor Jennifer Bean discussed Holmes's appeal with *Humanities* writer Janis Johnson. "As a movie star, Helen Holmes and her characters epitomized the modern new woman with stamina—'nerve strength' as courage was known at the time—and unbelievable physical action."

Continued with *Railroad Dramas*

After starring in 48 episodes of *Hazards of Helen,* Holmes and McGowan left Kalem for Universal Pictures in 1915. *Hazards* continued with Helen Gibson in the lead role and lasted 119 episodes, making it one of the longest-running serials ever filmed. The move to Universal, however, proved underwhelming as the studio failed to reunite the working team of Holmes and McGowan. Holmes was given the job of scenario writer and McGowan directed some shorts. They stayed only a few months, leaving after Samuel S. Hutchinson approached them with an offer to form the Signal Film Corporation with the intent to specialize in railroad dramas utilizing Holmes's talents. Distribution came through the Mutual Film Corporation, which was well-known as the home of Charlie Chaplin. Hutchinson had a share in Mutual.

The move to Signal marked the beginning of another highly successful period for Holmes, although the contracts McGowan negotiated with Signal left the two salaried employees facing an unrelenting schedule. Their first release was *The Girl and the Game,* which arrived in theaters in December 1915. *The Girl and the Game* was another serial, but unlike *Hazards,* each episode ended with a cliffhanger. The stunts were wilder, because with Mutual's backing McGowan and Holmes had a larger budget and could afford to do things like occasionally wreck a Pullman coach or two.

In 1916, McGowan and Holmes produced *The Diamond Runners,* which they wrote and filmed while on vacation in Hawaii. They followed with *Lass of the Lumberlands,* another well-liked series that followed a railroad motif with the added element of logging. *Lass* was shot in locations with breathtaking scenery, such as Yosemite National Park. *Lass* ran 15 episodes and reportedly grossed $2 million dollars. One episode of *Lass* called for Holmes to carry a baby across a river. After filming, newspapers reported that Holmes had fallen in love with the child, who had supposedly come from an orphanage. Papers recounted how Holmes and McGowan decided to adopt the girl, who became known as Dorothy Holmes McGowan. Other sources have indicated that the child, born in 1915, was actually the daughter of McGowan and his lover.

Holmes and McGowan continued their partnership and launched *The Railroad Raiders* in 1917. This serial offered Holmes the opportunity to continue her daredevil antics with all of the visual thrills and spills fans had come to adore. In one episode she raced a car across the San Pedro docks, then dropped the vehicle onto a barge some 30 feet away. It took her four tries to master the stunt. In another episode she rode a freight car off a ferry into the water.

With the brisk production pace and increasingly complicated stunts, the crew and the actors started having accidents. One crewman was injured in a scene that crashed a train into a warehouse. McGowan himself was hospitalized while shooting the series, forcing Holmes into the director's seat. *The Railroad Raiders* ran 15 episodes and reportedly grossed just as much as *Lass.* They followed with *The Lost Express,* which yielded several injuries and hospitalizations for various actors and crewmembers. Holmes evaded injury but had a few close calls. In one episode, she barely escaped a burning railcar. In another episode, she battled a villain on a runaway ore truck careening down a steep grade. When the brakes failed, the vehicle crashed, but Holmes lived to tell the tale.

Around this same time, the California State Fair cooked up the idea to have Holmes attempt a live action stunt for fairgoers. The fair announced a "Helen Holmes Day" with Holmes as the featured attraction. The live stunt involved two trains barreling toward each other on the same track. Naturally, Holmes rode clinging to the side of one. At the last instant, she jumped into a moving automobile. Moments after her departure from the locomotive, the steel hunks of the trains smashed and twisted together.

End of the Line

By June 1918, papers began reporting that McGowan and Holmes had split up. Around the same time, the Mutual Film Corp. went bankrupt, forcing Signal to close. The shuttering of the studio marked the end of a prolific period of output for Holmes and McGowan. Over a two-year period, they had produced 60 two-reel serial chapters and a handful of full-length features.

For Holmes, this marked the end of her journey to popularity and success. In 1918, Holmes did not make any films. In 1919, she appeared in *The Fatal Fortune,* playing a newspaper reporter searching tropical jungles for buried treasure. The 15-episode serial, produced by the S.L.K. Serial Corp., flopped because it failed to utilize Holmes in any hair-raising stunts. Next, she founded Helen Holmes Productions and produced *The Tiger Band,* which was released in 1920. She also produced a five-reel Western called *Ghost City* (1921), featuring herself and Leo Maloney in the starring roles. It was not very successful.

Sometime in 1921, Holmes and McGowan reconciled and began working together again. *Hills of Missing Men* (1922) was written and directed by McGowan with Holmes in a prominent role. They followed with a seven-reel feature, *One Million in Jewels* (1923), which starred McGowan as a jewel smuggler and Holmes in a supporting role. McGowan wrote and directed the drama. Next came *Stormy Seas* (1923), a ship-rescue action flick that showcased both McGowan and Holmes. After a handful of unsuccessful movies, the two returned to their previously popular Western railroad formula with 1925's *Blood and Steel,* followed by *Perils of the Rail* (1926), which was the last silent railroad melodrama the two would ever make.

In 1925, Holmes married Lloyd Saunders, a well-known stuntman and film cowboy. In 1926, they moved to a ranch near Sonora, California, and Holmes drifted away from acting. Unfortunately, they lost the ranch during the Great Depression and returned to Hollywood around 1932. Holmes took some bit roles, mostly uncredited. She appeared with W.C. Fields in *Poppy* (1936), another uncredited role.

Failing to make a comeback, Holmes and Saunders settled in the San Fernando Valley. Holmes spent her later years raising Irish terriers and training them for the movies. She also ran an antiques business. Saunders died in 1946. Holmes spent the reminder of her life battling numerous illnesses. Since contracting tuberculosis as a child, Holmes had struggled with lung problems and bouts of pneumonia. She died of pulmonary tuberculosis on July 8, 1950. In 2004, she enjoyed a small resurrection when *The Hazards of Helen* was chosen by the National Film Preservation Foundation for inclusion in a lengthy commemorative DVD anthology titled *More Treasures from American Film Archives, 1894-1931.*

Books

Lahue, Kalton C., *Winners of the West: The Sagebrush Heroes of the Silent Screen,* A.S. Barnes & Co., 1970.

McGowan, John J., *J.P. McGowan: Biography of a Hollywood Pioneer,* McFarland, 2005.

Rainey, Buck, *Serial Film Stars: A Biographical Dictionary, 1912-1956,* McFarland & Co., 2005.

Periodicals

Fort Wayne Journal-Gazette, July 8, 1917.

Humanities, January/February 2005. □

J

Glenda Jackson

Glenda Jackson (born 1936) was an award-winning actress on stage, screen, and television before being elected to the House of Commons as a member of the Labour Party in 1992. The winner of an Academy Award for her work in *Women in Love,* she was also admired for her appearances in the television miniseries *Elizabeth R* and *Marat/Sade.* Jackson formally retired from acting in the late 1990s and continued to serve in Parliament into the early 21st century.

Jackson was born May 9, 1936, in Hoylake, Merseyland, England, the first of four daughters born to Harry and Joan Jackson. Her family was working class. Her father was a bricklayer who served in the Royal Navy during World War II, while her mother was a charlady (house cleaner). She was educated at the West Kirby County Grammar School for Girls. After completing school when she was 16 years old with three school certificates, she spent two years working at the West Kirby branch of Boots, a well-known British pharmacy and drug store retailer. Jackson cleaned shelves as an employee in the medicine department.

Became Actress

By the time she was a teenager, Jackson was an amateur actor who participated in local theater groups. Very interested in acting, someone in the group told her she would be a good professional and she decided to pursue professional training. To that end, the 18-year-old Jackson attended the Royal Academy of Dramatic Art and trained for the stage. She served an apprenticeship in repertory work, appearing in productions at the Lyric Theatre and the Arts Theatre. In 1957, Jackson made her London debut in *All Kinds of Men.*

Joining the Royal Shakespeare Company (RSC) in 1963, Jackson was critically acclaimed for her role in the RSC's *The Persecution and Assassination of Jean-Paul Marat as Performed by the Inmates of the Asylum of Charenton under the Direction of the Marquis de Sade.* Directed by Peter Brook, the play was more commonly known as *Marat/Sade.* Jackson reprised the role on Broadway, making her Broadway debut in the process, and in the film version, released in 1967.

Jackson had made her film debut four years earlier in *This Sporting Life* (1963). She focused primarily on stage work in the 1960s, but appeared in a few films. They included *Tell Me Lies* and *Negatives,* both released in 1968.

Won Academy Award

Though Jackson continued to appear on stage in the 1970s, her professional focus shifted to film and television and she became internationally well known. In 1970, she played Gudrun Brangwen in *Women in Love,* an adaptation of a novel by D.H. Lawrence. She won numerous awards for her work in the Ken Russell film, including an Academy Award. Over the years, Jackson would appear in more films directed by Russell, including *The Music Lovers* (1971), playing the nymphomaniac wife of composer Tchaikovsky, *The Boy Friend* (1971), *Salome's Last Dance* (1988), and *The Rainbow* (1989). She also appeared in a 1992 television movie directed by him, *Secret Life of Sir Arnold Bax.*

Also in 1971, Jackson played Queen Elizabeth I in two different projects. In the film *Mary, Queen of Scots,* she depicted the British queen opposite Vanessa Redgrave's

Flying Colours/Getty Images

Mary Queen of Scots. Jackson portrayed the queen in the miniseries *Elizabeth R*, originally made for British television and airing in the United States. The role brought her two Emmy Awards and stardom in the United States.

Jackson continued to take on high profile, award-winning roles in the mid-1970s. She won two honors for portraying Alex Greville in *Sunday, Bloody Sunday* (1971). In 1973, Jackson won another Academy Award for her work in the role of Vicki Allession in the screwball comedy *A Touch of Class*. Though Jackson was considered quite a stylized, technique driven actress, she had a knack for certain types of comedies.

Took Diverse Roles

Jackson had roles in three other films in 1973, *Triple Echo*, *A Bequest to the Nation*, and *Il soriso del grande tentatore*. The following year, she appeared in one film, *The Maids*. She received wide acclaim for her work in the titular role in the stage play *Hedda Gabler*.

In the mid-1970s, Jackson's film roles became more diverse. She appeared in *The Romantic Englishwoman* (1975) and *Hedda*, the film version of the stage play *Hedda Gabler*. In 1976 Jackson memorably appeared in *The Incredible Sarah* as Sarah Bernhardt, and played a Richard Nixon-type nun in a comedy inspired by Watergate, *Nasty Habits*.

Though Jackson took on few stage roles in this period, the ones she took were often acclaimed. They included her

depiction of Cleopatra in Shakespeare's *Antony and Cleopatra* at Stratford in 1978. The production was directed by Peter Brook, who directed her in *Marat/Sade*. Also in 1978, Jackson was named a Commander, Order of the British Empire, a high honor.

Focused on Television and Stage Work

In the late 1970s and into the 1980s, Jackson's career focused more on television, and stage plays, than films. She appeared in only a few big spring productions in this period, including *Lost and Found* (1979), and Robert Altman's *Health* (1980). She would also appear in an Altman film in 1987, *Beyond Therapy*.

In 1981, Jackson won two awards for her work as poet Stevie Smith in the film *Stevie* (1978), a role she also played on stage. Also in 1981, she played actress Patricia Neal in the television movie *The Patricia Neal Story*. In 1982, Jackson appeared in the film *The Return of the Soldier* and the television movie *Giro City*. In 1984, Jackson similarly appeared in the film *And Nothing But the Truth* and the television movie *Sakharov*.

Jackson's extensive stage work in the 1980s included major roles in such plays as *Great and Small*, *Phedre*, and *Mother Courage*. In 1985, she appeared on stage in *Stranger Interlude*. The production moved from London to Broadway, and she was nominated for a Tony Award. In 1986, Jackson had another hit play with the West End production of *House of Bernarda Alba*.

In 1988, Jackson played a controversial Lady Macbeth in a production of *Macbeth*. It played in New York, and the actress was again honored with a Tony Award nomination for her work. After *Macbeth* ended its run in New York, Jackson traveled to Los Angeles to appear in *Who's Afraid of Virginia Woolf?*, then returned to London for *Scenes from an Execution*.

Ran for Political Office

In 1990, Jackson set aside her acting career for a time to focus on politics, an interest she had had since the age of 16 when she joined the Labour Party. She ran for a seat in Parliament, but lost the election and returned to work. In 1990, she appeared in the film *Doombeach* and television documentary *Open Space: Death on Delivery*. In 1991, Jackson had roles in two films *The Castle* and *A Murder of Quality* as well as a television movie *The House of Bernarda Alba*. Also in 1991, she appeared in a Glasgow production of Eugene O'Neill's *Mourning Becomes Electra*.

Despite her initial political setback, Jackson prepared to run again in 1991. She was concerned about the direction of Britain under Prime Minister John Major, a Conservative who had replaced the long-serving Conservative Margaret Thatcher. Jackson told Matt Wolf of the *New York Times*, "I never before felt ashamed of being English. And I have felt and still feel deeply ashamed of being English in many areas. I'm deeply ashamed of what our government is doing to its citizens."

When elections were held in 1992, Jackson triumphed, winning a seat representing a working class neighborhood in Hampstead and Highgate. She was the first Labour candidate to win the seat since the mid-1960s, and was re-elected to the same seat for nearly three decades. When Jackson made her first speech in the House of Commons, she was petrified. She told Anoosh Chakelian of the *New Statesman,* "It was the most frightening experience of my life. [I was] absolutely petrified...It suddenly struck me that here I was representing a constituency synonymous with some of the world's greatest exponents of the English language."

Played Active Role as MP

When Jackson took office, her presence was scrutinized and questioned, especially by the primarily male House of Commons, where nine of ten members were men. Not entering politics as an actress, she took her new role quite seriously, more so than the trappings that usually accompanied an acting career. She told Marianne MacDonald of the London *Independent* "I was never part of the glitzy, glamoury, showbizzy part of the entertainment world. I don't think I could ever have been. It wouldn't have interested in me and, you know...I wouldn't have been any good at it." Instead, she found a niche in politics.

Working hard as an MP, Jackson soon gained a position of power. In 1994, she was named the Labour Transport Team Campaigns Co-ordinator. Because of this post, when Labour gained control, Jackson was named Parliamentary Under-Secretary of State for Transport in the British government. She served from 1997 to 1999. She focused on responsibility for transport in London, airlines and airports, marine and shipping. Ports and railway issues were also her concern.

By this time, Jackson was indifferent to the arts. Talking to MacDonald of the London *Independent* in 1997, she said "I can't remember the last time I went to the theatre or cinema, and what I find particularly ironic is that my office looks directly over the South Bank, and the Tate Gallery is over there and the National Portrait Gallery, and I don't think I've ever been in any of them for the past four or five years. Scandalous, isn't it?" During this period, she announced her retirement from acting. Her last role came in 1999 in the television movie *Jerry Springer on Sunday.*

Expanded Political Role

As Jackson became more politically active, one of the issues she focused on was homelessness. From 2000 to 2004, she was a member of the Greater London Assembly advisory cabinet for homelessness. She worked to address issues such as meeting their medical needs.

Critical of the war in Iraq, Jackson was re-elected in 2010 by only 42 votes as her constituency was new, including Hampstead and Kilburn. She then joined the Work and Pensions Select Committee. There, she came out against cuts to housing benefits and the Incapacity Benefit, and attempted to detail how such cuts impacted women more than men.

Jackson was sometimes controversial. In 2013, upon the death of Thatcher, she did not give tribute to the former British prime minister as many others did in Parliament. Instead, she spoke out against her and said she damaged Britain through her policies.

Like Thatcher, Jackson left an important legacy, even as she spoke against the former prime minister. Katy Brand wrote in the London *Telegraph,* "During her time she has been a fiery and independent presence, even to her own party: she was a vocal protester against the Iraq war, and became so anti-Blair that she even threatened to challenge his leadership herself as a stalking horse candidate. She called for his resignation time and time again, and so, given her record on party-loyalty, why on earth would anyone expect her to be anything less than furious at the eulogising going on for Thatcher, a politician she opposed in every way?"

Overall, Jackson saw the world differently than most in acting, politics, and life. She told Tim Walker of the London *Daily Mail,* "This obsession with being happy is one of the curses of Western civilisation. I want to experience all the tears as well as all the laughter, and the last thing I want to be is content. I need to be discontented, I need stress, I need crises. It is, simply, the way I am." She added, "I found as an actress that it was easy indeed to act badly and inordinately difficult to act well. It is the same being a good constituency MP and being effective at the Department. All I have ever really wanted is to do my best. If I have a terror it is, perhaps, of letting myself down."

Books

International Dictionary of Films and Filmmakers, Vol 3: Actors and Actresses, edited by Sara Pendergast and Tom Pendergast, 4th ed., St. James Press, 2000.

Periodicals

Daily Mail (London, England), January 4, 1999.

Independent Education, November 16, 2006.

Independent (London, England), March 31, 1990; February 16, 1997.

New Statesman, August 15, 2014.

New York Times, December 15, 1991.

Telegraph (London, England), April 12, 2013.

Online

"About Glenda," Glenda Jackson MP, http://www.glenda-jackson.co.uk/about-glenda (December 20, 2014).□

Joe Jackson

One of the greatest natural hitters of all time, Shoeless Joe Jackson (1888–1951) exited major-league baseball after 13 seasons with a .356 career batting average, bested only by Ty Cobb and Rogers Hornsby. He was best remembered, however, for his connection to the 1919 Chicago White Sox game-fixing scandal in which players colluded with gamblers to take money for intentionally losing the World Series. Afterward, Jackson was banned from baseball, although he maintained his innocence for the remainder of his life.

oseph Jefferson Wofford Jackson was born into an illiterate sharecropper family on July 16, 1888, in Pickens County, South Carolina. Some sources cite 1887 as Jackson's birth year, which cannot be definitively identified because no birth certificate was ever issued and the family Bible, where dates were recorded, burned in a fire. Jackson was the eldest of eight children born to George Elmore and Martha Ann (Jenkinson) Jackson. At age six, in lieu of school, Jackson began working in the local cotton mill to support his family. After a series of illnesses at age 10, Jackson contracted the measles and was left paralyzed for two months with his knees locked up against his chest. He eventually recovered and returned to work.

Joined Mill-Sponsored Baseball Team

Jackson spent his childhood in a mill town near Greenville, South Carolina, called Brandon Mill. At the time, textile mills were plentiful and dotted the riverside. Company villages shot up around the mills. Mill owners maintained their own competitive baseball teams to provide a social outlet for workers and their families and to keep them engaged with the company town. Players were afforded a high social status, so competition to make the team was fierce.

In 1901, the teenage Jackson joined the Brandon Mill men's team and quickly proved he could outplay most of the adults in the league. Jackson became a local legend for his baseball antics, wowing spectators with his hitting and fielding. According to Kelly Boyer Sagert, author of *Joe Jackson: A Biography*, Jackson's glove was known as the "place where triples die." He also delighted fans by throwing the ball all the way home from the deepest part of the outfield.

Locals referred to Jackson's line drives as "blue darters," inferring that the ball traveled so fast off Jackson's bat that they could see blue flames spurting out behind. Jackson also hit a lot of home runs, which were known as "Saturday Specials." Whenever Jackson hit a homer, his brothers passed a hat through the stands, allowing fans to toss in coins and pay homage to their hometown hero. At times, Jackson's bat brought in almost as much money as his father made in an entire month at the mill. One local fan named Charlie Ferguson was so impressed with Jackson that he made Jackson a new bat. Ferguson crafted a 36-incher that weighed 48 ounces and rubbed it dark with tobacco juice, just the way Jackson liked. Jackson nicknamed the bat "Black Betsy."

Played Barefoot; Earned Nickname

In 1908, Jackson joined a minor league team called the Greenville Spinners. It was with the Spinners that Jackson earned the nickname "Shoeless," which he hated with a passion. Sagert offered this account: "While many stories exist to explain the nickname, they differ in detail but match in spirit. Joe had gotten a new pair of spikes, the legend goes, and he hadn't broken them in properly; his feet blistered in protest." According to Sagert, Jackson told his manager he could not play but the manager had no intention of benching his star, so Jackson went shoeless. Jackson only played shoeless that one time, but a fan

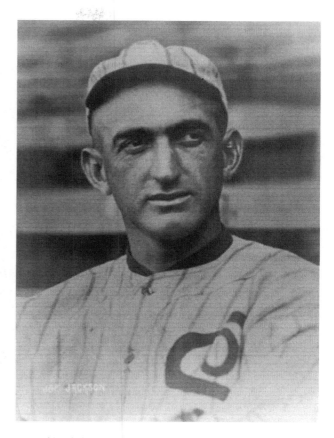

National Baseball Hall of Fame Library/Getty Images

razzed him for his lack of shoes. A reporter noted the incident and the name stuck. Jackson hated the moniker because it characterized his reputation as a Southern illiterate so poor he was forced to go barefoot.

While playing in Greenville, Jackson became good friends with Katie Wynn, who worked at the local drugstore. They married on July 19, 1908. Jackson was 20; Wynn was 15. The next day, he was back playing center field. Within a few weeks, their lives were uprooted after the Greenville manager sold Jackson's contract to Connie Mack, manager and part-owner of the Philadelphia Athletics. Mack's team stood no chance of making the postseason that year so he took the opportunity to try out some rookies and summoned Jackson north.

Called up to Major Leagues

A reluctant Jackson arrived in Philadelphia in 1908. During his initial trip north, Jackson changed his mind and hopped trains partway, buying a return ticket to South Carolina. Mack had to send outfielder Ralph Orlando "Socks" Seybold to South Carolina to fetch Jackson and escort him to Philadelphia. Jackson made his major league debut on August 25, 1908, but struggled in the big leagues. As a rural southerner, Jackson felt intimidated by the crowded northern city that teemed with extravagances like indoor plumbing, electricity and automobiles, all unknown back home. In addition, Jackson felt like an outsider, as anti-southern prejudices still lingered even though the Civil War was long over. Jackson's northern teammates made fun of his illiteracy and inability to read restaurant menus. Jackson deserted the team and escaped to Greenville once again in September. This time, he was lured back by the pleas of his former Greenville Spinners manager.

Jackson spent the off-season back home and returned to Philadelphia in the spring of 1909—not because he wanted to, but because he realized he had a contractual obligation to fulfill. Jackson batted .350 during spring training and was sent to the minor leagues to play in the South Atlantic League on a team based in Savannah, Georgia. His wife joined him and he seemed more comfortable on the southern circuit, batting .450 his first month in the league. Jackson ended the season by winning the league's batting title by hitting .358 in 118 games. He also stole 32 bases. In addition, Jackson proved he could nail runners on the base paths, throwing out 25 opponents from the outfield. Jackson made the league's all-star team. Once again, he was called up to the major leagues but turned in several lackluster performances and was sent back down.

In 1910, Mack dealt Jackson to the Cleveland Naps, now known as the Cleveland Indians. Jackson made his debut with the team on September 16, 1910, going one-for-four with a single. The next day, Jackson hit a two-run homer. Feeling more comfortable in Cleveland, Jackson's play improved. Jackson started the 1911 season on the Cleveland roster. During his rookie year, Jackson batted an impressive .408 but lost the batting title to Ty Cobb, who turned in the best batting average of his career, hitting .420. Jackson's .408, however, was the highest batting average recorded by a 20th century rookie. Jackson ended the season with 32 outfield assists and led the league with an on-base percentage of .468, which was better than Cobb's.

By now, interest in Jackson was growing and papers began reporting on his superstitions and eccentricities. For starters, Jackson traveled with a pet parrot that screeched "you're out." He also collected hairpins, which at the time were a popular fashion item for women. Jackson thought they brought him good luck. He preferred rusty ones and stuffed them into the back pockets of his uniform. When his batting slumped, he threw them out and started collecting again. Jackson did the same with bats, discarding them if he went into a slump. This rule did not apply to his original "Black Betsy." Jackson also rubbed his bats in sweet oil and wrapped them in clean cotton cloths. At every game, his wife, Katie, sat in the same spot in the stadium and always left in the seventh inning to go home and make dinner.

Jackson played some of his best seasons with Cleveland. In 1912, he batted .395 and led the league with 226 hits and 26 triples. In 1913, Jackson batted .373 and ended the season with a league high 197 hits and 39 doubles. In 1913, Jackson finished second in American League MVP voting. In 1914, however, Cleveland struggled with pitching issues, and finished last in the American League. Attendance waned and the club's finances took a turn for the worse. Cleveland lightened its payroll load by trading Jackson the following year.

Named in White Sox Scandal

Jackson joined the Chicago White Sox partway through the 1915 season. In 1916, Jackson was third best in the league in hitting, batting .341 and helping the Sox finish second in the American League. The team came alive in 1917, ending the season with 100 wins and 54 losses. They beat the New York Giants in the 1917 World Series. Jackson batted .304 in the series. In 1918, World War I disrupted the baseball season after the secretary of war issued a "work or fight" declaration for all able-bodied men of draft age. Jackson went to work for a shipbuilder in Delaware.

Jackson returned to Chicago and the Sox in 1919 and hit .351 during the regular season, leading his team to the World Series, which they lost to the Cincinnati Reds. Afterward, a scandal erupted as it came to light that several Chicago players, led by first baseman Arnold "Chick" Gandil, had conspired with gamblers to take money in exchange for losing the series. It was well-known that Sox owner Charles Comiskey was stingy with player salaries and infuriated the team by charging laundry fees for uniforms. The players stood to earn more in the gambling scheme than they did all season. In September 1920, a grand jury indicted eight players, including Jackson. They were all acquitted in court but banned from the game for life by the baseball commissioner. That meant Jackson remained ineligible for the Baseball Hall of Fame.

Historians agree that Jackson knew of the fix, but whether or not he participated has been widely debated. During the 1919 series, Jackson had 16 putouts in the outfield with no errors, and threw a runner out at home. He also led all players in the series with a batting average of .375, getting more hits than any other player on either team. Jackson's defenders noted that these statistics do not look like a man trying to throw the series. In his book, *Say It Ain't So, Joe!*, author Donald Gropman researched the scandal in detail and concluded, "I maintain that *Jackson was literally innocent of guilty involvement in the Black Sox scandal.* Furthermore, I contend that organized baseball, for reasons of its own or perhaps through relying on misinformation, has both perpetrated and perpetuated a lie."

Other researchers have said that the truth cannot be found. Sagert wrote, "Whether Shoeless Joe was a willing and active participant or a reluctant fellow traveler in the scheme simply cannot be known for sure." Researchers have concurred that Jackson knew about the scheme. Gandil approached Jackson and offered him $10,000 to throw the series; Jackson, however, refused. After realizing the fix was on, Jackson went to Comiskey and asked to be benched. Comiskey refused. Gandil, nonetheless, told the gamblers that Jackson was in on the scheme in an effort to make the plot seem more plausible. Gandil could not sell the fix if the team's best player was not in on it.

After the Sox lost the series, pitcher Lefty Williams delivered $5,000 to Jackson. Jackson refused the money, but Williams left it in his room anyway and Jackson's wife deposited it in their account. When Jackson testified before a grand jury in Chicago, he admitted that, yes, he had taken the $5,000, because the truth was that he had. During Jackson's "confession," he never admitted to botching plays. During later testimony from other players, it came to light that Jackson had never attended any pre-World Series meetings where the fix was discussed, suggesting he may not have been involved.

After being banned from baseball, Jackson played "outlaw" ball and coached semi-professional baseball. In 1933, he and his wife settled in Greenville, South Carolina. They opened a liquor store and barbeque restaurant. Later in life, Jackson suffered heart trouble and died on December 5, 1951, in Greenville. He was buried in the local Woodlawn Memorial Park cemetery. After his death, Jackson became a cult hero. Adaptations of his life story have been told in several books and movies, most notably 1988's *Eight Men Out* and 1989's *Field of Dreams*. Over the decades, politicians and fellow players have called for Jackson's reinstatement, but to no avail. His renown, though tarnished, has helped his family. In 2001, "Black Betsy" sold at auction for more than $575,000, the highest amount ever paid for a bat, even besting prices paid for the bats of Babe Ruth and Lou Gehrig.

Books

Gropman, Donald, *Say It Ain't So, Joe! The True Story of Shoeless Joe Jackson,* Carol Publishing Group, 1995.

Sagert, Kelly Boyer, *Joe Jackson: A Biography,* Greenwood Press, 2004.

Periodicals

Daily Herald (Arlington Heights, IL), September 13, 2009.

New Orleans Magazine, May 2010.

Online

"Shoeless Joe Jackson," *Baseball-Reference.com,* http://www.baseball-reference.com/players (November 8, 2014). ☐

Frank Jobe

In 1974, American orthopedic surgeon Frank Jobe (1925–2014) pioneered a career-saving elbow surgery for Major League baseball players. Dubbed "Tommy John" surgery after the pitcher who braved the initial surgical trial, the procedure revolutionized baseball by keeping players on the field.

Jobe is often referred to as one of the founding fathers of sports medicine. "He's touched more wins, more saves, more at-bats maybe, than anybody in baseball history," former MLB pitcher Orel Hershiser told Bill Shaikin of the *Los Angeles Times.* "He's extended the joy of every baseball fan, because he allowed great players . . . to get back on the field." Hershiser himself benefitted from Jobe's skill in 1990 when the surgeon conducted an innovative shoulder surgery to fix his ailing arm.

AP Images

Discovered Calling During War Service

Frank Wilson Jobe was born July 16, 1925, in Greensboro, North Carolina, to Lacy and Alma Jobe. Jobe's father, a World War I vet, worked as a postal clerk. An only child, Jobe grew up in a farmhouse with his parents and grandmother. He suffered a broken arm during childhood and became ambidextrous during the healing process. He played baseball during his youth, but never stood out enough to earn a starting position.

After high school, Jobe joined the U.S. Army and became a medical supply sergeant in the 326th Airborne Medical Company, which was part of the 101st Airborne Division. He landed in Europe and rode a glider into the Netherlands as part of Operation Market Garden. Later he was dispatched to Bastogne, Belgium. Jobe was asleep in a foxhole there when he awoke to German tanks and found himself surrounded by German troops. Jobe figured his capture was imminent; however, one of his fellow GIs shoved the German soldier who was attempting to round them up. Jobe took the opportunity to escape during the commotion, and narrowly evaded capture by hopping aboard an Allied truck.

The German invasion of Bastogne, or Siege of Bastogne as it came to be called, was part of the larger Battle of the Bulge offensive launched by the Germans in late 1944. As the battle waged on, Jobe supplied provisions to doctors patching up the wounded. He was plenty busy. During the attack, the 101st Division lost 312 enlisted men and 29 officers. More than 1,500 were wounded. Jobe earned several honors for his wartime service, including the Bronze Star, the Combat Medical Badge, and Glider Badge with one star.

Watching the military doctors operate while holed up in tents as bullets and shrapnel rained down around them inspired Jobe to attend medical school. "I don't want to make it something dramatic like they were my idols and I wanted to be just like them," Jobe told Mark Emmons of the *Orange County Register.* "But I watched them practice under shooting conditions, and I think that influenced me."

After his war service, Jobe enrolled at junior college in Tennessee, then moved to California to attend La Sierra University in Riverside. He completed his medical training at Loma Linda Medical School in 1956, then spent three years working in general practice. He used his income to pay off his medical school loans. Next, he completed an orthopedic residency at Los Angeles County Hospital.

During his residency, Jobe met a seasoned orthopedic surgeon named Robert Kerlan. The two hit it off and decided to form a practice together. In 1965, they started the Southwestern Orthopaedic Medical Group in Los Angeles. In 1985, they changed the name to the Kerlan-Jobe Orthopedic Clinic. By the 1990s, it had grown to include 16 doctors. The clinic became a recognized world leader in sports medicine rehabilitation, and trained hundreds of doctors to perform surgeries. The clinic served many major sports teams in the Los Angeles area, but Jobe focused his attention on the Dodgers. In 1964, he removed bone chips from the elbow of Dodgers pitcher Johnny Podres. No doctor had ever made that repair on a pitcher before.

Developed "Tommy John" Surgery

In 1968, the Dodgers made Jobe the team's designated orthopedic doctor. As such, he spent a great deal of time at Dodger Stadium and was in attendance on July 17, 1974, when Dodger ace Tommy John took the mound and disaster struck. Early in the game, John lost control of his pitches and instantly knew there was something terribly wrong with his arm. According to Matt Schudel of the *Washington Post,* John explained the event this way in his 1991 autobiography: "As I came forward and released the ball, I felt a kind of nothingness, as if my arm weren't there, then I heard a 'pop' from inside my arm, and the ball just blooped up to the plate."

Jobe examined John and determined that the 31-year-old pitcher had torn the ulnar collateral ligament. Pitchers had suffered this arm injury before, and it was considered a career-ending impairment. "You have to understand," Jobe told Emmons, "there was no known procedure to fix something like that. But Tommy told me, 'You've got to do something. I don't care what it is, but fix me.'"

John's determination to get back on the mound inspired Jobe to study the problem. The injury had never been fixed before. Such an injury had ended Dodger star Sandy Koufax's career in 1966. Jobe launched an investigation into the problem. He read books and medical journals and consulted with surgical specialists, and he knew surgeons had been successful in relocating tendons following a hand injury. Jobe himself had reinforced damaged

joints on polio victims by moving tendons. No one had ever done it with an elbow.

Jobe described the procedure to John, how he might be able to take a tendon from John's forearm and graft it into his pitching elbow. However, Jobe told John that the odds of the tendon transplant surgery working were slim to none. Despite the projected outlook, John wanted to proceed. Jobe performed the surgery on September 25, 1974. During the procedure, Jobe cut a six-inch tendon from John's right forearm. He also drilled holes into the largest two bones in John's left elbow, the ulna and humerus bones. Then he laced the tendon through the holes. He hypothesized that the tendon, if it took, would be able to support the joint just as the torn ligament had previously.

Initially, the outcome looked grim. John suffered numbness in his little finger and ring finger, which lingered several weeks after the surgery. A few months later, the situation was worse. His hand had begun to curl and the arm to atrophy. Jobe decided to perform another surgery, this one aimed at shifting the ulnar nerve to the back of the arm so it would not be "stretched" so far when the arm was in use. After the second surgery, John's arm improved and he was able to rebuild the muscles in both the arm and hand.

John worked through more than a year of rehabilitation under Jobe's care. He returned to baseball and won his first post-operative game on April 26, 1976. He had a 10-win season in 1976 and the surgery extended his career by an additional 14 seasons. He went on to play for the Yankees and never had trouble with the arm again. During his post-operative career, John had three 20-win seasons. In sum, he racked up 288 victories in his 26-year pitching career, with 164 coming after the surgery.

Kept Players on the Field

Two years after John's successful surgery, San Diego Padres pitcher Brent Strom sought out Jobe for a consultation on his persistent elbow pain. Strom became the second patient to have the procedure. The surgery added three more years and 20 victories to his career. Jobe never called it "Tommy John" surgery, but the name stuck. Technically, the procedure is called ulnar collateral ligament reconstruction surgery using the palmaris longus tendon. In the ensuing years, Jobe perfected the surgery and rehabilitation process.

By 2013, more than 1,000 baseball players had had the surgery. Most were pitchers. In 2013, ESPN studied Tommy John surgery and found that of all active pitchers, 124 of them had undergone the surgery at some point in their career. Some of baseball's biggest names have had the tendon transplant surgery, including pitchers Chris Carpenter, John Lackey, Francisco Liriano, John Smoltz, Stephen Strasburg, and Adam Wainwright. A 2014 study published in the *American Journal of Sports Medicine* found that of 179 pitchers who had the surgery, 83 percent returned to pitching in the major leagues.

In 1990, Jobe performed another groundbreaking procedure, this one on Dodgers pitcher Orel Hershiser, who suffered extensive cartilage damage in his right shoulder. Jobe rebuilt the shoulder by reconstructing the anterior capsule and tightening the ligaments. Jobe had performed a similar surgery before, but never on an athlete who relied on the shoulder. Before the Hershiser procedure, the surgery was done by drilling several holes and threading numerous sutures through the joint, which severely damaged the muscles. Jobe knew Hershiser would never pitch again with muscle damage, so he modified the surgery by separating Hershiser's muscle tendon to gain access to the shoulder joint and securing a toggle bolt to anchor the joint. The revolutionary operation extended Hershiser's career another decade and has been used on others.

Besides changing the lives of Major League pitchers, Jobe's surgeries affected the medical landscape as well. Jobe and Kerlan are often referred to as "the fathers of orthopedic medicine." Orthopedic surgeon James Andrews went on to become a big name in sports medicine, conducting reconstructive surgeries on high-profile sports figures. Andrews credited Jobe with revolutionizing sports medicine. "People [who] had elbow problems from pitching—sports medicine did not include any real treatment for them," Andrews told Jonah Keri of *Investor's Business Daily*. "Jobe initiated all of the things that have happened since then that have made elbow injuries both commonly recognized and treatable."

Launched Biomechanics Laboratory

Working with injured players inspired Jobe to pursue advancements in sports medicine. In 1979, he helped launch a biomechanics laboratory at Centinela Hospital Medical Center in Inglewood. One of the first studies he conducted there involved pitchers and rotator cuffs. The study involved placing electrodes in the arm muscle and taking pictures at hundreds of frames per second as a pitcher threw a ball. In this way, the team of researchers could conduct a motion analysis to see which parts of the arm were active at each point in a pitch. Jobe used the information to design exercises aimed at preventing rotator cuff injuries.

Later body-motion studies at the biomechanics lab involved running, tennis and swimming. Researchers at the lab used the data to develop exercise programs to prevent injuries. They also explored rehabilitation. Over the years, Jobe used his research to publish several books, including *The Official Little League Fitness Guide* (1984); *Thirty Exercises for Better Golf* (1986); *Operative Techniques in Upper Extremity Sports Injuries* (1995); and *Athletic*

Forever: The Kerlan Jobe Orthopedic Clinic Plan for Lifetime Fitness (1999). In total, he wrote 140 articles, seven books, and 24 professional book chapters on sports medicine and rehabilitation.

In addition, he worked as a clinical professor at the University of Southern California School of Medicine. He served as chairman of the American Orthopaedic Society for Sports Medicine, president of the Major League Baseball Physicians Association and was a diplomate of the American Board of Orthopedic Surgeons. Jobe also served as medical director of the PGA Tour and Senior PGA Tour and continued as a medical advisor to the Dodgers.

Jobe died on March 6, 2014, in Santa Monica, California. He left behind his wife of 54 years, Beverly (Anderson) Jobe, and sons Christopher, Meredith, Cameron, and Blair. Christopher Jobe followed his father into orthopedic surgery. The day after Jobe's death, Tommy John appeared on National Public Radio's *All Things Considered* to discuss the surgeon and the career-saving surgery that now carries John's name. The former pitcher told NPR's Melissa Block that Jobe was humble and mild-mannered. "He's not braggadocios. It's not 'I, I, I, me, me, me.'" John went on to say that he had once complimented Jobe on being a great surgeon but was rebuffed by Jobe, who replied, "'You know, really, I'm not a great surgeon.' He said, 'I'm kind of an average surgeon but I just have the best patients in the world, which makes me look like I'm a good surgeon.'"

Periodicals

Greensboro News & Record (NC), April 19, 2014.
Investor's Business Daily, April 16, 2009.
Los Angeles Times, June 30, 1991; March 7, 2014; March 8, 2014.
Orange County Register, September 21, 1999.
Washington Post, March 8, 2014.

Online

"Frank Wilson Jobe, M.D.," *Los Angeles Times,* http://www.legacy.com/obituaries/latimes/obituary.aspx?pid=170154737 (December 16, 2014).
"Tommy John Remembers Dr. Jobe, 'One of the Greatest Surgeons,'" NPR, http://www.npr.org/blogs/thetwo-way/2014/03/07/287291739/tommy-john-remembers-dr-jobe-one-of-the-greatest-surgeons (December 16, 2014).□

K

Ahmad Tejan Kabbah

Elected to two terms as president of Sierra Leone, Amhad Tejan Kabbah (1932–2014) was widely credited with bringing peace to the country after a long, destructive civil war. The first Muslim president of his country, Kabbah also was a trained barrister and spent two decades working for the United Nations Development Programme.

Amhad Tejan Kabbah was born on February 16, 1932, in the eastern Sierra Leonean city of Pendembu. He was the son of Abu Bakr Sidique Kabbah. His father was a businessman and trader who was ethnically a Mandingo. His mother was Mende and from a locally prominent family, the Coomber of the Mandu chiefdom. Both of his parents were Muslim.

Educated in Britain

Raised primarily in Sierra Leone's capital city of Freetown, Kabbah attended a Catholic secondary school, St. Edward's. For his higher education, Kabbah moved to Great Britain to attend the Cardiff College of Technology and Commerce, then the University of Wales, Aberystwyth. He earned his economics degree in 1959 from the latter institution.

Returning to Sierra Leone after graduation, he joined the civil service of the colonial British government still ruling the country. He began as a district commissioner. In 1961, Kabbah's country achieved independence from Great Britain. Because of his education, qualifications, and affiliation with the ruling Sierra Leone People's Party, he rose quickly in the ranks of the newly independent country's civil service. In 1962, he became a district commissioner, and by 1965,

he was the deputy permanent secretary at the Ministry of Trade and Industry. Kabbah was the youngest secretary to ever hold this post.

During his time in the latter post, Kabbah played a role in an event that would prove controversial in retrospect. When the Sierra Leone Produce Marketing Board was considering the purchase of a palm kernel oil mill and refinery, Kabbah advised that multiple vendors should be considered and costs compared. Ultimately, Kabbah's advice was ignored and an oil mill and refinery were purchased from a favored party at an extremely high price. When a commission of inquiry was called several years later, Kabbah was considered complacent in the deal. His property, including a house and land in Freetown, were seized and not returned until 1988.

Lived Abroad

After a military coup in 1967 and Sierra Leone People's Party losing elections in 1968, Kabbah was dismissed from his civil service position. As the All People's Congress party and prime minister Siaka Stevens took power, all of Kabbah's property was confiscated. Kabbah then returned to Great Britain. There, he studied law and was called to the bar at Gray's Inn in London in 1969. He briefly took up a new profession, barrister.

In 1970, Kabbah took on new challenges when he became employed by the United Nations Development Program (UNDP). The UNDP focuses on nation building and growth, poverty reduction, crisis prevention, sustainable development, and improving the quality of life. It works primarily in developing countries.

Spending more than two decades with UNDP, Kabbah first helmed operations in such African countries as Lesotho, Tanzania, Uganda, and Zimbabwe. He was later based

GEORGES GOBET/AFP/Getty Images

in the UNDP headquarters in New York City, and was the head of the Eastern and Southern African Division. He was directly responsible for the UNDP's work with liberation movements such as the African National Congress. Finally, Kabbah held senior administrative positions.

In Kabbah's home country, a civil war began in 1991 ignited by growing unrest in nearby Liberia. At that time, a rebel group, the Revolutionary United Front (RUF), challenged those in power and began a murderous insurrection. The group was helmed by Foday Sankoh, who had been trained by the regime of Colonel Muammar Gaddafi and backed by Liberian rebel leader Charles Taylor. RUF soon controlled much of the eastern Sierra Leone, which was rich in mineral wealth. By April 1992, Valentine Strasser oversaw a coup of the one-party dictatorship of Joseph Momoh in Freetown, while the RUF continued to rebel.

Returned to Sierra Leone

After retiring from the United Nations in 1992, Kabbah returned to Sierra Leone. He soon became involved in politics. He became the chairman and president of the National Advisory Council that had been organized by a military junta to ensure a return to constitutional rule, including multiparty politics and a new constitution. The political situation continued to intensify.

By early 1996, Strasser was overthrown, and elections were held for the first time in 23 years. Kabbah ran for president as the candidate for the Sierra Leone People's Party. Despite problematic voting in parts of Sierra Leone, elections continued. Kabbah was formally elected president in March 1996 after two rounds of voting. He gained nearly 60 percent of the vote.

When Kabbah took office, he was the first Muslim president of Sierra Leone. He immediately instituted a policy of inclusion, and his administration included representatives from the primarily political groups in the country. He also promised to end the still on-going civil war, which had resulted in so many deaths, created many refugees, and ruined the country's economy. This proved challenging, as another coup attempt occurred in September 1996. Those participating in the coup tried to put Major Johnny Paul Koroma in office. The coup failed, however, and Koroma was detained.

Forced Out by Rebels

Nine months after the election, the rebel leader, Sankoh, and Kabbah signed a peace accord in Abidjan, Ivory Coast. Stability was short-lived, however. Kabbah was overthrown in a coup led by rebels from the Sierra Leonean army, the Armed Forces Ruling Council, in May 1997, and he went into exile in nearby Guinea with the assistance of Ecomog. (Ecomog was a monitoring group of the Economic Community of West African States.)

A new junta took power in Sierra Leone, and it named Koroma the head of the Sierra Leonean government. This new group was aligned with the RUF. RUF gained further support when Taylor moved from rebel leader to elected president of nearby Liberia in 1997.

Fighting became intense over the next few years, but Kabbah gained wide diplomatic support at events like the Edinburg Commonwealth summit. Nigeria, the dominant country in Africa, also wanted his return, and acted with the diplomatic and logistical support of Great Britain. It was not until February 1998 that troops under Ecomog and backed by Nigerian leader Sani Abacha forced the new junta out of Freetown, and put Kabbah back into office, though he only controlled a small part of Sierra Leone around the capital. Rebels regrouped and paired with rebellious Sierra Leonean soldiers, attacked Freetown in January 1999.

Because the Nigerian and Ecomog troops were unable to fully defeat RUF, a new peace accord was signed by Kabbah and Sankoh in July 1999. This United Nations-sponsored treaty including power sharing, with RUF having a minority stake in a coalition government. Sankoh was given a minister's post.

As part of the treaty, soldiers from Ecomog were replaced by peacekeeping troops under the command of the United Nations. Sankoh gained more and more power, refusing to disarm or give up the areas it occupied. In May 2000, the Revolutionary United Front broke the accord and took 500 peacekeepers hostage. The escalation of the ongoing crisis compelled Great Britain to take action.

End to Civil War

While the United Nations increased its military force, British prime minister Tony Blair sent in British armed forces.

Though he publicly stated that the troops were needed to evacuate citizens of the United Kingdom, in reality they were there to quell the conflict. Over the next 18 months, a joint operation of the United Kingdom and the United Nations—with 17,000 foreign troops—worked to defeat Sankoh and the RUF.

The civil war was declared officially ended in January 2002. During the 11-year-long conflict, more than 50,000 people—mostly civilians—lost their lives. After Sankoh was imprisoned, Kabbah remained in power. When the war was brought to an end, Kabbah began a program to disarm the rebels and others involved in the conflict. This program was put into practice with the help of a United Nations peace-keeping force and military trainers from Great Britain.

Elected to Second Term

Elections were held again four short months later in 2002, and Kabbah was elected to his second five-year term as president with more than 70 percent of the vote. He defeated Ernest Bai Koroma of the APC (All Peoples' Congress). Though Kabbah was popular and widely respected, he was unable to eradicate hunger or poverty in his country.

By the end of Kabbah's second term, Sierra Leone remained quite impoverished, with the capital lacking electricity for at least two years and clean water for several more. He received criticism for failing to enact programs to lift the country and its people out of its economic straits. He was also accused of ignoring widespread corruption within his government. Yet, Kabbah did set up key governmental institutions in his second term. They included an Anti-Corruption Commission, and a National Revenue Authority. He also founded the Truth and Reconciliation Commission and the National Revue Authority. In addition, he sponsored laws that supported gender equality and protected children. Kabbah's intentions and actions were impressive enough that major creditors like the World Bank wrote off 90 percent of its foreign debt at the end of 2006.

Oversaw Power Transition

In 2007, Kabbah left office, unable to seek a third term because of constitutional limits. His opponent in the 2002 elections, Koroma, won the office, over Kabbah's vice president and his preferred successor, Solomon Berewa. Kabbah ensured a smooth transition out of power for his political power, without war or major conflict, though subsequent governments downgraded or got rid of some of his reforms. He later had to address rumors that he did not support Berewa, which he denied to Lansana Gberie of the *New African*. Kabbah stated, "I have kept quiet about these rumours. But the idea that I did not vote for my own party, that I did not support someone I nominated to succeed me, is simply outrageous."

When Kabbah departed the presidency, he was considered one of the most prominent and highly educated leaders in Africa of his generation. In this realm, the major criticism of Kabbah came from his lack of personal charisma. It was believed to have prevented him from becoming a transcendent statesman for the continent.

Published Memoir

After he left office, Kabbah lived quietly in his mansion in the far west-end of Freetown. He did some international work such as monitoring Kenyan elections as a representative of the African Union. Kabbah also monitored elections in Zimbabwe under similar circumstances. Additionally, he focused on writing his memoir. It was published in 2010 under the title *Coming Back from the Brink in Sierra Leone* by a Ghanaian publisher, EPP Books Services.

Kabbah died at his home in Freetown, Sierra Leone, on March 14, 2014. He was 82 years old. Lans Gberie of the *New African*, concluded of Kabbah, "though not at all a great man, Kabbah is (aside from Milton Margai, the country's first prime minister) without doubt the most successful as well as the most personable, leader Sierra Leone has had in five decades of independence."

Periodicals

Daily Telegraph (London, England), March 21, 2014.
Guardian (London, England), June 7, 2014.
New African, July 2009; February 2012.
New York Times, March 20, 2014.
Times (London, England), March 17, 2014.☐

Pauline Kael

American film critic Pauline Kael (1919–2001) spent more than two decades at the *New Yorker* writing highly controversial yet influential reviews of movies, actors and directors. Widely read, she was a pioneer in the art and craft of film criticism and the first to move away from objectivity, instead using a subjective lens and imposing her own personality into her writing.

"She had an enormous impact on a whole generation of critics," noted film reviewer David Denby, who followed Kael's work at the *New Yorker*. Denby explained Kael's far-reaching influence to *Los Angeles Times* writer Elaine Woo shortly after Kael died in 2001. "She opened a lot of doors to different ways of writing about movies. There was no simple set of rules for her. You had to respond with everything you had, not just what you knew about movies but what you knew about painting, literature, life, other people. That was what made the writing so three-dimensional, so engaging. People felt a need to argue with it, to rethink it themselves. She was enormously provocative in that way."

Raised in Rural California

Pauline Kael was born on June 19, 1919, at Petaluma General Hospital in California. Her parents were Polish immigrants, born and raised in Pruszków. Her father, Isaac Kael, immigrated to the United States in 1903, while her mother, Judith "Yetta" (Friedman) Kael followed two years later.

Everett Collection Inc/Alamy

Initially, the family settled in New York City, in a dirty, desolate, poverty-stricken neighborhood. In 1912, they headed to California after discovering that Petaluma had a large contingent of Jewish poultry farmers. The Kaels figured it would be easier to feed their family while operating a farm. They settled on a nine-acre plot just west of town, bought a flock of white Leghorns and entered the poultry business. By 1919, the family had grown to include five children. Pauline Kael was the last child born into the family.

From all accounts, Judith Kael despised farm life, was frequently unhappy and failed to form close relationships with her children. She had enjoyed a privileged upbringing in Poland and was frequently irritated by the dirty, back-breaking farm work. According to biographer Brian Kellow, author of *Pauline Kael: A Life in the Dark,* one of Kael's grandsons pronounced that his grandmother was someone whose "affection radiated at about two degrees above absolute zero."

Young Pauline learned to read early on. She spent her childhood devouring books and listening to discussions at the Jewish Community Center of Petaluma, which her father helped found. Though the area teemed with farmers, they were intellectuals, idealists and Zionists who came to the area to escape city life. Members of the community read and discussed Yiddish books and newspapers. Kael spent her formative years absorbing everything she could in this culture of learning. By 1928, the Kael farm had grown

to 25,000 chickens and the Kaels were well off. Isaac Kael, however, misplayed the stock market and lost the farm.

The family moved to San Francisco and Kael attended San Francisco Girls' High School. She played violin in the orchestra and participated on the debate team. As a teen, she lost herself in movies, watching the latest films at local picture palaces like the Fox, the Castro and the Roxie. She preferred the Ritz Brothers to the Marx Brothers and enjoyed films featuring Bette Davis, Katherine Hepburn, and Barbara Stanwyck.

Struggled to Find Way

Kael graduated from high school in 1936. She enrolled at the University of California at Berkeley as a philosophy major after earning an alumni-sponsored scholarship. Initially, she thought she would study philosophy and go to law school, but she became romantically involved with a fellow student and poet named Robert Horan. Spending time with Horan piqued Kael's interest in writing. Despite her fantastic grades, she left Berkeley a few credits shy of her degree and moved in with Horan. The two began writing essays together, hoping to sell them to literary magazines. In November of 1941, they hitchhiked to New York and arrived so broke they were forced to squat at Grand Central Station. Horan soon broke into New York's artistic circles and left Kael behind. After a stint as a governess, Kael gave up the struggle and went back to San Francisco to live with her mother.

Back in California, Kael fell in with an avant-garde literary circle. During the mid-1940s, artists flocked to San Francisco, which was becoming a bohemian center for writers and poets. Kael befriended poet James Broughton, who was known to take both male and female lovers. Kael did some minor production work for Broughton's 1948 experimental film *Mother's Day.* Their relationship quickly ended after Kael became pregnant. Kael moved to Santa Barbara and gave birth to Gina James on September 21, 1948. The birth certificate listed "Lionel James," a writer, as the baby's father and "Mrs. Pauline James" as the mother. Kael struggled financially, getting by with help from her sister and writing book reviews for the *Santa Barbara Star.* Eventually, she moved back to San Francisco and continued writing movie scripts and plays but struggled to sell them. To make ends meet, she tutored students, ran a laundry business and landed the occasional ghostwriting assignment.

Kael's first big break came in 1952, while she was sitting in a Berkeley coffeehouse discussing some recent films with a friend. *City Lights* founder Peter Martin sat nearby and listened in on the conversation. Impressed with Kael's banter and insight, he asked Kael if she would be interested in writing a review of Charlie Chaplin's new movie. In this first-ever published review by Kael, she showed a unique inclination to be scorchingly direct. Kael panned the film, titled *Limelight,* and titled her review "Slimelight," deriding the sentimental self-aggrandizement displayed by Chaplin's character.

Around 1955, Kael became a contributing film critic to Berkeley's KPFA-FM. The position did not pay, but offered Kael exposure, and she was soon contacted by Ed Landberg, owner and operator of the Cinema Guild and Studio, a Berkeley-based twin cinema. The Cinema Guild was one of the first repertory theaters in the United States. It presented foreign films with more serious topics than Hollywood covered at the time. After falling in with Landberg, Kael began writing the program notes for the Cinema Guild. The notes, complete with a calendar, pictures and descriptions of upcoming films, were mailed out to theater-goers and made available at local businesses. Kael's notes became popular and increased theater attendance. Kael eventually married Landberg and took over theater operations. The marriage, however, was based more on mutual interests than love, and the couple divorced after about a year.

Published Film Commentary

Through the 1950s and '60s, Kael continued her film commentary by contributing to periodicals such as *Film Quarterly, Kulchur, Moviegoer, Partisan Review,* and *Sight and Sound.* She worked incessantly, setting up a movie screen in her house so she could view 16mm films. According to Kael biographer Kellow, Kael often stayed up late at night, writing and watching movies with a cigarette in one hand and a shot of Wild Turkey in the other. Though she sold countless articles, they paid poorly. *Kulcher* paid about $2 per thousand words. "It was impossible to make a living at the kind of writing I was doing, particularly because I was on the West Coast, and when I got assignments from magazines and papers in New York, they would often reject what I wrote and not pay me any kill fee, because I was across the country and unlikely to bump into them," Kael told Francis Davis, author of *Afterglow: A Last Conversation with Pauline Kael.*

Kael broke into the limelight with 1965's *I Lost It At the Movies.* The book included reprints of movie reviews she had created between 1954 and 1965 (from both print and radio), as well as polemical essays in which she slammed analyses made by other critics. Reviewers panned the book for its breezy language and nonacademic, personal slant. However, the book propelled Kael to the forefront of American journalism. In the early 1960s, it was considered improper for reporters to impose their own personalities on a review. Kael turned that rule on its head.

Following the success of *I Lost It At the Movies,* Kael moved to New York and received lucrative assignments at the *Atlantic Monthly, Life,* and *New Republic.* She became a regular columnist at *McCall's* in 1966. The relationship was short-lived, as Kael was let go a few months later after criticizing *The Sound of Music.* According to Kellow, Kael's review called the movie a "sugarcoated lie that people seem to want to eat." Kael continued to pan popular films and was dismissed by the mass-audience magazine whose readers did not appreciate her perspective.

In 1967, Kael sold a defining essay to the *New Yorker,* a 7,000-word piece on *Bonnie and Clyde* and its relation to pop culture and the social climate. Many critics had condemned the film for glorifying bloodshed and crime. According to Kellow, in the essay, Kael wrote, "*Bonnie and Clyde* is the most excitingly American movie since *The Manchurian Candidate.* The audience is alive to it." She found the film to be a breath of fresh air in a

Hollywood era punctuated by few risks and populated by studios pandering to the mainstream. Kael felt the film was "real" in that it made viewers confront death in a way most films glossed over. Other critics had expressed her sentiment that American movies had typically failed to depict violence in graphic ways. She wrote, "The whole point of *Bonnie and Clyde* is to rub our noses in it, to make us pay our dues for laughing. The dirty reality of death—not suggestions but blood and holes—is necessary."

Joined *New Yorker* Staff

The *New Yorker* hired Kael as its chief film critic beginning in 1968. For the next 12 years, Kael would spend six months a year writing for the magazine, then head off to UCLA or other academic milieu to teach. With her film column at the *New Yorker,* Kael elevated the movie review as a form of literature with the capacity for social commentary. She left in 1979 to work briefly in Hollywood, hoping to shape the movie industry. However, she soon returned to the East Coast after a disastrous and humbling experience as a consultant with Paramount Pictures. She resumed her column with the *New Yorker* in 1980 and remained there until 1991.

During her years at the magazine, Kael earned a reputation for her acerbic tone. She was loved and loathed with equal measure. During the 1970s, Kael lauded Francis Ford Coppola's *The Godfather* (1972), Martin Scorsese's *Mean Streets* (1973), and *Taxi Driver* (1976). She loved Hal Ashby's *Shampoo* (1975), as well as Steven Spielberg's *Jaws* (1975) and Philip Kaufman's *Invasion of the Body Snatchers* (1978).

She was less enthusiastic about the highly popular Steve McQueen/Paul Newman action movie, *The Towering Inferno.* According to the *Daily Telegraph* Kael derided the film for being a misfire with good intentions, writing, "This movie has opened just in time to capture the Dumb Whore Award of 1974." Kael was equally underwhelmed by 1983's *Return of the Jedi.* According to the *Boston Globe's* Mark Feeney, Kael was frustrated with the commercial tie-ins. "If a filmmaker wants backing for a new project, there'd better be a video game in it. Producers are putting so much action and so little character or point into their movies that there's nothing for a viewer to latch on to. The battle between good and evil, which is the theme of just about every big fantasy adventure film, has become a flabby excuse for a lot of dumb tricks and noise." Lucas, in his turn, named a villain in 1988's *Willow* General Kael as an affront to the critic.

Kael left the *New Yorker* in 1991 as her struggle with Parkinson's disease escalated. Over her lifetime, Kael published collections of her work in several books, including *Kiss Kiss Bang Bang* (1968), *Reeling* (1976), and *Movie Love* (1991). *Deeper into Movies* (1973) was a National Book Award winner. A 1999 survey conducted by New York University ranked Kael's 1969 essay "Trash, Art and the Movies" as the 42nd best piece of journalism of the century on a list of the top 100. The piece originally appeared in *Harper's.* Kael died September 3, 2001, at her home in Great Barrington, Massachusetts.

Books

Davis, Francis, *Afterglow: A Last Conversation with Pauline Kael,* Da Capo Press, 2002.
Kellow, Brian, *Pauline Kael: A Life in the Dark,* Viking, 2011.

Periodicals

Boston Globe, September 4, 2001.
Daily Telegraph (London, England), September 5, 2001.
Los Angeles Times, September 4, 2001.
New York Times, September 4, 2001. □

Bob Kane

American comic book artist Bob Kane (1915–1998) is the legal, official creator of the popular superhero, Batman, as well as other cartoon characters and comic strips. Though the extent of Kane's role in creating Batman and the early Batman comics is disputed, Kane remained the public face of Batman's creation until his death in 1998.

AP Images/Anonymous

Bob Kane was born Robert Khan on October 24, 1915, in New York City. His family was Jewish and creative, with his father employed as an engraver and printer for a newspaper. Raised in a tough neighborhood in the Bronx, he was part of a childhood gang, the Crusading Zorros, and was once severely injured when a rival outfit beat him. In addition to losing several teeth and breaking his arm, they crushed his knuckles on his right hand, which was his drawing hand.

Had Early Interest in Drawing

From an early age, Kane loved to draw. His family, however, was concerned that Kane would not have much of a future despite his obvious talent. During summers, the teenaged Kane was sent to live with his uncle's family in Shrewsbury and work in his snack bar so that he might gain a work ethic. Kane remained more interested in drawing and cartoons. He attended DeWitt Clinton High School, and learned to draw in the film studios of Max Fleischer. Kane was also educated at the Cooper Union and Art Students League. Early in his career, he worked on animated cartoons featuring the character Betty Boop.

By 1936, Kane was making a living as a cartoonist. His early focus included funny comic strips like *Peter Pupp,* created for Eiser/Iger Studio, owned partially by cartoonist/agent Bob Iger. At the heart of this strip was a doggy hero with a sidekick named Tinymite. They had adventures like going to the moon and fighting Zula, the ruler of lunar men. Kane was paid five dollars per page to create *Peter Pupp.* For the same company, Kane also drew *Jest Laffs.*

Then, for *Circus Comics,* Kane created *Van Bagger* and *Side Streets of New York.* Moving on to National Periodical Publications (later and better known as DC Comics) on a fill-in basis, Kane's output continued to focus on humor. In

addition to fillers, he drew *Rusty and His Pals* and *Clip Carson* beginning in 1938. By this point, Kane was under exclusive contract with National.

Created Batman

In 1939, Kane was approached by an editor at National, Vincent Sullivan, to devise a new superhero along the lines of Superman, a newly popular superhero created for DC a year earlier. When coming up with the character who would become known as Batman, Kane drew on several influences, including a drawing by Leonardo da Vinci of a human-operated flying machine in a type of glider. In a book read by Kane of the artists' note-books, da Vinci included a quote, "Your bird shall have no other model but that of a bat." Kane read the book when he was 13 years old and never forgot the image. Another primary influence was a film featuring Douglas Fairbanks, Sr., *The Mark of Zorro* (1920), in which his Zorro was a count by day and a crime fighter at night. Other sources of inspiration included the radio program *The Shadow* and a 1930 film *The Bat Whispers* about a criminal with a bat insignia.

When appearing on the National Public Radio program *Fresh Air* years later, Kane explained to host Terry Gross, "I didn't want to emulate Superman and imitate it because I thought maybe they wouldn't want that. And I wanted to come up with something original . . . I felt that every person who doesn't have superpowers could relate to

Batman a lot easier than they could to Superman. In other words, you didn't have to come from another planet to be a superhero . . . ''

As originally conceived by Kane, the Bat-man, as the character was originally called, wore a domino mask, and had rigid batwings on his arms. His costume was bright red with black wings and trunks. Batman's mask was an homage to Zorro, who wore a mask to hide his identity. Bruce Wayne, Batman's real world identity, was an alliteration of Kane's name, and who he wanted to be in his daydreams. Kane asked fellow DeWitt Clinton graduate Milton ''Bill'' Finger to help him with the Batman, as Finger was starting his own career as a comic book writer and sometimes artist. Finger had already worked with Kane on *Rusty and Pals* and *Clip Carson.*

Collaborated with Finger

How the pair exactly developed the Batman as he is known today is unclear, but it is certain that Finger played a much larger role than Kane initially gave him credit for. Finger was the co-creator of Batman, despite Kane telling DC Comics that it was solely his idea and later legally claiming the title of creator. Initially meeting in New York's Edgar Allan Poe Park to collaborate on Batman comics, Kane wanted to make Batman as a vigilante with a violent streak. Batman debuted in *Detective Comics* issue 37 (1939) and *Batman #1* (1940) featured such a Batman, one who killed his enemies with an automatic pistol and machine guns.

When DC Comics stated it would not allow Batman to have firearms or kill anyone again, Finger brought a pulp detective magazine perspective to the Batman story. Finger made the sanitized Batman more of a private investigator dealing with a mystery and working with the law to some degree. Finger also developed many of the other aspects of Batman for which Kane took credit, including Batman's costume, Dick Grayson/Robin, the name of Gotham City, the Batcave, Batman's origin story, the Batman gadgets, and many of the villains like Catwoman. Though Finger was a writer, he also played a significant role in the comic's visual aspects as well. Kane contributed to the visual development as well—it was Kane who brought the dark images inspired by 1920s German Expressionism to the comic, among other concepts—but took credit for all of Finger's ideas.

Along with business acumen and a penchant for the business, Kane was a stronger assertive personality, while Finger was more passive, modest, and concerned about keeping his job. At first, when Kane presented his work to DC Comics, he claimed to have completed all the work, though Finger wrote or co-wrote the comics and Kane employed a number of ghost artists as well. As Marc Tyler Nobleman, the author of *Bill: The Boy Wonder: The Secret Co-Creator of Batman,* told *Premium Official News,* ''I talked to a lot of people who knew Bob and Bill personally. And none of them—literally none—framed Bob's legacy in a positive light, to put it delicately. I feel he did something that was hugely unethical. He started it when that 'type of practice' was rampant, when lots of people were taking credit for other people's work—it was just part of the relationship that writers and artists had in the day.''

Relied on Ghost Artists

By 1941, DC Comics learned of the situation and hired Finger away. Between 1941 and 1947, Kane used his assistant, Jerry Robinson, whom he had hired as a 17 year old in 1939, on Batman. Robinson only inked Kane's pencil drawings at first. Later, Robinson moved into drawing and inking his own stories for the comic. While Kane kept a more cartoon-like visual style, Robinson made the comic more polished before leaving in 1947 to work on other projects.

Kane himself had stopped drawing Batman comic books by 1943, to focus on illustrating the daily newspaper strip featuring Batman. Ghost writers and artists kept the comic book franchise going. He also tried to serve in World War II. He enlisted in the Navy after Pearl Harbor, but childhood injuries to his arm and hands prevented him from serving. After World War II, Kane resumed drawing the comic books again. At the same time, he again hired many ghost artists to work on the comic. By 1953, when Shelly Moldoff became the ghost illustrator of Batman, Kane essentially stopped drawing the comic.

Kane moved into television in the 1960s. He created an animated cartoon series, *Courageous Cat and Minute Mouse.* In 1966, when the campy television series *Batman* began airing, Kane gained even more fame as well as financial rewards because of his role as Batman's creator. He also became something of a celebrity during this period.

Signed Buy-Out with DC Comics

In 1967, Kane solidified the legal link between his name and the creation of Batman. That year, DC Comic gave him a buy-out deal worth millions of dollars. As part of the agreement, his name had to be credited as the creator of Batman on every Batman story. This aspect of the deal may have been agreed upon by both parties as early as 1946 before becoming part of a legal contract. After this deal was signed, Kane did not produce any more Batman-related art.

Publicly, many believed as they had for many years, that Kane was the sole creator of Batman. This illusion began to be shattered in the mid-1960s when Finger appeared at a comic convention and quietly stated his role in creating Batman. When an article summarizing Finger's appearance was printed in a fanzine in 1965, Kane responded with his own assertations that Finger played no role in Batman's development and made Finger seem like a liar. Later in life, Kane would publicly change this perspective.

In 1989, Kane published his autobiography, *Batman & Me.* In the book, Kane finally admitted that Finger had played a major role in Batman's development and had never received the credit he deserved. Kane stated that he wished he could go back and give Finger a byline.

Consulted on Batman Films

That year, Kane also became involved with the *Batman* films, serving as a consultant on several Batman projects. The first, *Batman,* was directed by Tim Burton and starred Michael Keaton as Batman. When the 1995 film *Batman Forever* came out, Kane again took overriding credit for Batman, telling Andy Seiler of *USA Today,* ''Imitation is the sincerest form of flattery. The main thing is that my name will go down as the creator and all the ghostwriters are forgotten. My imprint is left on the sands of time, and I'm very proud of that."

Still creative in the last decade of his life, Kane had been working on a screenplay featuring a new superhero under the working name Silver Fox when he died on November 3, 1998, in Los Angeles, California. At the time of his death, Batman remained one of the oldest comic book characters in continual production, along with Superman and Wonder Woman. Between 1940 and 1998, at least one new Batman comic was produced monthly.

Though Kane was remembered primarily for Batman, other characters created by Kane were memorable such as Courageous Cat, Minute Mouse, and Cool McCool. The president and editor in chief of DC Comics, Jenette Kahn, told Martin Wainwright of the London *Guardian*, "Bob Kane was a giant in the field of popular culture, one of a handful of people who launched the comic book industry and gave the world a group of characters so colourful and inventive that they continue to captivate every new generation."

Books

Icons of the American Comic Book: From Captain America to Wonder Woman, edited by Randy Duncan and Matthew J. Smith, Greenwood Press, 2013.

Periodicals

Associated Press State & Local Wire, November 6, 1998.
Guardian (London, England), November 7, 1998.
Independent (London, England), November 9, 1998.
National Post, February 7, 2014.
New York Times, November 7, 1998.
Premium Official News, November 6, 2012.
Telegram & Gazette (MA), July 21, 2014.

Transcripts

Fresh Air, National Public Radio, June 17, 2005. □

Jan Karski

Polish diplomat Jan Karski (1914–2000) risked his life on clandestine missions inside Nazi-occupied Poland during World War II. His eyewitness accounts served as the first reliable reports of Nazi genocide to reach the outside world. "I know that many people will not believe me, will not be able to believe me, will think I exaggerate or invent," Karski wrote in his 1944 book *Story of a Secret State: My Report to the World.* "But I saw it and it is not exaggerated or invented."

Jan Karski was born Jan Kozielewski in Łódź, a large city of majority-Polish population that at the time of his birth in 1914 was situated inside the Russian Empire. Two years later Łódź was returned to Polish self-rule and remained so until September of 1939, when Nazi Germany

Agencja Fotograficza

invaded Poland. "Karski" was a name he used later in his career as an undercover operative during the war.

The last of eight children, Karski was raised in a prosperous household and in the Roman Catholic faith. His father had a leather-goods manufacturing company and Karski's older brothers went on to careers with the independent Polish state. In his late teens Karski entered the University of Lwów (in present-day Lviv, Ukraine) to study law and, after graduating in 1935 entered the Polish Army's reserve officer cadet school. He was assigned to an artillery mounted unit that would be called up in the summer of 1939 to defend Poland from the Nazi invasion.

Proved Skilled Eluder

Before that pivotal event, however, Karski worked on a graduate degree in population studies and spent long stretches in Britain, Switzerland, and Germany conducting library research. His Polish Army regiment was called up in late August of 1939 and Karski was assigned to defend territory near Oświecim (Auschwitz). The unit was surprised to discover hostile Red Army units of the Soviet Union, which had invaded Poland from its eastern flank after signing a secret pact with Nazi Germany. Karski's regiment was defeated a few weeks after the start of the war on September 1, 1939.

Karski and his fellow Polish officers were detained as prisoners of war (POWs) by the Soviets and transported to an interment camp in Ukraine, but Karski managed to escape this grim situation by hiding with the non-commissioned soldiers in his unit, who were being sent back to German-held Łódź. It marked the first of several times that Karski eluded capture or escaped military detention. On his way back to Łódź Karski was seized again, this time by German forces, and on that occasion freed himself and a few other POWs by jumping out of a moving train. His survival in late 1939 made him one of a handful of Polish Army officers who escaped capture after World War II erupted; nearly all of those officers taken as POWs were slain in the infamous Katyń Forest massacre of 1940.

Already practiced in eluding military checkpoints and a gifted multilinguist from his recent graduate-school studies, Karski slipped into Nazi-occupied Warsaw to find his brother Marian, a top-ranking police official in the city before the German invasion. Both pledged their loyalties to the underground Polish resistance movement and Karski became a courier for this *Armia Krajowa* (AK), or Home Army. In the early months of 1940 he made his way into France to contact the leaders of the Polish government-in-exile. That journey was made south into Hungary, then across the Balkan states and Italy, and Karski's purpose was to report on conditions endured by Polish civilians in Warsaw, Łódź, and other cities and to request formal assistance for the AK's underground activities. The Polish government-in-exile appointed Karski to a post in its diplomat corps as a courier and envoy.

Botched Suicide Attempt

In the spring of 1940 Karski made a second trip to reach the government-in-exile in France but was betrayed in Slovakia, which by then had become a pro-Nazi puppet state. The German secret police, or Gestapo, subjected him to extreme interrogation tactics and Karski was so fearful that he would betray the names and activities of his fellow resistance fighters under duress that he attempted to commit suicide with a razor blade concealed in his shoe. He survived and learned that France, too, had capitulated to a Nazi invasion force in June of 1940. Hospitalized from his injuries somewhere in German-held Poland, he managed to send a message to the AK, and members of a local resistance cell found his room and persuaded him to jump, unclothed and still weakened from torture and his suicide attempt, from his window in the middle of the night. For several months Karski recuperated while posing as a servant on the estate of a sympathetic Polish landowner.

In 1941 Karski was assigned to work for the AK in the Polish city of Kraków, the seat of the German occupation government. There and in Warsaw later that same year he listened to secret radio broadcasts from London—a grave offense under Nazi occupation law—and disseminated the information gleaned to other members of the resistance movement. The situation in Poland worsened considerably in June of 1941 when the Soviet Union and Nazi Germany turned on one another, opening up a new Eastern Front in the war. Polish civilians lived under the direst of wartime restrictions, rations, and police-state fear, but Poland's sizable Jewish population suffered even worse deprivations. Roughly three million were forcibly relocated to walled-off

"Jewish Quarters" inside Warsaw, Łódź, Kraków, and other major cities after the Nazi invasion.

In 1942 Karski was asked to make another trip across Europe—nearly all of which was by then under German military occupation—to reach leaders of the Polish government-in-exile, who were now based in London. His mission was twofold: the AK asked him to first report on conditions inside Warsaw's Jewish Ghetto, then deliver those findings to senior leaders of the Polish government-in-exile and the British government in England.

Entered Warsaw Ghetto via Tunnel

Karski made plans to slip into the Warsaw Ghetto with the help of Leon Feiner, a leader in Jewish resistance movement inside Poland. Feiner and fellow activists in other Polish ghettoes were concerned about mass deportations of Jews that began in July of 1942. After suffering years of privation inside these barely supplied slums, Jews were ordered to report to railway-station transit points and roundups of the unwilling began in Warsaw and elsewhere. German authorities assured Jews they were to be resettled further east, away from battle lines, and that they would allowed to farm their own land. Yet Jewish leaders, along with AK resistance members, had long heard rumors of enormous internment camps that existed in top-secret locations in Poland and elsewhere in Nazi-occupied lands.

On a prearranged time and place in August of 1942, Karski met with a guide in Warsaw, who gave him shabby clothes to disguise himself inside the Ghetto. They entered the Jewish Quarter through one of the secret basement tunnels that ran between sections. Wearing the Star of David patch required by Nazi occupation law for all Jews, Karski entered a safe house protected by one of the Jewish militia groups working inside the Ghetto. He and Feiner walked outside, and what Karski saw was so shocking he did not trust his recollection and asked to re-enter the Warsaw Ghetto a few days later. On both occasions he saw emaciated, starving Polish Jews lying in the streets, near death or already dead, and hundreds of families waiting at transit points with what was left of their worldly belongings.

Feiner urged Karski to visit one of the camps and helped arrange a subterfuge for him to enter Bełżec, a concentration camp near Lublin. Through a series of underground-network connections and bribes, Karski pretended he was an Estonian national in a borrowed uniform. Estonian men of military-service age were among those recruited by the Nazis to round up Jews for transport and extermination. A bribed Estonian guard accompanied him. "About a mile away from the camp we began to hear shouts, shots, and screams," Karski wrote in *Story of a Secret State.*

Witnessed Horrific Event

Karski and his guide came to fences and entered what was probably a sorting area at Izbica Lubelska, not the actual camp at Bełżec. Even so, the situation was appalling. "The chaos, the squalor, the hideousness of it all was simply indescribable," Karski wrote in his book. "There was a suffocating stench of sweat, filth, decay, damp straw, and excrement." German guards randomly fired into the crowds while ordering detainees to board freight cars whose floor had been covered with quicklime. Karski watched for three hours as 46 train cars were filled with hundreds of Jews, then the doors sealed. "From one end to the other, the train, with its quivering cargo of flesh, seemed to throb, vibrate, rock, and jump as if bewitched," he reported in *Story of a Secret State*. "There would be a strangely uniform momentary lull and then, again, the train would begin to moan and sob, wail and howl." Inside the sealed cars the quicklime reacted with moisture to start a chemical process that dissolved flesh and other organic matter while also emitting noxious fumes. By this method Karski saw the Jews in the train cars both suffocate and burn to death.

At the end of the day Karski managed to return to a safe house near Lublin, slept fitfully, and began vomiting for days as he made his way to London. It took him 21 days to travel from Warsaw to Berlin, then Brussels, and through German-occupied France. After reaching Spain, a neutral country, he was ferried to Gibraltar, a British-held fortress on the Mediterranean Sea. From there he flew to London to meet with the Polish government-in-exile. Concealed on his person was a key that had been soldered so that rolls of microfilm could be tucked inside. The microfilm contained reports from Feiner and resistance-movement operatives inside Poland.

Met with U.S. President

Karski also met with Jewish leaders in London as well as British Foreign Minister Anthony Eden. The microfilm documents became the basis for a report by the Polish government-in-exile's Foreign Minister Edward Raczyński titled *The Mass Extermination of Jews in German Occupied Poland*. Karski then traveled across the Atlantic Ocean to meet with Jewish-refugee groups in the United States. He also discussed the dire situation separately with U.S. President Franklin Roosevelt and U.S. Supreme Court Justice Felix Frankfurter. As in London, in both Washington and New York City, Karski was informed that the Allied effort to defeat Nazi Germany was of primary importance, and that humanitarian operations to rescue concentration-camp detainees would be impossible.

The first edition of Karski's memoir *Story of a Secret State* appeared in 1944 and became an immediate best-seller. He helped publicize it on well-attended lecture tours. In 1952 he completed his doctorate at Georgetown University's School of Foreign Service and spent the next 40 years there as a professor of political science. In the 1970s he traveled back to his homeland to conduct research for a more scholarly look at Poland's recent history, *The Great Powers and Poland 1919–45*. The State of Israel honored his efforts in 1982 by naming him one of the Yad Vashem, or Righteous Among Nations, bestowed on non-Jews who risked their lives to save European Jews during the Holocaust. Karski died in Washington on July 13, 2000, at age 86.

Throughout his long and esteemed postwar career, Karski remained committed to publicizing Polish resistance during World War II against "the most formidable and ruthless war machine that ever existed, while all Europe was passive or compromising," he wrote in *Story of a Secret State*. He cited the efforts of the AK, the Warsaw Ghetto militants, and the ordinary civilians who aided him on his missions. He characterized this as "the first resistance staged not in the defense of Danzig or some corridor but for the moral principles without which nations could not live together."

Books

Karski, Jan, *Story of a Secret State: My Report to the World*, Houghton Mifflin, 1944, revised edition with foreword by Madeleine Albright, Georgetown University Press, 2013.

Periodicals

New York Times, July 15, 2000.
Times (London, England), July 17, 2000.□

Dost Mohammad Khan

The Afghan political leader Dost Mohammad Khan (1792–1863), also known as Amir Dost Mohammad or Amir Dost Mohammad Khan, was the ruler of Afghanistan from 1826 to 1838 and again from 1842 until his death in 1863. He essentially unified Afghanistan inside the boundaries it maintains today.

D
ost Mohammad ("Khan" is a title, meaning ruler) faced armed opposition from India's colonial British rulers, from the Sikhs of the northwestern Indian subcontinent, and from rivals within Afghanistan, an unstable patchwork then as now of conflicting tribal and religious loyalties. His reign was interrupted by three years of British imprisonment, but he was released and resumed his place on the throne. In the later years of his rule he even enjoyed cordial relationships with the British, who tried to set members of the complex web of regional powers against each other in what has been termed the Great Game. Dost Mohammad had 27 sons, one of whom succeeded him as Afghan ruler. He was the founder of the Barakzai dynasty that ruled the country until the 1970s, and Afghans called him *Amir-i-Kabir*, The Great Prince.

Father Killed

Dost Mohammad was born on December 23, 1792, in Kandahar, Afghanistan (at the time the Durrani Empire). He was part of a powerful family of the Barakzai tribe ("Barakzai" means son of Barak), but this did not prevent him from experiencing the cutthroat nature of Afghan tribal wars firsthand; his father, Painda Khan, the Barakzai chief and a member of the government of the ruling Durrani Empire, was killed by a rival, Shah Zaman, when he was only eight years old. According to the *Great Game Pashtun's History* website, "Dost Mohmmad Khan's mother is believed to have been a Shia from the Persian Qizilbash group." Dost Mohammad was raised mostly by his older brother, Fatteh Khan, who himself was an influential player in Afghan power struggles: Fatteh helped Mahmud Shah Durrani become the ruler of Afghanistan in 1800 and 1801 and again in 1809 after Mahmud had been deposed. Despite this help, Mahmud had Fatteh Khan killed in 1818. The angered Barakzai turned against the Durrani clan and finally defeated Mahmud after a bloody war. His lands were divided among Fatteh Khan's surviving brothers, bringing an end to the mighty Durrani Empire that had once rivaled the Ottoman Turks in splendor. It was in this way that Dost Mohammad began his rise to power.

Dost Mohammad became acting governor of the city of Ghazni in the east-central part of the country in the early 1820s. A crucial step came in 1824, when he succeeded in seizing power in Kabul, then as now the region's largest and richest city, after the death of its previous governor. When Dost Mohammad sought to expand his power to his home city of Kandahar, he faced the opposition of Shah Shuja (or Shuja Shah), a member of the rival Sadozai clain who would emerge as Dost Mohammad's most formidable opponent even though it was he who had made peace with the Barakzais and had helped bring them to power in the first place.

When Dost Mohammad's forces defeated those of Shah Shuja in Kandahar in 1826, he became a feared and dominant force everywhere in Afghanistan, and he gradually extended his rule over most of the country. His time as ruler of Afghanistan is generally understood to have begun with this victory, but he continued to face opposition from Shah Shuja, who made an alliance with the Sikh ruler Ranjit Singh. Dost Mohammad's army defeated the combined forces of Shah Shuja and Ranjit Singh in a battle at Kandahar in 1834, but Ranjit Singh took the opportunity, while Dost Mohammad was pinned down in southern Afghanistan, to seize the city of Peshawar. Although now in Pakistan, Peshawar was (and has remained) part of the cultural sphere of Afghanistan's Pashtun-speaking peoples.

Sought Alliance with British India

In the 1830s, Dost Mohammad tried to play his own Great Game. At first he spurned an alliance with Russia, which in both the 19th and 20th centuries had its own designs on Afghanistan and wanted to counter Western influence there. He received the Scottish traveler and unofficial diplomat Alexander Burnes in Kabul in 1837 and made a strong enough case for British help that Burnes returned George Eden, known as Lord Auckland and the British governor-general of colonial India, and argued that British troops should enter the Afghan-Sikh conflict on Dost Mohammad's side. Meanwhile, Dost Mohammad sent a force of 25,000 men to Jamrud, in the vicinity of the Khyber Pass, where they defeated a Sikh army at the Battle of Jamrud in 1837 and severely damaged Sikh military prospects. He issued coins (according to the *Encyclopedia Iranica*) bearing this verse: "Amir Dost Mohammad resolved to wage jihad / And to mint coins, may God grant him victory."

Burnes, however, failed to persuade Auckland, who instead merely promised to protect Afghanistan from a Sikh invasion (which was unlikely by this time anyhow), and demanded that Dost Mohammad abandon the attempt to recapture Peshawar. Now Dost Mohammad turned once again to the Russians and to the Persian Empire as well, receiving Russian agent Yan Vitkevich in Kabul. The alarmed Auckland ordered an invasion of Afghanistan in 1838, and in March of 1839 forces of British general Sir Willoughby Cotton entered Afghanistan through Bolan Pass in what is now Pakistan's Baluchistan province. By the summer Willoughby had conquered both Kandahar and Kabul, Shah Shuja had been restored to the Afghan throne, and Dost Mohammad fled into the mountains.

The fate of the British in Afghanistan in what became known as the First Anglo-Afghan War was similar to that which befell other global powers in the 20th century: although they conquered the cities easily, their supply lines were vulnerable to tribal guerrilla attacks, some of them instigated by Dost Mohammad, and Afghan tribes were further enraged when British reinforcements arrived and seemed to be occupying the country. Eventually Dost Mohammad gave up his personal struggle and submitted to being taken prisoner in November of 1840, but a partial British retreat back through the mountains proved disastrous as battalions were harassed by Afghan warriors. The British took extremely heavy casualties, and one magnificent battalion was reduced to a ragtag force of 40 men. Shah Shuja was never accepted as leader by the Afghan people, and Kabul fell once again into Afghan hands.

Released from British Custody

Dost Mohammad was held prisoner throughout the British retreat, and a new British force was sent to Kabul in 1842 with instructions to exact revenge. They razed the city, but at this point British leaders in London began to feel that the entire invasion had been a misadventure not worth its cost in money and British lives. Dost Mohammad was released. He arrived in Kabul to a hero's welcome and quickly reestablished his authority over the Kabul area. Shah Shuja was killed. It took Dost Mohammad some years to restore his authority over the rest of the country; Kandahar was not brought under his control until 1854, and Herat not until 1863.

After he returned to power, Dost Mohammad at first made peace with his old enemies the Sikhs, considering the British a common enemy. But as British control began to extend across Sikh lands in Punjab, Dost Mohammad signed a peace treaty with the colonial Indian government in 1855. He did so partly because he had a new enemy to the west, the Persian Empire, whose army began to move toward Kandahar in 1862. Calling this time on British help, Dost Mohammad led his own army into battle despite his advanced age, and repulsed the attack. Two weeks after his forces entered Herat, on June 9, 1863, Dost Mohammad died. He lived long enough to designate his son, Shere Ali Khan, as his successor, and to launch a new Afghan dynasty.

Books

Adamec, Ludwig W., *The A to Z of Afghan Wars, Revolutions and Insurgencies*, Scarecrow, 2010.

Vogelsang, Willem, *The Afghans*, Blackwell, 2002.

Online

"Amir Dost Mohammad Khan," *Afghanistan Online,* http://www.afghan-web.com/bios/yest/dost.html (January 8, 2015).

"Dost Mohammad Khan," *Encyclopedia Iranica,* http://www.iranicaonline.org/articles/dost-mohammad-kha (January 8, 2015).

"Dost Mohammad Khan," *Great Game Pashtun's History,* http://www.drksy.wordpress.com/2013/04/14/amir-dost-mohammed-khan/ (January 8, 2015).□

Thomas Kinsella

The Irish poet Thomas Kinsella (born 1928) has been regarded as one of the leading writers in the world of contemporary poetry, not only in Ireland but around the English-speaking world.

AP Images/Julien Behal

Kinsella's writing has evolved in both form and content over his long career, and after establishing his reputation in conventional genres of lyric poetry he embarked on a period of radical formal experimentation. For some years Kinsella produced poems of often extreme difficulty, seeming to concern himself with purely formal processes. Yet his poetry has always had consistent underlying themes, including death and the passage of time. Kinsella's publication history has been unorthodox and has been a key part of his creative effort: he has written poems that appear to be connected or mixed into other ones, and he has at times repeated poems from earlier books verbatim in later ones. In a way, much of Kinsella's later output seems to make up parts of one large poem whose ultimate shape remains elusive.

Took Gaelic-Language Classes

Thomas Kinsella was born in Dublin, Ireland, on May 4, 1928, and attended schools in the suburb of Inchicore. For a time he attended a school where classes were held in the Irish Gaelic language. Kinsella has said that he grew up in a typical Irish family; his father, John Paul, worked at the Guinness brewery and was politically oriented toward socialism. John Paul Kinsella was a member of a leftist-oriented book club, with the result that Thomas grew up with an exposure to literature that was unusually broad for a working-class family. He did well in school and earned scholarships and grants that enabled him to attend University College in Dublin, a level of education that his parents had never reached.

At the university, Kinsella switched his major from physics and chemistry to public administration, and even before graduating in 1949 he had landed a position in Ireland's civil service bureaucracy. He would remain a government employee until 1965, by which time his career as a poet was well underway. In an interview from *The Poet Speaks* (reprinted in *Contemporary Literary Criticism*) Kinsella said that he "never found any clash" between writing and government work, and that in fact "I've found

that my mental state when composing a particularly difficult minute is not unlike the process of writing a poem."

In 1955 Kinsella married Eleanor Walsh, an event he credited with inspiring him to devote himself seriously to poetry. Another influence was his university friend Seá Ó Riada, a composer and musician responsible for much of the revival of Irish folk music as it is known today. Kinsella published his first book of poetry, *Another September,* in 1958. The book won the annual Guinness Poetry Prize and earned Kinsella a reputation as a possible young successor to Ireland's greatest 20th-century poet, William Butler Yeats. Kinsella's early poetry, mixing love poems with reflective pieces of a more philosophical nature, was also influenced by that of W.H. Auden. Critics noticed the young writer's considerable formal ingenuity, which seemed to assert itself regardless of a poem's subject. Kinsella published a second book, *Moralities,* in 1960, and a third, *Downstream,* in 1962. These volumes gained attention in the United States as well as in the British Isles.

Moved to United States

In 1965 Kinsella retired from his government finance post and accepted a position as writer-in-residence at Southern Illinois University in Carbondale. In 1967 he became professor of English there, and in 1970 he moved to Temple University in Philadelphia as a professor. He established a Temple-in-Dublin program for the study of Irish culture there, serving from 1976 to 1990 as its director, and during his years in the United States he often divided his time between America and Ireland. "I admired the great modern American poets long before my move to the United States. They were a revelation in freeing the work from many obsolete understandings," he told JP O'Malley of the London *Sunday Times*.

Although Kinsella's work has drawn on several layers of Irish tradition, and he earned one of two Guggenheim Fellowships to work on a translation of the Old Irish epic *Taíin Bo Cualinghe*, living away from Ireland seemed to stimulate his creativity. In *Wormwood* (1966) and especially *Nightwalker and Other Poems* (1968) he struck out in new directions. He largely abandoned rhyme and let each poem take its own form. *Nightwalker and Other Poems* had a somber tone of preoccupation with death and the passage of time. For much of the rest of his career, Kinsella's poetry would have a meditative tone, in contrast to the lyric orientation of his earlier work. One of his few political poems was the long "Butcher's Dozen," written after the shooting of 13 Irish civil rights marchers by British forces in 1972. His poem "A Selected Life" memorialized O'Riada.

In 1973, in Dublin, Kinsella founded Peppercanister Press, a small publishing firm. This gave him the flexibility to issue his own work, which increasingly did not fall into such neat categories as small single work or full-length book. Kinsella sometimes published poems on the way to becoming parts of a longer work, and he began to develop new ideas whose shapes might become clear only over the course of several works. The press issued a long Kinsella poem, "Notes from the Land of the Dead," in 1972, following it with the volume *Notes from the Land of the Dead and Other Poems* in 1973, which included an untitled prologue to the earlier poem.

That prologue depicted a speaker's (perhaps the poet's) entrance into a psychic underworld, and a new feature of Kinsella's language beginning around this time was the use of a linked set of psychological symbols. In the words of Thomas H. Jackson, writing in the *Dictionary of Literary Biography*, "A hollow shape may be the female locus of male sexual ecstasy, a devouring mouth, a fearful dark cave, a womb, a grave–or, more exactly, any one of these is apt to be a murky version of any or all of the others. Here, then, Kinsella's images are less designative than resonant, and what they resonate with are the deepest desires, terrors, and confusions of the psyche." In the use of fragmentary, puzzling images that set a mood and might be linked over long stretches of text, Kinsella was influenced by the American-British poet T.S. Eliot.

"The Bard of Chaos"

Some critics found Kinsella's later poetry increasingly opaque, but even they tended to agree that it had a compelling quality. In such books as *One* (1974) and *Fifteen Dead* (1979), Kinsella appeared to be struggling toward a whole new poetic language. Such poems as "A Technical Supplement" (1976, published in a collection of the same title) could run to a length of 25 or 30 pages. *America* magazine characterized Kinsella as the "Bard of Chaos," observing that "in his quest for order he has gone from being a poet of elegant craft and

traditional form to one of structural innovation and incompleteness as the order he seeks . . . 'total theme—presented/to a full intense regard,' proves ever more internal and elusive." Kinsella continued to issue new and often experimental poems through the 1990s and into old age, as he returned to Ireland and settled in Killalane in County Wicklow.

Considered perhaps Ireland's greatest living poet, Kinsella has received several major awards. These included the Denis Devlin Memorial Award from his alma mater (1967, 1970, 1988, and 1994), the Before Columbus Foundation Award (1983), and the Freedom of the City of Dublin Award (2007). Among his many publications as editor or translator is *The New Oxford Book of Irish Verse* (1986).

In 2013, at the age of 85, Kinsella issued *Late Poems*, a collection of five Peppercanister volumes in pamphlet form, published between 2006 and 2011. The collection, he pointed out to O'Malley, "is introduced with a sentence from a sonnet by Michelangelo. It says, 'Where nature simply makes / you understand' Poetry is a powerful medium for the attempt to understand." In the words of *America*, "However fashions may change regarding poetic reputation, it seems likely that Kinsella's unique voice will continue to be heard in the only way it can—on its own terms."

Books

Contemporary Literary Criticism, Vol. 138, Gale, 2001.
Dictionary of Literary Biography, Vol. 27, Gale, 1984.
Harmon, Maurice, *The Poetry of Thomas Kinsella*, Wolfhound, 1974.
Lynch, David, *Confronting Shadows: An Introduction to the Poetry of Thomas Kinsella*, New Island, 2015.

Periodicals

America, March 18, 1995.
Guardian (London, England), July 7, 2007.
Sunday Times (London, England), September 8, 2013.

Online

"Biography of Thomas Kinsella," *PoemHunter.com*, http://www.poemhunter.com/thomas-kinsella/biography/ (November 1, 2014).
"Thomas Kinsella," *Carcanet*, http://www.carcanet.co.uk/cgi-bin/indexer?owner_id=38 (November 1, 2014).□

Margaret E. Knight

A prolific 19th-century American female inventor, Margaret Knight (1838–1914) was best known for engineering the machine that made feasible the manufacture of the flat-bottomed, freestanding paper bag. Over the course of her lifetime, Knight received 22 patents for her machines and mechanical inventions, mostly dealing with manufacturing processes and rotary engines. Her original, wooden bag-folding machine is housed at the Smithsonian Institution.

© Bettmann/Corbis

Knight was born in York, Maine, on February 14, 1838, to James and Hannah (Teal) Knight. She had two older brothers, Charlie and Jim. Knight's inventive nature showed up early on. As a youngster, she liked to tinker with tools. Knight made toys such as kites and sleds for her brothers and other neighborhood kids. In *Girls Who Rocked the World,* authors Michelle Roehm McCann and Amelie Welden included this quote from Knight: "As a child, I never cared for things that girls usually do; dolls never possessed any charms for me. I couldn't see the sense of coddling bits of porcelain with senseless faces: the only things I wanted were a jackknife, a gimlet, and pieces of wood."

Raised in Working-class Family

Knight's father died when she was young. Consequently, her mother moved the family to Manchester, New Hampshire, to find work in the local cotton textile mills. Knight's brothers and mother found work in the mills. Knight often brought her brothers lunch at the mill. On one visit she witnessed a loom malfunction, which caused a heavy steel-tipped shuttle to fly off like a missile and smack a worker. Afterward, Knight could not get the accident out of her mind. She invented a safety device to prevent such accidents from happening. Details about her invention remain sketchy. Some sources describe it as a stop-motion device that shut down the machine when it malfunctioned. Others describe it as a mechanism that kept the spindles moored to

the machine so they could not fly off. Whatever the case, her device was soon installed at the mill where the accident occurred and spread throughout the industry. Knight, who was about 12 at the time, received no money for her invention because she knew nothing about patents.

After finishing elementary school, Knight went to work to help support the family. During her late teens, she worked in several mills and also found employment at photography and engraving studios. At one point, she worked in house repair. All of these experiences allowed Knight to experiment with different tools and manufacturing processes, setting the stage for her later inventions.

Invented Bag-Making Machine

Around 1867, Knight moved to Springfield, Massachusetts, and found work at the Columbia Paper Bag Company. Knight worked as a bundler, meaning she collected, stacked and tied bunches of bags together so they could be shipped to merchants. At the time, paper bags were basically a cylinder glued together at the bottom. The hand-glued bags were hard to use and did not hold items very efficiently. Paper bag companies did offer flat-bottomed bags made with a box fold, but because such bags had to be cut and glued by hand, they cost a lot more to manufacture than the cylinder-type bags, so no one bought them. Knight took an interest in this design problem, realizing there must be a way to automate the manufacture of flat-bottomed bags.

For two years, Knight worked on her invention. She started by making sketches and paper models. Next, she took apart manufacturing machinery the bag company no longer used and retrofit the parts to match her design. Eventually, she came up with a wooden machine that could cut, fold and paste paper together to create the modern, flat-bottomed bag. By July of 1868, Knight had finished her wooden prototype and began making sample bags. Next, she hired a machinist to make a sturdier, iron version of her model. Later, she took her machine to Boston and hired another machinist to help her tweak the design.

Satisfied with her invention, Knight applied for a patent in February 1870 only to discover that a machinist named Charles Annan had submitted designs for a very similar manufacturing device and had already received the patent. Knight discovered that Annan had visited her machinist's shop several times to study her model. She took Annan to court and provided a mountain of evidence supporting her claims that she had been working on the machine first. Knight's roommate testified, noting that the young inventor had been working on the machine at home since early in 1867. Knight even produced diary entries and sketches to show she had experimented with the idea long before Annan. In addition, the machine shop workers testified that Annan had been hanging around the shop while they were working on the model. Knight won the trial and was awarded the patent on July 11, 1871, as patent number 116,842. Modern bag-making machines still utilize Knight's design principles.

Invention Felt 'Round the World

After winning her patent, Knight joined a local business-man in forming the Eastern Paper Bag Company in Hart-ford, Connecticut, putting her invention to work. Knight's machine worked from a roll of paper stock. The paper was fed into the machine, which bent it to create a tube, which the machine glued together. The machine then made sev-eral folds, cutting the ends into flaps that were trimmed into diamond shapes. These were folded and glued together to form a flat bottom. After the bag was completed, the machine cut it from the roll so the next bag could be made. Knight's bag found universal use and revolutionized the bags' manufacture and use.

Knight's invention greatly influenced the paper indus-try, as her flat-bottomed bags became the mode of choice for carrying and transporting goods. Merchants lauded the invention. The free-standing bag was easier for grocers to pack. In addition, department stores like Macy's and Lord and Taylor began utilizing her bags. Before they were available, department store workers had to wrap parcels with paper and twine for safe transporting. Knight's inven-tion so revolutionized the shopping world that in 1871 she received the Decoration of the Royal Legion of Honor from Britain's Queen Victoria.

While the bag-making machine was Knight's most notable invention, it was not her first patent. In 1870, Knight had received a patent for a pneumatic paper feeder that was utilized by printing presses and paper-folding machines. The bag-making machine, however, remained her most notable invention. It was also significant in that royalties from the invention gave Knight the opportunity to work full-time on her innovations, and she spent the rest of her life inventing things. Knight is credited with some 90 inventions, for which she received 22 patents. During her lifetime, she was profiled by a local newspaper, and the reporter referred to her as a "Woman Edison."

Held Several Patents

In the ensuing years, Knight received more patents for improvements to her bag-making machine, as well as five patents for cutting machines used in the manufacture of shoes, the first in 1890. She also held patents for a skirt protector (1883), a specialized clamp for holding robes (1884), a window frame and sash (1894), a barbecue spit for cooking meat (1885), a sewing machine reel (1894), a numbering mechanism (1894), a device for boring or plan-ing concave/cylindroidal surfaces (1903), a resilient wheel (1912), and a sleeve-valve rotary engine. At times, Knight was employed by different companies and sometimes assigned the patents to them. Several of her rotary engine designs were assigned to the Knight-Davidson Motor Com-pany of Saratoga, New York. Even though Knight was in her sixties when the automobile came around, she patented a series of engine designs beginning around 1902. Her sleeve-valve rotary engine was offered as an alternative to the poppet valve rotary engine and was utilized in some luxury cars. She also held a patent for an internal combus-tion engine.

Knight never married. She spent her last 25 years in Framingham, Massachusetts, and died on October 12, 1914, at the Framingham hospital, leaving an estate valued at under $300. She was buried in Newton, Massachusetts. While Knight was a savvy inventor, by most indications she was not an astute businesswoman. It is suspected that she sold many of the rights for her patents to the companies she worked for and therefore did not profit significantly from them. However, because Knight came from a working-class family, simply having enough money to live on without having to toil in a factory meant she had achieved success in her mind.

Having created so many revolutionary machines was impressive for Knight, a working-class girl who received little formal education. She was a self-taught inventor who learned mechanical engineering from observation, trial and error. Knight was inducted into the National Inventors Hall of Fame in 2006. A plaque noting her achievements was installed at Curry Cottage, her home in Framingham that still stands in homage to the hometown hero.

Book

Blashfield, Jean F., *Women Inventors,* Capstone Press, 1996.
McCann, Michelle Roehm, and Amelie Welden, *Girls Who Rocked the World,* Aladdin, 2012.
Stanley, Autumn, *Mothers and Daughters of Invention,* Scarecrow Press, 1993.

Periodicals

American Scholar, Autumn 2003.
Engineering & Technology, April 2013.
Tech Directions, January 2010.□

Jiří Kolář

Czech artist and writer Jirí Kolář (1914–2002) was a canny provocateur who spent much of his career working to subvert authoritarian Communist rule in the former Czechoslovakia. A poet whose own coun-try banned publication of his work, Kolář also cre-ated hundreds of works of collage art that remained hidden for decades.

Jirí Kolář was the son of a baker and born on September 24, 1914, in Protivín, South Bohemia. At the time, Czechoslovakia did not exist as a nation; instead the Czech-speaking regions of Bohemia and Moravia, plus the Slovak-speaking eastern provinces, were under the rule of the Austro-Hungarian Empire. Czechoslovakia emerged as an independent nation after Austro-Hungary's defeat at the end of World War I in 1918.

Self-Taught Collage Artist

In his youth Kolář attended a school in Kladno, a city near Prague, and from 1928 to 1934 trained as an apprentice

AP Images/Tomas Zelezny

carpenter and cabinetmaker. Eventually he opted to take menial-labor jobs in the construction trades so that he could devote more time to reading, writing, and creating art. He was deeply influenced by Filippo Tommaso Marinetti's decisive *Futurist Manifesto*. First published in France in 1909, the Manifesto was widely read across Europe and shaped several movements in modern art, chiefly Dadaism and Surrealism. The interplay between image and text that featured prominently in those two movements would become a hallmark of Kolář's art.

Because canvas rolls, paint, clay, and most other media were prohibitively expensive at the time, Kolář used the most readily available material: magazine images, art-reproduction books, and newspapers. Taking a surgeon's scalpel, he sliced precise vertical strips of one image and combined them with a similarly dissected second picture, calling the technique "rollage." He was aware that this was known as "collage," borrowed from the French verb *coller*, which means "to glue." In a clever twist, Kolář's surname was actually pronounced "collage" in the Czech language.

Czechoslovakia's brief period of independence came to a traumatic end in 1938 when neighboring Nazi Germany annexed a border region that was home to German-speaking Czechs. Czechoslovaks of Kolář's generation were fortunate to survive World War II, which erupted when Germany invaded Poland in September of 1939. Thousands of Czechs and Slovaks were conscripted into military service, sent to labor camps, or targeted for random reprisal-executions that were designed to instill maximum fear among the civilian population. Czechoslovak Jews fared much worse and were deported to Nazi death camps, where they counted among the six million victims of the Holocaust.

Formed Group 42

Kolář's first book of poems was *Křestný List* (Birth Certificate), published in 1941. He soon found a like-minded group of quietly subversive artists and they formed an underground collective that called themselves Skupina 42, or Group 42. Comprised largely of painters and writers who were favorably disposed toward their Nazi occupiers' chief nemesis, the Soviet Union, they waited out the war and hoped for a renewal of cultural experimentation and political independence once again.

The Soviet Red Army rolled across Nazi-occupied Poland and Czechoslovakia on its path to meet up with U.S. and British allies, who had invaded Europe from France, Belgium, and Italy. World War II ended in early May of 1945, which prompted Kolář to move to Prague to find work. He became an editor at a publishing house, Družstvo Dilo Publishers in Prague, which issued a collection of his verse titled *Ódy a variace* (Odes and Variations) in 1946. Now in his early 30s, Kolář hoped to pursue his art in a homeland that was both supportive of the arts and guaranteed freedom of expression. Soviet troops remained in Czechoslovakia, however, and a vicious battle began to impose one-party Communist rule across all of Eastern Europe. All hopes for a more balanced form of democratic socialism and political plurality were dashed in early 1948 when Czechoslovakia's Foreign Minister Jan Masaryk—a respected international diplomat as well as the son of the country's founding president—was found dead in the courtyard of the Prague castle building that housed the Foreign Ministry. An official investigation determined that Masaryk had committed suicide.

With Communist Party members firmly in control of all sectors, Družstvo Dilo was forced to shut down, and Kolář's poetry and other writings were officially banned under stringent new censorship rules. His chronicle of that period was published underground and circulated among friends as *Očitý svěek* (Eyewitness) in 1949. That same year he married Běla Helclová, an artist and a photographer. Among his friends were other writers and artists whose work had also been deemed objectionable according to socialist ideology. They included another Surrealist-inspired poet, Josef Hiršal, and Václav Černý, a prominent literary critic.

Jailed for Manuscript

In 1952 a leading figure in Czech Communist Party circles named Rudolf Slánský was arrested along with several others; all were deemed security risks to the state and Slánský—a hero to most leftists in Czechoslovakia since the 1920s—was hanged for treason. The purge of senior party figures included crackdowns on other suspected disloyalists, and Václav Černý's home was searched. Police discovered a sheaf of typeset poems from Kolář, and both men were taken into custody.

Kolář was held without trial for nine months for the poems in *Prométheova játra* (Prometheus' Guts). Jirí Holý, author of *Writers Under Siege: Czech Literature Since 1945,* quoted from one translated passage: "I really have no more hope/And I wouldn't know where to get any . . . [T]onight or tomorrow/I don't know/A man with a badge or in a leather coat/Might come and put an end to it all." Kolář was finally sentenced by a court to a nine-month sentence for subversion and immediately released for time served. *Prometheus' Guts* did not appear in English translation until 1985, when a Toronto press specializing in émigré literature issued a copy.

Called Himself 'Silent Poet'

For the next decade Kolář kept any new poems hidden to all but a trusted few friends and concentrated on visual art, which permitted him more freedom of expression. He had a regular table at a Prague landmark, the Café Slavia, which had long been a second home for Czech dissident artists and, remarkably, remained open until the early 1990s. In a small studio space he made painstaking collages using various methods, sometimes weaving strips of newspaper articles or cheap art prints together, or cutting out hundreds of words from newspapers and arranging them into figurative shapes. He had a noticeable gift for juxtaposing contemporary photographs of everyday life in Czechoslovakia with images torn from art-history books. "When I first combined two reproductions to make one, I couldn't believe my eyes," he once said, according to a Tate Museum catalog. "My mind seemed to explode at the multiple variations that appeared beneath my hands. From that time on I became penetrable, and so did the whole world. A non-illusory space could be produced and analogy could be pointed out with a finger."

Word of Kolář's growing trove of unseen art began to reach the West, and museums and galleries showed interest. In 1963, a selection was shown at a London gallery named after its American-born dealer, Arthur Jeffress. *The Visual Images of a Poet* served to introduce Kolář's art to international collectors. Meanwhile, behind the Iron Curtain that walled off Communist Czechoslovakia from the rest of Europe there were small, barely perceptible shifts occurring as hardliners died out and Moscow loosened some of its authoritarian grasp. A group of Czechoslovak Communist Party figures coalesced around a regional party secretary named Alexander Dubček, who was chosen to become the nation's newest president in early 1968. The move was a surprising one, as was Dubček's issuance of several domestic reforms known as the Action Programme, which included freedom of the press, freedom of movement, and freedom of speech.

Crushed by Oppressive Soviets

The liberalization program in Czechoslovakia became known as the Prague Spring and for a few months Kolář and other longtime underground writers flourished under the newly relaxed rules. The Prague Spring came to an end on orders of Moscow, which responded to fears from hardline leaders of Poland, Hungary, and East Germany that the Dubček regime would soon legalize the formation of long-banned political parties. On the night of August 20, 1968, Red Army tanks once again rolled westward across Europe. Demonstrations erupted in Prague and other cities in Czechoslovakia but were quickly put down by force. Dubček was forced onto a military plane, flown to Moscow under guard, and forced to sign a rescission of his Action Programme. He resigned a few months later and in 1970 was expelled from the Czechoslovak Communist Party.

The August invasion of Czechoslovakia made international headlines for days. In Europe and elsewhere, news photographs of Soviet tanks on the streets of Prague prompted widespread condemnation. A *Times* of London report from August 31, 1968, alleged that Czechoslovak intelligence-agency personnel were disguising themselves as emergency-response workers, complete with faux ambulances, and that Kolář was among the 11 literary figures who had been abducted and taken to an unknown location. One of the others was a rising young playwright named Václav Havel, whose own dissidence was shaped by long sessions with Kolář and other figures at the Café Slavia.

Feted by Guggenheim Museum

Kolář's art gained a wider audience when he was invited to participate at the Documenta 1968, an art fair showcasing international contemporary art in what was then West Germany. In December of 1969 a New York City gallery showed his collages, and *New York Times* art critic Hilton Kramer revealed that he had visited Kolář's small studio in Prague a few months earlier and saw hundreds of works. Kramer called him "an artist of remarkable gifts" and asserted that "many observers of the European art scene believe [him] to be the most accomplished visual artist in Czechoslovakia today."

In September of 1975 New York's Solomon R. Guggenheim Museum honored Kolář with a career retrospective. Two years later he added his name to *Charter 77,* a declaration of human rights spearheaded by Havel. In 1978 Kolář was granted permission to leave Czechoslovakia when he was offered a fellowship by the Deutscher Akademischer Austauschdienst (German Academic Exchange Service, or DAAD). The offer gave him an opportunity to work in freewheeling West Berlin, which in the Cold War era was a tightly guarded enclave protected by a cordon of Western military personnel deep inside Communist East Germany; entry and exit visas and stringent military checkpoints, along with a massive fortified wall, kept the taint of cosmopolitan West Berlin from East Berliners in the Communist zone. Kolář's wife came with him, but like several other prominent Czech dissidents during this period they were stripped of their citizenship and barred from returning. They settled in France in 1980.

In late 1989, in response to a liberalization program in the Soviet Union, East Germany began granting unrestricted access into West Berlin, and the situation quickly spiraled into joyous protests in which citizens of the city from both sides began dismantling the hated Berlin Wall themselves. Nine days later, demonstrators stood in Prague's Wenceslas Square and demanded the resignation of government officials of the Czechoslovak Communist Party. This was Czechoslovakia's Velvet Revolution, and Havel became the new president. Kolář and Helclová were able to return, though they kept their Paris apartment. Kolář died in Prague at age 87 on August 11, 2002. Havel, the 65-year-old president of Czechoslovakia, wrote an open letter to Kolář's widow in which he mourned the loss. "Jiří's death has stricken me deeply," Havel declared, according to the Edinburgh newspaper *The Scotsman.* "You well know what he meant to me. He was one of the pillars of the world I grew up in."

Books

Holý, Jiří, *Writers Under Siege: Czech Literature Since 1945,* Sussex Academic Press, 2008.
"Jiří Kolář: They Pass before Me, Those Electric Eyes Some Abstruse Angel Must Have Magnetized 1972," in *Tate Gallery: Illustrated Catalogue of Acquisitions 1986–88,* London 1996.

Periodicals

Guardian (London, England), September 10, 2002.
New York Times, December 20, 1969.
The Scotsman (Edinburgh, Scotland), August 14, 2002.
Times (London, England), August 31, 1968; August 26, 2002.□

Leslie Kong

The Jamaican music producer Leslie Kong (1933–1971) was a key figure in the Jamaican recording industry in the 1960s, nurturing the early careers of musical giants such as Bob Marley and Jimmy Cliff.

Creating an organization that could effectively identify emerging talent, Kong was in the forefront of developing cutting-edge Jamaican musical genres that would turn out to have international implications: rocksteady and, toward the end of his life, reggae. Kong has not become a widely recognized name in comparison with Marley, Cliff, or even later reggae producers such as Clement "Coxsone" Dodd. Yet the recordings he produced, released on his own Beverley's label, dominated Jamaican sales charts in the 1960s and formed the musical foundation out of which reggae emerged as an international phenomenon. "Was Kong the greatest of Jamaican producers?" asked Kevin O'Brien Chang and Wayne Chen in their book *Reggae Routes.* "Such arguments can never be settled, but he did produce more great singles than anyone else." In the opinion of more than one Jamaican commentator, Kong's reputation has not matched his influence in its dimensions.

Operated Ice Cream Shop

Chinese immigrants first came to British-ruled Jamaica in the 19th century as plantation laborers, with a large group arriving desperately ill with yellow fever in 1854 from Panama. Like Chinese immigrants elsewhere, later arrivals built small businesses in the Jamaican capital of Kingston. Among these were the members of the Kong family, into which Leslie Kong was born in Kingston in 1933. Little has been published about his early life. At the dawn of the 1960s he and two brothers, named Fats and Cecil, operated an ice cream shop called Beverley's at 135a Orange Street in downtown Kingston. Kong had one other brother who became a Catholic priest.

At the time, Kong had no special interest in music and no specific skills in creating it. But he recognized that the music industry in Jamaica was growing as the country approached independence from Great Britain in 1962—he could see that in the profusion of record stores that crowded Orange Street near his shop, and in the crowds of musically oriented young people who frequented them. And he knew that another Chinese-Jamaican businessman, hardware store owner Thomas Wong, had created and marketed a pioneering dance-hall sound system that had made possible one of the world's first nightclub DJ scenes. So, in 1961, when teenage customer James Chambers, later known as Jimmy Cliff, sang Kong "Dearest Beverley," a song of praise for the ice cream shop that Chambers hoped would attract Kong's sponsorship, Kong began thinking about new business possibilities. He had already joined forces with British-Jamaican entrepreneur Chris Blackwell to form a small label, Island Records, several years earlier.

However, Kong knew his limitations musically. He recruited singer and songwriter Derrick Morgan as a talent spotter and artist-and-repertoire expert for his new Beverley's label, luring him away from rival entrepreneur Prince Buster (Cecil Bustamente Campbell); an embittered Buster released the racially charged single "Black Head China-man" in response. Morgan listened to Chambers, was impressed, and suggested that the young artist write an up-tempo piece to replace the syrupy "Dear Beverley." Chambers, by then renamed Jimmie Cliff, complied, coming up with the infectious ska piece "Hurricane Hattie," and Morgan went on to write two new songs of his own. These three songs, plus one by another budding star, Owen Grey, became Beverley's first releases.

Signed Marley to Contract

Although he was learning production skills on the fly, with Morgan's help Kong was immediately successful. During one week in 1962, seven of Jamaica's top ten songs were Kong productions. His most influential signing that year was future reggae superstar Bob Marley, known first as Bobby Martell and then as Robert Marley. It was Kong who produced Marley's first two recordings, "Judge Not" and "One Cup of Coffee," and released them on the Beverley label. Marley was not an immediate success, but Cliff scored a hit with the Kong-produced "Miss Jamaica," and Morgan scored in a duet as Derrick & Patsy with "Housewife's Choice."

All these recordings were in the style known as ska, with often humorous or moralizing vocals over a gentle beat and quiet horn arrangement. As ska began to make inroads into British youth culture (its only American success, a moderate one, was the Island release "My Boy Lollipop" [1964] by Millie Small), Kong made his second crucial business decision: he licensed Beverley's singles for release on Island, which would distribute them in the United Kingdom. As Kong-produced singles began to proliferate in London record shops, the profile of Jamaican music was raised.

Kong's biggest British success was not Marley or Cliff, but Desmond Dekker (Desmond Adolphus Dacres), whose Kong-produced sides were consistent hits in Jamaica through the 1960s. Releasing Dekker's singles in Britain on the Trojan Records label (initially a partner of Island) beginning in 1968, Kong scored a major hit with the gangster (or "rudeboy")-flavored anthem "007 (Shanty Town)," a song (co-credited to Kong as songwriter) with a beat that, compared to that of ska, was deeper and heavier and had become known as rocksteady. The following year, in 1969, Dekker again stayed on top of musical trends with "Israelites," a song whose loping beat and spiritual theme exemplified the new reggae genre. Co-written by Dekker and Kong, and produced by Kong but remixed for British release on the Pyramid label, "Israelites" represented a key step in exposing reggae and Jamaican music generally to international audiences. The recording reached the top ten in the United States.

Kong continued to score hits in Jamaica and Britain as a producer. These included Dekker's "It Mek," which demonstrated that British audiences were open to songs recorded in Jamaican patois, and several singles by a new Jamaican band, the Maytals, whose singles "54-46," "Monkey Man," and "Pressure Drop" introduced another long-lasting reggae band. The Kong-produced "Rivers of Babylon," recorded by the Melodians, became a reggae classic and confirmed the genre's growing links to the Rastafarian religious sect; as a result the song was temporarily banned by the Jamaican government, which was leery of the sect's revolutionary political leanings. After Kong and others defended the song and pointed to the purely religious content of its lyrics, the ban was lifted.

Planned Film with Cliff

That song was included on the soundtrack of the 1972 film *The Harder They Come,* which featured Cliff in its story of Kingston's tough streets. The low-budget film, which earned many times its cost in international release, featured Kong-produced music and positioned him to ride the growing reggae wave; in the words of the *Jamaica Observer,* Kong "looked set to compete with younger rivals Lee 'Scratch' Perry and Winston 'Niney' Holness."

It was not to be; Kong died suddenly after a heart attack on August 9, 1971. According to reggae folklore, his unusually early death was the result of a curse laid by Bunny Wailer (Neville O'Riley Livingston), a member of Bob Marley's band the Wailers. Wailer, it is said, was irate over Kong's decision to issue a *Best of the Wailers* collection, a traditional career-ender in the music business, when the band's reputation was just gathering speed; Kong responded that the album had already been manufactured and slated for release. After his death, Kong's son and brother tried halfheartedly to continue his musical enterprises, without success.

Kong's role in reggae history remains somewhat underappreciated, and he lacks a full biographical treatment that would also shed light on the early careers of many of reggae's giants. The recordings he produced in the 1960s for the most part await reissue in digital form and have not been systematically documented. "In the midst of celebrating Reggae Month 2014," journalist Roy Black wrote in the *Jamaica Gleaner,* "Kong's contribution cannot be slighted or overlooked, as his work has, in no small way, contributed to the internationalisation of reggae."

Books

Chang, Kevin O'Brien, and Wayne Chen, *Reggae Routes: The Story of Jamaican Music,* Temple, 1998.
White, Timothy, *Catch a Fire: The Life of Bob Marley,* Holt, 1983.

Online

"Beverlys," *ReggaeCollector.com,* http://www.reggaecollector.com/en/feature/label.php?label_id=490' (October 7, 2014).
"Chinese Reggae Pioneers," *Danwei,* http://www.danwei.org/chinese_reggae_pioneers.php (October 7, 2014).
"Hits from an Ice Cream Parlor—Leslie Kong's Beverly's Plays Foundation Music Role," *Jamaica Gleaner* (February 9, 2014), http://www.jamaica-gleaner.com/gleaner/20140209/ent/ent3.html (October 7, 2014).
"Leslie Kong," *Allmusic,* http://www.allmusic.com (October 7, 2014).
"Leslie Kong's Reggae Pioneer," *Jamaica Observer* (July 20, 2012), http://www.jamaicaobserver.com/Entertainment/Leslie-Kong-s-reggae-pioneer_11989294 (October 7, 2014).□

Anton Kuerti

The Austrian-born Canadian pianist Anton Kuerti (1938–) has gained wide critical respect for his interpretations of the music of Beethoven and other 19th-century composers. Trained in the United States, Kuerti has also been active as a composer, journalist, and educator.

Moreover, unlike most classical musicians, Kuerti has been a strong political activist, speaking out in opposition to major aspects of Canadian and American foreign policy. Kuerti's musical and political activities have been linked by a sense of artistic idealism: he has aimed to make classical music accessible to a broad public, refusing to accept fees of the size a pianist of his stature could command, in order to keep ticket prices for his concerts low. Kuerti's writings on classical music and its performers have frequently graced the pages of the Toronto newspaper, the *Globe and Mail,* and his sharp opinions have appeared among its letters to the editor. For Kuerti, who has also amassed a long record as a teacher in several of Canada's leading music conservatories, being a musician is simply part of being an all-around artist and citizen.

Hiroyuki Ito/Getty Images

Played Abandoned Piano

Anton Emil Kuerti was born in Vienna, Austria, on July 21, 1938, shortly after Austria was annexed into Nazi Germany. Kuerti's parents, who were Jewish scientists, fled to the United States when he was a baby and settled first in Massachusetts. They had few resources, but they managed to find an apartment where someone had abandoned a piano, and Kuerti was given a few lessons by a nursery school teacher. In 1944 he was naturalized as a U.S. citizen. Though he showed talent, Kuerti was not pressured or treated as a prodigy by his parents. "I don't think I practiced more than an hour a day until I was at least 14," he recalled to Lindsay Key of the *Roanoke Times*. Even with this modest schedule, Kuerti was good enough by age 11 to perform Edvard Grieg's difficult Piano Concerto in A minor with the Boston Pops orchestra under legendary conductor Arthur Fiedler.

In his teens Kuerti got serious about practicing, and after he graduated from the Longy School in Cambridge, Massachusetts, at age 16, he won admission to the Cleveland Institute of Music. Partially paying his way through school by playing the organ at prison church services, he earned a bachelor of music degree in 1955 and moved on to the Curtis Institute in Philadelphia, one of the top music schools in the United States. He was influenced especially by teachers Arthur Loesser in Cleveland and Rudolf Serkin in Philadelphia, and as his own playing developed, it merged traits of both expressive and intellectual approaches.

As a student Kuerti was already becoming an experienced recitalist. After several appearances as a soloist in concertos for piano and orchestra, he gave recitals at two prestigious art museums, Boston's Isabella Stewart Gardner Museum and Washington's Phillips Gallery, in 1953. From 1953 to 1956 he performed at the summer Marlboro Festival in Vermont. The year 1957 marked Kuerti's breakthrough: he won several major prizes including the Leventritt Award, which carried with it appearances with several of the country's top symphony orchestras. Not yet 20 years old, Kuerti was a classical music star.

Emigrated to Canada

In the early 1960s Kuerti built relationships with several Canadian orchestras as well, and in 1965, disturbed at the proportion of U.S. tax revenues that were dedicated to the military, he moved to Canada permanently. He became a Canadian citizen in 1984.

In 1965 Kuerti immediately acquired the position of pianist-in-residence at the University of Toronto, and in 1968 he was elevated to associate professor there. In the 1970s he recorded a critically well-regarded set of all of Beethoven's 32 piano sonatas on Canada's Aquitaine Records, and his growing concert career put an end to his need to teach, although he continued to give master classes.

Kuerti's repertoire is varied but has generally centered on the period from Beethoven, in the early 19th century, to Russian composer Alexander Scriabin, in the early 20th. His playing has a somewhat intellectual cast, exploring deep structures and small details in the music he performs. "You came away feeling you know Beethoven far better than before," wrote David Patrick Stearns of the *Philadelphia Inquirer* in a review of a 2012 Kuerti concert. A *Toronto Star* review quoted in the *Canadian Encyclopedia* characterized the experience of a Kuerti concert this way: He "habitually pays his listeners the compliment of assuming that their ears come to him in search of stimulation rather than massage.... You can't just sit back and let the music wash over you. The playing is too intense, too probing. Almost in spite of himself, the listener becomes drawn into the action."

Kuerti's independent spirit manifested itself in the tangled history of the Aquitaine label Beethoven sonata recordings, which originally appeared in 1976. To get control of the master tapes of these recordings required a ten-year court battle on Kuerti's part—and then, when he finally had them in hand, he found that they were defective and could not be played without damaging them. After consulting with experts about a solution, Kuerti strengthened the tapes by baking them in a home food dehydrator. The tapes still suffered from print-through, a condition in which sonic images from one part of a tape appear on another as it is wound on a reel. Editing the tapes at first manually and then during the early years of digital editing, Kuerti painstakingly corrected these flaws. The remastered cycle finally appeared in 1997 and achieved strong sales.

Founded Music Festival

Kuerti had been interested in composition since his student days, and he wrote new music prolifically between the

1970s and 1990s. Some compositions were solo piano pieces and piano concertos that he performed himself, but others were in genres as varied as the string quartet, the violin-and-piano sonata, and the trio for clarinet, cello, and piano. Kuerti's compositions resembled those of Scriabin, Alban Berg, and other dissonance-oriented composers of the early 20th century. He premiered works by several other Canadian composers, and in 1980 he founded the Festival of the Sound in Parry Sound, Ontario, where new works were often given their debuts. He remained the festival's director until 1985.

The most controversial part of Kuerti's career lay not in his musical interpretations but in his political activities. In 1988, Kuerti attempted to put his political beliefs into action, running for a seat in Canada's parliament from the riding (or district) of Don Valley North in the Toronto area. He won the nomination as the candidate of Canada's socialist-oriented New Democratic Party but lost in the general election. Kuerti was a strong critic of Canadian and U.S. military involvement in Iraq in the early 2000s, and of Israel's invasion of the Gaza Strip in 2013. He disliked cars and could often be seen riding a bicycle on Toronto's crowded streets.

The Aquitaine Beethoven sonata cycle won the first Juno award (the Canadian counterpart to the Grammy) given in the classical field in 1976, and Kuerti subsequently garnered five more Juno nominations. He won major Canadian cultural and government awards, including recognition as an Officer of the Order of Canada in 1998, the Banff Centre's National Arts Award in 2007, and the Governor-General's Performing Arts Award in 2008. He is a recipient of Germany's Robert Schumann Prize. Kuerti married Hungarian-born cellist Kristine Bogyo in 1946; their son, Julian Kuerti, has gained recognition as a cellist and conductor.

In October of 2013, while performing in Miami, Florida, Kuerti suffered a medical emergency that caused him to begin playing the same piece repeatedly. Helped from the stage to a standing ovation, Kuerti was hospitalized and underwent several months of treatment. He was scheduled to resume performing, again in Florida, in January of 2015 in an appearance with the Pacifica Quartet, playing the Piano Quintet in F minor by Johannes Brahms.

Books

Slonimsky, Nicolas, editor emeritus, *Baker's Biographical Dictionary of Musicians,* centennial ed., Schirmer, 2001.

Periodicals

Globe and Mail (Toronto), March 11, 1986; September 2, 1988; February 12, 1994; February 18, 1995; January 18, 1997; October 1, 1999; April 2, 2001; June 21, 2008; February 26, 2009.

Philadelphia Inquirer, February 10, 2012.

Record (Kitchener, Ontario, Canada), March 23, 2012.

Roanoke Times (Roanoke, VA), May 3, 2007.

Toronto Star, January 9, 2009; January 10, 2009.

Online

"Anton (Emil) Kuerti," *The Canadian Encyclopedia,* http://www.thecanadianencyclopedia.com/en/article/anton-kuerti-emc/ (November 2, 2014).

"Anton Kuerti, piano," Jonathan Wentworth Associates, Ltd., http://www.jwentworth.com/pianists/anton_kuerti/index.htm (November 2, 2014).

"Canadian Pianist Anton Kuerti Hospitalized in Miami," *Toronto Star,* October 18, 2013, http://www.thestar.com/entertainment/2013/10/18/canadian_pianist_anton_kuerti_hospitalized_in_miami.html (November 2, 2014).

"A Rich Season of Orchestras, Mahler and Shostakovich Is On Tap for 2014–15," *South Florida Classical Review,* http://www.southfloridaclassicalreview.com/2014/09/a-rich-season-of-orchestras-mahler-and-shostakovich-is-on-tap-for-2014-15/ (November 2, 2014).□

L

Bartolomé des las Casas

Spanish friar Bartolomé de las Casas (c. 1484–1566) was one of the most vociferous critics of the Spanish Empire and its actions against the indigenous peoples of the Americas. A well-born soldier, landowner, priest, and later Bishop of Chiapas, de las Casas witnessed firsthand the horrors inflicted on Amerindian peoples in the Caribbean islands and, more crucially, wrote an extensive chronicle of the period of conquest following the arrival of Christopher Columbus. His 1552 work *The Devastation of the Indies* is one of the most frequently cited primary sources in European colonialism studies and the history of human rights.

Bartolomé de las Casas is so prominent a name in the record of European exploration and settlement in the Americas that debate over his exact date of birth was the subject of an entire scholarly article in a 1976 issue of the *Hispanic American Historical Review*. Its authors settled on November 11, 1484, as the likeliest date of the friar's birth. He was from Seville, a magnificent and influential city in Spain's Kingdom of Castile, which had only recently been united with the equally important Kingdom of Aragon through the marriage of Ferdinand II of Aragon and Isabella I of Castile. The jointly ruling monarchs were devout Roman Catholics and sought to expand their new kingdom's global presence. With this goal they financed the voyage of Genoese navigator Christopher Columbus in 1492, who returned to Spain in early 1493 with several Taíno Indians.

Family Close to Christopher Columbus

De las Casas's father Pedro was a merchant and his uncle Juan de Peñalosa was a government official who helped Columbus obtain two of the three ships used on that first voyage. Columbus had assured Ferdinand and Isabella that he knew a shorter passage to the fabled riches of Asia, and one that bypassed rival Portuguese mariners who had staked out a southward, easterly route to India by sailing around the African continent. Instead Columbus tried to reach the spice-rich islands of the East Indies via the Atlantic Ocean—but discovered the islands of the Caribbean, which became known as the West Indies.

Pedro de las Casas was among the hundreds of merchants, soldiers, and other Spaniards who sailed with Columbus on his second expedition in September of 1493. This was a much larger mission, with 17 ships in all, and enough supplies to build forts and trading posts across the large and fertile islands of the Caribbean sphere. The lands were well populated, but the indigenous Taíno appeared to pose little threat to Spanish expansion.

Another of de las Casas's Peñalosa uncles was a cleric attached to the Seville cathedral, and as a boy de las Casas attended the cathedral's rigorous academy. He began studies in Latin at a young age and showed a particular gift for the classical language, which was also the language of the Christian church. He was also a devout youth, fascinated by scripture, and likely encouraged to seek a role in the church as a future career. It is known that his father returned to Seville in 1498 or 1499 with a Taíno youth named Juanico, and from whom de las Casas was said to have picked up the indigenous language.

Made Early Voyage to Hispaniola

Even the most exhaustive of de las Casas's biographers note there are gaps in his schooling and career record. He is **231**

North Wind Pictures Archive/Alamy

thought to have attended the University of Salamanca for a time, where he may have studied law, and was possibly drafted into military service to stamp out a rebellion in Granada, a holdout of Spain's previous Moorish era. In February of 1502, he sailed for Hispaniola, the island Columbus had established as outpost of Spanish power in the Americas, aboard a ship that also carried a newly appointed governor of the Indies. Hispaniola is the name still used for the island that is home to both the Dominican Republic and Haiti.

On this first visit to the Americas, de las Casas participated in military expeditions to secure outlying territories in Hispaniola and place them under Spanish military control. He also supervised the income-producing parcel of land his father had been granted in the Cibao province of present-day Dominican Republic. Cibao was a fertile growing area and the land grant came with an appointed number of enslaved Taíno as field workers. This was the *encomienda* system used to establish Spanish control, and de las Casas later received his own income-providing parcel in Cienfuegos, Cuba.

In 1506, de las Casas returned to Spain and traveled to Italy with the younger brother of Columbus early the following year. In Rome he may have been ordained a priest—the exact date and place of his ordination remains unclear—and probably met with Pope Julius II. In the summer of 1509, de las Casas arrived back in Santo Domingo, the main city of Hispaniola. It is known that from 1512 to 1515 he went to

Cuba as part of the Spanish colonizing expedition that followed Diego Velásquez de Cuéllar's conquest of the island. De las Casas worked to convert Taíno to Christianity, an effort that had mixed success. The Taíno and neighboring peoples had been enslaved by the Spanish en masse: able-bodied men were sent to work in dangerous mines while women and children were conscripted for backbreaking agricultural labor in newly established sugar plantations. Some committed suicide, openly rebellious dissenters bled to death after their hands were publicly amputated by Spanish blades as punishment, and across both Hispaniola and Cuba the numbers of available forced laborers rapidly dwindled due to starvation and outbreaks of communicable diseases for which the Taíno had no natural immunities.

Moved by Plight of Taíno

De las Casas personally witnessed a massacre in Camagüey, Cuba, after an attempt was made to arrange a peaceful transfer of power between the cacique, or chieftain, in this part of Cuba. The remaining Taíno managed to flee to the hinterlands but later came back in small groups, as de las Casas later wrote, according to *Rivers of Gold: The Rise of the Spanish Empire, from Columbus to Magellan* by Hugh Thomas. "Men and women like sheep, each with his little bundle of poverty on his back," returned to the area, de las Casas recalled. "They were going back to their own homes which was what they wanted, and it caused me pity and great compassion, considering their meekness, humility, and poverty, and what they had suffered, their banishment and their weariness, brought upon them by no fault of their own."

De las Casas returned to Spain and urged its new King Charles I of Spain and one of the kingdom's most senior-ranking church officials, Cardinal Francisco Jiménez de Cisneros, to enforce more lenient laws that had recently been enacted regarding the treatment of non-Christians in the colonies. De las Casas made a convincing case, and the Cardinal even secured an official title for him, Protector of the Indians, inside the Spanish ministry responsible for the colonial administration. In 1520 de las Casas was granted permission to establish a small colony in what the Spanish called Tierra Firme, on what is the present-day Venezuelan mainland. His small community, sited near the mouth of the Cumaná River, was attacked by neighboring communities of indigenous peoples.

Entered Dominican Order

After this failure at Cumaná de las Casas took vows of the Dominican religious order in 1523. There was growing debate inside the Church, and inside the Kingdom of Spain, that the immense mortality rates of native peoples in the Americas was possibly a sign of grave moral failing of Spanish Catholicism. One of the more active voices in this ideological shift was a Spanish missionary and fellow Dominican, Fray Antonio de Montesinos. Montesinos had also campaigned against the genocidal Spanish policies in Hispaniola and de las Casas's entry into the Dominican order cemented his personal convictions. He had already given up his *encomienda* and freed his slaves, following the Dominicans friars' assertions that a Christian who enslaved others and participated in so brutal a system of human oppression was, in fact, living in a state of mortal sin.

The Spanish expansion into Tierra Firma was part of a series of conquests involving mainland Central and South America. Mexico, Guatemala, Colombia, and Peru were each home to fairly well-organized states like the Aztec in Mesoamerica and the Inca who held large parts of the South American continent. The Spanish defeated the Aztec by 1521, and the Incan conquest was completed in 1532.

Later in the 1520s, de las Casas began writing a definitive chronicle of the Spanish Conquest. He began working on it in 1527 while living in Puerto Plata (Silver Port) on Hispaniola. An inexhaustible scribe well-versed in Scripture and the writings of the Fathers of the Church, de las Casas laid out in specific detail all of the human-rights abuses committed by Spanish conquistadores who came after Columbus. These accounts of the Taíno and other Amerindians, their culture, and their reactions to Spanish invaders remain one of the most important documents in the history of relations between Europe and the Americas.

Text Used as Anti-Papist Propaganda

De las Casas's voluminous written works include *Brevísima relación de la destrucción de las Indias* (A Brief Account of the Destruction of the Indies), whose passages roiled Spain—and the rest of Europe—when it first appeared in print in 1552. "They are by nature the most humble, patient, and peaceable, holding no grudges, free from embroilments, neither excitable nor quarrelsome," he wrote of the Taíno, and also described them as receptive to the teachings of Christian missionaries. He contrasted this with the behavior of the Spanish, whom he likened to "ravening beasts, killing, terrorizing, afflicting, torturing, and destroying the native peoples, doing all this with the strangest and most varied new methods of cruelty, never seen or heard of before."

De las Casas traveled extensively in Latin America for a period that stretched nearly five decades, crossing the Atlantic on at least eight voyages. In Guatemala in the 1530s he worked with other Dominican friars to peaceably convert the Mayan and he later spent time in Oaxaca, Mexico, on the Isthmus of Panama. One of his most significant achievements came in 1542, when King Charles signed the *Leyes Nuevas,* or New Laws. These statutes specifically prohibited enslavement of Native Americans and abolished the *encomienda* system. In 1544 de las Casas was elevated to the rank of bishop and assigned the See of Chiapas, Mexico.

Spent Decade in Scholarly Seclusion

As Bishop of Chiapas, de las Casas wielded clear ecclesiastical supervision over all Christians living in this territory, which included a large part of southwestern Mexico. His pastoral flock included converted indigenous peoples and Spanish landholders, and of the latter some openly resisted enforcement of the New Laws. These holdouts were targeted by de las Casas and denied the sacrament of last rites upon their deathbed, which caused the bishop some trouble with his superiors in Spain and Rome. He took part in a major ecclesiastical assembly held in Mexico City in 1546

in which he argued his case before other bishops. In the spring of 1547, he was recalled to Spain by the Council of the Indies. Charles invited him to participate in a 1550 debate held at the Spanish monarch's court in Valladolid, Spain. The opposing side was presented by Juan Ginés de Sepúlveda, a humanist who argued that Spain's military conquest and enslavement of the indigenous peoples of Latin America was justified.

De las Casas never returned to his assignment of See in Chiapas, which he resigned in 1550. He spent a decade completing his magnum opus *Historia General de las Indias* and bequeathed it to the College of San Gregorio in Valladolid, where he had resided since 1551. He died in Madrid on July 18, 1566.

Books

Castro, Daniel, *Another Face of Empire: Bartolomé de Las Casas, Indigenous Rights, and Ecclesiastical Imperialism,* Duke University Press, 2007.

Clayton, Lawrence A., *Bartolomé de Las Casas: A Biography,* Cambridge University Press, 2012.

De Las Casas, Bartolomé, *The Devastation of the Indies: A Brief Account,* Johns Hopkins University Press, 1992.

Thomas, Hugh, *Rivers of Gold: The Rise of the Spanish Empire, from Columbus to Magellan,* Random House, 2004.☐

Tato Laviera

Through his writing, Puerto Rican poet Tato Laviera (1950–2013) offered a profound and meaningful reflection on ideas such as the Puerto Rican experience in New York City, multicultural life, immigration, cultural identity, and race. Formerly an activist and community organizer, the Nuyorican poet wrote in Spanish and English, and was known for his memorable poetry readings/performances. In addition to five collections of poetry, Laviera wrote at least 12 plays exploring topics similar to his poems.

He was born Jesús Abraham Laviera on May 9, 1950, in San Juan, Puerto Rico, the son of intellectual parents, a philosopher and a writer. In the late 1950s, the young Laviera was inspired to become a poet when he saw a reading given by Luis Palés Matos. Laviera's family moved from Puerto Rico to New York City's Lower East Side in 1960. Raised there, he attended Seward Park High School before graduating from Charles Evan Hughes High School with honors in 1968. Laviera received his higher education at Cornell University and Brooklyn College, but did not complete a degree.

Worked as an Activist and Organizer

Laviera's first career was as a community activist and organizer, activities he took part in from his teenage years. He was especially focused on youth and education causes,

Donna Ward/Getty Images

as a Puerto Rican and resident of New York City, exploring issues and topics central to these groups of people while creatively reflecting their rhythms and languages.

Sensitive and aware of the intricacies of communities, Laviera gave voice to the voiceless, reached and represented people in many environments through his words. New York University professor Juan Flores told Gonzalez of the *New York Times,* "I found his best poetry to be a jewel of New York Puerto Rican expression. His way of putting together the relationship between the island and the diaspora was more finely tuned and deeper than others. He took head on the issues of assimilation and cultural preservation and innovation."

In 1979, Laviera wrote the first of four poetry collections published by the Arte Público Press. Titled *La carreta made a U-Turn,* the poems therein were influenced by and based on ideas found in the 1953 play by René Marqués, *La carreta.* The iconic drama focused on a family moving from Puerto Rico to New York City, and their struggles and environmental adaptations. Laviera considered *La carreta made a U-Turn* to be the fourth act of the play.

The growing importance of Laviera was demonstrated in 1980, when President Jimmy Carter included him at the White House Gathering of American Poets. Within two decades, *La carreta made a U-Turn* became one of the most popular and widely read poetry collections penned by a Latino within the United States. Laviera followed *La carreta made a U-Turn* with *Enclave* in 1981. Featuring poems written in English, Spanish, and Spanglish, Laviera focused on the use of language and words as an expression of worldviews. The title has been interpreted to refer to the enclave of Puerto Ricans living in New York City, and the poems look at ideas of identity and expression among Puerto Ricans living in this enclave.

and actively encouraged the interests of others in these areas. Laviera worked as the director of the University of the Streets, which sought to support the efforts of adults to complete high school and go to college, and served as an administrator for the Association of Community Services. He was also employed in the arts, serving as the director of the Hispanic Drama Workshop.

Laviera worked in community organizing until the 1970s, when he shifted to poetry and began teaching at Livingston College. Community advocate Elizabeth Colón told David Gonzalez of the *New York Times* that Laviera's activism influenced his writing. She said, "His poetry and creativity came from that. It came from his involvement and his participation in the community's struggle, growing up on the Lower East Side, seeing the abuses and how others who were in charge had the power to intervene and did not. He deeply understood the need of people to participate in the future."

Focused on Poetry

Though Laviera was known as a performance poet, he also published five collections of poetry, contributed poems to numerous anthologies, and made hundreds of appearances at colleges, workshops, and literary events to share his words and encourage others to find their voice. A Nuyorican (New York-Puerto Rican) poet, Laviera wrote in Spanish, English, and Spanglish. His poetry reflected his life and experiences

Wrote Staged Plays

In addition to writing poetry, Laviera was also a playwright whose dozen or so works explored themes related to the Puerto Rican experience and Laviera's unique outlook. An early, successful play was based on the life of baseball legend Roberto Clemente; it was entitled *Olú Clemente.* In 1982, Laviera's play *Here We Come* made its debut at the Third Latin American Popular Theater Festival. The bilingual play explored key moments in the lives of four Latino students, beginning with a graduation ceremony. The play had social themes, and this production featured live music and employed dance as a way of underscoring these ideas.

Also in 1982, Laviera had another play staged, *La Chefa,* at the New Federal Theater in New York's Henry Street Settlement. *La Chefa* focused on a Puerto Rican family living in the Lower East Side in the 1950s. The close but struggling family had been living in the United States for many years; in addition to family issues, they are still grappling with what it means to live in the United States. Critics lauded the play, with Richard F. Shepard of the *New York Times* writing, "Mr. Laviera writes with knowledge, humor and a deep sensitivity to his subject." Shepard added, "Mr. Laviera has faith and hope in his people, and he spins a yarn that is realistic but optimistic." He would continue to produce plays for the rest of his life.

Laviera published his next volume of poetry in 1985, *AmeRícan*. This collection explored how he regarded Puerto Ricans and their place in the world as well as their racial background. Many poems looked at the diversity found in New York City, and called for Puerto Ricans to be recognized through all of American society. Laviera emphasized the need for a more humane America in which Latinos and minorities served as driving forces in the wider culture. Similar themes could be found in Laviera's 1988 poetry collection, *Mainstream Ethics (ética corriente)*. In his poems about Latinos in American culture, Laviera looked at ways Latinos are conventional Americans and how this occurs, including through language, religion, freedom, and poverty. He also expressed hope for transculturalism for Latinos and others.

Continued to Create Despite Blindness

Though Laviera produced a play entitled *Can Pickers* in 1995, his writing output was limited through the 1990s and first years of the 21st century. He continued to teach, lecture, and make appearances at schools like Wayne State University, Vanderbilt, Dartmouth College, Yale, and State University of New York at Binghamton. But he also suffered from ill health, primarily related to diabetes. By 2004, Laviera was legally blind because of his condition. Laviera used his diabetes to help others, forming the Jesús A. Laviera One-Day with Diabetes Project and putting on what he called Sugar Slams. These events were like poetry slams but intended to increase awareness about the effects of diabetes specifically on minorities.

Despite his blindness, Laviera continued to write and work. In 2008, he published *Mixturao and Other Poems*, his first poetry book in two decades. The poems therein covered such topics as the Spanish language, the increasing Mexican population in New York, gentrification, and abuses of people, and the legacy of the culture and people of Puerto Rico. According to Rigoberto González of the *El Paso Times*, the book "celebrates the varied linguistic forms of expression of U.S. Latinos." He also noted that its "pages erupt into a multilingual chorus...a blending not just of languages, but also of bloodlines, cultures and histories."

By 2009, Laviera had taught at more than 100 schools, colleges, universities, and communities centers. He had a project with Stephanie Alvarez, a professor at the University of Texas-Pan American, called Cosecha (Harvest) Voices. Held at Alvarez's college, the Cosecha Voices class consisted of oral history and intensive writing workshops, resulting in the creation of an original work of literature. It was primarily targeted at migrant students, and Laviera taught creative writing to help them express and better understand their life experiences. Laviera and Alvarez developed the course so it could be used by other schools and universities.

Suffered Ill Health

At the end of 2009, Laviera experienced a health setback that made his life quite difficult. In December 2009, he had to undergo emergency brain surgery after he developed water on the brain. After being hospitalized, he was not strong enough to return to his long-time home in Greenwich Village. Laviera checked into a nursing home for care and physical therapy, but left after two weeks because he could not tolerate the environment. He found the patients and residents drugged up and unengaged with life. Laviera had his sister get him out the situation, but he had no place to go as no one in his family could give him a home.

While Laviera looked for affordable housing, he connected with a group, the United Bronx Parents, who found him a temporary home in a shelter, the Casita Esperana (Little House of Hope), located in the Bronx. Living in this shelter, he participated in poetry readings with others who lived there and had the residents rehearse a play written by him *Chupacabra Sightings*. Laviera felt inspired by the experience and enjoyed the community as well. He told Gonzalez of the *New York Times*, "This has opened me up to even more feeling. I can create here, and that makes me feel liberated. Being here has given me the spirit of continuity and centrality, and that's better than a salary."

In 2012, Laviera's last play, *King of Cans*, had its premiere. The drama debuted at the Red Carpet Theater in New York City. This theater was located in the housing complex where he had made his home. Also in this period, Laviera completed a 700 page novel about East Harlem titled *El Barrio*. Though Laviera finished it in 2010, it was not published by the time of his death.

After slipping into a diabetic coma, Laviera died from complications from diabetes in New York City, on November 1, 2013, at the age of 63. Summarizing his importance, Laviera's friend William Luis, an academic and the editor of the *Afro-Hispanic Review*, wrote in his publication, "Tato will be remembered as a great poet, regardless of race, ethnicity, or nationality. He wrote in the tradition of other oral poets, such as Pedro Pietri and Miguel Pinero, and many, especially in New York, will recognize him as an 'AmeRican,' as the title of one of his most popular poems suggested."

Luis added, "Tato spoke not only to a Nuyorican public but also to a larger audience, represented by the multiethnic, racial, and religious groups known to the residents of New York City, as well as New York as a microcosm of a broader, world audience." Laviera's publisher, Nicolás Kanellos, concluded to the *New York Times*'s Gonzalez, "To him, poetry was the highest calling. Even though he lived in relative poverty, he was proud of being part of a tradition that went all the way back to the ancient, epic poets."

Periodicals

Afro-Hispanic Review, Spring 2013.

Centro Journal, Fall 2006.

El Paso Times, November 23, 2008.

New York Times, February 27, 1982; August 1, 1982; February 13, 2010; November 7, 2013.

Targeted News Service, December 7, 2009.

US Fed News, September 7, 2009.

Online

"Tato Laviera," Center for Puerto Rican Studies, http://centropr. hunter.cuny.edu/tato-laviera-bio (December 3, 2014).

"Tato Laviera," Poetry Foundation, http://www.poetryfoundation. org/bio/tato-laviera (December 2, 2014).□

Jerry Lee Lewis

American singer and pianist Jerry Lee Lewis (1935–) was one of the most important pioneers of rock and roll music.

With an outsized personality and musical talent to match, Lewis did not rival his mid-1950s rockabilly comrades Elvis Presley and Johnny Cash in terms of commercial success. He enjoyed only about a year at the top of the charts before his career was derailed after the first in what became a long series of controversies that plagued him. Lewis fought back from that episode of bad publicity—attending his marriage to his 13-year-old cousin—and has flourished over a 60-year-career as a performer. His raw, uninhibited vocal style might have made him a star, but his most distinctive contribution was as a pianist: his showy, brilliant style, marked by an alternation between pounding rhythmic passages and keyboard-spanning glissandos, resembled no one else's.

s_buckley/Shutterstock.com

Took Up Piano at Nine

Jerry Lee Lewis was born in Ferriday, Louisiana, on September 29, 1935. He was the second son of Elmo and Mary Ethel (Mamie) Lewis, in a poor family that lived in a rural shack on a small farm. The family had no money for musical activities, but there was piano music in the area in both white and black churches and taverns, and Jerry Lee began playing when he was nine. Two cousins, Mickey Gilley and future minister Jimmy Swaggart, also took up the instrument and became famous. Jerry Lee showed talent immediately, and according to a frequently told story that appears on Lewis's own website, his family took out a mortgage on their farm to buy him a piano. By the time he was 14, family members later agreed, he had gained the mastery that would be evident in his performances as an adult.

Lewis was influenced by the boogie-style country pianist Moon Mullican, by African-American piano players he heard at a local bar called Haney's Big House, by the yodel-country-blues fusion of singer Jimmie Rodgers, and by the high-volume, theatrically oversized vocals of vaudeville-era star Al Jolson. "There's only been four of us," Lewis was quoted as saying by Jimmy Guterman in the book *Rockin' My Life Away.* "Al Jolson, Jimmie Rodgers, Hank Williams, and Jerry Lee Lewis. That's your only four f---in' stylists that ever lived. " His mother insisted that he try to find a more respectable career than music, but her efforts came to nothing. Always a discipline problem (one account of his nickname "The Killer" holds that it came from an episode where he got into a fight with his eighth grade teacher), he enrolled at Waxahachie Bible College in Texas but was ejected after playing a hymn in boogie-woogie rhythms. He worked as a sewing machine salesman and auditioned unsuccessfully for several country record companies in Nashville and for the Louisiana Hayride Radio program.

Lewis's fortunes changed when he came to Memphis in 1956 and auditioned for the pioneer rock and roll label

Sun. Producer Jack Clement was impressed enough to record Lewis with a pair of backing musicians on a rhythmically intensified version of the Ray Price country hit "Crazy Arms;" it sold well regionally, and label owner Sam Phillips agreed to give Lewis studio work and to keep recording him. Lewis backed singer-guitarist Carl Perkins on the rock and roll classics "Matchbox" and "Your True Love" and recorded a session, not released until 1990, with Elvis Presley, Johnny Cash, and Perkins; they were dubbed the Million Dollar Quartet.

In the year 1957 Lewis matched the chart performance of those rockabilly giants. He scored major hits with "Whole Lotta Shakin' Goin' On," "Great Balls of Fire" (an Otis Blackwell composition whose sexualization of an image from Pentecostal Christian discourse proved explosive and prompted accusations that Lewis was playing the devil's music), and "Breathless." These songs not only reached top pop chart levels (though "Whole Lotta Shakin' was eclipsed by the Debbie Reynolds pop hit "Tammy") but were major hits in country and rhythm-and-blues markets as well.

Set Pianos Afire

Lewis had emerged as rock and roll music's newest star, and he appeared on the *Tonight Show* with host Steve Allen and on the music program *American Bandstand.* In person he was perhaps even more exciting than on recordings: his keyboard acrobatics, when they seemed to reach their maximum intensity, would explode into another level as he stood up, threw or kicked his piano bench aside and pounded the piano from a standing position. At the end of a set, he was known to set his piano on fire.

Riding high with a new self-penned hit "High School Confidential" and a role in a film of the same name, Lewis entered the year 1958 with his habitual confidence even higher than usual. He embarked on a tour of the United Kingdom, but journalists there discovered that he had married his 13-year-old first cousin once removed, Myra Gale Brown, in December of the previous year. Although the marriage was not illegal at the time, Lewis was vilified in the press and booed by fans. He returned to the United States to find the first wave of rock and roll in decline and his own reputation in tatters. Radio stations refused to play his music, and except for a 1961 cover of the Ray Charles hit "What'd I Say" he experienced only commercial failure for several years, during which his fee for a night's performance dropped from $10,000 to $250.

Supremely convinced of his own talent and creative worth, Lewis soldiered on, performing in any small club that would have him. A live performance he gave at the Star Club in Hamburg, Germany, was recorded and released, becoming one of rock and roll's classic live recordings. In 1963 Lewis signed with the Smash label, a subsidiary of the major label Mercury. Smash steered him toward country music, which Lewis had grown up with and recorded enthusiastically. He continued to perform wilder rock and roll shows on stage and occasionally explored side projects such as an appearance as Iago in a 1968 musical adaptation of William Shakespeare's play *Othello*.

Scored Country Hits

Lewis's country career, underrated in terms of reissues and journalistic attention, lasted from the mid-1960s into the early 1980s and produced 30 substantial hits, including "What Made Milwaukee Famous (Made a Loser Out of Me)" (1968), "She Even Woke Me Up to Say Goodbye" (1969), and "Would You Take Another Chance on Me" (1971). He continued to record songs such as "Meat Man" (1973) that pushed boundaries in country music's conservative culture. A biopic about Lewis, *Great Balls of Fire!*, was released in 1989; it featured actor Dennis Quaid as Lewis, but the singer, his powers undiminished, recorded many of his own classic songs for the soundtrack.

During the 1980s, Lewis experienced new problems and controversies. After he suffered a perforated ulcer in 1981, doctors gave him a 50-50 chance of survival, but he recovered. He was often at odds with the Internal Revenue Service and filed for bankruptcy in 1988. Most seriously, Lewis's fourth and fifth wives died under mysterious circumstances; a *Rolling Stone* magazine article raised questions about the investigation into the 1983 death of his fifth wife, Shawn Stephens, from a drug overdose, but Lewis was never charged with a crime. Since 2012 Lewis has been married to his seventh wife, Judith. He has had six children, two of whom died accidental deaths. In 1986 he was part of the first group of musicians inducted into the Rock and Roll Hall of Fame.

Remarkably, in view of a long history of alcohol abuse and prescription painkillers, Lewis remained a viable and enthusiastic performer into the 2010s. With several albums touted as his probable last, Lewis kept releasing new music, often in collaboration with the rock legends whom he had inspired; *Last Man Standing* appeared in 2006, *Mean Old Man* in 2010, and *Rock & Roll Time* in 2014. In that year, a biography based on Lewis's own words, *Jerry Lee Lewis: His Own Story*, was issued by author Rick Bragg. Jerry Lee Lewis was slated to appear at the New Orleans Jazz & Heritage Festival in 2015.

Books

Bragg, Rick, *Jerry Lee Lewis: His Own Story*, Harper, 2014.
Guterman, Jimmy, *Rockin' My Life Away: Listening to Jerry Lee Lewis*, Rutledge Hill, 1991.
Tosches, Nick, *Hellfire*, Grove, 1982.

Periodicals

Billboard, November 15, 2014.
Commercial Appeal (Memphis, TN), June 15, 2000.
Rolling Stone, March 1, 1984.
USA Today, September 7, 2010.
Virginian Pilot, April 9, 2007.

Online

"Biography," Jerry Lee Lewis Official Website, http://www.jerryleelewis.com (January 3, 2015).
"Biography," *Rolling Stone*, http://www.rollingstone.com/music/artists/jerry-lee-lewis/biography (January 3, 2015).
"Jerry Lee Lewis," *Allmusic*, http://www.allmusic.com (January 3, 2015).
"Jerry Lee Lewis Biography," Rock and Roll Hall of Fame, http://www.rockhall.com/inductees/jerry-lee-lewis/bio/ (January 3, 2015).□

Andro Linklater

Scottish journalist and historian Andro Linklater (1944–2013) wrote distinctive interpretations of American history through the lens of surveying, boundary lines, and property rights in such books as *Measuring America* (2002) and *The Fabric of America* (2007). In addition to writing for several British periodicals, Linklater penned many other noteworthy histories, biographies, nonfiction works, and books for children.

Linklater was born on December 10, 1944, in Edinburgh, Scotland, the son of Eric Linklater and Marjorie McIntyre. His father was a well known novelist and author, while his mother had been an actress. Raised in Orkney and Tain, Linklater and his three elder siblings were well educated and encouraged intellectually, yet allowed to develop a sense of independence by roaming freely around the family's property. After attending Belhaven Hill school and Winchester College, Linklater studied modern history at Oxford University.

Worked as a Teacher

After completing his degree, Linklater was not interested in becoming an academic. First, he spent a summer working as a tutor for the family of American jazz singer Josephine Baker. Linklater then went to the United States, where he traveled and attended the 1968 Democratic Convention. He also was employed at an art gallery in San Francisco. When he returned to Britain, he worked for the Liberal Party for a time, then entered a teacher's training course at Jordanhill College. Upon completing his training, Linklater worked as a teacher at a tough comprehensive school in west London.

Linklater's writing career began in the mid-1970s. At this time, his father had been working on a history of the Black Watch, the Royal Highland Regiment of Scotland, an infantry regiment of the British Army. When Linklater's father died in 1974 before completing the project, Linklater took it over and finished the book. Published in 1977, *The Black Watch: The History of the Royal Highland Regiment* was well received, and Linklater continued to write professionally.

Linklater's next book was for children, *Amazing Maisie and the Cold Porridge Brigade* (1978). This story focuses on a young girl who wanted to ride a camel, and discovers a camel named Amazing Maisie who can talk but not bend down to take on riders. By the end of the 1970s, Linklater's writing career also included journalism. At this time, he began writing features for the weekend magazine published by the British newspaper, the *Sunday Telegraph.* He wrote on a variety of topics, from pop star Cliff Richard to the nuclear incident at Chernobyl.

Wrote Biographies of Despard and Mackenzie

Linklater spent the 1980s writing biographies for an adult audience. The first, published in 1980, was of Charlotte Despard, a British suffragist who supported socialism and Irish republicanism through Sinn Fein. In 1987, Linklater published a memoir of Compton Mackenzie, a Scottish author who was a friend of Linklater's father. He completed *Compton Mackenzie: A Life* while living in isolation on a Scottish island, Isle Martin, for five years.

During the late 1980s, Linklater expanded his journalistic horizons. He began writing book reviews for the British publication, *The Spectator.* He also became a contributor to *Prospect* and *Reader's Digest* magazines. As a journalist, he liked to be challenged and wrote on many outdoor risk taking activities like powerboat racing around the Isle of Wright.

Linklater's next book saw him focus on a non-Scottish subject, the Iban tribe found in Sarawak on the island of Borneo. Time-Life had commissioned him to write about the head hunting tribe for a larger series about people groups living outside civilization. His 1991 book was entitled *Wild People,* and it humorously explored his experiences there as a journalist living among the now-Western influenced people group. After its publication, Linklater spent more time focused on journalism before penning his next book at the very beginning of the 21st century.

In 2001, Linklater published *The Code of Love.* This nonfiction work explored the relationship of a couple that was divided by World War II. Based on an article, the book looked at the lengths that a RAF (Royal Air Force) prisoner of war in Japan went to record his thoughts. He came up with a code that allowed him to write in a journal without his captors understanding its content. Though his British fiancée was unable to crack the code and understand his war turmoil during his lifetime, she was able to read the content years later after his death. *The Code of Love* was later turned into a musical.

Published *Measuring America*

Linklater's next books were on a very different topic: American history. When Linklater traveled to the United States in the 1990s on a book tour, he was inspired by what he saw from the plane. He observed how neatly divided the land was, which prompted the question for him of who was there first, the pioneers or the surveyors? Linklater's answer was the latter. Linklater also learned of French botanist and adventurer Joseph Dombey, who had been commissioned to take the metric system to America in 1794. Because Dombey was shipwrecked and captured by the British, his replica of the meter never made it to the United States in this time period. Despite the best efforts of metric system backer Thomas Jefferson, the British system of measurement was adopted. These incidents prompted Linklater to write *Measuring America: How an Untamed Wilderness Shaped the United States and Fulfilled the Promise of Democracy* (2002).

Essentially, Linklater investigated how the young federal government of the United States adopted both the British measurement of a chain (approximately 22 yards) and the Public Land Survey System to divide and register land across the continent. In doing so, the land could be sold to individuals, which facilitated westward expansion and development. Summarizing the appeal of *Measuring America,* the London *Daily Telegraph* stated, ''Linklater elaborated the story in fascinating style to show how, once land had been properly defined and registered, it became a commodity which could safely be bought and sold, thus playing a key role in the development of American democracy and enterprise. The frontier spirit, traditionally attributed exclusively to rugged individualism, was equally made possible by federal-financed surveyors.''

Unique and key to *Measuring America* is Linklater's argument that America's westward pioneers were not individualists who sought freedom in the ungoverned frontier. Instead, the author outlines his belief that pioneers greatly needed and depended on government support and security, through, for example, surveying, which divided the western lands often before the arrival of pioneers. Linklater also argues that pioneers would not have left their known confines if the government had not supported and invested in their efforts. Having land ownership and the backing of federal law and government was key to settlement. Linklater believes that these elements deeply shaped the development and character of the United States.

Completed *The Fabric of America*

Linklater followed *Measuring America* with *The Fabric of America* (2007). This book analyzes surveyors, focusing on the role Andrew Elliott played in creating the borders and boundaries of 11 states, the District of Columbia, and the United States itself. Central to Linklater's argument in both books are actions taken by the first American president, George Washington. Among the first projects Washington proposed to Congress for funding was the Public Land Survey. The president saw it as a means of paying off debts incurred by the government during the Revolutionary War. Instead, the survey, as interpreted by Linklater, became the starting point for westward expansion across the continent. There was an emphasis on drawing lines on ground that had not been chartered before. As much as the pioneers loved freedom, they also loved private property and government-enforced property rights, and the democratic process that supported these concepts.

Through *Measuring America* and *The Fabric of America*, Linklater attempted to discredit the popularly accepted Frontier Thesis proposed by American historian Frederick Jackson Turner. According to Turner, American pioneers, especially those who went west in the 19th century, represented key aspects of the American character by conquering the wilderness with the pursuit of freedom, creativity, will, and strength. Instead, Linklater argues, through his history and examination of the importance of the Public Land Survey System, that it was the surveyors who played a bigger role in conquering the west, more so than any conflict or pioneer movement. Law and order were important aspects of the pioneer experience in Linklater's estimation.

Because Linklater was not a professional historian, his perspectives and theories on American history were not taken as seriously as an academic. However, many American scholars found merit to his arguments and his original perspective bringing together settlement, land speculation, and surveying. Linklater also was a gifted, charming speaker, and made a well-received speaking tour of the United States discussing these books.

Focused on a Traitor, an Assassination

After *Measuring America* and *The Fabric of America*, Linklater's next book also looked at a topic in American history. In *An Artist in Treason: The Extraordinary Double Life of General James Wilkinson* (2009), he considers the life and times of an early American traitor, Wilkinson, who impacted early American democracy during the Revolutionary War and early Democratic period. A general by the age of 20, Wilkinson spent years in the employ of the Spanish as a spy on the Americans.

Turning to a British subject for his 2012 book, Linklater published *Why Spencer Perceval Had to Die*. In this tome, the author suggests that Perceval, who was a British prime minister, might have been assassinated in 1812 because of slave and trading interests. Though who killed Perceval is not in dispute—it was Liverpool businessman John Bellingham—Linklater explores the idea that he may have knowingly or unknowingly been used by these interests.

In 2013, Linklater returned to his fascination with the concept of private property in *Owning the Earth*. In this book, Linklater looks at how private property has impacted civilization. He explores the development of private property in the past 500 years, and considers how it has affected the growth of government in America, Europe, Asia, Russia, and the Middle East. Linklater uses stories of various people, the famous and not so famous, in these regions to illustrate his greater argument. Reviewing *Owning the Earth*, the publication *Scotsman* stated, "Even for a polymath like Linklater, this was an audacious undertaking. . . . The result is a sprawling, sparkling, off-the-wall political history of the globe."

Suffered Heart Attack During Research Trip

By October 2013, Linklater was researching his next book on the island of Eigg off the coast of Scotland. Considering the idea of land ownership from another perspective, the topic was an incident of mass starvation in the 19th century. In the Hebrides, an archipelago off the coast of Scotland, English landowners forced the removal of many Scots to create more space for sheep farming.

While on Eigg, Linklater suffered a heart attack, and because of transportation difficulties, was unable to receive proper medical treatment for two days. A week after the incident, Linklater had another massive heart attack and died at an Edinburgh hospital on November 3, 2013, at the age of 68. Upon his death, the London *Daily Telegraph* summarized his professional life by stating "Andro Linklater . . . was a versatile and courageous journalist, never frightened to take up a challenge, while as an author he had the alchemist's knack of transmuting whatsoever subject he tackled in literary—if rarely financial—gold."

Periodicals

Associated Press, October 6, 2009.
Daily Telegraph (London, England), November 12, 2013.
The Guardian (London, England), December 31, 2013.
New York Times, December 6, 2013.
Scotsman, November 7, 2013; January 18, 2014.
The Spectator, November 16, 2013.
The Times (London, England), November 8, 2013.
Washington Post, July 8, 2012.□

Anatole Litvak

Lacking a homeland, Russian émigré filmmaker Anatole Litvak (1902–1974) made films in five different countries. He was best known, however, for his contributions to French and U.S. cinema where he specialized in romantic melodramas and thrillers offered with a film noir flair. Career highlights included the French-made romantic tragedy *Mayerling* (1936) and the Hollywood-inspired *The Snake Pit* (1948).

Anatole Litvak was born in May 1902, in Kiev, Ukraine, to parents of Jewish descent. Ukraine became part of the Soviet Union when Litvak was a young man. As a teen, Litvak worked as a stage actor and

Pictorial Parade/Archive Photos/Getty Images

later earned assignments as a designer and director. He took classes at the State Theatre School in Leningrad. In 1923, Litvak began working for the Soviet branch of the Danish film studio Nordisk. Initially, Litvak was a set decorator or assistant director. Eventually, the studio handed Litvak the reins. Litvak was 22 when he directed his first film, *Tatiana* (1925).

Honed Film Skills in Paris, Berlin

In 1925, Litvak left the Soviet Union and went briefly to Paris before settling in Berlin. At the time, Berlin and Paris both had sizable populations of Russian emigres who had fled their homeland after the Bolshevik (Communist) Party came to power. With so many fellow Russians living in the two cities, Litvak had no trouble finding work and moved between Berlin and Paris for the next dozen years.

Litvak edited the 1925 German film *Die Freudlose Gasse* (The Joyless Street), which starred Greta Garbo. In Berlin, he found work with Ciné-Alliance and Albatros Films. For a time he worked for his uncle, Noë Bloch. Bloch had fled Russia after the revolution and became a noted producer in France. Litvak also worked with famed French director Abel Gance on 1927's *Napoléon*—an epic, multi-hour biopic of French leader Napoleon Bonaparte. In the film, Gance experimented with widescreen images and other technical innovations, such as taking the camera off the tripod and letting it remain in motion during much of

the shooting. For one snowball fight scene from Napoleon's childhood, Gance attached the camera to a cameraman's body, thus allowing the viewer to get right into the brawl. As Litvak worked under Gance and others, he picked up their tricks and developed his own twist on their styles.

Litvak also worked as an assistant to fellow Russian refugee and director Alexandre Volkoff, assisting with the French-made *The Loves of Casanova* (1927). In 1930, he helped Volkoff with the German-made *The White Devil*. He directed his first feature abroad in Berlin, the 1930 black and white musical *Dolly Macht Karriere* (Dolly Gets Ahead). He followed with a comedy, 1931's *Nie wieder Liebe!* (No More Love), also made for a German studio.

Earned Reputation for Visual Intricacies

Litvak returned to France and directed two films—1931's *Calais-Douvres* and 1932's *Coeur de Lilas* (Lilac). The latter film earned him critical praise for helping to influence the direction of the newly emerging French talkie film style. At the time Litvak made the film, directors in France were torn as to what creative style they should pursue. With the advent of "talkies," some directors began to pursue a more theatrical style, with movies resembling theatrical productions because the characters could now talk and sing.

Litvak, however, wanted to ensure that films remained a "visual" medium. He understood that films were different from theatrical stage performances because the camera was responsible for creating the intimacy between viewer and characters. Keeping this philosophy in mind, Litvak focused on the details of images and camera angles. He relied heavily on traveling shots and rhythmic editing and spent countless hours trying to find French-specific locations for the film. In one section of *Coeur de Lilas*, Litvak used a crane shot to capture the scene and set the atmosphere.

Litvak's films were noted for their visual sophistication. He paid special attention to the light, the rhythm and the images. He was known for his camera tracking and for utilizing pans and swoops. In the book *City of Darkness, City of Light,* author Alastair Phillips included a quote from Litvak discussing his 1932 film: "In *Coeur de Lilas*, my cast only speak when the situation demands. I simply want to make cinema; nothing more, nothing less." Next, the director went to Vienna, Austria, to film 1932's *Das Lied Einer Nacht* (The Song of Night).

In 1933, Litvak released another French film, *Cette Vieille Canaille*. He came to love Paris. Of the nearly 40 films he made, 13 were set in Paris. In addition to the atmosphere, he also preferred the personnel, noting that he did his best work there and found the actors and crew efficient. In *City of Darkness,* he was quoted as saying, "The French do the work in an instant that the English, who are nonetheless charming, take two hours to do with solemn slowness; or the Germans can only carry out with the most precise orders. The French may grumble but they do it so well!"

In 1935, *L'Équipage* (Flight into Darkness), hit theaters across France. Just as with *Coeur de Lilas*, this Litvak-directed film was artistically inspired. A high-class melodrama, it featured a love triangle set against the backdrop of World War I. In the film, two pilots team up for battle but are really fighting an internal war—one of them has become a lover to the other man's wife. The film starts out calmly with a romantic chiaroscuro-inspired mood. Chiaroscuro lighting was highly pervasive during Hollywood's film noir period, which started in the 1940s. It is bold and dramatic, with high contrast between the light and dark, thus offering a surreal nature to black and white films. In addition to the love scenes, the film took the viewer into battle. The movie earned praise for its battlefield scenes that keenly captured the cruelty of war. Litvak included dogfights with authentic German and French aircraft. The pace of the film got more frenzied as the pilot who committed the adultery faced his moral dilemma.

In 1936, French moviegoers were treated to another Litvak triumph, a film titled *Mayerling,* which became his first international hit. The cinematic love story was based on the true and tragic tale of Archduke Rudolph, onetime heir to the Austrian Habsburg dynasty. The archduke, however, has fallen for a baron's daughter, whom he prefers to his arranged-marriage wife. Rather than be separated from his mistress to take the throne, the Archduke forms a suicide pact with his lover. Writing on frenchfilmsite.com, movie reviewer James Travers credited Litvak for his delicate directing: "For a film of this era, *Mayerling* is visually stunning." Travers also noted that the "moody chiaroscuro cinematography conveys a chilling sense of oppression and transience that lends the tragic denouement an exquisite poignancy and poetry."

Moved to United States

Mayerling grabbed the attention of Hollywood, and offers to make films for U.S. studios soon rolled in. Litvak relocated to the United States in 1937. His first few years in Hollywood, he moved between dramas and comedies. The first film Litvak made on U.S. soil was the 1937 drama *The Woman I Love,* which was actually a remake of *L'Équipage.* After filming concluded, Litvak married the lead, Miriam Hopkins, but they divorced within two years. He followed with *Tovarich.* The storyline was right up Litvak's alley. It told the tale of Russian emigres (a prince and his wife) seeking a better life in Paris after escaping their homeland following the Russian Revolution. Litvak followed with another comedy, 1938's *The Amazing Dr. Clitterhouse,* a crime film starring Humphrey Bogart as a gangster. Next came *The Sisters* (1938), which featured Errol Flynn and Bette Davis.

Litvak switched gears with 1939's *Confessions of a Nazi Spy.* This Nazi expose was one of the first overtly anti-Hitler films made before the United States entered the war. The film's storyline was culled from articles published by a former FBI agent who had been tracking Nazi activity in the United States. The film proved highly unpopular. At the time, Hollywood studios for the most part were ignoring what was happening with Hitler, for fear of losing their European market. *Confessions of a Nazi Spy* was banned from many European nations. Though the movie flopped, it inspired Litvak to tackle films of a more serious nature.

Next, Litvak made *Castle on the Hudson* (1940), a prison feature about a mobster sent off to New York's infamous Sing Sing Correctional Facility. The year 1940 also saw the release of Litvak's *City for Conquest,* which featured James Cagney as a boxer. Litvak delved into social realism with *Out of the Fog* (1941). The film followed a young woman who falls for a

racketeer against the wishes of her father. The year 1941 also saw the release of *Blues In the Night,* which told the tale of an aspiring blues band helmed by bandleader Jigger Pine. The latter two films were widely classified as film noir, though other Litvak productions also fall within the style. Litvak directed 11 films during his first four years in Hollywood. It was rumored that he was a heavy gambler and needed to make a lot of films to pay off his debts.

Co-produced 'Why We Fight' War Series

After the United States entered World War II, Litvak found a new focus. In 1942, he joined Italian-born U.S. director Frank Capra at the Office of War Information, a newly created U.S. agency established to consolidate government information services. The agency's mission was to inform the public, both at home and abroad, about war events. Capra was put in charge of creating a series of documentary films called the *Why We Fight* series. The films, filled with both historical facts and propaganda, were shown to U.S. soldiers and citizens to help them understand why the United States was involved in the war in Europe. Between 1942 and 1945, the Office of War Information produced seven *Why We Fight* features. Litvak co-directed several productions and took charge of directing the *Battle of Russia* compilation under Capra's supervision. They also produced a segment on the D-Day Normandy Invasion, delving into the strategic framework for the invasion and exploring individual "hero" stories.

After the war, Litvak concentrated on "women's pictures." He directed the 1948 thriller *Sorry, Wrong Number,* which starred Barbara Stanwyck as a bedridden hypochondriac threatened by a hit man hired by her husband. The year 1948 also saw the release of Litvak's most well-known film, *The Snake Pit,* which starred Olivia de Havilland as an insane asylum inmate. Prior to filming, Litvak required the cast and crew to spend time in such an asylum. To prepare for her role, De Havilland viewed doctors administering electric shock treatments.

At the time of the film's release, *New York Times* reviewer Bosley Crowther called *The Snake Pit* "a mature emotional drama" and noted that "although it is frequently harrowing, it is a fascinating and deeply moving film." Though fiction, the drama brought to light the inhumane treatment faced by the mentally ill, prompting legislative reform across the United States. The film earned numerous Academy Award nominations, including best director and best picture. It won the award for best sound recording and in 1949 picked up the International Prize at the Venice Film Festival. Litvak's 1951 war drama *Decision Before Dawn* also earned an Academy Award best picture nomination.

Returned to Europe

In the early 1950s, Litvak had a falling out with 20th Century Fox. He was working on *Désirée,* a historical film involving Napoleon. Litvak told the studio he needed to shoot it on location in Europe, but 20th Century Fox preferred a cheaper, back-lot production. Litvak ended up quitting the production and returning to Europe. In 1955, he married costume designer Sophie Steur. The two had worked together on several projects.

He returned to the United States to direct the 1956 historical drama *Anastasia,* which rescued Ingrid Bergman's career. In the film, Bergman's character, an amnesiac, is involved in a swindle scheme to impersonate a Romanov princess who was rumored to have survived the execution of the entire family of Tsar Nicholas II. Litvak directed Bergman to an Academy Award for the role. He continued to work in Europe throughout the 1960s, but lost his popularity. He made his last film in 1970, *The Lady in the Car With Glasses and a Gun.* Litvak died in Neuilly-sur-Seine, France, on December 15, 1974.

Books

Brook, Vincent, *Driven to Darkness: Jewish Émigré Directors and the Rise of Film Noir,* Rutgers University Press, 2009.

Phillips, Alastair, *City of Darkness, City of Light: émigré Filmmakers in Paris, 1929-1939,* Amsterdam University Press, 2004.

Periodicals

Architectural Digest, April 1992.

Online

"Mayerling (1936)," *Frencfilmsite.com,* http://www.frenchfilmsite.com/review/1936-M/Mayerling.html (December 9, 2014).

"The Snake Pit," *New York Times,* http://www.nytimes.com/movies/movie/45324/The-Snake-Pit/overview (December 11, 2014).□

AFP/AFP/Getty Images

Raymond Loewy

French-born industrial designer Raymond Loewy (1893–1986) was hailed in his lifetime as the founder of modern American industrial design. Loewy invented or reimagined hundreds of products, from Pepsodent toothbrushes to the insignia of Air Force One. "I have only ever refused to design two things when asked," he told *Times* of London writer Alan Hamilton in 1981. "A hand grenade and a funeral casket."

Born Raymond Fernand Loewy in Paris on November 5, 1893, Loewy was the last of three sons in his family. His mother Marie was from the south of France while father Maximilian was originally from Vienna but had a long and successful career as a financial journalist in the French capital. The youngest Loewy boy displayed an almost preternatural aptitude for combining design with commerce: at age ten he launched his own self-published magazine, *Le Journal de Plombières,* filled with drawings of futuristic products and scenarios. In his teens he built a model aircraft for a competition near his home in Neuilly, a Paris suburb. It won first prize for staying aloft the longest, and out of that minor triumph the 15-year-old Loewy opened a small workshop to produce and sell the model flyer. "I learned about employment, sales, bookkeeping and writing manuals in three languages," his *New York Times* obituary quoted him as saying. "In two years I knew about business and knew it could be fun."

Carpeted His Trench

Loewy also took engineering courses at the École de Lanneau in Paris and briefly worked for an electrical engineering firm. When World War I erupted in the summer of 1914 the 20-year-old enlisted in the French Army and was assigned to a regiment that fought long and arduous trench battles against the German military. Loewy's mechanical skills proved adept enough to earn him a promotion to communications officer in charge of intercepting enemy telegraph transmissions. Already a rigorous aesthete, he also turned the communications dugout into a plush clubhouse, replete with bolts of fabric, rugs, and even pillows Loewy carried back from Paris while on leave.

Loewy was wounded in a mustard gas attack at Reims, and after the war ended in 1918 both of his parents died in the worldwide influenza pandemic of 1918–19. With French manufacturing at a postwar standstill he was unable to find work, and heeded his older brothers' invitation to join them in New York City. He hoped to land an engineering job at the General Electric Company in Schenectady, New York, but a war-relief charity auction aboard the ship brought him a lucky break: he drew a sketch of a stylishly dressed woman that received a high bid, and the buyer was a British diplomat who suggested he pursue a career in fashion illustration. Loewy arrived in New York City with two letters of introduction from the consul officer, one of them addressed to publishing titan Condé Nast.

Enthralled by New York City

In his 1951 autobiography *Never Leave Well Enough Alone,* Loewy recalled arriving in his French army uniform in Manhattan in September of 1919, and after his immigration paperwork was completed he and his brother took a cab to visit the observation deck of the new, 38-story Equitable Building skyscraper. In his first weeks in New York City he recalled feeling overwhelmed by "the giant scale of all things," as he wrote in *Never Leave Well Enough Alone,* especially anything that moved. "Their ruggedness, their bulk, were frightening. Lights were blinding in their crudity, subways were thundering masses of sinister force, streetcars were monstrous and clattering hunks of rushing cast iron; it was terribly impressive, gigantic, restless, and supervolted."

Loewy found success as a fashion illustrator for the Condé Nast magazine *Vogue* and other publications, and eventually parlayed his commercial illustration work into store-display and other design commissions. He created elegant print ads for Saks Fifth Avenue, the new luxury department store that opened in 1924, and designed spiffy uniforms for its elevator operators. The window display work led to store-interior jobs, but by the end of the Roaring Twenties Loewy was keen to move into product design, a relatively new profession at the time. He won his first commission from Gestetner, a British maker of duplicating machines. A precursor to the copier machine, the Gestetner mimeograph machine was a complicated piece of mechanical equipment that was difficult to maintain and often left ink stains on its users. Loewy's successful prototype encased the moving parts in Bakelite, an early form of plastic, and simplified other design elements. Loewy also worked for Westinghouse Electric Company as a radio set designer.

Loewy opened his own design consultancy firm in New York City in late 1933 with several business partners. It became Raymond Loewy Associates in 1944. Loewy's first wife Jean Thomson, whom he married in 1931, managed much of the daily operations at the Fifth Avenue office while the visionary Loewy spent long days at the drawing board or pitching new clients. He also traveled ceaselessly in an era before jet aircraft, a federal highway system, or even comfortable passenger-train seats. Loewy loved cars and designed several custom roadsters and sedans for personal use. His first automotive contract was with the Hupp Motor Company, who hired him as an interior-cabin consultant. He showed them a prototype car he had made at his own expense—for a stunning $18,000, revealing how much money Loewy was already earning from other clients in 1931—and it went into production but failed to keep Hupp in business.

Unveiled First Non-Riveted Train Body

In 1932 Loewy was hired by mass-retailing giant Sears Roebuck to design a new refrigerator under its Coldspot

brand of appliances, the predecessor of Kenmore. Loewy's first Coldspot refrigerator went into mass production in 1935 and began posting staggering sales numbers. Revealing both consumer demand and Sears' in-house manufacturing and shipping capacities, more than 5,000 of Loewy's refrigerators were sold some weeks at the tail end of the Great Depression.

Loewy also had a long history with Studebaker, another automotive pioneer. He designed several well-received models and lured top talent from General Motors and other competitors for the Studebaker design studio in South Bend, Indiana. Some of the Loewy touches on Studebaker's most popular models of the 1930s and '40s were the distinctive bullet-nosed front grill and a wraparound rear window. Another lucrative, symbiotic relationship Loewy's firm forged was with the Pennsylvania Railroad, operators of one of the most profitable overland transit routes of the mid-20th century. Loewy was first hired to solve a garbage-receptacle problem at busy Pennsylvania Station in New York City but by 1937 had overseen the production of the first all-welded locomotive, the sleep S-1.

Loewy and other colleagues formed the Society of Industrial Designers in 1944. He waited out the tough years of World War II, as manufacturing industries and all available material resources were directed toward the war effort. By the late 1940s Loewy had attained celebrity status as America's leading industrial designer, though there were other figures of equal importance whose products became ubiquitous but were less well-known to the general public. A skillful promoter and brand-identity theorist, Loewy courted mainstream media attention and invited journalists into his homes and office. A 1949 *Life* magazine profile mentioned listed a Fifth Avenue penthouse, a California desert home in Palm Springs with a swimming pool that extended from the rear yard into the living room, an estate in Sands Point, Long Island, plus three properties in France, one of them a seventeenth-century villa built for the mistress of French King Henry IV. Loewy also appeared later that year on the cover of *Time* magazine, the first industrial designer to achieve that place of honor.

Worked on Lever House

Loewy and his firm flourished in the 1950s. He created the popular Scenicruiser fleet for Greyhound, the long-distance passenger bus company, refined the iconic curves of the glass Coca-Cola bottle and devised a red-and-white diamond design for its newly introduced canned version, and created plush and modern interiors for the newly built Lever House, the first all-glass building on Park Avenue. Loewy worked with the architectural firm Skidmore, Owings & Merrill on the building that became an iconic Manhattan landmark not long after it opened in 1952. "Loewy's design expressed the hierarchical nature of mid-20th-century corporate culture," declared Donald Albrecht 50 years later in *Interiors.* "From street to pinnacle, like so many horizontal drawers, Loewy fashioned the building's interiors to convey gradual changes from public to private, open to closed, common to elite." Albrecht singled out the airy lobby, showing Lever brands, along with a "third-floor cafeteria...expressing a cheerful message of egalitarian corporate bonhomie.''

In the early 1960s Loewy returned to work for Studebaker once again as the automaker struggled to turn a profit. Working with a team of designers he produced the stunning Studebaker Avanti, a fiberglass sports coupe unveiled in 1962. One of the most cult-status cars ever built in the United States, the Avanti was ahead of its time by at least two decades. ''I alienated the automotive industry by saying that cars should be lightweight and compact,'' Loewy said in the late 1970s, according to his *New York Times* obituary. ''In those days they looked liked chrome-plated barges.''

Air Force One and Skylab

Loewy embraced the Jet Age with his characteristic verve and vision. U.S. President John F. Kennedy invited him to create the livery and logo for the official presidential plane, Air Force One, and in 1967 Loewy went to work for the U.S. National Aeronautics and Space Administration as a habitability consultant. He designed the interior and fittings for its Skylab spacecraft and once said that of all the products he designed over the decades, the zero-gravity toilet was the most challenging. There was also the matter of a porthole window, which vehicle-design engineers argued would be too expensive to make secure. Loewy contended that a window and view of their home planet was crucial for the astronauts.

Loewy devoted the final years of his career to designing iconic logos. His branding work in the 1970s included the new eagle emblem for the United States Postal Service and streamlined signage for petrochemical giants Shell Oil and Exxon. He finally retired in 1980, at age 87, and died on July 14, 1986, in Monte Carlo at age 92. His firm continued to operate its London and Paris offices for several more years. His survivors include second wife Viola Erickson Loewy and their daughter Laurence.

Loewy's Palm Springs house and its famous pool remain visible through Google Earth. In 2002 Johns Hopkins University Press reissued Loewy's autobiography *Never Leave Well Enough Alone* but maintained the original high-equality layout and bindings specified by the author. Its cover shows an egg against a gradient gray background. Loewy viewed the humble poultry product as the touchstone for all designers seeking to improve on the natural world or add to the human-built one. ''So beautiful in conception!,'' the *Life* magazine profile from 1949 quoted him as saying. ''The functionally perfect form, the symbol of progress! If the egg were any other shape, the life of the hen would be intolerable.''

Books

Loewy, Raymond, *Never Leave Well Enough Alone*, Simon & Schuster, 1951, reissued with new introduction by Glenn Porter, Johns Hopkins University Press, 2002.

Periodicals

Interiors, December 2000.
Life, May 2, 1949.
New York Times, July 15, 1986.
Times (London, England), June 13, 1981. □

Ludwig II, King of Bavaria

German King Ludwig II of Bavaria (1845–1886) endured a short but storied reign as hereditary ruler of his scenic principality. Not entirely engaged with the executive duties of state, the monarch later dubbed "Mad King Ludwig" devoted his energies to designing and furnishing extravagant, treasure-filled castles. Among them was the mountain aerie of Neuschwanstein, later used as the model for Sleeping Beauty's Castle at Walt Disney World theme parks.

udwig Otto Friedrich Wilhelm, Prince of Bavaria, was born on August 25, 1845, at Schloss Nymphenburg in Munich. At the time of his birth his father Maximilian was crown prince of Bavaria and his grandfather was King Ludwig I of Bavaria. They ruled through the powerful House of Wittelsbach, whose ducal lands and titles in southern Germany stretched back to 1180 and, like most European dynasties of the early medieval era, had ancestral links to the Charlemagne, founder of the Holy Roman Empire. Ludwig's mother was Princess Marie of Prussia, who came from Berlin and was of an equally august lineage as a daughter of the House of Hohenzollern, another dynastic power that controlled large parts of northern and central Europe for centuries.

Raised in Wittelsbachian Splendor

The marriage of Ludwig's parents produced just one other child, his younger brother Otto. The family home was a pretty castle, Schloss Schwansee (Swan Lake Castle), which had been built by his father over the ruins of a much older fortress at Hohenschwangau in the Bavarian Alps. Ludwig and Otto also spent happy hours at Schloss Berg, a smaller but equally splendid villa on Starnbergersee, a lake near Munich. Less pleasant, protocol-ruled days were demanded of them at court in the vast Residenz palace, the Bavarian royal seat, in the heart of Munich.

Ludwig was close to his zestful and eccentric namesake-grandfather, who had been forced to abdicate the throne in 1848 after political unrest but remained a popular figure in Bavaria. His grandfather lived to the age of 81, but Ludwig's father King Maximilian II of Bavaria died unexpectedly in March of 1864 at the age of 52. The 18-year-old crown prince reluctantly took the throne, and his unmarried status and particularly photogenic looks made him one of the first celebrity royals of the modern age. Photography was a new medium at the time and an early portrait of the handsome and dashing new king, looking pensive and slightly bohemian, was widely circulated across Europe and bolstered his image as one of the world's most eligible bachelors.

Suffered Anxiety in Crowds

The new King Ludwig II of Bavaria was said to have scarce inclination to involve himself in affairs of state. He kept his father's cabinet ministers and permitted them to carry on their duties with nominal interference from him. The hours-long military parades, holy-day processions, grand

De Agostini Picture Library/Getty Images

banquets for visiting dignitaries, and other displays of royal spectacle held even less interest for the new king, who found the pomp and protocol at court in the Munich Residenz stifling. He preferred a more relaxed lifestyle at Schloss Berg and began drawing up plans for other suitably private bolt-holes.

Ludwig was reluctantly drawn into schemes to find him a suitable wife. The winning candidate was his cousin Duchess Sophie Charlotte, with whom he shared a great-grandfather. The families had grown up near one another in the Lake Starnberg area and Ludwig had been close to Sissi, Sophie Charlotte's sister Elisabeth. Sissi went on to become Empress of Austria through her own marriage and achieved a similar level of press notoriety as Ludwig, also fueled by the emerging popular journalism in the latter decades of the 19th century.

Ludwig's engagement to Sophie Charlotte was announced in January of 1867, but by October the king had twice postponed their wedding date. Sophie's parents, becoming increasingly peeved, sent an emissary to make inquiries, and Ludwig responded with a letter to her father with profuse apologies, breaking off the engagement. He also wrote to Sophie, who was said to have been heartbroken but eventually married a French duke. Ludwig never married, but voluminous correspondence and personal diaries reveal him to have been internally conflicted about his romantic interest in other men. During his teen years he had become close to another prince, who served as his

aide-de-camp, and later traveled in the company who served as his chief equerry for nearly 20 years.

Became Wagner's Greatest Patron

The king's most enduring interest was his passion for classical music, specifically the Romantic *lieder* and operas of German composer Richard Wagner. Ludwig was an impressionable 15-year-old when he experienced his first Wagner opera, which were magnificent and stirring live spectacles that drew upon medieval Germanic legends and mythology. In awe of the composer's obvious gifts, Ludwig arranged to meet Wagner shortly after becoming king in 1864. The new Bavarian sovereign and the already-famous Wagner struck up a lasting, though platonic, relationship that shaped their subsequent careers and respective impact upon German culture. Ludwig agreed to fund Wagner's ambitious plans to complete more operas in his planned cycle, establish a world-renowned festival event, and premiere new works at an acoustically superior performance hall in the heart of Munich. Ludwig gave Wagner an annual stipend which helped the composer to complete *Tristan und Isolde*. That 1865 opera was the first to open on the stage of a new National Theater of Munich, a space whose layout and acoustic specifications were built to Wagner's exacting standards.

Both Wagner and the king experienced enormous trouble in the Bavarian capital. Wagner, born in 1813, had had a checkered career before Ludwig became his patron and was perpetually hounded by debt collectors. The composer also involved himself in political schemes and had at one point been banned from entering other German kingdoms. Ludwig paid off Wagner's debts but in Bavaria the opera creator imprudently became involved in an affair with the daughter of composer Franz Liszt, which scandalized conservative courtiers in Munich. Wagner was forced into exile once again and Ludwig arranged for the composer to live and work at a lakefront villa in Switzerland.

Began Building Neuschwanstein

Ludwig's private ambivalence about Munich and the ruthlessly judgmental scene at his court drove him back to his idyllic childhood playground around Schwansee. He began building a new, even more magnificent castle called Neuschwanstein in the late 1860s. It was massive in scale, opulent in design, and decadent in its interiors to the point of excess: Ludwig loved gold, mirrors, and the cherub-strewn allegorical art of the Baroque period

Early in his reign Ludwig's indifference to political leadership led to turmoil in Bavaria. In the Austro-Prussian War of 1866 he supported the Austrian side, and when Prussia emerged victorious after the seven-week conflict Ludwig was forced to sign a new defense treaty with the powerful northern German kingdom. Prussia then waged another war, this one against France, in its effort to create a new and powerful confederation of German states. Again, a superior Prussian military prevailed and Prussia's powerful minister-president Otto von Bismarck became chancellor of a new German Confederation united under Ludwig's Hohenzollern relation, the new Kaiser Wilhelm I. Ludwig's role in the unification of Germany survives in his signature on the infamous *Kaiserbrief* of 1870, which sanctioned Bismarck's unification plan for a new Reich, or empire.

Ludwig remained king of Bavaria, but the unification of Germany was deeply resented by many at court and among the general population. To forestall domestic unrest his ministers did win some special considerations for Bavaria in the German Constitution of 1871. The monarch, meanwhile, became increasingly reclusive. He spent much of the 1870s working on plans for new castles elsewhere in Bavaria. One was Schloss Linderhof, a splendidly constructed royal palace and park near Oberammergau in the Bavarian Alps. Linderhof featured an underground cave-lake, the Venus Grotto, which was illuminated by a special system of electricity-powered lamps developed for it by Siemens.

Resisted Pleas to Marry

The palace project that spelled the end for Ludwig was not the magical Linderhof nor even the gold-and-silver bedecked Neuschwanstein, but the instead his plans for an epic schloss on Chiemsee, Bavaria's largest lake. Planned as Germany's version of the Palace of Versailles in France, Schloss Herrenchiemsee was built on an island in the middle of the lake and the engineering work for the foundation alone proved so costly that Ludwig's family and ministers began to voice concerns. The king was independently wealthy on his own, with generous income provided by the ducal Wittelsbach lands, but he borrowed large sums from family members to finance these follies while resisting demands to marry a suitable bride and produce an heir to the throne.

There were other troubles in Ludwig's immediate family. Next in line to the throne was his younger brother Otto, who had began to display signs of mental illness in his late teens. The prince was kept under strict watch at Schloss Nymphenburg, but in one memorable incident Otto burst into Munich's landmark Frauenkirche Cathedral in the middle of a Roman Catholic holy-day Mass in 1875 and beseeched the Archbishop of Munich to forgive him his sins. The prince was under the care of a top physician-psychiatrist, Dr. Bernhard von Gudden, and Gudden was recruited into a scheme to remove Ludwig from power. The king's extravagant spending and desire for privacy came to be characterized as signs of his unfitness for office, and Bavarian cabinet ministers sought support from Prince Luitpold, the brother of Ludwig's late father Maximilian.

Prince Luitpold demanded firm proof that his other nephew was as mentally unstable as the piteous Otto. In early 1886 a cabal of anti-Ludwig officials recruited palace servants and other questionable figures to give secret testimony that the king had odd habits, including a preference for eating his meals in solitude and nighttime horseback rides through the countryside. Gudden signed off on the report, though he had met Ludwig only once 12 years earlier, and from that orders of deposition were drawn up.

Drowned in Shallow Water

In the early hours of June 10, 1886, Gudden brought an official committee to Schloss Neuschwanstein that included male psychiatric nurses ready to dose the king with chloroform and lace him into a straitjacket. Providentially, one of Ludwig's servants warned him ahead of time and he sent a detachment of guards to the castle gate to prevent them from entering. Later that day Luitpold was proclaimed prince regent of Bavaria. Supporters urged Ludwig to go to Munich and reassert his authority at court, but he resisted. Another armed commission was dispatched on June 12 and this time Ludwig, who seemed confused when guards found him, was taken into custody and into a waiting carriage in which Dr. Gudden sat.

Ludwig agreed to go to Schloss Berg, the family palace on Starnbergersee. The circumstances of his death there, and of Gudden the following day, remain part of the mystery and lore surrounding "Mad King Ludwig." Both men were seen walking along the shoreline of Lake Starnberg on the early evening of June 13, 1886. Later it began raining and a search party was sent out to find them. The king had apparently drowned in waist-deep water—though no water was in his lungs—and Gudden had purportedly died by strangulation. The most likely theories about the incident involve an escape plan Ludwig had attempted to carry out, probably with the help of sympathetic conspirators and a waiting rowboat. Five decades later, a local resident made a deathbed confession asserting that the official inquiry was a cover-up, and that the king had died of gunshot wounds.

The funeral of Ludwig in Munich was a testament to the passions the popular, job-creating prince stirred among Bavarians. Mourners lined up for hours in advance of the public viewing and openly wept at the sight of the 40-year-old deceased and deposed monarch; at one point armed guards had to be stationed at the casket. His uncle Luitpold ruled as regent for the still-secluded Prince Otto, who died in 1916. Luitpold's son became Ludwig III, the last king of Bavaria. The remaining family members, including the second Kaiser Wilhelm, lost their hereditary ruling rights with Germany's defeat in World War I. Luitpold's grandson bestowed Neuschwanstein and the other palace properties to the state of Bavaria in 1923.

Books

McIntosh, Christopher, *The Swan King: Ludwig II of Bavaria*, I.B. Tauris, 2012.

Periodicals

Der Spiegel, January 27, 2014.
Times (London, England), June 17, 1886.□

Béla Lugosi

The Hungarian-born Béla Lugosi (1882–1956) earned instant and immortal fame in 1931 for bringing Count Dracula to life in the original black and white film adaptation of Bram Stoker's vampire thriller. Lugosi's portrayal set the standard for big-screen bloodsucking vampires for decades to come, but forever left Lugosi relegated to the role of horror film villain.

Lugosi was born October 20, 1882, in the Hungarian city of Lugos. Today, the town is known as Lugoj and is part of Romania. Lugosi's birth name was Béla Ferenc Dezso Blaskó. Around age 20, he adopted the name "Lugosi," meaning "one from Lugos." Lugosi was the fourth and final child born to Paula Vojnits and Istvàn Blaskó. Lugosi's father was a successful baker in his early years, and in 1883 he used his earnings to become a partner in forming a savings bank called the Lugos Volksbank. As such, the Blaskó family was well-respected in Lugos.

Began Career As Stage Actor

From an early age, Lugosi was infatuated with theater, having seen local troupes pass through town. Growing up, Lugosi did not apply himself in school and eventually dropped out. His father died in 1894, ending the family's financial stability. Lugosi apprenticed with a locksmith but abandoned that career for acting around 1901. His first acting experiences came in the form of small roles supporting amateur theatrical troupes. In 1903, Lugosi began appearing at the Franz Joseph Theater of Temesvar. Besides plays, Lugosi earned roles in operettas because of his good baritone singing voice.

By the end of 1908, Lugosi had settled in the Hungarian city of Debrecen, which had a large theater. Lugosi became a featured attraction at the theater, earning lead roles as Pinkerton in Puccini's famed opera *Madame Butterfly* and as Antonio in a production of Shakespeare's *The Merchant of Venice*. In 1910, Lugosi starred as Romeo at the repertory theater in Szeged, Hungary. Lugosi appeared in several productions in Szeged before a Budapest director lured him away.

According to Arthur Lennig, author of *The Immortal Count: The Life and Films of Béla Lugosi,* Lugosi was well-received in Szeged. Lennig quoted an article from a May 1911 edition of the *Hungarian Theater News* in which the author lamented Lugosi's departure from Szeged and forecast a successful future for the young actor in Budapest. "The director will have good box-office with him, if Lugosi is given good parts. We can predict already that he will be loved the most by the women . . . [who] praise his manly beauty even beyond his acting talent."

Once in Budapest, Lugosi attended the Rákosi Szidi Acting School. Because of his weak academic background, Lugosi struggled to interpret foreign expressions and figures of speech. In 1913, Lugosi made his debut at the National Theater of Hungary, which had a reputation as one of the best theaters in Europe. That year, he appeared in 34 plays, though only in small roles. Lugosi's career was interrupted by the outbreak of World War I. In 1914, Lugosi stepped up to serve his country, becoming a lieutenant in the 43rd Royal Hungarian Infantry. He fought the Russians in the trenches and was twice wounded in battle, once in Rohatyn, now part of Ukraine, and also in the Carpathian Mountains. Lugosi left the service in the spring of 1916.

Turned to Film, Socialism

Lugosi returned to the National Theater and in 1916–17 played small roles in several Shakespearean plays. On June

Moviepix/Getty Images

25, 1917, Lugosi married his first wife, Ilona Szmik. Professionally, Lugosi struggled to find lead roles onstage and turned to film, a new, budding industry in Hungary. Lugosi made his first film in 1917 for the Star Film Company. In an effort to appeal to moviegoers outside of Hungary, the film company changed the actors' names, and Lugosi was credited as Arisztid Olt in several features.

Lugosi earned credit under his real name with a rival Budapest film company named Phoenix, appearing as the title character in 1917's *Az Ezredes* (The Colonel), which was directed by fellow Hungarian Mihály Kertész. Kertész later immigrated to the United States and made a name for himself directing as Michael Curtiz. Lugosi and Kertész made a handful of films together in Hungary. Lugosi gave an acclaimed performance in 1918, playing Lord Henry Wotton in *Az Elet Kiralya* (The King of Life), an adaptation of Oscar Wilde's 1890 novel *The Picture of Dorian Gray.*

During this time, civil tensions mounted in Hungary. Mihály Károlyi became president of the Hungarian Democratic Republic in 1918. A Socialist, Károlyi advocated for social change and land reform. Lugosi jumped on the Socialist bandwagon and became a leader of the Free Organization of Theater Employees, a labor union advocating for a socialized, state-run theater system. Lugosi spoke in favor of unions, urging every actor in the country to join. In 1919, the Communist-based Hungarian Soviet Republic was established and served to embolden Lugosi's Socialist leanings. However, a counter-revolution ensued and an ultra-conservative nationalist government took over. This new government banned the Communist Party and launched a reign of terror against those with Socialist inclinations. The very vocal and left-leaning Lugosi, finding himself on the wrong side of the government, fled for his life. Initially, Lugosi settled in Berlin with his wife but she soon left him and returned to Budapest, later filing for divorce.

Fled to United States

Lugosi, age 38 and penniless, headed for the United States. He arrived in New Orleans on December 5, 1920, and reported to Ellis Island on March 23, 1921, stating that he intended to become a U.S. citizen. In June 1931, Lugosi became a U.S. citizen. Because he had yet to learn English, Lugosi stood no chance of winning any acting roles at established theaters, so he formed his own acting troupe with other Hungarian emigres and began touring, performing for fellow Hungarian-Americans.

In 1922, a Greenwich Village theater manager contacted Lugosi for a role in *The Red Poppy*. Lugosi, who spoke no English, found a fellow cast member to tutor him on his lines and teach him the correct phonetic pronunciations. Positive reviews led to film offers. In 1923, Lugosi appeared in his first U.S. film, *The Silent Command,* playing a foreign saboteur. Over the next few years, Lugosi was cast for his dialect and offered the role of European spy, villain or lover in a number of films.

Lugosi's big break came in 1927 when he landed the role of Dracula in a Broadway adaptation of Stoker's gothic novel of the same name. While some reviewers criticized Lugosi for offering a stiff and deliberate yet flamboyant performance, others lauded the play as highly effective escapist entertainment. Whatever the case, Lugosi turned *Dracula* into a hit. It ran for 261 performances in New York before going on tour. Lugosi reprised the role for a West Coast tour, playing Dracula in Los Angeles and San Francisco, where he caught the attention of the Hollywood studios.

Earned Infamy as *Dracula*

In 1929, Lugosi made his talkie debut, starring as a nightclub owner in *Prisoners* and as a police inspector in *The Thirteenth Chair,* one of the first horror talkies ever made. The latter film was directed by Tod Browning, who would go on to direct *Dracula.* As Universal Pictures negotiated the film rights to Dracula, Lugosi was dispatched to bargain with Stoker's widow for a lower price. Lugosi assumed he would get the role, but Browning instead cast his friend Lon Chaney, who had earned acclaim as the disfigured apparition in the 1925 thriller *Phantom of the Opera.* Chaney, however, died before production began, which forced Browning to offer the role to Lugosi. Lugosi was so desperate for the part that he settled for a meager $500 a week and earned about $3,500 for the film, which had a budget of more than $350,000.

Dracula, which opened on Valentine's Day 1931, was an instant success, as brought to life by Lugosi with his slick-backed hair and hypnotizing eyes. Lugosi's thick Hungarian accent resulted in Dracula having a distinct, sinister voice, which, coupled with the actor's macabre mannerisms, made the vampire attractively disturbing. Lugosi's Dracula was eerie, yet chivalrous, and did not require a lot of makeup for effect. According to Lennig's book, *New York Times* movie critic Mordaunt Hall offered this review of *Dracula*: "Mr. Browning is fortunate in having in the leading role in this eerie work, Béla Lugosi.... What with Mr. Browning's imaginative direction and Mr. Lugosi's makeup and weird gestures, this picture succeeds to some extent in its grand, guignol intentions. This picture can at least boast of being the best of the many mystery films."

While critics lauded Lugosi's acting, they were quick to note the film's shortcomings. Critics complained about the slow pacing and grumbled that the storyline and scene architecture departed too heavily from Stoker's novel. Nonetheless, crowds flocked to the theater. At New York's famed Roxy Theater, *Dracula* brought in $120,000 over eight days. This was notable because a year before, *King of Jazz,* which starred the Paul Whiteman orchestra and had a production cost five times that of *Dracula,* brought in only $102,700 its first week at the Roxy. *Dracula* was Universal's biggest moneymaker of the year and kept the company out of Depression-era bankruptcy.

Struggled to Move Past Role

For Lugosi, playing Dracula proved to be both a fortune and a curse. It brought him the notoriety and recognition he yearned for, but also meant that Hollywood studios sought him out solely for weird, gruesome roles. In 1932 Lugosi played a mad, homicidal, female-abducting scientist in *Murders in the Rue Morgue,* an adaptation of an Edgar Allan Poe story. He also appeared as a voodoo sorcerer in 1932's *White Zombies.*

After Universal acquired the rights to Mary Shelley's *Frankenstein,* the studio cast Lugosi in the title role. After realizing that playing Frankenstein meant he would have to wear heavy makeup and speak in grunts rather than dialogue, Lugosi quit, opening the door for Boris Karloff to take on the role of Frankenstein. Lugosi later regretted the move, as the movie proved highly popular and boosted Karloff's reputation. Lugosi spent the next 25 years battling Karloff for the title of most popular horror film movie star.

In the ensuing years, Hollywood studios paired the two frequently because it boosted ticket sales. Lugosi and Karloff appeared together in 1934's *The Black Cat,* 1935's *The Raven,* 1936's *The Invisible Ray,* 1939's *Son of Frankenstein,* and 1945's *The Body Snatcher.* Karloff, however, got top billing because he had broken out into larger roles after Frankenstein. Lugosi, burdened with his Hungarian accent, was never offered larger roles. In 1948, Lugosi revived his Dracula character for *Abbott and Costello Meet Frankenstein.*

By the late 1940s, Lugosi was in bad health. He had developed severe sciatica as a result of his war injuries. Doctors prescribed morphine and methadone and Lugosi became addicted to narcotics. He was also known to drink heavily. Large studios quit offering roles, leaving Lugosi to find work with smaller, B-grade studios that gave him tiny, unchallenging roles in second-feature quickies. During this period, Lugosi appeared in films like *Béla Lugosi Meets a Brooklyn Gorilla* (1952).

Lugosi's career had a bit of a revival when eccentric filmmaker Ed Wood began casting Lugosi in his kitschy, low-budget sci-fi films. Lugosi narrated *Glen or Glenda* (1953) and starred in *Bride of the Monster* (1955). Lugosi also appeared in 1959's *Plan 9 From Outer Space,* playing a vampire raised from the dead by aliens. Wood inserted Lugosi into that film using footage he had taken for another project before the actor's death. Another actor filled in for Lugosi in some scenes, using a cape to obscure his face. The film became a cult classic, though some critics called it one of the shoddiest horror flicks ever made.

Lugosi died at his Los Angles home on August 16, 1956. He was nearly penniless, just as he had been most of his life. Lugosi's unsteady finances and flirty personality led to the dissolution of four of his five marriages. He left behind one son, Béla Lugosi, Jr., who was 18 when his father died. Lugosi was buried at the Holy Cross Cemetery in Culver City, California, wearing a high-collared Dracula cloak, medallion, and tux. For Lugosi, fame was fleeting. Ironically, Martin Landau won an Academy Award for best supporting actor for his portrayal of Lugosi in the 1994 Tim Burton biopic *Ed Wood.*

Books

Lennig, Arthur, *The Immortal Count: The Life and Films of Béla Lugosi,* University Press of Kentucky, 2003.

Periodicals

American Heritage, November 1998.

Entertainment Weekly, March 1, 1995.

Romanian Journal of Artistic Creativity, Spring 2014.□

Hunein Maassab

Scientist Hunein "John" Maassab (1926–2014) developed the science behind FluMist flu vaccine, the first nasal spray flu vaccine. A researcher and professor at the University of Michigan, he was also a respected academic in epidemiology.

Maassab was born on June 11, 1926, in Damascus, Syria. His father was employed as a jeweler. Maassab moved to the United States in 1947, primarily to further his education. At this time, he began using the first name John. He first entered the University of Missouri, where he studied biology. Maassab was granted his bachelor's degree in 1950. Pursuing graduate studies, he completed a master's degree in physiology and pharmacology in 1952.

Studied Epidemiology at Michigan

Next, Maassab entered the University of Michigan, where he first studied public health. He chose the school because of its appeal to medical doctors interested in public health and leading role in virus-related research. Maassab earned his master's degree in public health in 1954. Two years later, Maassab was granted his Ph.D. in epidemiology sciences, with a thesis that focused on influenza. While a graduate student there, he was a witness to history and events that inspired his future work in creating the FluMist vaccine.

As a Michigan graduate student, Maassab was a research assistant to Dr. Thomas Francis, Jr., who had founded the epidemiology department at the University of Michigan. Francis also had isolated the flu virus, developed the first killed-virus flu vaccine, and developed some early flu vaccines. Additionally, Francis had been in charge of the U.S. Army's flu vaccine program during the Second World War.

In April 1955, Francis announced the successful completion of human trials for a polio vaccine, indicating that the vaccine was safe and effective. The polio vaccine had been developed by Jonas Salk, who had been a lab researcher for Francis. Maassab had worked on the vaccine's field trials recording trial data through Francis, who played a major role in their operation.

Began Creating Flu Vaccine

When Maassab heard the results of the field trials being formally announced by Francis, he decided he would develop his own life-changing vaccine. This experience inspired his best known creation, the FluMist flu vaccine. Maassab focused on the flu because of Francis and Salk. He also was inspired by the Spanish flu pandemic of 1918, which lead to the deaths of 20 million of people worldwide.

As Maassab was developing his research on flu and his ideas for an effective vaccine, he began his professional career at the University of Michigan. After earning his Ph.D., he worked as an assistant in research in 1956 in the Epidemiology Department. In 1957, he became a research associate, and soon entered the tenure track. In 1960, he was named an assistant professor, then promoted to associate by 1965. By 1973, he had become a full professor.

After another flu pandemic hit the United States in 1958, resulting in 70,000 deaths, Maassab began working on the flu issue himself in 1960, though his idea would not reach production until 2003. Maassab came up with something different than previous versions of the flu vaccine. His vaccine was a nasal spray, not an injectable. An additional differece was that his nasal spray used a live but weakened

University of Michigan/Getty Images

version of the flu virus. Finally, Maassab ensured the vaccine acted quickly when it came into the body via the nasal passages, which were relatively cooler in temperature than other parts of the body.

Isolated Cold-Adapted Flu Virus

Maassab had several major accomplishments related to the development of the vaccine in the 1960s. First in 1960, he initially isolated the Influenza Type-A-Ann Arbor virus. It was the second cold-adapted flu virus ever isolated. The first had been isolated in Leningrad in 1957, was known as the Type-A Leningrad virus, and used in Russian vaccines.

Seven years later, Maassab had conquered a major issue in the delivery of the nasal spray vaccine. That is, he developed a live, but weakened, flu virus that stayed alive in the cool nasal passages but would not reproduce in the lungs which would cause infection. In 1967, Maassab published this milestone in an article in *Nature*. The article described how he adapted the flu virus for low-temperature growth in a culture.

Maassab continued to work on the vaccine in various ways until the early 21st century, sometimes with the help of colleagues like Dr. Brian R. Murphy of the National Institute of Allergy and Infectious Diseases. The pair worked together from 1975 to 1993 on live, weakened virus research. Maassab spent much time going through the development of many versions of the live, attenuated virus.

During the 1980s and early 1990s, Maassab, working with various colleagues, conducted research in many other areas related to flu vaccines. These include using genetic recombinant technology to help produce various types of flu viruses, both wild and cold adapted. He also had to develop a B strain of the virus.

Additionally, because the flu viruses are not the same each year, Maassab had to come up with means of quickly adjusting vaccines to the annual flu virus variations. As part of his ongoing flu vaccine project, Maassab had to record and verify the genetic composition of certain flu viruses. Through the 1970s and 1980s, the National Institutes of Health also played a major role in the development of the vaccine, including conducting early trials and coming up with needed technology.

Conducted Testing of Vaccine

Over the decades, Maassab's vaccine underwent many government reviews and test trials. Ultimately, more than 70 studies and trials were conducted with at least 24,000 volunteers. Tests that were conducted in the late 1990s showed that his vaccine had an effectiveness rate of 85 percent. This rate was better than injected vaccines made up of nonliving virus. Later tests showed that the flu vaccine nasal spray was even more effective than other flu vaccines, with a 93 percent effectiveness rate. These results were reported in 1998 in the *New England Journal of Medicine*.

It was not until 1991 that pharmaceutical companies became interested in developing the vaccine for market. By this time, Maassab was serving as the chair of the epidemiology department, a position he would hold from 1991 until 1997. He also founded and served as the first director of the epidemiology department's Hospital and Molecular Epidemiology Program.

Initially, the drug maker Wyeth purchased the rights to further develop the vaccine, then dropped the program a few years later. Beginning in 1995, Aviron in conjunction with the National Institutes of Health, completed its development. By 2002, FluMist was nearly ready for market, when Aviron was purchased by MedImmune. Ultimately, Wyeth and MedImmune brought Maassab's vaccine to market after government approval was gained despite some regulatory questions related to its safety.

Throughout this process, Maassab played an active role in getting his vaccine to market. A colleague at the University of Michigan, Rosemary Rochford, told Terence Chea of the *Washington Post*, "Every vaccine needs a champion to get it to market. John Maassab is FluMist's champion. It's been his life mission to see that the vaccine will be available to everyone. If it's approved, it would be a realization of his life's work." Maassab was named the professor emeritus of epidemiology in 2003.

Gained Government Approval for Vaccine

In December 2002, the U.S. Food and Drug Administration had declared that Maassab's flu vaccine in nasal spray form was safe for use in healthy, nonpregnant humans between the ages of five and 49. The vaccine was formally licensed as FluMist in June 2003. Soon thereafter, it was approved for use in children two and older. Concerns remained about the vaccine's safety and effectiveness in the very young and older because the live virus could, in theory, make those with weakened immune systems ill.

FluMist was put on the market in time for the 2003–04 winter flu season. Though it was not an instant success because of its high cost per dose (relative to a traditional flu shot) and need to be stored frozen, the limited availability of traditional vaccines helped push its sales and higher profile that year. Both Maassab and the University of Michigan received a percentage of the sales through royalties. Over the next decade, FluMist became commonly used in doctors' offices and is administered in place of injectable flu vaccines.

By the time FluMist was commercially available, Maassab had retired from the University of Michigan. He was honored with a career achievement award from the University of Michigan's School of Public Health in 2004. During the ceremony, Noreen Clark, the dean of the department, stated, according to Katie Marx of *Crain's Business Detroit,* "John Maassab is a true visionary. He did not stop until he had realized his dream."

Left Legacy at the University of Michigan

Maassab also had a significant legacy at the University of Michigan. There, he was a teacher and mentor to many in epidemiology. His name was attached to three programs at the University of Michigan School of Public Health. They included the H.F. Maassab Student Research Award and the Hunein F. Maassab Scholarship Fund. He and his wife also were named in the Hunein F. and Hilda Maassab Endowed Professorship in epidemiology. Maassab had married his wife in 1959, and the couple had twin sons, Sammy and Fred. Hilda Maassab died in 2006.

To many at the university, Maassab's project was motivating and important in many ways. According to an online obituary published by the University of Michigan School of Public Health, Ken Nisbet, the University of Michigan associate vice president for research-technology transfer, stated, "Dr. Maassab was an inspiration to many of us at the University and in the healthcare community. . . . The commercial success of FluMist allowed continual investments by the University into research and education, and inspired another generation of students and researchers. But the true value of his work lies in the millions of people who have, and will have, access to an innovative vaccine for the perils of influenza."

Shortly after retiring from the University of Michigan, Maassab died on February 1, 2014, in North Carolina. He was 87 years old. He considered FluMist his life's work. Rashid L. Bashshur, a friend and colleague, told William Yardley of the *New York Times,* "He always thought at the end of the day he was going to be able to perfect it. He just knew it. And he had to get the scientific data to support his position." Bashshur added, "You have to be smart, that goes without saying. But I think his unique characteristic was perseverance. Scientific discovery doesn't come easy. It's easy to give up, but he would just never give up."

Periodicals

Crain's Business Detroit, August 30, 2004.

New York Times, April 19, 2003; March 13, 2014.

USA Today, January 7, 2004.

Washington Post, March 18, 2002.

Online

"Hunein F. 'John' Maassab, Developer of Influenza Nasal-Spray Vaccine Known as FluMust, Dies at 87," University of Michigan School of Public Health, http://www.sph.umich.edu/news_events/031414Maassab.html (November 16, 2014).

"Timeline of the Work of Hunein 'John' Maassab, Professor of Epidemiology," University of Michigan School of Public Health, http://www.sph.umich.edu/news_events/flumist/timeline.html (November 6, 2014). □

Moms Mabley

A gifted comic and stage performer, Moms Mabley (1897–1975) gained notoriety as the first African-American woman to emerge as a single act in standup comedy. Mabley got her start on the black vaudeville circuit in the 1920s. She packed the house as a headliner at New York's famed Apollo Theater during the 1950s and in the 1960s landed on television variety shows, which turned her into a household name and top-selling comedienne for her recordings.

Moms Mabley was born Loretta Mary Aiken on March 19, 1897, in Brevard, North Carolina, to James and Mary (Smith) Aiken. Her father was a successful merchant and entrepreneur who ran a bakery, a barber shop, an undertaker's shop and a café/store. Mabley's father, a volunteer firefighter, died in 1908 as the result of a fire truck accident. Years later, her mother died after being run over by a mail truck. Besides her father's death, Mabley endured other hardships growing up. An older black man raped her when she was 11 and two years later she was raped by the town's white sheriff. Both times, she became pregnant, carried the babies to term and gave them away.

Mabley's grandmother, Jane Aiken Hall, encouraged her to overcome her circumstances. Grandmother Jane had spent her early life as a slave before her emancipation in 1861. Grandmother Jane encouraged Mabley to leave Brevard and make something of herself. Later, Mabley perfected a character based on her granny—her most beloved character was a feisty old woman who appeared onstage in a garish housedress with mismatched knee-high socks and slippers, dispensing anything-but-proper granny wit and wisdom.

Michale Oche Archive/Getty Images

Joined Vaudeville Circuit as Teen

When Mabley was just shy of her 14th birthday, she left Brevard to join a traveling minstrel show and initially landed in Cleveland, Ohio. At this time, she started using 1894 as her birthdate. Mabley secured bookings as a comedian through the Theater Owners Bookers Association, better known as TOBA. The performers, however, had another name, calling it the "Tough on Black Actors" circuit. TOBA booked black musicians, comedians, and other performers for venues that allowed black audiences. The venues were mostly in the East and South. Mabley spent her time traveling by train from city to city, perfecting her act.

Early on, Mabley had a boyfriend named Jack Mabley and assumed the stage name of Jackie Mabley after complaints from her family about her career choice. Wages with TOBA were much lower than on the white vaudeville circuit, and Mabley struggled to make a living. At one point she lived in a boarding house in Buffalo, New York, that was populated by theatrical wannabes. Luckily, Mabley's mother sent her a monthly letter that included money for food and rent. As Mabley quickly discovered, it did not matter how talented a person was—every black entertainer of the time was limited by skin color because Jim Crow segregation laws prevented them from performing at more prestigious venues. According to Elsie A. Williams, author of *The Humor of Jackie Moms Mabley*, Mabley once complained: "I don't care if you could stand on your head; if you was colored, you couldn't get no work outside the segregated black night club and theatrical circuits."

At one point, Mabley was working in Dallas for $14 a week. The black husband-and-wife comedy duo of Butterbeans and Susie caught Mabley's act and told her she was massively underpaid. They helped Mabley land an appropriate agent, and she was soon booked in Baltimore for $90 a week. Mabley's agent secured better and more regular bookings for her on the TOBA circuit. In the mid-1920s, during the Harlem Renaissance, Mabley entertained at prominent New York City nightspots like the Cotton Club, Connie's Inn, and the Savoy Ballroom.

The Cotton Club was an interesting venue, as it was a whites-only establishment that put black performers on the stage. At the Cotton Club, Mabley shared billings with famed black musicians like Louis Armstrong, Count Basie, Cab Calloway, Duke Ellington, and Benny Goodman. Mabley gained popularity for her unconventional act. At the time, there were many black female blues singers or women who were part of a standup duo. Mabley performed alone, perfecting her monologues and learning how to sell her suggestive humor about race, gender, age, and sexuality in the guise of an old granny.

Earned Nickname *Moms*

As Mabley gained success, she started mothering other struggling performers and earned the nickname "Moms." Oral historian and author Studs Terkel published an interview with Mabley in his 1999 book *The Spectator: Talk About Movies and Plays With The People Who Make Them*. In the interview, Mabley discussed how she came to be known as Moms. "The show people named me Moms. . . . Because, even though I was young, they would always bring their problems to me to settle. And then so many, sometimes, they get away from home and wouldn't be able to get back, and I'd send them home. Or I'd always put on a pot or something like that when I know that those ones that didn't have very much money, I'd see that they were fed. So they named me Moms."

Besides plying her own act, Mabley landed roles in musical comedy revues at black theaters. In 1919, she appeared in *Bowman's Cotton Blossoms*. The year 1927 found Mabley appearing in the musical *Miss Bandana* and *Look Who's Here,* where she performed in blackface using burnt cork makeup to darken her features. In 1932, Mabley appeared in a Broadway musical revue called *Blackberries,* which ran only 24 performances due to the ethnic humor that eluded white audiences.

One of Mabley's more noteworthy performances came in 1931, when she appeared in *Fast and Furious: A Colored Revue in 37 Scenes* at the New Yorker Theatre. Mabley worked with folklorist Zora Neale Hurston to write some of the scenes and the two appeared together in one skit as cheerleaders. Mabley played several different characters during the course of the revue. At the time, Broadway offered shows with all-black casts, but they were typically overseen by white producers and made for white audiences. This rare, black-produced Broadway show was aimed at black audiences and specifically tried to capture the African-American experience. The press singled out

Mabley's performance, though not in a positive light, instead making fun of the full-body gyrations she utilized while dancing. Panned by white critics, who once again failed to find the humor, the production quickly closed its doors.

In 1939, Mabley became the first female comedian to earn feature placement at Harlem's famed Apollo Theater. For the next 30 years, Mabley was a standby at the theater and appeared there more times than any other entertainer. She became the theater's star attraction and often closed down the show. Often billed as "The Funniest Woman in the World," Mabley earned 15-week bookings at the Apollo, switching her act each week so fans would return again and again. During the 1940s, she appeared at other venues on the segregated circuit, including the Royal Theatre in Baltimore and the Uptown in Philadelphia.

Perfected Cutting Comic Act

By the 1950s, Mabley had perfected her stage persona of Moms. She entertained audiences by coming onstage, often without her teeth, dressed as a frumpy old woman in a floral print housedress and floppy hat. She may have looked naïve, but once Moms opened her mouth, she was anything but a proper old lady. Instead, in the guise of Moms, Mabley hit touchy topics other comedians avoided, like sexism, racism, and misogyny. In *Women's Comic Visions*, Elsie A. Williams explored how Mabley's persona helped her connect with audiences and allowed her to comment on sensitive issues. "The adoption of the 'Moms' persona gave Mabley a natural platform for expounding folk wisdom, leveling world leaders and bigots, and instructing a society on what to teach its young," wrote Williams. Mabley characterized the FBI as "fat, bald and impossible" and made fun of U.S. presidents and other world leaders. Mabley demonstrated that comedians could make political and social statements in their work and still get laughs.

By appearing as a daft, unschooled granny, Mabley was able to talk about racism. Mabley had one joke, according to Williams, in which she complained about being pulled over by a police officer after running a red light in South Carolina. Her punchline: "I saw all the white folks driving on the green light; I thought the red light must have been for us." In this way, Mabley was able to offer cutting observations about racism. Mabley wrote her own material, sometimes with help from her brother, and also ad-libbed on stage. She acted out her jokes, tickling audiences with her expert use of the double entendre, metaphors, and misinterpretations. Mabley was so popular at the Apollo that she commanded a $10,000 weekly salary during the late 1950s. In 1962, she took "Moms" to Carnegie Hall.

Along the way, Mabley also earned small film roles. In 1933, she played a matron in *The Emperor Jones,* though her role was uncredited. Mabley earned a bigger role in 1947's musical comedy *Killer Diller,* a movie about a jewelry heist that takes place at a theater that's running a variety show. The star-studded cast included Mabley performing comedy and the Nat King Cole trio playing music, along with Andy Kirk and his orchestra. The film score was written by Count Basie. In 1948, Mabley landed the lead role in *Boarding House Blues,* playing a character loosely based on herself. In the movie, Mabley starred as Moms, the matron of a Harlem boarding house for theatrical entertainers.

Landed in Limelight

After more than four decades in the business, Mabley rose to prominence in the 1960s and received bookings for the top television variety shows of the day. She appeared on the *Smothers Brothers Comedy Hour,* and on the *Bill Cosby, Merv Griffin, Carol Burnett, Ed Sullivan,* and *Flip Wilson* shows, among others. Mabley's television work helped her find a wider audience. In addition, Mabley earned a recording contract with Chess Records and released 1961's live recording *On Stage (Funniest Woman in the World),* which earned gold certification after selling more than one million copies. Mabley signed with Mercury Records in 1966. In all, Mabley released more than 20 albums. Many of her recordings hit the *Billboard 200,* including 1961's *Moms Mabley at the 'UN.'* This album hit number 16 and made Mabley the highest-charting comedienne in *Billboard* history.

In 1974, Mabley landed the role she had yearned for—lead actress in a motion picture. That year Mabley filmed *Amazing Grace.* In the film, she starred as a widow trying to oust a crooked politician in Baltimore. Mabley suffered a heart attack during filming but managed to complete the movie after having a pacemaker installed. She died on May 23, 1975, in White Plains, New York. Mabley had three daughters: Yvonne, Christine, and Bonnie, as well as an adopted son, Charles. Writing in *The Humor of Jackie Moms Mabley,* Williams noted that Mabley complained about how long it took her to find her place in the entertainment business. Said Mabley, "Wouldn't you know it? By the time I finally arrived at the big money, I'm too old and sick to really enjoy it."

Mabley's story was captured in the 2013 HBO documentary *Whoopi Goldberg Presents Moms Mabley.* The film celebrated Mabley's life and achievements and included interviews with comedians who followed in her footsteps. The documentary also explored Mabley's sexual identity. Mabley was a lesbian who socialized with the lesbian and gay crowd in Washington, D.C., especially when appearing at the Howard. Black, lesbian, and female—Mabley pushed through barriers to achieve stardom during her lifetime. Speaking to Diane Anderson-Minshall of the *Advocate,* Goldberg explained her desire to make the documentary. "A lot of young people have no sense of history. No sense of history of the United States. Moms is a great magnifying glass into the past."

Books

Sochen, June (ed.), *Women's Comic Visions,* Wayne State University Press, 1991.

Terkel, Studs, *The Spectator: Talk About Movies and Plays With The People Who Make Them,* New Press, 1999.

Williams, Elsie A., *The Humor of Jackie Moms Mabley: An African American Comedic Tradition,* Garland Publishing, 1995.

Periodicals

Ebony, August 1, 1962; April 1974.
New Yorker, November 25, 2013.

Online

"Whoopi: First Female Comic Was A Lesbian," *Advocate,* http://
www.advocate.com/print-issue/current-issue/2013/11/06/
op-ed-moms-us-all?page=full (January 1, 2015). □

Antonio Machado

The Spanish writer Antonio Machado (1875–1939) is considered one of the greatest lyric poets active in Spain in the 20th century.

Intensely personal and even sometimes mystical, Machado nevertheless captured the spirit of Spain's landscapes and its people in his poetry. The Chilean poet Pablo Neruda (as quoted by Janice Valls-Russell in the *New Leader*) likened him to "an old tree of Spain." Machado spent most of his life as a teacher in small towns, avoiding the literary culture of the capital, Madrid. His poetry reflected his own spiritual attitudes and struggles, often dealing with the death of his young wife shortly after their marriage. But he also looked outward, to the land in which he lived and to the people who lived there, and sometimes, in his images of a Spain fundamentally divided between a progressive spirit and a dull traditionalism, he seemed to prophetically anticipate the destruction of the Spanish Civil War in the 1930s.

Wrote Comic Sketches

Antonio Machado, in full Antonio Machado y Ruiz, was born on July 26, 1875, at his family's estate, Palacio de las Dueñas, near Seville, Spain. His family was aristocratic but progressive; his father was a lawyer, and several members of his family were interested in Spanish poetry and music. Machado stayed long enough on the estate to acquire a feeling for the Spanish countryside, and to be able to write about it later, but in 1883 his family moved to Madrid. In the 1890s Machado's father and grandfather died within two years of each other, and Machado and his brother responded by taking up a low-cost, hipsterish lifestyle in the Spanish capital. Machado wrote comic sketches for a magazine, appeared in plays, and sometimes did translating and editing work to earn money.

Around the turn of the century Machado began to spread his literary wings. As he met other Spanish-language writers and the exiled British playwright Oscar Wilde, he began to focus more seriously on his own poetry. Machado's first creative efforts were difficult, and he apparently destroyed an entire book of poems, titled *Cantares.* In 1903, however, he issued a volume called *Soledades* (Solitudes). He continued to tinker with and expand the book, reissuing it in 1907 as *Soledades, galerías, y otros poemas*

Album/sfgp/Newcom

(translated into English as *Solitudes, Galeries, and Other Poems*). Combining a characteristically Spanish inward spirituality with contemporary influences, the book remains one of Machado's most popular.

Feeling that he should get a job that provided a regular income, Machado took a post as a French teacher in Soria, about 150 miles from Madrid, in 1907. At first he disliked the small town, but he soon became enamored with it and began to write poetry about it. Physical sites connected with his life there, including a classroom in a school built in 1585, remain a major Spanish tourist attraction. Machado made friends among local journalists and literary people. Most important was a romance with his landlord's 13-year-old daughter, Leonor Izquierdo. The pair married in 1909 when she was 16 and he was 34.

Suffered Wife's Death from Disease

In 1911 Machado and his wife enthusiastically moved to Paris so that he could take advantage of a fellowship for study there. But Leonor contracted tuberculosis, and the pair returned to Soria, hoping that the hometown surroundings and rural fresh air would help her to recover. Although Machado stayed with her during long months of illness, Leonor died on August 1, 1912. Devastated, Machado agreed to have his mother move in with him to help with his domestic affairs. Unable to cope with the constant reminders of his wife he encountered in Soria, he asked for and received a transfer to Baeza, some 300 miles away.

Despite the personal tragedy he faced there, Machado produced one of his best-known works during his time in Soria; *Campos de Castilla* (translated into English as *The Castilian Camp*) appeared in 1912 and contained many poems about Leonor, some of them written after she died. But its major theme was Spain itself, expressed through descriptions of its landscapes and through reflections on its glorious past and indifferent present. "Castilla miserable, ayer dominadora, / Envuelta en sus andrajos desprecia cuanto ignora" (Miserable Castille, yesterday dominant, / Wrapped in rags, it despises anything it does not know about), he wrote in one poem, "A las orillas del Duero" (On the Banks of the Duero). The book gained recognition for Machado as part of the so-called Generation of '98, a group of Spanish poets who reflected on Spain's national character and future direction in their work.

In Baeza Machado remained dissatisfied. Still depressed over Leonor's death, he contemplated suicide but told a friend that he felt a responsibility to continue using his poetic talent. He wrote more poems and enrolled at the University of Madrid, where in his 40s he resumed studies toward his college degree. After studying philosophy and literature with the influential philosopher and essayist José Ortega y Gasset, he finally received his degree in 1918. The following year he was able to get a new teaching job in Segovia, again a small town but one closer to Madrid.

Wrote Poems About Mystery Woman

In the mid-1920s Machado's poetry seemed to fall out of fashion, but he refused to accept this verdict and continued to produce important new work. In 1924 he published *Nuevas canciones* (New Songs), adding a second section, *De un cancionero apórifo* (From an Apocryphal Songbook) two years later. Although some of the 1924 poems dealt once again with Leonor, the newer ones alluded to a new love named Guiomar. Her identity remained a mystery for some time, but she was eventually identified as Pilar de Valderrama, a married woman with whom Machado communicated clandestinely. The exact nature of their relationship remains unknown.

Machado remained unusually active through the 1920s, collaborating with his brother Manuel on several plays and continuing to write poems about Guiomar. He created two new poetic identities, named Abel Martin and Juan de Mairena; the latter was a flamenco guitarist and later a professor. His poems of the 1930s, many of them collected in 1936 in a new edition of his *Poesías completas* (Complete Poems), fused poetic and philosophical ideas in unusual ways. The aging Machado gained increasing recognition and was elected to the Spanish Royal Academy in 1927, but he cared little for academic honors or literary high society. When his mother chided him for wearing clunky, unfashionable boots, he replied (according to Valls-Russell), "There are two kinds of people, those who look at your boots and those who look at your face."

A political liberal, Machado supported Spain's Republican government in the 1930s and put his talents at the government's service as civil war broke out with the fascist-supported Nationalists led by Francisco Franco. He moved first from Madrid to Valencia as Madrid was besieged by the Nationalists, and then tried to flee to France with a group of Republican sympathizers in 1939. During the journey, both Machado and his 85-year-old mother contracted pneumonia after going through a rainstorm in an open truck, and once they reached the fishing village of Collioure, France, near the Spanish border, he refused to continue. Machado died there on February 22, 1939, and his mother died three days later.

Spain's fascist government treated Machado's poetry coolly, but the reputation of his poetry continued to spread among ordinary Spaniards, and one 1986 study found that he was the poet most often read in Spanish prisons. His poetry has also been translated into Chinese. Machado's tomb in Collioure remains a popular destination for Spaniards of literary and progressive sensibilities; a mailbox attached to his tombstone receives about 500 letters annually.

Books

Cobb, Carl W., *Antonio Machado,* Twayne, 1971.
Dictionary of Literary Biography, Volume 108: Twentieth-Century Spanish Poets, First Series, Gale, 1991
Johnston, Philip, *The Power of Paradox in the Work of Spanish Poet Antonio Machado,* Mellen, 2002.

Periodicals

New Leader, March 20, 1989.
New York Times, August 24, 2008.
New Yorker, November 18, 1996.

Online

"Life & Works of Antonio Machado," *Classic Spanish Books,* http://www.classicspanishbooks.com/20th-cent-antonio-machado.html (November 20, 2014). □

Manuel II Palaeologus, Emperor of the East

Manuel II Palailogos (1350–1425) was the Byzantine Emperor from 1390 until he suffered a stroke in 1421. There were only two more emperors before the Byzantine Empire, successor to the societies of ancient Greece and Rome, met its final defeat in 1453.

Manuel ruled during a time when, despite periods when its fortunes temporarily improved, the empire was in decline. For the first part of his rule his domain was hardly larger than the city of Constantinople (today Istanbul) itself, and for years he labored valiantly but largely unsuccessfully to get help for the Byzantines in lifting a siege against their city put in place by the Ottoman Turks. Though a canny military tactician, Manuel was not a brilliantly charismatic leader: he was a somewhat bookish man who sometimes lamented that his responsibilities left him no time for scholarly pursuits. Yet he made the most of the one big break the empire received in its last years: the attack on the Ottoman sultanate by its Mongol rivals to the east. Thanks to Manuel's skillful management of the fallout from this development and his personal rapport with Ottoman leaders, the Byzantine world experienced a decade of peace under his leadership—the last such period it would ever have.

Accompanied Father on Fruitless Missions

Born on July 27, 1350, in Constantinople, Manuel was the second son of Emperor John V Palailogos (also transliterated from Greek as Palaeologus). Palailogos was a family name, Manuel his given name, and II denoted his place in the sequence of princes with that name. Under John's rule, the empire's decline accelerated, and the Turks began an incursion into southeastern Europe that would last for three centuries. John, an ineffectual ruler who was temporarily overthrown by his son and then by his grandson, traveled to Europe to ask for military help, and Manuel's world view was shaped by what he saw while accompanying him. John ran out of funds on the trip and was seized by authorities in the city-state of Venice; the 21-year-old Manuel had to pay a ransom for his father's release.

The biggest problem John faced, and that Manuel would face as emperor himself, was that the European powers who could have successfully fought the Turks and strengthened the empire all had their own agendas and could not be counted on for help. The popes (at the time there were two competing popes, in Rome and Avignon, France), who were the leaders of the western branch of the Christian church, regarded the encroachments of the Islamic Ottomans in Europe with concern but also viewed the Byzantines as heretics who, a thousand years earlier, had split from the true church in Rome. Mercantile Venice wielded a powerful navy but hesitated to disturb profitable trade routes. And kings from France, England, and Eastern Europe, though they longed to renew the era of crusades against the Islamic world, were often beset by conflicts among themselves.

Manuel backed his father against coup attempts by Manuel's older brother, Andronicus IV, and nephew, John VII. During the latter episode the two were imprisoned, and John was able to return to power only by asking for the help of the Turkish sultan Murad I, and agreeing to tax his own subjects to pay tribute to the Turk. Manuel, for his loyalty, was made co-emperor in 1373 and the ruler of the city of Thessaloniki, now in Greece, from 1382 to 1387. The Turks conquered that city, and Manuel fled across the Greek islands back to Constantinople, where he found John VII once again on the throne. Manuel succeeded in reinstalling his father as emperor, but both he and John VII had to consent to a humiliating hostage-like residence at the court of the sultan, who threatened to blind Manuel if his father went through with a planned reinforcement of Constantinople's city walls. Finally, in February of 1391, John V died. Manuel escaped from the sultan and was crowned emperor by the orthodox Patriarch Antony IV in a splendid ceremony.

Recorded Debates with Islamic Scholar

Well-educated by the famous Byzantine scholar Demetrius Kydones, Manuel enjoyed writing and debate. At the beginning of his reign, he still had to serve the Turkish sultan, and while accompanying him on a military campaign he fell into a discussion with the sultan's *kadi,* or religious judge. Manuel wrote this debate down, and by 1399 it had been made into a book, *Twenty-Six Dialogues with a Persian.* More than six centuries later this book made headlines when Pope Benedict XVI quoted one of its disparaging queries about Islam in a 2006 speech in Regensburg, Germany.

Under the aggressive new Turkish sultan, Bayazit (also transliterated Bajezid), the peace arrangements Manuel had negotiated broke down almost immediately. In 1394, following a series of military victories in Europe, Bayazit launched a siege against Constantinople. The siege lasted eight years. A campaign against the Ottomans by the Kingdom of Hungary ended in disaster. For a time, with the Byzantines and their French allies maintaining naval supremacy, grain made its way into the city, but finally supplies began to run short. There was talk of deposing Manuel in favor of John VII, who was still a prisoner of the sultan, and thus suing for peace, but Manuel kept to his course of resistance.

In 1399, with the help of French forces on the water, Manuel slipped out of Constantinople and embarked on a long trip to Europe to try once again to raise help for the besieged Byzantines. As a representative of what remained of the great European civilizations of the ancient world, he was treated as an honored guest and was the subject of considerable curiosity. France's King Charles VI, in Paris in 1400, welcomed Manuel and promised to send another force under Marshal Boucicaut, who had helped Manuel out of Constantinople. In London at the end of that year, King Henry IV ordered that a joust and masquerade be mounted in Manuel's honor.

No substantial military aid, however, was forthcoming. Finally help came, not from Europe, but from the East, as the Mongol general Tamerlane (also known as Timur), backed by renegade Turkish princes, inflicted a severe defeat on Bayazit's forces at the Battle of Ankara in 1402, where the Turks were no match for Timur's mounted archery brigades. Bayazit was captured, held prisoner in Samarkand, and died the following year, whereupon four of his sons fell to fighting among themselves.

Exploited Ottoman Defeat

Now it was Manuel's turn to play Ottoman adversaries against one another. Constantinople easily withstood another siege attempt from Bayazit's son Musa, who was captured and strangled in 1413. When Mehmed I emerged as sultan, the 63-year-old Manuel found a well-educated man like himself who, he rightly believed, would serve as a reliable negotiating partner. A peace treaty was agreed to later that year, and Manuel, according to a Greek historian (quoted by Donald M. Nicol in *The Last Centuries of Byzantium*), told assembled ambassadors from Serbia, Wallachia, Bulgaria, and Greece, "Tell your masters that I offer peace to all and accept peace from all. He who maliciously disturbs this peace, may the God of peace be against him."

The treaty restored some Greek lands to the Byzantines, and Manuel set about building a giant fortification, the Hexamilion Wall (parts of which still exist), at the base of the Peloponnese Peninsula. The aging Manuel scotched a plan to seize and murder Mehmed as he passed through Constantinople in May of 1421. A few days after that, however, Mehmed died, according to various accounts, by poison, after a hunting accident, or from dysentery. Mehmed's successor, Murad I, took a more aggressive attitude toward the Byzantines, as did Manuel's successor, John VIII, despite several attempts by Manuel to tamp the situation down. Later in 1421 Manuel entered a monastery and became a tonsured monk. He suffered a stroke but lived on until July 21, 1425. By that time, Turkish attacks had whittled down Byzantine holdings in Greece, and the trajectory toward the empire's final collapse was well underway.

The name of Manuel II Palailogos is not well known today, but he experienced a moment of celebrity in the contemporary 24-hour news cycle when, according to BBC News, Pope Benedict XVI, in a 2006 speech at Regensburg University in Germany, quoted Manuel's words from the *Twenty-Six Dialogues with a Persian*: "Show me just what Muhammad brought that was new, and there you will find things only evil and inhuman, such as his command to spread by the sword the faith he preached." Although the Pope had stressed that the sentiment was Manuel's and not his own, protests erupted across the Islamic world.

Books

Barker, John, *Manuel II Paleologus (1391–1425): A Study in Late Byzantine Statesmanship*, Rutgers, 1969.

Harris, Jonathan, *The End of Byzantium*, Yale, 2010.

Nicol, Donald M., *The Last Centuries of Byzantium*, Hart-Davis, 1972.

Online

"Manuel II PALAILOGOS," *De Imperatoribus Romanis: An Online Encyclopedia of Roman Emperors*, http://www.luc.edu/roman-emperors/manuel2.htm (December 20, 2014).

"Pope Sorry for Offending Muslims," *BBC News*, http://www.news.bbc.co.uk/2/hi/europe/5353208.stm (December 20, 2014).□

Richard Matheson

American science fiction author and specialist Richard Matheson (1926–2013) left his mark on U.S. pop culture with 28 novels, 88 short stories, and countless movie and television screenplays that seized on the paranoid psyche of post-World War II America. Matheson was well known for his contributions to the iconic 1960s television series *The Twilight Zone*. His novels spawned major motion pictures, including *The Incredible Shrinking Man* (1957), *What Dreams May Come* (1998), and *I Am Legend* (2007).

Raphael GAILLARDE/Gamma-Rapho/Getty Images

Richard Burton Matheson was born February 20, 1926, in Allendale, New Jersey, the son of Norwegian immigrants. His father, Bertolf Matheson, was a tile setter. His mother, Fanny Svenningsen, was orphaned as a child. She immigrated to the United States in her teens and changed her name to Swanson. Matheson's parents met in the United States; they both felt like outsiders in their new, adopted homeland. To deal with their insecurity, Matheson's father turned to alcohol and his mother turned to religion, becoming a Christian Scientist. Matheson's parents separated when he was about three and the family isolated itself. Matheson's mother was wary of the outside world and kept Matheson and his siblings close to home.

Matheson diverted his attention by turning to fantasy. "I found personal escape in writing," he told David Morrell, a contributor to *The Twilight and Other Zones: The Dark Worlds of Richard Matheson*. "Instead of imbibing drink, I imbibed stories. . . . Instead of turning to religion, I turned to fantasy . . . the creating of a new world of imagination in which I could work out any and all troubles. A therapeutic battlefield on which I could confront my enemies (my anxieties) and—in relative safety—deal with them in socially acceptable ways."

Explored Fantasy as Child

Matheson's fascination with fantasy began early on. At age seven, he got his own library card and checked out an adventure book about Pinocchio in Africa. The story inspired Matheson to write his own tale about a boy who befriends a bird and receives help from the bird in dealing with a neighborhood bully. By nine, Matheson had published several poems and short stories in the *Brooklyn Eagle*. In 1943, Matheson graduated from Brooklyn Technical High School and signed up for the U.S. Army, joining an infantry regiment in Germany during World War II. He contracted trench foot and received a medical discharge in June 1945. Matheson's military experience came forth in the 1960 novel *The Beardless Warriors,* a fast-paced drama about young draftees.

After leaving the military, Matheson attended the University of Missouri. During his time there, he joined a music fraternity and wrote concert reviews for the newspaper. He earned a journalism degree in 1949 but failed to secure a job at a newspaper or magazine as he hoped. Instead, he took a job in Brooklyn typing address plates and used his spare time to write. Within a few months he had sold his first story, *Born of Man and Woman,* to *The Magazine of Fantasy and Science Fiction.*

Born of Man and Woman appeared in the summer 1950 issue of the magazine. The story is about a mutant child who lives his life chained up in a basement. The story is told through the eyes of the boy, in six diary entries. The magazine editors were so impressed with the twists and structure of the story that they assumed it had been submitted by a seasoned writer using a pseudonym. *Born of Man and Woman* became a science fiction classic and has been reprinted in numerous anthologies.

Gained Success in Sci-Fi Market

Early in his career, Matheson focused on the science fiction market and explored the darker, twisted sides of reality. He placed stories in the leading digests of the day, including *Fantastic Universe, Galaxy, Wonder Stories,* and *Startling Stories.* Matheson was popular because he had a unique way of delving into people's everyday anxieties through "what-if" scenarios. Matheson's 1969 short story "The Prey" also made its way into numerous anthologies. "The Prey" is about a murderous Zuni doll who stalks a woman through her New York high rise.

In 1951, Matheson moved to California and joined a group called The Fictioneers, a collective of professional writers who met once a month to talk about their work. Many of the group's writers wrote westerns and mysteries, prompting Matheson to follow suit. He soon had his byline in publications like *Dime Western* and *Detective Story.* Once in California, Matheson settled down after meeting Ruth Ann Woodson, a recent divorcee with a daughter named Tina. They married in 1952. Their first son, Richard Christian Matheson, was born in October 1953. Another son, Christian, followed, along with two daughters, Bettina and Ali Marie. Three of Matheson's children became writers.

Matheson continued to publish short stories but found he could not support his family doing so. For a while, he worked at the post office and later took a night job at Douglas Aircraft in Santa Monica. Matheson's job as a machine parts operator was mindless. He cut airplane parts from a template, but he enjoyed the robot-like work because it allowed his mind to drift into fantasyland and ponder story ideas while at work. During the early 1950s, Matheson published dozens of short stories and also turned his attention to writing books.

Novels Adapted for Big Screen

Matheson's best known early novel, *I Am Legend,* was published in 1954. *I Am Legend* followed one man's quest to survive a pandemic that turned his fellow humans into vampire-like creatures. The protagonist finds himself to be the last human standing and struggles to survive each day as he researches ways to kill off the sub-humans occupying the planet. Well-researched in facts about bacteriology and psychiatry, the novel caught on with readers looking for the fright of well-written, pulse-pounding science fiction. As Matheson noted in *The Twilight and Other Zones*: "That I sometimes give alternative emphasis to the possibility that the male protagonist may be partially responsible for his own problems—that his real adversary is his own mind—does not alter the fact that he is, in the end, threatened by real outside forces. Or, to paraphrase an old joke, just because he's paranoid doesn't mean that someone isn't out to get him."

The storyline proved so powerful it was adapted for the big screen several times. The first movie version came in 1964 as *Last Man on Earth,* starring Vincent Price. *The Omega Man,* featuring Charlton Heston, appeared in 1971, followed by 2007's *I Am Legend,* with Will Smith. The novel fueled the emerging zombie genre. Horror film director George A. Romero credited *I Am Legend* as a major source of inspiration for his 1968 cult classic *Night of the Living Dead.* Some movie buffs say Matheson's work triggered the start of the monster-driven, post-apocalyptic film craze.

In 1956, Matheson published *The Shrinking Man,* a novel about a suburbanite who accidentally ingests an insecticide and subsequently gets exposed to a radioactive cloud, thus activating a bizarre molecular reaction that causes him to shrink one-seventh of an inch each day. Initially, people tease the man as he begins shrinking, and he literally loses his stature within his family and community. In time, his size proves downright dangerous as everything becomes a threat, and daily survival becomes his focus. The book proved so popular that Universal Studios came calling and tried to buy the rights. Matheson, however, refused to let go of the story and negotiated a deal that allowed him to write the screenplay. *The Incredible Shrinking Man* hit theaters in 1957 and was just as successful as the novel. The psychological science fiction film won a Hugo Award for Outstanding Film at the 1958 World Science Fiction Convention.

Turned to Screenwriting

Because Matheson's *Shrinking Man* screenplay worked out so well that Hollywood studios began offering jobs. In 1958, Matheson turned to television script-writing, beginning with the Western *Buckskin.* In 1959, Matheson wrote several episodes for *The D.A.'s Man* and began writing for *The Twilight Zone.* Between 1959 and 1964, Matheson wrote 16 episodes for the genre TV series that gained legions of fans for telling tales of the strange and extraordinary.

Matheson crafted some of *The Twilight Zone*'s most memorable storylines, including "Nightmare at 20,000 Feet," a 1963 episode that featured a young William Shatner traveling on an airplane. Shatner's character spies a gremlin on the wing fiddling with the aircraft. Scared the plane will crash, Shatner's character tries to persuade his wife and the crew of their imminent danger. However, the gremlin dashes out of view every time someone else looks out the window, and everyone thinks he has gone insane. The episode was actually an adaptation of Matheson's 1961 short story "Alone by Night."

Matheson was also well known for a 1962 episode titled "Little Girl Lost," which featured a little girl who falls out of bed and slips through a portal to another dimension. Her parents can hear her cries but are unable to locate her. Like most of his work, the story idea came from a real-life event, an incident in which Matheson's daughter had fallen out of bed and rolled underneath it. Matheson's *Twilight Zone* episode "Steel" was re-tooled for the big screen in 2011 as *Real Steel,* starring Hugh Jackman. During the 1960s, Matheson also contributed episodes to *The Alfred Hitchcock Hour* and *Star Trek.*

Matheson's stories piqued interest because, by focusing on unusual happenings in everyday places, they created a modern landscape of fear. His stories took place in common settings readers and viewers could relate to, like a mall or an airplane. Matheson also had a knack for turning routine anxieties into over-the-top thrillers. He was well-known for a short story titled "Duel," which appeared in *Playboy* in 1971. "Duel" captured one man's harrowing drive as he is traumatized by a tailgating tractor-trailer. Matheson pulled the idea from a real-life experience. Universal bought the rights to the story and handed Matheson's screenplay over to a young, unknown director named Steven Spielberg. The made-for-TV movie appeared on ABC in 1971 and was later released at the theater, with both versions starring Dennis Weaver. The movie helped Spielberg gain early recognition for his abilities.

Focused on Novels, Metaphysics

While Matheson was known for his thrillers, he hated it when the term "horror" was applied to his work. As he noted in *The Twilight and Other Zones,* "I was determined to fight against this image. Dammit, I never wrote 'real' horror to begin with! To me, horror connotes blood and guts, while terror is a much more subtle art, a matter of stirring up primal fears."

During the 1970s, Matheson concentrated on novels and all but gave up short story writing. He turned to metaphysics and published the time-travel romance *Bid Time Returns* in 1975. The book won a 1976 World Fantasy Award for best novel and was adapted for the big screen as the 1980's romantic fantasy *Somewhere in Time.* In 1978, Matheson published *What Dreams May Come.* This novel explored the afterlife, following one "dead" man's quest to locate his wife after both of their deaths. The book became 1998's Academy Award-winning *What Dreams May Come,* which starred Robin Williams and Cuba Gooding, Jr.

Matheson also dabbled with Western novels, publishing *Journal of the Gun Years* (1992) and *The Memoirs of Wild Bill Hickock* (1996). In 2002, he published a fairy tale aimed at young readers, titled *Abu and the 7 Marvels.*

Matheson died on June 23, 2013, at his home in Calabasas, California, and while his pen was silenced, his influence lives on. Gauntlett Press publisher Barry Hoffman predicted people would be reading Matheson for years to come. As Hoffman told *Publishers Weekly* writer Stefan Dziemianowicz: "He's written in every genre, but all of his books deal with the human condition. As much as he focuses on the plot, it's the characters in his books that are so unique and come so much to life that you remember them. He talks about things that all of us have experienced and can relate to, and will still 50 or 100 years from now. His books are timeless."

Books

Wiater, Stanley, Matthew R. Bradley, and Paul Stuve, eds., *The Twilight and Other Zones: The Dark Worlds of Richard Matheson,* Citadel Press Books, 2009.

Periodicals

Columbia Daily Tribune (MO), December 13, 2007.

Los Angeles Times, June 26, 2013.

Publishers Weekly, June 17, 2002.

Online

"Richard Matheson (1926-2013): The Wizard of What-If?," *Time.com,* http://www.entertainment.time.com/2013/06/28/richard-matheson-1926-2013-the-wizard-of-what-if/ (December 3, 2014). □

Huber Matos

Once an ally and supporter of Cuban revolutionary leader Fidel Castro, Huber Matos (1918–2014) became disillusioned when the young Castro regime became Communist. After the break, Matos suffered for 20 years in Cuban prison and later became a vocal leader of anti-Castro Cubans living in exile in Miami.

He was born Huber Matos Benítez on November 26, 1918, in Yara, Cuba. In this small community located in southeastern part of the island, Matos was raised in a family of modest means. His father was a farmer, while his mother was a school teacher. Matos followed in both his parents' footsteps. Matos first attended a teacher's college. He then completed a Ph.D. at the University of Havana in 1944. Professionally, Matos worked as a teacher. He also helped run a small-scale rice farm with his father and brothers.

ROBERT SULLIVAN/AFP/Getty Images

Protested Batista

It was Matos's experience as a teacher that informed his politics. He primarily taught in rural areas of Cuba, working among the impoverished and in areas such as Manzanillo. The desperate conditions profoundly affected Matos. Because of this experience, he became disenchanted with the regime of Fulgencio Batista. Though Batista had served as the elected president of Cuba in the early 1940s, he ruled as the island nation's dictator beginning in 1952 after overthrowing the democratically elected regime of President Carlos Prío Socarrás. Batista's regime was oppressive.

Matos opposed Batista and his regime, and encouraged his students to do the same. According to the London *Times,* Matos told his pupils, "We must go out and protest. We can't let this happen. Cuba is a democracy." His political affiliation was with the anti-Communist Partido Ortodoxo (the People's Party of Cuba), as was future Cuban revolutionary leader Fidel Castro. In 1953, Matos joined the 26th of July Movement helmed by Castro. Castro's group took up arms against Batista, and Matos played a key role in supporting Castro's efforts.

Early on, Matos arranged transportation for the first group of reinforcements received by what was then a small guerilla army. Matos went into exile in Costa Rica. In March 1958, he gained weapons, ammunition, and recruits in Costa Rica and flew the transport plane to Cuba himself. They were delivered to Cuban rebels located in the Sierra Maestra mountain range in southeastern Cuba.

Became Close to Castro

Because of such efforts, Matos was made a member of Castro's inner circle in the movement, and was named a major (comandante) in Castro's army. Matos was put in charge of a guerilla column, number nine. Matos later claimed he was the number three in the revolutionary hierarchy after Castro and his brother Raúl, ahead of Che Guevara.

Column 9 was in charge of the final attack on Santiago de Cuba. The rebels were victorious under Matos's leadership. In January 1959, Matos was with Castro when the rebels took Havana after Batista fled. A famous photograph showed Matos sitting next to Castro on a tank leading the parade into the city.

After Castro took power, Matos was given the position of military commander/governor of the province of Camagüey. In this post, he played a role in the trials and subsequent executions of Batista collaborators. Later, Matos stated he had no control over the executions.

In the first months of Castro's regime, Matos hoped that Castro would live up to his revolutionary promise of bringing back democratic government and elections to Cuba. Secretly, Castro was moving the country towards Marxism and Communism. Many involved with the revolution supported this shift.

Became Disillusioned with Castro

In his position as governor of Camagüey, Matos found himself sympathizing with those who were negatively impacted by the Marxist-influenced agrarian reforms implemented by Castro and the pro-Communist supporters. The central province of Camaguey had many cattle ranchers who believed that the reforms would lead to their cattle and ranches being taken away from them. Matos took their side over Castro's, leading to a rift with Castro.

Within six months, Matos was quite unhappy with the direction of Castro's leadership, and began speaking out about the lack of elections and ever increasing influence of Communism. Matos even asked Castro to address the infiltration of Communists in both the National Institute of Agrarian Reform and in the military. When Castro disregarded Matos's request, he tried to resign, but Castro would not let him. Though Castro admitted Raúl Castro and Che Guevara were toying with Marxism, Castro asked him to wait a while see if the situation would change and told Matos that men like him were still needed in the new Cuban government.

Matos waited a bit longer, but formally resigned from Castro's government by letter in October 1959 after Raúl Castro, the best known Communist in the Castro regime, was named the head of the army by Fidel. In Matos's resignation letter, he outlined his concerns that Communists were taking over the Cuban government. According to Lizette Alvarez of the *New York Times,* Matos once explained "I differed from Fidel Castro because the original objective of our revolution was 'Freedom or Death.' Once Castro had power, he began to kill freedom."

Matos was one of the first to question and break with Castro over the emergence of Communism in the revolutionary movement. When Matos sent his resignation letter, the pair exchanged a series of communications, and, at one point, Matos asked Castro to not see those who criticized his regime as counter-revolutionaries. Castro lashed out against Matos, however, and ordered him arrested.

Arrested and Tried by Castro's Government

Though Raúl Castro and Guevara wanted to shoot Matos, Castro instead ordered his arrest to avoid making Matos a martyr. Matos was put under arrest by another fellow revolutionary, Camilo Cienfuegos, who also took charge of Camagüey. Matos was placed in custody with 15 other officers who supported Matos's point of view and were declared enemies of the new Cuban government. They were imprisoned in La Cabana, a fortress.

In Camagüey, Castro made a speech denouncing Matos and accusing him of making plans for his own counter-revolutionary uprising. It was not until 1961 that Castro publicly admitted that Cuba was a socialist country. In the period around the arrest, tensions were high in Cuba, as more defectors from Cuba left and challenged Castro and the emerging Communism.

Matos and the other officers were put on trial in December 1959, all charged with treason. The trial took place in an army movie theater, witnessed by soldiers and newspaper representatives from around the world. When given a chance to speak, Matos declared the charges false. Raúl Castro demanded that Matos be put to death.

The trial was memorable for Castro's role in it. He served as the principal witness for the prosecution and gave a seven-hour speech, which aired on the radio in Cuba. In his remarks, he accused Matos and the others of attempting to cause a crisis in Cuba by resigning and implicitly supporting the interests of Cuba's enemies, namely the interests of the United States, what was left of the Batista government, and the major landowners in Cuba.

Suffered in Prison for Two Decades

Though the prosecutors wanted him sentenced to death by firing squad, he was given 20 years in prison. The years Matos spent imprisoned were difficult. He was regularly beaten and severely tortured. According to Chris Maume in the London *Independent*, Matos wrote in his autobiography, *Cómo Llegó la Noche*, "They were very cruel, to the fullest extent of the word.... I was subjected to all kinds of horrors, all kinds...."

Matos also spent about 16 of the 20 years in solitary confinement. During one three-year period, he was locked in a hot, insect-infected cell without windows. He would hear others tortured, sometimes killed, outside of his cell. Matos also suffered from years of illness as a result of his conditions.

Through it all, Matos protested his confinement and treatment therein with at least six hunger strikes. One lasted 165 days. During this hunger strike, he was force fed through his nose. He was not the only one speaking out about his imprisonment, though. Many groups stated their support, condemned his treatment, and called for his release. They included human rights groups, officials in the Roman Catholic church, and the U.S. government. Newspapers also stated their support for Matos, including the *New York Times*.

Moved to South America, then Miami

These efforts were in vain, however. Matos served his full twenty-year sentence. When it was completed in 1979, he was freed. Matos first went to Caracas, Venezuela, then moved to Costa Rica, where his wife, Maria Luisa Araluce, and four grown children lived. She had supported the family as a seamstress during her husband's imprisonment. While Matos was no longer imprisoned, violence still impacted his life in Costa Rica. One of his sons suffered grave injuries when his car was shot up by gunmen using machine guns soon after Matos's arrival. The perpetrators left Costa Rica for Panama before being caught.

Matos and his family soon moved to Miami, Florida, an American city that was home to many Cuban refugees and exiles, and established themselves in a working class suburb. By this time, Matos's left arm became partially paralyzed from the beatings suffered while in prison. Matos remained controversial in his new country. Though many from Cuba welcomed him as a former political prisoner of Castro's who had denounced Cuba and Communism, he was also distrusted, if not condemned, for his time and involvement with Castro. While living in Miami, Matos wrote and published his autobiography, *Cómo Llegó la Noche* (How Night Fell), in 2002. In the book, he detailed his experiences in Cuba and in exile, and explained his fervent anti-Communism.

Despite some antipathy towards him, Matos was a committed counter-revolutionary. He regularly denounced Castro from Miami and stayed in touch with supporters still living in Cuba. He founded and had leadership positions in two human rights organizations dedicated to supporting democracy in Cuba and Latin America, Cuba Independiente y Democrática and the Huber Matos Foundation for Democracy. Through such organizations, he never changed his stance against the Castro regime. In 2009, the 90-year-old Matos traveled to Honduras to take part in a protest against a proposal to allow Cuba back into the Organization of American States.

Five years later, Matos died on February 27, 2014, in Miami, after suffering a heart attack. He was 95 years old. Initially buried in Costa Rica, he left a letter stating his desire to be re-buried in his hometown of Yara when Cuba again became free. Even at the end of his life, Matos remained committed to his anti-Castro ideals. According to the London *Times*, "Even in his nineties he never gave up the fight against Castro and was vocal about what he regarded as his betrayal of the early ideals of the revolution. A prickly, loquacious man with a strong sense of historical drama and his role in it, his last words—according to his family—were 'the struggle continues. Long live free Cuba!'"

Periodicals

Associated Press, February 27, 2014.

Guardian (London, England), April 30, 2014.

The Independent (London, England), March 7, 2014.

New York Times, March 1, 2014.

The Times (London, England), March 5, 2014.

Washington Post, November 18, 1979; March 2, 2014.□

Tadeusz Mazowiecki

A journalist and activist, Tadeusz Mazowiecki (1927–2013) played an active role in the formation of the Solidarity movement that brought down the Communist government in Poland. He became the first non-Communist prime minster of Poland in 1989. Mazowiecki also served as the United Nations envoy to Bosnia during the Bosnian War in the early 1990s.

Forum/UIG/Getty Images

B orn April 18, 1927, in Plock, Poland, Mazowiecki's family had been Polish nobility and his father was a physician. The family's social rank did not prevent tragedy. Mazowiecki's brother died in a concentration camp during World War II. Mazowiecki was well-educated, however. He graduated from Marshal Stanislaw Malachowski Lyceum, then studied law at the University of Warsaw. Mazowiecki did not complete a degree.

Became Journalist and Activist

After leaving the university, Mazowiecki became a journalist and focused on social and political advocacy. He believed in a Catholic-inspired liberal activism that could challenge, if not subvert, the Communists in control of Poland after World War II. In 1947, Mazowiecki lost his first job in publishing because he supported what was deemed clericalism, which was unacceptable by Communist authorities.

In 1953, Mazowiecki became the editor of a weekly Catholic publication in southwest Poland. Because of his outspoken hostility towards the Communist party, he again was forced from his post. Also in this period, Mazowiecki was associated for a short time with the group PAX, which had been set up by Polish authorities but was somewhat independent. Many believed PAX existed to subvert lay Catholic activist groups in Poland. The number of Catholic intellectuals associated with PAX were few in number, and Mazowiecki moved on to his own organization.

By 1956, Poland had become temporarily more open and liberal under Communist leader Wladyslaw Gomulka, until he was forced out in 1959. During these years, Mazowiecki played a key role in establishing a unit of the Catholic Intelligentsia Club in Warsaw. The organization remained opposed to Communism and encouraged related political discussions. In 1958, Mazowiecki founded a new Catholic monthly magazine, *Wiez* (Bond) which emphasized an independent perspective and open debate. Through such forums, Mazowiecki challenged restrictions on individual rights in Poland. He remained *Wiez*'s editor until 1981.

Elected to the Polish National Assembly

From 1961 to 1972, Mazowiecki was elected to and served in Poland's National Assembly, in the lower house called the Sejm. Because he was a member of the legislature, he had immunity from prosecution. Mazowiecki also had some freedom of expression as the leader of the Znac, a

Catholic collective made up of independent deputies in the Sejm permitted by the Communists. Znac strived to bring democratic reforms, educational diversity, and autonomy to Polish universities.

During his tenure in the Sejm, Mazowiecki became a leader in the vocal opposition to the 1968 invasion of Czechoslovakia by the Soviet Union and the brutal actions employed by police against workers and students who were protesting the event in Poland. In 1971, Mazowiecki led a movement that sought to open an investigation into the police massacre of striking shipyard workers in Gdansk. Because of his outspokenness and support of such inquiries, the Polish government prevented Mazowiecki from seeking re-election in 1972.

Barred from elected office, Mazowiecki became more radical and outspoken. In the 1970s, he served as a lecturer in an illegal, underground college, the flying university, where classes were held in private apartments and flats. Mazowiecki also supported the Workers' Defense Committee. This organization focused on shielding activist workers from the Communist party.

Mazowiecki increasingly concentrated on bringing together the leftist intelligentsia and the small, but growing, Polish labor movement to challenge Communist rule in Poland. To that end, he backed the organization of a committee of intellectuals interested in defending the rights of workers. Mazowiecki also put together a hunger strike in support of the workers. The committee, KOR, was formed in the wake of protests by workers in 1976, and contributed to the eventual founding of the Solidarity movement.

Helped Found and Support Solidarity

Beginning in 1980, a number of labor incidents challenging the status quo occurred. Most were centered on the shipyard at Gdansk, and began with labor leader Lech Walesa leading a strike for better pay and the reinstatement of a worker who was fired. Mazowiecki supported Walesa's cause, and helped gather the support of academics, scientists, intellectuals, and other prominent people in Poland. Sixty-four in all signed a petition that stated their backing of Walesa and the laborers.

Mazowiecki assisted in writing an agreement that gave workers the right to form independent trade unions and the right to strike, on August 31, 1980. This was the formal establishment of Solidarity, which not only focused on workers rights but was a broader antibureaucracy and social movement. Led by Mazowiecki, Walesa, and others, Solidarity gained more support and influence in Poland. The Communist government felt threatened by the growing power of Solidarity, and soon outlawed such groups by declaring martial law. Leading figures in such pro-democracy groups were imprisoned, including Mazowiecki. He spent a year in prison.

Continued Activism After Prison

When Mazowiecki was released from detainment, he returned to Solidarity and his activism. He again served as an advisor to Walesa. Through *Wiez* and other publications Mazowiecki edited, the social values and beliefs of Solidarity were endorsed. Walesa chose him to edit a new Solidarity weekly periodical in 1981. Mazowiecki offered analysis of these events and a commentary of his life in this tumultuous era in his 1984 memoir *Internowanie.*

Over the next few years, Solidarity continued to work to bring changes to Poland. After the Polish economy took a turn for the worse, Mazowiecki and Walesa organized another strike at the shipyard in Gdansk in 1988. Mazowiecki played a key supportive role in the strike, remaining in the shipyards with the workers during the event. Though the first 1988 strike failed to force changes with the Polish government, another one later in the year was larger and compelled the government to negotiate with Solidarity.

In what came to be known as the Round Table talks, which began in February 1989, Solidarity, the Communist government, and the Roman Catholic Church worked towards an agreement. During the talks, Mazowiecki served as a mediator. Through the negotiations, an agreement was reached to make Solidarity legal again and permit Solidarity to put forward candidates in the elections. Somewhat free legislative elections were held, with open elections for all the seats in the Senate and 35 percent of the seats in Sejm open to non-Communist candidates. The office of president was also created.

Elected Prime Minister

When elections were held in June 1989, Communist officials were shocked by Solidarity's success. Solidarity won all its districts in which it put forth candidates, including all but one of the seats in the Senate and all 161 eligible seats in the Sejm. Walesa permitted the Sejm to select the Communist leader, General Wojciech Jaruzelski, as president.

After then forming alliances with the United People's Party and the Democratic Party, Solidarity essentially controlled the legislature. As a result, Mazowiecki was elected prime minister by the Sejm with a majority of 212. When he took office, Mazowiecki was the first leader of an Eastern Bloc country who was not a Communist since the immediate post-World War II era.

Though Mazowiecki was prime minster and Solidarity had much influence, the Communists remained in charge of key aspects of the Polish government. They controlled the military, the police, and the secret service. Mazowiecki was also not allowed to withdraw Poland from the Warsaw Pact, the military alliance between Eastern Bloc countries. Still, Mazowiecki promised to be true to his values and independent in thought.

Faced Challenges as Prime Minister

At the beginning of his term as prime minister, Mazowiecki faced many challenges and immediately focused on one of the biggest issues, the economy. The Polish economy was struggling with hyperinflation, as the rate was more than 300 percent. Poland also carried a large foreign debt and a treasury that had gone bankrupt. To gain a much needed $700 million loan from the International Monetary Fund, Mazowiecki had to agree to terms that were difficult. They included a freeze on wages and ended all subsidies to consumers.

At the same time, Mazowiecki did not seek to punish or castigate any Communists or officials in the previous Communist government. This stance created tension with Walesa, who believed that Mazowiecki should not be so lenient towards them. Mazowiecki also was able to put many reforms in place, including the introduction of a multiparty system of government and many civil liberties. Mazowiecki's government supported efforts to transition the economy from Communist to free market as well. In addition, the country's name changed from the People's Republic of Poland to the Republic of Poland. The changes in Poland helped inspire other revolts against Communist Eastern Bloc governments, the fall of the Berlin Wall, and the end of the Cold War in Europe.

Overall, Mazowiecki's time in office was not highly regarded and was increasingly difficult as time went on. As the London *Daily Telegraph* stated, "Far removed from the image of a radical, Mazowiecki's passionless pedantry and caution made him acceptable to the communists. But he lacked Walesa's charisma and as the year went on he came under criticism from radicals in Solidarity who accused him of going soft on former communists, who were still permitted to run for office. At the same time Walesa himself was increasingly frustrated at the way he was being sidelined, as he saw it, by a government he created." Mazowiecki found such pressures added to the challenges of his presidency.

Lost Presidential Election

In December 1990, elections were held again and the Solidarity movement was split. Mazowiecki and Walesa both ran for the office of president. Lacking deep economic knowledge and the magnetism that Walesa radiated, Mazowiecki was defeated. Walesa won the election with 40 percent of the vote while Mazowiecki finished third with 18 percent. After leaving office, Mazowiecki remained active in the Polish government. Beginning in 1991, for example, he served as the chairman of the Democratic Union Party. Mazowiecki also returned to the Polish legislature that year, serving from 1991 to 2001.

In 1992, Mazowiecki gained an international appointment, when he was named the United Nations envoy to Bosnia-Herzegovina. During this period, the brutal Bosnian War was taking place in the former Yugoslavia. The war began when Bosnia-Herzegovina declared its independence, and Bosnian Serb forces attacked and killed thousands of civilians, primarily Bosnian Muslims and Croatians. Mazowiecki produced a report on human rights violations during the war. He resigned in 1995 when he believed that there had been an inadequate international response to war crimes in the region.

Remembered as a Popular Leader

Mazowiecki continued to remain active in international and Polish affairs in the early 21st century. In 2003, he was elected to the Trust Fund for Victims' board of directors. The trust fund was sponsored by the International Criminal Court. The following year, he strongly supported Poland's entry into the European Union.

Though Mazowiecki had long been out of office and Poland had been a free country for many years, he was fondly remembered by the Polish people. In 2005, an opinion poll showed that Mazowiecki was regarded as the most popular leader in Poland's history. Also in 2005, Mazowiecki served as the co-founder of the Polish Democratic Party. Five years later, Mazowiecki served as an advisor to Polish president Bronislaw Komorowski.

On October 28, 2013, Mazowiecki died in a hospital in Warsaw, Poland, at the age of 86. Upon his death, the Polish government honored him by flying flags on government buildings at half staff and he was given a state funeral. Despite the difficult nature of Mazowiecki's time in office, his leadership and life still remained significant to his country.

According to the *Polish News Bulletin,* Bogdan Borusewicz, the speaker of the Polish senate, stated "We owe the fact that Poland is a democratic and independent country to Mazowiecki. He was PM for less than a year and a half, but during that time Poland made the transition from dictatorship to democracy, from a communist to a free market economy.... He was a man of compromise, dialogue, great honesty and moral integrity. His passing is a great loss and his life is something we should all look up to."

Periodicals

Associated Press, August 25, 1989; November 3, 2013.
Daily Telegraph (London, England), October 29, 2013.
Guardian (London, England), October 31, 2013.
New York Times, October 29, 2013.
Polish News Bulletin, October 31, 2013.
Times (London, England), October 29, 2013.□

Clyde McPhatter

The African-American vocalist Clyde McPhatter (1932–1972) was a major hitmaker in the rhythm-and-blues market in the 1950s, both in his solo releases and as part of the groups the Dominoes and the Drifters. Even more significant than his own sales track record was his influence, which loomed large over the next generation of singers who infused gospel passion into secular vocal music.

"He was one of the first guys I ever listened to," Motown label vocal star William "Smokey" Robinson was quoted as saying on the website of the Rock and Roll Hall of Fame. New Orleans crooner Aaron Neville also testified to McPhatter's direct influence, and echoes of his soaring tenor can be heard in the styles of other singers, from the smooth black pop of Sam Cooke to the athletic vocal leaps of McPhatter's successor in the Dominoes, Jackie Wilson. "Steeped in gospel music and endowed with the voice to employ all the musical devices of the preacher's art," in the words of historian Arnold Shaw in *Honkers and Shouters,* McPhatter was a linchpin of new developments in African-American music in the 1950s and 1960s.

Took Choir Solos as Child

Clyde Lensley (or Lensey) McPhatter was born on November 15, 1932, in Durham, North Carolina, and was exposed to gospel music almost from the cradle. His father, George McPhatter, was a minister at Mount Calvary Baptist Church, and his mother, Beulah, played the organ there. Clyde had joined the choir as a boy soprano by the age of five and was soon taking solos. Six of McPhatter's siblings, three brothers and three sisters, were also members of the choir. When the family joined the Great Migration north and settled in Teaneck, New Jersey, in 1945, McPhatter enrolled at Chelsior High School there and soon formed a gospel quartet of his own. Soon he was performing in New York's rich gospel scene, and by the late 1940s he had joined one of the top gospel groups in the eastern United States, the Mount Lebanon Singers. Working as a grocery clerk, McPhatter became well known as a rising gospel star in New York and New Jersey.

Entering the famed Amateur Night competitions at the Apollo Theater in Manhattan's Harlem neighborhood, McPhatter performed the Lonnie Johnson blues number "Tomorrow Night" and caught the ear of Billy Ward, a gospel singer who had made the leap to secular music with his new group, the Dominoes. Invited to join the group, McPhatter was sometimes billed as Clyde Ward, suggesting that he was Billy Ward's brother. The intention was to disguise the comparatively small vocal role played by Billy Ward; Bill Brown took lead vocals, with McPhatter singing harmony, on the racy "Sixty Minute Man," the song that got the Dominoes signed to the pioneering rhythm-and-blues label Federal in 1950.

Gilles Petard/Redferns/Getty Images

Soon McPhatter was taking lead vocals with the Dominoes himself, and he scored his first rhythm-and-blues number one hit as lead singer with "Have Mercy Baby" (1952). But McPhatter was restless under the leadership of Ward, who ran the group in a dictatorial way and collected all of its payments despite his own fairly modest musical role. In 1953 he quit the group; Jackie Wilson was chosen as his replacement. McPhatter had already gained an important fan in Atlantic Records co-founder Ahmet Ertegun, who on arriving at the Birdland jazz club and finding McPhatter missing from the band immediately set out in search of the young potential star. "He raced from bar to bar looking for Clyde and finally found him in a furnished room" in Harlem, Ertegun's business partner Jerry Wexler recalled to Shaw.

Formed Drifters

Auditioning for Ertegun and Wexler with a pickup group in June of 1953, McPhatter failed at first to hit his stride. The executives wisely suggested to McPhatter that he recruit a group of his own, and McPhatter gathered skilled gospel singers who reflected his musical skills and values: tenors Gerhart Thrasher and David Baughan, baritone Bubba Thrasher, and bass Willie Pinckney. This group went into Atlantic's studios as the Drifters on August 9, 1953, and recorded four songs: "Money Honey," "The Way I Feel," "Gone," and "Let the Boogie Woogie Roll."

The session was one of the more influential in the history of both rhythm-and-blues and rock and roll. It was successful for McPhatter and the Drifters themselves, as "Money Honey" became the top rhythm-and-blues hit of 1953, roosting in the number one chart position for 11 weeks. But the session also introduced McPhatter's voice to a wider audience that included other artists. Elvis Presley covered "Money Honey" in 1956, and the long list of later artists who recorded the song included Little Richard, Eddie Cochran, the Jackson 5, and Aaron Neville. Other group members made important contributions, but it was McPhatter, equally effective in ballads and in tougher, cynical numbers like "Money Honey," who was at the center of the Drifters' sound.

The Drifters remained a strong chart presence in 1954 and 1955 with other hits including "Honey Love," "Bip Bam," "What'Cha Gonna Do," "Such a Night" (also recorded by Presley), and the seasonal classic "White Christmas." Mainstream radio and promotional support often went to white artists who covered the Drifters' songs rather than to their originators. But McPhatter sensed that he was on the brink of crossover success, especially in pop-oriented pieces.

Like Presley, McPhatter was drafted into the United States Army in the midst of rising success. Entering the service in 1954, he was not sent overseas and was able to continue to record. Deciding that this was a propitious time to launch his solo career, he left the Drifters, who continued to notch hits under new lead singer Ben E. King. Wexler and Ertegun approved of his solo plans but favored the hard-edged rhythm-and-blues style McPhatter had mostly used up to that time. McPhatter himself set his sights on the orchestra-backed pop style that had brought success to Nat "King" Cole.

Scored Solo Hits

McPhatter released a duet with rhythm-and-blues belter Ruth Brown ("Love Has Joined Us Together") prior to his solo debut, "Seven Days," which appeared in August of 1955. With McPhatter's voice dancing arabesques above doo-wop vocals and a horn arrangement by pop composer Ray Ellis, the record marked a new sound for McPhatter and brought him both major rhythm-and-blues and limited pop chart success. McPhatter scored a string of hits in the middle and late 1950s, including three rhythm-and-blues chart-toppers, "Treasure of Love" (1956), "Long Lonely Nights" (1957), and "A Lover's Question" (1958). The last of these cracked the pop top ten at a time when few African Americans outside of the pure rock and rollers Little Richard and Chuck Berry had accomplished the feat. The song was co-composed by another black pop star-in-the-making whose music would reflect McPhatter's influence, Brook Benton.

The chemistry at Atlantic proved to be crucial to McPhatter's success. After his contract expired in 1959 he moved first to the MGM label and then to Mercury the following year. He scored hits with "Let's Try Again," "Ta Ta," and most successfully with "Lover Please" (1962, composed by future pop-soul star Billy Swan). But his stage appearances became increasingly erratic as a result of alcohol abuse, and increasingly his career suffered because of competition from singers he himself had largely inspired: Ben E. King, Sam Cooke, and later Smokey Robinson. The 1964 album *Live at the Apollo,* recorded for Mercury, gave a glimpse of what McPhatter had been like as a live artist in his prime.

McPhatter began to move in the direction of the rapidly emerging soul style in 1966 and 1967 but had little success. Increasingly frustrated, McPhatter moved in 1968 to Britain, where he had amassed a following after several concert tours. He lasted two years there, beset with the same problems that had plagued him in the United States, and in 1970 Britain refused to renew his visa. Back in the United States, he released the album *Welcome Home,* but this too failed, and on June 13, 1972, at age 39, he died from a cardiac episode associated with alcohol abuse. Despite his influence across multiple genres, he has not yet been the subject of a full-length biography.

Books

Contemporary Musicians, Vol. 25, Gale, 1999.

Shaw, Arnold, *Honkers and Shouters: The Golden Years of Rhythm and Blues,* Crowell-Collier, 1978.

Online

"Clyde McPhatter," *Allmusic,* http://www.allmusic.com (October 4, 2014).

"Clyde McPhatter," *Black Cat Rockabilly Europe,* http://www.rockabilly.nl/references/messages/clyde_mcphatter.ht (October 4, 2014).

"Clyde McPhatter," *Black History Now,* http://www.blackhistorynow.com/clyde-mcphatter/ (October 4, 2014).

"Clyde McPhatter Biography," Rock and Roll Hall of Fame, https://www.rockhall.com/inductees/clyde-mcphatter/bio/ (October 3, 2014).□

Steve McQueen

Known as the "King of Cool," American actor Steve McQueen (1930–1980) played tough, complex guys in such films as *The Great Escape* and *Bullitt.* McQueen was at the peak of his appeal and box office success in the 1960s and early 1970s, before his life and career were cut short by cancer and his death by the age of 50.

Terrence Stephen McQueen was born March 24, 1930, in Beech Grove, Indiana, the son of Bill McQueen and Julian Crawford. His father was an alcoholic drifter who abandoned his wife and son when McQueen was six months old, while his mother became a part-time prostitute when McQueen was a child. McQueen never saw his father again. As a young child, he was reared by his great uncle who owned a farm in the Missouri community of Slater. The family was middle class, but McQueen felt he did not fit in there nor in small town life. He also hated living on the farm.

John Kobal Foundation/Getty Images

Committed Petty Crimes, Went to Reform School

McQueen's mother would remarry twice. When he was nine, he went to live with his mother and a stepfather, first in Indianapolis, then in Los Angeles. McQueen clashed with at least one of his stepfathers, and was abused by one or both of them. McQueen also was getting in trouble for stealing. He then befriended and spent time with a group of kids who flouted the law.

When McQueen was 14 years old, he was given a choice to go to reform school or to a school for troubled boys. Located in Chino, California, the Boys' Republic was McQueen's choice. He went to the school briefly, ran away, went to jail, then returned. Once he spent significant time there, McQueen did well and decided to go straight. According to Christian Williams of the *Washington Post,* McQueen once wrote "One thing they taught me at Boys' Republic was discipline, and man it helped me when I started the acting scene." He would later endow a scholarship for the students there and visit on occasion when he became a famous actor.

After McQueen completed the ninth grade, he dropped out of school. After spending time working as a seaman on a Greek oil tanker, working on the deck, he drifted, working as a lumberjack in California, and on oil rigs in Texas. He even traveled in a carnival as a barker.

In 1947, McQueen joined the Marines and learned mechanics. Despite his experiences in reform school, McQueen struggled with the authority and discipline required in military service. During one incident, he had a weekend pass, but was gone for two weeks. As a result, he spent 41 days in a military prison. In all, McQueen spent three total years in the service and was demoted seven times from private first class to private.

Moved to New York, Became Actor

When McQueen was discharged in April 1950, he ended up in New York City. There, he took a series of odd jobs, including bartender, dockworker, and deliveryman. He repaired television sets, and sold encyclopedias and ball point pens. He was often quite poor and would convince young women to let him give them a tour of Greenwich Village. When they took him out to lunch, he would eat as much as possible.

McQueen also took advantage of the GI Bill, which led to him becoming an actor. A female friend was an actress and she suggested he try the craft. McQueen first took classes at the Neighborhood Playhouse, which was operated by famed acting teacher Sanford Meisner. He made his professional debut in a Yiddish-language production of *Nothing Will Help* in 1952. McQueen spent much of the next four years studying acting at the Uta Hagen-Herbert Berghof School and the Actors Studio.

During the summers, McQueen appeared in summer stock theater and small television roles. In 1956, he made his Broadway debut in *A Hatful of Rain,* replacing Ben Gazzara. McQueen's breakout role came on the television series *Wanted: Dead or Alive.* On the western, McQueen played the lead, a bounty hunter named Josh Randall. The series aired on CBS from 1958 to 1961.

As McQueen moved into film, his striking physical appearance translated well into the medium. Explaining his persona and its origins, Peter B. Flint of the *New York Times* wrote "The screen image of the short, wiry actor was a swaggering veneer he cultivated in his troubled youth and during a term in reform school. His disheveled, sandy hair framed an oddly innocent, slightly pummelled face with cool, blue eyes and an infectious grin that made the most outrageous action seem forgivable."

Made Film Debut

In 1958, McQueen made his film debut in the low-rent science fiction cult classic *The Blob.* By the early 1960s, McQueen was a film star and sex symbol, often playing tough guy convicts, soldiers, and cowboys with a lot of heart. Many of his characters were heroes with quiet determination, acting quickly when the situation called for it.

After appearing in the memorable western *The Magnificent Seven* (1960), McQueen's first big hit was *The Great Escape* (1963). In it, he played an audacious prisoner of war in a World War II German POW camp. As he would in many of his subsequent films, McQueen performed nearly all of his own stunts, including chase sequences.

McQueen appeared in a number of noteworthy films and roles in the early to mid-1960s. He played an indolent musician in *Love with the Proper Stranger* (1963), and Jackie Gleason's business partner in the comedy-drama *Soldier in the Rain* (1963). McQueen showed depth as a young gambler who loses his stake against an aging champion in *The Cincinnati Kid* (1965).

In 1966, McQueen was honored with an Academy Award nomination for his work in *The Sand Pebbles.* He played a sailor who does not get along with the rest of his crew and is only interested in the ship's engines. When the film was released, according to Bob Thomas of the Associated Press, McQueen summarized his career by stating, "I've done pretty well, considering I'm not the movie-star type. I'm not pretty by any means and I'm not that much of an actor. I should have been a character actor, but somehow it didn't turn out that way."

Made a Million Per Picture

By the late 1960s, McQueen was considered a major box office draw. He was paid more than a million dollars per film. He also owned his own film production company and a plastics manufacturing company. In 1968, McQueen appeared in one of his best known films, *Bullitt,* in which he played a cop in San Francisco charged with guarding a star witness for an important trial.

In addition to appearing in the 1969 adaptation of the William Faulkner novel *The Reivers,* McQueen took roles in some films that reflected his personal interests in the early 1970s. For example, McQueen enjoyed racing motorcycles and automobiles. He broke bones racing bikes in the desert, and won several auto races. He appeared in the film *Le Mans* (1971), about the famous endurance car race. McQueen also had a role in another adventure that year, *On Any Sunday.*

Because of his good looks and sex appeal, McQueen also appeared as the male romantic lead in a few films, beginning with *Love With the Proper Stranger* (1963). Even his romantic films were edgy, though these roles were generally considered his weaker parts. In 1968, McQueen played a dashing millionaire who robs a bank in *The Thomas Crown Affair.* Four years later, he played a recently released ex-convict who goes on the run with his wife after a failed heist in *The Getaway.* McQueen made his co-star in *The Getaway* his second wife. McQueen and Ali McGraw were married from 1973 to 1977.

After *Papillion* (1973)—a film about the darkness of imprisonment and escape set at Devil's Island—McQueen played a police chief in the commercially minded disaster flick, *The Towering Inferno* (1974). Though wealthy and respected, McQueen wanted to make quality films. After the release of *The Towering Inferno,* he stopped acting for two years. He spent the period reading books deeply for the first time in his life. He read the classic plays of such authors as William Shakespeare, Anton Chekhov, and Henrik Ibsen.

Failed Adaptation of Ibsen Play

It was in this period that McQueen decided he wanted to make a film of *An Enemy of the People,* by Ibsen. A chance meeting with respected British actor Alec Guinness solidified this decision as Guinness stated his belief that he should make it. McQueen played the lead and took no salary. He was upset that the resulting product was considered unreleasable by the other producers and financial backers, and financing for the release was blocked. *An Enemy of the People* was never shown to the general public after it was completed in 1976.

McQueen made only a few films at the end of his life. They included the western-influenced *Tom Horn* and his last film, *The Hunter,* both released in 1980. In the latter film, McQueen played a modern-day bounty hunter. Though he was already ill, McQueen continued to perform his own stunts by riding atop a train in Chicago. Both were box office failures, though the actor was well compensated for his appearance.

McQueen had been grappling with illness since 1978. That year, he developed a cough he could not shake, and was diagnosed with a rare type of lung cancer, mesothemelioma, in December 1979. The disease is usually fatal. Despite his illness, McQueen remained private about his condition. He only informed close friends and family of his cancer, and denied publicly that he had cancer until nearly the end of his life. He did not tell the press until shortly before his death so he could be left in peace.

Tried Controversial Cancer Therapy

To treat his mesothemelioma, McQueen underwent radiotherapy and chemotherapy. Because he was not making progress with treatments in the United States, he went to Mexico, where he received care considered uncommon and controversial at the time. It was developed by a Dallas-based dentist named Dr. William D. Kelley, who believed that cancers arose and grew from lack of certain pancreatic enzymes. His means of addressing cancer was considered unproven, and Kelly had received an injunction in Texas in 1969 for practicing medicine without a license.

Because Kelly was unable to fully treat patients at his center, International Health of Dallas, McQueen and other patients traveled to a hospital in Juarez, Plaza Santa Maria. Treatments included using drugs like Laetrile, a special diet, nutritional supplements, and animal cell injections. Massages and psychotherapy were also important. McQueen had tumors on his neck, lungs, abdomen, and chest that allegedly shrunk by 25 percent because of Kelly's treatments. Though by the end of October 1980 it seemed that McQueen was getting better, his overall condition was considered hopeless.

After undergoing surgery to remove a tumor from his body, McQueen died of a heart attack on November 7, 1980, in Juarez, Mexico, at Plaza Santa Maria. He was 50 years old. During his lifetime, McQueen was personally considered volatile, intense, and shrewd. Upon his death, respected critic Vincent Canby of the *New York Times* wrote that he had similarity qualities as an actor.

Canby stated, "McQueen didn't 'act in' a movie. His inhabited it. He wore it, as if it were an old, somewhat shabby, utterly comfortable jacket—without ostentation. His roles recall the sort of behavioral performances we now associate more with the great film actors of the 1930's and 1940's than with the often ethnic characterizations we expect today from Robert DeNiro, Al Pacino and Dustin Hoffman. Like Cooper and Gable, McQueen contributed, through his particular presence, far more to the films he was in than he ever received from them.''

Periodicals

Associated Press, November 7, 1980.
Mail on Sunday (London, England), April 1, 2007.
New York Times, November 8, 1980; December 7, 1980; November 15, 2005.
Washington Post, November 8, 1980.□

Myrtilla Miner

American educator Myrtilla Miner (1815–1864) founded the first school for educating African-American girls and women, located in Washington, D.C. A passionate believer in education, she worked tirelessly to educate African-American girls and teach them to become educators in their own right. Also a feminist and an abolitionist, Miner suffered from ill health for much of her life, which was cut short by injuries suffered in a carriage accident.

Myrtilla Miner was born in 1815, in North Brookfield, New York, the daughter of Seth and Eleanor Miner. Her parents were farmers who grew and picked hops. They were among the first to settle in New York's Madison County. Her parents were also deeply religious, and her father played a key role in the founding of the community's First Day Baptist Church. Seth Miner served in the local militia as well, fighting against British rule in the 18th century. Miner was one of 12 children born to the couple.

Had Early Interest in Education

From an early age, Miner was interested in pursuing more education than she had access to in Brookfield. Most women in this period were taught at home. If they attended school, it was quite unusual to receive more than an elementary school education. Though her father did not support her enthusiasm for education, she received all the schooling available in her home community, and read all the books she could acquire. To further her education, she picked hops during picking season to save money for more schooling and more books.

Advocacy was also a part of Miner's young life. She wrote to New York governor (later U.S. senator) William H. Seward, asking for his help and advice on her educational aspirations. She argued that the government should provide means for educating girls and women so they could teach children beyond what was required in Madison County. His reply was vague and not helpful, as women's education was not considered a priority by governments at the time.

Though she suffered from ill health, Miner taught in local schools by the age of 15 as a means of making money. She then gained admittance to the Clinton, New York-based Young Ladies Domestic Seminary, which had been founded by abolitionist Hiram H. Kellogg in 1833. The school allowed her to be a student on credit, and pay her tuition after becoming employed. She continued to struggle with a spinal issue while a student there, but would complete her lessons from her bed when necessary.

Became Teacher

Miner soon found work as a teacher, including a stint at Clover Street Seminary in Rochester, New York. For a two-year period beginning in 1844, she taught in Providence, Rhode Island, at public schools. While working in Providence, she came into contact with the ideas of Henry Barnard, who promoted the idea of educational awakening and expansion.

Inspired by Barnard's ideas and offered a job in Mississippi, Miner moved to the South to teach at the Newtown Female Institute in Whitesville in 1847. There, Miner came into contact with slavery for the first time and began to think as a reformer. Appalled by slavery and its effects, Miner protested the conditions of slavery and even came up with a plan to free slaves. She also wanted to educate African Americans, but was not allowed to do so. It was illegal to teach a slave to read in most of the South, including Mississippi. She spent two years trying to improve the lot of young female slaves in Mississippi to no avail.

The process of trying to affect change in Mississippi was not only frustrating for Miner but also deeply impacted her health. She returned home quite ill in 1849, and was believed to be near death. Instead of dying, however, Miner rallied and recovered. As she regained her health, she taught at a school in Friendship, New York. Miner also decided to focus her life on improving the circumstances of slaves and became determined to affect change through education. She came up with a new idea for an educational institution. She decided that she needed to establish a school located in the North that would teach African-American females and provide them with teacher training.

Opened a School in Washington

Miner's belief that every person had a right to education and achievement was radical for its time. Both a feminist and an abolitionist, she especially believed that education was a means of bettering the lives of the oppressed. As her educational institution idea developed, Miner decided that the school should be located in Washington, D.C. There, slavery was still legal and accepted, and its population was mostly pro-slavery. Yet there were also thousands of free African Americans in the Washington area who could legally be educated.

Determined to open her school, Miner was able to garner some financial support. Quakers were especially encouraging, including such nationally known abolitionists as Reverend Henry Ward Beecher and his daughter, author Harriet Beecher Stowe. Others worried about her safety. Among them was former slave and abolitionist leader Frederick Douglass, who initially tried to dissuade her from her pursuit. He eventually came to support and laud Miner's efforts.

Ignoring all concerns, Miner used the $100 given to her by Quakers to go to Washington, arriving in early December 1851. Renting a room from an African-American man for a small school, she began with six students. They were all daughters of freed slaves. Within two months, the number of pupils in her school had more than doubled to 40. Most of her students were from the city's more successful black families.

Miner's health began to suffer again as she taught for five days a week and tried to solicit support for the construction of a proper school house. She also had to take care of her own personal needs, including all her own sewing. In addition, she walked a mile to and from school daily as it was difficult to find closer lodgings in Washington because of her mission. This effort took a toll on her physical well being.

Protected Her School and Students

Over the next few years, Miner had to address those in Washington who were uncomfortable with, or even outright hostile, to her school. The school had to move three times in two years. There were many physical attacks on it. Stones were thrown at windows many nights, and fires set. Miner herself fended off a number of these assaults. To protect her school and herself, Miner learned how to shoot a pistol at a mark. She would shoot it out in the open to demonstrate her ability to take action. Miner also personally addressed groups of rowdy men who gathered near the school to hurl insults at the students and teachers as they walked home. Some of these protestors tried to enter the school, but Miner forbade it and once threatened to use her gun on the first man who came to the door.

Always highlighting her efforts and the school's success stories, Miner gained the support of leading abolitionists and Quakers. Her efforts to raise funding also paid off. Some of her donations were quite big, with Harriet Beecher Stowe sending $1,000 of the profits gained from her classic novel, *Uncle Tom's Cabin*. In 1858, Miner opened up a new school building located on the edge of Washington. The school—known as the Colored Girls School—had its own three acre lot, which had been purchased five years earlier. By this time, six graduates of the school had become teachers at other schools.

Stepped Down from Teaching

Before the new location of the Colored Girls School opened, however, Miner had stepped away from the day-to-day running of the school because of her continued poor health. By 1857, another abolitionist/educator, Emily Howland, had taken charge and Miner stopped teaching. Miner continued her fundraising efforts, but her health continued to worsen. Because of the beginning of the Civil War, the school temporarily closed in 1860.

To address her health problems, Miner went to California in October 1861. She initially stayed in San Francisco, before traveling to other parts of the state, including Petaluma. Her trip had a secondary agenda as well. She also hoped to raise funds to expand her school. When the Emancipation Proclamation was issued in 1863, the school was given a congressional charter with the support of Massachusetts senator Henry Wilson. It would be another eight years before the school reopened because of the reorganization efforts. Renamed the Institution for the Education of Colored Youth, the school's scope and purpose were expanded.

Miner was still in California during this period. In the spring of 1864, she was involved in a serious carriage accident and was critically injured, with damage to her right hip and lungs. Traveling via ship to New York and arriving in August, Miner returned to Washington, D.C., to attempt further recovery in early December. Staying at the home of the president of the school's board of trustees, Mrs. Nancy M. Johnson, Miner succumbed to her injuries on December 17, 1864. She was 49 years old. She was buried in Georgetown, in the Oak Hill Cemetery.

Left Important Legacy

Mary Treacy, a former librarian at the District of Columbia Teachers College, told Denise Roe of the *New York Archives,* that Miner "recognized the possibilities, established standards, and found the means to reach high goals... who lived by the principles that inspire 150 years later; all this shows what one energetic woman... can accomplish in the face of the most disheartening obstacles."

Despite her early death, Miner's vision was not forgotten and her school flourished. For five years beginning in 1871, the Institution for the Education of Colored Youth was affiliated with Howard University, a college dedicated to African Americans. Later in the decade, in 1879, the renamed Miner Normal School was incorporated into the public school system of the District of Columbia. Many graduates from Miner's teaching school taught in the first public high school for African Americans, which opened in 1870 and was funded in part by Miner's estate. It was the predecessor to D.C.'s Dunbar High School, which was still open in the early 21st century.

Miner's school remained intact in the 20th and 21st centuries as well. In 1929, her school became the Miner Teachers College. It was the subject of a merger in 1955, combining with the Wilson Teachers College to form the District of Columbia Teachers College. Two decades later, it was consolidated with the University of the District of Columbia, where it remained an active degree granting institution in 2014. Miner's name was also given to a public elementary school located in Washington.

Miner's legacy was considered profound even by her contemporaries. According to the State News Service, U.S. Secretary of Education Rod Paige said Douglass once wrote of Miner, "If we owe it to the generations that go before us and to those which come after us to make some record of the good deeds we have met with in our journey through life... we certainly should not forget the brave little woman who first invaded the city of Washington to establish here a school for the education of a class long despised and neglected."

Books

O'Connor, Ellen M., *Myrtilla Miner: A Memoir,* The Riverside Press, 1885.

Periodicals

New York Archives, Spring 2013.
State News Service, May 11, 2002.
Washington Post, January 19, 2014.

Online

"Myrtilla Miner: Educator (1815-1864)," *Biography.com,* http://www.biography.com/people/myrtilla-miner-39659#the-normal-school-for-colored-girls (December 20, 2014).
"Myrtilla Miner," National Abolition Hall of Fame and Museum, http://www.nationalabolitionhalloffameandmuseum.org/mminer.html (December 20, 2014).□

Ottavio Missoni

Ottavio Missoni (1921–2013) was the design maverick behind one of Italy's most successful designer-fashion brands. Largely self-taught, the former track star combined forces with his wife Rosita to create appealingly lightweight, multicolored knitwear in the signature Missoni zigzag pattern that became part of the cosmopolitan fashion uniform in the 1970s.

Ottavio Missoni was born on February 11, 1921, in Dubrovnik, a major Adriatic Sea port in what is present-day Croatia. In the 1920s, Dubrovnik was known by its Italian-language name of Ragusa and was a key maritime center and anchor of a tourist industry along its scenic Dalmatian coast. Missoni's sea-captain father Vittorio came from a seafaring family whose roots were in Breton, in northern France, and their surname was originally "Misson."

Competed in Olympics

Missoni's mother Teresa de Vidovich was a Countess of Capocesto and Ragosniza, an aristocratic house who were longtime landholders and prominent figures in Dalmatian Italy. She and Vittorio's son, called "Tai," preferred sports over schoolwork and emerged as a talented track and field athlete at an early age. He earned a spot on the Italian national team at age 16 and, in 1939, won first place in the 400-meter race at that year's International University Games in Vienna, Austria.

The first 20 years of Missoni's life were spent in an Italian Republic that was a right-wing, authoritarian dictatorship. Fascist Party leader Benito Mussolini sided with an increasingly aggressive Nazi Germany, whose bold territory grabs across the European continent prompted the outbreak of World War II just after Missoni's triumph at the Vienna student championships. Drafted into the Italian Army, he was sent to defend Italy's colonial holdings in Africa. He fought in a long and grueling campaign in the summer of 1942 to secure the region around the Suez Canal in Egypt, but the Battle of El Alamein ended in a stalemate and Missoni was taken as a prisoner of war by British forces. He spent four years in a detention facility in Egypt and returned to Italy in 1946.

Missoni returned to his athletic pursuits with a renewed vigor. Again, he won a place on the Italian national team and went to London for the 1948 Summer Olympics, the first postwar Games. By then Missoni had

Angelo Deligio/Mondadori Portfolio/Getty Images

started a small business in Trieste, another Adriatic seaport, making tracksuits and other athletic wear with a fellow Italian athlete, Giorgio Oberweger. Their company, called Venjulia, provided the uniforms for the Italian team at the London Games. In a keenly competitive field, Missoni placed just sixth in one men's event, the 400-meter hurdles, but he met his future wife, a fellow Italian, in London at the Olympics. Rosita Jelmini, from the northern Italian city of Varese, was staying in England for a language course chaperoned by the Roman Catholic nuns of her convent school. The couple were wed five years later in Golasecca, the town near Varese where she was raised.

Discovered Unusual Knitting Machine

The Jelmini family had a successful textile business in Varese that was by then several generations old. They made shawls and scarves from yarn spun from wool provided by sheep that grazed on the slopes of the Italian Alps in Lombardy. Missoni and his wife launched their company the same year they were wed, in 1953, with some yarn-spinning machines they set up in the basement of their first home in Gallarate, another city in the Lombardy region. They started small, with some striped dresses sold in a Milan department store under the label "Maglificio Jolly." Their three children—sons Vittorio and Luca, followed by daughter Angela—all arrived during this same five-year span when the company emerged as a fresh contender on

the Italian fashion scene. In 1958 the husband-and-wife team decided to change the company name and label to "Missoni."

In the early 1960s, Missoni and Rosita worked together to create the distinctive zigzag pattern that would become indelibly associated with their family name and fashion label. Its origins were in a knitting machine they rediscovered called the Raschel; Rosita's family had used it back in the 1920s to create shawls and other textiles with a distinctive pattern that let colored threads bleed over one another for an unusual effect. Missoni retooled one of the Raschel machines to knit with a lighter blend of yarn that used rayon, a synthetic fiber. The company's first zigzag-patterned item was introduced in 1963, and the novel women's items found an influential supporter in Italian fashion journalist Anna Piaggi. The Missonis also paired with a trend-setting Paris-based stylist, Emmanuelle Khanh, who designed some mini-skirt dresses for them that sold well. Missoni created the designs and oversaw the technical side of the family business. "His simple yet efficient system, a series of small colored lines drawn on checked paper with matching shreds of yarn to indicate the sequence for the looms, is still used," noted *WWD* writer Luisa Zargani in 2013.

The Missonis' first fashion shows were staged in Paris in the mid-1960s under the Missoni-Khanh label. In 1967 the Italian company garnered some terrific free publicity after a minor scandal erupted over a runway presentation in Florence—a city more fabled for its trove of Renaissance art than Milan, northern Italy's bustling commercial hub. Backstage at the opulent event space of the Palazzo Pitti, Rosita realized that the new viscose-blend knits they were about to present to store buyers and journalists were so lightweight that the models' undergarments showed through. She had the models remove their bras, but the high-wattage runway lighting had the unintended effect of making the sweaters see-through. The Missoni show at the august Palazzo Pitti caused a press sensation, and conservative Italian journalists compared the Missoni presentation to a lurid Paris nightclub scene.

Compared Colors to Music

Banned from the showing at the Palazzo Pitti again, Missoni and his company set up their presentations in Milan, which was closer to their Lombardy home anyway. Their presence helped Milan become a regular stop on the Fashion Week circuit, when journalists converge upon New York City, Paris, London, and the Italian commercial center for twice-yearly ready-to-wear previews of upcoming lines. Rosita handled the business and marketing side of the firm, while Missoni sketched out his mathematically precise designs on graph paper, with a barrage of hues that might seem to clash, but instead gave off a fresh tonal palette.

For creative inspiration Missoni looked to unusual sources, such as the textiles and designs of pre-Columbian indigenous culture of Central America, for example. As he wrote years later, "I like comparing color to music: Only seven notes and yet innumerable melodies have been composed with those seven notes," he explained, according to *New York Times* writer Eric Wilson. "How many basic colors are there? I don't remember exactly, seven perhaps, like the notes of the scale, but how many tones or shades does each color have? An infinite number, just as always endless are the hues and nuances composing a work of art."

Missoni and Rosita's children grew up in a thriving family business, which included a state-of-the-art factory they built in Sumirago, north of Milan, in 1968. In the 1970s, home textiles and menswear collections were introduced, as well as standalone boutiques across Italy. For years the Missoni name appeared regularly in *Vogue* and on the pages of other fashion magazines, and style-setting celebrities were photographed wearing the lightweight silk-blend sweaters, dresses, and accessories. "Though they did not bear a familiar logo," remarked Wilson in the *New York Times,* the Missoni "designs were so easily recognizable—and recognizably expensive—that they conveyed a peculiar social currency among the moneyed elite, like an updated varsity sweater for young preppies of the 1970s and '80s."

The genial Missoni and his equally lively wife were a favorite of the fashion pack, and regularly profiled by journalists who were welcomed cordially in Sumirago and at the family home. "I ask myself, 'Why is this working so successfully?'" Missoni pondered in a 1971 *New York Times* article by Bernadine Morris. "We try to find superior materials and new ways to use old materials. But I think our great asset is our simplicity of line. We make it possible for women to be dressed in fashion and still dress very simply."

Kept Control of Company

Despite that winning combination of luxe material and on-trend silhouettes, the Missoni company began to falter in the mid-1980s. Its signature zigzag and patchwork patterns began to look outmoded as fashion veered toward minimalist looks from designers like Giorgio Armani and Calvin Klein; on the other end of the scale, outlandish and extravagantly tailored fashions from Paris also captured attention. The Missoni label languished for a time, its name often grouped with Gucci, another once-dominant Italian fashion house that had failed to keep pace with the times. Unlike other Italian houses, however, the company remained privately held, thanks to the prudence of Missoni and Rosita.

As they passed their 40th wedding anniversary, the Missonis happily handed over daily operations of their business to their now-grown children in the mid-1990s. Daughter Angela became creative director, with the eldest son, Vittorio, holding the reins as chief executive officer: Luca was involved in reviving the menswear line and handled philanthropic projects.

Missoni stayed fit by throwing shot and discus well into his eighties. He also worked on textile art and penned his autobiography, *Una Vita sul Filo di Lana* (A Life on the Woolen Thread), published in conjunction with his 90th birthday celebration in 2011. Later in 2011, his granddaughter Margherita Maccapani Missoni became the latest brand ambassador for the family business when she promoted an enormously successful capsule line for U.S. retailing giant Target. The Missoni for Target collection prompted a shoppers' frenzy at some Target stores and demand was so intense that Target's Web site was unable to handle the Internet traffic at peak hours. Despite that success, the Missoni patriarch did not believe the company he built would become a giant like the revitalized Gucci. "We are not capable of creating a huge company," the descendant of 18th-century Breton corsairs told *WWD's* Zargani in 2011. "I always say you can launch a boat that weighs 100,000 tons, but then you must sail it and have the right crew. I'm pleased with the company: It's profitable, it gives us satisfaction and it hasn't lost prestige."

Two years later, tragedy struck the Missoni clan when 58-year-old Vittorio, their first-born child, went missing on January 4, 2013. The CEO, his wife Maurizia Castiglioni, and another couple had boarded a small plane on Los Roques, an island off the coast of Venezuela, and headed for Caracas, the Venezuelan capital. The plane vanished over open seas. Already in frail health, the 92-year-old Tai Missoni died five months later on May 9, 2013, at his home in Sumirago. His widow and children Luca and Angela, along with Vittorio's children, held out hope that the survivors of the plane crash would turn up somewhere in the Caribbean, but the wreckage was discovered in late June, six weeks after Missoni's death.

Periodicals

Guardian (London, England), May 10, 2013.

New York Times, November 24, 1971; May 10, 2013.

WWD, September 22, 2003; February 11, 2011; May 10, 2013. □

Chana Mlotek

An expert in Yiddish folksongs, Chana Mlotek (1922–2013) collected and archived such music from shtetls, ghettos, and Yiddish theater, and shared her encyclopedic knowledge in books and scholarly articles. Employed at the YIVO Institute for Jewish Research for 65 years, Mlotek also penned a column on Yiddish poetry for *The Forward* for more than four decades with her husband, Joseph.

Born Eleanor Chana Gordon on April 4, 1922, in Brooklyn, New York, she was the daughter of Russian immigrants. Her father was employed as a garment manufacturer, while her mother worked as a seamstress. Raised in the East New York section of Brooklyn and the North Bronx, her father had an appreciation of Yiddish theater songs and often sang them to her throughout her childhood. Yiddish was her first language. As a child, Mlotek was trained in piano by Jacob Helmann, who had studied with a student of Franz Liszt, the respected 19th-century Hungarian composer and pianist.

Immersed in Yiddish Culture

Mlotek learned about Yiddish culture by attending a Yiddish culture camp, Camp Boiberik, in the upstate New York village of Rhinebeck. She later served as a counselor and a teacher there. Mlotek also was educated at the Yiddish high school that was part of the Sholem Aleichem Folk Institute. In addition, Mlotek completed high school by attending Walton High School. Mlotek also earned a B.A. from Hunter College by attending the former Bronx campus.

In 1944, Mlotek became employed as a secretary to Max Weinreich. A respected scholar, he had co-founded the YIVO Institute for Jewish Research (originally known as the Yiddish Scientific Institute for Jewish Research) in Poland in 1925, and moved it to New York City in 1939. From its inception, YIVO focused on recording and studying the language, culture, and literature of Eastern European Jews. Mlotek was hired because she spoke outstanding Yiddish. In a later position, she was the assistant to Weinreich, the research director at YIVO.

After four years as Weinreich's employee, Mlotek won one of 12 scholarship to attend a seminar on Yiddish folklore and linguistics at the University of California Los Angeles (UCLA). The classes were taught by Weinreich, and marked the first time a Yiddish folklore class was taught there. The experience led Mlotek to focus on Yiddish folklore and folksongs. In 1949, she married Joseph Mlotek, a Polish Jew who had escaped during after Nazi Germany invaded Poland via a transit visa from Chiune Sugihara, a diplomat from Japan. The couple met at the seminar.

Served as Archivist at YIVO

Mlotek used her background and education at YIVO to serve as its music archivist for decades. She was considered a leading force in the re-establishment of Yiddish folksong research in the United States after World War II. By that time, YIVO again concentrated on folklore as the organization had in the years before the war.

Focusing on ethnographic investigation, Mlotek compiled and catalogued thousands of pieces of sheet music as part of her duties. She created many collections at YIVO, which inspired a number of guides and catalogs. Mlotek also was responsible was founding the Y.L. Cahan Folklore Club at YIVO early in her tenure. It published significant amounts of folklore material that had been collected at YIVO.

YIVO's senior archivist Fruma Mohrer stated in a press release by the institute, "Chana had every single piece of music from the YIVO Archives at her fingertips: every arrangement, every title, from the 19th century to the present. She was a woman of vast knowledge, and yet was unfailingly unassuming and unpretentious." Mlotek soon became recognized for her Yiddish music and folklore scholarship.

Developed Song Discerning Ability

Over the years, Mlotek also became widely known for her ability to discern Yiddish songs based on only a few words or lines, and shared this knowledge with scholars, writers, singers, and composers. In *The Forward,* Itzik Gottesman wrote of Mlotek's skill in this area, stating, "people would come to our archives and say, I only remember one Yiddish song from my mother, of that song I only remember one line. And, unfortunately, from that one line I only remember two or three words.... But Mlotek... almost always found what the person was looking for."

Because of her knowledge, enthusiasm, and ability to find obscure songs, Mlotek contributed to the revival of klezmer, a music genre of Ashkenazi Jews. Klezmer underwent a revival beginning in the 1970s and became popular outside of Yiddish speakers. Through Mlotek's work, she was able to find the song "Lid fun Titanik," a Yiddish lament about the sinking of the Titanic in 1912. It was later recorded by singer/actor Mandy Patinkin.

Wrote on Yiddish Music

Mlotek also wrote scholarly articles about Yiddish music, especially ballads and folksongs. Much of her research focused on folklorization, in which songs are changed by people to reflect their current lives and circumstances. Her first research paper examined a song entitled "The Beard." In the tune, the wife implores her husband as to why he cut off his beard because he no longer looks the same. Through her research, Mlotek found "The Beard" was based on an 1868 poem by Mikhl Gordon. Mlotek also had extensive knowledge of and wrote about Yiddish theater songs, art songs, and popular songs.

Some of Mlotek's writings were targeted at a wider audience. Beginning in 1970, Mlotek contributed "Perl fun der Yiddisher Poezie" (the "Pearls of Yiddish Poetry") to *The Forward*'s Yiddish edition. One feature of the column was "Readers Recall Songs," which asked readers to contribute songs or any part a reader remembered from Yiddish theater or Yiddish communities destroyed during the Second World War. Such letters and queries came from around the world. She would find or recreate many of the submitted songs, while information was also given on the origins and performances of these songs. Through the column, knowledge was gained and shared about the actual writers of many compositions previously believed to be traditional songs.

"Pearls of Yiddish Poetry" was co-written by Mlotek's husband, who did much of the actual column writing while Mlotek focused on research. Joseph Mlotek was the managing editor of the Yiddish edition of *The Forward* as well as the educational director of the Jewish fraternal organization and social services group, the Workmen's Circle. Before his death in 2000, no less of a personage than Isaac Singer, the winner of the 1978 Nobel Prize in Literature, compared them to Sherlock Holmes in their ability to locate Yiddish folk songs. Mlotek continued writing the column herself after her husband's demise.

Published Yiddish Songbooks

Over the years, the Mloteks published three songbooks of Yiddish music, both well known and obscure, under a Workmen's Circle imprint. These books included *Mir Trogn A Gezang* (We Are Carrying a Song), *Perl fun Yidishn Lid* (New Pearls of Yiddish Songs), and *Lider fun Dor tsu Dor* (Songs of Generations: New Pearls of Yiddish Songs).

Published in English translations in 1997, *Songs of Generations: New Pearls of Yiddish Songs* was based on their "Pearls of Yiddish Poetry" column. The anthology included 125 songs, both in Yiddish and translated into English by Barnett Zumoff. Explanations were included of each song's origins and any variations in existence. All the books sold well—they were among the best selling Yiddish songbooks worldwide—and contributed to the growth of knowledge about and interest in Yiddish songs in the late twentieth and early twenty-first centuries.

After Joseph Mlotek's death, Mlotek published another songbook in 2007. Cowritten with Mark Slobin and published by Wayne State University Press, it was entitled *Yiddish Folksongs from the Ruth Rubin Archive*. The book focused on the songs and research of Rubin, a leading early mid-20th century Yiddish folksong scholar. *Yiddish Folksongs from the Ruth Rubin Archive* received an honorable mention from the Modern Language Association in 2008. Mlotek also edited or co-edited several other books including *25 Geto-lider* (Twenty-Five Ghetto Songs) and *We Are Here: Forty Songs of the Holocaust*.

Overall, the work of Mlotek and her husband were considered invaluable in preserving and spreading Yiddish culture. The assistant director of Smithsonian Folkways Recordings, Amy Horowitz, told Richard F. Shepard of the *New York Times* that the work of the Mloteks was especially important "for new generations of singers who want to carry on these repertories. This is especially so with tradition like Yiddish, which was almost annihilated during World War II to have people who provide us not only with the songs themselves but with the context out of which the songs came and which really no longer exists in the rich and widespread form it was."

Mlotek's personal life also dominated her interest in Yiddish music and culture. The couple's home was a center of correspondence, with many people sending them requests for information about songs or people's remembrances of songs. Living in a three-bedroom apartment in the Bronx throughout most of her marriage, she stored her large and extensive music collection and related mail throughout her living space. Mlotek continued to play the piano throughout her life, and the couple hosted many gatherings of Yiddish writers and performers.

Worked Until Late in Life

Mlotek worked until very late in her life. Though Mlotek stepped away from YIVO for a time, she had returned under a National Endowment for the Arts grant in 1978, and became YIVO's full-time music archivist in 1984. She spent 65 total years with YIVO and 43 years penning the "Pearls of Yiddish Poetry" column. In 2004, Mlotek and her son Zalmen offered joint lectures on Yiddish music at KlezCamp, a family camp program, and helped in planning the YIVO's eightieth anniversary benefit. In this period, Mlotek was honored by the Milken Archive and the Jewish Theological Seminary with a lifetime achievement award. It was given in 2003.

Still actively and happily employed in 2012, Mlotek told the *New York Jewish Week*'s George Robinson, "My legs don't go as fast as they did. But I can still work three times a week at YIVO, I still write a column for the *Forverts*, and the work is interesting." She was working on her ninth book about Yiddish music when she lost her battle with cancer.

Mlotek died on November 4, 2013, at her home in the Bronx, New York at the age of 91. She was survived by her two sons, Zalmen and Mark, both of whom held high-profile positions in Jewish cultural organizations. A Juilliard-trained pianist, conductor, and composer, Zalmen Nosn became the artistic director of the National Yiddish Theater-Folksbiene, while Mark Elchonen served as the president of Folksbiene and was once the president of Workmen's Circle.

Afer her death, Mlotek was honored with a week-long arts festival, Kulturfest, being renamed in honor as The First Chana Mlotek International Festival of Jewish Performing Arts. For Mlotek, she felt the importance of her work in saving Yiddish culture and the wider history of Jews in Europe. She told Jennifer Siegel of *The Forward*, "We see what an important role music and songs played in the life of the people. They didn't have television or radio, so they sang songs to each other." Mlotek added that, "It's part of our cultural heritage. This is so rich and colorful, it should be part of everyone's knowledge and sensitivity."

Periodicals

Associated Press, November 5, 2013.

The Forward, December 3, 2004; November 15, 2013.

New York Times, December 28, 1997; November 5, 2013.

The Record (Bergen County, NJ), April 5, 2005.

Online

"Brief Introduction," YIVO Institute, http://www.yivoinstitute.org/about/ (November 28, 2014).

"Chamna Mlotek z"l," Yiddish Book Center, http://www.yiddishbookcenter.org/chana-mlotek (November 28, 2014).

"Mlotek, Slobin Receive Honorable Mention for YIVO Publication," YIVO Institute for Jewish Research, http://www.yivoinstitute.org (November 28, 2014).

"'The Queen' of Yiddish Song," *The New York Jewish Week*, http://www.thejewishweek.com/news/ (November 28, 2014).

"YIVO Mourns the Passing of Chana Mlotek, 1922-2013," YIVO Institute for Jewish Research, http://yivo.org/about (November 28, 2014). ☐

Charlotte Moon

Spending decades ministering in China, American missionary Charlotte "Lottie" Moon (1840–1912) is perhaps the best known Southern Baptist missionary. She founded the Lottie Moon Christmas Offering, which has helped fund Southern Baptist missionary work since the late 1800s.

Charlotte Diggs Moon was born December 12, 1840, in Crowe, Virginia, the daughter of Edward Harris Moon and his wife Anna Maria (Barclay). Her father was a plantation owner and she was raised in wealth and privilege. His estate, Viewmont, was located on the so-called "Road of the Presidents." Her uncle, Dr. James Barclay, bought Monticello after Thomas Jefferson's death.

Received Thorough Education

An impish, intelligent child, Moon received her early education at home from governesses. She then completed her higher education at two schools. She first attended Hollins College, a private Baptist girls' school in Virginia. She earned her B.A. there in 1856. Moon then entered the Charlottesville, Virginia-based Albermarle Female Institute.

Like Hollins, Albermarle was a female-only school organized by Baptists. There, Moon was intellectually challenged, studying Greek, Hebrew, Latin, Spanish, and French. She was mentored by and had a close friendship with one of her professors, Crawford Howell Toy. Later a missionary to Japan, Toy later became an early faculty member of the Southern Baptist Theological Seminary, was labeled a heretic, banished, and became a distinguished professor at Harvard. There is some speculation that Toy and Moon were once on the verge of engagement, though they never married. She earned her M.A. in 1861, and was one of the first women to earn a master's degree in the South.

Embraced Baptist Faith

During this period, Moon underwent a deeply religious experience. In her youth, she was quite hostile to the Baptist faith even though her parents were devout parishioners of the Scottsville Baptist Church. She remained skeptical even though she attended two Baptist institutions. While living in Charlottesville and attending Albermarle, Moon attended a student revival led by Dr. John A. Broadus in 1858. Though she intended to mock the event, she was moved, prayed all night, converted to the Southern Baptist faith, and was baptized by Broadus.

Moon soon expressed interest in becoming a foreign missionary, but it was not possible. Broadus made appeals to college students to serve as foreign missionaries, and several of Moon's friends in Charlottesville answered the call. However, Southern Baptists would not allow unmarried women to serve as missionaries after a failed experiment with one at an earlier date. To become a missionary, she would have to marry one.

After completing her master's degree, Moon returned home. Around the same time, the American Civil War began and Moon played a small role in helping the sick and wounded during the conflict. Moon's elder sister, Orianna, was one of the first female doctors in the South. She earned her medical degree from the Female Medical College of Pennsylvania in 1857 and used her skills as a physician in hospitals during the conflict. Moon assisted her sister, beginning in 1861. Moon also was a tutor to her younger sister Edmonia, and taught in Charlottesville.

Because of the Civil War, the Moon family lost its fortune while retaining Viewmont. Like other members of her family, Moon was forced to make her own way in the world and financially support herself. She also provided financial support for her mother until her death in 1870. In addition, Moon donated money to foreign missionary efforts of the Southern Baptist church. She supported the church through her own volunteer efforts as a church worker as well.

Worked as Educator

Continuing her employment in education, Moon served as a tutor for children in Alabama. She then taught in a girls' school in Danville, Kentucky, beginning in 1866. It was the predecessor to Centre College. In 1870, Moon was a co-founder of a school for girls in Cartersville, Georgia. She established the school with a close friend she met in Danville, Anna Cunningham Safford, a Presbyterian missionary who shared Moon's enthusiasm for missionary work. Moon and Safford ran the school for two years.

By the early 1870s, the Southern Baptist church perspective on unmarried women missionaries was changing. Groups of Baptist women were encouraging the foreign mission board of the Southern Baptist church to appoint single women missionaries. Support groups for women sprung up as well, and they brought funding for their cause. The mission board was nearly bankrupt by this time, and was finally convinced to allow unmarried women to go abroad as missionaries in 1872.

In September 1873, Moon traveled to China where her younger sister, Edmonia, had sailed the previous year to serve as a Southern Baptist missionary. Edmonia Moon had been active in the student missionary society at her school, the Richmond Female Institute. Through a correspondence with Tarleton Perry and Martha Forster Crawford, Baptist missionaries already in China, Edmonia was offered a position as their assistant. She left the United States in April 1872.

Became Missionary in China

Moon, too, wanted to live out her Christian life as a missionary. Inspired by a sermon she heard in Centerville and responding to calls from other missionaries in China, Moon asked to be sent to China as well. The Southern Baptist foreign mission board appointed her in 1873. After she arrived, she was able to acclimate quickly, including mastering Chinese and learning Chinese customs. The sisters lived in a home in Tengchow dubbed "The Home of the Crossroads." Tengchow had been the center of Southern Baptist missionary work in the Shantung Province since 1861.

Moon remained in Tengchow for the first few years of her mission, and the city would become her base of operations in subsequent years. Her assignment as a missionary was to evangelize to other women. She also ensured that women would not have any authority over men, including as teachers, preachers, or otherwise.

While Edmonia Moon was primarily a schoolteacher, her elder sister used school teaching, including supervising a girls' school, as a means of challenging Chinese culture and allowing women the freedom to become and live as Christians. With other missionaries, Moon became versed in the ways of personal evangelism, and would travel from village to village to teach children about the Bible.

Because Edmonia had a breakdown and declining health, she was compelled to return to the United States in 1876. Moon went with her to help get her home, but went back to China on her own the following year. She arrived there by Christmas of 1877, and re-established herself in Tengchow. Moon then resumed her teaching ministry.

Describing Moon's personal accomplishments in her first years as a missionary, Charlotte B. Allen wrote in *International Bulletin of Missionary Research*, "She learned to endure scrutiny and commentary by curious people who did not consider her human and gave her no privacy. She conquered fears of people who continually reviled her as 'Devil Woman,' she stayed courageous in the face of death threats, and she kept her poise in confrontations with soldiers. She came to accept the 'real drudgery' of mission life. She ennobled her view of the harsh realities by remembering that the Chinese peasants were living a simple existence with which the man Jesus would have been personally familiar."

Worked in Remote Location

Undistracted by controversies involving other missionaries and the foreign mission board, Moon made a bold move in the mid-1880s. Focusing on more remote villages and parts of China, she decided to move to Pingtu, although she retained a home in, and still considered Tengchow her home base. No missionary had previously spent any time in this area, located about 120 miles away from Tengchow. In addition to widening the scope of her work geographically, Moon wanted to increase efforts to support the education of Chinese women on a personal level. She no longer taught in schools but tried to make inroads into people's lives as their friend. She had little contact with non-Chinese people.

Because Moon lacked funding for even the most basic of needs, Moon contacted women affiliated with the Southern Baptist Church and challenged them to support the mission in China in 1888. The Southern Baptist Woman's Missionary Union responded by raising more than $3,000 in funds. This funding was used to provide three more female missionaries to the Pingtu region and establish a Baptist church there by 1889. The Lottie Moon Christmas Offering for Foreign Missions became an annual event.

An exhausted Moon was able to again return to the United States on her first two-year furlough between 1891 and 1893. She primarily focused on regaining her health, including addressing chronic headaches. Moon also made a few public appearances. During her time in America, she described the state of the Southern Baptist mission in China at events like the Southern Baptist Convention in Atlanta in October 1891 and the same event in Nashville in 1893. She also discussed her experiences with various women's groups in the South, attempting to garner their support.

Remained in China Despite Unrest

By October 1893, Moon was back in China and Tengchow. She spent the next seven years there, and saw the scope and size of the Southern Baptist mission expand greatly to include many new missionaries, a missionary hospital, a theological seminary, and schools of higher education. Moon was forced to leave temporarily in July 1900 because of the Boxer Rebellion. At this time, many in China were speaking out against the influences of the western world, including Christian culture. It was unsafe for missionaries such as Moon to be in the region.

Moon temporarily moved to Fukuola, Japan. By April 1901, she was able to return to Tengchow, leaving only to take another furlough in the United States from 1903 to 1904. Though Moon would remain in China for a more than a decade, the political situation in China grew more unstable because of the Russo-Japanese War of 1904 to 1905, and later because of the Chinese Revolution against the ruling Manchu Dynasty in 1911. Moon would not leave in this era despite the chaos and warnings of American officials that all Americans should leave China, suffering through bombing attacks during the war. In 1911, Moon helped organize the Woman's Missionary Union of North China to support women missionaries in the region.

By early 1912, Moon was ill from malnutrition, poor physical health, depression, and exhaustion. Mission medical personnel insisted that she return to the United States because of the terrible state of mental and physical well-being. Moon relented, donating her remaining funds to the Famine Relief Fund and Christians living in Pingtu.

Died on Ship to America

Setting sail from Shanghai to San Francisco on December 20, 1912, Moon was accompanied by a missionary nurse named Cynthia Miller. Weighing only 50 pounds, she died suddenly aboard the ship when it was docked in the harbor at Kobe, Japan, on Christmas Eve in 1912. Upon her death, Moon was cremated and her ashes were sent to her family in Virginia, where they were buried. Her estate consisted of $250 and a worn trunk of her personal items.

Perhaps Moon's most important legacy was the Lottie Moon Christmas Offering which continued in the early 21st century and is still administered by the Southern Baptist Woman's Missionary Union. As in the late 19th century, the offering funds the building of churches, hospitals, and schools at locations worldwide. It is also used to publish missionary tracts, and provide financial support for ministries working various countries. The offering is the largest funding source for Southern Baptist missionaries and raised more than a billion dollars overall by the end of the 20th century. As Terry G. Carter wrote in *Baptist History and Heritage*, "Arguably the convention's most famous missionary of all times, Lottie Moon is an icon for Southern Baptists."

Books

Dictionary of Women Worldwide: 25,000 Women Through the Ages, Volume 2, edited by Anne Commire and Deborah Klezmer, Yorkin Publications, 2007.

Women in World History: A Biographical Encyclopedia, Volume 11, edited by Anne Commire, Yorkin Publications, 2002.

Periodicals

Baptist History and Heritage, Spring 2013.
International Bulletin of Missionary Research, October 1993.□

P

Candace Pert

American neuroscientist Candace B. Pert (1946–2013) was a trailblazer in modern medicine best known for her breakthrough research in the 1970s on opiate receptors in the brain. Her subsequent findings revealed how endorphins and other naturally occurring peptides trigger neurological responses and even play a role in disease prevention. As she explained to television journalist Bill Moyers for the 1993 documentary *Healing and the Mind*, "your mind is in every cell of your body. We know that because so many cells of the body contain these molecules that we've been mapping."

Pert was born Candace Dorinda Beebe in New York City in 1946. Her father, Robert Beebe, was from a long line of New Englanders and worked as a commercial artist. His marriage to Pert's mother Mildred Rosenberg, whose parents were Lithuanian Jewish immigrants, caused a stir in both families and for this reason Pert's parents eschewed imposition of any religious affiliation on their three daughters.

Overcame Aversion to Lab-Animal Deaths

Growing up on Long Island, Pert and her two sisters were encouraged to pursue academic excellence, but her own college path stalled when she married in 1966, two years after graduating from Douglas MacArthur High School in Levittown, New York. She moved to the Philadelphia area when her husband began graduate school at Bryn Mawr College and she eventually began taking courses in biology

at the private college. As she recounted in her 1997 book *Molecules of Emotion: The Science Behind Mind-Body Medicine,* she was only able to pass her science requisites with the help of a rigorous Bryn Mawr instructor, Miss Oppenheimer, who cajoled Pert into tamping down her aversion to euthanizing and dissecting laboratory animals.

Pert went on to earn her Ph.D. in pharmacology in 1974 from the elite Johns Hopkins University in Maryland, a school she had chosen only because of its proximity to her husband's job at the Edgewood Arsenal of the U.S. Army Chemical Corps, which conducted sometimes-lurid psychopharmaceutical experiments on volunteer subjects. At Johns Hopkins she worked under pioneering neuropharmacologist Dr. Solomon H. Snyder, mentor to a long line of future scientists like Pert who made significant breakthroughs in neuroscience and pharmacology.

In the early 1970s, with increasing rates of illegal opiate abuse in the United States and the West, Pert was interested in why morphine and similar drugs derived from the opium plant were so demonstrably addictive. Snyder's lab was actively engaged in several areas of research around this, and Snyder signed off on one experiment Pert devised that used slice of rat brains and a radioactive agent to track chemical reactions in the tissue. At the time, scientists theorized that there were so-called "receptor" sites in brain tissue. In layperson's terms this idea of receptors was explained through the analogy of a lock and a key—that inside the brain was a receptor that was like a keyhole, and its activation response was triggered only when one specific key was inserted. In this case the key was morphine and other opiates, and Pert wanted to search for the receptor site.

Pert's initial research was also linked to the mystery behind the so-called "runner's high" which came during strenuous exercise, similar to the state of bliss she had

Archives du 7eme Art/Photos 12/Alamy

experienced after childbirth. The receptor onto which morphine and other opiates locked was also, Pert and other neuroscience researchers theorized, the place where the body produced the chemical that gave the same rush as an opiate.

Hailed for Breakthrough

Pert was 26 years old and working over a weekend in 1972 when she made the initial discovery, which she shared with other members of her team and Snyder, their supervisor. The first successful experiment had been done with some radioactive naloxone, an opioid antagonist she obtained with the help of her husband, she later revealed. Pert did receive credit as an author of the paper "Opiate Receptor: Demonstration in Nervous Tissue" that caused a sensation when it was published in the journal *Science* in March of 1973. A year later, Pert earned her Ph.D. and began a 13-year career at the National Institutes of Health (NIH) in Bethesda, Maryland.

Pert's discovery of the opiate-receptor site led to major advances in neuroscience over the next decade and she was widely credited as among the first wave of researchers who identified the chemical reactions tied to mood regulation, substance addiction, and even eating disorders. She explained this part of her career in a well-received 1993 Public Broadcasting Service (PBS) television documentary series hosted by Moyers, an esteemed journalist and author.

Her breakthrough at Johns Hopkins, she recalled, "led to the discovery that the brain makes its own morphine, and that emotional states are created by the release of the chemicals called endorphins, which is shorthand for 'endogenous morphines,'" she said in *Healing and the Mind,* which was also the title of a book by Moyers. "In the beginning, like many other neuroscientists, I was secretly interested in consciousness, and thought that by studying the brain I would learn about the mind and consciousness," she reflected.

Pert gained some notoriety in the late 1970s when she carried out a public media battle with Snyder, her former mentor, when he was one of the 1978 honorees for that year's Albert Lasker Award for Medical Research, a prestigious prize widely considered a precursor to the Nobel Prize. Snyder thanked her in his speech, and others noted that the standard practice of honoring the mentor, not the doctoral student who made the discovery, was commonplace in science and academia, which operated under a fairly inflexible set of protocols. On the other hand, Pert also received an outpouring of support from women scientists who had felt similarly slighted at times in their career.

Entered HIV/AIDS Field

In 1982 Pert was named director of the Brain Chemistry Section at the National Institutes for Mental Health. It was here that she and her colleagues made important breakthroughs in chains of peptides, the molecules that triggered reactions in the brain's most primitive, reactive part. Her work also expanded into immunology with the emergence of the acquired immune deficiency (AIDS) crisis that decade. AIDS was finally traced to an identifiable human immunodeficiency virus (HIV), and Pert and others looked into how certain peptides triggered AIDS in an HIV-positive person. She left her NIH job to devote her energies to researching the possibilities of threonine, an amino acid that showed some early promise in preventing wasting and dementia in AIDS patients. She and her second husband, immunologist Dr. Michael Ruff, founded a company to research and bring new drugs to the market through traditional U.S. Food and Drug Administration (FDA) clinical trials. At a time when mortality rates from AIDS were spiking, some patient-activists formed private clubs to acquire her company's drug, Peptide T, and another product that was not yet approved by the U.S. Food and Drug Administration. The 2013 feature film *Dallas Buyers Club* recounted the story of one AIDS sufferer and activist whose life was lengthened by Peptide T.

Pert's second husband was a specialist in a field of immunology called macrophages. Though Peptide T had not succeeded as an FDA-approved drug, the deeper connection between the brain and the body's response to outside triggers continued to fascinate her. "Why do I never get a cold on a ski trip? Because I love to ski and it makes me happy and excited," she explained to *Psychology Today* writer Jill Neimark. "The peptide norepinephrine is the chemical that stimulates excitement, and the cold virus uses the same receptors."

Pert's involvement in the 1993 PBS series had markedly increased her visibility outside the professional scientific community. She became more involved in researching so-called "alternative" medical practices such as chiropractic, acupuncture, and meditation. Her first book for a general readership, *Molecules of Emotion,* appeared in 1997 and drew upon some of the 200-plus scientific studies she had conducted over her years at the NIH and at Georgetown University Medical School, where she became professor in the department of biophysics and physiology in 1996. "There is more science to support complementary medicine than people realise," she told Eileen Fursland in the London *Guardian* in 1998, and added, "there is less science behind conventional medical practices than people realise."

Argued Against Cartesian Framework

In *Molecules of Emotion* Pert explained why there was such a dramatic divide between the two camps—regular F.D.A. approved remedies, for example, on one side, and "the mystical realm, where scientists have been officially forbidden to tread ever since the 17th century," she wrote. "It was then that René Descartes, the philosopher and founding father of modern medicine, was forced to make a turf deal with the Pope in order to get the human bodies he needed for dissection" of human corpses, a practice that had strong cultural taboos in European culture. "Descartes agreed he wouldn't have anything to do with the soul, the mind, or the emotions—those aspects of human experience under the virtually exclusive jurisdiction of the church at the time—if he could claim the physical realm as his own." Pert continued on, asserting the arrangement "set the tone and direction for Western science ... dividing human experience into two distinct and separate spheres that could never overlap, creating the unbalanced situation that is mainstream science as we know it today."

Pert and Ruff were partners in a second pharmaceutical company they established to find solutions to inflammation, a new frontier of health science believed to be key to the prevention and treatment of chronic diseases. Her second book, *Everything You Need to Know to Feel Go(o)d,* was published in 2006. In a tragic twist, Pert was felled by cardiac arrest at the surprisingly young age of 67 at her home in Potomac, Maryland, on September 12, 2013. Tributes around the world hailed her 40-year career as a pioneering researcher on neuroscience, and longtime fans remembered her well-received interview on Moyers' PBS series. "Clearly there's another form of energy that we have not yet understood," she discussed with Moyers in *Healing and the Mind.* "For example, there's a form of energy that appears to leave the body when the body dies. If we call that another energy that just hasn't been discovered yet, it sounds much less frightening to me than 'spirit.'"

Books

Pert, Candace B., *Molecules of Emotion: The Science Behind Mind-Body Medicine,* Simon & Schuster, 1997, 2010.

Periodicals

Globe & Mail (Toronto), April 23, 1993.
Guardian (London, England), March 17, 1998.
New York Times March 11, 1973; September 20, 2013.
Psychology Today, November-December 1997.
Sunday Times (London, England), October 16, 1977. □

Fritz Pollard

The African-American football player, coach, and entrepreneur Frederick Douglass "Fritz" Pollard (1894–1986) was the first black coach in the National Football League (NFL), and one of just a few African-American players active in the early days of professional football.

Although he achieved major accomplishments on the field and as a coach and was long active in promoting the interests of other black players, Pollard has lacked recognition as an African-American pioneer of the game. Partly his reputation has been obscured due to the fact that pro football in the 1920s, when he began his pro career, was in its infancy; few official records were kept of games and the league extended only to a group of Midwestern cities and was sparsely publicized nationally. Yet abundant testimony from the time has confirmed Pollard's talents as a player, and his role in resisting the de facto segregation enforced by the NFL in the 1930s and 1940s was significant. Pollard had a long life that contained several impressive careers after he left the game of football.

Aimed Toward Ivy League

Frederick Douglass Pollard, named for the 19th-century anti-slavery activist, was born in the northside Chicago neighborhood of Rogers Park on January 27, 1894, shortly after the area was annexed to the city of Chicago. His father, John, was a barber, his mother, Catherine, a seamstress, and his ancestors on his father's side were descended from slaves who had been freed during the Revolutionary War. Fritz was a neighborhood nickname that remained with him for his entire life. The seventh of eight children, Pollard attended Lane Technical High School, whose student body was almost exclusively white. In Pollard's middle class family, expectations ran high; his older brother Leslie attended Dartmouth College, and he began to look toward Ivy League schools himself.

He had an impressive high school athletic record as a credential: at Lane he played football and baseball and ran track, making all-county teams in all three sports and winning a state championship in the 440-yard dash in 1912. He hoped to attend Brown University in Providence, Rhode Island, in 1913 but had trouble with a foreign language requirement, eventually meeting it by attending classes at Springfield High School in Massachusetts. During this period, various schools including Brown, Dartmouth, Harvard, and Bates, enrolled him as a special student so that they could temporarily take advantage of his football skills, but he enrolled at Brown in the fall of 1915.

Pollard, a halfback, at first experienced hostility from his teammates but won them over with impressive performances on the field. Weighing just 148 pounds, he made up for his small size with (as the *New York Times* put it in an account quoted on Brown University's website), "the resiliency of a rubber ball," and was nicknamed The Human Torpedo. Pollard became the first African American to appear in the

AP Images/Anonymous

Rose Bowl on January 1, 1916, and that year he was also the first to make the All-American first team backfield. In the 1930s, famed sportswriter Grantland Rice named Pollard to his Dream Team of all-time college greats.

Set World Record

Pollard also set a world hurdles record as a member of Brown's track team and qualified for the 1916 U.S. Olympic team. All this activity apparently caused Pollard to neglect his studies, however, and he droppped out of Brown after being ruled academically ineligible for the football team. He bounced around for several years, serving as a trainer at an Army YMCA unit in Maryland and then, in 1918, he became head football coach at historically black Lincoln University in Pennsylvania. The following year he joined the Akron Indians professional football squad. In 1920 that team, renamed the Pros, joined the new American Professional Football Association (AFPA), which in 1922 was renamed the National Football League.

From the beginning he faced racial harassment. "There were a lot of Southerners in the league then, and besides that, a lot of the players were just bullies," he told Al Harvin of *The New York Times.* "They would say, 'We're going to get you on the playing field nigger and kill you.' I would say, 'If you can catch me.' They didn't, and after a while they stopped trying to scare me." Pollard had to shield himself with his arms against late hits, and he was

often unable to stay with his teammates in hotels. He even had to dress for games in an Akron cigar store instead of in the team locker room. His teammates began to defend him, though, as he led Akron to an undefeated record in the first 19 games he played with them, and to the first AFPA championship in 1920, the season capped by a thrilling game against a Canton, Ohio, squad led by Native American football star Jim Thorpe.

The role of coach was not fully defined during the early days of pro football, and it is difficult to specify exactly when Pollard became a head coach. In his first days at Akron he offered to show other Akron players some of the plays he had learned at Brown; they resisted, but he was backed by team owner Frank Neid. There and in other cities Pollard was in effect the coach but worked with a white co-coach who was kept on to avoid offending white fans. In 1923 he became head coach for the Hammond (Indiana) Pros franchise; at that point he was clearly the NFL's first black head coach.

He also played occasionally for Hammond, becoming the league's first black quarterback as well. He remained as coach at Hammond for several years, sometimes returning to the playing field for the Providence (Rhode Island) Steam Roller squad and for the Gilberton Cadamounts in the rival Pennsylvania Coal League. In 1926 he retired as a player, miraculously without ever having been seriously injured in an era when he was routinely subjected to physical abuse and when safety equipment was primitive. He remained active in football, forming and coaching an all-black Chicago Black Hawks team that played exhibition games against white squads as far away as the West Coast. In 1935 he organized the New York Brown Bombers and actively promoted team players to NFL owners, who responded with an informal ban on black players that lasted until the late 1940s.

Founded Investment Firm

Even before retiring as a player, Pollard had begun to expand his activities. In 1922 he founded F.D. Pollard and Co., perhaps the first black-owned investment firm; it lasted until the depths of the Great Depression before going bankrupt. Pollard established a tabloid newspaper, the *New York Independent News,* in 1935. Beginning with a stint as casting agent for the 1933 film *The Emperor Jones,* he was active in the entertainment industry, again making energetic efforts to promote African Americans in the field. He made short video-like films calls Soundies that featured black musicians, and in 1956 he produced a film of his own, *Rockin' the Blues,* which contained a treasure trove of 1950s rhythm-and-blues performances. For some years he was active as a booking agent for both clubs and broadcast media.

Pollard married Ada Laing in Providence in 1914. The marriage was not happy, and they separated in the early 1920s and were later divorced. But it produced four children; one son, Fritz Jr., won a bronze medal in track at the 1936 Olympics in Berlin, Germany, and became a football All-American at the University of North Dakota two years later. Pollard married Mary Ella Austin in 1947. In later years he worked as a tax consultant, retiring in 1975. He lived in the New York City suburb of New Rochelle for some time.

When African-American players and coaches finally began to enter the game of football, Pollard was dismayed to find that his pioneering role had often been forgotten. He had been inducted into the College Football Hall of Fame in 1954, becoming the first African American so honored, and he was honored with induction into the Rhode Island Heritage Hall of Fame (1967), the Brown Athletic Hall of Fame (1971), and the National Black Hall of Fame (1973). But induction into the Pro Football Hall of Fame eluded him during his lifetime. Pollard died on May 11, 1986, in Silver Spring, Maryland, and was buried in nearby Brentwood. He was finally inducted into the Pro Football Hall of Fame in 2005.

Books

Carroll, John M., *Fritz Pollard: Pioneer in Racial Achievement,* Illinois, 1999.
Contemporary Black Biography, vol. 53, Gale, 2006.

Periodicals

Jet, August 22, 2005.
New York Times, May 24, 1970; February 7, 1978; May 31, 1986; June 22, 1986.
USA Today, February 7, 2005.

Online

"Fritz Pollard," Brown University Library, http://www.library.brown.edu/cds/pollard/aboutpollard.html (December 1, 2014).
"Fritz Pollard," Pro Football Hall of Fame, http://www.profoot ballhof.com/hof/member.aspx?player_id=242 (December 1, 2014).
"Fritz Pollard and Early African American Professional Football Players," Brown University, http://www.brown.edu/Administration/News_Bureau/2003-04/03-078f.html (December 1, 2014).□

Francis Ponge

The French poet Francis Ponge (1899–1988) was among the most distinctive and original French writers of the middle 20th century.

Ponge's work is difficult to classify. He came of age artistically in the era of Surrealism, and he shared some goals with the Surrealist movement, including the aim of revolutionary change in the nature of artistic consciousness. But his poetry might be called hyperrealistic rather than surrealistic. Written mostly in prose rather than verse, it examined ordinary objects from a variety of perspectives, often seeming to give those objects a consciousness of their own or to link it to that of the reader. His style was sometimes dubbed a poetry of things, for it was generally about inanimate objects rather than human experiences or nature. Ponge's work had an intellectual, ingenious quality, but it abounded with humor, and Ponge himself believed it could be appreciated by ordinary readers.

AFP/Getty Images

Attended Law School in Paris

Francis Jean Gaston Alfred Ponge was born in Montpellier, France, on March 27, 1899, into a Protestant family. His father, Armand Ponge, was a bank director. Ponge was sent to Paris to top schools: the Sorbonne University and the Ecole de Droit law school. After several years of studying law, however, he found himself drawn more strongly to literature. He got a job with a publisher, Hachette, and began writing poetry. Working as a publisher's clerk and seeing that members of the company's workforce were poorly treated, Ponge became a member of France's Socialist Party. For the rest of his life he had a strong sympathy with leftist causes, although his poems had virtually no political content. Ponge served in the French military in 1918 and 1919.

In the 1920s Ponge worked for the publisher Gallimard as a production manager. Gallimard issued a literary magazine called the *Nouvelle Revue Français,* and some of Ponge's poems were published there; its editor, Jean Paulhan, became Ponge's friend and mentor. Gallimard would later issue most of his roughly 100 poems in book form. Ponge's first collection of poetry, *Douze petits érits* (12 Small Writings), was issued by Gallimard in 1926.

It would be 18 years before Ponge published another book. He wrote slowly, and he changed jobs several times; for six years in the 1930s he worked as a secretary for the publisher Hachette, and he was also employed as an insurance salesman in Paris in the late 1930s. Ponge seems to have flirted with the Surrealist movement in French poetry, signing the *Second Surrealist Manifesto* penned by writer André Breton in 1930, but the concrete nature of his writing was diametrically opposite to the distortions of reality practiced by the Surrealists, and to their attempt to draw on the subconscious through what they called automatic writing. In 1938 Ponge was drafted once again into the French military.

Served in French Resistance

The capitulation of the French to Nazi forces left Ponge free to work—and to serve in the French Resistance against Nazi rule. He did not participate in military actions but edited an underground publication, *Progress de Lyon.* In 1944 he moved to a post as literary editor of a Communist Party weekly called *L'Action.* There he became acquainted with and published the works of some of the writers who became leading figures in the postwar French intellectual scene: Jean-Paul Sartre, Paul Eluard, and Raymond Queneau, among others. Ponge parted ways with Communism in 1947.

Although he was well acquainted with some of the 20th century's most famous writers and lived through both world wars, none of these acquaintances and events seem to have made much of an impact on his own writing. The style of Ponge's poetry changed remarkably little over his 45-year career as a writer. Although he occasionally wrote verse poems, most of it was in prose, following a tradition that extended back to the early modernists Charles Baudelaire, Arthur Rimbaud, and Stéphane Mallarmé. Each poem was fairly long, and mostly they took ordinary objects for their topics: a pebble, a glass of water, a bar of soap.

One of Ponge's most famous books, *Le Parti pris des choses,* appeared in 1942 in the midst of World War II; it was translated into English as *The Voice of Things* and later issued in a revised and expanded edition in 1949, containing a new section called *Proêmes.* The term simultaneously suggested prose poetry and a term used in classical rhetoric, and the use of wordplay was typical of Ponge's style. In one of the proêemes, Ponge suggested that everyone be given the chance to create their own systems of rhetoric.

Another well-known book by Ponge, *Le Savon* (Soap), appeared in 1967 and was translated into English in 1969. The volume is unique yet typical of Ponge's method of exploring the inner essence of everyday objects. Each individual section in the book is written from the perspective of a bar of soap: one poem describes the soap in the act of being used for washing ("le savon écume, jubile," the soap foams, becomes jubilant), another evokes its resting, dried-out state. Unlike much other poetry of the 20th century, the meaning of the poetry is readily accessible to general readers, yet Ponge also is constantly reminding the reader that he is playing a kind of linguistic game.

Wrote Long Prose Poem About Orange

"L'Orange," from *Le parti pres des choses,* is typical of Ponge's poetry, although each of his poems develops according to its own logic. "Just as in a sponge, there is in the orange a yearning to recover its content after having been subjected to the ordeal of squeezing. But whereas the sponge always succeeds, the orange never does, for its cells have burst, its tissues have been torn," Ponge wrote, later asking, "Must we choose between these two ways of not tolerating oppression?" Ponge goes on to describe the juice of the orange, its rind, and finally its seeds, "in short, tiny, but with certainty, the fruit's reason for being."

In the late 1940s Ponge took an extended trip to Algeria, then a French colony. He wrote very little poetry but kept a diary with the English title *My Creative Method,* which is as idiosyncratic and original as the rest of his work. It was published in 1961. In the 1950s and early 1960s, Ponge made a living as a professor at the Alliance Française in Paris. Beginning in 1965, Ponge spent considerable time in the United States, teaching and lecturing at various universities. He was a visiting professor at Barnard College and Columbia University in the 1966–1967 academic year, and continued to lecture in France after that. During this period, his poetry often appeared in English translation; *Two Prose Poems* appeared in 1968 and *Rain: A Prose Poem* the following year. An American anthology of his work, *Things: Selected Writings of Francis Ponge,* was published in 1976 by White Pine Press.

Always an eccentric figure, Ponge became increasingly reclusive in later life and spent most of his time at his country house, called Mas des Vergers in the French Maritime Alps near Nice. He suffered from a variety of illnesses that have been described as psychosomatic in nature. He continued to write, however, and at his death he left a substantially complete and entirely characteristic prose poem called *La Table* (The Table). It ends: "O Table, ma console et ma consolatrice, table qui me console, ou je me consolide" (O Table, my console and my consoler, table that consoles me, where I consolidate myself).

Ponge married Odette Chabanel in 1931, and the couple had one child, Armande. Ponge was awarded several major prizes, including the International Poetry Prize (1959), the Grand Prize for Poetry from the French Academy (1972), and the French National Poetry Prize (1981), and he was made officer and commander in the French Legion of Honor. Ponge died in Le Bar-sur-Loup, France, on August 6, 1988.

Books

Greene, Robert W., *Six French Poets of Our Time: A Critical and Historical Study,* Princeton, 1979.

Reference Guide to World Literature, St. James, 1995.

Sorrell, Martin, *Ponge,* Twayne, 1981.

Periodicals

New York Times, August 9, 1988.

Times (London, England), August 11, 1988.

Online

Contemporary Authors Online, Gale, 2007. From *Literature Resource Center.*

"Francis Ponge," *Green Integer,* http://www.greeninteger.com/pipbios_detail.cfm?PIPAuthorID=143 (December 2, 2014).

"Francis Ponge," *Poetry Foundation,* http://www.poetryfoundation.org/bio/francis-ponge (December 2, 2014). □

Nadezhda Popova

During World War II, Russian aviator Nadezhda Popova (1921–2013) flew 852 successful sorties as a member of the all-female 588th Night Bomber Regiment. Dubbed "Night Witches" by the Germans, the women engaged in nightly harassment bombing of German military encampments.

RIA Novosti/Alamy

P opova was born December 17, 1921, in Shabanovka, Ukraine. During her childhood, Popova was thunderstruck one day when a pilot landed a plane in her village. She touched the wings of the plane and the pilot's leather jacket to make sure he was real. From that moment on, she was determined to reach the skies. At 15, she joined a flying club. At 16, she made her first solo flight, and in 1938 attended a school for parachute jumpers. After graduating from aviation school in Kherson, Ukraine, Popova became a flight instructor.

Joined Night Bomber Regiment

Popova's life took a radical shift after Hitler's armies attacked the Soviet Union in June of 1941 in one of the largest invasions in the history of warfare. Popova's 20-year-old brother, Leonid, died in action, and her anger only intensified as German troops swarmed her homeland. She watched as German planes flew overhead and saw the pilots follow the roads, shooting at women and children fleeing their homes.

Popova volunteered to join the Russian military, but was turned away like thousands of other women. However, as the German attack continued to devastate the Red Army, Russian dictator Joseph Stalin had to change the policy. Russian aviator Marina Raskova appealed to the Kremlin, asking that women be allowed to join the fight. She had already broken barriers as a teacher at the Zhukovsky Air Force Engineering Academy. Raskova received permission to form three all-female bomber regiments with the stipulation that the women fly only light bombers.

Popova, just 19, quickly joined and was placed with the 588th Night Bomber Regiment. Unlike Russian men, who were conscripted into service, the women were volunteers. The female pilots tended to be in their late teens and early twenties. The women of the 588th Night Bomber Regiment flew the Polikarpov Po-2, a primitive, plywood-framed fabric-wrapped biplane. The women engaged in nightly harassment bombing of German military encampments. They could not fly during the day because the slow-moving planes would have been easy targets. Over the course of the war, the regiment flew 24,000 night sorties, mainly bombing German forward positions, rear bases, and supply depots. Raskova was killed in action early on, and Popova rose to the position of deputy commander.

Nicknamed *Night Witches*

The women of the 588th carried out nearly the same mission every night. Flying in groups of three, they took their planes into enemy territory, cruising at low altitudes. Once over their destination, two pilots would dive full-throttle through enemy searchlights, acting as decoys. Once they had attracted attention, they would separate and go in opposite directions, swerving through anti-aircraft fire as the third pilot cut her engine and swooped into the darkness, dropping her payload of bombs. The pilots took turns until all of the bombs had been dropped. The planes were fitted with bomb racks that allowed them to carry a load of up to 800 pounds, typically with one bomb under each wing. The Germans called the female flyers the Nachthexen, or Night Witches, because the only thing they heard before the attack was the swishing glide of the silent, engine-cut planes, accompanied by a peculiar whistle caused by the wind rustling through the bracing wires on the wings. The Germans thought the sound resembled a witch's broom.

The night flights wore heavily on the Germans, keeping soldiers from getting any rest. It was rumored that if any German pilot or gunner downed a Night Witch, he would receive the Iron Cross. The missions of the 588th were fraught with danger. The Po-2 had no radio, no guns, no armor, and no parachute, because the military wanted a maximum payload of bombs and adding any extra night-flying equipment would exceed the plane's weight allowance. As such, there was always the danger of getting lost or failing to locate the airfield after completing a mission. In an interview with Albert Axell, author of *Russia's Heroes*, Popova complained about "those helpless moonless nights.... We had no special equipment for night flying and so we dreaded clouded nights or terribly bad weather. And almost every time we flew we had to sail through a wall of enemy fire while the Germans tried to blind us with their searchlights." In addition, because the plane was constructed of fabric, it burned quickly if struck by tracer bullets.

Another drawback included the open cockpit. To combat the elements, the women wore fur-lined helmets, boots and gloves, but when the temperatures fell below zero, their fingers and legs ached with the cold. At times, the bombs failed to deploy because they got stuck under the ice-covered wings and the pilots had to free them with their bare hands. Just like their male counterparts, the female pilots were allotted a small glass of vodka before each mission.

Despite the plane's shortcomings, the Po-2 proved effective for night bombing missions. The plane was highly dexterous and did not require an airfield for landing, thus adding versatility to locations where the plane could be deployed. The Po-2 could land on a village street or at the edge of a forest. In addition, the aircraft could fly at low altitudes and was so flimsy it passed through radar undetected. It was also highly maneuverable, allowing the women to skirt through anti-aircraft fire.

The German Messerschmitts were much faster, but this proved to be a disadvantage. Though the Messerschmitts were superior fighter planes, they had trouble shooting down the Po-2s because their light construction allowed them to stay aloft at a very slow flying speed. The heavier Messerschmitts required more lift and thus had to fly at faster speeds to stay in the air. The Messerschmitts were flying so fast in comparison to the Po-2s that by the time the German pilots locked in their aim on the lumbering aircraft, they were only seconds away from flying right past the craft they wanted to shoot down.

That is not to say that the Po-2 pilots did not face the danger of being shot down. As lead pilot in a mission over Taman on the Black Sea, Popova found herself pursued by Messerschmitts. She watched as the enemy planes downed her fellow fighters. The regiment lost 37 pilots that night. Popova herself, was shot down several times but managed to survive. She often said that she feared being taken prisoner more than she feared dying in action. One downing had an especially long-lasting impact. After being shot down one night in July 1942, Popova was headed back to base when she found herself caught in a swell of Russian soldiers and retreating civilians. She befriended a wounded pilot named Semyon Kharlamov, who was attempting to calm the crowd by reading aloud from Soviet author Mikhail Sholokhov's *And Quiet Flows the Don*. They had a long conversation that night and Popova recited some poetry to Kharlamov. They found each other after the war and married.

Typically, the Night Witches flew eight or so missions a night, but at times had to step up their game. During the Battle for the Caucasus in December 1944, the Night Witches were asked to fly as many sorties as possible one night. The women took off from an airstrip located four miles from the front line, dropped their bombs and returned to base. The female ground mechanics then refueled the planes and attached more bombs, getting the women back in the air as quickly as possible. The turnaround time was about five to seven minutes. They flew all night in this manner, and by the time the mission had ended, Popova had flown 18 sorties. She also found 42 bullet holes in her plane. In all, the regiment flew some 300 sorties that night.

Tapped for Special Missions

Because of her talent and skill, Popova was tapped for special missions. In the fall of 1942, she was asked to bomb a German crossing on the Terek River near Mozdok. The Germans guarded the crossing with anti-aircraft guns and searchlights. To get to the pass, Popova had to fly over cloud-covered mountains. When she and her navigator got near the area, they found visibility at zero. Popova had to fly through the clouds to try and locate a thin opening that would allow them to see. They finally succeeded in bombing the crossing as shots rang out.

In 1943, Popova was sent to deliver food, water, medicine, and ammunition to Russian troops trapped at the Soviet outpost at Malaya Zemlya. The Germans occupied nearby positions, meaning she had to hit her target within a dozen meters to avoid dropping the supply-filled canisters into enemy hands. She returned with a bullet-riddled wing but delivered the supplies accurately.

Another time, during the second year of the war, Popova was asked to find the front line of the invading Germans by flying over the area. The Russians knew the Germans were somewhere near the Azov Sea, near Rostov-on-the-Don. In order to see what kinds of units the enemy had stationed there, Popova had to fly at extremely low altitudes of 320 to 650 feet off the ground, making the mission extremely dangerous. She was completely on edge when she felt something hit one of the struts on her plane. It turned out to be a duck and not enemy fire. Flying with a map on her lap, Popova noted the positions of the enemy troops, tanks and artillery and escaped under a hail of machine-gun fire.

Three hours after landing, she was asked to deliver a message to a Russian commanding officer. The Russians lacked good communications, so messages to troop leaders had to be hand-delivered. Popova delivered the message, but was followed by two Messerschmitts on her way back to base. They hit her wing with bullets, but luckily she was almost back to base. She told Axell: "I flew straight back to my airstrip and, landing at the end of it, jumped from the plane before it came to a halt, meanwhile watching the flames envelop the fuselage. I ran as far from the plane as possible to avoid the blast. Meanwhile my plane continued moving slowly and the Messerschmitts, still following me, kept on shooting...completely destroying my little Po-2 plane. But I wasn't in it."

Earned Multiple Decorations

Over the course of the war, the female pilots and navigators of the 586th, 587th, and 588th regiments proved crucial in several key battles, such as in the Caucasus, Stalingrad, and Kursk. Their work in these areas helped turn the tide against the German invaders. Popova ended up flying missions over Berlin in the final days of the war as Russia beat back the German military and eventually overtook Berlin, raising the Soviet flag over the Reichstag, the German government building, in May of 1945.

After the war, Popova was reunited with Kharlamov and the two pilots married. They had one son, Aleksandr, who became a general in the Belarussian Air Force. They settled in Moscow, where Popova worked as a flying instructor. Kharlamov died in 1990. Popova and Kharlamov each received several honors for their war service. Popova earned designation as a Hero of the Soviet Union, the highest distinction awarded by the Soviet government. The honor came with a Gold Star Medal, given for heroic feats in service to her country. Kharlamov received the same award. Popova also received the Order of Lenin and Order of the Red Star (three times).

For the most part, Popova was pragmatic in recalling her wartime experience. "We bombed, we killed; it was all a part of war," she once told the Russian news service RIA Novosti, as reported by the *New York Times.* "We had an enemy in front of us, and we had to prove that we were stronger and more prepared." Popova died July 8, 2013, in Moscow. She was 91.

Books

Axell, Albert, *Russia's Heroes,* Carroll & Graf Publishers, Inc., 2001.

Periodicals

Daily Telegraph (London, England), July 11, 2013.
Economist, July 20, 2013.
New York Times, July 15, 2013.
Russian Life, September/October 2013.□

Miuccia Prada

Though Italian business executive and fashion designer Miuccia Prada (born 1950), took over her family company reluctantly in the late 1970s, she built the luxury firm of Prada into a fashion empire. She expanded the Prada firm's offerings into fashion, new labels (Miu Miu), new lines, and new markets worldwide, all while defining a certain look that brought together the past and the present in beautiful harmony.

Born May 10, 1950, in Milan, Italy, Miuccia Bianchi Prada was the daughter of Luigi Bianchi and Luisia Prada. Her father was a businessman who ran a mower manufacturing business. Her mother was the daughter of Mario Prada, the co-founder of Fratelli Prada. Established in 1913 by Mario Prada and his brother, Fratelli Prada designed, made, and sold luxury goods such as luggage, handbags, silver, and crystal for the elite of Italy and other wealthy clients throughout the world. Fratelli Prada had a well-appointed boutique in Milan at the

Stefania D'Alessandro/WireImage/Getty Images

Galleria Vittorio Emmaneule. Though the company competed with such French luxury good firms as Louis Vuitton, the Prada firm was fading as World War II reached its end in the mid-1940s.

Raised Around Family Business

When Prada, the second of three children, was born, her family was quite well-to-do, despite the struggles of the Prada company. Her grandfather continued to run his business until his death in the late 1950s, but did not allow any female members of his family to work at Prada during his lifetime. After his death, Luisia Prada was the only family member interested in taking over. After she took charge in 1958, the firm found new life under her leadership. She would remain in charge of the Prada firm for two decades.

In the meantime, Prada and her siblings were raised around the Prada firm, and became well-educated. Always passionate about fashion and self-expression through what she wore, Prada had a fashion forward sense. She told Sara Gay Forden of *Footwear News,* "When I was younger, I was always the first one to wear the miniskirt and then the long dresses. I began to realize that whatever I was wearing, others would start wearing after two or three years."

Prada also had other interests. She attended the University of Milan, where she earned a degree in political science in 1973. During the mid-1970s, she was an active member of the Italian Communist party, and enthusiastically participated in political demonstrations. Prada also was fascinated by the art of mime, spending five years on the art. She studied the craft with the Teatro Piccolo in Milan, and later joined a mime troupe there. Prada had aspirations to become an actress as well.

Took Over Prada

As a young adult, Prada's only exposure to the family business was a stint managing the Prada store in Milan beginning in 1970. This retail outlet specialized in luggage and handbag sales. When Luisa Bianchi retired in 1978, she asked Prada to take over the company despite her lack of experience. Prada took on the challenge.

By the early 1980s, Prada moved into designing items for her firm. She soon had her first hit item, a small handbag made out of a black nylon similar to that used to make military tents or parachutes. She added a shiny gold strap, and charged $450 for the bag. Considered the cutting edge of fashion, this bag brought new customers to Prada, and the attention of another bag maker, Patrizio Bertelli. His Florence-based company produced leather goods, and Prada had some of her company's bags made at his factory. Prada soon became personally as well as professionally involved with Bertelli. The couple married in 1987, and later had two sons.

Even before their marriage, however, Bertelli assisted Prada as she modernized the line of products produced by the Prada firm. Prada told Tina Gaudoin of the London *Times,* "I did everything I could not to be in fashion. I just wanted to make handbags and then Patrizio (Bertelli, her husband) said, 'You have to do fashion.'" In addition to identifying the Prada company name with exclusivity, the Prada store in Milan started only selling Prada products. The first clothing line designed by Prada were influenced by her interest in the concept of bohemian, but bad school girls. As she developed her own style, Prada was praised for designing timeless, quality pieces often using unexpected materials and influenced by various eras.

Added New Lines to Company

In the 1980s, Prada added new items to the Prada line. In addition to adding footwear in 1985, Prada designed her first ready-to-wear line for her company in 1989. The line was inspired by classic pieces produced in previous years and archived by the Prada family and firm. In this period, Prada was also making strides as a designer, making beautifully thought out, well-crafted items that reflected the past but were forward thinking and looking. This duality often resulted in very wearable, feminine yet flexible items, a trend that continued for the next few decades under her mindful leadership.

Prada also saw a duality in her company's customer base. Amidst the continued growth of her firm and prestige of her label, Prada was quite aware of what attracted people to it. She explained to Carl Swanson of *New York,* "You have some customers who are customers because they understand when you do something clever. For others, the brand is just a brand. It's just the name—who cares what you do. The two exist together."

In 1992, Prada launched a new label through her company, Miu Miu, taken from Prada's own nickname. This line was lower in price than items produced under the Prada company label, but was targeted at a younger, more hip shopper with a funkier, sometimes more whimsical look. Within a few years, Prada opened up Miu Miu stores in cites in the United States and Europe. The success of Miu Miu throughout the 1990s helped the Prada firm's overall growth during the decade.

Prada also expanded the firm's retail presence under her leadership in the mid-1990s. There were 47 Prada stores globally by 1995. She had opened her first store in London in 1994. Also in the mid-1990s, the Prada name was boosted unexpectedly when actress Uma Thurman wore a unique Prada dress to the Academy Awards. In addition, Prada added a men's line to her firm's offerings. Between 1998 and 1999, she added cosmetics, home furnishings, and athletic wear to the Prada line as well. Sales increased, reaching nearly $700 million in 1997.

Took Chances

In late 1990s, Prada continued to grow her company in unexpected, not always profitable ways. She bought a stake in Gucci in 1998, but sold it back to LVMH the following year. In 1999, Prada invested in a number of other fashion design companies, including Helmut Lang, Church, and Jil Sander. Together with LVMH, she bought Fendi in 1999, though she sold the stake to LVMH in 2001. The deals with Helmut Lang and Jil Sander also proved problematic when their namesake designers left their own firms.

By the early 2000s, Prada was poised to take her company public, but had to delay these plans when a global economic recession took hold in 2001. Prada would continue to consider the idea of taking her firm public for at least another decade. She even thought about listing it on the Hong Kong exchange in the early 2010s.

Growth continued in the new century, especially in terms of Prada's retail presence. The Prada firm had expanded to include 150 Prada stores by 2001. One of Prada's important retail projects was a Prada "epicenter" store in the Soho district of New York City. The store cost $40 million to build, and was designed by avant-garde designer Rem Koolhaas. It was a place for Prada to experiment and put her ideas forth to discuss within a flagship retail store. In 2006, for example, she displayed an exhibition of her skirts called "Waist Down" there.

New Focus on Asia, Miu Miu

Also in the early 2000s, Prada focused her firm's growth on China and other countries in Asia. By 2006, Prada had 12 stores in China, with more constructed in subsequent years. By 2010, revenues in China, Hong Kong, and Macau accounted for 30 percent of total company sales, and she opened up a design studio in Hong Kong. Reflecting Prada's commitment to expand in the region, the Prada label had its first runaway show ever in China in January 2011 at Beijing's Central Academy of Fine Arts Museum. As Prada told Amanda Kaiser of *WWD* about the Chinese market, "There are fashionable people here that you wouldn't even find in Paris, New York or London. They have already understood everything that they had to understand.''

Prada also further invested in the expansion of the ever popular Miu Miu line. In addition to better funding one of her favorite company projects, Prada continued to enjoy designing the fun, sophisticated, flirty, quirky clothes. She claimed she had more fun designing for Miu Miu than Prada, in part because of its subversion of classic ideas. Prada also laid plans to develop more stores and label-specific campaigns that focused on the Miu Miu buyer. To further differentiate Miu Miu from the Prada label, she placed Miu Miu fashion shows in different cites than Prada fashion shows beginning in 2006.

During the early 21st century, Prada devoted a significant amount of time to her foundation, Fondazione Prada, established in 2003. The foundation supported the arts and sponsored related events. In 2008, for example, it funded a project in London by Carsten Holler called the Double Club. Prada also opened her own nonprofit exhibition space in Milan.

In 2012, Prada was honored with a Costume Institute exhibition at New York's Metropolitan Museum of Art, which highlighted her own artistic contributions to fashion. Prada, however, saw a separation between art and commerce. She told Amy Larocca of *New York*, ''Art is for expressing ideas and for expressing a vision. My job is to sell. And I like very much my job.''

Expressed Interest in Politics

Though Prada had spent years at the head of her company, Prada still harbored political ambitions. As Prada told the *WWD*'s Kaiser, ''politics have always been a little of my passion. And now I *could* use my work as a tool to do things other than fashion.'' Prada was concerned, however, that her profession and status as a wealthy fashion designer would make her unacceptable to many.

Prada's desire to join Italian politics aside, she found fashion fulfilling in its own way. Though Prada took over her family's company—worth $5 billion by 2014—reluctantly, she always believed in herself about design. She told Samantha Conti of *Los Angeles Magazine*, ''I am very insecure about some things in my life, but I've always been sure about fashion—even in the beginning, when buyers told me they didn't like my designs and that an accessories house had no business designing clothes. For years they said awful things, but the criticism never got to me because I was always sure about what I was doing.'' She added, ''What I really enjoy is designing, and when I look at something I've made and say, 'Oh, my God—this is a really good piece of clothing,' that's what makes me happy.''

Books

Business Leader Profiles for Students, Volume 2, edited by Sheila Dow and Jaime E. Noce, Gale, 2002.

Contemporary Fashion, 2nd ed., edited by Taryn Benbow-Pfalzgraf, St. James Press, 2002.

Kellogg, Ann T., et al., *In an Influential Fashion: An Encyclopedia of Nineteenth- and Twentieth-Century Fashion Designers and Retailers Who Transformed Dress,* Greenwood Press, 2002.

Periodicals

Footwear News, May 29, 1995.
Harper's Bazaar, September 2014.
Los Angeles Magazine, September 1998.
New York, April 24, 2006; May 28, 2012.
WWD, January 25, 2011; January 26, 2011. □

Antonio Prohías

In 1960, Cuban political cartoonist Antonio Prohías (1921–1998) fled his Caribbean homeland after angering Communist leader Fidel Castro with his highly subversive cartoons. Prohías landed in New York and spent the next 26 years in exile, penning *Spy vs. Spy* cartoons for *MAD* magazine. The wordless strip featured two identical spies—one black, one white—locked in a perpetual battle neither side could ever win. The cartoon came to symbolize the absurdity of the Cold War and was one of *MAD*'s most popular regular features.

Antonio Prohías was born January 17, 1921, in Cienfuegos, Cuba. He was raised in Havana by three paternal aunts. Prohías gravitated toward drawing early on. By fourth grade he showed such aptitude that his teacher stepped aside and let the young student offer the art instruction. During class, Prohías drew caricatures and comic heroes, which he promptly sold to classmates during recess. Prohías attended a parochial school where the punishment for disruptive behavior was being sent to the chapel. When the school chapel was being repainted with religious scenes, Prohías started getting into trouble every day so he could go to the chapel and watch and discuss the progress with the artist at work. Prohías's father was a lawyer. He dismissed his son's artistic talents as a waste of time, which forced Prohías to hide his drawings.

Drew Political Cartoons

By age 17, Prohías had dropped out of school. He took a job in a fertilizer plant and used his paychecks to buy art supplies. Briefly, he had studied at Havana's San Alejandro Art School, but he disliked the rigidity of the instruction. Instead, he thought he might strike out on his own and began sketching vignettes. In 1938, Prohías sold his first piece, which appeared in the Cuban newspaper *Alerta*. The exposure helped him land a job as a staff cartoonist at *El Dia*, a new daily paper. Later, he moved to *El Diario de la Marina*. At this time, World War II had erupted, giving Prohías loads of material as fodder for his editorial cartoons. During this era, he also worked for the *Zig-Zag Libre* and *Informacion*.

In 1946, Prohías won the inaugural Juan Gualberto Gómez award. The award was the most prestigious journalism prize offered to cartoonists in Cuba. As the young artist's reputation spread, he fell into great demand.

He joined the editorial staff at *El Mundo* in 1947 and began using his drawing skills to parody political figures and offer satirical commentaries on the state of affairs in the world around him. He was known for his bite and wit, both flippantly displayed in his work. In his spare time, Prohías read psychology and history, which gave him background knowledge to effectively use his cartoons to comment with greater breadth and depth. While he worked primarily at *El Mundo,* Havana's leading daily, he also contributed to other publications. At one point, Prohías worked for five newspapers and magazines simultaneously.

In 1956, Prohías developed his first enduring character, a pointy-nosed charlatan dubbed "El Hombre Siniestro" (the Sinister Man). The callous character appeared regularly in *Bohemia,* a political magazine. The Sinister Man did sadistic things like chop the tales off dogs. In general, he was a happy-go-lucky trickster with an evil current. The Sinister Man was especially fond of swindling people out of their money. In one strip, he sells balloons to little kids, then pops them with a slingshot as the kids walk away. In another strip, he stands between a police officer and a little kid dressed as a cowboy, then switches their guns from their holsters while they are not looking. Prohías even created a companion character—the female "La Mujer Siniestra." Just as with Spy vs. Spy, these cartoons were wordless.

The Sinister Man struck a chord with Cuban citizens and became a beloved figure, despite his nasty streak. Prohías believed that the Sinister Man caught on because at the time, a collective sense of callousness pervaded the atmosphere as the Cuban Revolution dragged on. The reign of Cuban President Fulgencio Batista proved shaky as guerrillas tried to overthrow the government. "There was a feeling of impending doom," Prohías told the *Miami Herald's* Maria C. Garcia. "It was as if everyone was looking forward to something dreadful, all the time. It was morose, eerie."

Endured Character Assassination

As Castro rose to power, Prohías aimed his pen at the Cuban revolutionary leader. In the fall of 1959, Prohías published several anti-Castro/anti-Communist cartoons. After Batista's government fell, Castro was sworn in as prime minister in early 1959. Castro did not identify his regime as a Socialist establishment. Initially, Castro was popular with workers, students and peasants who benefitted from his government's programs. Prohías, however, had concluded Castro was clearly pushing Communist tenets. He had friends who were insiders, who warned him about Castro's dictatorial inclinations. Prohías's subversive cartoons appeared in *El Mundo* and *Bohemia.* One carried the caption, "I see the wolf" and depicted a sheep perched on the Communist hammer and sickle symbol. Another cartoon was titled, "Red Cutlery" and portrayed a skeleton attempting to eat with hammer-and-sickle utensils. The caption read, "Gentlemen, it's very difficult to eat with a hammer and sickle!"

Prohías's cartoons enraged Castro, who accused the cartoonist of being an agent for the U.S. Central Intelligence Agency. Castro agents began following Prohías, spying on him and frisking him on the street. At this time, Castro had legions of loyal followers who found new hope in his promises. At one point, Castro stood in front of a large crowd at the

presidential palace and thrust one of Prohías's cartoons into the air, denouncing him as a counterrevolutionary and scheming traitor. According to the *Spy vs. Spy Omnibus,* Castro got the crowd so worked up people began shouting, "Paredón para Prohías!" (execution for Prohías). After this, hostility toward Prohías escalated. In an interview with *National Public Radio's* Renee Montagne, Prohías' daughter, Marta Pizarro, discussed the difficulties of that time. "It was very dangerous.... He was really, really shunned by his peers. They kept talking that he should be sent to the wall to be shot." Newspapers refused to run his work and Prohías found himself unemployed. To make money, he started painting signs and trucks.

Fled to U.S.

Prohías fled Cuba on May 1, 1960, and arrived in New York with five dollars and little more than the clothes on his back. Once in the United States, Prohías sold a few cartoons that were critical of Castro to the Spanish language dailies *El Diario* and *La Prensa.* Afterward, his family was threatened, so he arranged for his wife and children to join him in New York. He took a job at a clothing factory pressing sweaters and began contemplating his next move. During the last year he spent in Cuba, Prohías had researched U.S. publications seeking a match for his style and had identified *MAD* magazine as a candidate for his work.

Prohías started working on a new portfolio. He studied the political climate in the United States, trying to figure out what might sell. As his daughter, Marta Pizarro, explained in the *Spy vs. Spy Omnibus,* "It was the time of the Cold War. Superpowers. There were bomb shelters, and anti-espionage stuff. He decided to reinvent the idea of 'The Sinister Man,' but rather than have him commit sinister acts on other people, my father created two characters, Spies, who would do unimaginable things to *one another.* And in that way people wouldn't complain about the violence. It was classic good guy versus bad guy, but neither one was totally good or totally bad, which is why he alternated victors."

Once Prohías had a few strips, he took them to *MAD* magazine's New York office with his 14-year-old daughter, Marta, in tow to act as a translator. Initially, the editors waved him away, saying there were no openings. Frustrated, Prohías told the editors the cartoons were drawn for *MAD* and for *MAD* alone. They decided to look. Impressed with the work, they paid Prohías for the cartoons. *MAD* magazine editor Nick Meglin told Montagne that he had no idea the strip would last so long. "I believed we were buying two or three pages, maybe. After selling us the two or three that we originally saw, he came back the next week with about 10 more sequences, and I was like a little embarrassed. I wanted to tell him, 'Gee, I don't know if we're going to run any more.' And I looked at them and about five of them were so ingenious and maybe better than the first ones.... I said, 'OK. Maybe a couple more. And maybe a couple more.'"

Landed at *MAD* Magazine

Spy vs. Spy became an instant success. The first installment of the series appeared in *MAD* #60 in January 1961.

The highly stylized strip featured two identical-looking espionage agents. The spies were constantly locked in battle, using bombs, daggers, torpedoes, machine guns, mallets, baited traps and various brutal gadgets to ensnare each other. Wounds were inflicted, but they never gave up. The characters had fedoras, long triangular noses, and shiny, black, insect-like eyes. In each installment, each spy sought to gain the upper hand, though in the end, they were doomed to an eternal standoff. Prohías rendered the spies as equally cunning, and each won 50 percent of the battles. Sometimes, they were joined by a third spy—a gray female—and the strip was christened *Spy vs. Spy vs. Spy.* Whenever the gray spy appeared, she always won. Prohías put his byline into the panels, using Morse code to spell out ''By Prohías.'' ''The sweetest revenge has been to turn Fidel's accusation of me as a spy into a money-making venture,'' Prohías once told the *Miami Herald.*

Prohías employed a unique work style. Back in Cuba, he had gotten used to working at night, trying to finish up editorial cartoons for the morning paper. He continued to keep unusual hours his whole life. He never wore a watch or used an alarm clock. Instead, he awoke at will, usually between 2 a.m. and 4 a.m., and got to work. He napped in the afternoons and returned to his work in the evening, usually wrapping up around 11 p.m. For a typical strip, he spent three to five days developing the storyline, then another week drawing. He split his time equally between New York and Miami, spending six months a year at each location. Prohías and his wife had divorced in the 1960s and she settled in Miami with the children, so Prohías liked to visit. He also liked Miami because he could speak Spanish there; he never learned English.

During his career, Prohías published several *Spy vs. Spy* paperback books. These were not reprints but contained all new material. The first volume was titled *The All New MAD Secret File on Spy vs. Spy* (1965). He published about nine books, and all sold well. During the 1980s, he could sell a half-million copies of a book because *Spy vs. Spy* was popular in the United States, Europe and South America. The timeless characters entered pop culture as they came to symbolize any endless, futile conflict. Nintendo and Milton Bradley placed the spies on video gaming systems and game boards. In 2001, Altoids launched a print campaign featuring the spies, and FOX's *MADtv* featured the antagonists in a cartoon segment. Even Mountain Dew used the spies to peddle pop in a 2004 TV commercial.

Prohías's last fully original strip appeared in March 1987 in *MAD* #269. His health and eyesight had declined to the point where he was no longer able to carry on with the strips. The series continued into the 21st century with ghostwriters. During his tenure, he had placed the spies in 241 installments of *MAD.* Prohías died of cancer on February 24, 1998, at a Miami hospital. Though the two had divorced, his ex-wife, Marta Leon, took care of him in his waning years.

Books

Prohías, Antonio, *Spy vs. Spy Omnibus,* E.C. Publications, 2011.
Reidelbach, Maria, *Completely MAD: A History of the Comic Book and Magazine,* Little, Brown & Co., 1991.

Periodicals

Miami Herald, December 4, 1983; February 25, 1998.
New York Times, March 2, 1998.

Other

Morning Edition, NPR, August 30, 2001. □

Alain Prost

One of the most successful Formula 1 drivers, French racer Alain Prost (born 1955), won the Formula 1 World Drivers' Championship four times by garnering the most points on the Grand Prix circuit in 1985, 1986, 1989, and 1993. In the history of the competition, only two other drivers have won more titles.

Alain Marie Pascal Prost was born February 24, 1955, in Lorette, France, to André and Marie-Rose Karatchian Prost. He grew up in Saint-Chamond alongside older brother Daniel. The Prost family ran a small manufacturing business that produced cycle racks, hi-fi stands and kitchen items. At one point the company employed nearly 20 workers and the business was successful enough that the Prost family could afford a vacation apartment in Cannes, on the French Riviera.

Discovered Karting on Vacation

Prost started playing soccer in 1963 and excelled at right wing. While he was growing up, his father took him and his brother to watch the professional team at Sainte-Étienne, and Prost dreamed of one day playing in the league. During the summer of 1970, the family vacationed in Cannes, with Prost nursing an injured knee and broken wrist from playing soccer. With his arm in a cast, Prost could not go swimming. Looking for entertainment the boy could participate in, the family found its way to an amusement park and ended up go-karting. The experience of racing around the track delighted Prost, and after the family returned home, he joined a local karting club.

Prost did not have enough money to buy a kart, so he began saving money. Whenever he received money to see a movie with friends, Prost instead skipped the film and pocketed the money. He offered to fetch groceries for the family and kept the meager change. He also saved the money he earned working in the family shop. After about a year, he had enough money to buy a used Mercadier-McCulloch kart. The kart needed frequent repairs to stay running but by constantly taking the machine apart and putting it back together, Prost learned about the technical aspects of racing.

In 1972, Prost gave up soccer and soon quit school to concentrate on racing. He began working in the family shop and hitting the karting circuit. He had limited success until he borrowed a chassis for a junior event in Hauteville,

Featureflash/Shutterstock.com

engines. Fabre invited Prost to test some of his vehicles and was impressed by the technical information Prost provided about the karts. He offered Prost a job as a distributor and engine-tuner. Driving with Fabre's machinery in 1974, Prost won the French Senior Karting Championship.

Next, Prost decided to fulfill his mandatory obligation to the French military. At the time, all young French men had to sign up for short-term conscription service to the country. Prost was sent to Treves, Germany, to do secretarial work.

In 1975, Prost enrolled at the Winfield Racing School, which offered driving lessons at the Paul Ricard motorsport track located near Marseille, France. The race sessions occurred on weekends. He was still in the military, stationed in Treves, and took weekend leave to attend. To get there, Prost left his garrison on Friday night. He met his mother around 1 a.m. at the railway station in Lyon, France. After a few hours of sleep, he took his mother's car and drove south to compete in the race sessions, which started on Saturday mornings. Initially, the instructors did not care for Prost's unconventional driving style of braking on the corners instead of the straights, but they found him to be a consistent driver who could ''read'' his car well and take tight lines around the track. As the fastest driver of the year, Prost won the school's Volant Elf competition in 1975. The winner of the Volant Elf got to drive a year in Formula Renault. In 1976, Prost won 12 of 13 races and ended the season as the champion of the French Formula Renault circuit. He moved into Formula 3 racing and in 1979 won both the French and European F3 championships.

France, and ended up winning. As Prost gained experience participating in league races, he refined his skills and soon realized his Mercadier-McCulloch would never get him to the front of the pack.

Found Success on Kart Circuit

In 1973, Prost acquired a better kart, this one with a French-made Vacquand chassis and an Italian-built Parilla engine. With his new machine, Prost won the 1973 French Junior Championship. That same year, he entered the European Junior Championship event in Oldenzaal, Netherlands. From the moment he arrived, he felt outclassed and did not expect good results after watching the competition unload. ''They already had trucks and trailers and we arrived with a trailer which I knocked together with the help of a handyman friend of my parents! I was not big headed and did not expect to be dominant. I had confidence, but I was already apprehensive about the next day and the next race,'' Prost recalled in the biography *Alain Prost: The Science of Racing*. However, Prost dominated, winning most of his heats and coming out the champion in the finals. ''It was from that race that realisation dawned,'' Prost noted in the biography. ''I told myself I might have a future ahead of me.''

On the race circuit, Prost met French motorsport enthusiast Michel Fabre. Fabre owned a shop in Paris that built a type of chassis for race karts and also imported

Joined Formula 1 Racing

In 1980, Prost made his Formula 1 debut with McLaren and showed great rookie talent by placing sixth at the Argentine Grand Prix, his first race in the circuit. Few racers score points in their first outing. Prost had a rough season, however, plagued by difficulties with his car. The suspension on his McLaren M29B failed on several occasions, causing Prost to hit barriers. Prost broke his wrist in one crash and injured his cervical vertebrae in another. Prost lost faith in his team's equipment and signed up to drive with Renault for the 1981 season.

In 1981, Prost enjoyed his first Formula 1 win by getting the checkered flag at the French Grand Prix. He won two more Grand Prix events that year, at Monza and in the Netherlands, and finished the year in fifth place. The 1982 season started out well for Prost. He won the first two events, at South Africa and Brazil, but did not earn the checkered flag again that year.

The 1983 season looked like it might be Prost's year. He won his third consecutive French Grand Prix and followed with wins in Belgium, Britain, and Australia. Heading into the 15th and final event of the season, which was held in South Africa, Prost led Brazilian racer Nelson Piquet by two points. However, mechanical issues forced Prost to drop out partway through, and Piquet took third in the race, capturing the championship title with 59 points to Prost's 57.

The South Africa race marked the third time that season that Prost's Renault had failed and forced him to exit a race early. He was critical of the car for not being competitive and was fired by Renault. Amid the controversy, Renault workers set Prost's car on fire outside his home. To escape the tension, Prost left France and moved his family to Switzerland in 1983. He had married in 1980 and had two sons and a daughter.

Prost went back to McLaren in 1984. His biggest rival was a teammate, Austrian Niki Lauda. The two battled it out all season. Prost won seven races, while Lauda won five. In the end, Lauda won the title, besting Prost by a mere half-point in the final standings. It was the closest finish in the history of Formula 1. Prost likely would have won the title if the Monaco Grand Prix, held earlier in the season, had not been called early for rain. Prost was leading that race but only received half of the nine points awarded for a win because the event ended early, and under controversy. Finally, in 1985 it all came together for Prost. He had five wins that season. In 16 races, Prost never finished lower than fourth and finally came out on top as the Formula 1 champion, marking the first time a Frenchman had ever won the title. He repeated as the Formula 1 World Drivers' Champion in 1986.

Sped Through Heated Rivalry

In 1988, Brazilian driver Ayrton Senna joined Prost at McLaren, touching off a heated driver rivalry. The two had opposing styles. Prost was called "the Professor" because of the cerebral approach he took to racing and the time he took with the technical aspects of his car. Engineer Steve Nichols worked with Prost at McLaren and discussed the racer's style in *Alain Prost: The Science of Racing.* "He was quite staggering when it came to the precision of his set-up on the chassis," noted Nichols. "He always chased the smallest detail which allowed him to make a difference. He was also equally demanding when it came to the engines and could spend hours testing different blocks and assessing their endurance. . . . His talent could obviously not do anything about a bad car and with that in mind he was always pushing us to improve the car and to strive for perfection."

Prost was a cunning driver. He set his car up to perform at its best, then drove a consistent race, conserving his tires and fuel for a final push near the end of the race. Senna, on the other hand, was a more explosive driver. Senna took more risks, which excited the public. The sparks started to fly at the 1988 Portuguese Grand Prix when, on lap 2, Prost passed Senna, who then pushed Prost into a pit wall. In the end, Prost finished the race in first with Senna in second, but an ugly rivalry ensued, bringing out the worst in each driver. Incredibly, Prost recorded seven wins and seven second places that year, yet lost the championship to Senna, who captured eight wins.

The 1989 season proved explosive between the two drivers. Prost complained that Honda had a preference for Senna and supplied Senna with superior engines. At the Japanese Grand Prix (the 15th of 16 races), Prost removed his gurney flap (unbeknownst to Senna) for more straight-line speed. Prost quickly moved into first in the race, though Senna had won the pole position. Senna caught up near the end of the race and made a move to pass, causing the two cars to collide. Prost left his car, figuring he had beat Senna. Senna, however, had the race marshals push his car down an

escape road and he re-entered the race, taking first after a pit stop to replace the nose cone on his car.

Senna was later disqualified for missing a chicane by going through the escape road, which led to Prost winning the Formula 1 championship. Senna and McLaren appealed the ruling, arguing that missing the chicane gave Senna no advantage. Having the win reinstated would have given Senna the title. The original decision was upheld at the appeal, and Senna was fined and banned for six months for dangerous driving. Race enthusiasts have long debated who was at fault in the collision. Some say Prost rammed Senna; others say Senna was to blame, overly ruthless in trying to overtake his rival.

In 1990, Prost went to drive for Scuderia Ferrari and ran Senna close all season. The title came down to the season finale in Japan. Senna attempted to take the lead at the first corner and the two drivers collided, knocking them both out of the race. Ultimately, this ensured the title for Senna. With only one race left, Prost could not catch Senna in points and Senna sailed on to his second consecutive Formula 1 championship. Prost had a terrible season in 1991. He failed to win a race all year and spent most of the season complaining about the shortcomings of his Ferrari 643. Prost was promptly fired at the end of the year, then sat out 1992.

In 1993, Prost joined the Williams-Renault race team and enjoyed a fabulous comeback by winning seven Grand Prix races and sailing to the Formula 1 championship to beat second-place Senna by 26 points. Prost decided to retire and go out at the top. Over the course of his Formula 1 career, he won four Formula 1 championships and 51 races. His record for most wins (51) stood for 14 years until Michael Schumacher achieved his 52nd win in 2001. In retirement, Prost worked as a TV commentator and an adviser for McLaren. In 1997, he bought the Ligier team and renamed it Prost Grand Prix. In 83 races, his drivers failed to win a single race. Prost shut down the team in 2001. Prost continued racing by competing for the Andros Trophy. The Andros is a French ice-racing event. Prost captured the title in 2007, 2008, and 2012. He also took up mountain-bike racing, competing in the Absa Cape Epic, a grueling stage race held in South Africa. Prost finished the race in 2012 and 2013.

Books

Ménard, Pierre, and Jacques Vassal, *Alain Prost: The Science of Racing,* Chronosports S.A., 2004.

Periodicals

Advertiser (Lafayette, Louisiana), November 1, 1991.
AutoWeek, January 6, 2003.
Sports Illustrated, November 15, 1993.

Online

"Alain Prost," *Formula1.com,* http://www.formula1.com/teams_and_drivers/hall_of_fame/36/driver_profile.html (December 22, 2014).
"Prost, 38, Announces Retirement," *Los Angeles Times,* http://www.articles.latimes.com/1993-09-25/sports/sp-38901_1_race-drivers (December 22, 2014). □

Yakov Protazanov

Russian filmmaker Yakov Protazanov (1881–1945) delivered one of cinema's landmark early works of science fiction in 1924 with *Aelita: Queen of Mars*. The first Russian-made science fiction movie, *Aelita* was conceived as a work of political propaganda but its stunning set design and imaginative costumes made it an early cult classic in the genre. Its avant-garde look was copied a few years later by the makers of *Flash Gordon,* a popular Hollywood serial.

Yakov Alexandrovich Protazanov was born in Moscow on January 23, 1881, a date sometimes reported as February 4, 1881, according to the older Julian calendar still in use in the Russian Empire at the time. His mother's family were the Vinokurovs, a prosperous merchant family in Moscow, and his father was thought to have been an accountant from Kiev, the Ukrainian city. As a child Protazanov lived with his mother at her family home in Moscow and learned French along with Russian at an early age. He loved attending theater performances and had additional contact with the performing arts through some Vinokurov cousins who worked in imperial Russia's thriving theater scene of the 1890s.

RIA Novosti/Alamy

Visited Pathé Paris Studio

As a young man, Protazanov duly followed a course charted for him by his family, enrolling at the Moscow Commercial School to earn his business degree. He graduated in 1900 and worked for a few years in an office, a job he loathed and quit as soon as he inherited a small sum from a Protazanov great-aunt in 1904. He spent some of the 5,000 ruble-sum traveling through Europe for the next three years, including an obligatory stop in Paris. A visit to the Pathé film studio in that city resurrected his interest in the performing arts. When he returned to Russia around 1907, he was hired at the Gloria Film studio, a Moscow outfit that was among the first such ventures in imperial Russia.

Protazanov learned camera arts, set lighting, scriptwriting, and even acted on screen with a small part in a 1909 drama *The Death of Ivan the Terrible*. His first film as director was *Bakchisarayskiy fontana,* based on the 1824 narrative poem by Alexander Pushkin. When the Gloria company folded, Protazanov went to work for Paul Thiemann, a Baltic German who had worked in Moscow as an agent for Gaumont, Pathé's rival studio. Thiemann and his business partner Friedrich Reinhardt took over the Moscow studio used by Pathé and began churning out silent-film versions of well-known works from Russian literature.

Protazanov's first film for the Thiemann and Reinhardt studio was *Pesn' katorzhanina* (The Prisoner's Song) in 1911, based on a script he wrote. His first completed work to gain notice was *Ukhod velikovo startza* (The Departure of a Grand Old Man), a 1912 semi-documentary film about the greatest Russian writer of the late 19th century, the world-famous Count Leo Tolstoy, author of *War and Peace.*

Tolstoy's widow Sofia was livid over the negative portrayal of her and successfully blocked its release in Russia. *The Departure of a Grand Old Man* played in European cinemas, however, and helped establish Protazanov's reputation as a talented young Russian filmmaker.

In the year just before World War I, Protazanov made 13 movies, most of them literary adaptations that were both profitable and popular with filmgoers and critics. One of these was *Klyuchishchastya* (The Keys to Happiness), based on a bestselling novel about a young Russian woman and her affair with an older man. Still with the Thiemann and Reinhardt outfit, Protazanov was paired with Vladimir Gardin to co-direct the first Russian film adaptation of Tolstoy's epic *War and Peace.* The silent-film version was released in early 1915 just as Russian troops were becoming mired in another potentially ruinous military debacle. This time, Russia was on the losing side and the turmoil led to the overthrow of Tsar Nicholas II, the last Romanov dynastic ruler of Russia. Protazanov was drafted in 1916 but apparently saw little action, for his film career continued apace.

Worked in Paris and Berlin

After the tsar's forced ouster in 1917, the combined Russian Communist and Socialist parties established a people's republic, or Soviet, and then a breakaway group, the Bolsheviks, seized full power later that year in what became known as the October Revolution. During the tumult of these years the Thiemann and Reinhardt studio was forced to shut down, civil war erupted across Russia, and the Romanov family was taken into custody and later executed by their guards.

By the time of the October Revolution of 1917 Protazanov had been working steadily at the film studio of Iosif Ermolev, a well-connected producer who turned out popular box-office fare and had a roster of respected stage actors on his payroll. One of them was Ivan Mozhukin, one of Russian cinema's first movie stars and sometimes called the Russian Rudolph Valentino; Mozhukin's name is sometimes spelled Mozzhukhin or Mosjoukine. For Ermolev and with Mozhukin Protazanov made two of his best-known works, *Satana likuiushchii* (Satan Triumphant), released in 1917, and *Otets Sergii* (Father Sergius) a year later. The latter was based on a classic—and controversial—Tolstoy work of the same title, and its film version was only possible once the tsar and his official government censors agency were ousted. Writing in the *International Dictionary of Films and Filmmakers,* film historian Liam O'Leary deemed this Protazanov's masterpiece. "Tolstoy's story of the spiritual struggles of a young officer of the Imperial Court who gives up a life of pleasure to become a monk was a tour de force for Mozhukin" wrote O'Leary. "The actor's transition from youth to age, the authenticity of the settings, and the cohesion of the film help to make it one of the great classics of the cinema."

The civil war continued after the end of World War I in 1918. White Russian pro-monarchist forces attempted to eliminate the Bolsheviks, whose Red Army returned firepower with equal vehemence. Ermolev moved his current film projects to safety in the Crimean peninsula, but as the fighting neared the Black Sea and its ports, Protazanov was among the many who decided to leave his homeland, perhaps forever. Like Ermolev, his middle-class background put him at risk in the new politically charged atmosphere that elevated ordinary workers and peasants to favored status. At Odessa, the Black Sea port, he boarded a British freighter that docked in Istanbul, where he began working on a new project from a script written by Mozhukin. They eventually moved on to Marseilles, France, and then worked with Ermolev, who was establishing himself in Paris. Protazanov remade a few of his previous films with French actors, and had some success after moving to Berlin to make *Der Liebe Pilgerfahrt* (The Pilgrimage of Love) for Germany's renowned UFA studio.

Invited to Return by Film Board

In 1923, Protazanov returned to the newly named Union of Soviet Socialist Republics (USSR) to work for a new state-financed studio, Mezhrabpom-Rus. The studio name was an acronym for the Workers' International Relief agency, or *Mezhdunarodny rabochy komitet pomoshchi,* and its workspace was a previous studio, Rus, in Moscow that dated back to the pre-revolutionary era. For Mezhrabpom-Rus Protazanov made ten silent films over the next seven years, including his most enduring work *Aelita: Queen of Mars.*

Aelita was an adaptation of a 1923 science-fiction tale by Alexei Tolstoy, a distant relative of the more famous Tolstoy and known as the "Comrade Count" for his leftist sympathies.

Protazanov's adaptation is the first feature-length Russian film to have space travel as its center. Its fictional protagonist is Moscow radio engineer Mstislav Los (the surname translates as "elk"), a man who murders his wife in a fit of jealousy. In a panic he sets to work on his dream of building a rocket ship and manages to launch the vehicle into space and toward the planet Mars.

Protazanov's version differed from the Tolstoy original in which Los was a depressed widower. On his journey to Mars the engineer's sidekick is Gusev, a staunch Bolshevik and Red Army veteran. Their rocket-ship landing on Mars has been anticipated by the Martian princess Aelita, who has spied on Los and his curiously affectionate human world through an advanced telescope device. Aelita belongs to a tightly guarded elite who rule Mars, while the majority of Martians are automatons who toil in grueling conditions to support the regime. Los and Gusev learn that the planet is approaching environmental catastrophe because of a coming freeze, and that millions of Martians will starve to death and die of cold. Los romances Aelita while Gusev leads a Martian revolution, which is brutally suppressed by the regime. Los must flee back to Earth, In the Tolstoy version he later hears transmission signals from Mars that hint the revolutionary spirit has indeed been seeded on the red planet. In the film version, the Muscovite's entire journey is revealed to have been a bad dream, as Los awakens in the morning and sees his wife still alive.

Aelita Provoked Sensation

Protazanov worked with highly regarded theater designer Alexandra Exter, who created a stunning visual set for *Aelita*'s palace and the Martian world. The film was released in 1924 in the Soviet Union but aroused some controversy from ideologically motivated film critics. It premiered in the United States in 1929 at the Film Guild Cinema of New York City, and *New York Times* reviewer Mordaunt Hall commented on the "queer settings and Martians sparsely costumed in spiked hats and celluloid or metal garments." The film marked the screen debut of Yuliya Solntseva in the title role and featured an array of Soviet-era screen talent of the era. Film historians note that *Aelita*'s cult status comes from the fairly generous budget Protazanov was given, which allowed him to work more slowly than most silent-era directors were permitted.

That budget, and the tidy nightmare-framework revealed at the end, prompted Russian film critics of the time to dismiss Protazanov's epic. *Kino-gazeta* and other publications deemed it insufficiently aligned with the revolutionary spirit, while other Soviet commentators argued that its lavish budget could have been better utilized on more ideologically sturdy films.

Protazanov was stunned by the negative reception of *Aelita* inside the Soviet Union. He made several more films for Mezhrabpom-Rus but ensured that they openly derided Western capitalism and decadence. In *Yevo prizyv* (His Call), a wealthy family stashes some treasure before fleeing the 1917 Revolution. A few years later the son comes back to Moscow to retrieve the gold, now hidden inside a communal apartment inhabited by a young woman and her grandmother. This 1925 film, wrote Russian cinema scholar Denise J. Youngblood in *Movies for the Masses: Popular Cinema and Soviet Society in the 1920s,* "had everything social critics wanted—contemporary subject-matter and precise details of everyday life, and everything the public wanted—love, violence and a happy ending."

Other films Protazanov made during this era include *Byelyi orel* (The White Eagle) from 1928 and *Tommy,* his first sound film, from 1931. Once again, he proved remarkably deft, quickly adapting to the new technical demands of sound film and continuing to make films popular with Russian filmgoers. In 1939 world war erupted again and the Soviet Union became enmeshed in a deadly conflict against Nazi Germany by 1941. Once more, Protazanov headed away from the action, going to Almaty in Kazakhstan to finish one movie shoot and completing what would be his last film, *Nasreddin v Bukhare* (Nasreddin in Bukhara), in 1943 in Uzbekistan. He died on the final day of World War II, August 8, 1945, in Moscow. Biographers report that in 1911 he married the sister of his first film-studio boss at Gloria. Many of his early prints have been lost, but *Aelita* remains a cult classic and is still cited as a work of merit in the history of science fiction film and literature.

In an essay that appeared in *Future Wars: The Anticipations and the Fears,* Robert Crossley called the 1924 classic "a more textured, challenging and intellectually consistent work of art than" Tolstoy's original story, and commended it as "a striking example of how the science fiction film could serve as a populist medium of skilful and effective propaganda."

Books

Crossley, Robert, "From Invasion to Liberation: Alternative Visions of Mars, Planet of War," in *Future Wars: The Anticipations and the Fears,* edited by David Seed, Liverpool University Press, 2012.

O'Leary, Liam, "Yakov Protazanov," in *International Dictionary of Films and Filmmakers,* Volume 2, Gale, 2000.

Youngblood, Denise J., *Movies for the Masses: Popular Cinema and Soviet Society in the 1920s,* Cambridge University Press, 1992.

Periodicals

New York Times, March 26, 1929.□

Q

Raymond Queneau

The French writer Raymond Queneau (1903–1976) was among the most noted novelists and poets of the post–World War II era in France.

Although Queneau earned a living at the center of the French literary establishment, serving as an editor at the large Gallimard publishing house, his fiction, especially, was resolutely experimental. Coming of age in a country with a strong set of traditional literary conventions, he disregarded many of them. He spelled words phonetically, coined words imaginatively, captured the colloquial speech of the French streets, and structured novels in original, playful ways. "After World War II," in the words of the *Books and Writers* website, "his work formed a bridge between the irrational world of Breton and other surrealists and the philosophical 'absurd' of existentialism." Some of his works reflect mathematical principles in their construction. Queneau's writing, unlike that of other experimentalists, enjoyed a measure of popular success; his 1959 novel *Zazie dans le métro* (Zazie in the Metro) became a major motion picture, and his poem "Si tu t'imagines" (If You Imagine) even became a hit for vocalist Juliette Greco. With his dry humor and his willingness to use the form of literature itself as a component in his expressive palette, Queneau has been hailed as a forerunner of the postmodern movement in the arts.

Served in Zouaves

Raymond Queneau (pronounced KENN-o) was born in Le Havre, France, on February 21, 1903. An only child, he described his childhood as unhappy, and he later underwent psychoanalysis in order to try to resolve his feelings about it. Queneau was an enthusiastic student of mathematics and philosophy as well as literature, and after graduating at age 19 from the *lycé* (an advanced secondary school) in Le Havre with majors in Latin, Greek, and philosophy, he headed for Paris, enrolled at the Sorbonne University, and earned several more degrees. His father, Auguste Queneau, who ran a clothing shop in Le Havre, had been a member of France's colonial army, and when the Rif War broke out in Algeria (a French colony) and Morocco, Queneau did military service there from 1925 or 1926 until 1927 as part of the traditional Zoauve infantry corps. While in Africa, he found it difficult to understand the colloquial French of his fellow soldiers; later he would try to incorporate colloquial speech into serious literature.

During this period Queneau was interested in the growing Surrealist movement and was close friends with its leader, poet André Breton, until the two had a falling-out in 1929. He married Breton's sister-in-law, Janine Kahn, and the pair had one son, Jean-Marie, later a visual artist. The marriage lasted until Queneau's death. Faced with the necessity of supporting his new family, Queneau worked at a wide variety of jobs: private tutor, translator, tablecloth salesman, and journalism; in the last-named capacity he wrote a daily column about the city of Paris from 1936 to 1938. In 1938 he was hired as a reader of manuscripts at Gallimard, and he spent much of his adult life there.

By that time, Queneau had published the first of his 16 novels, *Le Chiendent* (variously translated as *The Bark-Tree* and *Witch Grass*), in 1934. With its story of a man who develops a philosophical awareness of reality, *Le Chiendent* anticipated many of the themes of his later work. The novel features a large group of subsidiary characters whose appearances are determined by arithmetical principles and who all meet at the end. The book had 91 sections, 91 being

© Jacques Haillot/Sygma/Corbis

the product of 7 and 13, numbers that had personal significance for Queneau. He cited James Joyce as an influence; the details of Joyce's seemingly chaotic novel *Ulysses* are determined by extra-textual strategies.

Employed Mathematical Principles in Writing

Mathematical principles of the sort involved in *Le Chiendent* also appeared in later Queneau books. Mathematics as a discipline also played a role in the novel *Odile* (1936), in which the hero, Roland Travy, at first seeks to restrict his life to the world of mathematics but later falls in love with a woman. Many of Queneau's books consist of small fragments linked by some kind of mathematical principle. Queneau wrote several essays on mathematics. He was a member of France's mathematical society and joined the American Mathematical Society in 1963.

After publishing the 1939 novel *Un rude hiver* (A Rude Winter), which anticipated the coming world war, Queneau was drafted into the French army in August of that year. He served during most of the low-intensity so-called Phony War and returned to Paris after completing his service in the summer of 1940. He spent much of World War II in smaller French cities, contributing as a writer to underground publications connected with the French Resistance against Nazi rule, and he wrote a weekly column for the Resistance newspaper *Front National*. Queneau continued to write during the war and published several new novels,

including *Pierrot mon ami* (1942, translated as *Pierrot*) and *Loin de Rueil* (1944, translated as *The Skin of Dreams*).

Queneau's approach to literature perhaps reached its purest form in *Exercises de style* (1947, translated as *Exercises in Style*). The book was not a novel but a set of 99 separate descriptions of the same unimportant incident: a man boards a bus; his feet are stepped on by another passenger; he sits down; and he talks about one of his coat buttons with a friend. Queneau varies the order of the events, the tone and level of diction in which they are recounted, and the relative emphasis given to each part of the story. He gives each telling a label, such as "metaphoric," and he uses mathematical principles in their variations. Despite the rather obscure premise of the book—that writing is essentially about manner of expression rather than content—*Exercises de style* was popular with Queneau's growing following after the war.

Novel Filmed by Louis Malle

Still more popular was *Zazie dans le métro*, which was made into an acclaimed film by director Louis Malle in 1960. The novel tells of a girl, Zazie, who comes to visit her uncle, a drag queen, in Paris. Her dream is not to see the major sights of the city but rather to ride its Métro, or subway. Through the device of having Zazie imitate the speech of adults she meets, the book displays to maximum effect Queneau's experiments with colloquial French language. Queneau wrote this and several other ambitious books while serving as principal editor of the *Encyclopédie de la Pléiade*, a 49-volume universal encyclopedia issued by Gallimard.

Queneau's interests as a writer extended beyond his novels and his ten books of poetry. The film directors of the French New Wave saw in Queneau an ally of their own experiments with cinematic storytelling, and he worked on several film screenplays himself. He wrote several books, including *On est toujours trop bon avec les femmes* (1947, translated as *We Always Treat Women Too Well*), under the pen name Sally Mara, casting himself as "editor." Some of these books had elements of sex and violence, which may have caused him to use a pen name.

Athough Queneau distrusted mainstream literary organizations and schools of thought, he participated in groups of a more playful, fanciful nature, including the Collège de Pataphysique (where his title was Satrap) and later a subgroup of that group called the Ouvroir de Littérature Potentielle, (Oulpo, or Opening of Potential Literature), whose members set literary puzzles and games for themselves. He published journals at several points in his life; they show that he was interested in philosophy and religious ideas from both Western and Eastern traditions.

Queneau's 1965 novel *Les fleurs bleues* (translated as *The Blue Flowers*) was one of his most ambitious; it focused on a pair of time travelers, one who comes from the past to the present and the other who goes from present to past. Queneau continued to write into his last years, publishing a set of essays, *Morale elémentaire*, in 1975. He died in Paris on October 25, 1976. The French newspaper *Le Monde*, as quoted in *The New York Times*, memorialized him as "a philosopher hiding underneath fiction; a metaphysician disguising his tenderness; a scholar of language applying his experience to texts of irresistible humor."

Books

Cobb, Richard, *Raymond Queneau,* Clarendon, 1976.

Dictionary of Literary Biography, Vol. 72, Gale, 1988.

Guicharnaud, Jacques, *Raymond Queneau,* Columbia, 1965.

Henderson, Lesley, ed, *Reference Guide to World Literature,* 2nd ed., St. James, 1995.

Sanders, Carol, *Raymond Queneau,* Rodopi, 1984.

Periodicals

New York Times, October 25, 1976.

Online

''Raymond Queneau,'' *Books and Writers,* http://www.kirjasto.sci.fi/quene.htm (December 2, 2014).□

R

Rakoczi Ferenc II, Prince of Transylvania

Hungarian noble Ferenc Rákóczi II (1676–1735) led a briefly successful war of independence in Austrian-controlled Hungary in the early 1700s. The charismatic, multilingual, and visionary prince united fellow aristocrats and impoverished peasants into a Magyar rebel army determined to oust the oppressive authoritarian Habsburg regime from Hungarian lands in Central Europe. Known as Rákóczi's War of Independence, the short-lived restoration of Magyar authority marked the last significant uprising against Austrian domination of Hungary, which endured until 1918.

Ferenc Rákóczi was descended from a family of Hungarian nobility with a long record of military heroism. The first of note was Zsigmond Rákóczi, who became the first prince of a newly created, semi-independent Transylvanian state in the early 1600s. Zsigmond's son and grandson were both named György and each engaged in separate missions to reassert the political, economic, and religious rights guaranteed to Hungarian nobles that dated back to the Golden Bull of 1222. As an independent ethnic population—whose very language, classed as Finno-Ugric, linked them to Finns, Estonians, and a long-ago common ancestral tribe in Central Asia—Hungarians were wedged between two major world powers with imperialist aims. One was the Archduchy of Austria, ruled by the powerful Habsburg dynasty. The other was an immense and well-organized Ottoman Empire centered in Constantinople. At one point, between 1526 and 1686, Hungary was even divided into three distinct entities: Royal Hungary, Ottoman Hungary, and Transylvania.

Seventeenth-century Europe was roiled by bloody religious wars between Roman Catholics and supporters of the Protestant Reformation. The Rákóczis belonged to a cadre of Hungarian nobility who had accepted the terms of the Protestant Reformation and were followers of the French-Swiss theologian John Calvin. This pitted them against the staunch Roman Catholicism of the Austrian Habsburg rulers, and Rákóczi's grandfather György II had lost his lands and title in one campaign against the authoritarian Habsburg regime. In 1673, Emperor Leopold I of Austria, who also held the title Holy Roman Emperor, revoked all Hungarian self-rule, suspended the Hungarian constitution, and confiscated vast estates of other Protestant Hungarian nobles he suspected of disloyalty.

Never Knew Fabled Father

Rákóczi's father was Ferenc Rákóczi I, born in 1645 and wed to a Croatian countess, Ilona Zrínyi, daughter of the Ban of Croatia. Like the Transylvanian princes, the *bans* were minor aristocracy and had limited but autocratic power. Rákóczi's father set out to retrieve his power in Transylvania by teaming with Ilona's father Péter Zrínyi. The Croatian noble was taken prisoner and the elder Ferenc died in July of 1676, when his only surviving son was just four months old.

Rákóczi was born on March 27, 1676, when Ilona was living at a Rákóczi family holding in Borša, in present-day Slovakia. After the death of her husband, Ilona's status was imperiled, and technically Leopold could assert his right of legal guardianship of the disinherited prince of Transylvania.

INTERFOTO/Alamy

In June of 1682, when Rákóczi was six and his sister Julianna ten, the 39-year-old Ilona married Imre Thököly, another Hungarian noble whose estates had also been confiscated by Leopold. In 1683, Rákóczi's new stepfather joined forces with an Ottoman attempt to overtake Austrian rule in Hungary. The Muslim armies were turned back from their siege of Vienna, the capital of the Archduchy of Austria, but battles raged on in other parts of the realm. Thököly was forced to surrender in 1685 in Prešov, Slovakia. For his perfidy, Thököly was taken in chains to the Ottoman seat of power in Edirne, Turkey, near the present-day border with Bulgaria and Greece.

Confined to Besieged Castle

Rákóczi's mother, meanwhile, masterfully held off Austrian forces for nearly three years at one of last remaining outposts of the Hungarian nobility, Palanok Castle. This was located in what was then called Munkács but became the Ukrainian town of Mukacheve. The siege of the well-fortified castle, built in the 1300s, began in 1685 and finally ended when Ilona learned that Buda, the royal Hungarian city on the Danube held by the Ottomans, had fallen back into Austrian hands. She acquiesced to Leopold's order to bring her adolescent son and teenaged daughter to Vienna, where the young Rákóczi was placed under close watch and tutored by teachers of the Roman Catholic Jesuit order.

The teenage Rákóczi adapted well to the new setting. He studied at the renowned university in Prague and traveled through Italy, and was restored some lands and rights through the intercession of his sister, who had married into a Habsburg-loyalist family, the Aspremonts. In September of 1694 at age 18, he wed Charlotte Amalie von Hessen-Rheinfels-Wanfried, the daughter of a German landgrave, or duke. The wedding took place at the magnificent Gothic cathedral in Cologne, Germany. The couple moved to Sárospatak, one of Hungary's most famous castles and given to Rákóczi in return for his loyalty to Leopold.

Escaped from Military Detention

Rákóczi had spent scant time in Hungary until his adult years and was said to have known little of the piteous conditions endured by Hungarian peasants, who lived as serfs under the feudal noble class, who themselves were heavily taxed by the emperor. When the remnants of his stepfather's army contacted him and allegedly asked him to lead an uprising against the Habsburgs, Rákóczi initially declined. Hungarian historians surmise that his nationalist spirit was awakened when he made contact with another powerful Hungarian, Miklós Bercsényi, whose family seat had been adjacent to Munkács.

France and its powerful King Louis XIV also sought to curtail Austrian power in central Europe. When Rákóczi began secret correspondence with Louis to ascertain the monarch's willingness to support an ouster of the Habsburgs, the letter was intercepted and Rákóczi was jailed in April of 1700 in Wiener Neustadt, the fortress tow outside Vienna. His pregnant wife persuaded the German commander of the prison to help her husband escape, and Rákóczi fled to Poland to the protection of distant relatives, the Sienawski-Lubomirski noble family. The Rákóczis were tied to them through the marriage of Rákóczi's grandfather György II to Zofia Báthory, a daughter of this princely Polish-Lithuanian-Hungarian clan that ruled parts of Poland and Transylvania during the feudal era. Bercsényi joined him there and they made contact with Tamás Esze, a Hungarian serf, who also spoke of a waiting army of kurucs, or Hungarian peasants, willing to take up arms against oppressive Habsburg rule.

Around this same period, the Habsburg dynasty became enmeshed in an expensive War of the Spanish Succession, which lasted from 1701 to 1714. This pitted the Austrians against France—at the time, one of the world's best-equipped and most disciplined military powers—in a battle to control the Iberian peninsula and Spain's fabled colonial holdings abroad. Rákóczi and Bercsényi decided to act once massive deployments of Austrian troops were diverted to France and the Low Countries.

Restored as Prince of Transylvania

Funded in part by donations from the French treasury, Rákóczi's War of Independence began in June of 1703 at Munkács, the site of his mother's infamous standoff of the 1680s. Moving in a south and westerly direction Rákóczi's kurucs easily took majority-Hungarian cities and towns, and more soldiers and nobles joined its ranks. "His famous 1704 proclamation," wrote Miklós Molnár, author of A

Concise History of Hungary, was issued in Latin and "intended to unite the nobility and the people under his banner," wrote Molnár of Rákóczi's call to arms. "*Recrudescunt diutina indytae gentis Hungariae vulnera*—'Once again, the ancient wounds of the glorious Hungarian nation are open,'" Rákóczi reminded all.

The Hungarian nobility resurrected their Diet, or assembly, which had traditionally elected their own kings of Hungary until the Habsburgs usurped their power. The new Diet restored Rákóczi to his father's revoked title as Prince of Transylvania in 1704. A year later, with more victories in hand, the Diet elected Rákóczi the new King of Hungary. The 25-member Diet also sent word to the Habsburg throne in Vienna reasserting the restoration of their sovereignty and right to elect their own king.

When the War of Spanish Succession turned in the Habsburg favor, battalions were sent east to quash the Rákóczi revolt. General Siegbert Heister led the empire's forces against Rákóczi's men, which reached a peak force of about 70,000 in 1707. Heister and his troops reversed the significant territorial advances made by Rákóczi and Bercsényi's forces in 1707 and 1708.

Exiled to France

Again, Rákóczi requested help from France, but Louis XIV declined to involve his armies, having already decided that a peace treaty with Austria was in his kingdom's best interests. Rákóczi army was woefully outmatched and outmanned. Outbreaks of disease swept through the kuruc encampments and they were finally routed at Trencsén in 1711. The Emperor Leopold I had died by then, and his more liberal-minded son Joseph I ascended the throne that same year. Joseph offered an amnesty deal to the Hungarian nobles, many of whom accepted it. Rákóczi, meanwhile, had undertaken a mission to Poland to seek money and arms, hoping to enlist the support of Tsar Peter I of Russia, who was wary of involvement in the Hungarian cause. While Rákóczi was in Poland one of his generals, Sándor Károlyi, signed the Treaty of Szatmár on September 30, 1711, ending the Rákóczi War of Independence.

Rákóczi was enraged at what he viewed as Károlyi's treasonous action and refused to accept the amnesty deal. He made his way to Versailles, France, to the court of Louis XIV, and lived there with his wife and children for some years. He even wrote a volume of his *Mémoires* in French. In 1717, when tensions flared once again between the Habsburg empire and the Ottomans, Rákóczi sailed for Turkey to meet with Sultan Ahmed III. At the time, the Ottoman imperial ambitions had turned east and the Sultan was battling Russian forces, but by the time Rákóczi reached Constantinople, Ahmed had concluded a new treaty with Austria. Rákóczi spent the remaining 17 years of his life in Turkey at Rodosto, on the Sea of Marmara coastline. He died there on April 8, 1735, at age 59. His home there was preserved and became the Rákóczi Museum in the 1980s.

The Habsburg dynasty remained in power in Hungary until their defeat at the end of World War I. Many of the places Rákóczi lived still stand, including his birthplace of Rákóczi Castle in Borša, Slovakia. Palanok Castle, where his mother fended off Austrian forces, also remains a regional landmark, as does Sárospatak, where he lived with his bride and young children before the revolt. His wife Charlotte had been forced to stay in Vienna after her role in her husband's prison escape was discovered but later joined him in France. The couple had three sons, Lipot, József, and György, and a daughter given the Hungarian form of her mother's name, Sarolta. József inherited the right to the hereditary title prince of Transylvania, but failed in his attempt to have the lands and estate income restored. A Hungarian folk melody, Rákóczi's March, was used by Hungarian composer Franz Liszt in one of his 19 *Hungarian Rhapsodies*.

Books

Lendvai, Paul, *The Hungarians: A Thousand Years of Victory in Defeat*, Princeton University Press, 2003.

Molnár, Miklós, *A Concise History of Hungary*, Cambridge University Press, 2001.

Péter, Katalin, "The Later Ottoman Period and Royal Hungary," in *A History of Hungary*, edited by Peter F. Sugar, Péter Hanák, Tibor Frank, Indiana University Press, 1990.□

Franca Rame

Italian actress and playwright Franca Rame (1929-2013) was known for her bombshell looks, comedic timing, feminist writings, and passionate leftist politics. Usually collaborating with husband, playwright, actor, and director Dario Fo, they formed several theatrical companies, and created stage, television, and film works together. Rame wrote and performed a number of plays of her own, including the very personal *Lo Stupro* (The Rape, 1983), and served in the Italian parliament from 2006 to 2008.

Born July 18, 1929, in Parabiago, Italy, she was the daughter of Domenico and Emilia Rame. Her father was an actor and active socialist, while her mother was a teacher and fervent Catholic. Her family had been associated with performing since the 18th century and owned a theater company, Family Drama. They originally focused on puppeteering, before turning to stage acting when cinema appeared.

Made Stage Debut as an Infant

When Rame was eight days old, she made her stage debut, appearing on stage in her mother's arms. Educated in convent schools, she continued to act, especially revues, throughout her childhood and into young adulthood. Rame never formally studied the craft of acting.

By the age of 18, Rame had become known for her work in revues. By 1951, she was taking leading roles in productions. In the early 1950s, she appeared with a theater troupe based in Milan. Through this company, Rame

Elisabetta A. Villa/WireImage/Getty Images

met Dario Fo, an actor and playwright. At the time, he was a cabaret artist who created memorable satirical skits.

In 1954, Rame and Fo married. The couple had one son, Jacopo, in 1955; he would become a writer himself. In this period, Rame was appearing on stage and in several films. Perhaps the best known was *Lo Svitato* (The Screwball), released in 1956 and featuring a script penned by Fo. As an actress, she was becoming known for her comic timing and engaging presence.

Founded Theatrical Company with Fo

Four years after their marriage, Rame and Fo founded their first theater company together, the Dario Fo-Franca Rame Theater Company. While Rame was the leading actress and served in an administrative role, her husband was its primary director and playwright. Though Fo was the chief author of the plays they put, Rame was his muse and critic during the creative process. She played an important role in the development of plays, and was often Fo's informal co-author.

Fo's plays in the late 1950s and early 1960s were satires, often absurdist, but usually not political. Early works were entitled *Corpse for Sale* and *The Virtuous Burglar* (1958). Others included *Gli arcangeli non giocano a flipper* (Archangels Don't Play Pinball, 1959) and *Anyone Who Robs a Foot Is Lucky In Love* (1961).

Gli arcangeli non giocano a flipper was the first big theatrical success for the couple, performed at the Odeon in Milan. Pinball machines, then newly introduced to Italy, were used as a metaphor for concepts like mechanization, and conspicuous consumption. *Gli arcangeli* was the first of many plays the couple would put on and perform at the venue.

Gained Television Fame

In 1962, Rame and Fo became household names in Italy when they served as guest sketch writers and performers on *Canzonissima,* a popular variety show. The couple was the subject of controversy when they wrote and performed in a skit that emphasized how building site laborers were relatively unprotected under the law. It created an outcry in the Italian parliament and led to a wider discussion about censorship. Rame and Fo left the show over censorship and were essentially banned from television for the next 15 years.

Concentrating again on theater, the couple put on stage productions in unexpected locations such as factories and housing projects. Many of the works were quite political, a focus which only increased over time. Their next project together was written by Fo. Called *Isabella, Tre Caravelle e un Cacciaballe* (Isabella, Three Sailing Ships and a Con Man), it was set in Spain in the era of the Inquisition. In the production, Rame played Queen Isabella.

When political unrest and student protests occurred in the late 1960s, the couple became more political personally and their interests colored their work. Rame was especially radical. In 1967, she joined the Italian Community Party. In 1968, Rame and Fo began to see conventional theater as capitalist and founded a new cooperative theater, Nuova Scena, with the backing of the Communist Party. The Communists' support was short lived because the couple put on a production that attacked the party. It was a satirical pantomime with puppets that focused on the post-World War II history of Italy. In the production, Capitalism was depicted as a gorgeous woman who seduced Communism.

Established La Commune

Dissolving Nuova Scena, Rame and Fo founded another theater company in 1970. A similarly revolutionary theatrical collective, La Commune was based in Milan. It focused on raising awareness of the working classes and showing support of government overthrow to bring about a socialist state. As Rame and Fo became more politically active and political in their work, they increasingly became a target of scorn and acts of violence in Italy.

Despite the threats and violence, the couple persisted in their work. Critics believed that Rame played a role in writing two of Fo's most celebrated works, which were created in this period. They included Fo's best known works internationally: *Mistero Buffo* (Comic Mystery, 1969) and *Accidental Death of an Anarchist* (1970). *Mistero Buffo* offered a critique of the Roman Catholic church, Italian state, and abuses of power. Though fictional, *Accidental Death of an Anarchist* was inspired by an actual event. An anarchist being held at a police station as a suspect in a bombing died there under suspicious circumstances by falling from a window.

Turned Traumatic Event into Play

Rame's life and career were deeply impacted by one act of political violence in March 1973. She was kidnapped off a street in Milan at gunpoint by extremists affiliated with the far right. They cut her with razor blades, burned her with cigarettes, and gang raped her before dumping her in a park. Rame did not tell her husband about the attack until 1975, and she unexpectedly spoke details about the sexual assault during a stage production in 1979. Rame wrote a powerful play about the incident in 1983, *Lo Stupro* (The Rape).

In 1998, a judicial inquiry into the incident determined that the attack on Rame had been done on the order of the Italian federal police, the Carabinieri, in Milan. They were angry at Fame's role in putting together a group that supported leftists in police custody by giving them defense lawyers and sending them packages. The incident was also most likely intended to be a strike against the left movement as a whole, which was putting together protests against the Christian Democrats, then in power. There was no apology or charges brought because the statue of limitations had expired.

Though it took years for Rame to process the attack, she returned to the stage a few months after the incident. She appeared in a production of *Basta con i Fascisti* (Enough Now with the Fascists). In 1974, Rame had a major role in a La Commune production of *Can't Pay? Won't Pay!*, the first feminist play penned by Fo. She played a housewife who leads a group of women as they go on a shoplifting and looting spree in a supermarket. Though only credited to Fo, Rame most likely played a significant role in the writing of the play.

Began Writing Plays

Around this time, Rame began writing plays of her own, including *Lo Stupro*. Many, such as *Lo Stupro*, were monologues, and they were often feminist in nature. In her works, she discussed sexual politics, the Italian government, and the Roman Catholic church. Among the plays by Rame was *Orgasmo Adulto Escapes from the Zoo*, a group of monologues about the lives of women. Her plays were highly regarded in Italy and Europe.

A number of other plays were credited to both Rame and Fo. They included *A Woman Alone* and *Tutta Casa, Letto e Chiesa* (All Home, Bed and Church, 1977). The latter was a collection of feminist monologues, and its title referred to the lesser status given to Italian women. Another play written by both of them was most likely *Medea* (1977). An adaptation of the tragedy by Euripides with a feminist interpretation, the play focuses on the central character consciously deciding to kill her children to escape male-dominated society.

Rame and Fo continued to develop a similarly symbiotic relationship as performers. Rame appeared in many of her husband's plays, Fo appeared in his wife's plays. Sometimes, they appeared in the same production. One such play was one they wrote together, *The Open Couple* (1982). This one-act comedy was based on their own marriage and relationship. They had an open marriage, but the play showed that there were double standards about fidelity from the male perspective.

Denied Entry into the United States

Because of their political activities, Rame and Fo had difficulties in gaining entry to some countries, including the United States, to perform or speak. In both 1980 and 1983, Rame and Fo asked for visas to enter the United States. The couple was denied both times for leftist actions, including their role in a group called Soccorso Rosso (Red Aid). Rame helped establish the group, which helped the families of leftists who were jailed for crimes that were politically motivated.

It was not until 1984 that the United States finally allowed the couple entry. When they came to America, they attended a production of *Accidental Death of an Anarchist* in New York City. They also toured the country, appearing in theaters and at colleges. Two years later, in 1986, Rame and Fo performed in the United States. At New York City's Joyce Theater, Rame appeared in *Tutta Casa* and Fo in *Mistero Buffalo*.

Though Rame and Fo's professional and political careers continued through the 1980s and 1990s, the couple struggled at times. They nearly divorced in 1989, but were later able to reconcile. Rame also admitted that she attempted suicide. When Fo won the Nobel Prize for Literature in 1997, he dedicated his honor to Rame. It was suggested that the award should have gone to both of them. The couple decided together that most of the money that came with the prize would be donated to charities that worked with disabled people.

More Politically Active in Early 2000s

Rame and Fo again struck a strong political nerve in the early 2000s after Silvio Berlusconi took office as the Italian premier. In 2003, they wrote a new play, *L'anomalo bicefalo* (The Two-Headed Anomaly). In *L'anomalo bicefalo*, Berlusconi and Russian leader Vladimir Putin are the objects of assassination attempts in Sicily at a political rally. After the incident, Berlusconi receives what remains of Putin's brain so he can survive. Their consciousnesses meld, which results in much humor.

In 2006, Rame made a surprise run at politics when she ran for the Italian parliament under the Italy of Values Party. Elected to office as a senator, she was also nominated for Italy's presidency in 2006. Rame quit after two stressful, unproductive years. The following year, Rame and Fo published a memoir, *Una vita all'improvisa* (An Improvised Life). The couple was scheduled to appear in a production in Verona in the summer of 2013 of a new play by Fo, *Una Callas Dimenticata* (A Forgotten Callas).

However, by this time, Rame was suffering from ill health. She died on May 29, 2013, at her home in Milan at the age of 84. Summarizing her skills as an actress, Ronald S. Jenkins told the *New York Times'* Fox, "Whether she was telling stories in her kitchen or performing for thousands, she could cast spells that elicited tears, laughter or thoughtful indignation. Working onstage with her as a simultaneous translator was an impossible delight, like trying to find the words to translate Euripides, Goldoni, Brecht and Mae West all improvising next to me at once."

Periodicals

Associated Press, May 29, 2013.
Daily Telegraph (London, England), June 18, 2013.
The Guardian (London, England), May 30, 2013.
The Independent (London, England), June 3, 2013.
New York Times, June 3, 2013.
Times (London, England), June 3, 2013. □

Joey Ramone

American vocalist Joey Ramone (1951–2001) was a co-founder and the lead singer of the Ramones, the band that originated the punk rock style.

R amone started with the band as a drummer, but he very quickly became the Ramones' lead vocalist, and it was at that point that the group took on its familiar sound. "Joey Ramone's signature bleat was the voice of punk rock in America," wrote Steve Huey of *Allmusic*. With his sunglasses and long, dark hair, he helped shape the band's trademark look as well, with its unvarying outfit of leather jacket and torn jeans. Although the Ramones never had a chart-topping hit recording, they were one of the most influential bands of the last quarter of the 20th century, essentially originating and inspiring the entire punk movement, and it was Joey Ramone's tenor voice, unschooled but enthusiastic and clear in diction, that gave the movement its vocal sound.

Affected by Parents' Divorce

Joey Ramone was born Jeffrey Hyman on May 19, 1951, in Queens, New York. He was raised in the Jewish faith, and he grew up in the heavily Jewish neighborhood of Forest Hills. He had a younger brother, Mitchel, who later took the name Mickey Leigh and collaborated with Ramone on musical projects. When the Ramones were formed, all of them took the last name Ramone, suggested by a name in a 1950s gangster film that bassist Douglas Colvin (Dee Dee Ramone) had seen. Joey's father was a trucking company owner, and his mother, Charlotte, owned a Queens art gallery and was an artist herself. One central event in Ramone's childhood was his parents' divorce. Entering adolescence, he used rock music as an escape from emotional turmoil.

Ramone's problems were compounded by difficult times at Forest Hills High School, where he enjoyed art and music classes but was otherwise not a diligent student. "We were always on the outside, rejected by the girls—not by all girls, but by the pretty ones, who preferred guys with cars. Our protective shell was to shock people," Mickey Leigh was quoted as saying by John Leland of *The New York Times*. Ramone took up playing the drums, practicing in the basement of his mother's art gallery. He used LSD, was confined to a psychiatric hospital on two occasions, and only grew angrier. Ramone left home at 17, but his mother remained supportive, decorating his Manhattan apartment and giving him work at the gallery during lean times.

Ron Galella, Ltd./WireImages/Getty Images

In the early 1970s Ramone moved to the Greenwich Village neighborhood in lower Manhattan. He would live there for the rest of his life, except for short stints back home in Queens. For a time he performed with a band called the Snipers, adherents of the theatrical glam rock style popularized by British singer and songwriter David Bowie. But the music that had first inspired him was the raw rock and roll of the 1950s and 1960s, from rockabilly icon Gene Vincent to the Rolling Stones, music that made a statement with just voice, guitar, bass, and drums.

Moved from Drums to Vocals

In 1974, when he met guitarist John Cummings, bassist Douglas Colvin, and drummer-manager Tom Erdelyi, he was ready for a change. He and Cummings realized that they shared a background in Queens (Erdelyi was born in Hungary) and a variety of interests that included not only fast, simple rock music but also popular media and discourse oriented toward shock effects: horror films, comic books, and outrageous humor that advocated transgressive behavior. The band was originally a trio featuring Joey, Johnny, and Dee Dee Ramone; soon Erdelyi replaced Joey on drums, becoming Tommy Ramone, while Joey became lead vocalist.

Performing first at the Performance Studio and then repeatedly at the CBGB club, which became a central punk rock venue, the Ramones reached their characteristic sound quickly. It was fast, loud, and above all, compact. In an era when arena rock jams might extend for 20 minutes or more, an entire set by the Ramones might last that long—never more than half an hour, with a blistering sequence of two-minute songs barely separated by breaks. Yet, basic as they were, the Ramones' songs (mostly written by Dee Dee Ramone) were distinctive, with cartoonishly outrageous sentiments like "I Wanna Be Sedated" or "Teenage Lobotomy." The Ramones released the first of their 21 albums, *The Ramones,* in 1976, finishing it with a budget of just $6,000.

On July 4, 1976, the Ramones launched a tour of the United Kingdom at the Roadhouse club in London. The album and tour became enormously influential over the next quarter century, when the basic language of rock music shifted in the direction the Ramones had laid down and away from its roots in the blues. British followers of the Ramones, including the Sex Pistols, the Buzzcocks, and the Clash, were directly inspired by the 1976 tour. The Ramones quickly followed up their debut album with new music, and their first four albums, *The Ramones, Leave Home, Rocket to Russia,* and *Road to Ruin,* all appearing by the end of 1978, became classics of the new punk genre. Joey Ramone was the nearest thing the band had to a front man. He never married or had children.

Underwent Alcoholism Treatment

The Ramones never reached the top 40 of *Billboard* magazine's album sales chart; the Phil Spector–produced *End of the Century* (1980), their closest approach, reached number 44. The film *Rock & Roll High School,* with a soundtrack largely by the Ramones, raised their profile but still did not propel them to stardom. On the other hand, they never flamed out like most of the other early punk bands, and they continued to issue new music and tour indefatigably into the 1990s, with several changes in personnel but the core of Joey and Johnny Ramone remaining intact. Joey underwent successful treatment for alcoholism in the early 1990s. They played almost 2,400 shows over their 21-year performing career.

That career came to an end in 1996 after the release of the *Adios Amigos!* album, a farewell tour, and one final appearance at the Lollapalooza music festival in 1996. The band was no longer the commercial or creative force it once had been, but another factor was Joey Ramone's lymphoma diagnosis the previous year. He was given three to six months to live but recovered and remained active after the Ramones' breakup, working as a DJ and sponsoring music events in the New York area. Sometimes he appeared with pop vocalist Ronnie Spector, whose hit "Baby I Love You" (recorded with the Ronettes) the Ramones had covered, and who in turn admired the Ramones' music.

Living in his increasingly cluttered East Village apartment, Ramone became a familiar sight in the neighborhood. Often, when crossing a street, he would step down from the curb and return to touch it before proceeding. Observers were puzzled that in later life he became strongly interested in the stock market; Fox Business Network host Maria Bartiromo told the *New York Post* that

"most people don't know what a savvy investor Joey was." Ramone in turn wrote a song about her and performed it at CBGB. It was to be one of his last compositions.

Ramone worked on a solo album, but in 2000 he fell on an icy sidewalk and broke his hip as he was leaving a music event. The combined effects of cancer and hip surgery caused his condition to worsen, and he died on April 15, 2001, at the age of 49. His unfinished album was released under the title *Don't Worry About Me* the following year, but made little commercial impact despite the Ramones' recent induction into the Rock and Roll Hall of Fame. A block of Manhattan's E. 2nd St. was renamed Joey Ramone Place in 2003; the street sign had to be raised to a greater height than any other street sign in the city because of fans' repeated attempts to steal it. Other unfinished recordings, some of them reflecting Ramone's interest in early rock and roll, were assembled into the album " . . . Ya Know" in 2012.

Books

Beeber, Steven Lee, *The Heebie-Jeebies at CBGB's: A Secret History of Jewish Punk,* Chicago Review, 2006.

Leigh, Mickey, with Legs McNeil, *I Slept with Joey Ramone: A Family Memoir,* Simon & Schuster, 2009.

Periodicals

Billboard, May 26, 2012.

New York Post, September 27, 2010; February 27, 2014.

New York Times, April 22, 2001.

Orange County Register (Santa Ana, CA), April 23, 2001.

Washington Post, May 22, 2012,.

Online

"About," Joey Ramone Official Website, http://www. joeyramone.com/about/ (December 14, 2014).

"Joey Ramone," *Allmusic,* http://www.allmusic.com (December 14, 2014).

"Ramones," Rock and Roll Hall of Fame, https://www.rockhall. com/inductees/ramones/ (December 14, 2014).□

Horst Rechelbacher

Austrian-born entrepreneur Horst Rechelbacher (1941–2014) founded the enormously successful Aveda Corporation out of his Minneapolis hair salon and school back in the 1970s. Using formulations of fragrant botanical essences and nontoxic stabilizers, the company's first shampoos and other personal-care products developed a cult following and helped turn Aveda into a major retail brand that Rechelbacher sold to cosmetics giant Estée Lauder for an estimated $300 million in 1997.

ZUMA Press, Inc/Alamy

Horst Martin Rechelbacher was the last of three sons born to a financially struggling family in Klagenfurt, Austria, on November 11, 1941. At the time, Austria was part of Nazi Germany's Reich as a German-speaking land and Rechelbacher's father was drafted into military service on the brutal Eastern front during World War II. Captured by Soviet troops, Rudolf Rechelbacher was sent to Siberia as a prisoner of war. "He came back broken, a drinker," Rechelbacher once said of his father, according to his *Times* of London obituary.

Derailed by Car Accident

Rechelbacher's mother was a herbalist who worked at the local *apotheke* in their Klagenfurt neighborhood. Similar to a pharmacy, apothekes were a ubiquitous presence in German-speaking lands and became the basis of the modern-day pharmacy. In Austria and other European countries, licensed apothekers sold packaged medicines as well as homeopathic concoctions mixed on-site according to generations-old folk remedies. "Our house was filled with little bottles," Rechelbacher told Susannah Frankel, fashion writer for the London *Independent*, in 2002. "My mother sun-cooked everything. Every morning, we used to go out, pick species and bring them down. Then she would make tinctures, which she would put on shelves in the windows. She believed that the sun's energy helped the potency."

The Rechelbachers lived in a tiny apartment near a hairdresser's—a profession that looked alluring and glamorous to an impoverished adolescent. Rechelbacher started working at the salon at a young age, at first cleaning and lighting the fire at 6 a.m., and then entering a formal on-the-job apprenticeship program at age 14. He proved so skilled that his boss began sending him to Austrian hairdressing competitions and the teenager began winning top honors. Ambitious and creative, he landed in the Italian capital of Rome at age 17, which in the late 1950s was a locus for film stars and jet-setters from across Europe. He also worked in London and for Wella, the German haircare company.

Rechelbacher continued to enter professional hairstyling competitions in both Europe and North America. A 1963 visit to New York City for an American Beauty Association-sponsored event led to a job offer. "I was invited back for a seminar tour," he wrote in his 2008 business tome, *Minding Your Business: Profits That Restore the Planet.* "Within two months, I had made more money than I would have earned in an entire year in Europe. It was my first taste of the American Dream." He bought a sports car and one night, on business in Minneapolis, he was hit by a drunken driver on the highway. Because he had paid cash for the car, he had no auto insurance, and neither did the at-fault driver. Moreover, Rechelbacher had no health insurance, either, and faced a months-long recovery and rehabilitation period to mend broken vertebrae in his spine. "The hospital confiscated my passport, leaving me with no choice but to stay in Minneapolis and take a job at a salon to pay off my debt," he wrote in *Minding Your Business.*

Traveled to India

Once again, Rechelbacher rose quickly to the top of his game. He took as many client bookings as possible and soon became one of the Twin Cities' most in-demand stylists. With a $4,000 bank loan he opened his own salon, Horst of Austria, which eventually he renamed Horst & Friends as it expanded to several more sites in Minneapolis and St. Paul. Rechelbacher still liked fast cars and the fast life, however, and found himself in serious physical distress before his 30th birthday, which he later attributed to a combination of substance-abuse issues and daily proximity to the harsh chemicals used in salons. At the time, aerosol hair sprays contained propellants that were harmful to the Earth's ozone; nail polish was made with formaldehyde resin, and shampoos and conditioners used stabilizers and other ingredients that were of questionable safety and later were discovered to have endocrine-system disruptive properties—in other words, they had the potential to affect normal cell metabolism.

Rechelbacher learned how to make plant-based tinctures, again under his mother's tutelage, in the late 1960s. It was also during this period that he attended a lecture by a visiting Indian ayurvedic-medicine specialist, Swami Rama, that discussed the emerging science of biofeedback. Rechelbacher was so enrapt by Rama's explanation of the mind-body connection that he eventually made a pilgrimage to Rama's ashram in Rishkesh, India, to learn more about the ancient principles of ayurveda, a Sanskrit word meaning "the science of life."

By this time Rechelbacher had stepped away from the scissors and the mirror, and the grueling work of cutting and styling 30 to 40 heads a day at his salon. In 1970 he opened the Horst Institute, a cosmetology school in Minneapolis. The next step in his expansion was to convince an Indian herbalist he met at Rishkesh to come to Minnesota and help craft a line of hair-care products. After some trial and error, they came up with a fragrant clove shampoo, whose first batches were mixed in Rechelbacher's kitchen sink. That was the first product sold under the Aveda Corporation brand, which Rechelbacher formally registered in 1978. "Veda is also the Indian book of wisdom, and I placed an 'A' in front of that because it looked nice graphically," he later explained, according to his *Times* of London obituary.

Built Aveda into Elite Brand

Over the next several years Rechelbacher expanded Aveda's product range to other shampoos and conditioners, and sold the line himself via demonstrations at trade shows. In 1986 he bought an old Masonic Temple building on Central Avenue in downtown Minneapolis and renovated it to serve as his company headquarters and the new Aveda Institute for Beauty, Fashion, Wellness, and Art. Rechelbacher's products garnered a minor cult following among hair-styling professionals, with their signature fragrant scents and impressive performance, and he parlayed that into exclusivity contracts with salons across the United States branding themselves "Aveda Concept" businesses.

Never entirely content with managing a business empire, Rechelbacher hired others to serve as executives, including his 21-year-old son Peter. Rechelbacher was by then divorced from his wife, with whom he also had a daughter Nicole. Aveda entered into an ambitious expansion program in the late 1980s, opening its first freestanding store, on Madison Avenue in Manhattan, in October of 1989. More stores, salons, and products followed as Rechelbacher's concept grew alongside another cult-favorite, but less expensive retail line from Britain, the Body Shop. Both had a strong customer base, and the giants of the multibillion-dollar beauty sensed the shift to less toxic ingredients and environmentally friendly packaging. The U.S. based Estée Lauder company even created their own signature line, Origins, with standalone retail stores and a big-budget advertising campaign, but customers remained loyal to Aveda. In 1997 the Lauder family acquired Rechelbacher's company for an amount estimated at $300 million. Rechelbacher remained on board as a consultant for several more years. "It was a good transition for me," he told Frankel in the *Independent* interview a few years later. "My children didn't want to be in the business, and I never enjoyed management. I'm more the designer, the student, the mixer."

"Food as Medicine Is Real"

Years before, Rechelbacher's signature sales move was to trumpet the purity of his products by drinking his hairspray or ingesting a spoonful of his hair conditioner. "Don't put anything on your skin that you wouldn't put in your mouth," he often said, according to his *New York Times* obituary. One side project of his was Intelligent Nutrients, a vitamin and supplement company he launched in 1994 and kept for himself after the sale to Estée Lauder. He used some of his new fortune to expand it, buying a parcel of land in Osceola, Wisconsin, which he used as an organic farm, educational center, and palatial home powered by renewable energy. "When I sold Aveda, I became an activist, but what are you going to say to people if you don't practice what you teach?" he told Adam Spangler in *Vanity Fair* in 2009. "That's why I became a farmer . . . Food as medicine is real. Working with the medical profession, instead of just the hairdressers like I did with Aveda, gives me more credibility and people will pay more attention to my products."

Intelligent Nutrients (IN) grew over the years, just as Aveda had done, catching the consumer trend for healthier, organic products. In a *WWD* article that ran in 1999, Julie Naughton wrote that "Rechelbacher's pet Intelligent Nutrients project is the Wunderbar, something he calls a 'conceptual products experience center.' Others might simply call the setup a juice bar." He continued to serve as a consultant to Aveda, and spoke enthusiastically of its well-funded research and development division. "Lauder has a magical lab called the Sky Blue lab, filled with new innovations that don't step on Mother Nature's garments," he told Laughton. "When I was first exposed to that, I went berserk—I got so inspired."

Rechelbacher also established an eponymous foundation to support environmental awareness and sustainability issues, and was particularly vehement about cosmetic companies that branded their products as all-natural, arguing there was no certification mechanism in the United States to verify such claims. In addition to Deer View, the Wisconsin farm, Rechelbacher also had homes in Minneapolis and New York City. It was Osceola, however, that permitted him to indulge his love of nature and penchant for healthy living. "We are the soil," he explained to Sarah Ryle, a journalist for the *Guardian* newspaper. "We have the same percentage of water in our bodies as the earth. What we put into the soil, we eat because we eat what grows in the soil and so do the animals that we eat."

In that same interview, back in 1997, Rechelbacher discussed the toxicity in consumer products in modern society, with its reliance on chemically laden plastics and fossil fuels. "We can get cancer from the sun in the wrong amounts because the manufacturers have polluted the air," he told Ryle in the *Guardian*. "We can get cancer from the air. We can get cancer from the soil and from the water." Once again, Rechelbacher's pronouncements were prescient: despite a long commitment to healthy living, he was diagnosed with pancreatic cancer and died at his farm in Osceola on February 15, 2014. He was 72. His son and daughter survive him, and his second wife Kiran Stordalen, a former Aveda executive who co-managed the Intelligent Nutrients brand. "The most important thing about business is the intent behind it," Rechelbacher told Ryle back in 1997 in the *Guardian*. "I am interested in the long-term. Is the intent to serve beyond me? If it is only to enrich me, then it is certainly for nothing."

Books

Rechelbacher, Horst, *Minding Your Business: Profits That Restore the Planet,* Insight Editions, 2008.

Periodicals

Guardian (London, England), November 22, 1997.
Independent (London, England), June 13, 2002.
New York Times, February 23, 2014.
Times (London, England), February 20, 2014.
Vanity Fair, April 2009.
WWD, July 2, 1999.□

Bass Reeves

Bass Reeves (1838–1910) was the first African American to serve as a deputy U.S. marshal west of the Mississippi river. A former slave and illiterate, Reeves was a formidable tracker of wanted men, with knowledge of several Indian languages. Reeves was most likely the role model for the character, the Lone Ranger.

Reeves was born in Arkansas Territory in July 1838. (Some historians believe that he might have been born in Texas.) He was born into slavery, and spent his youth in north Texas. He was the property of Colonel George R. Reeves, who later served in the Texas legislature and as the speaker of the Texas house. After living in Lamar and Grayson counties in Texas as George Reeves' slave, Reeves allegedly got into conflict with his owner—perhaps even killing him after a card game—when he was a young adult.

Gained Familiarity with Indian Territory

Escaping into Indian Territory, Reeves lived among various tribes, including the Cherokee, Creek, and Seminole. He learned their ways of life and how to speak several of their languages. He also made money by serving as a bounty hunter for them. During the Civil War, Reeves most likely served in the Union Indian Home Guard Regiments. At the end of the war, Reeves returned to Arkansas where he bought land and was a farmer in the community of Van Buren.

While farming in Van Buren, Reeves would occasionally served as a guide for deputy U.S. marshals based at the federal court in Fort Smith, also located in Arkansas, who needed to enter Indian Territory. He would later offer these services to other peace officers. Because of his knowledge and skills, he was financially well-compensated for his services as a scout and tracker.

Became Deputy Marshal

In 1875, a new federal judge began presiding at the federal court in Fort Smith. When Isaac C. Parker took charge, he hired James F. Fagan as his U.S. marshal. Parker and Fagan commissioned 200 deputy marshals, including Reeves, whose reputation as a tracker and detective were widely known by law enforcement. Reeves was one of the first, if not the first, African American to receive this commission west of the Mississippi River. Reeves' grand nephew, Paul Brady, told Alex Hannaford of the London *Telegraph,* "At the time when Judge Parker appointed him, it was totally unheard of to give a black man a badge and a gun with jurisdiction to arrest white men. So a lot credit goes to Judge Parker. He was ahead of his time."

When Reeves joined the marshal service, the territory under Parker's jurisdiction was more than 75,000 square miles, including much of Indian Territory as well as Arkansas and parts of other adjacent regions. The deputy marshals, including Reeves, had to ride a circuit of more than 800 miles to Fort Reno, Fort Sill, and Anadarko. Because of the widespread landscape, pursuing and capturing outlaws usually required marshals to bring an entourage including a cook, a wagon, and at least one posse man with them for the journey. When Reeves had a posse man with him, it was usually a Native American.

Over the years, Reeves became even more well known for his skills as a peace officer. He was an expert marksman, and known for being a quick shot with both a pistol and rifle. He would travel the Indian Territory for months at a time executing his duties, on some occasions, and arrested both blacks and whites. During his duties, he concluded that there were three main types of outlaws in this region: murderers, horse thieves, and bootleggers. Some of his arrests became legendary. In 1882, Reeves arrested famous outlaw Belle Starr for horse theft, while in 1889 the threat of arrest by Reeves led to the end of the Tom Story gang's horse theft ring.

Had Sterling Reputation

Considered one of the best deputy marshals in the west, Reeves' reputation was sterling. He also created his own legend in terms of his appearance and image. His primary horse was a big red stallion with a distinctive white face. He also had two solid riding horses for pursuits, and a more common looking pony for undercover needs. A quality horse could give a criminal a tip off that the rider was a marshal.

Reeves' personal appearance was equally distinctive, and adaptive. He favored a large black hat with polished boots, and would use disguises when searching for his outlaws, including drover, cowboy, farmer, gunslinger, outlaw, and tramp. Some of his ploys would be elaborate. In one incident, to find and arrest a group of outlaw brothers, Reeves put together a tramp costume that included a hat that he shot into three times. He used his bedraggled appearance to gain entry into their home from their mother, claiming the shots came from a posse. She invited him in and told him he should join up with her sons. When her sons came home and agreed, Reeves spent the night. At night, after everyone went to sleep, Reeves cuffed them and took them into custody in the morning.

While making such arrests, Reeves did not fear for his own safety. In another widely publicized incident, which occurred while he traveled near the Osage Nation reservation, Reeves came upon a cattle rustler who was being hung by a lynch mob of cowboys near a big Oklahoma cattle ranch. Before the rustler could be strung up in a tree, but after the rope was on his neck, Reeves rode into the scene, cut down the man, and rode off with him in silence. The cowboys let him leave.

In 2006, young adult author Gary Paulsen, who wrote *The Legend of Bass Reeves*, told Anne Goodwin Sides of the *New York Times*, ''He'd ride alone into the center of hell and bring the men out, alive, if possible, or, if necessary, draped dead over a horse. He did this 3,000 times. Miraculously, he was never wounded. He rejected countless bribes . . . .''

Continued to Farm

While working as a deputy U.S. marshal, Reeves retained his farm in Van Buren. His grand-nephew, Paul Brady, told the *Canberra Times*, ''After he'd drop them [those he arrested or captured] off he'd clean up and go over to Van Buren where he lived on his farm. My father and his other kids always knew when Bass was expected back. They'd wait for him to arrive. Dad said Bass sat so tall in his saddle, and had such a large horse. His badge always shone brightly on his vest.''

After serving under Parker for 22 years, Reeves transferred to Wetumka in Indian Territory in 1897. When federal courts opened in Muskogee in 1898, Parker moved to this jurisdiction where he finished his career. In all, Reeves served as a deputy marshal for 32 years. During his tenure, he killed only 14 outlaws. He had a philosophy of not shooting a person unless it was absolutely necessary. He also arrested more then 3,000 violators of federal law, and during one incident brought in 17 men at once.

Though Reeves was responsible for capturing some of the most wanted criminals in the region, he once had to arrest a member of his family. When his own son was charged with murder for killing his wife in 1902, Reeves brought him in when the warrant arrived. Reeves spent two weeks looking for him to execute the warrant. His son was convicted of murder and sentenced to prison, but was later pardoned. Reeves himself had once been charged with murder. In 1877 he was charged with murdering the posse cook, William Leach, but was acquitted by Judge Parker. Reeves admitted to shooting him by accident while cleaning his gun.

Forced Out as Marshal

In 1907, Indian Territory became the state of Oklahoma. When Oklahoma became a state, Reeves was forced to retire as a marshal because of segregation and Jim Crow laws. Reeves spent the last years of his life as a member of the Muskogee police department. He was hired by Chief James Franklin ''Bud'' Ledbetter, who had also been a deputy U.S. marshal and was familiar with and respectful of Reeves. Ledbetter hired the reluctant Reeves because he needed assistance with his focus on bringing down bootleggers.

Reeves died on January 12, 1910, in Muskogee, Oklahoma. He was 71 years old. His funeral was a public event, widely attended. In the years after his death, Reeves lived on in folk songs written about his prowess as a marshal, but was eventually forgotten.

Considered Inspiration for Lone Ranger

By the 1980s, history professor Art Burton became interested in his story and was fascinated by the complexities of Reeves' stories. Burton told Alex Hannaford of the *Telegraph*, ''He was bigger than anything I'd seen in fiction. I always said when the public heard about Bass Reeves it was going to blow the lid off everything. He's actually like a combination of Sherlock Holmes, the Lone Ranger and Superman.''

In his book *Black Gun, Silver Star: The Life and Legend of Frontier Marshall Bass Reeves* (2008), Burton argued that Reeves was the actual inspiration for the Lone Ranger. In addition to a close name (Reid, similar to Reeves), Burton cited Reeves' use of Native American posse men, Tontos to his Lone Ranger. The Tonto character was a Potawatomi, a tribe that was forced to move to Oklahoma. Reeves also wore disguises like a black mask covering his face when he tracked down white fugitives, primarily because of his race. In addition, Reeves rode a white horse—as did the Lone Ranger—and used silver dollars as his calling cards, while the Lone Ranger used silver bullets. Finally, many of those arrested by Reeves were sent to Detroit, where the first Lone Ranger stories appeared on the radio in 1933. The prison system would have facilitated the spread of stories about Reeves.

Inspired Other Books

Burton also wrote another book in which Reeves was discussed, *Black, Red, and Deadly: Black and Indian Gunfighters of the Indian Territories* (1991). Other books and a film followed focusing on Reeves. A book by Reeves' grand-nephew Brady, was published in 2005, *The Black Badge*. A book for children, *Bad News for Outlaws: The Remarkable Life of Bass Reeves, Deputy U.S. Marshal* (2009), by Vaunda Micheaux Nelson received a Coretta Scott King Book Award in early 2010. News anchor/reporter turned filmmaker Nick Jones made an hour-long film on Reeves, *Bass Reeves: U.S. Deputy Marshal* (1994). It was filmed in Texas and Arkansas.

In the early 21st century, renewed attention on Reeves resulted in permanent honors. In November 2011, Muskogee, Oklahoma, named a bridge in honor of Reeves. The Bass Reeves Memorial Bridge spanned the Three Forks Harbor, crossing the Arkansas River between Muskogee and Fort Gibson. State senator Earl Garrison told Dylan Goforth of the *Muskogee Phoenix*, ''This is a fitting tribute to a true Muskogee legend.''

A few months later, in May 2012, a statute of Reeves was unveiled in a local park in Fort Smith, Arkansas. A group called the Bass Reeves Legacy Initiative group spent five years raising funds for the project and bringing it to fruition. Assistant director of the U.S. Marshall Service, Carl Caulk, spoke at its dedication. According to the Associated Press State & Local Wire's Lisa Hammersly, Caulk stated, ''He was one of our bravest and most legendary deputies.''

Periodicals

Associated Press State & Local Wire, May 27, 2012.
Canberra Times (Australia), August 16, 2013.
CNN Wire, August 6, 2013.
Muskogee Phoenix (OK), November 8, 2011.
New York Times, August 26, 2006.
South Bend Tribune (IN), April 1, 2005.
Telegraph (London, England), August 6, 2013.
Tulsa World (OK), March 10, 2007.

Online

"The Real-life Django: The Legendary African-American Wild
    West Marshal Who Arrested 3,000 and Killed 14 Men,"
    DailyMail.com, http://www.dailymail.co.uk/news/article-
    2264983/The-real-life-Django-black-Wild-West-marshal-
    Bass-Reeves-arrested-3-000-outlaws-killed-14-men.html
    (December 18, 2014).
"Reeves, Bass (1838-1910)," *Encyclopedia of Oklahoma History
    & Culture,* http://digital.library.okstate.edu/encyclopedia/
    entries/R/RE020.html (December 17, 2014).□

Robbie Robertson

Canadian guitarist and songwriter Robbie Robertson (born 1943) was best known as the lead guitarist in the rock group The Band, and he composed many of the group's most famous songs.

Jstone/Shutterstock.com

Robertson was highly influential as a guitarist in his own right. In an era filled with guitar heroics, he favored a precise, subtle approach in his recordings with The Band. "Instead of macho string bending and extended solos," noted *Guitar Player,* Robertson's playing became the ultimate servant to the song: sparse, funky, and ultra-melodic." Robertson was blamed by some for The Band's breakup in 1976, but he had been a member of the group since its beginnings in the late 1950s, through its stints accompanying Bob Dylan and its pathbreaking albums in the late 1960s and early 1970s; few other collections of musicians had worked together for so long. Robertson has remained active since The Band's breakup, releasing several solo albums and embarking on a significant second career as a film composer and film music producer.

Experienced Multireligious Upbringing

Robbie Robertson was born Jamie Royal Klegerman on July 5, 1943, in Toronto, Ontario, Canada. His father, Alexander David Klegerman, was a gambler and bookmaker active in Toronto's then-rough Cabbagetown neighborhood. Alexander Klegerman died when Robertson was young, and he took the surname of his mother's second husband. Nevertheless, he has said that he was influenced by the religious traditions of both his birth parents. "I always like to keep one hand in the tepee and the other hand in the synagogue," he told Robert Everett-Green of the Toronto *Globe & Mail.* "Wouldn't it be great if there was a combination of the two? You could go to synagogue, and it would be really hot in there."

Robertson spent summers with his mother on the Six Nations Reservation near Brantford, Ontario. There he heard Native Canadian music and songs from the country tradition in live shows, and he got relatives to teach him the guitar. He also began writing songs early in life, and back in Toronto he was heavily bitten by the rock and roll bug in the middle and late 1950s. Performing in a variety of bands including Little Caesar & The Consuls, Robbie Robertson and the Rhythm Chords, Robbie & the Robots, and Thumper and the Trambones, he eventually dropped out of school and began performing full-time.

Writing songs in Toronto, Robertson attracted the attention of the American-born Canadian rockabilly star Ronnie Hawkins, who recorded two of the teenager's songs ("Hey Boba Lu" and "Someone Like You"). That led to an invitation to Robertson to join Hawkins's band, the Hawks, as lead guitarist; the band already included drummer Levon Helm. The membership of the Hawks—Helm, Rick Danko, Richard Manuel, and Garth Hudson—would go on to form The Band a few years later. The group toured the United States and Canada with rock and roll legends Chuck Berry and Carl Perkins, and Robertson's guitar style developed rapidly, adding numerous unique moves to the classic blues structures of early rock and roll. His playing with Hawkins, *Guitar Player* noted, "showed [his] 6-string voice to be searing and ferocious, with over-the-top string bending and hedonistic pinch harmonics peppering his feral, [Telecaster]-centric style.''

Toured with Bob Dylan

By 1964 the Hawks were ready to strike out on their own. They recorded several tracks as the Canadian Squires in New York. The following year, having shocked the folk music world by adding electric instruments to his set at the Newport Folk Festival, Bob Dylan was in search of a band to accompany him on a tour featuring his new style. He met Robertson, who soon brought the rest of the Hawks aboard, and they toured with Dylan from September of 1965 through May of 1966. Robertson by this time had a reputation as a rising young guitarist, and he appeared on other albums during the period, including *So Many Roads* by the young blues prodigy John Hammond Jr. Rock critic Greil Marcus, quoted on Robertson's website, described Robertson's style on that album as ''all rough edges, jagged bits of metal ripping through the spare rhythm section.'' In 1967 the Hawks changed their name to The Band and were signed to the Capitol label.

The Band released their debut album, *Music from Big Pink*, in 1968, and its seemingly loosely structured jams and poetic treatment of Americana themes made it a founding document of roots-oriented rock styles. *Rolling Stone* magazine later ranked the album at number 34 on its list of the 500 greatest albums of all time. Four of its 11 tracks, ''To Kingdom Come,'' ''Caledonia Mission,'' ''The Weight'' (later featured in the film *Easy Rider*), and ''Chest Fever,'' were composed by Robertson, who did much to mix country flavors into the band's genre-crossing blend of rock, folk, and soul. In 1969 The Band performed at the giant Woodstock music festival and released a self-titled album, all of whose 12 songs were written or co-written by Robertson; his solo songwriting contributions included the heavily country-flavored standards ''The Night They Drove Old Dixie Down'' and ''Up on Cripple Creek.''

The Band released five more studio albums and several live albums, and continued to perform and record with Dylan on occasion.; their collaborative 1974 live album *Before the Flood* reached the top five on U.S. pop charts. The previous year the group had appeared before an estimated 650,000 people at the Watkins Glen music festival in New York State, reputed to be the largest rock concert in history. Robertson continued to exert strong control over The Band's creative direction, something not always welcomed by other members. But he wrote several more songs that have become rock music standards, including ''Ophelia,'' from the 1975 album *Northern Lights–Southern Cross*.

Performed Farewell Concert

The Band presented another famous live concert in 1976; held in San Francisco at the Winterland Ballroom, it was a swan song for the group and was titled *The Last Waltz*. Conceived by Robertson, the concert included a guest roster of the major artists who had influenced or been influenced by The Band, including Dylan, Hawkins, bluesman Muddy Waters, Canadian rock songwriters Neil

Young and Joni Mitchell, British guitar virtuoso Eric Clapton, country innovator Emmylou Harris, and many others. The concert was filmed by director Martin Scorsese and released as *The Last Waltz* in 1978; it is considered one of the greatest concert films of the rock era. Levon Helm blamed Robertson for the band's breakup, and the two remained on bad terms for many years.

Robertson's most significant activity since The Band's breakup has come in connection with films, several of them directed by Scorsese. He has approached each film as an individual project, composing music, producing recordings by others, or gathering preexisting tunes as desired. His film credits include Scorsese's *Raging Bull* (1980), *The King of Comedy* (1983), *The Color of Money* (1986), *Casino* (1995), *Gangs of New York* (2002), *Shutter Island* (2010), and *The Wolf of Wall Street* (2013). He also appeared opposite actress Jodie Foster in the 1980 drama *Carny*.

Robertson has also issued five solo albums: *Robbie Robertson* (1987), *Storyville* (1991, recorded in New Orleans with musicians from that city), *Music for the Native Americans* (1994, exploring the artist's Native musical heritage), *Contact from the Underworld of Redboy* (1998), and *How to Become Clairvoyant* (2011). He gave a dislike of touring as one of his reasons for leaving The Band, and he has rarely performed in public since then. But he has continued to play the guitar. ''I play guitar quite a bit, because I'm always in search of something,'' he told Everett-Green. ''I don't play to jam, but because I'm fishing. I'm looking for something, that I hope you can never find. If I do find it, I'm afraid I won't have a need to do this anymore.''

Robbie Robertson was inducted into the Canadian Songwriters Hall of Fame in 2011. He performed with the other members of The Band in 1994, except for Helm, upon the group's induction into the Rock and Roll Hall of Fame. Robertson and Helm were reconciled before Helm's death in 2012. Robertson is at work on an autobiography to be published by Random House and is the subject of a biography for children, *Rock and Roll Highway*, by his son, Sebastian Robertson.

Books

Hoskyns, Barney, *Across the Great Divide: The Band and America*, Hyperion, 1992.
Schneider, Jason, *Whispering Pines: The Northern Roots of American Music from Hank Snow to the Band*, ECW, 2009.

Periodicals

Globe & Mail (Toronto, Ontario, Canada), October 7, 2005, April 1, 2011.
Guardian (London, England), April 19, 2012.
Guitar Player, June 2011.
Maclean's, April 4, 2011.

Online

''Biography,'' Robbie Robertson Official Website, http://www.robbie-robertson.com (January 4, 2015).
''Robbie Robertson,'' *Allmusic*, http://www.allmusic.com (January 4, 2015).□

Mickey Rooney

American actor Mickey Rooney (1920–2014) had an eight-decade long career on stage, screen, and television, in which he did everything from song and dance to comedy to serious roles. Appearing in more than 300 film and television productions, Rooney's best known performances included Andy Hardy in the popular series of movies, musicals such as _Babes in Arms_ (1939), dramas like _The Human Comedy_ (1943), and family fare such as _The Black Stallion_ (1979). Married eight times and with an appetite for living large, Rooney's sometimes tumultuous personal life and financial issues also garnered headlines.

orn Ninian Joseph Yule, Jr., on September 23, 1920, in Brooklyn, New York, Rooney was part of a show business family. Both of his parents, Ninian Joseph Yule, Sr., and his wife Nell (nee Carter), were vaudeville performers. His father was a comedian, while his mother was a burlesque chorus line dancer. Rooney made his stage debut at the age of 17 months, and continued to perform in his parents' vaudeville act throughout his toddlerhood. By the age of two, Rooney had a starring role, appearing in a tuxedo and singing "Sweet Rosie O'Grady." From the first, he loved to perform, and never thought of acting as work.

Began Appearing in Films

Rooney's parents separated when he was four, and he continued to perform while living with his mother. She was a part of the chorus of vaudeville acts, while the young Rooney sang. As a young child, Rooney also made his film debut when his mother moved them to California. His first acting role came in _Not To Be Trusted,_ released in 1926. In the film, he played a dwarf pretending to be a child. His first role in a feature film came in 1927's _Orchids and Ermine,_ again playing a cigar-smoking dwarf.

In 1927, Rooney was cast in what would become a film series centered around the character Mickey McGuire, a naughty child. These shorts inspired Rooney's name change a few years later. The Mickey came from his film character, while Rooney was inspired by a vaudeville dancer named Pat Rooney. In 1932, Rooney legally changed his name from Joseph Yule to this moniker.

Signed by Metro-Goldwyn-Mayer

In 1934, Rooney's work in the film _Manhattan Melodrama_—he played Clark Gable's character, Blackie Gallagher, as a boy—resulted in a long-term contract with Metro-Goldwyn-Mayer (MGM). Setting the tone for his movie persona, Rooney played brash young characters in such films as _Ah, Wilderness!_ (1935), an adaptation of the Eugene O'Neill play. In _A Midsummer Night's Dream_ (1935), Rooney appeared as Puck, the same role he played in a stage version put on by director Max Reinhardt at the

Hollywood Bowl. Other film roles of note in this period came in _Little Lord Fauntleroy_ (1936) and _Captains Courageous_ (1937). While working at the studio, Rooney was educated at MGM studio school. Rooney also attended Pacific Military Academy and Fairfax High School.

In the mid-1930s, Rooney was cast as Andy Hardy in _A Family Affair_ (1937). This film would be the first in the long-running Andy Hardy series, which proved extremely popular with Depression-era film audiences in the United States and around the world. In the sentimental comedic films, Rooney's Hardy is the son of a small-town judge, who helps guide his offspring through his endless scrapes. Explaining the power of Hardy, Aljean Harmetz of the _International New York Times_ wrote, "As Andy Hardy, growing up in the idealized fictional town of Carvel, Mr. Rooney was the most famous teenager in America from 1937 to 1944; everybody's cheeky son or younger brother, energetic and feverishly in love with girls and cars." There were 15 Andy Hardy movies in all, and they earned a collective $80 million.

Built on Film Stardom

Because of the success of the Andy Hardy films, Rooney became a great earner, making $300,000 in 1938 alone. His role as Andy Hardy, in addition to his body of work as a juvenile, garnered Rooney a special Academy Award in 1939. Cementing Rooney's importance to the film industry in this period, Rooney was named the number one male box office star in the United States, as voted on by movie theater owners between 1939 and 1941.

In addition to playing Hardy, Rooney had other noteworthy roles which contributed to his reputation in this period. In 1938, he played a juvenile delinquent who becomes reformed in *Boys Town.* He also appeared in an adaptation of *The Adventures of Huckleberry Finn* (1939), and in the title role of the inventor biopic, *Young Tom Edison* (1940). Rooney became especially known for his work in musicals with Judy Garland, starting with *Babes in Arms* (1939). He was nominated for an Academy Award for his work in the role. In the MGM musicals Rooney made with Garland, the pair usually were in cahoots to put on a show. Other films in this genre starring Rooney included *Strike Up the Band* (1940) and *Girl Crazy* (1943).

In 1943, Rooney received another Academy Award nomination for his more serious work in *Human Comedy* (1943), written by William Saroyan. In this homefront drama, Rooney played a messenger who delivered telegrams, including those from the War Department informing families about the death of their loved ones. Another noteworthy early film for Rooney was *National Velvet* (1944), in which he played a jockey turned horse trainer for a young Elizabeth Taylor's horse-obsessed Velvet.

Completed Military Service

Rooney embarked on the first of his eight marriages. The first came in 1942, a brief marriage to sultry actress Ava Gardner. During these multiple marriages, Rooney had nine children and added two stepchildren. His propensity for marriage would gain the actor much notoriety over the years. Two years after marrying Gardner, Rooney joined the U.S. Army and spent much of his time in the service entertaining the troops. In all, Rooney spent 21 months in the military, and was discharged in 1946. He earned a Bronze Star for his contributions as a member of the military.

After leaving the service, Rooney faced many challenges. Not only were his savings stolen by a manager, but his contract with MGM ended. His last two MGM films under the deal came in 1948. That year, he played the lead in the musical version of *Ah, Wilderness,* titled *Summer Holiday.* Rooney also portrayed songwriter Lorenz Hart in the biopic *Words and Music.* In all, Rooney made 36 films while under contract with MGM.

As the studio system waned in Hollywood, Rooney spent much of the next few years working as a freelance actor. Though his popularity was declining over the decades, especially relative to his MGM years, he continued to work. In the late 1940s and early 1950s, Rooney explored his dramatic side in such films as *The Big Wheel* (1949) and *The Fireball* (1950). In 1954's *Drive a Crooked Road,* Rooney played a mechanic who becomes a criminal.

Rooney also moved into television. He starred in *The Mickey Rooney Show* in 1954. Though it lasted for only one season, he would go on to have many memorable small screen roles, including an Emmy nominated turn in *The Comedian.* This television play by Rod Serling, of *Twilight Zone* fame, aired as an episode of *Playhouse 90* in 1957.

Received Another Academy Award Nomination

Despite struggling with his waning fortunes, Rooney had a few high points in the 1950s and 1960s. In 1956, he was again nominated for an Academy Award for best supporting actor for *The Bold and the Brave.* In this role, he played a soldier who loses his life trying to protect the small fortune he wins playing craps. Rooney benefitted financially by gaining a percentage of the profits through his title role in 1957's *Baby Face Nelson.* Rooney also appeared in other major films of the decade, such as *The Bridges at Toko-Ri* (1954) and *The Last Mile* (1959).

Rooney appeared in a number of significant roles in the early 1960s as well. They included a small role in the Audrey Hepburn vehicle *Breakfast at Tiffany's* (1961). Rooney also appeared in *Requiem for a Heavyweight* (1962), starring Anthony Quinn, and was one of many stars who formed the ensemble in *It's a Mad Mad Mad Mad World.* Yet Rooney also suffered financial setbacks. Though he had earned $12 million by 1962, he declared bankruptcy after spending extravagantly, gambling, and poorly managing his finances. Essentially considered a has-been, Rooney starred in a number of B movies to pay off his accumulated debt, and the alimony from his seven marriages to date. These films included *How to Stuff a Bikini* (1965).

Underwent Career Revival

By the 1970s, Rooney underwent personal and professional changes which contributed to a career revival. After failing at more get-rich schemes, he quit drinking alcohol and converted to Christianity. In 1978, he married for the eighth and last time, to Jan Chamberlin. Unlike his other unions, this one lasted for more than three decades. Professionally, Rooney had two major performances in 1979. That year, he played a horse trainer in *Black Stallion* and landed his fourth Academy Award nomination. Also in 1979, Rooney made his Broadway debut in *Sugar Babies.* This homage to burlesque revues co-starred Ann Miller and led to a Tony Award nomination for Rooney. Rooney also toured in productions of *Sugar Babies,* spending nearly a decade affiliated with the revue.

Though he had reached his sixties, Rooney continued to work as he would, to a limited degree, until his death. In 1982, he won his first and only Emmy Award for his work in *Bill.* In this television movie, he played a developmentally delayed man who is forced to leave an institution and adjust to living in the outside world. The following year, Rooney was given an honorary Academy Award for his work in motion pictures to date. In the 1980s and beyond, Rooney regularly provided voice work for animated films like *The Fox and the Hound* (1981), *The Care Bears Movie* (1985), and *Little Nemo: Adventures in Slumberland* (1989). He took guest spots on hit series like *Full House* (1994) and *ER* (1998) as well.

In 1991, Rooney published his autobiography *Life Is Too Short* and, in 1996, again declared bankruptcy, owing nearly two million in back taxes. Highlights of his film career in the early 21st century included roles in *Night at the Museum* (2006) and its two sequels, playing a night watchman. He also had a cameo in *The Muppets* (2011).

In addition, Rooney still appeared on stage, appearing in productions of *Cinderella* in Britain playing Baron Hardup from 2007 to 2009. In 2007, Rooney and his wife toured in a performance called *Let's Put on a Show.*

Highlighted Elder Abuse Issue

Near the end of his life, Rooney returned to public attention under difficult circumstances. In early 2011, he took out a restraining order against a stepson, Christopher Aber, and his wife, Christina. Rooney accused them of elder abuse for withholding food and medication and the mismanagement of his finances after forcing him to sign over his assets. In addition to defrauding him of millions of dollars, he also charged that they made him think he was near poverty and compelled him to continue to work.

Filing a lawsuit against them in late 2011, Rooney testified before the U.S. Senate's Special Committee on Aging about the elder abuse issue a few weeks later. After giving his testimony, Rooney's finances were put under a conservatorship and Christopher and Christina Aber moved out of his home. When the suit was settled in 2013, Rooney was awarded $2.8 million from the Abers. Rooney also legally separated from Aber's mother, Rooney's eighth wife, in June 2012. Rooney was cared for by another stepson, Mark Rooney, and his wife, for the last two years of his life.

Rooney died of natural causes on April 6, 2014, at his home in North Hollywood, California, at the age of 93. Upon his death, noted author Neal Gabler summarized Rooney's appeal as an actor for CNN Wire. Gabler wrote, "Rooney had something that no other star had. Male stars—then as now—were largely figures of power: not just Cagney and Bogart, but Clark Gable, Errol Flynn, even Spencer Tracy. Moviegoers were attracted to their ability to dominate, to bend the world to their will. Rooney didn't exude power. He exuded pluck."

Periodicals

CNN Wire, April 7, 2014; April 8, 2014; May 9, 2014.

Globe & Mail, April 8, 2014.

Guardian (London, England), April 8, 2014.

International New York Times, April 8, 2014.

Times (London, England), April 8, 2014.□

Art Ross

Though Canadian hockey player, coach, and executive Art Ross (1886–1964) is most identified with the annually awarded Art Ross Trophy, he had a long, impressive career as a professional player, coach, and general manager. An innovative defenseman, Ross also made improvements to hockey nets and pucks that became National Hockey League standards for decades.

Arthur Howey Ross was born on January 13, 1886, in Naughton, Ontario, Canada. The son of Thomas Ross, he was the 12th of 13 children. At the time of Ross's birth, his father was the manager of the Whitefish Lake Trading Post. The trading post was owned by Hudson's Bay Company and it helped facilitate the on-going fur trade. As a child, Ross learned to skate on the local Simon Lake on skates with blades crafted from old metal files. He played hockey for fun with sticks made of out crooked tree limbs.

Emerged as Gifted Athlete

In the early 1890s, the trading post closed after the fur trade was supplanted by more profitable mining and lumber concerns in the region. Thomas Ross was transferred to Quebec at that time. The Ross family then moved to Westmount, Quebec, an English-speaking, well-to-do suburb of Montreal. There, Ross emerged as a talented athlete who played hockey, baseball, football, and lacrosse. He also raced motorcycles. An ambidextrous baseball player, he could pitch both right and left handed. The naturally gifted athlete later took up golf as an adult, and found he was skilled in this sport as well.

Though Ross had previous experience playing hockey in his youth, it was not until high school that he played formally organized hockey. His first experience came in Westmount High School in 1900. There his teammates included future Hockey Hall of Famers and brothers, Lester Patrick and Frank Patrick. All three were, by far, the best players on their team, and often played with local league teams as well. Ross played for bits of four seasons with the Canadian Amateur Intermediate Hockey League team, the Montreal Westmount.

In 1905, when Ross was 19 years old, he played in eight games for a Canadian Amateur Hockey League (CAHL) team. At the time, the CAHL was the best Canadian amateur league. While playing for this Montreal Merchants team—his first foray into this level of hockey—he scored ten goals in his eight games. He also showed his developing rushing defenseman skills.

Moved into Professional Hockey

Later in 1905, Ross moved to Brandon, Manitoba, to take a job as a bank clerk with the Merchant Bank. He continued to play amateur hockey as well. He began the 1905-06 season by playing in the senior Manitoba Hockey League's Brandon Wheat Cities. He played in eight games and scored five goals. Moving into professional hockey for the rest of the season, he played for the Brandon Elks.

Ross continued to be a bank teller by day and professional hockey player by night. Professional, semi-professional, and high amateur hockey was widespread in this period, with teams located in many small towns, and leagues that came and went on a regular basis. Ross emerged as a budding defenseman for the Elks. He was developing the unique ability to stickhandle and score in a manner similar to a forward. Unlike most defensemen of his era, he carried the puck into the offensive zone instead of passing it to a forward or shooting it down the ice.

While playing for Brandon in the 1905–06 and 1906–07 seasons, Ross's skills were noticed by opposing teams including the Kenora Thistles. This team in a very small Ontario town won its league championship and was in position to win the Stanley Cup—then given as a result of winning a challenge series, not via a playoff system—and arranged for the Brandon team to loan them Ross for the two-game Stanley Cup series against the Montreal Wanderers. Ross was paid $1,000 for his efforts.

In January 1907, Ross and the Thistles won the Cup. Ross did not score in the two Stanley Cup games but did contribute to the victory through a number of his signature offensive rushes. Because of his quality play in the Stanley Cup series, the Wanderers pursued Ross and bought his contract. Montreal was a better team than the Whistlers and he added depth to the team. Because of Ross's play in the 1907–08 season, Montreal finished first in the Eastern Canada Amateur Hockey Association.

Won Second Stanley Cup as Player

Ross repeated as Stanley Cup champion as a member of the Wanderers in 1908. He helped the team defeat squads from Winnipeg, Toronto, and Edmonton on its way to the championship. With his second Stanley Cup win in back-to-back years, he became only the second player to accomplish this feat after Jack Marshall, who did so in 1901 and 1902.

After the Stanley Cup victory, Ross signed to play and coach in the Canadian Hockey Association (CHA), a league that existed only for a few weeks in the 1909–10 season. He was a player-coach for All-Montreal Hockey Club. His team was able to play four games in the league's abbreviated season, and he scored four goals in them.

Also in the 1909–10 season, the National Hockey Association (NHA), a predecessor for the National Hockey League (NHL), had been founded. After All-Montreal and the CHA folded, Ross signed with an Ontario-based team, located in the mining community of Haileybury. He spent the rest of the 1909–10 season with the NHA Haileybury Comets, for which he earned $2,700. The Montreal Wanderers also joined the NHA. Ross then signed with his former team, and played there between 1911 and 1914. During the 1911–12 season, he scored a career high 16 goals on the season.

Fought for Better Salary

During this period, professionalization and player pay were emerging issues. In 1911, the players in the NHA attempted to gain what they considered a fair share of the revenues from the owners. Ross spoke up in these efforts, and articulately backed the players' position.

Three years later, Ross asked for an increase in his salary. Because the Wanderers did not seem open to giving him a raise, he attempted to convince other NHA stars to form a new league that would pay players higher salaries. For his efforts, the president of the NHA, Emmett Quinn, suspended Ross. In response, Ross stated he was a free agent and his Wanderers contract was no longer valid. Quinn, in turn, said Ross was suspended from organized hockey.

Though Ross signed a number of players, he was unable to form a new league. After that, Ross asked to be reinstated in the NHA. Because the owners understood that they could not just suspend Ross but would have to shelve all the players he signed and negatively impact their own league, Ross was allowed back into the NHA.

Released by the Wanderers at the beginning of the 1914–15 season, Ross joined the Ottawa Senators for two seasons. While playing for the Senators, he helped devise a new defensive strategy known as the "kitty bar the door." This formation—an early version of the neutral zone trap—was especially effective at a time when unstructured offenses were the norm. Ross's Ottawa squad bested the Wanderers for the right to play in the Stanley Cup finals in 1915, but lost to the Vancouver Millionaires of the Pacific Coast Hockey Association.

Played Briefly in NHL

Moving back to Montreal to run his sporting goods store, Ross re-joined the Montreal Wanderers for their last season in the NHA. He played in 16 games and scored six goals. The NHL was officially formed in 1917, and Ross again signed with the Montreal Wanderers, which had been a founding team in the new league. He was hired as both a player and the team's coach. After only three games, the Montreal Arena burned to the ground. The Wanderers had no place to play and disbanded. Ross's NHL career as a player reached an end as well.

Retiring from play, Ross had played professionally for 14 years in all. In his 167 regular season professional games, he scored 85 goals. In all, he played 192 high quality league games, with 102 goals and 34 assists. Ross scored one goal in his NHL games.

In retirement, Ross wanted to remain part of the game. He became a referee and an on-ice official. Next, Ross became a coach. His first coaching job, post-playing years, came with the senior club of the Hamilton Tigers. As he had on the ice, Ross demonstrated strong skills as a coach as well.

Hired as First Coach of Bruins

In 1924, millionaire Charles F. Adams brought an NHL franchise to Boston, Massachusetts, and hired Ross as his first coach. Ross later served as the team's general manager as well. He gained a reputation for discovering talent, bringing such iconic players as Eddie Shore, Milt Schmidt, Woody Dumart, and Bobby Bauer to the team. He led the Bruins to ten league championships and three Stanley Cups. Boston's Stanley Cup victories came in 1929, 1939, and 1941.

After Ross stepped down as coach of the Bruins in 1942, he was replaced by one of his former players, Dit Clapper. Ross then became Boston's vice president and general manager. At the same time, he became a governor of the NHL as well.

While Ross helped build the Bruins into a formidable team, he also made long-lasting contributions to the way the NHL game was played. He was the designer of the B-frame, or rounded back, goal net. This net was important because pucks were kept inside the netting more consistently than with the previous nets, the square goal nets. Ross's model also featured better mesh. Ross's net was used in the game until the 1980s.

Ross also played a key role in getting the NHL to use what became known as the Art Ross puck. This puck was more consistent than previous models. It featured a beveled edge, and was made of synthetic rubber instead of natural rubber. The Art Ross puck was used until the late 1990s. In addition, Ross was key in the introduction of the leather helmet, though such headgear were not consistently used in this era. Ross had also successfully supported and promoted the sport of hockey in Boston.

Inducted into the Hall of Fame

While still holding the general manager post for the Bruins, Ross received a number of honors from the NHL. During the 1947–48 season, Ross was honored for his many contributions to the game when the NHL introduced the Art Ross Trophy. The award has been given annually to the top scorer in the league each season ever since. In 1949, Ross was included in the inaugural class of the new Hockey Hall of Fame.

After 30 years with the Bruins, Ross retired as general manager of the Boston squad in 1954. In ill health at the end of his life, he spent his final years in a nursing home in Massachusetts. Ross died in Medford, Massachusetts, on August 5, 1964. He was 78 years old. In the years after his death, he received numerous additional tributes for his contribution to hockey, including being named to Canada's Sports Hall of Fame.

Periodicals

Globe and Mail, August 5, 2004.
Montreal Gazette, August 6, 1964.

Online

"Art Ross: Bigography," *The Official Site of the Hockey Hall of Fame,* http://www.legendsofhockey.net/LegendsOfHockey/jsp/ (January 3, 2014).
"Art Ross: Spotlight," *The Official Site of the Hockey Hall of Fame,* http://www.hhof.com/htmlSpotlight/ (January 3, 2014).
"Art Ross: Statistics," *The Official Site of the Hockey Hall of Fame,* http://www.legendsofhockey.net/LegendsOfHockey/jsp/ (January 3, 2014).
"Art Ross," Sudbury Heritage Museums, http://www.sudburymuseums.ca/(January 3, 2014).
"Honoured Member: Art Ross," Canada's Sports Hall of Fame, http://www.sportshall.ca/stories.(January 3, 2014). □

Porfirio Rubirosa

Dominican diplomat and jet-setter Porfirio Rubirosa (1909–1965) was a charming bon vivant whose romances with high-profile women made him a fixture in the tabloid press and gossip columns of the 1950s. His storied life came to a equally cinematic end in 1965 when the tuxedo-clad raconteur, returning home after a night celebrating a polo team victory, lost control of his Ferrari on a park lane in Paris at eight in the morning.

Hulton Archive/Getty Images

Porfirio Rubirosa Ariza came from a modest background in the Dominican Republic, where he was born on January 22, 1909, in the city of San Francisco de Macorís in Duarte Province. His father, known as Don Pedro, had served as head of a small mounted militia that controlled some valleys and mountain passes in the highlands of Cibao, and when a new regime came to power in Santo Domingo, the port city and capital, Rubirosa's father was rewarded with an ambassadorship to the Virgin Islands. In 1916 Don Pedro was posted to Paris and the young Rubirosa spent his formative years in the French capital.

Recruited as Presidential Bodyguard

The Rubirosa family, which included an older brother and older sister, lived at 6 Avenue Mac-Mahon in Paris and Rubirosa was sent to a series of elite schools in the city and surrounding environs. He was an admitted failure in nearly all academic pursuits but was sociable, athletic, and a surprisingly daring goaltender at the soccer net. His athletic prowess transitioned to the dance floor of Montmartre nightclubs, which he frequented with school friends in his teens. The young men took full advantage of the slightly debauched free-wheeling atmosphere of Paris in the mid-1920s. Rubi, as his friends and family called him, finished out his formal education in Calais, where he learned to box. At one point his father—by then a senior diplomat back in Santo Domingo—was believed to have stopped sending money to his youngest child when the hedonistic teen failed to pass his baccalaureate exam.

In 1928, Rubirosa returned to his family in Santo Domingo and tried to make the best of the situation, which grew dire after the death of his father. He made some attempt at studying for a law degree, as his family wished, but found an easier route to success when he met the country's newly installed dictator General Rafael Leonidas Trujillo. A ruthless and venal operator, Trujillo recruited the popular and athletic Santo Domingo law student to serve in his elite presidential guard. Rubirosa was surprised to find that he liked the athletics-focused discipline of the military and the respect his uniform commanded. When Trujillo's teenage daughter Flor de Oro returned home from a stint in France, Rubirosa impressed her with his fluent French and she was smitten by the young officer's attentions.

Flor Trujillo proved the first in a long list of women who capitulated to Rubirosa's attention, and she convinced her father to permit the two to wed. The couple were married in December of 1932 and Rubirosa began his diplomatic career that same year. The couple moved to Europe where Rubirosa's role was to represent Trujillo's government, but embassy records have scant evidence of his signature on any official documents or cables. At the 1936 Berlin Olympic Games Rubirosa and Flor sat with Nazi German leader Adolf Hitler in the chancellor's private viewing box.

Charmed French Film Star

Rubirosa was believed to have been sterile, perhaps from a childhood case of the mumps. In any case, an inability to father any children was the one element that made his complicated romantic life slightly less problematic. A profligate womanizer, he was unfaithful to Flor and resumed his nightclubbing habits once they settled in Paris. "He was out every night, and would come home at dawn, covered with lipstick," Flor once said of him, according to *Vanity Fair* journalist Gary Cohen.

The couple divorced in 1938 and Rubirosa briefly fell out of favor with Trujillo, now his ex-father-in-law. When World War II erupted in 1939 Rubirosa managed to remain in France even after it was occupied by Nazi Germany but had to leave Paris. He went to the city of Vichy, where right-wing French collaborationists were permitted a semblance of self-rule. Around this same period he met screen star Danielle Darrieux, a renowned beauty and reportedly the highest paid actress in France at the time.

The almost-divorced Darrieux was already a focus of media attention and her affair with the handsome Dominican with a sketchy past was a tabloid-ready wartime romance tale. Rubirosa was eventually sent to a luxury detention camp in Bad Nauheim, a German spa town, where Darrieux was permitted to visit him in exchange for agreeing to appear at a film premiere in Berlin, the Nazi capital. Rubirosa was released and the two married in September of 1942, but Darrieux paid a steep price for her transgression in visiting Berlin. She and Rubirosa became the target of French Resistance guerrillas, derided as collaborators, and in 1944 were victims of a sniper attack as their open-air car drove away from a Paris nightclub. Rubirosa took a bullet in the kidney but recovered his health with characteristic aplomb.

Married Duke Tobacco Heiress

After the war's end in 1945 Darrieux was able to resume her film career, and her husband accompanied her to Rome on one project. It was there he met the woman who would become his third wife, American heiress Doris Duke. Characterized since her teens as the richest woman in America, Duke inherited a vast tobacco and hydroelectric power fortune and was skittish of most suitors. She was also athletic, adventurous, and enjoying a brief career as a journalist during this period of her life. In that role she was sent to interview Darrieux for the fashion magazine *Harper's Bazaar*. Duke found Rubirosa intriguing but her legal advisors warned her about Rubirosa's slightly seedy past and still-strong ties to the Trujillo regime. On more than one occasion he was suspected of having used his international diplomatic immunity for personal gain or nefarious acts. One incident involved some missing jewels he had offered to retrieve in Madrid during the Spanish Civil War, and an earlier incident placed him in New York City around the time of an attempted assassination of one of Trujillo's exiled opposition leaders. "I asked Rubi straight out of the blue whether he would consider killing me to get my money," Duke recalled years later, according to Jeremy Scott's *The Irresistible Mr. Wrong*. He replied quietly, Duke said, with the words, "I have done much worse."

Duke reportedly paid Darrieux a $1 million sum for granting Rubi his second divorce. The Dominican diplomat became internationally famous almost overnight when he wed one of the world's wealthiest women on September 1, 1947. Even Trujillo was astonished by his ex-son-in-law's extraordinary postwar rise and offered Rubirosa any ambassadorial post he wished. He chose Argentina for its polo grounds, his newest fixation. The sport required a certain degree of physical risk and expensive equipment in the form of specially bred horses, which he began acquiring in rapid fashion with his new wealth. Both he and Duke were said to have been unfaithful in the marriage, and in Buenos Aires Rubirosa was said to have added the Argentinean president's equally formidable wife, Eva "Evita" Perón, to the long list of his romantic liaisons. In Paris Rubirosa bought a parcel of choice real estate, a three-story townhouse on the rue de Bellechasse, which Duke's team of interior decorators filled with expensive antiques. On its third floor Rubirosa had a regulation boxing ring set up, plus a full bar to host after-hours parties. From the four-year marriage to Duke he even acquired a private plane, a B-25 bomber refitted as a luxury long-distance aircraft.

Earned Millions from a Brief Marriage

After his divorce, Rubirosa fell out of favor with Trujillo once again after he was named in two separate but high-profile divorce cases in which the husband alleged infidelity on the part of the wife. In the early 1950s Rubirosa also dated Hollywood starlet Zsa Zsa Gabor, the former Miss Hungary. She was at the peak of her career when they met in 1952, but still married to British actor George Sanders and with a daughter from an earlier marriage to hotel tycoon Conrad Hilton. Rubirosa and Gabor carried on a highly public affair, and Gabor was divorced from Sanders in 1954. By then, however, Rubirosa had wed another enormously wealthy American woman, the Woolworth retail chain heiress Barbara Hutton. Hutton was 41 years old at the time—three years younger than Rubirosa—but already suffering from health and substance-abuse related issues by the time of their marriage, which lasted just 53 days. The entire debacle included a press conference summoned by Gabor, who sported a black eye she claimed Rubirosa had given her when she refused to marry him as prenuptial negotiations with Hutton were reaching a crucial stage.

As with Duke, Rubirosa had been compelled to sign an ironclad prenuptial agreement, but walked away from the seven-week escapade with a payout that earned him around $66,000 for every day of his fourth marriage. "He is the ultimate sorcerer," said Hutton of the man who was her fifth husband, according to Scott, author of *The Irresistible Mr. Wrong*. Gabor wrote extensively of Rubirosa in her own memoirs, and the U.S. Federal Bureau of Investigation even compiled what proved to be a detailed 20-year dossier on the Dominican charge d'affaires who rarely turned up at any embassy during daytime business hours. "He's an excellent diplomat," Trujillo once said of him, according to Cohen in the *Vanity Fair* profile, "because women like him and because he is a liar."

Guests of JFK

Rubirosa lived richly for a few years off the proceeds of his advantageous marriages. He skied in the Swiss resort of Gstaad, yacht-hopped on friends' boats on the French Riviera, exercised his ponies during polo season in Deauville, and was harassed by paparazzi in Palm Beach. In October of 1956, he married a 19-year-old French actress, Odile Rodin, and settled down in a villa outside Paris in Marnes-la-Coquette. Remarkably he remained still in service to Trujillo, who posted him to Havana, Cuba, as ambassador for a brief stint in 1957, just before the Cuban Revolution. Trujillo was assassinated in May of 1961, and Rubirosa spent a few weeks that summer as guests of the Kennedys, the American political dynasty with its own ties to the jet-set and Hollywood celebrities. He sailed with new U.S. President John F. Kennedy and First Lady Jacqueline Kennedy aboard the president's private yacht the *Honey Fitz,* unsuccessfully trying to convince the Kennedy and the U.S. State Department to back Trujillo's son as successor. Instead, the new regime in Santo Domingo stripped Rubirosa of his diplomatic status in 1962.

Rubirosa's fifth wife, nearly 30 years his junior, outmatched his notorious carousing. In the early morning hours of July 5, 1965, the pair were separated as Rubirosa and his polo teammates celebrated their victory earlier that day in the Coupe de France championship. By then Rubirosa had also attempted to break into an even more expensive sport, Formula One racing, and owned a prized Ferrari. He finally set off for Marnes-la-Coquette after leaving the nightclub Jimmy's on the Boulevard Montparnasse after the sun rose. He crossed the Seine River via the Ponte

de St. Cloud and entered the bucolic Bois du Boulogne, the park that borders the wealthier suburbs of Paris. On the Allée de la Reine Marguerite he lost control of the Ferrari and hit a stately chestnut tree. Rubirosa's thoracic cavity was crushed by the Ferrari's handcrafted wooden steering wheel and he died en route to the hospital.

Rubirosa's storied life has long been a subject of fascination. "My grandfather would just send him a blank check whenever Rubi needed it," Trujillo's grandson Ramfis Trujillo, Jr. told Cohen for the 2002 *Vanity Fair* article. "He was the best public relations money could buy for the regime, and the only condition for the money was that Rubi fly the Dominican colors whenever he had a party."

Books

Levy, Shawn, *The Last Playboy: The High Life of Porfirio Rubirosa,* Fourth Estate, 2005.

Scott, Jeremy, *The Irresistible Mr. Wrong,* Robson Press/Biteback Publishing, 2012.

Periodicals

New York Times, June 5, 1961; September 16, 2005.

Sunday Times (London, England), June 10, 2012.

Vanity Fair, November 2002.□

Olof Rudbeck

The Swedish scientist and physician Olof Rudbeck (1630–1702) was best known for his discovery of the human lymphatic system.

That discovery occurred almost by chance, early in Rudbeck's career, but he had the intelligence and the fresh eye to understand that what he was seeing was important. A professor of medicine at the University of Uppsala, Rudbeck later embarked on a variety of extremely ambitious projects, ranging from botany to comparative linguistics, horticulture, architecture, and even civil engineering. This later work, which included a vast attempt to demonstrate that Sweden was the cradle of civilization and the site of the lost civilization of Atlantis, was less significant than his work on the lymphatic system, and some of it was ridiculed. Taken as a whole, however, Rudbeck's life is one of the most fascinating and unusual in the annals of science.

Built Clock as Child

Olof (also known as Olaus) Rudbeck was born in 1630 in Västerås, Sweden. His father, Johannes Rudbeckius, was the Lutheran bishop of Västerås and had previously taught mathematics and theology at Uppsala. Rudbeck had a strongly religious upbringing (his mother, Malin, had read the Bible from cover to cover seven times), but he was a curious child who liked music and art and at one point built a wooden clock that would strike the hour with its

OLOF RUDBECK D. Ä.

Bookworm Classic/Alamy

own bell. Rudbeck's parents both died when he was in his teens, and he entered the University of Uppsala in 1648, majoring in medicine and attending basic lectures in anatomy and botany. He was frustrated that the school's small medical program and budget made it impossible for him to get permission to do experimental work himself.

In the fall of 1650, he happened to see two women butchering a calf at Uppsala's farmers' market, and he observed a milky substance, not blood, coming out of the slaughtered animal's chest. He asked the woman if he might cut the calf open further, and he found a blood-vessel-like tube that held a colorless liquid, connected to the calf's liver. What he had discovered was the lymphatic system, which regulates fluid levels and the presence of toxins in the body, and contributes to the functioning of the immune system. Working in a small shed on animals discarded by Uppsala butchers, he performed hundreds of dissections and began identify with considerable accuracy the functions of the glands, nodes, and vessels that make up the lymphatic system, in humans as well as animals.

Word of Rudbeck's discovery spread, and in the spring of 1652 he was invited to demonstrate his discoveries before Sweden's Queen Christina. Carrying out a dissection on a dog, he impressed the queen and her advisors, and the queen ordered that he be given a scholarship to study at the University of Leiden in the Netherlands. Before he departed for classes in the fall of 1653, he published his findings in a book,

Nova exercitatio anatomica (New Anatomical Exercises—academic writings at the time were generally in Latin).

Traded Charges with Danish Scientist

When he arrived in Leiden, he soon learned that the Danish scientist Thomas Bartholin had also made advances in studying the lymphatic system, and in fact had published his findings slightly in advance of Rudbeck's own book. One of Bartholin's students published a pamphlet that accused Rudbeck of plagiarism. Rudbeck, who had publicized his findings at the Swedish court well in advance of Bartholin's writings, fired back with a pamphlet of his own, and the dispute raged for several years. Aside from this issue, Rudbeck did well in the Netherlands; he received a botany degree and was admired for his skills as an anatomical researcher. Rejecting job offers in the Netherlands and in France, he returned to Sweden, where he joined the medical faculty at the University of Uppsala in 1655.

Rudbeck became a full professor in 1660, and "an enthusiast in all that he did," according to the *Dictionary of Scientific Biography.* He set about raising the university's prestige. He established a botanical garden that still exists (it was later renamed for Carolus Linnaeus, the creator of the Linnean system of classification of life forms, who was the student of Rudbeck's son), and designed and built a large anatomical auditorium, part of which is also still in existence. In 1658 he published a *Catalogum plantarum* (Catalogue of Plants), describing 1052 different plants. He served as professor at the university until 1691, and beginning in 1662 was its governor. He built a new chemistry lab at the university during this period, but he encountered disagreements with his colleagues after the university began running a budget deficit, and he resigned in 1670.

Greater efforts in cataloging plants were still to come for Rudbeck, but botany and medicine were just a small part of his interests. He built a machine shop and exhibit at the university, and he was active as an architect and builder of homes and bridges (for which he devised unique designs). Sometimes he did construction work on his buildings himself. An avid music lover, he composed several pieces and sang in a bass voice that, it was said, could drown out trumpets and drums. Rudbeck developed an unreliable but innovative system for measuring the age of monuments by noting the thickness of the moss on them. He printed his own books and dabbled in the philosophy of René Descartes, the hot intellectual topic at universities of his time.

Claimed Sweden as Site of Atlantis

Rudbeck was also an enthusiastic promoter of Sweden's natural and productive resources and for a time was employed to this end by the Swedish government. He was a patriotic supporter of all things Swedish, and it was this tendency that seems to have led him into the most questionable of his scientific enterprises: the four-volume work known as *Atlantica* (the Swedish title was *Atland eller Manheim*), which was written in Swedish and Latin and began appearing in 1679. Here Rudbeck argued that Sweden had been the cradle of civilization, the lost society of

Atlantis, from which all the great societies of the ancient world had evolved, and he found runic inscriptions and ruins in the north of Sweden that he thought supported his thesis. He believed that the language of the biblical Adam had in fact been a form of Swedish, which had spawned Greek, Latin, and other ancient languages. The book was satirized by later writers and even held up by the French encyclopedists as an example of how *not* to conduct etymological research, but it was one of the world's first attempts to systematically carry out what would now be called comparative linguistics.

An ingenious civil engineer, Rudbeck supervised the paving of Uppsala's streets with stones and even devised river wharves with a kind of early automatic doorway that opened when a ship approached. He designed a system of water pipes for the city of Uppsala and built some of the first greenhouses in northern Europe at the botanical garden. At the university, Rudbeck taught a course in the construction of military fortifications.

Around 1670 Rudbeck began to plan his magnum opus, a work describing all known plants, complete with illustrations. Over the next 30 years he hired graphic artists and engravers to make woodblocks, enlisting several of his own children in the enterprise. By the year 1700 3,200 woodblocks were ready, and the first two volumes of the work appeared under the title *Campus Elysius* (Elysian Field), featuring grasses, lilies, and orchids. The entire work was planned to cover 7,000 species.

But in 1702 a small fire in Uppsala quickly spread through the city's old buildings and burgeoned into a deadly conflagration. The aging Rudbeck, according to legend, stood on the roof of one of the university buildings and shouted instructions to firefighters and panicked residents below, but his own home, containing all his books and many of the woodcuts for the next volumes of his botanical masterwork, was destroyed. Soon after the fire, on September 17, 1702, Rudbeck died in Uppsala.

Books

Gillispie, Charles Coulston, ed., *Dictionary of Scientific Biography,* Scribner's, 1981.

King, David, *Finding Atlantis: A True Story of Genius, Madness, and an Extraordinary Quest for a Lost World,* Harmony, 2005.

Online

"From Anatomy to Atlantis," *Lost Manuscripts,* http://www.lostmanuscripts.com/tag/rudbeck/ (January 8, 2015).

"Rudbeck, Olof," *Galileo Project,* http://www.galileo.rice.edu/Catalog/NewFiles/rudbeck.html (January 8 2015).□

S

Carole Bayer Sager

Perhaps best known for penning such songs as "That's What Friends Are For" and "Arthur's Theme," American singer and lyricist Carole Bayer Sager (born 1947) was a prolific pop song writer beginning in the 1960s. She won numerous awards for her work, especially lyrics and songs written for films, and recorded three albums herself.

Born Carole Bayer on March 8, 1947, in New York City, she was the daughter of Elias and Anita (Nathan) Bayer. She enjoyed writing poetry as a child. She began her pursuit into songwriting as a teenager while attending the High School of Performing Arts in New York City. There, she concentrated her studies on piano and drama.

Became Interested in Songwriting

Sager soon became interested in songwriting. She attributed her interest in songwriting at such a young age to ventriloquism. She explained to Jim Bessman of *Billboard,* "It seemed to me like songwriting was the next step after the ventriloquism." To Bessman, Sager recalled the popularity of ventriloquist Paul Winchell and how speaking through a dummy "was another way to say things for me that I couldn't say for myself—and without having to take full responsibility."

At the age of 15, Sager wrote her first hit song, "A Groovy Kind of Love," for British pop group Wayne Fontana and the Mindbenders. With the song, she not only had a hit but also popularized the word groovy. Despite her early songwriting success, Sager attended New York University (NYU), where she studied Speech, English and Dramatic Arts. She completed a B.S. at NYU.

Married Record Producer

In her early twenties, Sager married record producer Andrew Sager in 1970, when she was in her early twenties. The couple divorced in 1978, but she kept her distinctive name, Carole Bayer Sager. At the same time, she began working in the theater, penning lyrics to George Fishchoff's music for the 1970 musical *Gregory.* Still, Sager struggled to match the success of her first pop song.

It was not until 1975, nine years after Sager's first number one smash hit, that "Midnight Blue," co-written and performed by fellow singer-songwriter Melissa Manchester, topped the charts. From there, Bayer Sager's writing, in collaboration with some of the biggest names in the music industry, established her as one of the most successful lyricists of the 1970s and 1980s. In this period, popular singers such as Frank Sinatra, Barbra Streisand, Dolly Parton, Elton John, Stevie Wonder, Aretha Franklin, Roberta Flack, Carly Simon, Bette Midler, and Michael Jackson performed Sager's lyrics or collaborated with her on pop songs.

Sager built on her popularity by recording and releasing her own album on the Elektra label in 1977. The self-titled release was popular worldwide. One single from *Carole Bayer Sager,* "You're Moving Out Today," was co-written by Bette Midler and Bruce Roberts, and became an international number one single. While many lauded *Carole Bayer Sager,* she was reluctant to perform in public at this stage in her career. She followed *Carole Bayer Sager* with her second album, *. . . Too,* in 1978.

Worked With Marvin Hamlisch

Also in the mid-1970s, Sager began what would become a fruitful professional, and later personal, relationship with award-winning composer Marvin Hamlisch in 1975. Early in their collaboration, the pair wrote the extremely

s bukley/Shutterstock.com

successful theme song for *The Spy Who Loved Me,* "Nobody Does It Better." For the song, Sager and Hamlisch received Academy Award and Golden Globe Award nominations in 1977. Another lauded composition written by the pair, "Through the Eyes of Love," the theme from the ice skating drama *Ice Castles* received the same nods.

In 1979, Sager and Hamlisch co-authored the book for the Broadway musical comedy, *They're Playing Our Song.* The comedy, also written with the assistance of Neil Simon, was a loose autobiography of Sager and Hamlisch's relationship. In *They're Playing Our Song,* a professional collaboration between female lyricist Sonia Walsk and composer Vernon Gersch turns romantic. The comedy ran for three years on Broadway and won several Tony Awards. Sager and Hamlisch's personal relationship soon reached an end as well.

Also in 1979, Sager began a new working relationship with pianist and composer Burt Bacharach. As with her collaboration with Hamlisch, it quickly turned romantic. The couple married and adopted a child in the early to mid-1980s. They also had professional success. Their song, "Arthur's Theme (The Best That You Can Do)" from the 1981 film *Arthur* won Sager her first Academy Award. Bacharach produced Sager's third solo album, *Sometimes Late at Night* later that same year. The release featured what became her biggest solo hit in America, "Stronger Than Before."

Wrote Novel

Feeling curbed by the limitations of songwriting, Sager dabbled in screenwriting before penning book-length fiction. She made her debut as a novelist in 1985, when Arbor House published *Extravagant Gestures.* This novel centered on a famous author, who is an expert on mother-daughter relationships. The story explores the character's high-flying lifestyle as well as her interactions with her eccentric mother, movie star best friend, and psychologist lover.

Writing *Extravagant Gestures* proved challenging to Sager. While her songs took about two hours to write, the novel consumed a year of time. Yet the experience was fulfilling. She told Megan Rosenfeld of the *Washington Post,* "My goal was to write something from me, that turned me on, that told a story. And I didn't even know what that story was until I was well into writing it. It was a growth experience for me. As a collaborative being, a person who has spent 20 years writing lyrics for composers, this was the first time I felt I could do something alone."

Won Grammy Award

Refocused on writing lyrics, Sager co-wrote two songs that attracted the attention of the Grammys in 1986. "On My Own," performed by Patti LaBelle and Michael McDonald, earned a Grammy nomination and simultaneously topped three different *Billboard* charts. "That's What Friends Are For," recorded by Elton John, Gladys Knight, Stevie Wonder, and Dionne Warwick, won the Grammy Award for best pop performance by a duo or group with vocal for the recording artists and song of the year for Sager and Bacharach. This marked the first time two co-written songs reached number one on two separate charts in the same year.

For Sager, these honors were secondary to the philanthropic reach of "That's What Friends Are For." All four of the recording artists on "That's What Friends Are For," Sager, and Bacharach donated their collected royalties—totaling nearly one million dollars—to AIDS research. The song remained popular, heightening AIDS awareness and eventually raised more than two million dollars towards research and treatment of the disease. Sager received numerous other honors. In 1986, the American Foundation for AIDS Research honored Sager and Bacharach with its Humanitarian Award. In 1987, she was inducted into the National Academy of Popular Music Songwriters Hall of Fame.

Despite years of success together, Sager and Bacharach's relationship was disintegrating under the pressures of being both personally and professionally involved. She told Rebecca Winters of *Time,* "It did become consuming. Burt's brilliant. But he can labor on a note for 40 minutes. 'Do you like this chord? Do you like that chord?' It was hard to leave the music room and just be Carole and Burt." In 1991, 12 years after Sager and Bacharach's initial artistic partnership began, the couple divorced.

Success with Film Songs

In the early 1990s, Sager was professionally focused on writing songs for films. The song "The Day I Fall in Love" from the 1992 film *Beethoven's 2nd* earned Sager an Academy Award nomination in 1993. The following year,

Sager's song "Look What Love Has Done" from *Junior* earned the same recognition. Sager told Dylan Siegler of *Billboard*, "Sometimes writing for a film is easier in a way. There's already a story and a theme, and you need to just find what you want to say about it. It's like collaborating with a movie."

Sager still wrote songs for other artists outside of film as well. In 1996, Sager was honored with two more Grammy nominations. Her songs "On My Own" and "When You Love Someone," recorded by Anita Baker and James Ingram, respectively, were so lauded.

In 1998, Sager had a strong career year. Celine Dion and Andrea Bocelli's recording of "The Prayer," co-written by Sager and David Foster for the Warner Bros. film, *The Quest for Camelot* earned an Academy Award nomination and won a Golden Globe Award. Dion featured the duet on her album released that year, *These Are Special Times.*

Also in 1998, Sager collaborated with one of her biggest idols, Carole King. For much of her career, Sager had credited King as a major influence on her work. Sager told Marilyn Beck and Stacy Jenel Smith of the Los Angeles *Daily News*, "It's a blessing we've come across each other this late in our careers. I'm thrilled, because Carole's one of the people who really inspired me to write." The pair co-wrote the song "Anyone At All" for Nora Ephron's film *You've Got Mail.* King also performed the song and included the track on her own album. Sager and King worked together again, writing the song "My One True Friend" for the Ephron film *One True Thing.*

Remained Active In Music and Art

Sager's collaborations with King continued into the 21st century. In 2001, Sager served as executive producer on King's album, *Love Makes the World.* The pair wrote four songs together for the album. Sager also made moves in her writing career. Having been affiliated with Warner/Chappell for much of her career, she signed with Universal Music Publishing Group in 2006.

Sager also pursued non-musical interests. A painter in her free time, she displayed her art works in Los Angeles in 2009 as part of an exhibit she curated at the L.A. Art House Gallery entitled "Wounded." The exhibit also featured three Chinese artists on the rise, Zhang Hui, Zhang Hiaying, and Zhang Peng. Serious about the visual arts, she became a trustee for the Los Angeles County Museum of Art in 2009 as well. In addition, she spent more time on other philanthropic activities in the early 21st century. Sager also capitalized on her fame by becoming the face of Binova skin care products in 2014.

Through it all, Sager continued to write songs, especially for film. In 2002, she was honored with a Hollywood Film Festival award for her songwriting for film. Five years later, Sager penned an award-winning song with director/actor Clint Eastwood entitled "Grace Is Gone," for his film of the same name. The song won a Satellite Award and was nominated for a Golden Globe Award. As David Renzer, the chairman and chief executive officer of the Universal Music Publishing Group, said of Sager's importance to *PR Newswire*, "Carole Bayer Sager is one of the true modern legends of the songwriting community."

Books

Contemporary Authors Online, Gale, 2007.
Contemporary Musicians, Volume 5, Gale, 1991.

Periodicals

Billboard, May 29, 1999; December 13, 2003.
Daily News (Los Angeles), December 24, 1998.
Daily News of Los Angeles, May 10, 2009.
PR Newswire, August 29, 2002; July 25, 2006; June 3, 2014.
Time, November 17, 2003.
Washington Post, September 30, 1985.

Online

"Carole Bayer Sager," Hollywood Walk of Fame, http://www.walkoffame.com/carole-bayer-sager (January 2, 2014).
Carole Bayer Sager Official Website, http://www.carolebayersager.com (January 3, 2014).
"LACMA Acquires Ten Artworks During Its Annual Collectors Committee Weekend, Raising More than $4.1 Million," Los Angles Count Museum of Art, http://www.lacma.org/sites/default/files/2014%20Collectors%20Committee%20Press%20Release%204.28.14.pdf (January 3, 2014).□

Milunka Savić

Known as the Serbian Joan of Arc, soldier Milunka Savić (1890–1973) served with honor in World War I and two Balkan wars. She was perhaps the most decorated woman soldier in World War I, if not history. Savić successfully hid her gender through 1913, but was allowed to remain a soldier after it was discovered and served six more years with valor.

Milunka Savić was born on June 24, 1890, in the village of Koprivnica, Serbia. Her home was located near Raska in the southwestern part of the country. It is unknown if she attended school at all. She was illiterate as an adult, and there was no record of her completing school.

Began Serving in Serbian Military

In 1912, Savić's brother was drafted to serve in the First Balkan War, which sought to liberate members of the Balkan League, including Serbia, from the Ottoman Empire. It is unknown if she went with him or assumed his identity to serve in his place. Either way, Savić went herself, and pretended to be male so she could serve in the Serbian military as a combatant. At the time, women could only be medical orderlies in the army.

Taking up arms, she assumed the name of Milun Savić. Savić served with valor through the first Balkan War, and received a number of military honors. The First Balkan War of liberation ended with an armistice in December 1912.

During the Second Balkan War—which occurred in 1913 and was fought between former allies over how to divide their territory gained in Macedonia in the First Balkan War—Savić kept her gender a secret and again served as a male soldier. The fact that she was female was only revealed when she suffered a grave injury from a Bulgarian grenade on her tenth military deployment during the Battle of the Bregalnica. Until that point, she feared her sex would be revealed by a gunshot wound to the chest; a chest wound ultimately betrayed her secret. The field surgeons who treated her reported the situation to her commanding officer.

Appearing before her superior officers after her recovery, Savić was not punished but was asked to explain how she evaded discovery. According to *Wieninternational.at,* Savić explained, "I am a woman, I know, but one who has fought on the front for the last few years, with bullets flying by my ears and with aching arms from all the hand grenades."

Allowed to Remain in Military

Savić's commanding officer told her that the army could not have a woman participating in combat. Savić was given the option of transferring to a nursing division, where women could serve. Savić's response was that she only wanted to serve in active fighting. When the officer said he needed a day to consider the situation, Savić stood at attention and planned to remain so positioned as long as he took to make that decision. After an hour, he agreed that she could again serve as a combat soldier.

Savić continued as a member of the Serbian Army during World War I, which began in 1914 and was caused in part by continued internal conflict in the Balkan region. When she began serving in the military at this time, she personally asked for a rifle from Serbian army leader Radomir Putnik when he advised her to be nurse so she would not die young. As a member of the Serbian army's Knjaz Mihailo, Savić wanted to join an elite infantry unit, the Iron Regiment.

During the war, Savić served with distinction in such areas as the Salonika Front. She took part in the battle of Kolubara and was said to have dashed through no man's land between the two sides of the battle and inflicted damage in several ways. She not only tossed hand grenades but also jumped into trenches with Austrian soldiers. Using only a bayonet, Savić allegedly captured 20 soldiers on her own. For her valor, she was honored with the Karadjordjevic Star with Swords. In other instances on the Macedonian front, she captured 43 Bulgarian soldiers alone, and in another, 60.

Showed Leadership During Retreat

Savić suffered at least four major war injuries, and nine wounded incidents in total. Acting as commander of the attack squad in December 1915 in Macedonia, she suffered major head wounds but led her squad through a massive retreat that took place through Albania to the Adriatic. Despite her weakened state, she kept her group going amidst trying circumstances.

More than one-third of the soldiers and civilians who took part on the trek—about 100,000 in all—died. Many were unburied, a scene which affected Savić and others deeply. According to Melissa Bokovoy in her essay "Scattered Graves, Ordered Cemeteries: Commemorating Serbia's Wars of National Liberation, 1912-1918" included in

Staging the Past: The Politic of Commemoration in Habsburg Central Europe, 1848 to the Present, Savić said, "My spirit ached, and this pain never ceased. Hundreds of people passed away. Quietly, without a word, without a prayer, without a candle, with their last though on their fatherland, mother, sister, children who would be waiting in vain for them." Recovery from her wounds took several months, but she returned to her post on the front in Macedonia as soon as she was physically able.

Because Serbia faced an internal decline during the conflict, its army was folded into the French military. Savić continued to serve, though she was sometimes challenged by officers on the veracity of her skills. Stories were told of her prowess throwing grenades. When stationed in Thessaloniki, a French officer did not believe she could accurately toss them. She proved it by smashing an expensive bottle of cognac on a post located 40 meters away with her first thrown grenade.

Decommissioned at War's End

In 1919, after the war's end, Savić was decommissioned as a soldier. By this time, she had reached the rank of sergeant. Throughout her three wars, she received numerous honors and citations from Serbia, France, Britain, and Russia. They included two French Légion d'Honneur medals, and the French Croix de Guerre with Golden Palm. She was the only woman to receive the Croix de Guerre with Golden Palm.

After Savić left the military, she was not a public figure. She married banker Veljko Gligorević, had a child, and was abandoned by him after the family moved to Belgrade. Savić later adopted three orphans and personally assisted 32 others so they could finish their educations.

To support her family, Savić worked as a cleaning lady, first at the Ministry of Foreign Affairs and later in the Mortgage Bank. Because she was a member of the Légion d'Honneur, the French government made her an offer of an apartment in France and a pension. Not wanting to leave Serbia long-term, she did not take up the offer of housing.

Savić's military service successfully brought her some financial gain, however. She was given a small piece of land in northern Serbia because she was a former soldier. Though she lived there for a time, she eventually settled permanently in Belgrade. She also had her French pension.

Held in Concentration Camp

During World War II, Savić founded a first aid outfit through which she offered medical assistance to Yugoslav Partisans (anti-Nazis) and Chetniks (anti-Axis powers). Because of her efforts, she was beaten by police and sent to a Nazi concentration camp in Banjica. Though Savić was scheduled to be killed by firing squad, she was released after ten months in captivity after her identity was discovered. After the war, French military officer Charles de Gaulle invited her to his inauguration as president because she had served with him during World War I. She was the only Serbian soldier to receive this honor.

Savić died October 5, 1973, in Belgrade, then part of Yugoslavia. Though she was essentially forgotten, a street in the city was named in her honor. Four decades after her

death, Savić's remains were moved from a family mausoleum to Belgrade's New Cemetery in the area known as the
Alley of the Greats. Here, the most distinguished Serbs
found their final resting place. A memorial ceremony was
held as part of the reinterment, which included both the
highest state and military honors. Among the attendees
were the leading citizens in Serbia, including the president,
vice president, and high church officials, representatives
from 19 other countries, and her family members.

Serbia continued to honor Savić's memory in 2014.
That year, several Serbian Cultural Centers in Europe
hosted events to highlight her contributions to Serbia and
the era in which she lived. In Paris, the center honored her
with an exhibit, "Milunka Savić—Female Face of the Great
War." A documentary, titled *Milunka Savić—A Heroine of
the Great War* was shown in Budapest.

During Savić's reburial ceremony in 2013, Serbian
president Tomislav Nokolic lauded her contributions to
Serbian history. He said, according to the Ministry of Foreign Affairs of the Republic of Serbia website, "By paying
homage to Milunka Savić on the eve of the celebration of
World War I Armistice Day, we, her grateful descendants,
are paying homage to all our heroic ancestors."

Books

*Staging the Past: The Politic of Commemoration in Habsburg
   Central Europe, 1848 to the Present,* edited by Maria Bucur
   and Nancy M. Wingfield, Purdue University Press, 2001.

Online

"Budapest: Screening of the Documentary Film *Milunka Savić—
   Heroine of the Great War,"* Ministry of Foreign Affairs of the
   Republic of Serbia, http://www.mfa.gov.rs/en/news-centenary/
   13547-budapest-screening-of-the-documentary-film-milunka-
   Savić-heroine-of-the-great-war- (January 2, 2014).

"The Five Fiercest One-Liners in History," *Mental_floss,* http://
   mentalfloss.com/article/52603/5-fiercest-one-liners-
   history#ixzz2eACe7vxl%20 (January 2, 2014).

"Funeral with Honors for Serbia's Balkan Wars, WWI Heroine,"
   Ministry of Foreign Affairs of the Republic of Serbia, http://
   www.mfa.gov.rs/en/component/content/article/64-daily-
   survey/12695-daily-survey-12112013 (January 2, 2014).

"The Hero Who Was a Heroine," *Wieninternational.at,* https://
   www.wieninternational.at/en/aktuell/the-hero-who-was-a-
   heroine-en (January 2, 2014).

"Milunka Savić, the Most Awarded Female Combatant in the
   History of Warfare," Ministry of Foreign Affairs of the
   Republic of Serbia, http://www.dijaspora.gov.rs/en/milunka-
   Savić-awarded-female-combatant-history-warfare/ (January 2,
   2014).

"Paris: 'Milunka Savić—Female Face of the Great War," Ministry
   of Foreign Affairs of the Republic of Serbia, http://www.mfa.
   gov.rs/en/news-centenary/13683-paris-milunka-Savić-female-
   face-of-the-great-war (January 2, 2014).

"Remains of Serbian Heroines Milunka Savić Transported to the
   Alley of Deserving Citizens in Belgrade," *InNews,* http://
   inserbia.info/today/2013/11/remains-of-serbian-heroine-
   milunka-Savić-transported-to-the-alley-of-deserving-citizens-
   in-belgrade/ (January 2, 2014).□

Sophia Scholl

**In 1942, German student activist Sophie Scholl
(1921–1943) joined the White Rose anti-Nazi resistance movement. Along with her brother, she
printed and distributed a series of leaflets denouncing Hitler's regime. Found guilty of high treason,
Scholl was executed in 1943 at the age of 21.**

Sophia Magdalena Scholl, better known as Sophie, was
born May 9, 1921, in Forchtenberg, Germany. She
was the fourth of six children born to Robert and
Magdalena Scholl. A staunch pacifist, Robert Scholl had
served as a medic during World War I and married a nurse
named Magdalena Müller around 1916. Robert Scholl
served as a "Bürgermeister," or mayor, in several small,
rural towns. At the time of Sophie Scholl's birth, he was the
mayor of Forchtenberg. Robert Scholl, however, was an
independent thinker and idealist who eventually lost his
political position when the country took a turn toward
conservatism. The family next settled in Ulm and Robert
Scholl opened a tax and business consulting office.

Grew Up During Nazi Takeover

Sophie Scholl was about 12 at the time the Nazi Party rose
to power in her homeland. Her older brother, Hans, was
14. Hans joined the Hitler Youth organization and Sophie
followed by signing up for the female branch, called the
Jungmädelbund (Young Girls League). At the time, adoles-
cents across Germany were joining in droves, caught up in
the thrill of the movement. Members got to attend rallies,
wear uniforms and go camping. At that moment, Germany
was a highly demoralized nation, still suffering from the
loss of World War I. Joining the Hitler Youth made young
people feel as if they could do something to help their
ailing nation. The Scholl children jumped on the National
Socialist bandwagon, even as their father quietly warned
them that he opposed the new regime and feared the Nazi
Party would abuse its power.

Hans, who was charismatic with natural leadership
abilities, became a squad leader of his Jungvolk (Young
Folk) unit, which had about 150 boys. He later became
disillusioned and was stripped of his rank for insubordina-
tion. Sophie also left the organization and her distrust for
the National Socialist movement turned toward opposition.
Sophie barely graduated from secondary school, nearly
failing the Abitur, or final exam, because she stopped participating after the academics gave way to a curriculum
promoting Nazi ideologies. In *Sophie Scholl & The White
Rose,* authors Annette Dumbach and Jud Newborn include
many of Scholl's own words, quoted through her letters to
others. According to the book, Scholl summed up her last
years of secondary school this way: "Sometimes school
seems like a film to me. I look on but for all intents and
purposes I'm excluded from performing."

Sophie's father fed her disillusionment. Robert Scholl
quietly opposed Hitler's war and found small ways to subvert the regime. He did small things that were against the

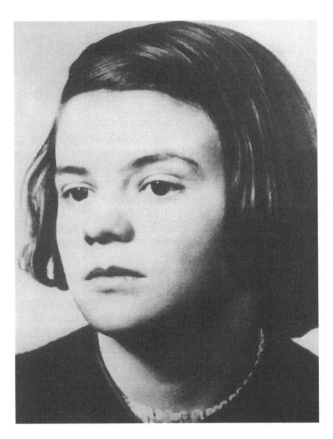

Akg-images/Newscom

law, such as tuning into the BBC or listening to Switzerland's National Public Radio station to learn what was going on with the war. He was interested in news that the Nazi Party did not report on its nationalized stations, and Sophie heard the reports as he listened.

After Sophie graduated from high school in 1940, she was supposed to serve a mandatory six months in the Reichsarbeitsdienst, or Reich National Labor Service. She found the prospect highly unappealing, so she enrolled at the Fröbel Institute in Ulm to become a kindergarten teacher, thinking this would get her out of conscription service. In the end, it only pushed back her work order. In March 1941, Sophie reported to a work camp for young women, to serve as an attendant in a kindergarten attached to a munitions factory. Sophie was housed in an old castle in Blumberg, near the Swiss border. Sophie hated her time there. She had to wear a uniform and attend sessions on ideological training. According to Dumbach and Newborn's book, Sophie wrote this: "We live like prisoners; not only work but leisure time is turned into duty-hours. Sometimes I want to scream 'My name is Sophie Scholl! Don't you forget it!'"

Joined Resistance Movement

In May 1942, Sophie enrolled at the Ludwig Maximilian University of Munich where her brother, Hans, studied medicine. Within a month of her arrival, Sophie found a leaflet published by the White Rose resistance group. It lay hidden under a desk

in the lecture hall. Sophie felt inspired and encouraged by the words, and to finally hear someone else express her own anti-Nazi sentiments. The leaflets of Die Weisse Rose (The White Rose) began appearing in Munich in June 1942. Its lengthy and passionate tracts urged the German people to fight Nazi oppression and tyranny. The leaflet was, in fact, written by her brother and his friend, Alex Schmorell.

According to a transcript of the leaflet, as published in *Sophie Scholl,* this first treatise began: "Nothing is so unworthy of a civilized nation as to allow itself to be 'governed' without any opposition by an irresponsible clique that has yielded to basest instincts. It is certainly the case today that every honest German is ashamed of his government." The leaflet went on to call for resistance before it was too late and "before the last youth of our nation bleeds to death on some battlefield because of the *hubris* of a sub-human." Sophie, naturally, brought the leaflet to the attention of her brother, and in the course of their discussion asked Hans if he had a connection. Initially, Hans denied his involvement but when pressed, admitted his role and told Sophie she could join the group.

The White Rose grew to include a handful of members, taking in fellow students Willi Graf and Christoph Probst, as well as Kurt Huber, a philosophy and musicology professor at the university, and a few others. While the origin of the name has never been fully revealed, historians speculate the name was chosen because it stood for purity and innocence blooming in the face of evil. Between June 1942 and February 1943, the White Rose published six different leaflets. The leaflets angered the Gestapo and caused a tremendous uproar because they represented the first time internal dissent had surfaced in Germany.

After the summer semester ended, Graf, Hans, and Schmorell were sent to Russia to serve as combat medics on the Eastern front of Hitler's campaign. They were only there about three months, but tending the wounded and dying all day long and watching how the Nazi soldiers treated their Russian prisoners ignited a deeper Nazi distaste in the young men. Sophie, meanwhile, went home to assist her mother. Her father had been sent to prison for making an anti-Hitler remark to one of his employees. The entire Scholl family was now placed under suspicion. Sophie, however, did not shy away from letting her feelings be known. According to *Sophie Scholl,* she told one friend: "If Hitler came walking by right now and I had a pistol, I would shoot. If the men don't do it, then a woman will have to. You have to do something to avoid being guilty yourself."

In August 1942, Sophie began mandatory war service at a factory in Ulm. She hated being forced to make parts for Hitler's weapons of war. "This spiritless, lifeless work, purely mechanical, these tiny little pieces whose whole we don't know, whose purpose is horrible. The work affects you not so much physically as mentally." Many of her co-workers were forced laborers from Russia who were housed behind barbed-wire barracks next door to the factory. At one point, Sophie embarked on her own private "strike" of sorts by working very slowly, hoping to slow down the factory. Reprimanded by a foreman, Sophie blamed the slowdown on her clumsiness.

Issued *A Call to All Germans*

By November 1942, Sophie and her brother were back at the university, ready for the winter semester. Members of the White Rose met to plan their upcoming verbal attacks. In January 1943, they began a fifth leaflet. By this time, the group had made contacts in other cities and received funding to help them expand their cause. They acquired a duplicating machine to speed up the process. Earlier tracts had been individually hand-typed. The fifth tract, titled "A Call to All Germans," spoke extensively about civil rights. The Gestapo reported that 8,000 to 10,000 of the tracts were handed out, representing a 20-fold increase over previous tracts.

By day, members of the White Rose carried on as students. By night, they printed their leaflets. Producing the copies proved tedious. The hand-cranked mimeograph machine made only one copy at a time and broke down often. To help them function, White Rose members took pep pills that were acquired by the medics in their group, who got them from military clinics where they worked.

While the production itself was risky, the dissemination of the leaflets was downright dangerous. To make their movement appear like a larger, consolidated effort, they began mailing their literature outside of Munich. Leaflets showed up in Augsburg, Frankfort, Linz, Salzburg, Stuttgart, Ulm, and Vienna. Not only did the White Rose mail leaflets to citizens who lived in those cities, they actually mailed the leaflets from many of those cities. To do this, members took turns transporting the leaflets by train in rucksacks and suitcases. They traveled at night under constant risk of being stopped by the Gestapo or military police who controlled the trains, streetcars and streets, and who frequently stopped travelers to check their identity papers or check for food smugglers and fugitives. White Rose members did their courier work alone, so as not to attract attention. Once they had arrived in their destination city, they looked for discreet mailboxes in low-pedestrian areas. Sophie made her runs to Augsburg, Ulm, and Stuttgart.

Caught in Act of Defiance

In early February, members produced a sixth tract—this one written by Huber and addressed to "Fellow Students." On February 18, 1943, Sophie and Hans brought a suitcase full of the new leaflets to the main lecture hall at the university and placed stacks of them at the entrances to the classrooms and in the stairways. Classes had not yet ended. As they were about to leave, the Scholls realized they had more handouts in the suitcase, so they strode up the stairwell to the upper floor atrium and flung them down from the balustrade just as classes ended. The falling leaflets attracted the attention of a custodian who tracked the young people through the crowd and ensured their arrest.

The Gestapo came to investigate and the lead interrogator, Robert Mohr, nearly let the brother and sister go. Because they were so calm and were such clean-cut kids, Mohr did not think they could possibly be behind the subversive acts of the White Rose. In time, the Gestapo collected all of the leaflets and discovered they fit perfectly in the suitcase. At this point, Hans and Sophie were arrested. Hour after hour, brother and sister were interrogated separately and

each denied involvement. Finally, after a second search of their apartment, the Gestapo turned up a large number of stamps and a letter from Probst. At the time of his arrest, Hans was carrying a draft for a seventh leaflet—this one written by Probst. Hans had tried to eat the letter at one point after his arrest. Seeing no way out, the brother and sister confessed, but each insisted he or she was solely responsible for the actions of the White Rose.

Probst was soon arrested and the three stood trial at Munich's Palace of Justice on February 22. They were found guilty of high treason. Three hours after the trial ended, Sophie was on her way to the guillotine. Hans and Probst were executed as well. Hans and Sophie were buried in a Munich cemetery next to the Stadelheim Prison. Graf, Huber, and Schmorell were later arrested and executed. Later, copies were smuggled out of Germany and given to Allied troops, who reproduced them and dropped them from planes all over Germany. Sophie's life was commemorated in a 2005 German film, titled *Sophie Scholl: The Final Days*. A "White Rose" monument was placed in the University of Munich building where the brother and sister made their final stand.

Books

Atwood, Kathryn J., *Women Heroes of World War II*, Chicago Review Press, 2011.
Dumbach, Annette, and Jud Newborn, *Sophie Scholl & The White Rose*, Oneworld Publications, 2006.

Periodicals

History Review, December 2005.
New American, April 3, 2006. □

Andrei Serban

In his theater and opera productions, Romanian-born American director and producer Andrei Serban (born 1943) created challenging stagings of classic works by Anton Chekhov and William Shakespeare, contemporary plays, and numerous operas. Launching his career in avant-garde theater in New York City, Serban retained his sense of experimentalism through nearly five decades as a professional.

Andrei Serban was born June 21, 1943, in Bucharest, Romania. Serban grew up in an oppressive period in Romanian history, when the country was part of the Soviet Union's sphere of influence and led by Communists, then ruled by dictator Nicolae Ceausescu. Serban's father was fired from his government economic advisor job by the Communists, but later became an award-winning art photographer.

Had Life-Long Interest in Theater

As a child, Serban created his own puppet shows and would put on battles with friends at a park in Bucharest.

According to Mel Gussow in the *New York Times,* Serban once explained, "I knew I always wanted to be in the theater. What fascinated me was the secret world behind the curtain and when the curtain went up, the secret would be revealed...another world on the other side."

Despite the repressive atmosphere in Romania, Serban's interest in theater also was impacted by available European influences. Though he began by studying acting and the Stanislavsky method, he eventually moved on to the Institute of Theatrical and Cinematographic Arts and the University of Bucharest. He began working professionally as a producer, staging plays in Romania. In 1966, Serban gained acclaim for his work on a production of *Ubu Roi* in Romania.

Serban's work was discovered by Ellen Stewart, the founder of the New York City-based experimental theater. Stewart gained a Ford Foundation grant for Serban so that he could come to the United States in 1969 to further his career at La MaMa. Serban told Eileen Blumenthal of the *American Theatre* about the culture shock he experienced when he arrived in New York. He said, "I was still wearing a Communist gray suit and gray tie. I'd never even seen a black person before. The first night, they put me up in the Chelsea Hotel, where Andy Warhol was filming a movie, and there were all these crazy transvestites in the lobby. I didn't know what planet I was on."

Made Theater Directing Debut

Serban made his directorial debut in 1970 with *Arden of Faversham,* and began working with Peter Brook at the International Center of Theatre Research later that year. Continuing his affiliation with La MaMa, Serban directed a production of the classic Anton Chekhov play *The Cherry Orchard* there in 1972.

Over the next few years, Serban would helm a number of productions for La MaMa, which would cement his reputation as a gifted director of avant-garde theater. In 1974, for example, Serban directed a memorable production of *Fragments of a Trilogy: Medea, Electra, and the Trojan Woman.* His five-hour *Fragments* took chances visually and packed emotional power, and was considered a breakthrough production of the play. This reinvention of Greek tragedy was later staged at many international festivals. Serban followed *Fragments* with another potent La MaMa production of the Bertolt Brecht play, *Good Woman of Setzuan* (1975).

Through the end of the 1970s, Serban continued to direct contentious versions of other classic plays. In 1977, he directed such a production of *The Cherry Orchard* at Lincoln Center. This production began a cycle of directing Chekhov works through the early 1980s. Also in 1977, Serban helmed his interpretation of August Strindberg's *Ghost Sonata* at Yale Repertory Theatre during his tenure as a visiting professor. Next, Serban directed Molière's *Sganarelle* at Yale Rep in 1978, then Samuel Beckett's *Happy Days* at the New York Shakespeare Festival in 1979. The production of *Sganarelle* emphasized the musicality of language.

Directed First Opera

In 1980, Serban took on new challenges, by producing and directing opera in addition to his staged theater work. He produced his first opera that year, at the Welsh National Opera in Cardiff, Wales. It was a production of Pyotr Ilyich Tchaikovsky's *Eugene Onegin.* Over the next few years, Serban would move between opera and stage productions. Opera would be a special focus at mid-decade. In 1984, he directed a staging of Giacomo Puccini's *Turandot* in both Los Angeles and London.

Serban produced *Fidelio* in London at Covent Garden, and directed a fantasy-laden, stylized production of Philip Glass's *The Juniper Tree* in 1985. The latter opera—based on a Grimm fairy tale—was put on at the American Reparatory Theatre in Cambridge, Massachusetts. The artistically challenging opera evoked many different reactions in critics and audiences, who had a range of opinions about the extremes in Serban's staging choices. Also in 1985, Serban staged a production of *Norma* for the New York City Opera.

As a stage director, Serban returned to Chekhov with a production of *The Seagull* in 1980 at the Public Theater in New York City. He then put on a memorable interpretation of Chekhov's *Three Sisters* at the American Reparatory Theatre in 1982. Serban's version removed the realism to emphasize memory and the idea of transcendence. The production also demonstrated the director's skill in creating smaller chamber pieces. As Mel Gussow wrote in the *New York Times,* "Each of the three productions, especially the first, has been a subject of controversy, a word that seems to have become synonymous with the work of the Rumanian-born director. Regarding his public, he says, 'I'm known as the director who destroys the classics.'"

Directed *Uncle Vanya*

Serban's last Chekhov play in English, *Uncle Vanya,* was helmed in 1983, This production was at the La MaMa Annex, and like its predecessors, was controversial. Featuring a small budget and resourceful staging, the production starred Joseph Chaikin and F. Murray Abraham. Despite the respect he gained from such production, Serban had no offers from Broadway and only found a few venues in New York—La MaMa and the Public Theater—interested in his work. Because of the lack of commercial theater interest, most of his theater projects were done regionally in the United States or abroad. As he told the Gussow of the *New York Times,* "Though I'm in the middle of my life. I'm still considered a dangerous child. I never meant to be—even when I was 20. To my complete surprise, I found I was creating an uproar. I don't do things to provoke. Life is full of negative steps, why be negative in the theater?"

Serban sometimes remained as experimental as he had been in the 1970s in his stage productions. During the mid to late 1980s, he became interested in and reinvented the idea of commedia dell'arte (an Italian form of theater with improvised dialogue and stock characters). As part of this interest, Serban staged theatrical allegories by Carlo Gozzi in the form of *King Stag* (1984) and *The Serpent Woman* (1988). Both plays were put on at the American Repertory Theater. Serban continued to emphasize intense visuals with *King Stag* featuring dance, masks, and life-size puppets as well as performances styles reminiscent of Asia. *King Stag* would tour the United States in 1986.

Became Head of National Theater

Also in the late 1980s, Serban began staging revolutionary interpretations of classic plays by William Shakespeare. The first came in 1989, with *Twelfth Night* at the American Repertory Theatre. In 1990, Serban returned to his native Romania to begin a three-year stint as the artistic director at the National Theater in Bucharest. He was invited by the new government put in place after the overthrow of dictator Ceausescu. Serban's homecoming production was of his *Fragments*.

While serving as artistic director, Serban also continued to produce and direct major operas worldwide. In 1990, he produced Alexander Borodin's *Prince Igor* at Covent Garden and directed Gaetano Donizetti's *Lucia di Lammermoor* at Chicago's Lyric Opera. Serban then directed Richard Strauss's *Elektra* in 1991, and Jacques Offenbach's *Les Contes d'Hoffmann* (The Tales of Hoffmann for the Vienna State Opera in 1993. In 1997, Serban was the producer of *Thaïs* in Nice, France.

In 1999, Serban took on perhaps one of the greatest challenges in operatic directing when he helmed a minimalist production of the *Ring* cycle for the San Francisco Opera. Two years later, Serban directed *Khovanshchina* at the Opéra de la Bastille. In 2003, he helmed a version of Giuseppe Verdi's grand opera *Falstaff* at the Vienna State Opera.

Directed Reinterpretations of Shakespeare

Serban directed a number of stage plays in the 1990s as well. In the late 1990s and early 2000s, Serban returned to his radical, sometimes controversial, versions of Shakespeare plays with *Cymbeline* at the New York Shakespeare Festival and *The Taming of the Shrew* at the American Repertory Theatre, both in 1998. Next came Serban's very divisive version of *Hamlet* for the New York Shakespeare Festival in 1999, *The Merchant of Venice* for American Repertory Theatre in 1999, and *Richard III* for La MaMa in 2001.

In a review of Serban's version of *The Merchant of Venice*, Peter Marks of the *New York Times* wrote of the director's work, "Mr. Serban is a restless experimenter, so his Shakespearean ventures tend to be jampacked with ideas good and less good. One of his best notions here is the decadent and sexually ambiguous world of Antonio, the merchant of the title, who takes the disastrous loan from Shylock, with its peculiar terms, to finance the effort of his friend Bassanio to romance Portia."

Also in the 1990s, Serban took up a regular position as an educator. In 1992, he became the head of the Oscar Hammerstein II Center for Theatre Studies at Columbia University. He later stepped down from that post but remained affiliated with Columbia as a theater professor through at least the early 2010s. Serban had previously taught at Carnegie Mellon, Sarah Lawrence College, the Paris Conservatoire d'Art Dramatique, and the American Reparatory Theatre Institute.

Remained Active Director

As Serban entered his sixth and seventh decades, he continued to work regularly in both theater and opera. In 2007, for example, he staged an adaptation of the abortion drama *4 Months, 3 Weeks and 2 Days*, based on the book by Romanian writer Tatiana Niculescu Bran, at La MaMa. He also directed numerous stage works in Romania and Hungary, including his versions of Chekhov plays in those languages at such events as the Festivalul National de Teatru in the early 2010s. His major operas included a problematic production of Charles Gounod's *Faust* in 2005 at the New York Metropolitan Opera and his take on Puccini's violent *Turandot* at London's Covent Garden in 2014.

Even late in his career, Serban carried an air of controversy with him. He claimed not to seek such a label, but viewed his stagings through wide lens. He told Martin Bernheimer of the *Opera News*, "It's so strange. I always think of myself as a conservative. When I approach a piece, I do my homework. But when I start to work, I let go, because I'm horrified by museum-theater. On the stage—and that includes opera, of course—everything somehow has to happen now. I don't mean now in terms of modern costumes. I don't need people singing in business suits, dark glasses or black raincoats, as they do in Germany. That's a stupid cliche. But it has to be now in terms of our sensitivity to history. One has to respect the past in order to interpret it."

Books

Baker's Biographical Dictionary of Musicians, Volume 5, edited by Nicolas Slonimsky and Laura Kuhn, Schirmer, 2001.
International Dictionary of Opera, Gale, 1993.
The Oxford Encyclopedia of Theater and Performance, Volume 2, edited by Dennis Kennedy, Oxford University Press, 2003.

Periodicals

American Theatre, October 2012.
Daly Telegraph (London, England), February 19, 2014.
New York Times, September 6, 1983; October 21, 1995; January 13, 1999; March 3, 2013.
Theatre Journal, October 1996.□

Chitra Singh

The Indian vocalist Chitra Singh (born c. 1945) was one half of a duet that recorded *The Unforgettables,* one of the best-selling albums in the history of Indian popular music, in 1976. She and her husband, Jagjit Singh, were known, according to Craig Harris of *Allmusic,* as "the king and queen of the ghazal world."

Ghazal was only a branch of Indian music, and a small branch at that, when Chitra and Jagjit Singh came on the scene in the 1970s. Forming first in a professional and then a personal partnership, they revived what was an ancient poetic form with roots in the Arabian peninsula and turned it into a contemporary popular genre with worldwide reach. Jagjit Singh is often credited with the development of this contemporary ghazal, but in the early years of their collaboration he and Chitra developed it

© Reporter#41763/Demotix/Corbis

together, shaping a duet sound that exploited the contrasting quality of their voices. Chitra's voice inspired compositional efforts from Jagjit that differed from the music he wrote for his own. They were one of the great creative partnerships in contemporary Indian music, and after she endured Jagjit's death and a series of other personal tragedies, Chitra Singh emerged as a curator of her husband's legacy.

Heard Indian Classical Music at Home

Details surrounding Chitra Singh's early life are scarce. Her birth name has been given as Chitra Shome. An only child, she has said that she was 22 when she met Jagjit Singh, an event whose date has been given as 1965 and 1967. This would place her birth around 1944 in Kolkata, India, then Calcutta. Her family was Bengali, and her mother, Krishna Roy, was trained as a singer of Indian classical music. Chitra soaked up the vocal techniques she heard around the house. Sources differ as to whether she herself had early vocal training in Indian classical music or in Rabindra Sangeet, a genre of vocal music based on the texts of Bengali poet Rabindranath Tagore; Singh herself stated that she never had classical training, and she always claimed to have learned to sing by ear. As an adult she absorbed influences from other singers, her husband above all.

Like so many other Indian girls, Chitra married very young. In the words of the Indian website *The Unforgettables*, "This child bride was a mother before she stopped

being a child herself." Nevertheless, she managed to finish school with an English honors degree. She married a man named Datta and moved with him to Bombay (now Mumbai), where he opened a recording studio. The couple had two children, Armaan and Monica.

Although her marriage was not a happy one, Chitra flourished in Bombay. Her husband recorded soundtracks for advertisements at his studio, and she picked up an education in how to sing on recordings in addition to her instinct for the refined vocals of Indian classical styles. Soon she was finding some success performing advertising jingles—the same profession a young Punjabi Sikh Jagjit Singh was pursuing in Bombay with intermittent success.

Thus, when the two met, they had a good deal in common; both were struggling young singers trying to break into the music industry. Their first duets were recorded for advertising jingles. The website *Jagjit Singh: The Ghazal King* reported that Chitra "appeared to be the most beautiful woman that he had ever seen," and in fact photographs of Chitra reveal a classic Indian beauty with long hair and high cheekbones. Despite religious differences—Jagjit, a Sikh, had cut off his traditional long hair and stopped wearing a turban—the pair fell in love. Chitra and her husband divorced, and she married Jagjit in 1969 or 1970. And, acccording to Jagjt's testimony (quoted on the *Ghazal King* site), it was Chitra who solidified his determination to pursue a musical career: "Chitra came from a very different world. She became my anchor, made me choose my way of life, my life style, my path as a musician."

Disliked Husband's Voice at First

The feeling was reciprocal, for as the two spent time together and talked about their dreams for the music business, Chitra, who ironically had disliked Jagjit's voice when she first heard it, learned musical lessons from him. Asked by Anand Holla of the *Mumbai Mirror* to specify the three most important musical lessons she had learned from her husband, Chitra Singh replied, in a mixture of Hindi and English, "It's hard to pick three. He would always say *riyaaz karo*... always hit the note on its head. Bahut singers *sur ke aaju baaju se gaate hain*. That is something he couldn't bear and he transferred that bug to me. The third thing he would repeat is *Ò zyaada ustaadi nahi maarneka* (smiles). Try out all your vocal fireworks at home. But when you sing, don't oversing." Jaghit emphasized, Chitra recalled, that the expression and meaning of the lyrics should be the most important, something that she thought many modern singers overlooked.

Both singers were interested in ghazal, which at the time had few exponents in the mainstream of Indian popular music. Ghazals had a classical form, and they sometimes were heard in films, but rarely on recordings. Most ghazal singers at the time were Muslim. Ghazals, which had their ultimate origin in the Middle East, had lyrics in a fixed poetic form, describing the importance of love even given the reality of pain, loss, and separation. Jagjit and Chitra modernized the form, adding such Western instruments as a guitar and setting the poetry to catchy melodies. "I would say that Jagjit Singh's biggest contribution to ghazals was that it drew the masses to the style, masses who till then only patronised filmi ghazals," singer Rekha Surya told Malini Nair of the *Economic Times.*

The spectacular result of this preparation was the album *The Unforgettables,* released in 1976 and for many years the best-selling album in the history of Indian popular music. It contained ten ghazals, one of which became a widely known anthem in which audiences would join at the "ahista, ahista" refrain. "Each of the songs," Nair commented, "was marked by a rare freshness and lilt, his voice deep and golden, hers clear and sharp."

Performed Worldwide

For the next 15 years, Jagjit and Chitra Singh were among the most popular acts in Indian music, performing popular music in several Indian languages as well as ghazals. Chitra Singh issued several albums of her own but never sang in public without her husband. They performed in more than 40 countries, including not only the United States and Britain but also places at the outer reaches of the Indian cultural orbit, such as Kenya, South Africa, Australia, and New Zealand. The pair had a son, Vivek.

Tragedy brought the duo's high-flying career to an end: Vivek was killed in an auto crash in 1990. They released one more album, *Someone Somewhere,* that had been recorded before the accident. After that, Chitra Singh gave up performing completely, and Jagjit turned to a darker, more serious tone in his music. Chitra suffered further tragedy when her daughter, Monica, committed suicide in 2009. Jagjit Singh died in 2011.

Her husband's death brought Chitra Singh out of a long period of seclusion. She supervised the release of *The Master and His Magic,* an album of eight unreleased Jagjit Singh tracks, and she launched a campaign to have her husband receive the Bharat Ratna, India's highest civilian award. Chitra organized and produced commemorative concerts, but she declined to perform herself. "I'm also 22 years older. It's physically impossible," she told Roshni Olivera of the *Times of India.* Even if I sit down for riyaaz every single day, it can't come back. It may do so, but in a completely different way. It will not be the same Chitra Singh that one has heard and I definitely don't want to spoil the memory that people have of me." Those memories, for Indians who listened to music in the last quarter of the 20th century, were numerous.

Books

Periodicals

DNA (Daily News & Analysis, India), October 7, 2012; August 28, 2014.

Economic Times (India), October 12, 2011.

Hindustan Times (New Delhi), August 11, 2012.

Times of India, October 10, 2012; October 13, 2013

Online

"Chitra Singh's daughter ends life at Bandra home," *Times of India,* http://www.timesofindia.indiatimes.com/Mumbai/Chitra-Singhs-daughter-ends-life-at-Bandra-home/articleshow/4595547.cms (December 1, 2014).

"'I am basking in Jagjit's glory,'" *DNA* (India), http://www.dnaindia.com/entertainment/report-i-am-basking-in-jagjit-s-glory-1126517 (December 1, 2014).

"I cannot indulge in any personal luxury: Chitra Singh," *Mumbai Mirror,* http://www.timesofindia.indiatimes.com/entertainment/hindi/music/news/I-cannot-indulge-in-any-personal-luxury-Chitra-Singh/articleshow/15431002.cms (December 1, 2014).

"Jagjit & Chitra Singh," *Allmusic,* http://www.allmusic.com (December 1, 2014).

"Jagjit & Chitra Singh: Biography," *The Unforgettables,* http://www.jagjitchitra.wordpress.com/about/biography/ (December 1, 2014).

"Jaghit Singh: The Ghazal King," http://www.orkut.google.com/c11829-t7ed4bfbc09c9f1e0.html (December 1, 2014).

"Jagjit Singh Obituary," *The Guardian* (London, England), October 25, 2011, http://www.theguardian.com/music/2011/oct/25/jagjit-singh-obituary (December 1, 2014).□

Sixtus IV

One of Christendom's most fabled landmarks is named after Pope Sixtus IV (1414–1484), the Italian cardinal who commissioned the Sistine Chapel for the Vatican City inside Rome. The former Francesco della Rovere was a theologian by training and one of the few members of the Franciscan religious order to serve as successor to St. Peter, one of the original 12 apostles.

Francesco della Rovere was born on July 21, 1414, in Celle Ligure, a coastal town on the Ligurian Sea. Before his term as pope, he used the name Francesco da Savona, referring to the Italian province of his birth. His father Leonardo was a merchant and minor landowner who was active in local Savonese politics. His mother Luchina Monteleoni was from a rich Genoese family, and she produced five daughters and a final son in an astonishingly short decade following her eldest son's birth.

Handed Over to Mendicant Monks

Sixtus's parents sent him into the Franciscan religious order around 1424, the year in which he turned ten. Founded in 1209 in Italy by St. Francis of Assisi, the Franciscans—formally known as the Order of Friars Minor, or Little Brothers—is a mendicant order, meaning that its members take a vow of poverty and live solely off charitable donations. By the time Sixtus entered the monastery, the Franciscans had grown in number and in influence in Italy, where they ran and staffed hospitals and institutions that served the poor.

According to standard church biographies, Sixtus's parents had delivered him to the Franciscan order after he became seriously ill and their prayers to St. Francis to intercede in his recovery had been granted. The youngster showed himself to be a studious, obedient young monk and attended a preparatory academy near Turin. He then entered the University of Padua, one of the world's oldest universities, and earned his licentiate degree in 1434. University records show he earned a doctorate in theology and philosophy in April of 1444, a few months before his 30th birthday.

At the universities of Padua and Perugia, Sixtus was a popular lecturer who taught classes in logic and philosophy. He emerged as one of the Franciscan order's most renowned theologians and debaters on doctrinal affairs, and was appointed assistant to the Minister General, or head of the Order of Friars Minor (Conventuals; abbreviated as O.F.M. [Conv.]). He later became the Franciscans' procurator general, or treasurer and financial officer of the order.

Sixtus became Minister General in 1464, the year he turned 50, and held that post for the next five years. In September of 1467, he was elevated to the rank of cardinal by Pope Paul II. He was assigned the see of Basilica of San Pietro in Vincoli and became eligible to take part in the next Conclave of Cardinals, which met in Rome on August 7, 1471, 12 days after the unexpected death of Paul II. The conclave was notably brief, and Sixtus's fellow cardinals elected him to lead the Roman Church on August 9. He chose the name Sixtus, an unusual choice that had not been used by the successors of St. Peter in nearly a thousand years. The name is Greek in origin and was originally spelled Xystus; it had first been used by the seventh pope, who headed the Holy See in Rome less than a century after the martyrdom of Christ. A second Sixtus II was beheaded in 258 CE, and a third bearer of the name, Pope Sixtus III, died in 440.

Continued Controversial Practice of Nepotism

Sixtus's formal consecration as the 212th head of the Roman Church took place in Rome on August 25, 1471. As with his predecessors, he was soon visited by a steady influx of relatives from Liguria and Savona, most of them sons of his sisters. He elevated a significant number of them—23 in all—to the rank of cardinal, and of that number a few went on to positions of enormous wealth and influence. One was Pietro Riario, the youngest son of his sister Bianca. Riario became archbishop of Florence and was succeeded in that post by his cousin Giuliano della Rovere, son of Sixtus's youngest brother Raffaele. Giuliano della Rovere later became Pope Julius II in 1503.

Sixtus also ennobled another Riario nephew, Girolamo, who in turn married into the Sforzas, a wealthy and influential Milanese family. That nephew lost his life for his role in the Pazzi plot, named after one of his co-conspirators. The scheme involved a highly public assassination attempt on the powerful Medici rulers of Florence. At Easter Mass at the famous *Duomo* cathedral of Florence in April of 1478, the instigators attempted to stab Lorenzo and his brother Giuliano. Lorenzo escaped the knife attack but his brother Giuliano bled to death on the church floor, interrupting a Holy Day Mass at which several thousand Florentines were in attendance. Correctly apprising the attack as a plot to overtake their city, Medici supporters quickly rounded up the conspirators and killed them. Girolamo was among the targets, as was the Archbishop of Pisa, Francesco Salviati, and for this treatment of a high-ranking church cleric Sixtus placed Florence under an interdict that lasted two years. A papal interdict prohibited Mass and the

sacrament of holy communion, and was a grave rebuke to the Florentines.

Sixtus issued other notable proclamations as pope. During his tenure the feast of St. Francis of Assisi became a day of holy obligation on the liturgical calendar, along with August 15, which was celebrated as the Feast of the Assumption of Mary. Sixtus also made that date—known as "Ferragosto" in Italian—another major church holiday. August 15 remains an official bank holiday in nations with large Roman Catholic populations well into the twenty-first century.

Commissioned Sistine Chapel

As pope, Sixtus made several significant contributions to the Italian Renaissance in the arts, as did junior members of his della Rovere family. His were focused on Rome and the Apostolic Palace, his official residence. He rebuilt churches, including the Basilica of Santa Maria del Popolo, an old Roman landmark dedicated to Mary, the Blessed Virgin mother of Christ. Seeking a more private and luxurious space in which he and the 200 clerics who served him could attend daily Mass, in 1477 he commissioned the restoration of *cappella papale*, or papal chapel, in the Apostolic Palace. The new space, later deemed the Sistine Chapel in Sixtus's honor, was also designed to ensure seclusion for future papal conclaves. Its ornate fittings, sculptures, and frescoes were the work of some of the Italian Renaissance era's most exalted artists, including Michelangelo, who executed the stunning series of ceiling frescoes for the Sistine Chapel several years after Sixtus's death.

During his lifetime Sixtus commissioned major works from the painters Sandro Botticelli and Pietro Perugino for the Sistine Chapel. Botticelli executed a fresco titled *The Trials of Moses* and Perugino created one of the more famous works of art associated with the papacy, *The Delivery of the Keys*, or *Christ Giving the Keys to St. Peter*. The title of Perugino's fresco refers to the handover of the keys to Christendom to St. Peter, the first pope and an original Apostle. In the painting, Christ passes to a kneeling Peter a key of gold, "from which hangs suspended the base-metal key of temporal power," explained Eamon Duffy in the book *Saints & Sinners: A History of the Popes*. The dual keys, Duffy continued, serve as "a deliberate evocation of the papal version of the 'two-powers' theory inherited from Gregory VII and Innocent III, in which the Pope possesses both spiritual and temporal power, exercising spiritual power directly, and the temporal power indirectly through obedient Christian rulers. The Pope, like Christ, is supreme in both spheres."

Sixtus became an enthusiastic urban planner once he became the Bishop of Rome, making significant improvements to the infrastructure of the ancient city. In the Middle Ages the number of religious pilgrims to Rome began to soar, and the increase in tourism strained resources. In 1450 one of the old Roman-built pedestrian bridges across the Tiber River partially collapsed, resulting in several fatalities. During his reign, Sixtus ordered construction of a new bridge, the first new span across the waterway since the Roman era. It remained in place more than five centuries later as the Ponte Sisto, or Sistine Bridge. This particular crossing also connected the more elite districts of Rome to Trastavere, a much older and less developed part of the city. Trastavere was home to many sailors and shipbuilders of Ligurian origin—like Sixtus himself—and was a fairly rough quarter. Sixtus ordered the streets of Trastavere to be paved for the first time. Elsewhere in the city he continued a predecessor's restoration of an aqueduct dating back to the time of Christ. The newly rebuilt Acqua Vergine brought a much-needed source of fresh water to Rome.

Indirectly Spurred Columbus' 1492 Expedition

Another significant achievement in Sixtus's papacy was his formal creation of the Vatican Library, a repository for some of the world's oldest and rarest manuscripts. As leader of all Christians in Western Europe, Sixtus also issued a few notable bulls, or official edicts, with far-reaching effects. One was *Exigit Sincerae Devotionis Affectus* on November 1, 1478, which authorized Spain's rulers, Ferdinand II and Isabella I, to create an official tribunal to root out suspected heretics. Collectively known as the Spanish Inquisition, this period of Spanish history forced longtime Muslim and Jewish residents of Spain to either leave or convert. Another bull from Sixtus was *Aeterni regis* (Eternal King's), which ratified a peace treaty between the formerly warring kingdoms of Spain and Portugal. There were several parts to this 1481 edict, but it assented to a dividing line in the Atlantic Ocean that granted Portugal—an earlier maritime pioneer than neighboring Spain—control of the already-explored southern lands like the African continent. In response, Ferdinand and Isabella acceded to a proposal by another notable Savonese figure, the explorer Christopher Columbus, to lead an exploratory mission to claim lands elsewhere for Spain.

It was Sixtus who hired the Vatican's longstanding elite protection unit, the Swiss Guards. These were well-trained and highly disciplined militia units he permanently installed to secure his safety and that of the Apostolic Palace. He died in Rome on August 12, 1484, at the relatively advanced age of 70. Gout was said to have been the cause of death. He was succeeded by Giovanni Battistia Cybo as Pope Innocent VIII, one of the many cardinals Sixtus created during his 13-year tenure. Several years later another cardinal elevated by Sixtus, his nephew Giuliano della Rovere, became Pope Julius II. In the introduction to *Patronage and Dynasty: The Rise of the Della Rovere in Renaissance Italy*, the scholar Ian F. Verstegen described the first della Rovere pope as "the greatest papal patron of the 15th century and single-handedly responsible for making Rome the papal capital it became." Verstegen quoted from one contemporary source of Sixtus, who hailed him as the Italian who "made Rome from a city of brick into stone just as Augustus of old turned the stone city into marble."

Books

Duffy, Eamon, *Saints & Sinners: A History of the Popes,* Yale University Press, 2006.

Lee, Egmont, *Sixtus IV and Men of Letters,* Edizioni di Storia e Letteratura, 1978.

Verstegen, Ian F. (editor), *Patronage and Dynasty: The Rise of the Della Rovere in Renaissance Italy,* Truman State University Press, 2007. □

Edith Södergran

The Swedish-speaking Finnish poet Edith Södergran (1892–1923) introduced a modernist style of poetry to the Scandinavian world and remains influential nearly a century after her slender body of work was composed.

Södergran was almost unknown in her own time. She lived in locations remote from the main centers of Scandinavian culture: St. Petersburg, Russia, and a village nearby that at the time was part of Finland. In addition to that, she was a woman in a society that at the time was heavily male dominated, and in some of her poems, influenced by German philosopher Friedrich Nietzsche, she adopted the persona of a hero with profound powers. Her poetry was met with incomprehension in the regional Swedish language publications in which it first appeared, and near the end of her life, under the influence of new philosophical beliefs, she declared, according to Stina Katchadourian, writing in the *Dictionary of Literary Biography,* that it was "complete trash." Yet, Katchadourian noted, "She is widely regarded as the harbinger of Nordic modernism, and her striking imagery and urgent poetic voice still influence new generations of poets." Her poems have been translated into more than 30 languages and have been read far beyond Scandinavia.

Spoke Seven Languages

Edith Irene Södergran was born in St. Petersburg, Russia, on April 4, 1892. Her family was part of Finland's Swedish-speaking minority, some of whom moved to St. Petersburg because of the declining influence of Swedes in Finland (which still consists of roughly 5 percent Swedish speakers). Södergran grew up speaking Swedish at home and also learned Russian and German as a child. She later mastered Finnish and spoke and read French, English, and Italian well. Södergran's father, Matts, worked for Swedish arms manufacturer Alfred Nobel (who later endowed the Nobel Prize) and later for a lumber mill in Raivola, Finland (now Roschino, Russia), northwest of St. Petersburg, where the family bought a home.

Södergran's mother, Helena, inherited a good deal of money, and Södergran received a top-notch education at a German language Catholic school in St. Petersburg where she was exposed to new trends in literature and the arts. But it was the dread disease of tuberculosis that shaped her teenage years: her father died from tuberculosis in 1907, and Södergran herself was diagnosed with it in early 1909. As her father's condition declined, Södergran wrote a large number of poems in a notebook. Most of them were in German, which she considered her best language, but she later switched to writing in Swedish.

After several unsuccessful attempts at a cure in Scandinavia, Södergran was sent in 1911 to a sanatorium in Davos, Switzerland. Her stay there was beneficial both physically and educationally; the sanatorium was home to a cosmopolitan group of patients from across Europe, and its director, Ludwig van Muralt (toward whom Södergran experienced one of her frequent bouts of unrequited love), was a leading Freudian psychiatrist, a tuberculosis sufferer himself, whose wife was American and may have introduced Södergran to the writings of American poet Walt Whitman. Whitman's combination of free verse and exuberant, spiritual writing influenced Södergran, as did the works of Swedish poet Jonas Love Almqvist. But her style, as it developed, was entirely her own.

Wrote Poetry at Family Villa

By 1914, although her health remained questionable, Södergran felt herself ready to return home to Raivola. Except for short trips, she spent the rest of her life there. She began to pay close attention to her surroundings, including a large garden running down to a nearby lake, and these provided material for her poems. But these were far from the orderly nature lyrics that up to then had been the standard for Swedish poetry. Södergran wrote in free verse (poetry without rhymes), and she often placed her own strong personality at the center of her poems. After another episode of unrequited love, she wrote in the poem "Violet Twilights": "Only sunbeams pay proper homage to a tender female body . . . / No man has yet arrived, has ever been, will ever be. / A man is a false mirror that the sun's daughter hurls against the cliffs in rage."

In 1916 Södergran's first book of poems, *Dikter* (Poems), was published. The reviews were mixed, with many of the Swedish publications in Finland misunderstanding the book's new style completely and even treating it as a kind of joke. The publisher, Holger Schildt, agreed to print the book without payment to Södergran on the grounds that paper during wartime was too expensive. Södergran agreed, saying that the chance to put her ideas out to the world was more important than payment.

That decision backfired as Bolshevik forces overthrew Russia's government in the fall of 1917 and instituted Communist rule in what became the Soviet Union. The remnants of Södergran's mother's family wealth were largely tied up in Russian and Ukrainian stocks that were suddenly rendered worthless. The reviews for *Septemberlyran* (The September Lyre, 1918) were even worse than those for Södergran's first book, thanks partly to a grandiose introduction, influenced by Nietzsche's outlandish individualism, in which she proclaimed that "my self-confidence stems from the fact that I have discovered my dimensions. It behooves me not to make myself smaller than I am." Some writers even suggested that she had gone insane.

Formed Friendship with Critic

Partly because of the poor critical reception of her writings and partly because of her deteriorating financial situation, Södergran increasingly began to withdraw from public appearances and to sequester herself in Raivola. However, she cultivated a close relationship with the critic Hagar Olsson, who had praised her works and who had had her own difficulties as a female literary critic. Olsson came to visit Södergran in Raivola, and the two women carried on a vigorous correspondence that was published by Olsson in 1956. Feeling that she had a devoted audience, even if it

was a small one, Södergran wrote rapidly in the late 1910s and early 1920s, despite the increasingly chaotic situation that surrounded her small village—both Russia and Finland endured civil war between Communist and non-Communist forces during this period.

Södergran's later books include two collections of poetry, *Rosenaltaret* (The Rose Altar, 1919) and *Framtidents skugga* (Shadow of the Future, 1920), as well as a book of aphorisms. The two books of poetry were not so much criticized as generally ignored, and in general they were known only to a small group of Södergran's friends and a few other poets. *Framtidents skugga* in particular, however, is regarded as a breakthrough in poetic language and attitude. In Katchadourian's words, "While, in comparison with *Septemberlyran* and *Rosenalteret*, *Framtidens skugga* is just as ecstatic in tone and equally visionary, it lacks the exhortations of the previous poetry books. In many of the verses the speaker—as if from a cosmic plateau—tells of the new dawn of mankind in words of almost mystical joy."

Around 1919 Södergran became interested in the ideas of Austrian philosopher Rudolf Steiner, whose system of thought, known as anthroposophy, posited the existence of a spiritual world that had implications for education, agriculture, dance, and many other fields of human endeavor. Södergran rejected her poetic writings up to that point, and tried in vain to interest Olsson in traveling to Switzerland to study at Steiner's center in the town of Dornach. Meanwhile, both her health and her financial situation were worsening, and she suffered from the so-called Spanish influenza that circulated in the late 1910s and early 1920s. She and her mother at times lacked money for food or medicine.

In the last year of her life, Södergran's circumstances grew increasingly dire. She searched for translation work but had little success in the war-devastated region. She sold off household items to make money and at one point went door to door selling used lingerie. Toward the end of her life she began to question Steiner's teachings and turned toward a Christian viewpoint. She wrote a few more poems that were collected into a book by poet Elmer Diktonius, who became one of the followers Södergran never knew she would have. Södergran died, partly from the effects of malnutrition, on June 24, 1923, in Raivola. English language editions of her poetry include those translated by Samuel Charters (also a scholar of blues music), Martin Allwood, Stina Katchadourian, and David McDuff.

Books

Dictionary of Literary Biography, Vol. 259, Gale, 2002.
Schoolfield, George, *Edith Södergran: Modernist Poet in Finland,* Greenwood, 1984.

Periodicals

Scandianvian Studies, Fall 1993.

Online

"Edith Södergran," *Books and Writers,* http://www.kirjasto.sci.fi/sodergra.htm (December 20, 2014).
"Edith Sodergran," *PoemHunter.com,* http://www.poemhunter.com/edith-sodergran/biography/ (December 20, 2014). □

"Södergran, Edith (1892–1923)," *Biografieakeskus,* http://www.kansallisbiografia.fi/english/?id=4814 (December 20, 2014).

"Södergran, Edith (1892–1923)," *Projekt Runeberg,* http://www.runeberg.org/authors/sodrgran.html (December 20, 2014). ☐

Aristides de Sousa Mendes

Portuguese diplomat Aristides de Sousa Mendes (1885–1954) is credited with saving the lives of thousands of refugees in the first year of World War II. As the Portuguese consul-general in the French city of Bordeaux, he deliberately ignored orders from the Foreign Ministry in Lisbon and instead spent several near-sleepless days issuing travel documents to French Jews and others fleeing Nazi Germany's march across France.

Aristides de Sousa Mendes do Amaral e Abranches came from a prosperous family of minor Portuguese aristocracy. He was born just after midnight on July 19, 1885, a few minutes following the birth of his twin brother César. The family seat was a Casa do Passal, a capacious villa in Cabanas de Viriato, a village near Coimbra. Both Sousa Mendes and his twin followed the career path of their father—an appellate court judge in Coimbra—and graduated from the University of Coimbra with law degrees in 1908.

Earned Law Degree

That same year, Sousa Mendes joined the Portuguese Foreign Service and was sent to British Guiana. A year later he wed a cousin, Maria Angelina Coelho, and their four-decade marriage produced an astonishing 14 children, some of them born in far-flung locales as Sousa Mendes moved up the ranks of the diplomatic corps in embassies and consulates that represented Portugal's interests abroad. He served in Brazil, Spain, and Belgium, and two of his children were born in California when their father was serving as the Portugal's consular official in San Francisco in the early 1920s.

Sousa Mendes's twin brother César had also entered the foreign service and was briefly a cabinet official for new Prime Minister António de Oliveira Salazar in the early 1930s. Salazar, head of the conservative National Union political party, established the right-wing *Estado Novo* (New State) regime, while Spain, Portugal's larger neighbor on the Iberian peninsula, fell into a period of civil war until it, too, succumbed to a right-wing military dictatorship under Generalissimo Francisco Franco. Both Salazar and Franco remained in power until the 1970s, unlike their Fascist counterparts in Italy and Germany. Italian leader Benito Mussolini moved aggressively into Africa to expand Italy's colonial holdings, while Nazi Party leader Adolf Hitler annexed German-speaking Austria, then occupied Czechoslovakia in 1938. The Nazi political ideology blamed much of contemporary Germany's woes on its

historically significant Jewish population, and Hitler's government began enacting stringent measures against Jews in Germany, even depriving them of their citizenship.

Sent to Bordeaux

In August of 1938, sensing the danger of a coming continental war, Sousa Mendes requested to be posted to China or Japan. Instead Salazar appointed him the new consul-general in Bordeaux, in the southwest corner of France. The city was a culturally significant site and close to the fabled vineyard regions of the same name, and Sousa Mendes moved into rather splendid quarters above the consulate at 14, Quay Louis XVIII, whose windows overlooked the Garonne River. Some of his younger children were with them, while others were already living abroad.

Sousa Mendes arrived in Bordeaux in late September of 1938. His brother César, meanwhile, was the Portuguese ambassador to Poland, a post he held from 1933 to September of 1939, when Germany invaded Poland. From Warsaw, the elder Sousa Mendes twin likely knew of Nazi atrocities, including the terrible conditions that Germany's and Czechoslovakia's Jews were enduring. After being stripped of legal protections, Jews were at first encouraged to immigrate, then rounded up in mass deportations. Falsely promised farmland in other parts of Eastern Europe, thousands of newly homeless Jewish families boarded actual cattle-transport train cars, which deposited them instead in labor camps like Bergen-Belsen, Treblinka, and Auschwitz. Few in the West knew of the brutal conditions in these camps, which were located deep inside Nazi-held territory.

Some of Europe's Jews had been able to flee to Britain, or the United States. When World War II erupted in the late summer of 1939, however, safe passage to either of those places became exceedingly difficult. Portugal and Spain were able to remain neutral noncombatants, and for this reason some ships carrying civilians were allowed to depart from ports like Lisbon and Bilbao to reach London or British coastal cities. Within a matter of months all transatlantic travel would become impossible when the sea, too, became a theater of war between Nazi Germany and the Allied powers. In the first months of the war, however, Sousa Mendes was permitted to grant transit visas to refugees, which allowed the bearer to enter Portugal and stay for a maximum of 30 days. Portugal could be reached via Spain, whose border with France was the Pyrenees Mountains, a relatively short distance from Bordeaux.

Ignored Circular No. 14

On November 11, 1939, the Salazar government issued the dire new directive known as Circular 14, which specifically forbade consular officials from issuing transit visas to those the Estado Novo termed dangerous to its stability, including Russians, stateless people, and Jews without travel documents showing they had been granted an entry visa from another country, such as the United States. The directive was in response to the stream of refugees who were attempting to enter neutral Portugal after Germany's invasion of Poland two months earlier. The stream turned into a river the following spring, when Nazi forces moved to occupy France and the Benelux countries of Belgium, the Netherlands, and Luxembourg.

Beginning in May of 1940, Sousa Mendes's picturesque adopted city of Bordeaux quickly became one of the last-chance destinations for Jews in all four countries, plus thousands of other politicians, journalists, and others who had railed against the Nazi threat in France and the Benelux nations. The German military moved westward in a multipronged attack, and the French capital Paris fell on June 14, 1940. Sousa Mendes had already made some attempts to evade the terms of Circular 14, sending a cable to Salazar on May 21 to ask what should be done about the onslaught of refugees asking the consulate in Bordeaux for aid; the response instructed him to do nothing.

Befriended Polish Rabbi

Sousa Mendes was distressed by the plight of the refugees desperate to escape the Nazi occupation of France, which took a little over a month to complete. He sometimes asked his chauffeur to take him around the city, and outside a synagogue he was moved by the encampment of families who had recently arrived. Among them was a Polish rabbi named Chaim Kruger, and Sousa Mendes invited him to stay at his home. As Kruger later recalled, Sousa Mendes had told him that one side of his Portuguese lineage were descended from Marranos, the Jews who had been compelled to convert to Christianity in the 1500s. Kruger told a Holocaust Memorial foundation that he visited Sousa Mendes at the consul's home, but that the rabbi's young children were frightened by the crucifixes and other icons of the Roman Catholic faith in the Sousa Mendes home. The rabbi beseeched Sousa Mendes for help in emigrating, and Sousa Mendes followed procedure and cabled the Foreign Ministry in Lisbon on June 13 to ask for permission to grant 30 Jews transit visas, including members of the Kruger family. The request was denied.

Sousa Mendes's sons recall that their father took to his bed for nearly three days. On June 16, 1940—the same day that France officially capitulated—he rose, dressed, and announced his intention to ignore Circular 14. "Our constitution clearly states that neither the religion nor the political beliefs of foreigners can be used as a pretext for refusing to allow them to stay in Portugal," he explained to his consular staff, according to Christian House in the *Independent on Sunday*. With that, he set up the necessary raft of papers, stamps, and ink to rapid-process applications for visas to enter Portugal via Spain. For the better part of two entire days, he processed paperwork and signed his name so many times that he shortened it to just "Mendes" to expedite the process.

On June 19 Sousa Mendes left for Bayonne, near the Spanish border, after learning that his Portuguese subordinate there, vice consul Faria Machado, was refusing to grant visas. He set up another makeshift visa-processing office, which was quickly flooded by desperate Jews, French Communist Party members, and others imperiled by the coming Nazi occupation. Machado complained to Spanish officials, and Franco's government reacted quickly to declare all visas issued by Sousa Mendes invalid for entering Spain. In one final act of bravery, Sousa Mendes drove to a less popular Pyrenees border crossing at Hendaye, with several cars of refugees behind him, and convinced the Spanish border guards on the other side in Irún to let them through. Sousa Mendes had correctly guessed that the little-used Irún crossing did not have a telephone, and thus the guards had not received instructions to turn back bearers of Portugal-issued transit visas. Among that last wave of entrants was the Kruger family.

Defended Himself in Court

The Germans entered Bordeaux on June 27. Sousa Mendes had already been formally recalled to Lisbon for his actions, and arrived on July 8, 1940. Disciplinary proceedings had commenced four days earlier, and he was indicted on August 2. In the written statement of defense he submitted, he argued that "it was indeed my aim to 'save all those people,' whose suffering was indescribable," he said, according to Mordecai Paldiel's 2007 book *Diplomat Heroes of the Holocaust*. "Some had lost their spouses, others had no news of missing children, others had seen their loved ones succumb to the German bombings which occurred every day and did not spare the terrified refugees. How many must have had to bury someone before continuing their frenzied flight! This filled me with commiseration for so much misfortune."

On October 19, 1940, Sousa Mendes was deemed guilty of disobedience in his role as the Portuguese consular-general in Bordeaux. The court's recommended punishment was overruled by Salazar, who stripped Sousa Mendes of his rank, pension, and even his license to practice law. Sousa Mendes spent the remainder of his life attempting to have these punitive measures reversed. Even in 1945, when the full extent of Nazi atrocities against Europe's Jews was revealed, Sousa Mendes was unable to win any recognition for the Salazar regime's boast that it had saved Jewish lives. The actual numbers have been debated by historians for decades, but Sousa Mendes was thought to have issued as many as 30,000 visas in May and June of 1940, of which 10,000 to 12,000 went to Jews of many nationalities. The list actually includes several well-known figures, among them the artist Salvador Dali; Otto von Habsburg, the last Crown Prince of Austria, along with the Luxembourg royal family; the entire cabinet of pre-invasion Belgium; noted interior designer Jean-Michel Frank; and the Reys, husband and wife creators of the *Curious George* children's books.

Among Gentiles Honored in Israel

Sousa Mendes spent his final years in poverty and isolation. His children, also prevented from finding employment in the Salazar regime, settled elsewhere. Sousa Mendes's wife died in 1948, and he remarried a year later to a French woman who had borne him a child a decade earlier. The couple lived at the rundown Casa do Passal, its furnishings sold off and even its interior doors chopped up for firewood. Sousa Mendes died in Lisbon on April 3, 1954, at a hospital for charity cases run by the monks of the Franciscan order. Rabbi Kruger survived to recount details of Sousa Mendes's bravery, and that testimony before Israel's Yad Vashem Holocaust Memorial panel earned Sousa

Mendes a posthumous designation as one of the Righteous Among the Nations in 1966. Though Casa do Passal was repossessed and became a notable area ruin for many years, it still stands and was restored to Sousa Mendes's descendants—including 39 grandchildren—by the Portuguese government.

Books

Fralon, Jose-Alain, *A Good Man in Evil Times: The Story of Aristides de Sousa Mendes, the Man Who Saved the Lives of Countless Refugees in World War II,* Penguin UK, 2000, Carroll & Graf, 2001.

Paldiel, Mordecai, *Diplomat Heroes of the Holocaust,* KTAV Publishing, 2007.

Periodicals

Independent on Sunday (London, England), October 17, 2010.

New York Times, May 4, 1986; July 10, 2013. □

E. G. Squier

Ephraim G. Squier (1821–1888) had a long and globe-trotting career as an American diplomat, journalist, and archeologist. As a newspaper editor in Ohio in the 1840s he became fascinated by the region's enormous earthen shapes, which had been abandoned in the pre-Columbian era by a Native American nation about whom little was known. Squier teamed with another amateur archeologist to write *Ancient Monuments of the Mississippi Valley,* a milestone in the fields of North American archeology and anthropology.

Ephraim George Squier was born on June 17, 1821, in Bethlehem, New York. The future journalist and diplomat spent his childhood traveling a circuit of towns in upstate New York and Vermont with his father Joel, a Methodist minister. His mother Katherine Kilmer Squier died when he was 12 and his father later married his late wife's sister Maria, a union that produced two half-brothers for Squier. In his mid-teens Squier attended the Troy Conference Academy in Poultney, Vermont, where he demonstrated a talent for mathematics. That led to a brief stint as a civil engineer, and for a time he shelved his youthful literary ambitions to work instead as a schoolteacher, a job he quickly came to loathe.

Moved to Southern Ohio

Ambitious and skilled in networking with more established figures in his chosen field, Squier moved into journalism in the early 1840s in Albany, New York. He was active in the state's landmark prison-labor reform movement and was also drawn into Whig Party politics. After serving as co-editor of the *Hartford Journal* he moved to Chillicothe,

Hulton Archive/Getty Images

Ohio, in early 1845 to take over at the *Scioto Gazette,* the oldest newspaper in the state.

Scioto County took its name from the Scioto River, which feeds into the Ohio River in the southern part of the state near present-day Kentucky and West Virginia. This region west of the Appalachian Mountains was also home to curious earthen structures that had been there for several centuries. Similar burial mounds had been found by fur trappers, settlers, and other Europeans as they moved into the mid-North American interior over the past three centuries, but those elsewhere were dwarfed by the enormous landscape shapes of the Ohio River Valley. Writing about them to his former newspaper colleague in Albany, Squier described them as "more perfect and more bewildering than any I ever before" seen in New England, according to Terry A. Barnhart's biography, *Ephraim George Squier and the Development of American Anthropology.* Squier added in his letter he found it "strange how these things have been overlooked!"

In Chillicothe, Squier met the physician Edwin Hamilton Davis, who was a decade his senior and also fascinated by the circles, squares, and even winding snake shapes created by the long-ago Mound Builder civilization, as it came to be called. At the time, the field of archeology was relatively new and just emerging as an academic and professional pursuit. The single work of scholarship on the Mound Builders was from an early Ohio settler and political figure named Caleb Atwater, whose 1820 paper had been published by the American Antiquarian Society. Atwater believed that the huge shapes like the Serpent Mound in Peebles, Ohio, were the work of a long-ago population descended from the "Hindoos" of India, as Atwater called them, who had come over to North America, stayed in the Ohio and Mississippi River Valleys for a time, then moved south to Mexico and Central America and evolved into the mighty nations of Mesoamerica discovered by Christopher Columbus. Atwater's theory was wrong, as were Squier's later conjectures about the origin of the Mississippian culture Mound Builders. Adherents of the Church of Jesus Christ of Latter-Day Saints, or Mormons, came across the landscape shapes on their journey west to Utah. Mormon leaders theorized they were earthen proof that the so-called Lost Israelites had come to America in ancient times, an idea discussed in the sect's 1830 holy tract *The Book of Mormon*.

Roused Interest in Pre-Columbian Era

Squier and Davis set out to document and sketch the mounds, and Squier presented some of their preliminary work at an 1846 meeting of the American Ethnological Society of New York. That led to the eventual publication of *Ancient Monuments of the Mississippi Valley*, a 300-page tome featuring 48 engraved plates and more than 200 maps and illustrations. The costs of printing and distribution were taken over in a deal with the recently established Smithsonian Institution in Washington, D.C. In their book, Squier and Davis grouped the mounds according to an assumed purpose. Some appeared to be works of strategic defense like the straight-line bluffs erected near river embankments. Others Squier and Davis described as effigies because of their resemblance to familiar animal shapes. The masterfully diametered circles located on higher elevations, their book surmised, were assumed to be temple mounds or sites of spiritual observance or homage.

Squier and his co-author also discussed possible origin theories in *Ancient Monuments of the Mississippi Valley*. Like Atwater, they believed the Serpent Mound and other sites were not the work of any known Native American peoples, but rather of an earlier population unrelated to local Shawnees and other Algonquian speakers who still lived in sparse pockets in the region. They assumed the earlier population had been forced off their lands by Algonquian-speaking First Nations from the eastern parts of the United States and Canada. "Though noting similarities in stone tools between Indians and Moundbuilders, the authors insisted that Indians of the east were 'hunters' rather than farmers," explained Paul D. Welch in the journal *Antiquity*, "and thus could have had neither the leisure time nor the impetus to devote so much labour to the calculation of geometry and piling of dirt." Squier and Davis also drew comparisons with other known ancient sites like Stonehenge in England, and the remnants of brutally demolished Aztec civilizations in Mexico and Central America.

Ancient Monuments of the Mississippi Valley caused a sensation when the Smithsonian published it in 1848. By that time, however, Squier and Davis had sundered their collaboration. The two disagreed about some theories of origin, which evolved into a battle over publication terms and payment. Their book was the first in the Smithsonian Institution's "Contributions to Knowledge" series, and Squier also fought bitterly with his editor Joseph Henry, the first Secretary of the Smithsonian and an esteemed scientist, over some claims in the text, which Henry excised due to his judgment that they were merely speculative. Nevertheless *Ancient Monuments of the Mississippi Valley* was well received and sparked interest in North American archeology and ethnology, or the study of human population groups. As Welch reported in the *Antiquity* essay, the book even incited general interest in the mainstream press of the era. "The Moundbuilder question became one of the most popular puzzles of the 19th century," Welch noted, "as popular then as have been questions in recent decades in the US about UFOs and who shot President Kennedy."

Appointed Envoy to Peru

Squier was just 27 years old when his first book was published, and he went on to a career of some note—and notoriety—as an explorer, writer, and even diplomat. In 1849 he headed south to Central America as the U.S. negotiator for a deal to build a canal across the Isthmus of Panama. At the time, Honduras, Nicaragua, and other parts of this land mass and vital strategic connector between the continents of North and South America were held by independent governments, like that of José Trinidad Cabañas, president of Honduras, or controlled by well-armed colonial authorities with trade interests. From Cabañas Squier secured access to the Gulf of Fonseca and its coal-rich Tigre Island. This irked the British, which sent troops in response to occupy the island. Squier was also involved in a scheme to build the Honduras Interoceanic Railroad, which ended in financial disarray.

During his time in Central America, Squier became involved in a notable but long-forgotten effort to establish English-speaking colonies in Central America. These were to eventually become slave-holding U.S. states, and thus tip the balance of power in the pre-Civil War United States. A Tennessee adventurer named William Walker led an army into Central America, declared himself president of Nicaragua in 1856, and was eventually shot by firing squad in Honduras. Squier, meanwhile, was appointed special charge d'affaires for Peru by the U.S. government. He made two extended trips to South America, one in the early 1850s and another again a decade later, and eventually produced two more works of archeological and anthropological merit, *The States of Central America* in 1858 and *Peru: Incidents of Travel and Exploration in the Land of the Incas*, an 1877 tome that took him more than a decade to complete.

Some of the delay was due to personal turmoil. Squier was 36 years old when he married a young woman destined to have an equally impressive career in nineteenth-century America. She was 21-year-old Miriam Folline of New Orleans, who spoke Spanish and French and had appeared onstage in a few American cities as the purported younger sister of notorious European cabaret artist Lola Montez. Squier and Miriam were married in 1857 and settled in New York City. A gifted, equally self-educated polymath, Miriam went with her husband to Peru in 1863, though she stayed in the capital of Lima instead of enduring the grueling archeological explorations into the Andes Mountains and its valleys.

Cuckolded by Tabloid Tycoon

Miriam tended to incite emotional turbulence in those who were close to her. In New York City she and Squier became friends with tabloid-newspaper founder Frank Leslie, who moved into the Squiers' Manhattan home at 205 East 10th Street as a tenant, then at some point may have become romantically involved with the new Mrs. Squier. Leslie was still married and the appearance of the trio at high-profile social events of the era—including President Abraham Lincoln's first inauguration ball—was a barely concealed scandal whispered about in elite circles. They even traveled to Europe together, where Squier spent two weeks in a Liverpool debtors' jail in a case of mistaken identity engineered by the underhanded Leslie, a powerful tabloid publisher of the era. Frank and Miriam spent two romantic weeks in London and Paris before returning to England and paying Squier's bail.

The situation tormented Squier and he succumbed to alcohol abuse and more trickery. He and Miriam were eventually divorced, as was Frank Leslie from his first wife, and the new Mrs. Leslie rather infamously began an affair with another man, a poet, while a New York courthouse declared Squier of unsound mind and confined him to the Sanford Hall Asylum in Flushing, New York. His half-brother eventually came to his aid and helped him restore his personal and professional reputation. While the Leslies became enormously successful newspaper and magazine publishers, Squier was thought to have extracted some revenge through the anonymous publication of a tell-all pamphlet about his ex-wife that bore the subtitle, *A Life Drama of Crime and Licentiousness.*

Squier died on April 17, 1888, at his brother's home on Lafayette Avenue in Brooklyn, New York. His passing was noted in both the *New York Times* and the *Times* of London, with the latter naming his extensive list of published books. These included *Waikna: Or, Adventures on the Mosquito Shore* and *Tropical Fibres: Their Production and Economic Extraction.* "The Spanish conquerors found in America nations far advanced in the arts," Squier had written in his 1877 volume *Peru,* "who had constructed great works of public utility, and who had founded imposing systems of government and religion.... The only modern nation that, in its polity, its aggressiveness, its adaptation, and, above all, its powers of assimilation, as well as in its utter disregard of traditions and of monuments at all comparable to the Incas is our own."

Books

Barnhart, Terry A., *Ephraim George Squier and the Development of American Anthropology,* University of Nebraska Press, 2005.

Squier, E.G., *Peru: Incidents of Travel and Exploration in the Land of the Incas,* Macmillan, 1877.

Periodicals

Antiquity, December 1998.

New York Times, April 18, 1888.

Times (London, England), April 20, 1888. □

Claus Von Stauffenberg

German military officer Claus von Stauffenberg (1907–1944) led a major assassination attempt on Adolf Hitler in 1944. Though his July 20 conspiracy failed to complete its goal, Stauffenberg came to be seen as a hero for his anti-Nazi stance. His plot was the subject of the 2008 film *Valkyerie.*

Claus von Stauffenberg was born November 15, 1907, in Jettingen-Scheppach, Germany, the youngest of three surviving sons of Alfred Schenk Graf von Stauffenberg and Caroline Gräfin von Üxküll-Gyllenband. (His twin, their fourth son, died at birth.) His family was aristocratic and Catholic, one of the most prominent in the region of Bavaria. Stauffenberg was born in the family's castle. Among his ancestors was August von Gneisenau who had played a prominent role in Prussia's fight against Napoleon Bonaparte.

In his youth, Stauffenberg was a gifted student and athlete. Academically, he enjoyed literature, especially poetry, and had a gift for learning languages. Athletically, Stauffenberg was a skilled equestrian. Because of his abilities, he earned a spot on a German Olympic team.

Joined German Military

As part of his aristocratic heritage, Stauffenberg's family emphasized the importance of serving one's country. Stauffenberg lived this out through military service. His family sponsored the Seventeenth Calvary Regiment, and Stauffenberg joined it in 1926. He soon began moving through the military ranks as a career military officer, reaching the rank of second lieutenant in 1932.

Stauffenberg's military career was impacted by the ascent of Adolf Hitler in 1933. When Hitler took power, Stauffenberg was initially supportive of the charismatic leader and his restoration of German nationalism. Germany struggled with harsh reparations and a bruised outlook after losing World War I.

Stauffenberg became disenchanted with Hitler almost immediately, and never joined the Nazi Party. Stauffenberg's attitude towards Hitler initially changed because of his attitudes and actions towards the Jews. In September 1934, Stauffenberg's soldiers were required to attend a party lecture that was imbued with anti-Semitism. Stauffenberg walked out.

Stauffenberg's career continued to progress, however. In 1936, he graduated first in his class from the Army Staff College. Upon completing this course, Stauffenberg was promoted to captain. He and the rest of the Seventeenth Calvary Regiment then joined the Sixth Panzer Division.

Became Disillusioned with Hitler

Stauffenberg continued to grow in his opposition to Nazi policy. In November 1938, Hitler implemented the Kristallnacht (Night of the Broken Crystal or Night of the Broken Glass), an evening of anti-Jewish pogroms in Germany.

Hulton Archive/Getty Images

Over the course of the night, thousands of homes and businesses owned by Jews were ransacked. Stauffenberg then became more openly repulsed by Nazi violence and cruelty. He considered such actions inane, and the actions of Kristallnacht, a marring of Germany.

Those in Germany who opposed Hitler had been organizing resistance groups and movements since he took power. Stauffenberg became more aware of and supportive of such efforts after Kristallnacht. Among those who were discussing resistance included Stauffenberg's cousin, Count Helmuth James von Moltke. He brought many, including Stauffenberg, into what was termed the Kreisau circle. Together, they discussed Germany's future after the Nazis. This group hoped that a new Germany would be built on Catholic principles and focus on small communities. Stauffenberg began thinking of the ways a coup could take place, including the murder of Hitler, and who would take power after the event.

By 1939, Stauffenberg's division was occupying the Sudetenland, a part of Czechoslovakia that included predominantly German speakers in its population. As World War II began in earnest in 1939, Stauffenberg took part in the invasion of Poland and the invasion of the Soviet Union, known as Operation Barbarossa. He also served in France, receiving two more promotions, and reaching the rank of colonel by the early 1940s. Over these years, Stauffenberg became more convinced that Hitler and the Nazis should be removed from power.

Suffered Major Injuries

In 1941, Stauffenberg was transferred to Tunisia in North Africa. He was part of the Afrika Korps led by General Erwin Rommel. During a military operation in April 1943, he suffered major injuries as a result of an Allied air offensive. They included the loss of his left eye, right hand, and two fingers on his left hand. Recovery from this near death experience took place at a hospital in Munich.

During his recuperation, Stauffenberg decided to go forward with a plot against Hitler and hoped to succeed where many had failed. (Over the course of his time in power, Hitler had lived through at least 15 and perhaps as many as 45 different assassination attempts.) Though Stauffenberg could have retired, he remained in the army. Because of his extensive injuries, he was transferred to Berlin and the General Army Office located in the Bendlerblock military building. There, because of his recent experiences and return to duty, he became a legend.

In Berlin, Stauffenberg served as the chief of staff to General Friedrich Olbritcht. The general also was already involved in the conspiracy against Hitler. As part of his new duties, Stauffenberg devised emergency plans if communication was broken between the high command and Berlin for any reason.

While stationed in Berlin, Stauffenberg began to actively plot the murder of Hitler and the overthrow of the Nazi regime. Serving in the Nazi military had only increased his negative feelings towards those in power, as Hitler and the Nazis represented all that he opposed as a Roman Catholic and career military officer. Picking only familiar conspirators, he overcame his initial resistance to armed action because he had taken the personal oath to Hitler required of all officers.

Devised Assassination Plot

By 1944, Stauffenberg overcame any personal qualms about assassinating Hitler. On July 1, 1944, Stauffenberg received a promotion, from lieutenant colonel to colonel. With it came a new position for Stauffenberg, as he became the chief of staff to General Friedrich Fromm, the Reserve Army's commanding officer. Fromm knew of the growing conspiracy, but was indifferent to it. Because of Stauffenberg's new post, he gained direct access to Hitler, allowing Stauffenberg to pull off an assassination plot with his group, which he dubbed "Secret Germany."

As part of the preparations, Stauffenberg and the other officers who formed the conspiracy prepared a list of well-known officers ready to take power in Berlin after Hitler died. Because of his position and duties in Berlin, Stauffenberg was in place to handle this type of responsibility for the conspiracy. Input and assistance also came from some of those involved with the Kreisau circle. Stauffenberg ultimately hoped a social democratic government would be formed after the Nazi regime was removed.

Stauffenberg's plan centered on the German army operational plan known as Operation Valkyrie. Under it, the Reserve Army was to be activated and used if there was a major event, such as Allied bombing or civil unrest. Those involved with the conspiracy changed the plan so that the Reserve Army gained the right to arrest Nazi and SS leadership if Hitler was assassinated. Thus, the plotters wanted to kill Hitler, ensure communications were impossible between the assassination site and headquarters, and launch Operation Valkyrie by stating that a coup within the Nazi Party had begun. Those involved with the conspiracy would then gain control of the Reserve Army and use it to take control of Germany from the Nazis. By this point, many in Nazi Germany knew and accepted that the war was lost.

Failure of Assassination Attempt

Stauffenberg's plot to kill Hitler went into motion on July 20, 1944. Stauffenberg played the key role in the plot. He carried two briefcases containing explosive charges on a timer to Hitler's military headquarters in Rastenburg, East Prussia. Because of limited time and his injuries, he only had time to set one bomb. Stauffenberg placed the case in the room where Hitler was attending a briefing with about 24 staff officers and their aides, and then left.

While the group was discussing the military situation, the bomb inside the case went off. Because it had been moved to one side by one of the attendees, Hitler survived. Four others were killed and 11 were wounded. Before the explosion, Stauffenberg was already on his way back to Berlin to activate the Reserve Army and seize power with his conspirators. Stauffenberg and his co-conspirators kept the plot going for several hours and seized control of certain aspects of the German government. Stauffenberg believed Hitler was dead until the Nazi leader communicated with some of his key staff via lines co-conspirators failed to cut or put under their control.

The coup lost more and more momentum by the evening of July 20. It ended when Stauffenberg and others still loyal to the cause were caught and exchanged gunfire with loyal representatives of the regime. Suffering a shoulder wound in the process, Stauffenberg was arrested by Fromm, who swung his support to Hitler during the coup attempt. Stauffenberg and three others were killed by firing squad under Fromm's orders later that night in the Bendlerblock courtyard. Stauffenberg died on July 21, 1944, in Berlin. He was 36 years old.

Legacy of Stauffenberg's Plot

In the years after Stauffenberg's death, the July 20 plot, as it came to be called, had a wide-ranging impact. Hitler sought out all who were conspiring or suspected of conspiring against him. In all, about 7,000 were arrested and about 2,000 were executed. Many were sent to concentration camps, and some committed suicide. Fromm was arrested and executed for failing to act against the plot early on.

Like many of the wives and children of conspirators, Stauffenberg's wife, Nina Freiin von Lerchenfeld, and their four children suffered indignities after his death. His wife and other relatives were arrested, while his children were left in the care of servants and officers from the Gestapo. The couple's fifth child was born while Stauffenberg's wife was held in confinement. Plans to send the children to Buchenwald, a concentration camp, never came to fruition as the U.S. Army reached them first.

Though much of Germany had a negative opinion of the conspirators for decades, attitudes changed significantly by 1970. In addition to being the subject of a number of books, the Stauffenberg plot was made into a Hollywood film, *Valkyrie*, in 2008, starring Tom Cruise as Stauffenberg. On July 20, 2014, the 70th anniversary of the plot was commemorated by the German government, with ceremonies led by President Joachim Gauck. About 200 people involved with the plot took part in the event and were celebrated for their courage. As Tim Hames wrote in the London *Times*, "The bravery and the principles of those involved in the July 20 plot can barely be overstated. They knew the dangers, and they knew that the penalty for failure would be gruesome."

Discussing the importance of Stauffenberg's plot, Stauffenberg's granddaughter, Sophie Bechtolsheim, told Elisabeth Braw of *Newsweek*, "Otherwise, how would we be able to look the victims of the Nazi regime in the eyes? We can learn [from the plotters] that taking a stand and taking the resulting action is not just necessary but possible."

Books

Europe Since 1914: Encyclopedia of the Age of War and Reconstruction, Volume 4, edited by John Merriman and Jay Winter, Charles Scribner's Sons, 2006.

Periodicals

The Express, August 23, 2008.

The Herald (Glasgow, Scotland), July 9, 1994.

The New American, March 2, 2009.

Newsweek, August 15, 2014.

The Times (London, England), July 19, 2004.

Washington Post, December 25, 2008.□

Josef von Sternberg

Best known for the seven films he made with German actress Marlene Dietrich, Austrian filmmaker Josef von Sternberg (1894–1969) directed her in such classics as *Der blaue Engel* (*The Blue Angel*, 1930) and *Shanghai Express* (1932). Sternberg imbued his films with a well-crafted, if not challenging, visual style that was often groundbreaking and breathtaking.

Born Jonas Sternberg on May 19, 1894, in Vienna, Austria, he was the son of Maurice Sternberg and Serafine Singer. His father was a businessman who emigrated to the United States in 1897. Maurice Sternberg's wife and son followed in 1901. The family briefly returned to Austria from 1904 to 1908. When in the United States, the family lived in New York City, where Sternberg attended Jamaica High School in Queens, New York, until dropping out in 1909. He spent the next two years working in the garment industry

DIZ Muenchen GmbH, Sueddeutsche Zeitung Photo/Alamy

Began Working in Film

By 1911, Sternberg was back in the United States, working in film. In this early era of silent films, he was employed by the Fort Lee, New Jersey-based World Film Company. Beginning as a splicer in his teens, Sternberg was employed as a patcher and spent much of the decade learning editing skills.

When World War I broke out, the United States Army used film technology for many purposes, including training. In 1917, Sternberg joined the U.S. Army Signal Corps so that he could make training films and gain more filmmaking experience. After World War I ended, he returned to the silent film industry.

In the post-war period, from about 1918 to 1924, Sternberg worked as a scenarist and assistant to several silent film directors. In 1919, Sternberg worked on three films, *The Mystery of the Yellow Room, By Divine Right,* and *Vanity Price* as an assistant director.

Also in this period, Sternberg added the "von" to his name. Sternberg did so by 1924 at the suggestion of Elliot Dexter. Around the same time, Sternberg made his way to Hollywood.

Directed First Film

In 1925, Sternberg directed his first film, *The Salvation Hunters.* This gritty social documentary feature starred and was mostly financed by British actor George K. Arthur. It gained the attention of silent film star Charlie Chaplin,

who was not only a film star but also a director and producer. Chaplin released *The Salvation Hunters* through the film company he co-owned, United Artists. *The Salvation Hunters* was never a widely popular success but helped move Sternberg's career forward.

After *The Salvation Hunters* was released, Sternberg signed an eight-picture contract with Metro-Goldwyn-Mayer in 1925. After his first two film projects failed to reach fruition under his guidance, however, the contract was terminated. The projects were *The Exquisite Sinner* and *The Masked Bride,* and both were completed by other filmmakers.

In 1926, Sternberg directed another film, *The Sea Gull,* also known as *Woman of the Sea.* The film was made for Chaplin, but Chaplin chose not to release it. The negative was lost or locked away, and the film was never shown publicly. Also in 1926, Sternberg was signed to a directing deal by Paramount. He would remain affiliated with Paramount for nearly a decade, well into the sound era.

Developed Visual Style

During his Paramount years, Sternberg was considered the leading visual stylist in Hollywood. As Tim Robey wrote in the London *Daily Telegraph,* "For Josef von Sternberg... light and shade were the only essential properties of movie art. Story and script had no value at all." Sternberg's films were lavish, with deep compositions created through an interplay of shadow and light. Emphasizing detail, sometimes to the point of clutter, to create a sense of place. Sternberg favored femme fatale central characters and often placed them in unusual love triangles. Films that best express this aspect of Sternberg's filmmaking include *Underworld* (1927), *The Last Command* (1928), and *Thunderbolt* (1929). The last film was the first talking picture by Sternberg.

Another example of Sternberg's early stylistic successes was *The Docks of New York* (1928). Both *Underworld* and *The Docks of New York* were considered masterpieces of the silent era. Starring George Bancroft and Evelyn Brent, *Underworld* was noteworthy as the first modern gangster film and featured elements of noir. In this film, a violent bank robber, played by Bancroft, deals with treachery in his ranks. Other films made by Sternberg in the 1920s, included *The Drag Net* (1928) and *The Case of Lena Smith* (1929).

Discovered Dietrich

Catching the attention of German actor Emil Jannings, Sternberg went to Germany in 1929 to make a film at his request for the UFA film studio. While in Berlin, he attended a cabaret production, where he saw actress Marlene Dietrich and found her look and skills suited to his style of filmmaking. Though he later claimed that he discovered the future film star, she had already taken roles in German silent films. Sternberg cast Dietrich as the female lead in his UFA film, *Der blaue Engel* (*The Blue Angel,* 1930). She played the role of Lola-Lola, a predator, who takes advantage of a lonely college professor played by Jannings. The film was a hit in Germany, and its English version was also somewhat popular.

Impressed by her presence on screen, Sternberg brought Dietrich to Hollywood, where they collaborated on six more films. As Dave Kehr wrote in the *New York*

Times, "The seven films in which Josef von Sternberg directed Marlene Dietrich constitute one of the most dazzling runs of creativity in the history of the movies. Released by Paramount Pictures between 1930 and 1935, these are works of breathtaking formal beauty, profound moral philosophy and devastating wit. In many ways they seem apart from, and perhaps in advance of, their time."

Dietrich continued to be a brilliant paradox, a woman who was masculine and superior to men. Through her work with Stenberg, Dietrich cemented her reputation as a sultry, mysterious film star. All the films they made together were exotic romances. In *Morocco* (1930), Dietrich played a cabaret singer, while in *Dishonored: An American Tragedy* (1931), she was an unflappable spy in the spirit of Mata Hari. For her work in *Morocco,* Dietrich would receive an Academy Award nomination

Had Hit with *Shanghai Express*

The most commercially successful film made by the Sternberg-Dietrich team was *Shanghai Express* (1932). The film's box office receipts were half the studio's earnings the year it was released. In the film, she played a martyr, as she would in *Blonde Venus* (1932). In the latter film, Dietrich is a former nightclub performer who marries an American scientist. Though she is a committed wife and mother, her husband becomes seriously ill. To pay medical bills, she returns to singing to pay the bills and becomes entangled with a millionaire, played by Cary Grant, to further cover her family's expenses.

Sternberg and Dietrich's creative partnership continued through the mid-1930s. *The Scarlet Empress* (1934) featured Dietrich playing the controversial Russian empress Catherine the Great. It was another masterwork of demented fantasy and fairytales. Though less popular and sometimes considered disappointing by critics, *The Devil is a Woman* (1935) featured Dietrich as a Spanish woman who is the obsession of an army captain. The film was ornate and extravagant, remembered for beautiful costumes and inventive sets.

Summarizing this stage of Sternberg's career, Richard Armstrong, Tom Charity, Lloyd Hughes, and Jessica Winter wrote in *The Rough Guide to Film,* "No one in this history of cinema has been photographed with such passionate intensity as Marlene Dietrich was by Josef von Sternberg. She was more than an inamorata, she was his creation. 'I am Marlene', he once famously declared. He then spent the rest of his career trying to prove that he was his own man." At the same time, Sternberg had developed a reputation for being an overbearing, contemptuous bully to his performers, including Dietrich. Many who knew Sternberg despised him. Dietrich, at least, would torment him back. The pair was rumored to be sexually involved as well.

Had Few Successes After Paramount

After leaving Paramount in 1935, Sternberg made no more films with Dietrich. His career had reached its peak and would never be as strong again. His first film post-Dietrich was an interesting adaptation of the Fydor Dostoevsky novel, *Crime and Punishment* (1935), followed by a poorly received comedy *The King Steps Out* (1936). In 1937, Sternberg had another aborted project with *I, Claudius.* Made for Alexander Korda in England, the film starred Charles Laughton as Claudius and actress Merle Oberon. During filming, Oberon was in a car crash and the project was canceled.

Sternberg continued to make films, and most were unmemorable, including *Sergeant Madden* (1939). As the *Daily Telegraph*'s Robey explained of this stage of his career, "Though he would continue to work, generally on films no one else wanted to make, von Sternberg's post-Dietrich career was diminished, and the stars with whom he was entrusted later—Gene Tierney, Jane Russell, Robert Mitchum—did not flourish under his autocratic baton."

During World War II, Sternberg returned to documentary work with *The Town* (1941). This film was made for the U.S. Office of War Information. His next feature was *The Shanghai Gesture* (1941), which he both directed and co-wrote. With *The Shanghai Gesture,* Sternberg consciously tried to produce a tour de force film that would prove he was capable of making such works without Dietrich.

Later in the 1940s, Sternberg directed several scenes in *Duel in the Sun* (1946). He also branched out into education in 1947, teaching a film directing class at the University of Southern California.

Made Two Films for Hughes

By the early 1950s, Sternberg was making films financed by eccentric billionaire Howard Hughes. *Macao* (1951) was later almost completely re-shot by Nicholas Ray, while the only film Sternberg made in color, *Jet Pilot* (1957), was totally re-edited. In between, Sternberg made a critically acclaimed, self-financed film, *The Saga of Anatahan* (1953; also known as *Anatahan*). The abstract melodrama focuses on a group of Japanese soldiers and a woman who have been stuck on an island since before the end of World War II who will not believe that the conflict has ended.

Sternberg's film directing career was essentially finished by the end of the 1950s. His contributions to film were not forgotten, however. In 1960, he was made an honorary member of Berlin's Akademie der Künste. Sternberg died on December 22, 1969, in Los Angeles, California. Summarizing Sternberg's legacy as a filmmaker, Gary Arnold wrote in the *Washington Times,* "Mr. Sternberg . . . left an indelibly entertaining mark on love stories that portray the consorts as worldly or shady types who find it advisable to act hard-boiled while proving susceptible to mutual attraction and capable of protective, sacrificial gestures. Before Howard Hawks could orchestrate the chemistry between Humphrey Bogart and Lauren Bacall, Mr. Sternberg was paving the way with George Bancroft and Evelyn Brent or Marlene Dietrich and Gary Cooper."

Books

Armstrong, Richard, Tom Charity, Lloyd Hughes, and Jessica Winter, *The Rough Guide to Film,* Rough Guides Limited, 2007.

Dictionary of American Biography, Charles Scribner's Sons, 1988.

International Dictionary of Films and Filmmakers, Volume 2, 4th ed., edited by Sara Pendergast and Tom Pendergast, St. James Press, 2000.

St. James Encyclopedia of Popular Culture, Volume 5, 2nd ed., St. James Press, 2013.

Periodicals

Daily Telegraph (London, England), December 5, 2009.
New York Times, March 4, 2012.
Washington Times, November 2, 2008. □

Sun Tzu

The Chinese general and military theorist Sun Tzu (c. 544 BCE–c. 496 BCE.) was reputedly the author of *The Art of War,* history's first compendium of military strategy. *The Art of War* is extraordinarily widely read today, not only in military circles but also in spheres of business, government, and even competitive sports.

Charlistoone Images/Alamy

As with most figures from the ancient world, little is known about Sun Tzu's life. There is even considerable debate over whether he actually existed, and, if he did, whether he wrote the book ascribed to him. About the influence of the book that bears his name, however, there is little dispute. It has been studied by military leaders from ancient China down to the modern United States. Numerous books and journalistic treatments offer ways of applying its lessons to business, management, or any other arena of human competition. The 13 chapters of *The Art of War* are carefully constructed, but at their most detailed level they consist of aphoristic single sentences—for example, "To subdue the enemy without fighting is the supreme excellence"—that can easily be generalized to other fields of human activity.

An Instant Classic

In the name Sun Tzu, Sun is a surname, as is usual in the Chinese naming system. Tzu is an honorific suffix, meaning "master." The traditional account of Sun Tzu's life comes from the writings of a Chinese historian named Sima Qian, also known as Szuma Chien or the Grand Historian, who lived from about 135 to 86 BCE. According to him, Sun's given name was Wu, and he was born in 544 BCE. China at the time consisted of a group of smaller kingdoms that were frequently at war with one another. Sun Tzu, according to Sima Qian's account, served a king, Ho-lu, of one of these lands, called Wu. According to Sima Qian, Sun Tzu was himself a native of Wu, but an official chronicle of the era, *The Spring and Autumn Annals,* states that he came from a different region, Qi.

According to Sima Qian, Sun Tzu was a general in Ho-lu's army. With Sun Tzu's help, the king emerged as a regional power, defeating the army of the strong Ch'u kingdom

in 506 BCE. and then conquering the more northerly states of Ch'i and Chin over the next few years. It was after these victories that he is said to have written *The Art of War.* A later military writer, Sun Bin, is thought to have been a descendant of Sun Tzu. Sun Tzu, in this traditional account, died in 496 B.C.E., and one chronicle, the *Yueh Chueh Shu,* stated that he was buried in a large tomb outside the city gate of Wu Shieh.

What is known for certain is that, whenever it was actually written, *The Art of War* began to circulate among Chinese leaders and military men during the so-called Warring States Period (476–221 BCE). By the time of the imperial Han Dynasty (206 BCE–220 CE) it was regarded as a classic, and tales about Sun Tzu himself had become well known. In one characteristic story, Sun Tzu agrees to demonstrate a military formation for the king. The king asks whether Sun Tzu can conduct the demonstration using women, and Sun Tzu replies that he can. The king summons a corps of 180 women, with the king's two favorite concubines in command.

Sun Tzu explains the formation, but when the women are told to carry it out, they begin to laugh instead. Sun Tzu repeats the instructions and orders, but once again the women laugh. Sun Tzu says (the translation of the chronicle *Sun Tzu Wu Ch'i Lieh Chuan* is by Samuel B. Griffith in his edition of *The Art of War*), "If instructions are not clear and commands not explicit, it is the commander's fault. But when they have been made clear, and are not carried out in accordance with military law, it is a crime on the part of the officers." Sun Tzu then orders the execution of the king's two favorite concubines. The king objects that without them, "my food will not taste sweet." But Sun Tzu retorts: "Your servant has already received your appointment as Commander and when the commander is at the head of the army he need not accept all the sovereign's orders." The concubines are executed, whereupon the other women carry out Sun Tzu's dictates.

Historical Accounts Questioned Authorship

As early as the 11th century, Chinese scholars challenged Sima Qian's life and even the fact of his very existence. They raised several objections. Chinese warfare around 500 BCE was not the brutal clash of armies that *The Art of War* depicted, they pointed out, but a more civilized affair marked by combat according to limiting rules. Some chronicles, the skeptics noted, had nothing to say about Sun Tzu as a general, including one covering the kingdom of Wu at that period in some detail. It was possible, they argued, that Sun Bin (also known as Sun Pin) could have written *The Art of War*; for him to have attributed the work to the older figure would not have been unusual in Chinese society at the time.

Defenders of the traditional account have made several counter-arguments: *The Art of War* says nothing about cavalry, they note, which it certainly should have if it were written around 300 BCE., as some of the skeptics assert. Further, given the uncertain transmission history of the text, it should be no surprise to find anachronistic elements in it; it may have been subject to editorial changes and additions at the hands of Sun Bin or other later writers. Sun Tzu's authorship has never been conclusively disproved, and at a distance of some 1,500 years the question may never be definitively solved.

Perhaps the best argument for the authenticity of the book as the product of a single author, whoever it may have been, is the text itself. Its 13 chapters are well-organized and pithy, accounting in large part for the continuing popularity of the book. At several points its advice is underlain by philosophical ideas: "Those skilled in war cultivate the Tao and preserve the laws and are therefore able to cultivate victorious policies," the author writes (as translated by Griffith). The book proceeds logically from Estimates through general evaluations of Waging War and Offensive Strategy, to more specialized chapters on maneuvers, weaknesses and strengths, "The Nine Varieties of Ground," and employment of secret agents. Even at a distance of well over a millennium, it reads clearly, with a minimum of topical reference or imagery peculiar to its own time.

As a result, *The Art of War* spread gradually but steadily around the world. Japanese shoguns and samurais are known to have studied Sun Tzu, whom they called Sonshi, as early as 700 CE. The first Western translation of the book was into French, in the late 18th century; the French general Napoléon Bonaparte, who conquered much of Europe, is thought to have read and applied it. An important early translation into English was by Lionel Giles, in 1910. By 2014 the work had been translated into English at least 18 times.

Several contemporary military leaders have applied the lessons of *The Art of War*. Japanese fleet admiral Togo Heihachiro, who led his naval forces to decisive victories in the Russo-Japanese War of 1905, studied *The Art of War* in detail. The Chinese Communist general Mao Zedong, the founder of the modern Chinese state, explicitly credited *The Art of War* with influencing his tactics in the Red Army's struggle with Nationalist Chinese forces. Vietnamese general Vo Nguyen Giap, who devised strategies that frustrated technologically superior American and French forces in Vietnam, is said to have been a Sun Tzu acolyte, and Americans in turn, subsequent to their defeat in Vietnam, have studied *The Art of War*: generals Norman Schwarzkopf, Jr. and Colin Powell ascribed aspects of American operations in the Persian Gulf War to precepts laid down in the book.

The most numerous examples of Sun Tzu's contemporary influence have come, however, not in military circles but in the world of business, where countless motivational articles have cited *The Art of War*'s highly adaptable formulations. Steven Michaelson's book *Sun Tzu for Execution: How to Use the Art of War to Get Results* is a representative example; Michaelson ascribes the success of companies such as Facebook and Twitter to their having followed Sun Tzu's maxim (quoted by Michael Mink in *Investor's Business Daily*): "Generally, he who occupies the field of battle first and awaits his enemy is at ease; he who arrives later and joins battle in haste is weary. And therefore, one skilled in war brings the enemy to the field of battle and is not brought there by him." Prospects for many centuries of further transmission of *The Art of War* appear promising.

Books

Griffith, Samuel B., *Sun Tzu: The Art of War: The New Illustrated Edition,* Watkins, 1963.

Mair, Victor, *The Art of War,* translation with essays and introduction, Columbia, 2007.

McNeilly, Mark R., *Sun Tzu and the Art of Business: Six Strategic Principles for Managers,* Oxford, 1996.

Sawyer, Ralph D., *The Essential Art of War,* Basic, 2005.

Periodicals

Investor's Business Daily, April 2, 2014.

Online

"Sun-Tzu," *Ancient History Encyclopedia,* http://www.ancient.eu/Sun-Tzu/ (December 2, 2014).

"Sun Tzu Biography," *The Famous People,* http://www.thefamouspeople.com/profiles/sun-tzu-261.php (December 2, 2014).

"Who Was Sun Tzu?" *Sonshi,* https://www.sonshi.com/who-was-sun-tzu.html (December 2, 2014).

"Who Was Sun Tzu?" *Sun Tzu Strategies,* http://www.suntzustrategies.com/about/who-was-sun-tzu (December 2, 2014). □

T

Teresa Teng

Taiwanese vocalist Teresa Tang (1953–1995) was popular not only in her home country but across East and Southeast Asia. Although her music was discouraged and at times even banned by the government of Communist mainland China, it circulated widely in that country as well.

A gifted linguist, Tang mastered several languages and performed in her native Mandarin Chinese, Cantonese, Taiwanese Hokier, Japanese, Indonesian, and English. At the height of her career she was a famous figure whose unsatisfied love life was splashed across newspaper headlines in multiple countries. Her music appealed equally to teenagers and adults, and she became something of a symbol of Chinese identity that could transcend political divisions. "To the Chinese who grew up with her music," noted *Billboard* magazine, "Teng was far more than a pop star. She became a symbol of unity between China, Taiwan, and Hong Kong in the '70s and '80s, when politics were pushing the three countries apart." Teng was a staunch opponent of Communism in mainland China, and she was kept at arm's length by its government as a result.

Practiced Singing at Riverside

Teresa Teng was born Teng Li-Yun on January 29, 1953, in Tien Yang Village, Baozhong Town, Yunlin County, Taiwan. Her family name, Teng, has also been transliterated as Deng, and she was sometimes known as Little Deng after Deng Xiaoping became the leader of mainland China in 1978. The only girl among five children, she grew up in an ordinary middle class family; her father, Teng Shu, was a veteran of the Nationalist Chinese war against the Communists in China in the late 1940s, and her mother, Zhao Sugui, was a government worker. Teng showed talent as a singer when she was as young as five, and she also had a flair for school performance events such as speech competitions. She would practice singing at the riverside, transported there by her father on a bicycle, and after she finished she was given a raw egg in the belief that it would help her develop a smooth vocal style.

At ten, Teng began performing with local bands and won first prize in a folk song contest sponsored by a local radio station. At 13 she won another prize, this one awarded by a radio station where she had taken a singing class; she appeared at a station event and sang a Chinese opera number from a film produced by Hong Kong's Shaw Brothers. The prize held the promise of potential success in the music business, but Teng's school would not allow her to continue missing classes for musical performances. So, at 14, and still a student in middle school, Teng decided to pursue a career in the music business. A year later she broke through to national awareness with an appearance on a music program on Taiwanese television.

With her mother serving as her manager, Teng rapidly became a Taiwanese teenage star. Between 1968 and 1970 she released several albums, signing with a succession of different labels. In 1970 she began to make an impact in Cantonese-speaking Hong Kong, performing at an event called the Pak Fa Yau Charity Fair and winning its top prize for two years in a row. By the early 1970s, still not yet 20 years old, Teng was a star across much of the Chinese-speaking world outside of mainland China; she toured widely in southeast Asia, where large populations of ethnic Chinese flocked to her shows.

Rachel Li/EyePress News EyePress/Newscom

Entered Japanese Market

Yet Teng had still greater ambitions, aiming to conquer the music market in what during the 1970s was by far Asia's largest democracy, Japan. Signing with the Japanese branch of the international Polydor conglomerate in 1974, she underwent another course of vocal and language training and then released the single "Airport," which won Japan's New Star Prize. For the next five years, Teng scored a succession of hits in Japan, winning a national cable television singing contest three consecutive times and mounting numerous tours. Between 1983 and 1995, by which time the brightest part of her career was over, Teng sold an estimated ten million recordings in Japan alone.

Possibly Teng's biggest impact, however, came in a country where her music was only intermittently available, at least officially. After the end of the Cultural Revolution, when mainland China opened to outside influences, her cassettes began to circulate there. They were later banned, but illicit copies continued to pass from hand to hand, and her music was widely known among ordinary Chinese, who reportedly would spend one-quarter of a month's sarlay to buy one of her tapes. She was offered several chances to perform on the mainland, but she refused, saying that she would perform there on the day the Communist system was replaced. Generally her music was romantic in nature, and she avoided political controversy, but she performed in 1989 at protest rallies in Hong Kong after China crushed the Tiananmen Square protests in Beijing. On the

mainland she was known as Teng Li-chun; she used the anglicized name Teresa Teng in Hong Kong and Taiwan.

In 1979 Teng moved to the United States because of immigration difficulties in Japan due to a breakdown in diplomatic relations between Japan and Taiwan. She acquired a questionable Indonesian passport and was barred from Japan for a year. She spent her time in the United States continuing to study languages. In the 1980s she divided her time between Taiwan, Hong Kong (where she could fill the city's three largest concert venues), and Paris. She retired from singing officially in 1989. Total legitimate sales of her albums between the early 1960s and the late 1980s were about 22 million copies; in a market where pirate recordings proliferated, those copies of her music numbered between 50 and 75 million.

Teng had girl-next-door good looks, which she augmented with up-the-leg slit dresses in Taiwanese style that fascinated Japanese audiences especially. But perhaps the biggest contributor to her success was her unique vocal style, which was often described (for example by Wei Hung-chin and Teng Sue-feng on the *Taiwan Panorama* website) as "seven parts sweetness, three parts tears". Teng's voice seemed simple, but it could take on inflections of many different vocal styles, including the sultry nightclub sound of mainland China before World War II, Japanese enka music, music influenced by Chinese opera, and limpid Taiwanese folk songs.

Resisted Demand to Abandon Career

As her high-flying career developed, Teng's love life was turbulent and was followed closely in the East Asian press. She was romantically linked to Hong Kong martial arts star Jackie Chan for a time, and in the early 1980s she was engaged to the wealthy Malaysian businessman Kuok-Khoon Chen. His family, however, demanded that Teng end her singing career, which she refused to do. Teng never married or had children, and she said that not marrying was one of her greatest regrets in life.

In Paris, Teng dated a Frenchman much younger than herself, and in May of 1995 the pair traveled to Chiang Mai, Thailand, for a vacation. Teng, who had struggled with asthma all her life, died suddenly there on May 8, 1995, at the age of 42. At the time, Hong Kong film director Peter Chan was at work with Teng on a script that incorporated her music, and showed her death on a television screen in a shop window. Teng's unexpected death caused a run on her CDs and laser discs, with some of the latter being sold for prices of more than $200 in Hong Kong.

Even a decade after her death, Teng's albums remained strong sellers, and Hong Kong's Phoenix Television produced a five-episode television series about her life. A wax bust of Teng was unveiled at the Hong Kong branch of Madame Tussauds museum, which mounted an exhibition titled "Thinking of Our Dear Teresa." The Teresa Teng Foundation, together with the Ming Pao Publishing House, issued a photo-heavy biography that included a ten-CD box set of Teng's music. Most strikingly, the California-based Digital Domain 3.0 firm created a "Virtual Teresa Teng" that performed in 2013 as part of a concert by Taiwanese pop star Jay Chou.

Periodicals

Billboard, May 20, 1995.
Entertainment Newsweekly, September 27, 2013.
New York Times, May 10, 1995.
Xinhua News Agency, May 8, 2005.

Online

"The Cultural Phenomenon of Teresa Teng," *Taiwan Panorama,*
http://www.taiwan-panorama.com/en/show_issue
(December 4, 2014).
"Deceased Taiwan Pop Star Makes Virtual Stage Comeback,"
Scene Asia (Wall Street Journal), http://www.blogs.wsj.com/
scene/2013/09/09/deceased-taiwan-pop-star-makes-virtual-
stage-comeback/ (December 4, 2014).
"Happy 60th, Teresa," *Global Times* (China), http://www.
globaltimes.cn/content/783245.shtml (December 4, 2014).
"Life of Teresa Teng," http://www.raymondleung.net/Tang/
Life.htm (December 4, 2014).
"Obituary: Teresa Teng," *Independent* (London, England), http://
www.independent.co.uk/news/people/obituary-teresa-teng-
1620611.html (December 4, 2014).
"Pop Diva Teresa Teng Lives On in Chinese Hearts," *China
Daily,* http://www.chinadaily.com.cn/english/doc/2005-05/
12/content_441430.htm (December 4, 2014).□

Bryn Terfel

**Emerging from Wales in 1990, opera singer Bryn
Terfel (born 1964) developed an international reputation as a vocalist and performer not only of operas
and operettas but also of popular forms of music,
including musical theater. Lauded for his charisma,
excellent technique, and memorable bass-baritone
voice, Terfel was an expressive, gifted actor and
singer. Some of his best known work came playing
the roles of Figaro and Falstaff in numerous operatic
productions.**

B orn Bryn Terfel Jones on November 9, 1964, in
Pantglas, North Wales, he was the son of Hefin and
Nesta Jones. His father was a sheep farmer, although
Terfel claimed his father's vocal abilities surpassed his own
but Hefin Jones did not have the same access to training.
Terfel was raised on the family's sheep farm in a small
Welsh village. His first language was Welsh, and he sang
throughout his childhood.

Competed in Local Singing Contests

D.G. "Selyf" Jones, a friend of his family, taught Terfel vocal
technique at an early age. In his youth, he sang in local
choirs. He also competed in amateur singing contests
throughout Wales called eisteddfods, often winning them.
As Terfel told Mary Campbell of the Associated Press, "Every
village in Wales has one on a certain Saturday once a year. I
think that's why so many talents come out of Wales.

Everett Collection/Shutterstock.com

Performing is a tradition from a very early age." Terfel would
use his cash winnings to buy shoes to play soccer.

Determined to pursue music, Terfel moved to London
in 1984 to enter the prestigious Guildhall School of Music
and Drama, after winning a scholarship. A gifted student, he
was honored with the Kathleen Ferrier Scholarship in 1988.
By the time he graduated in 1989, he had won the Best
Singer Gold Medal from the school. He also adopted the
name Bryan Terfel during this period because another professional singer in Equity, a trade union for those affiliated
with the performing arts, had the name Bryn Jones already.

Upon graduating, Terfel competed in the well-known
Cardiff Singer of the World Completion, which drew competitors from all over Europe. He placed second in the 1989
competition, after Russian Dmitri Hvorostovsky. Terfel did
win the Leider Prize and gained valuable publicity since the
competition airs throughout Europe. After the competition,
conductors and companies began seeking Terfel out to cast
him in opera performances. From this early stage in his
career, however, he generally chose supporting or small roles
so he could better develop his technique, stamina, and ability
to depict characters instead of taking the major roles he was
offered to capitalize on his instant popularity.

Made Opera Debut

In 1990, Terfel made his debut in opera, appearing in a
production of Wolfgang Amadeus Mozart's *Cosi fan tutte* at

the Welsh National Opera. Terfel performed the role of Gugliemo. Next, he appeared as Figaro in Mozart's *The Marriage of Figaro* for the same company. Figaro would become an important role for the singer, and he would regularly perform him in Salzburg, Hamburg, Vienna, Munich, Paris, Lisbon, Chicago, and London. He also made his debut at both New York's Metropolitan Opera and Milan, Italy's La Scala in the role. In his debut at the Met as Figaro in 1994, Mike Silverman of the Associated Press lauded Terfel, writing, "Terfel turned in a sophisticated performance brimming with confidence that belies his lack of experience. His was an energetic, intensely physical Figaro....Terfel, a strapping bear of a man, is a graceful actor as well....Vocally he was so on top of the role that he could have fun with it...."

After his appearances with the Welsh National Opera, Terfel's reputation spread to Britain, where he was already in demand. Terfel appeared in the Royal Opera House in London's Covent Garden. Though audiences wanted him to play Don Giovanni in Mozart's *Don Giovanni,* he chose to perform the smaller role of Masetto instead to further develop skills in a smaller role in 1991. He later played a slightly bigger role as Leporello. Also in 1991, Terfel made his first international appearance as the Speaker in *Die Zauberflöte* at Brussels' Théâtre de la Monnaie. Additionally, Terfel made his American operatic debut in *The Marriage of Figaro* at the Santa Fe Opera.

Terfel's international reputation was cemented in 1992 when he performed John the Baptist in *Salome* by Richard Strauss. Terfel made some more early American appearances as well. Appearing at the Ravinia Festival, he sang the Mahler Symphony No. 8 with the Chicago Symphony Orchestra. At the festival, Terfel also made his first appearance in an American recital. That year, he also was named the Young Singer of the Year by *Gramophone Magazine.*

Terfel would have a number of memorable performances in the United States in the mid-1990s that would compel David Patrick Stearns of *USA Today* to quip "Terfel emerged as a vocalist who can do almost anything." In 1993, for example, Terfel sang Donner in Richard Wagner's *Das Rheingold* with the Lyric Opera of Chicago. This marked the first time he performed Wagner.

Branched Out Musically

In this period, Terfel moved beyond opera in his recordings, demonstrating his versatility in the process. In 1996 he recorded a number of songs by the American musical theater composers Richard Rogers and Oscar Hammerstein II on his *Something Wonderful: Bryn Terfel Sings Rodgers and Hammerstein.* More recordings of Broadway songwriters would follow, including *If Ever I Would Leave You* (1998), which featured the songs of Alan Jay Lerner and Frederick Loewe. In 2003, Terfel recorded an album of duets made famous on Broadway with fellow opera singer, soprano Renée Fleming, *Under the Stars.* Of this aspect of his career, Terfel told the Associated Press's Campbell, he was not looking for a popular music career, but that "I know what music I enjoy singing. Therefore I create my own rules, and happily Deutsche Grammophon Records is very flexible with my choices."

In 1999, Terfel performed another iconic operatic character for the first time, the title role in Giuseppe Verdi's *Falstaff.* He had prepared for years to sing the role, including previously performing the smaller part of Ford at the Welsh National Opera. Terfel triumphed as Falstaff in Australia, Chicago, and London at the re-opening of Covent Garden. According to Joseph Stevenson of *Allmusic,* Terfel "has triumphed in Verdi's Falstaff, which he plays with notable humanity and restraint; his Falstaff is a braggart who overrates himself, but not the buffoon some other singers make him. He also sings the evil Scarpia in Tosca."

Terfel continued to expand his repertoire in the early 2000s. In 2000, he appeared at the Met, performing all four villains in Jacques Offenbach's *Tales of Hoffmann.* Terfel further showed his range by fulfilling composer Stephen Sondheim's request that the singer perform the title role in *Sweeney Todd,* appearing in a production of the musical theater stalwart in late 2002 and early at Chicago's Lyric Opera. As Charles Isherwood wrote in *Daily Variety,* "Even with his imposing physique, and made up to look as ghoulish as his teddy-bear face would allow, Terfel was not the most menacing of Sweeneys, but the richness and power of his voice brought their own natural intensity to his interpretation."

Appeared in More Wagner

Also by the first decade of the 2000s, Terfel had professionally matured to the point of taking on more challenging roles in Wagner operas. In the 2004-05 season of the Royal Opera House, he sang Wotan in two operas of Wagner's Ring Cycle, *Das Rheingold* and *Die Walkuere.* In February 2006, Terfel sang for the first time at a new Welsh venue, the Wales Millennium Centre in Cardiff Bay. There he appeared in the Welsh National Opera production of Wagner's *The Flying Dutchman.*

In 2007—the year after the British monarch honored Terfel with the Queen's Medal for Music—he removed himself from a production of Wagner's Ring Cycle at London's Royal Opera House only weeks before opening night. The Ring Cycle was a challenging production, a four-opera epic that took its storyline from ancient mythology of Germanic peoples. Tickets for this production had been sold out for a year. But the youngest of Terfel's three sons needed an operation on a seriously injured finger. Because he would have had to miss rehearsals to be with his child, Terfel felt he could not perform up to his high standards. It was to have been the first time Terfel had appeared in a complete production of the Ring Cycle, and he was widely criticized for the decision.

For much of 2008, Terfel took a sabbatical from performing in operas. Though there was speculation that he was considering retirement, Terfel insisted that he just needed time to recharge as an operatic performer. His only opera appearance came at the beginning of 2008 in a Welsh National Opera production of *Falstaff.* He spent the rest of the year doing a few concert performances, which were less demanding in terms of preparation and rehearsals. He also spent more time at his home with his family.

Among Terfel's concert appearances in 2008 was a performance at New York's Carnegie Hall, where he performed a program of pastoral music of Great Britain in the 20th century. Reviewing the recital, Bernard Holland of the *New York Times* wrote, ''With a towering physical presence that opera directors dream of, a clear, booming bass-baritone that can roar out Handel's 'Si, tra i ceppi e le ritorte' or croon 'Danny Boy' with great delicacy,... Mr. Terfel is also musician enough for the simple beauties of Mozart's 'Io ti lascio, o cara, addio'....''

Established Own Foundation

At the end of 2008, Terfel launched his own arts foundation, the Bryn Terfel Foundation, with gala concerts at St. David's Hall in Cardiff and the O2 Arena in London. Terfel had been funding a scholarship for Welsh music students since 1999 and hoped his new organization might help ease some students' debt loads after receiving a university music education.

In early 2009, Terfel returned to operas, performing in Wagner's *The Flying Dutchman* at the Royal Opera House in London. From 2010 to 2013, Terfel appeared in the four operas that make up the Ring Cycle at the Met at the rate of one per year. In 2011, Terfel returned to La Scala to appear in two operas to open its season. He sang Leporello in *Don Giovanni* and Scarpia in *Tosca*.

Wagner formed much of Terfel's operatic work in 2012. He performed in operas from the Ring Cycle not only at the Met but also the Royal Opera House. He also sang the title role in *Der fliegende Holländer* for the Zurich Opera. In addition, Terfel served as host of his own Brynfest, a four-day festival at London's Southbank Centre.

Recorded with the Mormon Tabernacle Choir

Terfel continued to add new firsts in his career in a productive 2013. He made his concert debut at the Abu Dhabi Festival in the United Arab Emirates, and Muscat, Oman's Royal Opera House. Terfel gave a number of performances in Australia and New Zealand, and performed four concerts at St. David's Hall in Cardiff, Wales, singing his favorite arias. In addition to singing Falstaff at the San Francisco Opera, he was an artist in residence for the first time at the Royal Liverpool Philharmonic Orchestra. He also released an album with the Mormon Tabernacle choir, *Homeward Bound*.

In 2014, Terfel maintained his career diversity by performing in a concert tour of South Africa and appearing in a semi-stage performance of *Sweeney Todd* that was put on at Lincoln Center and the Llangollen International Music Festival. Though Terfel had talked of retiring from opera by his mid-forties in 2008, because his voice would have reached the peak of its power, he planned to continue to challenge himself. In 2015, he was to make his debut as Tevye in *Fiddler on the Roof* for the Grange Park Opera.

Terfel believed he still had musical conquests to make, telling Helena de Bertodano of *The Telegraph*, ''There's a Schubert song cycle that I want to perform. And I'd love an opera—say *Citizen Kane*—to be written for me. Maybe a season in a West End theatre would be interesting, singing *Les Miserables* or *Sweeney Todd*. These are all wonderful singing opportunities.''

Books

Baker's Biographical Dictionary of Popular Musicians Since 1990, Volume 2, edited by Stephen Wasserstein, Ken Wachsberger, and Tanya Laplante, Schirmer Reference, 2004.

Periodicals

Associated Press, October 20, 1994; December 2, 1997; September 12, 1998; January 28, 2000; November 29, 2005; September 4, 2007.
Daily Variety, January 6, 2003.
New York Times, April 28, 2008.
San Jose Mercury News, October 9, 2013.
South Wales Argus, March 29, 2013.
USA Today, October 28, 1994.
The Western Mail, December 5, 2008.

Online

''Bryn Terfel,'' *Allmusic*, http://www.allmusic.com/artist/bryn-terfel-mn0000527469 (December 29, 2014).
''Bryn Terfel: Bass Baritone,'' Harlequin Agency, http://www.harlequin-agency.co.uk (December 29, 2014).
''Bryn Terfel Interview: 'Being an Opera Singer Is Easy','' *The Telegraph*, http://www.telegraph.co.uk/culture/music/10227815/ (December 29, 2014).□

Sigismond Thalberg

Swiss-born Sigismond Thalberg (1812–71) was widely recognized in the 19th century as a virtuoso piano player, touring in Europe and the Americas. He also had a public rivalry with fellow virtuoso piano player Franz Liszt, which culminated in a piano duel in 1837. Thalberg was also the composer of more than 100 works, including two operas and a number of pieces for the piano.

Sigismond Fortuné François Thalberg was born in Pâquis, Switzerland, on January 8, 1812. He was the son of Joseph Thalberg and Fortunée Stein. Both of his parents were natives of Frankfurt, Germany, but his mother resided in Geneva. Later, Thalberg would claim his birth parents were Prince Franz Josef Johann Dietrichstein and Baroness von Wetzlar. Though they were in charge of his education, his birth certificate listed his true parentage, Thalberg and Stein.

Educated in Vienna

When he was ten years old, Thalberg was moved from Geneva to Vienna to live with Dietrichstein and further his education. He was sent there so he could receive the training needed to become a diplomat at the Polytechnical Institute, which he attended beginning in 1822. As a child, Thalberg befriended the Duc de Reichstadt, a military officer.

Apic/Getty Images

Because of him, Thalberg seriously considered focusing on such a career for himself.

Studying music changed Thalberg's path, and Dietrichstein soon gave up his own ambassador training path to manage Thalberg's musical ambitions. His musical education began with the first bassoonist in the Court Opera orchestra, August Mittag. Soon after, Thalberg studied piano technique with Johann Nepomuk Hummel. He also was taught theory by Simon Sechter. Later Thalberg received additional musical training. In Paris, he studied with Johann Peter Pixis and Friedrich Kalkbrenner. In London, Thalberg was taught by Ignaz Moscheles in 1826.

Thalberg focused on becoming a virtuoso piano player. Throughout Vienna, the young Thalberg demonstrated his abilities on the piano in aristocratic salons by the age of 14. He appeared in the salon of Prince Metternich, among others. Thalberg began composing his own music as well, completing his first works by age 16. At the age of 18, he toured as a pianist in Germany and England, and other parts of Europe. During his German tour, he played his own Piano concerto in F minor op 5 in 1830.

Challenged Liszt

By 1834, Thalberg was selected to serve as a court musician for royalty. The following year, Thalberg returned to Paris, where he made his debut in November 1835. There, he performed at a private party hosted by Count Apponyi. By this point in history, Paris was considered the center of

piano virtuosity, and Franz Liszt was considered the best virtuoso piano player in Paris, but had left the city on what would be an 18-month tour. Liszt essentially invented the modern concept of solo piano performance. Before Liszt returned in the winter of 1836 to 1837, Thalberg successfully challenged Liszt's status as the leading virtuoso pianist in Paris.

As Vera Mikol wrote in the *Proceedings of the American Philosophical Society*, "Critics were claiming that Thalberg's playing was perfection itself; they raved about his extraordinary ease coupled with absolute certainty. Proclaimed one: 'His arpeggios at times rolled like the waves of the sea, at others resembled the airy and transparent folds of the finest lace.' Said another, 'From under his fingers there escape handfuls of pearls.'"

After Liszt's return, a rivalry played out based on their alleged mutual jealousy of the other's skills on the piano. Though there was some tension, it was a fabricated, consciously created feud between them. The enmity was created in the press, primarily *Revue et Gazette Musicale* with the assistance of people like Countess Marie d'Agoult, the mistress of Liszt. She penned many negative attacks on Thalberg, and signed Liszt's name to them. Thalberg had many of his own defenders, such as François Fètis, a composer and critic.

Publicly, the hostility between Thalberg and Liszt reached a peak in March 1837. That month, there were two public showdowns. Early in the month, they had consecutive solo concerts, with Liszt selling out a larger venue than Thalberg on the same day. On March 31, 1837, they appeared jointly at a charity recital concert held at the Paris salon of Cristina Trivulzio Belgiojoso, an Italian princess. The event was to determine who was the better of the two via a piano duel.

The Thalberg-Liszt duel at Belgiojoso's salon ended in a draw. As explained on the Kennedy Center website, "At that concert, Liszt's tempestuous, emotional virtuosity was technically superior (as Thalberg himself acknowledged), but Thalberg's repose and careful gradation of tone appealed to many who were put off by Liszt's passionate musical persona. The joint concert was nevertheless a symbolic reconciliation...." Thalberg became only more popular as a result of the competition, at least as a performer. After this point, a few critics viewed him as a lesser composer.

Composed with Liszt

This symbolic hatchet burying was further cemented when Thalberg and Liszt worked on a piece commissioned by the Princess Belgiojoso. The virtuoso piano players, along with other leading pianists/composers such as Pixis, Frédéric Chopin, Carl Czerny, and Henri Herz, created variations of the same piece of music. Within a few years, Thalberg and Liszt established a friendship. Thalberg became recognized as a piano virtuoso. Liszt even compared Thalberg's distinctive piano playing to a violin performance. Liszt was not the only one to admire Thalberg. His other admirers among lauded composers included Felix Mendelssohn, Gaetano Donizetti, and Eduard Hanslick.

What made Thalberg distinctive as a virtuoso piano player was his distinctive technique. While some admired his *legato sostenuto* (notes sustained without a break), he was primarily linked to what was called the third hand effect. As the *Irish Independent* explained, ''He thrilled the crowds with a unique style. He'd put the melody in the middle of the range and use his thumbs to play it. With his other fingers, he'd embark on ornate ornamentation. It made him sound as if he'd three hands. The flitting up and down the keyboard earned him the nickname 'Old Arpeggio'.'' Humorous cartoons of the day depicted Thalberg with three hands.

In Thalberg's third hand technique, the melody was divided between the right and left hands. As a result, the left hand played the bass line, while the right accompanied. The separation of melody, bass, arpeggios, and voices would make it seem like the pianist was using three hands simultaneously. Thalberg would notate music on three staves to capture its complexities.

Toured and Wrote Music

Building on his fame, Thalberg began touring more extensively in the late 1830s and into the 1840s, favoring performances of his own works. In 1839 alone he played in Belgium, Holland, England, and Russia. He appeared in Spain in 1845. Over the course of his touring career, he would appear with other leading musicians of his time, including Bernard Ullmann, Maurice Strakosch, and Henri Vieuxtemps.

Thalberg's personal life also impacted his touring. In 1843, Thalberg was married to Francesca, the eldest daughter of Luigi Lablanche, a bass-baritone singer from Naples. Thalberg then moved to the region. He used his home as his launching point for concert tours. He also worked in education, founding the Scuola Pianistica Napoletuna (Neapolitan School of Pianism).

Many of Thalberg's best-known compositions were created in the 1850s. Of his approximately 100 compositions penned over the course of his lifetime, he wrote a string trio, a duo for violin and piano, piano duets, songs, and two operas. The operas were *Florinda*, which was penned in London in 1851, and *Cristina di Suezia*, penned in Vienna in 1855. Neither were particularly successful.

Thalberg was most highly regarded for his 80 or so piano pieces. These include fantasies, variations, and arrangements based on the melodies of operas. Sixty were of paraphrases or transcriptions for the piano based on operatic melodies. He based such melodies on operas composed by Gioacchino Rossini, Vincenzo, Bellini, Giacomo Meyerbeer, Carl Maria von Weber, Wolfgang Amadeus Mozart, and Giuseppe Verdi. His fantasies based on famous opera arias were perhaps his best known works.

Thalberg also wrote nocturnes, including *Capricdes 2 Romances sans paroles*, *Grandes valses brillantes*, *Le Départ varié en forme d'étude*, and *Marche funébre variée*. In addition, Thalberg composed a piano concerto. The *Souvenirs de Beethoven: Grande Fantaisie pour le Piano sur la 7e Symphonie de Beethoven*, echoed both Beethoven's Fifth and Seventh Symphonies. Sheet music of his work sold quite well during his lifetime, especially in the United States.

Toured in the Americas

In the mid-1850s, Thalberg toured in the Americas. He first went to Brazil in 1855, then essentially lived in the United States from 1856 to 1858. During this period, he also made a concert appearance in Havana, Cuba, and in Canadian cities. During his extensive U.S. tour—conducted at a time when the country enthusiastically welcomed European musicians and singers—he appeared and shared accommodations with Henri Vieuxtemps, a Belgian composer and violinist.

In addition to his United States debut in New York City on November 1, 1856, Thalberg gave some 55 additional concerts in New York alone between 1856 and 1858. In New York, he would sometimes play three concerts per day; some of his appearances were concerts for children. He also put on 13 performances in Philadelphia and 15 in Boston, among other American cities. Thalberg taught and put on opera productions while in the United States as well.

Through the appearances of Thalberg and other European musicians, American music was greatly influenced by trends from the continent. As with his European performances, many of Thalberg's concerts and recitals focused on his own compositions. Yet Thalberg was able to expand his live repertoire. As Mark McKnight wrote in *Notes*, ''these performances, held in intimate settings and including more substantial works by Beethoven, Chopin, and others, allowed Thalberg to expand his repertoire beyond the usual flashy show pieces, and let the audience gain a greater appreciation of the performer's faultless technique.''

After his return from the United States, Thalberg purchased an estate, which included a villa and vineyard in the community of Posilippo, near Naples. Though he would tour occasionally and made appearances in Paris, London, and Brazil, they were fewer and far between. Thalberg also stopped composing by the early 1860s. After an 1863 visit to Brazil, Thalberg essentially retired to his estate and allowed no piano in his home. In his last years, his focus was on making quality wines.

Thalberg died on April 27, 1871, in Posilippo. After Thalberg's death, Liszt wrote a condolence letter to Thalberg's widow, underscoring Liszt's admiration of his one-time public rival. After a large funeral, a monument was erected in Thalberg's honor in a park in Naples.

Thalberg's compositions and techniques continued to be performed in the years after his death, and many recordings have been made of his work, primarily pieces for the piano. His orchestral, chamber, and operatic works have not retained their importance or popularity in the same way. The memory of Thalberg and his accomplishments was maintained by the American Thalberg Society and, after its founding in 1996, the Centro Studi Internazionale Sigismond Thalberg (the International Sigismond Thalberg Study Centre of Naples). The Naples-based organization hosts a major international piano competition named in Thalberg's honor.

Books

Baker's Biographical Dictionary of Musicians, Volume 6, edited by Nicolas Slonimsky and Laura Kuhn, Schirmer, 2001.
Encyclopaedia Judaica, Volume 19, 2nd ed., edited by Michael Berenbaum and Fred Skolnik, Macmillan Reference USA, 2007.

Periodicals

American Record Guide, September-October 1998; July-August 2000; March-April 2005; March-April 2013.

Irish Independent, March 31, 2012.

New York Times, December 7, 1987.

Notes (Second Series), June 2004.

Proceedings of the American Philosophical Society, October 20, 1958.

Toronto Star, July 19, 2011.

Online

"Sigismond Thalberg," *Allmusic,* http://www.allmusic.com/ artist/sigismund-thalberg-mn0001801365 (January 2, 2014).

"Sigismond Thalberg," *The Catholic Encyclopedia,* http:// www.newadvent.org/cathen/14553e.htm (January 2, 2014).

"Sigismund Thalberg," Centro Studi Internazionale Sigismund Thalberg, http://www.centrothalberg.it/Biography.htm (January 2, 2014).

"Sigismond Thalberg," The Kennedy Center, http://www. kennedy-center.org/explorer/artists/ (January 2, 2014).

"Sigismund Thalberg's Life," *Music of Yesterday,* http:// musicofyesterday.com/biographies/sigismund-thalberg/ (January 2, 2014).□

Ernest Lawrence Thayer

American poet and journalist Ernest Thayer (1863– 1940) is best known for writing the classic baseball poem "Casey at the Bat" (1888). The popular comic ballad became widely popular in the United States, though Thayer's authorship was not widely known until the early 20th century.

© Bettmann/Corbis

E rnest Lawrence Thayer was born on August 14, 1863, in Lawrence, Massachusetts, the son of Edward Davis and Ellen Darling Thayer. His father was the president of the American Woolen Mills, and was a descendent of early 17th century immigrants from England to the United States. The wealthy Thayer family had deep roots in Worcester, Massachusetts. One of his nephews, Scofield Thayer, was the creator of the Dial Collection of Modern Art. Thayer was raised in privilege and educated in private schools in the area.

Attended Harvard University

Continuing a family tradition, Thayer attended Harvard, entering in 1881. There, he studied philosophy, studying with William James, the brother of novelist Henry James (author of works including *The Turn of the Screw*). Though Thayer developed a lifelong interest in philosophy while at Harvard, he also was interested in humor and word play which was expressed through his involvement with the humor publication the *Harvard Lampoon*. Fellow workers on the *Lampoon* included George Santayana, who would become a well-known Spanish poet and philosopher. Santayana greatly admired Thayer's wit and way with words. In 1883, Thayer became the editor of the *Lampoon* and

remained so until he graduated from Harvard in 1885. His senior year, he also served as president of the publication.

After graduating summa cum laude with his under-graduate degree, Thayer toured Europe for several months. He spent much time in Paris, where he improved his knowledge of French. When he returned to the United States later in 1885, he found a job through one of his cohorts on the *Lampoon,* William Randolf Hearst. From a wealthy newspaper family, the Hearsts owned the *San Francisco Examiner.* By this time, Hearst had been expelled from Harvard for committing a number of pranks. Hearst's father gave him the newspaper, and Hearst became the publication's editor.

Hearst offered Thayer a position, and Thayer moved to the West Coast to join the staff of the *Examiner.* Beginning in 1886, Thayer was a member of the editorial staff, wrote obituaries and editorials, and sporadically contributed a humor column. Already interested in poetry as well, Thayer penned ballads that appeared in the *Examiner*'s Sunday editions. Much of his work was done under the pen name Phin, an abbreviation of his college nickname Phinny.

Falling severely ill in the winter of 1887, Thayer had to resign his position on the *Examiner* and return to his family home in Worcester, Massachusetts. As he recovered, he worked for his father's textile company, American Woolen Mills, for some months. He ran one of the mills himself. Thayer also continued to write pieces for the *Examiner* from his home.

Wrote "Casey at the Bat"

Among these works were poems that included "Casey at the Bat." Written in May 1888, it was originally published on June 3, 1888, under the Phin pseudonym. Thayer received five to ten dollars for the poem. Its original title was longer, "Casey at Bat: A Ball of the Republic Sung in the Year 1888." The epic-type ballad tells the story of a Mudville player named Casey, who may have been based on one of most popular players of the era, Mike "King" Kelly, or the captain of Harvard's baseball team in 1885, Samuel Winslow. Thayer had been close friends with Winslow at Harvard, and regularly attended his games.

According to Albert B. Southwick of the Worcester *Sunday Telegram,* Thayer once explained, "The poem has no basis in fact. The only Casey actually involved, I am sure about him, was not a ballplayer. He was a big, dour Irish lad of my high school days. While in high school I composed and printed myself a very tiny sheet, (in which) I ventured to gag, as we say, this Casey boy. He didn't like it and told me so . . . I suspect the incident, many years later, suggested the title for the poem. It was a taunt thrown to the winds. God grant he never catches me."

In "Casey at the Bat," Casey's team is losing near the end of a home game 4-2, and the situation seems dire as the last inning is reached. Even the crowd has given up. Casey, the team's hero and best hitter, is expected to bring life to the crowd. After two lesser players—Flynn and Blake—get on base, the crowd has reason to believe because Casey is up next. Though Casey acts confident in his abilities, the umpire is not calling the pitches in Casey's favor and both the crowd and Casey become more unruly. Thayer spends the last lines of the poem drawing out Casey's last at bat, which is a swing and miss for the strike out. The crowd reacts accordingly as Mudville loses the game.

Poem Made Famous By Hopper

When "Casey at the Bat" was first put in print, it was no more popular than Thayer's other Sunday ballads. Like some others, it was reprinted in other Hearst newspapers. The fate of "Casey at the Bat" was altered after it was printed in the *New York Sun* and brought to the attention of De Wolf Hopper, an actor and public speaker.

Later in the 1880s, Hopper performed a piece for two professional baseball teams, the Chicago White Stockings and the New York Giants, at New York's Wallack's Theatre. Hopper was appearing in a Broadway production of a farcical comic opera entitled *The Prince Methusalem.* The players were guests of the theater management, and Hopper decided to read "Casey at the Bat" to honor the guest players in between acts. The reading of the poem was widely lauded by audiences and critics, with those watching and listening at the end standing and cheering. Hopper incorporated "Casey at the Bat" into his repertoire, became deeply identified with it, reading it thousands of times over the course of his career and appearing as Casey in a 1916 silent film.

Also in this period of increased popularity, "Casey at the Bat" was reprinted in large numbers of newspapers and published in book form. The first bound publication of

Thayer's poem came in the Secretary's Report of the Harvard University Class of 1885, issued as a retrospective in 1901. There were also illustrated booklets put in print in 1901, 1902, and 1905. "Casey at Bat" was regularly published as a stand-alone book and included in poetry collections in the 20th and early 21st century.

Thayer's Authorship Established

As "Casey at the Bat" became a popular ballad read and performed regularly in public, authorship was claimed by many. Hopper was one of those who supported Thayer's claim to having written the poem, and his identity was firmly and widely established only around 1910. Hopper also claimed that in the 1890s, Thayer told him that Winslow was the inspiration for Casey. Thayer, however, wrote only a few more poems for publication in newspapers after "Casey at the Bat." He traveled to Europe again, and from 1896 to 1897, was an employee of the *New York Journal* in New York City.

By 1912, Thayer retired because of continued poor health. He returned to California, settling in Santa Barbara. He was married in 1913 to Rosalind Buel Hammett, whose grandfather, James William Buel, was a famous historian. Thayer was active in home service campaigns during World War I. Also in retirement, Thayer wrote scholarly tracts and essays on philosophical topics. Thayer's work from this period was generally unpublished.

Thayer died of a cerebral hemorrhage on August 21, 1940, in Santa Barbara, California. He was 77 years old. By the time of his death, "Casey at the Bat" was considered a popular masterwork, though the author himself did not think it was more or less well composed than his other pieces for the *Examiner.* According to Benno Isaacs of the *Saturday Evening Post,* Thayer distanced himself from the poem throughout his life and "continued insisting that Casey was not poetry at all. Stripped bare, he said, it was merely a simple rhyme with a vigorous beat. He had wanted to write an epic that could be read quickly, understood immediately, and be laughed at by newspaper readers who enjoyed baseball. Instead, he had written an American legend."

Poem Remained Popular After Thayer's Death

Thayer generally dismissed all of his newspaper work as having little value and most was lost over time. However, "Casey at the Bat" was immortalized in animated films, numerous recorded readings, television productions, and a 1953 opera. Mentioned in several popular songs, Casey was included in a 1996 United States Postal Service stamp collection of American folk heroes. Many other authors wrote sequels to the story of Casey, sometimes adding a more happy ending, while others penned parodies and alternate versions.

"Casey at the Bat" would remain a popular poem into the 21st century. Not only the subject of psychological analysis—of the crowd, the other players, the umpires, and Casey himself—the poem was a reminder for many baseball fans of the highs and the lows of the game. Upon Thayer's death, according to the *Saturday Evening Post's*

Isaacs, Yale English professor William Lyon Phelps stated, "The psychology of the hero and the psychology of the crowd leave nothing to be desired." Phelps added, "There is more knowledge of human nature displayed in this poem than in many of the works of our psychiatrists."

Of the staying power of "Casey at the Bat," Donald Hall wrote in the *New York Times Book Review*, "'Casey at the Bat' survives...because it crystallizes baseball's moment, the medallion carved at the center of the game, with pitcher and batter confronting each other." He continued, "Casey must strike out; Casey's failure makes the poem." Hal Bock of the Associated Press similarly felt that the poem is "a baseball ballad that perfectly captures the frustrations of the sport, its peaks and valleys, its joys and disappointments. The game, you see, is very much like life." Mudville could win again another day, like every other baseball team. There is also humor in Thayer's depiction of the mighty Casey, who never demonstrates the greatness accorded to him by the Mudville fans.

Thayer's poem has been examined from many angles, but "Casey at the Bat" remained poignant to audiences more than 150 years after its original publication. Describing the power of "Casey at the Bat," Michael Smith, a writing professor at James Madison University, told Larry Canale of *Sports Collectors Digest*, "Thayer's 'Casey at the Bat' is obviously all about anticipation. It's probably the best expression of the buildup, the rise that occurs in the spaces in between, and it's that rise that happens between lines, between the stanzas of the poem itself. But the poem's about something else, too: Failure and disappointment, which are integral to the game as well."

Books

Contemporary Authors Online, Gale, 2003.
EXPLORING Poetry, Gale, 2003.
Gale Contextual Encyclopedia of American Literature, Volume 4, Gale, 2009.
Poetry for Students, Volume 5, Gale Group, 2009.

Periodicals

Associated Press, July 8, 1987.
New York Times Book Review, June 5, 1988.
Saturday Evening Post, May-June 1988.
Sports Collectors Digest, November 16, 2012.
Sunday Telegram (MA), August 22, 2004. □

Tolui Khan

The Mongol prince Tolui Khan (1192–1232) was an important military leader of the Mongol Empire. He was the son of the celebrated Mongol leader, Genghis Khan, who initiated the empire's expansion, and the father of another, Kublai Khan, who established the long period of Mongol rule in China.

Tolui himself (the term "Khan" was a Mongol title for a king or military ruler, not a surname) was not selected as Genghis Khan's successor. As a result, his life was not documented as thoroughly as those of other Mongol leaders of the period; chronicles such as *The Secret History of the Mongols* tended to mention individual episodes in his career rather than exploring his life in detail. Nevertheless, his prowess as a military leader seems to have been considerable. He accompanied Genghis Khan on several important campaigns, and, together with an unnamed daughter of Genghis, laid waste to the Persian city of Nishapur in one of the crushing victories that contributed to the Mongols' fearsome military reputation. A ruler of a substantial part of the empire during the reign of his brother Ogedei, Tolui also contributed to Ogedei's military campaigns. He died young, and his death occasioned a momentous power struggle between the different branches of Genghis's family.

Enjoyed Special Status as Youngest Child

Born in 1192, Tolui was Genghis Khan's fourth and last son. The name Tolui referred to the three stones used to make a small fireplace in the center of a Mongol family's *gen,* or yurt, and in various other ways the youngest son had a special status in the family, for he was considered to have the closest connection to the past. His family called him *otchigen* or *otgon,* "the prince of the fire." From birth, Tolui was slated to inherit the Mongol lands closest to their seat of power, and he eventually did so. His mother was Borte, Genghis Khan's first wife, whom he had married when she was 16.

Tolui grew up amidst Genghis Khan's spectacular military campaigns, and several dramatic events from his childhood were recorded in chronicles. At one point, when he was four years old, he walked into the family *nger* during a sensitive negotiation with an angry Tartar king, who grabbed him and ran out the door. The kidnapping, had it succeeded, would have been an event with extremely serious consequences; in the words of Jack Weatherford, writing in *The Secret History of the Mongol Queens*, "Such a loss, akin to the departure of his ancestors' support and the blessing of the sky, carried enough supernatural importance to jeopardize the career of Genghis Khan."

The kidnapping, however, failed, and the failure was due to the fact that Mongol women, who enjoyed generally high status, were trained in the arts of war. Tolui's older sister Altani chased the kidnapper, who pulled out a knife and prepared to stab Tolui in the heart. Altani jumped on him, grabbed him by his braids with one hand, and pulled on his knife hand with the other, so hard that the Tatar dropped his knife. The Tatar continued to fight with her, but guards heard the commotion and quickly arrived, cutting the attacker up with an ax and knife. The guards claimed credit for foiling the kidnapping, but Altani objected, and Genghis Khan backed her account and presented her as a model of Mongol womanhood.

Climbed Walls of City

Tolui was betrothed in childhood to a woman named Sorghaghtani, the niece of the leader of a conquered Mongol tribe; she would become a powerful political leader in her own right. She and Tolui had four sons, known as Mongke Khan, Kublai Khan, Hulagu Khan, and Arik Boke. As he grew to adulthood, Tolui began to participate in and then lead Mongol military campaigns as Genghis expanded his empire. His four sons were raised largely by Sorghaghtani. In the east, as the Mongols began to make inroads into China, Tolui climbed the city walls of Dexing in battle against the forces of the Jin Dynasty.

In 1221, Genghis sent Tolui to the Khorasan region, straddling what is now Iran, Afghanistan, and Turkmenistan, where Islamic groups were resisting the Mongol conquest. An arrow fired from a rampart in the city of Nishapur killed the Mongol general Tokuchar, Genghis Khan's son-in-law and Tolui's brother-in-law. The Mongols' devastating response contributed to the empire's reputation for ferocity and total warfare, a reputation that often helped them, along with their superior command of cavalry warfare, to defeat numerically superior adversaries. In many accounts, Tolui has been credited with directing this response, but it may in fact have been masterminded by Tolui's sister (or half-sister), Tokuchar's widow. Chronicles of the event did not transmit her name.

Whoever directed the operation, it was brutal. The Mongols shut off the desert city's water supply and ordered its inhabitants to leave. Then Tolui's army entered the city to deal with those who refused. The Mongols spared skilled artisans but destroyed everyone else, including the rich. According to a Persian chronicle quoted by Weatherford, "[The unknown Genghis Khan daughter] left no trace of anything that moved." That chronicle reported that 1,747,000 people had been killed, probably an exaggeration but one that points to the scale of the massacre. Another Persian writer, Juvaini (as quoted by Weatherford), noted that "In the exaction of vengeance not even cats and dogs should be left alive," "dwelling places were leveled with the dust," and "rose gardens became furnaces."

Passed Over as Supreme Khan

Tolui is thought to have directed a similar massacre in the large Persian city of Merv, now a UNESCO World Heritage site in Turkmenistan. Genghis Khan had no doubts about Tolui's ability as a general, but as he entered old age, he began to favor his other sons when it came to choosing a successor. He believed that Tolui, although brave and valiant, would be too cautious as a political leader. Shortly before his death from unknown causes in a campaign against the Chinese in 1227, Genghis expressed his wish that Ogedei Khan become his successor.

In line with Mongol tradition, Tolui was given lands in the central part of the empire, and he emerged as commander of the greater part of the Mongol army. For two years he was the de facto ruler of the empire. He followed his father's wishes, however, and when the Mongol nobles met to choose the khagan, or supreme Khan, he agreed to their selection of Ogedei. Tolui continued to serve as Ogedei's top general, both in campaigns in the west, against Russia, and in the east, against China.

According to a story of the time that appeared in *The Secret History of the Mongols*, Tolui offered to sacrifice

himself to cure Ogedei of an illness he had contracted during the Chinese campaign. He drank a poisonous liquid, the story went, and died, whereupon Ogedei's condition dramatically improved.

It is more likely that the scourge of alcoholism, which plagued many of the Mongol leaders (who transmitted the technique of distilling alcoholic beverages to the Far East), was responsible for Tolui's death. He was known to have consumed large quantities of fermented mare's milk and, according to Weatherford, "One day in 1232, the forty-three-year-old Tolui had stumbled out of his *ger* and in a drunken tirade collapsed and died." One possibility is that he was poisoned by shamans in the service of Ogedei or another rival.

After Tolui died, Ogedei attempted to take Sorghaghtani as one of his wives, but she refused, successfully arguing that she had to raise the couple's four children. After Ogedei Khan's death during the Western campaign in 1241, a period of sustained uncertainty damaged the Mongol Empire and probably stopped it from overrunning Europe. The so-called Toluid Civil War ended in 1264 with the emergence of Kublai Khan as emperor, after which a long period of Mongol dominance in the Far East shaped the civilizations of the region fundamentally.

Books

Morgan, David, *The Mongols,* Wiley-Blackwell, 2007.
Rossabi, Morris, *Khubilai Khan: His Life and Times,* California, 1988.
Weatherford, Jack, *Genghis Khan and the Making of the Modern World,* Broadway, 2011.
Weatherford, Jack, *The Secret History of the Mongol Queens,* Broadway, 2010.

Online

"Tului Khan—Mongol Leader," *Epic World History,* http://www.epicworldhistory.blogspot.com/2012/09/tului-khan-mongol-leader.html (January 5, 2015). □

Peter Tosh

Jamaican musician Peter Tosh (1944–1987) helped bring reggae to an international audience as a founding member of the Wailing Wailers and later as a solo artist. A gifted singer, musician, and wordsmith, Tosh played an important role in the creation of such Wailers' albums as *Catch a Fire* (1983). Also an outspoken political activist and Rastafarian, Tosh was murdered at his home at the age of 42.

Born Winston Hubert McIntosh on October 19, 1944, in Westmoreland, Jamaica, Tosh was the son of James McIntosh and Alvera Coke. Tosh's father was a preacher, and Tosh's birth was illegitimate. McIntosh denied paternity and did not play a role in Tosh's life. Coke also did not actively participate in Tosh's upbringing.

Ebet Roberts/Redferns/Getty Images

Instead, Tosh was primarily raised by an aunt. In 1956, Tosh's aunt moved with her nephew to the Jamaican city of Kingston. They lived in Trenchtown, an impoverished neighborhood. She died soon after, however, leaving him without adult guidance.

Demonstrated Musical Skills

Despite instability in his life, Tosh showed musical ability from an early age. He could play music by ear, and played the music and musicians to which he was exposed. He was a self-taught guitarist and keyboardist. In his teens, Tosh met Bob Marley and Neville "Bunny" Livingston (later known as Bunny Wailer) at a gambling establishment in Trenchtown. Marley and Livingston had started a band, and asked Tosh to join because he could actually play.

By 1963, Tosh, Marley, and Livingston formed a ska band, the Wailing Wailers. When the band came together, only Tosh could play an instrument, and Tosh taught Marley and Livingston how to play guitar. Tosh also wrote songs for the band. Within a short period of time, the Wailing Wailers signed with a label, Studio One. In 1964, the Wailing Wailers had a hit song with "Simmer Down." This song was a call to Jamaican Rude Boys to change their ways. Most of the 30 songs recorded by the band between 1964 and 1967 were ska culture-focused, a popular musical form and lifestyle in Jamaica in this period. In 1966 alone, the Wailers had five singles in the top ten in Jamaica.

Converted to Rastafarianism

Tosh's life changed in 1966 when Haile Selassie I, the emperor of Ethiopia, came to Jamaica and introduced the Rastafarian religion to the island nation. The religion includes the worship of Haile Selassie as God, sees Ethiopia as Zion, and encourages the use of marijuana for spiritual reasons. Tosh, along with Marley and Livingston, became converts. An enthusiastic supporter of the use of marijuana, Tosh was jailed for marijuana possession in the mid-1960s.

As the trio saw their faith changing, the sound of their band evolved as well. Moving away from ska, they first incorporated rocksteady, then became a reggae outfit. In 1966, Tosh wrote the first song about Rastafarians for the Wailers, "Rasta Shook Them Up." At this point, Clement Dodd, the producer who had recorded and released the Wailing Wailers' hit ska singles to date, wanted them to continue to create the ska songs that had made the band successful. Tosh and his band mates did not, and left Dodd and his label to focus on their new musical direction. They founded their own label, which soon failed, produced some songs with Lee "Scratch" Perry, then wrote songs for Johnny Nash, a singer from America.

Signed with Island Records

The music career of Tosh and his band mates took off in the early 1970s, launched by their association with Nash. The Wailing Wailers became well-known when a song written by Tosh and Marley, "Stir It Up," became a hit for Nash. In 1972, the Wailing Wailers signed with Island Records, owned by wealthy Jamaican Chris Blackwell.

The Wailing Wailers released two albums on Island, including *Catch a Fire* (1973) and *Burnin'* (1973). The band also toured outside of Jamaica, in England and the United States, in support of *Catch a Fire*. Though it had slow initial sales, this album attracted a solid fan base and eventually brought reggae to an international audience. *Burnin'* brought Tosh and the band greater success, including songs that would become reggae standards such as "I Shot the Sheriff" and "Get up, Stand Up." More attention was brought to the band when a British rock star, Eric Clapton, had a number one hit in the United States with his version of "I Shot the Sheriff" in 1974.

Went Solo

After the release of *Burnin'*, however Tosh, along with Livingston, left the Wailers. Tosh's reasons were numerous. In 1973, he was involved in a serious car accident in which his girlfriend lost her life. Touring with the Wailers was also stressful for him. In addition, Tosh—who changed his name from Winston McIntosh to Peter Tosh at this time—had militant leanings which were more easily expressed as part of a solo career.

At the same time, Marley had became more of the leader and star of the Wailers, and Tosh believed that Marley was promoted by Blackwell because he was lighter skinned than the other members of the band. The differences in personality between Marley and Tosh were increasingly evident as well. As reggae historian Roger Steffens told the *Toronto Star*, "Peter was constantly in conflict: whether it was a reporter he didn't like or an audience that wasn't responding the way he wanted them to. Marley was a healer and Peter was a confronter."

Launching a solo career, Tosh more openly expressed his personal beliefs. In 1975, he wrote a song "Mark of the Beast," which took an anti-police stance and was banned from Jamaican radio. Albums soon followed, including *Legalize It* (1976) and *Equal Rights* (1977). On *Legalize It,* released on CBS Records, he offered his backing for legalizing marijuana. The album was also forbidden on Jamaican radio. Next, *Equal Rights* protested the inequalities and political unrest in Jamaican society and other countries around the world. The anti-authority *Equal Rights* included a version of "Get Up, Stand Up" as well as "Downpressor Man" and "Stepping Razor." Other tracks reflected Tosh's interest in Pan-Africanism, such as "Africa."

Spoke Out at Concert

Tosh's tangles with Jamaican authorities grew into physical harassment after he affronted the Jamaican prime minister and other politicos at the April 22, 1978, One Love Peace Concert. In a passionate performance, he spoke out against Jamaica's political leaders about such issues as police brutality, racism, economic divisions, and classism. Describing the event, Ian Burrell of the *Independent Magazine* wrote, "He knew what he was doing that charged evening as he strode to the microphone in his black martial arts uniform and put his life on the line in one of the most passionate and dangerous political speeches ever given by a musician. Addressing Jamaica's two leading politicians, Prime Minister Michael Manley and Edward Seaga, the Leader of the Opposition, as they sat before him at a time when the country was being rent apart by murderous political gun battles in its poorest districts, Tosh warned: 'Hungry people are angry people.'"

Five months after the concert, Tosh was jailed for having marijuana and nearly beaten to death by authorities after being taken into custody. The concert also led to expanded career opportunities for Tosh. The event brought him to the attention of Rolling Stones' lead singer, Mick Jagger, who signed him to his band's label, Rolling Stones Records. With this new label, Tosh released three records, *Bush Doctor* (1978), *Mystic Man* (1979), and *Wanted Dread and Alive* (1981), and gained wider exposure.

The musical limitations placed on him by the Stones were most evident in the poorly-received *Bush Doctor,* which included songs complied by both Tosh and his label owners. Upon its release, Tosh toured with the Stones on their dates in support of their iconic album *Some Girls. Mystic Man* marked a return to Tosh's outspokenness against war and oppression. The most musically relevant, and a long-term influence on reggae, was *Wanted Dread and Alive.* This album featured one of Tosh's best known songs, "Reggae-mylitis."

Released *Mama Africa*

In the early 1980s, Tosh's association with the Rolling Stones ended when he had a major disagreement with Stones' guitarist Keith Richards. Tosh went to Africa during this period, seeking a return to his roots and soul. When he

returned revitalized to Jamaica, he then re-committed to his career and political activism. His next album, *Mama Africa* (1983), was released on Capital Records. Another strong release for Tosh, it included his call for world peace with "Peace Treaty," and included other strong messages in "Glass House" and "Where You Gonna Run." In 1985, Tosh was nominated for a Grammy Award for the track, "Captured Live."

More intensely political was Tosh's last album, *No Nuclear War* (1987). Through such tracks as "No Nuclear War," "Fight Aprtheid," and "Vampire," Tosh protested the Cold War, the exploitation of Africa, and the elites of society, respectively. Other tracks had more positive messages, including "Come Together," and "Testify." Tosh was honored with a Grammy Award for the album, received after his untimely demise.

Murdered in His Home

As Tosh's life was reaching a professional peak, he was murdered on September 11, 1987, at his home in the Kingston suburb of St. Andrew. He was 42 years old. That night, four men, including an acquaintance, Dennis "Leppo" Lobban, tried to rob Tosh and the others present of money. The robbers believed that there was a large amount of cash in the home because Tosh had recently returned from the United States. Tosh was shot in the head and died from his wounds in a hospital in Kingston. Two other men, Wilton "Doc" Brown and Jeff Dixon, also died, while four others were wounded.

In the years after his death, Tosh was a highly regarded figure, especially in developing countries. In Jamaica, he was more contentious. Steffens told the *Toronto Star*, "He's a hero to the lower classes, the working classes, but he's still an embarrassment to the establishment. The powers that be still hate him; he told too much truth."

Subject of Posthumous Releases, Biography

A number of albums featuring Tosh's music were released posthumously, as his legacy continued to be defined and expanded. In 2000, Tosh's powerful set at the One Love Peace Concert finally saw the light of day as *Peter Tosh Live at the One Love Peace Concert. I Am That I Am* followed in 2001. A decade later, in 2011, Tosh's first two solo albums were re-issued, while in 2012, the Jamaican government honored him with the Order of Merit. In 2013, a well-researched biography of Tosh, *The Life of Peter Tosh: Steppin' Razor* by John Masouri, was published, while a feature film about the making of *Legalize It* was in the planning stages.

Summarizing Tosh's musical legacy, Daniel R. Vogel wrote in *Musicians & Composers of the 20th Century,* "As one of the forefathers of reggae, Tosh set the tone for Rastafarian ganja (marijuana) advocates and political activists. His musical subjects spanned many different topics, but he was foremost an activist like his Wailer brother Marley. It was their commitment to causes such as the Pan-African movement that set an example for other musicians, who started taking up their own campaigns. Tosh set an example for other performers, but foremost he was an excellent musician and a soulful vocalist, defining reggae and taking its popularity to an international level."

Books

Musicians & Composers of the 20th Century, edited by Alfred W. Cramer, Salem Press, 2009.

Periodicals

Associated Press, September 14, 1987; July 6, 1989.
Independent Magazine, November 2, 2013.
New York Times, September 13, 1987.
Toronto Star, July 19, 2000.

Transcripts

"Peter Tosh: Reclaiming a Wailer," *Weekend Edition,* National Public Radio, July 9, 2011. □

Georg Trakl

The Austrian poet Georg Trakl (1887–1914) was one of the most important German-language writers of the early modern period.

DIZ Muenchen GmbH, Sueddeutsche Zeitung Photo/Alamy

Trakl wrote poetry in a concentrated, terse style that seemed almost at odds with its profoundly gloomy vision, but was actually all the more effective because of that contrast. His work drew on several major styles of modern European poetry, including the anti-realistic Symbolist movement in France, the highly visual Imagist style from Britain and America, and the dark, emotionally oriented Expressionist style of Germany and Austria. Yet his poems were in the end entirely distinctive. His work had an orientation toward horror and disintegration that proved justified by his own experiences when he witnessed combat in World War I firsthand during the last year of his life. Yet in the very act of reducing the horrors he saw to concise poetic form, Trakl found something redemptive. He was, in the words of Herbert Lindenberger (quoted on the *Poetry Foundation* website), "with [Rainer Maria] Rilke, the last great representative of what could be called the sublime tradition in German."

Formative Relationship with Sister

Georg Trakl (pronounced GAY-org TROCK-el) was born in Salzburg, then part of Austria-Hungary, on February 3, 1887. His father, Tobias, was a metal dealer. Trakl's younger sister, Margarete, or Grete, was born in 1892, and the two children became very close and are thought by some to have had an incestuous relationship. Some of Trakl's poems include a mysterious figure called the Sister, who seems to reflect this period of his life. He attended Catholic schools, but his family arranged for him to receive Protestant religious teaching on the side, and an orientation toward spiritual imagery in his poetry began to set it apart from the work of the generally secular German and Austrian Expressionists. By 1900 Trakl had begun to write poetry.

An indifferent student who had to repeat fourth grade, Trakl struck his teachers as withdrawn and unsociable, perhaps because he had already begun, as early as 1902, to experiment with drugs. He was once again asked to repeat a grade at high school and dropped out after receiving an intermediate certificate, enrolling in a class at a local pharmacy instead. Trakl dedicated himself anew to writing, and in 1906 the Salzburg City Theater staged two of his short plays, *Totentag: Dramatisches Stimmungsbild in einem Akt* (Death Day: Dramatic Atmospheric Painting in One Act) and *Fata Morgana: Tragische Szene* (Fata Morgana: Tragic Scene). Both plays failed, and Trakl later renounced them.

In 1908 Trakl entered the University of Vienna and declared a major in pharmacy, giving him the means to facilitate his growing tendency toward drug abuse. His time in Vienna, however, exposed him to the city's vibrant creative scene, and he became interested in music, novels, painting, and architecture. He was encouraged by the publication of several of his poems. Leaving the university in 1910 with a pharmacy certificate, he was drafted into the Austro-Hungarian army and given a post in a medical corps. He completed his term of service, got a job in a pharmacy in Salzburg, found himself miserably bored, and enlisted for another stint in the military. In 1912, given the rank of second lieutenant as a medical assistant, he was stationed in the Austrian city of Innsbruck.

Mentored by Magazine Editor

There Trakl met Ludwig von Ficker, editor of a progressive Catholic magazine called *Der Brenner*. Von Ficker was impressed by the young man's poetry, agreed to publish it on a regular basis, and arranged for the publication of some of Trakl's poems in book form in 1913. The years 1912–1914 were, as a result, productive ones for Trakl, even after he enlisted once again in the army and was sent to the Eastern Front in the early days of World War I. He saw action as a medic in the area of Gródek, in southern Poland (now part of Ukraine), in the fall of 1914. But he experienced unimaginable horror as he found himself the sole caregiver of a troop of 90 wounded and dying men, in a barn.

Trakl broke down and attempted to shoot himself. He was stopped by comrades and attempted to keep working, but soon was hospitalized in the city of Kraków. During his hospitalization he completed his last and, according to some estimations his greatest, poem, titled ''Gródek,'' as well as several other major works. He wrote to Ficker about his growing depression, and the philosopher Ludwig Wittgenstein, a friend of the publisher's who was also serving in the army in the area of Krakó (and was later hospitalized there as well), agreed to visit Trakl. But the poet, fearing that he was about to be court-martialed, took an overdose of cocaine before Wittgenstein could get there, and he died on November 3, 1914. It was not definitely determined whether the overdose was accidental or intentional.

''The poems of Georg Trakl have a magnificent silence in them...,'' wrote Robert Bly in his introduction to the translation of 20 of Trakl's poems he made with Robert Wright. ''In a good poem made by Trakl images follow one another in a way that is somehow stately. The images have a mysterious connection with each other. The rhythm is slow and heavy, like the mood of someone in a dream.'' Even when they are about nature, Trakl's poems have a philosophical quality that sets them apart from the work of his contemporaries. ''The fish rises with a red body in the green pond. / Under the arch of heaven / The fisherman travels smoothly in his blue skiff,'' Trakl wrote in ''The Sun'' (all translations are by Bly and Wright).

The striking use of color in that poem is typical of Trakl's poetry. But in many of his earlier poems, descriptions of nature seem not peaceful but ominous. ''And the rats squeak eagerly as if insane / And go out to fill houses and barns / Which are filled full of fruit and grain. / Icy winds quarrel in the darkness,'' he wrote in ''The Rats.'' The natural world in the universe is often malevolent and threatening, in Trakl's view. In the poem ''In Venice,'' a rare contemporary poem about a homeless individual, he wrote: ''Black swarms of flies / Darken the stony space, / And the head of the man who has no home / Is numb from the agony / Of the golden day.''

Wrote About Depression

Trakl may have suffered from what today would be called depression, and he wrote about the experience directly in one poem, ''The Mood of Depression,'' using a military metaphor: ''Now the black horses rear / In the foggy pasture. / I think of soldiers! / Down the hill, where the dying sun lumbers, / The laughing blood plunges / Speechless / Under the oak trees.''

The darkest and yet the most mature poems Trakl wrote date from the last months of his life, as he was serving as a medic on the Eastern Front during World War I. His poems vividly yet somberly evoke an atmosphere of carnage. ''In the shade of the ash tree of autumn / The souls of the slain are sighing,'' he wrote in ''From the Eastern Front.'' His final poem, ''Gródek,'' is an antiwar classic. Its final lines may have been the last words he wrote: ''The hot flame of the spirit is fed today by a more monstrous pain, / The unborn grandchildren.''

''Gródek'' and Trakl's other war poems were published after his death, in 1915. His sister killed herself in Berlin in 1917, and in 1919 his complete poems were published. At Ludwig von Ficker's behest, Trakl's body was exhumed in 1925 and reburied in Innsbruck. His work remained little known until the 1950s, when interest began to grow in both the German-speaking and English-speaking worlds. Part of the reason was that Trakl was well known to other figures in the Viennese cultural flowering of the early 20th century, including composer Anton Webern, who set several of his poems as songs. The translation into English by Bly and Wright appeared in 1961.

Books

Henderson, Lesley, ed., *Reference Guide to World Literature*, 2nd ed., St. James, 1995.

Leiva-Merikakis, Erasmo, *The Blossoming Thorn: Georg Trakl's Poetry of Atonement*, Bucknell, 1987.

Lindenberger, Herbert, *Georg Trakl*, Twayne, 1971.

Periodicals

Daily Telegraph (London, England), April 28, 2001.

Online

''Chronology of Georg Trakl's Life,'' *Wersch's Website for Georg Trakl*, http://www.literaturnische.de/Trakl/english/material/material-f-e.htm (December 4, 2014).

''Georg Trakl: 1887–1914,'' Poetry Foundation, http://www.poetryfoundation.org/bio/georg-trakl (December 4, 2014).

''Twenty Poems of Georg Trakl: Translated and Chosen by James Wright and Robert Bly,'' http://www.dreamsongs.com/NewFiles/Trakl.pdf (December 4, 2014). □

U

Nick Ut

In 1972, Vietnamese photographer Nick Ut (born 1951) stunned the world with his haunting picture of a naked Vietnamese girl fleeing in agony after a napalm attack on her village. The photo, which appeared on front pages around the globe, won a Pulitzer Prize and became a seminal image from the Vietnam war.

Nick Ut's given name was Huỳnh Công Út. He was born March 29, 1951, in Long An, a province in the southern Mekong Delta. At the time, Long An was part of French Indochina, but later became part of Vietnam. Ut grew up in a warring nation. By the mid-1950s, North Vietnam and South Vietnam were locked in battle, with the north receiving backing from Communist allies (including the Soviet Union and China) and the south getting support from the United States and other anti-Communist allies.

Followed Brother to AP

Ut's brother, Huỳnh Thanh My (also known as La), worked as an Associated Press (AP) photojournalist. La had been a well-known Vietnamese actor before joining the press corps. He worked at the AP's Saigon bureau and took care of Ut, who had dropped out of school and gone to live with his older brother. Their mother was widowed and La figured if he left his teen brother home alone, either the Viet Cong or the government would try to recruit him. La joined the AP because he wanted to capture images that told the real story of the war. "My brother hated the war," Ut told the *Orange County Register*'s Theresa Walker. "He'd say, 'I want to make a picture someday to stop the war.'"

La never got the chance. As an AP photographer, he spent his time traveling into combat zones with the Army of the Republic of Vietnam (ARVN), taking cover in rice paddies next to soldiers armed with guns. In October 1965, La went to the Mekong Delta to photograph a battle between the ARVN and Viet Cong. He was wounded and awaiting a medical evacuation at a makeshift aid station when the Viet Cong reappeared and finished off the injured.

A few days after the funeral, 14-year-old Ut turned up at the AP office in Saigon asking for a job. AP editor Horst Faas told Ut to go home, but Ut refused to leave, saying he had nowhere to go. Faas hesitantly put Ut to work in the darkroom, where he processed film and made prints of other photographers' work. Ut began taking a camera home and practicing shots. Soon, he was out in the streets looking for photos. Ut never received any formal training in photography, but his time in the darkroom, printing pictures as taken through the eyes of veteran photographers, began to teach him about composition.

Became Combat Photographer

Ut could not escape the violence around him and was soon taking photos of the fighting factions. "I'd go out shooting by myself," Ut told Mark Edward Harris of the *Los Angeles Times*. "During the war you would see black smoke everywhere, so you knew where the fighting and where the bombing were. I didn't need a map. . . . I just had my Honda motorbike and wore an army uniform with Bao Chi written on it. Bao Chi means news media."

In this way, Ut fell into the role of combat photographer. In 1968, the Viet Cong and North Vietnamese Army joined forces in launching the Tet Offensive and the war

AP Images/Na Son Nguyen

intensified. Ut traveled the countryside covering the carnage. He usually carried several cameras, always his Leica and a couple of Nikon Fs. Ut liked the scooter because it allowed him to weave in and out of the traffic, avoiding the refugees and oxcarts that often clogged the streets. In addition, he could push the scooter to 50 miles an hour to escape bullet fire.

Former AP boss Hal Buell told *LA Weekly*'s Gendy Alimurung that Ut may have been young, but he was skilled at the job. "He scooted around making these pictures of battle scenes. He showed the adeptness and smarts you have to have to be a good combat photographer." But Ut was not immune from danger. He was wounded with shrapnel from a Russian B-40 anti-tank rocket. In another incident, he took a shot to the upper chest.

Captured Photo that Shook World

For Ut, June 8, 1972, started like any other day. He went to take pictures of another battle. In the morning, Ut headed toward Trang Bang, a village located 25 miles northwest of Saigon. The battle for the city had been going on for a few days between the South Vietnamese and the Viet Cong. As such, many villagers had gotten in the habit of leaving the city during the day and camping out on Route 1, where they milled about, eating and cooking their meals, waiting for the day's battle to end. Ut was stopped at a Route 1 roadblock outside the city.

Ut watched the battle from the outskirts of Trang Bang. Several other journalists were there, including Ut's competitor from UPI, a stringer for *Life* magazine and a *New York Times* writer, as well as several television crews. They all snapped away, taking pictures of explosions and planes all morning. Around midday, rain started to fall and the photographers began hiding their equipment under rain ponchos.

Ut considered leaving. The journalists knew the air strikes would likely stop with the rain because the cloud cover would prevent the planes from finding their targets. Ut was about to head back to Saigon when he noticed that a yellow smoke bomb had been set off. Intrigued, he grabbed his camera, then saw a South Vietnamese Skyraider fly over, followed by a second plane that dipped and seemed to be on course with Route 1. The soldiers, refugees and journalists hit the ground, then saw one of the planes drop a load of napalm bombs on the village. Ut captured the fiery explosion on film.

In the next moments, stunned villagers came pouring down the road. There was a grandmother carrying the charred body of her grandson. The photographers clicked away at the grim scene as the village emptied. Many photographers finished up their rolls of film capturing the grandmother and child. Several quiet moments passed before nine-year-old Kim Phuc came screaming out of the village. She was naked, having pulled off her burning clothes, and was yelling, "Nong qua! Nong qua!" (too hot! too hot!) as the burning flesh sloughed off her body. Ut clicked away as she approached. Many of the other photographers were busy reloading their film and missed the shot. In a time before there were motor rewinds, it took a few moments to manually rewind the film from a camera.

The girl's uncle begged for help, so Ut covered her with a poncho and put her in the AP van he had driven that day. He took her, along with several others, to a hospital. He was anxious to return to Saigon to see what he had captured on film. First, he wanted to beat his competitors, and second, he knew he had to be off the roads by dark or he would face attack by the Viet Cong. Ut told Harris that he sensed he might have something. "I was a very young Vietnamese photographer. I knew I had a good photo but I didn't know what a historic photo was. I took a few more pictures of her, but when she passed [me] and I heard her say 'too hot' and 'I think I'm going to die,' and I saw her skin coming off, I put my cameras down on the highway so I could help her. I didn't want to take any more pictures because I thought if I did she was going to die."

After Ut returned to the AP office in Saigon, he developed the day's film. The AP photo editors saw the picture of Phuc, but did not initially select it for transmission over the wire because of a clear policy against frontal nudity. Ut had captured the entire sequence on film, starting with the plane that had delivered the napalm. He also had the explosion and the villagers fleeing the aftermath. Plus the girl. His editor struggled over the decision, but eventually sent the photo. Television footage of the incident that appeared in news outlets on June 9 showed the naked girl from the side only. By June 12, Ut's photo had appeared on front pages across the globe and ended up on several magazine covers. The photo, which clearly captured the terrible consequences of war, helped turn the tide of public opinion against the conflict in Vietnam.

The 35mm Leica M2 that Ut used the day he took the picture later found a home at the Newsmuseum in Washington, D.C. Newsmuseum director Carrie Christoffersen discussed the photo's resonance with Walker: "It's the combination of complete and total innocence and the horrors of war in one frame, in one shot. It's sort of staring you in the face, and there's no capacity to deny the impact of the war on innocent citizens."

Survived War, Settled in Los Angeles

Ut was injured again in the months after he took the picture. He went to visit Phuc at her home, which was located near some supply routes used by the Viet Cong. On the way there he was hit in the leg by mortar fire. A soldier dragged Ut to safety and another AP photographer took him to the hospital. Despite being injured three times, Ut beat the odds. The AP's Faas estimated that 135 photojournalists died in the war. Ut once estimated that 90 percent of his AP colleagues had been shot.

By 1972-73, the United States had drastically reduced its troops in Vietnam and had virtually pulled out by March 1973, leaving a weak South Vietnam to its own defenses. By April 1975 it looked like Saigon was about to fall to the Viet Cong and evacuation orders went out. On April 22, 1975, Ut took a military flight out of Saigon. He was later transported to a tent city at Camp Pendleton in San Diego County, California. He stayed there for a month in the company of 20,000 fellow Vietnamese refugees. Back home, his family burned all of his possessions so as to leave no trace for the Viet Cong.

After leaving the camp, Ut found work with the AP and was placed at the Tokyo office. He met his future wife there. They had two children. In 1977, he moved to Los Angeles to work for the AP. Shooting general photography assignments in a large American city was a huge change of pace for the photographer. Editors dispatched him to an Angels game, but, knowing nothing about baseball, he failed to take any meaningful shots. Afterward, he studied the game.

Eventually, Ut found his way. Over the next three decades, he covered earthquakes, fires, and professional sports. He captured celebrities in their worst moments, covering the court trials of Robert Downey Jr. and capturing O.J. Simpson riding through Los Angeles on his way to be questioned by authorities after the double murder of his ex-wife and her friend in 1994. Many of the 1995 Simpson trial photos that went out over the AP and landed in papers across the country were his. He also covered the 1993 trial of the Menendez brothers and was unfazed taking pictures during the riots that followed the 1992 Rodney King verdict as the streets of Los Angeles burned for six days. He photographed the Alaska Airlines Flight 261 crash off Port Hueneme in 2000.

Despite the years that passed after the war, Ut continued to have nightmares about his days in Vietnam, and the war continued to come up in his work. In the late 1990s, he took a Veterans Day photo of a woman crying over a grave at the Los Angeles National Cemetery; her son had died in Vietnam. In 1989, Ut reunited with Phuc for the first time since leaving Vietnam. Phuc had defected to Canada, where she married, had two children and became a goodwill ambassador for UNESCO.

As of 2015, Ut had yet to retire. He often expressed annoyance at many of the young photographers he encountered in the business. He complained to Alimurung about photographers who shoot first, then look for the picture later, admonishing those who "shoot 15 frames a second. Too fast. Picture lousy. One frame. Show the best picture. That's how I learned. Look for the picture first."

Books

Associated Press, *Vietnam: The Real War*, Abrams, 2013.

Chong, Denise, *The Girl in the Picture: The Story of Kim Phuc, the Photograph, and the Vietnam War*, Viking, 2000.

Periodicals

Daily News (Los Angeles, CA), October 25, 2014.

Los Angeles Times, July 23, 2000.

Orange County Register (Santa Ana, CA), June 3, 2012.

Online

"Nick Ut's *Napalm Girl* Helped End the Vietnam War. Today in L.A., He's Still Shooting," *LA Weekly*, http://www.laweekly.com/news/nick-uts-napalm-girl-helped-end-the-vietnam-war-today-in-la-hes-still-shooting-4861747 (January 14, 2015). ☐

V

Tabare Vázquez

Leftist Uruguayan politician Tabare Vázquez (born 1940) became the president of his country in 2004 after losing two previous elections. A successful oncologist before entering politics, he won election to a second term in 2014. As president, Vázquez focused on the Uruguayan economy, crime and corruption, and education issues.

Tabare Vázquez Rosas was born on January 17, 1940, in Montevideo, Uruguay, in the La Teja neighborhood of the capital city. Vázquez's father was employed by the state-owned oil company, working in an oil refinery. His father also was a labor union leader and was particularly interested in politics. Vázquez was raised in a working class area of the city.

Became Medical Doctor

Deciding to pursue medicine, Vázquez attended the University of the Republic's medical school, funded by a government scholarship. He graduated in 1969. While deciding on his specialty, Vázquez found it hard to chose because of his wide interests. Because his mother and sister died of cancer in a very short period of time, he decided to become an oncologist. He began practicing medicine in 1972.

For more than 15 years, Vázquez focused on his medical career. While working in a poor neighborhood of Montevideo, he also was a professor of radiotherapy at his alma mater. Vázquez also launched social programs for poor children in Montevideo. He served as the manager of a local soccer club as well. In 1973, a brutal military dictatorship took control of Uruguay and ran the country until 1985. Though Vázquez did not fight against the regime, his brother did, as a guerilla fighter, and he was put imprisoned.

By the mid-1980s, Vázquez became more involved in politics, while continuing his oncology practice. In 1987, he joined the central committee of the Socialist Party. Two years later, he actively sought to squash a referendum to provide amnesty to the military. Though the referendum passed, Vázquez decided to run for elected office.

Elected Mayor of Montevideo

Vázquez ran for the position of mayor of Montevideo, and won, surprising even himself. He officially took office in 1990. During his time as mayor, he continued to practice medicine, as he would during the whole of his political career. Vázquez was lauded for his efforts in cleaning up the city's waterfront and parks. He also increased salaries for public service workers as well as property taxes. He served one term, ending in 1994.

That year, Vázquez ran for the Uruguayan presidency for the first time. He stood for office as the head of the left-leaning coalition known as Frente Amplio (Broad Front), which included such groups as Communists and Christian Democrats. He finished third with an impressive one-third of the vote. After losing the election, Vázquez returned to oncology.

Vázquez pursued the presidency again 1999, again representing Frente Amplio. As he pursued the presidency in 1999, he would practice medicine three days a week and campaign the other four. He ran as an outsider who planned on cleaning up the system, including the remnants of the brutal military dictatorship. Vázquez gained attention for being a strong campaigner and public speaker.

© Horacio Villalobos/Corbis

During his campaign, Vázquez vowed to cut taxes, create new jobs, and enact a $300 million emergency spending program. Though Uruguay had a relatively stable economy, unemployment had reached about 10 percent. According to Clifford Krauss of the *New York Times*, Vázquez said during one campaign stop, "In the 1940's, when we were known as the Switzerland of South America, we didn't have the unemployment we have today. We want to recuperate our old values and form of life."

Finished Second in 1999 Elections

When voting was held in 1999, Vázquez did not win the presidency but had a better showing than in 1994. His prediction that he would win the most votes in the first round came true, and he easily won the April primary. In the second round of voting, however, he lost to Jorge Batlle Ibanez, who represented the Colorado Party and garnered the support of the Blanco (National) Party to gain the presidency. During his time, Batlle pursued closer ties with the United States, a move that was criticized by many, including Vázquez.

The Frente Amplio candidate

During his campaign, he promised to enact major changes in Uruguay. By this time, Uruguay had been deeply affected by a four-year economic recession with high unemployment—as high as 20 percent at times—inflation of ten percent, a sinking currency value, and a major drop in exports. Vázquez promised to lessen government spending and reduce inflation, while encouraging economic growth. He also vowed to address corruption and issues

related to the social crisis in Uruguay created by these economic conditions, as many Uruguayans became impoverished. Vázquez wanted to implement a crisis program and wealth re-distribution.

Many voters viewed Vázquez quite positively, as someone who would protect and restore the welfare system and the laws related to social issues. Many believed he would improve Uruguay's educational system as well. Voter Gonzalo Mendoza told Larry Rohter of the *New York Times*, "The Front clearly has the best of the packages being offered to us, and Tabare Vázquez is obviously a balanced and capable leader."

Won First Term as President

When elections were held on October 31, 2004, Vázquez won in the first round of voting by gaining more than 50 percent of the total ballots. He officially began his five-year term in March 2005. Until his election, only two political parties had won in Uruguayan elections during its 170 years of independence, the Colorado Party and the White Party. Despite earlier impressive showings, Vázquez's victory in the 2004 political election was considered unexpected in the politically conservative country. It did reflect a wider trend in South America towards leftist national leadership.

According to Daniel Helft of the *Vancouver Sun*, Vázquez said upon his victory, "We should all celebrate. I promise to work intensely to bring about the needed changes for this country." Among his first goals was coming to an agreement with the International Monetary Fund and asking for its patience with his country so he could deal with the country's social emergency but not default on its foreign debt. While the Uruguayan economy was improving, Vázquez wanted to continue positive growth rather than create challenges to it.

During his inaugural address, Vázquez offered promises of changing the government's attitudes and actions and emphasizing economic and social policies. He also vowed to address human rights issues, develop Uruguayan society, and ensure that no outside countries, including the United States, would interfere in Uruguay's internal affairs. His first official action as president was announcing the Social Emergency Plan program. Costing $100 million, the plan was to help the extremely impoverished Uruguayans who had been impacted by recent economic difficulties. The program addressed such issues as food, health, jobs, and housing. Vázquez's second act involved restoring diplomatic relations with Cuba, broken by his predecessor in a dispute about human rights observers in the island nation.

Remained Part-Time Doctor

When Vázquez took office, he continued to practice medicine on a part-time basis. He spent one morning a week focusing on oncology and seeing patients. As he told Rohter of the *New York Times*, "Practicing medicine is not only my vocation, it gives me an opportunity to continue to be in direct contact with people, to see them and hear their needs.... But I'd feel empty and isolated if I couldn't practice my profession and had to give up that contact."

As president, Vázquez drew on diverse opinions, including representatives of six factions in his coalition plus an independent. His policies were also reform-oriented, favoring socialist and market-friendly solutions that resulted in less unemployment and poverty. The economy further rebounded and lead to more investor confidence. Focusing on a moderate agenda, he did not change Uruguay's constitution, nor did he introduce polices that would create a polarized, divided country.

One somewhat controversial area for the Vázquez administration was related to anti-tobacco legislation. Under his leadership, the country passed strict laws that banned smoking in enclosed public spaces. The laws also included a ban on tobacco advertising and sponsorships, and deemed that risk warnings had to cover 80 percent of cigarette packs. Uruguay became the first country in the Americas to prohibit smoking in all indoor public spaces. As a physician, Vázquez believed these laws would reduce cancer deaths and demands on his country's health system.

Unable to Seek Second Consecutive Term

Though Vázquez had high approval ratings—as high as 60 percent at times—the constitution of Uruguay did not allow re-election of the president to consecutive terms. In 2009, then, another Frente Amplio candidate ran. Former guerrilla fighter Jose Mujica, was elected president. The victory was seen as an endorsement of the success of Vázquez and his leftist policies. Part of Mujica's campaign promises included continuing Vázquez's policies and following in his footsteps as a consensus builder.

During Mujica's presidency, the economy continued to grow at a strong rate. Gay marriage and abortion also became legal. (Vázquez had vetoed the abortion law in 2008 when he was president.) Steps were also taken to form the first state-run marijuana marketplace in the world; related laws passed covered production, distribution, and sale of the drug.

In 2014, Vázquez was eligible to run for the presidency again, and did so. As Mujica did in the previous election, Vázquez used the popularity of his predecessor and his success in office to win the presidency himself. During his campaign, he promised to further improve the economy, while also addressing crime issues and investing in schools and education. Both crime and education had been the weak points of Mujica's government.

Though Vázquez did well in the first round of voting, he was unable to win the presidency outright with only 48 percent of the vote to 31 for National Party candidate Luis Lacalle Pou. He faced a run-off election with Lacalle Pou, a center-right candidate who vowed to alter Mujica's marijuana laws.

Won Second Term in Office

When the run-off vote was held on November 30, 2014, Vázquez again won the presidency with 53 percent of the vote to Lacalle Pou's 40 percent. As soon as the vote was completed, the second-term president reached out to his opposition and asked them to help form a national agreement to address such issues as public security and education. According to Leonardo Haberkorn of the Associated Press, Vázquez told his supporters "I want to be able to count on all Uruguayans, but not so they follow me but so they guide me, accompany me."

As president, Vázquez vowed to enforce the marijuana law, despite his personal opposition to certain aspects of it. He personally did not believe in consuming the drug, and was concerned about the potential impact on society caused by the laws. As a physician, Vázquez also was concerned with how marijuana sales would impact health. Before he took office, only two parts of the law had been enacted. People could legally grow six plants at home, and marijuana clubs were legalized so 45 people could form groups and produce the drug together. Vázquez had control of the implementation of the third aspect, selling state-controlled pot to registered consumers at pharmacies. Vázquez was concerned about pharmacy owners being attacked by drug traffickers when their sales lessened.

Vázquez's measured response to the marijuana laws demonstrated his continual balancing of his medical and political careers and perspectives. He told Rohter of the *New York Times,* "I don't see working in these two realms as schizophrenic, since both are forms of service to society. To me, politics is an extension of what I do in medicine. But society is also a human organism, and politics is a way of dealing with the pathologies that a society can have. You have to act on that society as you would a human being."

Periodicals

Associated Press, December 1, 2014.
Edmonton Journal, December 22, 2004.
Facts on File World News Digest, November 4, 2004.
The Guardian, December 2, 2014.
Hamilton Spectator (Ontario, Canada), October 30, 1999.
Malta Today, December 1, 2014.
Morning Star, August 30, 2004; November 16, 2004.
New York Times, July 18, 1999; November 1, 1, 2004; November 2, 2004; March 2, 2005; August 31, 2006; November 30, 2009; December 1, 2014.
Vancouver Sun (British Columbia, Canada), November 1, 2004.□

Emile Verhaeren

The French-language Belgian writer Emile Verhaeren (1855–1916) is considered one of his country's most important poets. Sometimes described as an important pioneer of the Symbolist movement, he wrote in a distinctive, personal style marked by great energy and spontaneity.

Verhaeren's writing, in fact, fell into none of the stylistic schools that developed on either side of the year 1900. Some of his poetry directly reflected his own life—a lengthy breakdown that he experienced in the late 1880s, his subsequent marriage, the landscapes of his Flemish homeland. Other works looked outward: to the

Lebrecht Music and Arts Photo Library/Alamy

conditions of working people, to the lives of monks, to world events. His epic, free-spirited portrayals of the people of Belgium have drawn comparisons to the works of the American poet Walt Whitman. Verhaeren was very widely read in the English-speaking world, including America, in the early 20th century; Horace B. Samuel wrote in *Modernities* (1914) that Verhaeren was "indisputably the most modern and the most massive force in the whole of contemporary European poetry." Since that time his reputation has declined somewhat.

Abandoned Priesthood Path for Poetry

Emile Verhaeren was born on May 21, 1855, in Saint-Amand (now Sint-Amands), Belgium, near Antwerp. Although he was of Flemish (Dutch-speaking) ancestry and grew up in a predominantly Flemish area, he spoke French at home and wrote exclusively in that language. His father was a cloth dealer. Verhaeren's Catholic family was strongly religious, and his parents hoped he would study for the priesthood. After attending schools in Saint-Amand he was sent to a Catholic school in the capital of Brussels and then to a Jesuit-run university, the Collège Saint-Barbe in Ghent. Despite his parents' hopes for their son as a priest, he was interested in poetry from the beginning and liked to discuss new poems with his friends.

The family worked out several compromises. First Verhaeren went to work for a year at an oil factory owned by an uncle, but this proved unsatisfactory on all sides. Then

he began studies toward a law degree at the University of Louvain, the country's premier French-speaking institution. There Verhaeren was able to pursue his interest in the arts: he was a member of a literary society and edited a magazine, *La Semaine* (The Week), of his own. He passed his bar exams and joined a law firm in Brussels in 1881.

Ironically, the move proved crucial for Verhaeren's literary ambitions: the lawyer for whom he went to work, Edmond Picard, was a writer himself and a member of a creative circle known as Young Belgium. Verhaeren soon became an active member of the group himself, began contributing poems to literary periodicals, and founded the magazine *Societé Nouvelle*. He published his first book of poems, *Les Flamandes* (The Flemish Women), in 1883; its critical reception was mixed, but it had an unrestrained, sometimes violent energy that gained the young poet a following. Verhaeren followed that up with *Les Moins* (The Monks, 1886), offering painterly descriptions of life in a monastery.

In the late 1880s, Verhaeren suffered from mental illness of some kind; given the antiquated terminology of the time it is difficult to determine exactly what he experienced. His mental state was reflected in three books of poetry he published during this period: *Les Soirs* (The Evenings, 1887), *Les Debâcles* (1888), and *Les Flambeaux noirs* (The Black Torches, 1891). The Austrian poet Stefan Zweig, in his biography of Verhaeren, noted that in these three works, "We have a document that must be priceless to pathologists as [well as] to psychologists. For here a deep-seated will to extract the last consequence of every phase of life has reproduced the stadium of a mental illness right to the verge of madness; here a poet has with the persistence of a physician pursued the symptoms of his suffering through every stage of lacerating pain, and immortalized in poems the process of the inflammation of his nerves." Verhaeren's formal experimentation, his concern with inner states, and his free treatment of language attracted attention from the poets of France's experimental Symbolist movement.

Wrote Poetry Inspired by Marriage

Verhaeren sought relief from these problems by taking to the road, traveling through France, Spain, England, and Italy. His parents both died in 1888. In 1891 Verhaeren married and settled in Brussels, which seems to have stabilized his life somewhat. His happy domestic life was reflected in a trilogy of poems to which he returned over the years: *Les Heures claires* (The Clear Hours, 1896), *Les Heures d'Après-midi* (Afternoon Hours, 1905), and *Heures du soir* (Evening Hours, 1911).

At about the time he married, Verhaeren became interested in the socialist movement. In his poetry of the 1890s, a concern with the effects of industrialization went hand in hand with increasing formal freedom. *Les campagnes hallucinées* (The Hallucinated Countryside, 1893) featured ghostlike figures in an emptied-out countryside, and *Les Villes tentaculaires* (The Tenticular Cities, 1895), written in free verse, was a vivid portrait of urban industry that envisioned the city as an octopus, stretching out its arms to drain the life's blood from the countryside.

In the late 1890s and early 1900s Verhaeren brought together the various strands of his work into a group of ambitious books that are often considered his best. In *Les Visages de la vie* (The Faces of Life, 1899), *Les Forces tumultueuses* (The Tumultuous Forces, 1902), and a five-part series, *Tout la Flandre* (All of Flanders), he drew exuberant, extensive portraits of Belgian society in images of individuals and landscapes. In an excerpt from *Contemporary Belgian Literature* appearing in *Twentieth-Century Literary Criticism*, Jethro Bithell wrote, "Following unconsciously in the track of Walt Whitman (his great forerunner whom he had not read), Verhaeren now turns his cosmic pain into cosmic joy, and strikes out into new paths of poetry which are destined to be the great highways of the verse to be."

Poems Widely Translated

Indeed, Verhaeren was an exceptionally well-known poet in his own time. He was the subject of a biography by Austrian poet Stefan Zweig, and that biography, as well as much of Verhaeren's work, was translated into English; for the first half of the 20th century there was an abundance of literary criticism applied to his work. His poems have been translated into 20 languages; Zweig translated many of them into German. In 1911 Verhaeren was said to be a finalist for the Nobel Prize for literature, but the prize went to his friend Maurice Maeterlinck instead. In the latter part of the 20th century, the amount of scholarly attention paid to Verhaeren, at least in the English-speaking world, began to decline.

Verhaeren was active in writing genres other than poetry. He wrote short stories, books on art (which influenced some of his poetry), and several plays in verse, including *Les Aubes* (The Dawn, 1898), *Le Cloître* (The Cloister, 1900), *Philippe II* (1901), and *Hélène de Sparte* (Helen of Sparta, 1912). Verhaeren was a hit on the lecture circuit in later life, appearing in many different countries, and Belgium's King Albert I proclaimed him the country's national poet.

Although a pacifist by nature, Verhaeren was deeply disturbed by the German invasion of Western Europe and turned to the writing of propaganda works during World War I. These included *Belgium's Agony* (1915), *Parmi les Cendres: La Belgique dévastéee* (Among the Ashes: Belgium Devastated, 1916), and *Ville Meurtries de Belgique* (Bruised Cities of Belgium, 1916). On November 27, 1916, in Rouen, France, Verhaeren was preparing to board a train in Rouen, France. He fell onto the tracks as the train began to move and was killed instantly.

Books

Contemporary Belgian Literature (*Twentieth Century Literary Criticism*, Vol. 12), Gale, 1984.

Encyclopedia of World Literature in the 20th Century, third ed., St. James, 1999.

Samuel, Horace B., *Modernities*, Dutton, 1914.

Zweig, Stefan, *Emile Verhaeren*, Constable, 1914.□

Georges Vézina

Known as the "Chicoutimi Cucumber," Canadian professional hockey player Georges Vézina (1887–1926) was an early star of the National Hockey League (NHL). An elite goalie who played in 328 straight games over the course of his 15 year career, Vézina led the Montreal Canadiens to two Stanley Cups. His playing days cut short because of his death from tuberculosis, an NHL trophy honoring the season's best goalie carries Vézina's name.

Born Joseph-Georges-Gonzague Vézina on January 21, 1887, in Chicoutimi, Quebec, Canada, he was the last of eight children born to Georges and Clara (Belley) Vézina. His father worked as a baker. Vézina was educated at the Petit Séminaire de Chicoutimi, attending from 1898 to 1902. Originally taking commercial courses, he dropped out of school to help his father run his bakery.

Began Playing Organized Hockey at 16

Though Vézina played street hockey in his youth, he did not play organized hockey on ice until he was 16 years old. Despite never having played on skates, he was put in goal for a local men's team, the Club de Hockey de Chicoutimi. Vézina proved a quick study of the game. Continuing to play in men's leagues in Chicoutimi for several years, Vézina landed his contract with the Canadiens in unusual fashion.

During the 1904–05 season, Vézina played in goal for Chicoutimi against the Montreal Nationals of the Canadian Amateur Hockey League. The locals won the game, impressing the team and its goaltender Joseph Cattarinich. Cattarinich went on to play professionally with the Montreal Canadiens (then known as the Club Athlétique Canadien). At the time, the team was part of the NHA (National Hockey Association). The NHA was the precursor to the National Hockey League, or NHL, which formed in 1917.

When Cattarinich was ready to retire as a player at the end of the 1909–10 season, he remembered Vézina. The goalie and one of his brothers, Pierre who played forward, were given try outs with the Canadiens before the 1910–11 season. The team asked Pierre Vézina to come to ensure the goalie would travel to Montreal and try out. Though Pierre did not make the cut, Georges Vézina was offered a contract worth $800 per year and signed with the team.

Became Professional Player

When Vézina turned professional in 1910, the game of hockey was quite different in many ways than its early twenty-first century counterpart. The league was more focused on offense, and goalies were forbidden from falling to the ice to make saves. Instead, goalies, including Vézina, played in a stand-up style. Over the course of his career, he would refine his version of stand up and become one of the dominant goalies of his era. He proved especially strong with his stick play.

Bruce Bennett Studios/Getty Images

Because Vézina was quiet and homesick, he was originally dubbed "le Chevrueil." As his calm, even tempered persona and style of play emerged, Vézina became known as "l'Habitant silencieux" (the quiet Hab) and the "Chicoutimi Cucumber." This nickname evolution took a little time as did his play, but he proved a strong, dependable goalie from the first for Montreal.

Vézina made his debut for the Canadiens in the opening game of the 1910–11 season of the NHA on December 31, 2010. From the first, Vézina proved dominant and helped build the struggling Montreal franchise. During the 1910-11 season, Vézina was the NHA leader in goals against average (GAA) with 3.80. He also had the fewest goals against in the league with 62. He repeated both feats during his second season, with only 66 goals allowed and a 3.57 GAA. During the off season, Vézina lived a quiet life and ran a tannery business in Chicoutimi. He would run this business through the whole of his professional career.

Denied, then Won Championship

Within a few years, Vézina put the Canadiens in the position to win championships. In the 1913–14 season, the team finished first in the NHA standings with an 11-9 record because of Vézina's strong play. It was the best record in the league. For a third time, Vézina also let in the fewest goals against in the NHA. The Toronto Blueshirts won the Stanley Cup that year, however.

After struggling in the 1914–15 season with only six wins and 14 losses, the Vézina-led Montreal squad again finished first in the NHA in the 1915–16 campaign with a 16-7-1 record. The Canadiens also won the team's first Stanley Cup that year. They defeated the Portland Rosebuds in five games to win the championship.

Still the acknowledged leader of the Canadiens, Vézina worked hard to bring Montreal back to the Stanley Cup finals. During the 1916–17 season in which the Canadiens posted a 10-10 record, he had the fewest goals against in the league with 80, but his team lost to the Seattle Metropolitans in the Stanley Cup finals that year. Despite the loss, Vézina remained one of the most respected players as the NHA transitioned into the NHL.

Vézina showed his prowess in other ways as well. A friendly match was held between the Canadiens and a team of soldiers in 1917 as a fundraiser to support Canadian efforts in World War I. To give the soldiers a chance of winning, Vézina played on their side against his Montreal teammates.

Posted First Shutout in NHL History

To many of the era, Vézina was the best netminder in the new league. During the inaugural NHL season of 1917–18, Vézina demonstrated his dominance with the best goals against average in the league at 3.93. The team had a 12-9 record overall. The season was memorable for other reasons as well. Vézina recorded the first NHL shutout, on February 18, 1918, in a 9-0 victory against the Toronto Arenas. Vézina also made the first assist by a goaltender in the NHL, in December 1918. This event also occurred against Toronto, when Vézina turned away a shot on goal by Toronto. Canadien Newsy Lalonde took the rebound down the ice for a goal.

In the 1918-19 season, Montreal posted a 10-8 record and again made the Stanley Cup finals. Scheduled to play against Seattle and Vézina's foe, Harry "Hap" Holmes, the Montreal team was denied the chance. The games were not played because of the ongoing influenza epidemic, in which 50 million people died worldwide. There were not enough players to complete the games because so many of them had become ill. One player and the Canadiens' owner died in the pandemic.

Though Montreal did not win the Stanley Cup and Vézina did not lead the league in GAA, the Canadiens had memorable seasons in the early 1920s as their goalie continued to perform at the peak of his game. In the 1921–22, the team posted a record of 12-11-1, with Vézina's GAA at 3.84. The following season was even better statistically, with Montreal reaching 13-9-2 in 1922–23, and Vézina lowering his GAA to 2.46.

Won Second Stanley Cup

Vézina led the NHL in GAA in the 1923–24 season with a dominant 1.84. Until this point, Clint Benedict of the Ottawa Senators had the best GAA in the NHL for five consecutive seasons. Vézina also backstopped Montreal to their second Stanley Cup championship. After defeating teams from Ottawa and Vancouver, the Canadiens defeated the Calgary Tigers in the best-of-three Stanley Cup finals to win the championship.

During the 1924–25 season, Vézina repeated as NHL GGA leader, lowering his mark to a mere 1.81. Though Montreal had a regular season record of 17-11-2, the Canadiens did not repeat as Stanley Cup champions. The team had high hopes for the 1925–26 season. However, during training camp in 1925, Vézina showed many signs of illness, including excessive sweating and obvious gauntness. Vézina played throughout the pre-season, but lost 35 pounds.

Despite being ill with a high fever and swollen joints, Vézina played in the season opener against the Pittsburgh Pirates, on November 28, 1925, in Montreal's new arena, Mount Royal. He played well in the first period. As he left the ice, he was bleeding from the mouth, then collapsed in the locker room. Vézina managed to return to the net, but crumbled on the ice and had to be carried off. He was replaced in the game by Alphonse Lacroix.

Died of Tuberculosis

On November 29, Vézina was diagnosed with advanced tuberculosis. The game against Pittsburgh would be his last and he was forced to retire. The disease continued to advance, and Vézina visited the Montreal locker room to say goodbye to his teammates on December 3 before returning home. Several months later, on March 27, 1926, Vézina died of tuberculosis in Chicoutimi, at the age of 39.

In all, Vézina played professional hockey for 15 years and played in every game for the Canadiens from 1911 until he collapsed on the ice in 1925. During the course of his career, he demonstrated his stamina by playing 328 consecutive games in the NHA (138) and NHL (190). He posted 15 shutouts, including the first one ever in the NHL. His career GAA was 3.49. During his tenure with Montreal, the team posted a record of 173-148-6. Vézina's playoff record was similarly impressive, at 22-12-1.

The owners of the Canadiens ensured that Vézina's name and greatness as a goalie would not be forgotten. Before the 1926–27 season, Leo Dandurand, Louis Letourneau, and Cattaranich founded the Vézina Trophy. Originally given annually to the goalie whose team allowed the fewest goals overall, the criteria changed in the 1981–82 season when the Vézina Trophy was given to the best goalie in the National Hockey League. The first winner of the Vézina was his replacement in the Canadiens' net, George Hainsworth. At least eleven more Canadiens goaltenders would follow in Hainsworth's footsteps, including William Ronald Duran, who won it six times, and Jacques Plante, who won it seven times.

Inducted into the Hockey Hall of Fame

Vézina was inducted into the Hockey Hall of Fame in 1945. He was included in the original class of 12 named to the Hall of Fame. Because of his stature in the game, the Vézina name had value into the 21st century. In 2000, the company that produced NHL trading cards, In the Game, acquired Vézina's pads from a private collector, cut them up, and attached a piece to cards included in a memorabilia set along with small bits of gear from other leading

players. In the Game was widely criticized for cutting up the pads, the only pair known to exist. The man who did the actual cutting, card consultant Ken Whitmell, told Kevin Allen of *USA Today,* that he appreciated the experience. Whitmell said, "You could feel they were Georges Vézina pads. I never saw Vézina play, but I could feel the importance. I didn't feel like I was doing anything terribly wrong."

When lists of the best hockey players of all time are compiled, Vézina's name is inevitably included. On the Official Hockey Hall of Fame website, Kevin Shea wrote of Vézina, "In the realm of extraordinary goaltenders through the NHL's long history, it is difficult to judge where Georges Vézina would rank. Hockey was a different game during Vézina's era—goaltenders were forbidden to drop to the ice to stop shots. Nevertheless, it is fair to make the claim that he is among the greatest the game has ever known."

Periodicals

USA Today, August 3, 2000.

Online

"Georges Vézina: Biography," The Official Site of the Hockey Hall of Fame, http://www.legendsofhockey.net/LegendsOfHockey/jsp/(December 13, 2014).

"Georges Vézina," *Dictionary of Canadian Biography,* http://www.biographi.ca/en/bio/vezina_georges_15E.html (December 13, 2014).

"Georges Vézina," *HockeyReference.com,* http://www.hockey-reference.com/players/v/vezinge01.html (December 13, 2014).

"Georges Vézina," The Original Hockey Hall of Fame, http://www.originalhockeyhalloffame.com/honoured-members/georges-vezina.html (December 13, 2014).

"Georges Vézina," The Official Site of the Montreal Canadiens, http://ourhistory.canadiens.com/player/Georges-Vezina (December 13, 2014).

"Spotlight: One on One with Georges Vezina," The Official Site of the Hockey Hall of Fame, http://www.hhof.com/htmlSpotlight/spot_oneononep194512.shtml (December 13, 2014). □

Gérard de Villiers

French author Gérard de Villiers (1929–2013) created the best-selling spy thriller series, S.A.S. At least 100 million copies of Villiers' 200 well-researched books featuring freelance intelligence operative Malko Linge were sold over five decades, primarily in the French-speaking world, Germany, Japan, and Russia. Villiers was France's most widely read author, and one of the best selling spy novelists of all time.

Foc Kan/Wireimage/Getty Images

the wake of the incident, Villiers gained an interest in conspiracies and spy schemes.

Developed Malko Linge

In the wake of this experience, Villiers began writing a detective novel in his free time. When Ian Fleming, the creator of the iconic spy novel character James Bond, died in 1964, an editor of Villiers' at *Plon* suggested that he should fill the void. Inspired, Villiers came up with Malko Linge in 1964, and wrote the first S.A.S. novel, *S.A.S. in Istanbul* (1965).

Villiers drew on several sources to formulate the French government spy, Linge. His character was a composite of the three men with whom he was acquainted. One was a French intelligence official, a chef de mission with the Service de Documentation Extérieure et de Contre-Espionage (SDECE, the External Documentation and Counter-Espionage Service). The second was a German baron who owned a Swabian castle, while the third was an Austrian arms dealer.

As created by Villiers, Linge is an aristocrat from Austria who does intelligence and espionage work for the American CIA (Central Intelligence Agency) on contract. He pursues this line of work primarily to fund the restoration and upkeep of his ancestral castle, a difficult undertaking because of his personal financial circumstances. Linge's life is a duality of Old World aristocracy and spy missions in sensitive areas around the world. In some of the novels, Linge has a fiancée but is rarely home and is often unfaithful to her. Describing Linge, Villiers told Edward Cody of the *Washington Post,* "He is a samurai. He is a mercenary with ethics. He may kill when he has to, but he would never change camps."

The name of Villiers' series came from Linge's code name, Son Altesse Sérénissime (His Serene Highness or His Most Serene Highness). The S.A.S. name was also intended to be an allusion to the British army unit of the same initials. The 200 S.A.S. novels that Villiers would pen became known for their formulaic writing and lurid covers featuring alluring women with fire arms, usually hand guns or assault rifles, in their hand. Villiers knew the limits to the sexy intrigue found in his novels. According to Pierre Perrone of the London *Independent,* "I never had any pretensions of being a literary writer. I consider myself a storyteller who writes to amuse people."

Developed Information Network

As Villiers' S.A.S. novels became a long-running series, he befriended Alexandre de Marenches. From 1970 to 1981, de Marenches served as the director of the French foreign intelligence service. De Marenches had many qualities that were similar to Linge's, and offered Villiers information on which to draw. Not only was Marenches from an aristocratic family, he was also charismatic and created a covert network of operatives in Africa and the Middle East used in French spy operations against the Soviets.

Through his friendship with Marenches, Villiers gained access to other French intelligence officers. These officers helped Villiers come into contact with and develop

Born in Paris on December 8, 1929, Gérard de Villiers was the son of a playwright known by the pen name Jacques Deval. His mother, Valentine Adam de Villiers, came from French aristocracy. A productive writer and serial womanizer, Deval married six times, had numerous children, and was absent for much of Villiers' childhood. By the time of Villiers' birth, however, the family was relatively impoverished and middle class. Villiers and his two sisters were raised by their mother.

Began Career in Journalism

Villiers received his education at the Institut d'Etudes Politiques (Sciences Po) and the Ecole Supérieure de Journalisme. He then completed military service, serving as an officer during the Algerian War. By the 1950s, Villiers pursued journalism, beginning with the far right wing publication *Rivarol.* Over the years, he wrote for *France Soir, Paris-Presse, France Dimanche,* and *Paris Match,* among other publications.

Over the course of his journalism career, Villiers covered events both deep and frothy. In addition to covering the Vietnam War, he wrote profiles of celebrities who were spending time on the French Riviera. It was Villiers' experience as a journalist that influenced his spy novels. While reporting from Tunisia, Villiers unwittingly became a player in an assassination plot involving a French intelligence officer after agreeing to do a favor for the government spy. In relationships with government spies from other countries, including the members of the C.I.A., the Soviet KGB, and the Israeli Mossad. Some of these relationships developed into real, close friendships. Villiers also built connections with others involved with major international events to gain information and an informed perspective. He cultivated relationships with diplomats, journalists, and military attachés, among others. Villiers would change details but included many of the colorful personalities he met along the way into his books. As a result, they trusted him enough to confidences knowing they would not be betrayed by the author.

Over the years, suggestions emerged that Villiers was part of the French intelligence setup. The SDECE was said to have used S.A.S. novels as a means of spreading disinformation. At the same time, Villiers had a personal rule to avoid all direct discussion of France, French operatives, and the French secret service in his novels to avoid any chance of betrayal.

Emphasized Research

Villiers' S.A.S. novels differed from Fleming's Bond books in his perspective. Greatly influenced by his long career as a journalist, he had a specific method for writing his novels, which included a certain flow of research and experiences. As the London *Times* explained, "Having chosen his country, de Villiers would study the political situation in the specialist press, CIA and Amnesty International reports, more recently Wikileaks, and talk to ambassadors and friends in the secret services. Then he would stay in the local hotel used by the international press and pursue his investigations, meeting as many government and opposition figures as he could. He recorded telling descriptive details, noted sounds and smells and took photographs. Then he put together his plot, correcting the typescript in pen."

Villiers especially emphasized the importance of doing research in the areas he wrote about to better understand a city or region's atmosphere and everyday culture. Before writing each S.A.S. novel, he spent about a week to ten days at the major settings before writing his book. Details were important to him, and every real street name, restaurant, and person's name was spelled correctly in the final product. In 2010, Villiers had a physical setback when he tore an aorta in a car accident. Though he susequently had to use a walker, Villiers did not let his disability hold him back. He still traveled to war zones, including Afghanistan and Libya, to do research.

Anticipated World Events

Villiers' thoroughness as an author—especially his use of real world people, secrets, and scenarios—and depth of knowledge and understanding about events and pressures worldwide allowed him to sometimes anticipate international incidents. The London *Independent*'s Perrone stated that Villiers once explained, "I'm not a prophet. I draw hypothetical conclusions about countries I know well and sometimes, they turn out to be true." There were numerous examples of his predictive abilities playing out in his novels.

In 1980, for example, an S.A.S. novel titled *Le Complot Du Caire* (The Cairo Plot) had Islamist militants assassinating Egyptian president Anwar el-Sadat. This event occured in 1981. Villiers' 1982 book *Red Grenada* included a scenario in which that island's government broke apart. Grenada's government did fall apart about 15 months later, leading to an invasion by the United States.

Villiers' prognostic skills continued in the 1990s and early 21st century. In 1994, *La Traque Carlos* (The Hunt for Carlos) anticipated the arrest of the elusive international terrorist, Carlos the Jackal. S.A.S. novels discussed civil wars in Syria and Libya that predicted the violent events in these regions. One such novel, *Les Fous de Benghazi* (The Madmen of Benghazi, 2012), anticipated the deep tensions in Libya after its revolution that resulted in the deaths of American ambassador Christopher Stevens and other personnel.

Because of the combination of formula and specific detail, Villiers' S.A.S. series were quite popular and believed to be the longest-running, perhaps best-selling, fiction series ever written by a single author. Always working on his own, Villiers pumped out four S.A.S novels each year, and could complete one in about six to eight weeks. Villiers typed his books on an IBM electric typewriter. For the last eight years of his life, he wrote five S.A.S. novels each year.

Self-Published

Beginning in 1998, Villiers added to his profitability by self-publishing his books. His profits were over one million dollars per year and contributed to his own lavish lifestyle. He lived in a large apartment on Avenue Foch, which included a view of the Arc de Triomphe, and had a vacation home in Saint-Tropez. Married four times with a son and daughter, Villiers' personal life often resembled that of his fictional creation.

Though Villiers had many fans, including politicians, spies, and warlords, he was not particularly respected by the French literary establishment or critics. His book were sold everywhere in France, including supermarkets and railway stations, but especially appealed to certain types of readers including those who favored a right-leaning political affiliation, or appreciated his geopolitical insights. Though such French luminaries as Jacques Chirac and Valéry Giscard d'Estaing enjoyed his books, his readership remained essentially limited—especially by the twenty-first century—and profits stagnated. Because he came to be seen as more politically incorrect as time went on—with unappealing, outspoken opinions on race, religion, and sexism—some readers were turned off by his books and perspective in the 2000s.

Villiers' novels were primarily popular in French-speaking parts of the world. Unlike the Bond franchise, which had a more universal popularity, S.A.S. novels did not sell particularly well outside of France, Germany, Japan, and Russia. The English-speaking world was particularly not interested in the books, though spies and those who worked in intelligence worldwide often read his works. A few of his novels were translated and published in the United States in the late 1970s, with poor sales.

Gained American Publisher

Despite the lack of English-speaking desire to read his S.A.S. novels, Villiers had an offer from a major American publisher to translate five of his novels and publish them in the United States shortly before his death. This offer came in early 2013, and was regarded as a means of achieving his career goal of breaking into the English-language market. Random House offered $350,000 for the rights to five books. Villiers hoped the deal would also eventually result in Hollywood adaptations of S.A.S. novels. In the 1980s, two French film adaptations of the novels had not been particularly popular worldwide.

Diagnosed with pancreatic cancer in early 2013, Villiers struggled with the effect of chemotherapy. Villiers died of the disease on October 31, 2013, in Paris, at the age of 83. He had published the 200th S.A.S. novel earlier in October, *La Vengeance du Kremlin* (The Kremlin's Vengeance). The following year, the Random House deal reached fruition, with three translated novels published in America beginning in July 2014. The titles were carefully chosen to appeal to American audiences and picked in consultation with Villiers before his death.

Of his reputation, Villiers told Robert F. Worth of *New York Times Magazine,* "I don't consider myself a literary man. I'm a storyteller. I write fairy tales for adults. And I try to put some substance into it."

Periodicals

Agence France Presse—English, November 1, 2013.
Independent (London, England), November 9, 2013.
New York Times, November 3, 2013; July 31, 2014.
New York Times Magazine, February 3, 2013.
Times (London, England), November 7, 2013.
Washington Post, November 18, 1987.□

Samuel Wallis

British navigator Samuel Wallis (1728–1795) was one of the Royal Navy's most able commanders. As captain of the HMS *Dolphin*, the veteran sailor logged 637 days at sea and on land in an historic circumnavigation to locate a mythical *Terra Australis,* or "South Land." Wallis found nothing but roiling and frigid seas hinting of an as-yet-undiscovered Antarctic continent, but his crew were the first Europeans of record to set foot on the particularly splendid tropical kingdom of Tahiti in the South Pacific Sea in 1767.

Samuel Wallis came from Cornwall, the southwest peninsular corner of England, and parish records list his place of birth at Fentonwoon, the estate that was the Wallis family seat. He was baptized in the parish of Lantegloss-by-Camelford on April 23, 1728, and was the third son of John Wallis and Sarah Barrett Wallis. Little is known of his early life, but he likely enlisted in the Royal Navy in his teens and had been promoted to the rank of lieutenant by the age of 20 in 1748. Wallis's entry in the British *Dictionary of National Biography* lists several postings and career milestones after this. In January of 1753 he came aboard the HMS *Anson* under Captain Charles Holmes, who was part of a successful naval campaign off the coast of Newfoundland against the French Navy. This was part of the Seven Years' War of 1756–63, and Wallis continued to earn merit for combat service as a lieutenant aboard the HMS *Torbay,* another famous warship. His career advanced rapidly as he served under Admiral Edward Boscawen, a noted British naval hero of the era. His first command post was that of a 14-gun sloop, the HMS *Swan,* a commission he received on June 30, 1756.

Spent Years at Sea, at War

Wallis's *Dictionary of National Biography* entry lists him as having received a new Royal Navy posting in April of 1757, this one aboard the *Port Mahon,* a 24-gun ship that headed west to North America as part of another campaign of the Seven Years' War. It was one of several warships that attacked the French fort Louisburg on Cape Breton Island but were forced into retreat. In September of 1758, Boscawen assigned Wallis the command of the HMS *Prince of Orange,* a 60-gun ship that had helped take the fort at Louisburg in a second, more successful attack that permanently ended French control of Canada's Maritime Provinces. Wallis helmed the warship in port in the St. Lawrence River region and later served with the Royal Navy's Channel Fleet in the early 1760s.

In 1766 the British Admiralty tapped Wallis for an ambitious new mission: to find the fabled Terra Australis, a Latin term that had appeared with a question mark on maps for centuries. Greek philosopher Aristotle theorized that because the known world of fourth-century BCE was so large, there was probably a correspondingly enormous land mass elsewhere on earth. The belief persisted for centuries, especially after Christopher Columbus landed on a large Caribbean island in 1492 and learned two vast continents lay above and below it. Columbus had actually been attempting to reach India by a westward route, but quickly claimed the Americas for his patrons, the King and Queen of Spain. Spanish voyagers and armies descended upon the New World and began mining its natural resources, which included seemingly limitless supplies of gold, silver, and copper.

To locate Terra Australis, Wallis was assigned to captain the HMS *Dolphin,* which had recently returned from a previous around-the-world mission. That was done in secret by John Byron, a fellow Brit and veteran of the Seven Years' War as well as future grandfather of the poet Lord Byron. The explorer Byron set a new record for sea circumnavigation when he returned after 23 months in May of 1766, during which he had staked Britain's claim to some windswept islands off the coast of Argentina, which Byron named the Falklands.

Survived Perilous Passage

The *Dolphin* was a solid vessel that had served Byron well in two particularly challenging passages: the one through the Strait of Magellan at the southern tip of South America, and another equally treacherous one off the southern coastline of Africa that led back to Atlantic Ocean waters. Accompanying Wallis on his mission was a smaller ship, the HMS *Swallow,* whose captain was Philip Carteret. The copper-hulled *Dolphin* had room for a crew of 150 men and carried more than a ton of citrus fruit, which was known to prevent scurvy. There was a metal forge aboard to make necessary ship repairs, plus a freshwater still and even a goat to provide fresh milk for Wallis and the other officers. The goat had actually gone with Byron, too, and became the first ungulate to make two consecutive circumnavigations of the earth.

Wallis's flotilla departed Plymouth, England, on August 22, 1766. His first stop was the island of Madeira, several hundred miles off the coast of Morocco, and then they visited Cape Verde Islands off the West African coast. Wallis then crossed the Atlantic to the Falklands before making a visit at a place the British had ominously named Port Famine, their naval base in Patagonia, Chile. Regarding Terra Australis, Admiralty officials briefed him on its purported location and suggested sailing toward the 100th meridian west—a line of longitude that bisects the earth from the North Pole through Nebraska, parts of Mexico, and then Pacific Ocean waters off the coast of South America—and on toward the 120th meridian west and look for land. If it was sighted, he was to return home and a fleet of supply ships and surveyors would be sent out to claim the new continent for King George III. If no land was visible, Wallis was told to keep heading west.

The *Dolphin* and *Swallow* entered the Strait of Magellan in early December of 1766, but it took four months of rough waters and bad storms to reach the other side. Carteret's ship lagged behind and sailors lost sight of each other's vessels in heavy fog. Wallis's log records the date of April 11, 1767, when the *Dolphin* sailed away from the treacherous Magellan passage. His captain's diary, later published as *Account of the Voyage Undertaken for Making Discoveries in the Southern Hemisphere,* mentions that both ships were in constant danger of shipwreck in the infamous straits, and also noted that rumors of extremely tall indigenous Patagonians were unfounded.

Delighted by Lush Paradise

Other British navy captains knew that once they reached Pacific waters they could sail up the coastline of Chile.

Instead, Wallis ordered sails to be set for a northwesterly direction into the unknown Pacific Ocean. The *Dolphin* went several weeks without sighting any landfall, but finally encountered the Tuamotus archipelago in early June. Both Magellan and Byron, plus Portuguese and Dutch mariners, had all stopped at this part of French Polynesia. Sailing on, Wallis and his crew were elated to see an enormous land mass that they assumed was the mythical South Land on June 18, 1767. It was actually Tahiti, the center of a rich Polynesian culture with a kingdom that extended over several other island groups.

Dolphin crew members were the first Europeans of record to set foot on Tahiti and establish formal diplomatic ties. Some 90 years earlier, a Spanish explorer named Juan Fernández made landfall on either Tahiti's main island or another one in its realm on another clandestine mission. The Tahitians of 1767 were curious about the enormous British vessel, and sent a flotilla of 800 men on 150 canoes to approach the *Dolphin.* After a discussion while British sailors waved strings of baubles from the deck to show they had friendly intentions, a party of Tahitians were invited aboard.

Wallis was granted permission to anchor his ship at Matavai Bay, and did so on June 24. He was ailing, however, and went ashore only twice. He dubbed the land King George III's Island and in his diary used the Polynesian word in describing the people and culture of "Otaheite." His men enjoyed the Tahitians' hospitality—famously chronicled in a later British mission under Captain William Bligh, whose crew mutinied in 1789, cast the punitive Bligh adrift, and returned the HMS *Bounty* to the main island, where they had taken Tahitian wives.

Returned to England

Wallis's second in command was Lieutenant Tobias Furneaux, who worked to foster cordial relations with representatives of Tahiti's Queen Obera, whom Wallis had met. The ship was repaired, fresh water and food acquired through trade deals, and plans were made for a departure date of July 27, 1767. Wallis was dismayed to learn that Tahiti was nothing more than a fairly large volcanic island and not an entire continent. From there the *Dolphin* visited Batavia, as the Indonesian capital of Jakarta was called at the time, where his crew fell ill from dysentery.

En route to Indonesia Wallis's ship "discovered" a pair of islands west of Samoa and north of Fiji; the smaller of the two is Wallis Island, later named in his honor. Both it and its larger neighbor, Futunua, became part of French Polynesia and remain an overseas territory of France in the 21st century. The *Dolphin* rounded the Cape of Good Hope in February of 1768 and arrived in the safe waters of The Downs near Dover, England, on May 18, 1768. Wallis had not lost any of his men to scurvy, which was considered an astonishing achievement in that era of epic sea voyages. He was back in London on May 20, and had set a new British naval record with the *Dolphin,* which became the first ship ever to circumnavigate the globe twice. Carteret eventually arrived back safely, too, several months later.

Wallis's superiors at the Admiralty were dismayed to learn there was probably no South Land in the South Pacific. A French party had also set out to explore the same route shortly after Wallis began his voyage. Its captain was Louis-Antoine de Bougainville, whose career had closely paralleled Wallis': both fought key battles in the Seven Years' War in Canada and visited the Falklands. Bougainville also stopped on Tahiti and claimed it for France, calling it *La Nouvelle Cythere.* His reports, too, described an island of intense natural beauty and one populated by friendly Polynesians, unlike some other parts of the region.

Excellent Recap Aided Cook

Wallis handed over his logs and charts to Alexander Dalrymple, a Scot who would eventually become the first Chief Hydrographer of the British Admiralty. Dalrymple was the most ardent proponent of the Terra Australis theory, and seized upon Wallis's notes that recounted that the *Dolphin* crew had seen spectacular sunsets on Tahiti; as dusk rolled in they thought they spotted mountain peaks far off in the distance, which was probably just an optical illusion. Dalrymple created new maps and ocean charts based on Wallis's findings, and these were used for an historic scientific mission to measure the Transit of Venus in 1769. The rare planetary alignment aided Royal Society astronomers in calculating the distance between the Earth and the sun. Captain James Cook was in charge of the South Seas expedition to measure the Transit and on that first trip discovered, explored, and charted New Zealand and Australia. On Cook's second trip his ship became the first to enter the Antarctic Circle, and on his third voyage in 1776–80 Cook followed Wallis's northwesterly route and discovered the Hawaiian Islands. Some veterans of the *Dolphin* went with Cook, among them Furneaux.

In 1770 Wallis went to war again, this time against Spain in the first of many conflicts England waged over the Falkland Islands. For his service he was made a commissioner of the Royal Navy in 1782. He died at his London home on Devonshire Street on January 21, 1795, at the age of 67. He and his wife, born Betty Hearle, had one daughter, also named Betty.

Books

Boase, George Clement, and William Prideaux Courtney, *Bibliotheca Cornubiensis,* Vol. 2, *P-Z,* Longmans, Green, Reader and Dyer, 1878.

Dictionary of National Biography, vol. LIX, *Wakeman–Watkins,* edited by Sidney Lee, Smith Elder, 1899.

Exploration and Exchange: A South Seas Anthology 1680–1900, edited by Jonathon Lamb, Vanessa Smith, and Nicholas Thomas, University of Chicago Press, 2000.

Wallis, Samuel, et al., *An Account of the Voyages Undertaken by the Order of His Present Majesty for Making Discoveries in the Southern Hemisphere, and Successively Performed by Commodore Byron, Captain Wallis, Captain Carteret, and Captain Cook, in the Dolphin, the Swallow, and the Endeavour,* edited John Hawkesworth, Strahan & Cadell, 1773.□

Y

Genrikh Grigoryevich Yagoda

Russian government official Genrikh Yagoda (1891–1938) spent a deadly two years as head of the Soviet Union's secret police in the 1930s. As head of the People's Commissariat for Internal Affairs, he worked closely with Soviet leader Josef Stalin to target and prosecute scores of high-ranking Communist Party officials in the notorious Moscow Show Trials, when veteran party figures and even senior military brass confessed to shocking acts of treason. Yagoda, too, fell victim to Stalin's Great Terror and was himself arrested, convicted, and executed by firing squad.

Genrikh Grigoryevich Yagoda was born on November 7, 1891, in Rybinsk, a city on the banks of the Volga River. On his father's side he was related to another Russian Jewish family, the Sverdlovs, and the Yagoda clan—a name sometimes spelled "Iagoda"—eventually moved to Nizhny Novgorod, a larger city, where Yagoda's father worked in a printing and engraving business with a Sverdlov cousin. In his youth Yagoda worked at the print shop, which had a profitable side business in forging new identity papers for those persecuted by the Tsarist regime.

Floundered in a Misspent Youth

Leftists, Social Democrats, and Communists were among the targeted political groups that agitated for reform in Tsarist Russia. By 1905 political unrest had brought Russia to the brink of full-scale revolution, but ruthless Cossack brigades were used to quash opposition and defend government buildings. Yagoda's older brother Mikhail was slain in one Cossack-led melee in Nizhny Novgorod, a death that traumatized the 13-year-old. A few years later Yagoda moved to live with his sister in Moscow, where he worked with her at a pharmacy. He came under police suspicion in 1912, accused in a conspiracy to set off a bomb, and was briefly exiled from Russia's chief city. He eventually found his way to the capital city, St. Petersburg, where he secured a job in the office of Putilov steel works, one of the largest industrial sites in the Russian Empire.

In 1914 Yagoda married Ida Averbakh, daughter of a prominent literary family in Nizhny Novgorod and also connected to the Sverdlov clan. Yagoda's family connections served him well when workers at the Putilov plant went on strike in early 1917 and pushed the country toward revolution once again. This time the leftists succeeded and Tsar Nicholas II was forced to abdicate. Among the high-ranking Russian Communists involved in these actions was Yakov Sverdlov, Ida's uncle. Sverdlov worked with Vladimir Lenin, Leon Trotsky, and other leaders to bring about the October Revolution of 1917, also known as the Bolshevik Revolution. This second action placed Russia's hard-line Communists firmly in control.

Joined Secret Police

Yagoda formally joined the Communist Party, but was able to backdate his documents to claim his membership application was approved ten years earlier, in 1907. Sverdlov, who had spent time in Siberian exile with several key Bolshevik figures before the February revolution, recommended Yagoda to Felix Dzerzhinsky, whom Lenin tasked

RIA Novosti/Alamy

with establishing a secret police force and intelligence bureau to safeguard the revolution's progress. This was called the *Vserossiyskaya Chrezvychaynaya Komissiya,* or All-Russia Emergency Commission, but was better known by the acronym VcheKA, which was shortened to Cheka. Yagoda rose quickly in the force, and when it was overhauled in 1922 and renamed the People's Commissariat of Internal Affairs (in Russian, *Narodnyy Komissariat Vnutrennikh Del,* or NKVD) he was promoted to second deputy under Vyacheslav Menzhinsky, Dzerzhinsky's second-in-command.

In 1924, Lenin died and Stalin outmaneuvered Trotsky and other party veterans to take control of the newly created Union of Soviet Socialist Republics (USSR). The power struggle between Stalin and the Old Bolsheviks, as leaders of the 1917 Revolution were known, continued to play out for years and Yagoda became deeply enmeshed within it. His NKVD boss, Menzhinsky, suffered ongoing health problems and Yagoda often represented Menzhinsky in meetings with Stalin. When Dzerzhinsky was moved to another ministry in 1924 and Menzhinsky promoted, Yagoda effectively became the de facto chief of the NKVD.

By the late 1920s Yagoda wielded immense power within the NKVD police and in a newly created intelligence service also headed by Menzhinsky, the OGPU, which replaced the Cheka. The *Obyedinyonnoye Gosudarstvennoye Politicheskoye Upravlenie,* or All-Union State Political Directorate, oversaw a newly created network of forced-labor camps known as the gulag. The camps expanded during the Great Terror of the 1930s and millions of Soviet citizens spent years in punitive, starvation-ration conditions.

Set Up Reeducation Camps

Yagoda was instrumental in carrying out Stalin's suppression of his most serious rival for power, Leon Trotsky. His office jailed the Old Bolshevik, sent him into internal exile in Central Asia, and finally arranged for Trotsky to be deported in 1929. As deputy director of the OGPU Yagoda also oversaw the use of forced labor to build the White Sea-Baltic Canal, which was completed in 1933. Under appalling conditions, more than 100,000 detainees were forced to dig earth and move rock by hand, and they competed in teams against one another for food. Some estimates place the infrastructure project's death toll as high as 25,000. For this Yagoda was awarded the prestigious Order of Lenin.

Through the Sverdlovs, Yagoda had some family connections to a revered Russian writer, Maxim Gorky. One of Russia's most famous living artists of the early 20th century, the novelist and playwright was also an ardent supporter of the Russian Communists during the pre-revolutionary era. When Gorky began to question the excesses of the Bolshevik regime, however, his works were censored and he finally left the country, citing health reasons. Gorky spent eight years in exile in Italy, but Yagoda was instrumental in persuading him to return for a visit in 1929. Stalin persuaded Gorky to stay permanently, become president of the Union of Writers, and use his talents to promote the Soviet Union, including an embarrassing propaganda piece about the White Sea-Baltic Canal.

Yagoda, who had but six years of formal education, idolized Gorky and inserted himself into the literary scene through this connection. In his own attempt at dazzling metaphor, Yagoda had once written to Gorky about his job at the NKVD. "Like a dog on a chain, I lie by the gates of the republic and chew through the throat of anyone who raises a hand against the peace of the Union," he asserted, according to Donald Rayfield's 2004 tome *Stalin and His Hangmen: The Tyrant and Those Who Killed for Him.*

Likely Arranged Kirov Assassination

Yagoda was married and the father of a young son, Garik, but rumored to have been infatuated with Gorky's daughter-in-law, Timosha Peshkov, who came to fear him after her husband Max died suddenly in May of 1934. That same month Yagoda's longtime boss, Vyacheslav Menzhinsky, also passed away. Two months later, the OGPU was folded into the NKVD and Stalin appointed Yagoda as its chief. With Yagoda firmly in charge of the domestic-intelligence apparatus, Stalin began a secret program to rid the party of all threats to his power, or perceived obstacles to his ambitious five-year plans to turn the Soviet Union into a global industrial power. This period became known as the Great Terror or Red Terror, and its onset was the mysterious death of an Old Bolshevik, Sergei Kirov, chief of the Communist Party organization in Leningrad, as St. Petersburg was now called. An assassin felled Kirov in the hallway of his office building, and the death of such a high-ranking figure in the Soviet Union prompted international headlines. Sovietologists surmise that Yagoda oversaw the unsavory details of the execution, finding a suspicious disgruntled ex-Communist Party member to commit the deed, and ensuring that Kirov's lone bodyguard died in a strange automobile accident shortly after the assassination while in police custody.

On the pretense of a national security threat, Yagoda ordered NKVD personal-protection units to be assigned to all senior party officials. The agents were also used as an informant network to keep tabs on members of the ruling Politburo elite. Next in line for reprisals were two more Old Bolsheviks, Lev Kamenev and Grigory Zinoviev, who had once allied with Stalin against Trotsky but had dually endured a long stretch of enmity with the tyrannical Soviet leader for nearly a decade. Arrested in January of 1935 by Yagoda's agents, Kamenev and Zinoviev were coerced to sign false confessions and were tried for treason and other state crimes, along with 14 others, in the summer of 1936. That was the first of the Moscow Show Trials, and in the first proceeding Kamenev and Zinoviev were found guilty, sentenced to death, and were shot by firing squad.

Wielded Enormous Police Power

As the head of the NKVD, Yagoda was responsible for the agents who made mass arrests, detained and tortured prisoners, and handed over signed confessions to state prosecutors, some of which were splattered in their victims' blood. Cleverly, many shocking admissions of treason and wrecking—a general term for actions or even inactions deemed an obstacle to the goals of the revolution—contained details that corresponded with those in statements made under duress by supposed co-conspirators. The middle-of-the-night roundups and trials continued through 1937 and 1938 and instilled fear at every level of Soviet society. People disappeared overnight, entire families vanished from their homes, and some feared the dreaded NKVD prison at Moscow's Lubyanka Square so intensely that they committed suicide when warned of a coming visit by Yagoda's agents. The writer Isaac Babel told his wife that he had once met Yagoda during this period. "Tell me, how should someone act if he falls into your men's paws?" Babel asked Yagoda, according to a *New York Times* review of Antonina Nikolaevna Pirozhkova's memoir *The Last Years of Isaac Babel.* Yagoda was said to have replied, "Deny everything, whatever the charges, just say no and keep saying no. If one denies everything, we are powerless."

Yagoda worked in tandem with Nikolai Yezhov, another ruthless operative who carried out Stalin's directives and ensured the party remained the moral center in the eyes of the Soviet citizenry. Yagoda was said to have been wary of Stalin's plan to eliminate General Mikhail Tukhachevsky, a famed military hero whose decisive moves in the Russian Civil War had been crucial to the Red Army victory in the early 1920s. Yagoda was ousted from his job as NKVD chief on September 26, 1936, on Stalin's orders for failing to act swiftly enough to root out treasonous elements in the party. His deputy, Yezhov, succeeded him. Technically, Yagoda was demoted and named the People's Commissar for Post and Communications. His arrest order was issued on March 31, 1937, and he was charged with diamond smuggling and espionage after a search of his homes turned up furs, cash, and a trove of expensive wines and pornographic photographs.

Abandoned by Stalin

Yagoda's trial in early 1938 was the last of the Moscow Show Trials. At one point, he warned one of the three-judge panel, "You can drive me, but not too far," he said, according to *The Great Terror: A Reassessment,* by historian Robert Conquest. "I'll say what I want to say," he continued, and likely hinting at the full scope of the Great Purge he could reveal in discussing the Kirov assassination, cautioned one judge in particular, "Do not drive me too far."

Yagoda was found guilty and sentenced to death by firing squad. He fell in the Lubyanka prison on March 15, 1938, at age 46. Yezhov, who had accused him of attempting to poison Yezhov's NKVD office with mercury, ordered Yagoda to be stripped and beaten before he died. Yezhov suffered the same ignominious end two years later. Yagoda's mother, father, and sisters disappeared into the gulag and presumably died there. His son Garik went into a special orphanage set up for children of high-ranking purge victims and it is not known if he survived World War II.

Books

Conquest, Robert, *The Great Terror: A Reassessment,* Oxford University Press, 1990.
Rayfield, Donald, *Stalin and His Hangmen: The Tyrant and Those Who Killed for Him,* Random House, 2004.

Periodicals

New York Times, November 25, 1996.
Times (London, England), March 9, 1938. □

Mandawuy Yunupingu

The Aboriginal Australian singer and songwriter Mandawuy Yunupingu (1956–2013) created a fusion between aboriginal traditional music and rock styles, bringing aboriginal music and culture to much wider audiences than had previously been exposed to these cultural influences.

Yunupingu was a groundbreaker in many ways. He was the first Aborigine from his home region (according to one account from remote Australia) to earn a university degree, and the first from any part of Australia to become a school principal. Yunupingu suggested new methods for the education of Aboriginal children, incorporating both Western and traditional materials. He was best known, however, for founding and fronting the band Yothu Yindi, whose music mixed rock and Aboriginal elements. With Yothu Yindi, Yunupingu toured Europe and

Caroline McCredie/Getty Images

the United States, and performed at the United Nations in New York; they were the first rock band ever to do so. Yunupingu was a familiar figure in Australia and a strong advocate for Aboriginal rights. Upon his death, Australian Prime Minister Julia Gillard said (as quoted by the *Bendigo Advertiser*): "We have lost a uniquely talented musician, a passionate advocate for Aboriginal people and a truly great friend. He leaves a great body of work to inspire us and we will need all of that inspiration."

Changed Name According to Cultural Norms

Yunupingu was born Tom Djambayang Bakamanana Yunupingu on September 17, 1956, in the small Aboriginal town of Yirrkala in northeast Australia's Arnhem Land region. His father, Mangurrawuy Yunupingu, was a clan leader. A member of the Yolngu people, Yunupingu was raised bilingually, in English and in an Aboriginal language called Gujamati. Until 1989 he used the name Bakmana, but in that year another Yolngu man with that name died, and in his culture it was impermissible to speak a dead person's first name. So Yunupingu began using the name Mandawuy, meaning clay. He had a sister, Gulumbu, who was a health worker and artist, and his brother, Galarrwuy, was an activist and musician.

As a teenager, Yunupingu saw his tribal lands, remote from the big Australian cities in the south, changing rapidly. Part of the Gove Peninsula where the Yolngu lived was taken away from the tribe and given to a mining firm,

which began producing bauxite and aluminum in a large factory complex on a beach. Yunupingu resolved not to simply keep to his own culture in an underground way as he had seen other Aboriginals do, but learn to function in the wider Australian society.

After earning a teaching certificate, Yunupingu began teaching at a school in Yirrkala in 1977. He later earned a bachelor's degree in educatoin from Deakin University, and got another degree, with honors, from the Queensland University of Technology. During this period he played in an all-Yolgnu band on the side. The group joined with a band of non-indigenous Australians called the Swamp Jockeys to form Yothu Yindi, which meant mother and child, in 1986. The band's name came from the fact that Yunupingu considered the didgeridoo (a wind instrument), which the Yolgnu called the yidaki, to be the band's mother.

Fused Aboriginal, Western Styles

The band's music combined the didgeridoo and Yunupingu's Yolgnu-style vocals with electric guitar and rock and pop beats. Yunupingu was not the first Aboriginal Australian musician to become popular; singer-songwriter and guitarist Jimmy Little had reached upper chart levels with country, pop, and gospel recordings in the 1960s, and Yunupingu's brother Galarrwuy had released a single, "Gurindji Blues," in connection with land rights protests in the 1970s. But the Aboriginal elements in Yothu Yindi's music were stronger than those in earlier efforts. Yuthu Yindi released its first album, *Homeland Movement*, in 1989, and it did not take them long to gain attention. The stylistically diverse Australian rock singer Paul Kelly heard their music and invited them to tour with him.

Music remained a part-time enterprise for Yunupingu, who in 1990 was appointed principal of the Yirrkala Community School, becoming the first Aboriginal anywhere in Australia to reach that rank. He began to develop a new educational philosophy known in English as "both ways" or "two ways," which involved mixing Western and Aboriginal teaching modes. He also campaigned in favor of bringing more Aboriginal teachers into Australia's educational system. For a time Yunupingu toured with Yuthu Yindi only during school vacations, but in 1991 he resigned his position in order to devote full time to his music.

The stimulus for that was the international success of Yothu Yindi's song "Treaty," which was included on an album called *Tribal Voice*. It topped Australian charts for 22 weeks, became a hit in Britain, and was performed by the band at the United Nations in New York to launch the UN's International Year for the World's Indigenous People. The song, composed by Yunupingu, Kelly, and Australian vocalist Peter Garrett of the band Midnight Oil, protested the broken promise of an Australian-Aboriginal treaty made in 1988 by Australian prime minister Bob Hawke. They toured with Midnight Oil and performed at Australia's Big Day Out festival, appearing above the new American band Nirvana on the bill. Performing with dancers in Aboriginal body paint, Yuthu Yindi made six albums and scored several more hit singles. Even at the height of their popularity the group experienced discrimination when they were asked to leave a bar in the town of St. Kilda.

Suffered Effects of Alcohol Abuse

In the mid-1990s Yunupingu was slowed by complications resulting from alcoholism; he himself admitted drinking up to four 24-can cartons of beer daily. He developed diabetes and then kidney failure, which necessitated undergoing dialysis three times weekly. He entered a rehabilitation program, telling Tracee Hutchison of the Melbourne *Age*: "As the saying goes with rock and roll, alcohol and drugs can take you to the road of no return, the road of despair. I now know how much damage excessive consumption of alcohol can do." Yuthu Yindi did not disband but began to focus its touring on Aboriginal communities close to Yunupingu's home in Arnhem Land.

Named Australian of the Year in 1992, Yunupingu saw his efforts toward recovery not only in personal terms, but also as a duty to those who had looked up to him and seen him as a leader. He continued to speak out on Aboriginal issues, such as a decision by the Australian government to lessen Aboriginal control over entry to ancestral lands. "[The government] are turning back the clocks to suit their needs, to suit their time frame in a way that we can't understand," he told Hutchison. Yunupingu received widespread support from both Aboriginal and non-Aboriginal musicians, and he was well enough to perform with Yuthu Yindi at the closing ceremony of the Summer Olympic Games in Sydney and at the opening of the Paralympics in 2000. They were backed by Midnight Oil, who wore outfits that bore the word "Sorry" on the front and back.

Yunupingu was married, and he and his wife, Yalmay, had six daughters. He continued to perform with Yuthu Yindi into the 2010s; the band addressed the issue of alcohol abuse in many of its shows. Yunupingu wrote his last song, "Healing Stone," in 2012; he had attempted to address his substance abuse issues with traditional Aboriginal healing methods as well as with Western rehabilitation. He was inducted into the ARIA (Australian Recording Industry Association) Hall of Fame in 2012, asking in his acceptance speech that Australia recognize Aboriginal peoples in its constitution.

Yunupingu died of complications from kidney disease on June 3, 2013, at his home in Yirrkala. His state funeral was marked by traditional Yolgnu rituals. His wife wore his trademark headband as family members carried his body toward a crowd of 500 mourners. His brother Duungatjunga Yunupingu recalled that Mandawuy had once told him to "catch the beauty, before it fades away."

Periodicals

Advertiser (Adelaide, South Australia), June 4, 2013.
Age (Melbourne, Australia), January 20, 1994; August 13, 2007; July 1, 2013.
Australian, June 4, 2013.
Bendigo Advertiser (Bendigo, Australia), June 4, 2013.
Daily Telegraph (London, England), July 19, 2013.
Daily Telegraph (Sydney, New South Wales, Australia), June 4, 2013.
Gold Coast Bulletin (Queensland, Australia), June 4, 2013.
New York Times, June 4, 2013.
Telegraph Online, July 18, 2013.
Western Daily Press (Bristol, England), June 4, 2013.
World News Entertainment Network, June 18, 2013.

Online

"Yothu Yindi's Mandawuy Yunupingu Dies at 56," *Billboard,* http://www.billboard.com/articles/news/1565597/yothu-yindis-mandawuy-yunupingu-dies-at-56 (January 4, 2015). □

Z

Yitzhak Zuckerman

During World War II, Nazi resistance leader Yitzhak Zuckerman (1915–1981) served as a key liaison between the Jewish and Polish undergrounds in Warsaw, Poland. Zuckerman, a Jewish Pole, played a prominent role in organizing fighters for the 1943 Warsaw Ghetto Uprising, which marked a turning point in Jewish resistance to German occupation and annihilation. The Warsaw Ghetto Uprising was the first Jewish act of aggressive armed resistance during the Holocaust and inspired more resistance.

Zuckerman was born in December 1915, in Vilna (now Vilnius, Lithuania). His mother, Rivka (Frenkel) Zuckerman, was from Lithuania, while his father, Shimon Zuckerman, was a Ukrainian immigrant who had grown up in Kiev. Zuckerman's paternal grandfather, Yohanan Zuckerman, was a rabbi. Zuckerman's father was an observant Jew and a Zionist. Zionism is a nationalist Jewish movement that calls for the return of the Jewish people to their homeland in Palestine. Zuckerman attended a Hebrew secular secondary school where many of the teachers were Zionists who fueled his interest in the movement. He graduated in 1933.

Joined Zionist Movement

In lieu of college, Zuckerman elected to join the He-Halutz Ha-Tza'ir (Young Pioneer) training kibbutz in Vilna. He-Halutz was a Zionist training organization. At this time, many adolescent Jews were joining Zionist youth movements, propelled by the anti-Semitic social climate

creeping across Eastern Europe. The pogroms that followed World War I, particularly in the Ukraine, served to heighten Zionist national consciousness. He-Halutz worked in the areas of organization, education, and political awareness. The group's ultimate goal was to recruit and train members to re-settle their long-abandoned Holy Land of Israel. He-Halutz ran an agricultural training program to prepare citizens to farm in the new settlement. The group also trained young women to become teachers. Zuckerman was appointed to the He-Halutz district council. In this capacity, he visited and lectured in the small towns around Vilna.

By 1936, Zuckerman was elevated to a role within the He-Halutz central committee. Over the next few years he worked in Warsaw, Poland; Lutsk and Lwów, Ukraine; and Kowel, a Soviet-occupied area of Eastern Poland. One of his activities involved putting out an underground newspaper. In early 1940, however, Zuckerman returned to Warsaw. Germany had invaded Poland in 1939. After defeating Poland a few months later, the Germans moved the Jewish people to a restricted, walled area known as the Warsaw Ghetto. Zuckerman was tasked with organizing a larger underground movement within the ghetto walls by continuing his education activities and setting up political cells. He became part of a resistance group known as Dror, which is Hebrew for freedom. He soon joined forces with other leaders of the Zionist-Socialist movement, including Mordechai Anielewicz of Ha-Shomer Ha-Tza'ir (The Young Guardians) and leaders of the Jewish Socialist Bund.

Zuckerman often stayed at an apartment in Warsaw where Dror had established a commune. Zuckerman was tall and did not look Jewish, so he was able to pass on the streets as a gentile Pole. Zuckerman made contacts in the ghetto by sneaking in and out, often bribing officials to let him pass from the Jewish ghetto into the Aryan, non-Jewish

Forum/UIG/Getty Images

side of the city. Zuckerman also traveled to areas outside of Warsaw, making connections with both the Jewish and Polish underground resistance movements. This was extremely dangerous because Jews caught riding the trains were executed on-site. Zuckerman got by with forged documents, street smarts, and luck.

Imprisoned at Work Camp

In April 1941, authorities came to the Warsaw apartment and Zuckerman and his comrades were taken to the Kampinos Camp. Each day, Zuckerman and his friends received 200 grams of bread and one bowl of soup per person. They were able to survive by buying food from the Polish villagers who came to the camp border. Zuckerman had money provided by the movement. After a few days, he was summoned to camp headquarters and interrogated because a woman had approached one of the guards and asked about him. Zuckerman figured it was a fellow Jewish member of the organization, Lonka Kozibrodska, who worked as a courier for Dror. She posed as a Polish girl, but aroused suspicion with her visit. The men at headquarters demanded to know if she was Jewish or Polish. Zuckerman responded that she was Polish; he feared they had already captured her and would execute her if her Jewishness was exposed.

Two of the camp officials beat Zuckerman but he declined to offer any incriminating evidence about himself or his visitor. They finally gave up and threw him in a water-filled pit. Later, Zuckerman was pulled from the pit

and placed in front of the entire camp. According to Zuckerman's memoir, *A Surplus of Memory: Chronicle of the Warsaw Ghetto Uprising,* the camp commandant told the crowd that Zuckerman was a criminal, then stated, "This man knows when he was born but he doesn't know when he will die. I can promise you only this: for three days his body will hang here as a warning to the entire camp."

Thrown back in the pit, Zuckerman awaited his execution, but it never came. Eventually he was returned to the camp, and his friends nursed him back to health. Zuckerman never learned why he had been spared. Later, when a transport came to take away the sick people too ill to work, Zuckerman offered a monetary bribe to one of the camp directors, suggesting he be added to that group. He also asked for the release of his friends, offering an even larger sum. The bribe was accepted, and when the group of sick and weak Jews left, Zuckerman and his comrades were included and returned to Warsaw.

Reinforced Resistance Movement

The stay at Kampinos increased Zuckerman's fury and desire to expand the resistance movement. While imprisoned at Kampinos, he witnessed countless deaths from starvation, execution, and typhus. He noted in his memoir, "During my few weeks in the camp, the Jewish population there shrank and the cemetery expanded." Every day he watched workers remove corpses from the camp. At this point, Zuckerman understood that being sent to a work camp meant near certain death. Because few people survived the work camps or ever returned to the ghetto, many were unaware of the horrors of being interned. As soon as Zuckerman returned to Warsaw, he published another newspaper. His article, about Kampinos, was translated into Polish and published in at least one Polish newspaper.

Over the next few months, Zuckerman and his comrades made connections with other resistance groups. Zuckerman soon established himself as a key liaison between the Jewish and Polish undergrounds. He soon heard the tale of a gravedigger who had escaped from a camp in Chelmno. The gravedigger provided stories about Jewish people being executed with poison gas. The picture became obvious to Zuckerman: the Germans intended to annihilate the Jews. Many people did not believe this could possibly be true. Zuckerman, having experienced the work camp, understood what was going on. Under his direction, Dror stepped up publication of its underground newspaper, no longer intending it for education purposes, but to tell the truth about what was happening to the Jews in Poland.

In July 1942, Zuckerman met with other resistance leaders and they formed the Jewish Fighting Organization or ZOB (Zydowska Organizacja Bojowa). He was included in the ZOB's command staff with Anielewicz as the leader. Initially, the ZOB's acts were small. The group began burning the homes of Jewish people who had died or been taken from the city, in an effort to keep the Germans from taking over or looting the homes. Next, the ZOB executed the head of the Jewish police because he continued to cooperate with German authorities to organize the transport of Jewish citizens to labor and concentration camps. To fund their resistance movement, the ZOB confiscated money from wealthy Jews. In another act of defiance, Zuckerman was sent to Krakow to join a Jewish underground attack at a café patronized by German officers. They threw grenades into the café, killing Gestapo agents. Afterward, they took their guns. During a covert operation one night, Zuckerman was shot in the leg, but managed to escape by slipping into a crowd. Meanwhile, the ZOB worked to stockpile weapons.

Led Resistance Fighters

By January 1943, the Germans came less frequently to patrol the ghetto for fear of getting shot by a sniper. They made their rounds hastily and retreated. This represented a shift in authority. Meanwhile, fighters with the resistance movement prepared to confront the Germans the next time they launched an *aktsia* roundup in the ghetto. During the previous aktsia that began in July 1942 and lasted several weeks, more than 250,000 Jews were moved from the Warsaw ghetto to the Treblinka death camp. This time, they wanted to be ready. The ZOB divided the ghetto into three sections, and Zuckerman was placed in charge of the Jewish fighters in the Többens-Schultz area.

On January 18, 1943, the Germans began rounding up Jews for deportation. Anielewicz, along with a few members of his unit, were among the first Jews taken. As they marched toward the collection point near the railway station, Anielewicz gave a sign and they threw their grenades, causing the crowd to scatter. Chaos ensued and the ghetto inhabitants fled for cover. Soon, the Germans began going door-to-door in small groups, attempting to round up more Jews. When they came to the home where Zuckerman was hiding, the Germans were shot and their guns confiscated. All over the ghetto, the Germans met resistance for the first time. They were surprised to find that the Jewish people had weapons. In another confrontation, Zuckerman hid on the roof of another building and when the Germans arrived, his unit attacked and took the German weapons. After about four days, the Germans retreated.

At this point, the armed underground began preparing for the next roundup. They knew the Germans would come back. They built bunkers inside the ghetto and worked to acquire more weapons. The Polish resistance group known as the Home Army sent about 50 pistols, several grenades, and some explosives to be smuggled into the ghetto. The ZOB also continued to purchase weapons by traveling undercover into the Aryan side of the city. The ZOB also acquired a recipe for Molotov cocktails. Zuckerman had the risky task of sneaking into the Aryan side and acquiring more weapons through contacts with the Home Army and the People's Army, a Communist-led guerrilla force. Zuckerman worked under the pseudonym "Antek."

Survived Warsaw Ghetto Uprising

Zuckerman was outside the ghetto walls when the final, fatal Warsaw Ghetto Uprising began on April 19, 1943. On this day, a large column of German soldiers marched through the ghetto. The ZOB was ready, with resistance fighters stationed in the windows of the upper stories along the street. They threw grenades, forcing a German retreat. The Germans came back with weapons drawn, creeping along the walls, but were easily picked off by ZOB snipers. The ZOB even managed to destroy some German tanks with Molotov cocktails.

The Germans had superior weapons and outnumbered the Jews, yet the fighting continued for weeks. Stuck on the outside, Zuckerman was unable to get any weapons inside to help his comrades. He did, however, manage to arrange for some of the last surviving ZOB fighters to be evacuated from the ghetto via the Warsaw sewer system. One of the survivors who made it out was Zivia Lubetkin, whom he later married. The uprising ended after the Germans set fire to the ghetto, forcing the Jewish fighters and imprisoned citizens to flee their bunkers. Many committed suicide rather than be taken by the Germans.

After the ghetto was destroyed, Zuckerman remained in Warsaw to aid Jewish survivors. He later fought in the Warsaw Uprising of 1944, leading a unit of Jewish fighters who joined the Home Army to liberate Warsaw from German occupation. After the war, Zuckerman helped organize an underground system for transporting illegal Jewish refugees into Palestine.

In 1947, Zuckerman and his wife immigrated to Palestine (to an area that later became part of Israel) and joined other Zionists and survivors in founding the Ghetto Fighters' Kibbutz. He also helped found a Ghetto Fighters' museum and spent the remainder of his life helping run a documentation center to collect stories and evidence on the Holocaust, the Jewish resistance movement, Nazi oppression, and the Warsaw Ghetto Uprising. Zuckerman died on June 17, 1981.

Books

Zuckerman, Yitzhak (translated and edited by Barbara Harshav), *A Surplus of Memory: Chronicle of the Warsaw Ghetto Uprising,* University of California Press, 1993.

Periodicals

Jerusalem Post, January 17, 2013.

New Republic, May 3, 1993.

New York Times, June 20, 1981; April 19, 2013. □

HOW TO USE THE *SUPPLEMENT* INDEX

The *Encyclopedia of World Biography Supplement (EWB)* Index is designed to serve several purposes. First, it is a cumulative listing of biographies included in the entire second edition of *EWB* and its supplements (volumes 1-34). Second, it locates information on specific topics mentioned in volume 35 of the encyclopedia—persons, places, events, organizations, institutions, ideas, titles of works, inventions, as well as artistic schools, styles, and movements. Third, it classifies the subjects of *Supplement* articles according to shared characteristics. Vocational categories are the most numerous—for example, artists, authors, military leaders, philosophers, scientists, statesmen. Other groupings bring together disparate people who share a common characteristic.

The structure of the *Supplement* Index is quite simple. The biographical entries are cumulative and often provide enough information to meet immediate reference needs. Thus, people mentioned in the *Supplement* Index are identified and their life dates, when known, are given. Because this is an index to a *biographical* encyclopedia, every reference includes the *name* of the article to which the reader is directed as well as the volume and page numbers. Below are a few points that will make the *Supplement* Index easy to use.

Typography. All main entries are set in boldface type. Entries that are also the titles of articles in *EWB* are set entirely in capitals; other main entries are set in initial capitals and lowercase letters. Where a main entry is followed by a great many references, these are organized by subentries in alphabetical sequence. In certain cases—for example, the names of countries for which there are many references—a special class of subentries, set in small capitals and preceded by boldface dots, is used to mark significant divisions.

Alphabetization. The Index is alphabetized word by word. For example, all entries beginning with *New* as a separate word (*New Jersey, New York*) come before

Newark. Commas in inverted entries are treated as full stops (*Berlin; Berlin, Congress of; Berlin, University of; Berlin Academy of Sciences*). Other commas are ignored in filing. When words are identical, persons come first and subsequent entries are alphabetized by their parenthetical qualifiers (such as *book, city, painting*).

Titled persons may be alphabetized by family name or by title. The more familiar form is used—for example, *Disraeli, Benjamin* rather than *Beaconsfield, Earl of.* Cross-references are provided from alternative forms and spellings of names. Identical names of the same nationality are filed chronologically.

Titles of books, plays, poems, paintings, and other works of art beginning with an article are filed on the following word *(Bard, The)*. Titles beginning with a preposition are filed on the preposition *(In Autumn)*. In subentries, however, prepositions are ignored; thus *influenced by* would precede the subentry *in* literature.

Literary characters are filed on the last name. Acronyms, such as UNESCO, are treated as single words. Abbreviations, such as *Mr., Mrs.,* and *St.,* are alphabetized as though they were spelled out.

Occupational categories are alphabetical by national qualifier. Thus, *Authors, Scottish* comes before *Authors, Spanish,* and the reader interested in Spanish poets will find the subentry *poets* under *Authors, Spanish.*

Cross-references. The term *see* is used in references throughout the *Supplement* Index. The *see* references appear both as main entries and as subentries. They most often direct the reader from an alternative name spelling or form to the main entry listing.

This introduction to the *Supplement* Index is necessarily brief. The reader will soon find, however, that the *Supplement* Index provides ready reference to both highly specific subjects and broad areas of information contained in volume 35 and a cumulative listing of those included in the entire set.

385

INDEX

A

"A"
see Arnold, Matthew

"A.B."
see Pinto, Isaac

AALTO, HUGO ALVAR HENRIK (1898-1976), Finnish architect, designer, and town planner **1** 1-2

AARON, HENRY LOUIS (Hank; born 1934), American baseball player **1** 2-3

ABACHA, SANI (1943-1998), Nigerian military leader **35** 1-3
Kabbah, Ahmad Tejan **35** 210-212

ABAKANOWICZ, MAGDALENA (Marta Abakanowicz-Kosmowski; born 1930), Polish sculptor **25** 1-3

Abarbanel
see Abravanel

ABBA ARIKA (c. 175-c. 247), Babylonian rabbi **1** 3-4

ABBAS I (1571-1629), Safavid shah of Persia 1588-1629 **1** 4-6

ABBAS, FERHAT (1899-1985), Algerian statesman **1** 6-7

ABBAS, MAHMOUD (Abu Masen; born 1935), Palestinian statesman **27** 1-3

Abbas the Great
see Abbas I

Abbasids (Islamic dynasty; ruled 750-1258)
caliphs
Abu al-Abbas As-Saffah **35** 4-6

Abbé Sieyès
see Sieyès, Comte Emmanuel Joseph

ABBEY, EDWARD (Edward Paul Abbey; 1927-1989), American author and environmental activist **27** 3-5

ABBOTT, BERENICE (1898-1991), American artist and photographer **1** 7-9

Abbott, Bud
see Abbott and Costello

ABBOTT, DIANE JULIE (born 1953), British politician and journalist **26** 1-3

ABBOTT, EDITH (1876-1957), American social reformer, educator, and author **26** 3-5

ABBOTT, GRACE (1878-1939), American social worker and agency administrator **1** 9-10

ABBOTT, LYMAN (1835-1922), American Congregationalist clergyman, author, and editor **1** 10-11

ABBOTT AND COSTELLO (Bud Abbott; 1895-1974, and Lou Costello; 1908-1959), American comedic acting team **32** 1-4

ABBOUD, EL FERIK IBRAHIM (1900-1983), Sudanese general, prime minister, 1958-1964 **1** 11-12

ABD AL-MALIK (646-705), Umayyad caliph 685-705 **1** 12-13

ABD AL-MUMIN (c. 1094-1163), Almohad caliph 1133-1163 **1** 13

ABD AL-RAHMAN I (731-788), Umayyad emir in Spain 756-788 **1** 13-14

ABD AL-RAHMAN III (891-961), Umayyad caliph of Spain **1** 14

Abd al-Rahman ibn Khaldun
see Ibn Khaldun, Abd al-Rahman ibn Muhammad

ABD AL-WAHHAB, MUHAMMAD IBN (Muhammad Ibn Abd al-Wahab; 1702-1703-1791-1792), Saudi religious leader **27** 5-7

ABD EL-KADIR (1807-1883), Algerian political and religious leader **1** 15

ABD EL-KRIM EL-KHATABI, MOHAMED BEN (c. 1882-1963), Moroccan Berber leader **1** 15-16

Abdallah ben Yassin
see Abdullah ibn Yasin

ABDELLAH, FAYE GLENN (born 1919), American nurse **24** 1-3

Abdu-l-Malik
see Abd al-Malik

ABDUH IBN HASAN KHAYR ALLAH, MUHAMMAD (1849-1905), Egyptian nationalist and theologian **1** 16-17

ABDUL-BAHA (Abbas Effendi; 1844-1921), Persian leader of the Baha'i Muslim sect **22** 3-5

ABDUL-HAMID II (1842-1918), Ottoman sultan 1876-1909 **1** 17-18

ABDUL RAHMAN, TUNKU (1903-1990), prime minister of Malaysia **18** 340-341

Abdul the Damned
see Abdul-Hamid II

ABDULLAH II (Abdullah bin al Hussein II; born 1962), king of Jordan **22** 5-7

ABDULLAH, MOHAMMAD (Lion of Kashmir; 1905-1982), Indian political leader who worked for an independent Kashmir **22** 7-9

'ABDULLAH AL-SALIM AL-SABAH, SHAYKH (1895-1965), Amir of Kuwait (1950-1965) **1** 18-19

ABDULLAH IBN HUSEIN (1882-1951), king of Jordan 1949-1951, of Transjordan 1946-49 **1** 19-20

ABDULLAH IBN YASIN (died 1059), North African founder of the Almoravid movement **1** 20

ABE, KOBO (born Kimifusa Abe; also transliterated as Abe Kobo; 1924-1993), Japanese writer, theater director, photographer **1** 20-22

ABE, SHINZO (born 1954), Japanese prime minister **28** 1-3

ABEL, FREDERICK (1827-1902), English chemist **35** 3-4

387

ALBERTUS MAGNUS, ST. (c. 1193-1280), German philosopher and theologian **1** 115-116

ALBRIGHT, MADELEINE KORBEL (born 1937), United States secretary of state **1** 116-118

ALBRIGHT, TENLEY EMMA (born 1935), American figure skater **23** 3-6

ALBRIGHT, WILLIAM (1891-1971), American archaeologist **21** 1-3

ALBUQUERQUE, AFONSO DE (c. 1460-1515), Portuguese viceroy to India **1** 118-119

Alcántara, Pedro de
see Pedro II

ALCIBIADES (c. 450-404 BCE), Athenian general and politician **1** 119-120

ALCORN, JAMES LUSK (1816-1894), American lawyer and politician **1** 120-121

ALCOTT, AMOS BRONSON (1799-1888), American educator **1** 121

ALCOTT, LOUISA MAY (1832-1888), American author and reformer **1** 122

ALCUIN OF YORK (c. 730-804), English educator, statesman, and liturgist **1** 122-123

ALDINGTON, RICHARD (1892-1962), English poet and novelist **35** 18-19

ALDRICH, NELSON WILMARTH (1841-1915), American statesman and financier **1** 123-124

Aldrin, Buzz
see Aldrin, Edwin Eugene, Jr.

ALDRIN, EDWIN EUGENE, JR. (Buzz Aldrin; born 1930), American astronaut **18** 15-17

ALDUS MANUTIUS (Teobaldo Manuzio; c. 1450-1515), Italian scholar and printer **21** 3-5

ALEICHEM, SHOLOM (Sholom Rabinowitz; 1859-1916), writer of literature relating to Russian Jews **1** 124-125

ALEIJADINHO, O (Antônio Francisco Lisbôa; 1738-1814), Brazilian architect and sculptor **1** 125-126

ALEMÁN, MATEO (1547-c. 1615), Spanish novelist **1** 126

ALEMÁN VALDÉS, MIGUEL (1902-1983), Mexican statesman, president 1946-1952 **1** 126-127

ALEMBERT, JEAN LE ROND D' (1717-1783), French mathematician and physicist **1** 127-128

ALESSANDRI PALMA, ARTURO (1868-1950), Chilean statesman,

president 1920-1925 and 1932-1938 **1** 128-129

ALESSANDRI RODRIGUEZ, JORGE (1896-1986), Chilean statesman, president 1958-1964 **1** 129-130

ALEXANDER I (1777-1825), czar of Russia 1801-1825 **1** 130-132

Alexander I, king of Yugoslavia
see Alexander of Yugoslavia

ALEXANDER II (1818-1881), czar of Russia 1855-1881 **1** 132-133

ALEXANDER III (Orlando Bandinelli; c. 1100-1181), Italian pope 1159-1181 **24** 12-14

ALEXANDER III (1845-1894), emperor of Russia 1881-1894 **1** 133-134

Alexander III, king of Macedon
see Alexander the Great

ALEXANDER VI (Rodrigo Borgia; 1431-1503), pope 1492-1503 **1** 134-135

ALEXANDER VII (Fabio Chigi; 1599-1667), Roman Catholic pope **25** 12-13

ALEXANDER, FRANZ (1891-1964), Hungarian-American psychoanalyst **35** 19-21

ALEXANDER, JANE (nee Jane Quigley; born 1939), American actress **26** 9-12

ALEXANDER, SADIE TANNER MOSSELL (1898-1989), African American lawyer **25** 13-15

ALEXANDER, SAMUEL (1859-1938), British philosopher **1** 141

Alexander Karageorgevich (1888-1934)
see Alexander of Yugoslavia

Alexander Nevsky
see Nevsky, Alexander

ALEXANDER OF TUNIS, 1ST EARL (Harold Rupert Leofric George Alexander; 1891-1969), British field marshal **1** 135-136

ALEXANDER OF YUGOSLAVIA (1888-1934), king of the Serbs, Croats, and Slovenes 1921-1929 and of Yugoslavia, 1929-1934 **1** 136-137

ALEXANDER THE GREAT (356-323 BCE), king of Macedon **1** 137-141

Alexeyev, Constantin Sergeyevich
see Stanislavsky, Constantin

ALEXIE, SHERMAN (born 1966), Native American writer, poet, and translator **1** 141-142

ALEXIS MIKHAILOVICH ROMANOV (1629-1676), czar of Russia 1645-1676 **1** 142-143

ALEXIUS I (c. 1048-1118), Byzantine emperor 1081-1118 **1** 143-144

ALFARO, JOSÉ ELOY (1842-1912), Ecuadorian revolutionary, president 1895-1901 and 1906-1911 **1** 144-145

ALFIERI, CONTE VITTORIA (1749-1803), Italian playwright **1** 145-146

ALFONSÍN, RAÚL RICARDO (1927-2009), politician and president of Argentina (1983-1989) **1** 146-148

ALFONSO I (Henriques; c. 1109-1185), king of Portugal 1139-1185 **1** 148

Alfonso I, king of Castile
see Alfonso VI, king of León

ALFONSO III (1210-1279), king of Portugal 1248-1279 **1** 148-149

ALFONSO VI (1040-1109), king of León, 1065-1109, and of Castile, 1072-1109 **1** 149

ALFONSO X (1221-1284), king of Castile and León 1252-1284 **1** 150-151

ALFONSO XIII (1886-1941), king of Spain 1886-1931 **1** 151

Alfonso the Wise
see Alfonso X, king of Castile and León

ALFRED (849-899), Anglo-Saxon king of Wessex 871-899 **1** 151-153

Alfred the Great
see Alfred, king of Wessex

Algazel
see Ghazali, Abu Hamid Muhammad al-

ALGER, HORATIO (1832-1899), American author **1** 153-154

Algeria, Democratic and Popular Republic of (nation, North Africa)
elections
Boudiaf, Mohammed **35** 79-81
French in
Bidault, Georges **35** 66-69
revolt and independence
Boudiaf, Mohammed **35** 79-81

ALGREN, NELSON (Abraham; 1909-1981), American author **1** 154-155

Alhazen
see Hassan ibn al-Haytham

ALI (c. 600-661), fourth caliph of the Islamic Empire **1** 155-156
Abu al-Abbas As-Saffah **35** 4-6

ALI, AHMED (1908-1998), Pakistani scholar, poet, author, and diplomat **22** 16-18

Ali, Haidar
see Haidar Ali

ALI, MUHAMMAD (Cassius Clay; born 1942), American boxer **1** 156-158

ALI, MUSTAFA (1541-1600), Turkish historian and politician **31** 1-2

ALI, SUNNI (died 1492), king of Gao, founder of the Songhay empire **1** 158-159

Ali Ber
see Ali, Sunni

Ali Shah (died 1885)
see Aga Khan II

Ali the Great
see Ali, Sunni

ALIA, RAMIZ (1925-2011), president of Albania (1985-1991) **1** 159

Alien (film)
Giger, H.R. **35** 166-168

ALINSKY, SAUL DAVID (1909-1972), U.S. organizer of neighborhood citizen reform groups **1** 161-162

All Russian Extraordinary Commission
see Cheka (secret police, Russia)

ALLAL AL-FASSI, MOHAMED (1910-1974), Moroccan nationalist leader **1** 162

ALLAN, HUGH (1810-1882), Canadian financier **35** 22-24

ALLAWI, IYAD (born 1945), Iraqi prime minister **25** 15-17

Allegri, Antonio
see Correggio

ALLEN, ELSIE (Elsie Comanche Allen; 1899-1990), Native American weaver and educator **27** 10-11

ALLEN, ETHAN (1738-1789), American Revolutionary War soldier **1** 163-164

ALLEN, FLORENCE ELLINWOOD (1884-1966), American lawyer, judge, and women's rights activist **1** 164-165

ALLEN, GRACIE (1906-1964), American actress and comedian **22** 18-20

ALLEN, MEL (1913-1996), American broadcaster **32** 10-12

ALLEN, PAUL (Paul Gardner Allen; born 1953), American entrepreneur and philanthropist **25** 17-19

ALLEN, PAULA GUNN (1939-2008), Native American writer, poet, literary critic; women's rights, environmental, and antiwar activist **1** 165-167

ALLEN, RICHARD (1760-1831), African American bishop **1** 168

ALLEN, SARAH (Sarah Bass Allen; 1764-1849), African American missionary **27** 12-13

ALLEN, STEVE (1921-2000), American comedian, author, and composer **22** 20-22

ALLEN, WOODY (born Allen Stewart Konigsberg; b. 1935), American actor, director, filmmaker, author, comedian **1** 169-171

ALLENBY, EDMUND HENRY HYNMAN (1861-1936), English field marshal **1** 171-172

ALLENDE, ISABEL (born 1942), Chilean novelist, journalist, dramatist **1** 172-174

ALLENDE GOSSENS, SALVADOR (1908-1973), socialist president of Chile (1970-1973) **1** 174-176

ALLEY, ALPHONSE (1930-1987), Dahomean statesman **35** 24-25

Alleyne, Ellen
see Rossetti, Christina Georgina

ALLSTON, WASHINGTON (1779-1843), American painter **1** 176-177

ALMAGRO, DIEGO DE (c. 1474-1538), Spanish conquistador and explorer **1** 177-178

ALMENDROS, NÉSTOR (Nestor Almendrod Cuyas; 1930-1992), Hispanic American cinematographer **27** 13-15

ALMODOVAR, PEDRO (Calmodovar, Caballero, Pedro; born 1949), Spanish film director and screenwriter **23** 6-9

Alompra
see Alaungpaya

Alonso (Araucanian chief)
see Lautaro

ALONSO, ALICIA (Alicia Ernestina de la Caridad dei Cobre Martinez Hoya; born 1921), Cuban ballerina **24** 14-17

ALP ARSLAN (1026/32-1072), Seljuk sultan of Persia and Iraq **1** 178-179

Alpetragius
see Bitruji, Nur al-Din Abu Ishaq al-

ALPHONSA OF THE IMMACULATE CONCEPTION, ST. (1910-1946), Indian nun and Roman Catholic saint **30** 1-3

Alphonse the Wise
see Alfonso X, king of Castile

ALTAMIRA Y CREVEA, RAFAEL (1866-1951), Spanish critic, historian, and jurist **1** 179

ALTDORFER, ALBRECHT (c. 1480-1538), German painter, printmaker, and architect **1** 179-180

ALTERMAN, NATAN (1910-1970), Israeli poet and journalist **24** 17-18

ALTGELD, JOHN PETER (1847-1902), American jurist and politician **1** 180-182

ALTHUSSER, LOUIS (1918-1990), French Communist philosopher **1** 182-183

ALTIZER, THOMAS J. J. (born 1927), American theologian **1** 183-184

ALTMAN, ROBERT (1925-2006), American filmmaker **20** 12-14

ALTMAN, SIDNEY (born 1939), Canadian American molecular biologist **23** 9-11

ALUPI, CALIN (Calinic Alupi; 1906-1988), Romanian artist **24** 18-19

Alva, Duke of
see Alba, Duke of

ALVARADO, LINDA (Linda Martinez; born 1951), American businesswoman **25** 21-23

Alvarez, Jorge Guillén y
see Guillén y Alvarez, Jorge

ÁLVAREZ, JUAN (1780-1867), Mexican soldier and statesman, president 1855 **1** 184-185

ALVAREZ, JULIA (born 1950), Hispanic American novelist, poet **1** 185-187

ÁLVAREZ, LILÍ (1905-1998), Spanish athlete **35** 25-27

ALVAREZ, LUIS W. (1911-1988), American physicist **1** 187-189

ÁLVAREZ BRAVO, MANUEL (1902-2002), Mexican photographer **31** 2-6

ALVARIÑO, ANGELES (Angeles Alvariño Leira; 1916-2005), Spanish American marine scientist **27** 15-17

AMADO, JORGE (1912-2001), Brazilian novelist **1** 189-190

AMBADY, NALINI (1959-2013), Indian-born social psychologist **35** 27-29

AMBEDKAR, BHIMRAO RAMJI (1891-1956), Indian social reformer and politician **1** 190-191

AMBLER, ERIC (1909-1998), English novelist **1** 191-192

Ambrogini, Angelo
see Poliziano, Angelo

AMBROSE, ST. (339-397), Italian bishop **1** 192-193

AMBROSE, STEPHEN E. (1936-2002), American historian **32** 12-14

AMENEMHET I (ruled 1991-1962 BCE), pharaoh of Egypt **1** 193-194

AMENHOTEP III (ruled 1417-1379 BCE), pharaoh of Egypt **1** 194-195

Amenhotep IV
see Ikhnaton

Amenophis IV
see Ikhnaton

American Academy of Psychoanalysis
Alexander, Franz **35** 19-21

AMERICAN HORSE (aka Iron Shield; c. 1840-1876), Sioux leader **1** 195-198

American literature
poetry
Estep, Maggie **35** 149-151

American Michelangelo
see Rimmer, William

American music
20th century
jazz and blues
Conover, Willis **35** 108-110
popular and show music
Sager, Carole Bayer **35** 321-323
punk
Ramone, Joey **35** 304-305

American Psychoanalytic Association
(established 1911)
Alexander, Franz **35** 19-21

American Rembrandt
see Johnson, Jonathan Eastman

American Woodsman
see Audubon, John James

AMES, ADELBERT (1835-1933), American
politician **1** 198

AMES, EZRA (1768-1836), American
painter **29** 1-3

AMES, FISHER (1758-1808), American
statesman **1** 199-200

AMHERST, JEFFERY (1717-1797), English
general and statesman **1** 200-201

AMICHAI, YEHUDA (Yehuda Pfeuffer;
Yehudah Amichai; 1924-2000),
German-Israeli poet **24** 19-21

AMIET, CUNO (1868-1961), Swiss
Postimpressionist painter **1** 201-202

AMIN DADA, IDI (c. 1926-2003),
president of Uganda (1971-1979) **1**
202-204

AMINA OF ZARIA (Amina Sarauniya
Zazzau; c. 1533-c. 1610), Nigerian
monarch and warrior **21** 5-7

AMIS, KINGSLEY (Kingsley William Amis;
1922-1995), English author **28** 5-8

Amitabha Buddha
see Buddha (play)

AMMA (Amritanandamayi, Mata;
Ammachi; Sudhamani; born 1953),
Indian spiritual leader **28** 8-10

AMMANATI, BARTOLOMEO (1511-1592),
Italian sculptor and architect **30** 3-5
Battiferri, Laura **35** 32-34

AMONTONS, GUILLAUME (1663-1705),
French physicist **29** 3-5

AMORSOLO, FERNANDO (1892-1972),
Philippine painter **1** 204

AMORY, CLEVELAND (1917-1998),
American author and animal rights
activist **26** 14-16

AMOS (flourished 8th century BCE),
Biblical prophet **1** 205

AMPÈRE, ANDRÉ MARIE (1775-1836),
French physicist **1** 205-206

AMPÈRE, JEAN-JACQUES (1800-1864),
French essayist **29** 5-7

AMUNDSEN, ROALD (1872-1928),
Norwegian explorer **1** 206-207

AN LU-SHAN (703-757), Chinese rebel
leader **1** 239-240

ANACLETUS II (c. 1090-1138), antipope
1130-1138 **29** 7-9

ANACREON (c. 570-c. 490 BCE), Greek
lyric poet **29** 9-11

ANAN BEN DAVID (flourished 8th
century), Jewish Karaite leader in
Babylonia **1** 207-208

ANAND, DEV (1923-2011), Indian actor
33 5-7

ANANDA MAHIDOL (1925-1946), king of
Thailand 1935-1946 **31** 7

Anarchism (political philosophy)
theorists
Berkman, Alexander **35** 57-59

Anatomy (science)
lymphatic
Rudbeck, Olof **35** 318-320

ANAXAGORAS (c. 500-c. 428 BCE), Greek
philosopher **1** 208-209

ANAXIMANDER (c. 610-c. 546 BCE),
Greek philosopher and astronomer **1**
209-210

ANAXIMENES (flourished 546 BCE), Greek
philosopher **1** 210

ANAYA, RUDOLFO ALFONSO (born
1937), Chicano American author **27**
17-19

ANCHIETA, JOSÉ DE (1534-1597),
Portuguese Jesuit missionary **1** 210-211

ANDERSEN, DOROTHY (1901-1963),
American physician and pathologist **1**
212

ANDERSEN, HANS CHRISTIAN (1805-
1875), Danish author **1** 212-214

ANDERSON, CARL DAVID (1905-1991),
American physicist **1** 214-215

ANDERSON, HERBERT L. (1914-1988),
American physicist **31** 7-8

ANDERSON, IVIE MARIE (Ivy Marie
Anderson; 1905-1949), African-American
singer **28** 10-12

ANDERSON, JUDITH (1898-1992),
American stage and film actress **1**
215-216

ANDERSON, JUNE (born 1953), American
opera singer **1** 216-218

ANDERSON, MARIAN (1902-1993),
African American singer **1** 218-219

ANDERSON, MAXWELL (1888-1959),
American playwright **1** 219-220

ANDERSON, REGINA M. (1901-1993),
Librarian and playwright **30** 5-7

ANDERSON, SHERWOOD (1876-1941),
American writer **1** 220-221

ANDERSON, SPARKY (1934-2010),
American baseball manager **33** 7-9

ANDO, TADAO (born 1941), Japanese
architect **18** 17-19

**ANDRADA E SILVA, JOSÉ BONIFÁCIO
DE** (1763-1838), Brazilian-born
statesman and scientist **1** 221-222

Andrade, Mário de, (1893-1945),
Brazilian poet, novelist, musicologist, art
historian and critic, and photographer
Guarnieri, Camargo **35** 175-176

ANDRÁSSY, COUNT JULIUS (1823-1890),
Hungarian statesman, prime minister
1867-1871 **1** 222-223

Andrea da Pontedera
see Andrea Pisano

ANDREA DEL CASTAGNO (1421-1457),
Italian painter **1** 223-224

ANDREA DEL SARTO (1486-1530), Italian
painter **1** 224-225

ANDREA PISANO (c. 1290-1348), Italian
sculptor and architect **1** 225-226

ANDREAS-SALOMÉ, LOU (Louise Salomé;
1861-1937), Russian-born German
author and feminist **28** 12-14

ANDRÉE, SALOMON AUGUST (1854-
1897), Swedish engineer and Arctic
balloonist **1** 226

ANDREESSEN, MARC (born 1972),
American computer programmer who
developed Netscape Navigator **19** 3-5

Andreino
see Andrea del Sarto

ANDREOTTI, GIULIO (1919-2013), leader
of Italy's Christian Democratic party **1**
226-228

ANDRETTI, MARIO (born 1940), Italian/
American race car driver **1** 228-230

ANDREW, JOHN ALBION (1818-1867),
American politician **1** 230-231

ANDREWS, BENNY (1930-2006), African
American artists **25** 23-25

ANDREWS, CHARLES MCLEAN (1863-
1943), American historian **1** 231

ANDREWS, FANNIE FERN PHILLIPS
(1867-1950), American educator,
reformer, pacifist **1** 231-232

ANDREWS, JULIE (Julie Edwards; born
1935), British singer, actress, and author
25 25-28

ANDREWS, ROY CHAPMAN (1884-1960),
American naturalist and explorer **33** 9-11

ANDREYEV, LEONID NIKOLAYEVICH (1871-1919), Russian author **29** 11-13

ANDRIĆ, IVO (1892-1975), Yugoslav author **24** 21-24

ANDRONIKOS II PALAIOLOGOS (1260-1332), Byzantine emperor **30** 7-9

ANDROPOV, IURY VLADIMIROVICH (1914-1984), head of the Soviet secret police and ruler of the Soviet Union (1982-1984) **1** 233-234

ANDROS, SIR EDMUND (1637-1714), English colonial governor in America **1** 234-235

ANDRUS, ETHEL (1884-1976), American educator and founder of the American Association of Retired Persons **19** 5-7

Angel of the Crimea
see Nightingale, Florence

Angelico, Fra
see Fra Angelico

ANGELL, JAMES ROWLAND (1869-1949), psychologist and leader in higher education **1** 236-237

Angelo de Cosimo
see Bronzino

ANGELOU, MAYA (Marguerite Johnson; born 1928), American author, poet, playwright, stage and screen performer, and director **1** 238-239

Angleton, James Jesus, (1917-1987), American intelligence agent
Golitsyn, Anatoliy **35** 170-172

Anglican King's College
see Toronto, University of (Canada)

Anglo-Saxons (British Saxons)
see England–5th century-1066 (Anglo-Saxon)

ANGUIANO, RAUL (1915-2006), Mexican artist **34** 9-11
Guerrero Galván, Jesús **35** 176-178

ANGUISSOLA, SOFONISBA (Sofonisba Anguisciola; c. 1535-1625), Italian artist **22** 22-24

Anheuser-Busch
Caray, Harry **35** 96-99

ANIELEWICZ, MORDECHAI (c. 1919-1943), Polish resistance fighter **34** 11-13
Zuckerman, Yitzhak **35** 382-384

Ankara, Battle of (1402)
Bayezid I **35** 38-40

Anna Comnena
see Comnena, Anna

ANNA IVANOVNA (1693-1740), empress of Russia 1730-1740 **1** 240-241

Annam (former kingdom; Indochina)
see Vietnam (state, Indochina)

ANNAN, KOFI (born 1938), Ghanaian secretary-general of the United Nations **18** 19-21

Annapolis Royal (Nova Scotia)
Broussard, Joseph **35** 91-93

ANNE (1665-1714), queen of England 1702-1714 and of Great Britain 1707-1714 **1** 241-242

ANNE OF BRITTANY (1477-1514), queen of France 1491-1498 and 1499-1514 **29** 13-15

ANNE OF CLEVES (1515-1557), German princess and fourth wife of Henry VIII **27** 19-21

ANNENBERG, WALTER HUBERT (1908-2002), American publisher and philanthropist **26** 16-18

ANNING, MARY (1799-1847), British fossil collector **20** 14-16

Annunzio, Gabriele d'
see D'Annunzio, Gabriel

ANOKYE, OKOMFO (Kwame Frimpon Anokye; flourished late 17th century), Ashanti priest and statesman **1** 242-243

ANOUILH, JEAN (1910-1987), French playwright **1** 243-244

ANSELM OF CANTERBURY, ST. (1033-1109), Italian archbishop and theologian **1** 244-245

ANSERMET, ERNEST (1883-1969), Swiss orchestral conductor **30** 9-11

Anson, Charles Edward
see Markham, Edwin

Anthoniszoon, Jeroen
see Bosch, Hieronymus

Anthony, Mark
see Antony, Mark

Anthony, Peter
see Shaffer, Peter Levin

ANTHONY, ST. (c. 250-356), Egyptian hermit and monastic founder **1** 246-248

ANTHONY, SUSAN BROWNELL (1820-1906), American leader of suffrage movement **1** 246-248

Anthony Abbott, St.
see Anthony, St.

Anthony of Egypt, St.
see Anthony, St.

ANTHONY OF PADUA, ST. (Fernando de Boullion; 1195-1231), Portuguese theologian and priest **21** 7-9

Anthropology (social science)
physical
Blumenbach, Johann Friedrich **35** 77-79

Anti-Semitism
Germany (19th century)
Bauer, Bruno **35** 36-38
Germany (20th century)
Stauffenberg, Claus von **35** 339-341
opponents
Stauffenberg, Claus von **35** 339-341
Russia
Beilis, Menaham Mendel **35** 47-49

ANTIGONUS I (382-301 BCE), king of Macedon 306-301 B.C. **1** 248-249

ANTIOCHUS III (241-187 BCE), king of Syria 223-187 B.C. **1** 249-250

ANTIOCHUS IV (c. 215-163 BCE), king of Syria 175-163 B.C. **1** 250

Antiochus the Great
see Antiochus III

ANTISTHENES (c. 450-360 BCE), Greek philosopher **1** 250-251

ANTONELLO DA MESSINA (c. 1430-1479), Italian painter **1** 251-252

Antoninus, Marcus Aurelius
see Caracalla

Antonio, Donato di Pascuccio d'
see Bramante, Donato

ANTONIONI, MICHELANGELO (1912-2007), Italian film director **1** 252-253

Antonius, Marcus
see Antony, Mark

ANTONY, MARK (c. 82-30 BCE), Roman politician and general **1** 253-254

Anushervan the Just
see Khosrow I

ANZA, JUAN BAUTISTA DE (1735-1788), Spanish explorer **1** 254-255

AOUN, MICHEL (born 1935), Christian Lebanese military leader and prime minister **1** 255-257

Apache Napoleon
see Cochise

APELLES (flourished after 350 BCE), Greek painter **1** 257

APESS, WILLIAM (1798-1839), Native American religious leader, author, and activist **20** 16-18

APGAR, VIRGINIA (1909-1974), American medical educator, researcher **1** 257-259

APITHY, SOUROU MIGAN (1913-1989), Dahomean political leader **1** 259-260

APOLLINAIRE, GUILLAUME (1880-1918), French lyric poet **1** 260

Apollo Theater (Harlem, New York)
Mabley, Moms **35** 252-255

APOLLODORUS (flourished c. 408 BCE), Greek painter **1** 261

APOLLONIUS OF PERGA (flourished 210 BCE), Greek mathematician **1** 261-262

Apostate, the
see Julian

Apostles
see Bible–New Testament

APPELFELD, AHARON (born 1932), Israeli who wrote about anti-Semitism and the Holocaust **1** 262-263

APPERT, NICOLAS (1749-1941), French chef and inventor of canning of foods **20** 18-19

APPIA, ADOLPHE (1862-1928), Swiss stage director **1** 263-264

APPLEBEE, CONSTANCE (1873-1981), American field hockey coach **24** 24-25

APPLEGATE, JESSE (1811-1888), American surveyor, pioneer, and rancher **1** 264-265

APPLETON, SIR EDWARD VICTOR (1892-1965), British pioneer in radio physics **1** 265-266

APPLETON, NATHAN (1779-1861), American merchant and manufacturer **1** 266-267

APULEIUS, LUCIUS (c. 124-170), Roman author, philosopher, and orator **20** 19-21

Apulia, Robert Guiscard, Count and Duke of
see Guiscard, Robert

Aquinas, St. Thomas
see Thomas Aquinas, St.

AQUINO, BENIGNO ("Nino"; 1933-1983), Filipino activist murdered upon his return from exile **1** 267-268

AQUINO, CORAZON COJOANGCO (1933-2009), first woman president of the Republic of the Philippines **1** 268-270

Arab Empire
see Islamic Empire

Arabi Pasha, (Colonel Ahmed Arabi)
see ORABI, AHMED

Arabia
see Islamic Empire; Saudi Arabia

ARAFAT, YASSER (also spelled Yasir; 1929-2004), chairman of the Palestinian Liberation Organization **1** 270-271

ARAGO, FRANÇOIS (1786-1853), French physicist **30** 11-14

ARAGON, LOUIS (1897-1982), French surrealist author **1** 271-272

ARAKCHEEV, ALEKSEI ANDREEVICH (1769-1834), Russian soldier and statesman **31** 9-10

ARAKIDA MORITAKE (1473-1549), Japanese poet **29** 287-288

ARÁMBURU, PEDRO EUGENIO (1903-1970), Argentine statesman, president 1955-1958 **30** 14-16

Arango, Doroteo
see Villa, Pancho

ARANHA, OSVALDO (1894-1960), Brazilian political leader **1** 272-273

ARATUS (271-213 BCE), Greek statesman and general **1** 273-274

ARBENZ GUZMÁN, JACOBO (1913-1971), Guatemalan statesman, president 1951-1954 **1** 274-276

ARBER, AGNES ROBERTSON (nee Agnes Robertson; 1879-1960), English botanist **28** 14-16

Arblay, Madame d'
see Burney, Frances "Fanny"

ARBUS, DIANE NEMEROV (1923-1971), American photographer **1** 276-277

ARBUTHNOT, JOHN (1667-1735), Scottish physician **31** 11-12

arcangeli non giocano a flipper, Gli (play) Rame, Franca **35** 301-304

ARCARO, EDDIE (George Edward Arcaro;1916-1997), American jockey **27** 21-23

Archaeology
see Archeology

Archeologist king
see Ashurbanipal

Archeology
United States
Squier, E.G. **35** 337-339

ARCHIMEDES (c. 287-212 BCE), Greek mathematician **1** 277-280

ARCHIPENKO, ALEXANDER (1887-1964), Russian-American sculptor and teacher **1** 280-281

Architecture
Baudot, Anatole de **35** 34-36
Bill, Max **35** 69-71

ARCINIEGAS, GERMAN (1900-1999), Colombian historian, educator, and journalist **24** 27-29

ARDEN, ELIZABETH (Florence Nightingale Graham; c. 1878-1966), American businesswoman **1** 281-282

ARDEN, JOHN (1930-2012), British playwright **33** 11-13

Ardler, Stella
see Adler, Stella

ARENDT, HANNAH (1906-1975), Jewish philosopher **1** 282-284

ARENS, MOSHE (born 1925), aeronautical engineer who became a leading Israeli statesman **1** 284-285

ARETE OF CYRENE (c. 400-c. 340 BCE), Grecian philosopher **26** 18-20

ARETINO, PIETRO (1492-1556), Italian satirist **29** 16-18

ARÉVALO, JUAN JOSÉ (1904-1951), Guatemalan statesman, president 1944-1951 **1** 285-286

ARGALL, SAMUEL (1580-1626), English mariner **29** 18-20

ARGÜELLES, JOSÉ (1933-2011), American philospher and art historian **32** 14-16

Ari Ha-qodesh
see Luria, Isaac ben Solomon

ARIAS, ARNULFO (1901-1988), thrice elected president of Panama **1** 286-287

ARIAS SANCHEZ, OSCAR (born 1941), Costa Rican politician, social activist, president, and Nobel Peace Laureate (1987) **1** 287-289

ARINZE, FRANCIS (born 1932), Nigerian Roman Catholic cardinal **26** 20-22

ARIOSTO, LUDOVICO (1474-1533), Italian poet and playwright **1** 289-290

ARISTARCHUS OF SAMOS (c. 310-230 BCE), Greek astronomer **1** 290-291

ARISTIDE, JEAN-BERTRAND (born 1953), president of Haiti (1990-1991 and 1994-1995); deposed by a military coup in 1991; restored to power in 1994 **1** 291-293

Aristio
see Unánue, José Hipólito

ARISTOPHANES (450/445-after 385 BCE), Greek playwright **1** 293-294

ARISTOTLE (384-322 BCE), Greek philosopher and scientist **1** 295-296

ARIUS (died c. 336), Libyan theologian and heresiarch **1** 297-298

ARKWRIGHT, SIR RICHARD (1732-1792), English inventor and industrialist **1** 298

ARLEDGE, ROONE (1931-2002), American television broadcaster **32** 16-18

ARLEN, HAROLD (born Hyman Arluck; 1905-1986), American jazz pianist, composer, and arranger **19** 7-9

ARLT, ROBERTO (Roberto Godofredo Christophersen Arlt; 1900-1942), Argentine author and journalist **23** 11-13

ARMANI, GIORGIO (1935-1997), Italian fashion designer **1** 299-301

Armia Krajowa (AK; Polish resistance movement)
Karski, Jan **35** 217-219

AYCKBOURN, ALAN (born 1939), British playwright **18** 23-25

AYER, ALFRED JULES (1910-1989), English philosopher **1** 391-393

AYLWIN AZÓCAR, PATRICIO (born 1918), leader of the Chilean Christian Democratic party and president of Chile **1** 393-395

AYUB KHAN, MOHAMMED (1907-1989), Pakistani statesman **1** 395-396

AZAÑA DIAZ, MANUEL (1880-1940), Spanish statesman, president 1936-1939 **1** 396-397

AZARA, FÉLIX DE (1746-1821), Spanish explorer and naturalist **1** 397-398

AZARA, JOSÉ NICOLÁS DE (c. 1731-1804), Spanish diplomat **29** 24-26

AZCONA HOYO, JOSÉ (1927-2005), president of Honduras (1986-1990) **1** 398-399

AZHARI, SAYYID ISMAIL AL- (1898-1969), Sudanese president 1965-1968 **1** 399-401

AZIKIWE, NNAMDI (1904-1996), Nigerian nationalist, president 1963-1966 **1** 401-402
    Akintola, Samuel **35** 13-16

Azorin
    see Ruíz, José Martinez

AZUELA, MARIANO (1873-1952), Mexican novelist **1** 402

B

BÂ, MARIAMA (1929-1981), Senegalese novelist **26** 25-27

BA MAW (1893-1977), Burmese statesman **1** 480-481

BAADE, WALTER (1893-1960), German astronomer **30** 24-26

BAADER AND MEINHOF (1967-1976), founders of the West German "Red Army Faction" **1** 403-404

BAAL SHEM TOV (c. 1700-c. 1760), founder of modern Hasidism **1** 404-405

BABA, MEHER (Merwan Sheriar Irani; 1894-1969), Indian mystic **24** 35-38

Babangida, Ibrahim, (born 1941), Nigerian politician
    Abacha, Sani **35** 1-3

BABAR THE CONQUEROR (aka Zahir-ud-din Muhammad Babur; 1483-1530), Mogul emperor of India 1526-1530 **1** 405-407

BABBAGE, CHARLES (1791-1871), English inventor and mathematician **1** 407-408

BABBITT, BRUCE EDWARD (born 1938), governor of Arizona (1978-1987) and United States secretary of the interior **1** 408-410

BABBITT, IRVING (1865-1933), American critic and educator **22** 36-37

BABBITT, MILTON (1916-2011), American composer **1** 410

BABCOCK, STEPHEN MOULTON (1843-1931), American agricultural chemist **1** 410-411

BABEL, ISAAC EMMANUELOVICH (1894-1941), Russian writer **1** 411-412

Baber
    see Babar the Conqueror

Babes in Arms (musical)
    Rooney, Mickey **35** 312-314

BABEUF, FRANÇOIS NOEL ("Caius Gracchus"; 1760-1797), French revolutionist and writer **1** 412

BABINGTON, ANTHONY (1561-1586), English Catholic conspirator **29** 27-29

Babrak Karmal
    see Karmal, Babrak

Babur, Zahir-ud-din Muhammed
    see Babar the Conqueror

BACA-BARRAGÁN, POLLY (born 1943), Hispanic American politician **1** 412-414

BACALL, LAUREN (1924-2014), American actress **29** 29-31

BACH, CARL PHILIPP EMANUEL (1714-1788), German composer **1** 414-415

BACH, JOHANN CHRISTIAN (1735-1782), German composer **1** 415-416

BACH, JOHANN SEBASTIAN (1685-1750), German composer and organist **1** 416-419

BACHARACH, BURT (born 1928), American composer **22** 38-39
    Sager, Carole Bayer **35** 321-323

BACHE, ALEXANDER DALLAS (1806-1867), American educator and scientist **1** 420

Baciccio
    see Gaulli, Giovanni Battista

BACKUS, ISAAC (1724-1806), American Baptist leader **1** 420-421

BACON, SIR FRANCIS (1561-1626), English philosopher, statesman, and author **1** 422-424

BACON, FRANCIS (1909-1992), English artist **1** 421-422
    Giger, H.R. **35** 166-168

BACON, NATHANIEL (1647-1676), American colonial leader **1** 424-425

BACON, PEGGY (Margaret Francis Bacon; 1895-1987), American artist and author **25** 29-31

BACON, ROGER (c. 1214-1294), English philosopher **1** 425-427

Bad Hand
    see Fitzpatrick, Thomas

BAD HEART BULL, AMOS (1869-1913), Oglala Lakota Sioux tribal historian and artist **1** 427-428

BADEN-POWELL, ROBERT (1857-1941), English military officer and founder of the Boy Scout Association **21** 16-18

BADINGS, HENK (Hendrik Herman Badings; 1907-1987), Dutch composer **23** 26-28

BADOGLIO, PIETRO (1871-1956), Italian general and statesman **1** 428-429

BAECK, LEO (1873-1956), rabbi, teacher, hero of the concentration camps, and Jewish leader **1** 429-430

BAEKELAND, LEO HENDRIK (1863-1944), American chemist **1** 430-431

BAER, GEORGE FREDERICK (1842-1914), American businessman **22** 39-41

BAER, KARL ERNST VON (1792-1876), Estonian anatomist and embryologist **1** 431-432

BAEZ, BUENAVENTURA (1812-1884), Dominican statesman, five time president **1** 432-433

BAEZ, JOAN (born 1941), American folk singer and human rights activist **1** 433-435

BAFFIN, WILLIAM (c. 1584-1622), English navigator and explorer **1** 435-436

BAGEHOT, WALTER (1826-1877), English economist **1** 436-437

BAGLEY, WILLIAM CHANDLER (1874-1946), educator and theorist of educational "essentialism" **1** 437-438

BAHÁ'U'LLÁH (Husayn-'Ali', Bahá'u'lláh Mírzá; 1817-1982), Iranian religious leader **28** 21-23

BAHR, EGON (born 1922), West German politician **1** 438-440

Baie des Anges, La (film)
    Demy, Jacques **35** 125-127

BAIKIE, WILLIAM BALFOUR (1825-1864), Scottish explorer and scientist **1** 440

BAILEY, F. LEE (born 1933), American defense attorney and author **1** 441-443

BAILEY, FLORENCE MERRIAM (1863-1948), American ornithologist and author **1** 443-444

BAILEY, GAMALIEL (1807-1859), American editor and politician **1** 444-445

BAILEY, JAMES A. (1847-1906), American circus owner **30** 26-28

BANDARANAIKE, SIRIMAVO RATWATTE DIAS (1916-2000), first woman prime minister in the world as head of the Sri Lankan Freedom party government (1960-1965, 1970-1976) **1** 486-488

Bandera de Provincias (Mexican artists group)
Guerrero Galván, Jesús **35** 176-178

Bandinelli, Orlando
see Alexander III, pope

BANERJEE, SURENDRANATH (1848-1925), Indian nationalist **1** 488

BANGS, LESTER (1948-1982), American journalist **32** 32-34

Bank of Montreal
Allan, Hugh **35** 22-24

BANKS, DENNIS J. (born 1932), Native American leader, teacher, activist, and author **1** 488-489

BANKS, SIR JOSEPH (1743-1820), English naturalist **1** 489-490

BANNEKER, BENJAMIN (1731-1806), African American mathematician **1** 490-491

BANNISTER, EDWARD MITCHELL (1828-1901), African American landscape painter **1** 491-493

BANNISTER, ROGER (born 1929), English runner **21** 18-20

BANTING, FREDERICK GRANT (1891-1941), Canadian physiolgist **1** 493-494

BAÑUELOS, ROMANA ACOSTA (born 1925), Mexican businesswoman and American government official **24** 40-42

BANZER SUÁREZ, HUGO (1926-2002), Bolivian president (1971-1979) **1** 494-496

BAO DAI (1913-1997), emperor of Vietnam 1932-1945 and 1949-1955 **1** 496-497

Baptists (religious denomination)
missions
Moon, Charlotte **35** 275-277

BAR KOCHBA, SIMEON (died 135), Jewish commander of revolt against Romans **2** 5

BARAGA, FREDERIC (Irenej Frederic Baraga; 1797-1868), Austrian missionary and linguist **27** 33-35

BARAK, EHUD (born 1942), Israeli prime minister **1** 497-498

BARAKA, IMAMU AMIRI (Everett LeRoi Jones; born 1934), African American poet and playwright **1** 498-499

Barakzai dynasty (Afghanistan)
Khan, Dost Mohammad **35** 219-221

BARANOV, ALEKSANDR ANDREIEVICH (1747-1819), Russian explorer **1** 499-500

BARBARA, AGATHA (1923-2002), Maltese politician **27** 36-38

BARBARO, FRANCESCO (1390-1454), Italian diplomat and author **31** 18-19

Barbarossa, Frederick
see Frederick I, (1657-1713)

BARBAULD, ANNA (MRS.) (nee Anna Laetitia Aiken; 1743-1825), British author **27** 38-40

BARBEAU, MARIUS (1883-1969), Canadian ethnographer, anthropologist, and author **24** 42-44

BARBER, RED (Walter Lanier Barber; 1908-1992), American broadcaster **31** 20-21

BARBER, SAMUEL (1910-1981), American composer **1** 500-501

Barbera, Joseph
see Hanna and Barbera

Barberini, Maffeo
see Urban VIII

BARBIE, KLAUS (Klaus Altmann; 1913-1991), Nazi leader in Vichy France **1** 501-503

Barbieri, Giovanni Francesco
see Guercino

BARBIROLLI, JOHN (Giovanni Battista Barbirolli; 1899-1970), British conductor **24** 44-46

Barbo, Pietro
see Paul II, pope

BARBONCITO (1820-1871), Native American leader of the Navajos **20** 25-27

BARBOSA, RUY (1849-1923), Brazilian journalist and politician **1** 503-504

BARCLAY, EDWIN (1882-1955), Liberian statesman, twice president **29** 44-45

BARCLAY, MCCLELLAND (1891-1943), American artist **33** 17-19

BARDEEN, JOHN (1908-1991), American Nobel physicist **2** 1-3

Bardi, Donato di Niccolò
see Donatello

BARENBOIM, DANIEL (born 1942), Israeli pianist and conductor **2** 3-4

BARENTS, WILLEM (died 1597), Dutch navigator and explorer **2** 4-5

Baring, Evelyn
see Cromer, 1st Earl of

BARING, FRANCIS (1740-1810), English banker **21** 20-22

BARKLA, CHARLES GLOVER (1877-1944), English physicist **29** 46-48

BARLACH, ERNST (1870-1938), German sculptor **2** 5-6

BARLOW, JOEL (1754-1812), American poet **2** 6-7

BARNARD, CHRISTIAAN N. (1922-2001), South African heart transplant surgeon **2** 7-8

BARNARD, EDWARD EMERSON (1857-1923), American astronomer **2** 8-9

BARNARD, FREDERICK AUGUSTUS PORTER (1809-1889), American educator and mathematician **2** 9-10

BARNARD, HENRY (1811-1900), American educator **2** 10
Miner, Myrtilla **35** 269-271

BARNES, DJUNA (Lydia Steptoe; 1892-1982), American author **2** 11-13

BARNETT, ETTA MOTEN (1901-2004), African American actress and singer **25** 34-36

BARNETT, MARGUERITE ROSS (1942-1992), American educator **21** 22-24

BARNEY, NATALIE CLIFFORD (1876-1972), American writer **33** 19-21

BARNUM, PHINEAS TAYLOR (1810-1891), American showman **2** 13-15

Barocchio, Giacomo
see Vignola, Giacomo da

BAROJA Y NESSI, PÍO (1872-1956), Spanish novelist **2** 15-16

BARON, SALO WITTMAYER (1895-1989), Austrian-American educator and Jewish historian **2** 16-17

BARONESS ORCZY (Emma Magdalena Rosalia Maria Josefa Orczy; 1865-1947), Hungarian-British author **28** 25-27

Barozzi, Giacomo
see Vignola, Giacomo da

BARRAGÁN, LUIS (1902-1988), Mexican architect and landscape architect **2** 17-19

BARRAS, VICOMTE DE (Paul François Jean Nicolas; 1755-1829), French statesman and revolutionist **2** 19

BARRE, RAYMOND (1924-1981), prime minister of France (1976-1981) **2** 19-20

BARRÉ-SINOUSSI, FRANÇOISE (born 1947), French scientist **34** 18-20

BARRÈS, AUGUSTE MAURICE (1862-1923), French writer and politician **2** 20-21

Barrett, Elizabeth
see Browning, Elizabeth Barrett

BARRIE, SIR JAMES MATTHEW (1860-1937), British dramatist and novelist **2** 21-22

BARRIENTOS ORTUÑO, RENÉ (1919-1969), populist Bolivian president (1966-1969) **2** 22-23

BARRIOS, AGUSTIN PÌO (1885-1944), Paraguayan musician and composer **28** 27-29

BARRIOS, JUSTO RUFINO (1835-1885), Guatemalan general, president 1873-1885 **2** 23-24

Barristers
see Jurists, English

Barrow, Joe Louis
see Louis, Joe

BARROWS, ISABEL CHAPIN (1845-1913), American missionary, stenographer, and physician **30** 34-36

BARRY, ELIZABETH (1658-1713), English actress **30** 36-38

BARRY, JAMES (Miranda Stuart Barry; 1795-1865), First British female physician **27** 40-41

BARRY, JOHN (1745-1803), American naval officer **2** 24-25

BARRY, JOHN (1933-2011), British film music composer **33** 21-23

BARRY, MARION SHEPILOV, JR. (1936-2014), African American mayor and civil rights activist **2** 25-28

BARRY, PHILIP (Philip James Quinn Barry; 1896-1949), American playwright **31** 22-23

BARRYMORES, American Theatrical Dynasty 2 28-30

Bartered Bride, The (opera)
Adler, Guido **35** 12-13

BARTH, HEINRICH (1821-1865), German explorer **2** 30-31

BARTH, KARL (1886-1968), Swiss Protestant theologian **2** 31-32

BARTHÉ, RICHMOND (1901-1989), African American sculptor **2** 33-34

BARTHOLDI, FRÉDÉRIC-AUGUSTE (1834-1904), French sculptor **28** 29-31

BARTHOLIN, THOMAS (1616-1680), Danish scientist **34** 21-23
Rudbeck, Olof **35** 318-320

BARTHOLOMAEUS ANGLICUS (Bartholomew the Englishman; Bartholomew de Glanville; flourished 1220-1240), English theologian and encyclopedist **21** 24-25

BARTIK, JEAN (1924-2011), American computer programmer **32** 34-36

BARTLETT, SIR FREDERIC CHARLES (1886-1969), British psychologist **2** 34-35

BARTÓK, BÉLA (1881-1945), Hungarian composer and pianist **2** 35-36

BARTON, BRUCE (1886-1967), American advertising business executive and congressman **2** 36-37

BARTON, CLARA (1821-1912), American humanitarian **2** 37-39

BARTON, SIR EDMUND (1849-1920), Australian statesman and jurist **2** 39-40

BARTRAM, JOHN (1699-1777), American botanist **2** 40-41

BARTRAM, WILLIAM (1739-1823), American naturalist **2** 41-42

BARUCH, BERNARD MANNES (1870-1965), American statesman and financier **2** 42-43

BARYSHNIKOV, MIKHAIL (born 1948), ballet dancer **2** 43-44

BARZIZZA, GASPARINO (1360-c. 1430), Italian humanist **30** 38-40

BARZUN, JACQUES (1907-2012), American writer **30** 40-42

BASCOM, FLORENCE (1862-1945), American geologist **22** 42-43

Baseball Hall of Fame (Cooperstown, New York)
Caray, Harry **35** 96-99
Cochrane, Mickey **35** 105-108

Baseball players
see Athletes

BASEDOW, JOHANN BERNHARD (1724-1790), German educator and reformer **2** 44-45

BASHO, MATSUO (1644-1694), Japanese poet **2** 45-48

BASIE, COUNT (William Basie; 1904-1984), pianist and jazz band leader **2** 48-49

BASIL I (c. 812-886), Byzantine emperor 867-886 **2** 49-50

BASIL II (c. 958-1025), Byzantine emperor 963-1025 **2** 50-51

BASIL THE GREAT, ST. (329-379), theologian and bishop of Caesarea **2** 51-52

Basil the Macedonian
see Basil I

Basketball players
see Athletes, American

BASKIN, LEONARD (1922-2000), American artist and publisher **22** 43-46

BASS, SAUL (1920-1996), American designer of film advertising **21** 25-27

BASSANI, GIORGIO (1916-2000), Italian author **30** 42-44

BASSI, LAURA (1711-1778), Italian physicist **20** 27-29

Bassianus
see Caracalla

BASTIAN, ADOLF (1826-1905), German ethnologist **30** 44-46

BATES, DAISY MAE (née O'Dwyer; 1861-1951), Irish-born Australian social worker **2** 52-53

BATES, HENRY WALTER (1825-1892), English explorer and naturalist **2** 53-54

BATES, KATHARINE LEE (1859-1929), American poet and educator **2** 54-55

BATESON, WILLIAM (1861-1926), English biologist concerned with evolution **2** 55-57

BATISTA Y ZALDÍVAR, FULGENCIO (1901-1973), Cuban political and military leader **2** 57-58
Hernández, Melba **35** 192-194
Matos, Huber **35** 260-262

BATLLE Y ORDÓÑEZ, JOSÉ (1856-1929), Uruguayan statesman and journalist **2** 58-59

Batman (comic, television, and film series)
Finger, Bill **35** 152-154
Kane, Bob **35** 215-217

BATTEN, JEAN (1909-1982), New Zealander aviatrix **26** 33-35

BATTIFERRI, LAURA (1523-1589), Italian poet **35** 32-34

BATTLE, KATHLEEN (born 1948), American opera and concert singer **2** 59-60

BATU KHAN (died 1255), Mongol leader **2** 60-61

BAUDELAIRE, CHARLES PIERRE (1821-1867), French poet and art critic **2** 61-63

BAUDOT, ANATOLE DE (1834-1915), French architect **35** 34-36

BAUER, BRUNO (1809-1882), German philosopher **35** 36-38

BAUER, EDDIE (1899-1986), American businessman **19** 13-14

Bauer, Georg
see Agricola, Georgius

Bauhaus (art school, Germany)
students
Bill, Max **35** 69-71

BAULIEU, ÉTIENNE-ÉMILE (Étienne Blum; born 1926), French physician and biochemist who developed RU 486 **2** 63-66

BAUM, ELEANOR (born 1940), American engineer **30** 47-48

BAUM, HERBERT (1912-1942), German human/civil rights activist **2** 66-73

BAUM, L. FRANK (1856-1919), author of the Wizard of Oz books **2** 73-74

Baumfree, Isabella
see Truth, Sojourner

BAUR, FERDINAND CHRISTIAN (1792-1860), German theologian **2** 74-75

BAUSCH, PINA (1940-2009), German dancer/choreographer **2** 75-76

Bavaria (state, Federal Republic of Germany)
politicians
Ludwig II of Bavaria **35** 244-246

BAWDEN, NINA (1925-2012), British author **34** 23-25

BAXTER, RICHARD (1615-1691), English theologian **2** 76-77

Bayern Munich (football team)
Beckenbauer, Franz **35** 43-45

BAYEZID I (Sultan of the Turks; 1354-1403), Turkish prince and warrior **35** 38-40
Manuel II Palaiologos **35** 256-258

BAYLE, PIERRE (1647-1706), French philosopher **2** 77-78

Bayley, Elizabeth
see Seton, Elizabeth Ann Bayley

BAYNTON, BARBARA (1857-1929), Australian author **22** 46-48

BAZAINE, ACHILLE FRANÇOIS (1811-1888), marshal of France **35** 40-43

BAZIN, ANDRÉ (1918-1958), French film critic **28** 32-33

BBC
see British Broadcasting Corporation (BBC)

BEA, AUGUSTINUS (1881-1968), German cardinal **2** 79

BEACH, AMY (born Amy Marcy Cheney; 1867-1944), American musician **23** 30-32

BEACH, MOSES YALE (1800-1868), American inventor and newspaperman **2** 79-80

Beaconsfield, Earl of
see Disraeli, Benjamin

BEADLE, GEORGE WELLS (1903-1989), American scientist, educator, and administrator **2** 80-81

BEALE, DOROTHEA (1831-1906), British educator **2** 81-83

BEAN, ALAN (born 1932), American astronaut and artist **22** 48-50

BEAN, LEON LEONWOOD (L.L. Bean; 1872-1967), American businessman **19** 14-16

BEARD, CHARLES AUSTIN (1874-1948), American historian **2** 84

BEARD, MARY RITTER (1876-1958), American author and activist **2** 85-86

BEARDEN, ROMARE HOWARD (1914-1988), African American painter-collagist **2** 86-88

BEARDSLEY, AUBREY VINCENT (1872-1898), English illustrator **2** 88-89

BEATLES, THE (1957-1971), British rock and roll band **2** 89-92

BEATRIX, WILHELMINA VON AMSBERG, QUEEN (born 1938), queen of Netherlands (1980-) **2** 92-93

BEAUCHAMPS, PIERRE (1636-1705), French dancer and choreographer **21** 27-29

BEAUFORT, FRANCIS (1774-1857), Irish naval officer and meteorologist **33** 23-25

BEAUFORT, MARGARET (1443-1509), queen dowager of England **20** 29-31

BEAUJOYEULX, BALTHASAR DE (Balthasar de Beaujoyeux; Baldassare de Belgiojoso; 1535-1587), Italian choreographer and composer **21** 29-30

BEAUMARCHAIS, PIERRE AUGUST CARON DE (1732-1799), French playwright **2** 93-94

BEAUMONT, FRANCIS (1584/1585-1616), English playwright **2** 95

BEAUMONT, WILLIAM (1785-1853), American surgeon **2** 95-96

BEAUREGARD, PIERRE GUSTAVE TOUTANT (1818-1893), Confederate general **2** 96-97

Beaverbrook, Lord
see Aitken, William Maxwell

BEBEY, FRANCIS (1929-2001), Cameroonian musician **32** 36-38

BECARRIA, MARCHESE DI (1738-1794), Italian jurist and economist **2** 97-98

BECHET, SIDNEY (1897-1959), American jazz musician **22** 50-52

BECHTEL, STEPHEN DAVISON (1900-1989), American construction engineer and business executive **2** 98-99

BECK, JÓZEF (1894-1944), Polish statesman **29** 48-50

BECK, LUDWIG AUGUST THEODER (1880-1944), German general **2** 99-100

BECKENBAUER, FRANZ (born 1945), German soccer player and coach **35** 43-45

BECKER, CARL LOTUS (1873-1945), American historian **2** 100-101

BECKET, ST. THOMAS (c. 1128-1170), English prelate **2** 101-102

BECKETT, SAMUEL (1906-1989), Irish novelist, playwright, and poet **2** 102-104

BECKHAM, DAVID (David Robert Joseph Beckham; born 1975), British soccer player **26** 36-38

BECKMANN, MAX (1884-1950), German painter **2** 104-105

BECKNELL, WILLIAM (c. 1797-1865), American soldier and politician **2** 105-106

BECKWOURTH, JIM (James P. Beckwourth; c. 1800-1866), African American fur trapper and explorer **2** 106-107

BÉCQUER, GUSTAVO ADOLFO DOMINGUEZ (1836-1870), Spanish lyric poet **2** 107-108

BECQUEREL, ALEXANDRE-EDMOND (1820-1891), French physicist **35** 45-47

Becquerel, Antoine César, (1788-1878), French physicist
Becquerel, Alexandre-Edmond **35** 45-47

BECQUEREL, ANTOINE HENRI (1852-1908), French physicist **2** 108-109
Becquerel, Alexandre-Edmond **35** 45-47

Becquerel, Jean Antoine, (1878-1953), French physicist
Becquerel, Alexandre-Edmond **35** 45-47

BEDE, ST. (672/673-735), English theologian **2** 109-110

BEDELL SMITH, WALTER (1895-1961), U.S. Army general, ambassador, and CIA director **18** 30-33

BEEBE, WILLIAM (1877-1962), American naturalist, oceanographer, and ornithologist **22** 52-54

BEECHAM, THOMAS (1879-1961), English conductor **24** 46-48

BEECHER, CATHARINE (1800-1878), American author and educator **2** 110-112

BEECHER, HENRY WARD (1813-1887), American Congregationalist clergyman **2** 112-113

BEECHER, LYMAN (1775-1863), Presbyterian clergyman **2** 113

Beer, Jakob Liebmann
see Meyerbeer, Giacomo

BEERBOHM, MAX (Henry Maximilian Beerbohm; 1872-1956), English author and critic **19** 16-18

BEETHOVEN, LUDWIG VAN (1770-1827), German composer **2** 114-117
influenced by
Arnim, Bettina von **35** 29-31
interpretations
Kuerti, Anton **35** 228-230

BOUTROS-GHALI, BOUTROS (born 1922), Egyptian diplomat and sixth secretary-general of the United Nations (1991-) **2** 457-458

BOUTS, DIRK (c. 1415-1475), Dutch painter **2** 458-459

Bouvier, Jacqueline Lee
see Kennedy, Jacqueline

BOVERI, THEODOR HEINRICH (1862-1915), German biologist **25** 60-62

BOW, CLARA (1905-1965), American actress **31** 37-38

BOWDITCH, HENRY INGERSOLL (1808-1892), American physician **2** 459-460

BOWDITCH, NATHANIEL (1773-1838), American navigator and mathematician **2** 460-461

BOWDOIN, JAMES (1726-1790), American merchant and politician **2** 461-462

BOWEN, EDWARD GEORGE (1911-1991), Welsh physicist **29** 84-86

BOWEN, ELIZABETH (1899-1973), British novelist **2** 462-463

BOWERS, CLAUDE GERNADE (1878-1958), American journalist, historian, and diplomat **2** 463

BOWIE, DAVID (David Robert Jones; born 1947), English singer, songwriter, and actor **18** 58-60

BOWIE, JAMES (1796-1836), American soldier **30** 71-73

BOWLES, PAUL (1910-1999), American author, musical composer, and translator **19** 31-34

BOWLES, SAMUEL (1826-1878), American newspaper publisher **2** 464

BOWMAN, ISAIAH (1878-1950), American geographer **2** 464-465

BOXER, BARBARA (born 1940), U.S. Senator from California **2** 465-468

Boxers
see Athletes–boxers

Boy bachelor
see Wolsey, Thomas

BOYD, LOUISE ARNER (1887-1972), American explorer **22** 73-74

Boyd, Nancy
see Millay, Edna St. Vincent

Boyd Orr, John
see Orr, John Boyd

BOYER, CHARLES (1899-1978), French-American actor **35** 87-89

BOYER, JEAN PIERRE (1776-1850), Haitian president 1818-1845 **2** 468-469

BOYER, PAUL DELOS (born 1918), American biochemist **25** 62-65

BOYLE, ROBERT (1627-1691), British chemist and physicist **2** 469-471

BOYLSTON, ZABDIEL (1679-1766), American physician **2** 471

Boz
see Dickens, Charles

BOZEMAN, JOHN M. (1837-1867), American pioneer **2** 471-472

Bozzie
see Boswell, James

BRACCIOLINI, POGGIO (1380-1459), Italian humanist **32** 48-50

BRACEGIRDLE, ANNE (c. 1663-1748), English actress **30** 73-75

BRACKENRIDGE, HUGH HENRY (1749-1816), American lawyer and writer **2** 472-473

BRACTON, HENRY (Henry of Bratton; c. 1210-1268), English jurist **21** 54-55

BRADBURY, RAY (1920-2012), American fantasy and science fiction writer **2** 473-474

Bradby, Lucy Barbara
see Hammond, John and Lucy

BRADDOCK, EDWARD (1695-1755), British commander in North America **2** 474-475

BRADFORD, WILLIAM (1590-1657), leader of Plymouth Colony **2** 475-476

BRADFORD, WILLIAM (1663-1752), American printer **2** 476-477

BRADFORD, WILLIAM (1722-1791), American journalist **2** 477

BRADLAUGH, CHARLES (1833-1891), English freethinker and political agitator **2** 478

BRADLEY, ED (1941-2006), African American broadcast journalist **2** 478-481

BRADLEY, FRANCIS HERBERT (1846-1924), English philosopher **2** 481-482

BRADLEY, JAMES (1693-1762), English astronomer **2** 482-483

BRADLEY, JOSEPH P. (1813-1892), American Supreme Court justice **22** 74-77

BRADLEY, LYDIA MOSS (1816-1908), American businesswoman and philanthropist **30** 75-77

BRADLEY, MARION ZIMMER (1930-1999), American author **18** 60-62

BRADLEY, OMAR NELSON (1893-1981), American general **2** 483-484

BRADLEY, TOM (1917-1998), first African American mayor of Los Angeles **2** 484-485

BRADMAN, SIR DONALD GEORGE (1908-2001), Australian cricketer **2** 485-486

BRADSTREET, ANNE DUDLEY (c. 1612-1672), English-born American poet **2** 486-487

BRADWELL, MYRA (Myra Colby; 1831-1894), American lawyer and publisher **24** 64-66

BRADY, MATHEW B. (c. 1823-1896), American photographer **2** 487-488

BRAGG, BRAXTON (1817-1876), American general **31** 39-41

BRAGG, SIR WILLIAM HENRY (1862-1942), English physicist **2** 488-489

BRAHE, TYCHO (1546-1601), Danish astronomer **2** 489-490

BRAHMAGUPTA (c. 598-c. 670), Indian mathematician and astronomer **26** 44-46

BRAHMS, JOHANNES (1833-1897), German composer **2** 490-492

BRAID, JAMES (1795-1860), British surgeon **31** 42-43

BRAILLE, LOUIS (1809-1852), French teacher and creator of braille system **2** 492-493

Brain (human)
Berger, Hans **35** 55-57
Pert, Candace **35** 278-280

BRAINARD, BERTHA (Bertha Brainard Peterson; died 1946), American radio executive **28** 47-48

BRAMAH, JOSEPH (Joe Bremmer; 1749-1814), English engineer and inventor **20** 58-59

BRAMANTE, DONATO (1444-1514), Italian architect and painter **2** 493-494

BRANCUSI, CONSTANTIN (1876-1957), Romanian sculptor in France **2** 494-496

BRANDEIS, LOUIS DEMBITZ (1856-1941), American jurist **2** 496-497

BRANDES, GEORG (Georg Morris Cohen Brandes; 1842-1927), Danish literary critic **23** 45-47

BRANDO, MARLON (1924-2004), American actor **2** 497-499

BRANDT, KARL (1904-1948), German physician **33** 44-46

BRANDT, WILLY (Herbert Frahm Brandt; 1913-1992), German statesman, chancellor of West Germany **2** 499-500

BRANSON, RICHARD (born 1950), British entrepreneur **19** 34-36

BRANT, JOSEPH (1742-1807), Mohawk Indian chief **2** 500-501

BRANT, MARY (MOLLY) (1736-1796), Native American who guided the Iroquois to a British alliance **2** 501-503

BRANT, SEBASTIAN (1457-1521), German author **2** 503-504

BRAQUE, GEORGES (1882-1967), French painter **2** 504-505

Braschi, Gianangelo
see Pius VI

BRATTAIN, WALTER H. (1902-1987), American physicist and co-inventor of the transistor **2** 505-507

Bratton, Henry de
see Bracton, Henry de

BRAUDEL, FERNAND (1902-1985), leading exponent of the *Annales* school of history **2** 507-508

BRAUN, FERDINAND (1850-1918), German recipient of the Nobel Prize in Physics for work on wireless telegraphy **2** 508-509

BRAVO, CLAUDIO (1936-2011), Chilean artist **33** 46-48

BRAY, JOHN RANDOLPH (1879-1978), American animator and cartoonist **21** 55-57

BRAZILE, DONNA (born 1959), American political strategist **32** 51-53

Brazilian music
Gil, Gilberto **35** 168-170
Guarnieri, Camargo **35** 175-176

BRAZZA, PIERRE PAUL FRANÇOIS CAMILLE SAVORGNAN DE (1852-1905), Italian-born French explorer **2** 509-510

BREASTED, JAMES HENRY (1865-1935), American Egyptologist and archeologist **2** 510-511

BRÉBEUF, JEAN DE (1593-1649), French Jesuit missionary **2** 511-512

BRECHT, BERTOLT (1898-1956), German playwright **2** 512-514

BRECKINRIDGE, JOHN CABELL (1821-1875), American statesman and military leader **22** 77-79

BRECKINRIDGE, MARY (1881-1965), American nurse **31** 44-45

Brède, Baron de la
see Montesquieu, Baron de

BREER, ROBERT (1926-2011), American artist **33** 48-50

BREGUET, ABRAHAM-LOUIS (1747-1823), French instrument maker **29** 86-88

BREMER, FREDRIKA (1801-1865), Swedish author **26** 46-48

BRENDAN, ST. (Brenainn; Brandon; Brendan of Clonfert; c. 486- c. 578), Irish Abbott and explorer **22** 79-80

BRENNAN, WILLIAM J., JR. (1906-1997), United States Supreme Court justice **2** 514-515

Brent of Bin Bin
see Franklin, Miles

Brentano, Bettina
see Arnim, Bettina von

BRENTANO, CLEMENS (1778-1842), German poet and novelist **2** 515-516

BRENTANO, FRANZ CLEMENS (1838-1917), German philosopher **2** 516-517

BRESHKOVSKY, CATHERINE (1844-1934), Russian revolutionary **2** 517-519

BRESLIN, JIMMY (born c. 1930), American journalist **33** 50-51

BRESSON, ROBERT (1901-1999), French filmmaker **25** 65-67

BRETON, ANDRÉ (1896-1966), French author **2** 519-520

Bretton, Henry de
see Bracton, Henry de

BREUER, JOSEF (1842-1925), Austrian physician **30** 77-79

BREUER, MARCEL (1902-1981), Hungarian-born American architect **2** 520-521

BREUIL, HENRI EDOUARD PROSPER (1877-1961), French archeologist **2** 521-522

BREWSTER, KINGMAN, JR. (1919-1988), president of Yale University (1963-1977) **2** 522-523

BREWSTER, WILLIAM (c. 1566-1644), English-born Pilgrim leader **2** 523-524

BREYER, STEPHEN (born 1938), U.S. Supreme Court justice **2** 524-527

BREYTENBACH, BREYTEN (Jan Blom; born 1939), South African author and activist **24** 66-68

BREZHNEV, LEONID ILICH (1906-1982), general secretary of the Communist party of the Union of Soviet Socialist Republics (1964-1982) and president of the Union of Soviet Socialist Republics (1977-1982) **2** 527-528

BRIAN BORU (c. 940-1014), Irish king **18** 62-64

BRIAND, ARISTIDE (1862-1932), French statesman **2** 528-529

BRICE, FANNY (1891-1951), vaudeville, Broadway, film, and radio singer and comedienne **3** 1-2

Bridge on the River Kwai, The (film)
Hayakawa, Sessue **35** 185-187

BRIDGER, JAMES (1804-1881), American fur trader and scout **3** 2-3

BRIDGES, HARRY A.R. (1901-1990), radical American labor leader **3** 3-5

BRIDGET OF SWEDEN (Saint Birgitta of Sweden; Birgitta Birgersdotter; 1303-1373), Swedish Catholic Saint **27** 53-55

BRIDGMAN, LAURA DEWEY (1829-1889), sight and hearing impaired American **29** 88-91

BRIDGMAN, PERCY WILLIAMS (1882-1961), American physicist **3** 5-6

BRIGHT, CHARLES TILSTON (1832-1888), English telegraph engineer **29** 91-93

BRIGHT, JOHN (1811-1889), English politician **3** 6-7

BRIGHT, RICHARD (1789-1858), English physician **3** 7-8

BRIGHTMAN, EDGAR SHEFFIELD (1884-1953), philosopher of religion and exponent of American Personalism **3** 8-9

BRILL, YVONNE (1924-2013), Canadian rocket scientist **35** 89-91

BRINK, ANDRE PHILIPPUS (1935-2015), South African author **22** 80-83

Brinkley, David
see Huntley and Brinkley

BRISBANE, ALBERT (1809-1890), American social theorist **3** 9

BRISBANE, ARTHUR (1864-1936), American newspaper editor **29** 93-95

BRISBANE, THOMAS MAKDOUGALL (1773-1860), Scottish military leader, colonial governor, and astronomer **30** 79-81

BRISTOW, BENJAMIN HELM (1832-1896), American lawyer and Federal official **3** 9-10

Britain, history of
see England

British Broadcasting Corporation (BBC)
Frost, David **35** 161-163

British India
see India (British rule)

BRITTEN, BENJAMIN (1913-1976), English composer **3** 10-11

BROAD, CHARLIE DUNBAR (1887-1971), English philosopher **3** 12

Broadcasting
drama
Corwin, Norman **34** 65-67
music
Conover, Willis **35** 108-110

CELLINI, BENVENUTO (1500-1571), Italian goldsmith and sculptor **3** 391-392

CELSIUS, ANDERS (1701-1744), Swedish astronomer **3** 392

CELSIUS, OLOF (1670-1756), Swedish botanist **32** 65-67

CELSUS, AULUS CORNELIUS (c. 25 BCE-c. A.D. 45), Roman medical author **3** 393

CENDRARS, BLAISE (1887-1961), Swiss-born poet **33** 69-71

Cenno de' Pepsi
see Cimabue

Censorship
China
Teng, Teresa **35** 346-348

CENTLIVRE, SUSANNA (Susanna Carroll; Susanna Rawkins; c. 1666-1723), British author **28** 65-67

Central America
see Latin America

Central Intelligence Agency (United States) counterintelligence
Golitsyn, Anatoliy **35** 170-172

Central Powers (WWI)
see World War I (1914-1918)

CEPEDA, ORLANDO (born 1937), Puerto Rican baseball player **34** 52-53

Cepeda y Ahumada, Teresa de
see Theresa, St.

Cephas
see Peter, St.

Cerenkov, Pavel
see Cherenkov, Pavel

CERETA, LAURA (Laura Cereta Serina; 1469-1499), Italian author and feminist **24** 75-77

CEREZO AREVALO, MARCO VINICIO (born 1942), president of Guatemala (1986-1991) **3** 393-395

CERF, BENNETT (1898-1971), American editor, publisher, author, and television performer **22** 98-100

CERNAN, GENE (Eugene Andrew Cernan; born 1934), American astronaut **22** 100-102

CERVANTES, MIGUEL DE SAAVEDRA (1547-1616), Spanish novelist **3** 395-398

Cervical cancer
Hausen, Harald Zur **35** 181-183

CÉSAIRE, AIMÉ (1913-2008), Martinican writer and statesman **30** 108-110

CÉSPEDES, CARLOS MANUEL DE (1819-1874), Cuban lawyer and revolutionary **3** 398-399

CESTI, PIETRO (Marc'Antonio Cesti; 1623-1669), Italian composer **3** 399-400

CETSHWAYO (Cetewayo; c. 1826-1884), king of Zululand 1873-1879 **3** 400

CÉZANNE, PAUL (1839-1906), French painter **3** 400-402

CHABROL, CLAUDE (1930-2010), French filmmaker **28** 67-69

CHADWICK, SIR EDWIN (1800-1890), English utilitarian reformer **3** 404-405

CHADWICK, FLORENCE (1918-1995), American swimmer **19** 64-66

CHADWICK, HENRY (1824-1908), American sportswriter **33** 71-73

CHADWICK, LYNN RUSSELL (1914-2003), English sculptor **18** 88-90

CHADWICK, SIR JAMES (1891-1974), English physicist **3** 405-406

CHAGALL, MARC (1887-1985), Russian painter **3** 406-407

CHAHINE, YOUSSEF (1926-2008), Egyptian filmmaker **25** 83-86

CHAI LING (born 1966), Chinese student protest leader **19** 67-68

CHAIN, ERNST BORIS (1906-1979), German-born English biochemist **3** 407-408

CHALIAPIN, FEDOR IVANOVICH (1873-1938), Russian musician **24** 77-79

CHALMERS, THOMAS (1780-1847), Scottish reformer and theologian **3** 408-409

CHAMBERLAIN, ARTHUR NEVILLE (1869-1940), English statesman **3** 409-411

CHAMBERLAIN, HOUSTON STEWART (1855-1927), English-born German writer **3** 411

CHAMBERLAIN, JOSEPH (1836-1914), English politician **3** 411-413

CHAMBERLAIN, OWEN (1920-2006), American physicist **25** 86-88

CHAMBERLAIN, WILT (1936-1999), American basketball player **3** 413-415

CHAMBERLIN, THOMAS CHROWDER (1843-1928), American geologist **3** 415-416

CHAMBERS, WHITTAKER (Jay Vivian; 1901-1961), magazine editor who helped organize a Communist spy ring in the United States government **3** 416-417

CHAMINADE, CÉCILE LOUISE STÉPHANIE (1857-1944), French composer and pianist **26** 62-64

CHAMOISEAU, PATRICK (born 1953), Martiniquais writer **32** 67-68

CHAMORRO, VIOLETA BARRIOS DE (born 1930), newspaper magnate, publicist, and first woman president of Nicaragua (1990) **3** 417-419

CHAMPLAIN, SAMUEL DE (c. 1570-1635), French geographer and explorer **3** 419-421

CHAMPOLLION, JEAN FRANÇOIS (1790-1832), French Egyptologist **3** 421

CHAN, JACKIE (Chan King-Sang; Sing Lung; born 1954), Chinese actor **27** 81-83

Chanakya
see Kautilya

CHANCELLOR, RICHARD (died 1556), English navigator **3** 422

CHANDLER, ALFRED DU PONT, JR. (1918-2007), American historian of American business **3** 422-423

CHANDLER, RAYMOND, JR. (1888-1959), American author **3** 423-425

CHANDLER, ZACHARIAH (1813-1879), American politician **3** 425-426

CHANDRAGUPTA MAURYA (died c. 298 BCE), emperor of India c. 322-298 **3** 426

CHANDRASEKHAR, SUBRAHMANYAN (1910-1995), Indian-born American physicist **3** 426-429

CHANEL, COCO (born Gabrielle Chanel; 1882-1971), French fashion designer **3** 429

CHANEY, LON (Alonzo Chaney; 1883-1930), American actor **19** 68-70

CHANG CHEH (c. 1923-2002), Chinese film director **31** 52-53

Chang Chiao
see Chang Chüeh

CHANG CHIEN (1853-1926), Chinese industrialist and social reformer **3** 429-430

CHANG CHIH-TUNG (1837-1909), Chinese official and reformer **3** 430-431

CHANG CHÜ-CHENG (1525-1582), Chinese statesman **3** 431-432

CHANG CHÜEH (died 184), Chinese religious and revolutionary leader **3** 432-433

CHANG HSÜEH-CH'ENG (1738-1801), Chinese scholar and historian **3** 433

Ch'ang-k'ang
see Ku K'ai-chih

CHANG PO-GO (died 846), Korean adventurer and merchant prince **3** 433-434

CLEMENT I (died c. 100 A.D.), Bishop of Rome, pope **23** 78-81

CLEMENT V (1264-1314), pope 1304-1314 **4** 101-102

CLEMENT VII (Giulio de Medici; 1478-1534), pope (1523-1534) **21** 81-83

CLEMENT XI (Giovanni Francesco Albani; 1649-1721), Italian pope 1700-1721 **24** 90-92
    Alberoni, Giulio **35** 16-17

CLEMENT OF ALEXANDRIA (c. 150-c. 215), Christian theologian **4** 102-103

Clement of Rome, St.
see Clement I, St.

CLEMENTE, ROBERTO (1934-1972), Hispanic American baseball player **19** 70-72

CLEOMENES I (flourished c. 520-490 BCE), Spartan king **4** 103

CLEOMENES III (c. 260-219 BCE), king of Sparta 235-219 **4** 103-104

CLEON (c. 475-422 BCE), Athenian political leader **4** 104-105

CLEOPATRA (69-30 BCE), queen of Egypt **4** 105-106

Cleophil
see Congreve, William

CLERIDES, GLAFCOS (1919-2013), Greek Cypriot diplomat **35** 101-103

CLEVELAND, FRANCES FOLSOM (1864-1947), American first lady **32** 77-79

CLEVELAND, JAMES (1932-1991), African American singer, songwriter, and pianist **4** 106-108

CLEVELAND, STEPHEN GROVER (1837-1908), American statesman, twice president **4** 108-110

CLIFF, JIMMY (born 1948), Jamaican singer **34** 61-62
    Blackwell, Chris **35** 74-77
    Dekker, Desmond **35** 121-123
    Henzell, Perry **35** 190-192
    Kong, Leslie **35** 227-228

CLIFFORD, ANNE (1590-1676), English author and philanthropist **27** 88-90

CLINE, PATSY (born Virginia Patterson Hensley; 1932-1963), American singer **4** 110-112

CLINTON, DEWITT (1769-1828), American lawyer and statesman **4** 112-113

CLINTON, GEORGE (1739-1812), American patriot and statesman **4** 113-114

CLINTON, SIR HENRY (c. 1738-1795), British commander in chief during the American Revolution **4** 114-115

CLINTON, HILLARY RODHAM (born 1947), American politician and first lady **4** 115-117

CLINTON, WILLIAM JEFFERSON ("Bill"; born 1946), 42nd president of the United States **4** 117-119

CLIVE, ROBERT (Baron Clive of Plassey; 1725-1774), English soldier and statesman **4** 119-120

CLODION (1738-1814), French sculptor **4** 121

CLODIUS PULCHER, PUBLIUS (died 52 BCE), Roman politician **4** 121-122

CLOONEY, ROSEMARY (1928-2002), American singer and actress **27** 90-93

Clopinel, Jean
see Jean de Meun

CLOUET, FRANÇOIS (c. 1516-c. 1572), French portrait painter **4** 122-123

CLOUET, JEAN (c. 1485-c. 1541), French portrait painter **4** 122-123

CLOUGH, ARTHUR HUGH (1819-1861), English poet **4** 123-124

CLOVIS I (465-511), Frankish king **4** 124

CLURMAN, HAROLD (1901-1980), American theater founder **35** 103-105

Clyens, Mary Elizabeth
see Lease, Mary Elizabeth Clyens

Cnut
see Canute I

COACHMAN, ALICE (Alice Coachman Davis; born 1923), African American athlete **26** 71-73

COANDĂ, HENRI (1886-1972), Romanian engineer **31** 54-55

COBB, JEWEL PLUMMER (born 1924), African American scientist and activist **22** 112-114

COBB, TYRUS RAYMOND (1886-1961), baseball player **4** 124-126

COBBETT, WILLIAM (1763-1835), English journalist and politician **4** 126-127

COBDEN, RICHARD (1804-1865), English politician **4** 127-128

COCHISE (c. 1825-1874), American Chiricahua Apache Indian chief **4** 128

COCHRAN, JACQUELINE (Jackie Cochran; 1910-1980), American aviator and businesswoman **18** 94-96

COCHRANE, MICKEY (1903-1962), American baseball player **35** 105-108

COCHRAN, JOHNNIE (1937-2005), African American lawyer **4** 128-131

COCHRANE, THOMAS (Earl of Dundonald; 1775-1860), British naval officer **20** 91-93

COCKCROFT, JOHN DOUGLAS (1897-1967), English physicist **4** 131-132

COCTEAU, JEAN (1889-1963), French writer **4** 132-133

Cody, William Frederick
see Buffalo Bill

COE, SEBASTIAN (born 1956), English track athlete **20** 93-95

COEN, JAN PIETERSZOON (c. 1586-1629), Dutch governor general of Batavia **4** 133

COETZEE, J(OHN) M. (born 1940), South African novelist **4** 133-135

COFFIN, LEVI (1789-1877), American antislavery reformer **4** 135

Coffin, Lucretia
see Mott, Lucretia Coffin

COFFIN, WILLIAM SLOANE, JR. (1924-2006), Yale University chaplain and activist **4** 135-137

COHAN, GEORGE MICHAEL (1878-1942), American actor and playwright **4** 137-138

Cohen, Bennett, (Ben Cohen; born 1951)
see Ben & Jerry

Cohen, George Morris
see Brandes, Georg Morris

COHEN, HERMANN (1842-1918), Jewish-German philosopher **4** 138-139

COHEN, LEONARD (born 1934), Canadian musician and writer **32** 79-81

COHEN, MORRIS RAPHAEL (1880-1947), American philosopher and teacher **4** 139-140

COHEN, WILLIAM S. (born 1940), American secretary of defense **18** 96-98

COHN, FERDINAND (1829-1898), German botanist **20** 95-97

COHN, HARRY (1891-1958), American movie industry executive **31** 56-59

COHN, MILDRED (1913-2009), American biochemist **32** 81-84

COHN, ROY MARCUS (1927-1986), American lawyer and businessman **29** 116-118

COHN-BENDIT, DANIEL (born 1946), led "new left" student protests in France in 1968 **4** 140-141

Coinage (metal currency)
    Boulton, Matthew **35** 83-85

COKE, SIR EDWARD (1552-1634), English jurist and parliamentarian **4** 141-142

DALEY, RICHARD J. (1902-1976), Democratic mayor of Chicago (1955-1976) **4** 373-375

DALEY, RICHARD M. (born 1942), mayor of Chicago **24** 102-104

DALHOUSIE, 1ST MARQUESS OF (James Andrew Broun Ramsay; 1812-1860), British statesman **4** 375-376

DALI, SALVADOR (1904-1989), Spanish painter **4** 376-377
 Giger, H.R. **35** 166-168

DALL, CAROLINE HEALEY (1822-1912), American reformer **31** 71-72

DALLAPICCOLA, LUIGI (1904-1975), Italian composer **4** 377-378

DALRYMPLE, ALEXANDER (1737-1808), Scottish hydrographer **34** 71-73
 Wallis, Samuel **35** 374-376

DALTON, JOHN (1766-1844), English chemist **4** 378-379

DALY, MARCUS (1841-1900), American miner and politician **4** 379-380

DALY, MARY (1928-2010), American feminist theoretician and philosopher **4** 380-381

DALZEL, ARCHIBALD (or Dalziel; 1740-1811), Scottish slave trader **4** 381-382

DAM, CARL PETER HENRIK (1895-1976), Danish biochemist **4** 382-383

DAMADIAN, RAYMOND (born 1936), American physician and inventor **35** 112-115

DAMIEN, FATHER (1840-1889), Belgian missionary **4** 383

DAMPIER, WILLIAM (1652-1715), English privateer, author, and explorer **4** 384

DAMROSCH, WALTER (1862-1950), American musical director **34** 73-75

DANA, CHARLES ANDERSON (1819-1897), American journalist **4** 384-385

DANA, RICHARD HENRY, JR. (1815-1882), American author and lawyer **4** 385-386

DANDOLO, ENRICO (c. 1107-1205), Venetian doge 1192-1205 **4** 386-387

DANDRIDGE, DOROTHY (1922-1965), African American actress and singer **18** 112-114

DANIEL, JACK (c. 1849-1911), American distiller **34** 75-77

DANIELS, JOSEPHUS (1862-1948), American journalist and statesman **4** 387

Daniels, W.
 see Wallace-Johnson, Isaac

D'ANNUNZIO, GABRIELE (1863-1938), Italian poet and patriot **4** 388

DANQUAH, JOSEPH B. (1895-1965), Ghanaian nationalist and politician **4** 388-389

DANTE ALIGHIERI (1265-1321), Italian poet **4** 389-391

DANTON, GEORGES JACQUES (1759-1794), French revolutionary leader **4** 391-393

DANTZIG, GEORGE BERNARD (1914-2005), American mathematician **26** 81-83

Danzig (city)
 see Gdansk (city; Poland)

DARBY, ABRAHAM (1677-1717), English iron manufacturer **20** 106-107

DARIN, BOBBY (1936-1973), American singer **34** 77-79

DARÍO, RUBÉN (1867-1916), Nicaraguan poet **4** 393-394

DARIUS I (the Great; ruled 522-486 BCE), king of Persia **4** 394-395

DARRIEUX, DANIELLE (born 1917), French actress **34** 79-81
 Decoin, Henri **35** 119-121
 Rubirosa, Porfirio **35** 316-318

DARROW, CLARENCE SEWARD (1857-1938), American lawyer **4** 396-397

DARWIN, CHARLES ROBERT (1809-1882), English naturalist **4** 397-399

DARWIN, ERASMUS (1731-1802), English physician, author, botanist and inventor **18** 114-116

DARWISH, MAHMUD (1942-2008), Palestinian poet **4** 399-401

DAS, CHITTA RANJAN (1870-1925), Indian lawyer, poet, and nationalist **4** 401-402

Dashti
 see Jami

DATSOLALEE (Dabuda; Wide Hips; 1835-1925), Native American weaver **22** 130-131

Datta, Narendranath
 see Vivekananda

Dau
 see Landau, Lev Davidovich

DAUBIGNY, CHARLES FRANÇOIS (1817-1878), French painter and etcher **4** 402

DAUDET, ALPHONSE (1840-1897), French novelist and dramatist **4** 402-403

DAUMIER, HONORÉ VICTORIN (1808-1879), French lithographer, painter, and sculptor **4** 403-405

DAVENANT, SIR WILLIAM (1606-1668), English poet laureate and dramatist **31** 73-75

DAVENPORT, JOHN (1597-1670), English Puritan clergyman **4** 405-406

DAVID (ruled c. 1010-c. 970 BCE), Israelite king **4** 406-407

DAVID I (1084-1153), king of Scotland **4** 407

DAVID, JACQUES LOUIS (1748-1825), French painter **4** 407-409

DAVID, ST. (Dewi; 520-601), Welsh monk and evangelist **23** 83-85

DAVID-NÉEL, ALEXANDRA (Eugenénie Alexandrine Marie David; 1868-1969), French explorer and author **28** 90-92

DAVIES, ARTHUR BOWEN (1862-1928), American painter **4** 409-410

DAVIES, MARION (1897-1961), American film star **29** 135-138

DAVIES, RUPERT (1917-1976), British actor **18** 116-117

DAVIES, WILLIAM ROBERTSON (1913-1995), Canadian author **18** 117-119

DAVIGNON, VISCOUNT (ETIENNE) (born 1932), an architect of European integration and unity through the Commission of the European Communities **4** 410-411

DAVIS, AL (1929-2011), American businessman **34** 81-84

DAVIS, ALEXANDER JACKSON (1803-1892), American architect **4** 411

DAVIS, ANGELA (Angela Yvonne Davis; born 1944), African American scholar and activist **4** 412-413

DAVIS, ARTHUR VINING (1867-1962), general manager of the Aluminum Company of America (ALCOA) **4** 413-414

DAVIS, BENJAMIN O., SR. (1877-1970), first African American general in the regular United States Armed Services **4** 414-415

DAVIS, BETTE (1908-1989), American actress **18** 119-121

DAVIS, COLIN REX (1927-2013), British conductor **22** 131-133

DAVIS, ELMER HOLMES (1890-1958), American journalist and radio commentator **22** 133-136

DAVIS, GLENN (1925-2005), American football player **21** 101-103

DAVIS, HENRY WINTER (1817-1865), American lawyer and politician **4** 415-416

EISELEY, LOREN COREY (1907-1977), American interpreter of science for the layman **5** 232-233

EISENHOWER, DWIGHT DAVID (1890-1969), American general and statesman, president 1953-61 **5** 233-236

EISENHOWER, MAMIE DOUD (1896-1979), American first lady **5** 236-237

EISENHOWER, MILTON (Milton Stover Esisenhower; 1899-1985), American adviser to U.S. presidents and college president **5** 237-238

EISENMAN, PETER D. (born 1932), American architect **5** 239-240

EISENSTAEDT, ALFRED (1898-1995), American photographer and photo-journalist **19** 100-102

EISENSTEIN, SERGEI MIKHAILOVICH (1898-1948), Russian film director and cinema theoretician **5** 240-242

EISNER, MICHAEL (born 1942), American businessman **19** 102-104

EITOKU, KANO (1543-1590), Japanese painter of the Momoyama period **5** 242

EKELÖF, GUNNAR (1907-1968), Swedish poet **35** 142-144

EKWENSI, CYPRIAN (1921-2007), Nigerian writer **5** 242-243

El-Hajj Malik El-Shabazz
see Malcolm X (film)

ELBARADEI, MOHAMED (born 1942), Egyptian diplomat **26** 98-100

Elchingen, Duke of
see Ney, Michel

ELDERS, JOYCELYN (born 1933), first African American and second woman U.S. surgeon general **5** 243-246

ELEANOR OF AQUITAINE (c. 1122-1204), queen of France 1137-52, and of England 1154-1204 **5** 246-247

Election monitoring
Kabbah, Ahmad Tejan **35** 210-212

Electrochemistry
Becquerel, Alexandre-Edmond **35** 45-47

Electroencephalogram (medicine)
Berger, Hans **35** 55-57

Electrolysis (chemistry)
Becquerel, Alexandre-Edmond **35** 45-47

Electromagnetism (physics)
theory
Biot, Jean-Baptiste **35** 73-74

Electrothermal hydrazine thruster (EHT)
Brill, Yvonne **35** 89-91

Elfgifu
see Emma of Normandy

ELGAR, SIR EDWARD (1857-1934), English composer **5** 247-248

ELGIN, 8TH EARL OF (James Bruce; 1811-63), English governor general of Canada **5** 248-249

Elia
see Lamb, Charles

ELIADE, MIRCEA (1907-1986), Rumanian-born historian of religions and novelist **5** 249-250

ELIAS, TASLIM OLAWALE (1914-1991), Nigerian academic and jurist and president of the International Court of Justice **5** 250-251

Eliezer, Israel ben
see Baal Shem Tov

ELIJAH BEN SOLOMON (1720-1797), Jewish scholar **5** 251-252

ELION, GERTRUDE B. (1918-1999), American biochemist and Nobel Prize winner **5** 252-254

ELIOT, CHARLES WILLIAM (1834-1926), American educator **5** 254

ELIOT, GEORGE (pen name of Mary Ann Evans; 1819-80), English novelist **5** 254-256

ELIOT, JOHN (1604-1690), English-born missionary to the Massachusetts Indians **5** 256-258

ELIOT, THOMAS STEARNS (1888-1965), American-English poet, critic, and playwright **5** 258-261

ELISABETH, EMPRESS OF AUSTRIA (1837-1898), German empress of Austria **28** 111-113

ELISABETH OF BOHEMIA (1618-1680), Palatine princess of Bohemia **35** 144-146

ELIZABETH (Elizabeth Petrovna; 1709-61), empress of Russia 1741-61 **5** 261-263

ELIZABETH I (1533-1603), queen of England and Ireland 1558-1603 **5** 263-266

ELIZABETH II (born 1926), queen of Great Britain and Ireland **5** 266-269

ELIZABETH BAGAAYA NYABONGO OF TORO (born 1940), Ugandan ambassador **5** 269-271

ELIZABETH BOWES-LYON (Elizabeth Angela Marguerite Bowes-Lyon; 1900-2002), queen of Great Britain and Ireland (1936-1952) and Queen Mother after 1952 **5** 261-263

ELIZABETH OF HUNGARY (1207-1231), saint and humanitarian **5** 271-272

ELLINGTON, "DUKE" EDWARD KENNEDY (1899-1974), American jazz composer **5** 273-274

ELLIS, HAVELOCK (Henry Havelock Ellis; 1959-1939), British psychologist and author **20** 126-128

ELLISON, RALPH WALDO (1914-1994), African American author and spokesperson for racial identity **5** 274-275

ELLSBERG, DANIEL (born 1931), U.S. government official and Vietnam peace activist **5** 275-277

ELLSWORTH, LINCOLN (1880-1951), American adventurer and polar explorer **5** 277

ELLSWORTH, OLIVER (1745-1807), American senator and Supreme Court Chief Justice **21** 115-117

ELON, AMOS (1926-2009), Israeli writer **32** 111-112

ELSASSER, WALTER MAURICE (1904-1991), American physicist **5** 277-278

ELSSLER, FANNY (1810-1884), Austrian ballet dancer **31** 107-108

ELUARD, PAUL (1895-1952), French poet **34** 108-109

ELWAY, JOHN (born 1960), American football player **23** 98-100

ELY, RICHARD (1854-1943), American economist and social reformer **21** 117-120

EMERSON, RALPH WALDO (1803-1882), American poet, essayist, and philosopher **5** 278-280
admiration of others' works
Arnim, Bettina von **35** 29-31

EMINESCU, MIHAIL (1850-1889), Romanian poet **5** 280-281

EMMA OF NORMANDY (c. 985-1052), wife of Ethelred II and of Canute I **35** 147-149

EMMET, ROBERT (1778-1803), Irish nationalist and revolutionary **5** 281-282

EMPEDOCLES (c. 493-c. 444 BCE), Greek philosopher, poet, and scientist **5** 282

ENCHI, FUMIKO UEDA (1905-1986), Japanese author **23** 100-102

ENCINA, JUAN DEL (1468-c. 1529), Spanish author and composer **5** 283

Encomienda system (Spanish America)
las Casas, Bartolomé de **35** 231-233

ENDARA, GUILLERMO (1936-2009), installed as president of Panama by the U.S. Government in 1989 **5** 283-284

ENDECOTT, JOHN (1588-1655), English colonial governor of Massachusetts **5** 284-285

ENDERS, JOHN FRANKLIN (1897-1985), American virologist **5** 285-286

Endorphins
Pert, Candace **35** 278-280

Enemy of the People, An (play)
McQueen, Steve **35** 267-269

ENGELBART, DOUGLAS (1925-2013), American inventor **31** 109-111

ENGELS, FRIEDRICH (1820-1895), German revolutionist and social theorist **5** 286-288
Bauer, Bruno **35** 36-38

England
5TH CENTURY-1066 (ANGLO-SAXON)
Normans and
Emma of Normandy **35** 147-149

ENGLAND, JOHN (1786-1842), Irish Catholic bishop in America **5** 288

Enigma (encryption system)
Cairncross, John **35** 94-96

ENNIN (794-864), Japanese Buddhist monk **5** 288-289

ENNIUS, QUINTUS (239-169 BCE), Roman poet **5** 289

ENRICO, ROGER (born 1944), American businessman **27** 111-112

ENSOR, JAMES (1860-1949), Belgian painter and graphic artist **5** 289-290

EPAMINONDAS (c. 425-362 BCE), Theban general and statesman **5** 291-292

EPÉE, CHARLES-MICHEL DE L' (1712-1789), French sign language developer **21** 120-122

EPHRON, NORA (1941-2012), American author, screenwriter and film director **18** 130-132

Epic (poetry)
English
Thayer, Ernest **35** 353-355

EPICTETUS (c. 50-c. 135), Greek philosopher **5** 292

EPICURUS (c. 342-270 BCE), Greek philosopher, founder of Epicureanism **5** 292-294

Epidemiology (medicine)
Maassab, Hunein **35** 250-252

Epilepsy (disease)
Berger, Hans **35** 55-57

Epimanes
see Antiochus IV (king of Syria)

Epistles (New Testament)
see Bible–New Testament (Epistolists)

EPSTEIN, ABRAHAM (1892-1945), Russian-born American economist **5** 294-295

EPSTEIN, SIR JACOB (1880-1959), American-born English sculptor **5** 295-296

Epstein-Barr virus
Hausen, Harald Zur **35** 181-183

EQUIANO, OLAUDAH (1745-c. 1801), African author and former slave **5** 296-297

ERASISTRATUS (c. 304 BCE- c. 250 BCE), Greek physician and anantomist **5** 297-298

ERASMUS, DESIDERIUS (1466-1536), Dutch author, scholar, and humanist **5** 298-300

ERASMUS, GEORGES HENRY (born 1948), Canadian Indian leader **5** 300-301

ERATOSTHENES OF CYRENE (c. 284-c. 205 BCE), Greek mathematician, geographer, and astronomer **5** 301-302

ERCILLA Y ZÚÑIGA, ALONSO DE (1533-1594), Spanish poet, soldier, and diplomat **5** 302

ERDOS, PAUL (1913-1996), Hungarian mathematician **22** 166-168

ERDRICH, LOUISE (Karen Louise Erdrich; born 1954), Native American author **23** 102-105

ERHARD, LUDWIG (1897-1977), German statesman, West German chancellor 1963-66 **5** 302-304

ERIC THE RED (Eric Thorvaldsson; flourished late 10th century), Norwegian explorer **5** 304

ERICKSON, ARTHUR CHARLES (1924-2009), Canadian architect and landscape architect **5** 304-306

ERICSON, LEIF (971-c. 1015), Norse mariner and adventurer **5** 306-307

ERICSSON, JOHN (1803-1889), Swedish-born American engineer and inventor **5** 307-308

ERIGENA, JOHN SCOTUS (c. 810-c. 877), Irish scholastic philosopher **5** 308-309

ERIKSON, ERIK HOMBURGER (1902-1994), German-born American psychoanalyst and educator **5** 309-310

ERLANGER, JOSEPH (1874-1965), American physiologist **5** 310-311

ERMAN, ADOLF (1854-1937), German Egyptologist and lexicographer **29** 154-156

ERNST, MAX (1891-1976), German painter **5** 311-312

ERNST, RICHARD (Richard Robert Ernst; born 1933), Swiss Chemist **27** 112-114

ERSHAD, HUSSAIN MOHAMMAD (born 1930), Bengali military leader and president of Bangladesh (1982-1990) **5** 312-314

ERSKINE, THOMAS (1750-1823), British lawyer **22** 168-170

ERTÉ (Romain de Tirtoff; 1892-1990), Russian fashion illustrator and stage set designer **5** 314-316

ERTEGUN, AHMET (1923-2006), Turkish-American record company executive **30** 162-164
McPhatter, Clyde **35** 265-267

ERVIN, SAM J., JR. (1896-1985), lawyer, judge, U.S. senator, and chairman of the Senate Watergate Committee **5** 316-317

ERVING, JULIUS WINFIELD (a.k.a. Dr. J.; born 1950), African American basketball player **5** 317-319

ERZBERGER, MATTHIAS (1875-1921), German statesman **5** 319-320

ESAKI, LEO (Reiona Esaki; born 1925), Japanese physicist **24** 127-130

ESCALANTE, JAIME (1930-2010), Hispanic American educator **5** 320-321

ESCHER, MAURITS CORNELIS (M.C. Escher; 1898-1972), Dutch graphic artist **18** 132-134

ESCOFFIER, AUGUSTE (Georges Auguste Escoffier; 1846-1935), French chef **21** 122-124

ESENIN, SERGEI ALEKSANDROVICH (1895-1925), Russian poet **5** 321

Española
see Hispaniola (island; West Indies)

Espionage Act (United States; 1917)
Berkman, Alexander **35** 57-59

ESQUIVEL, LAURA (born 1950), Mexican writer **31** 112-113

Essex, Earl of (circa 1485-1540)
see Cromwell, Thomas

ESSEX, 2D EARL OF (Robert Devereux; 1567-1601), English courtier **5** 321-322

Estabanico
see Estevan

Este, Leonello d', (died 1450), ruler of Ferrara
Bellini, Jacopo **35** 49-51

Este, Niccolo III d', (died 1441), ruler of Ferrara
Bellini, Jacopo **35** 49-51

Estée Lauder Companies
Rechelbacher, Horst **35** 305-308

Estenssoro, Victor Paz
see Paz Estenssoro, Victor

ESTEP, MAGGIE (1963-2014), American author and performer **35** 149-151

ESTES, RICHARD (born 1932), American realist painter **5** 322-323

Fair, A. A.
see Gardner, Erle Stanley

FAIR, JAMES RUTHERFORD, JR. (1920-2010), American chemical engineer and educator **20** 131-131

FAIRBANKS, DOUGLAS (Douglas Elton Ulman; 1883-1939), American actor and producer **19** 107-108

FAIRCLOUGH, ELLEN LOUKS (1905-2004), Canadian Cabinet minister **5** 367-368

FAIRUZ (née Nuhad Haddad; born 1933), Arabic singer **5** 368-369

FAISAL I (1883-1933), king of Iraq 1921-33 **5** 370-371

FAISAL II (1935-1958), king of Iraq, 1953-1958 **20** 132-132

FAISAL IBN ABD AL AZIZ IBN SAUD (1904-1975), Saudi Arabian king and prominent Arab leader **5** 371-372

FALCONET, ÉTIENNE MAURICE (1716-1791), French sculptor **5** 372

FALIERO, MARINO (1285-1355), Venetian doge, 1354 **34** 111-113

Falkland Islands (Southern Atlantic Ocean) Wallis, Samuel **35** 374-376

FALLA, MANUEL DE (1876-1946), Spanish composer **5** 372-373

FALLACI, ORIANA (1929-2006), Italian journalist **27** 115-117

FALLETTA, JOANN (born 1954), American conductor **5** 373-375

FALLOPPIO, GABRIELE (1523-1562), Italian anatomist **29** 157-159

Falstaff (opera)
Terfel, Bryn **35** 348-350

FALWELL, JERRY (1933-2007), fundamentalist religious leader who also promoted right-wing political causes **5** 375-376

FAN CHUNG-YEN (989-1052), Chinese statesman **5** 376-377

FANEUIL, PETER (1700-1743), American colonial merchant and philanthropist **5** 377

FANFANI, AMINTORE (1908-1999), Italian prime minister **5** 378-379

FANG LIZHI (1936-2012), Chinese scientist and dissident **34** 113-115

FANGIO, JUAN MANUEL (1911-1995), Argentine race car driver **33** 115-117

FANON, FRANTZ (1925-1961), Algerian political theorist and psychiatrist **5** 379-380

Fantasy (literary genre)
Matheson, Richard **35** 258-260

FARABI, AL- (Abou Nasr Mohammed ibn Tarkaw; 870-950), Turkish scholar and philosopher **22** 14-16

FARADAY, MICHAEL (1791-1867), English physicist and chemist **5** 380
influence of
Becquerel, Alexandre-Edmond **35** 45-47

FARAH, NURUDDIN (born 1945), Somali author **28** 114-116

FARGO, WILLIAM GEORGE (1818-1881), American businessman **5** 380-381

FARINA, MIMI (Margarita Mimi Baez Farina; 1945-2001), American singer and activist **27** 117-119

FARLEY, JAMES A. (1888-1976), Democratic Party organizer and political strategist **5** 381-383

FARMER, FANNIE MERRITT (1857-1915), American authority on cookery **5** 383

FARMER, JAMES (1920-1999), American civil rights activist who helped organize the 1960s "freedom rides" **5** 383-385

FARMER, MOSES GERRISH (1820-1893), American inventor and manufacturer **5** 385

Farnese, Alessandro (1468-1549)
see Paul III

FARNESE, ALESSANDRO (Duke of Parma; 1545-1592), Italian general and diplomat **20** 132-135

FARNSWORTH, PHILO T. (1906-1971), American inventor of the television **5** 386-387

FAROUK I (1920-1965), king of Egypt 1937-1952 **5** 387-388

FARRAGUT, DAVID GLASGOW (1801-1870), American naval officer **5** 388-389

FARRAKHAN, LOUIS (Louis Eugene Walcott, born 1933), a leader of one branch of the Nation of Islam popularly known as Black Muslims and militant spokesman for Black Nationalism **5** 389-390

FARRAR, GERALDINE (1882-1967), American opera singer **23** 106-108

FARRELL, EILEEN (1920-2002), American singer **27** 119-121

FARRELL, JAMES THOMAS (1904-1979), American novelist and social and literary critic **5** 390-391

FARRELL, SUZANNE (née Roberta Sue Ficker; born 1945), American classical ballerina **5** 391-393

FARRENC, LOUISE (Jeanne Louise Dumont; 1804-1875), French pianist **27** 121-122

FASSBINDER, RAINER WERNER (1946-1982), German filmmaker **26** 101-103

Fathers of the Church
see Religious leaders, Christian–Fathers

Fatih
see Mehmed the Conqueror

FAUCHARD, PIERRE (1678-1761), French dentist **26** 103-105

FAULKNER, BRIAN (1921-1977), prime minister of Northern Ireland (1971-1972) **5** 393-395

FAULKNER, WILLIAM (1897-1962), American novelist **5** 395-397

FAURÉ, GABRIEL URBAIN (1845-1924), French composer **5** 397-398

FAUSET, JESSIE REDMON (1882-1961), African American writer and editor **20** 135-138

FAUST, DREW GILPIN (Catherine Drew Gilpin; born 1947), American historian and university president **28** 116-118

FAVALORO, RENE GERONIMO (1923-2000), Argentine physician **24** 131-133

FAWCETT, MILLICENT GARRETT (1847-1929), British feminist **5** 398-400

FAWKES, GUY (Guido Fawkes; 1570-1606), English soldier and conspirator **27** 123-125

FAYE, SAFI (born 1943), Senegalese filmmaker and ethnologist **5** 400-401

FECHNER, GUSTAV THEODOR (1801-1887), German experimental psychologist **5** 401-402

FEE, JOHN GREGG (1816-1901), American abolitionist and clergyman **5** 402-403

FEIFFER, JULES RALPH (born 1929), American satirical cartoonist and playwright and novelist **5** 403-404

FEIGENBAUM, MITCHELL JAY (born 1944), American physicist **5** 404-405

FEIGL, HERBERT (1902-1988), American philosopher **18** 135-137

FEIJÓ, DIOGO ANTÔNIO (1784-1843), Brazilian priest and statesman **5** 405-406

Feiner, Leon, (1885-1945), Polish lawyer and activist
Karski, Jan **35** 217-219

FEININGER, LYONEL (1871-1956), American painter **5** 406-407

FEINSTEIN, DIANNE (Goldman; born 1933), politician, public official, and San Francisco's first female mayor **5** 407-408

FORD, HENRY (1863-1947), American industrialist **6** 5-6

FORD, HENRY, II (1917-1987), American industrialist **6** 6-7

FORD, JOHN (1586-c. 1639), English playwright **6** 7-8

FORD, JOHN SEAN O'FEENEY (c. 1890-1973), American film director **6** 8-9

FORD, PAUL LEICESTER (1865-1902), American bibliographer and novelist **6** 9-10

FORD, TOM (born 1961), American fashion designer and actor **25** 138-140

FORMAN, JAMES (1928-2005), writer, journalist, political philosopher, and leader of the Student Nonviolent Coordinating Committee **6** 10-11

FORMAN, MILOS (Tomas Jan Forman, born 1932), American screenwriter and film director **20** 143-145

Formula One (automotive racing)
Prost, Alain **35** 290-292

FORNÉS, MARÍA IRENE (born 1930), Cuban American playwright and director **24** 140-142

FORREST, EDWIN (1806-1872), American actor **6** 11-12

FORREST, JOHN (1st Baron Forrest of Bunbury; 1847-1918), Australian explorer and politician **6** 12-13

FORREST, NATHAN BEDFORD (1821-1877), American Confederate general **6** 13-14

FORRESTAL, JAMES VINCENT (1892-1949), American statesman **6** 14

FORSSMANN, WERNER (1904-1979), German physician **21** 140-141

FORSTER, EDWARD MORGAN (1879-1970), English novelist and essayist **6** 14-16

FORTAS, ABE (1910-1982), noted civil libertarian who served four years on the Supreme Court (1965-1969) **6** 16-17

FORTEN, JAMES (1766-1842), African American abolitionist and inventor **6** 17-18

FORTH, ELIZABETH DENISON (died 1866), African American landowner and philanthropist **27** 133-135

FORTUNE, DION (Violet Mary Firth; 1890-1946), British author and occultist **22** 180-182

FORTUNE, TIMOTHY THOMAS (1856-1928), African American journalist **6** 18-21

FORTUYN, PIM (Wilhelmus Petrus Simon Foruyn; 1948-2002), Dutch politician **28** 125-127

FOSCOLO, UGO (1778-1827), Italian author, poet, and patriot **6** 21

FOSDICK, HARRY EMERSON (1878-1969), American Presbyterian minister **6** 21-22

FOSS, LUKAS (1922-2009), American composer and conductor **31** 126-127

FOSSE, BOB (1927-1987), American director, choreographer, and dancer **6** 22-23

FOSSEY, DIAN (1932-1985), world's leading authority on the mountain gorilla **6** 23-24

Fossils
see Paleontology (science)

FOSTER, ABIGAIL KELLEY (1810-1887), American reformer **6** 25

FOSTER, MARIE (1917-2003), African American voting rights activist **25** 140-142

FOSTER, NORMAN (born 1935), British architect **19** 115-117

FOSTER, RUBE (Andrew Foster; 1879-1930), American baseball player and manager **24** 143-145

FOSTER, STEPHEN COLLINS (1826-1864), American composer **6** 25-27

FOSTER, WILLIAM ZEBULON (1881-1961), American Communist party leader **6** 27-28

FOUCAULT, JEAN BERNARD LÉON (1819-1868), French physicist **6** 28-29

FOUCAULT, MICHEL (1926-1984), French philosopher, critic, and historian **6** 29-30

FOUCHÉ, JOSEPH (1759-1820), French statesman **6** 30-31

Fountain (ready-made)
Freytag-Loringhoven, Elsa von **35** 160-161

FOUQUET, JEAN (c. 1420- c. 1480), French painter **6** 31

FOUQUET, NICOLAS (1615-1680), French superintendent of finance **31** 128-129

FOURIER, FRANÇOIS CHARLES MARIE (1772-1837), French socialist writer **6** 31-32

FOURIER, BARON JEAN BAPTISTE JOSEPH (1768-1830), French mathematical physicist **6** 32-33

FOWLES, JOHN (1926-2005), English novelist **6** 33-35

FOX, CHARLES JAMES (1749-1806), English parliamentarian **6** 35-37

FOX, GEORGE (1624-1691), English spiritual reformer **6** 37-38

FOX, VICENTE (born 1942), Mexican president **21** 142-143

FOX, WILLIAM (1879-1952), American film producer **21** 143-144

FOXX, JIMMIE (1907-1967), American baseball player **34** 124-128

FOXX, REDD (1922-1991), American comedian and actor **35** 156-158

FOYT, A.J. (born 1935), American race care driver **24** 145-147

FRA ANGELICO (c. 1400-1455), Italian painter **1** 235-236

FRACASTORO, GIROLAMO (Hieronymus Fracastorius; c. 1478-1553), Italian physician, poet, astronomer, and logician **21** 144-147

FRAENKEL, ABRAHAM ADOLF (Abraham halevi Fraenkel; 1891-1965), Israeli mathematician **23** 109-111

FRAGONARD, JEAN HONORÉ (1732-1806), French painter **6** 38-39

FRANCE, ANATOLE (1844-1924), French novelist **6** 39-40

France (French Republic; nation, Western Europe)
1815-70 (BOURBONS-2ND EMPIRE)
1848-52 (2nd Republic)
Bazaine, Achille François **35** 40-43

Francia
see France (French Republic; nation, Western Europe)

FRANCIS I (1494-1547), king of France 1515-1547 **6** 40-43

Francis I (emperor of Austria)
see Francis II (Holy Roman emperor)

Francis I Rákóczi
see Rákóczi Ferenc I

FRANCIS II (1768-1835), Holy Roman emperor 1792-1806 and emperor of Austria 1804-1835 **6** 43-44

Francis, Lydia Maria
see Child, Lydia Maria Francis

Francis Ferdinand
see Franz Ferdinand

FRANCIS JOSEPH (1830-1916), emperor of Austria 1868-1916 and king of Hungary 1867-1916 **6** 45-46

Francis of Angoulême
see Francis I (king of France)

FRANCIS OF ASSISI, ST. (1182-1226), Italian mystic and religious founder **6** 46-47
Sixtus IV **35** 331-333

FUENTES, CARLOS (1928-2012), Mexican author and political activist **6** 141-142

FUERTES, LOUIS AGASSIZ (1874-1927), American naturalist and artist **24** 152-153

FUGARD, ATHOL (born 1932), South African playwright **6** 142-143

FUGGER, JAKOB (Jacob Fugger; 1459-1525), German banker **21** 147-149

Fugitive slaves
see African American history (United States)

FUJIMORI, ALBERTO KEINYA (born 1938), president of Peru **6** 143-145

FUJITA, TETSUYA (Theodore "Ted" Fujita; 1920-1998), Japanese American meteorologist **27** 135-137

FUJIWARA KAMATARI (614-669), Japanese imperial official **6** 145

FUJIWARA MICHINAGA (966-1027), Japanese statesman **6** 145-146

Fujiwara-no Daijin
see Fujiwara Kamatari

Fukuda, Teiichi
see Shiba, Ryotaro

FUKUI, KENICHI (1918-1998), Japanese chemist **23** 111-112

FUKUYAMA, FRANCIS (born 1952), American philosopher and foreign policy expert **6** 146-147

FULBRIGHT, JAMES WILLIAM (1905-1995), American statesman **6** 147-149

FULLER, ALFRED (1885-1973), American businessman and inventor **19** 117-118

FULLER, JOHN FREDERICK CHARLES (1878-1966), British soldier and author **22** 185-186

FULLER, META WARRICK (1877-1968), American sculptor **23** 112-114

FULLER, MILLARD (1935-2009), American lawyer and social activist **18** 153-155

FULLER, RICHARD BUCKMINISTER (1895-1983), American architect and engineer **6** 149-150

FULLER, SARAH MARGARET (1810-1850), American feminist **6** 150-151

FULTON, ROBERT (1765-1815), American inventor, engineer, and artist **6** 151-152

Fulton, Ruth
see Benedict, Ruth Fulton

Fundy, Bay of (southeast Canada)
Broussard, Joseph **35** 91-93

FUNK, CASIMIR (1884-1967), Polish-American biochemist **22** 187-189

FUNKE, CORNELIA (born 1958), German author **30** 173-175

FURPHY, JOSEPH (1843-1912), Australian novelist **6** 152-153

FÜRÜZAN (Fürüzan Selçuk; born 1935), Turkish author and director **22** 189-190

FUSELI, HENRY (1741-1825), Swiss painter **6** 153-155

FUSTEL DE COULANGES, NUMA DENIS (1830-1889), French historian **6** 155

FUX, JOHANN JOSEPH (1660-1741), Austrian composer, conductor, and theoretician **6** 155-156

G

GABLE, WILLIAM CLARK (1901-1960), American film actor **6** 157-158

GABO, NAUM (1890-1977), Russian sculptor and designer **6** 158-159

GABOR, DENNIS (1900-1979), Hungarian-British physicist who invented holographic photography **6** 159-160

GABOR, ZSA ZSA (born c. 1917), Hungarian actress **33** 122-124
Rubirosa, Porfirio **35** 316-318

GABRIEL, ANGE JACQUES (1698-1782), French architect **6** 160-161

GABRIELI, GIOVANNI (c. 1557-1612), Italian composer **6** 161-162

Gabrini, Niccola di Lorenzo
see Rienzi, Cola di

GADAMER, HANS-GEORG (1900-2002), German philosopher, classicist, and interpretation theorist **6** 162-163

GADDAFI, MUAMMAR AL- (1942-2011), head of the revolution that set up the Libyan Republic in 1969 **6** 163-165

GADSDEN, JAMES (1788-1858), American soldier and diplomat **6** 165-166

GAGARIN, YURI ALEXEIVICH (1934-1968), Russian cosmonaut **6** 166-167

GAGE, MATILDA JOSLYN (1826-1898), American reformer and suffragist **6** 167-169

GAGE, THOMAS (1719/20-1787), English general **6** 169-170

GAGNÉ, ROBERT MILLS (1916-2002), American educator **6** 170

GAINES, WILLIAM M. (1922-1992), American publisher **34** 136-138

GAINSBOROUGH, THOMAS (1727-1788), English painter **6** 170-172

GAINSBOURG, SERGE (Lucien Gainsbourg; 1928-1991), French singer, songwriter and actor **27** 138-141

GAISERIC (died 477), king of the Vandals 428-477 **6** 172

GAITÁN, JORGE ELIÉCER (1898-1948), Colombian politician **6** 172-173

GAITSKELL, HUGH (1906-1963), British chancellor of the exchequer (1950-1951) and leader of the Labour Party (1955-1963) **6** 173-174

Gaius Sallustius Crispus
see Sallust

GAJDUSEK, CARLETON (1923-2008), American medical researcher and physician **34** 138-140

GALAMB, JOSEPH (Jozsef Galamb; 1881-1955), Hungarian-American engineer **24** 154-155

GALBRAITH, JOHN KENNETH (1908-2006), economist and scholar of the American Institutionalist school **6** 174-177

GALDÓS, BENITO PÉREZ (1843-1920), Spanish novelist and dramatist **6** 177-178

GALEN (130-200), Roman physician **6** 178-180

GALERIUS, EMPEROR OF ROME (Gaius Galerius Valerius Maximianus; c. 250-311), Thracian emperor **28** 132-134

Galilei, Galileo
see Galileo Galilei

GALILEO GALILEI (1564-1642), Italian astronomer and physicist **6** 180-183

GALL, FRANZ JOSEPH (1758-1828), German founder of phrenology **29** 165-167

GALLATIN, ALBERT (1761-1849), Swiss-born American statesman, banker, and diplomat **6** 183-184

GALLAUDET, THOMAS HOPKINS (1787-1851), American educator **6** 185

GALLEGOS FREIRE, RÓMULO (1884-1969), Venezuelan novelist, president 1948 **6** 185-186

GALLO, ROBERT CHARLES (born 1937), American virologist **22** 191-193

GALLOWAY, JOSEPH (c. 1731-1803), American politician **6** 186-187

GALLUP, GEORGE (1901-1984), pioneer in the field of public opinion polling and a proponent of educational reform **6** 187-189

GALSWORTHY, JOHN (1867-1933), English novelist and playwright **6** 189-190

GALT, SIR ALEXANDER TILLOCH (1817-1893), Canadian politician **6** 190-191

GRANT, MADISON (1865-1937), American conservationist and eugenics supporter **31** 145-146

GRANT, ULYSSES SIMPSON (1822-1885), American general, president 1869-1877 **6** 492-494

GRANVILLE, CHRISTINE (Krystyna Skarbek; c. 1915-1952), Polish secret agent **27** 153-154

GRANVILLE, EVELYN BOYD (born 1924), African American mathematician **6** 494-496

GRASS, GÜNTER (born 1927), German novelist, playwright, and poet **6** 496-497

GRASSELLI, CAESAR AUGUSTIN (1850-1927), third generation to head the Grasselli Chemical Company **6** 497-498

GRASSO, ELLA T. (1919-1981), American politician **32** 140-142

GRATIAN (died c. 1155), Italian scholar, father of canon law **6** 498-499

GRATTAN, HENRY (1746-1820), Irish statesman and orator **6** 499

GRAU SAN MARTIN, RAMÓN (1887-1969), Cuban statesman and physician **6** 499-500

GRAUNT, JOHN (1620-1674), English merchant and civil servant **21** 176-178

GRAVES, EARL GILBERT, JR. (born 1935), African American publisher **23** 130-132

GRAVES, MICHAEL (1934-2015), American architect **6** 500-502

GRAVES, NANCY STEVENSON (1940-1995), American sculptor **6** 502-504

GRAVES, ROBERT RANKE (1895-1985), English author **6** 504-506

GRAY, ASA (1810-1888), American botanist **6** 506-507

GRAY, ELISHA (1835-1901), American inventor **29** 176-178

GRAY, HANNAH HOLBORN (born 1930), university administrator **6** 507-508

GRAY, ROBERT (1755-1806), American explorer **6** 508-509

GRAY, THOMAS (1716-1771), English poet **6** 509-510

GRAY, WILLIAM H., III (1941-2013), African American politician **6** 510-511

Grayson, David
see Baker, Ray Stannard

Great Balls of Fire (song)
Lewis, Jerry Lee **35** 235-237

Great Britain (United Kingdom of Great Britain and Northern Ireland; island kingdom; northwestern Europe)

1603-1714 (STUART and COMMONWEALTH)
1649-1660 (Commonwealth and Protectorate)
Elisabeth of Bohemia **35** 144-146

Great Escape, The (film)
McQueen, Steve **35** 267-269

Great Purge (1936-38; Union of Soviet Socialist Republics)
perpetrators
Yagoda, Genrikh Grigoryevich **35** 377-379
victims
Yagoda, Genrikh Grigoryevich **35** 377-379

Greater New York
see New York City (New York State)

GRECO, EL (1541-1614), Greek-born Spanish painter **6** 511-514

GREELEY, ANDREW M. (born 1928), American Catholic priest, sociologist, and author **6** 514-515

GREELEY, HORACE (1811-1872), American editor and reformer **6** 515-517

GREELY, ADOLPHUS WASHINGTON (1844-1935), American soldier, explorer, and writer **6** 517-518

GREEN, CONSTANCE MCLAUGHLIN (1897-1975), American author and historian **6** 518-519

GREEN, EDITH STARRETT (1910-1987), United States congresswoman from Oregon (1954-1974) **6** 519-520

GREEN, HENRIETTA HOWLAND (1834-1916), American financier **30** 186-188

GREEN, THOMAS HILL (1836-1882), British philosopher **6** 520-521

GREEN, WILLIAM R. (1872-1952), American labor union leader **6** 521

Green Party (Brazil)
Gil, Gilberto **35** 168-170

GREENAWAY, KATE (Catherine; 1846-1901), English author and illustrator **18** 168-169

GREENBERG, CLEMENT (1909-1994), American art critic **6** 521-523

GREENBERG, HENRY BENJAMIN (Hank; 1911-1986), American baseball player **25** 161-165

GREENBERG, URI ZVI (1898-1981), Israeli author and activist **24** 158-159

GREENE, CATHERINE LITTLEFIELD (1755-1814), American inventor **22** 200-203

GREENE, DANNY (1929-2011), American mobster **34** 146-148

GREENE, GRAHAM (1904-1991), English novelist and dramatist **6** 523-524

GREENE, GRAHAM (born c. 1952), Canadian-Native American actor **6** 524-525

GREENE, NATHANAEL (1742-1786), American Revolutionary War general **6** 525-526

Greenfield, Jerry, (born 1951)
see Ben & Jerry

GREENSPAN, ALAN (born 1926), American economist **6** 526-528

GREENWICH, ELLIE (1940-2009), American songwriter, record producer and singer **32** 142-144

GREER, GERMAINE (born 1939), author and authoritative commentator on women's liberation and sexuality **6** 528-530

GREGG, JOHN ROBERT (1867-1948), American inventor of system of shorthand writing **21** 178-180

GREGG, WILLIAM (1800-1867), American manufacturer **6** 530-531

GREGORY I, ST. (c. 540-604), pope 590-604 **6** 531-532

GREGORY VII (c. 1020-1085), pope 1073-85 **6** 532-534

GREGORY IX (Ugo [Ugolino] di Segni; 1145-1241), Roman Catholic pope (1227-1241) **21** 180-183

GREGORY XII (Angelo Corrario; c. 1327-1417), pope 1406-1415 **18** 169-171

GREGORY XIII (1502-1585), pope 1572-1585 **6** 534

GREGORY XVI (Bartolommeo Alberto Cappellari; Mauro; 1765-1846), Roman Catholic pope 1831-1846 **25** 165-166

GREGORY, LADY AUGUSTA (1852-1932), Irish dramatist **6** 535-536

GREGORY, DICK (Richard Claxton Gregory; born 1932), comedian and civil rights and world peace activist **6** 536-537

GREGORY OF TOURS, ST. (538-594), Frankish bishop and historian **6** 534-535

Gregory the Great, Saint
see Gregory I, Saint

GRENE, MARJORIE (1910-2009), American philosopher **30** 188-190

GRENVILLE, SIR RICHARD (1542-1591), English naval commander **34** 148-150

GRETZKY, WAYNE (born 1961), Canadian hockey star **6** 537-539

GREUZE, JEAN BAPTISTE (1725-1805), French painter **6** 539

GREVER, MARIA (nee Maria de la Portilla; 1894-1951), Mexican musician **24** 159-161

HALE, GEORGE ELLERY (1868-1938), American astronomer **7** 72-74

HALE, SARAH JOSEPHA (née Buell; 1788-1879), American editor **7** 74-75

HALES, STEPHEN (1677-1761), English scientist and clergyman **7** 75

HALÉVY, ÉLIE (1870-1937), French philosopher and historian **7** 76

HALEY, ALEX (1921-1992), African American journalist and author **7** 76-78

HALEY, MARGARET A. (1861-1939), American educator and labor activist **7** 78-79

HALFFTER, CHRISTÓBAL (born 1930), Spanish composer **7** 79-80

HALIBURTON, THOMAS CHANDLER (1796-1865), Canadian judge and author **7** 80

HALIDE EDIP ADIVAR (1884-1964), Turkish woman writer, scholar, and public figure **7** 80-82

HALIFAX, 1ST EARL OF (Edward Frederick Lindley Wood; 1881-1959), English statesman **7** 82-83

HALL, ASAPH (1829-1907), American astronomer **7** 83-84

HALL, DONALD (born 1928), New England memoirist, short story writer, essayist, dramatist, critic, and anthologist as well as poet **7** 84-85

HALL, EDWARD MARSHALL (1858-1927), British attorney **22** 204-205

HALL, GRANVILLE STANLEY (1844-1924), American psychologist and educator **7** 85-86

HALL, LLOYD AUGUSTUS (1894-1971), American scientist and inventor **28** 154-156

HALL, PETER REGINALD FREDERICK (born 1930), English theater director **24** 162-165

HALL, PRINCE (c. 1735-1807), African American abolitionist and founder of the first black masonic lodge **26** 136-138

HALL, RADCLYFFE (Marguerite Radclyffe Hall; 1880-1943), British author **20** 168-170

HALLAJ, AL-HUSAYN IBN MANSUR AL (857-922), Persian Moslem mystic and martyr **7** 86-87

HALLAM, LEWIS, SR. AND JR. (Lewis Sr. c. 1705-1755; Lewis Jr. 1740-1808), American actors and theatrical managers **7** 87

HALLAREN, MARY AGNES (1907-2005), American army colonel **31** 153-154

HALLECK, HENRY WAGER (1815-1872), American military strategist **22** 205-207

HALLER, ALBRECHT VON (1708-1777), Swiss physician **7** 87-88

HALLEY, EDMUND (1656-1742), English astronomer **7** 88-89

HALLSTRÖM, LASSE (born 1946), Swedish film director **32** 147-149

HALONEN, TARJA KAARINA (born 1943), Finnish president **25** 178-180

HALS, FRANS (c.1581-1666), Dutch painter **7** 89-91

HALSEY, WILLIAM FREDERICK (1882-1959), American admiral **7** 91-92

HALSTED, WILLIAM STEWART (1852-1922), American surgeon **22** 207-209

HAMADA, SHOJI (1894-1978), Japanese potter **26** 138-140

HAMANN, JOHANN GEORG (1730-1788), German philosopher **7** 92

HAMER, FANNIE LOU (born Townsend; 1917-1977), American civil rights activist **7** 93-94

HAMILCAR BARCA (c. 285-229/228 BCE), Carthaginian general and statesman **7** 94-95

HAMILL, DOROTHY (born 1956), American figure skater **25** 180-183

HAMILTON, ALEXANDER (1755-1804), American statesman **7** 95-98

HAMILTON, ALICE (1869-1970), American physician **7** 98-99

HAMILTON, EDITH (1867-1963), American educator and author **22** 209-211

HAMILTON, SIR WILLIAM ROWAN (1805-1865), Irish mathematical physicist **7** 99-100

HAMLISCH, MARVIN (1944-2012), American composer and pianist **34** 151-153
    Sager, Carole Bayer **35** 321-323

HAMM, MIA (born 1972), American soccer player **30** 197-199

HAMM-BRÜCHER, HILDEGARD (born 1921), Free Democratic Party's candidate for the German presidency in 1994 **7** 101-103

HAMMARSKJÖLD, DAG (1905-1961), Swedish diplomat **7** 100-101

HAMMER, ARMAND (1898-1990), American entrepreneur and art collector **7** 103-104

HAMMERSTEIN, OSCAR CLENDENNING II (1895-1960), lyricist and librettist of the American theater **7** 104-106

HAMMETT, (SAMUEL) DASHIELL (1894-1961), American author **7** 106-108

HAMMOND, JAMES HENRY (1807-1864), American statesman **7** 108-109

HAMMOND, JOHN (1910-1987), American music producer **31** 155-156

HAMMOND, JOHN LAWRENCE LE BRETON (1872-1952), English historian **7** 108-109

HAMMOND, LUCY BARBARA (1873-1961), English historian **7** 109

HAMMURABI (1792-1750 BCE), king of Babylonia **7** 109-110

HAMPDEN, JOHN (1594-1643), English statesman **7** 110-111

HAMPTON, LIONEL (1908-2002), African American jazz musician **22** 211-213

HAMPTON, WADE (c. 1751-1835), American planter **7** 111-112

HAMPTON, WADE III (1818-1902), American statesman and Confederate general **7** 112

HAMSUN, KNUT (1859-1952), Norwegian novelist **7** 113-114

HAN FEI TZU (c. 280-233 BCE), Chinese statesman and philosopher **7** 124-125

Han Kao-tsu
    see Liu Pang

HAN WU-TI (157-87 BCE), Chinese emperor **7** 136

HAN YÜ (768-824), Chinese author **7** 136-137

HANAFI, HASSAN (born 1935), Egyptian philosopher **7** 114

HANCOCK, JOHN (1737-1793), American statesman **7** 114-116

HANCOCK, LANG (Langley George Hancock; 1909-1992), Australian industrialist **34** 153-155

HAND, BILLINGS LEARNED (1872-1961), American jurist **7** 116

Händel, Georg Friedrich
    see Handel, George Frederick

HANDEL, GEORGE FREDERICK (1685-1759), German-born English composer and organist **7** 116-119

HANDKE, PETER (born 1942), Austrian playwright, novelist, screenwriter, essayist, and poet **7** 119-121

HANDLER, ELLIOT (1916-2011), American toy manufacturer **34** 155-157

HANDLER, RUTH (Ruth Mosko; 1916-2002), American businesswoman **25** 183-185

HESBURGH, THEODORE MARTIN (1917-2015), activist American Catholic priest and president of Notre Dame (1952-1987) **7** 357-358

HESCHEL, ABRAHAM JOSHUA (1907-1972), Polish-American Jewish theologian **7** 358-359

HESELTINE, MICHAEL (born 1933), British Conservative politician **7** 359-361

HESIOD (flourished c. 700 BCE), Greek poet **7** 361-362

HESS, MYRA (1890-1965), British pianist **27** 169-171

HESS, VICTOR FRANCIS (1883-1964), Austrian-American physicist **7** 362-363

HESS, WALTER RICHARD RUDOLF (1894-1987), deputy reichsführer for Adolf Hitler (1933-1941) **7** 363-365

HESS, WALTER RUDOLF (1881-1973), Swiss neurophysiologist **7** 365

HESSE, EVA (1936-1970), American sculptor **7** 365-367

HESSE, HERMANN (1877-1962), German novelist **7** 367-369

HESSE, MARY B. (born 1924), British philosopher **7** 369-371

HEVESY, GEORGE CHARLES DE (1885-1966), Hungarian chemist **7** 371

HEWITT, ABRAM STEVENS (1822-1903), American politician and manufacturer **7** 371-372

HEYDLER, JOHN (1869-1956), American sports executive **32** 161-163

HEYDRICH, REINHARD (1904-1942), German architect of the Holocaust **20** 176-178

HEYERDAHL, THOR (1914-2002), Norwegian explorer, anthropologist and author **18** 194-196

HEYMAN, ABIGAIL (1942-2013), American photographer **35** 195-197

HEYSE, PAUL JOHANN LUDWIG (1830-1914), German author **7** 372-373

HEYWOOD, THOMAS (1573/1574-1641), English playwright **7** 373-374

HIAWATHA (c. 1450), Native American Leader **23** 143-145

HICKOK, JAMES BUTLER ("Wild Bill"; 1837-1876), American gunfighter, scout, and spy **7** 374-375

HICKS, BEATRICE (1919-1979), American engineer **31** 163-164

HICKS, EDWARD (1780-1849), American folk painter **7** 375

HIDALGO Y COSTILLA, MIGUEL (1753-1811), Mexican revolutionary priest **7** 375-377

HIDAYAT, SADIQ (1903-1951), Persian author **7** 377-378

Hideyoshi
see Toyotomi Hideyoshi

Higgins, Margaret
see Sanger, Margaret

HIGGINS, MARGUERITE (1920-1966), American journalist **7** 378-380

HIGGINSON, THOMAS WENTWORTH (1823-1911), American reformer and editor **7** 380

HIGHTOWER, ROSELLA (1920-2008), Native American dancer **26** 154-156

HIJUELOS, OSCAR (1951-2013), American author **35** 197-199

HILBERT, DAVID (1862-1943), German mathematician **33** 143-146

Hildebrand
see Gregory VII, Pope

HILDEBRANDT, JOHANN LUCAS VON (1663-1745), Austrian architect **7** 380-381

HILDRETH, RICHARD (1807-1865), American historian and political theorist **7** 382

HILFIGER, TOMMY (born 1952), American fashion designer **19** 144-146

HILL, ANITA (born 1956), African American lawyer and professor **7** 382-385

HILL, ARCHIBALD VIVIAN (1886-1977), English physiologist **7** 385-386

HILL, BENJAMIN HARVEY (1823-1882), American politician **7** 386-387

HILL, BENNY (Alfred Hawthorn Hill; 1924-1992), English comedian **28** 170-172

HILL, HERBERT (1924-2004), American scholar and civil rights activist **7** 387-388

HILL, JAMES JEROME (1838-1916), American railroad builder **7** 388-389

HILL, ROWLAND (1795-1879), British educator, postal reformer, and administrator **21** 202-204

HILLARY, EDMUND (1919-2008), New Zealander explorer and mountaineer **7** 389-390

Hillel Hazaken
see Hillel I

HILLEL I (c. 60 BCE -c. 10 A.D.), Jewish scholar and teacher **7** 390-391

HILLEMAN, MAURICE RALPH (1919-2005), American microbiologist **26** 156-158

HILLIARD, NICHOLAS (c. 1547-1619), English painter **7** 391-392

HILLMAN, SIDNEY (1887-1946), Lithuanian-born American labor leader **7** 392-393

HILLQUIT, MORRIS (1869-1933), Russian-born American lawyer and author **7** 393-394

HILLS, CARLA ANDERSON (born 1934), Republican who served three presidents as lawyer, cabinet member, and U.S. trade representative **7** 394-396

HILTON, BARRON (William Barron Hilton; born 1927), American businessman **19** 146-148

HILTON, CONRAD (1887-1979), American hotelier **20** 178-180

HIMES, CHESTER BOMAR (1909-1984), American author **22** 242-244

HIMMELFARB, GERTRUDE (born 1922), American professor, writer, and scholar **7** 396-398

HIMMLER, HEINRICH (1900-1945), German Nazi leader **7** 398-399
    Bernadotte, Folke **35** 60-62

HINDEMITH, PAUL (1895-1963), German composer **7** 399-400
    Guarnieri, Camargo **35** 175-176

HINDENBURG, PAUL LUDWIG HANS VON BENECKENDORFF UND VON (1847-1934), German field marshal, president 1925-1934 **7** 400-401

HINE, LEWIS WICKES (1874-1940), American photographer **28** 172-174

Hiner, Cincinnatus
see Miller, Joaquin

HINES, GREGORY OLIVER (1946-2003), American dancer and actor **7** 401-403

HINKLER, BERT (1892-1933), Australian aviator **34** 169-171

HINOJOSA, ROLANDO (born 1929), Hispanic-American author **7** 403-405

HINSHELWOOD, SIR CYRIL NORMAN (1897-1967), English chemist **7** 405-406

HINTON, SUSAN ELOISE (born 1950), American novelist and screenwriter **7** 406-407

HIPPARCHUS (flourished 162-126 BCE), Greek astronomer **7** 407-408

Hippius, Zinaida
see Gippius, Zinaida

HIPPOCRATES (c. 460-c. 377 BCE), Greek physician **7** 408-410

HOLLEY, ROBERT W. (1922-1993), American scientist **29** 191-193

Hollweg, Theobald von Bethmann
see Bethmann Hollweg, Theobald von

HOLLY, BUDDY (Charles Hardin Holley; 1936-1959), American singer, songwriter, and bandleader **22** 247-249

HOLM, HANYA (née Johanna Eckert; 1893-1992), German-American dancer and teacher **7** 454-455

HOLM, JEANNE M. (1921-2010), American military general **31** 168-169

Holm, Saxe
see Jackson, Helen Hunt

HOLMES, ARTHUR (1890-1965), English geologist and petrologist **7** 455-456

HOLMES, HELEN (1892-1950), American actress and stuntwoman **35** 199-201

HOLMES, JOHN HAYNES (1879-1964), American Unitarian clergyman **7** 456-457

HOLMES, OLIVER WENDELL (1809-1894), American physician and author **7** 457-458

HOLMES, OLIVER WENDELL, JR. (1841-1935), American jurist **7** 458-459

Holocaust
heroes
Sousa Mendes, Aristides de **35** 335-337
Zuckerman, Yitzhak **35** 382-384
survivors
Zuckerman, Yitzhak **35** 382-384
writers and writings
Karski, Jan **35** 217-219

HOLST, GUSTAV (1874-1934), English composer **7** 459-460

HOLT, BERTHA (1904-2000), American activist **32** 168-171

HOLTZMAN, JEROME (1926-2008), American sportswriter and author **31** 170-171

Holy Roman Empire
936-1024 (Saxon dynasty)
Adelheid, St. **35** 9-11

HOLYOAKE, KEITH JACKA (1904-1983), New Zealand prime minister and leader of the National Party **7** 460-462

HOLZER, JENNY (born 1950), American Neo-Conceptualist artist **7** 462-463

HOMANS, GEORGE CASPAR (1910-1989), American sociologist **7** 463-465

HOMER (ancient), Greek epic poet **7** 468-469

HOMER, WINSLOW (1836-1910), American painter **7** 468-469

HONDA, ISHIRO (Inoshiro Honda; 1911-1993), Japanese filmmaker **26** 158-160

HONDA, SOICHIRO (1906-1991), Japanese automaker **7** 469-470

HONECKER, ERICH (1912-1994), German Communist Party leader and head of the German Democratic Republic (1971-80s) **7** 471-472

HONEGGER, ARTHUR (1892-1955), Swiss composer identified with France **7** 472-473

HONEN (1133-1212), Japanese Buddhist monk **7** 473

HOOCH, PIETER DE (1629-c. 1684), Dutch artist **7** 473-474

HOOK, SIDNEY (1902-1989), American philosopher and exponent of classical American pragmatism **7** 474-475

HOOKE, ROBERT (1635-1703), English physicist **7** 475

HOOKER, HENRY CLAY (1828-1907), American rancher **29** 193-195

HOOKER, JOHN LEE (1917-2001), African American musician **23** 155-157

HOOKER, RICHARD (1554-1600), English theologian and Church of England clergyman **7** 475-476

HOOKER, THOMAS (1586-1647), English Puritan theologian, founder of Connecticut Colony **7** 476-477

HOOKS, BELL (born Gloria Jean Watkins; 1952), African American social activist, feminist, and author **7** 477-481

HOOKS, BENJAMIN LAWSON (1925-2010), executive director of the NAACP and first African American commissioner of the FCC **7** 481-483

HOOVER, HERBERT CLARK (1874-1964), American statesman, president 1929-1933 **7** 483-485

HOOVER, JOHN EDGAR (1895-1972), American lawyer, criminologist, and FBI director **7** 485-487

HOOVER, LOU HENRY (1874-1944), American translator and first lady **29** 195-197

HOPE, BOB (born Leslie Townes Hope; 1903-2003), entertainer in vaudeville, radio, television, and movies **7** 487-489

HOPE, JOHN (1868-1936), African American educator and religious leader **7** 489-490

HOPKINS, ANTHONY (Philip Anthony Hopkins; born 1937), Welsh actor **18** 196-198

HOPKINS, ESEK (1718-1802), American Revolutionary patriot **7** 490-491

HOPKINS, SIR FREDERICK GOWLAND (1861-1947), English biochemist **7** 496

HOPKINS, GERARD MANLEY (1844-1889), English Jesuit poet **7** 492-494

HOPKINS, HARRY LLOYD (1890-1946), American statesman **7** 494-495

HOPKINS, JOHNS (1795-1873), American financier and philanthropist **24** 178-180

HOPKINS, MARK (1802-1887), American educator **7** 495-496

HOPKINS, SAMUEL (1721-1803), American clergyman and theologian **7** 496

HOPKINSON, FRANCIS (1737-1791), American politician, writer, and composer **7** 496-497

Hopper, De Wolf, (1858-1935), American actor
Thayer, Ernest **35** 353-355

HOPPER, EDWARD (1882-1967), American realist painter **7** 497-498

HOPPER, GRACE (born Grace Brewster Murray; 1906-1992), American computer scientist **7** 498-500

HORACE (Quintus Horatius Flaccus; 65-8 BCE), Roman poet and satirist **7** 500-503

HORNE, HERMAN HARRELL (1874-1946), American philosopher and educator **7** 503-504

HORNE, LENA (1917-2010), American entertainer **7** 504-506

HORNE, MARILYN (born 1934), American opera singer **32** 171-172

HORNER, MATINA SOURETIS (born 1939), American scholar and administrator **7** 506-508

HORNEY, KAREN DANIELSEN (1885-1952), German-born American psychoanalyst **7** 508-509

HORNSBY, ROGERS (1896-1963), American baseball player and manager **21** 204-206

HOROWITZ, VLADIMIR (1904-1989), American pianist **7** 509-510

HORTHY DE NAGYBÁNYA, NICHOLAS (1868-1957), Hungarian admiral and statesman, regent 1920-1944 **7** 510-512

Horus Neteryerkhet
see Zoser

HORVÁTH, ÖDÖN VON (1901-1938), Hungarian author **26** 160-162

HOSEA (flourished 750-722 BCE), Hebrew prophet of the kingdom of Israel **7** 512

HOSTOS, EUGENIO MARÍA DE (1839-1903), Puerto Rican philosopher, educator, and writer **7** 513-514

HOUDINI, HARRY (born Erich Weiss; 1874-1926), American magician and illusionist **7** 514-516

HOUDON, ANTOINE (1741-1828), French sculptor **7** 516-517

HOUNSFIELD, GODFREY (1919-2004), English biomedical engineer **7** 517-519

HOUPHOUËT-BOIGNY, FELIX (1905-1993), Ivorian statesman 1960 **7** 519-520

HOUSE, EDWARD MANDELL (1858-1938), American diplomat **7** 520-521

HOUSMAN, ALFRED EDWARD (1859-1936), English poet **7** 521-522

HOUSSAY, BERNARDO ALBERTO (1887-1971), Argentine physiologist **7** 522-523

HOUSTON, CHARLES HAMILTON (1895-1950), African American lawyer and civil rights leader **7** 523-526

HOUSTON, SAMUEL (1793-1863), American statesman and soldier **7** 526-527

HOUSTON, WHITNEY (1963-2012), American singer and actress **19** 152-155

HOVHANESS, ALAN (1911-2001), American composer **29** 197-199

HOVLAND, CARL I. (1912-1961), American psychologist **7** 527-528

HOWARD, ELIZABETH JANE (1923-2014), British author **29** 200-202

HOWARD, JOHN WINSTON (born 1939), Australian prime minister **18** 198-200

HOWARD, OLIVER OTIS (1830-1909), American Union general **7** 528-529

HOWARD, RON (born 1954), American actor, director, and producer **19** 155-158

HOWE, EDGAR WATSON (1853-1937), American author and editor **7** 529

HOWE, ELIAS (1819-1867), American inventor **7** 529-530

HOWE, FLORENCE ROSENFELD (born 1929), feminist American author, publisher, literary scholar, and historian **7** 530-531

HOWE, GEOFFREY (Richard Edward; born 1926), British foreign secretary **7** 531-532

HOWE, GORDIE (born 1928), Canadian hockey player **7** 532-534

HOWE, JAMES WONG (1899-1976), Chinese-American cinematographer **30** 208-210

HOWE, JOSEPH (1804-1873), Canadian journalist, reformer, and politician **7** 534-535

HOWE, JULIA WARD (1819-1910), American author and reformer **7** 535-536

HOWE, RICHARD (Earl Howe; 1726-1799), English admiral **7** 536-537

HOWE, SAMUEL GRIDLEY (1801-1876), American physician and reformer **7** 537

HOWE, WILLIAM (5th Viscount Howe; 1729-1814), British general **7** 538-539

HOWELLS, WILLIAM DEAN (1837-1920), American writer **7** 539-541

HOWELLS, WILLIAM WHITE (1908-2005), American anthropologist **7** 541-542

HOXHA, ENVER (1908-1985), leader of the Communist Party of Albania from its formation in 1941 until his death **8** 1-3

HOYLE, EDMOND (1672-1769), English authority on card games **21** 206-208

HOYLE, FRED (1915-2001), English astronomer and author **18** 200-202

HRABAL, BOHUMIL (1914-1997), Czech writer **34** 173-176

HRDLIČKA, ALEŠ (1869-1943), American physical anthropologist **8** 3-4

HROTSVITHA OF GANDERSHEIM (Hrosvit/Roswitha; c. 937-c. 973), German author and nun **25** 202-204

HSIA KUEI (flourished 1190-1225), Chinese painter **8** 4-5

Hsiao Yen
see Liang Wu-ti

HSIEH LING-YÜN (385-433), duke of K'ang-lo, Chinese poet **8** 5-6

Hsien-tze
see Shih Ko-fa

Hsin-chien, Earl of
see Wang Yang-ming

Hsin Shun Wang
see Li Tzu-ch'eng

HSÜAN TSANG (c. 602-664), Chinese Buddhist in India **8** 6-7

HSÜAN-TSUNG, T'ANG (685-762), Chinese emperor **8** 7-8

HSÜN-TZU (Hsün Ch'ing; c. 312-c. 235 BCE), Chinese philosopher **8** 8

HU SHIH (1891-1962), Chinese philosopher **8** 63-65

Hu-t'ou
see Ku K'ai-chih

HUANG CH'AO (died 884), Chinese rebel leader **8** 8-9

HUANG TSUNG-HSI (1610-1695), Chinese scholar and philosopher **8** 9-10

HUBBARD, L. RON (1911-1986), American author and founder of Scientology **18** 202-204

HUBBLE, EDWIN POWELL (1889-1953), American astronomer **8** 10-11

HUBLEY, JOHN (1914-1977), American animator and filmmaker **21** 208-210

HUCH, RICARDA (1864-1947), German novelist, poet, and historian **8** 11-12

HUDSON, HENRY (flourished 1607-1611), English navigator **8** 12-13

Hueffer, Ford Madox
see Ford, Ford Madox

HUERTA, DOLORES (born 1930), Hispanic American labor activist **18** 204-207

HUERTA, VICTORIANO (1854-1916), Mexican general and politician **8** 13-14

HUGGINS, SIR WILLIAM (1824-1910), English astronomer **8** 14-15

HUGHES, CHARLES EVANS (1862-1948), American jurist and statesman **8** 15-16

HUGHES, HOWARD ROBARD (1905-1976), American entrepreneur **8** 16-17
Sternberg, Josef von **35** 341-344

HUGHES, JOHN JOSEPH (1797-1864), Irish-American Catholic archbishop **8** 17-18

HUGHES, LANGSTON (1902-1967), African American author **8** 18-19

HUGHES, RICHARD (1900-1976), English author **19** 158-160

HUGHES, TED (1930-1998), English poet laureate **8** 19-21

HUGHES, WILLIAM MORRIS (1864-1952), Australian prime minister 1915-1923 **8** 21-22

HUGO, VICOMTE VICTOR MARIE (1802-1885), French author **8** 22-25

Huguenots
Beza, Theodore de **35** 64-66

HUI-TSUNG (1082-1135), Chinese emperor and artist **8** 25

HUI-YÜAN (334-416), Chinese Buddhist monk **8** 25-26

HUIZINGA, JOHAN (1872-1945), Dutch historian **8** 26-27

HULAGU KHAN (Hüle'ü; c. 1216-1265), Mongol ruler in Persia **8** 27-28

HULBERT, WILLIAM AMBROSE (1832-1882), American baseball executive **30** 210-213

HULL, BOBBY (Robert Marvin Hull; born 1939), Canadian hockey player **20** 181-183

IVAN IV (1530-1584), grand duke of Moscow, czar of Russia 1547-1584 **8** 157-159

Ivan the Great
see Ivan III

Ivan the Terrible
see Ivan IV

IVANOV, LEV (Lev Ivanovich Ivanov; 1834-1901), Russian dancer and choreographer **24** 185-188

IVES, CHARLES EDWARD (1874-1954), American composer **8** 159-160

Ives, James Merritt, (1824-1895)
see Currier and Ives

IVORY, JAMES (born 1928), American film director and producer **20** 186-188

IWAKURA, TOMOMI (1825-1883), Japanese statesman **8** 160-161

IWERKS, UB (1901-1971), American animator **31** 178-179

IYENGAR, B.K.S. (Bellur Krishnamachar Sundararaja Iyengar; 1918-2014), Indian yoga educator and author **27** 178-180

IZETBEGOVIC, ALIJA (1926-2003), president of the eight-member presidency of the Republic of Bosnia-Herzegovina **8** 161-163

Izvekov, Sergei Mikhailovich
see Pimen I, Patriarch of Moscow

J

JA JA OF OPOBO (c. 1820-1891), Nigerian politician **8** 201-204

JABBAR, KAREEM ABDUL (Ferdinand Lewis Alcinor, Junior ; born 1947), American basketball player **8** 164-165

JABER AL-SABAH, JABER AL-AHMAD AL- (1926-2006), emir of Kuwait **8** 166-167

JABIR IBN HAYYAN (flourished latter 8th century), Arab scholar and alchemist **8** 167

JABOTINSKY, VLADIMIR EVGENEVICH (1880-1940), Russian Zionist **8** 167-168

JACKSON, ANDREW (1767-1845), American president 1829-1837 **8** 168-172

JACKSON, GLENDA (born 1936), English actress **35** 202-204

JACKSON, HELEN HUNT (1830-1885), American novelist **8** 172

JACKSON, HENRY MARTIN (Scoop; 1912-1983), United States senator and proponent of anti-Soviet foreign policy **8** 172-174

JACKSON, JESSE LOUIS (born 1941), U.S. civil rights leader and presidential candidate **8** 174-176

JACKSON, JOE (1887-1951), American baseball player ("Shoeless Joe") **35** 204-207

JACKSON, JOE (David Ian "Joe" Jackson; born 1954), British songwriter and musician **34** 189-190

JACKSON, JOHN HUGHLINGS (1835-1911), British neurologist **30** 214-216

JACKSON, MAHALIA (1911-1972), American singer **19** 166-168

JACKSON, MAYNARD HOLBROOK, JR. (1938-2003), first African American mayor of Atlanta, Georgia (1973-81 and 1989-1993) **8** 176-178

JACKSON, MICHAEL JOE (1958-2009), American singer **8** 178-180

JACKSON, NELL (1929-1988), American track and field athlete and coach **30** 216-218

JACKSON, PETER (born 1961), New Zealander actor and filmmaker **25** 211-213

JACKSON, RACHEL (Rachel Donelson Jackson; 1767-1828), American first lady **31** 180-181

JACKSON, REGINALD "REGGIE" MARTINEZ (born 1946), African American baseball player **8** 180-182

JACKSON, ROBERT HOUGHWOUT (1892-1954), American jurist **8** 182-183

JACKSON, SHIRLEY ANN (born 1946), African American physicist **8** 183-184

JACKSON, THOMAS JONATHAN ("Stonewall"; 1824-1863), American Confederate general **8** 184-185

JACKSON, WANDA (born 1937), American singer **34** 191-193

JACOB, JOHN EDWARD (born 1934), African American activist and president of the National Urban League **8** 185-188

JACOBI, ABRAHAM (1830-1919), American physician **8** 188-189

JACOBI, DEREK (born 1938), British actor **19** 168-170

JACOBI, FRIEDRICH HEINRICH (1743-1819), German philosopher **8** 189-190

JACOBI, MARY PUTNAM (1834-1906), American physician **8** 188-189

JACOBS, ALETTA HENRIETTE (1854-1929), Dutch physician and social reformer **26** 171-173

JACOBS, FRANCES (1843-1892), American activist **31** 182-184

JACOBS, HARRIET A. (1813-1897), runaway slave and abolitionist **8** 190-193

JACOBS, JANE (Jane Butzner; 1916-2006), Canadian author and urban planning activist **27** 181-183

JACOBSEN, JENS PETER (1847-1885), Danish author **8** 193-194

JACOBSON, DAN (1929-2014), South African author **22** 266-268

Jacopo, Giovanni Battista di
see Rosso, Il

JACOPONE DA TODI (c. 1236-1306), Italian poet and mystic **8** 194

JACQUARD, JOSEPH MARIE (1752-1834), French inventor **21** 216-218

JAELL, MARIE TRAUTMANN (1846-1925), French pianist and composer **24** 189-191

Jafar, Abu
see Mansur, al-

JAGGER, MICHAEL PHILIP ("Mick"; born 1944), lead singer for the Rolling Stones **8** 194-196
Tosh, Peter **35** 356-359

JAHAN, NUR (Mihrunnissa; Nur Mahal; 1577-1646), Indian queen **24** 191-193

JAHANGIR (1569-1627), fourth Mughal emperor of India **8** 196-199

JAHN, HELMUT (born 1940), German-American architect **8** 199-201

Jalal-ed-Din Rumi
see Rumi, Jalal ed-Din

Jamaica (nation, West Indies)
independence and after
Tosh, Peter **35** 356-359

Jamaican music
Blackwell, Chris **35** 74-77
Dekker, Desmond **35** 121-123
Henzell, Perry **35** 190-192
Kong, Leslie **35** 227-228
Tosh, Peter **35** 356-359

JAMERSON, JAMES (1936-1983), American bassist **30** 218-220

JAMES I (1394-1437), king of Scotland 1406-1437 **8** 206-207

JAMES I (James VI of Scotland; 1566-1625), king of England 1603-1625 **8** 204-206

JAMES II (1633-1701), king of England, Scotland, and Ireland 1685-1688 **8** 207-208

JAMES III (1451-1488), king of Scotland 1460-1488 **8** 208-209

James VI, king of Scotland
see James I (king of England)

James VII, king of Scotland
see James II (king of England)

JAMES, DANIEL, JR. ("Chappie"; 1920-1978), first African American man in the U.S. to become a four star general **8** 209-211

KHORANA, HAR GOBIND (1922-2011), Indian organic chemist **8** 537-538

KHOSROW I (died 579), Sassanid king of Persia 531-576 **8** 538-539

Khosru
see Khosrow I

KHRUSHCHEV, NIKITA SERGEEVICH (1894-1971), Soviet political leader **8** 539-540

KHUFU (ruled 2590-2568 BCE), Egyptian king **8** 540-541

Khurram
see Shah Jahan

Khusrau
see Khosrow I

KHWARIZMI, MUHAMMAD IBN MUSA AL- (died c. 850), Arab mathematician, astronomer, and geographer **8** 541

KIBAKI, MWAI (born 1931), Kenyan presidnet **25** 240-242

Kibo-no Mabi
see Makibi, Kibi-no

KIDD, WILLIAM (c. 1645-1701), Scottish pirate **21** 242-244

KIDDER, ALFRED VINCENT (1885-1963), American archeologist **8** 541-542

KIDMAN, SIDNEY (1857-1935), "The Cattle King" of Australia **8** 542-544

KIEFER, ANSELM (born 1945), German artist **8** 544-546

KIENHOLZ, EDWARD (1927-1994), American Pop artist **8** 546-547

KIERKEGAARD, SØREN AABYE (1813-1855), Danish philosopher **8** 547-549

KIESLOWSKI, KRZYSZTOF (1941-1946), Polish film director **25** 242-244

Kiev, Ukraine
Beilis, Menahem Mendel **35** 47-49

KILBY, JACK ST. CLAIR (1923-2005), American electrical engineer and inventor **25** 244-246

KILPATRICK, WILLIAM H. (1871-1965), American educator, college president, and philosopher of education **9** 1-3

KIM DAE-JUNG (1925-2009), worked for the restoration of democracy and human rights in South Korea after 1971 **9** 3-4

KIM IL-SUNG (1912-1994), North Korean political leader **9** 4-6

KIM JONG IL (1941-2011), leader of the Democratic People's Republic of Korea **9** 6-7

KIM OK-KYUN (1851-1894), Korean politician **9** 7-8

KIM PUSIK (1075-1151), Korean statesman, historian, and general **9** 8-9

Kim Song-ju
see Kim Il-sung

KIM YOUNG SAM (born 1927), South Korean statesman **9** 9-10

KINCAID, JAMAICA (Elaine Potter Richardson; born 1949), African American author **23** 196-199

KINDI, ABU-YUSUF YAQUB IBN-ISHAQ AL- (died 873), Arab philosopher **9** 10-11

KING, B. B. (born Riley B. King; 1925-2015, African American blues musician, singer, and songwriter **9** 11-14

KING, BILLIE JEAN (born 1943), international tennis star **9** 14-15

KING, CAROLE (born 1942), American singer and songwriter **32** 180-182
Sager, Carole Bayer **35** 321-323

KING, CLARENCE (1842-1901), American geologist and mining engineer **9** 15-16

KING, CORETTA SCOTT (1927-2005), American advocate of civil rights, nonviolence, international peace, full employment, and equal rights for women **9** 16-17

KING, ERNEST JOSEPH (1878-1956), American admiral **9** 17-18

KING, FREDERIC TRUBY (1858-1938), New Zealand doctor and founder of the Plunket Society **9** 18-19

KING, LARRY (born 1933), American journalist **34** 204-206

KING, MARTIN LUTHER, JR. (1929-1968), African American minister and civil rights leader **9** 20-22

KING, MARY-CLAIRE (born 1946), American geneticist **19** 182-183

KING, RUFUS (1755-1827), American statesman and diplomat **9** 22-23

KING, STEPHEN (a.k.a. Richard Bachman and John Swithen; born 1947), American horror novelist **9** 23-25

KING, WILLIAM LYON MACKENZIE (1874-1950), Canadian statesman **9** 25-26

King Curtis
see Ousley, Curtis

King of Bourges
see Charles VII (king of France)

KINGMAN, DONG (Dong Moy She Kingman; 1911-2000), Chinese American artist **27** 208-209

KINGSFORD SMITH, SIR CHARLES ("Smithy"; 1897-1935), Australian long-distance aviator **9** 26-28

KINGSLEY, CHARLES (1819-1875), English author and Anglican clergyman **9** 28

KINGSLEY, HENRY (1830-1867), British author **22** 278-280

KINGSLEY, MARY (1862-1900), English explorer and author **20** 201-204

KINGSTON, MAXINE HONG (Maxine Ting Ting Hong; born 1940), Asian-American feminist author **18** 231-232

KINNOCK, NEIL (born 1942), British Labour Party politician **9** 29-30

KINO, EUSEBIO FRANCISCO (1645-1711), Spanish missionary, explorer, and cartographer **9** 30-31

KINOSHITA, KEISUKE (1912-1998), Japanese screenwriter and film director/producer **24** 206-208

KINSELLA, THOMAS (born 1928), Irish poet **35** 221-222

KINSEY, ALFRED C. (1894-1956), American zoologist **9** 31-32

KINUGASA, TEINOSUKE (Teinosuke Kogame; 1896-1982), Japanese screenwriter and film director **24** 208-209

KIPLING, JOSEPH RUDYARD (1865-1936), British poet and short-story writer **9** 32-33

KIPNIS, ALEXANDER (1891-1978), Ukrainian American musician **24** 209-211

KIRBY, JACK (1917-1994), American comics artist **30** 240-242

KIRCH, MARIA WINCKELMANN (1670-1720), German astronomer **20** 204-205

KIRCHER, ATHANASIUS (c. 1601-1680), German polymath **27** 209-211

KIRCHHOFF, GUSTAV ROBERT (1824-1887), German physicist **9** 33-34

KIRCHNER, ERNST LUDWIG (1880-1938), German expressionist painter **9** 34-35

KIRCHNER, NÉSTOR (1950-2010), Argentine president 2003-2007 **34** 206-208

KIRKLAND, JOSEPH LANE (1922-1999), American labor union movement leader **9** 35-37

KIRKLAND, SAMUEL (1741-1808), American Congregationalist missionary **9** 37

KIRKPATRICK, JEANE J. (1926-2006), professor and first woman U.S. ambassador to the United Nations **9** 37-39

KIROV, SERGEI (1886-1934), Bolshevik leader **34** 208-211
Yagoda, Genrikh Grigoryevich **35** 377-379

Louis the Great
see Louis XIV (king of France)

Louis the Pious
see Louis I (Holy Roman emperor)

Louisiana Territory (United States history)
Broussard, Joseph **35** 91-93

LOVE, NAT (1854-1921), African American champion cowboy **10** 1-2

LOVE, SUSAN M. (born 1948), American surgeon and medical researcher **10** 2-3

LOVECRAFT, H. P. (1890-1937), American author **10** 3-6

LOVEJOY, ARTHUR ONCKEN (1873-1962), American philosopher **10** 6

LOVEJOY, ELIJAH PARISH (1802-1837), American newspaper editor and abolitionist **10** 6-7

LOVELACE, ADA BYRON (Countess of Lovelace, Augusta Ada King Byron; 1815-1852), English mathematician and author **18** 264-266

LOVELACE, RICHARD (c. 1618-c. 1657), English Cavalier poet **10** 7-8

LOVELL, SIR ALFRED CHARLES BERNARD (1913-2012), English astronomer **10** 8-9

LOW, JULIETTE GORDON (born Juliette Magill Kinzie Gordon; 1860-1927), American reformer and founder of the Girl Scouts **10** 10-11

LOW, SETH (1850-1916), American politician and college president **10** 11-12

LOWE, THADDEUS S.C. (1832-1913), American aeronaut **31** 215-217

LOWELL, ABBOTT LAWRENCE (1856-1943), American educator and political scientist **10** 12-13

LOWELL, AMY (1874-1925), American poet, critic, and biographer **10** 13

LOWELL, FRANCIS CABOT (1775-1817), American merchant and manufacturer **10** 13-14

LOWELL, JAMES RUSSELL (1819-1891), American poet and diplomat **10** 14-15

LOWELL, JOSEPHINE SHAW (1843-1905), American social reformer and philanthropist **10** 15-16

LOWELL, ROBERT TRAIL SPENCE, JR. (1917-1977), American poet **10** 16-17

LOWIE, ROBERT HARRY (1883-1957), Austrian-born American anthropologist **10** 18

LOWRY, MALCOLM (1909-1957), English author **19** 209-211

LOZIER, CLEMENCE SOPHIA HARNED (1813-1888), American suffragist, reformer, and physician **25** 273-275

LU CHI (261-303), Chinese poet and critic **10** 24

LU CHIU-YUAN (Lu Hsiang-shan; 1139-1193), Chinese philosopher **10** 24-25

LU HSÜN (pen name of Chou Shu-jen; 1881-1936), Chinese author and social critic **10** 35-37

Luang Pradit Manutham
see Pridi Phanomyong

LUBETKIN, ZIVIA (1914-1976), Polish resistance fighter **34** 242-244

LUBITSCH, ERNST (1892-1947), German-American film director **10** 18-19

LUCARIS, CYRIL (1572-1637), Greek Orthodox patriarch and theologian **10** 20

LUCAS, GEORGE (born 1944), American filmmaker **19** 211-213

LUCAS VAN LEYDEN (1494-1533), Dutch engraver and painter **10** 20-21

LUCE, CLARE BOOTHE (1903-1987), playwright and U.S. congresswoman **10** 21-23

LUCE, HENRY ROBINSON (1898-1967), American magazine editor and publisher **10** 23-24

LUCIAN (c. 120-c. 200), Greek satirist **10** 25-26

LUCIANO, LUCKY (Charles Luciano, Salvatore Lucania; 1897-1962), Italian American mobster **19** 214-215

LUCID, SHANNON (born 1943), American astronaut **19** 215-217

LUCRETIUS (Titus Lucretius Carus; c. 94-c. 55 BCE), Latin poet and philosopher **10** 26-27

LUDENDORFF, ERICH FRIEDRICH WILHELM (1865-1937), German general **10** 27-28

LUDLUM, ROBERT (a.k.a. Jonathan Ryder and Michael Shepherd; 1927-2001), American suspense novelist **10** 28-29

LUDWIG I OF BAVARIA (1786-1868), king of Bavaria 1825-1848 **34** 244-246

LUDWIG II OF BAVARIA (Ludwig Otto Friedrich Wilhelm; 1845-1886), king of Bavaria 1864-1886 **35** 244-246

LUDWIG, DANIEL KEITH (1897-1992), American shipping magnate **10** 29-31

LUDWIG, KARL FRIEDRICH WILHELM (1816-1895), German physiologist **10** 31

LUGARD, FREDERICK JOHN DEALTRY (1st Baron Lugard; 1858-1945), British soldier and colonial administrator in Africa **10** 31-32

LUGOSI, BELA (1882-1956), Hungarian-American actor **35** 246-249

LUHAN, MABEL DODGE (1879-1962), American writer, salon hostess, and patron of artists, writers, and political radicals **10** 32-34

LUHMANN, NIKLAS (1927-1998), German sociologist who developed a general sociological systems theory **10** 34-35

Luitpold, Prince Regent of Bavaria, (1821-1912), Regent of Bavaria 1886-1912
Ludwig II of Bavaria **35** 244-246

LUKÁCS, GYORGY (1885-1971), Hungarian literary critic and philosopher **10** 37-38

Lukar, Cyril
see Lucaris, Cyril

LUKASIEWICZ, IGNACY (1822-1882), Polish pharmacist and inventor of the kerosene lamp **28** 225-227

LUKE, ST. (flourished A.D. 50), Evangelist and biblical author **10** 38

LUKENS, REBECCA (née Rebecca Webb Pennock; 1794-1854), American industrialist **25** 275-277

LUKS, GEORGE BENJAMIN (1867-1933), American painter **10** 38-39

LULA DA SILVA, LUIZ INÁCIO (Lula; born 1945), president of Brazil **27** 244-247

LULL, RAYMOND (1232/35-1316), Spanish theologian, poet, and missionary **10** 39-40

LULLY, JEAN BAPTISTE (1632-1687), Italian-born French composer **10** 40-41

Lully, Raymond
see Lull, Raymond

LUMET, SIDNEY (1924-2011), American filmmaker and television director **22** 305-307

LUMIÈRE BROTHERS (Auguste Marie Louis, 1862-1954, and Louis Jean, 1864-1948), French inventors **10** 41-43

Luminescence (physics)
Becquerel, Alexandre-Edmond **35** 45-47

LUMMIS, CHARLES FLETCHER (1859-1928), American adventurer and journalist **33** 199-201

LUMUMBA, PATRICE EMERY (1925-1961), Congolese statesman **10** 43-45

LUNDY, BENJAMIN (1789-1839), American journalist **10** 45-46

MATTINGLY, GARRETT (1900-1962), American historian, professor, and author of novel-like histories **10** 342-344

MATZELIGER, JAN (1852-1889), American inventor and shoemaker **19** 232-234

MAUCHLY, JOHN (1907-1980), American computer entrepreneur **20** 250-252

MAUDSLAY, HENRY (1771-1831), British engineer and inventor **21** 286-288

MAUGHAM, WILLIAM SOMERSET (1874-1965), English author **10** 344-345

MAULBERTSCH, FRANZ ANTON (1724-1796), Austrian painter **10** 345

MAULDIN, BILL (1921-2003), cartoon biographer of the ordinary GI in World War II **10** 345-346

MAUPASSANT, HENRI RENÉ ALBERT GUY DE (1850-1893), French author **10** 347

MAURIAC, FRANÇOIS (1885-1970), French author **10** 347-348

MAURICE, JOHN FREDERICK DENISON (1805-1872), English theologian and Anglican clergyman **10** 349-350

MAURICE OF NASSAU, PRINCE OF ORANGE (1567-1625), Dutch general and statesman **10** 348-349
  Frederick Henry, Prince of Orange **35** 158-160

MAURRAS, CHARLES MARIE PHOTIUS (1868-1952), French political writer and reactionary **10** 350-351

MAURY, ANTONIA (1866-1952), American astronomer and conservationist **20** 252-254

MAURY, MATTHEW FONTAINE (1806-1873), American naval officer and oceanographer **10** 351-352

MAUSS, MARCEL (1872-1950), French sociologist and anthropologist **10** 352-353

MAWDUDI, ABU-I A'LA (1903-1979), Muslim writer and religious and political leader in the Indian sub-continent **10** 353-354

MAWSON, SIR DOUGLAS (1882-1958), Australian scientist and Antarctic explorer **10** 354-355

MAXIM, SIR HIRAM STEVENS (1840-1916), American-born British inventor **10** 355-356

Maximianus, Gaius Galerius Valerius
  see Galerius

Maximilian (emperor of Mexico)
  see Maximilian of Hapsburg

MAXIMILIAN I (1459-1519), Holy Roman emperor 1493-1519 **10** 356-357

MAXIMILIAN II (1527-1576), Holy Roman emperor 1564-1576 **10** 357-358

Maximilian II of Bavaria, (1811-1864), Elector of Bavaria 1848-1864
  Ludwig II of Bavaria **35** 244-246

MAXIMILIAN OF HAPSBURG (1832-1867), archduke of Austria and emperor of Mexico **10** 358-360
  Bazaine, Achille François **35** 40-43

MAXWELL, IAN ROBERT (née Ludvik Hock; 1923-1991), British publishing magnate **10** 360-361

MAXWELL, JAMES CLERK (1831-1879), Scottish physicist **10** 361-364

MAY, KARL (1842-1912), German author **26** 248-250

MAYAKOVSKY, VLADIMIR VLADIMIROVICH (1893-1930), Russian poet **10** 364-365

MAYBACH, WILHELM (1846-1929), German automobile builder **29** 274-277

MAYER, JEAN (1920-1993), nutritionist, researcher, consultant to government and international organizations, and president of Tufts University **10** 365-366

MAYER, LOUIS BURT (Eliezer Mayer; 1885-1957), American motion picture producer **19** 234-235

Mayerling (film)
  Boyer, Charles **35** 87-89
  Litvak, Anatole **35** 239-242

MAYFIELD, CURTIS (1942-1999), American musician **30** 273-275

MAYNARD, ROBERT CLYVE (1937-1993), African American journalist and publisher **10** 366-367

MAYO, WILLIAM J. AND CHARLES H. (1861-1939; 1865-1939), American physicians **10** 367-369

MAYO-SMITH, RICHMOND (1854-1901), American statistician and sociologist **10** 371-372

MAYOR ZARAGOSA, FEDERICO (born 1934), Spanish biochemist who was director-general of UNESCO (United Nations Educational, Scientific, and Cultural Organization) **10** 369-371

MAYR, ERNST (1904-2005), American evolutionary biologist **10** 372-374

MAYS, BENJAMIN E. (1894-1984), African American educator and civil rights activist **10** 374-376

MAYS, WILLIE (William Howard Mays, Jr.; born 1931), African American baseball player **10** 376-379

Mayson, Isabella Mary
  see Beeton, Isabella Mary

MAZARIN, JULES (1602-1661), French cardinal and statesman **10** 379-380

MAZEPA, IVAN STEPANOVICH (c. 1644-1709), Ukrainian Cossack leader **10** 381

MAZOWIECKI, TADEUSZ (1927-2013), Polish journalist and activist, and prime minister 1989-1991 **35** 263-265

Mazzarini, Giulio
  see Mazarin, Jules

MAZZINI, GIUSEPPE (1805-1872), Italian patriot **31** 224-225

Mazzola, Francesco
  see Parmigianino

M'BOW, AMADOU-MAHTAR (born 1921), director general of UNESCO (United Nations Educational, Scientific, and Cultural Organization) **10** 383-384

MBOYA, THOMAS JOSEPH (1930-1969), Kenyan political leader **10** 384-385

MCADOO, WILLIAM GIBBS (1863-1941), American statesman **10** 385-386

MCAULIFFE, ANTHONY (1898-1975), American army officer **19** 236-239

MCAULIFFE, CHRISTA (nee Sharon Christa Corrigan; 1948-1986), American teacher **20** 254-257

MCCAIN, JOHN SIDNEY, III (born 1936), American politician **25** 285-287

MCCANDLESS, BRUCE (born 1937), American astronaut **23** 243-246

MCCARTHY, EUGENE JOSEPH (1916-2005), American statesman **10** 386-388

MCCARTHY, JOHN (1927-2011), American computer scientist **34** 257-259

MCCARTHY, JOSEPH RAYMOND (1908-1957), American politician **10** 388-389

MCCARTHY, MARY T. (1912-2011), American writer **10** 389-391

MCCARTHY, NOBU (nee Nobu Atsumi; 1934-2002), Japanese actress and model **26** 250-252

MCCARTNEY, PAUL (James Paul McCartney; born 1942), British musician **24** 250-253

MCCAY, WINSOR (Zenas Winsor McKay; c. 1871-1934), American cartoonist and animator **21** 288-291

MCCLELLAN, GEORGE BRINTON (1826-1885), American general **10** 391-392

MCCLELLAN, JOHN LITTLE (1896-1977), U.S. senator from Arkansas **10** 392-393

MCCLINTOCK, BARBARA (1902-1992), geneticist and winner of the Nobel Prize in physiology **10** 393-394

MOHOLY-NAGY, LÁSZLÓ (1895-1946), Hungarian painter and designer **11** 82-83
Bill, Max **35** 69-71

Mohr
see Marx, Karl

MOI, DANIEL ARAP (born Daniel Toroitich arap Moi; born 1924), president of Kenya **11** 83-86

MOITESSIER, BERNARD (1925-1994), French sailor and author **28** 252-254

MOLIÈRE (1622-1673), French dramatist **11** 86-88

Molina, Rafael Leonidas Trujillo
see Trujillo Molina, Rafael Leonidas

MOLINARI, SUSAN K. (born 1958), American newscaster **18** 289-291

MOLINOS, MIGUEL DE (1628-1696), Spanish priest **11** 88-89

MOLOTOV, VYACHESLAV MIKHAILOVICH (1890-1986), Soviet statesman **11** 89-90

MOLSON, JOHN (1763-1836), English-Canadian entrepreneur **34** 268-270

MOLTKE, COUNT HELMUTH KARL BERNARD VON (1800-1891), Prussian military leader **11** 90-91

MOLTMANN, JÖURGEN (born 1926), German Protestant theologian **11** 91-92

MOMADAY, N. SCOTT (born 1934), Native American author **11** 92-94

MOMMSEN, THEODOR (1817-1903), German historian and philologist **11** 94-95

Momoh, Joseph, (1937-2003), Sierra Leonean president 1985-1992
Kabbah, Ahmad Tejan **35** 210-212

MOMPOU, FREDERIC (Federico Mompou i Dencausse; 1893-1987), Spanish composer **26** 261-263

MONAGHAN, TOM (Thomas Stephen Monaghan; born 1937), American businessman and philanthropist **19** 256-258

MONASH, JOHN (1865-1931), Australian soldier, engineer, and administrator **11** 95-96

MONCK, GEORGE (1st Duke of Albemarle; 1608-1670), English general and statesman **11** 96-97

MONDALE, WALTER F. (Fritz; born 1928), United States senator and vice president **11** 97-99

MONDAVI, ROBERT (1913-2008), American winemaker **19** 258-260

MONDLANE, EDUARDO CHIVAMBO (1920-1969), Mozambican educator and nationalist **11** 100-101

MONDRIAN, PIET (1872-1944), Dutch painter **11** 101-102

MONET, CLAUDE (1840-1926), French painter **11** 102-104

Monet, Jean Baptiste Pierre Antoine de
see Lamarck, Chevalier de

Money Honey (song)
McPhatter, Clyde **35** 265-267

MONGKUT (Rama IV; 1804-1868), king of Thailand 1851-1868 **11** 104

Mongol Empire
khans
Tolui Khan **35** 355-356

Monk, George
see Monck, George

MONK, MEREDITH (born 1942), American composer, entertainer, and critic **26** 263-265

MONK, THELONIOUS (1917-1982), African American jazz musician **11** 104-108

MONMOUTH AND BUCCLEUGH, DUKE OF (James Scott; 1649-1685), English claimant to the throne **11** 108-109

MONNET, JEAN (1888-1979), French economist and diplomat **11** 109-110

MONOD, JACQUES (1910-1976), French biologist who discovered messenger RNA **11** 110-111

Monophthalmos
see Antigonus I

MONROE, JAMES (1758-1831), American diplomat and statesman, president 1817-1825 **11** 111-113

MONROE, MARILYN (Norma Jean Baker; 1926-1962), film actress **11** 113-114

Mont Réal
see Montreal (city; Canada)

MONTAGNIER, LUC (born 1932), French virologist **11** 114-116

MONTAGU, ASHLEY (Israel Ehrenberg; 1905-1999), British-born American anthroplogist and author **22** 320-322

MONTAGU, JOHN, FOURTH EARL OF SANDWICH (1718-1792), English politician and first lord of the admiralty **21** 301-303

MONTAGU, MARY WORTLEY (1689-1762), English poet **18** 291-293

MONTAIGNE, MICHEL EYQUEM DE (1533-1592), French essayist **11** 116-117

MONTALE, EUGENIO (1896-1981), Italian poet and critic **11** 117-118

MONTALEMBERT, COMTE DE (Charles Forbes; 1810-1870), French political writer **11** 118-119

Montalte, Louis de
see Pascal, Blaise

MONTALVO, JUAN MARÍA (1832-1889), Ecuadorian writer **11** 119-120

MONTANA, JOE (born 1956), American football player **11** 120-121

MONTANUS (flourished 2nd century), Early Christian founder of schismatic sect **11** 122

MONTCALM DE SAINT-VÉRAN, MARQUIS DE (1712-1759), French general in Canada **11** 122-123

Montcorbier, François de
see Villon, François

Montefeltro, Federigo da, (1444-1482), duke of Urbino
Berruguete, Pedro **35** 62-64

Montefeltro, Guidobaldo da, (died 1508), duke of Urbino
Berruguete, Pedro **35** 62-64

MONTEFIORE, MOSES (1784-1885), English Zionist and philanthropist **20** 272-274

Montenevoso, Principe di
see D'Annunzio, Gabriele

Montereau, Pierre de
see Montreuil, Pierre de

MONTES, ISMAEL (Ismael Montes Gamboa; 1861-1933), president of Bolivia **24** 267-270

MONTESQUIEU, BARON DE (Charles Louis de Secondat; 1689-1755), French man of letters **11** 123-125

MONTESSORI, MARIA (1870-1952), Italian educator and physician **11** 125-126

MONTEVERDI, CLAUDIO GIOVANNI ANTONIO (1567-1643), Italian composer **11** 126-128

Montevideo (city, Uruguay)
Vázquez, Tabare **35** 364-366

MONTEZ, LOLA (1821-1861), Irish dancer and celebrity **33** 219-221

MONTEZ, MARÍA (1912-1951), Dominican actress **32** 261-263

MONTEZUMA I (Motecuhzoma I; Moctezuma I; 1397-1469), Aztec ruler **22** 322-324

MONTEZUMA II (c. 1466-1520), Aztec emperor 1502-1520 **11** 128-129

MONTEZUMA, CARLOS (born Wassaja; c. 1865-1923), Native American physician and political leader **11** 129-132

MONTFERRAND, JOSEPH (1802-1864), Canadian lumberjack **31** 236-237

MONTFORT, SIMON DE (6th Earl of Leicester; 1208-1265), English statesman and soldier **11** 132-133

NORMAN, JESSYE (born 1945), American singer **11** 425-427

NORMAND, MABEL (1895-1930), American actress **31** 251-253
Holmes, Helen **35** 199-201

Normandy, Duke of
see Charles V (king of France)

NORRIS, BENJAMIN FRANKLIN, JR. (1870-1902), American novelist and critic **11** 427-428

NORRIS, GEORGE WILLIAM (1861-1944), American statesman **11** 428-429

NORTH, FREDERICK (2nd Earl of Guilford; 1732-1792), English statesman **11** 429-430

NORTH, MARIANNE (1830-1890), English naturalist and painter **23** 268-270

Northern Nigeria
see Nigeria

NORTHROP, JOHN HOWARD (1891-1987), American biological chemist **11** 430-431

NORTHUMBERLAND, DUKE OF (John Dudley; c. 1502-1553), English soldier and statesman **11** 431-432

NORTHUP, SOLOMON (1808-c. 1863), American memoirist **34** 275-277

NORTON, ANDRE (Alice Mary Norton; 1912-2005), American science fiction and fantasy writer **28** 257-259

NOSTRADAMUS (born Michel de Notredame; 1503-1566), French physician, astrologist, and author **11** 432-434

NOTKER BALBULUS (c. 840-912), Swiss poet-musician and monk **11** 434-435

Nova Scotia (province; Canada)
Broussard, Joseph **35** 91-93

Novak, Joseph
see Kosinsky, Jerzy

NOVALIS (1772-1801), German poet and author **11** 435

Novanglus
see Adams, John

NOVELLO, ANTONIA (Antonia Coello; born 1944), Puerto Rican American pediatrician **18** 308-310

NOVOTNÝ, ANTONÍN (1904-1975), Czechoslovak politician **29** 291-293

NOYCE, ROBERT (1927-1990), American physicist and inventor **11** 436-437

NOYES, JOHN HUMPHREY (1811-1886), American founder of the Oneida Community **11** 437-438

NOZICK, ROBERT (1938-2002), American philosopher and polemical advocate of radical libertarianism **11** 438-439

N'si Yisrael
see Bar Kochba, Simeon

NU, U (1907-1995), Burmese statesman **11** 439-441

Nuclear magnetic resonance (NMR)
Damadian, Raymond **35** 112-115

NUJOMA, SHAFIIHUNA ("Sam"; born 1929), first president of independent Namibia **11** 441-443

Nukada-be, Princess
see Suiko

Núñez de Balboa, Vasco
see Balboa, Vasco Núñez de

NUNN, SAM (born 1938), United States senator from Georgia **11** 443-444

Nur-ad-Din
see Nureddin

Nur al-Din Abd al-Rahman, Maulana
see Jami

NUREDDIN (Malik al-Adil Nur-al-Din Mahmud; 1118-1174), sultan of Syria and Egypt **11** 444-445

NUREYEV, RUDOLPH (1938-1993), Russian-born dancer and choreographer **11** 445-446

NURI AL-SA'ID (1888-1958), Iraqi army officer, statesman, and nationalist **11** 446-447

NURMI, PAAVO (1897-1973), Finnish runner **19** 272-274

Nurse, Malcolm Ivan Meredith
see Padmore, George

NURSÎ, SAID (Bediüzzaman Said Nursî; 1876-1960), Turkish theologian **28** 259-261

NUSSLEIN-VOLHARD, CHRISTIANE (born 1942), German biologist **25** 314-316

Nuvolara, Count of
see Castiglione, Baldassare

NYE, GERALD (1892-1971), American senator **21** 320-323

NYERERE, JULIUS KAMBERAGE (1922-1999), Tanzanian statesman **11** 447-449

NYGREN, ANDERS (1890-1978), Lutheran bishop of Lund and representative of the so-called Lundensian school of theology **11** 449-451

NYKVIST, SVEN (Sven Vilhelm Nykvist; 1922-2006), Swedish cinematographer **28** 261-263

NYRO, LAURA (1947-1997), American singer-songwriter **31** 254-256

NZINGA, ANNA (Pande Dona Ana Souza; 1582-1663), queen of Angola **23** 270-271

Nzinga Mvemba
see Affonso I

NZINGA NKUWU (died 1506), king of Kongo **11** 451-452

O

OAKLEY, ANNIE (1860-1926), American markswoman and Wild West star **11** 453-454

OATES, JOYCE CAROL (born 1938), American author **11** 454-456

OATES, TITUS (1649-1705), English leader of the Popish Plot **11** 456

OBAMA, BARACK (born 1961), American president 2009- **32** 280-282

OBAMA, MICHELLE (born 1964), American first lady **33** 229-232

OBERTH, HERMANN JULIUS (1894-1989), Romanian physicist **29** 296-298

Objective school
see Historiography–objective school

OBOTE, APOLO MILTON (1925-2005), Ugandan politician **11** 457

OBRADOVIĆ, DOSITEJ (Dimitrije Dositej Obradović c. 1740-1811), Serbian author and educator **24** 282-284

OBRECHT, JACOB (1450-1505), Dutch composer **11** 457-458

OBREGÓN, ÀLVARO (1880-1928), Mexican revolutionary general and president **11** 458-459

O'BRIEN, WILLIS (1886-1962), American film special effects pioneer **21** 324-326

Obscure, the
see Heraclitus

O'CASEY, SEAN (1880-1964), Irish dramatist **11** 459-460

Occam, William of
see William of Ockham

OCHOA, ELLEN (born 1958), Hispanic American electrical engineer and astronaut **11** 460-461

OCHOA, SEVERO (1905-1993), Spanish biochemist **11** 461-464

OCHS, ADOLPH SIMON (1858-1935), American publisher and philanthropist **11** 464

OCKEGHEM, JOHANNES (c. 1425-1495), Netherlandish composer **11** 464-465

O'CONNELL, DANIEL (1775-1847), Irish statesman **11** 465-467

O'CONNOR, CARROLL (1924-2001), American actor **22** 343-345

O'CONNOR, JOHN JOSEPH (1920-2000), American Roman Catholic cardinal and archbishop **22** 345-347

PAYTON, WALTER (1954-1999), American football player **20** 294-296

PAZ, OCTAVIO (1914-1998), Mexican diplomat, critic, editor, translator, poet, and essayist **12** 161-162

PAZ ESTENSSORO, VICTOR (1907-2001), Bolivian statesman and reformer **12** 163-164

PAZ ZAMORA, JAIME (born 1939), president of Bolivia (1989-) **12** 165-167

PÁZMÁNY, PÉTER (1570-1637), Hungarian archbishop **12** 164-165

Pazzi conspiracy (Florence; 1478)
Sixtus IV **35** 331-333

PEABODY, ELIZABETH PALMER (1804-1894), American educator and author **12** 167-168

PEABODY, GEORGE (1795-1869), American merchant, financier, and philanthropist **12** 168

PEACOCK, THOMAS LOVE (1785-1866), English novelist and satirist **12** 169

PEALE, CHARLES WILLSON (1741-1827), American painter and scientist **12** 169-171

PEALE, NORMAN VINCENT (1898-1993), American religious leader who blended psychotherapy and religion **12** 171-172

PEALE, REMBRANDT (1778-1860), American painter **12** 172-173

PEARSE, PATRICK HENRY (1879-1916), Irish poet, educator, and revolutionary **12** 173-174

PEARSON, LESTER BOWLES (1897-1972), Canadian statesman and diplomat, prime minister **12** 174-175

PEARY, ROBERT EDWIN (1856-1920), American explorer **12** 175-176

Pecci, Vincenzo Gioacchino
see Leo XIII

PECHSTEIN, HERMANN MAX (1881-1955), German Expressionist painter and graphic artist **12** 176-177

PECK, ANNIE SMITH (1850-1935), American mountain climber **24** 304-306

PECK, MORGAN SCOTT (1936-2005), American author and psychologist **26** 288-291

PECK, ROBERT NEWTON (born 1928), American author of children's literature **12** 177-178

PECKINPAH, SAM (1925-1984), American film director **21** 338-340

PEDRARIAS (Pedro Arias de Ávila; c. 1440-1531), Spanish conqueror and colonial governor **12** 179

PEDRO I (1798-1834), emperor of Brazil and king of Portugal **12** 179-180

PEDRO II (1825-1891), emperor of Brazil 1831-1889 **12** 180-181

Pedro III (king, Aragon)
see Peter III, (Peter Feodorovich; 1728-62)

Pedro IV (king, Portugal)
see Pedro I (emperor, Brazil)

PEEL, JOHN (John Robert Parker Ravenscroft; 1939-2004), British disc jockey **27** 286-288

PEEL, SIR ROBERT (1788-1850), English statesman, prime minister 1834-35 and 1841-46 **12** 181-183

PÉGUY, CHARLES PIERRE (1873-1914), French poet **12** 183-184

PEI, I. M. (Ieoh Ming Pei; born 1917), Chinese-American architect **12** 184-187

PEIRCE, BENJAMIN (1809-1880), American mathematician **21** 340-342

PEIRCE, CHARLES SANDERS (1839-1914), American scientist and philosopher **12** 187-188

PEIXOTO, FLORIANO (1839-1895), Brazilian marshal, president 1891-94 **12** 188-189

PELAGIUS (died c. 430), British theologian **12** 189-190

PELE (Edson Arantes Do Nascimento Pele; born 1940), Brazilian soccer player **12** 190-191

PELLI, CESAR (born 1926), Hispanic American architect and educator **12** 191-192

PELOSI, NANCY (Nancy D'Alesandro; born 1940), American politician **25** 328-330

PELTIER, LEONARD (born 1944), Native American activist **12** 193-195

PEMBERTON, JOHN STITH (1831-1888), American inventor of Coca-Cola **28** 278-279

PEÑA, PACO (Francisco Peña Pérez; born 1942), Spanish guitarist and composer **23** 299-301

PENDERECKI, KRZYSZTOF (born 1933), Polish composer **12** 195-197

PENDERGAST, THOMAS J. (1872-1945), American political boss **29** 313-315

PENDLETON, EDMUND (1721-1803), American political leader **12** 197-198

PENDLETON, GEORGE HUNT (1825-1889), American politician **12** 198

PENFIELD, WILDER GRAVES (1891-1976), Canadian neurosurgeon **12** 198-200

PENN, WILLIAM (1644-1718), English Quaker, founder of Pennsylvania **12** 200-202

PENNANT, THOMAS (1726-1798), British naturalist, writer and antiquarian **31** 278-279

PENNEY, J. C. (James Cash Penney; 1875-1971), American chain store executive and philanthropist **12** 202-203

PENNINGTON, MARY ENGLE (1872-1952), American chemist **22** 352-355

PENROSE, BOIES (1860-1921), American senator and political boss **12** 203-204

PENROSE, ROGER (born 1931), British mathematician and physicist **12** 204-205

Pensador Mexicano, El
see Fernández de Lizardi, Josè Joaquin

PENSKE, ROGER (born 1937), American businessman and race car team owner **19** 280-282

PENZIAS, ARNO ALLEN (born 1932), German American physicist **23** 301-304

People's Commissariat for Internal Affairs (NKVD)
Yagoda, Genrikh Grigoryevich **35** 377-379

PEP, WILLIE (William Guiglermo Papaleo; 1922-2006), American boxer **21** 342-344

PEPPER, CLAUDE DENSON (1900-1989), Florida attorney, state representative, U.S. senator, and U.S. representative **12** 205-206

PEPPERELL, SIR WILLIAM (1696-1759), American merchant and soldier **12** 206-207

Peptides (molecules)
Pert, Candace **35** 278-280

PEPYS, SAMUEL (1633-1703), English diarist **12** 207-208

Perception (psychology)
Ambady, Nalini **35** 27-29

PERCEVAL, SPENCER (1762-1812), English statesman **34** 289-291
Linklater, Andro **35** 237-239

PERCY, WALKER (1916-1990), American author **19** 282-284

PEREC, GEORGES (1936-1982), French novelist **33** 241-243

PEREGRINUS, PETRUS (flourished 1261-69), French scholastic and scientist **12** 208

PEREIRA, ARISTIDES MARIA (1923-2011), Cape Verdean president **24** 306-308

PERELMAN, GRIGORY (Grisha Perelman; born 1966), Russian mathematician **27** 288-290

PETERSON, OSCAR (1925-2007), Canadian pianist **23** 304-306

PETIT, PHILIPPE (born 1949), French tightrope walker **33** 247-249

PETO, JOHN FREDERICK (1854-1907), American painter **12** 259

PETÖFI, SÁNDOR (1823-1849), Hungarian poet and revolutionary leader **23** 306-308

PETRARCH (Francesco Petrarca; 1304-74), Italian poet **12** 259-261

PETRIE, SIR WILLIAM MATTHEW FLINDERS (1853-1942), English archeologist **12** 261-262

PETRONIUS ARBITER (died c. 66), Roman author **12** 262-263

PEVSNER, ANTOINE (1886-1962), Russian sculptor and painter **12** 263-264

Pevsner, Naum Neemia
see Gabo, Naum

PEYO (Pierre Culliford; 1928-1992), Belgian cartoonist **28** 280-282

PFEIFFER, IDA (1797-1858), Austrian traveler and writer **33** 249-251

PHAEDRUS (c. 15 BCE-c. 50), Greek/Roman fabulists **20** 296-297

PHIBUN SONGKHRAM, LUANG (1897-1964), Thai statesman, prime minister 1938-44 and 1948-57 **12** 264-265

PHIDIAS (flourished c. 475-425 BCE), Greek sculptor **12** 265-267

Philadelphia Athletics (baseball team)
Cochrane, Mickey **35** 105-108

Philadelphos of Egypt
see Ptolemy II

PHILBY, KIM (1912-1988), British intelligence officer and spy **33** 251-253
Cairncross, John **35** 94-96
Golitsyn, Anatoliy **35** 170-172

PHILIDOR, FRANÇOIS-ANDRÉ (François-André Danican-Philidor; 1726-1795), French composer and chess player **21** 347-349

PHILIP (died 1676), American Wampanoag Indian chief 1662-76 **12** 267-268

PHILIP (Prince Philip; Philip Mountbatten; born 1921), Duke of Edinburgh and husband of Queen Elizabeth II of the United Kingdom **24** 308-310

Philip I (king of Portugal)
see Philip II (king of Spain)

PHILIP II (382-336 BCE), king of Macedon 359-336 **12** 269-271

PHILIP II (Philip Augustus; 1165-1223), king of France 1180-1223 **12** 268-269

PHILIP II (1527-1598), king of Spain 1556-1598 **12** 271-273

PHILIP III (1578-1621), king of Spain 1598-1621 **12** 273-274

PHILIP IV (the Fair; 1268-1314), king of France 1285-1314 **12** 274

PHILIP IV (1605-1665), king of Spain 1621-65 **12** 275

PHILIP V (1683-1746), king of Spain 1700-46 **12** 276-277
Alberoni, Giulio **35** 16-17

PHILIP VI (1293-1350), king of France 1328-50 **12** 277-278

Philip Augustus
see Philip II, king of France

Philip of Anjou
see Philip V, king of Spain

Philip the Fair
see Philip IV, king of France

PHILIP THE GOOD (1396-1467), duke of Burgundy 1419-67 **12** 278-279
staff and support
Binchois, Gilles **35** 71-73

PHILLIP, ARTHUR (1738-1814), English governor of New South Wales **12** 279-280

PHILLIPS, CLAIRE (1908-1960), American spy **30** 300-303

PHILLIPS, DAVID GRAHAM (1867-1911), American journalist and novelist **12** 280-281

PHILLIPS, SAM (1923-2003), American music producer **32** 298-301

PHILLIPS, WENDELL (1811-1884), American abolitionist and social reformer **12** 281-282

PHILLIPS, WILLIAM D. (born 1948), American physicist **32** 301-302

Philosphers, Bohemian
Elisabeth of Bohemia **35** 144-146

Philosophers, German
19th century
Bauer, Bruno **35** 36-38

PHIPS, SIR WILLIAM (1650/51-95), American shipbuilder and colonial governor **12** 283

Phosphorescence (physics)
Becquerel, Alexandre-Edmond **35** 45-47

PHOTIUS (c. 820-891), Byzantine patriarch **12** 283-284

Photojournalism
Ut, Nick **35** 361-363

Phuc, Kim, (born 1963), Vietnamese-Canadian war survivor
Ut, Nick **35** 361-363

Phya Kalyan Maitri
see Sayre, Francis

PHYFE, DUNCAN (1768-1854), American cabinetmaker **12** 284-285

Physical anthropology (social science)
Blumenbach, Johann Friedrich **35** 77-79

PIAF, EDITH (Edith Giovanna Gassion; 1915-1963), French music hall/cabaret singer **12** 285-287

PIAGET, JEAN (1896-1980), Swiss psychologist and educator **12** 287-288

PIANKHI (ruled c. 741-c. 712 BCE), Nubian king **12** 288-289

Piano (musical instrument)
Lewis, Jerry Lee **35** 235-237
Thalberg, Sigismond **35** 350-353

PIANO, RENZO (born 1937), Italian architect, lecturer, and designer **12** 289-291

PIATETSKI-SHAPIRO, ILYA (1929-2009), Russian-Israeli mathematician **30** 303-304

Piazza della Signoria (Florence)
Battiferri, Laura **35** 32-34

PIAZZOLLA, ASTOR (Astor Pantaleón Piazzolla; 1921-1992), Argentine musician **26** 291-293

Pibul Songgram, Luang
see Songgram, Luang Pibul

PICABIA, FRANCIS (1879-1953), French artist, writer, and bon vivant **12** 291-292

PICASSO, PABLO (1881-1973), Spanish painter, sculptor, and graphic artist **12** 292-295
associates
Hayter, Stanley William **35** 187-190

PICASSO, PALOMA (born 1949), Spanish fashion designer **12** 295-297

PICCARD, AUGUSTE (1884-1962), Swiss scientist **12** 297-298

PICCARD, JACQUES ERNEST JEAN (1922-2008), Swiss explorer, scientist, oceanographer, and engineer **18** 320-322

Piccolomini, Aeneas Sylvius de'
see Pius II

PICKENS, THOMAS BOONE, JR. (T. Boone Pickens; born 1928), American businessman **19** 284-286

PICKERING, EDWARD CHARLES (1846-1919), American astronomer **12** 298

PICKERING, TIMOTHY (1745-1829), American Revolutionary soldier and statesman **12** 298-299

PRÉVERT, JACQUES (Jacques Henri Marie Prevert; 1900-1977), French poet and filmmaker **27** 297-298

PREVIN, ANDRE (Andreas Ludwig Priwin; born 1929), German American composer and conductor **18** 333-334

PRÉVOST, ABBÉ (1697-1763), French novelist, journalist, and cleric **12** 445-446

Prévost d'Exiles, Antoine François
see Prévost, Abbé

PRICE, FLORENCE BEATRICE (nee Florence Beatrice Smith; 1887-1953), African American composer and music educator **26** 306-308

PRICE, LEONTYNE (Mary Leontyne Price; born 1927), American prima donna soprano **12** 446-447

PRICE, RICHARD (1723-1791), English Nonconformist minister and political philosopher **12** 447-448

PRICHARD, DIANA GARCÍA (born 1949), Hispanic American chemical physicist **12** 448-449

PRIDE, CHARLEY FRANK (born 1938), African American musician **23** 317-319

PRIDI PHANOMYONG (1901-1983), Thai political leader **12** 449

PRIEST, IVY MAUDE BAKER (1905-1975), treasurer of the United States (1953-1960) **12** 450-451

PRIESTLEY, J(OHN) B(OYNTON) (1894-1984), English author of novels, essays, plays, and screenplays **12** 451-452

PRIESTLEY, JOSEPH (1733-1804), English clergyman and chemist **12** 452-453

Prignano, Bartolomeo
see Urban VI

PRIMATICCIO, FRANCESCO (1504-1570), Italian painter, sculptor, and architect **12** 453-454

PRIMO DE RIVERA Y ORBANEJA, MIGUEL (1870-1930), Spanish general, dictator 1923-30 **12** 454-455

PRINCE, HAL (Harold Smith Prince; born 1928), American theatrical producer and director **19** 295-298

PRINCIP, GAVRILO (1894-1918), Serbian nationalist and assassin **21** 353-355

PRINGLE, THOMAS (1789-1834), Scottish author and abolitionist **23** 319-320

Prisoners of war
Bernadotte, Folke **35** 60-62
Karski, Jan **35** 217-219

PRITCHETT, V(ICTOR) S(AWDON) (1900-1997), English short story writer, novelist, literary critic, journalist, travel writer, biographer, and autobiographer **12** 455-457

Prizefighters
see Athletes

Pro Football Hall of Fame
Pollard, Fritz **35** 280-282

PROCLUS DIADOCHUS (410-485), Byzantine philosopher **12** 457

PROCOPIUS OF CAESAREA (c. 500-c. 565), Byzantine historian **12** 457-458

PROCTER, WILLIAM COOPER (1862-1934), American businessman **19** 298-300

PROHÍAS, ANTONIO (1921-1998), Cuban political cartoonist **35** 288-290

PROKOFIEV, SERGEI SERGEEVICH (1891-1953), Russian composer **12** 458-460

Prophets
see Bible–Old Testament

PROSSER, GABRIEL (c. 1775-1800), Afro-American slave rebel **12** 460-461

PROST, ALAIN (born 1955), French race car driver **35** 290-292

PROTAGORAS (c. 484-c. 414 BCE), Greek philosopher **12** 461

PROTAZANOV, YAKOV (1881-1945), Russian filmmaker **35** 293-295

Protestant Reformation
France
Beza, Theodore de **35** 64-66
Switzerland
Beza, Theodore de **35** 64-66

PROUDHON, PIERRE JOSEPH (1809-1864), French anarchist political philosopher and journalist **12** 461-463

PROULX, E. ANNIE (born 1935), American author **12** 463-465

PROUST, MARCEL (1871-1922), French novelist **12** 465-467

PROXMIRE, WILLIAM (1915-2005), Democratic senator for Wisconsin **12** 467-468

PRUDHOMME, SULLY (Rene Francois Armand Prudhomme; 1839-1907), French author and philosopher **25** 342-344

PRUD'HON, PIERRE PAUL (1758-1823), French painter **12** 469

PRUSINER, STANLEY BEN (born 1942), American biomedical researcher **23** 320-323

PRYOR, RICHARD (1940-2005), American entertainer **19** 300-302

PRZHEVALSKY, NIKOLAI MIKHAILOVICH (1839-1888), Russian general and traveler **12** 469-470

Psychoanalysis (medicine)
Alexander, Franz **35** 19-21
Deutsch, Helene **35** 127-129

Psychology (social science)
and gender
Deutsch, Helene **35** 127-129
social
Ambady, Nalini **35** 27-29

Psychology of Women, The (nonfiction work)
Deutsch, Helene **35** 127-129

Psychometry
see Psychology–testing

PTOLEMY I (367/366-283 BCE), Macedonian general, king of Egypt 323-285 **12** 470-472

PTOLEMY II (308-246 BCE), king of Egypt 285-246 **12** 472-473

PTOLEMY, CLAUDIUS (c. 100-c. 170), Greek astronomer and geographer **12** 473-474

Public Health (medicine)
Maassab, Hunein **35** 250-252

Public lands (United States)
settlers and
Linklater, Andro **35** 237-239

Public school (United States)
see Education (United States)

Publius Aelius Hadrianus
see Hadrian

PUCCINI, GIACOMO (1858-1924), Italian composer **12** 474-476

PUDOVKIN, V. I. (Vsevolod Illiarionovich Pudovkin; 1893-1953), Russian film director **24** 316-318

PUENTE, TITO (Ernesto Antonio Puente, 1920-2000), Hispanic American band leader, musician, and composer **12** 476-477 **30** 306-308

PUFENDORF, BARON SAMUEL VON (1632-1694), German jurist and historian **12** 477-478

PUGACHEV, EMELYAN IVANOVICH (1742-1775), Russian Cossack soldier **12** 478-479

PUGIN, AUGUSTUS WELBY NORTHMORE (1812-1852), English architect **12** 479-480

PULASKI, CASIMIR (1747/48-79), Polish patriot **12** 480-481

PULCI, LUIGI (1432-1484), Italian poet **12** 481

PULITZER, JOSEPH (1847-1911), American editor and publisher **12** 481-482

Pulitzer Prize winners
Hijuelos, Oscar **35** 197-199
Ut, Nick **35** 361-363

PULLMAN, GEORGE MORTIMER (1831-1897), American industrial innovator **12** 482-483

Pulse theory (light)
see Light–wave theory

SCHMITT, JACK (Harrison Hagan Schmitt; born 1935), American astronaut and geologist **22** 385-386

Schmitz, Ettore
see Svevo, Italo

SCHMOLLER, GUSTAV FRIEDRICH VON (1838-1917), German economist **14** 21

SCHNABEL, ARTUR (1882-1951), Austrian American pianist **27** 319-321

SCHNEERSON, MENACHEM MENDEL (The Rebbe; 1902-1994), Russian-American Hassidic Jewish leader **22** 386-388

SCHNEIDER, ROMY (Rosemarie Magdalena Albach-Retty; 1938-1982), Austrian actress **24** 350-352

SCHNEIDERMAN, ROSE (1882-1972), labor organizer and activist for the improvement of working conditions for women **14** 22-23

SCHNITZLER, ARTHUR (1862-1931), Austrian dramatist and novelist **14** 23-24

SCHOENBERG, ARNOLD (1874-1951), Austrian composer **14** 24-26

SCHOLASTICA, ST. (c. 480-547), Italian abbess **30** 314-316

SCHOLEM, GERSHOM (1897-1982), Jewish scholar **14** 26

SCHOLL, SOPHIE (1921-1943), German student activist **35** 325-327
Bill, Max **35** 69-71

SCHONGAUER, MARTIN (c. 1435-91), German engraver and painter **14** 26-28

SCHÖNHUBER, FRANZ XAVER (1923-2005), German right-wing political leader **14** 28-29

School of Paris (art)
see French art–School of Paris

SCHOOLCRAFT, HENRY ROWE (1793-1864), American explorer and ethnologist **14** 29

SCHOOLCRAFT, JANE JOHNSTON (1800-1842), Native American poet **30** 316-318

SCHOONMAKER, THELMA (born 1940), American film editor **30** 318-320

SCHOPENHAUER, ARTHUR (1788-1860), German philosopher **14** 29-31

SCHOUTEN, WILLIAM CORNELIUS (c. 1580-1625), Dutch explorer and navigator **14** 31

SCHRAMM, TEXAS ERNEST ("Tex"; 1920-2003), American football team owner **24** 352-355

SCHREINER, OLIVE (Olive Emilie Albertina Schreiner; Ralph Iron; 1855-1920), South African author **23** 362-364

SCHREMPP, JUERGEN (born 1944), German automobile industry executive **20** 331-332

SCHRODER, GERHARD (born 1944), German chancellor **19** 325-327

SCHRÖDINGER, ERWIN (1887-1961), Austrian physicist **14** 31-33

SCHROEDER, PATRICIA SCOTT (born 1940), first U.S. congresswoman from Colorado **14** 33-35

SCHUBERT, FRANZ PETER (1797-1828), Austrian composer **14** 35-37

SCHULLER, GUNTHER (born 1925), American musician **14** 37-38

SCHULZ, CHARLES M. (1922-2000), American cartoonist and creator of "Peanuts" **14** 38-39

SCHUMACHER, KURT (1895-1952), German socialist statesman **14** 40-41

SCHUMAN, ROBERT (1886-1963), French statesman **14** 41

SCHUMAN, WILLIAM HOWARD (1910-1992), American composer and educator **22** 388-391

SCHUMANN, CLARA (Clara Josephine Wieck Schumann; 1819-1896), German pianist and composer **26** 338-340

SCHUMANN, ROBERT ALEXANDER (1810-1856), German composer and critic **14** 41-43

SCHUMPETER, JOSEPH ALOIS (1883-1950), Austrian economist **14** 43-44

SCHURMAN, ANNA MARIA VAN (1607-1678), Dutch scholar **31** 321-322

SCHURZ, CARL (1829-1906), American soldier, statesman, and journalist **14** 44-45

SCHUSCHNIGG, KURT VON (1897-1977), Austrian statesman, chancellor of Austria 1934-38 **14** 45-46

SCHÜSSLER FIORENZA, ELIZABETH (born 1938), biblical scholar and theologian **14** 46-48

SCHÜTZ, HEINRICH (1585-1672), German composer **14** 48-49

SCHUYLER, PHILIP JOHN (1733-1804), American Revolutionary War general **14** 49-50

SCHWAB, CHARLES MICHAEL (1862-1939), American industrialist **14** 50-51

SCHWANN, THEODOR (1810-1882), German biologist **14** 51-52

SCHWARTZ, ANNA (1915-2012), American economic historian **33** 288-291

SCHWARTZ, DELMORE (1913-1966), American poet **19** 327-329

Schwartzerd, Philip
see Melancthon, Philip

SCHWARZKOPF, ELISABETH (Dame Olga Maria Elisabeth Friederike Schwarzkopf; 1915-2006), German opera singer **25** 378-380

SCHWARZKOPF, NORMAN (1934-2012), American army general **14** 52-54

SCHWEITZER, ALBERT (1875-1965), Alsatian-German philosopher and medical missionary **14** 55-56

SCHWENCKFELD, KASPER VON (1489/90-1561), Silesian nobleman and theologian **14** 56-57

SCHWIMMER, ROSIKA (1877-1948), Hungarian women's rights activist **14** 57-60

SCHWITTERS, KURT (1887-1948), German painter, collagist, typographer, and poet and creator of MERZ-art **14** 60-61

Science fiction
Matheson, Richard **35** 258-260
Protazanov, Yakov **35** 293-295

Scientists, American
archeologists
Squier, E.G. **35** 337-339
chemists (19th century)
Coston, Martha **35** 110-112
engineers
Loewy, Raymond **35** 242-244
engineers (electrical)
Dolby, Ray **35** 139-141
epidemiologists
Maassab, Hunein **35** 250-252
inventors (19th century)
Coston, Martha **35** 110-112
inventors (19th-20th century)
Knight, Margaret **35** 222-224
inventors (20th century)
Damadian, Raymond **35** 112-115
neurophysiologists
Pert, Candace **35** 278-280
physicians (20th century)
Damadian, Raymond **35** 112-115
physiologists
Maassab, Hunein **35** 250-252
psychiatrists and psychoanalysts
Alexander, Franz **35** 19-21
Deutsch, Helene **35** 127-129
surgeons
Jobe, Frank **35** 207-209

Scientists, Austrian
psychiatrists and psychoanalysts
Deutsch, Helene **35** 127-129

Scientists, Canadian
engineers (aeronautical)
Brill, Yvonne **35** 89-91

Scientists, English
chemists (19th century)
Abel, Frederick **35** 3-4
inventors
Abel, Frederick **35** 3-4

SELEUCUS I (c. 358-281 BCE), Macedonian general, king of Babylonia and Syria **14** 92-93

SELIGMAN, EDWIN ROBERT ANDERSON (1861-1939), American economist and editor **14** 93-94

SELIM I (c. 1470-1520), Ottoman sultan 1512-20 **14** 94-95

SELIM III (1761-1808), Ottoman sultan 1789-1807 **14** 95-96

Seljuks (Turkish dynasty; ruled 1055-1157) Bayezid I **35** 38-40

SELKIRK, 5TH EARL OF (Thomas Douglas; 1771-1820), Scottish colonizer in Canada **14** 96

SELLARS, WILFRED (1912-1989), American philosopher **14** 96-98

SELLERS, PETER RICHARD HENRY (1925-1980), British comedy genius of theater, radio, television, and movies **14** 98-99

SELZNICK, DAVID OLIVER (1902-1965), American filmmaker **20** 333-335

SEMENOV, NIKOLAI NIKOLAEVICH (1896-1986), Russian physicist and physical chemist **14** 101

SEMMELWEIS, IGNAZ PHILIPP (1818-1865), Hungarian physician **14** 101-102

SEMMES, RAPHAEL (1809-1877), American Confederate naval officer **14** 102-103

SEMPRÚN, JORGE (1923-2011), Spanish writer **33** 292-295

SEN, AMARTYA KUMAR (born 1933), Indian economist **24** 359-361

SEN, RAM CAMUL (1783-1844), Bengali intellectual and entrepreneur **13** 16-17

Senator, Flavius Magnus Aurelius Cassiodorus see Cassiodorus

SENDAK, MAURICE (1928-2012), American author, artist, and illustrator **19** 329-331

SENDER, RAMÓN JOSÉ (1901-1982), Spanish American author **24** 361-363

SENDLER, IRENA (Irena Sendlerowa; 1910-2008), Polish social worker **28** 318-320

SENECA THE YOUNGER, LUCIUS ANNAEUS (c. 4 BCE-A.D. 65), Roman philosopher **14** 103-105

SENESINO (c. 1686-1759), Italian singer **31** 331-332

SENFL, LUDWIG (c. 1486-c. 1543), Swiss-born German composer **14** 105-106

SENGHOR, LÉOPOLD SÉDAR (1906-2001), Senegalese poet, philosopher, and statesman **14** 106-107

SENNA, AYRTON (1960-1994), Brazilian race car driver **34** 326-328
Prost, Alain **35** 290-292

SENNACHERIB (ruled 705-681 BCE), king of Assyria **14** 108

SENNETT, MACK (1884-1960), American film producer and director **14** 108-109

Sepúlveda, Juan Ginés de, (1490-1574), Spanish historian and theologian las Casas, Bartolomé de **35** 231-233

SEQUOYAH (c. 1770-1843), American Cherokee Indian scholar **14** 110-111

SERBAN, ANDREI (born 1943), Romanian-American theater director **35** 327-329

Serbian Republic (former kingdom; former republic of Yugoslavia) Savić, Milunka **35** 323-325

Serial music Guarnieri, Camargo **35** 175-176

SERLING, ROD (1924-1975), American television writer and host **32** 313-315

SERRA, JUNIPERO (Miguel José Serra; 1713-84), Spanish Franciscan missionary, founder of California missions **14** 111-112

SERRANO ELÍAS, JORGE ANTONIO (born 1945), president of Guatemala (1991-1993) **14** 112-113

SERRÃO, FRANCISCO (Francisco Serrano; died 1521), Portuguese explorer **28** 320-321

SERTÜRNER, FRIEDRICH (Friedrich Wilhelm Adam Ferdinand Sertürner; 1783-1841), Prussian pharmacist **21** 379-381

SERVAN-SCHREIBER, JEAN-JACQUES (1924-2006), French journalist and writer on public affairs **14** 113-115

SERVETUS, MICHAEL (c. 1511-53), Spanish religious philosopher **14** 115-116

SESSHU, TOYA (1420-1506), Japanese painter and Zen priest **14** 116-117

SESSIONS, ROGER HUNTINGTON (1896-1985), American composer **14** 117-118

SETON, ELIZABETH ANN BAYLEY (1774-1821), American Catholic leader **14** 118-119

SETON, ERNEST THOMPSON (1860-1946), Canadian author and co-founder of the Boy Scouts of America **14** 119-120

SETTIGNANO, DESIDERIO DA (1428/31-1464), Italian sculptor **4** 509

SEURAT, GEORGES PIERRE (1859-1891), French painter **14** 120-122

Seuss, Dr. see Geisel, Theodor

SEVAREID, ERIC (Arnold Eric Sevareid 1912-1992), American broadcast journalist and author **22** 395-397

Seven Weeks War see Austro-Prussian War (1866)

SEVERINI, GINO (1883-1966), Italian painter **14** 122

SEVERUS, LUCIUS SEPTIMIUS (146-211), Roman emperor 193-211 **14** 109-110

SEVIER, JOHN (1745-1815), American frontiersman, soldier, and politician **14** 122-123

SÉVIGNÉ, MARIE DE (1626-1696), French writer **29** 263-265

SEWALL, SAMUEL (1652-1730), American jurist and diarist **14** 123-124

SEWARD, WILLIAM HENRY (1801-1872), American statesman **14** 124-125

SEXTON, ANNE (Anne Gray Harvey; 1928-74), American ''confessional'' poet **14** 125-126

Seymour, Edward see Somerset, Duke of

SEYMOUR, HORATIO (1810-1886), American politician **14** 126-127

SEYMOUR, JANE (1509-1537), third wife and queen consort of Henry VIII of England **18** 367-368

SEYMOUR, WILLIAM JOSEPH (1870-1922), African American religious leader **27** 323-325

SFORZA, LODOVICO (1452-1508), duke of Milan **14** 127-128

SHAARAWI, HUDA (Nur al-Huda Sultan; 1879-1947), Egyptian women's rights activist **24** 363-365

SHABAKA (ruled c. 712-c. 696 BCE), Nubian king, pharaoh of Egypt **14** 130

SHABAZZ, BETTY (1936-1997), African American educator, activist, and health administrator **14** 130-132

SHACKLETON, SIR ERNEST HENRY (1874-1922), British explorer **14** 132-133

SHADD CARY, MARY ANN (1823-1893), American and Canadian journalist, teacher, lawyer, and abolitionist **30** 324-326

SHAFFER, PETER LEVIN (born 1926), English/American playwright **14** 133-135

SHAFTESBURY, 1ST EARL OF (Anthony Ashley Cooper; 1621-83), English statesman **14** 135-136

SHEVCHENKO, TARAS GRIGORYEVICH (1814-1861), Ukrainian poet **24** 367-369

SHIBA, RYOTARO (1923-1996), Japanese novelist, historian, and journalist **30** 328-330

Shih-heng
see Lu Chi

SHIH KO-FA (died 1644), Chinese scholar-soldier **14** 194-195

SHIH LE (274-333), Chinese emperor 330-333 **14** 195

SHIHAB, FU'AD (1903-1973), Father of the Lebanese Army and president of Lebanon (1958-1964) **14** 193-194

SHILS, EDWARD ALBERT (1911-1995), American sociologist **14** 195-197

SHIMADA, SHIGETARO (1883-1976), Japanese naval admiral **30** 330-332

SHINRAN (1173-1262), Japanese Buddhist monk **14** 197

SHIPPEN, EDWARD (1728-1806), American jurist **14** 197-198

SHIRER, WILLIAM L. (1904-1993), American journalist and historian who wrote on the history of Nazi Germany **14** 198-199

SHIVAJI
see Śivaji

SHKLOVSKY, VIKTOR (1893-1984), Russian critic **30** 332-334

SHOCKLEY, WILLIAM (1910-1989), American physicist **14** 200-202

SHOEMAKER, GENE (Eugene Merle Shoemaker; 1928-1997), American geologist and planetary scientist **20** 335-338

SHOEMAKER, WILLIE (Billy Lee Shoemaker; 1931-2003), American jockey and horse trainer **21** 381-383

SHOLEM ALEICHEM (Sholem Rabinowitz; 1859-1916), Russian-born American author **14** 202-203

SHOLES, CHRISTOPHER LATHAM (1819-1890), American publisher, inventor, and social reformer **21** 383-385

SHOLOKHOV, MIKHAIL ALEKSANDROVICH (1905-1984), Russian novelist **14** 203-204

Shonekan, Ernest, (born 1936), Nigerian politician
Abacha, Sani **35** 1-3

SHORE, DINAH (1916-1994), American actress and singer **31** 333-334

SHORT, WALTER (1880-1949), American army officer **19** 337-339

SHOSTAKOVICH, DMITRI DMITRIEVICH (1906-1975), Russian composer **14** 204-205

SHOTOKU TAISHI (573-621), Japanese regent, statesman, and scholar **14** 205-207

SHOUSE, CATHERINE FILENE (1896-1994), American public servant **32** 317-320

Show Boat (musical)
Foley, Jack **35** 154-156

Showa Tenno
see Hirohito

SHREVE, HENRY MILLER (1785-1851), American steamboat designer and builder **14** 207

SHRIVER, EUNICE KENNEDY (1921-2009), American activist **19** 339-341

Shu Ch'ing-ch'un
see Lao Shê

Shu Maung
see Ne Win

SHUB, ESTHER (Esfir Ilyanichna Shub; 1894-1959), Ukrainian filmmaker **24** 369-371

SHUBERT BROTHERS (1883-1963), theatrical managers **14** 207-209

Shuja Shah, (1785-1842), Afghan ruler 1803-1809 and 1839-1842
Khan, Dost Mohammad **35** 219-221

SHULTZ, GEORGE PRATT (born 1920), labor and economics specialist, educator, businessman, and international negotiator **14** 209-211

Shunro
see Hokusai, Katsushika

Shuta
see Liang Wu-ti

SIBELIUS, JEAN JULIUS CHRISTIAN (1865-1957), Finnish composer **14** 211-212

Sicily, Duke of
see Guiscard Robert

SICKERT, WALTER RICHARD (1860-1942), English painter **14** 212-213

SICKLES, DANIEL EDGAR (1819-1914), American politician and diplomat **21** 385-388

SIDGWICK, HENRY (1838-1900), English philosopher and moralist **14** 213

SIDNEY, SIR PHILIP (1554-1586), English poet, courtier, diplomat, and soldier **14** 214-215

SIEBERT, MURIEL (1932-2013), American businesswoman **18** 368-370

SIEGEL, BENJAMIN ("Bugsy"; 1906-1947), American gangster **14** 215-216

SIENKIEWICZ, HENRYK (1846-1916), Polish novelist and short-story writer **14** 216-217

SIERRA, JUSTO (1848-1912), Mexican educator, writer, and historian **14** 217

Sierra Leone (nation, West Africa)
Kabbah, Ahmad Tejan **35** 210-212

Sierra Leone People's Party (established 1951)
Kabbah, Ahmad Tejan **35** 210-212

SIEYÈS, COMTE EMMANUEL JOSEPH (1748-1836), French statesman and political writer **14** 217-218

SIFTON, SIR CLIFFORD (1861-1929), politician who helped turn the Canadian West into a premier agricultural area **14** 219-220

SIGISMUND (1368-1437), Holy Roman emperor 1411-37, king of Bohemia 1420-37, and king of Hungary 1385-1437 **14** 220-221

SIGNAC, PAUL (1863-1935), French painter **23** 369-372

Signaling
Coston, Martha **35** 110-112

SIGNORELLI, LUCA (c. 1445/50-1523), Italian painter **14** 221-222

Sigüenza
see Ferrer, Gabriel Miró

SIHANOUK, PRINCE NORODOM (1922-2012), Cambodian nationalist and political leader **14** 222-223

SIKORSKI, WLADYSLAW (1881-1943), Polish military leader and prime minister **20** 338-340

SIKORSKY, IGOR (1889-1972), Russian-American aeronautical engineer, aircraft manufacturer, and inventor **14** 223-224

SILBER, JOHN (1926-2012), American philosopher and educator **14** 224-226

SILES ZUAZO, HERNAN (1914-1996), Bolivian politician **18** 370-373

SILKO, LESLIE (Leslie Marmon Silko; born 1948), Native American author and poet **14** 226-227

SILKWOOD, KAREN (1946-1974), American antinuclear activist **14** 227-229

SILLIMAN, BENJAMIN (1779-1864), American chemist, naturalist, and editor **14** 229-230

SILLS, BEVERLY (Belle Miriam Silverman; 1929-2007), American child performer, coloratura soprano, and operatic superstar **14** 230-231

SILONE, IGNAZIO (1900-1978), Italian novelist and essayist **14** 231-232

Silva, José Bonifácio de Andrada e
see Andrada e Silva, José Bonifácio de

X

Y